# Economic Impacts and Emergency Management of Disasters in China

Xianhua Wu · Ji Guo

# Economic Impacts and Emergency Management of Disasters in China

Springer

Xianhua Wu
School of Economics and Management
Shanghai Maritime University
Shanghai, China

Collaborative Innovation Center on Climate
and Meteorological Disasters
Nanjing University of Information Science
and Technology
Nanjing, China

Ji Guo
School of Economics and Management
Shanghai Maritime University
Shanghai, China

Collaborative Innovation Center on Climate
and Meteorological Disasters
Nanjing University of Information Science
and Technology
Nanjing, China

ISBN 978-981-16-1318-0 ISBN 978-981-16-1319-7 (eBook)
https://doi.org/10.1007/978-981-16-1319-7



This Springer imprint is published by the registered company Springer Nature Singapore Pte Ltd.
The registered company address is: 152 Beach Road, #21-01/04 Gateway East, Singapore 189721, Singapore

# Contents

# Part I
# Disaster and Economic Development

# Chapter 1
# Disaster Probability, Optimal Government Expenditure for Disaster Prevention and Mitigation, and Expected Economic Growth

**Abstract** As global climate warms, the occurrence frequency and loss of natural disaster are both increasing, posing a great threat to the sustainable development of human society. One of the most important approaches of disaster management is to prevent disaster and reduce disaster loss through fiscal expenditure of government; however, the optimal proportion of expenditure for disaster prevention and mitigation has always been a difficult issue that people concern about. First, this paper, after considering the impact of disaster on human capital, established a resident-manufacturer-government decision making model which contains the probability of disaster, and then solved the optimal proportion of government expenditure for disaster prevention and reduction as well as the expected economic growth rates under different conditions. Second, through numerical simulation method, this paper studied the impacts of such factors as coefficient of risk aversion and elasticity coefficient of substitution on the optimal proportion of disaster prevention and reduction expenditure. Third, through constant elasticity of sub-situation (CES) production function and ridge regression method, this paper verified the applicability of the proposed model with the data of the expenditures for disaster prevention and mitigation of Hunan Province in 2014. Finally, this paper summarized the research results and put forward corresponding suggestions on policy. The theoretical model proposed in this paper enriches the related researches of disaster economics, and the conclusions of empirical analysis can provide government departments with useful reference for the practice of disaster prevention and mitigation.

**Keywords** Government expenditure for disaster prevention and mitigation · Residents-manufacturer-government decision model · Probability of disaster · Expected economic growth rate

---

Guo Wei, Tingting Feng also made great contributions to this manuscript. We express our heartfelt thanks to them.

 
X. Wu and J. Guo, *Economic Impacts and Emergency Management of Disasters in China*,
https://doi.org/10.1007/978-981-16-1319-7_1

## 1.1 Introduction

In recent years, influenced by climate change and human activities, natural disasters have become more frequent, causing increasingly great losses (IPCC 2014). For example, natural disasters like the 2004 tsunami in Indonesia, the 2008 Wen chuan Earthquake in China and the 2011 Fukushima Earthquake in Japan have inflicted heavy losses on people's lives and property and caused great damage to socio-economic development. One important task of government in regard to disaster prevention and mitigation is to reduce damage loss and guarantee people's livelihood through fiscal expenditure. For this reason, the appropriate proportion of government's fiscal expenditure on disaster prevention and mitigation has become a difficult issue of public concern (Sawada and Takasaki 2017). If the proportion is too low, it is not conductive to the implement of disaster-preventing and mitigating measures; if the proportion is too high, it will crowd out other investment expenditures, which does not contribute to the sustainable development of economy and the continuity of government's disaster reduction work (Benalia et al. 2016). Therefore, the government's expenditure on disaster prevention and mitigation should be appropriate. However, few scholars have quantitatively analyzed the proportion of financial expenditure on disaster prevention and mitigation, which can't meet the needs of disaster prevention and mitigation.

After considering influencing factors like the impacts of disaster on capital stock and individual expected consumption, the distribution and constraints of fiscal policy, the complementary or substitutional relationship between private capital and government's productive expenditure, this paper establishes a resident-manufacturer-government decision making model which contains the probability of disaster. Aiming at the utility maximization of residents, this model is used to solve the optimal proportion of government expenditure on disaster prevention and reduction. Subsequently, this paper studies the impacts such factors as probability of disaster, residents' aversion to disaster risk, substitutional relationship between government's productive expenditure and private capital, input share of government's productive expenditure, and efficiency of disaster prevention and mitigation expenditure exert on the optimal proportion of government expenditure on disaster prevention and mitigation. Besides, the actual data of Hunan Province for disaster prevention and mitigation in 2014 are input into the proposed model to calculate the optimal proportion of government's expenditure on disaster prevention and reduction. The empirical results can provide government departments with useful reference for natural disaster prevention and mitigation and have good practical significance. The research findings of this paper not only enrich the related researches of disaster economics but also can provide government departments with theoretical support for the practice of disaster prevention and mitigation and the sustainable development of economic society.

The rest parts of the paper are arranged as follows: Sect. 1.2 is a literature review. Section 1.3 introduces the resident-manufacturer-government decision-making model and explains the specific steps. Section 1.4 is the numerical simulation and analysis of results. Section 1.5 is a case study, taking the flood disaster of Hunan Province in 2014 as an example. Section 1.6 is research conclusions and policy suggestions.

## 1.2 Literature Review

In recent years, many scholars have studied the role and scale of government expenditure on disaster prevention and mitigation from different perspectives. For example, Jena et al. (2020) thought that natural disasters caused severe damages to people's properties and lives. Therefore, they developed an urban seismic risk assessment model using the ANN-AHP integrated technique and the joint data of geomorphological, geological, and tectonic information and historical seismic data. The predictive models could effectively help government officials and policymakers to establish the strategic layout and planning of cities. From the EM-DAT database, Schumacher and Strobl (2011) found that natural disasters caused severe economic and human losses. The study showed different exposure levels of natural hazards and the stage of economic development with a non-linear relationship. The degree of risk of natural disasters was influenced by the relationship between disaster losses and the stage of socio-economic development. Yaron and Wilson (2020) proposed that floods were the most frequent and severe natural disaster; one of the maximum economic costs in emerging countries. The highest cost-benefit ratio could be generated by combining community and local government investment to build disaster prevention project infrastructure. Case study showed that the benefits of building flood prevention infrastructure far exceeded the costs. Wang et al. (2017) considered Typhoon disaster as a natural disaster with frequent occurrence and damage. Therefore, they proposed a combined static EC (econometric) and dynamic IO (input-output) model to estimate the direct and indirect economic losses caused by typhoons to related industries. The results of the research indicated that the total damage caused by typhoons to 17 industries in 2013 was 127,192.48 billion Yuan. The study revealed that the greater the cumulative economic damage caused by a hurricane, the longer the average time required resuming production in each industry. In short, natural disaster losses include both direct and indirect losses. Most direct losses could be expressed in physical form, and could be calculated directly or converted to monetary format to estimate approximate disaster losses. Disasters also caused more medium- to long-term hidden impacts that cannot be directly measured in monetary terms, especially non-structural indirect losses. Therefore, most scholars conducted their studies based on computable disaster losses. The value of measurable disaster losses reflects, to some extent, the scale of economic losses caused by disasters. Researches in this area emphasized the importance and irreplaceability of government involvement in disaster prevention and mitigation, and the necessity of government financial investment. Palm (1990) believed that government's investment in disaster prevention and mitigation was conductive to improving the human's ability to withstand natural disasters and was a major driving force for transforming people from passive defense to active mitigation when faced with disasters. Mileti (1999) put forward disaster control theory and believed that government's expenditure for pre-disaster prevention played a crucial role in controlling disasters, reducing disaster losses, and achieving sustainable development of economy. Alexander (1997) proposed that natural disaster not only destroyed capital stock and caused direct economic loss, but also affected individual's consumption expectation. Capital stock and expected consumption decision are important driving forces for economic development, thus it is of great significance to study government's expenditure on pre-disaster prevention. Haurie and Moresino (2006) argued that environmental disaster damage costs include productive physical capital, social costs, and investment capital. Hence, disaster prevention capital and government's investment could affect disaster preparedness. Capital stock and expected consumption decisions were crucial drivers of economic development, so it was significant to study government spending on disaster prevention. Meacher (2004), Hochrainer (2006), Hochrainer and Pflug (2009) et al., from the perspective of risk management, emphasized the necessity of increasing government's expenditure on disaster prevention and reduction. Anbarci et al. (2005) and Cohen and Werker (2008) believed that government's ability of disaster prevention played an important role in disaster mitigation even though the disaster risk was uncontrollable. Aldrich and Ono (2016) and Fraser et al. (2020) pointed out that the government carries out unified planning and coordination in disaster prevention and mitigation; develops assistance measures and emergency evacuation plans, implements disaster relief and reconstruction of infrastructure projects, and obtains the optimal disaster relief expenditures within limited resources. The government is the link and bridge of disaster management, as well as the leader, coordinator and organizer of disaster prevention, relief and reconstruction work. Through historical natural disaster cases in five dimensions, Ladds et al. (2017) analyzed the total disaster losses and impacts in Australia. The research showed that there were differences in the frequency and severity of damage caused by disasters. In addition to measuring the direct and indirect losses in monetary terms, it also included other intangible and non-measurable losses. The impact of natural disasters was widespread, and the value of the damage caused was severe. In conclusion, natural disasters had complex characteristics such as high frequency of occurrence, wide impact range, and severe economic losses. Hence, the government's investment in disaster management is necessary, and could reduce disaster losses, improve disaster defense capability, maintain regional stability, and restore regional economic development quickly. Based on this, the government must intervene in disaster risk management and invest in disaster prevention and mitigation.

Increasing government's investment in disaster risk reduction has many benefits, yet it is usually constrained by government budget. Besides, overinvestment will do no good from dialectic perspective (Wu et al. 2019). Keefer et al. (2011) found that the death rate of earthquakes can be greatly reduced by implementing anti-seismic construction regulations. However, some governments chose not to take corresponding disaster prevention measures. The root cause is that the scale of government's investment in disaster prevention and reduction is affected and restricted by the state budget as well as government's political motivation. To be more specific, low-income countries have higher opportunity costs of disaster prevention than middle- and high-income countries, and thus the scale of government's investment in disaster risk reduction is relatively small. Moreover, in some dictatorships and countries with serious corruption problems, the political motivation of government to offer public security expenditure is not to ensure people's welfare; consequently, the scale of government investment in disaster prevention and mitigation is small as well. Some scholars believe that the excessive increase of government's investment in disaster prevention and reduction is not conducive to the sustainable development of the country's social economy. Shi (2012) pointed out that the government, as a leader in disaster management, could improve disaster response capacity, enhance the overall welfare of society, and maintain social stability by integrating resources, organizations, culture, and workforce. Even in low-income countries and regions, under a limited situation, the government could build sustainable disaster reduction and emergency response systems, and heighten overall disaster preparedness capabilities. However, some governments have chosen not to take corresponding disaster prevention measures. The scale of government investment in disaster prevention and mitigation was influenced and limited by national budgets and government political motivations. To be more specific, low-income countries have higher opportunity costs of disaster prevention than middle- and high-income countries, and the scale of the government's investment in disaster risk reduction was relatively small. Natural disasters had spatial spillover effects that would affect adjacent regions. Under such circumstances, disaster mitigation and prevention policies were relatively passive, and the final results of disaster management measures were related to multiple factors such as neighboring regions, industries, and economies. From a global perspective of disaster prevention and mitigation management, Kumar et al. (2020) confirmed that international cooperation mechanisms between countries were restricted by national development stages, implementation efficiency, and economic goals. Mahmud and Prowse (2012) studied the issue of corruption in disaster management. The research found varying degrees of corruption in pre-disaster interventions, relief processes, and post-disaster interventions, and there were great differences in the degree of influence on different income groups. Hence, it suggested that the government should input anti-corruption policy in disaster reduction and prevention management. Some scholars believed that the excessive increase of government's investment in disaster prevention and reduction was not conducive to the sustainable development of the country's social economy. For instance, Kunreuther and Pauly (2006) proposed that if the government put extra investment in disaster prevention and mitigation, it would bring crowding out effect to other investment expenditures and reduce direct economic benefits. The Insurance Institute for Property Loss Reduction of Boston (1995) found that if the government excessively increased the scale of investment in disaster prevention and reduction, residents would be excessively dependent on the government's disaster prevention work. Howard also found that individuals generally had the inertia to avoid advance expenditure; if the government excessively intervened in the autonomous disaster prevention measures of people, for example, increasing investment in disaster prevention and mitigation, people's initiative to transfer risks and avoid losses would be reduced. Slavíková (2016) intended to assess the crowding-out effect on a macroeconomic perspective about the flood expenditure of central governments. The government's development of effective flood risk management had highlighted the importance of government self-involvement. The crowding-out effect was explored from a macroeconomic perspective, based on the case of the devastating floods that hit the central government of the Czech Republic in 1997 and 2002. Bachner et al. (2019) mentioned that government budgets for disaster prevention and mitigation, and climate adaptation were constricted by the tax base and government spending patterns. A higher account would lead to a corresponding reduction in post-disaster relief and unemployment benefits, resulting in higher tax revenues. Therefore, increasing government budgets for disaster risk management was not the best option. Disaster risk management with balanced government revenues and expenditures could achieve better management efficiency and a higher return on investment. Therefore, the government should consider the financial budget, the crowding out effect of disaster prevention and reduction expenditure, and people's inertia in disaster prevention while deciding the scale of investment in disaster prevention and mitigation (Klomp and Valckx 2014; Klomp 2016).

To sum up, the government's expenditure on disaster prevention and mitigation plays an important role in aspects like disaster loss reduction, but it is restricted by various factors, and excessive increase of investment in disaster prevention and reduction will not contribute to the sustainable development of society. To address this issue, some scholars have conducted researches on the optimal scale of government's disaster prevention and reduction expenditure. To solve this problem, some scholars studied the optimal scale of government expenditure on disaster prevention and reduction. The research focused on disaster prevention reserves, disaster mitigation investments, and post-disaster interventions. The whole process of disaster prevention and mitigation covered the household, enterprise and national levels. For example, Pindyck and Wang (2009) built a general equilibrium model which included production, capital accumulation, and family preference. This model assumes that in the coming decades, the United States is likely to experience a devastating earthquake that will significantly reduce the nation's capital stock, GDP, and wealth. In the case of known disaster risk distribution, this model takes taxes the major source of government's income for disaster prevention and mitigation to analyze how much tax residents are willing to pay to alleviate the impact of disasters. However, the obtained results mainly reflect residents' willingness rather than the optimal scale of government expenditure on disaster prevention and mitigation. Some other scholars studied the correlations among disaster prevention expenditure, disaster loss, and economic growth by establishing economic growth models so as to find the optimal scale of disaster prevention and reduction. For instance, Tian and Gao (2012) built a resident-government stochastic decision-making model to weigh-residents' welfare against financial gains and losses, and designed an optimal scale model of disaster relief which connected social environment with economic environment; yet this model failed to consider the crowing out effect the optimal scale of disaster prevention and reduction expenditure had on other investments. Liu et al. (2014) developed an observable and controllable urban seismic hazard risk model based on the system periphery theory. The system was applied to quantitatively analyze the relationship between urban seismic risk and system inputs, system state, and human seismic mitigation activities. The results showed that the model could achieve effective prevention, and control of urban seismic risk by analyzing the impact intensity of seismic hazard in peripheral systems and countries within the system. Several scholars studied the participation behavior and efficiency of government organizations in the disaster relief process. Based on the instant information obtained from social networks, they used disaster prediction tools to broadcast disaster damage in real-time. They found the optimal disaster relief solution through rational planning of funds, resources, labor and facilities.

Oloruntoba (2010) conducted an analytical study of the emergency relief chain and cyclone relief management process in disaster management agencies based on disaster management literature. This paper argued that a well-designed emergency response strategy and rescue plan could help managers understand and implement it. It was also an essential factor in achieving effective and comprehensive rescue operations, improving the efficiency of disaster rescue and reducing losses. Du and Qian (2016) explored the cooperation between governmental nonprofit organizations based on an evolutionary game model. The game model used the benefits of cooperation, incentives, the penalties for inaction, response efficiency, and coordination costs as the critical factor. With limited resources, they went to look for ways to optimize government spending on disaster prevention and response that could simultaneously improve the efficiency of the response system and the effectiveness of assistance. Other scholars established economic loss evaluation indexes from the macro level, and constructed a comprehensive economic loss model. From a global perspective, they evaluated the economic losses and government investments in disaster prevention and mitigation, and obtained optimal spending options for the government's investments in disaster risk management. For instance, Barro (2009, 2015) introduced lucas-tree asset pricing model and Epstein-Zin-Weil utility function to establish an economic model and studied the investment range of disaster risk reduction; nevertheless, this model didn't take social welfare maximization as the government's goal of disaster risk reduction expenditure. Zhuo and Duan (2012) built a two-sage economic growth model that had taken consumption expectations into account, and based on the endogenous economic growth theory with risk constraint, established the relationship between government expenditure on disaster prevention and mitigation and economic growth, and then, by using the expected utility and risk decision principles under uncertain conditions, studied the impact of investment expenditure for disaster prevention and reduction on recent capital stock, recent capital accumulation, and consumption expectation. However, this economic model neglected the role of human input and failed to consider the impact of the relationship between private capital and government productive expenditure on the optimal scale of disaster prevention and reduction expenditure.

Motoyama (2017) established an economic model which taken the maximization of social welfare as the goal of government expenditure. Meanwhile, in order to consider the crowding out effect of disaster prevention and reduction expenditure on other investment expenditures, a constraint condition, namely, the distribution relationship between fiscal expenditure on disaster prevention and mitigation and productive expenditure was introduced into the model. Nevertheless, the established economic model also failed to consider the role of human input as well as the influence of the relationship between private capital and government's productive expenditure on the optimal scale of disaster prevention and reduction expenditure. Yu et al. (2015) argued that the government should treat the cost of recovery and damage reduction inputs to the affected areas equally. According to Yu et al. (2015), the government should treat recovery costs and mitigation inputs to disaster areas equally. Estimated of disaster losses were used to obtain reconstruction costs, and serve as a measure of a country's or region's ability to rebuild. From the calculated recovery costs, they found the most vulnerable parts of the reconstruction system. Prioritize them for the post-disaster reconstruction process, i.e., rank the vulnerability of the reconstruction efforts. Based on historical disaster losses and recovery costs, the government could assess the sustainability of disaster management expenditures, and effectively manage disaster prevention and control budgets. He and Zhuang (2016) proposed to correlate disaster losses with pre-disaster preparedness, and construct a disaster management system to develop post-disaster relief measures. Through the optimized model to obtain the decision efficiency in the pre-disaster planning and post-disaster relief phases. The values of optimal disaster prevention and response were obtained using the inverse induction method. The obtained values enable us to find the balanced optimal strategy for disaster prevention and relief. Ye et al. (2016) proposed that the government should conduct a cost-benefit analysis in disaster reduction investment decisions. The essay discussed government investment options for typhoon disaster prevention and control in Shenzhen, and proposed a framework for comprehensive government investment in disaster reduction. A coordinated assessment of labor capital, a comparative study of structural government investments, showed that premium subsidies have the highest returns. The research also confirmed the mutual spillover effects in the overall risk management framework.

According to Wang et al. (2020), complex disasters had a process of transformation from natural disasters to social crises. The government would involve multiple stakeholders such as enterprises, residents, and local governments in the process of disaster prevention and relief management, and there were conflicts and conflicting interests among them. From a holistic perspective, this research constructed a three-stage dynamic game model. Research indicated that governments need to provide more environmental compensation as a risk premium, to mitigate multiparty conflicts of interest in the evolution of natural disasters to social crises and to achieve the goal of globally optimal complex disaster management. To sum up, disaster prevention and mitigation was an ongoing task for government departments. Based on historical data and current fiscal revenues, the government determined the scale of budgetary expenditures for disaster prevention and mitigation, thereby formulating a disaster management budget for integrated planning of disaster prevention and mitigation efforts. At the same time, the government needed to consider the limitations of financial budget, economic sustainability, and resource facilities. The process of developing a disaster prevention and mitigation plan did not allow for the creation of a disaster management model with all elements. An increasing number of studies had exploring optimal global solutions under certain constraints, or unconstrained local optimal solutions.

Based on the above researches, in this paper, we construct multi-factor optimal disaster prevention and mitigation model with human investment, producer contribution, capital and effective government expenditure as influencing factors. The model simulates the optimal strategy of government disaster relief under different conditions and analyzes, and discusses the optimal scale of disaster prevention and mitigation expenditures under various factors. Finally, a practical case is adopted for empirical study, which can be regarded as a beneficial supplement to the above researches.

## 1.3 Method and Model

### *1.3.1 Principle of Model*

The impact of disaster on economy is the key to establishing the model. The economic impact of disasters is mainly reflected in the following three aspects. First, disasters directly impact and reduce the social capital stock; second, disasters indirectly impact social capital stock by affecting residents' expected consumption. That's because the known disaster risk will increase the uncertainty of residents' future income and property. Thus, influenced by risk aversion, residents will be more cautious about making decisions. Specifically, without any external assistance or channel for diversification of risk, residents will take the initiative to spread the disaster risk. For instance, residents can realize inter-temporal risk sharing by choosing inter-temporal consumption and reducing the current consumption, thereby leading to the increase of capital stock. Third, the changes in disaster prevention and reduction expenditure affect socio-economic development. Increasing expenditure on disaster prevention and mitigation can not only enhance the ability of cities to resist disasters, but also reduce the direct economic loss caused by disasters. Moreover, it can save fiscal expenditures and ease the financial burden of the state in the case of emergency relief. It also can increase government procurement and improve infrastructures like water conservancy facilities. In addition, it contributes to changing the prudent consumption decisions of residents and increasing the current consumption. The disadvantages of increasing disaster prevention expenditures lie in that, under the constraints of fiscal budget, the government needs to reasonably allocate expenditures on disaster prevention and reduction and production; and excessive expenditure for the former will lead to the decrease of productive expenditure, which will possibly lead to more taxes, thereby affecting residents' saving level and retarding economic development.

Next, based on the impact of disaster on economy, the basic assumptions of the model are illustrated. To reflect the inter-temporal sharing of disaster risk, this paper constructed a two-phase economic model based on the closed economy of residents, manufacturers, and government. The model assumes that disasters occur after the production of manufacturers, consumption and saving of families, and tax collection of government. When a disaster occurs, a certain proportion of existing capital stock is destroyed. And the proportion of fiscal expenditure on disaster prevention and reduction ($h$) will influence the disaster loss ratio which is set as $D(h)$[1] ($D(h) \in [0, 1]$). When the government increases the proportion of fiscal expenditure on disaster prevention and reduction ($h$), the disaster loss ratio ($D(h)$) will decrease to some extent, then $D'(h) < 0$. Let the probability of disaster be $p$. As natural disasters are mostly inevitable but predictable (Nagasaka 2008), this paper assumes the probability of disaster ($p$) is an exogenous variable and meanwhile a known constant. Therefore, the social capital stock $s_{t+1}$ influenced by disaster risk can be formulated as:

$$s_{t+1} = p(1 - D_t)a_{t+1} + (1 - p)a_{t+1} \tag{1.1}$$

Where $s_{t+1}$ represents the social capital stock of the $(t + 1)$-th period under the influence of the $t$-th period disaster risk, $a_{t+1}$ represents the capital stock of the $(t + 1)$-th period that is not influenced by disaster risk, $D_t$ is the loss ratio of the $t$-th period caused by disaster, and $p$ is the probability of disaster.

### 1.3.2 Model Building

#### 1.3.2.1 Residents

Assuming that residents have an infinite life span and their utility function under budget constraints is maximized, so the discounted utility is:

$$U(C_t) = E_0 \sum_{t=0}^{\infty} \beta^t \frac{C_t^{1-\gamma}}{1-\gamma} \tag{1.2}$$

where $C_t$ is residents' consumption at moment $t$, and $u(C_t)$ is instantaneous utility function which represents the utility of residents' consumption at a set moment. The instantaneous utility function is in the form of $u(C_t) = \frac{C_t^{1-\gamma}}{1-\gamma}$, namely, CRRA (Coefficient of Relative Risk Aversion) model. It is a utility function determined by differential equation $\gamma = -Cu''(c)/u'(C)$. Here, $\gamma$ refers to the coefficient of relative risk aversion and is a constant.

Risk aversion coefficient determines the willingness of residents to transfer their consumption indifferent periods: when the coefficient of risk aversion ($\gamma$) is larger

[1]The disaster loss ratio is from the assumption of Motoyama (2017):$(h) = \frac{\hat{d}}{1-\bar{d}} - \frac{\hat{d}}{h-\bar{d}}$, where $\hat{d} = -\frac{1-\bar{d}}{\bar{d}}$, $\bar{d} \in (0, 1)$, $\bar{d}$ is the upper limit of disaster loss ratio, $D(0) = \bar{d}$, the lower limit of the loss ratio is zero $D(1) = 0$, and $h$ is the proportion of fiscal expenditure on disaster prevention and reduction.

than 0, it means risk aversion; and the larger the coefficient, the higher the degree of risk aversion, which means that residents are more concerned about the loss caused by disaster and tend to avoid risks through inter-temporal consumption. When the coefficient of risk aversion ($\gamma$) is equal to 0, it means risk neutral; it indicates that residents are neutral to disaster risk, that is, disaster has little impact on residents. In this case, the instantaneous utility function has two characteristics: First, if the coefficient of risk aversion ($\gamma$) is below 1, $C^{1-\gamma}$ increases along with $C$; if the coefficient of risk aversion ($\gamma$) is larger than 1, then $C^{1-\gamma}$ decreases as $C$ increases. Thus, $C^{1-\gamma}$ is divided by $1-\gamma$ to ensure that the marginal utility of consumption is positive whatever the coefficient of risk aversion ($\gamma$) is. Second, in special case where the coefficient of risk aversion γ is close to 1, the instantaneous utility function can be simplified into $lnC$. In Eq. (1.2), $E$ denotes expectation, and it is used due to the uncertainty of probability of disaster ($p$). $\beta$ is time preference rate whose value ranges between 0 and 1, it indicates residents will discount further consumption. According to Mehra and Prescott (1985), most residents are averse to disaster risk, so the coefficient of risk aversion $\gamma$ is assumed to range within 1–10 (Liu 2013) (risk aversion coefficient $\gamma > 10$ indicates residents' strong aversion to risk). The budget constraint faced by residents can be expressed as:

$$\tilde{a} = [1 + (1 - \tau_t)r_t - \delta_t] * s_t - c_t \tag{1.3}$$

where, capital stock $\tilde{a}$ is the capital stock of the $(t+1)$-th period that converted from the $t$-th period, $\delta_t \in (0, 1)$ is generalized capital depreciation rate, $s_t$ is the capital stock affected by disaster risk, $r_t$ is generalized return on capital, and $\tau_t$ is composite tax rate.

The utility value of residents' utility function after discount is denoted as $V(s)$. It is the discounted value of utility obtained after solving the utility maximization problem for residents on condition that the initial capital stock $s_0$ and government disaster prevention strategy $(\tau, g, h)$ are given. Residents' maximum utility value of $t$-th period can be formulated as:

$$V(s) = max_{\{C,\tilde{a}\}}\left\{\frac{1}{1-\gamma}C^{1-\gamma} + \beta E_t V(\tilde{s})\right\}$$

$$s.t.\begin{cases} \tilde{a} = [1 + (1-\tau)r - \delta]s - C = Rs - C \\ s_0, \pi(\tau, g, h) \end{cases} \tag{1.4}$$

where

$$\tilde{s} = \tilde{a}((1 - D(h))p + 1 - p) \tag{1.5}$$

$$R = [1 + (1 - \tau)r - \delta] \tag{1.6}$$

For the convenience of expression, the symbol for the $t$-th period is omitted. Superscript ~represents the value of variable for the next period, and $\tilde{s}$ is the capital stock after disaster. In Eq. (1.6), $R = [1 + (1 - \tau)r - \delta]$ represents the rate of return on savings, $p$ is the probability of disaster, and $D(h)$ is disaster loss ratio. By solving Eq. (1.4), the savings function and consumption function of residents can be obtained, and they are respectively formulated as:

$$\tilde{a} = R^{1/\gamma}\left[\beta(p\left(1 - D(h)\right)^{1-\gamma} + 1 - p)\right]^{1/\gamma} s = (R(\rho(h))^{1/\gamma} s = \sigma(\tau, h)s \quad (1.7)$$

$$C = (R - \sigma(\tau, h))s \quad (1.8)$$

In the above equations, $\rho(h) = \beta(p\left(1 - D(h)\right)^{1-\gamma} + 1 - p\big)$ is the discount rate after taking disaster risk into account, and $\sigma(\tau, h) = (R(\rho(h))^{1/\gamma}$ is the saving rate of the current capital of residents. Assuming that residents' consumption is larger than 0, then $R - \sigma(\tau, h) > 0$ (see Section "The Value Function of the Residents' Utility" for the details on the derivation process of Eq. (1.7)).

#### 1.3.2.2 Manufacturers

Manufacturers produce final product with the capital provided by residents. Considering the positive effect of government's productive expenditure on the production of manufacturers, this paper introduces government's productive expenditure into production function model. In terms of production function, this paper chooses CES (constant elasticity of substitution) production function rather than the C-D function model used by Motoyama (2017). Because the CES production function is conducive to studying the influence of the complementary or substitutional relationship between private capital and government's productive expenditure on the optimal scale of disaster prevention and reduction expenditure (Bucci and Bo 2012; Bom 2017). Here, the elasticity coefficient of substitution of private capital factor and government productive expenditure is the core parameter of the complementary or substitutional relationship, and the CES production function is formulated as:

$$Y = A(b_1\left(\theta_1 k^m + \theta_2 l^m\right)^{\frac{m_1}{m}} + b_2 G^{m_1})^{\frac{\alpha}{m_1}} \quad (1.9)$$

In this model, $Y$ represents total output, $\alpha$ represents the economies of scale of production function, $A$ is efficiency parameter which refers to the output efficiency of economic system, and $\theta, b \in (0, 1)$ is the efficiency of production factors that are put into the production process. The elasticity coefficient of substitution of material input and human input is $e = \frac{1}{1-m}$; and the elasticity coefficient of substitution of private capital and government productive expenditure is $x = \frac{1}{1-m_1}$ (see Section "Substitute Elasticity Derivation of CES Production Function" for the details on the derivation process of elasticity coefficient of substitution). In Eq. (1.8), $G$ is the productive input allocated by the government, and $g$ is the ratio of productive expenditure ($G = gY$, $g \in (0, 1)$).

Let $K = (\theta_1 k^m + \theta_2 l^m)^{\frac{1}{m}}$, where the private capital $K$ includes both material capital ($k$) and labor capital ($l$). The goal of manufacturers is to maximize the profit. Assuming that $\alpha = 1$, then Eq. (1.9) can be further transformed into (see Section "Conversion of CES Function Form" for the details on the transformation process of function):

$$Y = Ab_1^{\frac{1}{m_1}} K\left(1 - b_2 A^{m_1} g^{m_1}\right)^{-\frac{1}{m_1}} \tag{1.10}$$

#### 1.3.2.3 Government

After a disaster occurs, the government's responsibility is to reduce the welfare loss caused by risk aversion as well as the impact of disaster risk on residents' expected consumption behavior. Specifically, the government should, on the premise of known probability of disaster ($p$), reasonably allocate disaster prevention and reduction expenditure ($H$) and productive expenditure ($G$), and maximize the overall welfare of residents. In the present paper, $G = gY$, $g \in (0, 1)$; $H = hY$, and $h \in (0, 1)$. Disaster prevention and reduction expenditure ($H$) can reduce the loss of capital stock caused by disasters. Assuming that the government has a balanced budget in each period, then the budget constraint is:

$$\mathrm{\tau * r * s = (g + h)Y} \tag{1.11}$$

where $\tau$ denotes composite tax rate, $r$ denotes generalized return on capital, $s$ denotes social capital stock, $h$ is the ratio of fiscal expenditure on disaster prevention and reduction and $g$ is the ratio of productive expenditure.

### *1.3.3 Model Solution*

#### 1.3.3.1 Optimal Strategy for Disaster Prevention and Reduction

Based on the given government disaster prevention strategy $\pi = \{\tau, h, g\}$ and initial savings $s_0$, residents' consumption function (Eq. 1.7) and savings function (Eq. 1.8) after maximizing the inter-temporal utility of residents can be obtained. Assuming that the manufacturers' goal is to maximize profit, in the case of unchanged returns to scale ($\alpha = 1$), the marginal output of capital is equal to the capital return $r$, namely:

$$\mathrm{r = Ab_1^{\frac{1}{m_1}} (1 - b_2 A^{m_1} g^{m_1})^{-\frac{1}{m_1}} = Ab_1^{\frac{1}{m_1}} B(g)} \tag{1.12}$$

To simplify the expression, there is:

$$B(g) = (1 - b_2A^{m_1}g^{m_1})^{-\frac{1}{m_1}} \tag{1.13}$$

Under the condition of market equilibrium, the demand and supply of capital input are equal, i.e., $s = K$. Substituting $s = K$ and Eq. (1.11) into Eqs. (1.6) and (1.7), the consumption and savings functions under maximization of manufacturers' profit can be obtained, and they respectively are:

$$\tilde{a}^E = \sigma(\tau, h)K \tag{1.14}$$

$$C^E = (R - \sigma(\tau, h))K \tag{1.15}$$

where

$$R = 1 + (1 - \tau)Ab_1^{\frac{1}{m_1}}B(g) - \delta \tag{1.16}$$

Accordingly, the budget constraint of government (Eq. 1.11) can be simplified into:

$$\tau = g + h \tag{1.17}$$

Under given equilibrium conditions (Eqs. 1.14 and 1.15) and budget constraint of government (Eq. 1.17), expression $V^g(K)$ is regarded as the value function of utility function that maximizes the welfare of residents, and its dynamic programming problem is solved. Through the production function of government's productive expenditure $Y = Ab_1^{\frac{1}{m_1}}K(1 - b_2A^{m_1}g^{m_1})^{-\frac{1}{m_1}} = Ab_1^{\frac{1}{m_1}}B(g)K$ and $R = (1 - \tau)Ab_1^{\frac{1}{m_1}}B(g)$,[2] the government's dynamic programming expression can be obtained:

$$V^g(K) = max_\pi\left\{\frac{1}{1-\gamma}C^{1-\gamma} + \beta EV^g(\tilde{K})\right\}$$

$$s.t\begin{cases} \tilde{a}^E = \sigma(\tau, h)K \\ C^E = (R - \sigma)K \\ g = \tau - h \\ given\ K_0 \end{cases} \tag{1.18}$$

After taking the derivates of $\tau$ and $h$ at both sides of $V^g(K)$ equation (see more details in Section "Solving the Optimal Disaster Prevention and Mitigation Policy"), we get:

$$(R - \sigma)^{-\gamma}\left[(1 - \tau)B' - B\right] = 0 \tag{1.19}$$

---

[2]To simplify the calculation process, here the rate of depreciation $\delta$ is assumed to be 1.

$$(R-\sigma)^{-\gamma}\left[\frac{(1-\tau)B'}{B}-\sigma\frac{F(h)}{\rho}\right]=0 \tag{1.20}$$

By solving Eqs. (1.19) and (1.20), the optimal strategy for disaster prevention and reduction $\pi^*\{\tau^*, g^*, h^*\}$ can be obtained. Assuming that the rate of return on savings in production structure is constant, and the optimal strategy for disaster prevention and reduction $\pi^*$ is independent of state variables and time, then there isn't any sate variable in Eqs. (1.18) and (1.19). According to the budget constraint of government $g = \tau - h$, the optimal ratio of productive expenditure $g^*$ can be formulated with $\tau^* - h^*$. And the consumption and savings functions $(C^*, \tilde{a}^*)$ with given optimal disaster relief strategy $\pi^*$ respectively are:

$$C^* = \left(R^* - \sigma\left(\tau^*, h^*\right)\right)K \tag{1.21}$$

$$\tilde{a}^* = \sigma\left(\tau^*, h^*\right)K \tag{1.22}$$

*Here,* $R^* = (1-\tau^*)Ab_1^{\frac{1}{m_1}}B(g^*)$ *and* $\sigma(\tau^*, h^*) = (R^*\rho(h^*))^{1/\gamma}$.

By solving Eqs. (1.21) and (1.22), the optimal strategy for disaster prevention and reduction assumed in the present paper $\pi^*\{\tau^*, g^*, h^*\}$ can be formulated as:

$$\sigma\frac{F(h^*)}{\rho} = 1 \tag{1.23}$$

where $\sigma = (R^*\rho(h^*))^{1/\gamma}$, $\rho = \beta\left(p\left(1-D(h^*)\right)^{1-\gamma}+1-p\right)$, and $F(h^*) = \beta p\frac{-D'(h^*)}{(1-D(h^*))^{\gamma}}$, then Eq. (1.23) can be further transformed into:

$$\frac{\left(R^*\beta\left(p\left(1-D(h^*)\right)^{1-\gamma}+1-p\right)\right)^{1/\gamma} * \beta p\frac{-D'(h^*)}{(1-D(h^*))^{\gamma}}}{\beta\left(p\left(1-D(h^*)\right)^{1-\gamma}+1-p\right)} = 1 \tag{1.24}$$

#### 1.3.3.2 Expected Economic Growth Rate

The final production function model is:

$$Y = Ab_1^{\frac{1}{m_1}}K\left(1-b_2A^{m_1}g^{m_1}\right)^{-\frac{1}{m_1}} \tag{1.25}$$

Similar to the endogenous economic growth *AK* model, due to the randomness of disaster impact, the growth rate can be defined by the expected value. The expected economic growth rate is defined as the growth rate of generalized capital. Affected by the optimal strategy for disaster prevention and reduction $\sigma(\tau^*, h^*)$, the expected growth rate is:

$$Eg_t = E_t\frac{K_{t+1}}{K_t} \tag{1.26}$$

Because s = K and

$$s_{t+1} = p(1 - D_t)a_{t+1} + (1 - p)a_{t+1} \tag{1.27}$$

$$a_{t+1} = \sigma(\tau, h)s$$

Then,

$$\begin{aligned} Eg_t = E_t\frac{K_{t+1}}{K_t} &= \frac{p(1 - D(h^*))\sigma(\tau^*, h^*)K_t + (1 - p)\sigma(\tau^*, h^*)K_t}{K_t} \\ &= \left(1 - pD\left(h^*\right)\right)\sigma\left(\tau^*, h^*\right) \\ &= \left(1 - pD\left(h^*\right)\right)(R\left(\beta\left(p\left(1 - D\left(h^*\right) + 1 - p\right)\right)\right)^{1/\gamma} \end{aligned} \tag{1.28}$$

where

$$\begin{aligned} R &= (1 - \tau)Ab_1^{\frac{1}{m_1}}B(g) \\ &= \left(1 - \left[(1 - h) * A^{m_1}b_2\right]^{\frac{1}{1-m_1}} - h\right) * A * b_1^{\frac{1}{m_1}} * \left(1 - b_2^{\frac{1}{1-m_1}}A^{\frac{m_1}{1-m_1}}(1 - h)^{\frac{m_1}{1-m_1}}\right)^{-\frac{1}{m_1}} \end{aligned} \tag{1.29}$$

As can be known from the above equation, affected by disaster risk, the expected growth rate that has considered the optimal expenditure scale of disaster prevention and reduction is mainly affected by three aspects.

First, the increase of probability of disaster ($p$) affects the first term $1 - pD(h^*)$ in Eq. (1.27). If the probability of disaster ($p$) increases, with the optimal proportion of disaster prevention and reduction expenditure ($h^*$) given, the expected loss will increase as well. However, the fact is when the probability of disaster ($p$) increases, the optimal proportion of disaster prevention and reduction expenditure ($h^*$) will increase accordingly; consequently, the loss caused by disaster reduces. Therefore, the increase of probability of disaster ($p$) has an uncertain impact on $1 - pD(h^*)$.

Second, the proportion of expenditure on disaster prevention and reduction ($h$) that increases along with the probability of disaster ($p$) is at the price of more taxes or less government productive expenditures. Whether higher tax or lower productive expenditure will inevitably result in the decrease of return on capital and saving rate, thereby leading to the decline of expected growth rate $\left(E_g\right)$.

Third, residents increase their savings to prevent disasters. That is to say, when the probability of disaster ($p$) increases, residents will increase their savings. However, in practical situation, when the probability of disaster ($p$) increases, the expenditure on disaster prevention and reduction will increase accordingly. As a result, the expected disaster loss decreases, and residents may reduce their savings for disaster prevention, thereby leading to the decrease of economic growth rate. In short, when the probability of disaster ($p$) rises, the impact of residents' precautionary savings on economic growth rate is unclear. If the precautionary saving increases along with the probability of disaster ($p$), the economic growth will be promoted; if it decreases as the probability of disaster increases, the economic growth will be retarded. Meanwhile, the expected growth rate is affected by the coefficient of risk aversion ($\gamma$), the elasticity coefficient of substitution $\left(x = \frac{1}{1-m_1}\right)$, the input share of government's productive expenditure ($b_2$), and the upper limit of disaster loss ratio ($D(0)$). The influences of these factors will be analyzed in detail in the third part of this paper. In conclusion, affected by various factors, the trend of expected growth rate is not clear.

## 1.4 Numerical Simulation and Result Analysis

Although the correlation between the probability of disaster and the optimal proportion of disaster prevention and reduction is expressed in Eq. (1.24), we still cannot solve a fixed value. For this reason, numerical simulation is adopted in this paper. By assigning values to the parameters describing economic structure, the government's optimal strategy for disaster relief $\pi^*$ under different conditions can be simulated, and the impacts of different factors on the optimal scale of disaster prevention and reduction expenditure are analyzed in detail. Then, based on the simulation results, the expected economic growth rate is given, and the influence of natural disasters on the expected economic growth rate in the short term is discussed.

### *1.4.1 Parameter Setting*

According to the introduction to variables in the second part of this paper, we know that:

$$\begin{aligned} R &= (1-\tau)Ab_1^{\frac{1}{m_1}}B(g) \\ &= \left(1-\left[(1-h)*A^{m_1}b_2\right]^{\frac{1}{1-m_1}}-h\right)*A*b_1^{\frac{1}{m_1}}*\left(1-b_2^{\frac{1}{1-m_1}}A^{\frac{m_1}{1-m_1}}(1-h)^{\frac{m_1}{1-m_1}}\right)^{-\frac{1}{m_1}} \end{aligned} \tag{1.30}$$

All the parameters in the equation obtained by substituting Eq. (1.30) into Eq. (1.24) need value assignment, except for the probability of disaster ($p$) and the optimal proportion of disaster prevention and reduction expenditure ($h^*$). The parameters are total factor productivity ($A$), input share of government's productive expenditure ($b_2$), the elasticity coefficient of substitution of private capital and

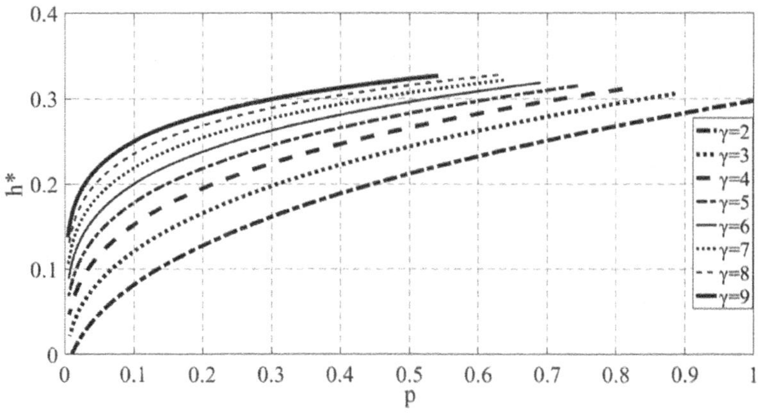


**Fig. 1.1** The correlation between the probability of disaster ($p$) and the optimal proportion of disaster prevention and reduction expenditure ($h^*$) under different coefficients of risk aversion ($\gamma$)

government productive expenditure ($x$), disaster loss ratio ($D(h^*)$), coefficient of risk aversion ($\gamma$), and discounted present value ($\beta$). In the present paper, the value of total factor productivity ($A$) is assigned to 3[3] (Ma 2016); discounted present value ($\beta$) is the loan rate of bank over the same period. Suppose there is a complementary relationship between private capital and government's productive expenditure, then $x$ is assigned to 0.625[4] (Qiu 2016; Lou 2012).

The values of the abovementioned parameters are as follows: $A = 3, b_2 = 0.2$, $x = 0.625$, $\beta = 0.952$, and $D(0) = 0.8$.[5] The value range of $p$ on x axis in Figs. 1.1, 1.2 and 1.3 is determined by constraint condition $R - \sigma > 0$ (see more details in Section "Solving the Optimal Disaster Prevention and Mitigation Policy").

### 1.4.2 *Impact of Risk Aversion Coefficient* $\gamma$

To illustrate the impact of coefficient of risk aversion ($\gamma$) on the optimal proportion of disaster prevention and reduction expenditure ($h^*$) under different probabilities of disaster ($p$), the correlation between the probability of disaster ($p$) and the optimal proportion of disaster prevention and reduction expenditure ($h^*$) under different coefficients of risk aversion ($\gamma$) is shown in Fig. 1.1, where the horizontal axis represents the probability of disaster $p$, and the vertical axis represents the optimal proportion of disaster prevention and reduction expenditure $h^*$.

[3] See Ma (2016) for the calculation of total factor productivity of technologically advanced region.

[4] According to the researches of Qiu (2016) and Lou (2012), though there is a complementary relationship between private capital and government's productive expenditure, the efficiency of government productive expenditure is decreasing, thus let $x = 0.625$.

[5] See Motoyama (2017) for parameter settings.

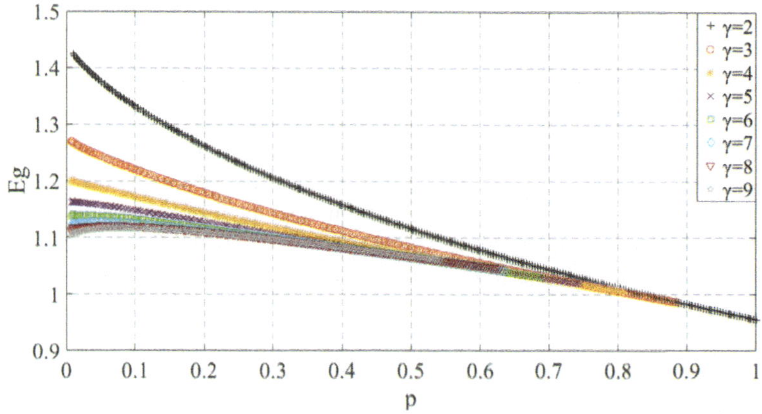


**Fig. 1.2** The expected growth rate $\left(E_g\right)$ under different coefficients of risk aversion $(\gamma)(0 \leq \mathrm{p} \leq 1)$

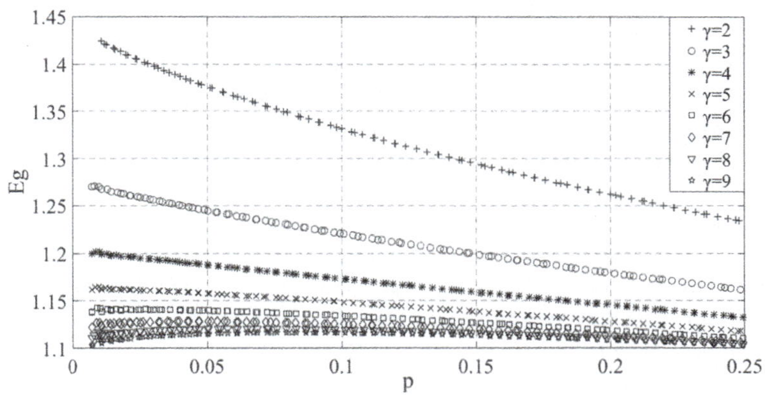


**Fig. 1.3** The expected growth rate $\left(E_g\right)$ under different coefficients of risk aversion $(\gamma)(0 \leq \mathrm{p} \leq 0.25)$

As can be known from Fig. 1.1, on condition that other parameters remain unchanged, the optimal proportion of disaster prevention and reduction expenditure $(h^*)$ increases monotonically along with the probability of disaster $(p)$. That is, under different coefficients of risk aversion $(\gamma)$, when the probability of disaster $(p)$ increases, the optimal proportion of disaster prevention and reduction expenditure $(h^*)$ will increase accordingly; besides, under the same probability of disaster $(p)$, the optimal proportion of disaster prevention and reduction expenditure $(h^*)$ will increase along with the coefficient of risk aversion $(\gamma)$. This indicates that residents' risk aversion will affect the optimal proportion of disaster prevention and reduction expenditure $(h^*)$; when the probability of disaster $(p)$ remains unchanged, residents' demand or dependence on expenditures for pre-disaster prevention and control varies with the degree of their aversion to disaster risk (Tian and Gao 2012). However, the increment of the optimal proportion of disaster prevention and reduction expenditure ($h^*$) caused by the change in residents' aversion to disaster risk gradually decreases as the probability of disaster ($p$) rises. It indicates that the optimal scale of disaster prevention and reduction expenditure is likely to be reduced through lowering residents' aversion to disaster risk if publicity and education lessons on disaster prevention and mitigation and disaster emergency management are taken by the public. But this method is obviously more suitable for situation with low probability of disaster ($p$). Because the gaps among the optimal proportions of disaster prevention and reduction expenditure ($h^*$) under different coefficients of risk aversion ($\gamma$) gradually narrow as the probability of disaster ($p$) increases. To be more specific, when the probability of disaster ($p$) is low, the differences among the optimal proportions of disaster prevention and reduction expenditure ($h^*$) under different coefficients of risk aversion ($\gamma$) are relatively large, so if science education is popularized in the public, residents' aversion to disaster risk, namely the coefficient of risk aversion ($\gamma$), is likely to be reduced, thereby indirectly affecting the optimal scale of disaster prevention and reduction expenditure and reducing the optimal proportion of disaster prevention and reduction expenditure ($h^*$). By contrast, when the probability of disaster ($p$) is high, the differences among the optimal proportions of disaster prevention and reduction expenditure ($h^*$) under different coefficients of risk aversion ($\gamma$) are small, in which case, it is not so effective to affect the optimal scale of disaster prevention and reduction expenditure by reducing residents' aversion to disaster risk.

With the same parameter setting, the expected growth rates $\left(E_g\right)$ under different under different coefficients of risk aversion ($\gamma$) can be obtained through Eq. (1.26), as shown in Figs. 1.2 and 1.3. The horizontal axis represents the probability of disaster $p$, and the vertical axis represents the expected growth rate $E_g$.

As can be known from Fig. 1.2, under different coefficients of risk aversion ($\gamma$), the expected growth rate $\left(E_g\right)$ decreases monotonically as the probability of disaster ($p$) increase, which is consistent with the conclusion that disasters retard economic development in the short term (Raddatz 2007; Hochrainer 2009). Meanwhile, the higher the coefficient of risk aversion ($\gamma$), the lower the expected growth rate $\left(E_g\right)$. It indicates that with the increase of risk aversion coefficient ($\gamma$), residents' aversion to disaster risks has a greater negative impact on the expected economic growth rate $\left(E_g\right)$. But as the probability of disaster ($p$) increases, the differences among the expected growth rates $\left(E_g\right)$ under different coefficients of risk aversion ($\gamma$) gradually decrease. This may mean that when residents have a strong aversion to disaster risk, the government's optimal expenditure on disaster prevention and reduction plays an important role in promoting the expected economic growth rate $\left(\mathrm{E_g}\right)$, effectively alleviating the negative impact of disasters on the expected economic growth.

Figure 1.3 shows the expected growth rates under different coefficients of risk aversion ($\gamma$) when the probability of disaster $p$ ranges within [0, 0.25]. As shown in Fig. 1.3, when the coefficient of risk aversion ($\gamma$) is equal to 2, the expected growth rate ($E_g$) keeps decreasing as the probability of disaster ($p$) increases; when the coefficient of risk aversion $\gamma$ is equal to 3, 4, 5, 6, 7, 8, or 9, the probability of disaster ($p$) and expected growth rate ($E_g$) do not always show a monotone decreasing relationship as the coefficient of risk aversion ($\gamma$) rises. In the event that the expected growth rate $\left(E_g\right)$ has an extreme point as the coefficient of risk aversion ($\gamma$) rises, the development of expected economic growth rate $\left(E_g\right)$ shows an inverted U-shaped trend (see Table 1.4 in Section "Expected growth rate ($E_g$) under different risk aversion coefficients ($\gamma$)" for more details). In other words, when the probability of disaster ($p$) is low, the optimal government expenditure on disaster prevention and mitigation has a stronger promoting effect on the expected growth rate $\left(E_g\right)$ as the coefficient of risk aversion ($\gamma$) rises; within a certain range, the expected economic growth rate $\left(E_g\right)$ will increase as the probability of disaster ($p$) rises.

### 1.4.3 Impacts of Other Parameters

Similarly, through Eq. (1.30), the impacts of other parameters, such as elasticity coefficient of substitution ($x$), input share of government's productive expenditure ($b_2$), upper limit of disaster loss ratio D(0), and efficiency of expenditure for disaster prevention and reduction can be analyzed. Due to the limitation of space, the analyzing process is neglected in this paper, and the main conclusions are presented as follows.

(1) In the case of fixed disaster probability, when the elasticity coefficient of substitution increases, the optimal proportion of government expenditure on disaster prevention and reduction will increase accordingly; however, the increment of the optimal proportion will reach its limit as the elasticity coefficient of substitution increases. In addition, when there is a complementary relationship between government's productive expenditure and private capital, the gaps among the expected economic growth rates under different elasticity coefficient of substitution will grow as the probability of disaster rises; yet this phenomenon is not obvious when the relationship becomes substitutional. It indicates that when the complementary relationship between government's productive expenditure and private capital is obvious, the probability of disaster has a great impact on the expected economic growth rates under different elasticity coefficients of substitution. This suggests that the socio-economic development of developing countries is more susceptible to disaster risks than that of developed ones.

(2) When there is a complementary relationship between government's productive expenditure and private capital, it is found that the reasonable control of input share of government's productive expenditure can reduce the optimal proportion of disaster prevention and reduction expenditure, but the expected economic growth will be retarded. By contrast, when there is a substitutional relationship between government's productive expenditure and private capital, if the optimal proportion of disaster prevention and reduction expenditure decreases with the increase of government's input share of productive expenditure, the expected growth rate will decrease as well.

(3) In the case of fixed probability of disaster, there is an inverted U relationship between the upper limit of disaster loss ratio and the optimal proportion of disaster prevention and reduction expenditure, indicating that reducing the upper limit of disaster loss ratio is of great significance for reducing the optimal proportion of disaster prevention and reduction expenditure and promoting the expected economic growth. When the disaster is extremely serious, the corresponding incremental expenditure for disaster prevention and reduction, after considering the opportunity cost of disaster prevention and reduction expenditure and weighing residents' welfare against financial gains and losses, is not the optimal strategy for disaster prevention and reduction. An excessive increase of expenditure on disaster prevention and reduction will increase the total social cost. On the contrary, an appropriate reduction of expenditure on disaster prevention and reduction can bring Schumpeter's creative destruction effect, promote the expected economic growth, and partly alleviate the resistance caused by disaster risk to economic growth.

(4) In the case of fixed probability of disaster, the higher the efficiency of disaster prevention and mitigation, the smaller the optimal proportion of disaster prevention and reduction expenditure. This indicates that improving the operational efficiency of disaster relief funds is conducive to easing the government's burden on disaster prevention and mitigation expenditure, thereby improving the level of social welfare.

## 1.5 Case Study

Taking the flood disaster of Hunan Province in 2014 as an example for case study, this paper first introduces the socio-economic impact of the flood disaster on Hunan Province, and then, briefly describes the data sources and processing approaches of the parameters required by the economic model. Finally, the optimal proportion of disaster prevention and reduction expenditure is simulated and compared with the actual proportion of disaster risk reduction expenditure of the government.

### *1.5.1 Flood Disasters in Hunan Province*

Located on the south bank of the Yangtze River, Hunan Province has a complex hydrographical condition and abundant water resources, but also suffers from flood disasters. In spring and summer, warm air and cold air frequently meet above Hunan Province, and most precipitation of a year is from April to July, coupled with the influence of the landform pattern which displays as high south and low north and high west and low east, so summer rainstorms concentrate in the middle and lower reaches of Xiang River, Zijiang River, Yuan River, and Lishui River and Dongting Lake area. In midsummer, the rainstorms caused by typhoon make these areas prone to flood disaster. Moreover, the rapid urbanization, accompanied by the inadequately developed flood control and drainage system, has made the cities in Hunan Province more vulnerable to flood disasters. Apart from that, the imperfect management of flood risk is another factor of flood disaster. The incomplete and infeasible disaster prevention and mitigation plans have also seriously affected the efficiency of disaster prevention and reduction (Yu et al. 2017; Li et al. 2014). These are the major factors that lead to the flood disasters in Hunan Province.

In 2014, Hunan Province suffered 8 flood disasters (among which the fourth and fifth rain processes are regarded as one flood disaster). A total of 10.247 million people in 1708 towns (villages) of 127 counties (including prefecture-lever cities, districts, and economic development zones) in 14 cities were affected by the floods, resulting in the death of 45 and the missing of 6. Besides, 27200 houses collapsed, and 1.1916 million people were evacuated in emergency; the direct economic loss reached RMB 15.226 billion (Hu 2015).

In recent years, Hunan Province has been improving its natural disaster defensing ability to reduce disaster loss. The defense methods, including defective reservoir reinforcement, comprehensive management of Dongting Lake, improvement of medium and small rivers, and reconstruction of dilapidated houses, are aimed at further improving large rivers' ability to prevent floods, reducing hidden dangers of geological disasters in densely populated areas and medium- and large-sized cities so as to enhance the overall defending ability of flood disasters (*2011–2015 Disaster Prevention and Mitigation Plan of Hunan Province*). In order to prevent flood disasters, Hunan Province has invested a lot in repairing and strengthening water conservancy projects and building flood control facilities. However, whether this is in line with the optimal proportion of disaster prevention and reduction expenditure will be evaluated by using the model proposed in this paper.

### 1.5.2 Parameter Estimation of CES Production Function

First, the parameters of the production function as shown in Eq. (1.9) need to be estimated. As the 2 Level-3 Factor CES is complicated, it is impossible to conduct a direct regression analysis. Therefore, based on the method proposed by Li (2012), the function in Eq. (1.9) is divided into first-order function and second-order function, as shown in Eqs. (1.31) and (1.32) respectively.

$$\mathrm{Y} = \mathrm{A}(\mathrm{b}_1\mathrm{K}^{\mathrm{m}_1} + \mathrm{b}_2\mathrm{G}^{\mathrm{m}_1})^{\frac{1}{\mathrm{m}_1}} \tag{1.31}$$

$$\mathrm{K} = (\theta_1\mathrm{k}^{\mathrm{m}} + \theta_2\mathrm{l}^{\mathrm{m}})^{\frac{1}{\mathrm{m}}} \tag{1.32}$$

According to direct estimation method, we take the logarithm of the two equations above, and apply the second order Taylor expression on $\rho_i = 0$ $(i = 1, 2)$:

$$\ln Y = \ln A + b_1 \ln K + b_2 \ln G + \frac{1}{2} m_1 b_1 b_2 \left[\ln\left(\frac{K}{G}\right)\right]^2 \tag{1.33}$$

$$\ln K = \theta_1 \ln k + \theta_2 \ln l + \frac{1}{2} m \theta_1 \theta_2 \left[\ln\left(\frac{k}{l}\right)\right]^2 \tag{1.34}$$

Substituting Eq. (1.33) into Eq. (1.34) and $b_2 = 1 - b_1$ and $\theta_1 = 1 - \theta_2$ into the above two equations, the following dependent linear equation can be obtained:

$$\begin{aligned}
\ln Y &= \ln A + b_1 \ln \frac{l}{G} + b_1\theta_1 \ln \frac{k}{l} + \frac{1}{2} m b_1 \theta_1 (1-\theta_1)\left[\ln\left(\frac{k}{l}\right)\right]^2 + \ln G + \frac{1}{2} m_1 b_1 (1-b_1) \\
&* [\theta_1^2\left[\ln\left(\frac{k}{l}\right)\right]^2 + \left[\ln\left(\frac{l}{G}\right)\right]^2 + \frac{1}{4} m^2 \theta_1^2 (1-\theta_1)^2 \left[\ln\left(\frac{k}{l}\right)\right]^4 + \theta_1 \ln \frac{k}{l} \ln \frac{l}{G} + m\theta_1^2 \\
&* (1-\theta_1)\left[\ln\left(\frac{k}{l}\right)\right]^3 + m\theta_1(1-\theta_1)\left[\ln\left(\frac{k}{l}\right)\right]^2 \ln\left(\frac{l}{G}\right)] + \varepsilon \\
&= \ln A + b_1 \ln \frac{l}{G} + b_1\theta_1 \ln \frac{k}{l} + \frac{1}{2} m b_1 \theta_1 (1-\theta_1)\left[\ln\left(\frac{k}{l}\right)\right]^2 \\
&+ \ln G + \frac{1}{2} m_1 b_1 (1-b_1) * \left[\theta_1^2 \ln \frac{k}{l} + \theta_2 \ln l + \frac{1}{2} m\theta_1\theta_2 \left[\ln\left(\frac{k}{l}\right)\right]^2 - \ln G\right]^2 + \varepsilon
\end{aligned} \tag{1.35}$$

Considering the effects of multicollinearity and computational complexity on parameter estimation, the higher order terms $\left[ln\left(\frac{k}{l}\right)\right]^2 \ln\left(\frac{l}{G}\right)$, $\left[ln\left(\frac{k}{l}\right)\right]^3$, and $\left[ln\left(\frac{k}{l}\right)\right]^4$ and cross term $ln\frac{k}{l}\ln\frac{l}{G}$ in the above equation are omitted. Then we get:

$$\begin{aligned}
lnY &= lnA + b_1 \ln \frac{l}{G} + b_1\theta_1 ln\frac{k}{l} + \frac{1}{2} m b_1 \theta_1 (1-\theta_1)\left[\ln\left(\frac{k}{l}\right)\right]^2 \\
&+ lnG + \frac{1}{2} m_1 b_1 (1-b_1)^* \left[\ln\left(\frac{1}{G}\right)\right]^2 + \varepsilon
\end{aligned} \tag{1.36}$$

After comparing Eq. (1.35) with Eq. (1.36), we believe that the coefficient of $\left[ln\left(\frac{k}{l}\right)\right]^2$ should include $\frac{1}{2} m_1 b_1 (1-b_1)\theta_1^2$ apart from $\frac{1}{2} m b_1 \theta_1 (1-\theta_1)$. If Eq. (1.33) is used for parameter estimation, then parameter $m$ may be overestimated. Therefore, Eq. (1.37) is used as the approximate form of Eq. (1.35).

$$\begin{aligned}
lnY &= lnA + b_1 ln\frac{l}{G} + b_1\theta_1 ln\frac{k}{l} + \left(\frac{1}{2} m b_1 \theta_1 (1-\theta_1) + \frac{1}{2} m_1 b_1 (1-b_1\right)\theta_1^2) \\
&\left[ln\left(\frac{k}{l}\right)\right]^2 + \ln G + \frac{1}{2} m_1 b_1 (1-b_1)\left[\ln\left(\frac{1}{G}\right)\right]^2 + \varepsilon
\end{aligned} \tag{1.37}$$

$$\begin{aligned}
ln\left(\frac{Y}{G}\right) &= lnA + b_1 ln\frac{l}{G} + b_1\theta_1 ln\frac{k}{l} + \left(\frac{1}{2} m b_1 \theta_1 (1-\theta_1) + \frac{1}{2} m_1 b_1 (1-b_1\right)\theta_1^2)\left[ln\left(\frac{k}{l}\right)\right]^2 \\
&+ \frac{1}{2} m_1 b_1 (1-b_1)\left[\ln\left(\frac{1}{G}\right)\right]]^2 + \varepsilon
\end{aligned} \tag{1.38}$$

**Table 1.1** Estimated results of parameters in CES production function

| Variable | Coefficient | Std. error | Prob. |
|---|---|---|---|
| $ln[l/G]$ | 0.296 ($\mu_1$) | 0.027 | 0.000 |
| $[ln(l/G)]^2$ | 0.043 ($\mu_2$) | 0.004 | 0.000 |
| $lnk/l$ | 0.176 ($\mu_3$) | 0.049 | 0.003 |
| $[ln(k/l)]^2$ | −0.068 ($\mu_4$) | 0.022 | 0.009 |
| Constant | 0.731 ($\mu_0$) | 0.093 | 0.000 |
| R-squared | 0.973 | | |
| Adjusted R-squared | 0.965 | | |
| S. E of regression | 0.066 | | |
| Prob (F-statistic) | 0.000 | | |

Through variable substitution, Eq. (1.38) can be formulated as:

$$Z = \mu_0 + \mu_1 X_1 + \mu_2 X_2 + \mu_3 X_3 + \mu_4 X_4 + \varepsilon \quad (1.39)$$

where $X_1 = \ln \frac{l}{G}$, $X_2 = \left[ln\left(\frac{l}{G}\right)\right]^2$, $X_3 = ln\frac{k}{l}$, $X_4 = \left[ln\left(\frac{k}{l}\right)\right]^2$, $\mu_0 = lnA$, $\mu_1 = b_1$, $\mu_2 = \frac{1}{2}m_1 b_1(1-b_1)$, $\mu_3 = b_1\theta_1$, and $\mu_4 = \frac{1}{2}mb_1\theta_1(1-\theta_1) + \frac{1}{2}m_1 b_1(1-b_1)\theta_1^2$. Then the estimated values of $\mu_0$, $\mu_1$, $\mu_2$, $\mu_3$, and $\mu_4$ can be obtained.

According to the methods mentioned above, relevant data from 1997 to 2015 were used to estimate the parameters in CES production function. The required data include GDP, material input, labor input, and government productive input. Material input $k$ was converted by base year 1997 by using the methods for calculating capital stock proposed by Zhang et al. (2004). Labor input $l$ is measured according to the employed people. Government productive input $G$ was converted by base year 1997; usually the productive expenditure includes fiscal education expenditure, capital construction expenditure,[6] expenditure on scientific research, and expenditures for medical care and public health. The data are from *China Statistical Yearbook*, and *Finance Yearbook of China* (see Table 1.2 for detailed data).

Due to the multicollinearity of model variables, parameter estimation based on OLS method is unreliable. To guarantee the identifiability of model (all variables must be preserved), the multicollinearity problem is solved by using ridged regression. The estimated results of parameters in CES production function are presented below (Table 1.1).

Based on the above empirical results, the following parameter values are obtained: $\mu_0 = 0.731$, $\mu_1 = 0.296$, $\mu_2 = 0.043$, $\mu_3 = 0.176$, and $\mu_4 = -0.068$. Because there is $\mu_1 = b_1$, $\mu_2 = \frac{1}{2}m_1 b_1(1-b_1)$, $\mu_3 = b_1\theta_1$, and $\mu_4 = \frac{1}{2}mb_1\theta_1(1-\theta_1) + \frac{1}{2}m_1 b_1(1-b_1)\theta_1^2$, through simultaneous equations, the values of parameters are obtained: $\theta_1 = 0.595$, $b_1 = 0.296$, $m_1 = 0.413$, $m = -2.33$, and $A = 2.077$.

[6]Due to the inconsistency in the statistical coverage of infrastructure expenditure in 2007 in the *Finance Yearbook of China*, the national budget in the stock of fixed assets is used as an alternative.

### 1.5.3 Estimation and Simulation Results of Other Parameters

With reference to the researches on the spatial and temporal distributions of floods in Human Province conducted by Wang et al. (2015) and Wang et al. (2003), the 14 cities or regions in Hunan Province are divided into five groups according to the frequency of flood disaster. They are Yiyang, Changde, and Yueyang; Xiangxi Autonomous Prefecture, Zhangjiajie, and Huaihua; Changsha, Xiangtan, Zhuzhou, and Loudi; Hengyang and Shaoyang; Chenzhou and Yongzhou. And their corresponding frequencies of flood are 80%, 40%, 30%, 27.5%, and 10%,[7] respectively. The upper limit of loss ratio $D(0)$[8] caused by flood disasters in Hunan Province was calculated with the frequencies of flood disaster of the 14 cities or regions and the proportions of GDP. According to the statistics of Wen et al. (2017) about the frequency of rainstorms and floods, the probability of disaster $p$ (including heavy rainstorms and large floods only) of Hunan Province is assumed to be 0.33 in this paper.

Taking the rainstorms and flood disasters in Hunan Province in 2014 as the research object, the values of parameters required in model (24) can be obtained by using the above data. Thus, there is $b_2 = 0.704, m_1 = 0.413, \beta = 0.980,$[9] $D(0) = 0.401$, and $\mathrm{A} = 2.077$. The optimal proportion of expenditure for disaster prevention and mitigation of Hunan Province obtained through simulation is 0.89%, yet the actual proportion in that year is 2.17%,[10] which is higher than the simulated results. It indicates that the expenditure on disaster prevention and reduction in that year is too high. It should be pointed out that the data collected mainly refer to the investment amount of water conservancy projects and expenditures for agriculture, forestry, and water affairs, and these expenditures are much larger than the disaster prevention and mitigation cost in that year.

## 1.6 Conclusions and Policy Suggestions

The innovations of the present paper are as follows. First, compared with the existing domestic and foreign studies which used economic models to simulate and analyze government expenditure on disaster prevention and reduction, this paper constructed a model which considered disaster's impact on human capital as well as its impact

[7] The data on the frequency of flood mainly come from the studies on the spatial and temporal distribution of flood in Hunan Province conducted by Wang et al. (2015) and Wang et al. (2003).

[8] It is obtained by multiplying the probability of disaster in each of the 14 cities by the city's GDP and then adding them up and dividing the sum by the total GDP of Hunan Province.

[9] The benchmark interest rate of one-year deposit in 2014 is used as the basis for discount.

[10] As some of the data on disaster prevention and reduction are unavailable, the proportion of investment in water conservancy construction and expenditures on agriculture, forestry and water affairs in the GDP of that year is regarded as the proportion of disaster prevention and reduction expenditure; the data come from *Hunan Statistical Yearbook* and *China Water Statistical Yearbook 2011* (see A6.2 for the detailed data).

on the optimal scale of government expenditure on disaster prevention and reduction when there was a complementary or substitutional relationship between government productive expenditure and private capital. Second, in numerical simulation, this paper, by assigning values to various parameters of the economic structure, obtained the optimal strategies for disaster prevention and reduction under different conditions. In this way, this paper not only analyzed the influencing factors of the optimal proportion of disaster prevention and reduction expenditure, but also simulated the expected economic growth rate and further discussed the impact of natural disasters on the expected economic growth rate in the short term. Third, to verify the reasonability of the model constructed in this paper, the model was used to calculate the optimal proportion of government expenditure on disaster prevention and mitigation of a practical case.

The policy suggestions of this paper are: First, the performance evaluation of disaster prevention and reduction expenditure should be carried out to test the effect of disaster prevention and mitigation work and improve the efficiency. In recent years, the focus of disaster management in many countries has shifted from post-disaster relief to pre-disaster prevention, but there still lacks practice in performance evaluation of disaster prevention and reduction expenditure. Thus, the content, index, and methods of performance evaluation on disaster prevention and reduction expenditure which are in line with the national conditions should be determined step by step. In addition, a regular working mechanism for evaluating the performance of disaster prevention and reduction expenditure should be established. In the stage of disaster prevention, disaster risk and disaster loss assessments shall be carried out so that the reasonable expenditure budget for disaster prevention and mitigation can be determined according to the levels of economic development and disaster risk in different places. Furthermore, the government should improve the supervision system, accelerate the process of legislation in natural disaster response and related fields, and improve the efficiency of use of disaster prevention and reduction funds.

Second, the disaster risk and loss assessment system should be improved to enhance the ability of predicting disaster. Disaster risk and disaster loss assessments are the major bases for the government to make budget for disaster prevention and mitigation. The comprehensive improvement of disaster risk and disaster loss assessment system can be started from the following two aspects: first, building professional teams for disaster evaluation, for example, establishing a training system for disaster evaluation professionals to promote the comprehensive risk assessment of natural disasters; second, based on the loss assessment cases of serious natural disaster around the world in recent years, building a standard content system for natural disaster loss assessment by means of consultation, expert forum, and simulation exercises in disaster-prone areas.

Third, the cooperation among government departments should be strengthened. Taking China as an example, a number of departments have been set up for disaster management, but these departments lack cooperation and the evaluation standard is oversimplified, so they cannot provide whole-process support for the improvement of disaster risk and disaster loss assessment system. Thus, it is suggested to use big date resources and analytical tools to build an integrated platform for disaster emergency management and disaster risk analysis so as to improve the cooperation abilities of government departments. In addition, developing countries should pay special attention to the transformation of production mode and lifestyle, so as to achieve the harmony between human and nature and reduce the probability of disaster and disaster loss ratio. Moreover, knowledge about disaster risk and response should be popularized among the public so as to create a good social and cultural atmosphere for the establishment of disaster risk guarantee system and to reduce residents' aversion to disaster risk and loss, thereby reducing the expenditure on disaster prevention and mitigation.

Last but not least, in future studies, the influence of multi-level catastrophe risk dispersion mechanism with financial support on the government's disaster prevention and reduction expenditure should be considered as well, for example, introducing catastrophe risk dispersion mechanism into model. Due to the difficulty in data acquisition, the expenditure on disaster prevention and reduction used in the case study was replaced by investment in water conservancy construction together with the expenditures on agriculture, forestry and water affairs. Next, the optimal scales of disaster prevention and reduction expenditure of different regions in Hunan Province can be obtained with the specific data of regions and industries.

**Acknowledgements** Zhijie Wang, Ge Gao, Peipei Xue, and Shaoli He also made great contributions to this manuscript. We express our heartfelt thanks to them. This research was supported by: National Social and Scientific Fund Program of China (18ZDA052; 17BGL142; 16ZDA047); The Natural Science Foundation of China (91546117, 71373131).

## Appendix: The Value Function of the Residents' Utility

According to formulas (1.4) and (1.5), $V(s) = max_{\{C,\tilde{a}\}}\left\{\frac{1}{1-\gamma}C^{1-\gamma} + \beta E_t V(\tilde{s})\right\}$ can be changed into the following form:

$$\mathrm{V(s)} = \max_{\{\tilde{a}\}}\left\{\frac{(\mathrm{Rs} - \tilde{a})^{1-\gamma}}{1-\gamma} + \beta p\mathrm{V}((1 - \mathrm{D(h)})\tilde{a}) + \beta(1 - p)\mathrm{V}(\tilde{a})\right\} \tag{1.40}$$

Assuming that $V(s) = \frac{(\alpha_1 s)^{1-\gamma}}{1-\gamma}$, $\alpha_1$ is unknown, we can get the following formula (1.41) if we add V(s) into the formula (1.40):

$$\frac{(\tilde{a}s)^{1-\gamma}}{1-\gamma} \max_{\{\tilde{a}\}} \left\{ \frac{(Rs-\tilde{a})^{1-\gamma}}{1-\gamma} + \beta p \frac{(\alpha_1(1-D(h))\tilde{a})^{1-\gamma}}{1-\gamma} + \beta(1-p)\frac{(\alpha_1\tilde{a})^{1-\gamma}}{1-\gamma} \right\} \tag{1.41}$$

Make $\rho(h) = \beta\big(p\big(1-D(h)\big)^{1-\gamma} + 1 - p\big)$, formula (1.41) can be simplified as follows:

$$(Rs-\tilde{a})^{1-\gamma} = (\alpha_1 s)^{1-\gamma} - \rho(\alpha_1\tilde{a})^{1-\gamma} \tag{1.42}$$

We can derive the first order derivative of $\tilde{a}$ on both sides of the formula, then the formula (1.43) is as follows:

$$\alpha_1 = (Rs-\tilde{a})^{\frac{-\gamma}{1-\gamma}} \rho^{\frac{-1}{1-\gamma}} \tilde{a}^{\frac{\gamma}{1-\gamma}} \tag{1.43}$$

Combining formula (1.42) can obtain the formula (1.44):

$$\tilde{a} = (R\rho)^{\frac{1}{\gamma}} s \tag{1.44}$$

## Solving the Optimal Disaster Prevention and Mitigation Policy

The formula 1.19 in the article

$$V^g(K) = max_\pi \left\{ \frac{1}{1-\gamma} C^{1-\gamma} + \beta E_t V^g\big(\widetilde{K}\big) \right\}$$

Can be changed into formula (1.45) as follows:

$$V^g(K) = \{ \frac{(R-\sigma)^{1-\gamma} K^{1-\gamma}}{1-\gamma} + \beta p V^g((1-D(h))\tilde{a}) + \beta(1-p)V^g(\tilde{a}) \} \tag{1.45}$$

By deriving K on both sides of the formula (1.45), the following formula can be obtained:

$$\frac{\partial V^{g}(K)}{\partial K} = (R-\sigma)^{1-\gamma} * K^{-\gamma} + \beta p V'^{g}((1-D(h))\tilde{a}) * ((1-D(h))\sigma) + \beta(1-p)V'^{g}(\tilde{a}) \tag{1.46}$$

By deriving τ on both sides of the formula (1.45), the following formula can be obtained:

$$0 = \frac{\partial(R-\sigma)^{1-\gamma}}{\partial\tau} * \frac{K^{-\gamma}}{1-\gamma} + \beta p V'^{g}((1-D(h))\tilde{a}) * (1-D(h))\frac{\partial\sigma}{\partial\tau} + \beta(1-p)V'^{g}(\tilde{a})\frac{\partial\sigma}{\partial\tau} \tag{1.47}$$

By deriving *h* on both sides of the formula (1.45), the following formula can be obtained:

$$0 = \frac{\partial(R-\sigma)^{1-\gamma}}{\partial h} * \frac{K^{-\gamma}}{1-\gamma} + \beta p V'^{g}((1-D(h))\tilde{a}) * \left((1-D(h))\frac{\partial\sigma}{\partial h} - D'(h)\sigma\right) + \beta(1-p)V'^{g}(\tilde{a})\frac{\partial\sigma}{\partial h} \tag{1.48}$$

Assuming that $V^{g}(K) = \frac{\alpha_2 K^{1-\gamma}}{1-\gamma} + \alpha_3$, $\alpha_2$ and $\alpha_3$ are unknown, add $V^{g}(K)$ into formula (1.45) can draw the following formula:

$\alpha_2 = R(R-\sigma)^{-\gamma}$, 即$V'^{g}(K) = R(R-\sigma)^{-\gamma} * K^{-\gamma}$

Therefore the formula (1.46), (1.47) can be transformed into formula (1.49) and (1.50) respectively:

$$0 = \frac{\partial(R-\sigma)^{1-\gamma}}{\partial\tau} * \frac{1}{1-\gamma} + (R-\sigma)^{-\gamma}\frac{\partial\sigma}{\partial\tau} \tag{1.49}$$

$$0 = \frac{\partial(R-\sigma)^{1-\gamma}}{\partial h} * \frac{1}{1-\gamma} + (R-\sigma)^{-\gamma}\frac{\partial\sigma}{\partial h} + (R-\sigma)^{-\gamma}\frac{\sigma F(h)}{\rho} \tag{1.50}$$

Among them, $F(h) = \beta p\frac{-D'(h)}{(1-D(h))^{\gamma}}$, $\sigma = (R\rho(h))^{1/\gamma}$, $\rho(h) = \beta\big(p(1-D(h))^{1-\gamma} + 1 - p\big)$, $R = (1-\tau)Ab_1^{\frac{1}{m_1}}B(g)$, so the formula (1.49), (1.50) can be simplified deeply as follows:

$$(R-\sigma)^{-\gamma}\big[(1-\tau)B' - B\big] = 0 \tag{1.51}$$

$$(R-\sigma)^{-\gamma}\left[\frac{(1-\tau)B'}{B} - \sigma\frac{F(h)}{\rho}\right] = 0 \tag{1.52}$$

Among them, $B' = \frac{\partial B}{\partial \tau}$, 因为 $(R-\sigma)^{-\gamma} > 0$, so $(1-\tau)B' = B$, 由于 $B(g) = (1 - b_2 A^{m_1} g^{m_1})^{-\frac{1}{m_1}}$, Considering $g = \tau - h$, so $B(g)$ can be transformed into a function which relates to h. Namely $B(h) = \left(1 - b_2^{\frac{1}{1-m_1}} A^{\frac{m_1}{1-m_1}} (1-h)^{\frac{m_1}{1-m_1}}\right)^{-\frac{1}{m_1}}$

Because of $(1-\tau)B' = B$, $(R-\sigma)^{-\gamma} > 0$, so formula (1.51) can be simplified as $\sigma \frac{F(h)}{\rho} = 1$.

## Substitute Elasticity Derivation of CES Production Function

When the return on scale is constant, the CES production function (Constant Elasticity of Substitution) usually gives the following forms:

$$Y = A\left(\theta_1 k^m + \theta_2 l^m\right)^{\frac{1}{m}} \tag{1.53}$$

$A$ is the efficiency parameter, representing the output efficiency of the economic system. $\theta_1, \theta_2 \in (0, 1)$ are the share of the input of production factors in the production process. These parameters are independent of substitution elasticity. The so-called substitution elasticity refers to the ratio of the relative change of input ratio of factors of production to the relative change of marginal substitution rate in a production system under the condition of constant output efficiency. The definition of alternative elasticity is as follows: $e = \frac{d(k/l)}{k/l} / \frac{d\left(\frac{\partial k}{\partial l}\right)}{\frac{\partial k}{\partial l}} = \frac{d(k/l)}{k/l} / \frac{d\left(\frac{\partial Y}{\partial l} / \frac{\partial Y}{\partial k}\right)}{\frac{\partial Y}{\partial l} / \frac{\partial Y}{\partial k}}$. Among the formula:

$$\frac{\partial \mathrm{Y}}{\partial \mathrm{l}} = \mathrm{A} * \frac{1}{\mathrm{m}} * (\theta_1 \mathrm{k}^{\mathrm{m}} + \theta_2 \mathrm{l}^{\mathrm{m}})^{\frac{1}{\mathrm{m}} - 1} * \theta_2 * \mathrm{m} * \mathrm{l}^{\mathrm{m}-1} \tag{1.54}$$

$$\frac{\partial \mathrm{Y}}{\partial \mathrm{k}} = \mathrm{A} * \frac{1}{\mathrm{m}} * (\theta_1 \mathrm{k}^{\mathrm{m}} + \theta_2 \mathrm{l}^{\mathrm{m}})^{\frac{1}{\mathrm{m}} - 1} * \theta_1 * \mathrm{m} * \mathrm{k}^{\mathrm{m}-1} \tag{1.55}$$

(1.51)/(1.52) can obtain the formula (1.56):

$$\frac{\partial \mathrm{Y}}{\partial \mathrm{l}} / \frac{\partial \mathrm{Y}}{\partial \mathrm{k}} = \frac{\theta_2}{\theta_1} * \left(\frac{\mathrm{k}}{\mathrm{l}}\right)^{1-\mathrm{m}} \tag{1.56}$$

Adding the formula (1.56) to the definition of alternative elasticity can get the formula (1.57):

$$\mathrm{e} = \frac{\mathrm{d(k/l)}}{\mathrm{k/l}} / \frac{\mathrm{d}\left(\frac{\partial \mathrm{Y}}{\partial \mathrm{l}} / \frac{\partial \mathrm{Y}}{\partial \mathrm{k}}\right)}{\frac{\partial \mathrm{Y}}{\partial \mathrm{l}} / \frac{\partial \mathrm{Y}}{\partial \mathrm{k}}} = \frac{\mathrm{dln(k/l)}}{\mathrm{dln(k/l)}^{1-\mathrm{m}}} = \frac{1}{1-\mathrm{m}} \tag{1.57}$$

From the above formula, we can see that the substitution elasticity coefficient of material capital and human capital is $e = \frac{1}{1-m}$. Similarly, we can infer that the substitution elasticity coefficient of private capital and government productive expenditure is $x = \frac{1}{1-m_1}$. When the coefficient of substitution elasticity approaches zero, it shows that the relationship between the two factors is close to complete substitution, which is similar to the fixed input proportional production function (Lyontyff production function); when the substitution elasticity tends to infinity, it shows that the two factors can be completely substituted, such as linear production function. When the substitution elasticity tends to be 1, it approximates the Cobb Douglas production function, which shows that there can be partial substitution between production factors.

## Conversion of CES Function Form

The CES function of the formula (1.9) in the article is as follows:

$$Y = A(b_1\left(\theta_1 k^m + \theta_2 l^m\right)^{\frac{m_1}{m}} + b_2 G^{m_1})^{\frac{\alpha}{m_1}}$$

Make $K = (\theta_1 k^m + \theta_2 l^m)^{\frac{1}{m}}$, Suppose $\alpha = 1$

$$\mathrm{Y} = \mathrm{A}(\mathrm{b}_1(\theta_1\mathrm{k}^{\mathrm{m}} + \theta_2\mathrm{l}^{\mathrm{m}})^{\frac{\mathrm{m}_1}{\mathrm{m}}} + \mathrm{b}_2\mathrm{G}^{\mathrm{m}_1})^{\frac{1}{\mathrm{m}_1}} = \mathrm{A}(\mathrm{b}_1\mathrm{K}^{\mathrm{m}_1} + \mathrm{b}_2\mathrm{G}^{\mathrm{m}_1})^{\frac{1}{\mathrm{m}_1}} \tag{1.58}$$

Because $\mathrm{G} = \mathrm{gY}$, so:

$$\mathrm{Y} = \mathrm{A}(\mathrm{b}_1\mathrm{K}^{\mathrm{m}_1} + \mathrm{b}_2\mathrm{g}^{\mathrm{m}_1}\mathrm{Y}^{\mathrm{m}_1})^{\frac{1}{\mathrm{m}_1}} \tag{1.59}$$

$$\mathrm{Y}^{\mathrm{m}_1} = \mathrm{A}^{\mathrm{m}_1}(\mathrm{b}_1\mathrm{K}^{\mathrm{m}_1} + \mathrm{b}_2\mathrm{g}^{\mathrm{m}_1}\mathrm{Y}^{\mathrm{m}_1})$$

$$= \mathrm{A}^{\mathrm{m}_1}\mathrm{b}_1\mathrm{K}^{\mathrm{m}_1}(1 - \mathrm{A}^{\mathrm{m}_1}\mathrm{b}_2\mathrm{g}^{\mathrm{m}_1})^{-1} \tag{1.60}$$

Finally, the CES function of formula (1.9) in the article can be transformed into formula (1.10):

$$Y = Ab_1^{\frac{1}{m_1}} K\left(1 - b_2 A^{m_1} g^{m_1}\right)^{-\frac{1}{m_1}}$$

## Constraint Conditions

$C = (R - \sigma(\tau, h))s$, $R = [1 + (1 - \tau)r - \delta]$ is the rate of return on savings. $\sigma(\tau, h) = (R(\rho(h))^{1/\gamma}$ is the savings rate of residents to current capital (current savings re-savings rate), Because it is assumed that household consumption is greater than 0, so make $R - \sigma > 0$. Among them:

$$R = (1 - \tau)Ab_1^{\frac{1}{m_1}} B(g)$$

$$= \left(1 - [(1 - h) * A^{m_1} b_2]^{\frac{1}{1-m_1}} - h\right) * A * b_1^{\frac{1}{m_1}} * \left(1 - b_2^{\frac{1}{1-m_1}} A^{\frac{m_1}{1-m_1}} (1 - h)^{\frac{m_1}{1-m_1}}\right)^{-\frac{1}{m_1}} \quad (1.61)$$

$$\sigma(\tau^*, h^*) = \left(R^* \rho(h^*)\right)^{1/\gamma} \quad (1.62)$$

$$\rho(h^*) = \beta(p(1 - D(h))^{1-\gamma} + 1 - p) \quad (1.63)$$

## Data

See Tables 1.2 and 1.3.

## Expected Growth Rate $(E_g)$ Under Different Risk Aversion Coefficients $(\gamma)$

See Table 1.4.

**Table 1.2** Data used in CES model (Data GDP, employees and capital stock refer to the 1997–2015 China Statistical Yearbook, and data productive expenditure refers to the 1997–2015 China Financial Statistics Yearbook. These data are converted based on 1997)

| Years | GDP(billion yuan) | Employees (thousand people) | Capital stock (billion yuan) | Productive expenditure (billion yuan) |
|---|---|---|---|---|
| 1997 | 2993.00 | 35602.90 | 3801.20 | 167.76 |
| 1998 | 3247.39 | 36031.70 | 4199.46 | 197.39 |
| 1999 | 3520.11 | 36013.90 | 4502.32 | 401.07 |
| 2000 | 3836.90 | 35775.80 | 5128.38 | 345.56 |
| 2001 | 4182.19 | 36079.60 | 5711.78 | 405.59 |
| 2002 | 4558.60 | 36445.20 | 6387.07 | 456.77 |
| 2003 | 4996.19 | 36947.80 | 7108.39 | 527.05 |
| 2004 | 5600.80 | 37471.00 | 8065.71 | 480.43 |
| 2005 | 6284.14 | 38014.80 | 9111.09 | 535.94 |
| 2006 | 7088.44 | 38421.70 | 10473.30 | 607.10 |
| 2007 | 8151.75 | 38834.10 | 12088.08 | 854.16 |
| 2008 | 9284.85 | 39100.60 | 14021.59 | 1359.39 |
| 2009 | 10556.93 | 39352.10 | 16405.27 | 1900.72 |
| 2010 | 12098.24 | 39827.30 | 19847.20 | 1935.46 |
| 2011 | 13646.82 | 40050.30 | 24282.64 | 1931.96 |
| 2012 | 15188.91 | 40193.10 | 28654.77 | 2567.87 |
| 2013 | 16722.99 | 40364.50 | 33924.11 | 2565.19 |
| 2014 | 18311.67 | 40441.30 | 39201.99 | 3052.83 |
| 2015 | 19868.16 | 39803.00 | 44959.82 | 3473.41 |

**Table 1.3** Expenditure Ratio for Waterlogging Prevention in Hunan Province in 2014 (Data GDP, expenditure on agriculture, forestry and water affairs came from the Hunan Statistical Yearbook in 2014, and data investment in water resources construction came from the China Statistical Yearbook of Water Resources in 2014)

| Years | GDP (billion yuan) | Investment in water conservancy construction (billion yuan) | Expenditure on agriculture, forestry and water affairs (billion yuan) | Waterlogging control expenditure Ratio |
|---|---|---|---|---|
| 2014 | 27037.32 | 147.33 | 423.72 | 2.17% |

**Table 1.4** Expected growth rate $(E_g)$ under different risk aversion coefficients $(\gamma)$

| R = 2 | | R = 3 | | R = 4 | | R = 5 | | R = 6 | | R = 7 | | R = 8 | | R = 9 | |
|---|---|---|---|---|---|---|---|---|---|---|---|---|---|---|---|
| *p* | *Eg* | *p* | *Eg* | *p* | *Eg* | *p* | *Eg* | *p* | *Eg* | *p* | *Eg* | *p* | *Eg* | *p* | *Eg* |
| 0.010641 | 1.423512 | 0.007200 | 1.269935 | 0.007229 | 1.199981 | 0.007200 | 1.161646 | 0.007229 | 1.137821 | 0.007200 | 1.122080 | 0.007229 | 1.111280 | 0.007229 | 1.103307 |
| 0.010843 | 1.422799 | 0.008201 | 1.270841 | 0.008733 | 1.202324 | 0.008441 | 1.164398 | 0.007413 | 1.138370 | 0.009070 | 1.127058 | 0.008110 | 1.114137 | 0.007455 | 1.104128 |
| 0.013036 | 1.420551 | 0.009819 | 1.270250 | 0.010061 | 1.201891 | 0.009840 | 1.165160 | 0.009302 | 1.142445 | 0.010171 | 1.127058 | 0.009719 | 1.117153 | 0.009401 | 1.109440 |
| 0.014458 | 1.417569 | 0.010790 | 1.267346 | 0.010822 | 1.199173 | 0.010608 | 1.162988 | 0.010318 | 1.141704 | 0.010721 | 1.124471 | 0.010518 | 1.115787 | 0.010372 | 1.109031 |
| 0.015236 | 1.416867 | 0.010800 | 1.267306 | 0.010843 | 1.199065 | 0.010800 | 1.161898 | 0.010843 | 1.138843 | 0.010800 | 1.123813 | 0.010843 | 1.113360 | 0.010816 | 1.106189 |
| 0.017776 | 1.413212 | 0.012997 | 1.267268 | 0.012917 | 1.200286 | 0.012215 | 1.163526 | 0.010851 | 1.138856 | 0.012538 | 1.126489 | 0.011344 | 1.114365 | 0.010843 | 1.105905 |
| 0.018072 | 1.412616 | 0.014400 | 1.264966 | 0.014257 | 1.198696 | 0.013743 | 1.163270 | 0.012967 | 1.141449 | 0.013893 | 1.126258 | 0.013285 | 1.116713 | 0.012873 | 1.109360 |
| 0.020708 | 1.409567 | 0.014468 | 1.264973 | 0.014458 | 1.198233 | 0.014400 | 1.161898 | 0.014175 | 1.140385 | 0.014400 | 1.125004 | 0.014316 | 1.115392 | 0.014108 | 1.108891 |
| 0.021687 | 1.407951 | 0.016882 | 1.264238 | 0.016403 | 1.198767 | 0.015255 | 1.162569 | 0.014458 | 1.139646 | 0.015405 | 1.126142 | 0.014458 | 1.114950 | 0.014458 | 1.107915 |
| 0.023768 | 1.405680 | 0.018000 | 1.262779 | 0.018049 | 1.197257 | 0.017227 | 1.162683 | 0.016080 | 1.141027 | 0.017299 | 1.126688 | 0.016416 | 1.117001 | 0.015854 | 1.109658 |
| 0.025301 | 1.403457 | 0.019052 | 1.262571 | 0.018072 | 1.197222 | 0.018000 | 1.161769 | 0.017736 | 1.140529 | 0.018000 | 1.125870 | 0.017911 | 1.116390 | 0.017618 | 1.109980 |
| 0.027031 | 1.401634 | 0.021383 | 1.260817 | 0.020593 | 1.197234 | 0.019185 | 1.162310 | 0.018072 | 1.140063 | 0.019202 | 1.126786 | 0.018072 | 1.116149 | 0.018072 | 1.109419 |
| 0.028916 | 1.399127 | 0.021600 | 1.260547 | 0.021687 | 1.196314 | 0.021261 | 1.161812 | 0.019978 | 1.141057 | 0.021242 | 1.126800 | 0.020323 | 1.117686 | 0.019781 | 1.110861 |
| 0.030530 | 1.397457 | 0.024192 | 1.259397 | 0.022946 | 1.196385 | 0.021600 | 1.161496 | 0.021687 | 1.140264 | 0.021600 | 1.126506 | 0.021687 | 1.117125 | 0.021649 | 1.110589 |
| 0.032530 | 1.394943 | 0.025200 | 1.258449 | 0.025301 | 1.195230 | 0.023819 | 1.161866 | 0.021866 | 1.140364 | 0.023778 | 1.127443 | 0.022359 | 1.117596 | 0.021687 | 1.110558 |
| 0.034273 | 1.393155 | 0.027071 | 1.257687 | 0.025326 | 1.195232 | 0.025200 | 1.161185 | 0.024536 | 1.140879 | 0.025200 | 1.127011 | 0.024885 | 1.118119 | 0.024467 | 1.111914 |
| 0.036145 | 1.390885 | 0.028800 | 1.256357 | 0.028306 | 1.194649 | 0.026323 | 1.161396 | 0.025301 | 1.140482 | 0.026233 | 1.127461 | 0.025301 | 1.117926 | 0.025301 | 1.111669 |
| 0.038252 | 1.388726 | 0.030118 | 1.255839 | 0.028916 | 1.194254 | 0.028800 | 1.160744 | 0.027225 | 1.140954 | 0.028800 | 1.127330 | 0.027755 | 1.118804 | 0.027246 | 1.112584 |
| 0.039759 | 1.386940 | 0.032400 | 1.254306 | 0.031389 | 1.193813 | 0.028947 | 1.160772 | 0.028916 | 1.140518 | 0.028824 | 1.127340 | 0.028916 | 1.118590 | 0.028916 | 1.112516 |
| 0.042454 | 1.384168 | 0.033388 | 1.253915 | 0.032530 | 1.193222 | 0.032046 | 1.160501 | 0.030012 | 1.140780 | 0.032006 | 1.127775 | 0.030742 | 1.119201 | 0.030200 | 1.113075 |

(continued)

**Table 1.4** (continued)

| R = 2 | | R = 3 | | R = 4 | | R = 5 | | R = 6 | | R = 7 | | R = 8 | | R = 9 | |
|---|---|---|---|---|---|---|---|---|---|---|---|---|---|---|---|
| *p* | *Eg* | *p* | *Eg* | *p* | *Eg* | *p* | *Eg* | *p* | *Eg* | *p* | *Eg* | *p* | *Eg* | *p* | *Eg* |
| 0.043373 | 1.383093 | 0.036000 | 1.252299 | 0.034647 | 1.192839 | 0.032400 | 1.160337 | 0.032530 | 1.140464 | 0.032400 | 1.127662 | 0.032530 | 1.119109 | 0.032530 | 1.113233 |
| 0.046861 | 1.379484 | 0.036907 | 1.251929 | 0.036145 | 1.192170 | 0.035351 | 1.160121 | 0.033021 | 1.140570 | 0.035361 | 1.128011 | 0.033976 | 1.119536 | 0.033465 | 1.113590 |
| 0.046988 | 1.379336 | 0.039600 | 1.250332 | 0.038127 | 1.191783 | 0.036000 | 1.159877 | 0.036145 | 1.140365 | 0.036000 | 1.127881 | 0.036145 | 1.119539 | 0.036145 | 1.113858 |
| 0.050602 | 1.375677 | 0.040680 | 1.249872 | 0.039759 | 1.191111 | 0.038854 | 1.159619 | 0.036328 | 1.140397 | 0.038943 | 1.128130 | 0.037530 | 1.119877 | 0.037103 | 1.114162 |
| 0.051642 | 1.374716 | 0.043200 | 1.248399 | 0.041849 | 1.190656 | 0.039600 | 1.159371 | 0.039759 | 1.140230 | 0.039600 | 1.128018 | 0.039759 | 1.119898 | 0.039759 | 1.114404 |
| 0.054217 | 1.372093 | 0.044698 | 1.247726 | 0.043373 | 1.190048 | 0.042584 | 1.159024 | 0.039960 | 1.140256 | 0.042783 | 1.128157 | 0.041422 | 1.120206 | 0.041123 | 1.114740 |
| 0.056623 | 1.369823 | 0.046800 | 1.246493 | 0.045814 | 1.189448 | 0.043200 | 1.158830 | 0.043373 | 1.140061 | 0.043200 | 1.128089 | 0.043373 | 1.120191 | 0.043373 | 1.114873 |
| 0.057831 | 1.368577 | 0.048947 | 1.245476 | 0.046988 | 1.188978 | 0.046550 | 1.158336 | 0.043917 | 1.140104 | 0.046800 | 1.128105 | 0.045640 | 1.120470 | 0.045497 | 1.115241 |
| 0.061446 | 1.365128 | 0.050400 | 1.244609 | 0.050013 | 1.188142 | 0.046800 | 1.158257 | 0.046988 | 1.139857 | 0.046921 | 1.128121 | 0.046988 | 1.120416 | 0.046988 | 1.115264 |
| 0.061805 | 1.364815 | 0.053404 | 1.243107 | 0.050602 | 1.187900 | 0.050400 | 1.157681 | 0.048177 | 1.139887 | 0.050400 | 1.128122 | 0.050150 | 1.120607 | 0.050173 | 1.115587 |
| 0.065060 | 1.361746 | 0.054000 | 1.242743 | 0.054217 | 1.186822 | 0.050869 | 1.157653 | 0.050602 | 1.139615 | 0.051573 | 1.128204 | 0.050602 | 1.120571 | 0.050602 | 1.115573 |
| 0.067332 | 1.359714 | 0.057600 | 1.240908 | 0.054490 | 1.186767 | 0.054000 | 1.157104 | 0.052707 | 1.139555 | 0.054000 | 1.128088 | 0.054217 | 1.120705 | 0.054217 | 1.115859 |
| 0.068675 | 1.358421 | 0.058156 | 1.240670 | 0.057831 | 1.185771 | 0.055533 | 1.156938 | 0.054217 | 1.139331 | 0.056471 | 1.128108 | 0.055172 | 1.120805 | 0.055441 | 1.116023 |
| 0.072289 | 1.355153 | 0.061200 | 1.239107 | 0.059369 | 1.185398 | 0.057600 | 1.156499 | 0.057467 | 1.139068 | 0.057600 | 1.127999 | 0.057831 | 1.120815 | 0.057831 | 1.116109 |
| 0.073057 | 1.354505 | 0.063230 | 1.238167 | 0.061446 | 1.184708 | 0.060404 | 1.156061 | 0.057831 | 1.139000 | 0.061200 | 1.127868 | 0.060588 | 1.120906 | 0.061072 | 1.116291 |
| 0.075904 | 1.351936 | 0.064800 | 1.237317 | 0.064423 | 1.183863 | 0.061200 | 1.155863 | 0.061446 | 1.138678 | 0.061681 | 1.127886 | 0.061446 | 1.120858 | 0.061446 | 1.116280 |
| 0.079057 | 1.349200 | 0.068400 | 1.235537 | 0.065060 | 1.183629 | 0.064800 | 1.155221 | 0.062715 | 1.138625 | 0.064800 | 1.127750 | 0.065060 | 1.120877 | 0.065060 | 1.116447 |
| 0.079518 | 1.348774 | 0.068454 | 1.235514 | 0.068675 | 1.182565 | 0.065615 | 1.155124 | 0.065060 | 1.138337 | 0.067407 | 1.127677 | 0.066469 | 1.120939 | 0.067347 | 1.116580 |
| 0.083133 | 1.345653 | 0.072000 | 1.233795 | 0.069837 | 1.182277 | 0.068400 | 1.154588 | 0.068226 | 1.138025 | 0.068400 | 1.127578 | 0.068675 | 1.120879 | 0.068675 | 1.116566 |

(continued)

**Table 1.4** (continued)

| R = 2 | | R = 3 | | R = 4 | | R = 5 | | R = 6 | | R = 7 | | R = 8 | | R = 9 | |
|---|---|---|---|---|---|---|---|---|---|---|---|---|---|---|---|
| *p* | *Eg* | *p* | *Eg* | *p* | *Eg* | *p* | *Eg* | *p* | *Eg* | *p* | *Eg* | *p* | *Eg* | *p* | *Eg* |
| 0.085362 | 1.343801 | 0.074109 | 1.232834 | 0.072289 | 1.181507 | 0.071179 | 1.154117 | 0.068675 | 1.137948 | 0.072000 | 1.127388 | 0.072289 | 1.120823 | 0.072289 | 1.116649 |
| 0.086747 | 1.342582 | 0.075600 | 1.232062 | 0.075507 | 1.180573 | 0.072000 | 1.153922 | 0.072289 | 1.137570 | 0.073525 | 1.127356 | 0.072767 | 1.120842 | 0.074122 | 1.116733 |
| 0.090361 | 1.339552 | 0.079200 | 1.230343 | 0.075904 | 1.180433 | 0.075600 | 1.153259 | 0.074223 | 1.137410 | 0.075600 | 1.127188 | 0.075904 | 1.120779 | 0.075904 | 1.116713 |
| 0.091911 | 1.338310 | 0.079953 | 1.230020 | 0.079518 | 1.179378 | 0.077102 | 1.153030 | 0.075904 | 1.137169 | 0.079200 | 1.126947 | 0.079518 | 1.120676 | 0.079518 | 1.116738 |
| 0.093976 | 1.336564 | 0.082800 | 1.228647 | 0.081583 | 1.178820 | 0.079200 | 1.152591 | 0.079518 | 1.136741 | 0.080063 | 1.126924 | 0.079616 | 1.120678 | 0.081504 | 1.116787 |
| 0.097590 | 1.333618 | 0.086097 | 1.227117 | 0.083133 | 1.178319 | 0.082800 | 1.151900 | 0.080553 | 1.136659 | 0.082800 | 1.126714 | 0.083133 | 1.120585 | 0.083133 | 1.116749 |
| 0.098730 | 1.332731 | 0.086400 | 1.226961 | 0.086747 | 1.177257 | 0.083331 | 1.151823 | 0.083133 | 1.136320 | 0.086400 | 1.126440 | 0.086747 | 1.120445 | 0.086747 | 1.116729 |
| 0.101205 | 1.330705 | 0.090000 | 1.225294 | 0.087937 | 1.176948 | 0.086400 | 1.151226 | 0.086747 | 1.135865 | 0.087105 | 1.126413 | 0.087077 | 1.120446 | 0.089529 | 1.116726 |
| 0.104819 | 1.327836 | 0.092591 | 1.224136 | 0.090361 | 1.176206 | 0.089952 | 1.150534 | 0.087310 | 1.135817 | 0.090000 | 1.126174 | 0.090361 | 1.120311 | 0.090361 | 1.116691 |
| 0.105830 | 1.327067 | 0.093600 | 1.223641 | 0.093976 | 1.175148 | 0.090000 | 1.150522 | 0.090361 | 1.135422 | 0.093600 | 1.125873 | 0.093976 | 1.120140 | 0.093976 | 1.116633 |
| 0.108434 | 1.324992 | 0.097200 | 1.222000 | 0.094627 | 1.174981 | 0.093600 | 1.149836 | 0.093976 | 1.134947 | 0.094688 | 1.125813 | 0.095162 | 1.120114 | 0.097590 | 1.116551 |
| 0.112048 | 1.322192 | 0.099370 | 1.221056 | 0.097590 | 1.174102 | 0.097013 | 1.149171 | 0.094543 | 1.134893 | 0.097200 | 1.125576 | 0.097590 | 1.119967 | 0.098285 | 1.116554 |
| 0.113219 | 1.321320 | 0.100800 | 1.220375 | 0.101205 | 1.173049 | 0.097200 | 1.149127 | 0.097590 | 1.134482 | 0.100800 | 1.125254 | 0.101205 | 1.119768 | 0.101205 | 1.116461 |
| 0.115663 | 1.319416 | 0.104400 | 1.218761 | 0.101688 | 1.172925 | 0.100800 | 1.148428 | 0.101205 | 1.133992 | 0.102813 | 1.125102 | 0.103846 | 1.119640 | 0.104819 | 1.116344 |
| 0.119277 | 1.316678 | 0.106456 | 1.217880 | 0.104819 | 1.172007 | 0.104400 | 1.147712 | 0.102271 | 1.133875 | 0.104400 | 1.124928 | 0.104819 | 1.119560 | 0.107833 | 1.116256 |
| 0.120895 | 1.315493 | 0.108000 | 1.217162 | 0.108434 | 1.170961 | 0.104467 | 1.147702 | 0.104819 | 1.133506 | 0.108000 | 1.124587 | 0.108434 | 1.119337 | 0.108434 | 1.116219 |
| 0.122892 | 1.313966 | 0.111600 | 1.215573 | 0.109134 | 1.170779 | 0.108000 | 1.147005 | 0.108434 | 1.133003 | 0.111455 | 1.124253 | 0.112048 | 1.119098 | 0.112048 | 1.116074 |
| 0.126506 | 1.311284 | 0.113860 | 1.214613 | 0.112048 | 1.169922 | 0.111600 | 1.146285 | 0.110487 | 1.132745 | 0.111600 | 1.124234 | 0.113229 | 1.119043 | 0.115663 | 1.115914 |
| 0.128854 | 1.309589 | 0.115200 | 1.213999 | 0.115663 | 1.168882 | 0.112394 | 1.146146 | 0.112048 | 1.132499 | 0.115200 | 1.123877 | 0.115663 | 1.118854 | 0.118243 | 1.115817 |

(continued)

**Table 1.4** (continued)

| R = 2 | | R = 3 | | R = 4 | | R = 5 | | R = 6 | | R = 7 | | R = 8 | | R = 9 | |
|---|---|---|---|---|---|---|---|---|---|---|---|---|---|---|---|
| *p* | *Eg* | *p* | *Eg* | *p* | *Eg* | *p* | *Eg* | *p* | *Eg* | *p* | *Eg* | *p* | *Eg* | *p* | *Eg* |
| 0.130120 | 1.308636 | 0.118800 | 1.212432 | 0.116965 | 1.168536 | 0.115200 | 1.145568 | 0.115663 | 1.131984 | 0.118800 | 1.123505 | 0.119277 | 1.118591 | 0.119277 | 1.115748 |
| 0.133735 | 1.306005 | 0.121586 | 1.211253 | 0.119277 | 1.167848 | 0.118800 | 1.144844 | 0.119167 | 1.131482 | 0.120814 | 1.123319 | 0.122892 | 1.118322 | 0.122892 | 1.115560 |
| 0.137089 | 1.303612 | 0.122400 | 1.210882 | 0.122892 | 1.166814 | 0.120748 | 1.144479 | 0.119277 | 1.131463 | 0.122400 | 1.123130 | 0.123329 | 1.118299 | 0.126506 | 1.115362 |
| 0.137349 | 1.303419 | 0.126000 | 1.209336 | 0.125173 | 1.166189 | 0.122400 | 1.144121 | 0.122892 | 1.130939 | 0.126000 | 1.122741 | 0.126506 | 1.118041 | 0.129543 | 1.115206 |
| 0.140964 | 1.300834 | 0.129600 | 1.207811 | 0.126506 | 1.165785 | 0.126000 | 1.143393 | 0.126506 | 1.130405 | 0.129600 | 1.122347 | 0.130120 | 1.117747 | 0.130120 | 1.115162 |
| 0.144578 | 1.298295 | 0.129630 | 1.207799 | 0.130120 | 1.164755 | 0.129506 | 1.142686 | 0.128494 | 1.130135 | 0.130771 | 1.122237 | 0.133735 | 1.117451 | 0.133735 | 1.114937 |
| 0.145660 | 1.297558 | 0.133200 | 1.206283 | 0.133735 | 1.163734 | 0.129600 | 1.142665 | 0.130120 | 1.129871 | 0.133200 | 1.121947 | 0.134257 | 1.117417 | 0.137349 | 1.114704 |
| 0.148193 | 1.295766 | 0.136800 | 1.204776 | 0.133742 | 1.163732 | 0.133200 | 1.141933 | 0.133735 | 1.129326 | 0.136800 | 1.121534 | 0.137349 | 1.117140 | 0.140964 | 1.114472 |
| 0.151807 | 1.293267 | 0.138079 | 1.204264 | 0.137349 | 1.162708 | 0.136800 | 1.141199 | 0.137349 | 1.128781 | 0.140400 | 1.121121 | 0.140964 | 1.116818 | 0.141864 | 1.114426 |
| 0.154514 | 1.291436 | 0.140400 | 1.203273 | 0.140964 | 1.161689 | 0.138834 | 1.140807 | 0.138340 | 1.128647 | 0.141425 | 1.121018 | 0.144578 | 1.116495 | 0.144578 | 1.114221 |
| 0.155422 | 1.290799 | 0.144000 | 1.201780 | 0.142812 | 1.161192 | 0.140400 | 1.140467 | 0.140964 | 1.128229 | 0.144000 | 1.120699 | 0.146059 | 1.116379 | 0.148193 | 1.113955 |
| 0.159036 | 1.288335 | 0.146836 | 1.200632 | 0.144578 | 1.160673 | 0.144000 | 1.139728 | 0.144578 | 1.127671 | 0.147600 | 1.120267 | 0.148193 | 1.116163 | 0.151807 | 1.113689 |
| 0.162651 | 1.285913 | 0.147600 | 1.200303 | 0.148193 | 1.159656 | 0.147600 | 1.138993 | 0.148193 | 1.127115 | 0.151200 | 1.119835 | 0.151807 | 1.115815 | 0.155241 | 1.113442 |
| 0.163675 | 1.285245 | 0.151200 | 1.198823 | 0.151807 | 1.158650 | 0.148613 | 1.138801 | 0.148794 | 1.127032 | 0.152824 | 1.119657 | 0.155422 | 1.115466 | 0.155422 | 1.113425 |
| 0.166265 | 1.283497 | 0.154800 | 1.197365 | 0.152243 | 1.158536 | 0.151200 | 1.138253 | 0.151807 | 1.126549 | 0.154800 | 1.119397 | 0.158730 | 1.115155 | 0.159036 | 1.113130 |
| 0.169880 | 1.281106 | 0.155964 | 1.196912 | 0.155422 | 1.157636 | 0.154800 | 1.137511 | 0.155422 | 1.125978 | 0.158400 | 1.118946 | 0.159036 | 1.115120 | 0.162651 | 1.112831 |
| 0.173135 | 1.278991 | 0.158400 | 1.195906 | 0.159036 | 1.156629 | 0.158400 | 1.136776 | 0.159036 | 1.125412 | 0.162000 | 1.118496 | 0.162651 | 1.114749 | 0.166265 | 1.112534 |
| 0.173494 | 1.278749 | 0.162000 | 1.194458 | 0.162143 | 1.155781 | 0.158911 | 1.136679 | 0.159902 | 1.125288 | 0.164980 | 1.118136 | 0.166265 | 1.114375 | 0.169815 | 1.112248 |
| 0.177108 | 1.276387 | 0.165429 | 1.193101 | 0.162651 | 1.155631 | 0.162000 | 1.136030 | 0.162651 | 1.124835 | 0.165600 | 1.118048 | 0.169880 | 1.114004 | 0.169880 | 1.112241 |

(continued)

**Table 1.4** (continued)

| R = 2 | | R = 3 | | R = 4 | | R = 5 | | R = 6 | | R = 7 | | R = 8 | | R = 9 | |
|---|---|---|---|---|---|---|---|---|---|---|---|---|---|---|---|
| *p* | *Eg* | *p* | *Eg* | *p* | *Eg* | *p* | *Eg* | *p* | *Eg* | *p* | *Eg* | *p* | *Eg* | *p* | *Eg* |
| 0.180723 | 1.274062 | 0.165600 | 1.193029 | 0.166265 | 1.154623 | 0.165600 | 1.135285 | 0.166265 | 1.124254 | 0.169200 | 1.117580 | 0.172432 | 1.113754 | 0.173494 | 1.111914 |
| 0.182934 | 1.272668 | 0.169200 | 1.191589 | 0.169880 | 1.153626 | 0.169200 | 1.134548 | 0.169880 | 1.123677 | 0.172800 | 1.117112 | 0.173494 | 1.113630 | 0.177108 | 1.111585 |
| 0.184337 | 1.271755 | 0.172800 | 1.190169 | 0.172503 | 1.152921 | 0.169766 | 1.134440 | 0.171680 | 1.123404 | 0.176400 | 1.116649 | 0.177108 | 1.113233 | 0.180723 | 1.111258 |
| 0.187952 | 1.269454 | 0.175308 | 1.189203 | 0.173494 | 1.152635 | 0.172800 | 1.133800 | 0.173494 | 1.123094 | 0.177990 | 1.116456 | 0.180723 | 1.112837 | 0.184337 | 1.110935 |
| 0.191566 | 1.267188 | 0.176400 | 1.188760 | 0.177108 | 1.151634 | 0.176400 | 1.133052 | 0.177108 | 1.122502 | 0.180000 | 1.116176 | 0.184337 | 1.112444 | 0.185702 | 1.110821 |
| 0.193036 | 1.266287 | 0.180000 | 1.187345 | 0.180723 | 1.150645 | 0.180000 | 1.132313 | 0.180723 | 1.121914 | 0.183600 | 1.115691 | 0.187166 | 1.112146 | 0.187952 | 1.110592 |
| 0.195181 | 1.264929 | 0.183600 | 1.185951 | 0.183318 | 1.149953 | 0.181193 | 1.132080 | 0.184121 | 1.121370 | 0.187200 | 1.115208 | 0.187952 | 1.112049 | 0.191566 | 1.110234 |
| 0.198795 | 1.262684 | 0.185549 | 1.185216 | 0.184337 | 1.149662 | 0.183600 | 1.131565 | 0.184337 | 1.121331 | 0.190800 | 1.114732 | 0.191566 | 1.111630 | 0.195181 | 1.109878 |
| 0.202410 | 1.260473 | 0.187200 | 1.184561 | 0.187952 | 1.148668 | 0.187200 | 1.130814 | 0.187952 | 1.120728 | 0.191856 | 1.114600 | 0.195181 | 1.111212 | 0.198795 | 1.109524 |
| 0.203457 | 1.259846 | 0.190800 | 1.183171 | 0.191566 | 1.147687 | 0.190800 | 1.130071 | 0.191566 | 1.120128 | 0.194400 | 1.114239 | 0.198795 | 1.110797 | 0.202410 | 1.109175 |
| 0.206024 | 1.258261 | 0.194400 | 1.181800 | 0.194605 | 1.146877 | 0.193192 | 1.129592 | 0.195181 | 1.119535 | 0.198000 | 1.113739 | 0.202410 | 1.110387 | 0.202938 | 1.109127 |
| 0.209639 | 1.256068 | 0.196173 | 1.181142 | 0.195181 | 1.146713 | 0.194400 | 1.129328 | 0.197345 | 1.119192 | 0.201600 | 1.113242 | 0.203034 | 1.110321 | 0.206024 | 1.108796 |

## References


Alexander, D. (1997). The Study of natural disasters, 1977~1997: Some reflections on a changing field of knowledge. *Disasters, 21*(4), 284–304. https://doi.org/10.1111/1467-7717.00064.

Aldrich, D. P., & Ono, Y. (2016). Local politicians as linking social capital: An empirical test of political behavior after Japan's 3/11 disasters. *Natural Hazards, 84*(3), 1637–1659.

Anbarci, N., Escaleras, M., & Register, C. A. (2004). Earthquake fatalities: The interaction of nature and political economy. *Journal of Public Economics, 52*, 1907–1933. https://doi.org/10.1016/j.jpubeco.2004.08.002.

Bachner, G., Bednar-Friedl, B., & Knittel, N. (2019). How does climate change adaptation affect public budgets? Development of an assessment framework and a demonstration for Austria. *Mitigation and Adaptation Strategies for Global Change, 24*, 1325–1341.

Barro, R. J. (2009). Rare disasters, asset prices, and welfare costs. *American Economic Review, 99*, 243–264. https://doi.org/10.1257/aer.99.1.243.

Barro, R. J. (2015). Environmental protection, rare disasters, and discount rates. *Economica, 82*, 1–23. https://doi.org/10.1111/ecca.12117.

Benalia, N., Abdelkafib, I., & Fekib, R. (2016). Natural disaster shocks and government's behavior: Evidence from middle-income countries. *International Journal of Disaster Risk Reduction, 27*, 1–6. https://doi.org/10.1016/j.ijdrr.2016.12.014.

Bom, P. R. D. (2017). Factor-biased public capital and private capital crowding out. *Journal of Macroeconomics, 52*, 100–117. https://doi.org/10.1016/j.jmacro.2017.03.002.

Bucci, A., & Bo, C. D. (2012). On the interaction between public and private capital in economic growth. *Journal of Economics, 106*(2), 133–152. https://doi.org/10.1007/s00712-011-0239-3.

Cohen, C., & Werker, E. D. (2008). The political economy of "natural" disasters. *Journal of Conflict Resolution, 52*, 795–819. https://doi.org/10.1177/0022002708322157.

Du, L., & Qian, L. (2016). The government's mobilization strategy following a disaster in the Chinese context: An evolutionary game theory analysis. *Natural Hazards, 80*(3), 1411–1424.

Fraser, T., Aldrich, D. P., Small, A., et al. (2020). In the hands of a few: Disaster recovery committee networks. *SSRN Electronic Journal*. https://doi.org/10.2139/ssrn.3544373.

He, F., & Zhuang, J. (2016). Balancing pre-disaster preparedness and post-disaster relief. *European Journal of Operational Research, 252*(1), 246–256.

Hochrainer, S. (2009). *Assessing the macroeconomic impacts of natural disasters—Are there any?*. World Bank: Washington, D. C.

Hochrainer, S. (2006). *Macroeconomic risk management against natural disasters*. Wiesbaden, Germany: German University Press.

Hochrainer, S., & Pflug, G. (2009). Natural Disaster risk bearing ability of governments: Consequences of kinked utility. *Journal of Natural Disaster Science, 31*(1), 11–21.

Hu, X. X. (2015). Review of the flood and waterlogging disasters in Hunan Province in 2014. *China Flood & Drought Management, 25*(2), 74–76. https://doi.org/10.16867/j.cnki.cfdm.2015.02.023.

Institute for Business and Home Safety. (1995). *Homesand hurricanes: Public opinion concerning various issues relating to home builders*. Boston: Building Codes and Damage Mitigation.

IPCC. (2014) Climate change 2014: Impacts, adaptation, and vulnerability. IPCC, Work Group II Contribution to the IPCC Fifth Assessment Report (AR5).

Haurie, A., & Moresino, F. (2006). A stochastic control model of economic growth with environmental disaster prevention. *Automatica, 42*(8), 1417–1428.

Jena, R., Pradhan, B., Beydoun, G., et al. (2020). Integrated model for earthquake risk assessment using neural network and analytic hierarchy process: Aceh province. *Indonesia. Geoence Frontiers, 11*(2), 613–634.

Keefer, P., Neumayer, E., & Plümper, T. (2011). Earthquake propensity and the politics of mortality prevention. *World Development, 39*(9), 1530–1541. https://doi.org/10.1016/j.worlddev.2011.02.010.

Klomp, J., & Valckx, K. (2014). Natural disasters and economic growth: A meta-analysis. *Global Environmental Change, 26*,183–195. https://doi.org/10.1016/j.gloenvcha.2014.02.006.

Klomp, J. (2016). Economic development and natural disasters: A satellite data analysis. *Global Environmental Change, 36*, 67–88. https://doi.org/10.1016/j.gloenvcha.2015.11.001.

Kumar P., Debele S. E., Sahani J., et al. (2020). Towards an operationalization of nature-based solutions for natural hazards. *Science of the Total Environment*. https://doi.org/10.1016/j.scitotenv.2020.138855.

Kunreuther, H., & Pauly, M. (2006). Rules rather than discretion: Lessons from Hurricane Katrina. *Journal of Risk and Uncertainty, 33*(1–2), 101–116. https://doi.org/10.1007/s11166-006-0173-x.

Ladds, M., Keating, A., Handmer, J., et al. (2017). How much do disasters cost? A comparison of disaster cost estimates in Australia. *International Journal of Disaster Risk Reduction, 21*, 419–429.

Li, M. J., Wang, M., & Shi, P. M. (2014). Spatial and temporal characteristics and influencing factors of rainstorm and flood disaster Loss in Hunan Province. *Journal of Beijing Normal University (Natural Science), 50*(4), 429–434.

Li, Z. N. (2012). Advanced applied econometrics. Tsinghua University.

Liu, C. F., Su, J. Y., Wang, W., et al. (2014). An observability–controllability model of urban earthquake disaster risk based on system periphery theory. *Natural Hazards, 73*(2), 303–315.

Liu, C. Y. (2013). The mystery of disaster and risk premium: A review of recent research progress. *Chinese Review of Financial Studies, 5*(3), 100–111.

Lou, Z. H. (2012). Research on the dynamic relationship between public investment and private investment in China since 1978. Nankai University.

Ma, W. J. (2016). Research of Technological progress skill bias and productivity promotion in China under the new normal. Jilin University.

Mahmud, T., & Prowse, M. (2012). Corruption in cyclone preparedness and relief efforts in coastal Bangladesh: Lessons for climate adaptation? *Global Environmental Change, 22*(4), 933–943.

Mechler, R. (2004). Natural disaster risk management and financing disaster losses in developing countries. *Doctoral Dissertation Universit at Friderician a Zu Karisruhe, 2*(6), 1479–1484.

Mehra, R., & Prescott, E. C. (1985). The Equity Premium: A Puzzle. *Journal of Monetary Economics., 15*(2), 145–161. https://doi.org/10.1016/0304-3932(85)90061-3.

Mileti, D. S. (1999). *Disasters by Design A Reassessment of Natural Hazards in the United States*. Washington, D. C.: Joseph Henry Press.

Motoyama, T. (2017). Optimal disaster-preventive expenditure in a dynamic and stochastic model. *Journal of Macroeconomics, 51*, 28–47. https://doi.org/10.1016/j.jmacro.2016.11.005.

Nagasaka, T. (2008). New problems in the study of disaster prevention based on disaster risk governance. *Quarterly Review, 27*, 77–92.

National Disaster Reduction Commission. Long-term plan for the development of national disaster prevention and mitigation talents (2010–2020). http://www.Mca.Gov.cn/article/zwgk/jhgh/201508/20150800865101.Shtml.

Oloruntoba, R. (2010). An analysis of the Cyclone Larry emergency relief chain: Some key success factors. *International Journal of Production Economics, 126*(1), 85–101.

Palm, R. I. (1990). *Natural hazards: An integrative framework for research and planning*. Baltimore: The Johns Hopkins University Press.

Pindyck, R. S., & Wang, N. (2009). The economic and policy consequences of catastrophes. *American Economic Journal Economic Policy, 5*(4), 306–339. https://doi.org/10.1257/pol.5.4.306.

Qiu, L. H. (2016). A study of the non-linear effects of Fiscal expenditure: An analysis from economic growth, private consumption and private investment perspective. Yunnan University.

Raddatz, C. (2007). Are external shocks responsible for the instability of output in low income countries? *Journal of Development Economics, 84*(1), 155–187. 10.1016/j.jdeveco.2006.11.001.

Sawada, Y., & Takasaki, Y. (2017). Natural disaster, poverty, and development: An introduction. *World Development, 94*, 2–15. https://doi.org/10.1016/j.worlddev.2016.12.035.

Schumacher, I., & Strobl, E. (2011). Economic development and losses due to natural disasters: The role of hazard exposure. *Ecological Economics, 72*(12), 97–105.

Shi, P. (2012). On the role of government in integrated disaster risk governance—Based on practices in China. *International Journal of Disaster Risk science, 3*(3), 139–146.

Slavíková, L. (2016). Effects of Government Flood Expenditures: The Problem of Crowding-out. *Journal of Flood Risk Management, 11*(2018), 95–104. https://doi.org/10.1111/jfr3.12265.

Tian, L., & Gao, J. (2012). Disaster risk, welfare loss and government's optimal assistance plan. *Economic Management, 34*(1), 184–192. https://doi.org/10.19616/j.cnki.bmj.2012.01.020.

Wang, C. H., Wang, K. L., Xiong, Y., et al. (2003). Vulnerability assessment and disaster mitigation strategy of heavy rain and flood disasters in Hunan Province. *Resources and Environment in the Yangtze Basin, 12*(6), 586–592. 10.1004-8227(2003)06-0586-07.

Wang, G., Chen, R., & Chen, J. (2017). Direct and indirect economic loss assessment of typhoon disasters based on EC and IO joint model. *Natural Hazards, 87*(3), 1751–1764.

Wang L., Zhao N., & Liu D. Complex disaster management: A dynamic game among the government, enterprises, and residents. *Journal of Cleaner Production.* https://doi.org/10.1016/j.jclepro.2020.122091.

Wang, P., Zhang, C., Chen, Y., et al. (2015). Rainstorm, flood and waterlogging disasters and assessment of agricultural disasters in Hunan Province. *Journal of Beijing Normal University, 51*(1), 75–79. 10.16360j.cnki.Jbnuns.2015.01.017.

Wen, Q. P., Zhou, Y. H, Huo, Z. G., et al. (2017). Risk changes of storm flood disasters in southeast China under climatic warming. *Chinese Journal of Ecology, 36*(2), 483–490. https://doi.org/10.13292/j.1000-4890.201702.005.

Wu, X. H., Xu, Z., Liu, H., Guo, J., & Zhou, L. (2019). What are the impacts of tropical cyclones on employment?—An analysis based on meta-regression. *Weather, Climate and Society, 11*(2), 259–275.

Yaron, G., & Wilson, D. (2020). Estimating the economic returns to community-level interventions that build resilience to flooding. *Journal of Flood Risk Management*, (13):1–11. https://doi.org/10.1111/jfr3.12662.

Yu, J. J., Wan, J. H., & Chen, G. Y. (2017). Causes of flood and waterlogging disasters in the Yangtze River Basin and suggestions for disaster reduction. *Studies and Discussions, 27*(1), 84–87. https://doi.org/10.16867/j.cnki.cfdm.20170116. 008.

Ye, T., Wang, Y., Wu, B., et al. (2016). Government investment in disaster risk reduction based on a probabilistic risk model: A case study of typhoon disasters in Shenzhen, China. *International Journal of Disaster Risk science, 7,* 123–137.

Yu, S., Kim, S. W., Oh, C. W., et al. (2015). Quantitative assessment of disaster resilience: An empirical study on the importance of post-disaster recovery costs. *Reliability Engineering & System Safety, 137*(5), 6–17.

Zhang, J., Wu, G. Y., & Zhang, J. P. (2004). The estimation of China's provincial capital: 1952–2000. *Economic Research Journal, 10,* 35–44.

Zhuo, Z., & Duan, S. (2012). Investment expenditure for disaster prevention and mitigation, disaster control and economic growth: Economic analysis and empirical study in China. *Management World, 4,* 1–8. https://doi.org/10.19744/j.cnki.11-1235/f. 2012.04.001.

# Chapter 2
# A Multi-scale Periodic Study of $PM_{2.5}$ Concentration in the Yangtze River Delta of China Based on Empirical Mode Decomposition-Wavelet Analysis

**Abstract** With the acceleration of industrialization and urbanization, the problem of air pollution in China has become increasingly serious. Particulate matter (PM) is a representative indicator of pollutants, and it is of great significance to carry out targeted treatment by studying its periodicity of concentration. In this paper, as a data mining information technology, the Empirical Mode Decomposition-Wavelet Analysis (EMD-WA) model is used to conduct a multi-scale periodic study of the $PM_{2.5}$ concentration time sequence in the Yangtze River Delta region in China and it is found that: (1) through the decomposition and reconstruction of the EMD-WA model, the period characteristics of four scales from short to long can be obtained, which are seasonal, short, medium and long period terms respectively; (2) the $PM_{2.5}$ concentration in the Yangtze River Delta region shows obvious multi-scale periodicity for the four scales, which includes a seasonal cycle of 46 days (about 1.5 months), a short cycle of 101 days (about 3.5 months), a medium cycle of 294 days (about 10 months), and a long cycle of 671 days (about 22.5 months), respectively. (3) The results are consistent in terms of season, short and middle cycle scales, in north (Jiangsu), east (Shanghai), south (Zhejiang) and west (Anhui) of the Yangtze River Delta region, but there are significant differences in the terms of long cycle scales. (4) The $PM_{2.5}$ concentration still shows obvious periodicity within 240 h during severe haze in the Yangtze River Delta region. This paper provides a framework for the government to make policies on energy conservation, emission reduction and air pollution control, and also provides a strong basis for haze prediction.

**Keywords** $PM_{2.5}$ · Empirical mode decomposition · Wavelet analysis · Multi-scale period · Prediction

## 2.1 Introduction

In recent years, $PM_{2.5}$ pollution has become a critical challenge faced by all countries in the world in the process of industrial development. In China, $PM_{2.5}$ pollution is particularly severe in the economically developed Beijing-Tianjin-Hebei region, the Yangtze River Delta and the Pearl River Delta. $PM_{2.5}$ contains a variety of toxic and harmful substances, which greatly impact the respiratory health of the public and



X. Wu and J. Guo, *Economic Impacts and Emergency Management of Disasters in China*,
https://doi.org/10.1007/978-981-16-1319-7_2

directly harm people's physical health (Wang and Wang 2014; Bao and Fang 2007; Li et al. 2007). Moreover, $PM_{2.5}$ has a significant impact on atmospheric visibility (Shen et al. 2005; Malm et al. 1994) and climate change (Hansen et al. 2005). The scope of influence of $PM_{2.5}$ on the environment and the harm to human health is more severe than that of $PM_{10}$ and $PM_{100}$. The United States, the European Union and other developed countries have listed $PM_{2.5}$ as a typical air pollutant (Yang et al. 2012). The factors leading to and influence the concentration of $PM_{2.5}$ in the atmosphere are very complex. Studies have proved that the variation of $PM_{2.5}$ concentration is closely related to the law of human production activities and local meteorological changes (Liang et al. 2007), and these factors tend to be cyclical. For example, the seasonal characteristics of the concentration of the main chemical components of $PM_{2.5}$ in autumn and winter are significantly higher than those in spring and summer (Zhang et al. 2013), and the time series data of $PM_{2.5}$ should also have an implicit periodicity (Zheng et al. 2010).

To control PM, one of the feasible ways is to find the periodic law of PM time series, which will help government management departments to implement targeted measures before the peak of PM, such as shutting down key pollution sources and reminding the public to deal with the negative impact of PM. For example, Some of China's northern cities, such as Beijing and Xi'an, have implemented "coal-to-gas" projects, which wanted to avoid the peak PM emission in winter and spring caused by the burning of coal for heating. In 2015, Shanghai implemented a "temporary air quality control scheme in winter" to avoid the peak of PM emissions in winter. However, few researchers currently use common methods in the information and communication technologies (ICT) field to study the PM cycle. This article combines classical methods in the ICT field, such as EMD and WA, to study the periodic characteristics of PM from different scales, which can master the periodic operation characteristics of $PM_{2.5}$, controlling $PM_{2.5}$ concentration, and introducing targeted governance measures to optimize air quality.

The decomposition method of EMD (Empirical Mode Decomposition, hereinafter referred to as EMD) does not need to be given a basis function in advance. It carries out adaptive decomposition based on the data sequence, and the results can better reflect the fluctuation characteristics of the original sequence in different time scales. This paper uses the empirical mode decomposition and wavelet analysis to construct the EMD-WA (Empirical Mode Decomposition-Wavelet Analysis, hereinafter referred to as the EMD-WA) model, and multi-scale periodicity of $PM_{2.5}$ in the Yangtze River Delta is studied with the method of measurement after decomposition. The innovation is that: (1) Previous studies on the periodicity of $PM_{2.5}$ often used filtering methods directly. In wavelet analysis, it is necessary to manually set parameters and give basis functions, so it is difficult to avoid subjectivity. The EMD decomposition method applied in this paper does not need to set parameters and a given basis function, but it is an adaptive decomposition process based on the data. The results of decomposition can well reflect the local time characteristics of the original data. (2) When selecting the period length of the Morlet wavelet analysis sequence, the Morlet wavelet analysis has the characteristics of the period study in Fourier analysis, accurately reflecting the original sequence's multi-time-scale periodic fluctuation.

The rest is as follows. The second part is a literature review; the third part introduces the principle and characteristics of EMD decomposition and wavelet analysis. The fourth part constructs EMD-WA model and explains the specific steps. The fifth part is the empirical analysis of EMD-WA model and cycle measurement of each city. The last part is the conclusion and the research prospect.

## 2.2 Literature Review

Scholars have conducted extensive studies in the fields of EMD decomposition, wavelet analysis and period research of $PM_{2.5}$, but there are relatively few studies on combining EMD decomposition and wavelet analysis to analyze the multi-scale period of $PM_{2.5}$. The following part will summarize the study of $PM_{2.5}$ period and the quantitative analysis method of time series period.

### 2.2.1 *Periodic Study of $PM_{2.5}$*

At present, there are in-depth studies on the time series of $PM_{2.5}$ concentration. For example, Zhao (2008) studied the seasonal and daily variation characteristics of $PM_{2.5}$ concentration in urban areas and suburbs of Beijing, and Li et al. (2011) pointed out the variation characteristics of $PM_{2.5}$ concentration in urban areas of Beijing, etc. Studies in the Yangtze River Delta region mainly analyze the correlation between $PM_{2.5}$ and meteorological factors. For example, Gu et al. (2015) studied the relationship between the variation characteristics of $PM_{2.5}$ concentration and meteorological conditions in Chongming island of Shanghai in the past three years, and pointed out that the seasonal characteristics of $PM_{2.5}$ concentration are obvious. However, in terms of research methods, conventional statistical analysis is used. For example, Mao et al. (2017) studied the spatial and temporal pattern of $PM_{2.5}$ in cities in the Yangtze River Delta region in 2015 and its influencing factors, and pointed out that the seasonal changes of $PM_{2.5}$ concentration generally showed a high seasonal cycle in spring and winter and low in summer and autumn. By time series models, Cekim (2020) forecasted $PM_{10}$ concentrations in most polluted cities in Turkey. Used Generalized Additive Models, Fiffer et al. (2020) assessed the Long-term impact of $PM_{2.5}$ mass and sulfur reductions on ultrafine particle trends in Boston from 1999 to 2018. Li et al. (2018) found that there are significant periodic changes in the $PM_{2.5}$ mass concentration in Beijing urban area, and the main periods include about 24 h, 8 and 14 days; Zhou et al. (2018) analyzed the periodic changes of $PM_{2.5}$ in Taiyuan City from January 1, 2014 to May 31, 2016. The results show that there are significant cycles of 2–8 days and 10–16 d in the $PM_{2.5}$ concentration change in Taiyuan. However, because each research city is different and the research period is also different, the period of each time series is not exactly the same. But on the whole, from the seasonal trend, the PM cycle is more significantly affected by the season, and there are generally high data in winter and spring, and low data in summer and autumn. Looking at the micro data again, the "Sunday" effect is widespread, such as the cycle being about 7–8 days. Tis shows that people emit more PM in their production and life, and that the reduction in production and life on weekends will also reduce PM. This paper finds that the PM time series in the Yangtze River Delta has more abundant features from other scales in addition to the above "seasonality" and "Sunday" characteristics.

For the systematic study of variation period of $PM_{2.5}$ concentration, the method of wavelet analysis is mostly applied directly. For example, Li et al. (2017) used Morlet continuous wavelet to study the period of $PM_{2.5}$ at different time scales in the urban area of Beijing, and concluded that the primary period was about 24 h, 8 and 14 days. Wang et al. (2017) used Morlet continuous wavelet to study and found that the change periods of the $PM_{10}$ and $PM_{2.5}$ time series are mainly short periods of 4–8 days. From the perspective of the authors, the current literatures on the periodic research of PM time series are not comprehensive enough. This article innovatively combines the commonly used methods in the ICT field, such as EMD and WA technology, to study the characteristics of PM in terms of season, short cycle, medium cycle and long cycle, and try to find the law, not only enriching existing research, but also providing countermeasures and suggestions for PM governance.

### 2.2.2 *Quantitative Analysis Method of Periodicity of Time Series*

In the past, the main idea of analyzing the periodicity of time series was to process the original sequence, extract the sub-sequence containing periodic fluctuations, usually called the period term, and then calculate the period length of the sub-sequence. This process of extracting periodic items is mainly realized by filtering or decomposition. Pedregal (2003) designed the HP (hodrick-prescott) filter model and analyzed the trend part obtained by the Gross National Product (GNP) serial low-pass filter and the periodic part obtained by the band-pass filter. Mohr (2006) used a trans conduction-capacitor (TC) filter to analyze the cycles and trends of gross domestic product (GDP) in various European countries, and verified that the TC filter was more convenient than the HP filter through empirical analysis. He and Song (2013) used HP filtering and BP (band-pass) filtering to study the periodic variation of the marine economy. Cendejas et al. (2017) concluded that after economic globalization, all economies have a common business economic cycle based on the 4–7 year cycle determined by HP filter model. Carvalho et al. (2012) decomposed GDP of U.S. by singular spectrum analysis. Sella et al. (2010) verified the synchronicity of economic cycle based on singular spectrum analysis (SSA for short), Multi Taper Method (MTM for short) and Maximum Entropy Method (MEM for short). The study of Yogo (2008) showed that wavelet decomposition could decompose GDP time series into three parts: white noise, period and trend. Most of the above studies extract the period term from the original time series through the methods of sequence noise reduction, trend term filtering or sequence decomposition, but these methods also have their own limitations. For example, the filtering method is often subjective in the selection of parameters, resulting in a large gap in the cycle measurement results of the same time series; a basis function is needed in the decomposition method, and it is easy to appear false fluctuation scale in the decomposition process.

The research on the calculation of the length of the fluctuation cycle has evolved several times, from the initial analysis of variance to the spectrum analysis (Kuo and Lee 1988), and then into the field of wavelet analysis (Cui 1995). It is a development process from time domain to frequency domain. Baubeau and Cazelles (2009) used continuous wavelet transform analysis. Addo et al. (2014) proved that the wavelet analysis can analyze hidden period fluctuations of time series more effectively. Berdiev and Chang (2015) adopted wavelet analysis to discuss the synchronicity of economic development cycles in China, Japan, the United States and other Asia–Pacific countries. Marczak and Gomez (2015) extracted the original sequence period term through wavelet analysis, and studied the periodicity of behavior of producers and wages of consumers. The above method for measuring the period length indicates that wavelet analysis solves the problem of low time–frequency resolution of Fourier transform spectrum method to a certain extent, and can effectively measure the time scale of the period term.

The Empirical mode decomposition (EMD) method was proposed by Huang et al. (1998, 1999). This method has advantages in dealing with nonlinear and non-stationary time series. Flandrin et al. (2004) proved that the empirical mode decomposition method could be used as a method similar to wavelet decomposition, which is an adaptive high-pass filtering process and suitable for the analysis of nonlinear time series. It can be seen that from the EMD decomposition principle, its filtering process is based on the characteristics of the analyzed time series instead of artificial function. The decomposed IMF (Intrinsic Mode Function) can represent fluctuations on different time scales, so that each IMF component can characterize the original sequence more accurately and comprehensively. Based on the above advantages, the empirical mode decomposition method is popular in the fields of time series prediction (Yu et al. 2008; Zhang et al. 2008; Wang et al. 2010; Li et al. 2012) and multi-scale periodic analysis (Zhang 2014; Wu et al. 2018a, b; Wang et al. 2020).

In recent years, rapid developments and applications of modern ICT have created more and more opportunities for air pollution control (Wu et al. 2018a, b). For example, online monitoring instruments can more accurately monitor and predict the emission of air pollutants. The modern information analysis technologies used in this article, such as EMD and WA technologies, are commonly used to reduce noise and find rules for data information. This article combines the two and analyzes the periodic characteristics of PM, which is the application of ICT technology in environmental governance and has a good typical demonstration significance.

## 2.3 Research Methods

### 2.3.1 *Empirical Mode Decomposition*

The core objective of empirical mode decomposition is the process of decomposing a nonlinear non-stationary sequence into a finite number of IMF components and a trend term. The specific steps of EMD decomposition are as follows:

(1) Search for all local extremum (maximum and minimum) points of the original data sequence.
(2) Choose a curve interpolation method (cubic spline interpolation method is applied in this paper), connect all local maxima to get the upper envelope $x_{\max}(t)$, and connect the local minima to get the lower envelope $x_{\min}(t)$. It can be known that the upper and lower envelope should cover all local maxima and minima of $x(t)$, namely

$$x_{\min}(t) \le x(t) \le x_{\max}(t) \tag{2.1}$$

where, t is time. In the part of "5. Empirical analysis", t is the day data.

(3) The upper and lower envelope $x_{\max}(t)$, $x_{\min}(t)$ and mean value $m_{11}(t)$ can be calculated, namely

$$m_{11}(t) = \frac{x_{\max}(t) + x_{\min}(t)}{2} \tag{2.2}$$

(4) Then subtract $m_{11}(t)$ from sequence $x(t)$, and the new sequence $h_{11}(t)$ is obtained, namely

$$x(t) - m_{11}(t) = h_{11}(t) \tag{2.3}$$

(5) Finally, check whether the new sequence $h_{11}(t)$ meets the two conditions in the definition of the eigenmode function. If satisfied, $h_{11}(t)$ is selected as the first IMF component $c_1(t)$ of $x(t)$; If not, the new sequence $h_{11}(t)$ should be used as the original data sequence $x(t)$ to repeat steps (1) to step (4) until the envelope mean of the new sequence approaches zero. Repeat the operation for $k$ times to get the first IMF component of $x(t)$, namely

$$c_1(t) = h_{1k}(t) = h_{1(k-1)}(t) - m_{1k}(t) = x(t) - \sum_{i=1}^{k} m_{1k}(t) \tag{2.4}$$

Taking the difference between the original data sequence $x(t)$ and the first IMF component $c_2(t)$ as the original signal, repeat steps (1) to (5) to get the remaining IMF components $c_2(t)$, $c_3(t)$ ... $c_n(t)$. After repeating for $n$ times, the last margin

$r_n(t)$ is obtained, which represents the trend information of the original data sequence $x(t)$, in which there is only one extreme point. $r_n(t)$ is called the trend term of $x(t)$.

$$r_1(t) = x(t) - c_1(t) \tag{2.5}$$

$$c_n(t) = r_{n-1}(t) - r_n(t) \tag{2.6}$$

In steps (1) to (5), the process of decomposition of IMF from the original data sequence $x(t)$ is called the "filtering" process of EMD method.

The condition for EMD algorithm to stop filtering is determined by the difference between two consecutive filtering results, Standard deviation (SD), and the threshold value of SD is set as the judging basis for stopping the filtering process. The formula of SD is as follows

$$\mathrm{SD} = \sum_{t=0}^{T} \frac{\left|h_{1(k-1)}(t) - h_{1k}(t)\right|^2}{h_{1(k-1)}^2(t)} \tag{2.7}$$

The selection of SD threshold value is subjective to some extent, and the selection is mostly determined by experience. When the magnitude of the original sequence data is 10, the value of SD is usually [0.2, 0.3] (Zheng 2010). The length of the data sequence in the study is about 2000, so the value of SD is 0.003.

From the above empirical mode decomposition principle, it can be known that the decomposed IMF can fully and clearly reflect the different time scales of the original sequence, so the study of the periodic characteristics of each IMF component can clearly understand the periodic characteristics of the original sequence.

### 2.3.2 *Wavelet Analysis*

In the analysis of time series, we usually start from the two directions of time domain and frequency domain. The time domain exists objectively in reality and develops linearly according to time, while the frequency domain is a description of frequency, which can be obtained by the time domain through the Fourier transform. Common time domain analysis and frequency domain analysis are usually suitable for stationary time series. However, the fluctuation of $PM_{2.5}$ concentration has a multi-time-scale structure. In the early 1980s, the wavelet analysis with time–frequency multi-resolution function proposed by Jean Morlet provided a solution to the problem of multi-time-scale periodic change hidden in time series.

#### 2.3.2.1 Wavelet Function

The definition of the wavelet function is as follows: suppose $\psi(t)$ is a square integrable function in the real number domain, that is $\psi(t) \in L^2(R)$; if its Fourier transform $\hat{\psi}(t)$ satisfies formula (2.8), $\psi(t)$ is called a basic wavelet function

$$\int_R \frac{|\hat{\psi}(t)|^2}{\omega} d\omega < 0 \tag{2.8}$$

It can be seen that the value of $\hat{\psi}(t)$ is zero when $\omega = 0$, so it means that the integral of the wavelet function in its time domain is also zero, namely:

$$\int_{-\infty}^{+\infty} \psi(t) d_t = 0 \tag{2.9}$$

The volatility shown in formula (2.9), combined with the characteristic of rapid attenuation to zero in the definition of wavelet function, indicates that the wavelet function is convergent.

$\psi(t)$ can form a family of continuous wavelet functions through translation and scaling, also known as subwavelet, denoted as $\psi_{ab}(t)$, and expressed as follows:

$$\psi_{ab}(t) = |a|^{\frac{1}{2}} \psi(at - b) \tag{2.10}$$

In the formula, $a$ is the scale scaling factor, and the change of $a$ can reflect the period length of different time scales; $b$ is the translation factor, and represents the translation in time.

#### 2.3.2.2 Wavelet Transform

The definition of wavelet transform is as follows:

If there are a sequence $x(t)$ and a wavelet $\psi_{ab}(t)$, then

$$W_x(a, b) = \int_{-\infty}^{\infty} x(t)\overline{\psi}_{ab}(t)dt = |a|^{\frac{1}{2}} \int_{-\infty}^{\infty} x(t)\overline{\psi}(at - b)dt \tag{2.11}$$

is the continuous wavelet transform of the sequence $x(t)$, $W_x(a, b)$ is the wavelet coefficient, $\overline{\psi}_{ab}(t)$ is the complex conjugate function of $\psi_{ab}(t)$.

From the above definition of wavelet transform, it can be known that wavelet analysis is an integral transformation that maps a one-dimensional linear time series to a two-dimensional time-scale plane, which is conducive to extracting the hidden multi-time-scale information.

The modulus $\|\psi_{ab}(t)\|_0^2$ of $\psi(t)$ calculated according to formula (2.10) can be obtained as follows:

$$\begin{aligned}\|\psi_{ab}(t)\|_0^2 &= \int_R |\psi_{ab}(t)|^2 \mathrm{d}t = \int_R \left|a^{1/2}\psi(at-b)\right|^2 \mathrm{d}t \\ &= \int_R |\psi(at-b)|^2 \mathrm{d}(at-b) \\ &= \int_R |\psi(t)|^2 \mathrm{d}t = \|\psi(t)\|_0^2\end{aligned} \tag{2.12}$$

It indicates that after translation and scaling, the modulus of $\psi(t)$ is unchanged after being transformed into Eq. (2.10). Therefore, the multi-time scale of the original sequence can be grasped by scaling and changing the scale parameters $a$ to obtain the information of high and low frequencies in the sequence.

At the same time, under different values of $a$, continuous wavelet transform has the adaptive ability of time-window and frequency-window, that is, the wavelet function has the adaptive short-term analysis effect on both high and low frequency sequences. The specific analysis is as follows:

$$\begin{aligned}\hat{\psi}_{ab}(\omega) &= \int_R a^{1/2}\psi(at-b)\mathrm{e}^{\mathrm{i}at}\mathrm{d}t \\ = a^{-1/2} &\int_R \psi(at-b)\mathrm{e}^{-i\frac{\omega}{a}(at)-b}\mathrm{e}^{-i\omega\frac{b}{a}}\mathrm{d}(at-b) \\ &= a^{-1/2}\mathrm{e}^{-i\omega\frac{b}{a}}\hat{\psi}_{ab}\left(\frac{\omega}{a}\right)\end{aligned} \tag{2.13}$$

From formula (2.10) and formula (2.12), it can be seen that, when $a < 1$, from the perspective of time domain, the time window is widened and the fluctuation amplitude is compressed after transforming $\psi(t)$ to $\psi_{ab}(t)$. From the perspective of frequency domain, the frequency window is narrower than before, and the time–frequency window is flatter than before after transforming $\psi(t)$ to $\psi_{ab}(t)$, so it can adapt to the localization requirements of the lower frequency sequence. When $a > 1$, from the perspective of time domain, after transforming $\psi(t)$ to $\psi_{ab}(t)$, the time window is compressed and the fluctuation amplitude is enlarged; From the perspective of frequency domain, after transforming $\psi(t)$ to $\psi_{ab}(t)$, the frequency window is wider than before, and the time–frequency window is taller and thinner than before, so it can adapt to the localization requirements of higher frequency sequences.

#### 2.3.2.3 Wavelet Variance

The wavelet coefficient can demonstrate the variation characteristics of the original sequence at a specific time scale. Different wavelet coefficients correspond to different time scales, and the larger the absolute value of the wavelet coefficient is, the more significant the time scale is. Therefore, the square of all wavelet coefficients related to $a$ in the time domain is integrated in the $b$ domain to obtain the wavelet variance:

$$\mathrm{Var}(a) = \int_{-\infty}^{\infty} |W_x(a, b)|^2 \mathrm{d}b \tag{2.14}$$

Since $a$ is a scaling factor, its change can reflect the periodicity of the original sequence at different time scales, and Var($a$) can reflect the strength of the fluctuation period at this time scale. Therefore, the main time scale, namely the primary period, can be determined through the peak of its wavelet variance. In order to avoid the multiple local peaks of wavelet variance when determining the period with the peak of wavelet variance, the primary period is usually analyzed by combining the wavelet variance graph.

## 2.4 Model Design and Data Description

### 2.4.1 Model Design

Firstly, the empirical mode decomposition method is used to decompose the variation sequences of $PM_{2.5}$ concentration of 41 cities, and then the decomposed IMF is reconstructed in groups. Finally, the wavelet analysis method is used to calculate the reconstructed IMF period as the period of the original sequence.

In terms of grouping reconstruction, although the empirical mode decomposition method can be widely used to analyze multi-scale time series, it has limitations. Firstly, in the process of applying the empirical mode decomposition method, spurious modes are easy to appear, that is, the waveform superposed by the real mode and error, and periodic calculation of the spurious mode will obtain the false cycle. Secondly, generally speaking, the main fluctuation information of the original sequence is often concentrated in a few decomposed IMF. If each of the decomposed IMF is subjected to period measurement, it cannot accurately reflect the multiscale period features implied in the original sequence. In view of the above limitations, the orthogonality of empirical mode decomposition is used to reconstruct the IMF groups.

To sum up, the EMD-WA model applied in this paper can be summarized into four steps: decomposition, reconstruction, measurement and analysis. In the decomposition step of the model, the empirical mode decomposition method enables the decomposed sequence to cover all the local time domain features of the original sequence, which effectively overcomes the defect of ignoring some local time domain features of the sequence due to the subjective selection of specific wavelet basis functions in the study of periodicity of time series by wavelet analysis.

The steps of decomposition, reconstruction, measurement and analysis of EMD-WA model are as follows:

(1) Decomposition: the $PM_{2.5}$ concentration data sequence $x(t)$ is decomposed by EMD. The specific steps of EMD decomposition are shown in steps (1) to (6) in 2.1. to obtain the IMF sequence $\{c(t)\}$ and trend item sequence $\{r(t)\}$.

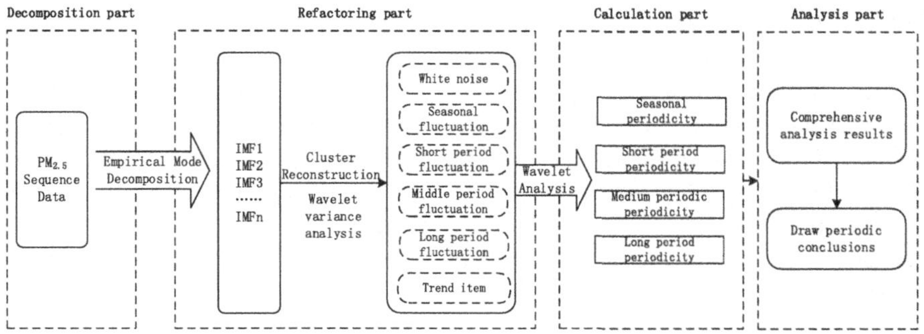


**Fig. 2.1** Cycle decomposition and analysis process of $PM_{2.5}$

(2) Reconstruction: the IMF decomposed by the $PM_{2.5}$ concentration sequence of each city is applied to wavelet analysis for periodic analysis. The morlet wavelet is selected as the basis function in the form of $\psi(t) = e^{kt}e^{\frac{-t^2}{2}}$. After calculating the wavelet coefficient $W_x(a, b)$, the primary period of each IMF component in each city is calculated with the wavelet variance $\mathrm{Var}(a)$ in formula (2.12). Then, clustering analysis is conducted according to the main cycle length of each IMF, and clustering results are used as the basis for grouping. According to the orthogonality of the EMD method, the same group of the IMF is added as the reconstruction result, so as to obtain more accurate and comprehensive multi-scale periodic result of the sequence.

(3) Measurement: wavelet analysis method is used to calculate the cycle length of IMF series in various cities after reconstruction.

(4) Analysis: combined with geographical location, high concentration period and other information, the results of various cities are compared to comprehensively analyze the multi-scale period characteristics of $PM_{2.5}$ in the Yangtze River Delta.

The periodic decomposition and prediction analysis process of $PM_{2.5}$ are shown in Fig. 2.1.

### *2.4.2 Data Description*

In October 2019, when the *19th Yangtze River Delta urban economic coordination meeting* was held, 7 cities including Huangshan, Bengbu, Lu'an, Huaibei, Suzhou, Bozhou, and Fuyang in Anhui were recruited as new members of the Economic Coordination Committee of the Yangtze River Delta, and 41 prefecture-level cities in Shanghai, Jiangsu, Zhejiang, and Anhui all became new members in the Yangtze River Delta. Therefore, the Yangtze River Delta includes: Shanghai, Nanjing, Wuxi, Xuzhou, Changzhou, Suzhou, Nantong, Lianyungang, Huaian, Yangzhou, Zhenjiang, Taizhou, Suqian, Hangzhou, Ningbo, Wenzhou, Jiaxing, Huzhou, Shaoxing,

Jinhua, Quzhou and Zhoushan, Taizhou, Lishui, Hefei, Wuhu, Huainan, Maanshan, Tongling and Anqing, Chuzhou, Xuancheng, Chizhou, Huangshan, Bengbu, Luan, Huaibei, Suzhou, Bozhou, Fuyang.

This paper collected 1,795 hourly $PM_{2.5}$ concentration data of 41 cities in the Yangtze River Delta from January 1, 2015, to November 30, 2019 from Website of https://www.aqistudy.cn/historydata/. In the study, the average concentration of $PM_{2.5}$ from 0 AM to 23 Afternoon in each city was taken as the $PM_{2.5}$ concentration of that day. $PM_{2.5}$ concentration data is measured as $\mu g/m^3$ and can be input the models directly.

## 2.5 Empirical Analysis

### *2.5.1 Periodic Analysis of Daily $PM_{2.5}$ Concentration in the Yangtze River Delta Region*

The daily $PM_{2.5}$ concentration data of 41 prefecture-level cities in Shanghai, Jiangsu, Zhejiang and Anhui in the Yangtze River Delta from January 1, 2015 to November 30, 2019, and the EMD-WA model constructed above are used to conduct periodic analysis of daily $PM_{2.5}$ concentration data of various cities. In order to show the analysis process in detail while avoiding repeated descriptions, this section takes the $PM_{2.5}$ daily concentration data in Shanghai as an example to show the empirical process in detail, and summarizes the results of other cities (the conclusions please see Part of "6.1 Conclusion") (Fig. 2.2).

First, decompose step (1) of the daily $PM_{2.5}$ concentration in Shanghai processed by the EMD-WA model, and steps (1) to (6) of the empirical mode decomposition method are specifically used. The fluctuations or trends of different scales in the Shanghai's daily $PM_{2.5}$ concentration data sequence $x(t)$ are decomposed one by one to obtain the new series containing a trend term $r_n(t)$, namely formula (2.5), and the intrinsic modal function $c_n(t)$, which is formula (2.6).

Figure 2.3 above shows the obtained IMF after the daily $PM_{2.5}$ concentration

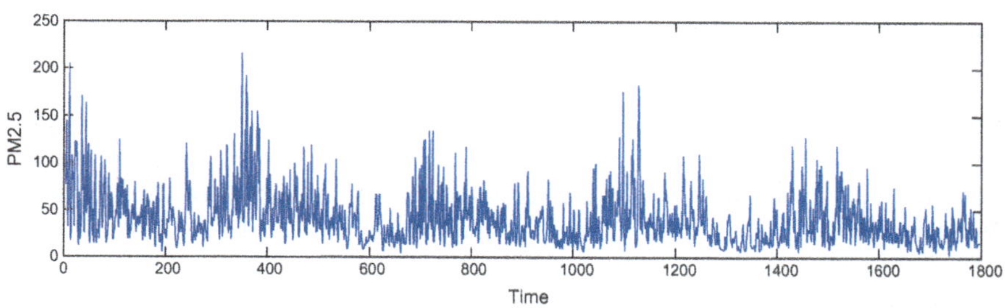


**Fig. 2.2** Daily concentration sequence of $PM_{2.5}$ in Shanghai

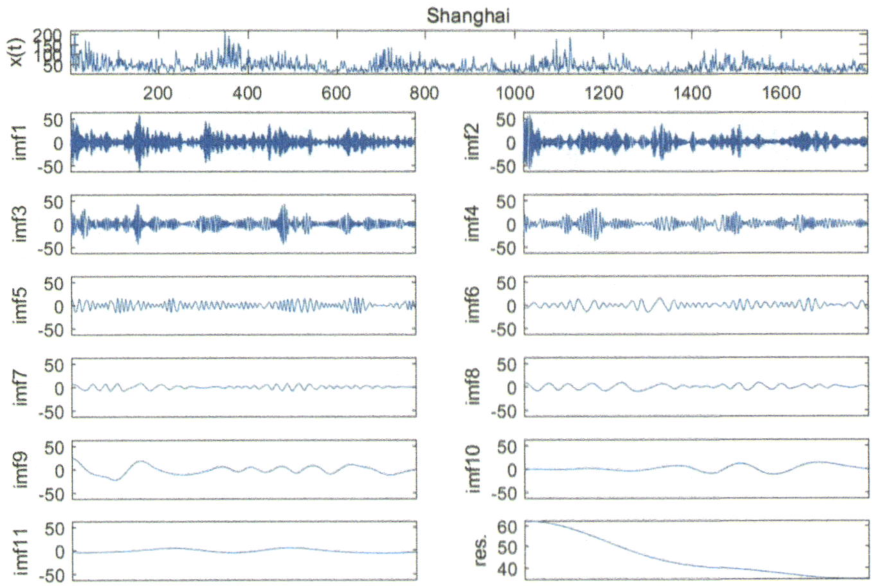


**Fig. 2.3** $PM_{2.5}$ EMD decomposition results of concentration series in Shanghai

sequence $x(t)$ in Shanghai was decomposed by EMD. Among them, a total of 11 IMF sequences and 1 trend item sequence were decomposed. For the convenience of description, the 12 sequences were denoted as $c(i), i = 1, 2, ..., 12$. As can be seen from Fig. 2.3, the frequency of each IMF sequence is arranged from high to low. Therefore, compared with the earlier IMF sequence $c(i - n), i > n$, the later IMF sequence $c(i)$ has the characteristics of slower fluctuation and longer cycle. Until it is decomposed to the last sequence, it can be called the residual component or the trend term, which is characterized by the extreme slowdown of fluctuations and the absence of periodicity. It can represent the long-term trend of the daily concentration of $PM_{2.5}$ in Shanghai.

After completing the decomposition of EMD-WA, the IMF sequences $c(i)$ decomposed from the daily concentration sequences $x(t)$ of $PM_{2.5}$ in Shanghai were reconstructed to eliminate the false modes in the eigenmode function, so as to make the cycle more accurate. Therefore, the morlet wavelet in form of $\psi(t) = e^{kt}e^{\frac{-t^2}{2}}$ is used as the basic wavelet function, and wavelet analysis method is used to obtain the wavelet coefficient $W_x(a, b)$ according to formula (2.11), and then calculate the wavelet variance $\mathrm{Var}(a)$ according to formula (2.14). When determining the primary period with the wavelet variance, the time when the maximum value appears is selected as the primary period. In practice, it is often analyzed by combining the wavelet variance graph to avoid the problem of partial and unobjective selection of the primary period caused by maxima in multiple positions. After the wavelet analysis of IMF sequences $c(i)$ decomposed by step (1) of the EMD-WA model, the wavelet variance graph obtained is shown in Fig. 2.4.

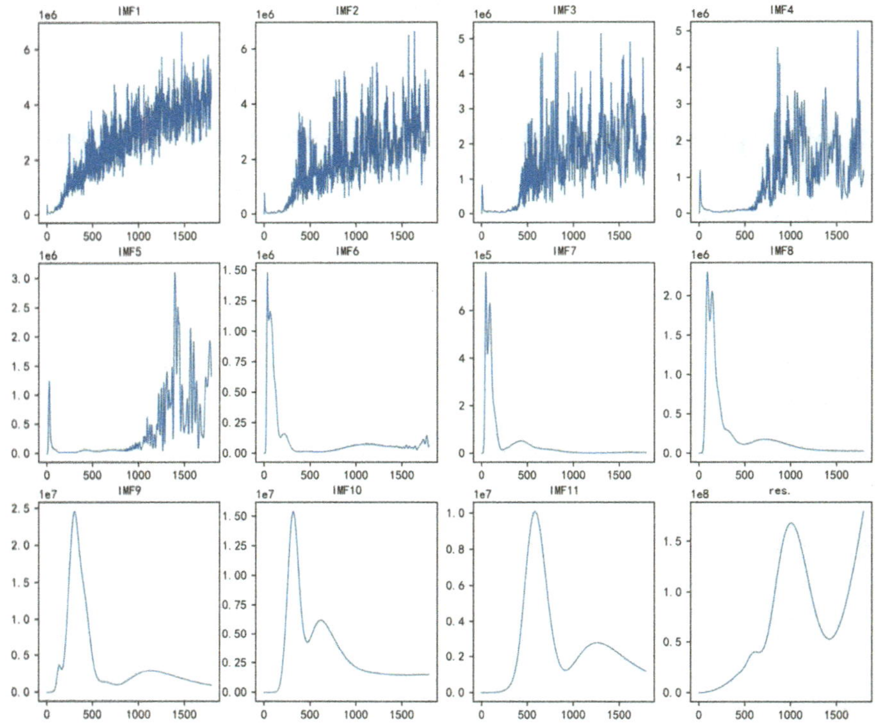


**Fig. 2.4** IMF wavelet variance in Shanghai

It can be seen intuitively from Fig. 2.4, the wavelet variance map corresponding to $c(1), \cdots, c(5)$ is not smooth with violent, dense and no obvious trend of fluctuations. The wavelet variance can reflect the strength of the fluctuation cycle under the time scale, for $c(1), \cdots, c(5)$ without obvious maximum value, it can be identified that the first five IMFs $c(1), \cdots, c(5)$ decomposed by $x(t)$ through EMD method have the random fluctuation characteristic of white noise, so there is no obvious primary period.

In this paper, after morlet wavelet analysis, one or more IMF sequences that are relatively "front" (that is, relatively high frequency) will be converted into the white noise part of the original sequence if the corresponding wavelet variance has a sharp fluctuation and no obvious maximum value. The periodic characteristics will not be analyzed. The first five IMFs $c(1), \cdots, c(5)$ decomposed from the original sequence $x(t)$ are the white noise part of the daily $PM_{2.5}$ concentration in Shanghai. Starting from $c(6)$, the wavelet variance graphs obtained by morlet wavelet analysis in subsequent sequences $c(i), i \geq 6$ all show obvious maximum values. However, there are still some unsmooth parts in the wavelet variance graphs of $c(6)$, $c(7)$, and $c(8)$, indicating that relatively high-frequency IMF sequences other than white noise may have the limitation of empirical mode decomposition (that is, spurious modes). The main cycle results of each IMF sequence are shown in the Table 2.1.

**Table 2.1** Main period of IMF series in Shanghai

| Name | Cycle/Day | Name | Cycle/Day |
|---|---|---|---|
| $c(1)$ | No main period | $c(7)$ | 48 |
| $c(2)$ | No main period | $c(8)$ | 91 |
| $c(3)$ | No main period | $c(9)$ | 305 |
| $c(4)$ | No main period | $c(10)$ | 318 |
| $c(5)$ | No main period | $c(11)$ | 576 |
| $c(6)$ | 35 | $c(12)$ | 1794 |

The reconstruction of the decomposed IMF sequence can eliminate the spurious mode generated by the EMD decomposition of the daily $PM_{2.5}$ concentration sequence $x(t)$ in Shanghai and centralize the similar cycle information hidden in each IMF. In combination with Yogo's (2008) study on the periodicity of time series, the multi-scale periodicity of $PM_{2.5}$ was divided into four categories: seasonal cycle, short cycle, medium cycle and long cycle. Among them, the seasonal cycle refers to the repeatability of a trend line within a short cycle of time, so it is defined as the shortest period in this paper.

It can be seen from Table 2.1 that $c(6)$ and $c(7)$ are relatively close in Shanghai's results, with a period difference of about 13 days. Their shape of the wavelet variance graphs are also very similar; $c(8)$ is unique, and it is not close to the period before and after; the period of $c(9)$ and $c(10)$ are relatively close and the difference is also 13 days; $c(11)$ is a unique category with the longest period; $c(12)$ is trend item and shows a long-term trend, so the period length is almost equal to the sequence length. It can be seen from wavelet variance graph that; it also presents an obvious rising trend. It cannot find longer cycle characteristics due to the length of data set in this paper, which is also a limitation of this paper.

The classification above is based on the analysis of the wavelet variance graph and the subjective judgment of the difference in spans between cycles. However, in order to avoid the reconstruction caused by too subjective classification, K-means clustering method is used to cluster the cycle length of $c(6)$ to $c(11)$ of IMF series except white noise and trend items, and the objective is to divide it into four categories for reconstruction. The purpose of clustering is to verify the subjective classification results and provide references for the reconstruction of IMF sequences. The clustering used in this paper is based on the principle of minimization of Euclidean distance. Finally, $c(6)$ and $c(7)$ are put into a category, $c(8)$ is put into a category, $c(9)$ and $c(10)$ are put into a category, and $c(11)$ is put into a category. The result of K-means clustering is consistent with that of subjective classification, verifying the subjective classification result combined with the analysis of the wavelet variance graph. Therefore, we have decomposed 12 IMF sequences from the daily $PM_{2.5}$ concentration in Shanghai, and divided them into 6 categories according to the characteristics of different cycle scales:

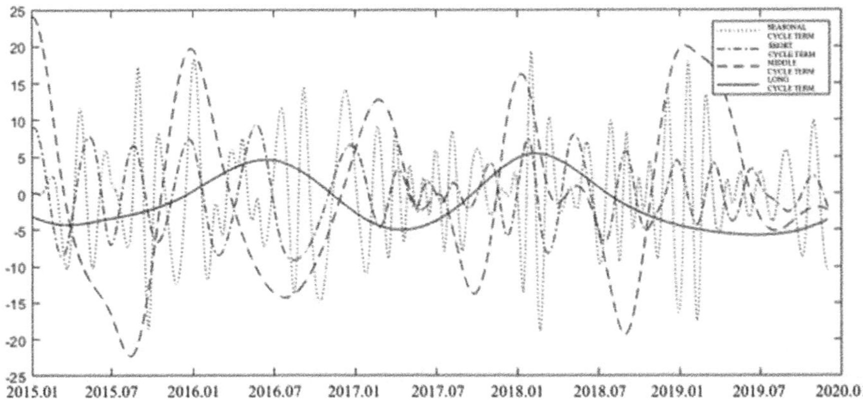


**Fig. 2.5** The seasonal, short, medium and long-term terms of IMF reconstruction in Shanghai

(1) The part with no obvious primary period of $c(1), \cdots, c(5)$ is defined as the white noise of the sequence $x(t)$, which is defined as the white noise item after reconstruction.
(2) $c(6)$ and $c(7)$ have the shortest period length measured by wavelet analysis. They are defined as the seasonal cycle of the sequence $x(t)$ after reconstruction.
(3) $c(8)$ is defined as the short cycle term of the sequence $x(t)$.
(4) After $c(9)$ and $c(10)$ are reconstructed, they are defined as the medium cycle of the sequence $x(t)$.
(5) $c(11)$ is defined as the long cycle item of the sequence $x(t)$.
(6) According to the decomposition principle of EMD, $c(12)$ shows the long-term trend of the sequence $x(t)$, so it is defined as the trend term of the sequence $x(t)$.

As shown in Fig. 2.5, the seasonal cycle term, short cycle term, medium cycle term and long cycle term formed by the reconstructed $c(6)$ to $c(11)$ can reflect the multi-scale periodic fluctuation characteristics hidden in the original sequence $x(t)$ as scheduled from high to low in frequency. Therefore, it is reasonable to take the period length of these periodic terms as the multi-scale periodic characteristics of the original sequence $x(t)$.

After the decomposition and reconstruction of steps (1) and (2) of the EMD-WA model, four sequences with cycle characteristics of different time scales, namely, seasonal cycle term, short cycle term, medium cycle term and long cycle term, are obtained. The cycle measurement of step (3) of the EMD-WA model is carried out in the following part. The wavelet analysis is used to analyze the four sequences to obtain the wavelet coefficients $W_x(a, b)$ according to formula (2.11), and the wavelet variance $\mathrm{Var}(a)$ is calculated according to formula (2.14). The time scale corresponding to the maximum point is found by combining the wavelet variance graph, which is the primary period of the sequence. The wavelet variance graph is shown below.

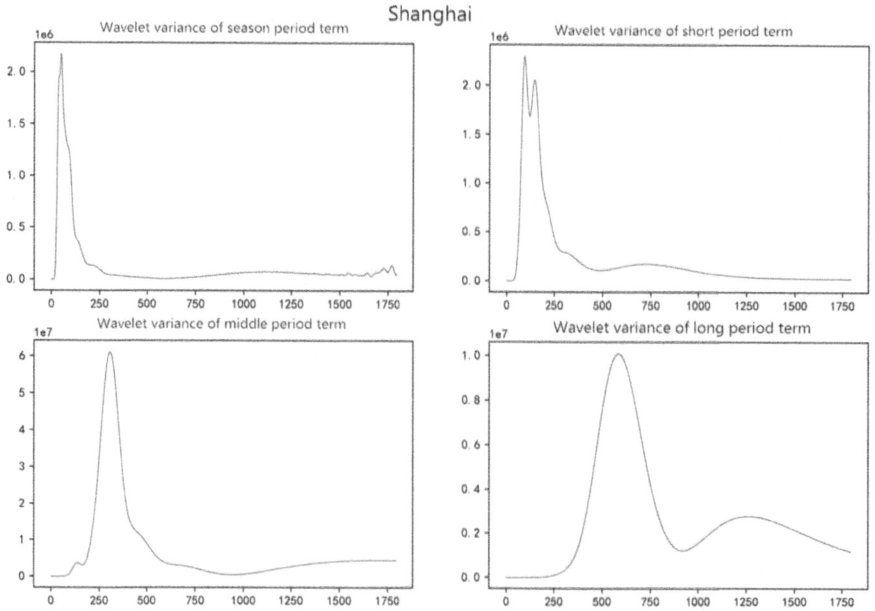


**Fig. 2.6** Wavelet Variance of Seasonal Periodic, Short-term, Mid-period and Long-period Terms of Shanghai $PM_{2.5}$ Sequence

According to Fig. 2.6 and wavelet analysis, the following conclusions can be drawn:

(1) The seasonal cycle of the daily $PM_{2.5}$ concentration sequence $x(t)$ in Shanghai is about 49 days.
(2) The short cycle of the daily $PM_{2.5}$ concentration sequence $x(t)$ in Shanghai is about 91 days.
(3) The medium cycle of the daily $PM_{2.5}$ concentration sequence $x(t)$ in Shanghai is about 305 days.
(4) The long cycle of the daily $PM_{2.5}$ concentration sequence $x(t)$ in Shanghai is about 575 days.

After the cycle measurement of step (3) of the EMD-WA model is completed, a comprehensive analysis is needed to reach a conclusion. Moreover, in order to verify the validity of the conclusion, Therefore, it is of more practical value to study the multi-scale periodicity of $PM_{2.5}$ concentration in the Yangtze River Delta.

### 2.5.2 Comprehensive Analysis of Empirical Results Based on the EMD-WA Model

In the previous section, taking Shanghai as an example, the operation process of the EMD-WA model was elaborated to analyze the multi-scale periodicity of the daily $PM_{2.5}$ concentration in Shanghai. This paper aims to analyze the multi-scale periodicity of $PM_{2.5}$ in the Yangtze River Delta. In the previous studies on periodicity of $PM_{2.5}$, its periodicity of a city is only analyzed. This paper analyzes the periodicity of a region, because $PM_{2.5}$ exists objectively, and its concentration distribution is not discrete, but the values obtained by each monitoring station are discrete due to measurement errors, recording errors, missing data, etc. Since $PM_{2.5}$ in neighboring areas is correlated to a certain extent, this paper intends to eliminate the errors and one-sidedness of the results of the periodic study on $PM_{2.5}$ in a single city through the periodic results of neighboring areas. The results of 41 prefecture-level cities in the Yangtze River Delta through the EMD-WA model are shown below.

As shown in Table 2.2, the daily $PM_{2.5}$ concentration sequence of 41 prefecture-level cities in the Yangtze River Delta region was decomposed by the EMD-WA model, and morlet wavelet analysis was used to measure the primary period of the decomposed IMF sequence of each city.

According to Fig. 2.7, the number of IMF in each city ranges from 11 to 14, and the number of IMF in most cities is 12 or 13. To some extent, the number of IMF can reflect the fineness of EMD decomposition in filtering the original sequence. The number of IMF can be controlled by setting the SD value in the EMD method (formula 2.7). Too many decomposed IMF will generate more spurious modes, resulting in increased difficulty of grouping during IMF reconstruction. However, if the number of decomposed IMF is too small, it means that the filtering original sequence fluctuation is not refined enough. It is impossible to study the periodicity of the time series on multiple scales. The number of IMF obtained in this paper is relatively moderate, indicating that the setting of $SD = 0.003$ is reasonable.

What is shown in Table 2.3 is as follows: (1) In addition to the white noise and the sequence trend item, the IMF sequence of 41 cities is classified by K-means clustering for its primary period length; (2) The reconstructed seasonal cycle item, short cycle item, medium cycle item, long cycle item is calculated according to the classification results.

According to the multi-scale cycle length of various cities shown in Table 2.4, the boxplot of seasonal period item, short period item, medium period item and long period item is made. As shown in Fig. 2.8, there is more overlap between each period item, and the length of each scale period is not concentrated enough, indicating that there may be cases where different time scale period items are grouped into a group during IMF reconstruction, so it is not effective to take clustering results as the basis for reconstruction grouping. Therefore, combined with the wavelet variance graph of each city's IMF sequence and the principle of cycle length concentration, after several reasonable attempts, the reconstruction grouping was corrected, and the results are shown in the following table.

**Table 2.2** Main period of IMF sequence in 41 cities of three provinces and one city

| City | IMF Cycle/Day | | | | | | | | | | | | | |
|---|---|---|---|---|---|---|---|---|---|---|---|---|---|---|
| | 1 | 2 | 3 | 4 | 5 | 6 | 7 | 8 | 9 | 10 | 11 | 12 | 13 | 14 |
| Shanghai | * | * | * | * | * | 35 | 48 | 91 | 305 | 318 | 576 | 1794 | None | None |
| Nanjing | * | * | * | * | * | 38 | 62 | 93 | 240 | 303 | 662 | 1794 | None | None |
| Zhenjiang | * | * | * | * | * | 31 | 50 | 65 | 238 | 303 | 814 | 1794 | None | None |
| Yangzhou | * | * | * | * | * | 29 | 50 | 149 | 303 | 325 | 586 | 1794 | None | None |
| Taizhou | * | * | * | * | * | 28 | 51 | 137 | 300 | 300 | 637 | 1003 | None | None |
| Changzhou | * | * | * | * | * | 28 | 50 | 70 | 253 | 297 | 671 | 1021 | None | None |
| Wuxi | * | * | * | * | * | 50 | 60 | 101 | 296 | 459 | 894 | 1794 | None | None |
| Suzhou | * | * | * | * | * | 53 | 57 | 93 | 238 | 305 | 1794 | None | None | None |
| Nantong | * | * | * | * | * | 36 | 78 | 156 | 305 | 319 | 1064 | 1794 | None | None |
| Huaian | * | * | * | * | * | 28 | 51 | 96 | 212 | 297 | 612 | 799 | 1794 | None |
| Yancheng | * | * | * | * | * | 33 | 43 | 53 | 169 | 307 | 1794 | None | None | None |
| Lianyungang | * | * | * | * | * | 59 | 38 | 50 | 106 | 287 | 320 | 456 | 1033 | 1794 |
| Suqian | * | * | * | * | * | 41 | 48 | 206 | 297 | 311 | 542 | 782 | 1794 | None |
| Xuzhou | * | * | * | * | * | 33 | 62 | 126 | 290 | 463 | 1404 | 1794 | None | None |
| Hangzhou | * | * | * | * | * | 32 | 60 | 95 | 155 | 296 | 492 | 1020 | 1794 | None |
| Huzhou | * | * | * | * | * | 49 | 69 | 101 | 310 | 448 | 566 | 1794 | None | None |
| Jiaxing | * | * | * | * | * | 39 | 107 | 262 | 318 | 488 | 1794 | None | None | None |
| Shaoxing | * | * | * | * | * | 36 | 70 | 104 | 300 | 419 | 960 | 1794 | None | None |
| Jinhua | * | * | * | * | * | * | 46 | 62 | 125 | 292 | 475 | 1794 | None | None |
| Quzhou | * | * | * | * | * | 36 | 57 | 70 | 111 | 290 | 637 | 1794 | None | None |
| Lishui | * | * | * | * | * | 38 | 91 | 134 | 294 | 945 | 1794 | None | None | None |
| Wenzhou | * | * | * | * | * | 36 | 51 | 106 | 280 | 309 | 927 | 1794 | None | None |
| Taizhou | * | * | * | * | * | 55 | 73 | 113 | 295 | 448 | 879 | 1794 | None | None |
| Ningbo | * | * | * | * | * | 37 | 68 | 95 | 137 | 305 | 320 | 501 | 766 | 1794 |
| Zhoushan | * | * | * | * | * | 35 | 58 | 101 | 287 | 301 | 431 | 851 | 1794 | None |
| Hefei | * | * | * | * | * | 41 | 65 | 160 | 292 | 419 | 1794 | None | None | None |
| Chuzhou | * | * | * | * | * | 35 | 54 | 101 | 290 | 484 | 744 | 1794 | None | None |
| Maanshan | * | * | * | * | * | 35 | 57 | 90 | 318 | 327 | 735 | 1794 | None | None |
| Bengbu | * | * | * | * | * | 46 | 47 | 147 | 297 | 532 | 1794 | None | None | None |
| Suzhou | * | * | * | * | * | 27 | 57 | 101 | 291 | 525 | 595 | 1124 | 1794 | None |
| Huaibei | * | * | * | * | * | 33 | 51 | 101 | 300 | 656 | 879 | 1794 | None | None |
| Haozhou | * | * | * | * | * | 34 | 57 | 96 | 307 | 599 | 677 | 1213 | 1794 | None |
| Huainan | * | * | * | * | * | 27 | 108 | 96 | 354 | 521 | 624 | 595 | 1794 | None |
| Fuyang | * | * | * | * | * | * | 51 | 101 | 404 | 320 | 519 | 960 | 1794 | None |
| Liuan | * | * | * | * | * | 36 | 58 | 107 | 280 | 788 | 799 | 735 | 1794 | None |

(continued)

**Table 2.2** (continued)

| City | IMF Cycle/Day | | | | | | | | | | | | | |
|---|---|---|---|---|---|---|---|---|---|---|---|---|---|---|
| | 1 | 2 | 3 | 4 | 5 | 6 | 7 | 8 | 9 | 10 | 11 | 12 | 13 | 14 |
| Anqing | * | * | * | * | * | 55 | 74 | 96 | 297 | 311 | 547 | 1794 | None | None |
| Chizhou | * | * | * | * | * | 36 | 55 | 101 | 287 | 525 | 1794 | None | None | None |
| Tongling | * | * | * | * | * | 28 | 60 | 96 | 262 | 357 | 287 | 814 | 1794 | None |
| Huzhou | * | * | * | * | * | * | 57 | 101 | 150 | 300 | 548 | 814 | 1794 | None |
| Xuancheng | * | * | * | * | * | 32 | 60 | 72 | 106 | 290 | 799 | 1794 | None | None |
| Huangshan | * | * | * | * | * | 41 | 70 | 125 | 291 | 559 | 973 | None | None | None |

*Note* * Indicates that the white noise part of the IMF is no main period

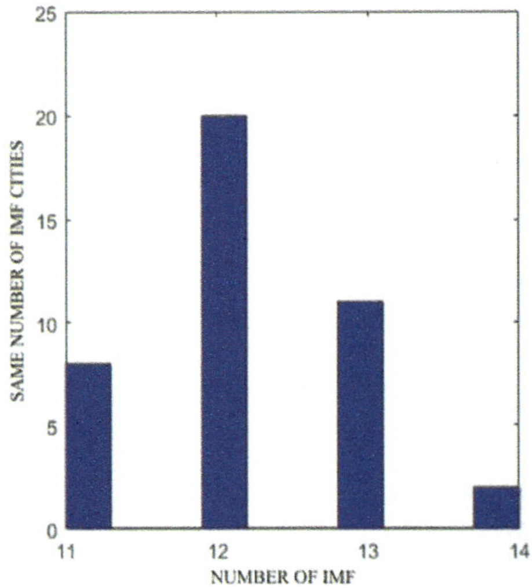


**Fig. 2.7** Frequency histogram of IMF number in different cities

As shown in Fig. 2.9, after the correction and reconstruction grouping based on the wavelet variance graph, the overlap between seasonal cycle items, short cycle items, medium cycle items and long cycle items is significantly reduced, and the cycle length of seasonal cycle items, short cycle items and medium cycle items are quite concentrated in various cities, showing good effectiveness. Although the concentration degree of the long-cycle term is slightly improved, its upward and downward range is still large, so it is not effective enough. Because the insufficient data length used in this paper leads to a longer period fluctuation hidden in the trend term during the EMD operation, resulting in a higher degree of dispersion in the range of long periods and poor effectiveness.

The research objective of this paper is to study the multi-scale period characteristics of $PM_{2.5}$ in the Yangtze River Delta region. In order to take into account, the overall macroscopicity and local specificity, the above cycle results are analyzed in two parts: (1) The cycle length of 41 prefecture-level cities in the Yangtze River

**Table 2.3** IMF clustering results of 41 cities in three provinces and one city and the main period after IMF reconstruction

| City | Seasonal cycle term | | Short cycle term | | Middle cycle term | | Long cycle term | |
|---|---|---|---|---|---|---|---|---|
| | Cluster results | Cycle/Day | Cluster results | Cycle/Day | Cluster results | Cycl/Day | Cluster results | Cycle/Day |
| Shanghai | [6,7] | 49 | [8] | 91 | [9,10] | 305 | [11] | 576 |
| Nanjing | [6,7,8] | 62 | [9] | 240 | [10] | 303 | [11] | 662 |
| Zhenjiang | [6,7,8] | 50 | [9] | 238 | [10] | 303 | [11] | 814 |
| Yangzhou | [6,7] | 39 | [8] | 149 | [9,10] | 295 | [11] | 586 |
| Taizhou | [6,7] | 41 | [8] | 137 | [9,10] | 299 | [11] | 637 |
| Changzhou | [6,7,8] | 57 | [9] | 253 | [10] | 297 | [11] | 671 |
| Wuxi | [6,7,8] | 53 | [9] | 296 | [10] | 459 | [11] | 894 |
| Suzhou | [6,7] | 36 | [8] | 93 | [9] | 238 | [10] | 305 |
| Nantong | [6,7] | 36 | [8] | 156 | [9,10] | 296 | [11] | 1064 |
| Huaian | [6,7,8] | 49 | [9,10] | 294 | [11] | 612 | [12] | 799 |
| Yancheng | [6] | 33 | [7,8] | 50 | [9] | 169 | [10] | 307 |
| Lianyungang | [6,7,8,9] | 101 | [10,11] | 300 | [12] | 456 | [13] | 1033 |
| Suqian | [6,7] | 41 | [8,9,10] | 294 | [11] | 542 | [12] | 782 |
| Xuzhou | [6,7,8] | 96 | [9] | 290 | [10] | 463 | [11] | 1404 |
| Hangzhou | [6,7,8,9] | 96 | [10] | 296 | [11] | 492 | [12] | 1020 |

(continued)

**Table 2.3** (continued)

| City | Seasonal cycle term | | Short cycle term | | Middle cycle term | | Long cycle term | |
|---|---|---|---|---|---|---|---|---|
| | Cluster results | Cycle/Day | Cluster results | Cycle/Day | Cluster results | Cycl/Day | Cluster results | Cycle/Day |
| Huzhou | [6,7,8] | 58 | [9] | 310 | [10] | 448 | [11] | 566 |
| Jiaxing | [6] | 39 | [7] | 107 | [8,9] | 310 | [10] | 448 |
| Shaoxing | [6,7,8] | 93 | [9] | 300 | [10] | 419 | [11] | 960 |
| Jinhua | [7,8] | 65 | [9] | 125 | [10] | 292 | [11] | 475 |
| Quzhou | [6,7,8] | 45 | [9] | 111 | [10] | 290 | [11] | 637 |
| Lishui | [6] | 38 | [7,8] | 104 | [9] | 294 | [10] | 945 |
| Wenzhou | [6,7] | 41 | [8] | 106 | [9,10] | 295 | [11] | 927 |
| Taizhou | [6,7,8] | 95 | [9] | 295 | [10] | 448 | [11] | 879 |
| Ningbo | [6,7,8,9] | 101 | [10,11] | 297 | [12] | 501 | [13] | 766 |
| Zhoushan | [6,7,8] | 99 | [9,10] | 305 | [11] | 431 | [12] | 851 |
| Hefei | [6,7] | 46 | [8] | 160 | [9] | 292 | [10] | 419 |
| Chuzhou | [6,7,8] | 95 | [9] | 290 | [10] | 484 | [11] | 744 |

(continued)

**Table 2.3** (continued)

| City | Seasonal cycle term | | Short cycle term | | Middle cycle term | | Long cycle term | |
|---|---|---|---|---|---|---|---|---|
| | Cluster results | Cycle/Day | Cluster results | Cycle/Day | Cluster results | Cycl/Day | Cluster results | Cycle/Day |
| Maanshan | [6,7] | 55 | [8] | 90 | [9,10] | 299 | [11] | 735 |
| Bengbu | [6,7] | 44 | [8] | 147 | [9] | 297 | [10] | 532 |
| Suzhou | [6,7,8] | 55 | [9] | 291 | [10,11] | 431 | [12] | 1124 |
| Huaibei | [6,7,8] | 50 | [9] | 300 | [10] | 656 | [11] | 879 |
| Haozhou | [6,7,8] | 95 | [9] | 307 | [10,11] | 381 | [12] | 1213 |
| Huainan | [6,7,8] | 62 | [9] | 354 | [10] | 521 | [11,12] | 331 |
| Fuyang | [7,8] | 53 | [9,10] | 294 | [11] | 519 | [12] | 960 |
| Liuan | [6,7] | 55 | [8] | 107 | [9] | 280 | [10,11,12] | 311 |
| Anqing | [6,7] | 62 | [8] | 96 | [9,10] | 292 | [11] | 547 |
| Chizhou | [6,7] | 41 | [8] | 101 | [9] | 287 | [10] | 525 |
| Tongling | [6,7,8] | 60 | [9,10] | 305 | [11] | 287 | [12] | 814 |
| Huzhou | [7,8,9] | 150 | [10] | 300 | [11] | 548 | [12] | 814 |
| Xuancheng | [6,7,8] | 62 | [9] | 106 | [10] | 290 | [11] | 799 |
| Huangshan | [6,7] | 43 | [8] | 125 | [9] | 291 | [10] | 559 |

*Note* The number in [] indicates the IMF serial number decomposed by EMD of PM2.5 daily concentration series of the city; the period is the main period calculated after IMF reconstruction in []

**Table 2.4** IMF restructuring groups and the main period after IMF restructuring

| City | Seasonal cycle term | | Short cycle term | | Middle cycle term | | Long cycle term | |
|---|---|---|---|---|---|---|---|---|
| | Cluster results | Cycle/Day | Cluster results | Cycle/Day | Cluster results | Cycle/Day | Cluster results | Cycle/Day |
| Shanghai | [6,7] | 49 | [8] | 91 | [9,10] | 305 | [11] | 576 |
| Nanjing | [6,7] | 58 | [8] | 93 | [9,10] | 297 | [11] | 662 |
| Zhenjiang | [6,7] | 45 | [8] | 65 | [9,10] | 300 | [11] | 814 |
| Yangzhou | [6,7] | 39 | [8] | 149 | [9,10] | 295 | [11] | 586 |
| Taizhou | [6,7] | 41 | [8] | 137 | [9,10] | 299 | [11] | 637 |
| Changzhou | [6,7] | 48 | [8] | 70 | [9,10] | 293 | [11] | 671 |
| Wuxi | [6,7] | 53 | [8] | 101 | [9,10] | 297 | [11] | 894 |
| Suzhou | [6,7] | 36 | [8] | 93 | [9] | 238 | [10] | 305 |
| Nantong | [6,7] | 36 | [8] | 156 | [9,10] | 296 | [11] | 1064 |
| Huaian | [6,7] | 47 | [8] | 96 | [9,10] | 294 | [11,12] | 666 |
| Yancheng | [6] | 33 | [7,8] | 50 | [9] | 169 | [10] | 307 |
| Lianyungang | [6,7,8] | 53 | [9] | 106 | [10,11,12] | 302 | [13] | 1033 |
| Suqian | [6,7] | 41 | [8] | 206 | [9,10] | 292 | [11,12] | 606 |
| Xuzhou | [6,7] | 58 | [8] | 126 | [9] | 290 | [10,11] | 1404 |
| Hangzhou | [6,7] | 57 | [8,9] | 95 | [10,11] | 297 | [12] | 1020 |

(continued)

**Table 2.4** (continued)

| City | Seasonal cycle term | | Short cycle term | | Middle cycle term | | Long cycle term | |
|---|---|---|---|---|---|---|---|---|
| | Cluster results | Cycle/Day | Cluster results | Cycle/Day | Cluster results | Cycle/Day | Cluster results | Cycle/Day |
| Huzhou | [6,7] | 49 | [8] | 101 | [9,10] | 300 | [11] | 566 |
| Jiaxing | [6] | 39 | [7] | 107 | [8,9] | 310 | [10] | 448 |
| Shaoxing | [6,7] | 36 | [8] | 104 | [9,10] | 294 | [11] | 960 |
| Jinhua | [7,8] | 65 | [9] | 125 | [10] | 292 | [11] | 475 |
| Quzhou | [6,7,8] | 45 | [9] | 111 | [10] | 290 | [11] | 637 |
| Lishui | [6] | 38 | [7,8] | 104 | [9] | 294 | [10] | 945 |
| Wenzhou | [6,7] | 41 | [8] | 106 | [9,10] | 295 | [11] | 735 |
| Taizhou | [6,7] | 70 | [8] | 113 | [9,10] | 294 | [11,12] | 879 |
| Ningbo | [6,7] | 38 | [8,9] | 137 | [10,11] | 297 | [12,13] | 735 |
| Zhoushan | [6,7] | 46 | [8] | 101 | [9,10,11] | 303 | [12] | 851 |
| Hefei | [6,7] | 46 | [8] | 160 | [9] | 292 | [10] | 419 |
| Chuzhou | [6,7] | 41 | [8] | 101 | [9,10] | 294 | [11] | 744 |

(continued)

**Table 2.4** (continued)

| City | Seasonal cycle term | | Short cycle term | | Middle cycle term | | Long cycle term | |
|---|---|---|---|---|---|---|---|---|
| | Cluster results | Cycle/Day | Cluster results | Cycle/Day | Cluster results | Cycle/Day | Cluster results | Cycle/Day |
| Maanshan | [6,7] | 55 | [8] | 90 | [9,10] | 299 | [11] | 735 |
| Bengbu | [6,7] | 44 | [8] | 147 | [9] | 297 | [10] | 532 |
| Suzhou | [6,7] | 55 | [8] | 101 | [9,10,11] | 292 | [12] | 1124 |
| Huaibei | [6,7] | 35 | [8] | 101 | [9] | 300 | [10,11] | 542 |
| Haozhou | [6,7] | 33 | [8] | 96 | [9,10,11] | 297 | [12] | 1213 |
| Huainan | [6,7] | 59 | [8] | 96 | [9] | 354 | [10,11,12] | 297 |
| Fuyang | [7] | 51 | [8] | 101 | [9,10,11] | 294 | [12] | 960 |
| Liuan | [6,7] | 55 | [8] | 107 | [9] | 280 | [10,11,12] | 311 |
| Anqing | [6,7] | 62 | [8] | 96 | [9,10] | 292 | [11] | 547 |
| Chizhou | [6,7] | 41 | [8] | 101 | [9] | 287 | [10] | 525 |
| Tongling | [6,7] | 57 | [8] | 96 | [9,10,11] | 287 | [12] | 814 |
| Huzhou | [7] | 57 | [8,9] | 149 | [10,11] | 301 | [12] | 814 |
| Xuancheng | [6,7] | 58 | [8,9] | 96 | [10] | 290 | [11] | 799 |
| Huangshan | [6,7] | 43 | [8] | 125 | [9] | 291 | [10] | 559 |

*Note* The number in [] indicates the IMF serial number decomposed by EMD of PM2.5 daily concentration series of the city; the period is the main period calculated after IMF reconstruction in []

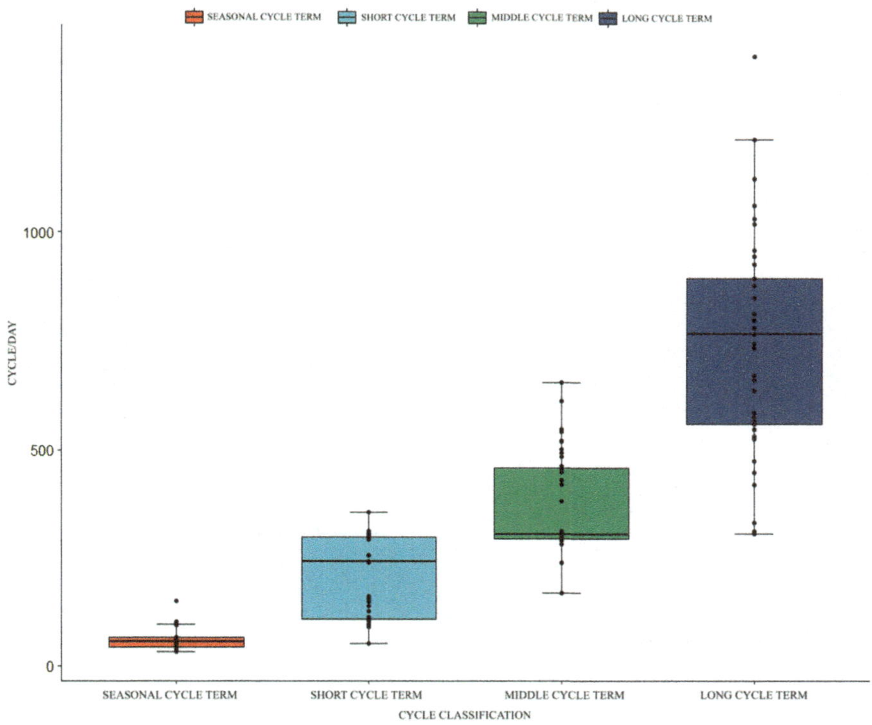


**Fig. 2.8** Boxplot of each period determined by clustering results

Delta is analyzed; (2) Taking the province as the unit, statistical analysis is carried out for different provinces to study the local multi-scale periodic characteristics of the Yangtze River Delta region more clearly.

The above table provides a statistical summary of the seasonal cycle items, short cycle items, medium cycle items, and long cycle items in all prefecture-level cities in the Yangtze River Delta from six aspects: including median, upper quartile, and lower quartile, average, minimum and maximum, all indicators are rounded. In combination with Fig. 2.9, in order to objectively measure the period length and reduce the influence of extreme values, the median is adopted as the period length of each period item. The following conclusions are drawn:

(1) The seasonal cycle of daily $PM_{2.5}$ concentration in the Yangtze River Delta is 46 days (about 1.5 months).
(2) The short cycle of daily $PM_{2.5}$ concentration in the Yangtze River Delta is 101 days (about 3.5 months).
(3) The medium cycle of the daily $PM_{2.5}$ concentration in the Yangtze River Delta is 294 days (about 10 months).
(4) The long cycle of daily $PM_{2.5}$ concentration in the Yangtze River Delta is 671 days (about 22.5 months).

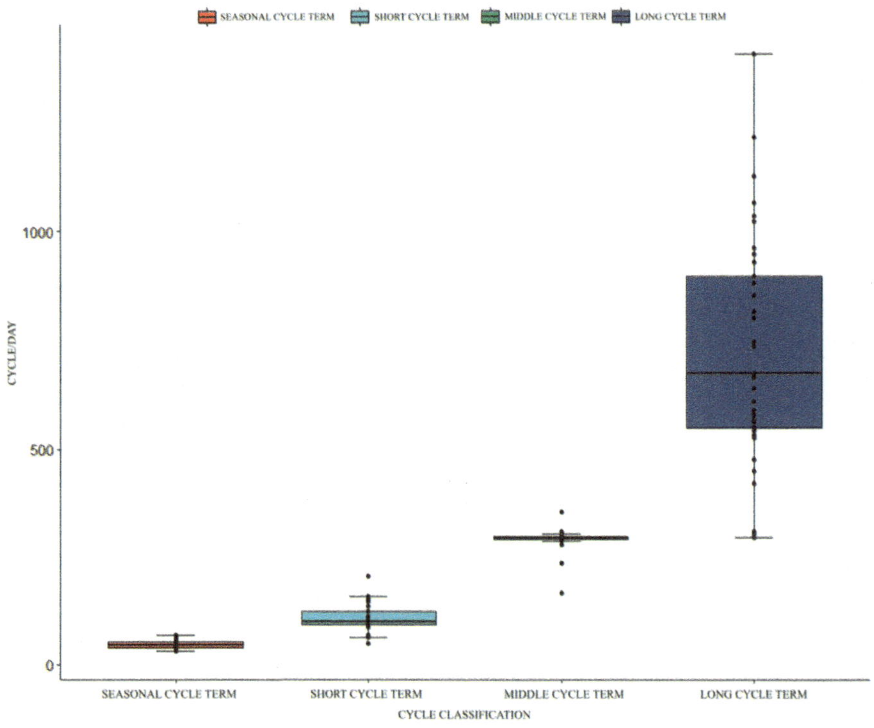


**Fig. 2.9** Box line diagram of each period determined after modification and reconstruction grouping

Among all the periodicity scales, the medium cycle is the most significant. Not only is the cycle length concentration high in all cities, but the results are basically consistent with that of 298 days of cycle results of Chen et al.'s (2020) study on $PM_{2.5}$ in Chengdu.

After obtaining the overall multi-scale periodicity in the Yangtze River Delta region, we still want to know whether there is consistency or specificity in the local multi-scale periodicity in the Yangtze River Delta region. In order to facilitate the research, elaboration and analysis of relevant results, this paper divides the Yangtze River Delta region into four parts according to the provincial administrative regions: Jiangsu, Shanghai, Zhejiang and Anhui, which can roughly correspond to the north, east, south and west of the Yangtze River Delta region. Except for Shanghai, the statistical analysis is carried out in the other three provinces according to the multi-scale cycle results of cities in Table 2.4 based on the statistical caliber in Table 2.5. The statistical results are shown in Tables 2.6, 2.7 and 2.8.

According to the above three tables and the results of multi-scale cycle in Shanghai (east of Yangtze River Delta), it can be found that the period length is roughly consistent on the seasonal, short and medium cycle scales; however, there are large differences on the long cycle scale: (1) The median and average of the long cycle term in the south of the Yangtze River Delta (Zhejiang) are higher than that in other regions

**Table 2.5** Multi scale periodic overall statistical analysis of all cities in the Yangtze River Delta

| Periodic scale | Median/day | Upper quartile/day | Lower quartile/day | Average/day | Min/day | Max/day |
|---|---|---|---|---|---|---|
| Seasonal cycle term | 46 | 41 | 55 | 48 | 33 | 70 |
| Short cycle term | 101 | 96 | 125 | 110 | 50 | 206 |
| Middle cycle term | 294 | 292 | 299 | 292 | 169 | 354 |
| Long cycle term | 671 | 547 | 894 | 722 | 297 | 1404 |

**Table 2.6** Multi scale periodic statistical analysis of the Northern Yangtze River Delta (Jiangsu)

| Periodic scale | Median/day | Upper quartile/day | Lower quartile/day | Average/day | Min/day | Max/day |
|---|---|---|---|---|---|---|
| Seasonal cycle term | 45 | 39 | 53 | 45 | 33 | 58 |
| Short cycle term | 101 | 93 | 137 | 111 | 50 | 206 |
| Middle cycle term | 295 | 292 | 297 | 282 | 169 | 302 |
| Long cycle term | 666 | 606 | 894 | 742 | 305 | 1404 |

**Table 2.7** Multi scale periodic statistical analysis of cities in the south of Yangtze River Delta (Zhejiang)

| Periodic scale | Median/day | Upper quartile/day | Lower quartile/day | Average/day | Min/day | Max/day |
|---|---|---|---|---|---|---|
| Seasonal cycle term | 45 | 39 | 53 | 48 | 36 | 70 |
| Short cycle term | 106 | 103 | 112 | 109 | 95 | 137 |
| Middle cycle term | 295 | 294 | 299 | 297 | 290 | 310 |
| Long cycle term | 851 | 602 | 936 | 768 | 448 | 1020 |

of the Yangtze River Delta; (2) In the west of the Yangtze River Delta (Anhui), the dispersion degree of the long period term is relatively large, and the minimum value of the long period term even overlaps with that of the middle period term.

To sum up, the EMD-WA model was applied to carry out an empirical study of multi-scale periodic of $PM_{2.5}$ in the Yangtze River Delta region to comprehensively analyze its overall and local characteristics. The results are summarized in Table 2.9.

**Table 2.8** Multi scale periodic statistical analysis of Western Yangtze River Delta (Anhui)

| Periodic scale | Median/day | Upper quartile/day | Lower quartile/day | Average/day | Min/day | Max/day |
|---|---|---|---|---|---|---|
| Seasonal cycle term | 53 | 43 | 57 | 50 | 33 | 62 |
| Short cycle term | 101 | 96 | 112 | 110 | 90 | 160 |
| Middle cycle term | 293 | 291 | 298 | 297 | 280 | 354 |
| Long cycle term | 647 | 530 | 814 | 683 | 297 | 1213 |

**Table 2.9** Summary of multi-scale periodic results in the Yangtze River Delta and its parts

| Periodic scale | Yangtze River Delta (overall) / day | Northern Yangtze River Delta (Jiangsu) / day | Eastern Yangtze River Delta (Shanghai)/day | Southern Yangtze River Delta (Zhejiang)/day | Western Yangtze River Delta (Anhui) / day |
|---|---|---|---|---|---|
| Seasonal cycle term | 46 | 45 | 49 | 45 | 53 |
| Short cycle term | 101 | 101 | 91 | 106 | 101 |
| Middle cycle term | 294 | 295 | 305 | 295 | 293 |
| Long cycle term | 671 | 666 | 575 | 851 | 647 |

### 2.5.3 *Short Periodic Analysis in Yangtze River Delta During Heavy Haze*

This section intends to study the periodic characteristics of hourly $PM_{2.5}$ concentration within 10 days in the most severe haze days (240 h) in the Yangtze River Delta region. The data set selected is from January 1, 2015 to November 30, 2019. The moving average maximum value of hourly $PM_{2.5}$ concentration in cities in the Yangtze River Delta during the 240 window periods. The results of 41 prefecture-level cities are shown in Table 2.10.

As shown in Table 2.10, the moving average value of the 240 window periods of the hourly $PM_{2.5}$ concentration in Xuzhou city is the largest in all cities. The most polluted period is from 0:00 on January 13, 2018 to 23:00 on January 22, 2018, with a total length of 240 h. The results of using the EMD-WA model are as follows.

**Table 2.10** Average maximum value of PM2.5 hourly concentration in 240 window periods in different cities

| City | PM2.5 | City | PM2.5 | City | PM2.5 | City | PM2.5 |
|---|---|---|---|---|---|---|---|
| Shanghai | 107 | Lianyungang | 142 | Taizhou | 100 | Fuyang | 171 |
| Nanjing | 131 | Suqian | 167 | Ningbo | 100 | Liuan | 128 |
| Zhenjiang | 145 | Xuzhou | 210 | Zhoushan | 65 | Anqing | 128 |
| Yangzhou | 118 | Hangzhou | 118 | Hefei | 130 | Chizhou | 130 |
| Taizhou | 127 | Huzhou | 135 | Chuzhou | 139 | Tongling | 119 |
| Changzhou | 129 | Jiaxing | 106 | Maanshan | 138 | Huzhou | 154 |
| Wuxi | 123 | Shaoxing | 117 | Bengbu | 147 | Xuancheng | 118 |
| Suzhou | 114 | Jinhua | 121 | Suzhou | 167 | Huangshan | 66 |
| Nantong | 122 | Quzhou | 98 | Huaibei | 161 | | |
| Huaian | 147 | Lishui | 89 | Haozhou | 160 | | |
| Yancheng | 128 | Wenzhou | 96 | Huainan | 152 | | |

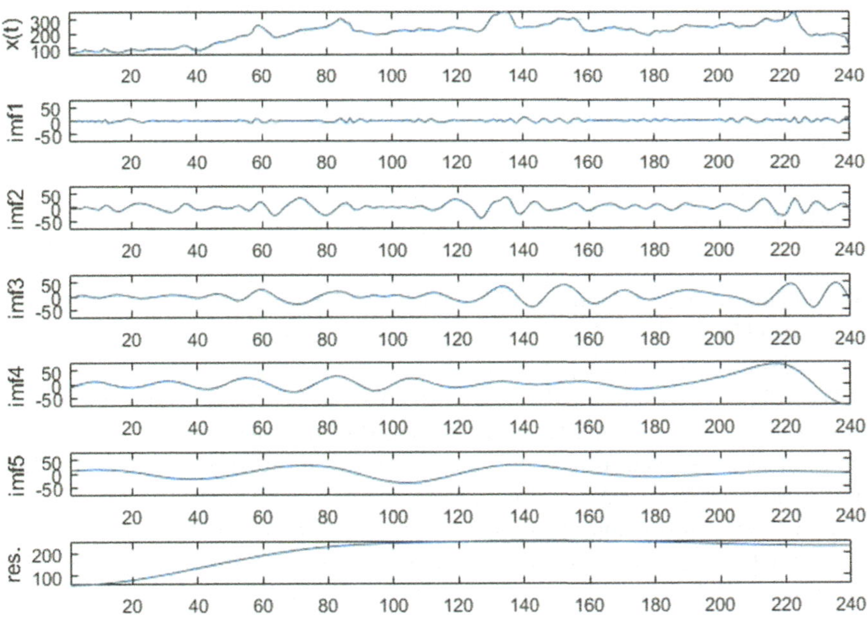


**Fig. 2.10** Timing chart of $PM_{2.5}$ concentration in Xuzhou City and IMF

## 2.5.4 *Short Periodic Analysis in Yangtze River Delta During Heavy Haze*

The length of the data set applied in this section is only 240, so the stop filter condition of the EMD method is set as SD = 0.03. As shown in Fig. 2.10, IMF $c(1), \cdots, c(5)$

**Table 2.11** Main cycle of IMF sequence in Xuzhou

| Name | Cycle/hour | Name | Cycle/hour |
|---|---|---|---|
| $c(1)$ | No main period | $c(4)$ | 47 |
| $c(2)$ | 9 | $c(5)$ | 55 |
| $c(3)$ | 14 | $c(6)$ | 240 |

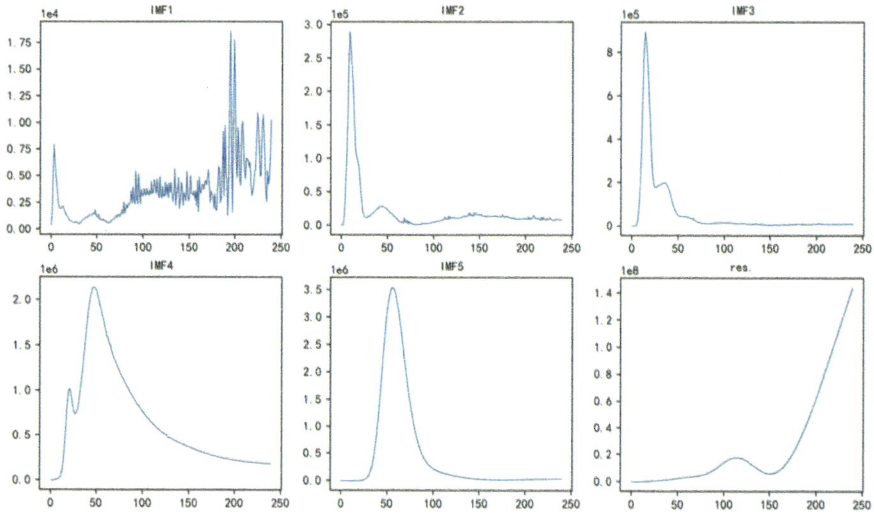


**Fig. 2.11** IMF wavelet variance in Xuzhou

and trend item $c(6)$ are decomposed through the EMD method, and their cycle length is calculated by morlet wavelet analysis for reconstruction.

The results are shown in Table 2.11.

According to the cycle length of each IMF in Table 2.11, combined with Fig. 2.11 corresponding to the wavelet variance graph of IMF sequence, it is divided into two groups of short cycle term and long cycle term for reconstruction, and $c(2)$, $c(3)$ are short cycle term, and $c(4)$, $c(5)$ are long cycle term.

After the reconstruction, the period is calculated and the results are as follows: (1) During the 240 h with the most severe haze in Xuzhou, the short cycle is 14 h. (2) During the 240 h with the most severe haze in Xuzhou, its long cycle is 55 h.

Therefore, in the short period during severe haze in the Yangtze River Delta, the variation of $PM_{2.5}$ concentration still has a significant periodicity. However, due to its short sequence, the periodicity may be more inclined to the oscillation period, and the trend period is not obvious.

## 2.6 Conclusion and Outlook

In this article we attempt to apply ICT technology to PM time series, and verifies the feasibility and practicability of these methods in PM time series analysis.

In this paper, EMD and WA are combined to analyze the following two data sets: *a*. the daily $PM_{2.5}$ concentration in 41 prefecture-level cities in the Yangtze River Delta from January 1, 2015 to November 30, 2019; *b*. The hourly $PM_{2.5}$ concentration sequence during the heavy haze region of the Yangtze River Delta from 0 on January 13, 2018 to 23 on January 22, 2018. The multi-scale periodicity of $PM_{2.5}$ in the Yangtze River Delta is analyzed and the main conclusions are as follows:

(1) In the analysis of data set *a*, through the decomposition and reconstruction of the EMD-WA model, cycle characteristics of four scales from short to long can be obtained, which are seasonal, short, medium and long cycle terms respectively.
(2) The $PM_{2.5}$ concentration in the Yangtze River Delta region has an obvious multi-scale periodicity on the whole, with a seasonal cycle of 46 days (about 1.5 months), a short cycle of 101 days (about 3.5 months), a medium cycle of 294 days (about 10 months), and a long cycle of 671 days (about 22.5 months).[1]
(3) There is good consistency in terms of seasonal, short and medium cycle scales in the north (Jiangsu), east (Shanghai), south (Zhejiang), and west (Anhui) of the Yangtze River Delta, but there are significant differences in terms of long cycle scales.
(4) Based on the analysis of data set b, it is proved that in the 240 h with severe haze in the Yangtze River Delta region, $PM_{2.5}$ concentration still has a relatively obvious periodicity, showing a short cycle of 14 h and a long period of 55 h.

According to the findings above, policy suggestions can be given as follows:

(1) According to the short-term periodic characteristics of the PM sequence, it is possible to strengthen the detection of key pollution sources, shut down and reduce pollution sources before the arrival of PM peaks such as winter and spring or working days; Early warning of high-polluting weather is issued to remind the public to prevent the impact of haze on health, to remind the transportation industry to deal with the possible impact of severe haze on vehicle driving and aircraft travel, and to remind hospitals of the negative effects of the surge in respiratory diseases caused by PM.
(2) According to the long-term periodic characteristics of the PM sequence, the most important thing is to reduce pollution emissions in industrial production, improve the environmental standards of fuels used, reduce vehicle exhaust emissions, and strengthen urban greening work; It is necessary to advocate the implementation of a low-carbon lifestyle, and to gradually eliminate the use of fireworks or firecrackers to celebrate holidays. Only by starting with systems

[1]These conclusions are basically consistent with the other study. For example, Wang et al. (2020) found hourly concentrations of $PM_{2.5}$ from 2015 to 2018 in the cities of the Yangtze River Delta have two dominant periods: an annual cycle on the time scale of 250–480 days and a semi-annual cycle on the time scale of 130–220 days.

and regulations and persevering, can we achieve sound haze reduction effects (Wu et al. 2020).

Future researches include:

During the analysis of the long-cycle term, it is found that there are abnormal points in the period length. A possible reason is that the insufficient length of the selected sequence makes it impossible to find fluctuation trends with longer cycle lengths (Song and Wang 2018).

(1) When judging the period of multi-scale period results of the Yangtze River Delta region at present, we find that the data of only one city may not be able to represent the Yangtze River Delta region, but this paper has not found a better method to study this point-to-face problem.
(2) When analyzing the multi-scale period of $PM_{2.5}$, little information about the causes of haze is mentioned, but this period characteristic is closely related to a series of factors such as geographical conditions, weather, climate, human production activities (Wu et al. 2019a, 2019b). It is necessary to consider the joint analysis of the geographic characteristics, climatic characteristics, economic composition, and policy orientation of the research area under the premise of studying the concentration sequence of $PM_{2.5}$ to study the periodicity of $PM_{2.5}$ more accurately.

**Acknowledgements** Shaoli He, Weihang Sun also made great contributions to this manuscript. We express our heartfelt thanks to them. This research was supported by: National Social and Scientific Fund Program of China (18ZDA052; 17BGL142; 16ZDA047); The Natural Science Foundation of China (91546117, 71373131).

## References

Addo, P. M., Billio, M., & Guégan, G. (2014). *Nonlinear dynamics and wavelets for business cycle analysis*. Berlin: Springer International Publishing.

Bao, C., & Fang, C. L. (2007). Water resources constraint force on urbanization in water deficient regions: A case study of the Hexi Corridor, arid area of NW China. *Ecological Economics, 62*(3–4), 508–517.

Baubeau, P., & Cazelles, B. (2009). French economic cycles: A wavelet analysis of French retrospective GNP series. *Cliometrica, 3*(3), 275–300.

Berdiev, A. N., & Chang, C. P. (2015). Business cycle synchronization in Asia-Pacific: New evidence from wavelet analysis. *Journal of Asian Economics, 37*, 20–33.

Carvalho, M. D., Rodrigues, P. C., & Rua, A. (2012). Tracking the us business cycle with a singular spectrum analysis. *Economics Letters, 114*, 32–35.

Cendejas, J. L., Muñoz, F. F., & Fernández-de-Pinedo, N. (2017). A contribution to the analysis of historical economic fluctuations (1870–2010): Filtering, spurious cycles, and unobserved component modeling. *Cliometrica, 11*(1), 93–125.

Cekim, H. O. (2020). Forecasting PM10 concentrations using time series models: A case of the most polluted cities in Turkey. *Environmental Science and Pollution Research, 27*, 25612–25624.

Chen, X. B., Yin, L. R., Fan, Y. L., Song, L. H., Ji, T. T., Liu, Y., Tian, J. W., & Zheng, W. F. (2020). Temporal evolution characteristics of PM2. 5 concentration based on continuous wavelet transform. *Science of the Total Environment,* 699, 134244.

Cui, J. T. (1995). *Wavelet Analysis.* Xian: Xi'an Jiaotong University Press.

Fiffer, M., Kang, Choong-Min., Requia, M. J., & Koutrakis, P. (2020). Long-term impact of PM2.5 mass and sulfur reductions on ultrafine particle trends in Boston, MA from 1999 to 2018. *Journal of the Air & Waste Management Association, 70*(7):700–707.

Flandrin, P., Rilling, G., & Gonçalves, P. (2004). Empirical mode decomposition as a filter bank. *IEEE Signal Processing Letters, 11*(2), 112–114.

Gu, K. H., Shi, H. X., Zhang, S., Fan, S. X., Xu, J. M., & Tan, J. G. (2015). Variation characteristics of PM2.5 levels and the influence of meteorological conditions on Chongming Island in Shanghai. *Resources and Environment in the Yangtze Basin, 24*(12), 2108–2116.

Hansen, J., Sato, M. K. I., Ruedy, R., Nazarenko, L., Lacis, A., Schmidt, G. A., & Bell, N. (2005). Efficacy of climate forcings. *Journal of Geophysical Research: Atmospheres, 110*(D18).

He, J. L., & Song, W. L. (2013). Measurement and analysis of ocean economic cyclical changes based on filtering method. *Marine Science Bulletin, 32*(1), 1–7.

Huang, N., Shen, Z., Long, S. R., & Wu, M. C. (1971). The empirical mode decomposition and the Hilbert spectrum for nonlinear and non-stationary time series analysis. *Proceedings of the Royal Society A-Mathematical Physical & Engineering Sciences, 1998*(454), 903–995.

Huang, N. E., Shen, Z., & Long, S. R. (1999). A new view of nonlinear water waves: The Hilbert spectrum. *Annual Review of Fluid Mechanics, 31*(1), 417–457.

Kuo, S. M., & Lee, B. H. (1988). Fast Fourier transform and its applications.

Li, C. G., Tian, Y. X., & He, J. R. (2012). Prediction model of AC algorithm based on EMD decomposition combined with GMDH and its application. *Journal of Systems & Management, 21*(1), 105–110.

Li, X. F., Chu, J. H., Yu, L. D., Zhu, G. H., & Wang, G. F. (2011). Variational characteristics of PM2.5 concentration in a monitoring site in Beijing urban area. *Journal of Beijing Normal University (Natural Science), 47*(3), 258–261.

Li, X. Y., Jin, M. J., Chen, K., Xiang, H. Q., & Liu, Q. M. (2007). The case-crossover studies of air particulate matter pollution and cardiovascular disease death. *China Environmental Science, 27*(5), 657–660.

Li, Z. M., Sun, Z. B., S. X., Liao, X. N., Zhang, X. L., Xiong, Y. J., & Ma, X. H. (2017). Using Morlet wavelet analysis to analyze multiple time scale periodically in PM2.5 in Beijing. *China Environmental Science, 37*(2), 407–415.

Liang, M. Y., Dong, L., & Tao, J. (2007). Pollution Level of the Airborne Particulate Matter (PM2.5) During the Haze Period in Winter in Guangzhou. *Environmental Monitoring in China,* (5), 52–54 + 70.

Mao, W. L., Xu, J. H., Lu, D. B., Yang, D. Y., & Zhao, J. N. (2017). An analysis of the spatial-temporal pattern and influencing factors of PM2.5 in the Yangtze River Delta in 2015. *Resources and Environment in the Yangtze Basin, 26* (2), 264–272.

Pedregal, D. J. (2003). Filter-Design and Model-Based Analysis of Economic Cycles. Documento de trabajo, 13.

Shen, L., Cheng, S., Gunson, A. J., & Wan, H. (2005). Urbanization, sustainability and the utilization of energy and mineral resources in China. *Cities, 22*(4), 287–302.

Sella, L., Vivaldo, G., Ghil, M., & Groth, A. (2010). Economic cycles and their synchronization: Spectral analysis of macroeconomic series from Italy, The Netherlands, and the UK. *EGU General Assembly Conference Abstracts, 12,* 11847.

Song, M., & Wang, S. (2018). Market competition, green technology progress and comparative advantages in China. *Management Decision, 56*(1), 188–203.

Malm, W. C., Sisler, J. F., Huffman, D., Eldred, R. A., & Cahill, T. A. (1994). Spatial and seasonal trends in particle concentration and optical extinction in the United States. *Journal of Geophysical Research: Atmospheres, 99*(D1), 1347–1370.

Marczak, M., & Gomez, V. (2015). Cyclicality of real wages in the USA and Germany: New insights from wavelet analysis. *Economic Modelling, 47,* 40–52.

Mohr, M. F. (2006). The missing cycle in the HP filter and the measurement of cyclically-adjusted budget balances. *SSRN Electronic Journal,* 73–111.

Wang, F., Han, Y. L., & Zhao, Y. (2017). Spatial-temporal variations of PM10 and PM2.5 on different time-scales in Taiyuan. *Ecology and Environmental Sciences, 26*(9), 1521–1528.

Wang, G. C., & Wang, P. C. (2014). PM2.5 Pollution in China and Its Harmfulness to Human Health. *Science & Technology Review, 32*(26), 72–78.

Wang, J. J., Lu, X. M., Yan, Y. T., Zhou, L. G., & Ma, W. C. (2020). Spatiotemporal characteristics of PM 2.5 concentration in the Yangtze River Delta urban agglomeration, China on the application of big data and wavelet analysis. *Science of The Total Environment,* 724.

Wang, W. B., Fei, P. S., & Yi, X. M. (2010). Prediction of China stock market based on EMD and neural network. *Systems Engineering Theory & Practice, 30*(6), 1027–1033.

Wu, H. H., Kuang, H. B., Meng, B., & Feng, W. W. (2018). Study on the periodic characteristics of BDI index based on EMD-WA model. *Systems Engineering C Characteristics, 38*(06), 1586–1598.

Wu, X. H., Cao, Y. L., Xiao, Y., & Guo, J. (2018b). Finding of urban rainstorm and waterlogging disasters based on microblogging data and the location-routing problem model of urban emergency logistics. *Annals of Operations Research,* 1–32.

Wu, X. H., Chen, Y. F., Zhao, P., Guo, J., & Ma, Z. X. (2019). Study of haze emission efficiency based on new co-opetition data envelopment analysis. *Expert Systems, 3,* 1–12.

Wu, X. H., Wang, Z. J., Gao, G., Guo, J., & Xue, P. P. (2020). Disaster probability, optimal government expenditure for disaster prevention and mitigation, and expected economic growth. *Science of the Total Environment, 709,* 135888.

Wu, X. H., Xu, Z., Liu, H., Guo, J., & Zhou, L. (2019b). What are the impacts of tropical cyclones on employment? An analysis based on meta-regression. *Weather, Climate, and Society, 11*(April), 259–275. https://doi.org/10.1175/WCAS-D-18-0052.1.

Yang, X. X., Feng, L. H., & Wei, P. (2012). Air particulate matter PM2.5 in Beijing and its harm. *Frontier Science, 6*(1), 22–31.

Yogo, M. (2008). Measuring business cycles: A wavelet analysis of economic time series. *Economics Letters, 100,* 208–212.

Yu, L., Wang, S., & Lai, K. K. (2008). Forecasting crude oil price with an EMD-based neural network ensemble learning paradigm. *Energy Economics, 30*(5), 2623–2635.

Zhang, W. A. (2014). Study on the dynamic and mechanism of regional economical disparity in western china—Multi-scale analysis based on EMD Method. *Journal of Applied Statistics and Management, 33*(6), 951–964.

Zhang, Z. S., Tao, J., Xie, S. D., Zhou, L. D., Song, D. L., Zhang, P., Cao, J. J., & Luo, L. (2013). Seasonal variations and source apportionment of PM2.5 at urban area of Chengdu. *Acta Scientiae Circumstantiate, 33*(11), 2947–2952.

Zhao, X. J. (2008). Seasonal and daily variation characteristics of PM2.5 concentration in urban and suburban areas of Beijing. *China Meteorological Society: China Meteorological Society,* 11.

Zhang, X., Lai, K. K., & Wang, S. Y. (2008). A new approach for crude oil price analysis based on empirical mode decomposition. *Energy Economics, 30*(3), 905–918.

Zheng, Z. G. (2010). *Empirical modal analysis and wavelet analysis* (pp. 1–2). Beijing: Meteorological publishing house.

Zhou, J., Zhang Y. J., Xiang, D., & Han, Z. Y. (2018). The periodicity and cause analysis of PM2.5 in Taiyuan. *Ecology and Environmental Sciences, 27*(3), 527–532.

# Chapter 3
# Natural Disasters and Economic Growth—An Empirical Study Using Provincial Panel Data of China

**Abstract** Natural disasters have been happening more frequently in the world in recent years. Different groups of economists have different opinions towards the economic impact after these natural disasters. One group believes that natural disasters will promote the economic growth in the area where natural disasters occurred and the other believes strongly that natural disasters will hinder economic growth. In this paper, we based on the provincial panel data between 2000 and 2010 in China including 31 provinces and categorized natural disasters into two different groups, i.e. meteorological and geological disasters. It has been found that meteorological disasters promote economic growth through the accumulation of physical capital, while the geological disasters have been found with no significant relationship economic growth of the local economy.

**Keywords** Economic growth · Geological disasters · Meteorological disasters · Physical capital · Human capital

## 3.1 Introduction

On the 11th of March 2011, a magnitude 9.0 earthquake struck Japan's northeastern coast, along with a tsunami, which caused 19,846 deaths, 368,820 injuries and over \$210 billion damage. Other natural disasters, such as the 2004 Indian Ocean tsunami, the 2005 Hurricane Katrina, and the earthquakes in Haiti and Chile in 2010 are the natural disasters which went the headlines in last decade. EM-DAT statistics indicate that since 2000, global natural disasters have occurred nearly twice as often as from 1990 to 1999.

China, on the other hand, is also frequently affected by natural disasters. The wide distribution and high frequency of different types of natural disasters have resulted in a massive loss of lives and their belongings. On the 12th of May 2008, a catastrophic earthquake struck Wenchuan in Sichuan province. It took 87,476 lives and caused 845.2 billion RMB (\$1 = 6.3 RMB) damage. During the period of September 2009 to May 2010, Yunnan, Guizhou and Sichuan Provinces were all suffered severe droughts which caused significant damages to farming, forestry, livestock and fisheries. On the 14th of April 2010, Yushu County in Qinghai Province was struck by an earthquake



X. Wu and J. Guo, *Economic Impacts and Emergency Management of Disasters in China*,
https://doi.org/10.1007/978-981-16-1319-7_3

which left thousands of people homeless. On the 21st of July 2012, Beijing suffered an unprecedented storm which caused over 80 deaths. The list can go on. Each disaster will not only link with the human and economic loss, however, they are almost certainly lead to the rebuild and recovery of these disasters. The impact of such natural disasters on the social economy is therefore becoming one of the research topics.

After analyzing data collected from 115 countries between 1960 and 1993, Benson (2003) found that those countries with more frequent natural disasters have a lower economic growth rate. Using household data, Dercon (2004) reported that floods caused by storms in rural Ethiopia had a persistent negative impact on household consumption over time without any sign of economic recovery. Using five-year data collected from 95 countries, Noy and Nualsri (2007) identified a negative correlation between natural disasters and long-term economic growth rate. Raddatz (2009) reached similar conclusions by using panel time series techniques, in which a meteorological disaster would lead to a reduction in real GDP per capita by at least 0.6% over the long run. Further, based on satellite images of the night-time light (NTL) intensity data, Klomp (2016) indicated that natural disasters would put an adverse impact on the region's economic development both in the short and long run. Similarly, Fabian et al. (2019) also used night-time light data. They found that natural disasters reduced light growth and light level in the disaster areas. Taking the housing market in the USA as an example, Coulson et al. (2020) treated the spatial and temporal variations as shocks to economic system in disaster areas. They concluded that the diversity of economic dampened the negative effect of natural disasters. Utilizing tunnel-construction data in South Korea and taking inherent risks and various property into account, Yum et al. (2020) found geological hazards caused by natural disasters also had negative impact on society and economy.

After examining the Schumpeterian "creative destruction" hypothesis proposed by Skidmore and Toya (2002), using an empirical approach, Cuaresma et al. (2008) found that disasters had a negative impact on knowledge spillover between developing and developed countries. They also pointed out that the "creative destruction" process only happens in developed countries. Utilizing a calibrated theoretical endogenous growth model, Hallegatte and Dumas (2009) found that natural disasters have no positive impact on the economy and that big natural disasters can even lead to poverty traps. To calculate the economic losses by windstorms in Central America, Ishizawa and Miranda (2019) used socioeconomic indicators and then computed the hurricane damages both in macro and micro levels. Their findings pointed out that windstorm decreased the growth of total per capita gross domestic product by 0.9 to 1.6% and reduced the total income and labor income by 3%. Khan (2020) used the generalized method of moment (GMM) and proposed that economic growth declined by 0.016 after natural disasters. Utilizing Difference-in-Differences (DID) model, Lima and Barbosa (2019) also found that natural disasters as flash flood decreased GDP per capita by 7.6% in Brazil.

Gassebner et al. (2010) tested the influence of disasters on imports and exports with a gravity model and concluded that smaller and less democratic countries suffer more losses from disasters. Boris (2012) analyzed factors that have affected both international and Russian economic vulnerabilities and found that natural disasters have a negative impact on the social economy. The research of Eric (2012) noted that the output in Central American and Caribbean regions dropped at least 0.83% after being hit by hurricanes. Strulik and Trimborn (2019) constructed a novel economic theory and emphasized that if natural disasters badly destroyed the productive capital, the economic growth would considerably decline. Using newly available data, Breckner et al. (2016) provided new evidence to prove the natural disasters had negative impact on economic. They also found that insurance penetration was conducive to mitigate the adverse effects of natural disasters. By combining the information from different comparative natural disasters case studies, Cavallo et al. (2013) examined the causal impact of catastrophic natural disasters on economic growth. The computation results showed that extremely large natural disasters had negative impacts on economic output both in the short and long run.

Rodriguez-Oreggia et al. (2010) and Mechler (2009) supplemented traditional standard growth variables by utilizing Human Development Index (HDI) in one study and consumption data in another. The former study found that natural disasters increased poverty by 1.5–3.6% and had a significant negative impact on HDI in affected cities in Mexico, while the latter showed that household consumption is reduced slightly in poor countries after disasters. Felbermayr and Groeschl (2014) compared the natural disasters in different countries and then studied the relationship between natural disasters and economic in different countries. They concluded that poor countries were more negatively affected by geophysical disasters and rich countries were more impacted by meteorological events. de Oliveira et al. (2019) used data from the Damage Assessment Reports to assess the association of natural disaster's damage with local economic development. The results confirmed that the economic development level and the impact of natural disasters had a convex relationship.

Since little research focused on subnational level data of natural disasters, Tang et al. (2019) and Zhou et al. (2014) both used subnational data in China. The former concluded that the damage's degree of natural hazard-induced disasters to regional economic growth depended on the regional economic development levels and the types of disasters. The latter study stunningly found economic development level could mitigate the damages of natural disasters. The conclusion of Zhou et al. (2014) was similar to Padli et al. (2018). For examining the correlation of economic growth per capita with natural disasters, Klomp and Valckx (2014) used meta-analysis method and confirmed that natural disasters existed even more significant negative effect on the economic growth of developing countries. Haddad and Teixeira (2015) remeasured the relationship between natural disasters and economic in Brazil. The relationship obtained by the study showed the adverse effect of the flood on city economic growth and resident's welfare. Using panel data of 187 countries from 1960 to 2010, Shabnam (2014) found that the people affected by floods disasters significantly decreased the annual GDP per capita growth rate and the death toll caused by floods had no effects on the annual GDP per capita growth rate.

Because of the natural disasters and fiscal problems frequently occurred in India, Panwar and Sen (2020) studied the effect of natural disasters on the fiscal situation and economic activities. They confirmed that natural disasters always created fiscal problems by destroying economic activities. Albuquerque and Rajhi (2019) also focused on the financial problem affected by natural disasters. They used three panels data in developing countries and concluded that natural disasters would cause significant economic and financial disruption. Using the country-year level data, McDermott et al. (2014) constructed a two-period economic development model and found that the countries with low levels of financial market development would suffer more severe negative impact of natural disasters. Based on micro-data in Bangladesh, Karim (2018) certified the relationship between economic growth and natural disasters. The results showed that recurrent flooding had substantial negative impacts on income and expenditure of agriculture. Using dynamic propensity score matching method, Bondonio and Greenbaum (2018) found counties affected by natural disasters would experience a short economic recession after natural disasters in the USA.

More detailed, there was increasing numerous studies about the impact of natural disasters on specific sectors in a particular economic system. For example, using Vector Autoregressive (VARX) model, Mohan et al. (2018) studied the impacts of natural disasters on different economic components and then justified that export, import, public consumption, investment, and private consumption were adversely affected by natural disasters. Moreover, Khan et al. (2019) focused on the impact of natural disasters on different parts of an economic system. Their results proposed that natural disasters increased migration, the incidence of poverty and price level in disaster areas. de Oliveira (2019) also studied the impacts of natural disasters on economic sectors and stressed that the GDP growth, the agricultural and service sectors of the municipal economy were negatively affected by natural disasters in the state of Ceara, Northeast Brazil. Boudreaux et al. (2019) and Luo and Kinugasa (2020) analyzed entrepreneurs and household behavior after natural disasters. They found that entrepreneurship activities were limited after natural disasters in low and middle-income countries and the household saving rate of the rural and urban population declined after natural disasters. To investigate the impact of small and moderate disasters on child health and investments, Datar et al. (2013) used the Indian National Family and Health Survey data and natural disaster's data from an international database of natural disasters (EM-DAT). They pointed out that the adverse effects of natural disasters on investments growth were much smaller than the negative impact on child health in disaster areas.

By applying the simultaneous equation approach, Anuchitworawong and Thampanishvong (2015) studied the effect of natural disasters on foreign direct investment (FDI) in Thailand and expressed that natural disasters reduced FDI flows and then had negative impact on economic growth. After investigated the disasters data from 1970 to 2010, Mukherjee and Hastak (2018) concluded that openness to trade and government's consumption share of purchasing power parity (PPP) were the most vulnerable economic factors in the regions affected by natural disasters. Cole et al. (2019) and Verschuur et al. (2020) studied the effect of natural disasters on the manufacturing plants and port economy. The first study found that natural disaster's damages significantly increased the local manufacturing plant's likelihood of failure. Meanwhile, the other research discovered that natural disasters caused ports disruptions and logistics disruptions in multi ports. To design a systems approach for mitigating the economic losses of natural disasters and reducing the risks of natural disasters, Harrison and Williams (2016) reviewed the recent natural disasters and proposed a comprehensive approach that was useful for decreasing economic losses and promoting reconstruction after natural disasters.

In contrast with the negative impacts, some researchers have found that natural disasters could promote economic growth with the argument that when the tangible assets have been destroyed by natural disasters, parts of productive capital will be used for post-disaster reconstruction, which can stimulate both the recovery and economic growth in that affected areas. A book entitled "The Economics of Natural Disasters" by Dacy and Kunreuther (1969) concluded that GDP is increased in affected areas after a disaster. Albala-Bertrand (1993) collected data from 28 unforeseen natural events from 26 countries between 1960 and 1979 and analyzed the macroeconomic dynamic of natural disasters. It has been concluded that GDP, agricultural and construction output, capital formation, fiscal and trade deficits were all higher after disasters while exchange rates and inflation remained the same. The research of Otero and Marti (1995) reported that the GDP of both Latin America and Caribbean countries grew after disasters. Tol and Leek (1999) similarly found natural disasters had a positive impact on macroeconomic variables in the short run.

Skidmore and Toya (2002) researched the data from of 89 sample countries from 1960 to 1990 and concluded that natural disasters promote economic growth with the reason that the frequency of meteorological disasters had a positive and significant relationship with accumulation of human capital, growth of per capita GDP and total factor productivity. On the basis of the Schumpeterian "creative destruction" process, they point out that capital stocks may have to be updated following natural disasters therefore leading to the adoption of new technologies. Okuyama (2013) and Okuyama et al. (2004) also found that old facilities are more vulnerable when natural disasters struck. Replacing those old facilities will have a positive impact on overall economic growth and productivity in the long run. Wang (2008) analyzed the long-term relationship between natural disasters, human capital and economic growth and showed that natural disasters will promote the accumulation of human capital, thus positively affect the economic activities. Based on the data from 1990 to 2004, Kim (2010) examined the hypothesis of "creative destruction" also concluded that natural disasters promote economic growth, in which meteorological disasters might be advantageous for the accumulation of human capital and economic growth. Doytch and Klein (2018) measured energy consumption changes after meteorological and geophysical disasters. The findings supported "creative destruction" and found that natural disasters improved renewable energy consumption in high-income countries. They also proposed that natural disasters increased residential energy consumption in middle-income countries and enhanced industrial energy consumption in low-income countries after natural disasters.

For economic reconstruction after natural disasters was highly related to public debt, Benali et al. (2018) used 15-years panel data and Granger non-causality test to verify the relationship between natural disasters, public debt and economic reconstruction. Their findings showed that increasing public debt would promote economic reconstruction after natural disasters. Attary et al. (2020) concluded that if the government provided financial assistance after natural disasters, the disaster areas would not decrease the economic outcomes in the short run. Using 400 violent earthquakes data from 85 countries, Klomp (2020) pointed out that the short-run policy interest rate would fall after earthquake disasters. The fall in interest rate would stimulate economic recovery and was good for fighting inflationary pressure. From a particular view on a Pacific small island state, Zhang and Managi (2020) attested that economy system with high internal financing capabilities could effectively improve the disasters resilience and island state's economic growth. Cheng and Zhang (2020) constructed an index system of economic resilience and utilized the quantile regression method. Their research results showed that tourism development of disaster areas could improve economic growth rate after natural disasters.

A number of studies have shown inconclusive relationship between natural disasters and economic growth. From the macroeconomic perspective, Horwich (2000) found that the catastrophe like Kobe earthquake in Japan in 1995, which caused as high as $100 billion damage, just destroyed 0.08% of capital stock. Using the Harrod-Domar model to examine the relationship between natural disasters and economic growth in China, Zou (2009) found that natural disasters in China have had a negative impact on short-term economic growth but did not show influence on long-term growth. Leiter et al. (2009) used European firm-level data and a difference-in-difference (DID) approach to test the effect of floods on capital stock, employment and productivity. They found that companies in regions hit by floods showed a higher growth in total assets and employment than those in unaffected regions but that there was also a negative impact on productivity. Noman (2012) also found that natural disasters do not always have negative impacts on economic growth; in developing countries storms and earthquakes may actually promote industrial growth. Moderate floods can have a positive impact on agriculture and other economic industries in developing countries.

Comparing the impact of two earthquake disasters on economic growth, Barone and Mocetti (2014) underlined that natural disasters caused adverse effects on economic growth in the short run but had no negative impact on the long run. Based on a meta-analysis, Lazzaroni and van Bergeijk (2014) proposed that natural disasters had direct adverse impacts but no significant indirect negative impacts on economy. Siodla (2015) studied the urban redeveloping land after natural disasters. They demonstrated that natural disasters caused differential economic growth in disaster areas and non-disaster areas. Using panel data from 1965 to 2016 in Malaysia, Qureshi et al. (2019) found that natural disasters such as flood, storm and epidemic disasters had negative impacts on economic growth in the short run, but exhibited positive effects on economic growth in the long run. Atsalakis et al. (2020) used panel data from more than 100 countries and then concluded a mixed result that natural disasters had negative impacts on most countries, but there also were some exceptional countries in which natural disasters caused positive effects on economic growth. Since the different types of natural disasters had differentiated influences on the economic, Fomby et al. (2013) compared the effect of four types of natural disasters, such as droughts, floods, earthquakes and storms. Their findings showed that most natural disasters had adverse impacts on economic but also some natural disasters put positive effects on economic growth.

According to the theory of creative destruction by Schumpeterian, when disasters destroy the existing social and economic bases, they also create new opportunities for innovation. For example, in the short run, both capital and facilities after disasters can be updated with the support of aids. In the long run, society will pay more attention to human capital and investment in education in order to improve both technological and production efficiency, thus promoting endogenous growth in the economy.

This paper focuses on China with the data collected from 31 provinces between 2000 and 2010. China is not only the most populous country but also in the process of fast economic growth. Over the last decade, China suffered from many serious natural disasters including the Wenchuan earthquake in 2008 and the Yunnan-Guizhou-Sichuan drought in 2010. Due to culture and ethical characteristics, the fast economic development period and its different governing system, it would be interesting to know how natural disasters would affect the economic growth in China.

## 3.2 Data and Hypotheses

All data related to economy, education and population are sourced from "China Statistical Yearbook" (2001–2011). Disaster related data are found from the Emergency Events Database (EM-DAT), which is maintained by the Center for Research on the Epidemiology of Disasters (CRED) at the Catholic University of Louvain, Belgium.

In this study, we used the method developed by Skidmore and Toya (2002) and grouped natural disasters into two groups: meteorological disasters and geological disasters. Meteorological disasters are those created by deviations in the normal water cycle and atmospheric processes, including floods, cyclones, hurricanes, storms, snow storms, tornadoes, typhoons, and storms. Geological disasters are those caused by geological process, including volcanic eruptions, natural explosions, avalanches, landslides, and earthquakes. The reason for this classification is that meteorological disasters and geological disasters have different characteristics. Meteorological disasters happen more frequently, more predictable and more regular than geological disasters. On the other hand, geological disasters are more difficult to predict, which limits evacuation of the population. Skidmore and Toya (2002) stated that climatic disasters are a reasonable proxy for risk to physical capital and geological disasters may be perceived as a threat to both life and property.

EM-DAT records the number of disasters, death toll, people affected and the estimated loss in USD. Skidmore and Toya (2002), however, analyzed the number

**Table 3.1** Top 5 natural disasters in China (1990–2010)

| | Date | Type | Killed | Affected | Loss ($ million) |
|---|---|---|---|---|---|
| 1 | May 2008 | Wenchuan earthquake | 87,476 | 45,976,596 | 85,000 |
| 2 | July 1998 | Extraordinary flood | 3656 | 238,973,000 | 30,000 |
| 3 | Jan. 2008 | Ice and snow disaster in the South | 129 | 77,000,000 | 21,100 |
| 4 | May 2010 | Extraordinary rainstorm in the South | 1691 | 134,000,000 | 18,000 |
| 5 | Jan. 1994 | Drought | 0 | 82,000,000 | 13,755.2 |

of disasters only from this database, as they believed accurate figure is hard to obtain on death toll and economic losses.

Although the number of disasters is the most objective information in the EM-DAT, such a number alone would be difficult to represent the real impact of disasters. According to EM-DAT, Hurricane Katrina in 2005 and a local storm which killed 10 people are both recorded as one disaster, but their impact on society and the local economy are totally different. Table 3.1 contains the list of top 5 natural disasters in China (1990–2010). It shows that property and casualty losses caused by the Wenchuan earthquake are more than the sum of all the other 4.

To measure more accurately the degree of impact of natural disasters, we need to synthesize all three disaster indicators (number of disasters, death toll and economic losses). This research uses the entropy weight method to obtain an index weight from each disaster indicator. First, we calculate the proportion of disaster indicator $j$ in region $i$:

$$y_{ij} = \frac{x_{ij}}{\sum_{i=1}^{n} x_{ij}} (i = 1, 2, \cdots n;\ j = 1, 2, \cdots, m) \tag{3.1}$$

$i$ are the 31 Chinese provinces and central municipalities, $j$ are the indicators of natural disasters (the number of disasters, death toll and economic loss), $x_{ij}$ is the value of the disaster indicator $j$ in region $i$.

Then, we calculate the value of information entropy about the disaster indicator $j$:

$$e_j = -K \sum_{i=1}^{n} y_{ij} \ln y_{ij} \tag{3.2}$$

$K$ is a constant, $K = \frac{1}{\ln n}$, $n$ is the number of regions, in this paper $n = 31$. The information utility value of disaster indicator $j$ is:

$$d_j = 1 - e_j \tag{3.3}$$

The bigger the information utility value, the more important the evaluation is. The weight of the disaster indicator $j$ is:

$$w_j = \frac{d_j}{\sum_{j=1}^{m} d_j} \tag{3.4}$$

Using a weighted summation method:

$$U = \sum_{j=1}^{m} x_{ij} w_j \tag{3.5}$$

$U$ is the synthetic calculated value from the three-natural disaster indicators. The weight of the entropy weight method is more objective and totally determined by the data. Finally, we use a weighted model to get a new indicator to measure the degree of natural disasters. In the following empirical analysis, the new disaster indicators will be named $ND$ as the degree of total natural disasters, $GD$ as the degree of geological disasters, and $MD$ as the degree of meteorological disasters.

As discussed in the introduction section, natural disasters may hinder or promote economic development. To determine the role of natural disasters in regional economic growth, this paper includes all three measures of natural disasters (*ND*, *MD*, and *GD*). Specifically, we add ND or MD and GD into the classical growth model and use provincial panel data to test the following hypotheses.

$H_1$: Meteorological and geological disasters may affect economic growth with different mechanisms.

Natural disasters may affect investment decisions on production thus affect the economic growth. It is believed that physical capital investment may be reduced because of the immediate impact of disasters. However, since China's economic growth remains investment-driven, governments may rapidly increase physical capital investment afterward. Foreign aid and a higher saving rate in the short run may promote the accumulation of physical capital. In addition, old facilities destroyed may also need to be reinstalled or upgraded to resume production, thus increasing physical capital investment. Accordingly, lead to our second hypothesis.

$H_2$: The accumulation of physical capital may promote economic growth.

Further, we look at the long term impact of natural disasters on human capital investment. When an economy suffers from natural disasters, new equipment and technologies may be introduced and adopted, which may improve the efficiency of the laborers. Furthermore, people may choose investment between human capital and physical capital in the endogenous growth framework. When people are threatened by natural disasters, they may reduce the expectation of investment in physical capital and turn to investing in human capital. The economy may allocate more resources to improve the human capital. Accordingly, we propose the third hypothesis.

$H_3$: The accumulation of human capital may promote economic growth.

Geological disasters like earthquakes are hard to predict. Their durations are short and the range of influence is relatively small. On the other hand, meteorological disasters are more frequent, predictable and regular than geological disasters. So, we have the following fourth hypothesis

$H_4$: Different types of natural disasters may have different impacts on economic growth. Compared with geological disasters, meteorological disasters may have more obvious influence on economic growth.

## 3.3 The Empirical Analysis

According to the number of disasters in EM-DAT, we summarize the frequency and distribution of natural disasters in China. Figure 3.1 shows the number of meteorological and geological disasters from 2000 to 2010. For this period, the average number of meteorological disasters was 23 each year. The lowest frequency was 16 in 2003 and the highest was 30 in 2006. Compared with the number of meteorological disasters in China, geological disasters were much less frequent. The average number of geological disasters was 5. The lowest frequency was one in 2007 and the highest one was 11 in 2003. The numbers of other years were all less than 8.

Figure 3.2 presents the distribution of meteorological and geological disasters in China from 2000 to 2010. All provinces in China suffered meteorological disasters. The greatest number of meteorological disasters was 47 in Guangdong and the least was 1 in Tianjin. When looking at most to least, the numbers of meteorological disasters were more than 16 in 16 provinces, including Guangdong, Sichuan, Zhejiang, Fujian, Hubei, Yunnan, Anhui, Hunan, Guizhou, Guangxi, Chongqing, Jiangxi, Henan, Shaanxi, Xinjiang and Jiangsu. Most of these provinces are located in the coastal and central regions of China. Figure 3.3 shows that, from most to least, 11 provinces suffered from geological disasters; Yunnan, Sichuan, Gansu, Xinjiang, Inner Mongolia, Qinghai, Guizhou, Liaoning, Jiangxi, Hubei and Guangdong. Only

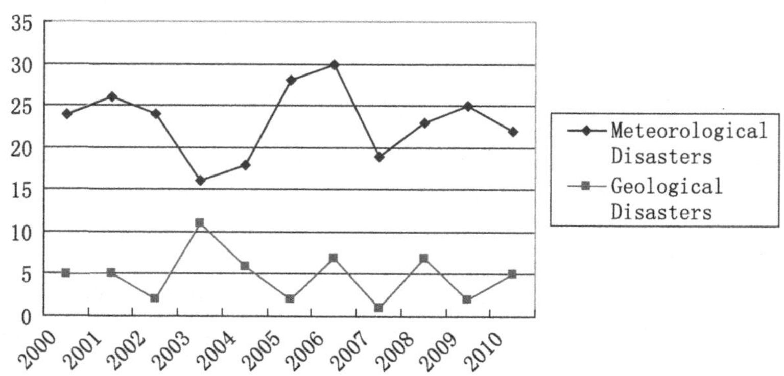


**Fig. 3.1** The frequency of natural disasters in China in 2000–2010

Fig. 3.2 Distribution of meteorological disasters in China in 2000–2010

Fig. 3.3 Distribution of geological disasters in China in 2000–2010

Yunnan had more than ten geological disasters, a very high 23. One disaster occurred in Liaoning, Jiangxi, Hubei and Guangdong respectively; these provinces are located in the inland and eastern regions of China. Many provinces had no geological disasters which may adversely affect the accuracy of the following regression analysis.

To empirically investigate the relationship between natural disasters and economic growth, we did regression analysis using data concerning different disasters and using a number of economic variables. After reviewing Skidmore and Toya (2002), Wang (2008), Kim (2010), Gassebner et al. (2010), Guo (2005) and Liu (2009), we have chosen investment growth rate, openness (total volume of foreign trade/GDP), SOE (the number of state-owned enterprises), and birth rate during 2000–2010 as control variables.

We first perform the unit root tests with ADF methodology in order to avoid spurious regression. As we can see in Table 3.2, parts of variables are rough at the initial level. After the 1st difference they return to smoothness.

Based on the test results in Table 3.2, we then use the following panel regression model to examine the determinants of economic growth rate:

$$G_{it} = c_1 + c_2 ND_{it} + c_3 I_{it} + c_4 \Delta O_{it} + c_5 S_{it} + c_6 B_{it} + \varepsilon_{it},\ (i = 1, 2, \ldots, 31;\ t = 1, 2, \ldots, 11) \tag{3.6}$$

$G_{it}$ is the per capita GDP growth rate in region $i$ in period $t$(The base year is 2000). $ND_{it}$ is the degree of natural disasters in region $i$ in period $t$. $I_{it}$ is the investment (investment in the fixed assets) growth rate in region $i$ in period $t$(The base year is 2000). $\Delta O_{it}$ is the degree of openness (total volume of foreign trade/GDP) at the 1st difference level in region $i$ in period $t$. $S_{it}$ is the number of SOE (the number of state-owned and state-holding industrial enterprises) in region $i$ in period $t$. $B_{it}$ is the birth rate in region $i$ in period $t$. $c_z (z = 1, 2, \ldots, 6)$ is the regression coefficient, and $\varepsilon_{it}$ is the error term.

Based on the F test (Table 3.3 row 1) and the Hausman test (Table 3.4 row 1), a fixed regression model is used. Table 3.5 presents the OLS results. It shows that the estimated coefficient of *ND* is statistically insignificant. Therefore, when meteorological and geological disasters are grouped together, natural disasters neither hinder nor promote economic growth. All other control variables have the expected results. Both investment and international trade promote economic growth, while SOE and birth rate hinder economic growth.

To examine the different impacts of different disasters on economic growth, we separate natural disasters into meteorological disasters and geological disasters. Accordingly, Eq. 6 becomes,

$$G_{it} = c_1 + c_2 MD_{it} + c_3 GD_{it} + c_4 I_{it} + c_5 \Delta O_{it} + c_6 S_{it} + c_7 B_{it} + \varepsilon_{it}, (i = 1, 2, \ldots, 31; t = 1, 2, \ldots, 11) \tag{3.7}$$

**Table 3.2** Unit root tests

| Variable | | Method | Statistic | Prob | Result |
|---|---|---|---|---|---|
| Per capita GDP growth rate *G* | level | ADF—Fisher Chi-square | 122.603 | 0.0000 | smooth |
| | | ADF—Choi Z-stat | −5.02789 | 0.0000 | |
| Degree of natural disasters *ND* | level | ADF—Fisher Chi-square | 191.972 | 0.0000 | smooth |
| | | ADF—Choi Z-stat | −7.98315 | 0.0000 | |
| Degree of geological disasters *GD* | level | ADF—Fisher Chi-square | 76.8110 | 0.0000 | smooth |
| | | ADF—Choi Z-stat | −5.80939 | 0.0000 | |
| Degree of meteorological disasters *MD* | level | ADF—Fisher Chi-square | 190.793 | 0.0000 | smooth |
| | | ADF—Choi Z-stat | −7.84935 | 0.0000 | |
| Investment growth rate *I* | level | ADF—Fisher Chi-square | 90.9102 | 0.0098 | smooth |
| | | ADF—Choi Z-stat | −2.55968 | 0.0052 | |
| Degree of education *E* | level | ADF—Fisher Chi-square | 154.046 | 0.0000 | smooth |
| | | ADF—Choi Z-stat | −6.09306 | 0.0000 | |
| Birth rate *B* | level | ADF—Fisher Chi-square | 193.387 | 0.0000 | smooth |
| | | ADF—Choi Z-stat | −6.37075 | 0.0000 | |
| Openness *O* | level | ADF—Fisher Chi-square | 55.8987 | 0.6938 | rough |
| | | ADF—Choi Z-stat | −0.25433 | 0.3996 | |
| D (Openness)$\Delta O$ | 1st difference | ADF—Fisher Chi-square | 206.881 | 0.0000 | smooth |
| | | ADF—Choi Z-stat | −9.58559 | 0.0000 | |
| SOE *S* | level | ADF—Fisher Chi-square | 180.921 | 0.0000 | smooth |
| | | ADF—Choi Z-stat | −6.90409 | 0.0000 | |

(continued)

**Table 3.2** (continued)

| Variable | | Method | Statistic | Prob | Result |
|---|---|---|---|---|---|
| Income level $IN$ | level | ADF—Fisher Chi-square | 42.4335 | 0.9728 | rough |
| | | ADF—Choi Z-stat | 1.71087 | 0.9564 | |
| D (Income level)$\Delta IN$ | 1st difference | ADF—Fisher Chi-square | 286.952 | 0.0000 | smooth |
| | | ADF—Choi Z-stat | −11.6077 | 0.0000 | |

In Eq. 3.7, the new independent variables are $MD_{it}$ and $GD_{it}$. $MD_{it}$ is the degree of meteorological disasters in region $i$ in period $t$. $GD_{it}$ is the degree of geological disasters in region $i$ in period $t$. Other variables are same with ones in Eq. 3.6.

Similar to Eq. 3.6, both the F test (Table 3.3 Row 2) and Hausman test (Table 3.4 Row 2) suggested that a fixed regression model should be used. Table 3.6 shows the results. It indicates that *MD* has a positive but marginally significant (at 15% level) estimated coefficient. This finding provides weak evidence that meteorological disasters could promote economic growth. The insignificant result on *GD* suggests that there is no relationship between GDP growth rate and degree of geological disasters. The possible reason of this finding could be that only a few geological disasters occurred in China from 2000–2010 and most of them occurred in only two or three provinces, thus affecting the statistical significance of the regression coefficient.

To further examine whether natural disasters affect economic growth through physical capital, we analyze the relationship between natural disasters and physical

**Table 3.3** $F$ tests

| | F Statistic | Threshold | Result |
|---|---|---|---|
| Equation 3.6 | 1.606612363 | $F_{0.05}(30, 305) = 1.4967029$ | fixed regression model |
| Equation 3.7 | 1.580522771 | $F_{0.05}(30, 304) = 1.4968262$ | fixed regression model |
| Equation 3.8 | 2.092598 | $F_{0.05}(30, 307) = 1.496459$ | fixed regression model |
| Equation 3.9 | 59.94449 | $F_{0.05}(30, 306) = 1.49658$ | fixed regression model |

**Table 3.4** Hausman test

| | Chi-Sq. Statistic | Chi-Sq. d.f | Prob | Result |
|---|---|---|---|---|
| Equation 3.6 | 21.623663 | 5 | 0.0006 | fixed regression model |
| Equation 3.7 | 21.378078 | 6 | 0.0016 | fixed regression model |
| Equation 3.8 | 20.301236 | 3 | 0.0001 | fixed regression model |
| Equation 3.9 | 17.425064 | 4 | 0.0016 | fixed regression model |

**Table 3.5** Dependent variables is per capita GDP growth rates $G$

| Variable | Coefficient | Std. Error | t-Statistic | Prob |
|---|---|---|---|---|
| C | 0.247683 | 0.044216 | 5.601638 | 0.0000 |
| Degree of natural disasters $ND$ | 0.000622 | 0.000717 | 0.867920 | 0.3862 |
| Growth rate of investment $I$ | 0.133333 | 0.037490 | 3.556525 | 0.0004 |
| D (openness)$\Delta O$ | 0.000130 | 3.33E–05 | 3.896037 | 0.0001 |
| SOE $S$ | −0.000433 | 9.74E−05 | −4.443667 | 0.0000 |
| Birth rate $B$ | −0.007647 | 0.003633 | −2.105012 | 0.0362 |
| Cross-section fixed (dummy variables) | | | | |

| | | | |
|---|---|---|---|
| R-squared | 0.329225 | Mean dependent var | 0.153916 |
| Adjusted R-squared | 0.243543 | S.D. dependent var | 0.060989 |
| S.E. of regression | 0.053045 | Akaike info criterion | −2.926531 |
| Sum squared reside | 0.770980 | Schwarz criterion | −2.492606 |
| Log likelihood | 489.6122 | Hannan-Quinn criter | −2.753066 |
| F-statistic | 3.842371 | Durbin-Watson stat | 2.386057 |
| Prob (F-statistic) | 0.000000 | | |

capital. We choose investment growth rate as the dependent variable to measure physical capital. The theory of Accelerated-Figure developed by Clark (1917) indicates that national income is the decisive factor which affects the level of investment. Higher national income can raise the level of savings, thus promoting the growth of investment. On the other hand, higher national income can also increase the growth of consumption, which can further stimulate investment. The two main indexes which can reflect national income are gross domestic product (GDP) and gross national product (GNP). Due to data availability, we choose per capita GDP growth rate as control variables and use the following panel regression model:

$$I_{it} = c_1 + c_2 MD_{it} + c_3 GD_{it} + c_4 G_{it} + \varepsilon_{it}, (i = 1, 2, \ldots, 31; t = 1, 2, \ldots, 11) \tag{3.8}$$

$I_{it}$ is the investment (in the fixed assets) growth rate in region $i$ in period $t$(The base year is 2000). $MD_{it}$ is the degree of meteorological disasters in region $i$ in period $t$. $GD_{it}$ is the degree of geological disasters in region $i$ in period $t$. $G_{it}$ is the per capita GDP growth rate in region $i$ in period $t$(The base year is 2000). $c_z(z = 1, 2, \ldots, 4)$ is the regression coefficient, and $\varepsilon_{it}$ is the error term.

**Table 3.6** Dependent variables is per capita GDP growth rates *G*

| Variable | Coefficient | Std. Error | t-Statistic | Prob |
|---|---|---|---|---|
| C | 0.246604 | 0.044139 | 5.587021 | 0.0000 |
| Degree of meteorological disasters $MD$ | 1.563728 | 1.053280 | 1.484627 | 0.1388 |
| Degree of geological disasters $GD$ | 0.051057 | 0.088511 | 0.576841 | 0.5645 |
| Growth rate of investment $I$ | 0.128178 | 0.037592 | 3.409707 | 0.0007 |
| D (openness)$\Delta O$ | 0.000127 | 3.33E−05 | 3.804531 | 0.0002 |
| SOE $S$ | −0.000424 | 9.74E−05 | −4.349956 | 0.0000 |
| Birth rate $B$ | −0.007734 | 0.003627 | −2.132665 | 0.0338 |
| Cross-section fixed (dummy variables) | | | | |
| R-squared | 0.334205 | Mean dependent var | 0.153916 | |
| Adjusted R-squared | 0.246408 | S.D. dependent var | 0.060989 | |
| S.E. of regression | 0.052945 | Akaike info criterion | −2.927530 | |
| Sum squared reside | 0.765256 | Schwarz criterion | −2.481552 | |
| Log likelihood | 490.7672 | Hannan-Quinn criter | −2.749247 | |
| F-statistic | 3.806558 | Durbin-Watson stat | 2.391694 | |
| Prob (F-statistic) | 0.000000 | | | |

Again, both the F test (Table 3.3 Row 3) and Hausman test (Table 3.4 Row 3) suggested that a fixed regression model should be used. The results of regression (Table 3.7) indicate that there is a significant and positive relationship between investment growth rate and meteorological disasters, but that there is no relationship between investment growth rate and geological disasters. The empirical analysis shows that meteorological disasters possibly affect economic growth by increasing physical capital investment.

Skidmore and Toya (2002) argued that meteorological disasters may promote the investment in human capital. Suppose that a society can choose the level of investment for factors of production. Human capital investment will be more attractive because society will invest more in human capital when physical capital is destroyed by meteorological disasters. Human capital investment mainly includes educational investment, health investment, training investment and labor force flow investment. Human capital investment can contribute to improving the abilities of workers to use new technologies and equipment which can enhance the output efficiency of physical capital thus promoting economic growth. In return, economic development can help workers gain more human capital investment and further promote the accumulation

**Table 3.7** Dependent variables is investment growth rates $I$

| Variable | Coefficient | Std. Error | t-Statistic | Prob |
|---|---|---|---|---|
| C | 0.140058 | 0.013944 | 10.04439 | 0.0000 |
| Degree of meteorological disasters $MD$ | 3.586480 | 1.781984 | 2.012633 | 0.0450 |
| Degree of geological disasters $GD$ | −0.061124 | 0.152739 | −0.400187 | 0.6893 |
| Per capita GDP growth rate $G$ | 0.597244 | 0.088668 | 6.735711 | 0.0000 |
| Cross-section fixed (dummy variables) | | | | |
| R-squared | 0.329386 | Mean dependent var | | 0.234772 |
| Adjusted R-squared | 0.257300 | S.D. dependent var | | 0.106454 |
| S.E. of regression | 0.091742 | Akaike info criterion | | −1.845299 |
| Sum squared resid | 2.583883 | Schwarz criterion | | −1.463234 |
| Log likelihood | 348.6234 | Hannan-Quinn criter | | −1.693078 |
| F-statistic | 4.569371 | Durbin-Watson stat | | 1.436648 |
| Prob (F-statistic) | 0.000000 | | | |

of human capital. It therefore follows that human capital and economic growth are inseparable.

We use education degree to measure human capital because education is one of the main ways to form human capital. The higher the levels of education individual workers accept, the more human capital there is. According to the household production function model, birth rate is negatively related to economic development. Higher birth rates will increase the burden on society and family, thus affecting education levels (Guo 2005). Income levels are also a key factor since income is the foundation of education investment. Lu (2005) points out that low income will lead families to face credit constraints, which will further reduce education levels. We use education degree as the dependent variable and birth rate and income level as control variables in examining the relationship between human capital and natural disasters.

$$\begin{aligned} E_{it} =& c_1 + c_2 MD_{it} + c_3 GD_{it} + c_4 B_{it} + c_5 \Delta IN_{it} \\ &+ \varepsilon_{it}, (i = 1, 2, \ldots, 31; t = 1, 2, \ldots, 11) \end{aligned} \tag{3.9}$$

$E_{it}$ is the education degree in region $i$ in period $t$. In this paper, the education degree is defined as the average education years.

$$E = \frac{\sum P_h \cdot N_h}{\sum P_h}, (h = 1, 2, \ldots, 5) \tag{3.10}$$

$E$ is the average education years. $P_h$ is the population of each education level. $N_h$ is the education years of each education level. $h$ is the education level including

**Table 3.8** Dependent variables is education degree $E$

| Variable | Coefficient | Std. Error | t-Statistic | Prob |
|---|---|---|---|---|
| C | 8.740422 | 0.248857 | 35.12229 | 0.0000 |
| Degree of meteorological disasters $MD$ | 13.08233 | 6.192561 | 2.112587 | 0.0355 |
| Degree of geological disasters $GD$ | 0.161549 | 0.522123 | 0.309408 | 0.7572 |
| Birth rate $B$ | −0.098940 | 0.021489 | −4.604249 | 0.0000 |
| D (income level)$\Delta IN$ | 17.08515 | 1.687697 | 10.12335 | 0.0000 |
| Cross-section fixed (dummy variables) | | | | |
| R-squared | 0.933340 | Mean dependent var | | 7.620672 |
| Adjusted R-squared | 0.925098 | S.D. dependent var | | 1.141238 |
| S.E. of regression | 0.312336 | Akaike info criterion | | 0.616529 |
| Sum squared resid | 26.82725 | Schwarz criterion | | 1.038400 |
| Log likelihood | −60.56205 | Hannan-Quinn criter | | 0.785176 |
| F-statistic | 113.2474 | Durbin-Watson stat | | 1.057345 |
| Prob (F-statistic) | 0.000000 | | | |

illiteracy, primary education, lower secondary education, upper secondary education, tertiary education. $MD_{it}$ is the degree of meteorological disasters in region $i$ in period $t$. $GD_{it}$ is the degree of geological disasters in region $i$ in period $t$. $B_{it}$ is the birth rate in region $i$ in period $t$. $\Delta IN_{it}$ is the income level (general budget revenue/GDP) at the 1st difference level in region $i$ in period $t$. $c_z(z = 1, 2, \ldots, 5)$ is the regression coefficient, and $\varepsilon_{it}$ is the error term.

Similar to Eq. 3.8, both the F test (Table 3.3 Row 4) and Hausman test (Table 3.4 Row 4) suggested that a fixed regression model should be used. As shown in Table 3.8, there is a positive and significant relationship between meteorological disasters and degree of education. Geological disasters, however, still have no significant relationship to education levels. There are many natural disasters, especially meteorological disasters, in China, and physical capital is easier to be destroyed by meteorological disasters. It follows more investment is put into potential human capital. Long run economic growth will be promoted through the accumulation of human capital. In addition, natural disasters may provide more chances for introducing new technologies, which further raising the efficiency of human capital.

Tables 3.7 and 3.8 conclude that meteorological disasters have a positive and significant relationship with both physical capital and human capital, while geological disasters do not. To check the robustness of our empirical finding and further explore the relationship between meteorological disasters and economic growth, we examine the causal relationship between variables using the Granger causality test. We use the AIC (Akaike Info Criterion) to determine the optimal lag. Table 3.9 shows the results of Granger causality test.

Several findings are observed. First, meteorological disasters are the Granger cause of GDP growth rate (economic growth), but not vise visa. Second, meteorological disasters are the Granger cause of investment growth rate (physical capital), but

**Table 3.9** Granger test

| Null hypothesis | Lags | Obs | F-Statistic | Prob | Result |
|---|---|---|---|---|---|
| GDP growth rate is not Granger cause of meteorological disasters | 5 | 186 | 0.63649 | 0.6721 | There is not enough evidence to reject the null hypothesis |
| Meteorological disasters are not Granger cause of GDP growth rate | | | 2.39688 | 0.0393 | Reject the null hypothesis |
| Education is not Granger cause of GDP growth rate | 2 | 279 | 6.58917 | 0.0016 | Reject the null hypothesis |
| GDP growth rate is not Granger cause of education | | | 15.8314 | 3.E−07 | Reject the null hypothesis |
| Education is not Granger cause of meteorological disasters | 3 | 248 | 0.33086 | 0.8030 | There is not enough evidence to reject the null hypothesis |
| Meteorological disasters are not Granger cause of education | | | 0.78102 | 0.5056 | There is not enough evidence to reject the null hypothesis |
| GDP growth rate is not Granger cause of investment growth rate | 7 | 124 | 2.79653 | 0.0103 | Reject the null hypothesis |
| Investment growth rate is not Granger cause of GDP growth rate | | | 4.65037 | 0.0001 | Reject the null hypothesis |
| Meteorological disasters are not Granger cause of investment growth rate | 5 | 186 | 2.11228 | 0.0661 | Reject the null hypothesis |
| Investment growth rate is not Granger cause of meteorological disasters | | | 0.46614 | 0.8011 | There is not enough evidence to reject the null hypothesis |

not vise visa. Third, investment growth rate and GDP growth rate are mutual Granger cause of each other. Fourth, education and GDP growth rate are mutual Granger cause of each other. Fifth, meteorological disasters and education are not Granger cause to each other. These findings suggest that meteorological disasters could promote economic growth through physical capital investment rather than human capital investment. Because meteorological disasters change the original industrial layout and planning to some extent by destroying roads, electricity, water supply and plant buildings, people need to reinvest and reallocate resources to arrange the production and residential areas, thus increasing physical capital investment.

## 3.4 Conclusions

This paper used China's provincial panel data from 2000 to 2010 to examine the relationship between natural disasters and long-term economic growth. The results show an inconclusive relationship between natural disasters and economic growth. Then we separate natural disasters into meteorological disasters and geological disasters to test different impacts of different disasters on economic growth. The results show a positive and marginally significant relationship between meteorological disasters and economic growth. Geological disasters, on the other hand, have no significant relationship to economic growth. One possible reason why there is no significant relationship between geological disasters and economic growth could be that the small number of geological disasters happened during the period 2000–2010 and most geological disasters occurred in western China. The sample size could be too small to be statistically valid.

This paper also tested Granger causality to examine causal relationships between variables. The results show that meteorological disasters are the Granger cause of investment growth rate and GDP growth rate but not of education, both physical and education are reciprocal causalities of GDP growth rate. Therefore, we conclude that meteorological disasters promote economic growth through physical capital investment, not through human capital investment.

Two caveats need to be acknowledged. One is that some data from EM-DAT don't have economic loss data. The duration of most natural disasters is short but the time-span of economic statistics data is long. For example, earthquakes occur over minutes, while most economic statistics data are measured in months, quarters or years. Also, natural disasters often happen in one province but its reconstruction involves other provinces' supports. Crowding-out could occur. Consequently, it is difficult to get accurate and reliable data. The other caveat is that the data of death toll and economic losses have a certain relationship with income level and are not the most exogenous factors. For example, with more advanced medical treatment, stricter building laws and other safety rules, the impact caused by natural disasters may be reduced in developed regions. Thus, future research needs to explore a new indictor which is not only determined by income levels but reflects the actual level of disasters.

**Acknowledgements** Hui Liu, Xianhua Wu, Jiong Gu, Shunfeng Song, Yinshan Tang, Huai Deng also made great contributions to this manuscript. We express our heartfelt thanks to them. This study was supported by the National Social and Scientific Fund Program (18ZDA052; 17BGL142;16ZDA047; 11CGL100), Natural Science Foundation of China(91546117,71373131; 71140014, 91024020), National soft Scientific Fund Program(2011GXQ4B025), National Industry-specific Topics (GYHY200806017), Ministry of Social Science Project Youth Fund (09YJC 630128) and China Postdoctoral Foundation(20090461132). This study was also supported by the Priority Academic Program Development of Jiangsu Higher Education Institutions.

## References


Albala-Bertrand, J. M. (1993). *Political economy of large natural disasters: With special reference to developing countries*. Oxford, United Kingdom: Clarendon Press.

Anuchitworawong, C., & Thampanishvong, K. (2015). Determinants of foreign direct investment in Thailand: Does natural disaster matter? *International Journal of Disaster Risk Reduction, 14*(3), 312–321.

Attary, N., Cutler, H., Shields, M., et al. (2020). The economic effects of financial relief delays following a natural disaster. *Economic Systems Research, 32*(3), 351–377.

Atsalakis, G. S., Bouri, E., & Pasiouras, F. (2020). Natural disasters and economic growth: A quantile on quantile approach. *Annals of Operations Research*. https://doi.org/10.1007/s10479-020-03535-6.

Albuquerque, P. H., & Rajhi, W. (2019). Banking stability, natural disasters, and state fragility: Panel VAR evidence from developing countries. *Research in International Business and Finance, 50*, 430–443.

Benson, C., & Clay, E. (2003). *The impact of drought on sub-saharan African economies: A preliminary examination*. Washington, DC: World Bank Technical Paper.

Barone, G., & Mocetti, S. (2014). Natural disasters, growth and institutions: A tale of two earthquakes. *Journal of Urban Economics, 84*, 52–66.

Boudreaux, C. J., Escaleras, M. P., & Skidmore, M. (2019). Natural disasters and entrepreneurship activity. *Economics Letters, 182*, 82–85.

Bondonio, D., & Greenbaum, R. T. (2018). Natural disasters and relief assistance: Empirical evidence on the resilience of US counties using dynamic propensity score matching. *Journal of Regional Science, 58*(3), 659–680.

Benali, N., Abdelkafi, I., & Feki, R. (2018). Natural-disaster shocks and government's behavior: Evidence from middle-income countries. *International Journal of Disaster Risk Reduction, 27*, 1–6.

Breckner, M., Englmaier, F., Stowasser, T., et al. (2016). Resilience to natural disasters Insurance penetration, institutions, and disaster types. *Economic Letters, 148*, 106–110.

Clack, J. M. (1917). Business acceleration and the law of demand. *Journal of Political Economy, 25*(3), 217–235.

CRED. (2012). EM-DAT. Retrieved 18 May, 2012, from www.emdat.be.

Cuaresma, J. C., Hlouskova, J., & Obersteiner, M. (2008). Natural disasters as creative destruction? Evidence from developing countries. *Economic Inquiry, 46*(2), 214–226.

Cavallo, E., Galiani, S., Noy, I., et al. (2013). Catastrophic natural disasters and economic growth. *Review of Economics and Statistics, 95*(5), 1549–1561.

Coulson, N. E., McCoy, S. J., & McDonough, I. K. (2020). Economic diversification and the resiliency hypothesis: Evidence from the impact of natural disasters on regional housing values. *Reginal Science and Urban Economics*. https://doi.org/10.1016/j.regsciurbeco.2020.103581.

Cole, M. A., Elliott, R. J. R., Okubo, T., et al. (2019). Natural disasters and spatial heterogeneity in damages: The birth, life and death of manufacturing plants. *Journal of Economic Geography, 19*(2), 373–408.

Cheng, L., & Zhang, J. (2020). Is tourism development a catalyst of economic recovery following natural disaster? An analysis of economic resilience and spatial variability. *Current Issues in Tourism, 23*(20), 2602–2623.

Dacy, D. C., Kunreuther, H. (1969). The economics of natural disasters-implications for federal policy. The Free Press.

Dercon, S. (2004). Growth and shocks: Evidence from rural Ethiopia. *Journal of Development Economics, 74*(2), 309–329.

Datar, A., Liu, J., Linnemayr, S., et al. (2013). The impact of natural disasters on child health and investments. *Social Science & Medicine, 76*, 83–91.

Doytch, N., & Klein, Y. L. (2018). The impact of natural disasters on energy consumption: An analysis of renewable and nonrenewable energy demand in the residential and industrial sectors. *Environmental Progress & Sustainable Energy, 37*(1), 37–45.

de Oliveira, V. H. (2019). Natural disasters and economic growth in Northeast Brazil: Evidence from municipal economies of the Ceara State. *Environmental and Development Economics, 24*(3), 271–293.

de Oliveira, V. H., de Franca, J. M. S., & Martins, F. M. V. (2020). The influence of local development on the impact of natural disasters in Northeast Brazil: The case of droughts and floods in the state of Ceara. *Papers in Reginal Science, 99*(4), 1019–1043.

Fomby, T., Ikeda, Y., & Loayza, N. V. (2013). The growth aftermath of natural disasters. *Journal of Applied Econometric, 28*(3), 412–434.

Felbermayr, G., & Groschl, J. (2014). Naturally negative: The growth effects of natural disasters. *Journal of Development Economics, 111,* 92–106.

Fabian, M., Lessmann, C., & Sofke, T. (2019). Natural disasters and regional development-the case of earthquakes. *Environmental and Development Economics, 24*(5), 479–505.

Gassebner, M., Keck, A., & The, R. (2010). Shaken, Not Stirred: The impact of disasters on international trade. *Review of International Economics, 18*(2), 351–368.

Guo, J. X. (2005). Human capital, the birth rate and the narrowing of the urban-rural income gap. *Social Sciences in China, 3,* 27–38.

Hallegatte, S., & Dumas, P. (2009). Can natural disasters have positive consequences? Investigating the role of embodied technical change. *Ecological Economics, 68*(3), 777–786.

Horwich, G. (1997). Economic lessons of the Kobe earthquake. Purdue CIBER Working Papers, p. 128.

Haddad, E. A., & Teixeira, E. (2015). Economic impacts of natural disasters in megacities: The case of floods in Sao Paulo. *Brazil. Habitat International, 45,* 106–113.

Harrison, C. G., & Williams, P. R. (2016). A systems approach to natural disaster resilience. *Simulation Modelling Practice and Theory, 65,* 11–31.

Ishizawa, O. A., & Miranda, J. J. (2019). Weathering storms: Understanding the impact of natural disasters in Central America. *Environmental & Resource Economics, 73*(1), 181–211.

Kim, C.-K. (2010). The effects of natural disasters on long-run economic growth. *The Michigan Journal of Business, 41,* 15–49.

Klomp, J. (2020). Do natural disasters affect monetary policy? A quasi-experiment of earthquakes. *Journal of Macroeconomics*. https://doi.org/10.1016/j.jmacro.2019.103164.

Klomp, J., & Valckx, K. (2014). Natural disasters and economic growth: A meta-analysis. *Global Environmental Change-Human and Policy Dimensions, 26,* 183–195.

Khan, K. A., Zaman, K., Shoukry, A. M., et al. (2019). Natural disasters and economic losses: Controlling external migration, energy and environmental resources, water demand, and financial development for global prosperity. *Environmental Science and Pollution Research, 26*(14), 14287–14299.

Karim, A. (2018). The household response to persistent natural disasters: evidence from Bangladesh. *World Development, 103,* 40–59.

Klomp, J. (2020). Do natural disasters affect monetary policy? A quasi-experiment of earthquakes. *Journal of Macroeconomics*. https://doi.org/10.1016/j.jmacro.2019.103164.

Khan, A., Yang, C. G., & Khan, G. (2020). The dilemma of natural disasters: Impact on economy, fiscal position, and foreign direct investment alongside Belt and Road Initiative countries. *Science of the Total Environment*. https://doi.org/10.1016/j.scitotenv.2020.140578.

Lai, M. Y., Zhang, X., Peng, S. J., et al. (2005). The source of economic growth: Human capital, R & D and technical spillovers. *Social Sciences in China, 2,* 32–46.

Leiter, A. M., Oberhofer, H., & Raschky, P. A. (2009). Creative disasters? Flooding effects on capital, labor and productivity within European firms. *Environmental and Resource Economics, 43*(3), 333–350.

Liu, J. R. (2009). Impact of Meteorological disasters on economic development and countermeasures. *Journal of Shanxi Finance and Economics University, 31*(2), 25–26.

Liu, R. M., & Shi, L. (2010). The dual efficiency loss of state-owned enterprises and economic growth. *Economic Research Journal, 1,* 127–137.

Loayza, V. N., Olaberria, E., & Rigolini, J. (2012). Natural disasters and growth: Going beyond the averages. *World Development, 40*(7), 1317–1336.

Lu, M., Chen, Z., & Wan, G. H. (2005). Equality for the sake of growth: The Mexus of inequality, investment, education and growth in China. *Economic Research Journal, 12,* 4–14.

Lazzaroni, S., & van Bergeijk, P. A. G. (2014). Natural disasters' impact, factors of resilience and development: A meta-analysis of the macroeconomic literature. *Ecological Economics, 107,* 333–346.

Luo, K., & Kinugasa, T. (2020). Do natural disasters influence long-term saving?: assessing the impact of the 2008 sichuan earthquake on household saving rates using synthetic control. *China-An International Journal, 18*(3), 59–81.

Lima, R. C. D., & Barbosa, A. V. B. (2019). Natural disasters, economic growth and spatial spillovers: Evidence from a flash flood in Brazil. *Papers in Regional Science, 98*(2), 905–924.

Munasinghe, M., Clarke, C. (1995). Disaster prevention for sustainable development: Economic and policy issues. Geneva and New York, pp. 11–40.

Mechler, R. (2009). A risk management approach for assessing adaptation to changing flood and drought risks in Europe.

Hulme, M., Neufeldt, H. (2009). Making climate change work for Us: European perspectives on adaptation and mitigation strategies. Cambridge.

McDermott, T. K. J., Barry, F., & Tol, R. S. J. (2014). Disasters and development: Natural disasters, credit constraints, and economic growth. *Oxford Economic Papers-New Series, 66*(3), 750–773.

Mohan, P. S., Ouattara, B., & Strobl, E. (2018). Decomposing the macroeconomic effects of natural disasters: A national income accounting perspective. *Ecological Economics, 146,* 1–9.

Mukherjee, S., & Hastak, M. (2018). A novel methodological approach to estimate the impact of natural hazard-induced disasters on country/region-level economic growth. *International Journal of Disaster Risk Science, 9*(1), 74–85.

Noy, I., Nualsri, A. (2007). What do exogenous shocks tell us about growth theories? University of Hawaii Working Paper, pp. 7–28.

Okuyama, Y. (2013). Economics of natural disasters: A critical review. Philadelphia, PA: Research Paper.

Okuyama, Y., Hewings, G. J. D., Sonis, M. (2004). Measuring economic impacts of disasters: Interregional input-output analysis using sequential interindustry model. *Advances in Spatial Science,* 77–101.

Otero, R., & Marti, R. (1995). The impacts of natural disasters on national economies and the implications for the international development and disaster community.

Porfiriev, B. (2012). Economic issues of disaster and disaster risk reduction policies: International vs. Russian perspectives. *International Journal of Disaster Risk Reduction.* doi: 10.1016/j.ijdrr.2012.05.005.

Panwar, V., & Sen, S. (2020). Fiscal repercussions of natural disasters: stylized facts and panel data evidences from India. *Natural Hazards Review.* https://doi.org/10.1061/(ASCE)NH.1527-6996.0000369.

Padli, J., Habibullah, M. S., & Baharom, A. H. (2018). The impact of human development on natural disaster fatalities and damage: Panel data evidence. *Economic Research-Ekonomska Istrazivanja, 31*(1), 1557–1573.

Qureshi, M. I., Yusoff, R. M., Hishan, S. S., et al. (2019). Natural disasters and Malaysian economic growth: Policy reforms for disasters management. *Environmental Science and Pollution Research, 26*(15), 15496–15509.

Raddatz, C. (2009). The wrath of god: macroeconomic costs of natural disasters. Washington, DC: World Bank Policy Research Working Paper Series.

Rodriguez-Oreggia, E., de la Fuente, A., de la Torre, R., et al. (2010). The impact of natural disasters on human development and poverty at the municipal level in Mexico. Cambridge, MA: Center for International Development Working Paper.

Skidmore, M., & Toya, H. (2002). Do natural disasters promote long-run growth? *Economic Inquiry, 40*(4), 664–687.

Strobl, E. (2012). The economic growth impact of natural disasters in developing countries: Evidence from hurricane strikes in the central American and Caribbean regions. *Journal of Development Economics, 97*(1), 130–141.

Shabnam, N. (2014). Natural disasters and economic growth: A review. *International Journal of Disaster Risk Science, 5*(2), 157–163.

Siodla, J. (2015). Razing San Francisco: The 1906 disaster as a natural experiment. *Journal of Urban Economics, 89,* 48–61.

Strulik, H., & Trimborn, T. (2019). Natural disasters and macroeconomic performance. *Environmental & Resource Economics, 72*(4), 1069–1098.

Tol, R., & Leek, F. (1999). *Economic analysis of natural disasters*. Climate: Change and Risk. London.

Tang, R. M., Wu, J. D., Ye, M. Q., et al. (2019). Impact of economic development levels and disaster types on the short-term macroeconomic consequences of natural hazard-induced disasters in China. *International Journal of Disaster Risk Science, 10*(3), 371–385.

Verschuur, J., Koks, E. E., & Hall, J. W. (2020). Port disruptions due to natural disasters: Insights into port and logistics resilience. *Transportation Research Part D-Transport and Environment.* https://doi.org/10.1016/j.trd.2020.102393.

Wang, Y. M., Chen, M. L., & Wang, X. (2008). The impacts of natural disasters on long-term growth: Theoretical and empirical study. *Economic Management, 30*(19–20), 144–150.

Xin, J. W., Xu, X. C., & Chen, M. (2009). A study on meteorological disaster management model and defense mechanism. *China Soft Science, S2,* 276–283.

Okuyama, Y., Chang, S. E. (2004). Modeling the spatial and economic effects of disasters. New York, pp. 77–101.

Yum, S. G., Ahn, S., Bae, J., et al. (2020). Assessing the risk of natural disaster-induced losses to tunnel-construction projects using empirical financial-loss data from South Korea. *Sustainability.* https://doi.org/10.3390/su12198026.

Zhang, F. (2000). Physical capital and human capital estimation in China. *Economic Research Journal, 8,* 65–71.

Zhang, X. D., & Shen, R. F. (1995). The quantitative study on the relationship between disasters and economic growth. *Journal of Natural Disasters, 4*(4), 23–26.

Zhu, C. L., Shi, P., Yue, H. Z., et al. (2011). The study on bind of human capital, human capital structure and regional economic growth efficiency. *China Soft Science, 2,* 110–119.

Zou, X. H. (2009). *Research on the influence of natural disasters on economic growth in China.* Xiamen: Xiamen University.

Zhou, Y., Li, N., Wu, W. X., et al. (2014). Socioeconomic development and the impact of natural disasters: Some empirical evidences from China. *Natural Hazards, 74*(2), 541–554.

Zhang, D. Y., & Managi, S. (2020). Financial development, natural disasters, and economics of the Pacific small island states. *Economic Analysis and Policy, 66,* 168–181.

# Chapter 4
# Comprehensive Economic Loss Assessment of Disaster Based on CGE Model and IO model—A Case Study on Beijing "7.21 Rainstorm"

**Abstract** The economic loss evaluation of disaster is the basis for disaster prevention and disaster emergency management and thus needs to be solved urgently. Computable general equilibrium (CGE) model and input–output (IO) model are the major disaster assessment methods, which each have their own strengths and weaknesses currently. However, few comparative researches have been conducted on the economic losses of one disaster evaluated by CGE Model and IO Model based on the same disaster impact. Therefore, this paper, taking the Beijing "7.21 Rainstorm" in 2012 as an example, from the direct loss of agricultural and transportation sectors, used CGE Model and IO Model to calculate the comprehensive economic loss ratios of sectors and the final output loss of economic system, and then determined the range of the economic loss caused by the rainstorm. The results showed that: (1) CGE Model has a greater spillover effect upon sectors and a wider distribution of disaster-affected sectors than IO Model; (2) the range of economic loss determined by the assessment results of CGE Model and IO Model is [67.9396, 74.2739] (100 million yuan); (3) agricultural, transportation, and mining sectors are high-sensitivity sectors to rainstorm disasters. Through the comparison of the two models, the accurate economic loss of disaster can be obtained, according to which governments can take targeted measures for the prevention and early warning of disasters.

**Keywords** Computable general equilibrium model · Input–output model · Comprehensive economic loss · "7.21 Rainstorm"

## 4.1 Introduction

The climate warming and the frequent occurrence of meteorological disasters have posed a serious challenge to the sustainable development of the world as well as the safety of human life and property. Thus, the reasonable assessment on the economic losses of disaster and the selection of high-sensitivity sectors and regions have aroused wide concern among the government, academics and public so that targeted disaster prevention and damage reduction measures can be taken (Okuyama 2004; Heatwole and Rose 2013). In terms of the studies on the economic loss assessment of disaster, many scholars have demonstrated the importance of comprehensive

 
X. Wu and J. Guo, *Economic Impacts and Emergency Management of Disasters in China*,
https://doi.org/10.1007/978-981-16-1319-7_4

economic loss and believe it can reflect the overall influences of disasters in a wider space and a longer period and thus is conductive to mobilizing the whole society to prevent and mitigate disasters with concerted effort (Hallegatte 2008; Hu et al. 2014; Li et al. 2017). However, these studies mostly focus on the overall influence of disaster on a specific industry or a certain region. Quite a few researches have been conducted on the assessment of the comprehensive economic loss the disasters caused to the industrial-economic system based on quantitative model, not to mention the comparative studies based on various methods.

This paper attempts to go deep into the two major methods for assessing the comprehensive economic loss of disaster, i. e., computable general equilibrium (CGE) model and input–output (IO) model. This paper takes Beijing "7.21 Rainstorm" as an example, from the direct losses of agricultural and transportation sectors, introduces the same disaster impact value into production function and conducts a contrastive analysis on the comprehensive economic losses of industrial sectors, and then, with the range of comprehensive economic loss of disaster determined through the assessment models, manages to reduce the uncertainties of evaluated results (see the details in Fig. 4.1). This paper is not only a comparative research on the comprehensive economic loss assessment methods but also an intensive study on the mechanism and process of disaster in affecting socio-economic development and provides empirical reference for disaster preventing and alleviating measures.

## 4.2 Literature Review

Due to the connections among the industrial sectors, the shutdown or output reduction of a certain sector often will influence the upstream and downstream sectors, which will further affect the whole industrial-economic system (Rose and Lim 2002; Helbing 2013; Hallegatte 2015). For this reason, the comprehensive influences disasters exert on the whole industrial-economic system should be considered rather than the losses of certain sectors in one or several regions when evaluating the socio-economic loss caused by disasters (Haimes and Jiang 2001; Santos and Haimes 2010). Currently, the methods for assessing the economic influences of disasters can be mainly grouped into two types.

The first type is CGE Model. For instance, Narayan (2003) used the CGE Model to evaluate the short-term macroeconomic impact upon Fiji after hit by Hurricane Ami in 2003. Rose and Liao (2005) improved the production function of CGE Model by introducing the concept of resilience and then, taking the supply disruption of the urban water system in Portland after an earthquake as an example, simulated and evaluated the indirect economic loss caused to associated sectors and regions by the earthquake. Pauw et al. (2011) combined stochastic hydrometeorological crop-loss models with a regionalized computable general equilibrium model to estimate losses for the full distribution of possible weather events in Malawi. Carrera et al. (2015) combined space model with CGE Model to evaluate the direct and indirect economic influences of flood on different sectors and regions. Cui et al. (2018)

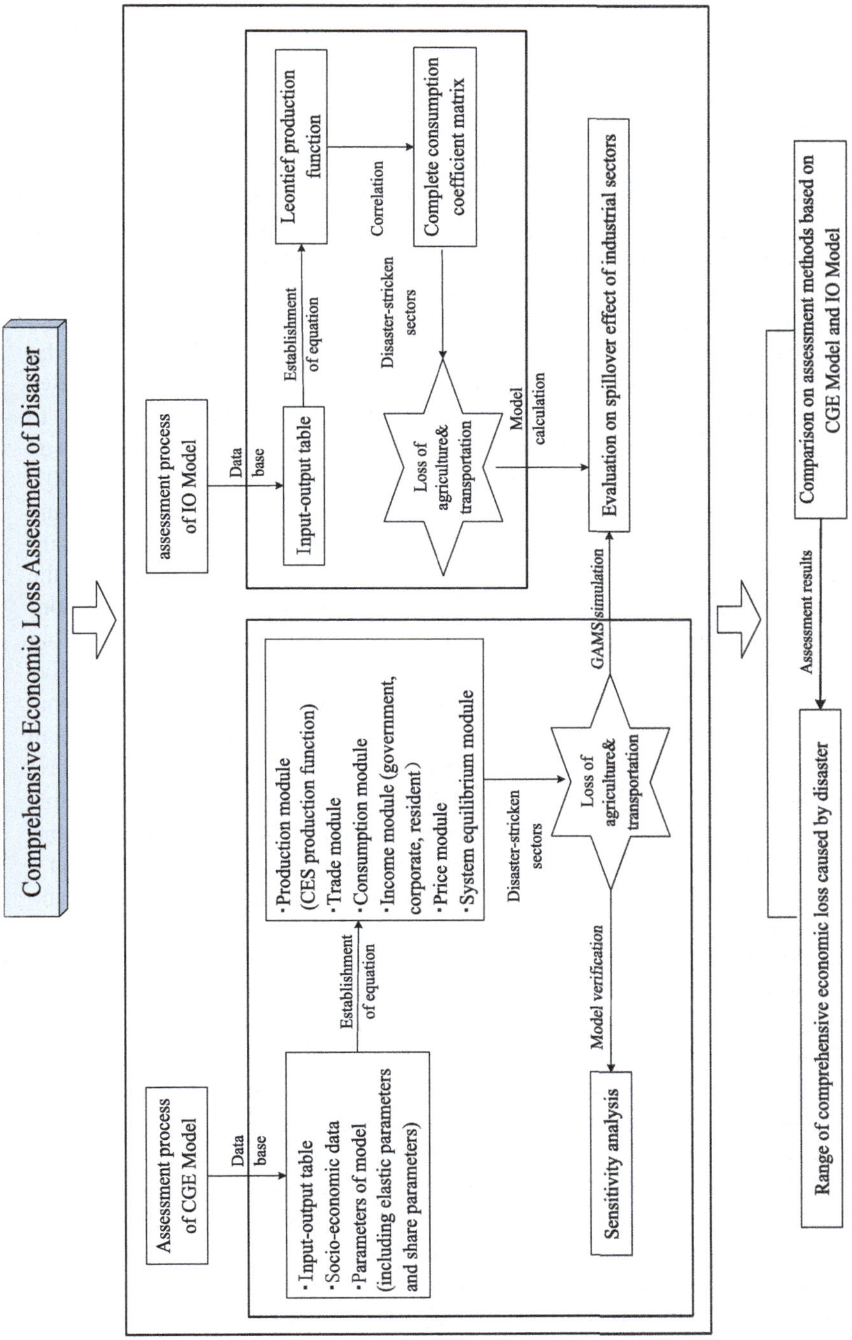


**Fig. 4.1** Flow chart of comprehensive economic loss assessment process of disaster

established a multi-region CGE Model for evaluating the economic impacts of sea level rise on the coastal cities in China. Xie et al. (2018) linked the disaster relief policies to the dynamic economic resilience of disaster-stricken area and used CGE Model to evaluate the comprehensive economic loss caused by 2008 Wenchuan Earthquake as well as the disaster loss reduced due to resilience. Wang et al. (2016) introduced labour losses and excess medical expenditure into the CGE model. He combined the CGE model with an exposure–response function to evaluate the adverse effects of PM2.5 pollution various industries as well as the entire economic system in Beijing. Taking the power disruptions caused by the 2008 Hunan snowstorm as an example, Hu et al. (2014) compared the indirect economic losses estimated by the CGE and other output models. In attentional, he discussed how the elasticity of the regional economy could reduce financial losses through market replacement and price fluctuations. Fung et al. (2020) examined the "resilience dividends" in Cedar Rapids, USA, after disaster reconstruction. He constructed CGE models for two separate periods, before the 2007 floods and after the 2015 disaster investments, to illustrate how co-benefits were distributed across the economy. The results showed that the co-benefits of critical economic indicators were better in 2015 than in 2007.

To quantitatively assess the non-market damage of extreme weather, Hoffmann (2019) developed a new model. He scaled up a static CGE model to the standard Auerbach-Kotlikoff model. He then simulated the effects of a Swiss heatwave on the cohort effects in an unadapted economy. The results implied that young and non-vulnerable groups profited from the disaster. Gertz et al.(2019)used a forward-looking and dynamic CGE model to study the losses induced by economic disruptions in five towns in Vancouver, British Columbia, caused by flooding. The results suggested that GDP loss relative to the no-flood scenario relatively persistent. Hurricane Katrina in 2012 caused an outward migration of the population of Orleans Parish. Therefore, Fan and Davlasheridze (2019) incorporated the hurricane-induced brain drain into a CGE model to examine the impact of migration and permanent loss of skilled labour in the region. The study found that skill loss caused a further loss in GRP than a population decline. To validate the CGE with a short-term case, Kajitani and Tatano (2018) used a spatial CGE model to divide Japan into nine regions and then estimated the elasticity of substitution after the 2011 earthquake and tsunami. Comparing the calculated values with the observed values revealed that the estimation results were consistent regardless of the degree of damage. Using a multiregional and dynamic CGE model, Mcdonald et al. (2017) calculated the adverse effects of economic disruptions under three volcano scenarios. The findings implied that different phases of a volcanic crisis could cause quite different economic impacts. For example, the economic structure of the most affected areas might be permanently altered. Thirawat et al. (2017) studied the effects of floods on resource losses and the impact of resource losses on real GDP through a dynamic CGE model. Based on the calculations, he suggested that ex-ante risk financing instruments such as insurance funds and catastrophe bonds could be used to improve the government's resilience to disaster losses. Wang and Li (2015) incorporated the disaster impact parameters of the four most severely affected sectors of the 2012 Beijing rainstorm into a regional CGE model. He then measured the direct and indirect economic losses caused by the disaster to

Beijing. Unexpectedly, the results showed that the rainstorm caused a total loss of about $30 billion, but stimulated both social employment and fixed asset investment. Xie and Li (2015) constructed a time-recursive dynamic CGE model by linking post-disaster reconstruction investment and reconstruction funding sources. Using the 2008 Wenchuan earthquake in China as an example, He compared various investment measures to reduce business interruption losses. He also analyzed the relative importance of pre-disaster mitigation investments and post-disaster reconstruction investments. To account for the negative impact of the earthquake on the economy and the positive effects of reconstruction investment, Xie and Li (2014a, b) incorporated disaster shocks and reconstruction investment shocks into the CGE model. Taking the 2008 Wenchuan earthquake as an example, he studied the economic losses under three scenarios: no disaster, disaster but reconstruction investment, and disaster but no reconstruction investment. Taking the 2008 snowstorm in Hunan Province as an example, Li et al. (2013) used a CGE model to quantify the cascading effects of a single industry failure on other related industries. The analysis showed that large-scale disasters induce more substantial cascading effects than small-scale disasters and that post-disaster recovery measures effectively prevented the spread of cascading effects. Other similar researches were conducted by Enke (2007), Tatano and Tsuchiya (2008) and Antimiani et al. (2015).

The second type is IO Model. For example, Hallegatte (2008) introduced disaster impact modules into IO Model to dynamically evaluate the indirect loss caused by Hurricane Katrina and to analyze the output variation trends of different industrial sectors. Mackenzie et al. (2012), by using multi-region IO Model, assessed the indirect economic losses caused by earthquakes and tsunamis in Japan and quantitatively evaluated the influences of enterprises' production facility breakdown, yield reduction, and break of global product supply chain. Haque and Jahan (2015) investigated induced effects of flood disaster scenarios on national and regional output, income and employment through Input–Output model. Mendoza-Tinoco et al. (2017), after introducing the concept of flood footprints into input–output method, calculated the comprehensive economic losses of Yorkshire and Humber River region caused by the summer floods in England in 2007. Oosterhaven (2017) used the inoperability input–output model (IIM) to assess the indirect economic impact of disasters and pointed out the limitations of the model in assessing disaster losses. Avelino et al. (2007) compared the assumptions and results of single-region IO Model with those of more complicated methods like rebalancing algorithms and sequential interindustry model and assessed the economic loss of flood on Chehalis River in 2007. Xia et al. (2018) developed an interdisciplinary approach by combining a supply-driven IO model with meteorology and epidemiology. Through this approach, he examined the impact of the 2013 heatwave on Nanjing and found that heatwaves lead to degradation of productive time and human capital. This finding highlighted the importance of including industrial dependencies and indirect economic losses in the study.

Wang et al. (2017) extended the IO model by combining the uncertainty of the economy and the sectoral breakdown structure. He also developed static and dynamic models to assess the direct financial losses and indirect economic losses caused by typhoons. Earthquakes not only reduce production in the affected regions but also disrupt supply chains in other areas. Using inter-regional input–output tables, Tokui et al. (2017) studied the impact of supply chain disruptions on GDP and the role of multiple supply chains in mitigating losses after the 2011 earthquake in Japan. The results showed that while multiple supply chains could reduce the losses caused by disasters, they might also reduce the productivity of firms. Bonfiglio et al. (2020) used a multi-regional IO model to quantify the economy-wide impact of the earthquake sequence that hit rural central Italy in 2016–2017. The study suggested that rural influences were transmitted more diffusely to surrounding areas due to a higher dependence on trade. In the context of the COVID-19 pandemic, Santos (2020) explored the impact of the epidemic on the workforce by the IO model. First, he generated attack rates by identifying the source of the epidemic curve. He then hypothesized that attack rates could reflect sector-specific labour classifications. Finally, he used IO data to assess the effects of several anti-epidemic measures. Floods can impact the entire production chain of a regional economy, and ignoring this knock-on cost may affect the effectiveness of disaster prevention. Thus, Zeng et al. (2019) introduced the concept of flood footprint into the IO model and focused on assessing the indirect impact of flooding on the regional economy. Further, he also simulated the economic recovery of the entire production supply chain after a flooding event. Krichene et al. (2020) constructed a credit-based adaptive ARIO model. He analyzed the negative impact of exogenous shocks such as the Lehman Brothers bankruptcy in 2008 and the Japanese earthquake in 2011 on the credit network of bank firms through the supply chain. The 2015/2016 Pseudo-nitzschia australis bloom resulted in a five-month delay in the opening of the California coastal fishery. Holland and Leonard (2020) used the IO model to calculate the loss of revenue and employment caused by the delayed onset of the fishery statewide. He also discussed what options and initiatives might be available to reduce direct and indirect losses if future large-scale blooms cause delays or even closures of the fishery. Climate change can lead to different industrial structures in other regions. Using an inter-country IO model, Lin et al. (2020) investigated the comprehensive economic loss caused by natural disasters to various industries on both sides of China during 2005–2017. The results showed that the value-added losses caused by natural disasters mainly involved agriculture, forestry, and fisheries.

Taking the 2008 Wenchuan earthquake as an example, Wu et al. (2019) used the IO model to study how much aid amount countries should provide to China. The results showed that countries with more significant indirect economic losses and the ability to pay should donate more. Comparing the actual amount donated by 41 countries with the estimated value, he found that six countries, such as Indonesia, contributed too much. In comparison, 23 countries, such as India, presented too little. To explore the impact of coastal disasters on the island, Yu et al. (2019) used a supply-driven IO model to analyze the substantial damage caused by Typhoon Fanapi to agriculture in Taiwan Province. The empirical results showed that the multiplier effect of output reduction was 1.33 and the unemployment rate increased by 0.06%. Faturay et al. (2020) used the MRIO model to measure regional and sectoral spillover effects when disasters occurred. Using Taiwan as an example, he calculated the negative impact on business operations from multiple disasters such as the 1999 and 2016 earthquakes and the 2009 and 2016 typhoons. The results of the study targeted key sectors vulnerable to the impact and provided a reliable reference for government decision-making. Sieg et al. (2019) combined the direct economic effects with a supply-side IO model to estimate the indirect economic impact of the 2013 German floods on 19 local sectors. He drew three conclusions. First, the manufacturing and financial sectors had the highest indirect economic effects. Second, the indirect economic impact was as high as the direct economic impact. Third, it was inappropriate to measure indirect financial losses in all economic sectors by a single factor. Khalid and Ali (2019) combined IO tables with Dynamic Inoperability Input–Output Model to study the indirect economic losses caused by the 2011–2012 floods to the Pakistani economic system. The results showed that the strongest linkages with key industries were in agriculture and services. This finding had significant implications for disaster management authorities to make decisions. Using a multi-regional IO model, Lenzen et al. (2019) examined the impact of the 2017 Tropical Cyclone Debbie on the number of jobs and GDP in Australia. The results implied that the disaster resulted in approximately 4,800 full-time jobs and $150 million in losses. Moreover, he analyzed how industries located upstream in the supply chain and not directly affected by the disaster suffered losses.

Other similar studies based on IO Model were carried out by Crowther and Haimes (2007), Barker and Santos (2010), Li et al. (2013), Baghersad and Zobel (2015), and Galbusera and Giannopoulos (2018).

It can be known form the previous researches that CGE Model and IO Model are the most widely used methods at present which have played important roles in simulating the spillover effects of disasters upon industrial sectors as well as evaluating the comprehensive economic loss caused by disasters. However, it should be pointed out that there are several issues in loss evaluation that are worthy of further investigation. The first problem is that the evaluation models, taking the industrial sectors as a whole, can only analyze the overall impact of disaster upon stricken area through the correlations among the sectors; there lacks targeted study on the loss of single or several sectors in macro industrial economic system. The second problem is that CGE Model and IO Model both have strengths and weaknesses in economic impact assessment (Okuyama 2007; Weitzman 2009; Ring et al. 2010). A case in point is that the disaster loss evaluated by IO Model is slightly higher as the variables of IO Model, though being measurable and verifiable, are characterized by linearity and rigidity and thus little consideration is given to the inherent elasticity in economic system. As for CGE Model, although it successfully reflects the interdependence of economic factors and production activities and avoids such shortcomings as lack of behavioral responses and market prices, and linear characteristics; yet the assumption of behavior optimization and the elasticity setting in the model equation may lead to the extreme changes of parameters like price and quantity; as a result, the overall impact of disaster upon economy is underestimated (Rose 2004; Koks et al. 2015). For example, Zhou and Chen (2020) tested the reliability of the CGE model through a meta-analysis of 253 CGE simulations. Three conclusions were obtained. First, elasticity could significantly reduce the disturbance of disasters to the firm. Second, the results obtained using real or hypothetical data were influenced by the type of disaster. Third, the results were sensitive to model assumptions and structure. Husby and Koks (2017) argued that IO and CGE models had limitations in describing household migration under disaster risk. Therefore, he combined IO and CGE models with agent-based models to study the effects of changes in the spatial distribution of population caused by disasters on local labour and housing markets. Using the impact of the Chehalis River flood on three Washington counties as an example, Avelino and Dall'erba (2019) compared the differences between the loss values estimated by a single-region IO model, a balanced algorithm, a continuous inter-industry model, and a dynamic inoperable input–output model.

The previous comparative researches on IO Model and CGE Model mostly remain at the theoretical level (Rose 2004; Okuyama 2010), and the empirical studies on the comparison of the two models are quite limited. The only example is that Kokset al. (2016), using both IO Model and CGE Model, from the perspective of labor and capital damaged by disaster, assessed the overall economic loss of the north and south of Po Valley in northern Italy resulted from flood; nevertheless, the data analysis and disaster impact of this study were inevitably affected by the underlying assumptions because it focused on the macro-economic loss and was carried out under the background of a simulated disaster. At present, few researches have been conducted, with both IO Model and CGE Model, to comparatively analyze the loss ratio of particular sector and the comprehensive economic loss of a typical extreme disaster. For this reason, the present paper, attempts to conduct a comparative study on the assessment results of IO Model and CGE Model based on Beijing "7.21 Rainstorm" in 2012.

## 4.3 Model Building

### *4.3.1 Structure of CGE Model*

CGE Model, based on general equilibrium theory, describes the correlations between the sectors of national economy and the national economic accounting through equations. Under the constraints of account balance and resources, the economic entities can realize the optimization of behavior through price response. With a deepening understanding of disaster-causing mechanism and post-disaster recovery process, CGE Model is able to show the importance of economic factors like production substitution and price elasticity in disaster and has become a major method for quantitatively simulating the economic loss caused by disasters.

In terms of the setting of CGE Model, this paper has consulted the research of Rose et al. (2005); as for the sectorial structure of Beijing and data processing, the studies of Xu (2009) and Yan et al. (2007) have provided certain information for reference. Labor and capital are used as the essential production factors for describing the production activities of model; and the economic system is divided into 12 industrial sectors according to the impact of disaster. They are agricultural sector, mining sector, manufacturing sector, production and supply of electricity and fuel gas and water, construction sector, wholesale and retail, transportation and storage and post service, accommodation and catering, finance, real estate, education and health and public administration, and technical, commercial and other services and are denoted by subscript i in CGE Model. The production activity of each sector is described through a two-level nested function: the total output in the first level is represented by the CES production function which is composed of intermediate input and value added; the intermediate input in the second level is represented by Leontief production function and the value added is represented by the Cobb–Douglas (CD) function which contains labor input and capital input. The functions are written as:

$$X_i = A_i\left[\delta_i V_i^{\rho_i} + (1-\delta_i) IT_i^{\rho_i}\right]^{1/\rho_i} \tag{4.1}$$

$$V_i = AV_i L_i^{\alpha_i} K_i^{1-\alpha_i} \tag{4.2}$$

$$WLDISTI_i \times \text{WL} = \frac{a_i \cdot PV_i \cdot V_i}{L_i} \tag{4.3}$$

$$WKDISTI_i \times \text{WK} = \frac{(1-a_i) \cdot PV_i \cdot V_i}{K_i} \tag{4.4}$$

where $X_i$ is the total output of all sectors, $V_i$ is value added, $IT_i$ is intermediate input, $L_i$ is labor input, $K_i$ is capital input, $WLDISTI_i$ is the distribution rate of return on labor employed, $WKDISTI_i$ is the distribution rate of sector of return on invested capital, $PV_i$ is the price of value added, WK is the price of capital, WL is price of labor, $A_i$ is the scale efficiency of total output function, $\delta_i$ is the share of total output function, $\rho_i$ is the correlation coefficient of elastic parameters of total output function, $AV_i$ is the scale efficiency of value added function, and $a_i$ is the share of input factor.

To show the impact effect of disaster on the agricultural and transportation sectors of Beijing, this paper has introduced disaster impact parameters $\alpha_{agr}$ and $\alpha_{tra}$ into the production activity simulation of economic system. Before the disaster, $\alpha_{agr} = \alpha_{tra} = 1$; the disaster impact parameters will change accordingly after the disaster. The corresponding equations are:

$$X_{agr}^{'} = \left(1 - \alpha_{agr}\right) \times X_{agr}^{0} \tag{4.5}$$

$$X_{tra}^{'} = (1 - \alpha_{tra}) \times X_{tra}^{0} \tag{4.6}$$

where $X_{agr}^{'}$ and $X_{tra}^{'}$ are the output values of agricultural and transportation sectors of Beijing after the disaster, respectively, $\alpha_{agr}$ and $\alpha_{tra}$ are disaster impact parameters, and $X^0_{agr}$ and $X^0_{tra}$ respectively are the original output values of agricultural and transportation sectors, namely, the output values before the disaster.

### 4.3.2 Structure of IO Model

IO model, through a simultaneous system of linear equations, assembles the whole economic system, and based on the data from input–output table, is able to reflect the economic relationships between the sectors of national economy and the links of social reproduction process. Since the 1970s, scholars both home and abroad have developed the traditional IO Model into dynamic IO model (Cochrane 1997a, b), Adaptive Regional Input–Output Model (ARIO) (Hallegatte 2008), and Inoperability Input–output Model (Haimes et al. 2005a, b). and have used them to evaluate the comprehensive economic loss caused by disasters like earthquakes and hurricanes. In general, the input–output table is composed of three parts, i. e., intermediate use matrix X, final use matrix Y, and value added matrix Z. The correlations among the industrial sectors are shown through the equilibrium relationships of row and column:

(1) The equation ($\Delta$ Q = (B + I)$\Delta$Y) shown to indicate that the research on disaster loss is from the perspective of total requirement coefficient in this paper. The damage caused by the disaster was not just considered as the loss of the final product, it also included the loss due to the reduction of indirect consumption. The equation B = $(I - A)^{-1} - 1$ shown the correspondence between the direct input co-efficient and the total requirement coefficient.

(2) The transformation of supply constraints estimated turned to final demand decline has been added as follows:

Row equilibrium relationship: intermediate use + final use = total output, namely:

$$\sum_j X_{ij} + Y_i = Q_i \tag{4.7}$$

Column equilibrium relationship: intermediate input + increased value = total input, namely:

$$\sum_i X_{ij} + Z_j = Q_j \tag{4.8}$$

Total output = total input, namely:

$$Q_i = \sum_j X_{ij} + Y_i = \sum_i X_{ij} + Z_j = Q_j \tag{4.8}$$

where $X_{ij}$ refers to the product value of the intermediate input of all sectors consumed during the production, $Y_i$ refers to the product value for final use of sector i, $Q_i$ is the gross output of sector i, $Z_j$ is the increased value of sector j, and $Q_j$ is the gross output of sector j.

This paper is based on the row equilibrium, that is, the formula (4.7) to calculate the economic losses of sectors, namely:

$$Q_{ij} = \sum_{j} a_{ij} Q_{ij} + Y_i, (i, j = 1, 2, \ldots, n) \tag{4.10}$$

where $Q_{ij}$ represents the total output of the sector i, $a_{ij}$ is the direct input coefficient.

The relationship between the final use of the product and the total output can be obtained by matrix transformation:

$$Q = (I - A)^{-1} Y \tag{4.11}$$

$$\Delta Q = (I - A)^{-1} \Delta Y \tag{4.12}$$

where $\Delta$ Q is the economic loss of disaster-stricken sector, $\Delta Y$ is the final product loss of disaster-stricken sector, A is direct input coefficient matrix, I is identity matrix.

In order to analyze the relevant economic losses of each sector comprehensively, this paper assessed disaster losses from the perspective of total requirement coefficient. The damage caused by the disaster was not just considered as the loss of the final product, it also included the loss due to the reduction of indirect consumption.

The correspondence between the direct input coefficient and the total requirement coefficient can be expressed as:

$$B = (I - A)^{-1} - I \tag{4.13}$$

where B is the total requirement coefficient matrix which stands for the total amount of direct and indirect input when the production unit uses products ultimately.

$$AQ + Y = Q \tag{4.14}$$

Then the comprehensive economic losses caused by changes in output of agriculture and transportation sectors to other related sectors can be expressed as:

$$\Delta Q = (B + I) \Delta Y \tag{4.15}$$

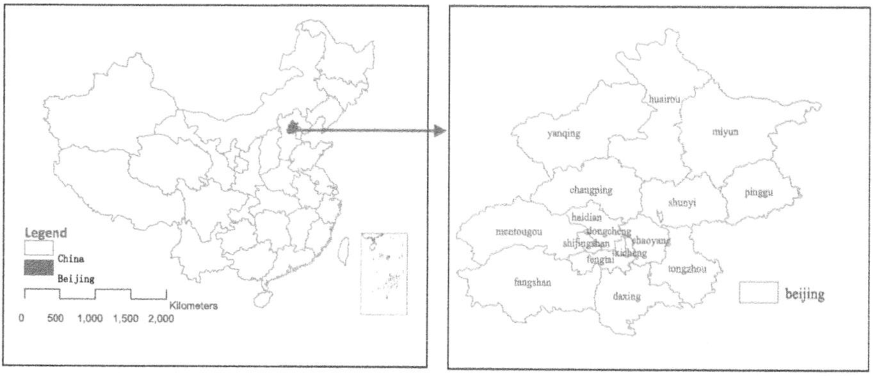


**Fig. 4.2** Location of Beijing city in China

## 4.4 Case Introduction and Data Sources

### *4.4.1 Case Introduction*

An extraordinary heavy rainstorm whipped Beijing on July 21, 2012, resulting in an average rainfall of 170 mm across Beijing, an average rainfall of 215 mm in the urban areas of Beijing, and a regional maximum rainfall of 460 mm. According to the relevant news reports, the rainstorm lasted for nearly 16 h and incurred a series of flood disasters which affected nearly 1.9 million people and caused the death of 79 people as well as the collapse of 10,660 houses; the flood-stricken area and flood-inundated area respectively are 16,000 km$^2$ and 14,000 km$^2$; and the direct economic loss hits RMB 11.64 billion *yuan*.[1,2] As announced by the Beijing Municipal Flood Prevention Office, this rainstorm is rare in history with its large rainfall, high intensity, and long duration, and severe local floods.[3]

Beijing has received the largest rainfall from "7.21 Rainstorm" since complete meteorological records began in 1951. The rainstorm had great adverse impacts on the infrastructures in agriculture, forestry and transportation as well as on the daily life of citizens. It is a typical extreme climate disaster which can provide good research materials for this paper (Fig. 4.2).

[1]CNTV: https://news.cntv.cn/china/20120723/101507.shtml.

[2]CHINANEWS: https://www.chinanews.com/gn/2012/08-06/4085857.shtml.

[3]CNTV: https://news.cntv.cn/china/20120723/101507.shtml

### 4.4.2 Data Sources

(1) Data of disaster. According to the relevant reports of Sohu Business,[4] the direct economic loss of the agricultural sector in Beijing caused by "7.21 Rainstorm" is close to RMB 0.45 billion *yuan*. The data of the specific losses of other sectors are unavailable owing to the lack of statistical information. It can be known from the researches of Nakanishiet al. (2014), Fotouhi et al. (2017), Wei et al. (2018), and Yücelet al. (2018) and the reports from various news media that the impact of the rainstorm upon transportation sector cannot be ignored either. Thus, this paper used the monthly and quarterly statistical data on the profit gap of transportation sector (transportation, storage, and post service) between the second quarter and the third quarter in 2012 obtained from the Beijing Municipal Bureau of Statistics to calculate the loss of transportation sector; and the calculated economic loss of transportation sector is approximately RMB 0.64 billion yuan.

(2) Input–output table. Input–output table is the data source of IO Model. This paper has made an assessment with the data of 42 sectors obtained from the *2012 Input–Output Table of Beijing* released by the Beijing Municipal Bureau of Statistics.[5] The input–output relationships among the sectors in 2012 are assumed to be stable.

(3) Social accounting matrix (SAM). SAM is the most important data source of CGE Model. The SAM of Beijing in the present paper is established using 2012 as the base year. The data obtained from the *2012 Input–Output Tables of Beijing*, *China Statistical Yearbook of 2013*, *Beijing Statistical Yearbook of 2013*, and *2013 Finance Yearbook of China* are processed by using RAS method. The parameters involved in CGE Model are divided into two types, i. e., elastic parameters and scale parameters, which can be worked out directly. The elasticity of substitution in CES production function and trade function has consulted the studies of He et al. (2002) and Zhai and Hertel (2005); and thus, the elastic parameter values of 12 sectors can be obtained. The scale parameters, share parameters, and relevant tax rate parameters are calculated directly or obtained by calibration method with the base year data in SAM and the parameters given exogenously. The relevant parameters are given in Section "Values of Related Parameters" (Table 4.1).

---

[4] Sohu Business: https://business.sohu.com/20120724/n348852792.shtml.

[5] Beijing Municipal Bureau of Statistics: https://www.bjstats.gov.cn/tjsj/zxdcsj/trccdc/dcsj_4603/.

**Table 4.1** The macro social accounting matrix of Beijing in the year 2012 (Unit: RMB100 million *yuan*)

| | | Activities | Commodities | Factors | | Residents | Enterprises | Government | Foreign | Domestic | Savings and investment |
|---|---|---|---|---|---|---|---|---|---|---|---|
| | | | | Labor | Capital | | | | | | |
| Activities | | | 45,434 | | | | | | 7078 | | |
| Commodities | | 34,632 | | | | 6203 | | 4452 | | 64,730 | 7410 |
| Factors | Labor | 9023 | | | | | | | | | |
| | Capital | 5925 | | | | | | | 261 | | |
| Residents | | | | 9023 | 618 | | 2313 | 424 | | | |
| Enterprises | | | | | 5569 | | | | | | |
| Government | | 2931 | | | | 282 | 821 | | | | 842 |

## 4.5 Analysis on the Comprehensive Economic Loss of Rainstorm

### *4.5.1 Analysis Based on CGE Model*

(1) CGE Model building. The production activity is described through a two-level nested function: the total output in the first level is represented by the CES production which contains intermediate input and value added; the intermediate input in the second level is represented by Leontief production function, and value added is represented by the CD function which is composed of labor input and capital input. In the labor market, China is a developing country with a large surplus of labor currently, so this paper assumed that wages were rigid and the labor market was not fully regulated, that is, full employment was not necessarily achieved, and unemployment was allowed. In the capital market, considering that the strengthening of China's economic system reform, the industry's entry barriers are gradually reduced, and the industry monopoly is weakened. This paper assumed that enterprises can adjust the enterprise inventory and change the investment direction, that is, capital can flow and conversion freely between sectors.

Generally, the commodities sold on regional market are purchased by economic entities like enterprises, governments, and residents either for consumption or investment. The consumption of residents, which is restricted by their incomes, is determined through the utility maximization of CD production function; the consumption and investment demand of government are shown through the function of fixed share expenditure. The incomes of residents and enterprises come from the factor rewards as well as the received transfer payment, while the government revenue includes the indirect taxes and the income taxes of residents and corporates. In the equilibrium module of CGE Model, all commodities are cleared through price so as to achieve the balance of investment and savings and the balance of foreign exchange receipts and payments. The specific functions of CGE Model are presented in Section "Construction of CGE Model".

(2) Impact of rainstorm on economic system. The trigger and impact mechanisms of disaster for economic system should be determined before evaluating the economic influences of disaster with CGE Model. The losses of agricultural sector and transportation sector are deemed as impact variables. The disaster impact parameters $\alpha_{agr}$ and $\alpha_{tra}$ were added to the production activities. Then with the introduction of the associated losses in Beijing economic system caused by rainstorm disaster, the calculation equations of disaster impact parameters can be expressed as:

$$\alpha_{agr} = \left(1 - \frac{X'_{agr}}{X^0_{agr}}\right) \times 100\% \tag{4.16}$$

$$\alpha_{tra} = \left(1 - \frac{X'_{tra}}{X^0_{tra}}\right) \times 100\% \tag{4.17}$$

Based on the total product losses of agricultural sector and transportation sector, which are RMB 0.56799 billion yuan and 1.72723 billion yuan, respectively, the disaster impact parameters can be obtained: $\alpha_{agr} = 98.5648$; $\alpha_{tra} = 99.4571$.

(3) Structure effect of rainstorm disaster on sectors. Rainstorm disaster can damage infrastructures and cause direct economic losses. It will, through the internal correlations in economic system, impair the productivity and reduce the output of enterprises, and will decrease the purchasing power and demand of residents by reducing incomes, thereby eventually affecting the regional economy.

According to the statistics, the disaster loss ratios of sectors are presented in Table 4.2 and can be ranked from top to bottom as: agricultural sector > mining sector > transportation, storage, and postal service > manufacturing sector > production and supply of electricity, fuel gas, and water > real estate > finance > technical, commercial and other services > wholesale and retail > education, health and public administration > construction sector. The total loss of the sectors caused by rainstorm disaster is up to RMB 6.79396 billion *yuan*.

**Table 4.2** Comprehensive economic losses of sectors assessed by CGE model

| Sector | Loss/RMB 100 million *yuan* | Loss ratio of disaster /%[6] |
|---|---|---|
| Agricultural sector | 2.0570 | 0.5198 |
| Mining sector | 6.7528 | 0.4642 |
| Manufacturing sector | 26.2736 | 0.1914 |
| Production and supply of electricity, fuel gas, and water | 3.0673 | 0.0816 |
| Construction sector | 0.6040 | 0.0145 |
| Wholesale and retail | 2.1289 | 0.0539 |
| Transportation, storage, and postal service | 13.9789 | 0.4394 |
| Accommodation and catering | 0.7270 | 0.0610 |
| Finance | 2.8335 | 0.0708 |
| Real estate | 1.4961 | 0.0714 |
| Technical, commercial and other services | 6.5260 | 0.0688 |
| Education, health and public administration | 1.4947 | 0.0293 |
| Total | 67.9396 | 0.0013 |

[6]"Loss ratio of disaster" mean economic losses value of each sector caused by disaster/ the total output of each sector in no-disaster scenario.

### 4.5.2 Analysis Based on IO Model

(1) Calculation of total requirement coefficient matrix (B). Through the *2012 Input–Output Table of Beijing*, the direct input coefficient of all sectors is calculated firstly and $(\mathrm{I}-\mathrm{A})^{-1}$ can be obtained. Then the total requirement coefficient matrix for the merged 12 sectors is obtained by the correlation equation of total requirement coefficient and direct input coefficient $\mathrm{B}=(\mathrm{I}-\mathrm{A})^{-1}-1$:

$$\begin{bmatrix}
0.2844 & 0.0288 & 0.0777 & 0.0226 & 0.0616 & 0.0151 & 0.0368 & 0.1454 & 0.0159 & 0.0149 & 0.0323 & 0.0430\\
0.1980 & 2.0054 & 0.4053 & 0.6587 & 0.3756 & 0.0730 & 0.2013 & 0.2128 & 0.0618 & 0.0951 & 0.1417 & 0.1633\\
1.0526 & 0.9939 & 1.8565 & 0.7472 & 1.9223 & 0.4207 & 1.2412 & 1.1744 & 0.3713 & 0.4060 & 0.8993 & 0.9717\\
0.2091 & 0.1981 & 0.1906 & 2.1256 & 0.1669 & 0.0913 & 0.2049 & 0.2921 & 0.0662 & 0.1823 & 0.1204 & 0.1667\\
0.0063 & 0.0074 & 0.0097 & 0.0149 & 0.0242 & 0.0057 & 0.0134 & 0.0129 & 0.0067 & 0.0144 & 0.0081 & 0.0416\\
0.1462 & 0.1920 & 0.2627 & 0.1216 & 0.2351 & 0.1220 & 0.1565 & 0.1719 & 0.0520 & 0.0560 & 0.1264 & 0.1288\\
0.1358 & 0.2477 & 0.1650 & 0.1155 & 0.1717 & 0.1357 & 0.4555 & 0.1176 & 0.0614 & 0.0537 & 0.1212 & 0.1358\\
0.0190 & 0.0217 & 0.0300 & 0.0221 & 0.0336 & 0.0278 & 0.0321 & 0.0236 & 0.0460 & 0.0306 & 0.0411 & 0.0508\\
0.0605 & 0.1163 & 0.0861 & 0.1700 & 0.1071 & 0.1172 & 0.1675 & 0.0951 & 0.1093 & 0.1854 & 0.1062 & 0.0812\\
0.0144 & 0.0191 & 0.0218 & 0.0278 & 0.0210 & 0.0437 & 0.0259 & 0.0667 & 0.0513 & 0.0569 & 0.0318 & 0.0498\\
0.1469 & 0.1261 & 0.1762 & 0.1451 & 0.1748 & 0.2388 & 0.2084 & 0.2116 & 0.2127 & 0.1461 & 0.2465 & 0.1955\\
0.0462 & 0.0103 & 0.0125 & 0.0162 & 0.0128 & 0.0113 & 0.0139 & 0.0182 & 0.0271 & 0.0205 & 0.0233 & 0.0949
\end{bmatrix}$$

(2) Analysis on the associated loss of multi-sectors. Based on the direct economic losses of agricultural and transportation sectors caused by disaster, the comprehensive economic losses of industrial sectors can be deduced:

$$\begin{bmatrix}\Delta Q_1\\ \Delta Q_2\\ \vdots\\ \Delta Q_n\end{bmatrix}=\begin{bmatrix}b_{11} & b_{12} & \cdots & b_{1n}\\ b_{21} & b_{22} & \cdots & b_{2n}\\ \vdots & \vdots & \vdots & \vdots\\ b_{n1} & b_{n2} & \cdots & b_{nn}\end{bmatrix}\begin{bmatrix}\Delta Y_1\\ \Delta Y_2\\ \vdots\\ 0\end{bmatrix}+\begin{bmatrix}\Delta Y_1\\ \Delta Y_2\\ \vdots\\ 0\end{bmatrix} \tag{4.18}$$

The changes of the total products of agricultural and transportation sectors can be obtained by the following equations respectively:

$$\Delta Q_{agr}=\sum_{i=1} b_{ij}\Delta X_n+\Delta Y_{agr} \tag{4.19}$$

$$\Delta Q_{tra}=\sum_{i=2} b_{ij}\Delta X_n+\Delta Y_{tra} \tag{4.20}$$

Considering the time pressure on collecting the statistical data of disaster loss, the losses of the two disaster-stricken sectors (i. e., agricultural and transportation sectors) are regarded as the final product losses in this paper. The total product losses of agricultural and transportation sectors calculated by Eqs. (4.19) and (4.20) are RMB 0.56799 billion *yuan* and 1.72723 billion *yuan*, respectively. Based on Eq. (4.18), the associated economic loss of any other industrial sector can be calculated by:

$$\Delta Q_n=b_{n1}\Delta Y_{agr}+b_{n2}\Delta Y_{tra} \tag{4.21}$$

**Table 4.3** The associated comprehensive economic losses of industrial sectors assessed by IO Model

| Sector | Loss/RMB 100 million *yuan* | Loss ratio of disaster/%[7] |
|---|---|---|
| Agricultural sector | 6.3147 | 1.5956 |
| Mining sector | 4.6025 | 0.3164 |
| Manufacturing sector | 27.4166 | 0.1997 |
| Production and supply of electricity, fuel gas, and water | 4.7273 | 0.1257 |
| Construction sector | 0.2671 | 0.0064 |
| Wholesale and retail | 3.5337 | 0.0895 |
| Transportation, storage, and postal service | 18.0438 | 0.5671 |
| Accommodation and catering | 0.6620 | 0.0555 |
| Finance | 3.2416 | 0.0810 |
| Real estate | 0.5285 | 0.0252 |
| Technical, commercial and other services | 4.4340 | 0.0467 |
| Education, health and public administration | 0.5022 | 0.0098 |
| Total | 74.2739 | 0.0014 |

[7]"Loss ratio of disaster" mean economic losses value of each sector caused by disaster/ the total output of each sector in no-disaster scenario.

Then with the results calculated by Eq. (4.21), the sum of the losses of different sectors, namely, the comprehensive economic loss caused by disaster, is obtained.

The economic losses and loss ratios of the industrial sectors obtained through IO Model are given in Table 4.3. In the short run, the output values of the sectors have been decreased by the rainstorm disaster at different degrees. The sectors, from top to bottom, ranked according to the loss ratios of disaster are: agricultural sector > transportation, storage, and postal service > mining sector > manufacturing sector > production and supply of electricity, fuel gas, and water > Wholesale and retail > finance > technical, commercial and other services > real estate > Education, health and public administration > construction sector. Generally speaking, the agricultural and transportation sectors have suffered the most severe disaster loss. The total loss of the sectors caused by rainstorm is up to RMB 7.42739 billion yuan.

### 4.5.3 Comparison of Assessment Results of CGE Model and IO Model

Considering the time pressure on collecting the statistical data of disaster loss, the losses of the agricultural and transportation sectors (i. e., RMB 0.45 billion yuan and 0.64 billion yuan) were regarded as the final product losses in this paper, then the total product losses of the two disaster-stricken sectors were calculated as RMB 0.56799 billion yuan and 1.72723 billion yuan respectively. The disaster impact parameters of agricultural and transportation sectors were introduced in the CGE model. The comprehensive economic loss was obtained by comparison of no-disaster scenario and with-disaster scenario. In the no-disaster scenario, the disaster impact parameter was 1, and the with-disaster scenario, the disaster impact parameter of agricultural and transportation sectors have become 98.5648% and 99.4571%. In the IO model, the total product losses in the agricultural and transportation sectors were RMB 0.56799 billion yuan and 1.72723 billion yuan respectively, then the change of output can be calculated through the correlations among the sectors. By comparing the changes in the output between sectors of no-disaster scenario and with-disaster scenario, the disaster loss rate and the total disaster economic loss value of each sector can be obtained. The comprehensive economic losses of the 12 sectors caused by Beijing "7.21 Rainstorm" are shown in Fig. 4.3.[8]

(1) Overall, the economic losses evaluated by IO Model are higher than those assessed by CGE Model, which partly verifies the research findings concerning economic loss evaluation model conducted by Rose (2004) and Okuyama (2007). Specifically, the evaluated results of IO Model and CGE Model can be deemed as the upper and lower limits of economic loss, respectively. Thus, according to the assessment results of IO Model and CGE Model, the range of the comprehensive economic loss caused by Beijing "7.21 Rainstorm" is [67.9396, 74.2739] (RMB 100 million *yuan*).
(2) In the economic loss assessment based on IO Model, the loss ratios of disaster of agricultural and transportation sectors are much higher than those of other sectors, indicating that IO Model focuses particularly on the evaluation of the sectors divided by this paper. However, according to the evaluated results of CGE Model, there are more sectors being affected by the disaster, indicating a greater spillover effect in economic system and a wider distribution of disaster-affected sectors. The reason lies in that the input–output coefficient of IO Model is fixed, while the input elements of CGE Model can replace each other.
(3) The assessment results of CGE Model and IO Model both show that agricultural sector, transportation sector, and mining sector are the three sectors with relatively high comprehensive economic losses among the 12 sectors; and the corresponding disaster losses range within [2.0570, 6.3147], [13.9789, 18.0438], and [4.6025, 6.7528] (RMB 100 million *yuan*), respectively. As for

[8]In the Fig. 4.3, the X-axis indicates the sectors affected by the disaster, and the Y-axis indicates the economic loss rate of the affected sectors.

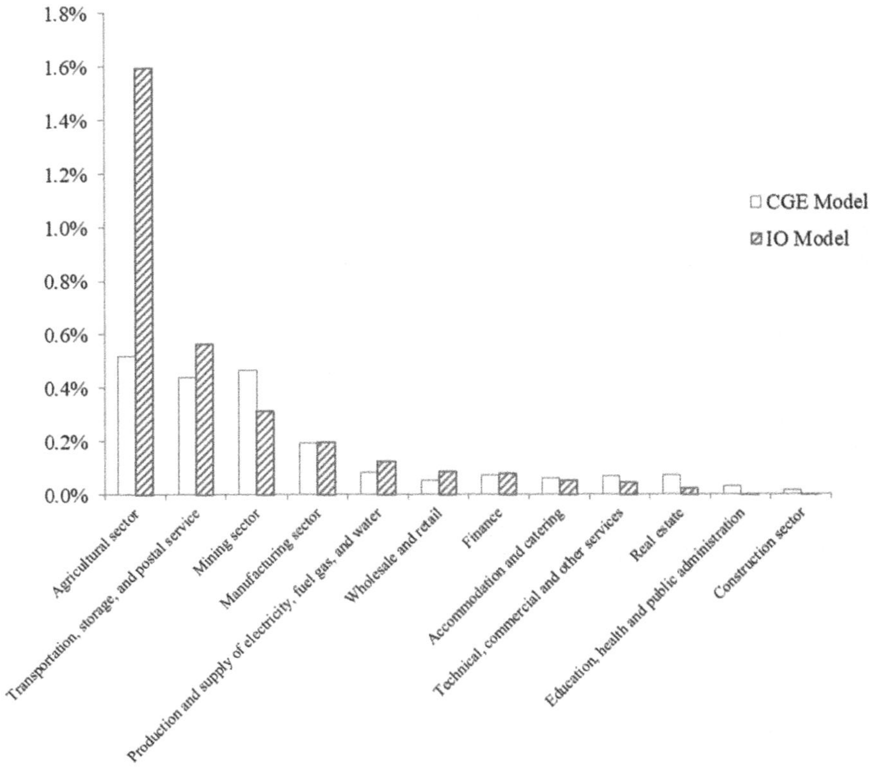


**Fig. 4.3** Comparison of comprehensive economic losses assessed by IO Model and CGE Model

agricultural sector, rainstorm and flood generally will inundate vast areas of cropland and destroy plenty of crops, thereby leading to the reduction of agricultural products or even crop failure. Meanwhile, mechanical damages like soil and sand sediment in cropland and vegetation deterioration will inevitably exert huge adverse impact on agricultural production. As for transportation sector, rainstorm will destroy transportation infrastructures, which often leads to traffic interruption or even traffic accidents. There are two reasons for the large losses to the mining industry caused by the disaster. On the one hand, the major influence of rainstorm on mining sector lies in the decline of production which resulted from the halt in production and shutdown of mines caused by site damage. On the other hand, the relationship between the mining industry and other industrial sectors is closely related in the Beijing economic system, which may not only be affected by disasters directly, but also be implicated in the decline of output in other sectors. Therefore, conclusions can be drawn from the abovementioned analyses that greater emphasis should be given to these sectors as they are more severely affected by rainstorm.

## 4.6 Sensitivity Analysis

The simulated results may be affected when the elastic parameters in the function of CGE Model vary. Therefore, a sensitivity test should be performed on the relevant parameters of CGE Model. Mahmood and Marpaung (2014) introduced high elasticity (increases by 20%) and low elasticity (decreases by 20%) into the elastic parameters and then, through the simulation based on new elastic parameters, obtained the change rate of relevant economic indicators. This paper, based on the method proposed by Mahmood et al., has tested the elasticity of the parameters in production function. That is to say, a sensitivity analysis has been conducted on the elasticity of substitution of production function through a 20% increase (high elasticity) and a 20% decrease (low elasticity), respectively. The change rates of relevant economic variables are presented in Table 4.4.

The results of the above sensitivity test show that, the change of the elastic parameters of total output function has a slight influence on the output indicators of the industrial sectors. Taking the total output of the sectors as an example, the change rate of the total output is 0.3362% when the substitution of elasticity of CES function is increased by 20% (high elasticity), while the change rate is −0.4904% when the substitution of elasticity is decreased by 20% (low elasticity). Thus, the results

**Table 4.4** Sensitivity analysis on the elastic parameters of production function

| Indicator: output of sector | Elastic parameters of production function | |
|---|---|---|
| | High elasticity (increases by 20%) | Low elasticity (decreases by 20%) |
| Agricultural sector | 0.3802 | −0.6167 |
| Mining sector | 0.1077 | −0.0716 |
| Manufacturing sector | 0.0998 | −0.1279 |
| Production and supply of electricity, fuel gas, and water | 0.0115 | −0.0962 |
| Construction sector | 0.1481 | −0.1581 |
| Wholesale and retail | 0.6855 | −0.9280 |
| Transportation, storage, and postal service | 0.1619 | −0.3409 |
| Accommodation and catering | 0.3102 | −0.4905 |
| Finance | 0.6237 | −0.8769 |
| Real estate | 0.5602 | −0.8862 |
| Technical, commercial and other services | 0.5580 | −0.8261 |
| Education, health and public administration | 0.5687 | −0.8439 |
| Total | 0.3362 | −0.4904 |

of CGE Model have a low sensitivity to the values of elastic parameters and are acceptable, indicating that the CGE Model is robust.

## 4.7 Conclusions and Prospect

The quantitative evaluation on the comprehensive economic loss of economic system caused by disaster and the corresponding targeted disaster preventing and alleviating measures have become urgent and difficult issues in disaster risk management (Wagner and Bode 2006; Levermann 2014). CGE Model and IO Model, as quantitative analysis models of economic loss assessment, have played important roles in simulating the spillover effect of disaster and guiding the post-disaster reconstruction and allocation of funds, and are the most widely used methods currently. For this reason, this paper, taking the Beijing "7.21 Rainstorm" as an example, compared and analyzed the comprehensive economic losses of rainstorm evaluated by CGE Model and IO Model. The conclusions are as follows:

(1) The CGE Model and IO Model, with different characteristics, have their own emphases on the assessment results. In terms of the data requirements and model building, the data base of IO Model is the input–output table of the study area which has simple structure and equation and is easy to process; while the data base of CGE Model is SAM which not only contains the correlations among the sectors in input–output table but also the connections among economic entities, commodities, and factor markets showed through plenty of external data. Besides, the elastic parameters of CGE Model need to be determined exogenously. Furthermore, the establishment of structural equation and simulation are quite complicated. For this reason, IO Model is more suitable for the quick evaluation of comprehensive economic loss caused by disaster while CGE model is more appropriate for the overall analysis of economic loss.

(2) The comprehensive economic loss caused by disaster should not be neglected. With the acceleration of economic integration and the specialization of industrial division, the correlations among the industrial sectors and links have become increasingly close, thereby leading to the formation of a complex association network. Any damage to the local critical points or infrastructures will possibly affect the whole industrial economic system through forward and backward diffusion, giving rise to systematic risks (Wagner and Bode 2006). In the Beijing "7.21 Rainstorm", the total economic loss of the sectors evaluated by CGE Model is RMB 6.79398 billion *yuan* while that assessed by IO Model is RMB 7.42739 billion *yuan*. Therefore, according to the assessment results of CGE Model and IO Model, the range of the comprehensive economic loss is [67.9398, 74.2739] (RMB 100 million *yuan*).

(3) Agriculture, transportation, and mining sectors are high-sensitivity sectors which need special attention. The simulation results of CGE Model and IO Model both show that Beijing "7.21 Rainstorm" has a greater impact on agricultural, transportation, and mining sectors than on other sectors. In disaster prevention and alleviation, full consideration should be given to the structural features of industrial sectors which are highly sensitive to disasters, so that targeted measures can be taken for the effective post-disaster recovery and reconstruction according to different sectors. Meanwhile, preferential policy support should be given to disaster-stricken sectors so as to minimize the comprehensive economic loss caused by disasters.

It should be pointed out that further studies are necessary owing to the limitations of this paper. For instance, this paper only compares the short-term economic losses evaluated by CGE Model and IO Model; consequently, it fails to investigate the evolutionary tracks of the two models during disaster loss assessment through consistent dynamic modules. Furthermore, the direct economic losses of different sectors cannot be obtained through the assessment method proposed in this paper. For this reason, only the exogenous impact of agricultural and transportation sectors upon economic system havebeen simulated. The above shortcomings are to be further discussed.

## 4.8 Appendix: Values of Related Parameters

See Tables 4.5 and 4.6.

## 4.9 Construction of CGE Model

### 1. Model equations

(1) Production module

1. $X_i = A_i\left[\delta_i V_i^{\rho_i} + (1-\delta_i) IT_i^{\rho_i}\right]^{1/\rho_i}$
2. $V_i = AV_i L_i^{\alpha_i} K_i^{1-\alpha_i}$
3. $IT_{j,i} = a_{j,i} \cdot IT_i$
4. $WLDISTI_i \times \mathrm{WL} = \frac{a_i \cdot PV_i \cdot V_i}{L_i}$
5. $WKDISTI_i \times \mathrm{WK} = \frac{(1-a_i) \cdot PV_i \cdot V_i}{K_i}$

(2) Trade module

6. $X_i = AT_i\left[\delta T_i E_i^{\rho T_i} + (1-\delta T_i) D_i^{\rho T_i}\right]^{1/\rho T_i}$
7. $E_i = D_i\left[\frac{PE_i(1-\delta T_i)}{PD_i \delta T_i}\right]^{1/(\rho T_i - 1)}$

**Table 4.5** Values of elastic parameters in production and trade modules (12 sectors)

| Sectors | Equations of production functions (CES) | | Equations of the Armington import functions (CES) | | Equations of the Armington export functions (CET) | |
|---|---|---|---|---|---|---|
| | Elastic parameters $\varepsilon$ | Correlation coefficient $\rho_i$ | Elastic parameters $\varepsilon Q_i$ | Correlation coefficient $\rho Q_i$ | Elastic parameters $\varepsilon T_i$ | Correlation coefficient $\rho T_i$ |
| Agricultural sector | 0.1 | 9 | 3.020 | −0.669 | 3.60 | 1.278 |
| Mining sector | 0.1 | 9 | 3.720 | −0.731 | 4.60 | 1.217 |
| Manufacturing sector | 0.1 | 9 | 3.240 | −0.691 | 4.51 | 1.222 |
| Production and supply of electricity, fuel gas, and water | 0.1 | 9 | 2.80 | −0.643 | 3.80 | 1.263 |
| Construction sector | 0.1 | 9 | 1.90 | −0.474 | 3.80 | 1.263 |
| Wholesale and retail | 0.1 | 9 | 1.90 | −0.474 | 2.80 | 1.357 |
| Transportation, storage, and postal service | 0.1 | 9 | 1.90 | −0.474 | 2.80 | 1.357 |
| Accommodation and catering | 0.1 | 9 | 1.90 | −0.474 | 2.80 | 1.357 |
| Finance | 0.1 | 9 | 1.90 | −0.474 | 2.80 | 1.357 |
| Real estate | 0.1 | 9 | 1.90 | −0.474 | 2.80 | 1.357 |
| Technical, commercial and other services | 0.1 | 9 | 1.90 | −0.474 | 2.80 | 1.357 |
| Education, health and public administration | 0.1 | 9 | 1.90 | −0.474 | 2.80 | 1.357 |

8. $Q_i = AQ_i\left[\delta Q_i M_i^{-\rho Q_i} + (1-\delta Q_i)D_i^{-\rho Q_i}\right]^{1/\rho Q_i}$
9. $M_i = D_i\left[\frac{PD_i\delta Q_i}{PM_i(1-\delta Q_i)}\right]^{1/(1+\rho Q_i)}$

(3) Consumption module

10. $PQ_i \times CD_i = \beta H_i[YH(1-t_h)] \times (1-mps)$
11. $GD_i = \beta G_i \times GC$
12. $DST_i = dstr_i \times X_i$
13. $DK_i = Kshr_i \times (INVEST - \sum_i DST_i)$

**Table 4.6** Values of share parameters and scale parameters in the production and trade module (12 sectors)

| Sectors | Equations of production functions (CES) | | Equations of the Armington import functions (CES) | | Equations of the Armington export functions (CET) | |
|---|---|---|---|---|---|---|
| | Share parameters $\delta_i$ | Scale parameters $A_i$ | Share parameters $\delta Q_i$ | Scale parameters $AQ_i$ | Share parameters $\delta T_i$ | Scale parameters $AT_i$ |
| Agricultural sector | 0.194 | 1.304 | 0.778 | 2.743 | 0.641 | 2.382 |
| Mining sector | 0.038 | 1.058 | 0.979 | 1.604 | 0.576 | 2.292 |
| Manufacturing sector | 0.048 | 1.072 | 0.389 | 5.254 | 0.539 | 2.537 |
| Production and supply of electricity, fuel gas, and water | 0.023 | 1.035 | 0.000 | 1.516 | 0.000 | 1.000 |
| Construction sector | 0.064 | 1.096 | 0.000 | 1.004 | 0.000 | 1.000 |
| Wholesale and retail | 0.295 | 1.512 | 0.000 | 2.029 | 0.626 | 2.490 |
| Transportation, storage, and postal service | 0.103 | 1.153 | 0.122 | 2.450 | 0.592 | 2.525 |
| Accommodation and catering | 0.159 | 1.243 | 0.030 | 1.985 | 0.671 | 2.514 |
| Finance | 0.278 | 1.472 | 0.007 | 1.133 | 0.745 | 2.850 |
| Real estate | 0.269 | 1.452 | 0.000 | 1.104 | 0.000 | 1.000 |
| Technical, commercial and other services | 0.260 | 1.433 | 0.092 | 1.549 | 0.592 | 2.556 |
| Education, health and public administration | 0.264 | 1.442 | 0.030 | 1.294 | 0.753 | 2.905 |

(4) Income module

14. $YH = \sum_i WLDISTI_i \times WL \times L_i + GTP + ETP$
15. $YC = \sum_i WKDISTI_i \times WK \times K_i$
16. $YCTAX = (YC - DEPREC) \times t_{ye}$
17. $DEPREC = \sum_i depr_i \times WK \times K_i$
18. $INDTAX = \sum_i PX_i \times X_i \times tx_i$

19. $\mathrm{HTAX} = \mathrm{YH} \times \mathrm{t_h}$
20. $\mathrm{GR} = \mathrm{INDTAX} + \mathrm{YCTAX} + \mathrm{HTAX}$
21. $\mathrm{CSAV} = \mathrm{YC} + \mathrm{GTE} - \mathrm{DEPREC} - \mathrm{YCTAX}$
22. $\mathrm{HSAV} = \mathrm{mps}[\mathrm{YH}(1 - \mathrm{t_h}) + \mathrm{GTP}]$
23. $\mathrm{GSAV} = \mathrm{GR} - \mathrm{GTP} - \mathrm{GTE} - \sum_{\mathrm{i}} \mathrm{PD_i} \times \mathrm{GD_i}$
24. $\mathrm{SAVING} = \mathrm{HSAV} + \mathrm{GSAV} + \mathrm{CSAV} + \mathrm{DEPREC} + \mathrm{FSAV}$

(5) Price module

25. $PX_i \times X_i = PV_i \times V_i + PIT_i \times IT_i$
26. $PV_i \times V_i = \mathrm{WL} \times L_i + \mathrm{WK} \times K_i$
27. $PIT_i = \sum_i a_{j,i} \cdot PX_i$
28. $PE_i = PWE_i \times (1 - te_i) \times R$
29. $PM_i = PWM_i \times (1 + tm_i) \times R$

(6) System equilibrium module

30. $\sum_i L_i = LS$
31. $\sum_i K_i = KS$
32. $\sum_i PWM_i \times M_i \times R = \sum_i PWE_i \times E_i \times R + FSAV$
33. $\mathrm{SAVING} = \mathrm{INVEST}$

**2. Variable description of the Model**

See Table 4.7.

**Table 4.7** Symbols and meanings of endogenous variables, exogenous variables and parameters

| | | |
|---|---|---|
| Endogenous variables | | |
| $X_i$: Total output | $V_i$: Value added | $IT$: Intermediate input |
| $L_i$: Labor input | $K_i$: Capital input | $E_i$: Export |
| $D_i$: Goods for domestic market sales | $Q_i$: General use of goods | $M_i$: Import |
| $CD_i$: Residents' consumption | $GD_i$: Government's consumption | $DK_i$: Fixed-assets investment |
| DEPREC: Depreciation of fixed assets | $DST_i$: Added inventory | YH: Residents' income |
| YC: Corporate income | YCTAX: Corporate direct tax | HTAX: Residents' personal income tax |
| GR: Government's income | INDTAX: Indirect tax | HSAV: Residents' savings |
| GSAV: Government savings | CSAV: Corporate savings | SAVING: Total savings |
| INVEST: Total investment | LS: Total labor | KS: Total capital |
| $PX_i$: Products' output prices | $PV_i$: Products' added value prices | $PIT_i$: Intermediate input' prices |
| $PQ_i$: Composite products' prices | $PM_i$: Domestic prices of imports | $PE_i$: Domestic prices of exports |
| $PD_i$: The domestic prices | WK: Capital prices | |
| Exogenous variables | | |
| $WLDISTI_i$: Departmental distribution rate of labor | $WKDISTI_i$: Departmental distribution rate of capital | GTP: Profit distribution of government to residents |
| $ETP$: Profit distribution of corporate to residents | $PWE_i$: International prices of exports | $PWM_i$: International prices of imports |
| $R$: Exchange rate | $FSAV$: Foreign savings | WL: Labor prices |
| GC: Total government expenditure | | |
| Parameters | | |
| $A_i$: The scale efficiency parameter of the Total output function | $\delta_i$: The share parameter of the total output function | $\rho_i$: The elastic parameter correlation coefficient of the total output function |
| $AV_i$: The scale efficiency parameter of CD function | $a_i$: The share parameter of CD function | $a_{j,i}$: The direct input coefficient |

(continued)

**Table 4.7** (continued)

| Parameters | | |
|---|---|---|
| $AT_i$: The scale efficiency parameter of CET function | $\delta T_i$: The share parameter of CET function | $\rho T_i$: The elastic parameter correlation coefficient of CET function |
| $AQ_i$: The elastic parameters of composite product function | $\delta Q_i$: The share parameter of composite product function | $\rho Q_i$: The elastic parameter correlation coefficient of composite product function |
| $\beta H_i$: The residents' consumption share | $t_h$: The rate of residents' personal income tax | mps: The rate of residents' marginal savings |
| $\beta G_i$: The Government's consumption share | $dstr_i$: The rate of inventory | $Kshr_i$: The share parameter of Actual investment |
| $depr_i$: Depreciation rate of fixed assets | $t_{ye}$: The rate of corporate tax | $tx_i$: The rate of indirect tax |
| $te_i$: The rate of export subsidies | $tm_i$: The rate of import tariff | |

**Acknowledgements** Ling Tan, Zeshui Xu, Lianshui Li, Shaohan Jiang also made great contributions to this manuscript. We express our heartfelt thanks to them. This research was supported by: National Social and Scientific Fund Program of China (18ZDA052; 17BGL142; 16ZDA047); The Natural Science Foundation of China (91546117, 71373131).

## References

Antimiani, A., Costantini, V., & Paglialunga, E. (2015). The sensitivity of climate-economy CGE models to energy-related elasticity parameters: Implications for climate policy design. *Economic Modelling, 51,* 38–52.

Avelino, A. F. T., & Dall'erba, S. (2019). Comparing the economic impact of natural disasters generated by different input-output models: An application to the 2007 Chehalis River Flood (WA). *Risk Analysis, 39*(1), 85–104.

Avelino, F. T. A., Dall'erba, S. C. (2018). Comparing the economic impact of natural disasters generated by different input-output models: An application to the 2007 Chehalis River Flood (WA). *Risk Analysis*. https://doi.org/10.1111/risa.13006.

Baghersad, M., & Zobel, C. W. (2015). Economic impact of production bottlenecks caused by disasters impacting interdependent industry sectors. *International Journal of Production Economics, 168*(10), 71–80.

Barker, K., & Santos, J. R. (2010). Measuring the efficacy of inventory with a dynamic input–output model. *International Journal of Production Economics, 126*(1), 130–143.

Bonfiglio, A., Coderoni, S., et al. (2020). The role of rurality in determining the economy-wide impacts of a natural disaster. *Economic Systerms Research*. https://doi.org/10.1080/09535314.2020.1814206.

Carrera, L., Standardi, G., Bosello, F., et al. (2015). Assessing direct and indirect economic impacts of a flood event through the integration of spatial and computable general equilibrium modelling. *Environmental Modelling & Software, 63*(11), 109–122.

Cochrane, H. C. (1997a). Economic impacts of a Midwestern earthquake. The quarterly publication of NCEER (National Center for Earthquake Engineering Research), 11(1), 1-55.

Cochrane, H. C. (1997b). Forecasting the economic impact of a Midwest earthquake. Economic Consequences of Earthquakes: Preparing for the Unexpected, 223–247

Crowther, K. G., & Haimes, Y. Y. (2007). Systemic valuation of strategic preparedness through application of the inoperability input-output model with lessons learned from Hurricane Katrina. *Risk Analysis, 27*(5), 1345–1364.

Cui, Q., Xie, W., & Liu, Y. (2018). Effects of sea level rise on economic development and regional disparity in China. *Journal of Cleaner Production, 176*(1), 1245–1253.

Enke, D. (2007). Case study: Applying a regional CGE model for estimation of indirect economic losses due to damaged highway bridges. *Engineering Economist, 52*(4), 367–401.

Fan, Q., & Davlasheridze, M. (2019) Economic impacts of migration and brain drain after major catastrophe: the case of hurricane katrina. *Climate Change Economics, 10*(1), 1950004. https://doi.org/10.1142/S2010007819500040.

Faturay, F., Sun, Y. Y., et al. (2020). Using virtual laboratories for disaster analysis—A case study of Taiwan. *Economic Systerms Research, 32*(1), 58–83.

Fotouhi, H., Moryadee, S., & Miller-Hooks, E. (2017). Quantifying the resilience of an urban traffic-electric power coupled system. *Reliability Engineering & System Safety, 163,* 79–94.

Fung, J. F., Helgeson, J. F., et al. (2020). Does resilience yield dividends? Co-benefits of investing in increased resilience in Cedar Rapids. *Economic Systerms Research, 12,* 1–27.

Galbusera, L., & Giannopoulos, G. (2018). On input-output economic models in disaster impact assessment. *International Journal of Disaster Risk Reduction, 30,* 186–198.

Gertz, A. B., Davies, J. B., & Black, S. L. (2019). A CGE framework for modeling the economics of flooding and recovery in a Major Urban area. *Risk Analysis, 39*(6), 1314–1341.

Haimes, Y.Y., Horowitz, B.M., Lambert, J.H., et al. (2005a). Inoperability input-output model for interdependent infrastructure sectors. I: Theory and methodology. *Journal of Infrastructure Systems, 11*(2), 67–79.

Haimes, Y.Y., Horowitz, B.M., Lambert, J.H., et al. (2005b). Inoperability input-output model for interdependent infrastructure sectors. II: Case studies. *Journal of Infrastructure Systems, 11*(11), 80–92.

Haimes, Y. Y., & Jiang, P. (2001). Leontief-based model of risk in complex interconnected infrastructures. *Journal of Infrastructure Systems, 7*(1), 1–12.

Hallegatte, S. (2008). An adaptive regional input-output model and its application to the assessment of the economic cost of Katrina. *Risk Analysis, 28*(3), 779–799.

Hallegatte, S. (2015). The indirect cost of natural disasters and an economic definition of macroeconomic resilience. *Policy Research Working Paper Series, 151*(1), 155–160.

Haque, A., & Jahan, S. (2015). Impact of flood disasters in Bangladesh: A multi-sector regional analysis. *International Journal of Disaster Risk Reduction, 13,* 266–275.

He, J. H., Shen, K. T., & Xu, S. L. (2002). CGE model for carbon tax and carbon dioxide emission reduction. *the Journal of Quantitative & Technical Economics, 19*(10), 39–47 (in Chinese).

Heatwole, N., & Rose, A. (2013). A reduced-form rapid economic consequence estimating model: Application to property damage from U. S. earthquakes. *International Journal of Disaster Risk Science, 4*(1), 20–32.

Helbing, D. (2013). Globally networked risks and how to respond. *Nature, 497,* 51–59.

Hoffmann, C. (2019). Estimating the benefits of adaptation to extreme climate events, focusing on nonmarket damages. *Ecological Economics*, 106250. https://doi.org/10.1016/j.ecolecon.2019.02.014.

Holland, D. S., & Leonard, J. (2020). Is a delay a disaster? Economic impacts of the delay of the california dungeness crab fishery due to a harmful algal bloom. *Harmful Algae*, 101904. https://doi.org/10.1016/j.hal.2020.101904.

Hu, A., Xie, W., Li, N., et al. (2014). Analyzing regional economic impact and resilience: A case study on electricity outages caused by the 2008 snowstorms in southern China. *Natural Hazards, 70*(2), 1019–1030.

Husby, T. G., & Koks, E. E. (2017). Household migration in disaster impact analysis: Incorporating behavioural responses to risk. *Natural Hazards, 87*(1), 287–305.

Kajitani, Y., & Tatano, H. (2018). Applicability of a spatial computable general equilibrium model to assess the short-term economic impact of natural disasters. *Economic Systems Research, 30*(3), 289–312.

Khalid, M. A., & Ali, Y. (2019). Analysing economic impact on interdependent infrastructure after flood: Pakistan a case in point. *Environmental Hazards, 18*(2), 111–126.

Koks, E. E., Carrera, L., Jonkeren, O., et al. (2015). Regional disaster impact analysis: comparing input-output and computable general equilibrium models. *Natural Hazards & Earth System Sciences Discussions, 3*(11), 7053–7088.

Koks, E. E., Carrera, L., Jonkeren, O., et al. (2016). Regional disaster impact analysis: Comparing input–output and computable general equilibrium models. *Natural Hazards and Earth System Sciences, 16*(8), 1911–1924.

Krichene, H., Inoue, H., et al. (2020). A model of the indirect losses from negative shocks in production and finance. *PLos One, 15*(9). e0239293. https://doi.org/10.1371/journal.pone.0239293.

Lenzen, M., Malik, A., et al. (2019). Economic damage and spillovers from a tropical cyclone. *Natural Hazards and Earth System Sciences, 19*(1), 137–151.

Levermann, A. (2014). Climate economics: Make supply chains climate-smart. *Nature, 506*(7486), 27.

Li, J., Crawford-Brown, D., Syddall, M., et al. (2013). Modeling imbalanced economic recovery following a natural disaster using input-output analysis. *Risk Analysis, 33*(10), 1908–1923.

Li, N., Zhang, Z. T., Chen, X., et al. (2017). Importance of economic loss evaluation in natural hazard and disaster research. *Progress in Geography, 36*(2), 256–263 (in Chinese).

Lin, H. C., Chou, L. C., & Zhang, W. H. (2020). Cross-Strait climate change and agricultural product loss. *Environmental Science Pollution Research, 27*(12), 12908–12921.

Mackenzie, C. A., Santos, J. R., & Barker, K. (2012). Measuring changes in international production from a disruption: Case study of the Japanese earthquake and tsunami. *International Journal of Production Economics, 138*(2), 293–302.

Mahmood, A., & Marpaung, C. O. P. (2014). Carbon pricing and energy efficiency improvement—why to miss the interaction for developing economies? An illustrative CGE based application to the Pakistan case. *Energy Policy, 67,* 87–103.

McDonald, G. W., Cronin, S. J., et al. (2017). Computable general equilibrium modelling of economic impacts from volcanic event scenarios at regional and national scale, Mt. Taranaki, New Zealand. *Bulletin Volcanology, 79*(12), 87.

Mendoza-Tinoco, D., Guan, D., Zeng, Z., et al. (2017). Flood footprint of the 2007 floods in the UK: The case of the Yorkshire and The Humber region. *Journal of Cleaner Production, 168*(1), 655–667.

Nakanishi, H., Black, J., & Matsuo, K. (2014). Disaster resilience in transportation: Japan earthquake and tsunami 2011. *International Journal of Disaster Resilience in the Built Environment, 5*(4), 341–361.

Narayan, P. K. (2003). Macroeconomic impact of natural disasters on a small island economy: Evidence from a CGE model. *Applied Economics Letters, 10*(11), 721–723.

Okuyama, Y. (2004). Modeling spatial economic impacts of an earthquake: Input-output approaches. *Disaster Prevention & Management, 13*(4), 297–306.

Okuyama, Y. (2007). Economic modeling for disaster impact analysis: Past, present, and future. *Economic Systems Research, 19*(2), 115–124.

Okuyama, Y. (2010). Globalization and localization of disaster impacts: An empirical examination. *General Information, 11*(2), 56–66.

Oosterhaven, J. (2017). On the limited usability of the inoperability IO model. *Economic Systems Research, 29*(3), 452–461.

Pauw, K., Thurlow, J., Bachu, M., et al. (2011). The economic costs of extreme weather events: A hydrometeorological CGE analysis for Malawi. *Environment and Development Economics, 16*(2), 177–198.

Ring, I., Hansjürgens, B., Elmqvist, T., et al. (2010). Challenges in framing the economics of ecosystems and biodiversity: The TEEB initiative. *Current Opinion in Environmental Sustainability, 2*(1), 15–26.

Rose, A. (2004). Economic principles, issues, and research priorities in hazard loss estimation. In: Y. Okuyama & S. E. Chang (Eds.), *Modeling spatial and economic impacts of disasters* (pp. 13–36). New York: Springer.

Rose, A., & Liao, S. Y. (2005). Modeling regional economic resilience to disasters: A computable general equilibrium analysis of water service disruptions. *Journal of Regional Science, 45*(1), 75–112.

Rose, A., & Lim, D. (2002). Business interruption losses from natural hazards: Conceptual and methodological issues in the case of the Northridge earthquake. *Global Environmental Change Part B Environmental Hazards, 4*(1), 1–14.

Santos, J. (2020). Using input-output analysis to model the impact of pandemic mitigation and suppression measures on the workforce. *Sustainable Production and Consumption, 23,* 249–255.

Santos, J. R., & Haimes, Y. Y. (2010). Modeling the demand reduction input-output (I-O) inoperability due to terrorism of interconnected infrastructures. *Risk Analysis, 24*(6), 1437–1451.

Sieg, T., Schinko, T. et al. (2019). Integrated assessment of short-term direct and indirect economic flood impacts including uncertainty quantification. *PLos One, 14*(4), e0212932. https://doi.org/10.1371/journal.pone.0212932.

Tatano, H., & Tsuchiya, S. (2008). A framework for economic loss estimation due to seismic transportation network disruption: A spatial computable general equilibrium approach. *Natural Hazards, 44*(2), 253–265.

Thirawat, N., Udompol, S., & Ponjan, P. (2017). Disaster risk reduction and international catastrophe risk insurance facility. *Mitigation & Adaptation Strategies for Global Change, 22*(7), 1021–1039.

Tokui, J., Kawasaki, K., & Miyagawa, T. (2017). The economic impact of supply chain disruptions from the Great East-Japan earthquake. *Japan and the World Economy, 41,* 59–40.

Wagner, S. M., & Bode, C. (2006). An empirical investigation into supply chain vulnerability. *Journal of Purchasing and Supply Management, 12*(6), 301–312.

Wang, G. Z., Chen, R. R., & Chen, J. B. (2017). Direct and indirect economic loss assessment of typhoon disasters based on EC and IO joint model. *Natural Hazards, 87*(3), 1751–1764.

Wang, G. Z., Li, X., et al. (2015). The rainstorm comprehensive economic loss assessment based on CGE model: Using a July heavy rainstorm in Beijing as an example. *Natural Hazards, 76*(2), 839–854.

Wang, G. Z., Gu, S. J., et al. (2016). Assessment of health and economic effects by PM2.5 pollution in Beijing: A combined exposure-response and computable general equilibrium analysis. *Environmental Technology, 37*(24), 3131–3138.

Wei, F., Koc, E., Soibelman, L., et al. (2018). Disaster economics and networked transportation infrastructures: Status quo and a multi-disciplinary framework to estimate economic losses. *Advanced Computing Strategies for Engineering*: 3–22.

Weitzman, M. L. (2009). On modeling and interpreting the economics of catastrophic climate change. *Review of Economics & Statistics, 91*(1), 1–19.

Wu, X. H., Guo, J., Gonzalez, E. D. R. S. (2019). Determining the amount of international aid that countries should donate after a disaster to alleviate sustainable implications: A new framework for analysis. *Journal of Cleaner Production*, 118285. https://doi.org/10.1016/j.jclepro.2019.118285.

Xia, Y., Li, Y., et al. (2018). Assessment of the economic impacts of heat waves: A case study of Nanjing China. *Journal of Cleaner Production, 171,* 811–819.

Xie, W., Li, N., et al. (2015). Disaster risk decision: A dynamic computable general equilibrium analysis of regional mitigation investment. *Human and Ecological Risk Assessment, 21*(1), 81–99.

Xie, W., Li, N., et al. (2014). Modeling the economic costs of disasters and recovery: Analysis using a dynamic computable general equilibrium model. *Natural and Hazards & Earth System Sciences, 74*(4), 757–772.

Xie, W., Li, N., et al. (2014). Quantifying cascading effects triggered by disrupted transportation due to the Great 2008 Chinese Ice Storm: Implications for disaster risk management. *Natural Hazards, 70*(1), 337–352.

Xie, W., Rose, A., Li, S., et al. (2018). Dynamic economic resilience and economic recovery from disasters: A quantitative assessment. *Risk Analysis, 38*(6), 1306–1318.

Xu, Z. S. (2009). Modeling principles, parameter estimation methods and applications of computable general equilibrium model. Jilin University.

Yan, D., Zhou, J. Z., & Wang, X. G. (2007). Evaluation on effects of water price reform using CGE model—A case study in Beijing. *China Population, Resources and Environment, 17*(5), 70–74 (in Chinese).

Yu, J. Y., Hu, P., & Chou, L. C. (2019). Apply supply-driven input-output model to evaluate economic losses from Coastal Typhoons. *Journal of Coastal Research, 96,* 26–31.

Yücel, E., Salman, F. S., & Arşik, İ. (2018). Improving post-disaster road network accessibility by strengthening links against failures. *European Journal of Operational Research, 269*(2), 406–422.

Zeng, Z., Guan, D. B., et al. (2019). Flood footprint assessment: A new approach for flood-induced indirect economic impact measurement and post-flood recovery. Journal of Hydrology, 124204. https://doi.org/10.1016/j.jhydrol.2019.124204.

Zhai, F., & Hertel, T. W. (2005) Impacts of the Doha Development Agenda on China: The role of labor markets and complementary education reforms. World Bank Policy Research Working Paper, 187(22): 7727–7737.

Zhou, L., & Chen, Z. H. (2020). Are CGE models reliable for disaster impact analyses? *Economic Systems Research.* https://doi.org/10.1080/09535314.2020.1780566.

# Chapter 5
# Impacts of Tropical Cyclones on Employment—An Analysis Based on Meta-regression

**Abstract** Tropical cyclones are one of the serious environmental disasters. However, researcher's opinions are divided as to the impacts of tropical cyclones on labor employment. In order to investigate the general principle of tropical cyclones' impact on employment, explore the reason of the divergence among existing research conclusions and put forward some suggestions for post-disaster reconstruction, this paper employed quantitative analysis of the literature—meta-regression analysis based on the existing literature. This paper studies the impact of tropical cyclones on the quantity of labor employed and employee remuneration from four aspects: industry dimension, time dimension, income dimension and tropical cyclone intensity, which clarifies the impact direction and intensity of the disaster in each dimension. The results show that: (1) Tropical cyclone disasters have greater impact on the employment of the primary industry, that is, the primary industry suffers the heaviest loss of employee remuneration. The impact of tropical cyclones on the employment quantity in the second and tertiary industries is greater, and the impact on the secondary industry is greater than the tertiary industry. (2) In the short term, the impact of tropical cyclones on employment is negative and the impact intensity is strong; in the medium and long term, the impact is positive and the intensity of impact is decreasing. Thus, through post-disaster restoration and reconstruction, the negative impact of tropical cyclones on the employment is gradually reduced. (3) Although Tropical cyclone disasters increased the quantity of labor employed from the low-income groups, it reduces their employment remuneration. In addition, the impact of disasters on the employment number of high-income groups is relatively small compared to that of low-income groups. (4) The higher the category of the tropical cyclone, the greater the positive impact on the employment of labor force. In the final part of the paper, the causes of these phenomena are analyzed, and suggestions are given on how to carry out post-disaster restoration and reconstruction activities. This paper is a useful supplement to the study of natural disasters' impact on employment. The conclusions can provide reference for the emergency management of the disaster and the improvement of the labor market.

**Keywords** Tropical cyclone · Employment · Meta-regression analysis

 
X. Wu and J. Guo, *Economic Impacts and Emergency Management of Disasters in China*,
https://doi.org/10.1007/978-981-16-1319-7_5

## 5.1 Introduction

The fifth report of the IPCC (Intergovernmental Panel on Climate Change) states that the future impact of global warming on the climate system will continue and the change rate would be faster than previously estimated (Qin and Stocker 2014). The frequency and intensity of the tropical cyclones tend to further increase, on account of global warming (Qin 2008, Qin and Luo 2008). Of course, the study showed that we cannot further increase the frequency and intensity of tropical cyclones in the current historical data backtracking. Because the radiative forcing of greenhouse gases and aerosols had the opposite effect. However, with the increase of greenhouse gas emissions, the warming caused by greenhouse gases would further exceed the rate of aerosol cooling. Based on the above reasons, the global temperature would continue to warm in the future, which would lead to the increasing intensity of tropical cyclones (Sobel et al. 2016). Bruyère et al. (2019) used the HWCM model to analyze. They simulated the model on a 12-km horizontal grid covering a large area of Australia and the southwest Pacific Ocean. The results showed that the area affected will continue to expand in the future. For example, the future climate scenario triples the area of land subject to high rainfall and five times the land area subject to strong winds. Due to its high frequency and devastating effects, the United Nations has classified tropical cyclones as one of the most destructive environmental disasters second only to floods (Baez and Santos 2008). The tropical cyclone poses a great threat to the construction and sustainable development of human society (Shi 1996), which not only destroys traffic grid, communication facilities, warehousing and so on, causing large amounts of property damage, but also causes human casualties, spread diseases and jeopardizes the physical and mental health of human. Assessing the impact of tropical cyclones on social and economic development and mastering the general principle of the disaster's impact on social development has become an important topic for the government, academia and the public. What are the impacts of tropical cyclones on employment? Because of the differences in the research samples and methods, the scholars' conclusions are quite different. The results can be divided into the following two categories. Some researchers hold the view that the tropical cyclones have brought a positive impact on employment. Scholars explain their stance mostly from the following three aspects. First is about the post-disaster reconstruction financing, technical assistance and support. Guimaraes et al. (1992) took hurricane Hugo that struck South Carolina in the United States in 1989 and studied the impact of natural disasters on social wealth and income. They found that during the economic recovery of the afflicted area, billions of dollars of insurance and South Carolina's public funds has created a short-term economic boom in the area. The biggest beneficiaries are industries like construction, agriculture, trade, retail, transportation and public services and facilities. Porcelli and Trezzi (2019) analyzed output and employment data after 22 earthquakes in Italy from 1986 to 2011. The evidence showed that reconstruction activities funded by public donations were generally conducive to support the local economy. And this economic impact was unsustainable and would not spill over to neighboring countries. Second is about the post-disaster restoration and reconstruction activities. Ewing et al. (2003, 2009) and Eduardo (2013) think that the post-disaster reconstruction of industrial areas, commercial areas, residential areas and infrastructure will create many job opportunities. The soaring prices and labor costs will lead to rising costs of reconstruction and rehabilitation. The surging demand will attract labor force flooding in, thus increasing employment rate. Mohan et al. (2019) used the output, capital, and labor data of Caribbean countries for research. They pointed out that when natural disasters happened, strikes have a devastating impact on capital and labor. But it also provided opportunities to upgrade capital, increase labor demand and training opportunities. Zander et al. (2020) conducted a questionnaire survey in Australia and analyzed the data using the RO-RPL model. They believed that natural disasters would not affect people's choice of employment and settlement, and people were more willing to choose places with good employment prospects. And the reconstruction after the disaster would inevitably produce a good prospect. Strobl and Walsh (2009) studied the impact of hurricanes on the employment of American construction industry and found that hurricanes increased the employment rate by an average of 25%. Julie and Karoly (2010) found that a year after Hurricane Katrina, Louisiana and Mississippi developed a relatively high rate of self-employment. The researchers believe that independent entrepreneurship is an important factor in post-disaster economic recovery. How and Kerr (2019) used the discrete dependent variable logistic regression model. They analyzed the changes in employment data before and after the Christchurch earthquake. Results confirmed that the employment of the construction industry increased significantly after the earthquake. Unlike the number of low-end occupations that increased dramatically after the New Orleans earthquake, Christchurch had increased the number of highly skilled occupations. At the same time, the Christchurch earthquake also greatly accelerated the existing mode of migration in Christchurch. Eduardo (2013) made use of the micro-data from 32 regions of Mexico to study the impact of hurricanes on worker with various educational background. The results indicate that hurricanes had a positive impact on employment and wages for workers who are less educated. Kirchberger (2017) combined data from the Indonesian household life survey, the Desinventar database, the US Geological Survey, and data from various regional employment indicators. Research showed that the labor market has a significant resistance to the impact of natural disasters. On average, there was no significant difference in wage growth among workers living in the earthquake-affected areas. Third is about Schumpeter's theory of "creative destruction". Skidmore and Toya (2002) and Leiter et al. (2009) argue that natural disasters have a positive impact. Although disasters would undermine the existing social and economic foundations to some extent, at the same time they also provide opportunities for innovation. What's more, enterprises will prioritize the technology that is more disaster-resistant during their maintenance of the updated capital. In addition, the disaster may also reduce the return on investment in material capital, pushing society to invest in human capital, thus accelerating its accumulation. Martínez et al. (2020) used the data after the Biobio earthquake in Chile for analysis. The results showed that although natural disasters had a negative impact on the quantity and quality of employment in the short term. However, some public policies and rehabilitation plans may have mitigated or eliminated the adverse effects in some affected areas in the long run. Therefore, with the implementation of these policies and plans, the labor market began to show signs of recovery.

Other researchers believe tropical cyclones have a negative impact on the employment. There are three main reasons: First, the disaster causes a large-scale population migration. Climate and environmental changes have led to frequent occurrence of disasters and have become a driving force of population migration. Areas with better conditions of employment opportunities, living environment and risk protection have become the target areas for people to migrate (Zheng 2013). Belasen and Polachek (2007, 2008) studied the impact of hurricanes on the employment in Florida during the period of 1988–2005, and found that the composition of the workforce in the hurricane-affected areas changed, with high-income groups moving to areas of low-hazard potential and low-income workers being left behind in the disaster area, resulting in a decrease in the rate of employment. Kondo (2018) studied the post-disaster situation in Japan. This study found that supply chain disruption increased after the disaster and did not lead to inter-industry flow. On the contrary, this phenomenon had led to migration to other areas. At the same time, they also found that the degree of influence of workers' self-report was significantly related to negative factors (such as high unemployment rate). Cui et al. (2020) analyzed the employment data of chambers county. The study found that hurricanes' impact on the employment level can be divided into long-term and short-term. In the short term, the employment rate would drop rapidly after the disaster, but this phenomenon would not last long. In the long run, disasters had an unchangeable impact on the mean value of time series data. Felsenstein and Grinberger (2020) used simulation to understand the long-term cascading effect of disasters on the labor market. In this effect, the labor market lag leads to new jobs always vacant, so the employment rate rises. With the rebalancing of labor distribution after the disaster, the market supplied exceeds the demand, so the employment rate decreased. As a result, a large number of unemployed people began to migrate to other places. Groen and Polivka (2008) found that two months after Hurricane Katrina, New Orleans' urban employment decreased by 35%. Ouattara and Strobl (2014) applied a vector autoregression model to study the impact of hurricanes on coastal urban migration in the United States, and found that hurricanes increased the outward mobility of the wealthier population. In places affected by hurricanes, in absolute terms, the rich may be more affected. However, in terms of household expenditure, the negative impact had a greater impact on low-income families' expenditure. As a result, the hurricane had exacerbated economic inequality in the affected areas. In general, because the increase of inequality in the region was less than the decrease, the degree of inequality would eventually decrease (Warr and Aung 2019). Second, the disaster led to a decline in the purchasing power of individuals. Disasters have reduced family property, affected people's health, and changed household consumption behavior. Ye et al. (2020) used tropical cyclone records from 2000 to 2015 in mainland China to quantify. The regression model was used to analyze the data. Ye et al. quantified the relationship between the direct economic loss induced by a tropical cyclone and the maximum wind speed, asset value, and GDP per capita. With the increase of urban asset value, the direct economic loss caused by tropical cyclones will increase sharply. Some researchers (Geiger et al. 2016) had found a superlinear relationship between the loss caused by a hurricane and per capita income in the United States. In the study of Abdullah et al. (2016), in developing countries, hurricanes narrowed the gap between the rich and the poor in the short term. They collected and analyzed the household income data of Sandarban in Bangladesh by questionnaire. The results showed that, compared with the income before the disaster, the income of low-income families increased by 16%, the income of middle-income families decreased by 4%, and the income of rich families decreased by 50%. Therefore, most middle and high-income families had to reduce their consumption to cope with life after the disaster. After analyzing the medium and long-term effects of disasters on wages, Groen et al. (2015) pointed out that evacuees would face higher reemployment and relocation costs, which could lead to involuntary unemployment and changes in budget constraints. Katayanagi et al. (2020) used questionnaires to investigate the unemployment situation in Japan after the earthquake. In the survey of old coastal communities dominated by primary industry, they found that 19% of the people are unemployed, and the unemployment rate of the elderly is the highest. Unemployment rose from 150000 to 190000 after the earthquake. The results also show that 27.1% of the people's income decreased after the earthquake, and 67.5% of the people's income did not change compared with that before the earthquake. When addressing the impact of disasters on wages, Mueller and Rquisumbing (2011) also argue that natural disasters reduce the purchasing power in rural areas for non-agricultural goods and services. Third, the disaster widened the income gap. Chou et al. (2020) used the maximum entropy principle to estimate the disaster loss. They analyzed the temporal and spatial variation, interannual variation, and intensity of disasters induced by tropical cyclones landing in China's coastal areas from 1990 to 2016. As crop losses and building losses decrease, direct economic losses are becoming more and more serious, the study said. The impact of tropical cyclone disaster had gradually shifted from the primary industry to the secondary and tertiary industries. On the one hand, poor areas are more vulnerable to losses due to the loss of disasters are closely linked to the initial economic situation in the affected areas (Masozera et al. 2007).

According to Adam and Bevan (2020), using the general equilibrium model of a small open economy, they found that many developing countries lack external financing. When natural disasters destroyed public capital, the indirect losses caused by the reduction of private output in the reconstruction process would aggravate these direct losses. However, due to the high price of disaster risk insurance, its role in developing countries' reconstruction process was limited. On the contrary, developed countries often have perfect disaster risk insurance. On the other hand, low-income people relatively lack the ability of disaster recovery, and they tend to reduce education expenditure to make up for the losses caused by disasters, which further hinders low-income families' effective improvement in abilities to prevent and mitigate the impact of disasters, thus lapsing into a vicious circle. High income people tend to adopt various measures such as moving to low-risk areas, increasing insurance investment, learning advanced knowledge and skills and so on to mitigate the damage caused by natural disasters (Sadowski and Sutter 2005). Therefore, compared to high-income groups, low-income people suffered more losses. Kim and Marcouiller (2015) analyzed the impact of hurricanes on tourism from 1979 to 2004. From the perspective of vulnerability and resilience of the disaster, the researcher pointed out that the material and human capital losses caused by disasters were negatively correlated with income levels. The losses in developed areas were relatively less, and the tropical cyclones have a negative impact on the local economy and people's income. Mottaleb et al. (2013) studied the impact of Typhoon Aila in 2009 on household income and expenditure of rural households in Bangladesh. The result shows that tropical cyclone disasters cause a decrease in household income and a reduction in education expenditure.

It is evident that different scholars have different conclusions based on different research samples and methods for the impact of tropical cyclones on the employment. In order to find out the general rule of the impact of tropical cyclones on the quantity of labor employed as well as employee remuneration, this paper puts forward the research hypothesis on the basis of analyzing the mechanism of the tropical cyclones' impact on employment. Then the paper adopted meta-regression analysis to study the sample data from the four aspects, which include industry dimension, time dimension, income dimension and intensity of tropical cyclone. The conclusions can provide some suggestions for the tropical cyclone management. The difference between this paper and the previous studies are as follows: First, through meta-regression analysis, the paper is the first to review the literatures related to the impact of tropical cyclones on labor employment using quantitative analysis; second, based on labor market segmentation and disaster attributes, the paper analyzed the origin of the divergence in research conclusions in the existing literature from the perspectives of industry dimension, time dimension, income dimension and tropical cyclone intensity; Third, it analyzed the direction and intensity of the tropical cyclones' impact on employment from multiple perspectives using probit model and multiple regression model.

The rest of this paper is as follows: The second part is about the mechanism and research hypothesis that the disasters' impact on the employment; the third part is the explanation of research method, data and variables; the fourth part is the result of the meta-regression analysis, and the last part presents the conclusion and the discussion.

## 5.2 The Mechanism and Research Hypothesis of Disasters Affecting the Employment

Based on the research of Groen et al. (2015), this paper first analyzes the mechanism of tropical cyclone's impact on employment from the aspects of labor supply and demand. Then, from the aspects of labor market segmentation and disaster attributes, the paper analyzes the impact of disasters on labor employment (as shown in Fig. 5.1), and gives the assumptions of the study.

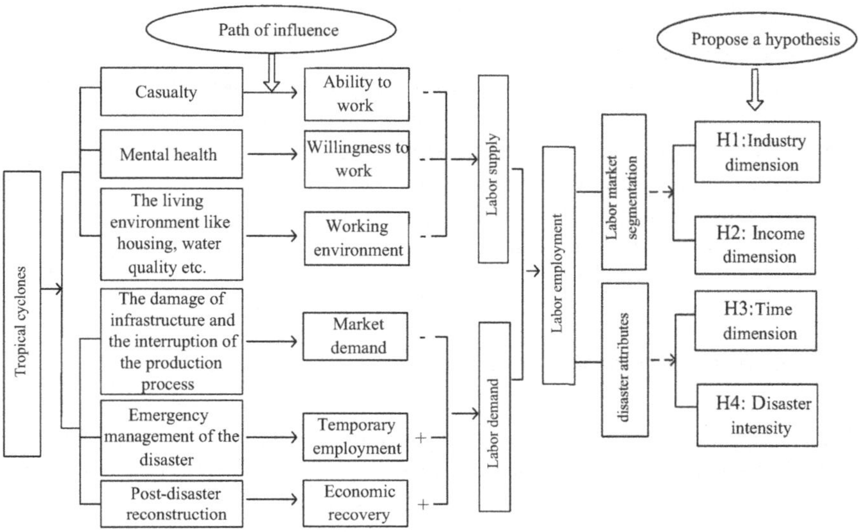


**Fig. 5.1** The logical framework of the study. *Note* the symbols "+" and "−" from the figure above represents "positive" and "negative" impact respectively

## 5.2.1 *Changes in Labor Supply Under Disaster Conditions*

The labor supply refers to the sum of labor ability the decision-making body of labor supply, like individuals or families is willing to provide, under certain market conditions. Labor supply is mainly affected by factors such as labor ability, willingness and employment environment (Li 2007). Disasters not only lead to casualties, evacuation of residents, a direct reduction in the quantity of labor employed, they may also cause pessimistic emotion like anxiety and depression which has a negative effect on people's mental health and job performance (Qin and Jiang 2011). In addition, disasters damage the key lifelines such as transportation, communication, water supply and power supply, deteriorate the living environment such as water quality and air quality, which drives people to relocate themselves in areas of low-hazard potential and superior environment (Zheng 2013), resulting in a decline in the supply of labor force in the affected areas.

## 5.2.2 *Changes in Labor Demand Under Disaster Conditions*

Labor demand is derived demand, while the demand for material goods or services is direct demand. The demand for labor is influenced by the direct demand of the market as well as the products and services it provides; besides other factors such as national policies and capital supply also count (Li 2007). When the disaster strikes, the demand for labor is reduced due to the damage to road traffic, water and power supply, and buildings, causing disruption of the production process and decline in commercial services and retail sales (Groen et al. 2015). However, in the process of disaster response and post-disaster reconstruction, the rehabilitation of industries like manufacturing, construction, transportation and so on demand for a large number of labor. During this time, government departments will also increase investment and promote the prosperity of other industries, which acts as an expanded indirect demand for labor (Eduardo 2013). The two factors compete with each other, leaving the demand for labor in an uncertain state.

### *5.2.3 Labor Market Segmentation Theory*

Labor market segmentation theory is put forward by American economists Dorlinger and Pioli in the 1960s, which generally refers to the phenomenon of labor market stratification caused by the social and institutional factors. Labor market segmentation falls into two categories: one is horizontal labor market segmentation, such as unit division of labor, industrial segmentation, urban-rural segmentation and regional segmentation; The other is vertical labor market segmentation, which involves the objective boundary of the occupational level of labor force, also called technical division, which originates from the gap in the individual qualities of the workers as well as their education and training (Yang 2001). The impact of disasters on employment varies with labor market segmentation. Since the present study is an inductive analysis of the existing literature which has the limitation of indicators and data, the vertical study focuses on industrial segmentation of the labor market, while the division caused by the income gap of labor market is the main concern for horizontal study. It is generally acknowledged that people whose job requires more skill and knowledge receive a relatively high wage compared with those whose job is not that skill-intensive. Therefore, in the aspect of technical division, the income is taken as a substitute variable for technology. The research hypothesis is as follows:

H1: The impact of disasters on employment varies along with different industrial sectors.

H2: The impact of disasters on employment varies along with employees of different income.

### *5.2.4 Disaster Attributes*

Disasters are external factors that affect social and economic development. The perturbation to the employment system will stimulate imbalance between labor supply and demand. Nevertheless, the labor market is adaptive. Moreover, government intervention could facilitate its gradual restoration. This recovery process can be defined as a process that the labor market of the disaster area transits from one equilibrium state to another when faced with destruction of the disaster (Wu et al.

2013). As time passes by, the process of the disaster's impact is featured with phase characteristics. The demand for labor is reduced at the beginning of the disaster, but it has risen again during the response and post-disaster reconstruction phases. Therefore, the following hypothesis is proposed:

H3: The impact of disasters on employment varies along with different time period.

Moreover, Skidmore and Toya (2002) believe that only the most destructive natural disasters will have an impact on the economy, on the basis of which they came to the fourth hypothesis:

H4: The impact of disasters on employment varies along with their intensity scale.

To sum up, the process and mechanism of disaster's impact on labor market can be described as follows in Fig. 5.1.

## 5.3 Explanation of Research Methods, Data and Variables

### *5.3.1 Research Methods*

Meta-regression analysis was first put forward by Stanley and Jarrell in 1989 and then introduced into the field of economic. It is a quantitative method of literature analysis which could not only synthesize all the research results, but also identify the source of the differences. At present, some scholars have applied meta-regression analysis to the field of natural disaster economics. For example, Klomp and Valckx (2014) synthesized 750 samples to study the relationship between natural disasters and economic growth using meta-regression analysis; Lazzaroni and Bergeijk (2014) analyzed the direct and indirect effects of natural disasters on the macro economy through meta-regression analysis; Bergeijk and Lazzaroni (2015) combined the meta-regression analysis and the traditional literature review to study the macroscopic effect brought by the natural disaster, and compared the advantages and disadvantages of the two research methods. Compared with traditional literature review, meta-regression analysis combines qualitative and quantitative analysis to achieve more objective results, as well as identifies the impact of different sample sources and methods on the conclusions (Bergeijk and Lazzaroni 2015). Without doubt meta-regression analysis does have limitations, such as the coverage of the literature is relatively narrow, which makes it impossible to analyze the literature outside the scope of the measurement method, i.e. the literature that could be studied by using computable general equilibrium model and input-output method.

In order to study the general law of the impact of tropical cyclone disasters on the employment, this paper referred to the method and framework of meta-regression analysis put forward by Klomp and Valckx (2014), Chen and Wang (2014) to find out the causes of different conclusions and clarify the direction and strength of the differences. Taking the characteristic variables of the existing literature as explaining variable and the estimated results[1] as explained variable, the basic model is as follows:

$$y_i = \beta + \sum_{k=1}^{k} \alpha_k Z_{ik} + e_i (i = 1, 2, \ldots, N) \tag{5.1}$$

In the model, $y_i$ indicates the direction (the positive impact value is 1, otherwise 0) and the value(the absolute value of the estimation coefficient) of tropical cyclone disasters' impact on the quantity of labor employed and the employee remuneration. $Z_{ik}$ is the $i$th characteristic variable in the $i$th literature, which includes the characteristic variable of the sample data appeared in the literature, the research method and the publication situation; $\beta$ symbolizes the true value of the coefficient of the impact of tropical cyclones on the quantity of labor employed or the remuneration of employment;$\alpha_k$ is a regression coefficient, reflecting the influence coefficient of the $k$th characteristic variable on $y_i$; $e_i$ represents random disturbance item.

On the basis of model (5.1), the sample model (5.2), the method model (5.3), the publication model (5.4) and the total variable model (5.5) are established respectively:

$$y_i = \beta_1 + \sum_{k1=1}^{k1} \alpha_{k1} S_{ik1} + e_i (i = 1, 2, \ldots, N) \tag{5.2}$$

$S_{ik1}$ indicates the characteristic variable of the $k_1$th sample model in the $i$th literature, the remaining is the same with model (5.1).

$$y_i = \beta_2 + \sum_{k2=1}^{k2} \alpha_{k2} M_{ik2} + e_i (i = 1, 2, \ldots, N) \tag{5.3}$$

$M_{ik2}$ shows the characteristic variable of the $k_2$th method model in the $i$th literature, the remaining is the same with model (5.1).

$$y_i = \beta_3 + \sum_{k3=1}^{k3} \alpha_{k3} P_{ik3} + e_i (i = 1, 2, \ldots, N) \tag{5.4}$$

$P_{ik3}$ shows the characteristic variable of the $k_3$th publication model in the $i$th literature, the remaining is the same with model (5.1).

$$y_i = \beta_4 + \sum_{k1=1}^{k1} \alpha_{k1} S_{ik1} + \sum_{k2=1}^{k2} \alpha_{k2} M_{ik2} + \sum_{k3=1}^{k3} \alpha_{k3} P_{ik3} + e_i (i = 1, 2, \ldots, N) \tag{5.5}$$

[1]The estimation results of the selected literature were all significant at the level of 10%, 5%, or 1%. Finally, the results were all included in meta regression analysis regardless of their significance to test their robustness.

### 5.3.2 The Data

Meta-regression analysis requires a comprehensive and complete collection of literature. The literature collected is all but English ones, owing to the fact that the tropical cyclones are mainly distributed in the United States, Mexico, Bangladesh, and the Philippines etc. Besides, few Chinese studies are found on the topic of tropical cyclones' impact on employment. Moreover, theoretical studies, review studies and qualitative studies are excluded. It should be noted that literatures like research reports, working papers, and dissertations are all included in the meta-analysis, due to the relatively small number of researches on the tropical cyclones' impact on the employment. By searching the titles, keywords, abstracts, 22 documents were found, with a total of 357 sample observations; Among which 148 influences the quantity of employment and 209 affects the employee remuneration. The detailed information of the literature is shown in Table 5.1.

### 5.3.3 Variables Description

Explained variables. (1) Using probit binary choice model, the effect of tropical cyclone on the quantity of employment or employee remuneration is taken as a binary explained variable. If it is positive, the value is 1, otherwise it is 0. (2) By using the ordinary least squares (OLS) ordinary least squares, the absolute value of the influence coefficient of the tropical cyclone on the quantity of employment or employee remuneration is taken as the explained variable to estimate the intensity of the impact of the tropical cyclone on the quantity of employment or employee remuneration.

Explaining variables. (1) The Characteristics of the sample and data. The "developed country" is set as a dummy variable, that is, whether or not the data is from the developed countries or developing countries; "macro data" is set as a dummy variable, which means whether the data is a macro data; "industry data" is set as a dummy variable, meaning whether or not the research data belongs to the industry data; in the industry dimension, the "primary industry", "secondary industry" and "tertiary industry" are set as dummy variables respectively; In the time dimension, in order to study the dynamic change of the impact of tropical cyclones on labor employment, the authors set "observation duration "variable and "short term effect", "medium term effect" and "long term effect" according to Groen's et al. (2015) division of short, medium and long; in terms of disaster intensity, Nordhaus (2006) argued that hurricane losses were related to wind speed and set the tropical cyclone rating variable with the Saffir-Simpson Hurricane Wind Scale. Moreover, the "wind speed variable" is set, the maximum wind speed of tropical cyclone center (one nautical mile per hour); In the income dimension, in order to detect whether not the impact of disasters vary with different income groups, dummy variables like "low-income groups", "middle-income groups", and "high-income groups" are set. (2) Research methods.

**Table 5.1** The literature analyzed through meta-regression

| Number | Author | Region | Tropical cyclone | Time period |
|---|---|---|---|---|
| 1 | Ewing et al. (2003) | Fort Worth | Tornadoes on March 27, 2000 | 1980–2002 |
| 2 | Ewing et al. (2005a) | Corpus Christi | Hurricane Bret in August 1999 | 1990–2003 |
| 3 | Ewing et al. (2005b) | Oklahoma City | Tornadoes on May 3, 1999 | 1990–1999 |
| 4 | Ewing et al. (2004) | Nashville | Tornadoes on April 16, 1998 | 1981–2002 |
| 5 | Anttilahughes and Hsiang (2013) | Philippines | 411 tropical cyclones | 1985–2000 |
| 6 | Kim et al. (2015) | Southeastern United States | Hurricane Allen, Diana, Elena, Emily, Charley, Gloria, Hugo, Andrew | 1979–2004 |
| 7 | Kugler and Yuksel (2008) | United States | Hurricane Mitch in October 1998 | 2000–2005 |
| 8 | Chaganti and Waddell (2015) | New Orleans | Hurricane Katrina on 29 August 2005 | 2006–2007 |
| 9 | Andrade (2013) | Houston | Hurricane Katrina on 29 August 2005 | 2005–2006 |
| 10 | Deryugina et al. (2014) | New Orleans | Hurricane Katrina on 29 August 2005 | 1999–2010 |
| 11 | Liliedahl (2009) | Houston and Baton Rouge | Hurricane Katrina on 29 August 2005 | 2003–2008 |
| 12 | Kaegi et al. (2013) | Louisiana | Hurricane Lili, Cindy, Humberto, Gustav Ike, Katrina, Rita | 2001–2010 |
| 13 | Akter and Mallick (2013) | Bangladesh | Typhoon Aila on May 25, 2009 | 2009–2010 |
| 14 | Strobl and Walsh (2009) | United States | Several tropical cyclones from the HAZUS software database | 1988–2005 |
| 15 | Eduardo (2013) | Mexico | Hurricane Keith, Juliette, Isidore, Kenna, Claudette, Ignacio, Emily, Wilma, John, Lane, Norbert, Alex, Karl | 2000–2011 |
| 16 | Mottaleb et al. (2013) | Bengal | Typhoon Aila on May 25, 2009 | 2000–2010 |

(continued)

**Table 5.1** (continued)

| Number | Author | Region | Tropical cyclone | Time period |
|---|---|---|---|---|
| 17 | Mcintosh (2008) | Houston | Hurricane Katrina on August 29, 2005 | 2000–2006 |
| 18 | Groen and Polivka (2008) | New Orleans | Hurricane Katrina on August 29, 2005 | 2004–2006 |
| 19 | Ewing et al. (2009) | Oklahoma City | Tornadoes on May 3, 1999 | 1980–2002 |
| 20 | Belasen and Polachek (2007) | Florida | 19 tropical cyclones | 1988–2005 |
| 21 | De Silva et al. (2010) | Houston | Hurricane Katrina on August 29, 2005 | 2004–2007 |
| 22 | Groen et al. (2015) | United States | Hurricane Katrina, Rita | 2003–2006 |

The dummy variables of panel data, ordinary least squares (OLS) and autoregressive moving average models (ARMA) are set. (3) The publication of the literature. The "year of publication" variable and "whether published" are set as dummy variables. Finally, the logarithm of the observed number of samples (lnobs) is taken as a control variable. The explaining variables are described in Table 5.2.

## 5.4 Results of Meta-regression Analysis

### *5.4.1 The Impact of Tropical Cyclones on the Direction of Employment Quantity Change*

In model 1 and 2, the sample variable is added; in model 3, method variable is added; in model 4, literature variable is added for meta-regression[2]. In order to further test the stability of the model results, models 5 and 6 are used for regression of the

[2]The results of Meta-regression analysis were obtained by using software Stata11. Heteroskedasticity all eliminated by robust analysis; as for multicollinearity problem: since the significant correlation between industry variable and secondary industry variable is 0.592, and the significant correlation between industry variable and tertiary industry variable is 0.681, added that the secondary industry and tertiary industry variables are the core variables, the industry dummy variable is eliminated. In addition, short-term effects dummy variable, medium-term effects dummy variable and long-term effects dummy variable are also highly correlated. Therefore, the medium-term effects dummy variables are regarded as the base variables. The short-term effects dummy variables and the medium-term effects dummy variables are set as one group, and the medium-term effects dummy variables and the long-term effects dummy variables are set as another to carry out regression analysis. The analysis is also performed within the group consisting of the short-term effects dummy variables and the long-term effects dummy variables. The results show that in the short term, the impact of tropical cyclones on employment quantity is enormous, while the impact is marginal in the long run. This result is consistent with the conclusion of the study.

**Table 5.2** Descriptions of the explaining variables

| Level | Dimension | Variables | Description |
|---|---|---|---|
| Sample data | | Developed country | If the research sample is from developed countries, the value is 1, otherwise 0 |
| | | Macro data[a] | If the research sample belongs to macro data, the value is 1, otherwise 0 |
| | | Industry data | If the research sample belongs to industry data, the value is 1, otherwise 0 |
| | Industry dimension | Primary industry | If the research sample is from primary industry, i.e. agriculture, fishery, then the value is 1, other wise 0 |
| | | Secondary industry | If the research sample is from secondary industry, like construction, manufactory, mining etc., then the value is 1, otherwise 0 |
| | | Tertiary industry | If the research sample is from tertiary industry, like finance and insurance, real estate, wholesale and retail trade, services etc., then the value is 1, otherwise 0 |
| | Time dimension[b] | Observation period | The time span of the study period. If the study period is from 1980 to 2002, then the observation period is 23 years |
| | | Short-term effects | The lower limit of the time span of the study period—the year of disaster occurrence <3, then the value is 1, otherwise it is 0 |
| | | Long-term effects | 3 ≤ the lower limit of the time span of the study period—the year of disaster occurrence <6, the value is 1, otherwise 0 |

(continued)

**Table 5.2** (continued)

| Level | Dimension | Variables | Description |
|---|---|---|---|
| | | Long-term effects | The lower limit of the time span of the study—the year of disaster occurrence ≥6, then the value is 1, otherwise it is 0 |
| | Disaster intensity | Disaster level | Rated according to the Saffir-Simpson Hurricane Wind Scale |
| | | Wind speed | The maximum wind speed of tropical cyclone center after landing(one nautical mile per hour) |
| | Income dimension[c] | Low-income groups | If the sample of literature research objects are of low skill, low education and with earnings less than or equal to $28.5K, then the value is 1, otherwise 0 |
| | | Middle-income groups | If the sample of literature research objects are of medium skill, medium education and with earnings greater or equal to $28.5K and less than $50 K, then the value is 1, otherwise 0 |
| | | High-income groups | If the sample of the literature research objects are of high skill, high education and with earnings greater or equal to $50K, then the value is 1, otherwise 0 |
| Method characteristics | | Panel data | If the sample data belongs to panel data, then the value is 1, otherwise 0 |
| | | OLS | If OLS is employed, then the value is 1, otherwise 0 |
| | | ARMA | If ARMA is employed, then the value is 1, otherwise 0 |
| Publication characteristics | | Publication year | The year in which the document was published or publicly released |

(continued)

**Table 5.2** (continued)

| Level | Dimension | Variables | Description |
|---|---|---|---|
| | | Whether published | If the literature published in journal, then the value is 1, otherwise 0, such as work papers and research reports |

[a]Here the macro data refers to the data that takes region as a statistical unit; micro data refers to the data that takes individual or household as a statistical unit
[b]The division of time period is based on Groen's et al. (2015) criteria for short, medium and long term division
[c]The division of income dimension is based primarily on literature's verbal and numerical description of income. As for numerical description, its lower limit of low, middle and high income referred to Groen's et al. (2015) criteria for division; as for verbal description, then low-income group are of low skill and low education background. Middle income group are of medium skill and medium education background. High income group are of high skill and high education background

whole variable model. The results show that: (1) From the sample aspect, "developed country" and "macro data" have no significant impact on the positive and negative effects of employment quantity; In terms of industry dimensions[3], industry disparities have no significant impact on the positive and negative effects of the employment quantity during hurricane occurrence. In time dimension, the "short-term effects" tend to have a negative relationship, while the "medium-term effects" and "long-term effects" tend to have a positive relationship; it is clear that tropical cyclones cause a series of damage, such as casualties, massive evacuation, transportation paralysis and communications failure, infrastructure damage, business interruption and suspension from work etc., which influences employment quantity in a short term. In a medium and long term, due to post-disaster recovery and reconstruction work, a lot of manpower, material and financial resources is needed, which will lead to a surge in labor demand; With regard to disaster intensity, the higher the hurricane category, the more likely to get a positive relationship. A higher hurricane category means a greater wind speed, resulting in a greater destructive force. Therefore, post-disaster reconstruction requires a greater amount of human capital and material, which leads to an increase in the number of available jobs; In regard to income dimension, low-income groups are more likely to get a positive employment relationship. On the one hand, in the aftermath of a tropical cyclone, people tend to cut household budget (Groen et al. 2015). For low-income families, household consumption expenditure tends to be food and medical treatment, and relocation and reemployment costs are higher, therefore households bear a relatively heavier financial burden. However, workers with high-paying jobs or high-skill have relatively more available budget and are more likely to evacuate to relatively safer areas, while low-paid workers have no choice but to stay in the local area (Belasen and Polachek 2007, 2008). On the other

[3]None of the literatures dealing with tropical cyclones' impact on employment has data on the primary industry, so neither Table 5.3 nor Table 5.4 shows the dummy variables of the primary industry.

hand, the relocation of some people reduces labor supply, however, post-disaster restoration and reconstruction requires a large amount of labor. The gap of labor supply and demand leads to an increase in employee remuneration, thus attracting a large number of low-income groups (Eduardo 2013). (2) From the method aspect, OLS was used to adjust the negative employment. (3) From the literature aspect, "year of publication" and "whether published" have no significant influence. The results of Probit analysis are shown in Table 5.3.

### 5.4.2 *Impact of Tropical Cyclones on Intensity of Employment Quantity Change*

The impact of tropical cyclones on intensity of employment quantity change was analyzed by multiple regression model and the results are shown in Table 5.4 below. (1) From the sample aspect, the developed countries have no significant influence on the intensity of employment quantity change; if the macro data is employed, the change of the employment quantity is then relatively mild; In the industry dimension, the industry differences will lead to a relatively significant change in intensity of employment quantity, and the second industry employment intensity is greater than that of the tertiary industry. On the one hand, the sensitivity of various sectors to the disaster intensity and their ability of disaster prevention and reduction vary. On the other hand, post-disaster reconstruction and industrial rehabilitation include rebuilding damaged buildings, roads, bridges and other facilities (Jiang 2012), which inevitably leads to a greater demand for labor in the secondary industry. Nevertheless, due to the lack of primary industry data, the change of the employment intensity in the primary industry cannot be observed; In the time dimension, the impact of the disaster on short-term employment quantity is greater, while the change in medium-term and long-term employment is insignificant and mild respectively. Along with the post-disaster restoration and reconstruction, the society and economy gradually return to normal, which would gradually restore to normal labor market conditions. Thus, the impact of the hurricane on the employment quantity is gradually abated; In terms of disaster intensity, the higher the hurricane' category, the greater its impact on employment quantity, though the statistics are not robust; in the income dimension, the change in employment quantity of high-income groups is relatively mild, while the statistics of high-income groups are not robust (model 7, 8 is inconsistent with the significance of the results of the robustness testing model 11, 12). (2) From the method aspect, using panel data model can reduce the intensity of employment quantity change. (3) From the literature aspect, there are differences between model 10 and models 11, 12, which indicates "year of publication" and "whether published" are not significant.

**Table 5.3** The positive and negative meta-regression results of tropical cyclones' impact on employment quantity

| Variables | Model 1 | Model 2 | Model 3 | Model 4 | Model 5 | Model 6 |
|---|---|---|---|---|---|---|
| | Sample aspect | Sample aspect | Method aspect | Publication aspect | Robustness test | Robustness test |
| Control variable | 0.0778 | 0.0778 | 0.195*** | 0.0719** | 0.0908 | 0.0908 |
| | (0.0753) | (0.0753) | (0.0674) | (0.0366) | (0.178) | (0.178) |
| Developed country | −0.290 | −0.290 | | | −1.068 | −1.068 |
| | (0.491) | (0.491) | | | (0.970) | (0.970) |
| Macro data | 0.282 | 0.282 | | | −5.484*** | −5.484*** |
| | (1.068) | (1.068) | | | (1.532) | (1.532) |
| The secondary industry | 0.611 | 0.611 | | | 0.217 | 0.217 |
| | (0.656) | (0.656) | | | (0.823) | (0.823) |
| The tertiary industry | 0.534 | 0.534 | | | −0.0702 | −0.0702 |
| | (0.634) | (0.634) | | | (0.768) | (0.768) |
| Observation period | −0.0081 | −0.0081 | | | 0.0162 | 0.0162 |
| | (0.0407) | (0.0407) | | | (0.0892) | (0.0892) |
| Short-term effects | −0.847** | | | | −1.009** | |
| | (0.384) | | | | (0.439) | |
| Medium-term effects | −0.233 | 0.614* | | | −0.181 | 0.828** |
| | (0.375) | (0.341) | | | (0.408) | (0.372) |
| Long-term effects | | 0.847** | | | | 1.009** |
| | | (0.384) | | | | (0.439) |
| Cyclone intensity | 0.350*** | 0.350*** | | | 0.319** | 0.319** |
| | (0.127) | (0.127) | | | (0.147) | (0.147) |
| Low-income | 1.057** | 1.057** | | | 1.387** | 1.387** |
| | (0.492) | (0.492) | | | (0.621) | (0.621) |
| Middle income | 0.331 | 0.331 | | | 0.613 | 0.613 |
| | (0.619) | (0.619) | | | (0.685) | (0.685) |
| High-income | −0.145 | −0.145 | | | 0.0113 | 0.0113 |
| | (0.519) | (0.519) | | | (0.575) | (0.575) |
| Panel data | | | −0.184 | | −0.640 | −0.640 |
| | | | (0.533) | | (1.138) | (1.138) |
| OLS | | | −1.354*** | | −6.283*** | −6.283*** |
| | | | (0.472) | | (0.724) | (0.724) |
| ARMA | | | −0.0952 | | −0.680 | −0.680 |
| | | | (0.599) | | (1.822) | (1.822) |
| Year of publication | | | | −0.0355 | −0.131 | −0.131 |
| | | | | (0.0500) | (0.112) | (0.112) |

(continued)

**Table 5.3** (continued)

| Variables | Model 1 | Model 2 | Model 3 | Model 4 | Model 5 | Model 6 |
|---|---|---|---|---|---|---|
| | Sample aspect | Sample aspect | Method aspect | Publication aspect | Robustness test | Robustness test |
| Whether published | | | | −0.185 | −1.357 | −1.357 |
| | | | | (0.249) | (0.881) | (0.881) |
| Constant | −2.042** | −2.889*** | −1.084** | 70.78 | 270.1 | 269.1 |
| | (1.028) | (1.000) | (0.473) | (100.5) | (227.2) | (227.1) |
| Pseudo $R^2$ | 0.1657 | 0.1657 | 0.0635 | 0.0203 | 0.2399 | 0.2399 |
| Sample size | 135 | 135 | 148 | 148 | 135 | 135 |

*Note* The numbers in the brackets are the corresponding regression coefficient robust standard error, * indicates a significance level of 10%, ** indicates a significance level of 5%, *** indicates a significance level of 1%

### *5.4.3 The Impact of Tropical Cyclones on the Direction of Employee Remuneration*

Probit model was used to analyze the impact of tropical cyclones on employee remuneration. The results are shown in Table 5.5. (1) From the sample aspect, developed countries are more likely to have a positive effect on employee remuneration; Since the developed countries have higher levels of disaster resilience, for example, the construction of disaster mitigation facilities, infrastructure and houses are more resilient than the counterparts in developing countries; Moreover, the enterprises and residents possess more disaster mitigation knowledge and the response measures are optimized compared with the situation in developing countries. Therefore, the disaster is relatively less destructive and more conducive to the recovery of the labor market in developed countries. In the industry dimension, there's no significant change in employee remuneration of primary industry[4], which is most likely due to the limited data from primary industry, therefore its impact is not reflected. The coefficient of the tertiary industry is negative. The tertiary industry mainly consists of leisure tourism industry, retail trade etc. The hurricane will lead to a slump in leisure tourism industry tourism. In addition, tropical cyclones disrupt the normal operation

[4]When using the binary selection model to analyze the positive and negative effects of employee remuneration, the authors find that the estimation coefficient of the primary industry is missing; this could be explained by two reasons. First, there is a serious collinearity problem between the primary industry and other explaining variables in the model. Correlation analysis shows that the primary industry is highly correlated with industry variable, which however has already been excluded from all the models. Second, the positive and negative regression coefficient between the primary industry and wage is very small, thus ignored by the Stata program automatically. In the first industry, the regression coefficient is very small, and it is ignored by the Stata program. It is classified as the second reason. It is the same with the panel data variables. Since the literature which involved with the impact of disasters on employee remuneration didn't employ autoregressive moving average model, there is no ARMA variables in Tables 5.5 and 5.6.

**Table 5.4** The meta-regression results of the tropical cyclone's impact on the intensity of employment change

| Variable | Model 7 | Model 8 | Model 9 | Model 10 | Model 11 | Model 12 |
|---|---|---|---|---|---|---|
| | Sample aspect | Sample aspect | Method aspect | Publication aspect | Robustness testing | Robustness testing |
| Control variable | −0.109*** | −0.109*** | 0.00983 | −0.0465** | −0.0475 | −0.0475 |
| | (0.0378) | (0.0378) | (0.0171) | (0.0189) | (0.0717) | (0.0717) |
| Developed country | −0.0781 | −0.0781 | | | 0.0865 | 0.0865 |
| | (0.119) | (0.119) | | | (0.318) | (0.318) |
| Macro data | −1.246** | −1.246** | | | −1.381** | −1.381** |
| | (0.531) | (0.531) | | | (0.560) | (0.560) |
| The secondary industry | 0.993** | 0.993** | | | 1.324*** | 1.324*** |
| | (0.410) | (0.410) | | | (0.475) | (0.475) |
| The tertiary industry | 0.602* | 0.602* | | | 0.984** | 0.984** |
| | (0.331) | (0.331) | | | (0.433) | (0.433) |
| Observation period | 0.0655** | 0.0655** | | | 0.0876*** | 0.0876*** |
| | (0.0261) | (0.0261) | | | (0.024) | (0.024) |
| Short-term effects | 0.238* | | | | 0.144* | |
| | (0.125) | | | | (0.0863) | |
| Medium-term effects | 0.0647 | −0.174 | | | 0.00812 | −0.136 |
| | (0.105) | (0.177) | | | (0.0753) | (0.139) |
| Long-term effects | | −0.238* | | | | −0.144* |
| | | (0.125) | | | | (0.0863) |
| Cyclone intensity | 0.0547* | 0.0547* | | | 0.0141 | 0.0141 |
| | (0.0323) | (0.0323) | | | (0.026) | (0.026) |
| Low-income | −0.160 | −0.160 | | | −0.107 | −0.107 |
| | (0.119) | (0.119) | | | (0.0953) | (0.0953) |
| Medium-income | −0.248** | −0.248** | | | −0.174* | −0.174* |
| | (0.115) | (0.115) | | | (0.0954) | (0.0954) |
| High-income | −0.226* | −0.226* | | | −0.103 | −0.103 |
| | (0.114) | (0.114) | | | (0.0956) | (0.0956) |
| Panel data | | | −0.357*** | | −0.790** | −0.790** |
| | | | (0.121) | | (0.384) | (0.384) |
| OLS | | | −0.224 | | −0.0921 | −0.0921 |
| | | | (0.195) | | (0.165) | (0.165) |
| ARMA | | | 0.706 | | −1.158** | −1.158** |
| | | | (0.460) | | (0.464) | (0.464) |
| Year of publication | | | | −0.0678** | −0.0718 | −0.0718 |
| | | | | (0.0336) | (0.073) | (0.073) |

(continued)

**Table 5.4** (continued)

| Variable | Model 7 | Model 8 | Model 9 | Model 10 | Model 11 | Model 12 |
|---|---|---|---|---|---|---|
| | Sample aspect | Sample aspect | Method aspect | Publication aspect | Robustness testing | Robustness testing |
| Whether published | | | | 0.0000579 | 0.144 | 0.144 |
| | | | | (0.0968) | (0.403) | (0.403) |
| Constant | 0.773*** | 1.012*** | 0.492*** | 137.1** | 145.0 | 145.2 |
| | (0.268) | (0.309) | (0.151) | (67.64) | (147.7) | (147.7) |
| R-squared | 0.429 | 0.429 | 0.323 | 0.223 | 0.492 | 0.492 |
| Sample size | 135 | 135 | 148 | 148 | 135 | 135 |

*Note* The numbers in the brackets are the corresponding regression coefficient robust standard error, * indicates a significance level of 10%, ** indicates a significance level of 5%, *** indicates a significance level of 1%

of enterprises; a drop in output will also affect export trade, thus employee remuneration in tertiary industry is relatively reduced; In the time dimension, the short-term tropical cyclones will reduce the employee remuneration, while the employee remuneration tends to increase in the long run. Olsen and Porter (2013) also pointed out that prices and labor costs will rise after a large-scale natural disaster, which might be a reason why the employee remuneration increases. From cyclone intensity aspect, the higher the hurricane category, the more likely it will get a positive employee remuneration relationship; In the income dimension, the employee remuneration of the middle- and low-income groups are even lower. The low-income people relatively lack post-disaster recovery ability, and after experiencing severe natural disasters, they tend to reduce the education expenses to make up for the losses caused by the disaster. This, in turn stops the family's ability of disaster prevention and reduction from being effectively improved, resulting in a reduced ability of low-income families to withstand disasters, thus entering a vicious circle. Moreover, the places where the majority of low-income groups live are disaster-prone region. By contrast, high-income groups tend to take various measures to mitigate the damage caused by natural disasters (Sadowski and Sutter 2005), therefore, disasters will cause more damage to the low-income people. (2) From the method aspect, the research method employed has no significant influence on positive and negative regulation of employee remuneration. (3) From the literature aspect, neither "year of publication" nor "whether published" has statistical significance.

### *5.4.4 The Impact of Tropical Cyclones on the Intensity of Employee Remuneration Change*

The impact of tropical cyclones on the intensity of employee remuneration change is analyzed by using multiple regression models. The results are shown in Table 5.6. (1)

**Table 5.5** The meta-regression results of positive and negative effects of tropical cyclones on employee remuneration

| Variables | Model 13 | Model 14 | Model 15 | Model 16 | Model 17 | Model 18 |
|---|---|---|---|---|---|---|
| | Sample aspect | Sample aspect | Method aspect | Publication aspect | Robustness testing | Robustness testing |
| Control variable | 0.459*** | 0.459*** | 0.209*** | 0.174*** | 0.286 | 0.286 |
| | (0.157) | (0.157) | (0.0442) | (0.0418) | (0.200) | (0.200) |
| Developed country | 2.124* | 2.124* | | | 2.213** | 2.213** |
| | (1.102) | (1.102) | | | (1.101) | (1.101) |
| Macro data | 0.769 | 0.769 | | | 0.065 | 0.065 |
| | (1.069) | (1.069) | | | (1.399) | (1.399) |
| The primary industry | 0 | 0 | | | 0 | 0 |
| | (0) | (0) | | | (0) | (0) |
| The secondary industry | −0.127 | −0.127 | | | 0.189 | 0.189 |
| | (0.921) | (0.921) | | | (0.826) | (0.826) |
| The tertiary industry | −1.555** | −1.555** | | | −1.195* | −1.195* |
| | (0.766) | (0.766) | | | (0.656) | (0.656) |
| Observation period | 0.425** | 0.425** | | | 0.427*** | 0.427*** |
| | (0.166) | (0.166) | | | (0.161) | (0.161) |
| Short-term effects | −0.778* | | | | −0.855* | |
| | (0.424) | | | | (0.442) | |
| Medium-term effects | 1.568*** | 2.346*** | | | 1.348*** | 2.203*** |
| | (0.514) | (0.529) | | | (0.441) | (0.485) |
| Long-term effects | | 0.778* | | | | 0.855* |
| | | (0.424) | | | | (0.442) |
| Cyclone intensity | 0.267* | 0.267* | | | 0.403** | 0.403** |
| | (0.148) | (0.148) | | | (0.189) | (0.189) |
| Low-income | −0.973** | −0.973** | | | −0.991* | −0.991* |
| | (0.493) | (0.493) | | | (0.536) | (0.536) |
| Middle income | −1.353** | −1.353** | | | −1.328** | −1.328** |
| | (0.574) | (0.574) | | | (0.570) | (0.570) |
| High-income | −0.363 | −0.363 | | | −0.196 | −0.196 |
| | (0.616) | (0.616) | | | (0.630) | (0.630) |
| OLS | | | −0.517 | | −0.341 | −0.341 |
| | | | (0.344) | | (0.536) | (0.536) |
| Year of publication | | | | −0.0078 | −0.0604 | −0.0604 |
| | | | | (0.0574) | (0.190) | (0.190) |
| Whether published | | | | 0.0201 | 1.073 | 1.073 |
| | | | | (0.239) | (0.796) | (0.796) |

(continued)

**Table 5.5** (continued)

| Variables | Model 13 | Model 14 | Model 15 | Model 16 | Model 17 | Model 18 |
|---|---|---|---|---|---|---|
| | Sample aspect | Sample aspect | Method aspect | Publication aspect | Robustness testing | Robustness testing |
| Constant | −10.02*** | −10.80*** | −1.384*** | 14.24 | 112.9 | 112.1 |
| | (3.351) | (3.221) | (0.446) | (115.4) | (385.1) | (385.2) |
| Pseudo $R^2$ | 0.3717 | 0.3717 | 0.0954 | 0.0931 | 0.3812 | 0.3812 |
| Sample size | 171 | 171 | 208 | 209 | 170 | 170 |

*Note* The numbers in the brackets are the corresponding regression coefficient robust standard error, * indicates a significance level of 10%, ** indicates a significance level of 5%, *** indicates a significance level of 1%

From the sample aspect, the impact of tropical cyclones on employee remuneration in developed countries is relatively mild. In the industrial dimension, employee remuneration in the primary industry suffers a relatively greater loss. The primary industry mainly includes agriculture and fishery. These industries are of weak resilience, thus vulnerable to tropical cyclones, resulting in relatively heavily affected employee remuneration in the primary industry. The change intensity of employee remuneration of the secondary industry is less than that of the primary industry, though the result is not stable. The change of employee remuneration in the tertiary industry is not significant; In the time dimension, the change intensity of employee remuneration in the short and long term is not significant, while the change of the mid-term employee remuneration is relatively mild; from the cyclone intensity aspect, the category of hurricane has no significant impact on the change intensity of the employee remuneration; in the income dimension, the employee remuneration of the low-income groups changes a lot but didn't have statistical significance. The middle-income group's employee remuneration changes mildly, though the result is not stable. (2) From the method aspect, model 21 is different from model 23 and 24, therefore the adoption of the research method has no significant influence on the positive and negative regulation of the employee remuneration. (3) In the literature aspect, neither "year of publication" nor "whether published" has statistical significance.

### 5.4.5 Robustness Analysis

In order to test the stability of the results of meta-regression analysis, robustness analysis is applied to all the regression results from both variables and data aspects. (1) The regression of the total variables is conducted, which means the characteristic variables from the sample aspect, the method aspect, the published aspect are all included in the meta-regression model. The estimated results are shown in the last columns of Tables 5.3, 5.4, 5.5 and 5.6, the last two columns, in which the main regression results remains basically unchanged. (2) The estimated values, regardless

**Table 5.6** Meta-regression results of tropical cyclones' impact on the intensity of employee remuneration change

| Variable | Model 19 | Model 20 | Model 21 | Model 22 | Model 23 | Model 24 |
|---|---|---|---|---|---|---|
| | Sample aspect | Sample aspect | Method aspect | Publication aspect | Employee remuneration | Employee remuneration |
| Control variable | −0.0108*** | −0.0108*** | −0.0227 | −0.0542 | −0.011** | −0.011** |
| | (0.00304) | (0.00304) | (0.0189) | (0.0414) | (0.00436) | (0.00436) |
| Developed country | −0.0527*** | −0.0527*** | | | −0.0445* | −0.0445* |
| | (0.0125) | (0.0125) | | | (0.0254) | (0.0254) |
| Macro data | −0.0411** | −0.0411** | | | −0.0742*** | −0.0742*** |
| | (0.0204) | (0.0204) | | | (0.0272) | (0.0272) |
| The primary industry | 0.0652*** | 0.0652*** | | | 0.0664*** | 0.0664*** |
| | (0.0114) | (0.0114) | | | (0.0125) | (0.0125) |
| The secondary industry | 0.0265* | 0.0265* | | | 0.028 | 0.028 |
| | (0.0151) | (0.0151) | | | (0.0173) | (0.0173) |
| The tertiary industry | −0.00997 | −0.00997 | | | −0.00766 | −0.00766 |
| | (0.00879) | (0.00879) | | | (0.0124) | (0.0124) |
| Observation period | −0.00252 | −0.00252 | | | 0.000509 | 0.000509 |
| | (0.00162) | (0.00162) | | | (0.00175) | (0.00175) |
| Short-term effects | −0.00315 | | | | 0.00638 | |
| | (0.00856) | | | | (0.00823) | |
| Medium-term effects | −0.0145** | −0.0114 | | | −0.00834 | −0.0147* |
| | (0.00575) | (0.00789) | | | (0.00593) | (0.00777) |
| Long-term effects | | 0.00315 | | | | −0.00638 |
| | | (0.00856) | | | | (0.00823) |
| Cyclone intensity | 0.00323 | 0.00323 | | | 0.00373 | 0.00373 |
| | (0.00267) | (0.00267) | | | (0.00256) | (0.00256) |
| Low-income | 0.00622 | 0.00622 | | | 0.00181 | 0.00181 |
| | (0.00972) | (0.00972) | | | (0.0116) | (0.0116) |
| Middle income | −0.0177* | −0.0177* | | | −0.0187 | −0.0187 |
| | (0.0103) | (0.0103) | | | (0.0117) | (0.0117) |
| High-income | −0.00389 | −0.00389 | | | −0.00486 | −0.00486 |
| | (0.0117) | (0.0117) | | | (0.0124) | (0.0124) |
| Panel data | | | 0.0286 | | −0.0598 | −0.0598 |
| | | | (0.148) | | (0.0479) | (0.0479) |

(continued)

Table 5.6 (continued)

| Variable | Model 19 | Model 20 | Model 21 | Model 22 | Model 23 | Model 24 |
|---|---|---|---|---|---|---|
| | Sample aspect | Sample aspect | Method aspect | Publication aspect | Employee remuneration | Employee remuneration |
| OLS | | | −0.200 | | −0.0343** | −0.0343** |
| | | | (0.305) | | (0.0141) | (0.0141) |
| Year of publication | | | | 0.0198 | −0.00183 | −0.00183 |
| | | | | (0.0206) | (0.00387) | (0.00387) |
| Whether published | | | | 0.221 | −0.00319 | −0.00319 |
| | | | | (0.200) | (0.024) | (0.024) |
| Constant | 0.247*** | 0.244*** | 0.547* | −39.26 | 3.996 | 4.002 |
| | (0.0457) | (0.0452) | (0.311) | (41.04) | (7.808) | (7.809) |
| R-squared | 0.302 | 0.302 | 0.032 | 0.044 | 0.359 | 0.359 |
| Sample size | 174 | 174 | 209 | 209 | 174 | 174 |

*Note* The numbers in the brackets are the corresponding regression coefficient robust standard error, * indicates a significance level of 10%, ** indicates a significance level of 5%, *** indicates a significance level of 1%

of whether or not it is significant are all put into Meta-regression analysis. The results are shown in appendixes 1 to 4, and the results of the main regression remain almost unchanged. Thus, it might be concluded that the result is robust.

## 5.5 Conclusion and Discussion

Through reviewing the literature and based on the analysis of disaster impacts on the mechanism of labor market, this paper explored the impacts of tropical cyclones on the quantity of labor employed and employee remuneration from the following four dimensions: industry, time, income and cyclone intensity, using meta-regression analysis. Final conclusions are:

(1) In the industry dimension, industry differences have a significant impact on change intensity of the quantity of labor employed and employee remuneration. The quantity of labor employed in the secondary and tertiary industries varies greatly due to the tropical cyclones. Moreover, the change in the secondary industry is greater than that of the tertiary industry. In addition, the employee remuneration of the primary industry is strongly influenced by the tropical cyclones. Therefore, the employee remuneration of the primary industry suffers a great loss.

(2) In the time dimension, the impact of tropical cyclones on labor employment is negative, and the impact intensity is large in the short term. The long-term impact is positive and decreases gradually. Therefore, it can be seen that the

negative impact of tropical cyclones on labor employment is gradually restored through post-disaster restoration and reconstruction.

(3) In the income dimension, the disaster promoted the employment rate of the low-income group, but reduced the low-income group's employee remuneration. Moreover, the change in the quantity of labor employed caused by disasters in the medium and high-income groups is relatively mild. Therefore, the low-income people are more vulnerable when faced with tropical cyclones, while the disaster has less impact on the high-income group.

(4) In the intensity of disaster dimension, the higher the category of tropical cyclones, the greater its impact on the quantity of labor employed and employee remuneration.

According to the above research findings, the following recommendations are proposed for the post-disaster restoration and reconstruction in the aftermath of the natural disasters like tropical cyclones:

(1) Post-disaster assistance policy should favor the low-income group. Investment in health care and education for low-income people should be increased, in order to improve their consciousness of disaster prevention and mitigation and also improve their disaster response ability.

(2) During post-disaster restoration and reconstruction, attention should be paid to secondary industry development such as construction and housing. Restore road traffic and resume the normal operation of other key lifelines, like water and electricity as soon as possible.

(3) Take low-income groups as the key protected group. Great attention must be paid to assist and support the industries in the less developed areas, especially the primary industry.

(4) Build a sound labor employment insurance system of natural disasters. In the short-term, disaster insurance can reduce the huge risk caused by tropical cyclones and alleviate the economic burden of afflicted people and enterprises through economic compensation. In the long run, disaster insurance system can achieve full potential in financing, which can inject funds into post-disaster restoration and reconstruction activity, thus accelerate the reconstruction work in the aftermath of the disaster.

**Acknowledgements** Zhe Xu, Hui Liu, Ji Guo, Lei Zhou, Zheng Fu also made great contributions to this manuscript. We express our heartfelt thanks to them. This research was supported by: National Social and Scientific Fund Program of China (18ZDA052; 17BGL142; 16ZDA047); The Natural Science Foundation of China (91546117, 71373131).

## References


Abdullah, A. N. M., Zander, K. K., Myers, B., Stacey, N., & Garnett, S. T. (2016). A short-term decrease in household income inequality in the Sundarbans, Bangladesh, following Cyclone Aila. *Natural Hazards, 83*(2), 1103–1123.

Adam, C., & Bevan, D. (2020). Tropical cyclones and post-disaster reconstruction of public infrastructure in developing countries. *Economic Modelling, 93,* 82–99.

Akter, S., & Mallick, B. (2013). The poverty–vulnerability–resilience nexus: Evidence from Bangladesh. *Ecological Economics, 96*(C), 114–124.

Andrade, J. B. (2013). *Labor market assimilation: Evidence from hurricane Katrina evacuees.* Syracuse, New York: Syracuse University.

Anttilahughes, J., & Hsiang, S. (2013). *Destruction, disinvestment, and death: economic and human losses following environmental disaster.* SSRN. http://ssrn.com/abstract=2220501.

Baez, J., & Santos, I. (2008). On Shaky Ground: The Effects of Earthquakes on Household Income and Poverty, RPP LAC-MDGs and Poverty-02/2008, RBLACUNDP, New York.

Belasen, A. R., & Polachek, S. W. (2007). How hurricanes affect local labor markets—The effects of hurricanes in Florida. *The Journal of Human Resources, 44,* 251–276.

Belasen, A. R., & Polachek, S. W. (2008). How hurricanes affect wages and employment in local labor markets. *American Economic Review, 98*(2), 49–53.

Bergeijk, P., & Lazzaroni, S. (2015). Macroeconomics of natural disasters: Strengths and weaknesses of meta-analysis versus review of literature. *Risk Analysis, 35*(6), 1050–1072.

Bruyère, C. L., Done, J. M., Jaye, A. B., Holland, G. J., Buckley, B., Henderson, D. J., et al. (2019). Physically-based landfalling tropical cyclone scenarios in support of risk assessment. *Weather and Climate Extremes, 26,* 100229.

Chaganti, S., & Waddell, J. (2015). Employment change among hurricane Katrina evacuees: Impacts of race and place. *Journal of Public Management & Social Policy, 22*(2), Article 3.

Chen, L. M., & Wang, L. X. (2014). Whether international strategy will help firm improve their performance. *China Industrial Economics, 320*(11), 102–115.

Chou, J., Dong, W., Tu, G., & Xu, Y. (2020). Spatiotemporal distribution of landing tropical cyclones and disaster impact analysis in coastal China during 1990–2016. *Physics and Chemistry of the Earth, Parts A/B/C, 115,.*

Cui, Y., Liang, D., & Ewing, B. (2020). Analysis of employment change in response to hurricane landfalls. *Natural Hazards and Earth System Sciences, 20*(2), 413–424.

De Silva, D. G., Mccomb, R. P., Moh, Y. K., et al. (2010). The effect of migration on wages: Evidence from a natural experiment. *American Economic Review, 100*(2), 321–326.

Deryugina, T., Kawano, L., & Levitt, S. (2014). *The economic impact of hurricane Katrina on its victims: Evidence from individual tax returns.* http://www.nber.org/papers/w20713.pdf.

Eduardo, R. O. (2013). Hurricanes and labor market outcomes: Evidence for Mexico. *Global Environmental Change, 23,* 351–359.

Ewing, B. T., Kruse, J. B., & Thompson, M. A. (2003). A comparison of employment growth and stability before and after the Fort Worth tornado. *Environmental Hazards, 5,* 83–91.

Ewing, B. T., Kruse, J. B., & Thompson, M. A. (2004). Employment dynamics and the Nashville tornado. *Regional Analysis & Policy, 34*(2), 47–60.

Ewing, B. T., Kruse, J. B., & Thompson, M. A. (2005a). Empirical examination of the Corpus Christi unemployment rate and hurricane Bret. *Natural Hazards Review, 6*(4), 191–196.

Ewing, B. T., Kruse, J. B., & Thompson, M. A. (2005b). Transmission of employment shocks before and after the Oklahoma city tornado. *Global Environmental Change Part B: Environmental Hazards, 6*(4), 181–188.

Ewing, B. T., Kruse, J. B., & Thompson, M. A. (2009). Twister! Employment responses to the 3 may 1999 Oklahoma City tornado. *Applied Economics, 41,* 691–702.

Felsenstein, D., & Grinberger, A. Y. (2020). Cascading effects of a disaster on the labor market over the medium to long term. *International Journal of Disaster Risk Reduction, 47,.*

Geiger, T., Frieler, K., & Levermann, A. (2016). High-income does not protect against hurricane losses. *Environmental Research Letters, 11*(8),

Groen, J. A., & Polivka, A. E. (2008). The effect of hurricane Katrina on the labor market outcomes of evacuees. *American Economic Review: Papers & Proceedings, 98*(2), 43–48.

Groen, J. A., Kutzbach, M. J., & Polivka, A. E. (2015). *Storms and jobs: The effect of hurricanes on individuals' employment and earnings over the long term.* https://ssrn.com/abstract=2648980.

Guimaraes, P., Hefner, P. L., & Woodward, D. P. (1992). *Wealth and income effects of natural disasters: an econometric analysis of hurricane Hugo.* Working Paper, College of Business Administration, University of South Carolina, College of Business Administration, Columbia, South Carolina.

How, S. M., & Kerr, G. N. (2019). Earthquake impacts on immigrant participation in the Greater Christchurch construction labor market. *Population Research and Policy Review, 38*(2), 241–269.

Jiang, L. (2012). *Innovation research on post-disaster restoration and reconstruction projects management*. Nanjing, China: Nanjing University.

Julie, Z., & Karoly, L. A. (2010). Employment and self-employment in the wake of hurricane Katrina. *Demography, 47*(2), 345–367.

Kaegi, R., Voegelin, A., Sinnet, B., Zuleeg, S., Hagendorfer, H., Burkhardt, M., et al. (2013). The impact of hurricanes on wages and employment: the case of Louisiana. *SSRN Electronic Journal, 45*(9), 3902–3908.

Katayanagi, M., Seto, M., Nakaya, N., Nakamura, T., Tsuchiya, N., Narita, A., et al. (2020). Impact of the Great East Japan earthquake on the employment status and mental health conditions of affected coastal communities. *International Journal of Environmental Research and Public Health, 17*(21), 8130.

Kim, H., & Marcouiller, D. W. (2015). Considering disaster vulnerability and resiliency: The case of hurricane effects on tourism-based economies. *The Annals of Regional Science, 54*(3), 945–971.

Kim, H., Woosnam, K. M., & Marcouiller, W. (2015). Spatial and temporal contours in economic losses from natural disasters: a case study of Florida. *KSCE Journal of Civil Engineering, 19*(3), 457–464.

Kirchberger, M. (2017). Natural disasters and labor markets. *Journal of Development Economics, 125,* 40–58.

Klomp, J., & Valckx, K. (2014). Natural disasters and economic growth: A meta-analysis. *Global Environmental Change, 26,* 183–195.

Kondo, A. (2018). The effects of supply chain disruptions caused by the Great East Japan earthquake on workers. *Japan and the World Economy, 47,* 40–50.

Kugler, A., & Yuksel, M. (2008). *Effects of low-skilled immigration on U.S. natives: Evidence from hurricane Mitch.* Working Paper, Centre for Research and Analysis of Migration Department of Economics, University College London Drayton House, 30 Gordon Street, London.

Lazzaroni, S., & Bergeijk, P. (2014). Natural disasters' impact, factors of resilience and development: A meta-analysis of the macroeconomic literature. *Ecological Economics, 107,* 333–346.

Leiter, A. M., Oberhofer, H., & Raschky, P. A. (2009). Creative disasters? Flooding effects on capital, labour and productivity within European firms. *Environmental Resource Economy, 43,* 333–350.

Li, Z. B. (2007). *Labor economics*. Beijing, China: China Social Science Press.

Liliedahl, E. (2009). *The impact of hurricane Katrina migration on low-wage labor markets.* Washington, DC: Georgetown University.

Martínez, M. J., Martínez, M. J., & Romero-Jarén, R. (2020). How resilient is the labour market against natural disaster? Evaluating the effects from the 2010 earthquake in Chile. *Natural Hazards, 104*(2), 1481–1533.

Masozera, M., Bailey, M., & Kerchner, C. (2007). Distribution of impacts of natural disasters across income groups: A case study of New Orleans. *Ecological Economics, 63*(2–3), 299–306.

Mcintosh, M. F. (2008). Measuring the labor market impacts of hurricane Katrina migration: Evidence from Houston, Texas. *American Economic Review: Papers & Proceedings, 98*(2), 54–57.

Mohan, P. S., Spencer, N., & Strobl, E. (2019). Natural hazard-induced disasters and production efficiency: Moving closer to or further from the frontier? *International Journal of Disaster Risk Science, 10*(2), 166–178.

Mottaleb, K., Mohanty, S., Hoang, H., et al. (2013). The effects of natural disasters on farm household income and expenditures: A study on rice farmers in Bangladesh. *Agricultural Systems, 121*(C), 43–52.

Mueller, V., & Rquisumbing, A. (2011). How resilient are labour markets to natural disasters? The case of the 1998 Bangladesh flood. *Journal of Development Studies, 47*(12), 1954–1971.

Nordhaus, W. (2006) The economics of hurricanes in the United States. http://nber.org/papers/w12813.pdf.

Olsen, A., & Porter, K. (2013). Storm surge to demand surge: Exploratory study of hurricanes, labor wages, and material prices. *Natural Hazards Review, 14*(4), 247–257.

Ouattara, B., & Strobl, E. (2014). Hurricane strikes and local migration in US coastal counties. *Economics Letters, 124,* 17–20.

Porcelli, F., & Trezzi, R. (2019). The impact of earthquakes on economic activity: Evidence from Italy. *Empirical Economics, 56*(4), 1167–1206.

Qin, D. H. (2008). Latest progress on climate change research. *Science & Technology Review, 7,* 3.

Qin, X., & Jiang, Y. X. (2011). The impact of natural disaster on absenteeism, job satisfaction, and job performance of survival employees: An empirical study of the survivors in Wenchuan earthquake. *Research Article, 5*(2), 219–242.

Qin, D. H., & Luo, Y. (2008). Causes of global climate change and change trend in the future. *Impact of Science on Society, 2,* 16–21.

Qin, D. H., & Stocker, T. (2014). Highlights of the IPCC working group I fifth assessment report. *Progressus Inquisitions De Mutatione Climatis, 5301*(10), 1–6.

Sadowski, N. C., & Sutter, D. (2005). Hurricane fatalities and hurricane damages: Are safer hurricanes more damaging? *South Economic Journal, 72,* 422–432.

Shi, P. J. (1996). Theory and practice of disaster study. *Journal of Natural Disasters, 4,* 6–17.

Skidmore, M., & Toya, H. (2002). Do natural disasters promote long-run growth? *Economic Inquiry, 40*(4), 664–687.

Sobel, A. H., Camargo, S. J., Hall, T. M., Lee, C. Y., Tippett, M. K., & Wing, A. A. (2016). Human influence on tropical cyclone intensity. *Science, 353*(6296), 242–246.

Stanley, H., & Jarrell, S. (1989). Meta-regression analysis: A quantitative method of literature survey. *Journal of Economic Surveys, 3*(2), 161–170.

Strobl, E., & Walsh, F. (2009). The re-building effect of hurricanes: Evidence from employment in the US construction industry. *Economics Bulletin, 29*(4), 3059–3066.

Warr, P., & Aung, L. L. (2019). Poverty and inequality impact of a natural disaster: Myanmar's 2008 cyclone Nargis. *World Development, 122,* 446–461.

Wu, J. D., Li, N., Zhou, Y., Gu, X. T., & Hao, X. L. (2013). Disaster recovery measurement framework: An application case of disaster recovery after hurricane Katrina. *Journal of Natural Disasters, 4,* 58–64.

Yang, Y. Y. (2001). Administrative division of labor market. *Review of Economic Research, 27,* 30–37.

Ye, M., Wu, J., Liu, W., He, X., & Wang, C. (2020). Dependence of tropical cyclone damage on maximum wind speed and socioeconomic factors. *Environmental Research Letters, 15*(9),

Zander, K. K., Wilson, T., & Garnett, S. T. (2020) Understanding the role of natural hazards in internal labour mobility in Australia. *Weather and Climate Extremes* 100261.

Zheng, Y. (2013). Environmental migration: Concepts, theories and policy implications. *China Population, Resources and Environment, 4,* 96–103.

# Chapter 6
# Impacts of Ttyphoons on Local Labor Markets Based on GDD: An Empirical Study of Guangdong Province, China

**Abstract** What impacts do typhoons have on local labor markets? Few empirical researches have been conducted in China. By collecting the data of 23 quarters of Guangdong province from 2009 to 2014 and using generalized difference-in-difference (abbreviated GDD), this paper analyzes the impacts of typhoons on labor markets from the perspectives of general effect, regional effect, intensity effect and time effect respectively. In addition, a comparative analysis is carried out between this study and similar studies of developed countries. The results show that: (1) though the effects of typhoons on employment are insignificant, high-strength typhoons can cause a 5.15% decline in per capita labor remuneration; (2) the effects of typhoons on labor remuneration, with cyclical characteristics, circle every four quarters. The negative impacts in the current quarter are followed by two quarters of positive adjustment and the final quarter of the recovery to pre-disaster levels; (3) the results of this study are different from those of the studies whose subjects are developed countries, which may be caused by the distinctiveness of China's labor market. Finally, conclusions and corresponding suggestions are presented.

**Keywords** GDD · Typhoon disasters · Labor market

## 6.1 Introduction

In 2015, as the twenty-first United Nations Climate Change Conference took place in Paris, France, climate change and its effects aroused ongoing heated discussions. In its fifth assessment report, IPCC points out that due to global warming, natural disasters happen more intensely and frequently. Under the extensive impact of global warming, there is an apparent global rise in the number of natural disasters such as landslides and extreme rainfall, at the same time they incur catastrophic and significant economic and human losses (Haque et al. 2019). The destruction of human socio-economic system caused by natural disasters is manifold, including casualties, epidemic spreading, infrastructure and material capital directly damaged, decreasing residents' income and consumption capacity, and slowing-down human capital accumulation (Baez and Sontos 2008). Worldwide, China is one of the countries that are

 
X. Wu and J. Guo, *Economic Impacts and Emergency Management of Disasters in China*,
https://doi.org/10.1007/978-981-16-1319-7_6

affected by natural disasters in the most serious way. Qin (2008a), Qin and Luo (2008) believe that in the context of global warming, the frequency and intensity of typhoons will be further increased. Luo and Kinugasa (2020) investigated the short- and long-term effects of the 2008 Sichuan earthquake on saving behavior. The result found that the quake had no discernible long-run influence on the saving propensity of the affected population at the aggregate level. Among several major natural disasters concerned by international community and the United Nations major, tropical cyclone (typhoon) causes destruction and losses only after flood disasters, due to such features as high frequency and wide coverage (Shi 1996). To summarize, typhoons are an environmental threat that mainly affects coastal regions among the world. Based on previous cases, the direct losses caused by typhoon disasters on natural and socioeconomic factors are difficult to be measured and evaluated (Zhang et al. 2020). The massive energy of a mature typhoon can be imagined, as it is equivalent to the energy released by hundreds of thousands of Hiroshima atomic bombs. For instance, No. 14 strong tropical storm "Rananim" of 2014 made landfall on Taizhou, Zhejiang, released within 96 h the energy of about half a million Hiroshima atomic bombs,[1] and caused a lot of human and material losses. In August 2015, typhoon "Soudelor" hit 33 cities and 191 counties (cities, districts) of 5 provinces in China's coastal areas, with 5,655,000 people affected, 26 deaths and direct economic losses as much as 13.77 billion Yuan.[2] The existing cases showed that the typhoon had a large area of influence and was exceptionally destructive, so the methods of prevention and risk assessment on natural disasters have started to increase. For example, Ye et al. (2020) used the technique relies on GIS (Geographic Information System) and RS(Remote Sensing) technology to simulate typical natural disaster risk scenarios in the scenic area in the future, and established the corresponding relationship between the intensity of specific hazards and disaster risk scenarios to prevent potential natural disasters.

Due to great destructiveness and negative impacts, the socio-economic effects of typhoon disasters have become an international research focus, and quite a few research results have been achieved based on different methods. In recent years, the methods on the research of the socio-economic effects caused by typhoons are increasing, such as a multi-attribute decision-making method for the decision-making problems with attributes and sub-attribute based on information entropy and the evaluation based on distance from average solution (Tan and Zhang 2020). According to the classification method of Xiao (2011), current relevant literature can be divided into two categories: input–output and quantitative regression analysis, from the perspective of research methods.

Based on the great compatibility of Input–output techniques, there are many factors can be added to improve the model to evaluate the related socio-economic issues such as the emission intensity and total emission of industries (Lirong et al. 2020). Input–output techniques can be divided into the input–output table model and CGE model. Input–output model analyzes the comprehensive effects caused by

[1]https://www.safehoo.com/Live/Alert/Typhoon/201210/287243.shtml.

[2]https://www.weather.com.cn/zt/tqzt/368537.shtmls.

disasters based on "input–output table", which is proposed by Leontief, an American economist. For instance, Ning Ai and Polenske (2008) improved the input–output techniques and analyzed the socio-economic impacts of Beijing's sandstorms in 2000. Results showed that the indirect effects of the sandstorms are much higher than direct ones. Akhtar and Santos (2013), by applying the dynamic inoperational input–output model (DIIM) proposed by Haimes et al. (2005), evaluated the economic losses caused by the hurricane to various economic sectors and made a sequence according to the sensitivity of industries. Long et al. (2020) found that due to the lack of multi-regional input–output tables for most cities in research, there is a comprehensive application of single regional input–output tables, so they highlighted the difference of carbon footprint accounting between these two types of input–output tables with the Data for Tokyo, Japan. Zhai et al. (2019) take Guangdong, China, as a particular case to study. They use the input–output analysis to edit the physical input–output table through the embodied energy element intensity to elucidate the effect of energy classification differences on the energy metabolism system. At the same time, they introduced the concepts of "urban metabolism", and viewed sectors and energy flows as nodes and paths in a network model. Wu and Xu (2014) took Jiangsu's typhoon disasters in 2008 as an example. They evaluated the effects of typhoons on labor remuneration, national income and employment in Jiangsu Province in 2008, with the application of input–output model and multiplier principle. Similar studies have also been conducted by Rose et al. (2007), Lin et al. (2012), In den Bäumen (2015).

The evaluation of natural disasters can be divided into various classes. Ha (2020) proposed that qualitative content analysis has been utilized as the principal methodology when evaluating the relationships between the natural disasters and other objects such as the role of ecosystems in the field of natural disaster management. There are many kinds of literature about the loss assessment of natural disasters by statistical and quantitative methods. For example, Asadul et al. (2020) investigated how natural disasters impact risk-sharing behaviours, showing that disaster-affected individuals were less likely to defect from risk-sharing groups, no matter what the level of ex-ante commitment was. Crawford et al. (2020) made empirical assessments on tornado damage in a sample area of Tuscaloosa, Alabama. They used satellite imagery collected at numerous time steps after the tornado, and the result showed that combining publicly available imagery and deep learning approaches could make more robust empirical models that would aid in identifying physically vulnerable locations within communities and cause more risk-informed decision-making. Based on percentile rankings, Khan et al. (2020) investigated the damages and population influenced by natural disasters. They analyzed the effect on the economy, per capita, fiscal balance, and foreign direct investment. Their purpose was to seek better financial decisions for the policymakers, to attract FDI inflows and preparedness after natural disasters. Bănică et al. (2020) developed a risk-disaster-opportunity framework for a territorial system and analyzed the socio-economic impacts of natural shocks from a resilience perspective. They concluded that whether natural disasters necessarily lead to a structural deprivation of the affected area depends on the effectiveness of public management of natural disaster phenomena. Skidmore and Toya

(2002) studied the long-term relationship between natural disasters and capital accumulation, total factor productivity and economic growth and found out that natural disasters have promoted economic growth. Dalbyu and Katrin (2020) studied the effect of a natural disaster on neighborhood poverty rate and its different impact according to neighborhood socioeconomic traits, indicating that natural disasters cause a shift in the pattern of the neighborhood poverty rate trajectory and that disasters' effects on neighborhood poverty rates differ across neighborhoods. In particular, natural disasters impacted the poverty rates of low-income neighborhoods most greatly. Attary et al. (2020) replicated the damage from a tornado that devastated the community in 2011 and examined the costliness of delay by linking an economic model of the Joplin, Missouri economy to a civil engineering model. The result showed that delaying financial assistance could have significant, irretrievable adverse outcomes in the short run. As for typhoons and tornado, Ewing et al. (2009) analyzed the total-employment changes of eight industrial sectors in Oklahoma City before and after the tornado on May 3rd, 1999 and believed that after the tornado, the reconstruction of commercial and residential areas and infrastructure stimulated labor market and increased the average employment rate. Zissimopoulos and Karoly (2010) found that a year after Hurricane Katrina, there appeared in Louisiana and Mississippi relatively higher self-employment rate, and that self-employment is an essential factor in the post-disaster recovery. Rodríguez-Oreggia (2013) studied the impacts of hurricane on the income of workers with different education level by using microdata from 32 regions of Mexico and pointed out that the hurricane had a positive effect on the wages of low-education formal workers. Still, the impact of hurricane intensity was uncertain. Ouattara and Strobl (2014) studied the effect of hurricanes on the migration of coastal cities of the United States by using vector autoregression model and found that in the wake of hurricanes the outward migration rate of the wealthy increased, but inward migration rate had no significant changes. González et al. (2020) found that being exposed to natural disasters during the first year of life would significantly reduce the number of years of schooling achieved in 0.03 years and increased the opportunities of being unemployed and living in a multidimensionally poor household when adult. Also, Mcintosh (2008), Groen and Polivka (2008), Olsen and Porter (2013), Asad (2015), Hamilton et al. (2016) and so on also did related researches.

From the perspective of research trends, the researches on the impacts of disasters have gradually transferred from economic property and other material capital to such human capital as labor markets and physical and mental health. Most researches of developed countries found that hurricane (typhoon) disasters could make labor flee the area, so employing units had no choice but to increase wages to attract enough labor. Besides, the impact of typhoons on workers of different income groups also varies, for the reason that there are differences in human capital among the workers. Hurricane (typhoon) disasters had a negative impact on the employment rate, but a positive one on wages. For instance, Belasen and Polachek (2007) took the effects of the hurricane in Florida as an example and believed that changes could take place in the industrial structure of the labor markets of hurricane-stricken areas. High-paid workers moved to relatively safe areas, and most of those who stay in disaster areas were low-paid workers, and thus the employment rate there fell by 4.76% while wages grew by 4.35%.

In recent years, there are more and more studies on the impact of disasters on the labor market. Felsenstein and Grinberger (2020) put forward an economic definition of cascading effects of a disaster on the labor market over the medium to long term. They found that a strong cascading impact in the labor market lied on severe functional change in the physical environment such as land-use change. When considering the labor market in the aftermath of a disaster, there were two opposite perspectives. The first imagined a production sector which is non-tradeable and a labor market with total mobility, and the second imagined a production sector which is fully tradeable and a labor market which is entirely immobile. In the case of a disaster, outcomes are very different (Grinberger and Samuels 2018). Kirchberger (2017) combined data from the Indonesia Family Life Survey, the DesInventar database, the U.S. Geological Survey, and district-level employment indicators to explore how a large earthquake in Indonesia affected labor market outcomes. The result found that labor shifted out of the agricultural sector into the construction sector, raising the marginal product of labor in agriculture.

However, few researches on the impacts of natural disasters on labor market have been conducted, especially in China. Is there a similar phenomenon in China, a developing country? In light of this, by using GDD and taking 21 prefecture-level cities of Guangdong Province as basic research units, this paper evaluates the impacts of typhoon disasters on the employment and wages of labor markets during 23 quarters from 2009 to 2014 from four effects of typhoons– general effect, regional effect, intensity effect and time effect, and compares itself with current similar studies of developed countries, so as to analyze the reasons behind the phenomenon and try to get some new inspirations.

## 6.2 Methods, Data and Variable Descriptions

### *6.2.1 Methods*

Difference-in-difference, emerging in the 1980s, is usually used to study the effects of some external interventions such as the implementation of a policy or a project on research objects. There are also many domestic and foreign scholars introducing difference-in-difference method into disaster economics. For instance, Belasen and Polachek (2007) conducted studies about the effects of the hurricanes on the local labor market, Xiao (2011) about those of the flood disaster in the American Midwest in 1993 on the local economy and Zhang et al. (2015) about those of Wenchuan-earthquake reconstruction policy on economy. The prominent characteristic of this method is regarding an external intervention or event as a natural experiment and making two dimensions of analysis to examine the effects of an external intervention. From the longitudinal view, the differences between the observed objects before and after an external intervention are measured; from the horizontal view, the differences between experimental group and control group differences before and after an external intervention are measured, so as to exclude the impacts of macro-environment-system differences and to isolate the net impacts of the external intervention. In addition, assuming that external interventions affect two groups (experimental group and control group) at the same time, this method eliminates the influence of external interventions, thus solving the problem of endogeneity.

Of course, there are also difficulties in difference-in-difference, one is how to select control groups, as control groups may also be affected to a certain extent by natural experiments and unobservable individual heterogeneity may have an impact on dependent variables, causing deviation in estimated results; the other is that representative and general results can hardly be obtained based on a single natural experiment (Belasen and Polachek 2007). By referring to generalized difference-in-difference (abbreviated GDD)[3] proposed by the Belasen and Polachek (2008), this paper controls the impacts of unobserved individual heterogeneity on dependent variables through panel data of samples (Chen and Wu 2015), selects several groups of typhoon disasters as external interventions, or makes multiple randomized natural experiments to measure the effects of typhoon disasters on labor markets, thus making a random selection of control groups and overcoming the difficulties in the process of difference-in-difference. In addition, as typhoon-disaster variables adopted in the paper (evaluating to 1 if typhoon happens, otherwise, to 0) belong to typical exogenous variables, the endogeneity brought by the typhoons as an independent variable can be avoided and the interaction between typhoons and with the variables in labor markets can be effectively controlled. Therefore, GDD can objectively identify the impacts of typhoon disasters on labor markets.

Assuming that Y is the observed variable of experimental group T (hit by typhoons) and control group $T^C$ (not hit by typhoons), namely, the total amount of unit employment and per capital labor remuneration, $E[Y_{i,k}|T^C]$ represents the expected value of Region i at the point of k when it is not attacked by typhoons while $E[Y_{i,k}|T]$ represents the value when it is attacked by typhoons, and the net impact of external interventions $\delta$ can be expressed as:

$$\delta = E\left[Y_{i,k}|T\right] - E\left[Y_{i,k}|T^C\right] = \delta_i + \delta_k \tag{6.1}$$

In the model, $\delta_i$ represents the differences between the observed variables of experimental group and control group in the horizontal dimension, while $\delta_k$ in the longitudinal dimension.

[3]The main differences between GDD and difference-in-difference are presented as below: (1) the two have different number of natural experiments—difference-in-difference has only one experiment, while GDD many; (2) the two have different ways of expressing the differences in the longitudinal dimension—difference-in-difference measures through dummy variables (evaluating to 1 after natural experiments and to 0 before) (Chen and Wu 2015), while GDD through differentials, which are the variations between the value before and after the natural experiments (Belasen et al. 2007).

### 6.2.2 Data

To study the impacts of natural disasters on the local labor market needs to select appropriate types of natural disasters in the first place. Sui and Tang (2012) pointed out that different natural disasters had different attributes and effects, which could not be added up. If one of the natural disasters needs to be taken as an example, it needs to ensure that in the larger region, there is no great difference in the frequency of occurrence of the disaster in each sub region, otherwise the comparability might be lost. Typhoon is an appropriate choice. First, typhoons occur quite frequently and commonly each year, thus meeting the requirements of GDD that random natural experiments need to be done many times. Second, Wei and Tang (2011) believed that the path of typhoons had strong randomness, so in the long run external influences on different cities and counties are roughly the same. This can improve the matching degree between experimental group and control group in GDD. Third, with wide coverage, typhoons can affect several areas simultaneously, thus providing more experimental groups in GDD to ensure the reliability of experimental results. Fourth, given the strong destructiveness of typhoons, it is of good practical significance to conduct studies on the impacts of typhoon disasters.

The disastrous weather events of typhoons come from the EM-DAT database, which is built and maintained by the Center for Research on Epidemiology of Disaster (CRED) of Katholieke Universiteit Leuven of Belgium. The records in EM-DAT database must meet the following conditions: (1) 10 or more deaths have been reported; (2) 100 or more people have been reported affected, wounded or homeless; (3) disaster-stricken areas have declared a state of emergency; (4) a call for international assistance. From the EM-DAT database 15 disastrous weather events of typhoons have been selected that hit Guangdong from 2009 to 2014. According to the national standard classification of tropical cyclones (GBT19201-2006) issued by China Meteorological Administration, tropical cyclones are divided into the following six levels: (1) super typhoon: the maximum wind speed of the ground near the center reaches more than 51.0 m/s (equivalent to wind grade 16 or above); (2) severe typhoon: the maximum wind speed of the ground near the center reaches 41.5–50.9 m/s (equivalent to wind grade 14–15); (3) typhoon: the maximum wind speed of the ground near the center reaches 32.7–41.4 m/s (equivalent to wind grade 12–13); (4) severe tropical storm: the maximum wind speed of the ground near the center reaches 24.5–32.6 m/s (equivalent to wind grade 10–11); (5) tropical storm: the maximum wind speed of the ground near the center reaches 17.2–24.4 m/s (equivalent to wind grade 8–9); (6) tropical depression: the maximum wind speed of the ground near the center reaches 10.8–17.1 m/s (equivalent to wind grade 6–7). The first three grades can be categorized as high-intensity typhoons, while the later three as low-intensity typhoons. Details are shown in Table 6.1.

Besides, the reason why research area is restricted to Guangdong Province is based on the following considerations: first, from the point of view of research methods, GDD has a prerequisite for the estimation the parameters (Zhang et al. 2015): were there no typhoon disasters, the economic growth of treatment group and control group

**Table 6.1** Descriptions of Typhoons affecting Guangdong during 2009–2014

| Landing time | Name of Typhoon | Affected areas | Level of tropical cyclones | Intensity | Death toll | Economic loss (million dollars) |
|---|---|---|---|---|---|---|
| 2009.8.1 | Goni | Zhanjiang | STS | L | 9 | 70 |
| 2009.9.14 | Koppu | Jiangmen, Yangjiang | TY | H | 13 | 295.001 |
| 2009.10.13 | Parma | Zhanjiang | TS | L | 3 | 35 |
| 2010.9.20 | Fanapi | Yunfu, Meizhou, Zhaoqin, Yangjiang, Shanwei, Maoming, Chaozhou, Zhanjiang | STY | H | 75 | 298.285 |
| 2011.6.19 | Haima | Zhanjiang, Yangjiang, Zhuhai | TS | L | 0 | 0 |
| 2012.7.24 | Vicente | Shenzhen, Zhuhai, Foshan, HeYuan, Meizhou, Jiangmen, Zhongshan, Yangjiang, Shanwei, Maoming, Zhaoqing, Jieyang, Yunfu | TY | H | 8 | 329 |
| 2012.8.17 | Kai-tak | Zhanjiang | TY | H | 2 | 262 |
| 2012.10.28 | Son-Tinh | Zhanjiang | STS | L | 1 | 197 |
| 2013.7.14 | Soulik | Zhanjiang | STY | H | 9 | 460 |
| 2013.8.15 | Utor | Zhanjiang, Maoming, Yangjiang | STY | H | 88 | 2120 |
| 2013.9.22 | Usagi | Shantou, HeYuan, Meizhou, Shanwei, Chaozhou, Jieyang | STY | H | 20 | 0 |
| 2013.9.30 | Wutip | Zhanjiang, Maoming | TS | L | 74 | 0 |

(continued)

**Table 6.1** (continued)

| Landing time | Name of Typhoon | Affected areas | Level of tropical cyclones | Intensity | Death toll | Economic loss (million dollars) |
|---|---|---|---|---|---|---|
| 2014.6.14 | Hagibis | Shantou, Shanwei | TS | L | 0 | 131 |
| 2014.7.18 | Rammasun | Yangjiang, Maoming, Zhanjiang | Super TY | H | 71 | 4232.973 |
| 2014.9.10 | Kalmaegi | Zhanjiang, Maoming | STY | H | 9 | 2900 |

*Note* Affected municipal areas come from Baidu Encyclopedia, levels of tropical cyclones from Information Center for Tropical Cyclones of China Meteorological Administration, death toll and economic loss from EM-DAT

would have the same average change, or the time change-path of the two would be parallel. This is a strong assumption, so when it fails, the estimated coefficient of difference-in-difference may be biased. To select cities in the same province can basically satisfy the hypothesis. In addition, under the jurisdiction of Guangdong Province are 21 prefecture-level cities: Guangzhou, Shaoguan, Shenzhen, Zhuhai, Shantou, Foshan, Jiangmen, Zhanjiang, Maomen, Zhaoqing, Huizhou, Meizhou, Shanwei, HeYuan, Yangjiang, QingYuan, Dongguan, Zhongshan, Chaozhou, Jieyang and Yunfu, thus providing quite a few basic research units.

Second, seen from the situation of disasters, Guangdong Province is located at a special geographical position subjected to the threat of typhoons, with low latitudes and marked monsoon climate, facing South China Sea on the south and the Pacific on the East and having the coastline up to 8500 km which accounts for more than one third of the total of the country. According to incomplete statistics, from 1985 to 2006, typhoon disasters of Guangdong have caused 667 deaths, 20,873 injuries, 1,699,150 collapsed buildings and the economic loss as much as 250 billion Yuan. In the horizontal comparison, almost each disaster indicator of Guangdong ranks highest in the country, so the place can be considered as the province that has been most affected by the typhoon disasters in China (Den 2011).

Three, seen from the social conditions, Guangdong province, adjacent to Hongkong and Macao, has distinct location advantages and is one of China's economically developed coastal provinces. Each year Guangdong attracts a wealth of labor resources that have the following characteristics: first, the majorities are migrant workers. According to the results of the sixth national census in 2010, Guangdong is the province with the largest inflow of population (Zhang 2005); second, with fast economic development and relatively developed labor market, Guangdong is a typical developed region and a development benchmark for relatively backward provinces. Therefore, the study on the impacts of natural disasters on Guangdong's employment and labor remuneration has great demonstrative significance.

Due to data availability, the quarterly data of unit employment and per capita remuneration of 21 prefecture-level cities of Guangdong from the first quarter of 2009 to the third quarter of 2014 have been selected to reflect the changes in the labor market. The statistical scope of labor forces includes state-owned units, urban collective-owned units, joint ventures, joint-stock economy, foreign investment economy and the economy invested by Hong Kong, Macao and Taiwan, etc. The descriptive results of data are shown in Table 6.2.

Seen from the table above, from 2009 to 2014, Guangdong Province was hit by 15 severe typhoons. Zhanjiang is the city that suffered typhoon invasions most frequently, 11 times; Shaoguan, QingYuan, Huizhou, Guangzhou, Dongguan were not attacked; the number of prefecture-level cities hit by typhoons reached 11. During the 23 quarters from 2009 to 2014, Shenzhen had the most employment, reaching

**Table 6.2** Quarterly data of unit employment and per capita remuneration of the cities in Guangdong during 2009–2014

| | Unit employment (million persons) | | | Per capita remuneration (Yuan) | | |
|---|---|---|---|---|---|---|
| | Maximum | Minimum | Mean | Maximum | Minimum | Mean |
| Chaozhou | 20.09 | 11.78 | 13.55 | 10,383.24 | 5297.11 | 7107.14 |
| Dongguan | 243.86 | 21.29 | 58.78 | 16,888.33 | 1275.67 | 9550.53 |
| Foshan | 168.63 | 52.43 | 75.22 | 12,716.34 | 3954.63 | 8826.70 |
| Guangzhou | 366.39 | 219.77 | 284.97 | 16,780.07 | 11,159.49 | 13,153.12 |
| HeYuan | 25.36 | 23.13 | 24.27 | 12,891.77 | 5407.38 | 7871.83 |
| Huizhou | 92.80 | 70.87 | 83.36 | 12,121.49 | 5685.06 | 8349.14 |
| Jiangmen | 60.33 | 34.71 | 48.03 | 9437.70 | 5563.57 | 6848.64 |
| Jieyang | 37.74 | 20.52 | 23.79 | 8873.78 | 4410.33 | 6206.42 |
| Maoming | 43.59 | 29.61 | 34.64 | 8764.91 | 5147.35 | 6929.25 |
| Meizhou | 29.38 | 22.49 | 24.36 | 10,272.33 | 5002.22 | 7410.66 |
| QingYuan | 31.07 | 24.30 | 27.46 | 11,852.57 | 6099.43 | 8373.55 |
| Shantou | 52.48 | 30.74 | 38.34 | 8427.53 | 5605.02 | 6960.66 |
| Shanwei | 23.23 | 13.24 | 16.15 | 12,906.81 | 3950.15 | 7119.44 |
| Shaoguan | 37.98 | 29.67 | 32.36 | 11,189.00 | 6193.13 | 8350.32 |
| Shenzhen | 462.31 | 200.94 | 278.95 | 17,341.22 | 8158.15 | 12,078.78 |
| Yangjiang | 23.33 | 16.67 | 18.77 | 10,710.24 | 4512.41 | 6913.63 |
| Yunfu | 21.52 | 16.16 | 17.78 | 8741.08 | 5024.75 | 7086.26 |
| Zhanjiang | 49.66 | 24.24 | 41.68 | 12,047.24 | 5356.49 | 7520.97 |
| Zhaoqing | 40.77 | 27.06 | 31.07 | 12,347.61 | 3946.95 | 8005.26 |
| Zhongshan | 86.01 | 23.40 | 37.94 | 14,331.60 | 3903.16 | 9072.80 |
| Zhuhai | 73.29 | 52.08 | 62.01 | 15,189.64 | 6954.69 | 9427.16 |

*Note* Data come from Statistical Information Network of Guangdong Province. Among the data, per capita remuneration is obtained by dividing total remuneration and the number of employees and goes through price deflator processing, with 2009 as the base period

4,623,100 while Chaozhou had the least, 200,900; Guangzhou had the most average employment at 2,849,700 while Chaozhou had the least, 135,500; from per capita remuneration per quarter, Guangzhou's average topped the list, reaching 13,153.12 Yuan while Yangjiang's average has the minimum, 6913.63 Yuan.

### 6.2.3 *Variable Descriptions*

To study the relationship between typhoon disasters and Guangdong's employment and labor remuneration, a regression model has been established with GDD. Based on the previous studies on labor markets (like Belasen and Polachek 2007, 2008; Groen and Polivka 2008; Ewing et al. 2009, etc.) and taking into account data availability, the following variables have been selected as the control varibales of regression from the economic, seasonal and policy factors affecting labor markets.

Economic factors. The employment of labor markets is closely related to economic development. With economic growth, investment, production and consumption will increase accordingly, thus creating more employment opportunities and stimulating rising employment rate, otherwise it will lead to a decline in employment rate. For instance, Zhang (2009) believed that gross domestic product (GDP) is the preferred measure of economic development. Therefore, GDP[4] is chosen as a control variable, the data of which come from Statistical Information Network of Guangdong. In order to eliminate the impacts of such price factors as inflation, GDP data goes through the price deflator processing, with 2009 as the base period.

Seasonal factor. The supply and demand of labor can be affected by seasonal variations, especially in Guangdong Province that is rich in migrant labor resources. In the new year and the Spring Festival of the first quarter, a large number of labor return led to a substantial reduction in the number of labor. Therefore, seasonal dummy variables are applied to exclude the impacts of seasonal labor return.

Policy factor. The labor market of our country, different from common commodity markets, is greatly influenced by the country's intervention. For example, as an important method adopted by the government to the protect the rights and interests and labors, minimum wage standard plays a significant role in the relationship of labor supply and demand objectively. Ma et al. (2012) believed that every 10% increase in the minimum wage gave rise to a decline about 0.6% in the employment of manufacturing enterprises. However, what this paper adopts are quarterly data, so in different quarters within a year of the minimum wage standard basically remained unchanged. In other words, the minimum wage standard for each area after the occurrence of every typhoon disaster was the same as before, and the longitudinal-dimension change value of GDD is 0, so policy variables are not included in the empirical analysis.

[4]Since there is no data of cities' quarterly GDP per capita and the only data available is GDP, this paper adopted cities' quarterly GDP.

## 6.3 Empirical Analysis

According to the analysis above, the unit employment and per capita remuneration of the cities of Guangdong Province are selected as dependent variables, typhoon disasters as an independent variable, economic factor (GDP) and seasonal factor (seasonal dummy variable) as control variables, and regression analysis is carried out based on the establishment of panel model. Specific models are shown as below:

$$\begin{aligned} Q_{it} &= \alpha_{10} + \alpha_{11} TC_{it} + \alpha_{12} GDP_{it} \\ &\quad + \alpha_{13} S_{it} + \nu_{it}, (i = 1, 2, \ldots, 21; t = 1, 2, \ldots, 23) \end{aligned} \tag{6.2}$$

$$\begin{aligned} PW_{it} &= \alpha_{20} + \alpha_{21} TC_{it} + \alpha_{22} GDP_{it} \\ &\quad + \alpha_{23} S_{it} + \upsilon_{it}, (i = 1, 2, \ldots, 21; t = 1, 2, \ldots, 23) \end{aligned} \tag{6.3}$$

In the models, $Q_{it}$ represents the unit employment[5] of region i in the period t; $PW_{it}$ the per capita remuneration of region i in the period t; $TC_{it}$ the dummy variable of typhoon, whose value is 1 when it is in experimental group where region i in the period t is hit by typhoons and 0 when it is in control group free from typhoons; $GDP_{it}$ the gross product of region i in the period t; $S_{it}$ the seasonal dummy variable, whose value is 1 when period t is the first quarter in region i and 0 when it is other quarters; $\alpha_{mn}$ (m = 1,2; n = 0,1,2,3) coefficient of regression and both $\nu_{it}$ and $\upsilon_{it}$ are error terms.

In order to avoid the pseudo regression generated by data instability, ADF method has been applied to test data stability for all the variables to enter the model and shown that all the variables are stable (specific results omitted and the same below). Based on the Models (6.2) and (6.3) above, the effects of Typhoon on the labor market are calculated from four aspects: general effect, regional effect, intensity effect and time effect.

### 6.3.1 General Effect of Typhoons on Labor Market

Referring to the principle of GDD proposed by Belasen and Polachek (2008), as the direct impacts of typhoons last for a short time, this paper makes differential analysis of Eqs. (6.2) and (6.3)[6] and obtained the impacts of typhoons on unit employment and per capita remuneration. In addition, to avoid heteroscedasticity and multicollinearity

[5]The unit employment refers to the total number of the employed who work in state-owned units, urban collective-owned units, joint ventures, joint-stock economy, foreign investment economy and the economy invested by Hong Kong, Macao and Taiwan, etc.

[6]Other equations in this paper are differential treatment of Eqs. (6.2) and (6.3) in order to eliminate the instability of the data (Belasen et al. 2008).

in the process of regression analysis, continuous variables go through log processing and the results are presented as below:

$$\Delta \ln Q_{it} = \alpha_{10} + \alpha_{11}\Delta TC_{it} + \alpha_{12}\ln GDP_{it} + \alpha_{13}\Delta S_{it} + v_{it}, (i = 1, 2, \ldots, 21; t = 1, 2, \ldots, 23) \quad (6.4)$$

$$\Delta \ln PW_{it} = \alpha_{20} + \alpha_{21}\Delta TC_{it} + \alpha_{22}\ln GDP_{it} + \alpha_{23}\Delta S_{it} + v_{it}, (i = 1, 2, \ldots, 21; t = 1, 2, \ldots, 23) \quad (6.5)$$

According to F test and Hausman test (specific results omitted and the same below), Models (6.4) and (6.5) select mixed-effect model and fixed effect model respectively. The regression result of column 1 of Table 6.3 shows that the typhoon has no significant effect on local-unit employment, the reason of which may be that China's abundant labor resources can compensate the negative impacts of the typhoon disasters in a timely manner. Especially in Guangdong, a place with relatively developed economy and a large number of migrants, the threat of typhoon disasters is still not enough to cause local labor shortage. On the other hand, as the inflow of labor forces in Guangdong comes basically from underdeveloped areas (Liu 2004), they are willing to assume the risk of typhoon disasters for their survival (Belasen and Polachek 2008). Therefore, the typhoons in Guangdong Province have no significant impacts on the total employment.

The column 3 of Table 6.2 shows that typhoons can lead to a decline in per capita labor remuneration of employees by 5.6%. The labor remuneration of enterprises is composed of basic salary, performance pay, bonus and welfare. Among them, performance pay and bonus mainly depend on the performance of staff. Typhoon damaged plants, high voltage transmission lines, communication lines and other infrastructure, causing widespread blackout or suspension of water supply and paralysis in transportation, power grid and so on. Therefore, enterprises' normal operation is interrupted and staff's effective work time reduced, work performance affected, thereby affecting employees' performance pay and bonus.

### 6.3.2 *Regional Effect of Typhoons on Labor Market*

Typhoon disasters are often accompanied by storm surge, heavy rains, strong winds and other destructive disaster chains. Do series of interference generated by typhoons affect the surrounding areas and result in spillover effects? This paper further divides typhoon variable into $TC_{it}^{D}$, a variable directly affected by the typhoon, and $TC_{it}^{D}$, a variable indirectly affected by typhoon (neighboring areas of typhoon-stricken areas), so as to discuss the regional effects of typhoons on labor markets. The models are shown as follows:

**Table 6.3** Regression results of GDD

| Independent variable | Dependent variable | | | | | | | |
|---|---|---|---|---|---|---|---|---|
| | General effect | | Regional effect | | Intensity effect | | Time effect | |
| | Employment | Per capita remuneration | Employment | Per capita remuneration | Employment | Per capita remuneration | Employment | Per capita remuneration |
| Constant Term | −0.0207** [0.0679] | −1.2940*** [0.0000] | −0.0594** [0.0305] | −1.6020*** [0.0000] | −0.0590** [0.0479] | −1.2984*** [0.0000] | 0.0270*** [0.0000] | −0.0030*** [0.0000] |
| GDP | 0.0062*** [0.0019] | 0.2130*** [0.0000] | 0.0032*** [0.0017] | 0.2638*** [0.0000] | 0.0140** [0.0171] | 0.2137*** [0.0000] | | |
| Seasonal Variable | 0.0028 [0.2152] | −0.0846*** [0.0000] | 0.01563 [0.2177] | −0.0916*** [0.0011] | 0.0156 [0.1756] | −0.0854*** [0.0000] | | |
| Typhoon | −0.0011 [0.7599] | −0.0560***[0.0030] | | | | | 0.0087 [0.5432] | −0.0190*** [0.0000] |
| Direct Impacts of Typhoons | | | 0.0032 [0.7619] | −0.0659* [0.0624] | | | | |
| Indirect Impacts of Typhoons | | | 0.0041 [0.7238] | −0.0516 [0.1624] | | | | |
| High-intensity Typhoons | | | | | 0.0023 [0.8752] | −0.0515*** [0.0000] | | |
| Low-intensity Typhoons | | | | | 0.0074 [0.8160] | −0.0808 [0.1100] | | |
| One-phase Lagged Typhoons | | | | | | | 0.0114 [0.4827] | 0.0423*** [0.0000] |
| Two-phase Lagged Typhoons | | | | | | | −0.0127 [0.3853] | 0.0603*** [0.0000] |
| Number of Observed Value | 462 | 462 | 462 | 462 | 462 | 462 | 420 | 420 |
| $R^2$ | 0.0234 | 0.2945 | 0.0198 | 0.1080 | 0.0322 | 0.2956 | 0.0020 | 0.2186 |

*Note* In the brackets are corresponding P-values, *, **, and *** represent the significant levels of 10%, 5% and 1% respectively

$$\Delta \ln Q_{it} = \alpha_{10} + \alpha_{11}\Delta TC_{it}^{D} + \alpha_{12}\Delta TC_{it}^{I} + \alpha_{13}\ln GDP_{it} + \alpha_{13}\Delta S_{it} + v_{it}, (i = 1, 2, \ldots, 21; t = 1, 2, \ldots 23) \quad (6.6)$$

$$\Delta \ln PW_{it} = \alpha_{20} + \alpha_{21}\Delta TC_{it}^{D} + \alpha_{22}\Delta TC_{it}^{I} + \alpha_{23}\ln GDP_{it} + \alpha_{23}\Delta S_{it} + v_{it}, (i = 1, 2, \ldots, 21; t = 1, 2, \ldots 23) \quad (6.7)$$

In the models, $TC_{it}^{D}$ represents the variable of whether region i in the period of t is directly affected by typhoons; $TC_{it}^{I}$ the variable of whether region i in the period of t is indirectly affected by typhoons (or of whether the neighboring areas of region i is directly affected).

According to F test and Hausman test, Models (6.6) and (6.7) are consistent with the models above. The results in the columns of Table 6.3 that describe regional effects show that in the regions either directly or indirectly affected by typhoons, the total employment is not affected, but the per capita labor remuneration in directly affected areas has fallen by 6.59%. Besides, no effects have been found on the labor remuneration of neighboring areas; in other words, spillover effects of typhoons do no exist.

### 6.3.3 Intensity Effect of Typhoons on Labor Market

Skidmore and Toya (2002) believed that only high-intensity disasters had impacts on economy. Is this true concerning Guangdong's typhoon disasters? Therefore, typhoon variable is further divided into high-intensity typhoons and low-intensity typhoons, so the impacts of typhoons of different intensity will be discussed. The models are shown as below:

$$\Delta \ln Q_{it} = \alpha_{10} + \alpha_{11}\Delta HTC_{it} + \alpha_{12}\Delta LTC_{it} + \alpha_{13}\ln GDP_{it} + \alpha_{13}\Delta S_{it} + v_{it}, (i = 1, 2, \ldots, 21; t = 1, 2, \ldots, 23) \quad (6.8)$$

$$\Delta \ln PW_{it} = \alpha_{20} + \alpha_{21}\Delta HTC_{it} + \alpha_{22}\Delta LTC_{it} + \alpha_{23}\ln GDP_{it} + \alpha_{23}\Delta S_{it} + v_{it}, (i = 1, 2, \ldots, 21; t = 1, 2, \ldots, 23) \quad (6.9)$$

In the models, $HTC_{it}$ represents the variable of whether region i in the period of t is affected by high-intensity typhoons; $LTC_{it}$ the variable of whether region i in the period of t is affected by low-intensity typhoons.

Likewise, models are selected according to the results of F test and Hausman test. The regression results in the columns of Table 6.3 that describe intensity effects show that either high-intensity or low-intensity typhoons have no impacts on total employment. Though high-intensity typhoons lead to a decline in per capita labor remuneration by 5.15%, low-intensity typhoons have no impacts on remuneration.

The reason may be that the small destructiveness of low-intensity typhoons is not enough to affect normal order of production, nor can it have any negative impacts on labor remuneration.

### 6.3.4 Time Effect of Typhoons on Labor Market

The United Nations International Strategy for Disaster Reduction (UN/ISDR 2004) points out that in the face of the pressure of weather and other natural disasters, restoring force is an important factor in the disaster prevention and mitigation, the vulnerability reduction and the sustainable development of both nature and human society, which is worthy of further studies. In 1984, Pimm (1984) proposed that restoring force, the characteristic of the system to resist disturbance, can be measured by the speed or the time of the recovery to the original equilibrium state when the system is disturbed.[7] So, typhoon lagged variables are introduced—$TC_{it-1}$ and $TC_{it-2}$, which represent the one-phase and the two-phased lagged variables of region i in the period of t respectively. Models (6.10) and (6.11) are established to analyze the recovery time of the labor market after disasters, so as to measure the restoring force of Guangdong's labor market hit by typhoon disasters.

$$\begin{aligned}\Delta \ln Q_{it} &= \alpha_{10} + \alpha_{11}\Delta TC_{it} + \alpha_{12}\Delta TC_{it-1} \\ &\quad + \alpha_{13}\Delta TC_{it-2} + v_{it}, (i = 1, 2, \ldots, 21; t = 1, 2, \ldots, 23)\end{aligned} \quad (6.10)$$

$$\begin{aligned}\Delta \ln PW_{it} &= \alpha_{20} + \alpha_{21}\Delta TC_{it} + \alpha_{22}\Delta TC_{it-1} \\ &\quad + \alpha_{23}\Delta TC_{it-2} + v_{it}, (i = 1, 2, \ldots, 21; t = 1, 2, \ldots, 23)\end{aligned} \quad (6.11)$$

After the regression of the equation above (the selection of regression model according to F test and Hausman test), the time-effect column of Table 6.3 shows that typhoons have no significant impacts on total employment, which is consistent with the results obtained by the models of general effect, regional effect and intensity effect. However, typhoons have caused a decline in labor remuneration of employees by 1.85% in the quarter t, a rise by 4.23% in the quarter t + 1, and another rise by 6.03% in the quarter t + 2. Then, what effects will the typhoon in the period of t + 3 have on per capita remuneration? When three-phase lagged variable $TC_{it-3}$ is further introduced into Model (6.11), it is found that its coefficient of influence on per capita remuneration is 0.006, but it fails to pass T test (t-Statistic = 0.178, Prob. = 0.859). Therefore, it is concluded that the typhoon in the period of t + 3 cannot have a significant impact on per capita remuneration. In that period, per capita remuneration returns to normal levels. In brief, the delayed negative effects of

[7]The best lagged phase of typhoon variables is 2, accoring to Akaike Information Criterion (AIC) and Schwarz Criterion (SC).

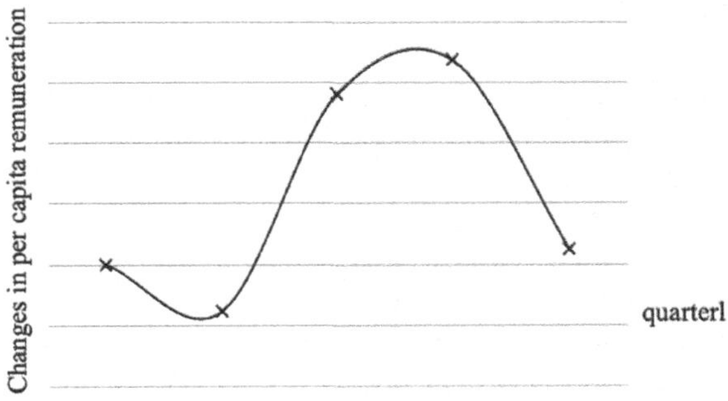


**Fig. 6.1** Time effect of typhoons on per capita labor remuneration

typhoons on labor remuneration last for no more than three quarters. After several months of adjustments, the damages caused by typhoons can gradually be restored over time. The details are given as below (Fig. 6.1).

## 6.4 Conclusions and Discussions

Based on the quarterly data of unit employment and labor remuneration of 21 prefecture-level cities of Guangdong from 2009 to 2014, this paper applies GDD to establish a regression model between disastrous weather events of typhoons and such variables as employment and per capita labor remuneration, and does calculations from four aspects of the impacts of typhoons on labor markets—general effect, regional effect, intensity effect and time effect. The results are presented as below: first, typhoons have no significant impacts on the total employment of Guangdong Province; second, high-intensity typhoon disasters give rise to a 5.15% fall in per capita labor remuneration; third, with time going by, the negative impacts of typhoons are gradually on the decline. The first and the second conclusions are markedly different from those obtained by current studies abroad. For instance, Mcintosh (2008), Zissimopoulos and Karoly (2010), and Belasen and Polachek (2007, 2008) believed that hurricanes reduced the local employment rate; Ewing et al. (2009), Olsen and Porter (2013) and Belasen and Polachek (2008) pointed out that disasters increased the local per capita remuneration.

The reasons that lead to the different conclusions of the studies may lie in the uniqueness of the labor market in Guangdong Province. First, in Guangdong Province, the number of labor forces does not decrease in disaster-stricken areas. It may be explained that the abundant and relatively cheap labor resources flowing into Guangdong can timely make up for the "labor shortage" brought by typhoon disasters. In contrast, the "labor shortage" in developed countries can only be resolved by rising labor remuneration. Second, there is a difference in the mobility of the labor market between China and developed countries. Because of better mobility of labor markets in developed countries, it is easier for high-paid workers flee the area and leave low-paid ones, resulting in inadequate labor supply and accordingly rising labor remuneration. In China, however, there is regional segmentation in such parts as household registration system, medical security system and normal enrollment, so labor mobility is impeded by many institutional obstacles and the cost of movement is quite high. Therefore, facing the threat of typhoon disasters, employment will not change accordingly. Third, Sui and Tang (2012) found that different from the typhoons in developed countries, China's typhoon disasters are more likely to bring more serious impacts on less developed areas. As underdeveloped areas have worse capability of disaster prevention and mitigation, inadequate disaster-mitigation infrastructure, the infrastructure and buildings with worse capability of disaster resistance than those of developed countries and the enterprises and residents having relatively inadequate knowledge and measures of disaster prevention, high-intensity typhoons is likely to affect normal production and operation, interrupt business operations and reduce the performance pay and labor remuneration of staff by transportation, the lines of water and power supply, logistics and warehousing, plant facilities and other means. In developed countries, however, the negative impacts of typhoons mainly lie in inadequate labor supply, which fails to meet the demand and results in rising labor remuneration (Rodríguez-Oreggia 2013; Belasen and Polachek 2007, 2008).

Based on the research above, this paper puts forward the following three suggestions from such aspects as the construction of facilities for disaster prevention and mitigation, the popularization of catastrophe insurance and the construction of disaster emergency system:

First, the construction of facilities for disaster prevention and mitigation should be strengthened in a targeted manner. Since the 18th CPC National Congress, the Central Committee and the State Council has proposed the basic policy of poverty alleviation. In disaster prevention and mitigation, "disaster alleviation" should also be carried out. Typhoon disasters in Guangdong Province often have impacts on those areas with relatively slow development, such as Shaoguan, HeYuan, Meizhou (Sui and Tang 2012). These areas are located in inland mountainous areas where secondary disasters including flood, waterlogging, landslides and debris flows are extremely easy to be triggered by typhoons. The infrastructure of disaster prevention and mitigation and the awareness of disaster prevention are relatively backward, often making enterprises suspend their production and migrant workers stricken by poverty because of disasters. Therefore, in terms of either the investment in disaster mitigation, or the training and education of disaster prevention and mitigation, particular attention should be paid to backward areas, thus breaking their vicious circle of "insufficient investment in disaster prevention and mitigation—stricken by poverty—insufficient investment in disaster prevention and mitigation".

Second, the catastrophe insurance should be popularized in agriculture and small and medium sized enterprises. Because of the uncertainty in the path and the influence of typhoons, the threat of high-intensity typhoons is difficult to resist by the long-term project construction of disaster prevention and mitigation and daily measures. Therefore, the popularization of catastrophe insurance is a feasible way to reduce the losses in typhoon disasters. Those who are vulnerable to the negative impacts of high-intensity typhoon disasters on labor remuneration tend to group in the agriculture with poor natural conditions and the small and medium sized enterprises with inadequate infrastructure. The government can consider the promotion of catastrophe insurance in these sectors, as well as appropriate subsidies. Catastrophe insurance can be achieved in a variety of forms, such as the insurance of agricultural production drop and the insurance of enterprise production suspension. To reduce the negative impacts of typhoons is to secure abundant labor for the areas frequently stricken by typhoons to stabilize the normal production of agriculture and small and medium sized enterprises.

Third, the loss assessment of typhoon disasters and the construction of emergency management system should be strengthened. It is a useful experience from developed countries to carry out disaster prevention and mitigation by scientific and technological means. With the aid of computer simulation technology and 3S technology, western developed countries have successfully developed a multi-disaster assessment model and system with wide application, strong functions and strong timeliness, such as HAZUS-MH, a multi-disaster joint assessment model developed by the United States, SLOSH, a tropical storm (surge) model and RADIUS, a risk assessment tool for urban earthquake disasters. At present, academic circles have made great achievements in the cause and the forecast and early warning of typhoons and, but the loss assessment of typhoon disasters and the construction of emergency management system in mainland China develop relatively slowly. In fact, whether the construction of facilities for disaster prevention and mitigation or the popularization of catastrophe insurance is based on the loss assessment of typhoon disasters. We should combine the knowledge including meteorology, geography, economics, management science and computer science, conduct investigation and research concerning the socio-economic value of property in categories, with "hazard-bearing body" of typhoon disasters as the basic unit, gather the information including the forecast information of disaster-causing factors, disaster-pregnant environment, historical disasters and the cases of emergency decision-making, and construct the loss assessment and the emergency management system of typhoon disasters based on multi-source heterogeneous data. In this regard, the relevant government departments should increase investment for scientific researches and establish advanced loss assessment and emergency management system of typhoon disasters, thus effectively reducing the negative impacts of typhoon disasters on society and economy.

**Acknowledgements** Lei Zhou, Ji Guo, Hui Liu, Dongyu Xi also made great contributions to this manuscript. We express our heartfelt thanks to them. This research was supported by: National Social and Scientific Fund Program of China (18ZDA052; 17BGL142;16ZDA047); The Natural Science Foundation of China (91546117, 71373131).

## References

Ai, N., & Polenske, K. R. (2008). Socioeconomic impact analysis of yellow-dust storms: An approach and case study for Beijing. *Economic System Research, 20*(2), 187–203.

Akhtar, R., & Santos, J. R. (2013). Risk-based input–output analysis of hurricane impacts on interdependent regional workforce systems. *Natural Hazards, 65*(1), 391–405.

Asad, A. L. (2015). Contexts of reception, post-disaster migration, and socioeconomic mobility. *Population and Environment, 36*, 279–310.

Asadul, I., Matthew, L. C., Minhaj, M., & Paul, A. R. (2020). Natural disaster and risk-sharing behavior: Evidence from rural Bangladesh. *Journal of Risk and Uncertainty, 61*(1).

Attary. N., Cutler. H., Shields. M., & van de Lindt, J. W. (2020). The economic effects of financial relief delays following a natural disaster. *Economic Systems Research, 32*(3), 351–377.

Baez, J., & Santos, I. (2008). On shaky ground: The effects of earthquakes on household income and poverty. Document prepared for the ISDR/RBLAC Research Project on Disaster Risk and Poverty.

Bănică. A., Kourtit. K., & Nijkamp P. (2020). Natural disasters as a development opportunity: a spatial economic resilience interpretation. *Review of Regional Research, 40*(prepublish).

Belasen, A. R., & Polachek, S.W. (2007). How hurricanes affect local labor markets-the effects of hurricanes in Florida. *The Journal of Human Resources, 44*, 251–276.

Belasen, A. R., & Polachek, S. W. (2008). How hurricanes affect wages and employment in local labor markets. *American Economic Review, 98*(2), 49–53.

Chen, L., & Wu, H. J. (2015). Research status and potential problems of differences-in-differences method in China. *The Journal of Quantitative & Technical Economics, 7*, 133–148.

Crawford, P. S., Hainen, A. M., Graettinger, A. J, van de Lindt. J. W., & Powell, L. (2020). Discrete-outcome analysis of tornado damage following the 2011 Tuscaloosa, Alabama, Tornado. *Natural Hazards Review, 21*(4).

Dalbyul, L., & Katrin, B. A. (2020). The impact of natural disasters on neighborhood poverty rate: A neighborhood change perspective. *Journal of Planning Education and Research, 40*(4), 447–459.

Den, Z. W. (2011). Research on the assessment of Typhoon risk in Guangdong Province. Central China Normal University.

Ewing, B. T., Kruse, J. B., & Twister, M. A. (2009). Employment responses to the 3 May 1999 Oklahoma City tornado. *Applied Economics, 41*, 691–702.

Felsenstein. D., & Grinberger. A. Y. (2020). Cascading effects of a disaster on the labor market over the medium to long term. *International Journal of Disaster Risk Reduction, 47*.

González. F. A. I., Santos. M. E., & London, S. (2020). Persistent effects of natural disasters on human development: quasi-experimental evidence for Argentina. *Environment, Development and Sustainability* (prepublish).

Grinberger. A. Y., & Samuels, P. (2018). Modeling the labor market in the aftermath of a disaster: Two perspectives. *International Journal of Disaster Risk Reduction, 31*, 419–434.

Groen, J. A., & Polivka, A. E. (2008). The effect of hurricane Katrina on the labor market outcomes of evacuees. *American Economic Review: Papers & Proceedings, 98*(2), 43–48.

Ha, K. (2020). Evaluating ecosystem-based natural disaster management. *Human and Ecological Risk Assessment: An International Journal, 26*(7), 1896–1906.

Haimes, Y. Y., Horowitz, B. M., Lambert, J. H., Santos, J. R., Lian, C., & Crowther, K. G. (2005). Inoperability input-output model for inter dependent infrastructure sectors. II: Case study. *Journal of Infrastructure Systems, 11*(2), 82–92.

Hamilton, L. C., Saito, K., Loring, P. A., Lammers, R. B., & Huntington, H. P. (2016). Climigration? Population and climate change in Arctic Alaska. *Population & Environment, 38*(2), 115–133.

Haque, U., Da Silva, P. F., Devoli, G., Pilz, J., Zhao, B., Khaloua, A., et al. (2019). The human cost of global warming: Deadly landslides and their triggers (1995–2014). *Science of the Total Environment, 9*, 673–684.

In den Bäumen, H. S., Többen, J., & Lenzen, M. (2015). Labour forced impacts and production losses due to the 2013 flood in Germany. *Journal of Hydrology, 527*, 142–150.

Khan. A., Yang C.G., Khan. G., & Muhammad. F. (2020). The dilemma of natural disasters: Impact on economy, fiscal position, and foreign direct investment alongside Belt and Road Initiative countries. *Science of the Total Environment, 743.*

Kirchberger, M. (2017). Natural disasters and labor markets. *Journal of Development Economics, 125,* 40–58.

Lin, H. C., Kuo, Y. L., Shaw, D., Chang, M. C., & Kao, T. M. (2012). Regional economic impact analysis of earthquakes in northern Taiwan and its implications for disaster reduction policies. *Natural Hazards, 61*(2), 603–620.

Lirong, L., Gordon, H., Brian, B., Guanhui, C., Scott, M. P., & Siyue, P. (2020). Input-output modeling analysis with a detailed disaggregation of energy sectors for climate change policy-making: A case study of Saskatchewan, Canada. *Renewable Energy, 151,* 1307–1317.

Liu, H. (2004). On "to Raise the Proportion of the Middle-income Group". Guangxi University.

Long. L., Yoshida. Y., Liu. Q. L., Zhang. H. R., Wang. S. Q., & Fang, K. (2020). Comparison of city-level carbon footprint evaluation by applying single- and multi-regional input-output tables. *Journal of Environmental Management, 260.*

Luo, K., & Kinugasa, T. (2020). Do natural disasters influence long-term savings?: Assessing the impact of the 2008 Sichuan earthquake on household saving rates using synthetic control. *China: An International Journal, 18*(3).

Ma, S., Zhang, J., & Zhu, X. (2012). The effect of minimum wage on average wage and employment. *Economic Research Journal, 5,* 132–146.

Mcintosh, M. F. (2008). Measuring the labor market impacts of hurricane Katrina migration: Evidence from Houston, Texas. *American Economic Review: Papers & Proceedings, 98*(2), 54–57.

Olsen, A., & Porter, K. (2013). Storm surge to demand surge: Exploratory study of hurricanes, labor wages, and material prices. *Natural Hazards Review, 14*(4), 247–257.

Ouattara, B., & Strobl, E. (2014). Hurricane strikes and local migration in US coastal counties. *Economics Letters, 124,* 17–20.

Pimm, S. L. (1984). The complexity and stability of ecosystems. *Nature, 307,* 321–326.

Qin, D. H. (2008). Latest progress on climate change research. *Science & Technology Review, 7,* 3.

Qin, D. H., & Luo, Y. (2008). Reasons and future trends of global climate change. *Impact of Science on Society, 2,* 16–21.

Rodríguez-Oreggia, E. (2013). Hurricanes and labor market outcomes: Evidence for Mexico. *Global Environmental Change, 23,* 351–359.

Rose, A., Oladosu, G., & Liao, S. Y. (2007). Regional economic impacts of a terrorist attack on the water system of Los Angeles: A computable general disequilibrium analysis. In H. Richardson, P. Gordon, & J. Moore (Eds.), *Economic costs and consequences of a terrorist attack* (pp. 291–316). Cheltenham, UK: Edward Elgar.

Shi, P. J. (1996). Theory and practice of disaster study. *Journal of Natural Disasters, 4,* 6–17.

Skidmore, M., & Toya, H. (2002). Do natural disasters promote long-run growth? *Economic Inquiry, 40*(4), 664–687.

Sui, G. J., & Tang, D. L. (2012). Typhoon disasters and regional economic divergence: Evidence from Guangdong. *Reform, 06,* 18–25.

Tan, R. P., & Zhang. D. W. (2020). Decision-making method based on new entropy and refined single-valued neutrosophic sets and its application in Typhoon disaster assessment. *Applied Intelligence* (prepublish).

UN/ISDR. (2004). *Living with risk: A global review of disaster reduction initiatives.* Geneva: United Nations.

Wei, Z. J., & Tang, D. L. (2011). A statistical study of origin and intensity of tropical cyclone on the North Western Pacific. *Journal of Applied Statistics and Management, 3,* 512–521.

Xiao, Y. (2011). Local economic impacts of natural disasters. *Regional Science, 51*(4), 804–820.

Ye, X., Wen, J., Zhu, Z., & Sun, R. (2020). Natural disaster risk assessment in tourist areas based on multi scenario analysis. *Earth Science Informatics* (prepublish), 1–12.

Zhai, M. Y., Huang, G. H., Liu, L. R., & Zhang, X. (2019). Ecological network analysis of an energy metabolism system based on input-output tables: Model development and case study for Guangdong. *Journal of Cleaner Production, 227*, 434–446.

Zhang, J. (2005). The employment structure analysis of Guangdong province–based on the perspective of industrial structure. South China Normal University.

Zhang, J. W. (2009). Economic growth and employment in China: Pursuing for flexicurity in Chinese labor markets. *China Industrial Economics, 1*, 18–28.

Zhang, W. B., Li, G. P., & Peng, S. Q. (2015). The empirical study between reconstruction policy of Wenchuan earthquake and economic growth. *Soft Science, 1*, 24–28.

Zhang, X. X., Nie, J., & Cheng, C. X. (2020). Natural and socioeconomic factors and their interactive effects on house collapse caused by Typhoon Mangkhut. *International Journal of Disaster Risk Science, 11*(prepublish).

Zissimopoulos, J., & Karoly, L. A. (2010). Employment and self-employment in the wake of hurricane Katrina. *Demography, 47*(2), 345–367.

# Part II
# Disaster Emergency Management

# Chapter 7 Urban Flood Depth-Economic Loss Curves and Their Amendment Based on Resilience: Evidence from Lizhong Town in Lixia River and Houbai Town in Jurong River of China

**Abstract** Resilience is a key term in disaster economic loss assessment. The flood loss rates in different scenarios for the residence, industry, commerce, infrastructure, and agriculture are calculated and the original depth-damage curves are drawn by collecting the socio-economic data of Lizhong Town in Lixia River and Houbai Town in Jurong River. Thereafter, by fully considering the resilience factor to draw the new depth-economic loss curves, which are in line with the actual situation, the results show: (1) the disaster reduction capability correction loss rate of different receptors in Lizhong Town is in the range of 16 to 74%, and in Houbai Town is in the range of 20 to 79%. The residential flood loss, commercial loss, infrastructure loss and industry loss were reduced by 74, 54.8, 38 and 16%, respectively in Lizhong Town, and the residential flood loss, commercial loss, and industry loss were reduced by 79, 60, and 20%, respectively in Houbai Town. (2) Residential property types and their display heights in families with different income levels have similar flood-damage rate curves in mainland China and Taiwan (Su et al. 2002); (3) The loss rate reached the maximum at the depth of 3 m, and the sum of the five receptors' damage are 6.98 million Yuan (RMB) and 2.2 million Yuan (RMB) in Lizhong Town and Houbai Town, respectively. At last, in this paper, several approaches to improving resilience were proposed and possibilities in future researches were put forward. This study is a useful complement to flood economic loss evaluation literature and provides reference for disaster prevention and mitigation decisions in similar areas.

**Keywords** Depth-economic loss curve · Flood risk · Resilience · Amendment · Lixia river · Jurong river

## 7.1 Introduction

China's urban environments are particularly vulnerable to flooding because of climate change and rapid urbanization. With the global climate changing, the intensity and frequency of extreme meteorological events have been increased (IPCC 2013). At the same time, ongoing urbanization amplifies the adverse effects of floods by increasing the runoff from impervious surfaces and blocking water flow. A wide range of sources have caused urban flood with considerable economic losses and casualties in many



X. Wu and J. Guo, *Economic Impacts and Emergency Management of Disasters in China*,
https://doi.org/10.1007/978-981-16-1319-7_7

Chinese towns, such as the heavy rains in Beijing, China, on July 21, 2012, and the rainstorm in Shenzhen, China, on May 30, 2014. The evaluation of the economic losses caused by floods, proposing corresponding disaster prevention, and implementing reduction risk management countermeasures have an important theoretical value and the practical significance.

With the deepening of disaster prevention and mitigation work, as one of vulnerability assessment methods, the synthetic depth-damage curves scenario analysis by establishing vulnerability curves (loss rates function) has become a disaster research with the focus on loss estimation (Penning et al. 1977; Kelman 2002; Turner et al. 2003; Dutta et al. 2003; Füssel and Klein 2006; Fuchs et al. 2007; Shi et al. 2009, 2011; Papathoma-KÖhle et al. 2012; Field et al. 2012; Dong et al. 2012; Liu et al. 2011; Yin et al. 2010). The majority of the studies of vulnerability assessment are actually scenario analyses because historical disaster data are limited and the indicator system is still highly uncertain with index selection and weight calculation. The analyses are based on the damage (rate) curves, which are characterized by the strength after natural disasters for different urban land uses or assets, and the data collection and evaluation results via field survey and interview are accurate and reliable; the depth-damage curves have been plotted for urban flooding in many areas.

Field survey is an effective method for the assessment of the detailed basic data for constructing flood-damage functions (Shi et al. 2009; Wu et al. 2016), and water depth is a key factor to flood-damage (rate) (Kelman 2002). Many institutions and scholars have conducted similar studies of building flood-damage (rate) curves. For example, the 168 stage-damage curves of residential buildings in the United Kingdom were plotted by dividing the houses into 84 categories according to the type of residence, time of construction, owner's social status, and so on (Penning et al. 1977). Three different stage-damage curves were built in two administrative regions in Bangkok, Thailand, on the basis of the investigation and evaluation of the monetary values for the structure of buildings, indoor property, and outdoor property (Dutta et al. 2003). The United States Army Corps of Engineers (USACE) also investigated 140 flood cases in California and divided the flood losses into 3 parts: structure, internal property, and non-physical losses. Vulnerability functions were established for residential properties by the regression equation. Furthermore, on the basis of other major flood events from 1996 to 2001, USACE also constructed two residential flood-damage curves to distinguish the houses with basements from those without basements (USACE 2000). Malgwi et al. (2020) developed a framework that incorporated vulnerability indices and regional damage ratings. This framework could support flood damage assessment in data-scarce areas. By investigating the main characteristics of flash floods, Khajehei et al. (2020) presented a county-level socioeconomic vulnerability index based on socioeconomic data from the US Bureau of the Census and Social Analysis. The study showed that more severe flash floods occurred in the southwestern United States than in the northern Great Plains. Based on damage data from the 2010 Veneto floods in Italy, Scorzini et al. (2017) proposed new site-specific depth damage function. They focused on the uncertainty of this function due to the lack of flood data or building information. Albano et al. (2017)

compared the losses obtained from the actual survey of the June 2006 floods in the Ilisua basin with losses estimated by the UNRC loss function. They found that the choice of vulnerability curves would influence the flood losses assessment. Taking into account the differences between various building structures, McGrath et al. (2019) introduced probabilistic depth loss curves based on the depth loss curves derived in southern Ontario. Probabilistic depth loss curves assessed the damage to buildings of different materials and structures. Bignami et al. (2018) estimated economic losses in flooded areas based on a survey of more than 7000 refund applications and constructed damage curves based on field observation data from the 2000 floods in Piedmont, Italy. They found that a strong nonlinear relationship between damage and water depth. Marc et al. (2016) applied a coupled 1D-2D model to obtain flood depths. Then, they simulated stage-damage curves and estimated flood damage in the Raval district of Barcelona based on survey data and losses reported by Spanish reinsurance. Englhardt et al. (2019) presented specific vulnerability curves based on a survey of the built environment and building materials to distinguish between urban and rural losses from flood risk. Besides, they used Ethiopia as a case study to show the importance of flood hazard loss studies in rural areas. Hofflinger et al. (2019) demonstrated the Social Vulnerability Response Index (ReTSVI) by investigating the time of population evacuation during natural disasters. They used the ReTSVI in the Huaraz severe flood event in Peru as a case study to reveal that areas with higher social vulnerability had lower population evacuation rates. Szewranski et al. (2018) constructed socio-environmental vulnerability mapping with the use of a location intelligence system. They conducted this method to identify residential areas that were vulnerable to flooding hazards.

In China, some scholars quoted and amended mature flood-damage curves by employing actual events (Dong et al. 2012), whereas others constructed different vulnerability curve functions by using survey data. For example, vulnerability loss rates were estimated for housing properties and commercial assets in Wenzhou, Zhejiang (Liu et al. 2011). Stage-damage curves were plotted for different land uses in Shanghai city (Yin et al. 2010). Based on text data, Wu et al. (2016) developed vulnerability curves to represent the relationship between the storm index and the composite hazard index. The results indicated that there was a significant exponential correlation between the storm index and the mixed hazard index. Given that the local spatial dependence of adjacent areas, Chen et al. (2019) proposed an uncertainty-based vulnerability assessment for different land-use types. Chen et al. (2015) constructed a hyperbolic tangent function based on hazard class. They evaluated flood losses in the Yangtze River Delta region to explain the configuration process of this function. The evaluation results revealed that the hyperbolic tangent function was valid. Li and Cheng (2016) presented an S-shaped function for assessing flood hazard losses. The function contained three parameters: maximum flood losses, critical return period and integrated loss factor. They applied the model to flood loss assessment in the Taihu Lake basin. The results found that the economic development level and urbanization level played a significant role in the improvement of flood control capacity. Feng et al. (2017) quantified infrastructure vulnerability based on the duration of the flood by surveying tidal sites. However, the samples employed in these studies are not enough to cover most types of receptors. Moreover, research on damage rate curve and resilience is not considered in the above research. Turner et al. (2003) and Shi et al. (2011) presented that resilience is an important part of general vulnerability; it forces disaster relief capacity that reflects the social system's ability to self-regulate, ablation of indirect losses, and return to normal development level as soon as possible. Being conducive to finding the weak links in the process of disaster recovery and developing a plan for post-disaster recovery and reconstruction, resilience should be fully taken into account when designing the damage rate curve.

The existing approaches for resilience assessment in the international community can be divided into two categories. The first is the quantitative method using data and indices. For example, Bruneau et al. (2003) built a conceptual framework to describe resilience. According to the theory, resilience consists of four interrelated dimensions, namely, technology, organization, society, and economy (TOSE), and has four properties, namely, robustness, rapidity, redundancy, and resourcefulness (4Rs). Having applied input–output analysis to a 90-day disruption of a seaport, Rose (2012) found that regional output could decline by as much as $13 billion at the port region level and that resilience can reduce these impacts by nearly 70%. Therefore, resilience is significant in restoring the stability of the regional economic system. Considering the response to emergency events and the implementation of emergency measures, Rumson et al. (2020) created a set of indicators to assess dynamic coastal resilience. Taking a region in East Anglia, the UK as a case study, they defined the scope for incorporating evolving data collection and dissemination methods in dynamic coastal resilience assessment. From the perspectives of the social, economic and natural environment, Yang et al. (2020) performed a comprehensive disaster resilience index system for evaluating the resilience of 17 counties in the Three Gorges reservoir area. The results indicated significant regional differences in disaster resilience in the Three Gorges reservoir area. By using secondary data across the country, Parsons et al. (2016) described the ANDRI (Australian Natural Disaster Resilience Index). This index measured people's ability to cope with disasters through available resources and their adaptive capacity to disasters through learning. Asadzadeh et al. (2017) applied a survey approach to resilience assessment indicators, which incorporated four criteria: community-based, multifaceted, quantitative, and operationalized. Galbusera et al. (2018) improved the input–output model by considering quantification of multi-regional losses to serve economic resilience assessment. Tan et al. (2020) constructed a three-dimensional framework based on resilience at the household level. Then, they conducted a questionnaire survey of representative rural households in disaster-prone areas of Chongqing, China. The results illustrated the low resilience of most households, as well as significant differences in the resilience of households in different regions. Cutter (2016) examined existing quantitative methods for resilience assessment in four areas: assessment focus, spatial orientation, methodology, and domain. The results found that economic, social, environmental, infrastructure, and social capital were the most common influencing factors in all assessment methods. Kim et al. (2018) proposed a two-stage approach to quantify resilience based on community baseline resilience indicators. They validated the approach with a case study about resilience assessment of Korean ports in response to hazardous substance spills. Joyce et al. (2018) investigated the relationship between flood risk and resilience of drainage infrastructure in low-lying areas of coastal cities. They classified the risks of flooding in low-lying areas and constructed functions to predict flood hazard, vulnerability and resilience. Wang et al. (2019) discussed the flood resilience of urban drainage based on a grid cell-based resilience metric, which was measured as the ratio of the number of unflooded grid cells in the urban drainage catchment to the total number of grid cells. They validated the metric with an urban drainage catchment in Dalian, China. The results showed that the high-resolution resilience assessment could identify areas vulnerable to urban flooding. Adeniyi et al. (2019) assessed the resilience of firms to flooding by constructing a conceptual model of capability maturity. The study provided technical support to improve the flood resilience of enterprises. Kim et al. (2018) defined resilience as the ability to prevent flooding after a significant rainfall and to return to expected levels as soon as practicable. Then, they built a resilience assessment framework, which estimated the maximum possible flood volume and discharge of the dam to quantify the damage. Wang et al. (2019) proposed a new resilience assessment index and constructed a resilience curve for urban drainage systems based on the synthesis of continuous and short-duration rainfall. The curve integrated the measures of sewer inundation and property inundation, as well as the concepts of reliability and resilience. Taking into account social, institutional, community capital and economic aspects, Moghadas et al. (2019) composed an index of community resilience, combining data from the Statistical Center of Iran and the Tehran government. The research emphasized that place-based assessment could document community resilience performance over time.

The other is qualitative analysis. Gaetano and Rose (2014) analyzed resilience and sustainability in relation to disasters and described their characteristics, application measures, and contribution to sustainable development. Mustafa et al. (2003) suggested that the aid to the receptors from the disaster through field investigation and disaster statistics is the key to resilience. Emmanuel et al. (2013) employed data gathered from the interview of 120 households. The results show that indigenous knowledge system is an indispensable component of disaster resilience because it can assist the community in rescuing lives and protecting household items, crops, and poultry. Thomas et al. (2010) constructed a depth-damage function of buildings by considering the factor of enhancing resilience, including obtaining a long-lasting and durable structure, and moving vulnerable elements to higher stories. The results reveal that the measures are characterized by the function's diminished slope, thus resulting in lesser damages at the same depth. Qualitative methods can provide insight into the nature of resilience when society, organizations, and individuals are faced with disasters (Vogel et al. 2007; Ceccato et al. 2011). Choptiany et al. (2017) introduced a method for self-evaluation of the resilience of farmers and herders. Self-evaluation could help farmers and herders understand the threats and opportunities posed by climate change through a participatory approach. The research proved that farmers and herders, through self-evaluation, could prioritize actions that would contribute to collective resilience. Taking two communities in

Cambodia as case studies, Jacobson (2020) constructed a framework for assessing the capacity of communities to respond to climate change on their own. The capacity was measured primarily by the achievements of communities in taking effective action. He found that aid dependency and family ties would affect the assessment of community resilience. By use of the insurance industry's approach to technical risk grading, Hochrainer-Stigler et al. (2020) proposed a standardized indicator for measuring community resilience from a quantitative perspective. Besides, they validated the indicator from a qualitative perspective. The results showed that resilience grades related to capacity and perception were more dependent on expert judgment than on collected data.

Cox et al. (2015) provided a qualitative tool applicable to assessing disaster resilience in rural and remote areas. The tool emphasized the importance of community-based and citizen-centered action for resilience building. They argued that improving overall community resilience required full utilization of local resources and services, the timely implementation of emergency management planning and the stockpile of relevant knowledge. Following a review of the resilience framework of coastal communities, Almutairi et al. (2020) established 64 critical resilience criteria through an analysis of the similarities and differences among the assessment indicators in the framework. The framework focused primarily on governance and institutions, infrastructure and socioeconomic, yet there was a lack of consideration of environmental impacts and potential risks from climate change. Spialek et al. (2019) examined the role of citizen communication about disasters and neighborhood belonging on community resilience by looking at different stages before and after a disaster. The results indicated that neighborhood communication of disaster information and correction of disaster rumors contributed to the overall community resilience. Coetzee et al. (2018) advocated an integrated and flexible approach to resilience building rather than a one-size-fits-all approach. They argued for a non-linear effect of different social contexts on resilience and validated that effect with data from communities in southern Africa. Via simple random sampling, Hamidi et al. (2020) conducted a household questionnaire survey in flood-prone areas of Khyber Pakhtunkhwa Province. The results found that susceptibility and exposure factors had strong impacts on vulnerability.

This study has two contributions. First, the division of samples in Lizhong Town and Houbai Town into residential, industrial, commercial, infrastructure, and agricultural receptors enabled the construction of flood deeps-economic losses curves based on the detailed investigation and research on these five different receptors in two towns, which are typical low-lying town in the flood area. The flood loss rates in different water depths were calculated and the original depth-damage curves were drawn on the basis of the investigation and evaluation of the monetary values for different receptors. Second, the new depth-damage curves were constructed on the basis of the actual situation by fully considering the resilience. Few previous studies have explored depth-damage curves, and this study is a scarce research effort that explores this topic.

These goals will be achieved with the following four steps: (1) Overview of the research area was introduced (Sect. 7.1). (2) The scene, data and research approaches were utilized detailedly (Sect. 7.2). (3) The Flood depth-damage curves of residential indoor property from different incomes and Receptors' damage rate regression functions were developed (Sect. 7.3). Finally, the summary is provided in Sect. 7.4.

## 7.2 Overview of the Research Area

### *7.2.1 Lizhong Town*

As the central part of Jiangsu Province, China, region of Lixia River is a vast low-lying plain and comprises Xinghua City, Huai'an City, Yancheng City, Taizhou City, Yangzhou City, and Nantong City (Fig. 7.1). The altitude at the fringe of the plain is higher than that at the center. With its inter weaved river network, low-lying topography, and frequent water logging, it has been known as a "water town". Xinghua, Jianhu and Qingtong low-lying lands are scattered at the center of the plain, which has an elevation from 1.0 to 1.5 m. The region is obviously covered by the monsoon climate. The average annual rainfall is 1025 mm/year and is impacted by plum rains and typhoons. From May to September, rainfall accounts for approximately 70% for the whole year (Ye et al. 2009; Tian et al. 1998). Several severe floods occurred in the region of Lixia River. For example, the long duration of plum rains in 1954, 1991, 2003, and 2006 and the typhoon rainstorms in 1962 and 1965 (Chen et al. 2008; Ye et al. 2011) led to huge economic losses.

As a vast low-lying plain at the northwest of Xinghua City, Lizhong Town has an area of 80.27 $km^2$ (Fig. 7.2) with 15 administrative villages. The population density of Lizhong is 400 people per $km^2$. Its GDP per capita is approximately 27,400 Yuan (RMB) by the end of 2014. The favorable factors to urban resilience include the following: (1) The structure is relatively simple, dominated by agriculture,

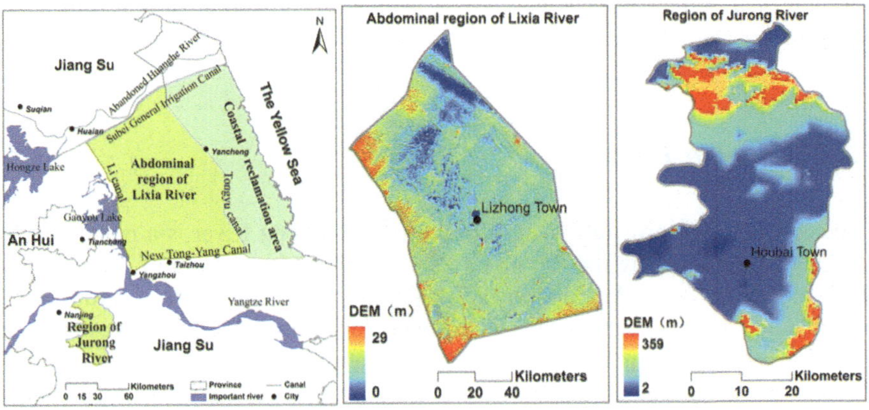


Fig. 7.1 Location and DEM of Lixia River and Jurong River

**Fig. 7.2** Location of the research areas

while the industrial and commercial scales are small; (2) The buildings with bricks and concrete structures have flood performance. The adverse factors include the following: (1) Low income and high population density in the area; (2) Many young adults go to work in the city, thus leaving the old ones and the children with poor disaster prevention and mitigation abilities; (3) Inter weaved river network with many varieties of agricultural plants in the area. Agricultural economic loss is difficult to recover after a flood impact.

### *7.2.2 Houbai Town*

Located in the southwest of Jiangsu province, the Jurong River is a branch of the Qinhuai River. Crossing the Jurong city and the Jiangning district of Nanjing city, the Jurong River is 64.8 km long and 25–100 m wide. The basin area of Jurong River is 1262 km$^2$. Alongside the river is a lowland polder area of 262 km$^2$, whose ground elevation is 6–8 m; the mountainous and hilly area is 1000 km$^2$ and the ground elevation below 300 m. Being in the subtropical monsoon climate, it is easily influenced by natural disasters, such as typhoon, rainstorm, etc. With fast flow concentration, there is a large increase in the flood level and a high flood peak. Influenced by the backwater effect of the tide of the Yangtze River, the river's flood discharge capacity is poor and the waterlogging is hard to drain, leading to a high flood risk. For example, heavy rainfall in 1974, 1991, 2003 and 2015 had all caused serious flood disasters (Sha et al. 1994; Shi et al. 2011).

Being a typical town in the Jurong River basin, Houbai Town, with the total area being 160 $km^2$, is located in a low mountain-hill region. The southeast of Houbai Town are hills and mound land, and the northwest lowland polder areas. There are 21 administrative villages and 2 neighborhood committees, with the population density being 350 people per $km^2$ and per capital GDP 40,081 RMB in 2014. Characteristics shared by Lizhong Town and Houbai Town are as follows: (1) For the geographical position, they are all low lying towns located in flooded areas; (2) Being in the "central Jiangsu" region, the economic development is on a middle level in Jiangsu province, i.e. the medium high level in the country. For the industrial structure, they are dominated by agriculture, forestry and fishery, while the second and third industry is not very developed; (3) For disaster prevention and mitigation capability, the waterlogging-preventing facilities are relatively perfect owing to severe flood disasters suffered in the history. However, the disaster prevention and mitigation capability is relatively weak, because young adults were out for work, leaving elderly people and children behind.

## 7.3 Disaster Scenario, Data and Methodology

### *7.3.1 Disaster Scenario*

Given the lack of the database of historical disasters taking place at Lizhong Town and Houbai Town and the absence of typical floods in recent years, it is difficult to conduct field researches after disasters. Therefore, this research draws on the scenario analysis implemented by Coto et al. (2002), Dutta (2003), Kleist (2006), Shi et al. (2009) and other researchers with reference of the flood brought by the plum rains which occurred at Lixia River in 2006 and Jurong River in 2015.

Flood disaster scenario of Lizhong Town. In 2006, the plum rain period in region of Lixia River, beginning on June 21st and ending on July 12th, lasted for as long as 22 days. During this period, two heavy precipitation processes took place in the area from June 21st to 24th and from June 29th to July 4th, and the latter led to a flood (Ding et al. 2010). At 8 a.m. on July 5th, the water level of Lizhong Town dramatically rose to about 2.5 m. A great many houses were drowned and the unmovable belongings on the first floor soaked in the water, which was a heavy loss.

Flood disaster scenario of Houbai Town. On June 26–28th, 2015, two rounds of heavy rainfall led to dyke breaking, causing flood disaster. The water level soaring to 1.6 m, more than 30,000 people were trapped, 4000 dwellings flooded and 26.67 $km^2$ crops influenced, with fishery suffering particularly serious losses.

This research regards the flood mentioned above as the hypothetical scenarios. Though they are latent disasters caused by plum rains, they also have the features of accidental disasters, because the region suffers heavy precipitation on the set-in of the plum rain and the majority of left-behind residents are the elderly, sick and disabled. Combined with the interviews of the local dwellers, the hypotheses of the research and the calculation are presented below:

(1) The issue of property transfers. What are categorized into unmovable belongings are such bulky and undetachable items as sofas, wardrobes, beds, air-conditioners and refrigerators in residential areas, the raw materials and stocks in industrial areas, the quantitative and scattered commodities in commercial areas, the air-conditioners, refrigerators together with office desks and chairs in departments of public facilities as well as crops.
(2) The issue of elevation. As the two towns are low-lying, flat and gentle in elevation, the difference in elevation is not taken into consideration. Besides, only the property losses on no higher than the first floor (3 m) is taken into account.

## *7.3.2 Data Descriptions*

With local government assistance, data were collected through a questionnaire survey from 7th July to 14th July, 2014 in Lizhong Town and 19th Jan. to 21th Jan., 2016 in Houbai Town. Questionnaire surveys were prepared to collect damage data covering the following aspects. (1) The systematical investigation covered 15 administrative villages and one residents' committee in Lizhong Town and 21 villages and two residents' committees in Houbai Town. According to the receptors' property types, different questionnaires were designed to calculate the economic losses in different inundation depths. (2) We also collect demographic details, annual income, economic structure, industry output values, and geographic information from the government departments.

For residence properties, a typical sampling method was adopted to collect data. First, each administrative village was divided into five types according to the annual income: high, medium and high, medium, low and medium, and low income households. Second, two households of every type were investigated. Thus, 145 effective samples, which accounted for 1.50% of the total households (the town has 9637 families), were gathered from Lizhong Town and 10 effective samples, which accounted for 0.053% of the total households (the town has 18,700 families), were gathered from Houbai Town. The investigation of residence properties is mainly divided into five categories: vehicles, furniture, household appliances, daily necessities, and reserve supplies.

For agricultural properties, one village was identified for the questionnaire survey to collect agriculture data. A total of 17 villages (15 and 2 in Lizhong Town and Houbai Town, repectively) were surveyed. Agricultural crops mainly include rice, wheat, cotton, corn, soybeans, and vegetables, with large breeding areas of fish, shrimp, and crab existing. Information on each economic crop in every village, cultivated area, estimated price per unit weight, annual yield per unit area, and attachment value of assets were collected from the statistics personnel within the administrative villages.

For the commercial and industrial properties, 36 valid questionnaires (34 and 2 in Lizhong Town and Houbai Town, respectively) were obtained according to the different types of enterprises. In Lizhong Town, the questionnaires respectively accounted for 15.38% of the whole industry and 50.00% of the whole commercial enterprises (the whole town has 26 industrial and 60 commercial enterprises in 2014). In Houbai Town, the questionnaires respectively accounted for 0.49% of the whole industry and 0.11% of the whole commercial enterprises (the whole town has 206 industrial and 900 commercial enterprises in 2014). Detailed property information, which includes internal property values (equipment value, inventory value), vehicles, and commercial indices (turnover), and so on, were collected through social investigation in the two towns.

For infrastructure properties, 28 valid questionnaires (all in Lizhong Town) were collected for schools, nursing homes, hospitals, and governments, in different water depths, economic losses of vehicles, furniture, home appliances, equipment, office supplies, and so on.

The sample sizes and proportions are shown in Table 7.1.

### 7.3.3 *Research Approaches*

The calculation is divided into several steps as follows: first, estimate the total value of the properties; second, estimate the loss under different water depths and obtain the loss rate by having the loss divided by the total loss; third, make loss-rate curves of various properties, with water depths as the horizontal axis and loss rates of properties as the vertical axis; fourth, considering the competence of disaster prevention and mitigation, the loss rates of different properties are recalculated and new loss-rate curves are constructed. The detailed methods and process of calculation are presented as follows.

### 7.3.4 *Assessment of Flood Damage for Receptors in Agriculture*

(1) Assessment of property value

The estimation of property values mainly refers to the costs to restore to the original state, without considering the structure damages. Asset value refers to market price and considers the depreciation ratio. Asset value is obtained from the maximum

**Table 7.1** Sample variable description

| Receptors | Statistic unit | Research object | The sample size | | The total number | | Percentage of total number | |
|---|---|---|---|---|---|---|---|---|
| | | | Lizhong Town | Houbai Town | Lizhong Town | Houbai Town | Lizhong Town (%) | Houbai Town (%) |
| Residence | Household | Resident | 145 | 10 | 9000 | 18,700 | 1.50 | 0.053 |
| Agriculture | Administrative village | The head | 15 | 2 | 15 | 21 | 100 | 9.5 |
| Industry | Factory | Manager | 4 | 1 | 26 | 206 | 15.38 | 0.49 |
| Commerce | Retail store | Manager | 30 | 1 | 60 | 900 | 50 | 0.11 |
| Infrastructure | Institution | The head | 28 | – | 32 | – | 87.5 | – |

difference between the net and estimated present market values. The net value was calculated by the straight-line depreciation method.

The receptors are indexed by $i = 1, 2, 3, 4$. The samples of receptor $i$ are indexed by $s = 1, 2, \ldots, f^{i}$. $f^{i}$ is the sample sizes of receptor $i$. The assets of receptor $i$ are indexed by $k = 1, 2, \ldots, g^{i}$. $g^{i}$ is the number of all types of assets of receptor $i$.

For the sample s from receptor i, the net value of its asset k is calculated by the following formula:

$$N_{sk}^{i} = N_{sk0}^{i} \times \left(1 - n_{sk}^{i}/t_{sk}^{i}\right) \quad (7.1)$$

where:

$N_{sk}^{i}$ is the net value of asset $k$ of sample $s$ of receptor $i$, $N_{sk0}^{i}$ is the purchase price of asset $k$ of sample $s$ of receptor $i$, $n_{sk}^{i}$ is the depreciation years of asset $k$ of sample $s$ of receptor $i$, and $t_{sk}^{i}$ is the life expectancy of the asset $k$ of sample $s$ of receptor $i$.

The present value of each asset was obtained from the maximum difference between the net value and the estimated present value:

$$P_{sk}^{i} = \text{Max}[N_{sk}^{i}, M_{sk}^{i}] \quad (7.2)$$

where:

$P_{sk}^{i}$ is the present value of asset $k$ of sample $s$ of receptor $i$ and $M_{sk}^{i}$ is the estimated present market value of asset $k$ of sample $s$ of receptor $i$.

On the basis of the present value of each asset, the total value of each sample is obtained from the sum of the assets' present values in each sample. The average value of each sample is calculated by the following formula:

$$V^{i} = \sum_{s=1}^{f^{i}} \sum_{k=1}^{g^{i}} P_{sk}^{i}/f^{i} \quad (7.3)$$

where:

$V^{i}$ is the average value of each sample of receptor $i$.

(2) Estimation of the loss rate at different depths

The flood loss rate of each asset is related to the height of the asset placed. In the calculation of the loss rate of different assets at different depths, distinguishing whether the asset loss is total or partial is important. Some assets are not completely lost once it flounders. For example, gradual loss occurs when a refrigerator floods from the bottom to drown all. However, some assets are completely lost once they founders. For example, once water floods the operating panel of a TV, microwave oven, and induction cooker, their value would be lost totally. Therefore, the estimation of the asset loss rates at different depths is based on asset characteristics.

Asset loss at different depths was obtained for each asset as the present value multiplied by the asset loss rate was at different depths. On the basis of each asset loss at different depths, the average loss of each receptor sample at different depths was calculated by the following formula:

$$D_j^i = \sum_{s=1}^{f^i} \sum_{k=1}^{g^i} [P_{sk}^i r_{skj}^i]/f^i \tag{7.4}$$

where:

$D_j^i$ is the average loss of each sample of receptor $i$ at depth $j$, and $r_{skj}^i$ is the loss rate of asset $k$ of sample $s$ of receptor $i$ at depth $j$.

The loss rate of each sample of receptors at different depths was obtained from the average loss of each sample of receptors at different depths divided by the average value of each sample of receptors. The loss rate of each sample of receptors at different depths was calculated by the following formula:

$$R_j^i = D_j^i / V^i \tag{7.5}$$

where:

$R_j^i$ is the loss rate of each sample of receptor $i$ at depth $j$.

(3) Construction of depth-damage curves

The depth-damage curve was drawn on the basis of the information collected from the questionnaire survey and can be employed to derive the relationship of the loss rate with flood depths. The loss rate curves of different income families' properties were constructed (Figs. 7.3 and 7.4). Residence damage rate functions and the corresponding trend lines were also obtained using the regression method (Figs. 7.5a and 7.6a).

(4) Construction of new depth-damage curves considering the resilience factor

Once threatened by the flood disaster, residents will be spontaneous and actively perform self-help and mutual aids, such as transferring of important properties (such as vehicle) or vulnerable properties (such as home appliances). Primary data were collected through household surveys in Lizhong Town and Houbai Town. The following question was asked.

*What property will you primarily transfer to a safe place when the flood hits?*

Survey results show that people give priority to transferring movable goods/properties, such as vehicles, TVs, microwave ovens, induction cookers, washing machines, fixed telephones, bed sheets, food, and clothing. Some large and bulky items, such as sofa, wardrobe, bed, air conditioner, and refrigerator are difficult to transfer. Excluding the movable items, the new depth-damage curves considering resilience factor were constructed.

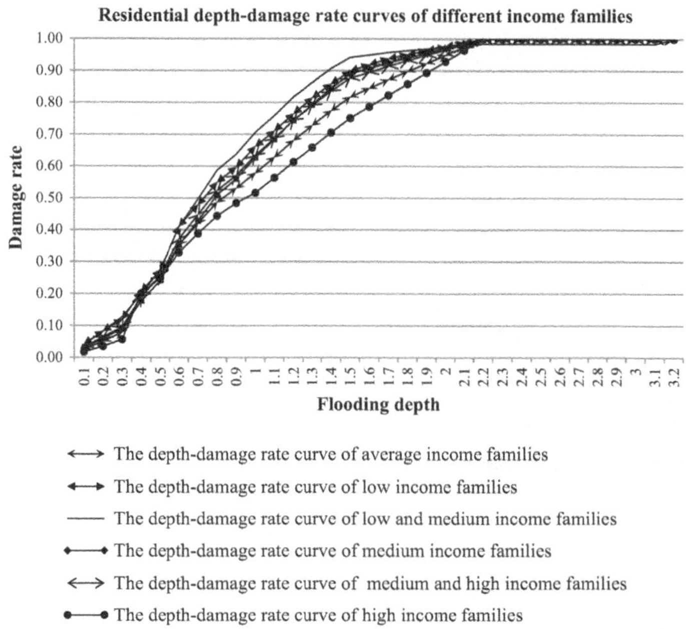


**Fig. 7.3** Residential depth-damage rate curves of different income families in Lizhong Town

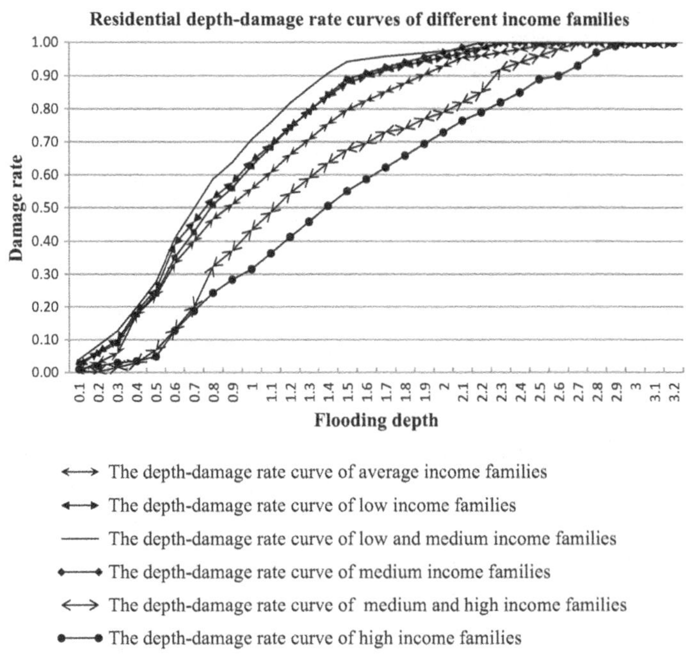


**Fig. 7.4** Residential depth-damage rate curves of different income families in Houbai Town

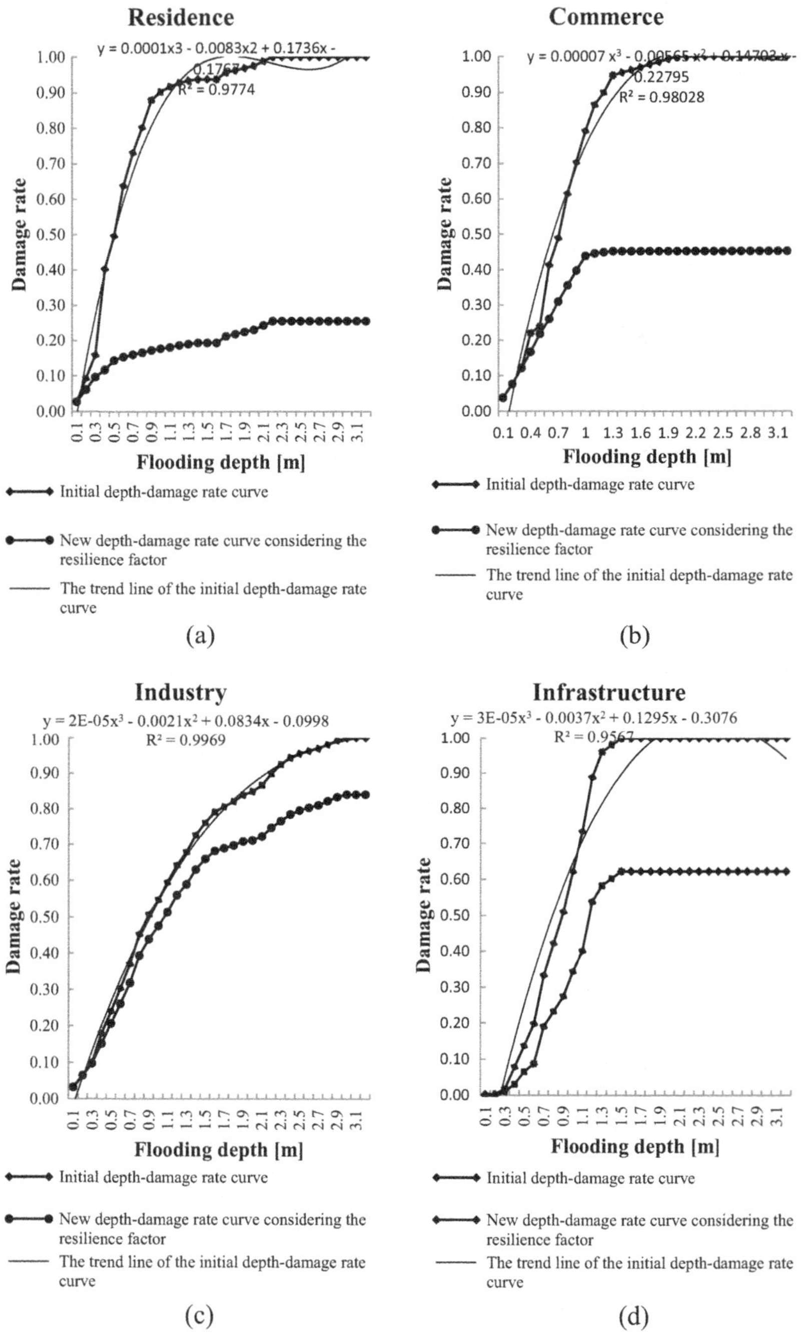


**Fig. 7.5** Receptors initial depth-damage rate curve and the new depth-damage curve considering the resilience factor in Lizhong Town. **a** Residential depth-damage rate curve, **b** Commercial depth-damage rate curve, **c** Industrial depth-damage rate curve, **d** Infrastructure depth-damage rate curve, **e** Agriculture depth-damage rate curve, **f** Receptors depth-damage rate curve

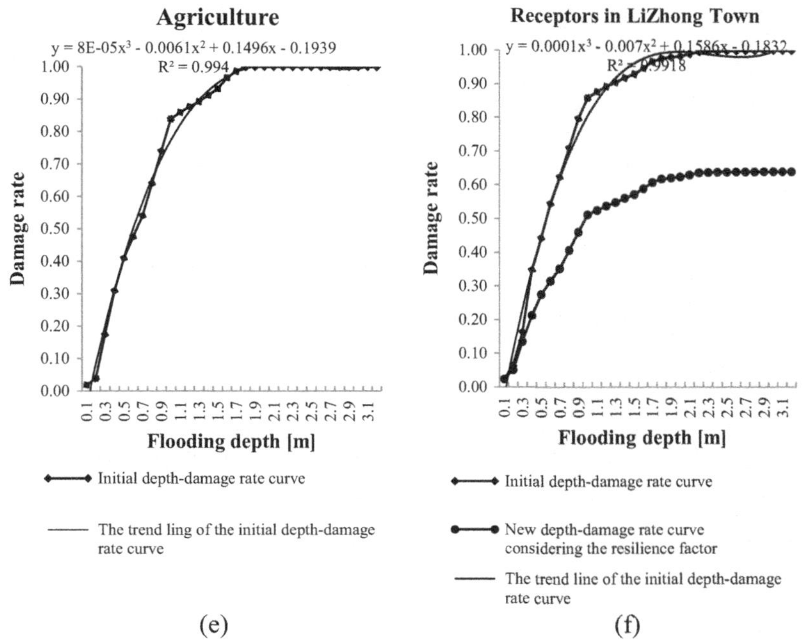


**Fig. 7.5** (continued)

Commercial receptors were classified into non-movable items because the inventory is relatively scattered and plentiful. Excluding the movable items, including vehicles, computers, and telephones, the new depth-damage rate curves considering resilience were constructed (Figs. 7.5b and 7.6b).

For industrial receptors, priority transfer items include vehicle, computer, telephone, and so on. Meanwhile, items such as bulky inventory and raw materials cannot be transferred because floods are usually overwhelming (Figs. 7.5c and 7.6c).

For infrastructures, priority movable items include TV, microwave oven, computer, printer, and so on. Air conditioners, refrigerators, office desks, chairs, and so on are classified as non-movable items (Fig. 7.5d).

#### 7.3.4.1 Assessment of Flood Damage for Agriculture

Data were collected through field research. Several of the major agricultural indices were collected on the basis of the farmers' description of the crop loss rate under different inundation depths and reference to the article *A Study on the Technology and Method of Flood and Water logging Disaster Loss Assessment Based on RS and GIS* (in Chinese) (Ding 2004) to estimate the loss rate of each crop at different water depths. The annual loss of each crop can be calculated from the loss rate multiplied

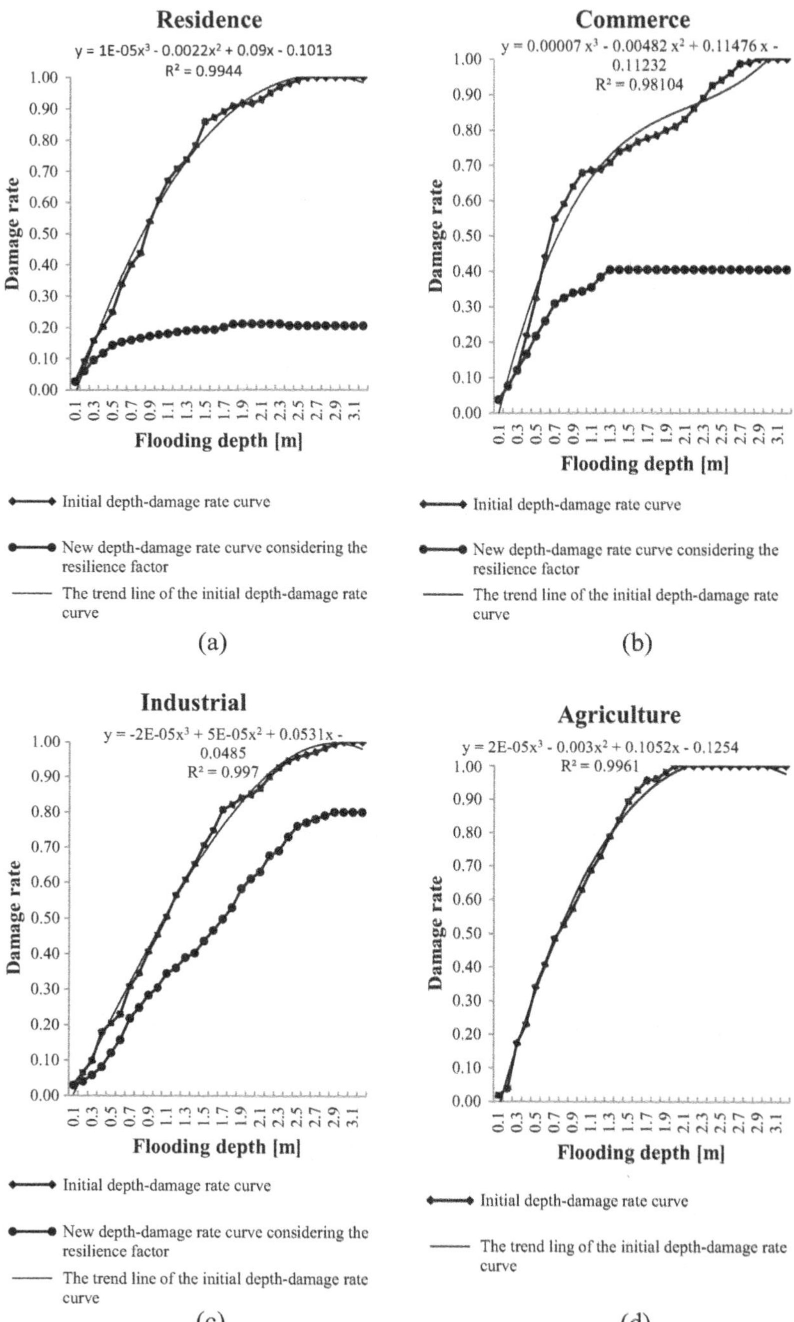


**Fig. 7.6** Receptors initial depth-damage rate curve and the new depth-damage curve considering the resilience factor in HoubaiTown. **a** Residential depth-damage rate curve, **b** Commercial depth-damage rate curve, **c** Industrial depth-damage rate curve, **d** Agriculture depth-damage rate curve

by the annual output value. Economic crops are indexed by $c = 1, 2, 3, \ldots, q$. The total agriculture value can be evaluated by the following equation:

$$AV = \sum_{c=1}^{q} V_c \; and \; V_c \; P_c Y_c A_c \tag{7.6}$$

where:

$AV$ is the total agriculture value, $q$ is the number of all types of crops, $V_c$ is the annual output value for the $c$ types of crops, $P_c$ is the estimated price per unit weight of crop $c$, $Y_c$ is the annual yield per unit area for crop $c$, and $A_c$ is the cultivated area of crop $c$.

The agriculture losses at different depths can be measured as follows:

$$AD_j = \sum_{c=1}^{q} [V_c r_{cj}], \tag{7.7}$$

where:

$AD_j$ is the agriculture loss at depth $j$ and $r_{cj}$ is the loss rate of crop $c$ at depth $j$.

The loss rate is the ratio of loss value to the original value of the property. Residential, commercial, and industrial properties, and infrastructure are calculated per unit loss rate. For example, residential loss rate is measured by the average family's loss rate, and industrial loss rate is measured by average factory's loss rate. However, agricultural loss rate cannot be measured by the average village loss rate as a unit because of the considerable differences in economic crop planting areas and species in each village. For the agricultural loss rate under different inundation depths calculated from the losses at different depths divided by the total annual output value of agriculture, the agriculture loss rate is calculated by the following formula:

$$AR_j = AD_j / AV \tag{7.8}$$

where:

$AR_j$ is the agriculture loss rate at depth $j$.

According the results of the agriculture loss rate at different depths, agriculture depth-damage rate curve is constructed through the excel table and the flood-damage rate functions is calculated by using SPSS regression analysis (Figs. 7.5e and 7.6d). Research founded that villagers can hardly conduct crop rescue work facing with the floods hit, so the estimation of agricultural disaster loss rate is not considered by resilience factors.

#### 7.3.4.2 Assessment of Flood Damage for All Receptors

In the above calculation, gross loss calculation is adopted for agriculture, while unit loss calculation is adopted for the others, and receptors in addition to agriculture are indexed by $i$. Water depths are indexed by $j$, and the total value can be measured as follows:

$$TV = \sum_{i=1}^{4} \left[V^i Q^i\right] + AV \tag{7.9}$$

where:

$TV$ is the total value of all receptors, and $Q^i$ is the flood affected number of receptor $i$.

$$TD_j = \sum_{i=1}^{4} \left[D^i_j Q^i\right] + AD_j \tag{7.10}$$

where:

$TD_j$ is the total losses of all receptors at depth $j$.

The total loss rates at different water depths can be calculated from the total losses at different depths divided by the total value of the five receptors, and the total loss rate was calculated by the following formula:

$$TR_j = TD_j / TV \tag{7.11}$$

where:

$TR_j$ is the total loss rates at different depths of $j$.

The construction of the flood depth-damage rate curve through the Excel table and calculation of the flood loss rate functions by using SPSS regression analysis are shown in Fig. 7.5f. On the basis of the calculation process above, the flood loss rate concerning the resilience factor can also be calculated, with the new depth-damage rate curves drawn.

**Table 7.2** Fitting results of the relationship between loss rate and water depth

| Function | | Constant | $b_1$ | $b_2$ | $b_3$ | $R^2$ |
|---|---|---|---|---|---|---|
| Polynomial-3ord | Lizhong town | $-0.173^{***}$ | $1.711^{***}$ | $-0.813^{***}$ | $0.124^{***}$ | 0.978 |
| | Houbai town | $-0.135^{***}$ | $0.882^{***}$ | $-0.192^{***}$ | $0.08^{***}$ | 0.998 |
| Function | Lizhong town | (0.035) | (0.090) | (0.063) | (0.013) | – |
| | Houbai town | (−0.101) | (0.09) | (−0.002) | (0.0001) | – |

*Notes* (1) Standard deviations are reported in brackets. (2) The symbol *** stands for 1% significant

## 7.4 Results

### *7.4.1 Flood Depth-Damage Curves of Residential Indoor Property from Different Incomes*

The flood depth-economic loss curves of the five different family types (Figs. 7.3 and 7.4) display S-shaped curves. The loss rate increased slowly from depths 0.1 to 0.3 m. It increased sharply from depths 0.3 to 1.5 m, and slowed down from depths 1.5 to 2.2 m. Thereafter, the loss rate gradually reached the maximum of one.

From the family income differences perspective, the depth-damage rate curve of high- income families are steeper than those of low-income families. However, the overall growth trends of flood depth-damage rate curves for different types of income families are similar. Meanwhile, the shape of the curves constructed in this article is almost the same with those of the curves constructed by Su et al. (2002) and Shi (2010). This result indicates that residential property types and their display heights have little difference in mainland China and Taiwan.

### *7.4.2 Receptors' Damage Rate Regression Functions*

Different function types, such as liner, polynomial-2ord, polynomial-3ord, exponential, logarithmic, and power functions were analyzed to investigate the uncertainty share linked to the damage rate curve shape adopted in the analysis. By taking a residential area as an example, the damage rate is the dependent variable and water depth the independent variable. From the fitting coefficient of all functions, the polynomial-3ord function presents the best results (Table 7.2).

### *7.4.3 Receptors Flood Depth-Damage Rate Curves*

It can be seen from the disaster loss rate curves that the shapes of the disaster loss rate curves of disaster bearing bodies were all close to "S", whether considering the resilience factor or not. With the water depth growing, the disaster loss rate monotonically increased. Nevertheless, the change rate of disaster loss rate to water depth went through a "small-large-small" process, dividing into the primary stage, developmental stage and declining stage. At the primary stage, change rates of losses of various kinds of disaster bearing bodies were relatively small; at the developmental stage, with the water depth growing, change rates of losses rapidly increased; at the declining stage, when the water depth reached a certain level, change rate of losses gradually decreased and the situation tends to be stable.

Significant differences between receptors' flood loss rates at different depths exist, as exemplified by Lizhong Town. For the commerce, flood loss rate increased slowly from depths of 0 to 0.4 m and increased sharply from depths of 0.4 to 1.3 m. Subsequently, the loss rate increased slowly and gradually reached the maximum of one. For the industry, flood loss rate increased sharply from depths of 0 to 1.3 m. Thereafter, the loss rate increased slowly and gradually reached the maximum value. For the infrastructure, the loss rate was almost zero at depths of 0 to 0.3 m. The loss rate increased sharply from depths 0.3 to 1.3 m. Subsequently, the loss rate increased slowly and gradually reached the maximum. For the agriculture, flood loss rate increased slowly from depths of 0 to 1.0 m. It increased sharply from depths 1.0 to 1.8 m. Subsequently, the loss rate gradually reached the maximum of one.

The loss rates of all receptors decreased when resilience factor was considered, and the reductions were different, as exemplified by Lizhong Town. With the increase of the water depth, the total flood loss rate of all the receptors decreased by 34%. The residential, commercial, industrial, and infrastructural receptors were reduced by 74, 54.8, 16, and 38%, respectively. The degrees of reduction were remarkably different and were related to the characteristics of the receptors' properties. Most residential and commercial properties are small and easy to move, whereas items in industry are too heavy to move. These items include inventory, raw materials, and machines. Therefore, the resilience factor is of more significance to residential and commercial properties than to industrial properties. The damage rate curves of receptors are shown as follows (Figs. 7.5a–f).

It can be seen from the investigations of the two towns that disaster loss rate curves of various disaster bearing bodies were closely related to the bodies' characteristics, such as the height of the putting position, water resistance, the convenience of transfer, etc. For example, in residential areas, business districts and infrastructure areas, the heights of articles were relatively low, resulting in weak water resistance. With the increase of water depth, the change rate of losses grew relatively large. But when it was beyond certain level of water depth, the change rate of losses became smooth; in spite of this, these disaster bearing bodies were convenient to move owing to their small volumes, and considering the resilience factor, the disaster loss rate could be lowered to a large degree.

It was also found that in industrial areas, it was dominated by enterprises like clothing factory and so forth. Raw materials and inventories were put high and thus water resistance was relatively weak. For this reason, with the growth of water depth, disaster loss rate increased. These articles being cumbersome and difficult to move, the disaster loss rate could only be lowered to a small extent in consideration of the resilience factor.

In agroforestry areas, it was dominated by fishery breeding, trees and flowers planting, etc. When the water depth went beyond a certain height, the loss rate would keep stable. These types of disaster bearing bodies being difficult to move, the disaster loss rate almost remained to be constant, whether considering the resilience factor or not.

The difference of disaster loss rate was obtained by subtracting the disaster loss rate with the resilience being considered from the initial disaster loss rate. This value reflected the effects of the resilience when disaster bearing bodies are in different water depth. The larger the difference value was, the more obvious the effect of the resilience would be, and the smaller the difference value, the less obvious the effect of the resilience. With the increase of the water depth, the difference value grew larger. The reason was that with the increase of the water depth, victims had more time to transfer their property, and thus the effect of the resilience growing more obvious.

From the perspective of the disaster loss rate with resilience being considered, in the residential area, industrial area, business district and infrastructure area, the disaster loss rates all decreased. However, the range of the decrease was inconsistent. Among these areas, the residential area had the largest decreasing range. With different water depth, the difference was the largest, indicating that, in the residential area, the transformability of property easily waterlogged was relatively large and the effect of the resilience the most obvious; the industrial area had the least difference, showing that it was difficult to transfer property easily waterlogged in this area. This was related to property features of various disaster bearing bodies. In residential areas, owing to the small unit value of indoor property, indoor property was easy to move; in industrial areas, however, property such as machines being cumbersome, raw materials and inventories being large, they were very difficult to move. Therefore, in the residential area, the resilience had a more obvious influence on economic losses caused by flood disasters.

## 7.5 Conclusion

This paper conducted researches on the typical towns of Lizhong in the Lixia River and Houbai in Jurong River to collect data via field survey and household interview. Subsequently, the flood loss rates in different water depths were calculated for the residential, industrial, commercial, infrastructure, and agricultural properties. Damage rate functions were fitted on the basis of the regression method, with the original depth-economic loss curves drawn. Then, considering the resilience factor fully to draw the new depth-economic loss curves, which were more in line with the actual situation, the main conclusions are as follows.

(1) This paper plotted the flood depth-economic loss curves for different income levels of residential households. The results show that the damage values of different family income levels are not identical, but they have similar flood-damage rate curves.
(2) We can see that the five receptors depth-economic loss curves are all shaped like an S. The loss rate reached the maximum at the depth of 3 m, and the sums of the five receptors' damage are 6.98 million Yuan (RMB) and 2.2 million Yuan (RMB), respectively. The property damage on agricultural and residential properties accounted for a large proportion of the five receptors' damage because Lizhong Town and Houbai Town are predominantly agricultural towns.
(3) This analysis emphasizes that the resilience correction loss rate of different receptors in Lizhong Town is in the range of 16 to 74%, and in Houbai Town is in the range of 20 to 79%. The residential flood loss, commercial loss, infrastructure loss and industry loss were reduced by 74, 54.8, 38 and 16%, respectively in Lizhong Town, and the residential flood loss, commercial loss, and industry loss were reduced by 79, 60, and 20%, respectively in Houbai Town.

It can be seen from the above study that resilience, as a crucial factor of reducing economic losses caused by rainstorm and flood, should be brought to the forefront widely by sectors of the society. The restoring force of disaster reduction can be strengthened from the following aspects. Firstly, departments, such as the meteorological one, should further improve the ability of early warning against and forecasting disasters like typhoon, rainstorm, etc. For instance, the longer the advanced period of early warning and forecasting is, the less disaster losses will be, because that victims' preparation for disaster prevention will be more adequate; secondly, as regards disaster reduction, local governments and communities should improve publicity, mobilization, organization, coordination and so forth. For example, labor force, i.e., young adults, and vehicles should be gathered to transfer victims, important property, etc.; thirdly, victims' mutual assistance and self-salving. This always saves lives and major property losses of victims at the critical moment in the first scene.

According to social investigation as the main method for evaluating the economic damage of the different receptors in two towns and construct the depth- economic loss curves, it is of significance in flood-damage prevention and reduction. However, because of research time and data limitations and the complexity of the receptors and disaster environment, flood-economic loss assessment is subject to uncertainties from various sources. This paper is just a study of the economic loss of flood disaster under a static situation. Future research should be carried out on the following aspects.

(1) Flood-damage assessment should consider flood hazard and exposure analyses. These factors include rainfall intensity, water flow, submerged duration, and terrain.
(2) The research process should be more specific and reasonable to minimize errors brought about by human factors. The research steps should be further refined, and the questionnaire should be designed on the basis of multiple preliminary

investigation. In addition, the research team should be trained to ensure the validity of the survey data.

(3) In addition to the investigation and evaluation of receptors based on different urban land uses or assets, more attention should be given to conducting field survey in each flood spot because the economic loss at the flood point accounts for the majority in all areas.

(4) Considering resilience, the main factors affecting all receptors' resilience should be classified and deeply excavated to provide a reference for the government's and people's disaster prevention and reduction measures.

(5) In the future, other types of towns, i.e. those showing great difference in economic developmental degree, disaster prevention and mitigation facilities and industrial structures, should be compared to obtain results having typical significance by comparing disaster loss rate curves of various disaster bearing bodies.

**Acknowledgements** Lei Zhou, Ge Gao, Ji Guo, Zhonghui Ji, Rongrong Gu also made great contributions to this manuscript. We express our heartfelt thanks to them. This research was supported by: National Social and Scientific Fund Program of China (18ZDA052; 17BGL142;16ZDA047); The Natural Science Foundation of China (91546117, 71373131).

## References

Adeniyi, O., & Perera, S. (2019). Developing maturity levels for flood resilience of businesses using built environment flood resilience capability areas. *Sustainable Cities and Society, 51,* 101778. https://doi.org/10.1016/j.scs.2019.101778.

Albano, R., Craciun, I., et al. (2017). Flood damage assessment and uncertainty analysis: The case study of 2006 flood in Ilisua basin in Romania. *Carpathian Journal of Earth and Environmental Sciences, 12*(2), 335–346.

Almutairi, A., Mourshed, M., & Ameen, R. F. M. (2020). Coastal community resilience frameworks for disaster risk management. *Natural Hazards, 101*(2), 595–630.

Bignami, D. F., Rulli, M. C., & Rosso, R. (2018). Testing the use of reimbursement data to obtain damage curves in urbanized areas: The case of the Piedmont flood on October 2000. *Journal of Flood Risk Management, 11*(2), 575–593.

Bruneau, M., Chang, S., Eguchi, R., et al. (2003). A framework to quantitatively assess and enhance seismic resilience of communities. *Earthquake Spectra, 19*(4), 733–752.

Ceccato, L., Giannini, V., & Giupponi, C. (2011). Participatory assessment of adaptation strategies to flood risk in the Upper Brahmaputra and Danube river basins. *Environmental Science and Policy, 14,* 1163–1174.

Chen, M., Ma, J., et al. (2015). Is the S-shaped curve a general law? An application to evaluate the damage resulting from water-induced disasters. *Natural Hazards, 78*(1), 497–515.

Chen, W., Wang, X. L., et al. (2019). Integrated urban flood vulnerability assessment using local spatial dependence-based probabilistic approach. *Journal of Hydrology, 575,* 454–469.

Chen, X. L., Wen, Y. H., Huang, L. Y., et al. (2008). Multiple-time scale analysis of precipitation in Lixiahe region. *Journal of China Hydrology, 03,* 83–85. (in Chinese).

Choptiany, J. M. H., Phillips, S., et al. (2017). SHARP: Integrating a traditional survey with participatory self-evaluation and learning for climate change resilience assessment. *Climate and Development, 9*(6), 505–517.

Coetzee, C., Van Niekerk, D., & Raju, E. (2018). Reconsidering disaster resilience: A nonlinear systems paradigm in agricultural communities in Southern Africa. *Natural Hazards, 90*(2), 777–801.

Coto, E. B. (2002). Flood hazard, vulnerability and risk assessment in the city of Turrialba, Costa Rica. International Institute for Geo-information Science and Earth Observation (ITC), pp. 1–102.

Cox, R. S., Hamlen, M., et al. (2015). Community disaster resilience and the rural resilience index. *American Behavioral Scientist, 59*(2), 220–237.

Cutter, S. L. (2016). The landscape of disaster resilience indicators in the USA. *Natural Hazards, 80*(2), 741–758.

Ding, Z. X. (2004). A study on the technology and method of flood and waterlogging disaster loss assessment based on RS and GIS (in Chinese).

Ding, J. G., Xu, M., Fu, G. S., et al. (2010). Yang tai 2006 Storm floods analysis in Lixia river region in 2006 Meiyu period. *Jiangsu Water Resources,* (7), 22–23+25 (in Chinese).

Dong, Z. N., Jiang, L. P., Zhang, J. Q., et al. (2012). Research on flood vulnerability curves of rural dwellings based on "3S" technology. *Journal of Catastrophology, 02*(34), 38–42. (in Chinese).

Dutta, D., & Tingsanchali, T. (2003). Development of loss functions for flood urban flood risk analysis in Bangkok. Proceedings of the 2nd international symposium on new technologies for urban safety of Mega Cities in Asia, ICUS, The university of Tokyo, pp. 229–238.

Emmanuel, M., Siambabala, B. M., Andrew, E., et al. (2013). Indigenous knowledge, coping strategies and resilience to floods in Muzarabni, Zimbabwe. *International Journal of Disaster Risk reduction,* 38–48.

Englhardt, J., Moel, H. D., et al. (2019). Enhancement of large-scale flood risk assessments using building-material-based vulnerability curves for an object-based approach in urban and rural areas. *Natural Hazards and Earth System Sciences, 19*(8), 1703–1722.

Feng, Y., Brubaker, K. L., et al. (2017). New view of flood frequency incorporating duration. *Journal of Hydrologic Engineering, 22,* 11.

Field, C. B., Barros, V., Stocker, T. F., Qin, D., Dokken, D. J., Ebi, K. L., Mastrandrea, M. D., Mach, K. J., Plattner, G. -K., Allen, S. K., Tignor, M., & Midgley, P. M. (2012). Managingthe risks of extreme events and disasters to advance climate change adaptation. A special report of working groups I and II of the intergovernmental panel on climate change. Cambridge University Press, Cambridge, UK, and New York, NY, USA, 582.

Fuchs, S., Heiss, K., & Hübl, J. (2007). Towards an empirical vulnerability function for use in debris flow risk assessment. *Natural Hazards and Earth Systems Sciences, 7*(5), 495–506.

Füssel, H.-M., & Klein, R. (2006). Climate change vulnerability assessments: Anevolution of conceptual thinking. *Climatic Change, 75*(3), 301–329.

Gaetano, M., & Rose, A. (2014). Resilience and sustainability in relation to disasters: A challenge for future cities: C. Springer briefs in earth sciences.

Galbusera, L., & Giannopoulos, G. (2018). On input-output economic models in disaster impact assessment. *International Journal of Disaster Risk Reduction, 20,* 186–198.

Hamidi, A. R., Wang, J. W., et al. (2020). Flood vulnerability assessment using MOVE framework: A case study of the northern part of district Peshawar, Pakistan. *Natural Hazards, 101*(2), 385–408.

Hochrainer-Stigler, S., Laurien, F., et al. (2020). Standardized disaster and climate resilience grading: A global scale empirical analysis of community flood resilience. *Journal of Environmental Management, 276,* 111332. https://doi.org/10.1016/j.jenvman.2020.111332.

Hofflinger, A., & Somos-Valenzuela, M. A. (2019). Response time to flood events using a social vulnerability index (ReTSVI). *Natural Hazards and Earth System Sciences, 19*(1), 251–267.

IPCC. (2013). Approved summary for policymakers. In: L. Alexander, S. Allen, & L.B. Nathaniel et al. (Eds.), Climate change 2013: The physical science basis summary for policymakers. Contribution of working Group I to the fifth assessment report of the intergovernmental panel on climate change. Cambridge: Cambridge University Press, Cambridge.

Jacobson, C. (2020). Community climate resilience in Cambodia. *Environmental Research, 186,* 109512. https://doi.org/10.1016/j.envres.2020.109512.

Joyce, J., & Chang, N. B. (2018). Coupling infrastructure resilience and flood risk assessment via copulas analyses for a coastal green-grey-blue drainage system under extreme weather events. *Environmental Modelling & Software, 100,* 82–103.

Joyce, A., Kotter, T., et al. (2017). Operationalizing a concept: The systematic review of composite indicator building for measuring community disaster resilience. *International Journal of Disaster Risk Reduction, 25,* 147–162.

Kelman, I. (2002). *Physical flood vulnerability of residential properties in coastal, eastern England*. UK: University of Cambridge.

Khajehei, S., Ahmadalipour, A., et al. (2020). A place-based assessment of flash flood hazard and vulnerability in the contiguous United States. *Scientific Reports, 10*(1), 448. https://doi.org/10.1038/s41598-019-57349-z.

Kim, E., & Park, H. (2018). Two-stage approach to quantify the resilience of maritime hazardous and noxious substance spill accidents. *International Journal of Disaster Risk Reduction, 28,* 595–601.

Kim, B., & Shin, S. C. (2017). A resilience loss assessment framework for evaluating flood-control dam safety upgrades. *Natural Hazards, 86*(2), 805–819.

Kleist, L., Thieken, A. H., Koehler, P., et al. (2006). Estimation of the regional stock of residential buildings as a basis for a comparative risk assessment in Germany. *Natural Hazards and Earth System Sciences, 6*(4), 541–552.

Li, C. C., & Cheng, X. T. (2016). A three-parameter S-shaped function of flood return period and damage. Advances in Meteorology, 6583906. Doi: https://doi.org/10.1155/2016/6583906.

Liu, Y. L., Chen, Z. L., Wang, J., et al. (2011). Study on Property (Capital) vulnerability of houses in regular rainstorm water-logging areas–taking wenzhou city as example. *Journal of Catastrophology, 26*(2), 66–71. (in Chinese).

Malgwi, M. B., Fuchs, S., et al. (2020). A generic physical vulnerability model for floods: Review and concept for data-scarce regions. *Natural Hazards and Earth System Sciences, 20*(7), 2067–2090.

Marc, V., Àngels, C., & Beniamino, R. (2016). Flood damage assessment in urban areas. Application to the Raval district of Barcelona using synthetic depth damage curves. *Urban Water Journal, 13*(4), 426–440.

McGrath, H., ElEzz, A. A., & Nastev, M. (2019). Probabilistic depth-damage curves for assessment of flood-induced building losses. *Natural Hazards, 97*(1), 1–14.

Moghadas, M., Asadzadeh, A., Vafeidis, A., Fekete, A., & Ktter, T. (2019). A multi-criteria approach for assessing urban flood resilience in Tehran, Iran. *International Journal of Disaster Risk Reduction, 35,* 101069. https://doi.org/10.1016/j.ijdrr.2019.101069.

Mustafa, D. (2003). Rein forcing vulnerability? Disaster relief recovery, and response to the 2001 flood in Rawalpind, Pakistan. *Global Environmental Change Part B: Environmental Hazards, 5*(3–4), 71–82.

Papathoma-KÖhle, M., Totschnig, R., Keiler, M., & Glade, T. (2012). A new vulnerability function for debris flow e the importance of physical vulnerability assessment in alpine areas. In G. Koboltschng, J. Hübl, & J. Braun (Eds.), *Internationales Symposion Interpraevent, Genoble, April 23e26, 2012* (pp. 1033–1043). Internationale Forschungsgesellschaft Interpraevent: Klagenfurt.

Parsons, M., Glavac, S., et al. (2016). Top-down assessment of disaster A conceptual framework using coping and adaptive capacities. *International Journal of Disaster Risk Reduction, 19,* 1–11.

Penning-Rowsell, E. C., & Chatterton, J. B. (1977). *The benefits of flood alleviation: A manual of assessment techniques*. Alder shot England: Gower Technical Press.

Rose, A. (2012). Estimating the economic consequence of a port shutdown: The special role of resilience. *Economic Systems Research, 25*(2), 212–232.

Rumson, A. G., Garcia, A. P., et al. (2020). The role of data within coastal resilience assessments: An East Anglia, UK, case study. *Ocean & Coastal Management, 185,* 105004. https://doi.org/10.1016/j.ocecoaman.2019.105004.

Scorzini, A. R., & Frank, E. (2017). Flood damage curves: New insights from the 2010 flood in Veneto, Italy. *Journal of Flood Risk Management, 10*(3), 381–392.

Sha, R., & Zhen, H. (1994). Morphological analysis of flood in the Qinhuai river basin[J]. *Journal of Nanjing Normal University (National Science), 17*(3), 47–53. (in Chinese).

Shi, Y. (2010). Research on vulnerability assessment of cities on the disaster scenario. East China normal university (in Chinese).

Shi, Y., Xu, S. Y., Shi, C., et al. (2009). A review on development of vulnerability assessment of floods. *Progress in Geography, 28*(01), 41–46. (in Chinese).

Shi, Y., Xu, S. Y., Shi, C., et al. (2011). Progress in research on vulnerability of natural disasters. Journal of natural disasters, 2009, 20 (2): 131–137. (in Chinese).

Shi, Y., Xu, Y., & Cai, J. (2011). Analysis of the impact of urbanization on flood risk in the middle and lower reaches of Qinhuai river. *Research of Soil and Water Conservation, 05,* 26–31. (in Chinese).

Spialek, M., & Houston, J. B. (2019). The influence of citizen disaster communication on perceptions of neighborhood belonging and community resilience. *Journal of Applied Communication Research, 47*(1), 1–23.

Su, D. M., et al. (2014). Flood damage assessment and related database Implementation for KeeLung River Basin (II), Special research report of National Science Council (See Taiwan). Retrieved 1 August, 2014, from http://ntur.lib.ntu.edu.tw/items-by-author?author=&collectionid=44 (in Chinese).

Szewranski, S., Swiader, M., et al. (2018). Socio-environmental vulnerability mapping for environmental and flood resilience assessment: The case of ageing and poverty in the city of Wrocaw, Poland. *Integrated Environmental Assessment and Management, 14*(5), 592–597.

Tan, J., Peng, L., & Guo, S. L. (2020). Measuring household resilience in hazard-prone mountain areas: a capacity-based approach. *Social Indicators Research, 152*(3), 1153–1176.

Thomas, N., Johannes, N., et al. (2010). Resilience and resistance of buildings and built structures to flood impacts—approaches to analysis and evaluation. German annual of spatial research and policy.

Tian, H., Huang, W. C., & Ma, K. Y. (1998). Possible anomaly and changing rule of precipitation during mei-yu period in Lixiahe region. *Science Meteorological Sinics, 03,* 262–265. (in Chinese).

Turner, B. L., Kasperson, R. E., & Matsonp, A. (2003). A frame work for vulnerability analysis in sustainability science. *Proceedings of the National Academy of Sciences of the United States of America, 100*(14), 8074–8079.

USACE. (2000). Economic Guidance Memorandum (EGM) 01–03, Generic Depth-Damage Relationships, US Army Corps of Engineers Memorandum, CECW -PG4, Washington, DC.

Vogel, C., Moser, S. C., Kasperson, R. E., & Dabelko, G. D. (2007). Linking vulnerability, adaptation, and resilience science to practice: Pathways, players, and partnerships. *Global Environmental Change, 17*(3–4), 349–364.

Wang, Y., & Meng, F. L. (2019). Assessing catchment scale flood resilience of urban areas using a grid cell-based metric. *Water Research, 163,* 114852. https://doi.org/10.1016/j.watres.2019.114852.

Wang, S., Fu, J., & Wang, H. (2019). Unified and rapid assessment of climate resilience of urban drainage system by means of resilience profile graphs for synthetic and real (persistent) rains. *Water Research, 162,* 11–21.

Wu, X. H., Zhou, L., Gao, G., et al. (2016). Flood depth-damage curves for urban properties considering disaster prevention and mitigation capabilities: Evidence from Lizhong Town, Lixiahe region, China. *Progress in Geography, 35*(2), 223–231. (in Chinese).

Wu, Z. N., Shen, Y. X., Wang, H. L., et al. (2020). Quantitative assessment of urban flood disaster vulnerability based on text data: Case study in Zhengzhou. *Water Science and Technology-Water Supply, 20*(2), 408–415.

Yang, Y. Y., Guo, H. X., et al. (2020). Multiattribute decision making for the assessment of disaster resilience in the three gorges reservoir area. *Ecology and Society, 25*(2), 5. https://doi.org/10.5751/ES-11464-250205.

Ye, Z. W., Xu, Y. P., & Xu, J. T. (2009). Flood changing trend and flooding mechanism in Lixiahe region, Jiangsu, China. *Scientia Geographica Sinica, 06,* 880–885. (in Chinese).

Ye, Z. W., Xu, Y. P., & Pang, G. B. (2011). Relationship between flood rainfall and water level in a Jianghuai plain river network region: A case study in the inner Lixiahe. *Jiangsu Geographical Research, 06,* 1137–1146. (in Chinese).
Yin, Z. E., Xu, S. Y., Yin, J., et al. (2010). Small-scale based scenario modeling and disaster risk assessment of urban rainstorm water-logging. *Actageographicasinica, 65*(5), 11–22. (in Chinese).

# Chapter 8
# Finding of Urban Rainstorm and Waterlogging Disasters Based on Microblogging Data and the Location-Routing Problem Model of Urban Emergency Logistics

**Abstract** Due to the climate change and the rapid progress of urbanization, extreme weather disasters such as urban rainstorm and waterlogging are frequent. Therefore, how to find the waterlogging points in the presence of disasters and how to optimize the distribution of urban emergency logistics and reduce the negative impact of disasters have become a hot and difficult issue for government departments and scholars. First of all, the idea and method of using the big data of microblogging to obtain urban rainstorm and waterlogging disasters and public sentiment are put forward. In addition, this thesis constructed the location-routing problem (LRP) model of urban emergency logistics in the situation of rainstorm and waterlogging disaster, and found out the dynamic emergency distribution path of Nanjing in the situation of waterlogging disaster by using NSGA-III algorithm. Research shows that the risk management of urban rainstorm and waterlogging disasters, together with social media data, is a feasible way to obtain on-site data of disasters and carry out risk assessment of disasters. At the same time, the emergency logistics location-positioning model and algorithm can provide a reference for similar disaster emergency logistics distribution network and the conclusion can provide empirical reference for cities to cope with rainstorm and waterlogging disasters.

**Keywords** Microblogging data · Urban rainstorm and waterlogging disasters · Location-routing problem · NSGA-III algorithm

## 8.1 Introduction

In recent years, meteorological disasters have become increasingly frequent as a result of global warming. In the meanwhile, compared with the rapid urbanization process, the less developed water system planning and underground pipe network construction in China lead to frequent rainstorms and waterloggings, imposing a serious effect on the traffic, tourism, routine work and life, even bringing huge threats to the personal safety of inhabitants. For instance, the extraordinary rainstorm, happened in Beijing on July 21st, collapsed 10,660 houses, exerted significant influence on 1,602,000 people and even killed 79 people, causing CNY11.64 billion financial loss. Therefore, urban rainstorm waterlogging has become a common



X. Wu and J. Guo, *Economic Impacts and Emergency Management of Disasters in China*,
https://doi.org/10.1007/978-981-16-1319-7_8

concern in all sectors of society, since it may lead to congestion and submergence of areas that are prone to be submerged. The formidable site condition makes it difficult for governments and emergency organizations to know the detail about the disaster site and the public emotion, which also poses a difficulty in carrying out emergency rescue work targeted at the high-risk places. All these have been hot and difficult issues in the process of the disaster emergency management.

However, the bloom of social media big data, such as microblog, and data mining technologies, provides a viable channel for us to know disaster details and the public emotion. China owns the most netizens in the world: by the December 2015, Chinese citizens had amounted to 731 million and the popularity rate of the Internet had reached 53.2%; phone netizens had amounted to 620 million, the percentage of which increases to 90.1%. With the enlargement of netizen scale, the usage of social platforms, like microblog and wechat, shows a gradually rising trend, for example, Sina Weibo, launched in China in August, 2009. In 2010, four largest portal websites dedicated to the development and publicity of microblog, especially Sina Weibo, achieving the greatest success, with active users amounting to 50 million within one year in 2010. Statistics suggest that the number of microblog messages that Chinese netizens post and forward every day are 250 million. As a kind of social tool, microblog has become a major platform for more and more people to express personal emotions and record their life. Featured by real time and timeliness, microblog serves as a platform for the extremely rapid spread of hot issues. Therefore, microblog contents could be a valid source for the public opinion analysis, emotion extraction and personal opinion mining. Owing to the low efficiency of information dissemination of traditional media, in the case of waterlogging disaster brought by rainstorm, relevant departments are unable to obtain the first-hand information and elicit quick response. With strong timeliness, microblog could be employed by the public to post disaster details once natural disaster happens, which would provide a means to extract the disaster information through social big data.

Meanwhile, with global warming and the rapid progress of urbanization in China, urban rainstorm and waterlogging disasters have become frequent, which has drawn scholars' attention to the emergency management of urban waterlogging disasters (Kaur and Singh 2016; Song and Du 2017).

However, once a rainstorm disaster occurs in the city, the finding of the disaster and the waterlogging points in the emergency situation and the building of the traffic emergency network are undoubtedly important theoretical and practical problems in the emergency management of the disaster. In this paper, the waterlogging points can be found in the presence of rainstorm disasters by using the microblogging data. When the rainstorm results in breaks of roads, the optimization model of the road traffic is put forward, and the new road traffic route is designed. The methods are of great significance for their novelty and integrity.

The rest of the paper is as follows: the second part is the literature review; the third part is the research of finding the waterlogging points and the disasters by using microblogging data; the fourth part is the model construction; the fifth part is the simulation calculation; and the last is the summary.

## 8.2 Literature Review

### 8.2.1 Disaster Information Extraction of Microblogs

Currently, studies on the microblog disaster extraction mainly center on the earthquake area. Once an earthquake happens, rescue must be conducted within the shortest time in order to reduce the loss to the minimum. Due to the lack of timeliness of traditional media, it is difficult for relevant departments to control the disaster and rescue in time and accurately. Microblogs enjoy strong timeliness. After an earthquake, the public generally post various conditions that they are facing through microblog and other social media. By analyzing microblog big data, disaster details could be known, including the location and casualty of the earthquake.

However, research on using microblog big data to extract disaster information is quite rare at home and abroad. Xu et al. (2015) was the first person who put forward the concept of position microblog. Sakaki (2010) and other researchers put forward the real-time earthquake monitoring system based on the Twitter through the Bayesian Decision Method: take keywords as the evidence. In practical application, the system has successfully detected more than 80% earthquakes and forecasted earlier than the local earthquake organizations. The system can not only detect the occurrence of earthquakes, but also can estimate the location of the earthquake on account of the location information contained in the microblog data. Choi and Bae (2015) introduced how Social Big Board, a real-time monitoring system based on the social big data, represented the disaster and its spreading trend on the map for further disaster estimation, forewarning and precaution development by analyzing earthquake-relevant contents posted on Twitter after the Haiti Earthquake happened in 2010. Because the losses caused by the earthquake are affected by many factors, Avvenuti et al. (2017) referred to users of social media as social sensors, and the ground observations transmitted by Twitter as the input of predictive models. Then they used predictive models to nowcast the perceived intensity of earthquakes. Hoang et al. (2018) thought that although the location information of disasters can be extracted from Twitter, the problems about linguistically incorrect and too numerous of tweets were important to be solved. They introduced a model to analyze whether the tweets contain the location information and to improve the accuracy of location. Cresci et al. (2018) developed a big data crisis mapping system (CrisMap) to quickly collect and analyze social media data. The maps generated by the system can identify areas of severe damage and estimate the impacts of disaster events in the early stages. Yan et al. (2010) believed that microblog contents play a vital role in extracting disaster information by analyzing the microblog message, developing trend of various themes and propagation process through various analysis methods by the example of Yushu Earthquake in 2010. Li et al. (2018) proposed a Multinomial Naïve Bayes Classifier to classify microblog posts forwarded during the Yiliang Earthquake. They discussed the propagation patterns of the different types of Weibo information in different periods after the earthquake. The results showed that the type of information has important effect on propagation patterns and the social media data can be used for efficient emergency management. Xing et al. (2019) put forward a spatial distribution detection method based on emergency information, and used acharacter-level convolutional neural network classifier to mine the spatio-temporal changes of emergency rescue information. Taking the Jiuzhaigou earthquake as an example, the research showed that combining classification and spatio-temporal analysis can effectively dig out the emergency demand information.

In a word, by mining microblog data, earthquake information could be known and it is efficient to prevent and reduce the loss that might be caused by earthquakes. Nevertheless, the microblog big data has not been applied to the emergency management research of urban rainstorm waterlogging disaster.

### 8.2.2 Emotion Analysis of Microblogs

By mining and analyzing microblog contents, relevant departments could know the emotion of the public timely so that they could take corresponding measures to control the public emotion. By now some scholars have developed relevant research by taking advantage of microblog big data. For instance, Zheng et al. (2012) raised an integrated microblog data process method and detecting algorithm about news topics. Li et al. (2013) presented the topic propagation evolution 74 model that could describe the fissionpropagation mode with immunization rate. Hou (2013) made an integrated analysis on the evolution process of the public emotion about the unexpected group events by the example of Shenfang Lindgrenite Event. Yang (2014a, b) raised the method to monitor the public emotion about the emergency on the internet on the basis of the microblog data. Lin et al. (2017) studied the relationship between emotions and emoticons, then they established a multi-modality emotion learning framework by using emoticons as emotional signals. The results of the research showed that their approach has obvious superiority. Based on studying the emoticons in Weibo posts, Yang et al. (2019) built the emotion-semantic-enhanced convolutional neural network (ECNN) model, a convolutional neural network model that can enhance emotional semantics, to improve the sentiment analysis of Weibo content. The consequences demonstrated that this model is easier to recognize emotional semantics and is outperforms other models. Xie et al. (2019) proposed an algorithm that combines geographic information with fine-grained public sentiment information extracted from social big data. Deep learning and further analysis of the disaster were used to study the laws of emotional movement in the disaster-affected areas and optimize disaster reduction strategies by the example of Ya'an Earthquake in 2013. Li et al. (2020) studied the evolution of public emotion on social networks during COVID-19. They tracked the evolutionary patterns of public emotion over time and extracted details of major social events. It turned out that the public's attention has shifted to other aspects of the event over time.

Microblog emotion analysis is conducted through three steps: text preprocessing, emotion information extraction and emotion classification. This kind of research is quite common. For instance, Zheng (2014) came up with the concept of emotion polarity: classify the emotion polarity into positive, neutral and negative by comparing the number of positive and negative emotion vocabularies in the text. Zhou et al. (2013) put forward the method to build Chinese emotion dictionary based on the HowNet and SentiWordNet. The experiment represented that the dictionary is superior to those emotion dictionary with general polarity, which provides valid dictionary resources for emotion analysis studies. Preethi et al. (2015) introduced a generalized model that could be adopted to determine the possibility of an event happens in the future by estimating the causal relationship between the event and its corresponding emotion reaction on the basis of timeliness emotion analysis of Twitter. Take the Sandy Hurricane happened in October, 2012 as an example, Neppalli et al. (2016) visualized the hurricane-related emotions on the map based on the Twitter big data. The study showed that the public emotions are not only related to their geographical position, but also the distance range that the hurricane has affected. Karyotis et al. (2017) proposed an emotional fuzzy model to integrate emotions into intelligent computer systems and explored the feasibility of processing large-scale data based on a hybrid cloud intelligent infrastructure model. Madani et al. (2018) introduced two new methods to classify tweets. One is to calculate the semantic similarity between tweets and the three types of emotions, and the other is to calculate the semantic similarity between the words in the tweet and the words "positive" and "negative". They also used the Hadoop framework and the programming model MapReduce to solve the problem of computing time in the case of very large data sets in tweets. Karmegam and Mappillairaju (2020) used the sentiment dictionary of the National Research Council to extract and classify different sentiments in tweets released during the floods in Chennai in 2015. They evaluated the changes in the rate of negative emotions over time and concluded that there were great differences in the rates of negative emotions among the three periods before, during and after the flood disaster. Finally, they found that spatial analysis of sentiment in tweets during disasters are useful for identifying disaster geographic regions. Although currently there are abundant studies about emotion analysis on the microblog big data, the emotion analysis on the urban rainstorm waterlogging based on the microblog big data are quite rare.

On the basis of the above research, the paper extracts and analyzes the Sina Weibo data during the heavy rain occurrence to further analyze the disaster information and the public emotion, select urban rainstorm waterlogging areas with high risks and provide empirical support for disaster emergency management by the example of the heavy rainfall on June 18th and July 7th in 2016.

### *8.2.3 Urban Emergency Logistics in Waterlogging Disasters*

The decision-making in the presence of urban rainstorm disasters is a focus of attention for scholars. People like Chen et al. (2016) build an urban waterlogging disaster emergency shelter to improve the flexibility and capacity for decision making in emergency management departments; Deng et al. (2016) put forward suggestions on how Shanghai could prevent and cope with waterlogging. Hu et al. (2015) constructed the two-stage stochastic mixed integer programming model at the aim of minimizing the total cost of logistics; Su et al. (2016) presented an integrated simulation method to analyze the effects of urban rainstorm and waterlogging on traffic congestion. Using Weibo data, Xiao et al. (2018) introduced a real-time identification method to analyze urban rainstorm disasters. They used the naive Bayes, support vector machine, and random forest text classification algorithms to train the classification model, then compared the classification performance of the three methods. Research proved that the naive Bayes algorithm they used has higher macro-average accuracy than the two others. Yu et al. (2018) studied how the spatial pattern of impervious surfaces produced in the process of urbanization affects urban waterlogging. Due to the heterogeneity of urban impervious surface effects on waterlogging, they used the Geographically Weighted Regression (GWR) model to evaluate the spatiotemporal changes of the impact of impervious surface expansion on urban waterlogging. The results meant that cities should have different optimization strategies for the spatial pattern of impervious surfaces in different runoff areas. Zhu et al. (2019) put forward a method for evaluating the dynamic impact of heavy rain and waterlogging. This method used land-use data to simulate waterlogging disasters and the performance of the method is assessed by evaluating the socioeconomic impact, object impact, industry impact, regional impact, and comprehensive of the disaster. Huang and Jin (2019) presented a 2-D submergence analysis method combining geographic information system (GIS) and Storm Water Management Model (SWMM). In order to improve the accuracy, the submergence algorithm and the geometric form of the watershed division were also introduced. Hou and Du (2020) proposed a water diffusion algorithm which uses geographic information system (GIS) and remote sensing (RS) technology to build Storm Water Management Model (SWMM). The results obtained can help Emergency Management Department predict urban rainstorms and design drainage networks. However, the research on how to carry out disaster relief material delivery on flooded roads after urban rainstorm and waterlogging is rare. But it is a key issue that needs to be solved in real life as well as a difficult and hot issue that people are concerned about. Therefore, this paper, by proposing an optimization model of post-disaster material delivery and carrying out the demonstration by taking Nanjing as an example, is of great theoretical and practical significance.

Disaster relief supplies can be classified as a sort of location-routing problem. In 1970s, Cooper (1972, 1976) combined the distribution center location problem with the vehicle routing problem, and put forward the transportation-positioning problem. People like Rahman and Smith (2000) suggested that the key to solving the location-routing problem was constructing a reasonable optimization model. During the delivery of emergency supplies, the effect of the relief effort depends on the ability to deliver emergency supplies to affected areas with the minimum amount of time and minimal cost of emergency relief. People such as Li and Zhou (2014) and Moshref and Lee (2016) constructed the rescue model aiming at spending the shortest time; people like Pramudita et al. (2014) constructed the model with the aim of minimizing the total cost; people including Wei and Özdamarb (2007), Rath and Gutjahr (2014), Wang et al. (2014), Burkart et al. (2016), Khalipourazari and Khamseh (2017), Tayal and Singh (2017), Chang et al. (2017), Song and Du (2017) constructed multi-objective models considering a variety of mixing factors to solve the multi-objective problems. Shahparvari et al. (2018) founded a mixed integer programming model to establish emergency rescue resource allocation strategies. In the research, a programming method was used to minimize the risk of transportation interruption. The results showed that mixed integer programming model could effectively allocate resource under emergency situations. Vahdani et al. (2017) built a two-stage, multi-objective mixed-integer, multi-period and multi-commodity mathematical model to effectively distribute relief supplies after an earthquake. Gao (2020) believed that in the event of a large-scale disaster, the surplus materials of the disaster relief center should be used validly. And then, he designed a bi-level random mixed-integer nonlinear programming model and took Sichuan earthquake as an example. Taking into account the urgency of the injured, the fairness of blood distribution and other various risks, Cheraghi and Hosseini-Motlagh (2020) carried a dual-objective algorithm based on mixed-integer robust equity. Experimental results showed that the algorithm was helpful to design a blood transport plan in a disaster.

The difficulty of research lies in how to obtain optimal or satisfactory solutions of these models. Scholars often use heuristic algorithms, among which the two-stage heuristic algorithms are used more frequently (Mete and Zabinsky 2010; Han et al. 2011; Ahmadi et al. 2015). Some other algorithms such as simulated annealing algorithm and ant colony algorithm are also used by scholars (Jotshi et al. 2009; Yu et al. 2010; Dalfard et al. 2013; Ting and Chen 2013). Genetic algorithm is one of the most common used algorithms, but the hybrid optimization algorithm is more adopted by combining basic genetic algorithm with other algorithms due to the complex design and long running time of basic genetic algorithm (Wu et al. 2002; Wang et al. 2015; Asgari et al. 2017). Taking into account the location and route of emergency facilities, Zhang et al. (2018) aimed to solve the location-routing problem of emergency warehouses with uncertain information. By using a combination of a genetic algorithm and uncertainty simulation algorithm, researchers formed a multi-target location planning model that considers time, cost and carbon dioxide emissions for emergency response. Zhou et al. (2019) held that the design of the last mile delivery system is very useful to serve customers economically and effectively, so they designed a bi-level multisized terminal location-routing problem (BL-MSTLRP), and adopted a combination of genetic algorithm and simulated annealing algorithm called self-adaptive (SGA). Based on the cold chain logistics, Yan et al. (2020) established a two-stage distribution location model with minimum total cost as the objective function, and used a hybrid genetic algorithm. In addition, by comparing and studying, scholars (Rabiee et al. 2012; Fallah-Mehdipoura et al. 2012; Bandyopadhyay and Bhattacharya 2013; Kalaivani et al. 2013; Pasandideh et al. 2013; Pramudita et al. 2014; Song et al. 2017) found that non-dominated sorting genetic algorithm had obvious advantages among the current multi-objective optimization algorithms; The improved NSGA-III algorithm, in particular had great advantage in running time and solution quality. Therefore, in recent years, the improved NSGA-III algorithm has been applied to the research of emergency and other multi-objective planning in many literatures (Mohapatra et al. 2015; Duan et al. 2016; Yu et al. 2017; Zhou et al. 2019, 2017b; Feng et al. 2017). Zhang et al. (2019) improved the NSGA-III algorithm was useful for multiple objective function minimization problems. Ma et al. (2020) considered various factors such as the utilization rate of computing and storage resources and load balancing rates of the resource service center; hence they designed a multi-objective optimization model and used a knowledge-driven evolutionary algorithm (Multi-Generations Reference NSGA-III, MGR-NSGA-III) to pick the optimal solution of the model. The results of the study proved that this evolutionary algorithm (MGR-NSGA-III) was faster than NSGA-III to find out the optimal solution of the model. Based on the above considerations, the algorithm was also selected in this paper.

Based on the existing literature review, there exists very little research in which a city in taken as an example to study emergency material delivery under the circumstance of rainstorm flood disaster. As far as the researchers' vision is concerned, there has not yet been research of building the LRP model based on the disaster information obtained via the microblogging. Therefore, in the paper, information on the disasters is obtained through microblogging data for the first time, and then the paper presented the LRP model in the context of rainstorm and waterlogging disaster, and by taking Nanjing as an example, used non-dominated sorting algorithm NSGA-III to get solutions. The strategy and method of the research has enriched the existing research literature of disaster management, and the conclusion has provided an empirical reference for Nanjing to cope with the rainstorm and waterlogging disaster.

## 8.3 Obtainment of Disaster Information via Microblogging Data

### *8.3.1 Research Steps*

On the basis of the Sina Weibo content, take the following three steps to extract the urban rainstorm water blogging information from microblogs of numerous users:

First step: data extraction and IP address translation. Take the persistent strong rainfall from the mid-June to the beginning of July in 2016 as an example, 6,385 microblogs are extracted from June 18th to July 7th. Owing to the longtime quantum, microblog contents are divided into two parts and processed separately to specifically reflect the variation trend of waterlogging during this period in Nanjing: from June 18th to June 30th and from July 1st to July 7th. The paper will analyze the seriousness level of waterlogging in all administrative regions of Nanjing and find out areas prone to be submerged during this strong rainfall via microblog contents. Since the IP address contained by the microblog cannot directly reflect the administrative region of the blogger, all IP addresses are translated into physical addresses through IP address convertor. Then all microblogs can be classified according to administrative regions for further analysis.

Second step: repetition and noise elimination, word segmentation and index establishment. It is necessary to eliminate the repetition and noise, segment words and establish the index because of the loud noise and plenty of invalid repetition in the original microblog data. ICTCLAS is used for word segmentation to process microblog contents. The result of the word segmentation is classified according to the rainfall reasons, the description about the ponding of the public, the effect of the waterlogging on traffic and the emotion reaction of the public (see the attachment Table 8.9 for details); the waterlogging information and emotion description are rated and coded in order to compare the strong rainfall information and emotion reaction in various administrative regions of Nanjing (see attachment Tables 8.10 and 8.11 for details).

Third step: contrastive analysis of these two phases. According to the word segmentation result, for one thing, the variation trend of the waterlogging in the two phases and water logging differences in various administrative regions of Nanjing can be determined and areas prone to be submerged can also be found; for another, the varying regularity of the public's emotions during the urban waterlogging could be analyzed and the emotion difference of the public in various administrative regions could be achieved.

Targeting at the urban rainstorm waterlogging disaster, the paper designs the following extraction process (Fig. 8.1).

## *8.3.2 Research Methods*

The present paper adopts the word segmentation to analyze the enormous microblog text data. Words are processed by the currently universal ICTCLAS, which enjoys high accuracy and can label the part of speech and its corresponding weight and frequency of each word. The main purpose of the paper is to distinguish the disaster degree of waterlogging in all administrative regions of Nanjing. After the word segmentation, the urban rainstorm waterlogging reflecting table and disaster classification coding table could be established and then disaster values of all administrative regions could be normalized by the word frequency and weight of the strong rainfall description.

## *8.3.3 Empirical Results*

### 8.3.3.1 Brief Introduction About the Disaster

Nanjing began to rain form June 18th, 2016 and it did not stop until the beginning July. From the mid-June to the end of June, the rain was normal, mainly thundershower

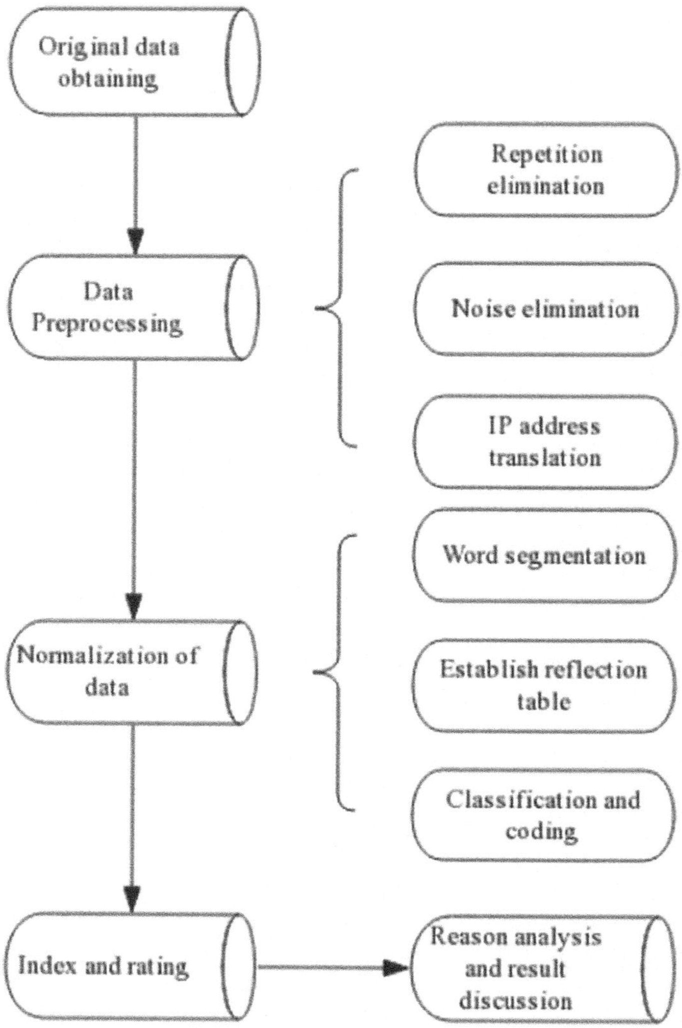


**Fig. 8.1** The extraction process of urban rainstorm waterlogging information based on the microblog big data

and moderate rain; at the beginning of July, the rain started to be stronger, mainly moderate and torrential rain. This persistent rain refreshed the rainfall amount record of Nanjing, amounting to 441 mm on June 27th.

The persistent strong rainfall directly caused serious ponding in urban areas of Nanjing, so that the emergency office of municipal government kept raising the rating of flood prevention and emergency response. There were numerous ponding in urban areas: the depth of ponding in Nanjing University of Science and Technology amounted to 1.5 m; the rainwater submerged the garage in the Yinchengdongyuan housing estate; numerous cars were submerged; the metro station of the Mingfa

Square was submerged by rainwater, the depth of ponding on the Saihongqiao Street amounted to almost 2 m, which imposed great negative influence on citizens' property safety and transportation.

From the result of word segmentation of microblogs, people gave the following description: convective weather, convection, violent typhoon, Nepartak, plum rains, plum, and so on. Since June belongs to rainy seasons, adding to that strong convective weather and typhoon are common in summer, these two factors led to the lasting rainstorm with huge amount of rainfall. People also offered the following description about the disaster: water level rises of Qinhuaihe River; dragon water on the city wall; traffic paralysis; the Yangtze River exceeds the warning level; rapid increase of water level of Xuhe River. The disaster brought huge challenge to the city water prevention system of Nanjing.

#### 8.3.3.2 Contrastive Analysis on the Waterlogging Level

How to evaluate the waterlogging level in various administrative regions of Nanjing is an important issue for research. Generally, people regard disaster degree as the rating standard to measure the loss of the natural disaster. Cheng et al. (2011) put forward the synthetical disaster index (SDI), which can be used to normalize a series of disaster evaluation factors and obtain quantitative disaster evaluation index by weighted addition. Ma (2006) advocated to adopting the disaster degree rating standard of dual-factor evaluation at the early stage: the death roll and the value of the social property loss in a disaster. In the study of the disaster degree of floods, some scholars presented indicators that reflect the size of the disaster area (including the size, population and the number of counties that the disaster has affected). By three-factor analysis, Mao (2000) built the flood disaster index (including the affected area, affected population and food reduction) to evaluate the disaster degree of flood, waterlogging and flood-waterlogging disaster in Dongtinghu Region.

It can be known from the microblog content that this torrential rain did not cause any casualties; however, the direct and indirect economic loss caused by waterlogging was unlikely to be calculated through microblog contents. Therefore, the disaster rating of the urban rainstorm waterlogging is mainly influenced by the amount of rainfall, ponding range, ponding depth and traffic jam. Based on the previous research, the paper summarizes the following formula to calculate the disaster rating of urban rainstorm waterlogging:

$$\begin{aligned}\text{Disaster index} = {} & \text{ponding range} \ast 30\% + \text{ponding depth} \ast 30\% \\ & + \text{traffic jam} \ast 40\%\end{aligned}$$

Based on the above formula, the value of rainstorm waterlogging disaster is quantized and classified into five ratings: low-grade, mild, ordinary, serious, grave. The results can be seen in the following two figures (Figs. 8.2 and 8.3).

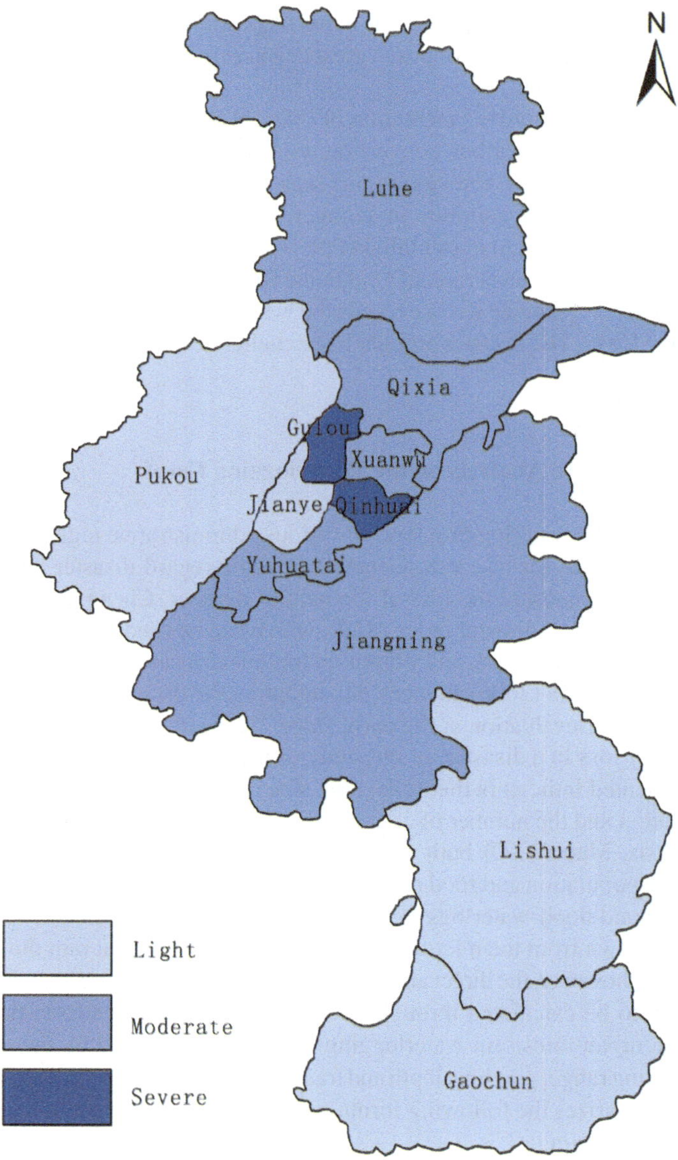


**Fig. 8.2** The rainstorm waterlogging disaster from June 18th to June 30th

In the last ten days of June, ponding in Qinhuai Region and Xuanwu Region was ordinary- even more serious than the other regions; ponding in Pukou Region, Lishui Region and Gaochun Region was mild. In the first ten days of July, the rain became strong, mainly heavy rain, rainstorm and heavy rainstorm. Adding to the previous persistent rain, the increase of rainfall directly led to severe ponding in various

**Fig. 8.3** The rainstorm waterlogging disaster from July 1st to July 7th

administrative regions of Nanjing. There were plenty of direct descriptions about the waterlogging in contents of microblogs. For instance, see the sea; the deepest depth of ponding amounts to 1.5 m; hundreds of cars were submerged; and so on. The ponding in Nanjing was more serious than before as whole: the ponding in Qinhuai Region, Gulou Region and Jiangning Region was grave; the ponding in Jianye Region and Yuhuatai Region was serious; the ponding in Pukou Region, Gaochun Region and Lishui region was mild. At the same time, urban places prone to be submerged can be determined by the ponding depth based on the direct description of ponding depth on specific streets in the microblog, such as "the deepest depth of ponding was 1.5 m", "the deepest depth of ponding was more than 2 m", "the depth of ponding was from 60 to 80 cm", and so on. Areas prone to be submerged mainly centered in Xuanwu Region, Qinhuai Region, Gulou Region, Jianye region, Yuhua Region and Pukou Region. Among these areas, the ponding in Saihongqiao Street was the most grave, with depth of 2 m; the ponding depth in Nanjing University of Science and Technology was 1.5 m; the rainwater submerged the metro station in Mingfa Square, which greatly affected the normal function of metro system.

The ponding in Qinhuai Region was the most serious. Nanjing University of Science and Technology, Zijin East Road and HoubiaoYing Road all become places prone to be submerged. Located at the south part of Zijin Mountain, all these places were low-lying. Adding to the enormous flood from the Zijin Mountain, lots of ponding failed to discharge in time, which made the ponding worse. The layout of areas prone to be submerged is showed as follows (Fig. 8.4).

#### 8.3.3.3 The Subjective Emotion of the Public

After the urban rainstorm waterlogging, the emotion of the public can be estimated by analyzing contents of microblogs, so that corresponding emergency management could be conducted on the basis of the public opinion. After the strong rain happened in June 2016 and subsequent ponding, microblog users expressed their emotion reactions immediately, for example: "smile", "titter", "full of tears", "cry", "curse in rage", and so on. Based on the emotion analysis on microblog contents, the present paper divides the emotion reaction of the public into five categories: exultant, happy, ordinary, unhappy and terribly upset.

From June 18th to June 30th, the public basically had no negative emotions. Although there were some negative vocabularies, such as "tears", "cry", "heartbroken", and the like, the percent of these words was quite small. Instead, there appeared some positive vocabularies like "haha", "titter", "smile" and "handclap". It can be seen that there was not obvious negative emotion among the public during this phase.

From July 1st to July 7th, the public began to show strong negative emotions compared with the previous phase: "whine", "sad", "fear", "full of tears" and "sorrow". The percentage of negative vocabularies was large. There were a few positive vocabularies with low percentage. Therefore, the public expressed intense negative emotion during this phase, mainly shown as anger, panic, fear, sadness, and annoyance. The negative emotion in Qinhuai Region and Gulou Region was the most intense, rating as terribly upset; the negative emotion in Jianye Region and Xuanwu Region rating as unhappy; the negative emotion in Lishui Region and Gaochun Region was the least intense, rating as exultant.

The emotion reactions of the public toward the urban rainstorm waterlogging in June and July can be seen in the following figures (Figs. 8.5 and 8.6).

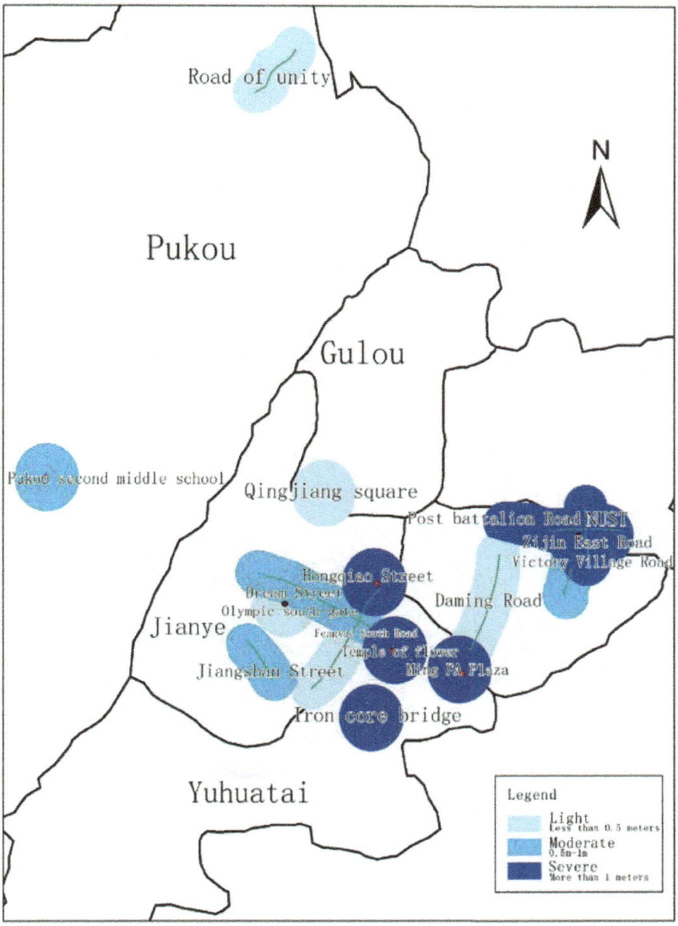


**Fig. 8.4** The layout of areas prone to be submerged from July 1st to July 7th

## 8.4 Construction of Location-Routing Problem Model

According to the disaster information obtained in the third part, the LRP model is built, and then the road traffic data of Nanjing is used to optimize the road traffic after interruption.

### *8.4.1 Problem Description*

The location-routing problem of emergency logistics after rainstorm and waterlogging disaster is described as follows. The location of emergency logistics distribution

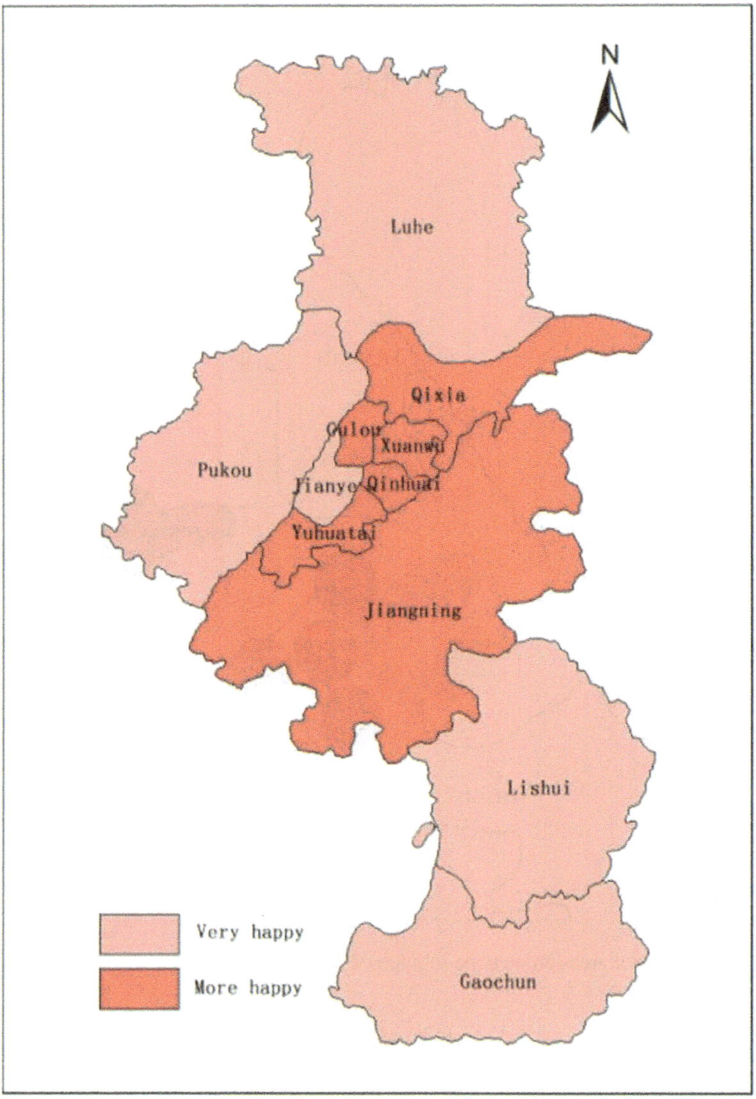


**Fig. 8.5** Emotion reactions of the public from June 18th to June 30th

center, the construction cost and capacity, the capacity of distribution vehicle and the location of the affected point (area) of material rescue have been known. Besides, the demand for various materials can be collected and predicted by the logistics information platform. Based on the information above, the emergency distribution center needs to be determined to make sure that the total demand of the affected points on each distribution route starting from a distribution center is less than the capacity of the distribution center, and that the amount of transport supplies on a single route

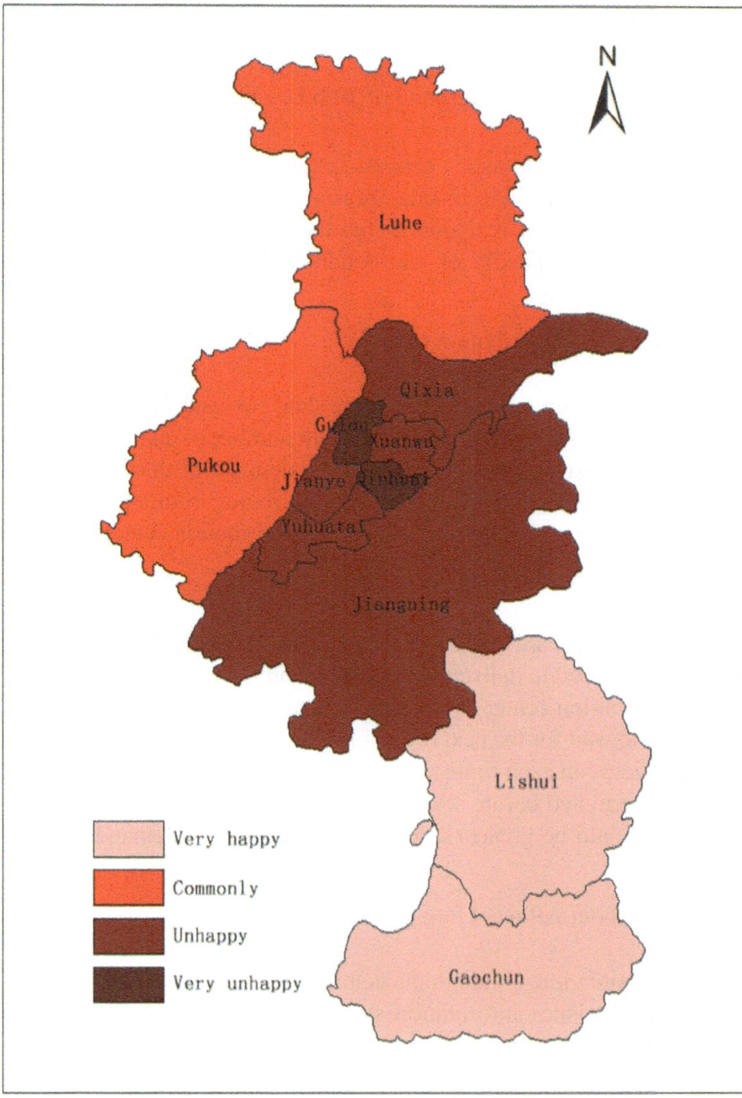


**Fig. 8.6** Emotion reactions of the public from July 1st to July 7th

is less than the total capacity of all the vehicles on the route. Transportation route should be planned reasonably based on the above-all two premises with an aim of making sure the transport time is the shortest and the cost is the least in the whole transport network.

### 8.4.2 Basic Hypotheses and Symbol Description

(1) Hypothesis about the Background of Web Design

In the design of the city's logistics network, exclusive areas which the urban road network can reach are taken into consideration, and the road transport is the exclusive choice for transportation. It is assumed that the road network condition is static; however, due to the complexity of real condition, network circuitous factors are added to the model.

(2) Hypothesis about Distribution Centers

Assume that the distribution centers are more than two and the capacity is limited and known. After waterlogging disaster, a certain number of distribution centers are started for material distribution according to the demand of the affected areas; the total demand of affected points on all distribution routes from a distribution center should be less than the maximum capacity of the distribution center.

(3) Hypothesis about Transport Vehicles

Assume that the vehicles are of the same size and have limited capacity and that the same vehicle can be used to deliver different demand materials; the transport vehicle starts from a distribution center and returns to it after distributing to all the affected points on a route to wait for the next round of delivery. For the sake of simplification, the transport vehicles on each route are considered as a whole, and the total demand of the route is determined before allocating specific number of vehicles; the vehicle load on a route should be greater than or equal to the total demand of all affected points on the route.

(4) Hypothesis about Affected Points

According to real situation, although the demand of affected points can be predicted by corresponding logistics information system, it is not accurate. Therefore, the material demand of affected points can be signified by triangular fuzzy numbers and be transformed into real numbers in the interval [0, 1] by function in operations (Fig. 8.7).

The established model symbols are illustrated below:

(1) Collection Setting

$P$: Distribution Center Collection, $P = \{1, 2, \ldots, p\}$;
$Q$: Affected Points Collection, $Q = \{p + 1, p + 2, \ldots, p + q\}$;
$R$: Node Collection, $R = P \cup Q = \{1, 2, \ldots, p + q\}$;
$V$: Vehicle Collection, $V = \{1, 2, \ldots, k\}$.

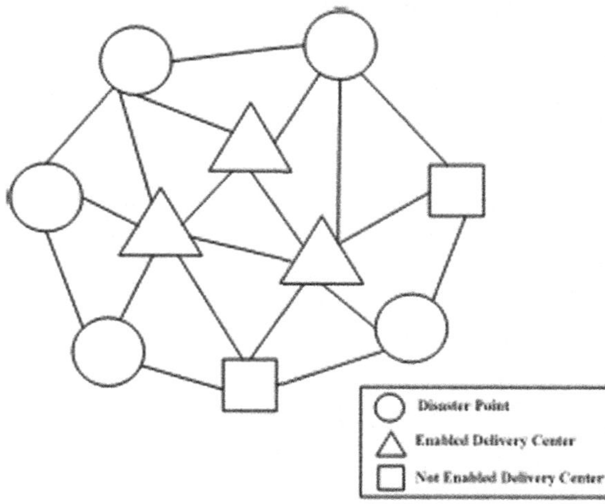


**Fig. 8.7** Conceptual model

(2) Parameter Setting

$F_i$: Construction cost of material distribution center $i$,$i \in P$;
$\delta_i$: Maximum storage capacity of $i$, $i \in P$;
$n_k$: Maximum carrying capacity of vehicle $k$, $k \in V$;
$C_k$: Fixed use cost of vehicle $k$, $k \in V$;
$d_{ij}$: Distance between $i$ and $j$, $i, j \in R$;
$v_k$: The average travel speed of vehicle $k$, $k \in V$;
$c_{ijk}$: The transportation cost of per unit distance of vehicle $k$ from $i$ to $j$, $i, j \in R$, $k \in V$;
$\partial_{ij}$: The circuitous factor of node $i$ to node $j$, $\omega_{ij} \geq 1, i, j \in R$, when $i, j \in R$,$\partial_{ij} = 0$;
$MT_j$: The time limit for the delivery of goods to affected point $j$, $j \in Q$;
$T_{jk}$: The time when vehicle $k$ reaches node $j$, $j \in R$, when $j \in P$, $T_{jk} = 0$;
$t_{ijk}$: The time vehicle k takes from node $i$ to node $j$, $i, j \in R, k \in V, t_{ijk} = d_{ij}/v_k$;
$\tilde{D}_j$: The demand of affected point $j$ is expressed by triangular fuzzy numbers $\tilde{D}_j(\alpha_j, \beta_j, \gamma_j)$;$\alpha_j, \beta_j$ and $\gamma_j$ can be collected by the emergency logistics information system under the circumstance of disaster;
$p_1$: Confidence coefficient limited by emergency vehicle capacity, $p_1 \in [0, 1]$;
$p_2$: Confidence coefficient limited by distribution center,$p_2 \in [0, 1]$.

(3) Variable setting

When emergency distribution center $i$ ($i \in P$) is started, $x_i = 1$, or else $x_i = 0$;

When delivery vehicle $k$ is called from emergency distribution center I ($i \in P$,$k \in V$), $y_{ik} = 1$, or else $y_{ik} = 0$;

When the delivery vehicle drives from node $i$ to node $j$ ($i \neq j$, $i \in P$,$k \in V$), $z_{ijk} = 1$, or else $z_{ijk} = 0$.

### 8.4.3 Model Establishing

Objective functions:

$$\min Z_1 = \sum_{i \in Q} \sum_{k \in V} MT_{ik} \tag{8.1}$$

$$\sum \tag{8.2}$$

Constraint conditions:

$$V_1\left(\sum_{i \in R} \sum_{j \in Q} z_{ijk} \tilde{D}_j \le n_k\right) \ge p_1, \forall k \in V \tag{8.3}$$

$$V_2\left(\sum_{i \in R} \sum_{j \in Q} \sum_{k \in V} y_{lk} z_{ijk} \tilde{D}_j \le \delta_l x_l\right) \ge p_2, \forall l \in P \tag{8.4}$$

$$T_{jk} = T_{ik} + t_{ijk} z_{ijk}, \forall i, j \in R, \forall k \in V \tag{8.5}$$

$$MT_j \ge T_{jk}, \forall j \in Q, \forall k \in V \tag{8.6}$$

$$\sum_{j \in Q} \sum_{k \in V} z_{ijk} - x_i \ge 0, \text{ when } x_i = 1 \text{ and } \forall i \in P \tag{8.7}$$

$$\sum_{j \in Q} z_{ijk} - x_i \le 0, \text{ when } x_i = 0 \text{ and } \forall i \in R, \forall k \in V \tag{8.8}$$

$$\sum_{j \in R} z_{ijk} - \sum_{j \in R} z_{jik} = 0, \forall i \in R, \forall k \in V \tag{8.9}$$

$$\sum_{k \in V} z_{ijk} = 0, \forall i, j \in P \tag{8.10}$$

$$\sum_{i \in R} \sum_{k \in V} z_{ijk} > 0, \forall j \in R \tag{8.11}$$

$$x_i = \{0, 1\}, \forall i \in P \tag{8.12}$$

$$y_{ik} = \{0, 1\}, \forall i \in P, \forall k \in V \tag{8.13}$$

$$z_{ijk} = \{0, 1\}, \forall i, j \in R, \forall k \in V \tag{8.14}$$

Objective functions (8.1) and (8.2) are the general goals of the LRP model.

In the main objective function, (8.1) represents the total amount of time of delivering all materials, but the time of returning to the distribution center is not included. Condition (8.2) represents the total cost of emergency rescue including the construction cost of the emergency distribution center and the cost of transport vehicles. The constraint condition (8.3) ensures that the demand of the affected point is not greater than the probability of the vehicle capacity but is not less than the given probability $P_1$. Condition (8.4) ensures that the demand of affected points is not greater than the probability of the capacity of the emergency distribution center and not less than the given probability $P_2$. Condition (8.5) gives explanation for $T_{jk}$. Condition (8.6) ensures that the time that the vehicle actually reaches the affected point is less than the specified time limit. Condition (8.7) ensures that the distribution center must deliver supplies to the affected areas after started. Condition (8.8) ensures that the distribution center does not deliver supplies without being started. Condition (8.9) ensures that the vehicle starting from a distribution center eventually returns to it. Condition (8.10) ensures that there is no more than one emergency distribution center on an independent rescue route. Condition (8.11) ensures that every affected point can get supplies. Conditions (8.12), (8.13) and (8.14) are integer variables, which stipulate the value of the variable is zero or one.

Constraint conditions (8.3) and (8.4) contain the triangular fuzzy number $\tilde{D}_j$, which needs to be processed by real numbers. Suppose the demand of affected point $j$ to be $\tilde{D}_j(\alpha_j, \beta_j, \gamma_j)$, the remaining capacity of transport vehicle $k$ after delivering to be $\Delta\tilde{\Lambda}_k$, and the remaining capacity of distribution center $i$ after serving all the affected points within to be $\Delta\tilde{\Omega}_i$. $\Delta\tilde{\Lambda}_k$ and $\Delta\tilde{\Omega}_i$ are both triangular fuzzy numbers, namely,

$$\begin{aligned}\Delta\tilde{\Lambda}_k &= (\Delta\Lambda_{k1}, \Delta\Lambda_{k2}, \Delta\Lambda_{k3}) \\ &= \left(n_k - \sum_{l\in R}\sum_{j\in Q} z_{ljk}\gamma_j, n_k - \sum_{l\in R}\sum_{j\in Q} z_{ljk}\beta_j, n_k - \sum_{l\in R}\sum_{j\in Q} z_{ljk}\alpha_j\right)\end{aligned} \tag{8.15}$$

$$\begin{aligned}&\Delta\tilde{\Omega}_i = (\Delta\Omega_{i1}, \Delta\Omega_{i2}, \Delta\Omega_{i3}) \\ &= \left(\delta_i x_i - \sum_{l\in R}\sum_{j\in Q}\sum_{k\in V} z_{ljk}\gamma_j, \delta_i x_i - \sum_{l\in R}\sum_{j\in Q}\sum_{k\in V} z_{ljk}\beta_j, \delta_i x_i - \sum_{l\in R}\sum_{j\in Q}\sum_{k\in V} z_{ljk}\alpha_j\right)\end{aligned} \tag{8.16}$$

and:

$$V_1\left(\Delta\tilde{\Lambda}_k \geq 0\right) = \begin{cases} 1, & \Delta\Lambda_{k2} > 0 \\ \frac{\Delta\Lambda_{k3}}{\Delta\Lambda_{k3} - \Delta\Lambda_{k2}}, & \Delta\Lambda_{k2} \leq 0 \leq \Delta\Lambda_{k3} \\ 0, & \Delta\Lambda_{k3} < 0 \end{cases} \tag{8.17}$$

$$V_2\left(\Delta\tilde{\Omega}_i \geq 0\right) = \begin{cases} 1, & \Delta\Omega_{k2} > 0 \\ \frac{\Delta\Omega_{k3}}{\Delta\Omega_{k3}-\Delta\Omega_{k2}}, & \Delta\Omega_{k2} \leq 0 \leq \Delta\Omega_{k3} \\ 0, & \Delta\Omega_{k3} < 0 \end{cases} \tag{8.18}$$

By the above transformation, constraint conditions (8.3) and (8.4) are respectively equivalent to:

$$V_1\left(\Delta\tilde{\Lambda}_k \geq 0\right) \geq p_1, \forall k \in V \tag{8.19}$$

$$V_2\left(\Delta\tilde{\Omega}_i \geq 0\right) \geq p_2, \forall l \in P \tag{8.20}$$

## 8.5 Stimulation Application

### *8.5.1 Algorithm*

Non-dominated sorting genetic algorithm NSGA, based on the optimality concept of Pareto, was proposed by Srinivas and Deb (1995). Deb et al. (2000) proposed the improved algorithm NSGA-II, which expanded the sample space, by introducing the elite strategy and reduced the computational complexity of the algorithm by using rapid non-dominated sorting method. The steps are taken as follows.

(1) Supposing that there is a population A of size N, after applying genetic operators (selection, recombination and mutation) to which, population B of size N is obtained. Population C of size 2 N can be obtained by combining population A and B.
(2) Rank population C in a non-dominant way to obtain individuals of non-dominant layers 1, 2, 3, …, and add all the individuals in order to set D of the next generation until the size of set D is larger than N. Record the non-dominant layer as L, and then select K individuals from layer L to make the sum of K and all of the previous layer individuals equal to N.
(3) Operation of Function Standard Quantization

First, calculate the minimum on each target dimension i in M objective functions to obtain the corresponding minimum $z_i$ of the goal i. The set of $z_i$ is the ideal point set, perform quantitative operations on which and the formula is: $f_i^{'}(x) = f_i(x) - z_i^{\min}$. Then seek for the extreme point by traversing each objective function with $ASF(X, W) = MAX_{i=1:m} \frac{f_i^{'}(x)}{W_i}$ to obtain individuals of the minimum ASF, which are the extreme points. Based on the specific function values of these points, the intercepts on the corresponding axes are calculated and recorded as $a_i$. Finally, the normalization operation is carried out according to the following formula: $f_i^n(x) = \frac{f_i'(x)}{a_i}$.

(4) Associating Individuals with Reference Points

The corresponding divisiory reference points are obtained with recursive method to construct the vector quantity of the reference points. The individual of each population is then traversed to find the nearest reference point for each population and meanwhile record the information of reference points and the corresponding shortest distance.

(5) Selecting the Sub-generation and deleting Reference Points

After non-dominated sorting, assume that from the first non-dominated layer to layer L the total number of members of a population is larger than population size N, and then define St + 1 as a collection that contains all the individuals in L. St + 1 needs to be screened because its number is larger than the pre-set number of members of the population. First, traverse each reference point to view the times that it is cited by St + 1 except layer L, and then find out the reference point with the least cited times, which is the one that is associated with least amount of population individuals, and record the cited times as $p_i$. Next, the following points need to be discussed. (1) Assuming $p_i = 0$, if individuals in layer 1, 2, ..., L are associated with the vector quantity of the reference point, find out the point of the shortest distance and extract and then add it to the selected next population, setting $p_i = p_i + 1$; otherwise, delete the vector quantity of the reference point. (2) If $p_i > 0$, select the reference point of the shortest distance. The program does not end until the size of population becomes N.

### 8.5.2 Application Background Analysis

In 2016, affected by El Nino, the rainfall in the Yangtze River basin was significantly more than that in previous years, and the water level was much higher than the annual average. Since June 27, there had been a wide range of continuous heavy rain in areas along and southwest parts of the middle and lower reaches of the Yangtze River, which had stricken 2.772 million people from Jiang Su and other 10 provinces (municipalities directly under the central government), 37 cities (autonomous prefecture) and 133 counties (cities or areas). The rainstorm caused 14 dead and 20 missing as well as direct economic loss of 3.14 billion yuan. Nanjing was one of the most affected cities in the rainstorm, where the rainfall was of high and sudden intensity and long duration. The precipitation in many areas including the main urban area, Gaochun and Lishui all surpassed the peak of the same period in history. By July 7, the rainfall in the main urban area reached 235.5 mm. At least dozens of sections of road were encountered with traffic interruption because of serious seeper in urban area; subway line 3 was forced to shut down for water inflow; the water surface in serious water logging-stricken areas even drew close to the height of traffic light. Water flowed backward in parts of the road, which had caused serious threat to people's life and property. Under this circumstance, how to carry out the distribution of emergency supplies became an important problem to be solved urgently.

### 8.5.3 *Data Collecting and Dealing*

Assume under the rainstorm waterlogging disaster, each candidate distribution center has been established. The only question is to decide which centers are to be started supposing that the distribution center has enough supplies to meet the demand of the whole city.

Demand Data of the Affected Areas

After severe rainstorm and waterlogging, the number of people affected by the disaster determines the amount of supplies. The higher the population intensity is, the greater the demand for supplies is. The eleven districts of Nanjing were selected as the affected areas, and the regional permanent population, administrative area and population density were shown in Table 8.1.

According to the density of affected population and the number of resident population as well as the actual data, the demand for all sorts of materials that the affected areas of Nanjing needed in rainstorm could be predicted. Rainstorms typically occur during summer, so the supplies needed are food, water, tents and emergency medicine. Referring to Yang Yang's design (Yang 2014a, b), considering both the minimum and maximum amount of these items per person needed per day and the number of the resident population of each district, the demand for all sorts of materials that the affected points in each area needed were figured out as shown in Table 8.2.

Data of Emergency Distribution Center

According to the actual situation of Nanjing, the five districts of Qinhuai, Gulou, Jianye, Pukou and Jiangning were selected to build candidate emergency distribution centers. Old urban areas of Nanjing including Qinhuai and Gulou district, owing to its large resident population and outdated planning of drainage systems, the occurrence of waterlogging is really frequent. Jianye district, which is near the Yangtze River and located in the west of Qinhuai River, was low-lying and the pressure on drainage system was high. However, it has developed into the vice center of Nanjing. Pukou and Jiangning districts, respectively located at the core of the north and south of Nanjing, can radiate the surrounding areas. The commissioning cost and inventory capacity of the candidate emergency distribution centers are assumed data, and the location is where each district government lies. The specific data are shown in Table 8.3.

**Table 8.1** Data of population and area of district in Nanjing

| No | Area code | Resident population (10 thousand) | Affected population* (10 thousand) | Administrative area (sq. km) | Population density (people/sq. km) |
|---|---|---|---|---|---|
| 1 | Xuanwu district A | 65.24 | 1.30 | 75.46 | 8645.64 |
| 2 | Qinhuai district B | 102.24 | 2.04 | 49.11 | 20,818.57 |
| 3 | Jianye district C | 45.45 | 0.91 | 81.75 | 5559.63 |
| 4 | Gulou district D | 127.56 | 2.55 | 54.18 | 23,543.74 |
| 5 | Pukou district E | 74.94 | 1.50 | 910.51 | 823.06 |
| 6 | Qixia district F | 67.98 | 1.36 | 395.38 | 1719.36 |
| 7 | Yuhuatai district G | 42.69 | 0.85 | 132.39 | 3224.56 |
| 8 | Jiangning district H | 119.14 | 2.38 | 1563.33 | 762.09 |
| 9 | Liuhe district I | 93.44 | 1.87 | 1471.00 | 635.21 |
| 10 | Lishui district J | 42.44 | 0.85 | 1063.68 | 398.99 |
| 11 | Gaochun district K | 42.47 | 0.85 | 790.23 | 537.44 |

*Note* (1) *: Referring to Yang Yang's [44] method, 2% of the resident population is selected as the proportion of the affected people. (2) Data Source: *Nanjing Statistical Yearbook—2016*

It is assumed that the location of each distribution center and the affected point is determined, as shown in Fig. 8.8. Code A-K corresponds to the affected points of eleven districts.

According to Baidu map, the shortest practical distance between points is figured out by kilometer, among which, 1–5 in Table 8.4 are the corresponding candidate emergency distribution centers in Table 8.3. Since there is only one distribution center per route, it is assumed that the distance between each distribution center is finite. The data of distance between each node is shown in Table 8.4.

According to the actual situation of Nanjing, other parameters are set. The average speed of the vehicle is set as $v_k = 50km/h$, the driving cost of unit distance as $c_{ijk} = 10.5$ yuan/km, vehicle carrying load as $n_k = 20$ tons, fixed using cost of vehicle as $C_k = 450$. And set $p_1 = 0.88$, $p_2 = 0.85$, $\partial_{ij} = 1.2$.

**Table 8.2** Supplies demand of the affected areas (tons)

| No | Area | Supplies demand | | | |
|---|---|---|---|---|---|
| | | Food | Water | Tents | Emergency medicine |
| 1 | Qinhuai district | (28.2,33.6,37.5) | (40.3,45.1,48.6) | (11.2,13.5,15.4) | (8.3,9.1,11.6) |
| 2 | Jianye district | (42.4,58.2,63.5) | (60.3,64.7,67.8) | (25.6,27.2,30.8) | (13.5,16.4,18.4) |
| 3 | Gulou district | (11.5,12.5,13.1) | (12.0,13.5,16.9) | (6.8,7.6,8.3) | (4.9,5.4,6.0) |
| 4 | Pukou district | (58.9,62.3,67.1) | (71.2,74.5,77.6) | (31.2,33.5,36.8) | (16.4,18.6,21.5) |
| 5 | Qixia district | (31.3,36.4,40.2) | (43.7,47.8,51.2) | (12.9,15.7,17.3) | (10.6,11.5,12.8) |
| 6 | Yuhuatai District | (29.2,35.1,38.6) | (41.9,46.3,49.7) | (11.8,14.3,16.2) | (9.2,10.1,12.0) |
| 7 | Jiangning district | (9.1,11.2,13.0) | (10.3,12.5,15.1) | (5.5,6.2,7.4) | (3.6,4.2,5.1) |
| 8 | Liuhe district | (56.4,59.8,64.2) | (68.3,72.5,76.7) | (29.6,22.1,35.8) | (15.5,17.3,20.9) |
| 9 | Lishui district | (37.8,42.7,46.3) | (46.7,50.4,53.5) | (15.4,17.8,19.1) | (11.8,13.2,15.3) |
| 10 | Gaochun district | (9.8,10.2,11.0) | (10.9,12.7,15.3) | (6.0,6.8,7.7) | (4.1,4.8,5.5) |
| 11 | Qinhuai district | (10.1,10.5,11.3) | (11.2,12.9,16.0) | (6.3,7.2,7.9) | (4.4,5.0,5.8) |

**Table 8.3** Data of candidate emergency logistics distribution center

| No | Location of distribution center | Commissioning cost (Yuan) | Inventory capacity (tons) |
|---|---|---|---|
| 1 | Qinhuai district | 48,000 | 620 |
| 2 | Gulou district | 55,000 | 490 |
| 3 | Jianye district | 40,000 | 520 |
| 4 | Pukou district | 38,000 | 500 |
| 5 | Jiangning district | 42,000 | 620 |

### 8.5.4 Solution to Model Application

(1) First, assume that all routes are accessible. The shortest time is the main objective function, so the calculation result of the shortest time is the final result. With Java programming, after the iteration of 10,000 times, the time required for delivery was 1.974 h and the total cost was 175,294.75 yuan. The emergency distribution center,

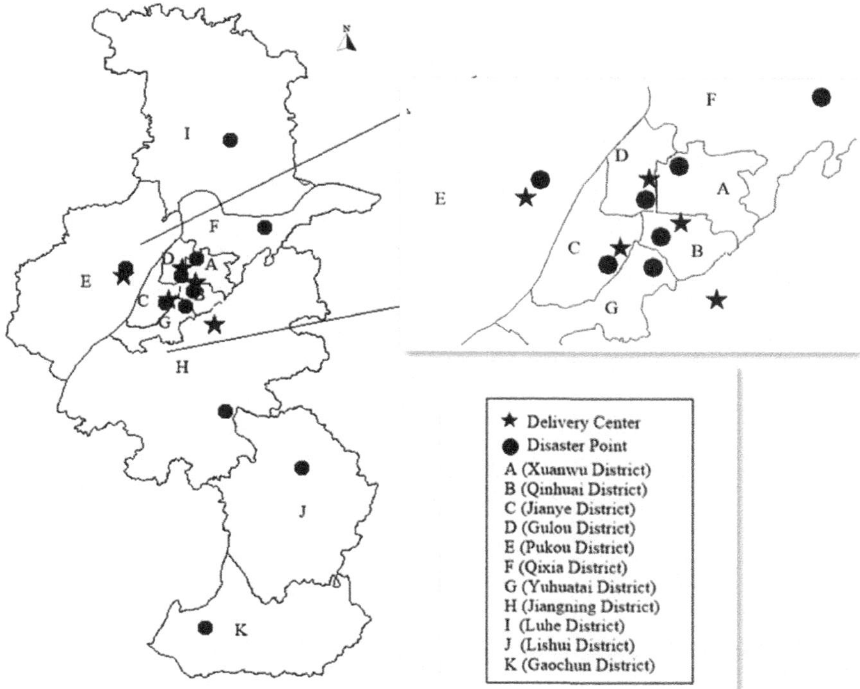


**Fig. 8.8** Location of distribution center and affected points

route arrangement as well as the maximum material demand and the needed relief vehicles of each route are shown in Tables 8.5 and 8.6.

The unloading time of vehicles after reaching the affected points should be taken into consideration. If there are multiple affected points on a route, the relief vehicles required on this route are the sum of the vehicles needed for these affected points. For instance, on route 6, five vehicles are issued from the distribution center of Jiangning district, of which two stop and are unloaded at the affected point of Lishui district, and the other three continue to transport to Gaochun district. The route arrangement is shown in Fig. 8.9.

(2) According to the actual situation analyzed above, the old urban areas of Nanjing such as Qinhuai and Gulou districts are vulnerable to waterlogging. It is assumed that the road between the affected point of Qinhuai district and the affected point of Gulou district is interrupted by the south road, which causes the road between the two affected points is not directly accessible, so the route needs to be re-planned and re-calculated. The time needed for the delivery is 1.974 h, and the total cost is 19,0566.7 yuan, which is 1,5271.95 yuan more than the cost of the initial calculation. The emergency distribution center, route arrangement as well as the maximum material demand and required relief vehicles of each route are shown in Tables 8.7 and 8.8. The route arrangement is shown in Fig. 8.10.

**Table 8.4** Distances between each node

| No | 1 | 2 | 3 | 4 | 5 | A | B | C | D | E | F | G | H | I | J | K |
|---|---|---|---|---|---|---|---|---|---|---|---|---|---|---|---|---|
| 1 | 0 | ∞ | ∞ | ∞ | ∞ | 12.6 | 8.8 | 10.1 | 2.8 | 20.2 | 21.9 | 7.2 | 33.1 | 61.4 | 53.6 | 107.6 |
| 2 | ∞ | 0 | ∞ | ∞ | ∞ | 6.2 | 2.2 | 10.1 | 5.0 | 17.8 | 22.0 | 11.1 | 37.3 | 59.0 | 62.6 | 116.6 |
| 3 | ∞ | ∞ | 0 | ∞ | ∞ | 14.4 | 7.3 | 1.3 | 7.8 | 16.3 | 32.4 | 6.1 | 33.0 | 57.5 | 55.0 | 109.0 |
| 4 | ∞ | ∞ | ∞ | 0 | ∞ | 21.7 | 18.1 | 15.3 | 17.6 | 1.1 | 37.4 | 18.6 | 45.9 | 42.3 | 67.6 | 121.6 |
| 5 | ∞ | ∞ | ∞ | ∞ | 0 | 20.1 | 10.7 | 14.4 | 16.3 | 26.7 | 28.8 | 8.5 | 22.9 | 67.9 | 44.7 | 98.7 |
| A | 12.6 | 6.2 | 14.4 | 21.7 | 20.1 | 0 | 4.0 | 15.9 | 1.2 | 23.1 | 18.2 | 13.1 | 39.2 | 40.0 | 58.2 | 98.1 |
| B | 8.8 | 2.2 | 7.3 | 18.1 | 10.7 | 4.0 | 0 | 8.6 | 2.8 | 18.3 | 24.2 | 4.4 | 30.4 | 51.2 | 54.1 | 89.4 |
| C | 10.1 | 10.1 | 1.3 | 15.3 | 14.4 | 15.9 | 8.6 | 0 | 8.0 | 15.0 | 31.0 | 6.7 | 31.6 | 50.8 | 53.7 | 91.0 |
| D | 2.8 | 5.0 | 7.8 | 17.6 | 16.3 | 1.2 | 2.8 | 8.0 | 0 | 16.0 | 24.6 | 8.7 | 35.7 | 46.8 | 57.4 | 94.6 |
| E | 20.2 | 17.8 | 16.3 | 1.1 | 26.7 | 23.1 | 18.3 | 15.0 | 16.0 | 0 | 38.2 | 19.8 | 46.0 | 41.2 | 67.4 | 104.6 |
| F | 21.9 | 22.0 | 32.4 | 37.4 | 28.8 | 18.2 | 24.2 | 31.0 | 24.6 | 38.2 | 0 | 28.2 | 50.6 | 35.1 | 65.1 | 120.1 |
| G | 7.2 | 11.1 | 6.1 | 18.6 | 8.5 | 13.1 | 4.4 | 6.7 | 8.7 | 19.8 | 28.2 | 0 | 27.8 | 56.2 | 49.1 | 86.3 |
| H | 33.1 | 37.3 | 33.0 | 45.9 | 22.9 | 39.2 | 30.4 | 31.6 | 35.7 | 46.0 | 50.6 | 27.8 | 0 | 75.7 | 23.6 | 61.0 |
| I | 61.4 | 59.0 | 57.5 | 42.3 | 67.9 | 40.0 | 51.2 | 50.8 | 46.8 | 41.2 | 35.1 | 56.2 | 75.7 | 0 | 94.2 | 146.1 |
| J | 53.6 | 62.6 | 55.0 | 67.6 | 44.7 | 58.2 | 54.1 | 53.7 | 57.4 | 67.4 | 65.1 | 49.1 | 23.6 | 94.2 | 0 | 54.0 |
| K | 107.6 | 116.6 | 109.0 | 121.6 | 98.7 | 98.1 | 89.4 | 91.0 | 94.6 | 104.6 | 120.1 | 86.3 | 61.0 | 146.1 | 54.0 | 0 |

**Table 8.5** Emergency distribution centers and route arrangement

| Emergency distribution centers | Route arrangement |
|---|---|
| Qinhuai district | Route 1: → Qinhuai district → Gulou district → Xuanwu district |
| | Route 2: → Xixia district |
| Jianye district , | Route 3: ,→ Jianye district → Pukou district → Liuhe district |
| | Route 4: →Yuhuatai district |
| Jiangning district *f* | Route 5: *f* → Jiangning district |
| | Route 6: *f* → Lishui district → Gaochun district |

**Table 8.6** Distributed materials and vehicles required on each route

| Route | Maximum material demand (tons) | Relief vehicle required |
|---|---|---|
| Route 1 | 496.6 | 27 |
| Route 2 | 116.5 | 6 |
| Route 3 | 300.0 | 17 |
| Route 4 | 40.6 | 3 |
| Route 5 | 197.6 | 10 |
| Route 6 | 80.5 | 5 |

## 8.6 Conclusion

With the approaching big data and rapid development of big data analysis technologies, microblog and other social media will gradually become an important source of disaster information extraction due to its timeliness, huge data amount and abundant contents.

The present paper introduces the process and methods to analyze the urban rainstorm waterlogging and its corresponding emotions of the public on the basis of microblog big data. First of all, eliminate the repetitive contents of original microblogs, translate all IP addresses into physical location and classify all microblogs according to administrative regions of Nanjing. Second, Segment words and label the part of speech of each word of all microblogs by ICTCLAS. Third, establish the urban rainstorm waterlogging reflecting table and waterlogging disaster and subjective emotion classification coding table. Last but not least, divide microblogs of all administrative regions into two phases: from June 18th to June 30th and from July 1st to July 7th, extract the rainstorm waterlogging and emotion vocabularies and calculate their percentages separately to determine the disaster degree of waterlogging and the emotion reaction of the public in various administrative regions of Nanjing. On the ground of descriptions about the ponding depth of a certain location that frequently appeared in microblogs, areas prone to be submerged during rainstorm can be determined by classifying the depth of ponding.

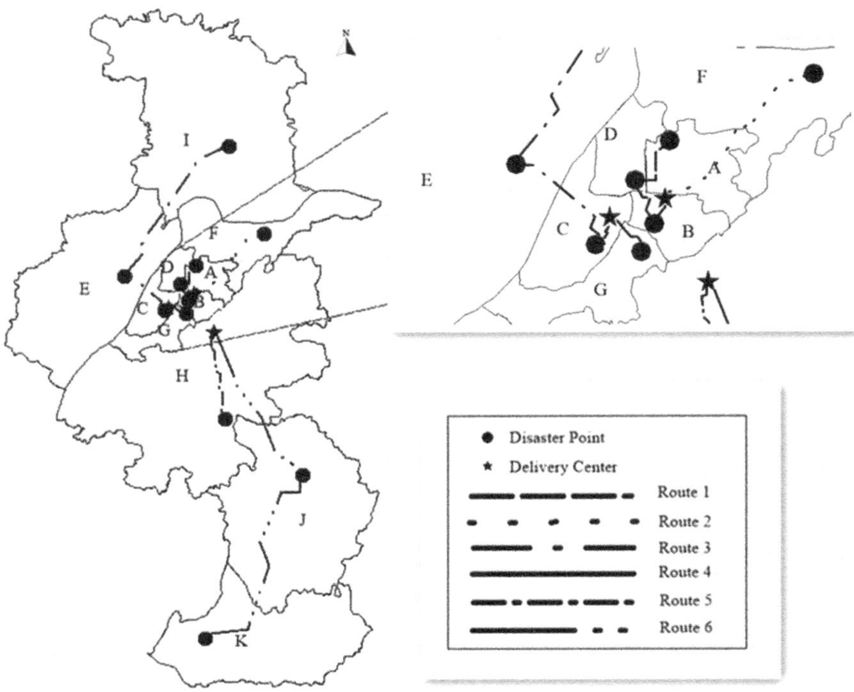


**Fig. 8.9** Route arrangement without route interrupts

**Table 8.7** Emergency distribution centers and route arrangement

| Emergency distribution centers | Route arrangement |
|---|---|
| Gulou district | Route 1: → Affected points in Gulou district |
| | Route 2: → Affected points in Jianye district |
| | Route 3: → Affected points in Yuhuatai district |
| | Route 4: → Affected points in Xixia district |
| Qinhuai district , | Route 5: → Affected points in Qinhuai district → Affected points in Xuanwu district |
| | Route 6: → Affected points in Pukou district → Affected points in Liuhe district |
| Jiangning district *f* | Route 7: *f* → Affected points in Jiangning district |
| | Route 8: *f* → Affected points in Lishui district → Affected points in Gaochun district |

With the waterlogging points in the presence of disasters found in the first part, the re-optimization is made to develop traffic road. This paper constructed the location-routing problem model of urban emergency logistics in the situation of rainstorm and waterlogging disaster, and by taking Nanjing as an example, found out the dynamic

**Table 8.8** Distributed materials and required vehicle

| Route | Maximum material demand (tons) | Required relief vehicles |
|---|---|---|
| Route 1 | 203.0 | 11 |
| Route 2 | 44.3 | 3 |
| Route 3 | 40.6 | 3 |
| Route 4 | 116.5 | 6 |
| Route 5 | 293.6 | 16 |
| Route 6 | 255.7 | 14 |
| Route 7 | 197.6 | 10 |
| Route 8 | 80.5 | 5 |

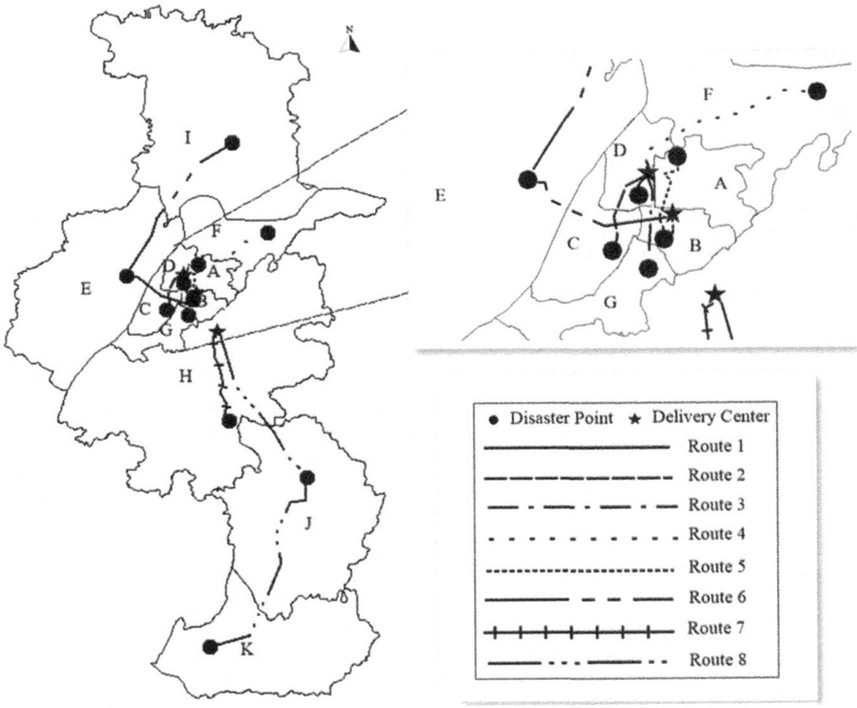


**Fig. 8.10** Route arrangement with route interrupts

emergency distribution path of Nanjing in the situation of waterlogging disaster with NSGA-III algorithm. Meanwhile, assuming that the route between Gulou and Qinhuai is interrupted, the paper re-planned and re-calculated the distributing route. The feasibility of the location-routing problem model was verified in the case.

Finally, what needs to be noted is that the design of the model contains many hypotheses such as distribution centers are fixed, route network are closed, and that a vehicle can only running between the distribution center and its destination. However, in reality, there exists temporary distribution centers, much wider road network and changeable parameter values, therefore, the orientation of future research be targeted on how to make the model more realistic.

**Acknowledgements** Yaru Cao, Yang Xiao, Ji Guo, Qi Cao also made great contributions to this manuscript. We express our heartfelt thanks to them. This research was supported by: Key Project of National Social and Scientific Fund Program (18ZDA052; 17BGL142; 16ZDA047); The Natural Science Foundation of China (91546117, 71373131); The Ministry of Education Scientific Research Foundation for the returned overseas students (No.2013-693, Ji Guo). This research was also supported by the Priority Academic Program Development of Jiangsu Higher Education Institutions and the Flagship Major Development of Jiangsu Higher Education Institutions.

## Appendix

See Tables 8.9, 8.10 and 8.11.

**Table 8.9** Urban rainstorm waterlogging reflecting table

| Category | Description vocabulary |
|---|---|
| Reasons of rain | Convective weather, convective strong typhoon, Nepartak, plum rain and plum |
| Ponding | Spill, ponding, serious ponding, easily to form ponding, rise, submerge, get submerged, flood, sea, seascape, waterlogging, waterlog, fill, metro station filled with water, cars submerged into water, city surrounded by water, deluge, 30 mm higher than the line, warning, excessive rain, flood resistance, be drowned, travel far away across the sea, boundless seas, rubber dinghy canoe and kayak, kayak, raft, 235 m higher than the warning level, depth, swim, sharp rise of water level, rapid rise, universal rise, swift rise, wall collapse, serious ponding in low-lying sections, the height of ponding arrives at the waist, row the door plank, take a boat, rowing, row the friend-ship, inundation, a world of waters, wade, roaring waves, drainage, flood mode, become a sea, sea, ship, from driver to captain, feel powerless and frustrated, flood discharge, flood disaster, ocean, crop failure, submerged crop, collapsed road, the Jungle Book, filled with rain, the rapid rise of the water level of brook, deep ponding, one-meter ponding, road ponding, buy a boat, become Venice the City of Water, water filled in the pathway, half shank submerged into water, the deepest ponding amounts to 15 cm, soak, dragon water on the city wall, 0.42 m higher than the warning level, 0.06 m higher than the warning level, ponding fails to discharge within short time, household appliances soaked into rainwater, the ponding area amounts to roughly 200 m, large-scale ponding, approximately one-meter ponding, over twenty persistent ponding areas, hundreds of cars submerged, house becomes an isolated island, ponding reaches the thigh, the deepest ponding reaches 0.7 m, thirty-two sections prone to ponding, ponding fills into the basement and the deepest ponding reaches the waist |

(continued)

**Table 8.9** (continued)

| Category | Description vocabulary |
|---|---|
| Traffic | Congestion, traffic jam, bad traffic jam, refund, ferry suspension, enlarging train distance, late, late for work, road blocking, traffic paralysis, block up, paralysis, fault in Tianlongsi section, train outage, line 3 repair, line 3 outage, stop, connection, slow down, slow-moving, behind the schedule time, flight canceled, delay, metro faults, road congestion and road closure |
| Rain conditions | Extraordinary rainstorm, rainstorm, shower, thunderstorm, downpour, heavy rain, roaring waves, thundershower, rain falls in torrents, small to moderate rain, stormy weather, moderate rain, windy and rainy, raining dogs and cats, tempest, overcast and rainy, occasional drizzles, thunderstorm rainfall, small rain, moderate rain, sunny rain, plum rains, pouring, thunderstorm rain, time brings a great change to the world, break in full fury, downpour, gurgle, break in full fury and thunderstorm wind and cloudburst |
| Emotion reactions | Anger: anger, rage, curse in rage, indignantly resent, furious, resentment, angry and sulky<br>Worry: worried, grievance, sad, sadness, chagrin, pitiful, struggle, unhappy, depressed, worry about, anxious, anxiety, alas, nervous and disturbed<br>Sadness: sad, tragedy, tears, cry, want to cry, purr, cry, grieved, pain, feel sad, anguished, injury, unfortunate, breakdown, miserable, weep, hurt, whine, disappoint, heartbroken, uncomfortable, alas and desolate<br>Fear: frighten to death, in shock, terrifying, be afraid of, horrific, horrible, scare, frightening and threaten<br>Panic: surprise, wake due to fear, wow and astonish<br>Annoyance: annoyance, irritable, go crazy, impatient, distressed, bewilderment, hurry, fluster, gloomy, bother and repression<br>Chillax: cool, ho ho and ho<br>Others: love dearly, faint, embarrassed, ache, smile, laugh, too happy, tired, likes, haha and joyful<br>Emoticons: [roll eyes], [lacrimation], [sweating], [ tearful], [ control], [ tears of laugh], [bye-bye], [hopeless], [stunned], [candle], [hum], [haha], [fist], [titter], [smile], [raining], [sunshine], [Meowth], [smirk], [lightning], [shy], [make a wish], [ pick nose], [surprised], [thinking], [gluttonous], [good], [shut up], [thunderbolt], [chuckle], [ heart], [microphone], [enjoy oneself], [onlooker], [laughingly], [cute], [love you], [handshake], [sun], [music], [flower], [coming], [yeah], [recommend], [handclap], [rose], [hee hee], [why], [nothing], [wink], [great], [screw you], [oh yeah], [speechless], [bravo], [bow], [prove wrong], [despise], [disappoint] and [curl lips] |

**Table 8.10** Waterlogging rating coding table

| Code category | Rating | Description |
|---|---|---|
| The rainfall amount | 1 | Small to moderate rain, sunny rain, shower, overcast and rainy, occasional drizzles, small rain, thundershower and plum rains |
| | 2 | Rainstorm, thunderstorm, heavy rain, moderate rain, windy and rainy and tempest |

(continued)

**Table 8.10** (continued)

| Code category | Rating | Description |
|---|---|---|
| | 3 | Downpour, roaring waves, rain falls in torrents, stormy weather, raining dogs and cats, thunderstorm rainfall, pouring, cloudburst, thunderstorm rain, time brings a great change to the world, break in full fury, downpour, gurgle, break in full fury and thunderstorm wind |
| Traffic | 1 | No description |
| | 2 | Congestion, traffic jam, late, late for work, enlarging train distance, block up, slow down, slow-moving, behind the schedule time, delay, connection, road blocking and fault in Tianlongsi section |
| | 3 | Bad traffic jam, ferry suspension, refund, traffic paralysis, paralysis, train outage, stop, flight canceled, subway faults, road closure, line 3 outage and line 3 repair |
| Ponding range | 1 | No description |
| | 2 | Sea, seascape, rowing, row the door plank, take a boat and road ponding |
| | 3 | Travel far away across the sea, a world of waters, feel powerless and frustrated, ocean, over twenty persistent ponding areas, the ponding area amounts to toughly 200 m and hundreds of cars submerged |
| Ponding depth | 1 | 0.5 m and below |
| | 2 | 0.5–1 m |
| | 3 | 1 m and above |

**Table 8.11** Subjective emotion rating coding table

| Rating | Description |
|---|---|
| 1 | Surprise, wake due to fear, wow, astonish, cool, ho ho, ho, [roll eyes], [sweating], [control], [stunned], [hum], [haha], [fist], [titter], [smile], [sunshine], [Meowth], [ smirk], [lightning], [shy], [make a wish], [ pick nose], [surprised], [thinking], [gluttonous], [good], [shut up], [thunderbolt], [chuckle], [heart], [microphone], [enjoy oneself], [onlooker], [laughingly], [cute], [love you], [shake hands], [sun], [music], [flower], [coming], [yeah], [recommend], [handclap], [rose], [hee hee], [oh yeah], [speechless] and [bravo] |
| 2 | Annoyance, irritable, go crazy, impatient, distressed, bewilderment, hurry, fluster, gloomy, bother, repression, alas, nervous, disturbed, worried, grievance, sad, sadness, chagrin, pitiful, struggle, unhappy, depressed, worry about, anxious, anxiety, [tears of laugh], [bye-bye], [raining], [despise] and [curl lips] |
| 3 | Sad, tragedy, tears, cry, want to cry, purr, cry, grieved, pain, feel sad, anguished, injury, unfortunate, breakdown, miserable, weep, hurt, whine, disappoint, heartbroken, uncomfortable, alas, desolate, love dearly, ache, [hopeless], frighten to death, in shock, terrifying, be afraid of, horrific, horrible, scare, frightening, threaten, [lacrimation], [tearful], [candle], [bow], [disappoint] and [screw you] |

# References

Ahmadi, M., Seifi, A., & Tootooni, B. (2015). A humanitarian logistics model for disaster relief operation considering network failure and standard relief time: A case study on San Francisco district. *Transportation Research Part E 75*,145–163.

Asgari, N., Rajabi, M., Jamshidi, M., et al. (2017). A memetic algorithm for a multi-objective obnoxious waste location-routing problem: A case study. *Annals of Operations Research, 250,* 279–308. https://doi.org/10.1007/s10479-016-2248-7.

Avvenuti, M., Cresci, S., Polla, M. N. L., Meletti, C., & Tesconi, M. (2017). Nowcasting of earthquake consequences using big social data. *IEEE Internet Computing, 21*(6), 37–45.

Bandyopadhyay, S., & Bhattacharya, R. (2013). Solving multi-objective parallel machine scheduling problem by a modified NSGA-II. *Applied Mathematical Modelling, 37*(10–11), 6718–6729.

Burkart, C., Nolz, P. C., & Gutjahr, W. J. (2016). Modelling beneficiaries' choice in disaster relief logistics. *Annals of Operations Research.* https://doi.org/10.1007/s10479-015-2097-9.

Chang, K. L., Zhou, H., Chen, G. J., & Chen, H. Q. (2017). Multiobjective location routing problem considering uncertain data after disasters. *Discrete Dynamic in Nature and Society, 3,* 1–7.

Cheng, L. H., Hong, T., Zhou, T. G., et al. (2011). Evaluation method of natural disaster intensity and its application: A research based on comprehensive disaster condition index. *Journal of Natural Disasters, 20*(1), 46–50.

Chen, P., Zhang, J., Sun, Y., & Liu, X. (2016). Wargame simulation theory and evaluation method for emergency evacuation of residents from urban waterlogging disaster area. *International Journal of Environmental Research & Public Hearth, 13*(12), 1260.

Cheraghi, S., & Hosseini-Motlagh, S. M. (2020). Responsive and reliable injured-oriented blood supply chain for disaster relief: A real case study. *Annals of Operations Research, 291,* 129–167.

Choi, S., & Bae, B. (2015). The real-time monitoring system of social big data for disaster management. In *Computer science and its applications* (809–815). Springer Berlin Heidelberg,

Cooper, L. (1972). The transportation-location problem. *Operations Research, 20,* 94–108.

Cooper, L. (1976). An efficient heuristic algorithm for the transportation-location problem. *Journal of Regional Science, 16*(3), 309–315.

Dalfard, V. M., Kaveh, M., & Nosratian, N. E. (2013). Two meta-heuristic algorithms for two-echelon location-routing problem with vehicle fleet capacity and maximum route length constraints. *Neural Computing & Applications, 23*(7–8), 2341–2349.

Deb, K., Agrawal, S., & Pratap, A., et al. (2000). A fast elitist nondominated sorting genetic algorithm for multi-objective optimization: NSGA-II. In *Proceedings of the Parallel Problem Solving From Nature VI Conference* (pp. 849–858). Paris.

Deng, J. L., Shen, S. L., & Xu, Y. S. (2016). Investigation into pluvial flooding hazards caused by heavy rain and protection measures in Shanghai, China. *Natural Hazards, 83,* 1301–1320. https://doi.org/10.1007/s11069-016-2369-y.

Duan, P. Y., Wang, Y., & Sang, H., et al. (2016). A developed NSGA-II Algorithm for multi-objective chiller loading optimization problems. In: D. S. Huang, V. Bevilacqua, & P. Premaratne (Eds.), *Intelligent computing theories and application.* ICIC 2016. Lecture Notes in Computer Science, vol. 9771. Springer, Cham.

Fallah-Mehdipoura, E., Haddad, O. B., & Tabari, M. M. R. (2012). Extration of decision alternatives in construction management projects: Application and adaptation of NSGA-II and MOPSO. *Expert Systems with Applications, 39,* 2794–2803.

Feng, Y. Y., Wu, I. C., & Chen, T. L. (2017). Stochastic resource allocation in emergency departments with a multi-objective simulation optimization algorithm. *Health Care Management Science, 20*(1), 55–75.

Gao, X. H. (2020). A bi-level stochastic optimization model for multi-commodity rebalancing under uncertainty in disaster response. *Annals of Operations Research.*

Han, Y. Y., Guan, X. H., & Shi, L. Y. (2011). Optimization based method for supply location selection routing in large-scale emergency material delivery. *IEEE Transactions on Automation Science and Engineering, 8*(4), 683–693.

Hoang, T. B. N., & Mothe, J. (2018). Location extraction from tweets. *Information Processing & Management Libraries & Information Retrieval Systems & Communication Networks an International Journal.*

Hou, W. Y. (2013). An analysis of public opinion evolution of microblogging in group incident. Harbin Institute of Technology.

Hou, J., & Du, Y. (2020). Spatial simulation of rainstorm waterlogging based on a water accumulation diffusion algorithm. *Geomatics, Natural Hazards and Risk, 11*(1), 71–87.

Huang, M., & Jin, S. (2019). A methodology for simple 2-d inundation analysis in urban area using swmm and gis. *Natural Hazards, 97,* 15–43.

Hu, S. L., Han, C. F., & Meng, L. P. (2015). A scenario planning approach for propositioning rescue centers for urban waterlog disasters. *Computers & Industrial Engineering, 87,* 425–435.

Jotshi, A., Gong, Q., & Batta, R. (2009). Dispatching and routing of emergency vehicles in disaster mitigation using data fusion. *Socio-Economic Planning Sciences, 43*(1), 1–24.

Kalaivani, L., Subburaj, P., & Iruthayarajan, M. W. (2013). Speed control of switched reluctance motor with torque ripple reduction using non-dominated sorting genetic algorithm (NSGA-II). *Electrical Power and Energy Systems, 53,* 69–77.

Karmegam, D., & Mappillairaju, B. (2020). Spatio-temporal distribution of negative emotions on twitter during floods in Chennai, India, in 2015: A post hoc analysis. *International Journal of Health Geographics, 19*(1), 19.

Karyotis, C., Doctor, F., Iqbal, R., James, A., & Chang, V. (2017). A fuzzy computational model of emotion for cloud based sentiment analysis. *Information Sciences.*

Kaur, H., & Singh, S. P. (2016). Sustainable procurement and logistics for disaster resilient supply chain. *Annals of Operations Research.* https://doi.org/10.1007/s10479-016-2374-2.

Khalipourazari, S., & Khamseh, A. A. (2017). Bi-objective emergency blood supply chain network design in earthquake considering earthquake magnitude: A comprehensive study with real world application. *Annals of Operations Research.* https://doi.org/10.1007/s10479-017-2588-y.

Lin, D., Li, L., Cao, D., Lv, Y., & Ke, X. (2017). Multi-modality weakly labeled sentiment learning based on explicit emotion signal for Chinese microblog. *Neurocomputing, 272,* 258–269.

Li, S. Y., & Zhou, H. J. (2014). Optimization model of fuzzy location-routing problem of victim search in flood disaster. *Journal of Chemical and Pharmaceutical Research, 6*(6), 2080–2085.

Li, Q., Zhu, H. M., & Yang, D. C. (2013). The evolution model of public opinion topic in microblogging network. *New Technology of Library and Information Service, 12,* 74–80.

Li, L., Zhang, Q., Tian, J., & Wang, H. (2018). Characterizing information propagation patterns in emergencies: A case study with yiliang earthquake. *International Journal of Information Management, 38*(1), 34–41.

Li, Q., Wei, C., Dang, J. N., Cao, L., & Liu, L. (2020). Tracking and analyzing public emotion evolutions during COVID-19: A case study from the event-driven perspective on microblogs. *International Journal of Environmental Research and Public Health, 17,* 18.

Ma, Z. J. (2006). China's natural disasters and disaster mitigation countermeasures (2). *Journal of Disaster Prevention Science and Technology, 4,* 1–5.

Madani, Y., Erritali, M., & Bengourram, J. (2018). Sentiment analysis using semantic similarity and hadoop mapreduce. *Knowledge & Information Systems, 59*(8), 413–436.

Mao, D. H. (2000). Assessment and analysis of flood-waterlogging disaster condition in Dongting lake region. *Journal of Natural Disasters, 3,* 46–53.

Ma, W., Wang, R., Gu, Y., Meng, Q., & Wu, Y. (2020). Multi-objective microservice deployment optimization via a knowledge-driven evolutionary algorithm. *Complex & Intelligent Systems.*

Mete, H. O., & Zabinsky, Z. B. (2010). Stochastic optimization of medical supply location and distribution in disaster management. *International Journal of Production Economics, 126*(1), 76–84.

Mohapatra, P., Nayak, A., Kumar, S. K., & Tiwari, M. K. (2015). Multi-objective process planning and scheduling using controlled elitist non-dominated sorting genetic algorithm. *International Journal of Production Research, 53*(6), 1712–1735.

Moshref-Javadi, M., & Lee, S. (2016). The latency location-routing problem. *European Journal of Operational Research, 255*(2), 604–619.

Neppalli V. K., Caragea C., & Squicciarini A., et al. (2016). Sentiment analysis during Hurricane Sandy in emergency response. *International Journal of Disaster Risk Reduction, 21*, 213–222.

Pasandideh, S. H. R., Niaki, S. T. A., & Sharafzadeh, S. (2013). Optimizing a bi-objective multi-product EPQ model with defective items, rework and limited orders: NSGA-II and MOPSO algorithms. *Journal of Manufacturing Systems, 32,* 764–770.

Pramudita, A., Taniguchi, E., & Qureshi, A. G. (2014). Location and routing problems of debris collection operation after disasters with realistic case study. *Procedia-Social and Behavioral Sciences, 125,* 445–458.

Preethi, P. G., Uma, V., & Kumar, A. (2015). Temporal sentiment analysis and causal rules extraction from tweets for event prediction. *Procedia Computer Science, 48,* 84–89.

Rabiee, M., Zandieh, M., & Ramezani, P. (2012). Bi-objective partial flexible job shop scheduling problem: NSGA-II, NRGA, MOGA and PAES approaches. *International Journal of Production Research, 50*(24), 7327–7342.

Rahman, S. U., & Smith, D. K. (2000). Use of location-allocation models in health service development planning in developing nations. *European Journal of Operational Research, 123*(3), 437–452.

Rath, S., & Gutjahr, W. J. (2014). A math-heuristic for the warehouse location-routing problem in disaster relief. *Computers & Operation Research, 42,* 25–39.

Sakaki, T. (2010). Earthquake shakes twitter users: real-time event detection by social sensors. In Proceedings of the 19th International Conference on World Wide Web, WWW 2010, Raleigh, North Carolina, USA, April 26–30, 2010.

Song, M., & Du, Q. (2017). Analysis and exploration of damage-reduction measures for flood disasters in china. *Annals of Operations Research, 3,* 1–16.

Song, M., Peng, J., Wang, J., & Zhao, J. (2017). Environmental efficiency and economic growth of china: A ray slack-based model analysis. *European Journal of Operational Research.* https://doi.org/10.1016/j.ejor.2017.03.073.

Srinivas, N., & Deb, K. (1995). Multiobjective function optimization using nondominated sorting genetic algorithms. *Evolutionary Computation,* 2(3), 221–248.

Su, B. N., Huang, H., & Li, Y. (2016). Integrated simulation method for waterlogging and traffic congestion under urban rainstorms. *Natural Hazards, 81,* 23. https://doi.org/10.1007/s11069-015-2064-4.

Tayal, A., & Singh, S. P. (2017). Formulating multi-objective stochastic dynamic facility layout problem for disaster relief. *Annals of Operations Research.* https://doi.org/10.1007/s10479-017-2592-2.

Ting, C. G., & Chen, C. H. (2013). A multiple ant colony optimization algorithm for the capacitated location routing problem. *Int. J. Production Economics, 141,* 34–44.

Vahdani, B., Veysmoradi, D., Noori, F., & Mansour, F. (2017). Two-stage multi-objective location-routing-inventory model for humanitarian logistics network design under uncertainty. *International Journal of Disaster Risk Reduction, 27,* 290–306.

Wang, H. J., Du, L. J., & Ma, S. H. (2014). Multi-objective open location-routing model with split delivery for optimized relief distribution in post-earthquake. *Transportation Research Part E, 69,* 160–179.

Wang, L. Z., Wang, D. W., & Wu, S. L., et al. (2015). Study on multi-depots vehicle transshipment scheduling problem and its genetic algorithm and ant colony algorithm hybrid optimization. In E. Qi, J. Shen, & R. Dou (Eds.), *Proceedings of the 22nd International Conference on Industrial Engineering and Engineering Management 2015.* Atlantis Press, Paris.

Wei, Y., & Özdamarb, L. (2007). A dynamic logistics coordination model for evacuation and support in disaster response activities. *European Journal of Operational Research, 179*(3), 1177–1193.

Wu, T. H., Low, C., & Bai, J. W. (2002). Heuristic solutions to multi-depot location-routing problems. *Computers & Operations Research, 29*(10), 1393–1415.

Xing, Z., Su, X., Liu, J., Su, W., & Zhang, X. (2019). Spatiotemporal change analysis of earthquake emergency information based on microblog data: A case study of the "8.8" Jiuzhaigou earthquake. *International Journal of Geo-Information, 8*(8), 359.

Xu, J. H., Chu, J., Nie, G., et al. (2015). Earthquake disaster information extraction based on location microblog. *Journal of Natural Disasters, 5,* 12–18.

Yang S. N. (2014a). Research on method of network public opinion monitoring of emergency based on micro-blog. Dalian University of Technology.

Yang, Y. (2014b). Research on the emergency logistics location-path of urban emergency. Harbin Institute of Technology. (In china).

Yang, T., Xie, J., Li, G., Mou, N., Li, Z., & Tian, C., et al. (2019). Social media big data mining and spatio-temporal analysis on public emotions for disaster mitigation. *International Journal of Geo-Information, 8*(1).

Yan Q., Huang C., & Zhang P., et al. (2010). Microblogging after a major disaster in China: A case study of the 2010 Yushu earthquake. In *ACM Conference on Computer Supported Cooperative Work, CSCW 2011* (pp. 25–34). Hangzhou, China, March. DBLP.

Yan, L., Grifoll Colls, M., & Zheng, P. (2020). Model and algorithm of two-stage distribution location routing with hard time window for city cold-chain logistics. *Applied Sciences, 10*(7), 2564.

Yu, V. F., Lin, S. W., Lee, W., & Ting, C. J. (2010). A simulated annealing heuristic for the capacitated location routing problem. *Computers & Industrial Engineering, 58*(2), 288–299.

Yu, S. W., Zhang, S. H., Gao, S. W., & Yang, J. (2017). A multi-objective decision model for investment in energy and mission reductions in coal mining. *European Journal of Operational Research, 260*(1), 335–347.

Yu, H., Zhao, Y., Fu, Y., & Li, L. (2018). Spatiotemporal variance assessment of urban rainstorm waterlogging affected by impervious surface expansion: A case study of Guangzhou, China. *Sustainability, 10*(10), 3761.

Zhang, B., Li, H., Li, S., & Peng, J. (2018). Sustainable multi-depot emergency facilities location-routing problem with uncertain information. *Applied Mathematics and Computation, 333,* 506–520.

Zhang, J., Wang, S., Tang, Q., Zhou, Y., & Zeng, T. (2019). An improved NSGA-III integrating adaptive elimination strategy to solution of many-objective optimal power flow problems. *Energy, 172,* 945–957.

Zheng, Y. (2014). Emotional analysis of Chinese microblogging based on emotional dictionary. Sun Yat-sen University.

Zheng, F. R., Miao, D. Q., Zhang, Z. F., et al. (2012). News topic detection approach on Chinese microblog. *Computer Science, 1,* 138–141.

Zhou, Y. M., Yang, J. N., & Yang, A. M. (2013). A method on building Chinese sentiment lexicon for text sentiment analysis. *Journal of Shandong University, 6,* 27–33.

Zhou, Y. W., Liu, J., Zhang, Y. T., Gan, X. H. (2017). A multi-objective evolutionary algorithm for multi-period dynamic emergency resource scheduling problems. *Transportation Research Part E, 99,* 77–95.

Zhou, L., Lin, Y., Wang, X., Zhou, F. (2019). Model and algorithm for bilevel multi-sized terminal location-routing problem for the last mile delivery. *International Transactions in Operational Research, 26,* 131–156.

Zhu, X., Zhou, B., Qiu, X., Zeng, Y., & Jin, Y. (2019). A dynamic impact assessment method for rainstorm waterlogging using land-use data. *Journal of Integrative Environmental Sciences, 16*(1), 163–190.

# Chapter 9
# A New Economic Loss Assessment System for Urban Severe Rainfall and Flooding Disasters Based on Big Data Fusion

**Abstract** **Background and Purpose**: Increasingly frequent meteorological disasters have brought severe challenges that should be urgently handled in the sustainable development. However, meteorological data, loss data, social economic data and so forth relating to meteorological disasters rarely be effectively fused, failing to generate, rapidly and efficiently, economic losses and thus hindering the emergency management of disasters. **Methods**: A new economic losses evaluation information system has been developed for monitoring severe rainfall and flooding disasters in cities. The data mining method, econometric regression model and input–output model are implemented in the system, on the basis of multi-source data including hourly rainfall, geographical conditions, historical and real-time disaster information, socioeconomic data, and defense countermeasure. **Results**: Combined with the weather forecast information, this system can has the capability for reporting the real-time direct and indirect economic losses incurred by urban heavy rainfall and flooding disasters, automatically generating defense countermeasure reports for typical rainstorm and flooding points, and providing the spatial distribution of disasters. **Conclusions**: Finally, the system is conducive to improving the ability to manage disaster emergencies and eventually reducing the economic losses from the disaster.

**Keywords** Big data · Rainfall and flooding · Disasters · Economic loss evaluation · Information system

## 9.1 Introduction

In recent years, with the acceleration of global warming and urbanization, together with the relatively outdated planning of urban water systems and construction of underground pipe networks, some developing countries have frequently experienced adverse effects of heavy rains and flooding in urban areas (Huang 2012; Huang and Huang 2018). For instance, a heavy rainstorm in Beijing, China, on July 21 2012, killed 79 individuals, affected 1.602 million people and destroyed 10,660 houses, causing an economic loss of 11.64 billion yuan. Incurred by rainfall, fatal flooding's lead to not only casualties but also huge economic losses, and this has aroused wide spread concerns from all sectors of society, creating a difficult issue

 
X. Wu and J. Guo, *Economic Impacts and Emergency Management of Disasters in China*,
https://doi.org/10.1007/978-981-16-1319-7_9

for the government and scholars. The economic loss from natural disasters such as rainstorms should be quickly evaluated and effective countermeasures of emergency management should be advanced (Wang et al. 2016).

In mainland China, however, there is a lack of research on methods for the comprehensive loss assessment of natural disasters, as well as a corresponding lack of evaluation systems and software. This seriously restricts the work of disaster prevention and risk management and is thus worthy of further studies and discussion. On one hand, flooding disaster data includes meteorological data (disaster-causing factor), loss data (hazard-inducing factors) and social statistics data. Among them, meteorological data alone is of a large amount of 4PB-5PB with an annual increment of 1PB, exchanged frequently among countries all over the world and typically characterized by big data's 4 V features (Wang et al. 2014): Volume (large quantity), Variety (multiple modes), Velocity (fast generation) and Value (huge value with very low density). Nevertheless, various types of data scatter at different levels and departments, hardly to be fused on high risk spots. On the other hand, under the complicated natural and social environment, and owing to the intensifying of the internal connection of the social and economic system, losses caused by extreme climate events have grown larger, bringing tremendous obstacles to emergency decision-making. Therefore, how to fuse big data and evaluate comprehensive economic losses of meteorological disasters has become urgent and necessary fundamental problems.

In this study, we will choose the Longhua district, Shenzhen city, as the research object to illustrate the feasibility and rationality of the system developed in this study, integrate the information of meteorology, disaster science, statistics, economics and other disciplines, and collect and analyze the basic data according to the characteristics such as disaster factors, disaster environment and the degree of exposure. With the help of advanced and applicable data filtering algorithm and input–output models, an economic loss assessment system with human–computer interaction and distributed data acquisition has been constructed based on WebGIS, which is capable of assessing the direct and indirect economic loss of heavy rainfall and flood disasters. This system possesses the following functions: (1) Communities in the study area act as system's basic units, and (2) Preventive countermeasures for heavy rainfall and flood critically affected areas are automatically generated, and this has both theoretical value and practical significance.

There are two innovations in this new economic loss assessment system. The first innovation takes rainstorm and flooding points as the research objects, whose geographic scopes are determined by investigators. A survey questionnaire is then used to investigate the economic value of different types of properties. The second innovation is trying to integrate the data of different sources and different formats for evaluating economic losses and generating defense countermeasures. There are three kinds of data: socioeconomic property value, precipitation data, and the text data of defense strategy.

## 9.2 Literature Review

This paper mainly estimates the direct economic loss, indirect economic loss and the construction of disaster system. The research progress in this area will be reviewed below.

### 9.2.1 *Evaluation Direct Economic Losses of Meteorological Disasters*

In the current literature scholars mainly assess the direct economic losses of meteorological disasters, and the methods are primarily limited to the following two categories:

(1) Loss evaluation model based on mathematical methods. For example, Dias et al. (1988) comprehensively analyzed the effects of water depth, flooding duration, water flow speed, and forecast time on flood economic loss assessment, and proposed a non-traditional water depth-loss curve method to calculate the economic losses caused by the severe flood. Tang et al. (1992) investigated the data of more than 3,000 units in the residential areas, industrial areas, agricultural areas and commercial areas of Bangkok, Thailand, and then fitted the relationship curve between the economic loss of the flood and the submergence depth and submergence time according to the regional nature. Oliveri et al. (2000) proposed an empirical frequency-loss curve to assess the economic losses caused by flood disasters. Kazama et al. (2010) based on map data and flood control economy investigation manual investigated by the Ministry of Land, Infrastructure, Transportation, and Tourism, employed numerical simulations to estimate the cost of flood damage. Middelmann (2010) studied a combinatorial model to assess the economic losses caused by floods. Notaro et al. (2014) evaluated the uncertainty of water depth loss curve in flood loss analysis, and utilized a variety of water depth loss curves to calculate the flood loss in Cappalermo, Italy. Dabbeek et al. (2020) constructed an earthquake hazard model and a flood hazard model, and assessed the direct economic impacts of earthquakes, rivers floods and rainstorms on the residential building stock in 12 regions in the Middle East. Based on spatial analysis, Kefi et al. (2018) integrated several kinds of data, including the flood depth, land-use category, attribute value and damage rates, to estimate the impacts of climate change on the economic losses of floods. D'Ayala et al. (2020) proposed a multi-scale flood vulnerability model to assess the flood vulnerability and risk of residential buildings characterized by traditional wooden houses in Kuala Lumpur, Malaysia, and developed a universally applicable damage function to calculate the economic losses of a single building and sample levels. Establishing equations about the values of the disaster-bearing body with inundation and the disaster loss rate, Zheng et al. (2020) quantitatively estimated the

economic losses of floods along the Pearl River Estuary in China. Considering water depth, Pinos et al. (2020) developed a univariate deterministic flood loss model. They then estimated the economic losses caused by floods in different return periods in urban and agricultural areas. Pang et al. (2020) developed three typhoon carrier indexes by using principal component analysis, and further developed a typhoon disaster loss index to calculate the economic losses, and applied the index to evaluate the losses of 54 typhoons in Guangdong province from 2001 to 2018. Rahman et al. (2020) proposed a new Disaster Vegetation Damage Index (DVDI) to assess the specific crops damage caused by flooding. And then they applied this method to the assessment of the losses of severe storm and flood in Iowa, Nebraska and Texas. Constructing equations about the damage ratio of building structure, the direct economic loss ratio of indoor property, the building replacement unit price and the total construction surface area, Zhou et al. (2020) obtained the direct economic loss of Xiamen earthquake disaster by respectively calculating the building structure loss and the indoor property loss. Hisamatsu et al. (2020) proposed a random storm surge risk assessment program, and used a stochastic method to estimate the economic loss along the Tokyo Bay coast due to extreme flooding caused by storm surges. By using 1,000 typhoon inundation depth data sets, the spatial distribution of assets and damage function, they estimated the economic losses caused by typhoon with risk exceeding probability. Hou et al. (2019) analyzed the loss mechanism of drought disasters, and developed a general function of physical loss based on the hyperbolic tangent function to estimate the direct economic losses caused by drought in Southwest China in 2014. Using depth-damage curves, Cobb–Douglas production functions and input–output models, Li et al. (2019) comprehensively assessed the economic losses of Shanghai enterprises caused by extreme storms and floods.

(2) Loss functions were developed. According to the types of the global buildings, Komolafe et al. (2019) developed a loss function. First, empirical damage data were obtained by questionnaire survey, and then a loss function was generated for residential buildings that integrated multiple damage factors by using multiple linear regressions analysis. In addition, a function of water depth was established to estimate the economic damage of flooding in the Chao Phraya River Basin in Thailand. Based on the flood characteristics (usually flood depth) and land-use data, Amadio et al. (2016) estimated the flood economic losses in northern Italy by using an improved stage damage curve (SDC) model. Use Geographic Information System (GIS) and Remote Sensing (RS) technology to assess the economic losses. For example, Jonge et al. (1996) simulated the flood depth and loss based on GIS technology, and established a flood disaster loss assessment model. Haq et al. (2012) combined with socio-economic data, assessed flood losses by using RS and GIS technologies to determine the flooded range. Mohammadi et al. (2014) proposed a comprehensive loss model to calculate the economic loss of floods based on GIS model, HEC-RAS, HEC-GEORAS software and hydraulic conditions when assessing the economic loss of floods in the Neckar basin of Iran. Combining

multi-dimensional flood damage analysis (MD-FDA) and geographic information system (GIS), Jeon et al. (2018) assessed the damage losses from flood in building scale. Ye et al. (2020) used GIS (Geographic Information System) and RS (Remote Sensing) technology to simulate typical natural disaster risk scenarios, and established a comprehensive disaster loss model for scenic spots by fitting the risk curve to predict the average annual losses of the scenario. They used this model to assess the natural disaster risk of Jiuzhaigou Tree Zhengjing Group. Zhang et al. (2019) introduced a process of GIS-based rapid earthquake disaster assessment, this process integrated the isoseismal attenuation model, building damage model, economic loss model and death toll model into the geographic information system (GIS), and they used this method to assess the losses of four earthquake disasters.

According to the existing literature, it is a common and applicable assessment method to first obtain the loss rate curve of disaster bearing body on the basis of field investigation, and then calculate the direct economic loss of flood disaster by combining the submergence depth. The method is also adopted in this study, and the specific calculation formula is provided in Sect. 4.2.

### 9.2.2 *Indirect Economic Losses Evaluation of Meteorological Disasters*

In the economic system, due to the correlation between various industrial sectors, when some industries are hit by disasters, the impact tends to spread to the upstream and downstream industries and then to the entire industrial economic system as the ripple effect, which is the indirect economic loss caused by disasters (Rose 2002; Helbing 2013; Hallegatte 2015). At present, many scholars adopt input–output method to calculate the indirect economic loss. From the perspective of evaluation methods, it can be divided into the following two categories.

One is the CGE (Computable General Equilibrium model). For example, Narayan (2003) used the CGE model to assess the short-term macroeconomic impact of Fiji island hit by hurricane Ami in 2003. Tan et al. (2019) employed the CGE model to assess the comprehensive economic loss of “7.21” rainstorm in Beijing. Gao et al. (2020) combined Analytic Hierarchy Process (AHP) and spatial analysis with the use of geographic information system (GIS) to generate a comprehensive weighted risk assessment with 11 indicators from three different aspects: disaster, vulnerability and resilience, and then proposed a new method of risk calculation based on the cumulative pattern of typhoon-induced flood disasters in time and space. They incorporated these direct effects into a computable general equilibrium (CGE) model to simulate the indirect economic losses based on the local level, regional level, national level and global level. Tanoue et al. (2020) developed a global modeling framework that used a computable general equilibrium (CGE) model and a global river and flood model to estimate the direct and indirect economic losses associated with floods, and applied this framework to estimate the 2011 floods Economic losses in Thailand. Wang et al. (2015) used a general equilibrium model to assess the economic losses caused by the 2012 Beijing rainstorm. Using a forward-looking, dynamic computable general equilibrium (CGE) model, Gertz et al. (2019) assessed the impacts caused by flooding on the local economy, and applied the CGE model to Vancouver. Kilimani et al. (2018) used a computable general equilibrium model to assess the impacts of drought on agricultural productivity and the damage of the entire economy. Thirawat et al. (2017) used a dynamic computable general equilibrium (CGE) model to evaluate the resource losses caused by floods. Other representative literature includes the researches of Rose et al. (2005), Carrera (2015), Cui (2018) and Xie et al. (2018).

The other is the IO (Input–output) model. For example, Hallegatte (2008) used the abnormal input–output table to calculate the indirect economic losses caused by hurricane Katrina in the United States. Wu et al. (2019) used the abnormal input–output table to evaluate the indirect economic losses caused by the Wenchuan earthquake to other countries in the world. Xia (2018) used the IO model to calculate the indirect economic loss caused by the heat wave in Nanjing city in China in 2013. Jin et al. (2020) compiled the input–output table with ten sectors, and then they calculated the direct and indirect consumption coefficients to assess the indirect economic losses of the storm surge disaster in Guangdong from 2007 to 2017. Liu et al. (2019) proposed an adaptive regional input–output (ARIO) model, and then applied this model to assess the indirect economic losses caused by sea ice disasters in Liaoning, China. Mendoza-Tinoco et al. (2017) used the flood footprint method based on the input–output method to assess the production factors' damages caused by the summer floods in the United Kingdom in 2007, and the overall economic impacts on Yorkshire and the Humber. The ordinal regression model and the K-means clustering method were used to directly measure the intensity of snowfall, low temperature and frost disasters in non-pastoral areas, and then Wang et al. (2016) used static and dynamic input–output models to assess the indirect economic losses caused by snowfall, low temperature and frost in Beijing in 2010. Zhang et al. (2019) assumed that an earthquake was similar to the Wenchuan earthquake occurred in Beijing, and used an improved input–output model to assess the indirect economic losses, and then compared the difference in the indirect economic losses between Beijing and Wenchuan earthquake at the same loss rate. Sieg et al. (2019) developed an innovative modeling procedure, and considered the uncertainties related to the disasters and their vulnerability to assess the direct economic losses, and then input the direct economic losses to the supply side output model to estimate the indirect economic losses. Based on an input–output model, Tinoco et al. (2018) proposed a method to assess the economic losses caused by flood disasters, and then applied this method to estimate the flood losses in Sheffield, the UK in 2007. Using an adaptive regional input–output model, Zhang et al. (2017) assessed the indirect economic losses caused by the Wenchuan earthquake in Beijing. Wu et al. (2017) combined the inter-regional input–output model (IRIO) with the elasticity index, used the index system of the provincial economic resilience, and developed the indirect economic loss measures based on IRIO to assess the indirect economic loss. Wang et al. (2017) constructed static and dynamic input–output models to evaluate the direct and indirect economic losses caused by typhoon disasters in four dominant departments. Other representative literature includes the researches of Mackenzie et al. (2012), Menza-Tinoco (2017) and Avelino et al. (2018). According to the existing literature, CGE model and IO model have their own advantages and disadvantages in evaluating the impact on economy. The CGE model requires a large amount of basic data, a large amount of calculation, and the calculated value is lower, which is not suitable for embedding into disaster loss assessment system. IO model requires less data and has a clear structure, making it easy to calculate the indirect economic losses of various industrial sectors, and is more suitable for the disaster losses evaluation system (Okuyama 2007; Weitzman 2009; Ring 2010). Based on the above considerations, this paper adopts input–output model to calculate, and the specific calculation steps are given in Sect. 4.3.

### *9.2.3 Big Data Fusion and its Application to Meteorological Disasters*

According to BostrÖm et al. (2007), information fusion is a process in which effective methods are used for transforming, automatically or semi-automatically, information from different sources and time points into a unified expression, so as to support decisions made manually or automatically. Data may come from different databases, sensors, simulated data and human activities, and the data format may be diverse (number, text, image and video). Khaleghi et al. (2013) reviewed the front edge of multi-source data fusion technology. They considered two data sources of information fusion. One is hard data, produced by electronic sensors; and the other is soft data, by human activities. Yet most studies on information fusion took hard data, instead of soft data, as the research object, which went against to the fact that the volume of soft data increases exponentially at present. Under the background of information retrieval, Wu and Crestani (2015) came up with the idea to handling information fusion by utilizing geometric principles. Sun et al. (2014) summarized the algorithm of data training and test in multi-source information fusion.

In the field of big data applications to meteorological disasters, the data fusion technology is concentrated mainly on the fusion of meteorological remote sensing observation data, which is multi-source, multi-scale, multi-dimension and multi-temporal. Research and applications concerning multi-source data fusion oriented to disaster emergencies are tough problems, owing to the diverse data sources. Llinas (2002) put forward earlier the concept and scheme of information fusion geared to natural and man-made disasters, and applied fusion with the consideration of both disaster scenario and influencing data, as exemplified by earthquake disaster. Launched by the Federal Emergency Management Agency (FEMA) (Scawthorn et al. 2006; Vickery et al. 2006; MRI 2003; Ploeger et al. 2010, Kappes et al. 2012), the HAZUS-MH (Multi-Hazard) series, as the software platform of standard application applicable to the country, was able to assess potential losses brought by earthquake, flood and hurricane. As a combination of fundamental geospatial information data, social economic data, historical loss data, seismic and meteorological data by real-time observation, this system provided essential evidence for early warning and evaluation decisions of disasters. In addition, Goodchild (2009, 2011, 2015), an academician of geographic information science in the American Academy of Sciences, who is specialized, for a long time, in fusing spatial data from fields of meteorology, geology, hydrology, vegetation, zoology, limnology, computer science and remote sensing, proposed a grid-based algorithm model of multi-dimensional data fusion, and has developed an uncertainty measurement, contributing significantly to the development of spatial big data fusion.

Research concerning the fusion theories and technologies of big data of meteorological disasters theories started relatively late in China. It is until the end of the 1980s that studies of multi-sensor information fusion technology appeared and were applied to the national defense and military affairs. After the 1990s, information fusion was applied to robots and industrial process monitoring and control system. Studies concerning information fusion in the field of emergency decision-making were relatively rare, owing to the complexity of multi-variate and multi-dimensional information as well as of problems such as information fusion, self-learning mechanism and the mining and treatment of historical data. As regards the application practice, the meteorological hardware facilities have been continuously improved, the prediction ability promoted, and the meteorological service ability and the emergency management enhanced. However, the application of data information resources in the field of disaster emergency need to be further explored, and the technology and method of multi-variate data fusion and treatment analysis are also insufficiently studied. Multi-source data fusion oriented to disaster emergency has been applied to emergency decision-making in geological and earthquake disasters (Zhu 2010), but it has seldom been used in meteorological disasters. For example, Yang et al. (2005) fused data of agrometeorological losses, crops observation, agricultural economic statistics and soil humidity into a database, so as to serve the agrometeorological disaster prevention and decision-making in Anhui Province. It can be seen from the present research that most studies concerned fusion based on certain hard data (data that collected by remote sensing, sensor, etc.), but hardly any of them fused hard data with soft data, for instance, research concerning the fusion technology and method of meteorological data, loss data and social statistics data (Wu et al. 2018a, b). Based on D-S evidence theory and fuzzy mathematics multi-sensor data fusion algorithm, Zhang (2020) realized the integration of multi-dimensional heterogeneous geological monitoring data, and designed a geological disaster monitoring and early warning system. Anbarasan et al. (2020) proposed a flood disaster detection method based on the Internet of Things, Big data and Convolutional Deep Neural Network (CDNN). Puttinaovarat et al. (2020) proposed a new flood forecasting system which integrated meteorological, hydrological, geospatial and crowdsourced data in an adaptive machine learning framework. Wu et al. (2020) established the vulnerability curve, and they used web searchers to extract flood-related text information from the Internet and social platforms. Based on the three indicators of rainfall intensity, duration and coverage area, they calculated the heavy rainfall index. And based on the affected population, areaand direct economic losses, they calculated the comprehensive disaster index. Then they took the rainstorm index as the independent variable and the comprehensive disaster index as the dependent variable, they established the vulnerability curve of flood disasters, and then compared with the actual situations to verify this model's performance.

## 9.3 Construction Plans

### *9.3.1 System Architecture*

The overall system architecture diagram is illustrated in Fig. 9.1, composed of data layer, service layer and application layer. The system uses the web development framework of MapGIS IGServer as the development platform, and combines it with the logic process of specific business to build the application system.

(1) Data layer: This provides the system foundation for data support. The system data consists of two parts: the basic map data, and the corresponding business data.

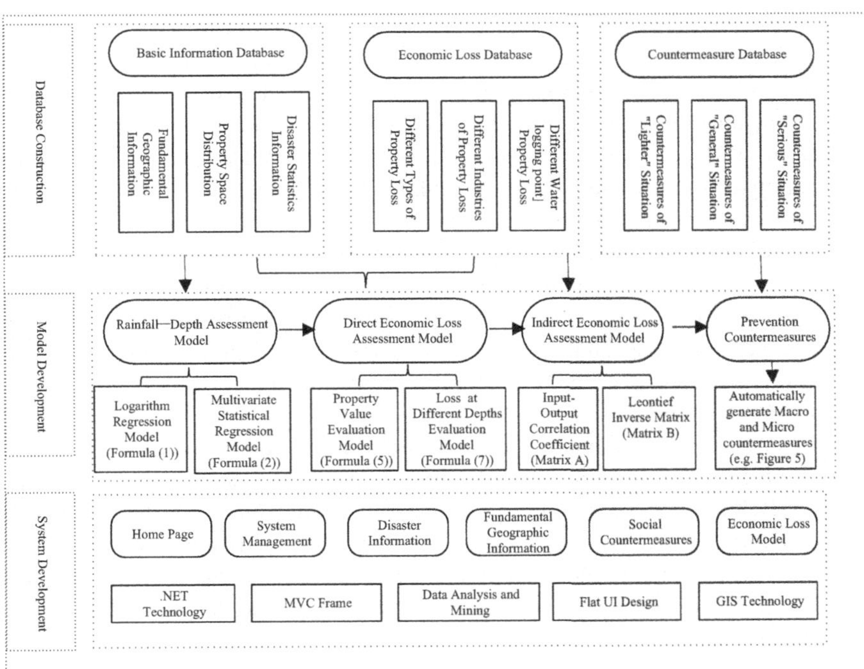


**Fig. 9.1** Overall system architecture diagram

(2) Service layer: Located on the data layer, this layer uses the MapGIS IGServer development platform as an application support, and accesses system data through the MapGIS data engine and relational database engine, respectively. The service layer provides GIS data services and functional services, releases administrative commands through the service management module and achieves business functions when called by the application system. With the REST (Representational State Transfer) services, the communication on the GIS platform and the GIS functions can be realized.

(3) Application layer: Based on data support and the GIS development platform, an economic loss evaluation system for urban rainstorm and flood disasters has been constructed, including social and economic data management, data management of historical disasters, data management of disaster countermeasures, economic loss assessment, and generation of assessment reports, user management, system management and other functional modules.

This is illustrated in Fig. 9.1.

### 9.3.2 Data Organization

(1) Map data: This system is composed of two types of data format. The first is the base maps for the system, and it directly uses the third-party free map data provided by the Map World Corporation. With web map technology, it provides users with smooth map roaming, seamless zoom, fast graded display and other online operating experiences. The second is vector data, which is stored in the form of MapGIS local data sources, including administrative divisions and a variety of infrastructure data. Through the layer control panel, it is possible to achieve free setting of the display and hiding all factors, and browsing both the spatial distribution and related attribute information of administrative divisions, places, roads, infrastructure, water systems, water conservancy facilities, and other surface features. Incorporating a variety of information from business databases and map data into the unified base map of geographic framework, the system can form a complete database of geographic frameworks, thus providing support for business analysis.

(2) Business data: This mainly consists of the information about historical rainstorm and flood disasters, the distribution of population density, the distribution of GDP density, community property value, individual buildings, defensive countermeasures, etc. As most of the data contain spatial information and attribute information, for a query in the application system the spatial location and attribute information are acquired from the business database, and then the spatial position information points are drawn on the client-side maps.

## 9.4 Models and Data

### 9.4.1 *Rainfall—Flood Depth Assessment Model*

The evaluation model makes use of the historical data of urban waterlogging sites to construct a statistical regression model. When developing the regression model, multiple regression models such as linear, logarithm (single logarithm and double logarithm), exponential, quadratic and cubic are considered, and then compare the values of decision coefficients $R^2$ to choose the best model of fit.

Taking the linear regression equation as an example, the relationship between rainfall and water depth can be expressed by the following equation:

$$Y_{ct} = \alpha_1 + \alpha_2 \times X_{ct} + \mu_{ct}, \quad \forall c, t \tag{9.1}$$

In the equation, $X_{ct}$ and $Y_{ct}$ are the rainfall and flood depth of waterlogged site c at time t, $\alpha_1$ is the intercept, $\alpha_2$ is the coefficient and $\mu_{ct}$ is the residual.

Taking Longhua District in Shenzhen as an example, the research area of this paper, fifty-eight sets of historical data were obtained by collecting the rainfall data of the automatic weather station in or closest to each waterlogging site during each rainstorm and flood disaster. $Y_{ct}$ is accumulated precipitation for one hour, and $X_{ct}$ is the water depth. After repeated fitting, the following expression can be obtained:

$$\widehat{Y_{ct}} = 0.06813 \times \log_2(X_{ct}) \tag{9.2}$$

The confidence level is 95%, $R^2 = 0.523$.

This expression can be regarded as the relation curve between the water depth of waterlogging site *c* in Longhua District, Shenzhen and the precipitation in one hour. For waterlogging site *c*, once a rainstorm occurs, the flood depth $\widehat{Y_{ct}}$ of the waterlogging site can be predicted by substituting the hourly rainfall $X_{ct}$ into Formula (9.2).

### 9.4.2 *Direct Economic Loss Assessment of Disasters*

By combining census and sampling surveys, the properties suffering urban rainstorms and flood disasters are divided into 15 categories, including residential houses, office buildings, parking lots, commercial enterprises, industrial enterprises and public facilities. The corresponding tables are designed for different types of property and the data of socioeconomic losses are obtained through surveys. With the aid of mathematical statistics, the disaster loss rates of various types of objects subject to hazard effects in different situations are calculated according to the water depth, and the curve reflecting disaster loss rates is constructed. Finally, according to the survey data and the data in the official statistical yearbook, the economic losses of different types of properties affected by different water depths are calculated.

The calculation is divided into three steps as follows: first, estimate the total value of the properties; second, compute the losses at different water depths and obtain the loss rates by dividing the loss by the total loss; third, calculate the loss rates of various types of properties. Take one property as example, the detailed methods and process of calculation are presented as follows.

(1) Assessment of property value

Data of seventy-three waterlogging sites are collected by field investigation, and each waterlogging site is defined as $c = 1, 2 \ldots 73$. The properties at each waterlogging site are divided into six disaster zones: residential area, office building, commerce, industry, traffic road and ground (underground) parking.

The category of disaster zone is distinguished by $i$; The labor (a number) of sample of the disaster bearing body in disaster zone is denoted by $s$. The label (a number) of internal properties (such as computer, television, refrigerator, etc.) in disaster bearing body i distinguished by $k$. $i,s,k$ are all natural numbers.

For investigating sample $s$ from hazard-affected body $i$, the net value of its asset $k$ is calculated by straight-line depreciation method using the following formula:

$$N_{sk}^{i} = N_{sk0}^{i} \times \left(1 - n_{sk}^{i}/t_{sk}^{i}\right) \tag{9.3}$$

where $N_{sk}^{i}$ is the net value of asset $k$ of sample $s$ of hazard-affected body $i$, $N_{sk0}^{i}$ is the purchase price of asset $k$ of sample $s$ of hazard-affected body $i$, $n_{sk}^{i}$ is the depreciation years of asset $k$ of sample $s$ of hazard-affected body $i$, and $t_{sk}^{i}$ is the life expectancy of the asset $k$ of sample $s$ of hazard-affected body $i$.

The present value of each asset was obtained from the arithmetic mean value of the net value and the estimated present value:

$$P_{sk}^{i} = (N_{sk}^{i} + M_{sk}^{i})/2 \tag{9.4}$$

where $P_{sk}^{i}$ is the present value of asset $k$ for the sample $s$ of hazard-affected body $i$, and $M_{sk}^{i}$ is the estimated present market value of asset $k$ *of* hazard-affected body $i$.

For example, there are seventy-three waterlogging sites in Longhua District, Shenzhen, and the Junzibu is the No.1 waterlogging site. Suppose that there are only four types of properties in Junzibu ($c = 1$): residential area ($i = 1$), office buildings ($i = 2$), commerce ($i = 3$), and industrial area ($i = 4$). Suppose further that Junzibu has one hundred residences, and the author investigates the second residence($s = 2$). In this residence, the television is the third property ($k = 3$), and its service life is assumed to be $t$ years, which has been used for $n$ years. Then the net present value of television is:

$$N_{23}^{1} = N_{230}^{1} \times \left(1 - n_{23}^{1}/t_{23}^{1}\right) \tag{9.5}$$

In (5), $N_{23}^{1}$ is the net present value of the third property television ($k = 3$) for the second residential house ($s = 2$) in Junzibu at the first waterlogging site ($i = 1$) of Longhua District, Shenzhen city; $N_{230}^{1}$ represents the initial value of the television, and $M_{23}^{1}$ is the estimated value of the present value of the television; $n_{23}^{1}$ represents its service time so far; $t_{23}^{1}$ represents its life expectancy. Suppose the purchase price of the television is 2,000 yuan, and it has been used for four years with a total life expectancy ten years. In the survey, the user's valuation of the television is 1500 yuan, and according to Formula (9.4), the actual present value of the television can be calculated as:

$$P_{23}^{1} = \frac{\left(2000 \times \left(1 - \frac{4}{10}\right) + 1500\right)}{2} = 1350 \tag{9.6}$$

On the basis of the present value of each asset, the total value of each sample is obtained from the sum of the assets' present values in each sample. The average value of each sample is calculated by the following formula:

$$V^{i} = \sum_{s=1}^{f^{i}} \sum_{k=1}^{g^{i}} P_{sk}^{i} / f^{i} \tag{9.7}$$

where $V^{i}$ is the average value of each sample of hazard-affected body $i$, $f^{i}$ is the size of hazard-affected body $i$ , $g^{i}$ is the size of asset $k$ *of* hazard-affected body $i$.

(2) Estimation of the loss rate at different depths

Asset loss at different depths was obtained for each asset as the present value multiplied by the asset loss rate at different depths (Wu et al. 2016). On the basis of each asset loss at different depths, the average loss of each sample of hazard-affected body sample at different depths was calculated by the following formula:

$$D_{j}^{i} = \sum_{s=1}^{f^{i}} \sum_{k=1}^{g^{i}} [P_{sk}^{i} r_{skj}^{i}] / f^{i} \tag{9.8}$$

where $D_{j}^{i}$ is the average loss of each sample of hazard-affected body $i$ at depth $j$, and $r_{skj}^{i}$ is the loss rate of asset $k$ of sample $s$ of hazard-affected body $i$ at depth $j$.

The loss rate of each sample of hazard-affected body at different depths was calculated by the following formula:

$$R_{j}^{i} = D_{j}^{i} / V^{i} \tag{9.9}$$

where $R_{j}^{i}$ is the loss rate of each sample of hazard-affected body $i$ at depth $j$.

### 9.4.3 Indirect Economic Loss Assessment of Disasters

(1) Indirect economic loss

According to the Standardization Administration of China (2011) and Wu et al. (2019), indirect economic loss is defined as follows: After an industry is directly impacted by a disaster, it subsequently causes damages to other industry sectors due to ripple effects, which will then be transmitted to the entire industrial economic system. Scholars mainly adopted input–output model (hereinafter referred to as IO Model) to substitute the demand side reduction value of some industries into the input–output coefficient matrix to calculate the indirect economic loss caused by disaster impact (Wu et al. 2019).

(2) The input–output model (IO)

Input–output table provides a quantitative analysis method, and it was proposed by American economist Wassily Leontief in 1936 to explore the quantitative interdependence among various sectors and reproduction links of the national economy. The input–output table is the basis for calculating the indirect economic losses of disasters. It is a crisscrossed matrix balance table, describing the economic links and distribution relationships between regions and sectors from the source of production inputs and the distribution of products, comprehensively and systematically reflecting the complete social reproduction process of production, distribution, exchange and consumption in different regions and different sectors. The specific form is shown in Table 9.1, in which there are $n$ different departments.

From the input–output table, input and output cross each other to form a line equilibrium relationship and a column equilibrium relationship that reflect the equilibrium relationship between the same department and the entire society. The line equilibrium relationship reflects the identity relationship between the consumption of a product by various production sectors and the consumption of that product as the final product.

$$\sum_{v=1}^{n} a_{uv} + B_u = G_u \quad \forall u, v \tag{9.10}$$

In the expression, $u$, $v$ are the serial number of row and column in the Input–output table, respectively. $a_{uv}$ represents the product value of the $u$-th department consumed by the department $v$ in the production process; $B_u$ represents the product value of the department $u$ for final use; $G_u$ represents the total output of sector $u$.

Direct consumption coefficient $a^*_{uv}$ and direct consumption coefficient matrix $A$ are introduced into the line equilibrium relation,

$$a^*_{uv} = a_{uv}/G_u \tag{9.11}$$

**Table 9.1** Basic structure of input–output table

| Output | | Intermediate use | | | Final use | | Gross output |
|---|---|---|---|---|---|---|---|
| Input | | Department 1 | Department 2 | ... | Department $w$ | | |
| Intermediate input | Department 1 | $a_{11}$ | $a_{12}$ | ... | $a_{1w}$ | $B_1$ | $G_1$ |
| | Department 2 | $a_{21}$ | $a_{22}$ | ... | $a_{2w}$ | $B_2$ | $G_2$ |
| | ... | ... | ... | ... | ... | ... | ... |
| | Department w | $a_{w1}$ | $a_{w2}$ | ... | $a_{ww}$ | $B_w$ | $G_w$ |
| Value added | Remuneration for workers | $L_1$ | $L_2$ | ... | $L_w$ | | |
| | Net production tax | $T_1$ | $T_2$ | ... | $T_w$ | | |
| | Depreciation of fixed assets | $F_1$ | $F_2$ | ... | $F_w$ | | |
| | Operating surplus | $S_1$ | $S_2$ | ... | $S_w$ | | |
| Total input | | $G_1$ | $G_2$ | ... | $G_w$ | | |

$$A = \begin{pmatrix} a_{11}^* & a_{12}^* & \cdots & a_{1w}^* \\ a_{21}^* & a_{22}^* & \cdots & a_{2w}^* \\ \cdots & \cdots & \cdots & \cdots \\ a_{w1}^* & a_{w2}^* & \cdots & a_{ww}^* \end{pmatrix} \tag{9.12}$$

Then Formula (9.10) becomes

$$AG + B = G \tag{9.13}$$

$$G = (I - A)^{-1} B \tag{9.14}$$

In the formulas, $G$ is the total output of each industry, $B$ is the final use, and $A$ is the direct consumption coefficient matrix.

Suppose an industry is hit by a disaster, and the final demand decreases by $\Delta B$. The indirect loss $\Delta G$ can be calculated by multiplying $\Delta G$ with the Leontief inverse matrix.

The calculation formula of this module is shown as follows:

$$\Delta G = (I - A)^{-1} \Delta B \tag{9.15}$$

In the formula, $(I - A)^{-1}$ is the Leontief inverse matrix calculated based on the Shenzhen input–output table (Liu 2015), and it represents the change in the total output of each department when the final output of a certain sector changes by a unit. $\Delta G$ expresses the change amount of the final output of the industry affected by rainstorm and flood disaster, while $\Delta G$ indicates the change amount of the indirect output of the related industries.

### 9.4.4 Data and Database

(1) Data Collection

(1) Basic map data. It is from *baidu map.*
(2) Basic property information. In May 2014, under the guidance of the staff of Shenzhen meteorological bureau, the author and others conducted a survey on the property value of waterlogging sites in Longhua District, Shenzhen. A total of seventy three waterlogging sites were investigated. According to the actual situation, the disaster bearing bodies of each waterlogging site were divided into different types of properties, with a maximum of fifteen types. Then we investigate the value of each property at different immersed water depth.
(3) Input–output table. Data of the input–output table of Shenzhen city are from literature of Liu (2015).

(4) Rainfall data. It is from observational data from the Shenzhen meteorological bureau.
(5) Information on defense countermeasures. Through the investigation, we obtained 3050 copies of "clearly-understood card of community weather disaster prevention" in Longhua District, Shenzhen. Then the data were sorted out and the defense countermeasures of each waterlogging site were obtained. According to the severity of economic losses, the defense countermeasures are divided into three grades: "general", "medium" and "severe". From the macro and micro levels, corresponding defense countermeasures are proposed for different objects such as the public, industry and government departments.

Once the direct and indirect economic loss values of a waterlogging site are calculated, we add them up to get the total economic loss. The total loss value of all waterlogging sites is divided into three intervals, "general", "medium" and "severe". Then based on the calculated sum of the economic losses of a research object (direct economic losses plus indirect economic losses), the defense countermeasures at different levels of scenarios can be automatically extracted.

To be clear, the current defense countermeasures are sorted out and stored in the database. One part is fixed, for example, for different public, industry, street, government, etc., under "severe, medium and general" situation, there are different schemes, which can be automatically extracted. But the other part is non-fixed, for example, which industries should be focused on? Which are automatically screened according to the degree of the industry's losses. If the loss rate of industry $u$ is the highest, industry $u$ is automatically selected as the industry to be focused on.

(2) Database Construction.

Database is the foundation of system design. The first step is the construction of the basic database for the economic loss evaluation of rainstorm and flood disasters, whose data can be collected through investigation, outsourcing, remote sensing and other methods. The content covers the basic geographic information, disaster statistics, economic statistics and disaster countermeasures from the Longhua District in Shenzhen. At the same time, the basic data are systematically summarized, so via database recording and storage, the query, additions, calls, and statistical analysis can be achieved at any time.

## 9.5 Case Analysis

Shenzhen city is located on the east coast of Pearl River Delta and is under the jurisdiction of Guangdong Province. Shenzhen has a total area of 1,953 km$^2$ and an average elevation of 70 to 120 m. Shenzhen enjoys the subtropical oceanic climate and frequently experiences meteorological disasters, such as storm, typhoon,

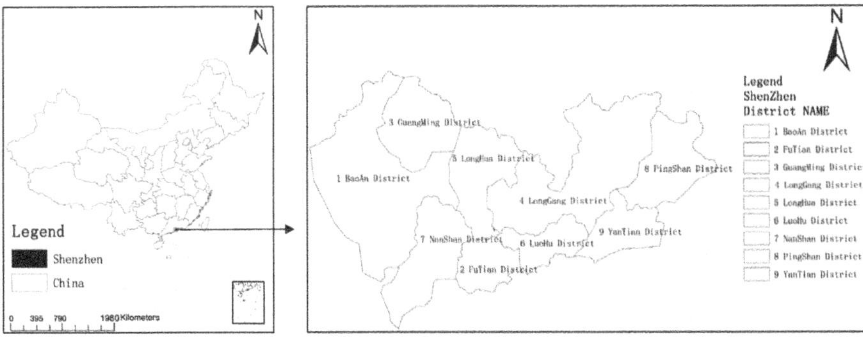


**Fig. 9.2** Location of Longhua District and Shenzhen city in China

thunderstorm, higher temperature, cold weather, heavy fog, dust-haze, drought, and hail.

Longhua district, belonging to Shenzhen, is located in the geographical center of Shenzhen and the urban development axis, adjacent to "six districts and one city", Dongguan city and Guangming district in the north, Longgang in the east, Futian, Luohu, Nanshan in the south, Baoan in the west. The total area is 175.6 square kilometers.

In 2018, Longhua district has jurisdiction over six sub-districts. In 2017, Longhua district had a permanent resident population of 1.6037 million, with a gross regional product (GDP) of 213.016 billion yuan, including 123.559 billion yuan added value of the secondary industry and 89.439 billion yuan added value of the tertiary industry. The proportion of the three industries was 0.01:58.00:41.99. Per capita GDP is 135,100 yuan, which is about 20,000 US dollars at the 2017 average exchange rate.

The locations of Longhua district and Shenzhen city are showed as follows (Fig. 9.2).

### *9.5.1 "8.29" Rainstorm and Flooding Disaster of Shenzhen in 2018*

From 12:00 on August 28 to 18:00 on August 30, 2018, the average accumulative rainfall in Shenzhen was 355.8 mm, the maximum rainfall in one hour was 112.4 mm (Tiantou station, Pingshan district), and the maximum accumulative rainfall was 678.1 mm (Chishi da an primary school station).

During August 28 to 30, 2018, Shenzhen was hit by the consecutive days of heavy rain, and the whole city suffered from various degrees of danger. Road traffic was almost paralyzed because of the severe flooding in a large area. "8.29 rainstorm disasters" caused different degrees of flood in the four street jurisdictions of Longhua District. According to preliminary investigation, the total number of rainstorm and flooding points increased to 27 in the whole Longhua District.

Taking the worst-affected rainstorm and flooding points—Junzibu Community in the Guanlan Street—as an example, in the "8.29" storm disaster in 2018, the maximum sliding rainfall within 3 h was 90.4 mm, with the average water depth of 607 mm and the longest flooding time of 7 h. The heavy rain trapped more than 300 residents; more than 100 cars and 400 shops flooded and more than 25 companies were affected. There were even three small landslides, which, luckily, did not cause any casualties. The direct property losses amounted to 760,000 yuan. The main reasons of the flood were prolonged rainfall, low-lying land, underdeveloped drainage facilities and delayed drainage.

### *9.5.2 Economic Loss Assessment of the "8.29" Rainstorm Disasters of Shenzhen in 2018*

The economic loss assessment of the "8.29" rainstorm in Shenzhen in 2018 can be divided into two parts: direct economic loss assessment and indirect economic loss assessment. According to Formulas (9.8) and (9.15), direct loss and indirect loss of Junzibu community were calculated, respectively. The spatial loss distribution of each flood point caused by the storm is shown in Fig. 9.3.

The point that suffered most was the Junzibu community: The direct economic losses amounted to 516,000-yuan, indirect economic losses to 43,107,000 yuan, and the total economic loss to 43,623,000 yuan. From the perspective of the direct

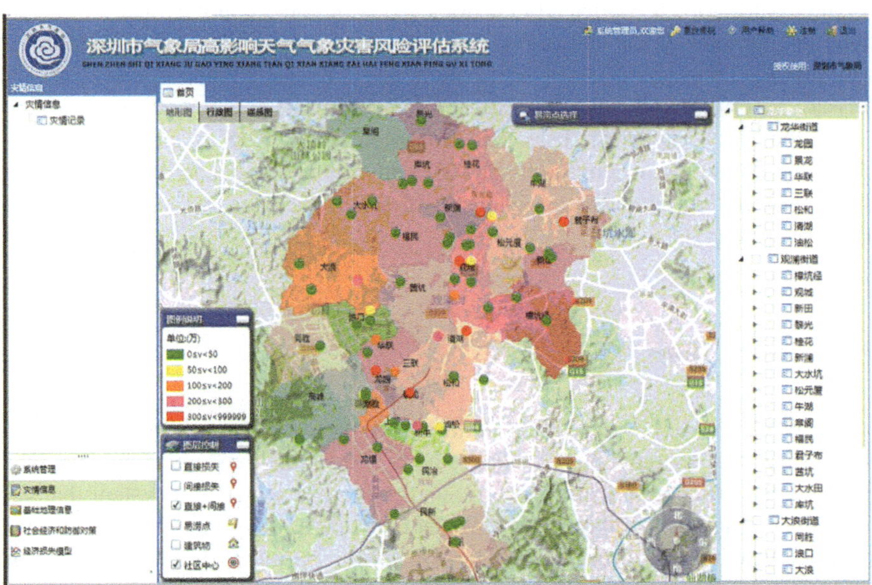


**Fig. 9.3** Economic losses of all waterlogged points during the natural disaster on August 29, 2018

economic losses of objects of hazard effect, the residential-area losses were around 15,400 yuan, the business-district losses around 150,000 yuan, the industrial area losses around 280,000 yuan, and the office building losses around 7,000 yuan.

The five industries that suffered the most direct economic losses were wood processing and furniture manufacturing (58,000 yuan), wholesale and retail (76,428 yuan), accommodation and catering (37,300 yuan), real estate (15,300 yuan), and the garment and textile industry (14,200 yuan). The five industries with the most indirect economic losses were chemical (1,270,200), electricity, heat production and supply (1,131,700 yuan), leasing and business services (1,115,600 yuan), farming (1,513,300 yuan), and the financial industry (1,175,000 yuan).

### *9.5.3 Countermeasures of the "8.29" Rainstorm and Flooding Disaster of Shenzhen in 2018*

Based on human–computer interaction and distributed data acquisition, this system can be used to automatically generate not only the direct economic losses and the disaster-reduction efficiency of different types of properties as well as the indirect economic losses of different industries and regions, but also the disaster prevention report of typical rainstorm and flood points. The report includes six parts: basic information about the disaster, assessment ideas, direct economic losses, indirect economic losses, disaster description, and defensive countermeasures. The countermeasures are chosen from both macro and micro levels. At the macro level, attention is paid to the seriously damaged industries and their corresponding disaster prevention interventions. At the micro level, the classification of disaster losses is achieved based on the historical disaster information, and different countermeasures are put forward according to the characteristics of rainstorm and flooding points.

For the "8.29" rainstorm disaster in Shenzhen city in 2018, in terms of the rainstorm and flooding points of the Junzibu Community and based on the severity level of the disaster, the system has automatically extracted the defensive countermeasures, as shown in Fig. 9.4.

## 9.6 Conclusions

In this research, we have collected multi-source data covering meteorology, geography, disaster, economy, public management, and so on, constructed models, integrated with waterlogging site as a unit, and developed a platform system that can be used in practice. Combined with weather forecasts, this system can be used to calculate instantly the direct economic losses of the rainstorm and flood disaster in the Longhua District of Shenzhen, obtain the indirect economic losses of the related industries, regions and departments, and generate automatically the economic loss

1. At the macro level, the countermeasures are as follows:

(1) Strengthen disaster prevention in the industrial zone, commercial district and residential area.

(2) Enhance disaster prevention in wood processing and furniture manufacturing, wholesale and retail trades, accommodation and catering, the real estate industry, textile and clothing industry, shoes, hats, leather and feather product industry.

2. At the micro level, the countermeasures are shown below:

(1) Relevant officials should be available on a 24-hours/day basis.

(2) Suspend classes in primary and secondary schools as well as kindergartens. The school should be equipped with professionals to ensure the children's safety in school.

(3) Teach students how to avoid dangers on their way to and from school.Schools should protect the safety of students during school hours (including students on the school bus and boarding students).

(4) Inform people outdoors to move away from trees, billboards, overhead lines, towers, transformers and other areas of high-risk. Never touch the wires blown down by wind. Find a safe place to shelter nearby.

(5) Personnel out on patrol should check dangerous slopes, simple scaffolding, flood-prone areas and precarious houses. Once any sign of disaster is seen, it should be promptly reported to a sub-district office.

**Fig. 9.4** Storm disaster prevention countermeasures that were used on August 29, 2018

evaluation and the countermeasure reports for typical rainstorm and flood points. All these can provide decision-making references for disaster prevention and the disaster emergency management of the municipal government and the Shenzhen Meteorological Bureau. At the same time, the interactive data collection of this system can facilitate the staff working for the communities, the streets and the municipal government to acquire data and evaluate disaster losses, saving labor and material costs for the staff at all levels of government. In addition, real-time updates of the database can be used for other disaster management. Finally, this system can be extended to the municipal and provincial ministry of environmental protection and civil affairs and other government departments as a norm of disaster economic loss assessment, to provide supplementary information for the natural disaster emergency management of Shenzhen and other similar cities. In this way, the risks of natural disasters can be drastically reduced, management costs lowered, and social welfare prioritized.

It is important to note that the system constructed in this paper has some limitations. First, the underlying basic information and data need to be updated in a timely manner. For example, land use, distribution of waterlogging sites and property value of waterlogging sites need to be updated in time. At present, the defense countermeasures are sorted out and stored in the database, which also need to be updated in time. The second is about the data of input–output table: If the system is to be applied to other cities, the input–output table of that city needs to be obtained. The creation of the table is time-consuming, labor-intensive, and more difficult. The third is that the case study in this paper is based on the data collected and stored in the system in 2014. According to the "8.29" rainstorm disaster data of 2018, the results which generated automatically by substituting it into the system do not fully match the reality. Since the main purpose of this paper is to introduce the idea of system construction, the case is only used as an auxiliary verification to illustrate the method. Finally, how to obtain and update the data stored in the system automatically and regularly with the help of social media, government documents and big data of high-precision real-time map in the future remains not only the research difficulty, but also the direction of further research.

**Acknowledgements** Guo Wei, Tingting Feng also made great contributions to this manuscript. We express our heartfelt thanks to them. This research was supported by: National Social and Scientific Fund Program of China (18ZDA052; 17BGL142;16ZDA047); The Natural Science Foundation of China (91546117, 71373131).

## Appendix

See Table 9.2.

**Table 9.2** Description of symbols in this paper

| Symbols | Description | Location of first occurrence |
|---|---|---|
| $Y$ | Flood depth of waterlogged site | Formula (9.1) |
| $X$ | Rainfall of waterlogged site | Formula (9.1) |
| c | Serial number of waterlogged site | Formula (9.1) |
| t | Time | Formula (9.1) |
| $\alpha_1$ | Intercept in the regression equation | Formula (9.1) |
| $\alpha_2$ | Coefficient in the regression equation | Formula (9.1) |
| $\mu_{ct}$ | Residual in the regression equation | Formula (9.1) |
| $\widehat{Y_{ct}}$ | Estimated flood depth of waterlogged site | Formula (9.2) |
| i | Serial number of disasters bearing body | Formula (9.3) |
| $s$ | Sample size of the disaster bearing body $i$ | Formula (9.3) |
| $k$ | The number of internal properties of each disaster bearing body $i$ | Formula (9.3) |

(continued)

**Table 9.2** (continued)

| Symbols | Description | Location of first occurrence |
|---|---|---|
| *N* | Net value of asset | Formula (9.3) |
| *n* | Depreciation years of asset | Formula (9.3) |
| t | Life expectancy of asset | Formula (9.3) |
| P | present value of asset | Formula (9.4) |
| *M* | Estimated present market value of asset | Formula (9.4) |
| V | Average value of each sample | Formula (9.7) |
| f | Size of i | Formula (9.7) |
| g | Size of k | Formula (9.7) |
| *D* | Average loss of hazard-affected body | Formula (9.8) |
| r | Loss rate of asset | Formula (9.8) |
| j | Immersed water depth | Formula (9.8) |
| R | Loss rate of each sample of hazard-affected body | Formula (9.9) |
| u | serial number of rows in the Input–output table | Formula (9.11) |
| v | serial number of column in the Input–output table | Formula (9.11) |
| A | Direct consumption coefficient matrix | Formula (9.12) |
| w | Serial number of departments in the Input–output table | Formula (9.12) |
| a | Intermediate use | Table 9.1 |
| B | Final use | Table 9.1 |
| *L* | Remuneration for workers | Table 9.1 |
| *T* | Net production tax | Table 9.1 |
| *F* | Depreciation of fixed assets | Table 9.1 |
| *S* | Operating surplus | Table 9.1 |
| G | Gross output | Table 9.1 |

**Table 9.3** Description of abbreviations in this paper

| Abbreviation | Full Name | Location of first occurrence |
|---|---|---|
| PB | Petabyte | 1. Introduction |
| WebGIS | Web-based Geographic Information System | 1. Introduction |
| GIS | Geographic Information System | 0.1 2.1 Evaluation direct economic losses of meteorological disasters |
| RS | Remote Sensing | 0.2 2.1 Evaluation direct economic losses of meteorological disasters |
| HEC-RAS | Hydrologic Engineering Center's River Analysis System | 0.3 2.1 Evaluation direct economic losses of meteorological disasters |
| HEC-GEORAS | Hydrologic Engineering Center's Geometry River Analysis System | 0.4 2.1 Evaluation direct economic losses of meteorological disasters |

(continued)

**Table 9.3** (continued)

| Abbreviation | Full Name | Location of first occurrence |
|---|---|---|
| CGE | Computable General Equilibrium | 0.5 2.2 Indirect Economic losses evaluation of meteorological disasters |
| IO | Input–output | 0.6 2.2 Indirect Economic losses evaluation of meteorological disasters |
| FEMA | Federal Emergency Management Agency | 0.7 2.3 Big data fusion and its application to meteorological disasters |
| HAZUS-MH | Multi-Hazard | 0.8 2.3 Big data fusion and its application to meteorological disasters |
| MapGIS IGServer | | 0.9 2.3 Big data fusion and its application to meteorological disasters |
| REST | Representational State Transfer | 0.10 2.3 Big data fusion and its application to meteorological disasters |
| MVC Frame | Model View Controller Frame | Figure 9.1 |

# References


Amadio, M., Mysiak, J., Carrera, L., & Koks, E. (2016). Improving flood damage assessment models in Italy. *Natural Hazards, 82*(3), 2075–2088.

Anbarasan, M., Muthu, B., Sivaparthipan, C. B., Sundarasekar, R., Kadry, S., Krishnamoorthy, S., et al. (2020). Detection of flood disaster system based on loT, big data and convolutional deep neural network. *Computer Communications, 150,* 150–157.

Antimiani, A., Costantini, V., & Paglialunga, E. (2015). The sensitivity of climate-economy CGE models to energy-related elasticity parameters: Implications for climate policy design. *Economic Modelling, 51,* 38–52.

Avelino, F. T. A., & Dall'erba, S. (2018). Comparing the economic impact of natural disasters generated by different input-output models: An application to the 2007 chehalis river flood (WA). *Risk Analysis, 13006,* 85–104.

Baghersad, M., & Zobel, C. W. (2015). Economic impact of production bottlenecks caused by disasters impacting interdependent industry sectors. *International Journal of Production Economics, 168*(10), 71–80.

Barker, K., & Santos, J. R. (2010). Measuring the efficacy of inventory with a dynamic input–output model. *International Journal of Production Economics, 126*(1), 130–143.

Boström, H., Andler, S., Brohede, M., Johansson, R., Karlsson, A., Laere, J. V., Niklasson, L., Klingegard, M., Persson, A., & Ziemke, T. (2007). On the definition of information fusion as a field of research. Informatics Research Centre, University of Skovde, Tech. Rep. HS-IKI-TR-07–006. Retrieved from https://urn.kb.se/resolve?urn=urn:nbn:se:his:diva-1256.

Carrera, L., Standardi, G., & Bosello, F. (2015). Assessing direct and indirect economic impacts of a flood event through the integration of spatial and computable general equilibrium modelling. *Environmental Modelling & Software, 63*(11), 109–122.

Crowther, K. G., & Haimes, Y. Y. (2007). Systemic valuation of strategic preparedness through application of the inoperability input-output model with lessons learned from hurricane Katrina. *Risk Analysis, 27*(5), 1345–1364.

Cui, Q., Xie, W., & Liu, Y. (2018). Effects of sea level rise on economic development and regional disparity in China. *Journal of Cleaner Production, 176*(1), 1245–1253.

D'Ayala, D., Wang, K., Yan, Y., Smith, H., Massam, A., Filipova, V., & Pereira, J. J. (2020). Flood vulnerability and risk assessment of urban traditional buildings in a heritage district of kuala lumpur, malaysia. *Natural Hazards and Earth System Sciences, 20*(8), 2221–2241.

Dabbeek, J., Silva, V., Galasso, C., & Smith, A. (2020). Probabilistic earthquake and flood loss assessment in the middle east. *International Journal of Disaster Risk Reduction, 49,* 101662.

Das, S., & Lee, R. (1988). A nontraditional methodology for flood stage-damage calculations. *Jawra Journal of the American Water Resources Association, 24*(6), 1263–1272.

De, Jonge, T., Kok, M., & Hogeweg, M. (1996). Modelling floods and damage assessment using GIS. Iahs publication, 299–306.

Enke, D. (2007). Case study: Applying a regional CGE model for estimation of indirect economic losses due to damaged highway bridges. *Engineering Economist., 52*(4), 367–401.

Galbusera, L., & Giannopoulos, G. (2018). On input-output economic models in disaster impact assessment. *International Journal of Disaster Risk Reduction, 3,* 0186–0198.

Gao, Z. Q., Richard, G., & Tao, M. (2020). Direct and indirect economic losses using typhoon-flood disaster analysis: An application to Guangdong province, China. *Sustainability, 12*(21), 8980.

Gertz, A. B., Davies, J. B., & Black, S. L. (2019). A CGE framework for modeling the economics of flooding and recovery in a major urban area. *Risk Analysis, 39*(6), 1314–1341.

Haimes, Y. Y., & Jiang, P. (2001). Leontief-based model of risk in complex interconnected infrastructures. *Journal of Infrastructure Systems, 7*(1), 1–12.

Hallegatte, S. (2008). An adaptive regional input-output model and its application to the assessment of the economic cost of Katrina. *Risk Analysis, 28*(3), 779–799.

Hallegatte, S. (2015). The indirect cost of natural disasters and an economic definition of macroeconomic resilience. World Bank Policy Research Working Paper, 1–37.

Haq, M., Akhtar, M., & Muhammad, S. (2012). Techniques of remote sensing and GIS for flood monitoring and damage assessment: A case study of Sindh province, Pakistan. *The Egyptian Journal of Remote Sensing and Space Science, 15*(2), 135–141.

Helbing, D. (2013). Globally networked risks and how to respond. *Nature, 497,* 51–59.

Hisamatsu, R., Tabeta, S., Kim, S., & Mizuno, K. (2020). Storm surge risk assessment for the insurance system: A case study in Tokyo Bay, Japan. *Ocean and Coastal Management, 189,* 105147.

Hou, W., Chen, Z. Q., Zuo, D. D., & Feng, G. L. (2019). Drought loss assessment model for southwest China based on a hyperbolic tangent function. *International Journal of Disaster Risk Reduction, 33,* 477–484.

Huang, C. F. (2012). Risk analysis and management of natural disaster. Beijing: Science Press. (in Chinese).

Huang, C. F., & Huang, Y. D. (2018). An information diffusion technique to assess integrated hazard risks. *Environmental Research, 161,* 104–113.

IPCC. (2014). IPCC[R]. https://www.ipcc.ch.

Jeon, H., Eem, S. H., & Park, J. (2018). Flood damage assessment in building scale caused by the coastal inundation height at Haeundae beach, Busan. *Journal of Coastal Research,* 1561–1565.

Jin, X., Rashid, S., & Kedong, Y. (2020). Direct and indirect loss evaluation of storm surge disaster based on static and dynamic input-output models. *Sustainability, 12*(18), 7347.

Kappes, M. S., Keiler, M., Von, E. K., & Glade, T. (2012). Challenges of analyzing multi-hazard risk: A review. *Natural Hazards, 64,* 1925–1958.

Kazama, S., Sato, A., & Kawagoe, S. (2010). Evaluating the cost of flood damage based on changes in extreme rainfall in Japan. Adaptation and Mitigation Strategies for Climate Change. Springer Japan, 3–17.

Kefi, M., Mishra, B. K., Kumar, P., Masago, Y., & Fukushi, K. (2018). Assessment of tangible direct flood damage using a spatial analysis approach under the effects of climate change: Case study in an urban watershed in Hanoi, Vietnam. *ISPRS International Journal of Geo-Information, 7*(1), 29.

Khaleghi, B., Khamis, A., Karray, F. O., & Razavi, S. N. (2013). Multisensor data fusion: A review of the state-of-the-art. *Information Fusion, 14,* 28–44.

Kilimani, N., van, Heerden, J., Bohlmann, H., & Roos, L. (2018). Economy-wide impact of drought induced productivity losses. *Disaster Prevention and Management, 27*(5), 636–648.

Koks, E. E., Carrera, L., & Jonkeren, O. (2015). Regional disaster impact analysis: Comparing input-output and computable general equilibrium models. *Natural Hazards & Earth System Sciences Discussions, 3*(11), 7053–7088.

Koks, E. E., Carrera, L., & Jonkeren, O. (2016). Regional disaster impact analysis: Comparing input–output and computable general equilibrium models. *Natural Hazards and Earth System Sciences, 16*(8), 1911–1924.

Komolafe, A. A., Herath, S., & Avtar, R. (2019). Establishment of detailed loss functions for the urban flood risk assessment in Chao Phraya River basin, Thailand. *Geomatics Natural Hazards and Risk, 10*(1), 633–650.

Liu, H. B. (2015). A study on economic loss assessment of heavy rain and waterlogging disaster in Shenzhen city from the perspective of highway traffic industry. Nanjing University of Information Science & Technology.

Liu, X. Q., Yuan, S., Chen, Z. H., Song, L. N., Ma, Y. X., Wang, C. L., & Wu, J. D. (2019). Assessing the indirect economic losses of sea ice disasters: An adaptive regional input-output modeling approach. *International Journal of Offshore and Polar Engineering, 28*(4), 415–420.

Li, W. J., Wen, J. H., Xu, B., Li, X. D., & Du, S. Q. (2019). Integrated assessment of economic losses in manufacturing industry in shanghai metropolitan area under an extreme storm flood scenario. *Sustainability, 11*(1), 126.

Llinas, J. (2002). Information fusion for natural and man-made disasters. Information Fusion, Proceedings of the Fifth International Conference on Information Fusion. *IEEE, 1,* 570–576.

Mackenzie, C. A., Santos, J. R., & Barker, K. (2012). Measuring changes in international production from a disruption: Case study of the Japanese earthquake and tsunami. *International Journal of Production Economics, 138*(2), 293–302.

Mendoza-Tinoco, D., Guan, D., & Zeng, Z. (2017). Flood footprint of the 2007 floods in the UK: The case of the Yorkshire and The Humber region. *Journal of Cleaner Production, 168*(1), 655–667.

Mendoza-Tinoco, D., Guan, D. B., Zeng, Z., Xia, Y., & Serrano, A. (2017). Flood footprint of the 2007 floods in the UK: The case of the Yorkshire and The Humber region. *Journal of Cleaner Production, 168,* 655–667.

Middelmann-Fernandes, M. H. (2010). Flood damage estimation beyond stage–damage functions: An Australian example. *Journal of Flood Risk Management., 3*(1), 88–96.

Mohammadia, S. A., & Nazarihaa, M. (2014). Flood damage estimate (quantity), using HEC-FDA model. Case study: The Neka river. *Procedia Engineering, 70,* 1173–1182.

MRl, H. M. H. (2003). Multi-hazard loss estimation methodology: Earthquake model. Department of Homeland Security, FEMA, Washington, DC.

Narayan, P. K. (2003). Macroeconomic impact of natural disasters on a small island economy: Evidence from A CGE Model. *Applied Economics Letters, 10*(11), 721–723.

Notaro, V., De, Marchis, M., & Fontanazza, C. M. (2014). The effect of damage functions on urban flood damage appraisal. *Procedia Engineering, 70,* 1251–1260.

Okuyama, Y. (2007). Economic modeling for disaster impact analysis: Past, present, and future. *Economic Systems Research, 19*(2), 115–124.

Okuyama, Y. (2010). Globalization and localization of disaster impacts: an empirical examination. *General Information, 11*(2), 56–66.

Oliver, E., & Santoro, M. (2000). Estimation of urban structural flood damages: The case study of Palermo. *Urban Water., 2*(3), 223–234.

Pang, S. L., Li, S. H., & Hu, X. F. (2020). Typhoon carrier disaster loss index models and application based on principal component analysis. *Journal of Coastal Research,* 68–72.

Pinos, J., Orellana, D., & Timbe, L. (2020). Assessment of microscale economic flood losses in urban and agricultural areas: Case study of the santa Bárbara river, Ecuador. *Natural Hazards, 103*(2), 2323–2337.

Ploeger, S. K., Atkinson, G. M., & Samson, C. (2010). Applying the HAZUS-MH software tool to assess seismic risk in downtown Ottawa, Canada. *Natural Hazards, 53,* 1–20.

Puttinaovarat, S., & Horkaew, P. (2020). Flood forecasting system based on integrated big and crowdsource data by using machine learning techniques. *IEEE Access, 8,* 5885–5905.

Rahman, M. S., Di, L. P., Yu, E., Lin, L., & Yu, Z. Q. (2020). Remote sensing based rapid assessment of flood crop damage using novel disaster vegetation damage index (dvdi). International Journal of Disaster Risk Science.

Ring, I., Hansjürgens, B., & Elmqvist, T. (2010). Challenges in framing the economics of ecosystems and biodiversity: The TEEB initiative. *Current Opinion in Environmental Sustainability, 2*(1), 15–26.

Rose, A. (2004).Economic principles, issues, and research priorities in Hazard Loss estimation. In: Y. Okuyama & S. E Chang (Eds.), Modeling Spatial and Economic Impacts of Disasters (pp. 13–36). New York: Springer.

Rose, A., & Liao, S. Y. (2005). Modeling regional economic resilience to disasters: A computable general equilibrium analysis of water service disruptions. *Journal of Regional Science, 45*(1), 75–112.

Rose, A., & Lim, D. (2002). Business interruption losses from natural hazards: Conceptual and methodological issues in the case of the Northridge earthquake. *Global Environmental Change Part B Environmental Hazards, 4*(1), 1–14.

Scawthorn, C., Blais, N., Seligson, H., Tate, E., & Jones, C. (2006). Hazus-mh flood loss estimation methodology. I: overview and flood hazard characterization. *Natural Hazards Review, 7*(2), 72–81.

Sieg, T., Schinko, T., Vogel, K., Mechler, R., Merz, B., & Kreibich, H. (2019). Integrated assessment of short-term direct and indirect economic flood impacts including uncertainty quantification. *PLoS ONE, 14*(4), e0212932.

Sun, S., Shi, H., & Wu, Y. (2014). A survey of multi-source domain adaptation. *Information Fusion, 24,* 84–92.

Tang, J. C. S., Vongvisessomjai, S., & Sahasakmontri, K. (1992). Estimation of flood damage cost for Bangkok. *Water Resources Management, 6*(1), 47–56.

Tanoue, M., Nabe, S., Fujimori, S., Hirabayashi, Y. Estimation of direct and indirect economic losses caused by a flood with long-lasting inundation: Application to the 2011 Thailand flood. *Water Resources Research,* 56(5), e2019WR026092.

Tan, L., Wu, X. H., & Xu, Z. S. (2019). Comprehensive economic loss assessment of disaster based on CGE Model and IO Model—A case study on Beijing "7.21 Rainstorm". *International Journal of Disaster Risk Reduction,* 39, 101246.

Tatano, H., & Tsuchiya, S. (2008). A framework for economic loss estimation due to seismic transportation network disruption: A spatial computable general equilibrium approach. *Natural Hazards, 44*(2), 253–265.

Thirawat, N., Udompol, S., & Ponjan, P. (2017). Disaster risk reduction and international catastrophe risk insurance facility. *Mitigation and Adaptation Strategies for Global Change, 22*(7), 1021–1039.

Tinoco, D. M. (2018). Alba Verónica Méndez Delgado. Evaluación de los costos económicos totales de los desastres naturales: inundación en la ciudad de sheffield, 2007. *Estudios Demográficos y Urbanos, 33*(3), 699.

Vickery, P. J., Skerlj, P. F., Lin, J., Twisdale, J., Young, M. A., & Lavelle, F. M. (2006). Hazus-MH hurricane model methodology. II: Damage and loss estimation. *Natural Hazards Review, 7,* 94–103.

Wang, C. H., Chen, W. N., Zhang, J., Song, S., & Lu, R. Q. (2014). Challenging scientific problems for technologies and applications of big data. *Bulletin of National Natural Science Foundation of China, 2*, 92–98.

Wang, G. Z., Li, X., Wu, X. H., & Yu, J. (2015). The rainstorm comprehensive economic loss assessment based on CGE model: Using a July heavy rainstorm in Beijing as an example. *Natural Hazards, 76*(2), 839–854.

Wang, D., Huang, C., & Mai, B. (2016). To facilitate the advance of risk analysis and crisis response in China. *Environmental Research, 148*, 547–549.

Wang, G. Z., Wu, L. Y., & Chen, J. B. (2016). Intensity and economic loss assessment of the snow, low-temperature and frost disasters: A case study of Beijing City. *Natural Hazards, 84*(1), 293–307.

Wang, G. Z., Chen, R. R., & Chen, J. B. (2017). Direct and indirect economic loss assessment of typhoon disasters based on EC and IO joint model. *Natural Hazards, 87*(3), 1751–1764.

Weitzman, M. L. (2009). On modeling and interpreting the economics of catastrophic climate change. *Review of Economics & Statistics, 91*(1), 1–19.

Wu, S., & Crestani, F. (2015). A geometric framework for data fusion in information retrieval. *Information Systems, 50*, 20–35.

Wu, X. H., Zhou, L., & Gao, G. (2016). Urban flood depth-economic loss curves and their amendment based on resilience: Evidence from Lizhong Town in Lixia River and Houbai Town in Jurong River of China. *Natural Hazards, 82*, 1981–2000.

Wu, X. H., Xue, P. P., Guo, J., Ji, Z. H., Wei, G., & Ning, X. Q. (2017). On the amount of counterpart assistance to be provided after natural disasters: From the perspective of indirect economic loss assessment. *Global Environmental Change Part B Environmental Hazards, 16*(1), 50–70.

Wu, X.H., Cao, Y. l., Xiao, Y., & Guo, J. (2018). Finding of urban rainstorm and waterlogging disasters based on microblogging data and the location-routing problem model of urban emergency logistics. *Annals of Operations Research*, 1–32.

Wu, X. H., Xu, Z., Liu, H., Guo, J., & Zhou, L. (2018). What are the impacts of tropical cyclones on employment? An analysis based on meta-regression. *Weather Climate & Society, 11*(2), 259–275.

Wu, X. H., Guo, J., & Gonzalez, E. D. R. S. (2019). Determining the amount of international aid that countries should donate after a disaster to alleviate sustainable implications: A new framework for analysis. *Journal of Cleaner Production, 241*(12), 118285.

Wu, Z. N., Shen, Y. X., Wang, H. L., & Wu, M. M. (2020). Quantitative assessment of urban flood disaster vulnerability based on text data: Case study in Zhengzhou. *Water Science and Technology-Water Supply, 20*(2), 408–415.

Xia, Y., Li, Y., Guan, D. B., David, T., Xia, J. J., Yan, Z. W., et al. (2018). Assessment of the economic impacts of heat waves: A case study of Nanjing, China. *Journal of Cleaner Production, 171*, 811–819.

Xie, W., Rose, A., & Li, S. (2018). Dynamic economic resilience and economic recovery from disasters: a quantitative assessment. *Risk Analysis, 38*(6), 1306–1318.

Yang, T. M., Chen, J. H., & Chen, X. Y. (2005). Study on the knowledge base system of agricultural meteorological disasters and Defense Countermeasures in Anhui Province. *Journal of Anhui Agricultural Sciences, 33*, 1682–1683.

Ye, X. L., Wen, J. H., Zhu, Z. F., & Sun, R. H. (2020). Natural disaster risk assessment in tourist areas based on multi scenario analysis. Earth Science Informatics.

Zhang, W. H. (2020). Geological disaster monitoring and early warning system based on big data analysis. *Arabian Journal of Geo Sciences, 13*(18), 946.

Zhang, Z. T., Li, N., Wei, X., Yu, L., Feng, J. L., Xi, C., & Liu, L. (2017). Assessment of the ripple effects and spatial heterogeneity of total losses in the capital of china after a great catastrophic shock. *Natural Hazards and Earth System Ences, 17*(3), 1–21.

Zhang, S. H., Yang, K., & Cao, Y. B. (2019). GIS-based rapid disaster loss assessment for earthquakes. *IEEE Access, 7*, 6129–6139.

Zhang, Z. T., Li, N., Xu, H., Feng, J. L., Chen, X., Gao, C., & Zhang, P. (2019). Allocating assistance after a catastrophe based on the dynamic assessment of indirect economic losses. *Natural Hazards, 99*(1), 17–37.

Zheng, G. G. (2014). Annual 2000–3000 billion yuan of economic losses caused by meteorological disasters in China. Retrieved from https://www.ce.cn/.

Zheng, Y., & Sun, H. (2020). An integrated approach for the simulation modeling and risk assessment of coastal flooding. *Water, 12*(8), 2076.

Zhou, S. T., Zhai, G. F., Shi, Y. J., & Lu, Y. W. (2020). Urban seismic risk assessment by integrating direct economic loss and loss of statistical life: An empirical study in Xiamen, China. *International Journal of Environmental Research and Public Health, 17*(21), 8154.

Zhu, Z. H. (2010). Study of data warehouse and data mining application on geohazard in three gorges reservior area. Ph. D. dissertation (in Chinese), Institute of Engineering, China University of Geosciences, 121.

# Chapter 10
# Design of Temperature Insurance Index and Risk Zonation for Single-Season Rice in Response to High-Temperature and Low-Temperature Damage: A Case Study of Jiangsu Province, China

**Abstract** Disaster insurance is an important tool for achieving sustainable development in modern agriculture. However, in China, the design of such insurance indexes is far from sufficient. In this paper, the single-season rice in Jiangsu Province of China is taken as an example to design the high-temperature damage index in summer and the low-temperature damage index in autumn to construct the formula calculating the weather output and single-season rice yield reduction. The daily highest, lowest and average temperatures between 1999 and 2015 are selected as main variables for the temperature disaster index to quantitatively analyze the relationship between the temperature index and the yield reduction rate of the single-season rice. The temperature disaster index can be put into the relevant model to obtain the yield reduction rate of the year and determine whether to pay the indemnity. Then, the burn analysis is used to determine the insurance premium rate for all cities in Jiangsu Province under four-level deductibles, and the insurance premium rate can be used for the risk division of the Province. The research provides some insights for the design of agricultural weather insurance products, and the empirical results provide a reference for the design of similar single-season rice temperature index insurance products.

**Keywords** Single-season rice · Agricultural weather index-based insurance · Premium rate determination · Jiangsu Province

## 10.1 Introduction

Climate warming increases the possibility of weather disasters for agriculture (Field et al. 2012). It is a recurring subject of human society, particularly how agriculture draws on advantages and avoids weather disasters (Lesk et al. 2016). China is located in the middle latitudes of the northern hemisphere, with various and complex weather system and frequent weather related disasters. Over the past 30 years, weather disasters such as cold spring, drought and flood, cold wind in autumn, and frost have affected one-third of China's arable land, causing significant economic losses (Huang 2006). Thus, how to avoid losses and maintain farmers' incomes with weather insurance for agricultural products draws considerable attention from the government, academia and the public (Zhang et al. 2018a, b).

 
X. Wu and J. Guo, *Economic Impacts and Emergency Management of Disasters in China*,
https://doi.org/10.1007/978-981-16-1319-7_10

"Good harvests in Jiangsu and Zhejiang, enough food for old and young" (E L 1999). Jiangsu Province has been a traditional rice producer, with the largest area of japonica rice plantation in southern China. The *japonica* rice in Jiangsu is dominated by single-season rice (Zuo et al. 2014), which is susceptible to abnormal temperature during the growing season. During the flowering period of single-season rice, more than two days of temperature greater than 35 °C may cause up to 25% of empty seed (Xu et al. 2001). The temperature above 35 °C for single-season rice in the booting, heading and flowering stages may lead to a sharp decline in photosynthesis and rise in transpiration, resulting in flower and fruit abortion (Luo et al. 2005). Low-temperature damage in autumn for single-season rice in the filling and ripening period may delay maturity. Since the 1990s, the frequency of low-temperature damage has increased in Jiangsu. In August and September, many districts experience such damage with an average temperature of less than 20 °C for more than three consecutive days, increasing the chance of empty rice shell at the heading and filling stages. The listed risks justify the development of weather index-based insurance to protect the income of rice farmers in Jiangsu.

Policy-oriented agricultural insurance is effective tools to promote agricultural development, however, policy-based agricultural insurance takes actual disaster losses as the basis for compensation and the operation for compensation is very complicated. In addition, a high level of disagreement exist between insurance company and insurance applicant for check danger, decide loss, manage compensate and etc., which limited the implementation of the insurance business. The deficiency of policy-based agricultural insurance provides market space for the design and application of weather index insurance. The core of weather index agricultural insurance is the design of weather index.

The indemnity for weather index insurance is determined based on the value of the weather index, and the indemnity amount is based on the estimated loss distribution. Once the weather index parameter reaches the trigger value (if the cumulative rainfall falls below a certain threshold), all policyholders of insurance companies will obtain indemnity (World Bank 2013). According to Gommes and Kayitakire, although the index-based insurance have advantages, such as the design basis risk, spatial basis risk and idiosyncratic basis risk (Leblois et al. 2014), agricultural weather index-based insurance can partly help avoid problems in traditional insurance such as asymmetric information and high transaction costs, and transfer the risk of weather disasters to insurance companies, which is of significance for promotion. However, at present, there are no weather insurance products specifically targeting single-season rice in Jiangsu. To fill this gap, this paper intends to design a single-season rice weather index based on local conditions to effectively transfer agricultural production. It not only enriches the theoretical research of the weather insurance index, but also provides the reference for the practical application of the weather insurance index in Jiangsu and similar regions in the world.

The rest of this paper is as follows: the second part is research summary, the third part is research data and methods, the fourth part is results analysis, and the last part is conclusions.

## 10.2 Research Summary

Scholars have paid attention to the study of theories and methods of weather index-based insurance design. For example, Skees et al. (1999) designed the calculation method of the insurance payout, and divided the difference between the trigger index and the weather index and the lower limit of the trigger index to determine the corresponding rate. Zanini et al. (2004) fitted the detrended per unit yield of soybeans and corn in 26 farms and determined the actuarially fair premium rate in different regions with different statistical models. Turvey and Weersink (2005) eliminated the factors that affected crop yield such as altitude and latitude and longitude, and only considered the weather index that had a major impact on Canadian grape production. Turvey et al. used the Monte Carlo model to estimate the premium rate of grapes. Clarke et al. (2012) completed the design and pricing of the weather index-based insurance product portfolio with the Bayesian model, and improved the accuracy of the model. Norton et al. (2012) found that the spatial–temporal characteristics of the area affected the accuracy of their weather index, resulting in an increased risk of basis error. Miranda et al. (1999) designed a new type of insurance to divide a weather index-based insurance contract into multiple equal parts. The standard unit of insurance has the same rate payment time, and farmers can choose to purchase the insurance according to the area of the crop. Castaneda et al. (2014) assessed the insurance coverage and claims in rainfall-related risks in processing tomato in Western Spain. Marco et al. (2016) assessed the economic effect of increased thermal stress on the expected insurance expenditures for durum wheat in the Mediterranean Basin. The insurance model results showed that the modification of the probability density function of crops induced by thermal stress led to an overall increase in expenditure under stress-free conditions. Ayala et al. (2017) utilized the weather data classified by time and space as well as three types of household data to understand the impact of extreme weather on family welfare. We found that all severe weather types affect family well-being, although the effects of income and calorie estimates will sometimes be different. Okpara et al. (2017) collected 52 years of monthly precipitation data to propose a weather index-based insurance that relies on SPI to alleviate the negative impact of insured farmers' payouts in the event of a drought. Tam et al. (2017) studied the impact of hurricanes and deforestation on Vietnam's three major grains. The results showed that grain loss was the highest, tuber second, and other crops lost the least. Deforestation has a negative impact on these food crops. Aditya et al. (2018) structured a region-specific index based on the estimation of a panel geographic weighted regression model. They quantified the applicability, feasibility, and possible weather index-based insurance cost to introduce drought index into Indonesian rice production. By incorporating adaptive capacity and sensitivity indicators, Patrick et al. (2019) established an empirical model of the relationship between extreme weather disasters and agricultural output from 1995 to 2010. The results can be used to infer crop yields at different levels of adaptability under climate change. Koshi et al. (2019) researched the economic damage caused by the weather to land crops such as sugar cane and cassava. The findings suggested mixing sugarcane and cassava to stabilize agricultural incomes during periods of drought. Thong et al. (2019) utilized the C-vine method to simulate the joint insurance losses caused by the simultaneous circumstances of drought events in different locations and consecutive occurrences in different growing seasons. Thierry et al. (2020) explored the impact of climate change and natural disasters on African countries' total agricultural output and distinguished these countries based on income levels. The conclusion was that temperature is the main climatic factor affecting agricultural production. Kenneth and Matin (2020) analyzed the effect of weather index-based insurance by using observed data from maize farmers in Kenya. They concluded that expanding the weather index-based insurance program may help stimulate agricultural development on small farms. Andrea et al. (2020) solved the current pricing and operational challenges of some rainfall-derived products by applying the experience of Comunidad Valenciana in Spain. The calculation results showed that when the correlation between adjacent observation stations is not strong, rainfall risk hedging measures may depend on multiple adjacent observation stations. José et al. (2020) addressed some of the problems in agricultural insurance and described the drawbacks of the bonus-fraud system (BMS) method used in Spain and many other EU countries. And scholars developed an experience-based alternative rate discount system.

From the above reviews, it can be observed that most of the authors used historical distributions to estimate the models and calculate actuarially fair premiums. However, in this research, the burn analysis is used to determine the insurance premium rate due to data restriction.

In China, scholars have mainly studied the impact of single or integrated weather disaster factors such as continuous rain, drought, high-temperature damage, low-temperature damage, and strong wind on per unit yield, and designed different types of weather index-based insurance products according to local conditions. For example, Wang and Zhang (2010) used cotton per unit yield data from three counties in Xinjiang to fit different distribution models and obtained different premium rates. They concluded that only the optimal per unit yield risk distribution model could determine the relatively accurate pure rate. Wu et al. (2010) considered many weather factors to establish the rice yield reduction model and designed the premiums of three risk areas under different deductibles. Lu (2010) obtained the relations between weather index and grain yield through panel data modeling. With the probability distribution of the disaster, he designed the grain weather index insurance contract. Zhou (2014) determined that low-temperature damage was the main weather disaster for apples in Shandong Province. After the yield and trend output were separated with a reasonable low-temperature damage index, the linear relation between Qixia City's annual per unit yield and low-temperature damage index was determined, and the risk zoning and rate determination were finally determined. Liu et al. (2015) selected agricultural statistics and monthly Southern Oscillation Index from 1961 to 2007 to assess regional agrometeorological disasters. The results showed that during the El Niño period, the seasonal trends in the drought-affected areas had been mixed. However, in the La Niña era, the upward trend in all seasons is consistent. Yang et al. (2015a, b) first identified the factors affecting farmers' participation in soybean insurance. Then these scholars estimated the willingness to pay (WTP) for soybean insurance to promote the management of soybean crop insurance in Jilin Province. The results showed that the diversity of disaster types and the importance of insurance significantly impact farmers' willingness to participate in insurance. Sun et al. (2015) adopted copula function, growth model, and natural disaster risk assessment technology to put forward drought risk analysis of different irrigation levels in cities. The results showed that the reduction in drought resulted from the increase in the irrigation water supply rate. Jia et al. (2016), based on the crop model of the erosive impact calculator, the EPIC (Environmental Policy Integrated Climate) model of the maize drought risk assessment model in the southwest karst area is proposed. The results revealed that the southwest maize belt has a high level of damage risk. Li et al. (2017) developed a weather risk management system based on mobile Internet according to the concept of the weather disaster early warning model. The system could analyze the relationship between crops and meteorological events for farmers and workers. Wang et al. (2017) used the coverage risk index to analyze agro-meteorological disasters' variability characteristics and calculated the risk background of climate change in Gansu Province based on the information diffusion method. Zhang et al. (2017) selected Jilin and Henan provinces to represent two different corn-growing regions. They assessed the risks in terms of hazard and vulnerability. The results explored that the drought hazard and sensitivity of Jilin are much higher than that of Henan, and Henan's irrigation capacity is better. Sun et al. (2018) proposed a new method to estimate the premium rate of grain sprout cold weather index insurance. Two years of manual control experiments were used to develop logarithmic and linear yield loss models. The results revealed that the pure premium rate determined by the logarithmic return loss model has lower risk and higher efficiency. Chen et al. (2018) considered the spatial heterogeneity of disaster and yield datasets in mainland China from 1949 to 2015 and studied the impact of flood disasters on crop production. And through the Bayesian hierarchical model to determine the impact of drought and flood intensity on various types of food production. Zhang et al. (2018a, b) collected and analyzed conventional meteorological data and agricultural statistics and outlined the drought trend and the decline in agricultural output per unit area. The results showed that China's agricultural loss rate due to drought has increased. Over the past 50 years, it has decreased by about 0.5% every ten years. Wang et al. (2018) utilized the CERES-Rice model to conduct a detailed case study of early rice in Hunan Province. This study's conclusions indicated that the effects of extreme events and fluctuations are more severe than those caused by climate trends. Yu et al. (2020) adopted the theory of information diffusion and analyzed the impact of five frequent natural disasters in five selected regions from 2001 to 2006. Three agricultural indicators to illustrate the economic losses caused by natural disasters. A method based on the Analytic Hierarchy Process (AHP) framework calculates the weights of the five disaster categories. Wang et al. (2020), according to the spatial clustering analysis of maize yield, the study area was divided into three different locations. It turned out that the best climate for maize growth in various regions is different.

From our research perspective, few papers studied the agricultural weather disaster insurance of single-season rice of Jiangsu. To fill this gap, this paper will therefore investigate the actuarially fair premium rate under different deductibles, and then classify different weather disaster risk regions.

The details of the design, application and marketing of index-based insurance varies between countries (Wu et al. 2018). Examples include Thailand's Coffee Rainfall Insurance, Rwanda's Tomato Weather Index-based Insurance, Ethiopia's Grain Rainfall Index-based Insurance, and Canadian Forage Index-based Insurance. After Shanghai introduced the first agricultural weather index-based insurance in 2007, the Watermelon Plum Rain Index-based Insurance, other provinces began to promote weather index-based insurance. For instance, in 2008, Anhui Province developed a drought-flood weather index-based insurance for rice in vulnerable rural areas; in 2009, Shaanxi Province carried out a weather index-based insurance for apples; Fujian Province launched a pilot typhoon disaster weather index-based insurance in 2010; in 2016, insurance companies launched "Wind Index-based Insurance for Crops" purchased through Alipay. Overall, as most of China's weather index-based insurance models adapted from foreign countries, so it is necessary to adjust them according to local conditions. As a national grain-producing province, Jiangsu has not yet promoted the use of agricultural weather index-based insurance, and has not applied the temperature weather index-based insurance for rice (Wu et al. 2018). This paper thus establishes the summer high-temperature damage index and the autumn low-temperature damage index to quantify the relationship between the single-season rice temperature index and the yield reduction rate. And then, the single-season rice weather insurance index is constructed.

## 10.3 Research Data and Methods

### *10.3.1 Data Sources*

The weather data mainly includes the daily minimum, maximum, and average temperature of 8 weather stations in Jiangsu from 1999 to 2015. The data comes from the National Meteorological Information Center and the Meteorological Observatory of Nanjing University of Information Science and Technology. The total production and area of single-season rice come from the statistical yearbooks of Jiangsu.[1] Figure 10.1 shows the location of Jiangsu Province in China.

[1]This is the data set available at the present, the statistics of prefecture level cities are unavaliable.

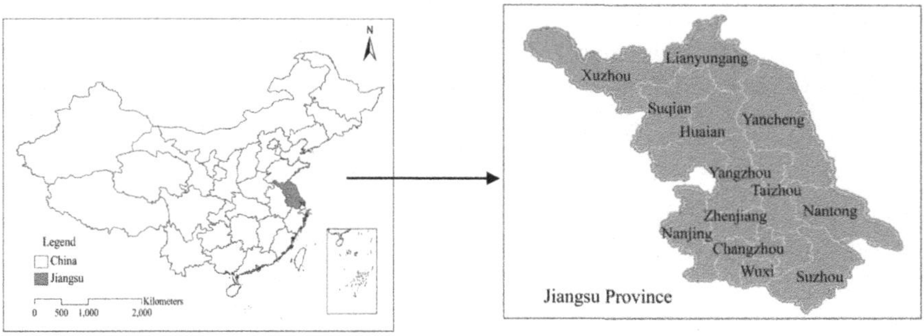


**Fig. 10.1** Location of Jiangsu Province in China.[2]

---

[2]Of China's 9.6 million km$^2$, Jiangsu covers 107,200 km$^2$. The area of 13 cities in Jiangsu are as follows: Nanjing with a total area of 6587 km$^2$, Wuxi with 4628 km$^2$, Xuzhou with 11258 km$^2$, Changzhou with 4385 km$^2$, Nantong with 8544 km$^2$, Suzhou with 8488.42 km$^2$, Lianyungang with 7615 km$^2$, Huaian with 10072 km$^2$, Yancheng with 17000 km$^2$, Yangzhou with 6591.21 km$^2$, Zhenjiang with 3848 km$^2$, Taizhou with 5787.26 km$^2$, Suqian with 8555 km$^2$.

### *10.3.2 Determination of Weather Production and Yield Reduction*

In general, crop yields consist of trend output, weather output, and random error terms. Trend output is determined by factors such as productivity and agricultural technology (Lu 2010). Weather output is affected by weather factors such as drought, flood, rainfall, and temperature. Random error terms are caused by sporadic incidents such as insect pests. According to the actual production data of eight cities like Nanjing in Jiangsu from 1999 to 2015, the yield data is processed with the 5-year moving average method, and the single-season rice yield series are divided into trend yield and weather yield, as shown in the following formula:

$$Y = Y_t + Y_w + \varepsilon \tag{10.1}$$

$Y$ represents the actual production, $Y_t$ the trend output, and $Y_w$ the weather output. $\varepsilon$ is the random error terms, which are generally omitted in the calculation. The actual output $Y$ minus the trend output $Y_t$ is the weather output $Y_w$. When $Y_w$ is greater than 0, it means that the weather conditions are beneficial to increase the yield of single-season rice. When $Y_w$ is less than 0, it means that the current weather conditions will reduce single-season rice production.

The ratio of the difference between the actual output of each city and its trend production to the trend output is defined as the relative weather output $S_i$:

$$S_i = \frac{Y_i - Y_{it}}{Y_{it}} \times 100\%, \; i, \; t = 1, 2, \ldots, n \tag{10.2}$$

$S_i$ is the relative weather output that is not subject to productivity and time constraints. When $S_i$ is less than 0, it means that the single-season rice yield reduces due to the weather, and its absolute value is defined as the yield reduction rate $x_i$:

$$x_i = \begin{cases} |S_i|, & S_i < 0 \\ 0, & S_i > 0 \end{cases}, \; i = 1, 2, \ldots, n \tag{10.3}$$

## 10.3.3 Weather Index Selection and Design

### 10.3.3.1 Single-Season Rice High-Temperature Damage Index

High-temperature damage is a common weather disaster in Jiangsu in summer (Zhang 2012). Since the 1970s, the frequency of high-temperature damage in Jiangsu has risen steadily. It concentrates in July and August when the rice are in jointing and flowering stages. Continuously rising temperature above 35 °C may lead to a decrease in stamen pollen activity, which inhibits fertilization, affects grouting, and increases the empty seed rate. This is the phenomenon of heat-forced maturity (Zhang 2012).

According to the data of 57 weather stations in Jiangsu, since the 1980s, the frequency of daily maximum temperatures greater than 35 °C for three or more consecutive days has been increasing. It peaked in the 1990s, with an average of 1.57 times per year. From the spatial distribution, the occurrence of extreme high-temperature in the south of Huaihe River is greater than the north of the river. The daily maximum temperature higher than 35 °C for three consecutive days or more in the north of the river is least in frequency. The average frequency in Ganyu and Dongtai of Lianyungang is the lowest, and the average annual number in Xuzhou, Huai'an, and Nantong is about 0.9. Nanjing, Suzhou, Wuxi and Changzhou have the averaging of over 2 times per year (Long 2008). Qiang concluded that 35 °C is the critical temperature to mark the high-temperature damage (Qiang 2011). In addition, when the daily average temperature is higher than 30 °C and the maximum is greater than 35 °C, a 3–4 day duration causes slight high-temperature damage, 5–7 day duration causes medium high-temperature damage, and longer than 8 day causes severe high-temperature damage. The cumulative value of the high-temperature difference is used as an evaluation index of high-temperature damage:

$$HT = \begin{cases} 0, & else \\ \sum_{i=d1}^{d2} \Delta T = \sum_{i=d1}^{d2} (T_i - 35), & T_i \geq 35, T \geq 30 \end{cases} \tag{10.4}$$

The onset time for high-temperature damage in Jiangsu is set at July 15 and the end time is set at August 19. $T_i$ is the maximum temperature at the start date, and once the threshold value is triggered during the statistical period, $T_i$ will be put in the index $HT$.

#### 10.3.3.2 Single-Season Rice Low-Temperature Damage Index

An abnormally low-temperature during the reproductive period may destroy the physiological structure of the crops, preventing the timely opening of anthers, increasing empty seeds and reducing production (Meng et al. 2005). Such low-temperature damage is called "sterile-type low-temperature damage", which often occurs in September. For the single-season rice in Jiangsu, only the low-temperature damage in September should be considered. At this time, the critical temperature for single-season rice flowering and maturation is 20 °C. Below this temperature, the number of tillers will be reduced and even though the pollen grains can be fertilized normally, they cannot develop into normal full grains.

According to the *technical specifications for evaluation of rice cold damage* [QX/T 182-2013], one of industry standard of China Meteorological Administration (Long 2008), the average daily temperature lower than 20 °C for 3–4 days causes slight low-temperature damage, 5–6 days causes moderate low-temperature damage, and longer than 7 days causes severe damage. Since the 1980s, the average number of slight low-temperature damage in the single-season rice growing season in Jiangsu is between 0 and 11, with the maximum number happed in 1988. Severe low-temperature damage reached 7 times in 1997. In terms of spatial distribution, the southern areas such as Nanjing, Suzhou, Changzhou, and Wuxi have more low-temperature damage and less serious low-temperature damage than the northern areas, while the northern areas such as Xuzhou, Lianyungang, and Yancheng have more severe low-temperature damages than the southern areas.

Since the grain heading and filling period of single-season rice in Jiangsu is from August 21 to September 27, given the influence of the low-temperature damage index on the yield, the temperature below 20 °C during the statistical period is recorded as a time of low-temperature damage. The formula for calculating the low-temperature damage index in autumn for single-season rice is as follows:

$$LT = \begin{cases} 0, & else \\ \sum_{j=1}^{n} \left(T_0 - T_j\right), & T_j \leq 20,\ j = 1, 2, \ldots, n \end{cases} \tag{10.5}$$

In above formula, $T_0$ is the minimum temperature at the stage of the grain heading and filling; $T_j$ the daily average temperature below the lower limit; $n$ the number of days below 20 °C.

### 10.3.4 Design of Single-Season Rice Temperature Index-Based Insurance in Jiangsu

#### 10.3.4.1 Relations Between the Yield Reduction and Weather Disaster Index in Single-Season Rice

In order to analyze the influence of high-temperature damage index and low-temperature damage index on yield reduction rate, the yield reduction rate is used as explained variable, and high-temperature damage index and low-temperature damage index are used as explanatory variables; For the curve effect of these two explanatory variables on dependent variables, the quadratic terms of high-temperature damage index and low-temperature damage index are taken as explanatory variables to construct the following regression equation:

$$S_i = F\left(HT, LT, HT^2, LT^2\right) = a + \sum_{i=1}^{n} b_i y_i + \mu_i,\ i = 1, 2, \ldots, n \tag{10.6}$$

In this formula, $S_i$ is the yield reduction rate of single-season early rice in 8 cities in Jiangsu, *HT* is the high-temperature damage index, *LT* is the low-temperature damage index, $a$ and $b_i$ are regression coefficient, and $y_i$ is the weather disaster index.

#### 10.3.4.2 Determination Method of Pure Insurance Premium Rate

The actuarially fair premium rate of crop insurance is equal to loss expectancy, which is the value of actuarially fair premium minus the amount of insurance (Ker and Goodwin 2000). The formula for actuarially fair premium rate of single-season rice index insurance is:

$$R_c = \frac{E[loss]}{\lambda\mu} E[loss] \tag{10.7}$$

$\lambda$ is the index insurance scope of coverage of crops, $\mu$ the expected per unit yield, and $E[loss]$ represents the expected loss of single-season rice. According to the Jiangsu's policy-oriented agricultural insurance pilot program, both $\lambda$ and $\mu$ can be assumed as 100% (Lou et al. 2011).

In weather index insurance products, the calculation formula of the single crop rice insurance index is:

$$W = \begin{cases} 0,\ x \le x_c \\ x,\ x > x_c \end{cases} \tag{10.8}$$

In the formula, $W$ is the single-season rice insurance index in a certain region of Jiangsu, $x_c$ the deductible of the region and $x$ the yield reduction rate in an area caused by weather disasters.

By establishing a model of single-season rice and temperature disasters, the corresponding temperature index can be found at the end of the growth period of single-season rice. Then the single-season rice yield reduction rate can be calculated through the temperature index. Based on the regional deductible, whether to implement the indemnity will be determined. The single-season rice insurance index is shown in formula (10.8), and the calculation formula for pure rice premium of single-season rice under different deductibles is as follows:

$$P_c = R_c \times Q \tag{10.9}$$

$R_c$ is the actuarially fair premium rate for different deductibles, and $Q$ the insurance amount. According to Jiangsu's policy-oriented agricultural insurance (You 2008), the single-season rice insurance is recommended with the amount of CNY 6000 per Ha in this paper, namely, $Q = 6000\ CNY/Ha$.

The premium rate has the following formula:

$$R_g = R_c * (1 + r_s)(1 + r_p)(1 + r_b) \tag{10.10}$$

$R_g$ represents the gross rate, $r_s$ the safety coefficient, $r_p$ the profit rate, and $r_b$ the operating cost coefficient. Except the actuarially fair premium rate, the formula is determined by the regional risk and the operating conditions of the insurance company. The following discussion focuses on the determination of the actuarially fair premium rate.

The premium rate of the weather index is determined by the index model method and the burn analysis (Yang et al. 2015a, b; Jewson and Brix 2005). The index model method uses a distribution to fit historical payouts and estimates the model parameters, thereby calculating actuarially fair premiums. The per unit yield distribution model is a common derivation method for an actuarially fair premium rate. However, it is difficult to verify per unit yield distribution function of each region, and it is error-prone. The burn analysis is used to determine the insurance premium rate. This method assumes that the expected loss rate in the future and the past loss distribution are the same.[3] The expected loss rate is estimated through historical production data:

$$S_i = \frac{1}{n} \sum \frac{Y - Y_t}{Y_t}, Y - Y_t < 0; i, t = 1, 2, \ldots, n \tag{10.11}$$

[3]According to Jewson and Brix (2005), burn analysis uses historical data to evaluate the value of derivative contracts. When use the burn analysis, the basic hypothesis includes: (1) the time series data of temperature is stable; (2) the data of each year are independent and subject to the same distribution. Therefore, the burn analysis is regarded as a simplified pricing method, which can estimate price conveniently (Jewson and Brix 2005).

$$R_c = E[loss] = \frac{1}{n}\sum |S_i|,\ S_i < 0, i = 1, 2, \ldots, n \tag{10.12}$$

*E[loss]* is the expected yield reduction rate of each city, n the length of time series, and $R_c = E[loss]$ is the actuarially fair premium rate of each city in Jiangsu. According to above formula, the yield reduction rate of the corresponding year in each city, namely, the indemnity rate can be obtained:

$$L_t = \begin{cases} 0,\ x \le x_c \\ x,\ x > x_c \end{cases} \tag{10.13}$$

In this case, the average indemnity rate of 17 years is:

$$L = \frac{1}{17}\sum_{t=1}^{17} L_t \tag{10.14}$$

In the past, the determination of the premium rate was usually made by the average rate of indemnity, because the average loss rate of crops has sound stability, and the fluctuation of the loss rate is small, which is a relatively good estimate of the actuarially fair premium rate. However, the insurance indemnity and crop loss in different regions are different, and the average loss rate fluctuates. Therefore, the determination of actuarially fair premium is improved in this paper:

$$R_c = L(1 + \delta) \tag{10.15}$$

$$\delta = \frac{\sigma}{\overline{L}} \tag{10.16}$$

In the formula, $\sigma$ and $\overline{L}$ are the standard deviation and the mean of $L$, respectively. $\delta$ is the coefficient of variation, which reflects the degree of dispersion of the average yield reduction rate in several years.

## 10.4 Results and Analysis

### *10.4.1 Regression Analysis*

Taking the year-by-year yield reduction rate as the dependent variable, and the high-temperature damage and the low-temperature damage as the independent variables to establish the regression model for the single-season rice yield reduction rate and temperature index in each city of Jiangsu. Using Rand SPSS for stepwise regression,

**Table 10.1** Regression report on yield reduction rate of single-season rice and temperature index in Jiangsu

| City | High-temperature damage index | Square of high-temperature index | Low-temperature damage index | Square of low-temperature damage index | Adjusted R Square |
|---|---|---|---|---|---|
| Xuzhou | −0.00468 | −0.00361 | −0.041866** | −0.003416** | 0.539 |
| | (0.165) | (0.258) | (0.026) | (0.024) | |
| Yancheng | −0.00033 | −0.00842** | −0.008343** | −3.89E−05* | 0.543 |
| | (0.241) | (0.186) | (0.048) | (0.061) | |
| Lianyungang | −0.022362** | −0.004589** | 0.003008*** | −5.05E−05** | 0.492 |
| | (0.047) | (0.037) | (0.009) | (0.004) | |
| Nanjing | 0.000712*** | −0.000873*** | −0.009874** | −0.000401** | 0.506 |
| | (0.006) | (0.002) | (0.049) | (0.059) | |
| Nantong | 0.003358** | −0.000108** | 0.006685*** | −0.000381*** | 0.450 |
| | (0.015) | (0.046) | (0.001) | (0.005) | |
| Changzhou | 0.0273 | −0.000912** | 0.010007* | −0.000771*** | 0.422 |
| | (0.155) | (0.037) | (0.055) | (0.002) | |
| Wuxi | −0.002780** | −0.039 | −0.013001** | −0.042 | 0.616 |
| | (0.049) | (0.127) | (0.042) | (0.131) | |
| Suzhou | −0.00745 | −0.00631 | −0.005343** | −3.89E−05** | 0.639 |
| | (0.26) | (0.142) | (0.024) | (0.024) | |

*Note* (1) In the brackets are the P value; (2) * indicates the significance level at 10%, ** the significance level at 5%, and *** the significance level at 1% Jiangsu

the regression models of the eight cities[4] are significant overall (the P-value of the F-test value is less than 5%).[5] The effect of temperature index on single-season rice yield in Jiangsu is significant at a 10% confidence level. The regression correlation coefficient of each city and the P value of the correlation index are shown in the Table 10.1. The single-season rice yield reduction in Xuzhou, Yancheng, Changzhou, and Suzhou has a significant relation with low-temperature damage. The weather disasters in the southern region are mainly sight low-temperature damage. In other words, the single-season rice yield reduction rate in Lianyungang, Nanjing and Nantong has a significant relation with high-temperature damage and low-temperature damage. See the Table 10.1 for detail.

[4]Due to the lack of data from five cities in Taizhou, Suqian, Huai'an, Yangzhou and Zhenjiang, only regression analysis for 8 cities including Nanjing and Suzhou in Jiangsu Province is conducted.

[5]In model (6), the potential multicollinearity, heteroscedasticity and autocorrelation of variables are tested by Pearson correlation analysis, Whiter test and Durbin- Watson test, respectively. We found the multicollinearities between independent variables are not existed. Heteroscedasticity or autocorrelation of variables are eliminated through Generalized Least Square (GLS). Limited to space, the results are not reported here.

### 10.4.2 Analysis on the Pure Insurance Premium Rate of Cities in Jiangsu Under the Deductibles at All Levels

In order to fully calculate the actuarially fair premium rates for cities in Jiangsu, the actuarially fair premium rates for deductibles of 2.5%, 5%, 7.5%, and 10% respectively will be calculated below. According to the regression results and the actual production of single-season rice in Jiangsu, the safety surcharge rate is set as 20%, the profit rate 5%, and the operating cost surcharge rate 15%, then the gross insurance premium rate = actuarially fair premium rate × 1.45 (Yang et al. 2015a, b). The *Kriging* interpolation method and *Arcgis* software mapping are used to intuitively describe the classification of actuarially fair premium rates under various deductibles for each city in the province, and then different risk areas are divided.[6]

From Fig. 10.1, with a 2.5% deductible, the province's single-season rice actuarially fair premium rate is between 1.902 and 6.180%. The rates in Xuzhou and Yancheng are high, more than 4%; the rates in southeastern Jiangsu are low. The rates in the central region are between those of the north and the south.

From Fig. 10.2, with a 5% deductible, the province's actuarially fair premium rate is between 1.80 and 6.12%, which is lower than the 2.5% deductible. The actuarially fair premium rate in the southeast region of Jiangsu is still the lowest, lower than 2.7%.

From Fig. 10.3, with a 7.5% deductible, the province's actuarially fair premium rate continues to fall, from 1.781 to 6.010%. The premium rates in the northeast are still the highest, but it is clear from the figures that the range of high rates has narrowed.

From Fig. 10.4, under a 10% deductible, the actuarially fair premium rate fluctuates from 1.51% to 6.01%. Only Xuzhou city with an actuarially fair premium rate of more than 4%, in many other cities, the actuarially fair premium rates even drop below 2% (Fig. 10.5).

Through the analysis of the actuarially fair premium rates under different deductibles above, it is found that the risk of yield reduction with the deductibles at all levels in the northwestern region of Jiangsu is higher and the rates are higher than those in other regions, while the rates in the southeastern cities are lower. According to the distribution of actuarially fair premium rates with the deductibles at all levels and the actual conditions of agricultural insurance Jiangsu, different deductibles can be set in different risk regions to reduce the probability of adverse selection and opportunistic behaviour(Table 10.2).

The single-season rice insurance premium rate is affected by weather disasters, and the greater disaster risk means greater single-season rice premium rate. On the whole, the risks of high-temperature damage and low-temperature damage are not too high, but the deductible cannot be set to the same in different cities. Although

[6]Based on the data of seven other prefecture-level cities such as Nanjing and Suzhou in Jiangsu Province, this paper interpolates and estimates the actuarially fair premium rates of the five cities of Taizhou, Suqian, Huai'an, Yangzhou and Zhenjiang.

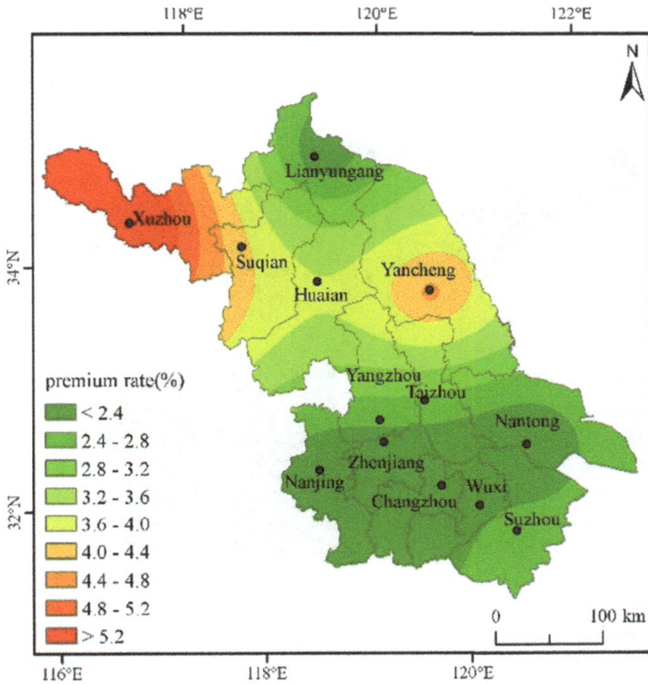


**Fig. 10.2** Distribution of actuarially fair premium rate for each city when the deductible amount is 2.5%

the same deductible is beneficial to the management of insurance companies, the probability of occurrence of risks in each region is entirely different, and it is easy to cause basis risk. It is proposed to divide Jiangsu into two risk areas, where Xuzhou and Yancheng are the first risk area, and Lianyungang, Nanjing, Changzhou, Nantong, Wuxi, and Suzhou are the second category of high risk area. Xuzhou's rates are the highest with various deductibles. The main reason is that Xuzhou's low-temperature index is higher than those of other cities. That is, the number of days with an average daily temperature below 20 degrees during the autumn grouting period is the highest, resulting in high yield reduction rates. Yancheng's actuarially fair premium rate is slightly lower than that of Xuzhou, but it is significantly higher than in other cities. The same deductible of 5% can be set to reduce management costs. For other cities, such as Lianyungang, Nanjing, Changzhou, and Nantong, both the actuarially fair premium rate and the total premium rate are very close. Therefore, in determining the actuarially fair premium rate, the same deductible for the other cities may be set at 2.5% to reduce the insurance company's management costs.

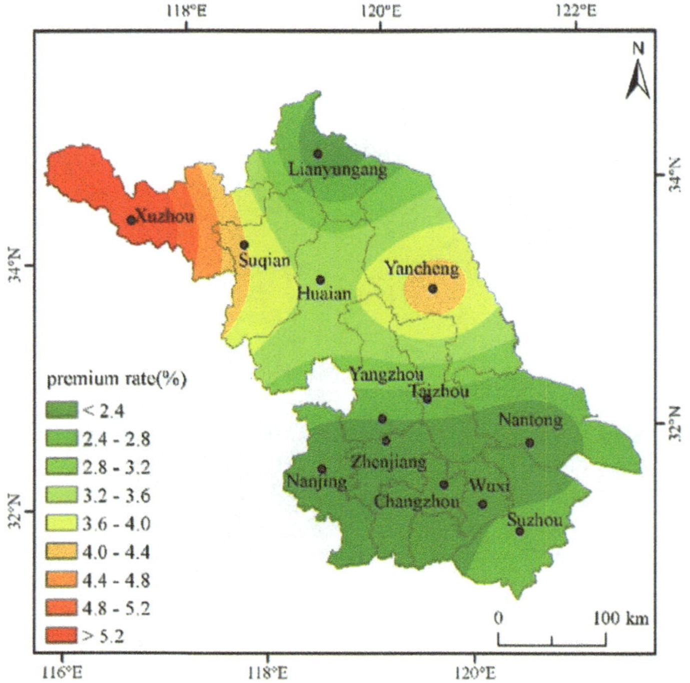


**Fig. 10.3** Distribution of actuarially fair premium rate for each city when the deductible amount is 5%

## 10.5 Conclusions and Discussions

### *10.5.1 Research Conclusion*

The single-season rice high-temperature and low-temperature indices of Jiangsu are designed based on daily weather data and single-season rice production data from eight cities from 1999 to 2015. The relations between single-season rice yield reduction rate and temperature index are studied, the actuarially fair premium rates of single-season rice temperature index-based insurance in Jiangsu are determined, the single-season rice temperature index insurance in Jiangsu is designed, and the risk area of single-season rice in Jiangsu is divided. This paper proposes to take Xuzhou City as Risk Area One, and other cities as Risk Area Two. These results can provide a reference for the application and extension of agricultural insurance in Jiangsu or beyond.[7] In addition, for the managerial implications, it is necessary to pay attention to the differences of temperatures in different cities and regions. For

[7] We sent the results to three officials of the development and reform commission of Jiangsu province. They thought that this research could improve their work and be of significant.

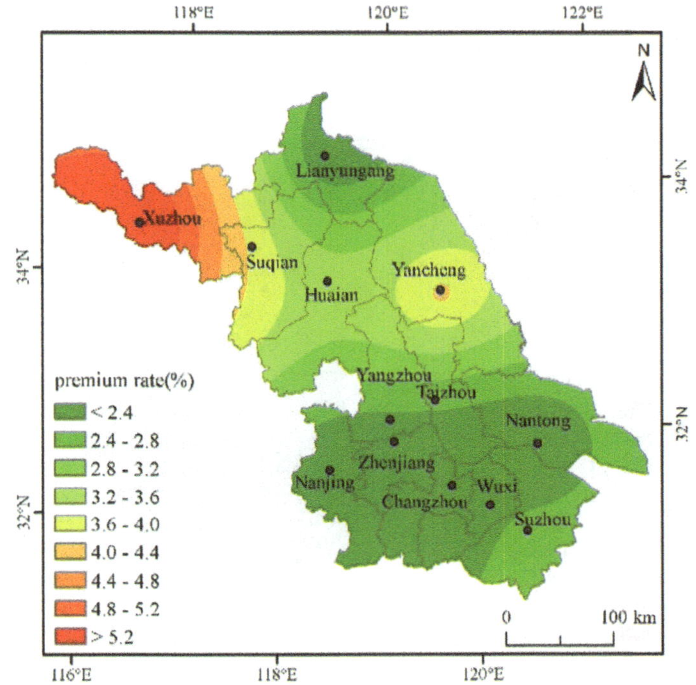


**Fig. 10.4** Distribution of actuarially fair premium rate for each city when the deductible amount is 7.5%

example, ground sensors and remote sensors can be used to obtain grid data, and then local agricultural meteorological disaster insurance can be formulated.

### *10.5.2 Research Prospect*

The following aspects can be further studied in the future:

(1) Due to the lack of data on single-season rice production in some cities before 2005 in Jiangsu, data from eight cities from 1999 to 2015 is selected for empirical analysis, so the data is incomplete. In addition, the lack of county-level city data makes the actuarially fair premium rate only determined based on prefecture-level cities, so there is still a certain basis risk.

(2) The weather output is separated through the moving average method, losing some production data. In the future, better models can be selected by comparing other models such as the Autoregressive Integrated Moving Average (ARIMA) model and the linear moving average method.

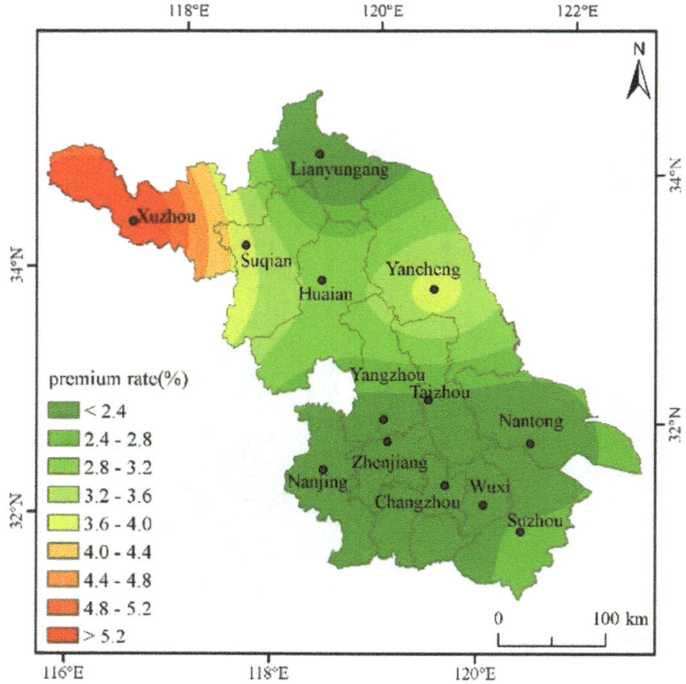


**Fig. 10.5** Distribution of actuarially fair premium rate for each city when the deductible amount is 10%

(3) Many factors are affecting the fertility of single-season rice. In this paper, only the high-temperature damage and low-temperature damage indexes are included in the model, which can be further enriched in the future.

**Table 10.2** Premium rates of each city under different deductibles

| City | 2.5% deductible | | 5% deductible | | 7.5% deductible | | 10% deductible | |
|---|---|---|---|---|---|---|---|---|
| | Actuarially fair premium rate (%) | Actuarially fair premium (CNY) | Actuarially fair premium rate (%) | Actuarially fair premium (CNY) | Actuarially fair premium rate (%) | Actuarially fair premium (CNY) | Actuarially fair premium rate (%) | Actuarially fair premium (CNY) |
| Xuzhou | 6.18 | 370.80 | 6.12 | 367.20 | 6.01 | 360.60 | 6.01 | 360.60 |
| Yancheng | 4.53 | 271.80 | 4.41 | 264.60 | 4.12 | 247.20 | 3.91 | 234.60 |
| Lianyungang | 2.04 | 122.40 | 1.98 | 118.80 | 1.89 | 113.40 | 1.51 | 90.60 |
| Nanjing | 1.90 | 114.12 | 1.80 | 108.12 | 1.78 | 106.86 | 1.53 | 92.04 |
| Changzhou | 1.91 | 114.66 | 1.89 | 113.16 | 1.82 | 109.38 | 1.59 | 95.10 |
| Nantong | 1.85 | 111.06 | 1.85 | 111.00 | 1.85 | 110.94 | 1.72 | 103.26 |
| Wuxi | 2.22 | 133.38 | 2.21 | 132.84 | 2.01 | 120.72 | 2.00 | 120.06 |
| Suzhou | 2.71 | 162.54 | 2.70 | 161.88 | 2.68 | 161.04 | 2.55 | 152.82 |

**Acknowledgements** Jiajia Jin, Yinshan Tang, Zili Tai also made great contributions to this manuscript. We express our heartfelt thanks to them. This research was funded by The National Social and Scientific Fund Program (17BGL142; 18ZDA052; 16ZDA047); Natural Science Foundation of China (91546117, 71373131); The Ministry of Education Scientific Research Foundation for the returned overseas students (No. 2013-693). This research was also supported by the Priority Academic Program Development of Jiangsu Higher Education Institutions.

**Conflicts of Interest** The authors declare no conflict of interest.

## References

Aditya, K., Bethanna, J., & Ilan, N. (2018). A viable and cost-effective weather index insurance for rice in Indonesia. *The Geneva Risk and Insurance Review, 43,* 186–218.

Andrea, M. S., Maria, A., & Tarrazon, R. (2020). Approaching rainfall-based weather derivatives pricing and operational challenges. *Review of Derivatives Research, 23,* 163–190.

Ayala, W., Nicole, M. M., Justus, O., & Lilian, K. (2017). Weather extremes and household welfare in rural Kenya. *Food Security, 9,* 281–300.

Castaneda, V. A., Barrios, L., & Garrido, A. (2014). Assessment of insurance coverage and claims in rainfall related risks in processing tomato in Western Spain. *European Journal of Agronomy, 59,* 39–48. https://doi.org/10.1016/j.eja.

China Meteorological Administration. (2013). Technical specifications for evaluation of rice cold damage [QX/T 182-2013]. Beijing.

Clarke, D. J., Clarke, D., Mahul, O., & Verma, N. (2012). *Index Based Crop Insurance Product Design and Ratemaking: The Case of Modified Nais in India.* Policy Research Working Paper.

Chen, H. L., Liang, Z. Y., Liu, Y., Jiang, Q. S., & Xie, S. G. (2018). Effects of drought and flood on crop production in China across 1949–2015: Spatial heterogeneity analysis with Bayesian hierarchical modeling. *Natural Hazards, 92,* 525–541.

E L. (1999). *Records of song poems 100.* Shanghai: Shanghai Ancient Books Publishing House.

Field, C. B., Barros, V., Stocker, T. F., Qin, D., Dokken, D. J., Ebi, K. L., et al. (2012). Managing the risks of extreme events and disasters to advance climate change adaptation: IPCC special report on working groups I and II of the intergovernmental panel on climate change. *Journal of Clinical Endocrinology and Metabolism, 18,* 582. https://doi.org/10.1017/CBO9781139177245.

Huang, R. H. (2006). Progresses in research on the formation mechanism and prediction theory of severe climatic disasters in China. *Advances in Earth Science, 21,* 564–575.

Jia, H. C., Pan, D. H., Li, J., Zhang, W. C., & Rasul, G. (2016). Risk assessment of maize drought disaster in southwest China using the Environmental Policy Integrated Climate model. *Journal of Mountain Science, 13,* 465–475.

Jewson, S., & Brix, A. (2005). *Weather derivative valuation: The meteorological, statistical, financial and mathematical foundations.* Cambridge: Cambridge University Press.

José, L. V., Antonio, H., & de Estela, F. (2020). An average model approach to experience based premium rates discounts: An application to Spanish agricultural insurance. *European Actuarial Journal, 10,* 361–375.

Kenneth, W. S., & Matin, Q. (2020). Weather index insurance, agricultural input use, and crop productivity in Kenya. *Food Security, 12,* 151–167.

Ker, A. P., & Goodwin, B. K. G. (2000). Nonparametric estimation of crop insurance rates revisited. *American Journal of Agricultural Economics, 82,* 463–478. https://doi.org/10.2307/1244665.

Koshi, Y., Mallika, S., Supranee, S., Desell, S., & Naruekamon, J. (2019). Weather-induced economic damage to upland crops and the impact on farmer household income in Northeast Thailand. *Paddy and Water Environment, 17,* 341–349.

Leblois, A., Quirion, P., & Sultan, B. (2014). Price vs. weather shock hedging for cash crops: Ex ante evaluation for cotton producers in Cameroon. *Ecological Economics, 101,* 67–80.

Lesk, C., Rowhani, P., & Ramankutty, N. (2016). Influence of extreme weather disasters on global crop production. *Nature, 529,* 84–87.

Li, M., Chen, S. N., Liu, F., Zhao, L., Xue, Q. Y., Wang, H., et al. (2017). A risk management system for meteorological disasters of solar greenhouse vegetables. *Precision Agriculture, 18,* 997–1010.

Liu, Y., Liu, B. C., Yang, X. J., Bai, W., & Wang, J. (2015). Relationships between drought disasters and crop production during ENSO episodes across the North China Plain. *Regional Environmental Change, 15,* 1689–1701.

Long, Z. X. (2008) Research on System of Agricultural Insurance in Jiangsu Province. Soochow University.

Lou, W. P., Ji, Z. W., & Qiu, X. F. (2011). Design of tea frost weather index insurance. *Chinese Journal of Natural Medicines, 26,* 2053–2059. https://doi.org/10.1007/s11769-011-0450-8.

Lu, P. (2010). Design of Weather Index Crop Insurance Contract for Northeast China. Tsinghua University.

Luo, L. H., Liu, G. H., Xiao, Y. H., Tang, W. B., & Chen, L. Y. (2005). Influences of high-temperature stress on the fertility of pollen, spikelet and grain-weigh in rice. *Journal of Hunan Agricultural University, 31,* 593–596.

Marco, M., Giovanni, A., Roberto, F., Camilla, D., Giacomo, T., & Marco, B. (2016). Heat stress and crop yields in the Mediterranean basin: Impact on expected insurance payouts. *Regional Environmental Change, 16,* 1877–1890.

Meng, Z. H., Wang, Y. J., Sun, Z. S., Meng, Q. X., Liu, Y. W., Lei, C. G., & Zhang, J. L. (2005). The research of rice sterile-type chilling injury and irrigation technique. *Chinese Agricultural Science Bulletin, 21,* 197–201.

Miranda, M., Skees, J. R., & Hazell, P. (1999). *New Approaches to Public/Private Crop Yield Insurance.* EPTD Discussion Papers.

Norton, M. T., Turvey, C., & Osgood, D. (2012). Quantifying spatial basis risk for weather index insurance. *J Credit Risk, 14,* 20–34. https://doi.org/10.1108/15265941311288086.

Okpara, J. N., Afiesimama, E. A., Anuforom, A. C., Owino, A., & Ogunjobi, K. O. (2017). The applicability of Standardized Precipitation Index: Drought characterization for early warning system and weather index insurance in West Africa. *Natural Hazards, 89,* 555–583.

Patrick, M. R., Hyun, K., & Emily, M. (2019). Climate change, adaptation, and agricultural output. *Regional Environmental Change, 19,* 113–123.

Qiang, H. T. (2011). Study on High Temperature Induced Heat Damage and its Impacts on Rice Production in Jiangsu Province. NUIST.

Skees, J. R., Hazell, P. B. R., & Miranda, M. (1999). New approaches to crop yield insurance in developing countries. *EPTD Discussion Papers, 55,* 18–23.

Sun, Q., Yang, Z. Q., Che, X. C., Han, W., Zhang, F. M., & Xiao, F. (2018). Pricing weather index insurance based on artificial controlled experiment: A case study of cold temperature for early rice in Jiangxi, China. *Natural Hazards, 91,* 69–88.

Sun, Z. Y., Zhang, J. Q., Yan, D. H., Wu, L., & Guo, E. L. (2015). The impact of irrigation water supply rate on agricultural drought disaster risk: A case about maize based on EPIC in Baicheng City, China. *Natural Hazards, 78,* 23–40.

Tam, B. V., Eric, I. I., Karla, H., & Ryan, T. (2017). Cyclones, deforestation, and production of food crops in Vietnam. *Economics of Disasters and Climate Change, 1,* 245–262.

Thierry, C., Moinul, I., & Shunsuke, M. (2020). The impacts of climate change and natural disasters on agriculture in African countries. *Economics of Disasters and Climate Change, 4,* 347–364.

Thong, N., Ravinesh, C. D., Shahbaz, M., Jarrod, K., & Shahjahan, K. (2019). Copula statistical models for analyzing stochastic dependencies of systemic drought risk and potential adaptation strategies. *Stochastic Environmental Research and Risk Assessment, 33,* 779–799.

Turvey, C. G., & Weersink, A. (2005). Pricing weather insurance with a random strike price: An Application to the Ontario ice wine harvest. *American Journal of Agricultural Economics, 88,* 696–709. https://doi.org/10.1111/j.1467-8276.2006.00889.x.

Wang, K., & Zhang, Q. (2010). Influence of flexible crop yield distributions on crop insurance premium rate: A case study on cotton insurance in three counties of Xinjiang Province. *Journal of China Agricultural University, 15,* 114–120. https://doi.org/10.1097/ICO.0b013e3182000add.

Wang, Y., Wang, C., & Zhang, Q. (2020). Synergistic effects of climatic factors and drought on maize yield in the east of Northwest China against the background of climate change. *Theoretical and Applied Climatology, 143*(3–4), 1017–1033.

Wang, Y., Zhang, Q., Wang, S. P., Wang, J. S., & Yao, Y. B. (2017). Characteristics of agro-meteorological disasters and their risk in Gansu Province against the background of climate change. *Natural Hazards, 89,* 899–921.

Wang, Z., Shi, P. J., Zhang, Z., Meng, Y. C., Luan, Y. B., & Wang, J. W. (2018). Separating out the influence of climatic trend, fluctuations, and extreme events on crop yield: A case study in Hunan Province, China. *Climate Dynamics, 51,* 4469–4487.

World Bank. (2013). *Weather index insurance for agriculture: Guidance for development practitioners* (pp. 50–54). Washington, D.C.: Agriculture and Rural Development Discussion.

Wu, L. H., Lou, W. P., Yao, Y. P., Mao, Y. D., & Su, G. L. (2010). Design of products for rice agro-meteorological index insurance: A case in Zhejiang Province. *Scientia Agricultura Sinica, 43,* 4942–4950. https://doi.org/10.1097/MOP.0b013e3283423f35.

Wu, X. H., Cao, Y. R., Xiao, Y., & Guo, J. (2018). Finding of urban rainstorm and waterlogging disasters based on microblogging data and the location-routing problem model of urban emergency logistics. *Annals of Operations Research* 1–18. https://doi.org/10.1007/s10479-018-2904-1.

Xu, H. B., Wang, G. M., et al. (2001). Correlation analysis of the characters of pollen grains and seed-setting of rice under high temperature stress. *Journal of Southwest Agricultural University, 23,* 205–207.

Yang, X. J., Liu, Y., Bai, W., & Liu, B. C. (2015). Evaluation of the crop insurance management for soybean risk of natural disasters in Jilin Province, China. *Natural Hazards, 76,* 587–599.

Yang, T. M., Sun, X. B., & Liu, B. C. (2015). Design on weather indices model for insurance of rice heat damage in Anhui Province. *Journal of Agrometeorology, 36,* 220–226.

You, Z. X. (2008). Research on System of Agricultural Insurance in Jiangsu Province. Soochow University.

Yu, X. B., Li, C., & l., Huo T. Z., & Ji Z. H., (2020). Information diffusion theory-based approach for the risk assessment of meteorological disasters in the Yangtze River Basin. *Natural Hazards.* https://doi.org/10.1007/s11069-020-04418-6.

Zanini, F. C., Sherrick, B. J., Schnitkey, G. D., & Lrwin, S. H. (2004). Crop insurance valuation under alternative yield distributions. *American Journal of Agricultural Economics, 86,* 406–419. https://doi.org/10.2307/30139564.

Zhang, F. F. (2012). The spatial and temperature distribution of rice heat injury Hubei Province. *Journal of Huazhong Agricultural University.*

Zhang, Q., Zhang, J. Q., & Wang, C. Y. (2017). Risk assessment of drought disaster in typical area of corn cultivation in China. *Theoretical and Applied Climatology, 128,* 533–540.

Zhang, J., Zhang, S., Cheng, M., Jiang, H., Zhang, X., Peng C., et al. (2018). Effect of drought on agronomic traits of rice and wheat: A meta-analysis. *International Journal of Environmental Research and Public Health, 15,* 839. https://doi.org/10.3390/ijerph15050839.

Zhang, Q., Han, L. Y., Lin, J. J., & Cheng, Q. Y. (2018). North–south differences in Chinese agricultural losses due to climate-change-influenced droughts *Theoretical and Applied Climatology, 131,* 719–732.

Zhou, J. W. (2014). Product design of apple low temperature freezing injury index insurance-Shandong Qixia City as an example. *Journal of Shandong Agricultural University.*

Zuo, J., Wang, X. J., Guo, Y. L., et al. (2014). Weed species in a transgenic rice field at the plant breeding base of Hainan Province. *Weed Science, 32,* 40–44.

# Chapter 11
# Determining the Amount of Sustainable International Aid that Countries Should Donate After Disaster: A New Frame, Indices and Method

**Abstract** Disasters are a serious challenge to human development and because climate change natural disasters are becoming more frequent. International aid, which can effectively alleviate resultant losses, has become an important way for humans to resist disasters cooperatively. Relevant research on how much each country should donate sustainably is barely seen. Against such a background, by taking into account indirect economic loss to and payment ability of donors, this paper propose the novel frame and detail input-output model for determining the amount of international aid that countries and multilateral organizations should allocate to disaster-stricken countries. To validate our method, the May 12th Wenchuan earthquake of 2008 is taken as example, and the indirect economic loss to each country is calculated based on the world input-output tables. Assuming that the total amount of aid is unchanged, the greater the indirect economic loss and payment ability are, the larger the amount of aid should be. Otherwise, the smaller the amount of aid should be. Based on the China's Ministry of Foreign Affairs statistics, the results show that among the 41 donors, 6 countries including Indonesia, Australia, South Korea, Spain, Turkey, and Japan donated too much while 23 countries such as India donated too little. Next, the recommended amount of aid is given by considering the indirect economic loss to and payment ability of each country. The advantage of this framework and method lines in that the calculation results are objective and concise, while the disadvantage is that the indirect economic loss is relatively large and the recommend donate is uncertain. This paper demonstrates a new perspective for the study of standards for determining the amount of international aid that countries and multilateral organizations should provide.

**Keywords** Natural disaster · International aid · Indirect economic loss · Standard · Input-output model

## 11.1 Introduction

Natural disasters such as earthquakes, volcanoes, debris flows, tsunamis, typhoons, tornadoes, and floods are natural phenomena harmful to human survival or to the human living environments, impacting also the sustainable development of society

 
X. Wu and J. Guo, *Economic Impacts and Emergency Management of Disasters in China*,
https://doi.org/10.1007/978-981-16-1319-7_11

and economy (Cao et al. 2018). For instance, the May 12th Wenchuan earthquake of 2008 in China caused 69,227 deaths, 374,643 injured and 17,923 missing, thus becoming the most destructive earthquake in China since 1949 and the earthquake with greatest casualties after the Tangshan earthquake in 1976; the March 11th earthquake of 2011 in Japan caused 11,232 deaths and 16,361 missing. The India Ocean tsunami on December 26th, 2004, which resulted in at least 156,000 deaths, is possibly the worst tsunami disaster in the world nearly 200 years. In recent years, extreme weather events and natural disasters are increasingly frequent due to global warming. In fact, the number of natural disasters increased thousands of times from 2000 to 2009 compared with that from 1920 to 1929 (UNISDR, 2005–2011). According to United Nations International Strategy for Disaster Reduction (UNISDR): during 2000–2017 over 193.000 million of people each year were impacted by earthquakes, drought, and flood among others. Natural disasters have undoubtedly become one of the most severe challenges in the development of human society.

In the process of constantly fighting against natural disasters, mutual assistance between humans has effectively reduced casualties and disaster losses. After the Second World War, foreign aid was gradually institutionalized. A case in point is the Office of Foreign Disaster Assistance (OFDA) established by the United States. Since 1964, USAID's OFDA has responded to more than 2500 disasters in over 80% of the world. International aid aimed at fighting against natural disasters mainly starts from humanitarian principles, but sometimes is mingled with strategic interests of the donors. In the meanwhile, it is also closely related to institutional conditions of the done. So, how much should donor countries give to ensure sustainability (that is, both the fairness and feasibility) of donations? According to the present author's view, few scholars have ever studied this fundamental and interesting question (Wu et al. 2017).

We study the standards of international aid from a novel angle. Once a disaster happens, other countries will inevitably be indirectly affected because each country is interrelated with others in many aspects such as international trade, human migration. Donations of these countries, in essence, should reduce economic losses that a disaster-stricken country would bring to them. Therefore, the relative amount of aid can be determined according to the indirect economic loss caused by the disaster. Furthermore, the reasons why indirect economic losses to donors should be duly considered is as follows. (1) According to systems theory, all countries in the world form an interrelated system. When a natural disaster strikes a country, causing loss of life and property, disrupting vital lines such as transportation and electricity, reducing local production and consumption capacity, inevitably shall bring indirect economic losses to other related countries and regions (Wu et al. 2017). The participation of donors in disaster relief, in essence, abates indirect economic losses that the disaster would bring to them. Sooner participation and higher aid will help donors avoid more indirect economic losses. Therefore, in the design of international aid standards, indirect economic losses caused by natural disasters to donors should be fully assessed. (2) In line with the theory of reciprocal altruism, there are conflicts of interests between donors and doneness (Birkland 1997; Drabek 2003). Peters (1998) pointed out that the integration of emergency responses among several parties is a political process; though voluntary is best, all parties still weigh the interests of their own and others in the actual rescue process. Haraoka et al. (2012) proposed giving enough incentives and guarantees to donors so that international rescue can be sustained. When a natural disaster occurs in a country, other related countries carry out international aid action according to their indirect economic losses. Lending aid in accordance with indirect economic losses can help donors become conscious of their obligations and enjoy their rights. That is to say, donors are supposed to receive aid from other related countries when stricken by a disaster in the future. (3) From the viewpoint of equity theory, different types of natural disasters tend to occur in different countries. Some countries are frequently stricken while others are not. If a few fixed countries are lending aid for a long time, countries with fewer disasters will not be willing to aid those with more disasters in the long run. For this reason, the degree of participation of each donor should be dynamically adjusted according to the amount of its indirect economic loss. The ideal aid amount can be estimated by objectively measuring indirect economic losses to donors, thereby eliminating donors' "sense of injustice". Accordingly, the amount of indirect economic losses can be used as an index to evaluate the amount of international aid.

Of course, it is worth mentioning that the amount of aid not only depends on the indirect economic loss but also on the payment ability of a donor country. The stronger the payment ability of a donor country is, the higher the aid amount it should grant. In view of this, this paper will measure the amount of aid by considering both indirect economic loss and payment ability of each donor.

Based on the above considerations, this paper proposes the idea, steps, indices and method to determine sustainable aid standards through the assessment of the donor's indirect economic loss and payment ability of the donor country. Also, the proposed method is empirically proved by taking the May 12th Wenchuan earthquake as an example, thereby not only enriching the theoretical research on disaster emergency management, but also providing an example for the practice of international disaster assistance. The remaining parts of this paper are as follows: the second part presents a literature review; the third part gives the working definitions and research steps; the fourth part offers the input-output model and evaluative indices; the fifth part consists of an introduction of the May 12th Wenchuan earthquake and a description of relevant data; the sixth part contains the results of the empirical analysis; a conclusion comes in the last.

## 11.2 Literature Review

The following is a brief review of the literature on international aid and indirect economic losses caused by disasters.

### *11.2.1 International Aid After Disaster*

International aid is an important issue in the field of disaster research. Relevant studies can be roughly divided into four categories: the motivations for aid, the ways of aid, the social and economic effects of aid, and the standards of aid.

There is an abundant research on the motivations that countries and multilateral organizations have for aid after a natural disaster hit a country. Overall, the motivations for aid include humanitarian needs (Fink and Redaelli 2011): strategic interests of the donor (Bermeo 2007; Copelovitch 2010): democracy degree of the donee (Burnside and Dollar 2004; Svensson 2010): and geographical proximity between the donor and the donee (Fink and Redaelli 2011). According to Dollar (2000): foreign aid is mainly determined by the political and strategic interests of the donor as well as the economic needs and policies of the donee; in the meantime, colonial history and political alliance are also vital determinants; other conditions being equal, the more democratic the donee is, the more aid it can receive. Dreher and Jensen (2007) found that aid from multilateral organizations is influenced by political factors. There are also scholars who studied motivations of different donors. For illustration, Maizels and Nissanke (1984) investigated motivations for aid flowing to developing countries, and found the motivations was shifted from recipient need over the 1970s towards donor interest in the 1980s.

Doucouliagos and Manning (2009) studied motivations for aid from Luxemburg, Huang and Jianmei (2020) summarized the four core motives of China' s foreign aid: economic motive, political motive, diplomatic and strategic motive, development motive and humanitarian motive. Greece, and Portugal and the results indicate that humanitarian concerns are not an important factor. To efficiently distribute relief materials and evacuate the wounded to health centers, Mahbubeh et al. (2017) established a multi-objective planning model to determine the location of relief material distribution centers and health centers from a humanitarian perspective. Raschky and Schwindt (2012) applied a dataset on international post-disaster assistance between 2000 and 2007 and suggested that the choice of the channel (bilateral vs. multilateral) and type (cash vs. in-kind) of disaster assistance is mainly determined by humanitarian aspects, strategic interests and institutional quality. Lauren et al. (2020) used the method of case comparison, revealing a phenomenon: the assistance requiring the labor of donee was not aimed at stimulating economic development, in fact, the assistance restrained the poor but supported aid organizations. Furuoka (2017) noted that there was no significant difference in motivations for aid to Africa from China or from Japan. Richey and Ponte (2020) pointed out that even though brand aid forms promised to supply work assistance outside the enterprise, donors actually served the interests of the enterprise and celebrities.

Other scholars conducted empirical research on needs of the donee, strategic and political needs of the donor and amount of foreign aid (Neumayer 2003; Kuziemko and Werker 2006; Höffler and Outram 2008; Younas 2008; Liam 2017; Hallwright and Handmer 2019). Suyeon et al. (2020) insisted that the main effects of renewable energy official assistance varied with the degree of political democracy, and political democracy also brought policy influence to the distribution of renewable energy assistance. Taking ethnic, religious and political distortions into account, Andreas et al. got the result that aid distribution was associated with geophysical estimates of earthquake damage. Mao Suzuki (2020) used analysis of dyadic panel data of 23 OECD donors and 149 recipient countries, showing the assessment of specific activities were contributed to analyze the real economic motivations of donors. Overall, different studies show that the motivations for aid vary widely from country to country and time to time.

The main ways of aid include official and private aid, bilateral and multilateral aid, in-kind aid and financial aid. For example, Dudley and Montmarquette (1976) constructed a supply model of bilateral international aid. Cingranelli and Pasquarello (1985) and Neumayer (2003) explored the role of human rights performance in allocating bilateral aid. Robin Shields (2019) regarded the bilateral aid just like a network which was reducing dependence on donors, for recipients in the network were connected with an increasing number of donors. Clemens et al. (2004) and Neanidis and Varvarigos (2009) analyzed the effectiveness of international aid tools. Habibzadeh et al. (2008) believed that cultural habits, religious beliefs, and geographical factors will all affect the effectiveness of international aid. Michael et al. (2020) questioned the effectiveness of bilateral aid to improve the natural environment. Liao et al. (2020) believed IDA (international development aid) good to promote FDI (foreign direct investment) in recipient countries, while IDA in the physical form might discourage FDI in recipient countries.

In addition, Nunnenkamp and Öhler: taking Germany as an example, made a distinction between private and official aid, and argued that aid from a different source tends to have a dissimilar motivation. Lewin (2020) considered the assistance would not increase, because this year's economic was hit by the COVID-19, therefore, author insisted to establish a better system distribution system to make full use of the resources. Ryan et al. explored policy reforms without additional expenditures, for COVID-19 not only increased the demand for international food aid, but also interrupted the normal supply and delivery of food aid.

There exist plenty of studies of the social and economic effects of aid. These studies focused on the effects of aid on regional economic growth (Albala-Bertrand 1993; Skidmore and Toya 2002; Noy 2009): on industrial sectors (Loayza et al. 2012; Bulte et al. 2018) and on victims (Townsend 1994; Udry 1994; Nakhaei et al. 2015). Via studying the effect of financial sector assistance in nearly 70 developing countries, Admasu et al. (2019) found the financial sector assistance had a significant positive impact on financial development. By studying whether international assistance could reduce international migration, Mauro et al. found that investment in capacity-building in the agricultural sector did good to reduce the migration in developing countries. Xiaoli et al. (2020) built a mediation model to study the influence of climate aid, and concluded that climate aid reduced carbon dioxide in some way. Through the data of India's carbon dioxide from 1978 to 2004, Mantu et al. got the conclusion that foreign aid, globalization and energy consumption had significantly reduced carbon dioxide emissions, in contrast, foreign energy assistance, remittance aid and foreign direct investment had increased carbon dioxide emissions.

Nonetheless, no uniform conclusion has been reached. For instance, Rajan and Subramanian (2008) studied the influence of aid on economic growth, but failed to find either positive or negative effect of received aid on economic growth; they argued that there is no evidence that aid plays a greater role under a better policy or in an improved geographical environment or that aid in one form is more effective than that in another form. For another example, through analyzing the Chinese aid and overseas direct investment (FDI) in 47 African countries between 2003 and 2013, Yan et al. found that China's assistance had a significant positive impact on African economic growth. In addition, the relationship between aid and economy growth varied by different types of aid. Scobie (2020) argued that deficiencies in international aid governance had led to inequity in international trade, aid and investment. What is more, some scholars had discussed that international aid had partially undermined the peace process from a political perspective. For example, Ghanem (2020) insisted international aid helping Israel to strengthen grip on East Jerusalem, but had undermined efforts to reach reconciliation in the Holy city. Koch (2017) noticed the gap between aid policy and implementation, and found that policy makers often changed their agendas in line with donor priorities, but did not necessarily put new policies into practice.

Scholars also touched upon the issue of aid amount. For example, Dowling and Hiemenz (1985): who studied more than 90 countries' models of bilateral and multilateral foreign aid in the 1970s, found that while low-income countries receive more foreign aid than middle-income countries, extremely impoverished countries often fail to secure enough aid. Besides, Fink and Redaelli (2011) analyzed the determinants of international emergency aid on the basis of data on 270 natural disasters. They argued that donors prefer small neighboring oil exporters, and tend to support those politically inconsistent countries and their former colonies. Raschky and Schwindt (2012) held that the ways and forms of aid are influenced by many factors, such as humanitarianism, strategic interests, institutional quality, and that donors prefer to lend aid in kind to neighboring disaster-stricken countries.

A different stream of research focuses on the problem of designing a relief distribution network to quickly alleviate and support victims and mitigate post-disaster deaths. Readers interested on this topic are pointed to Cao et al. (2018) and Haghi et al. (2017) for further details. While the relief distribution network design problem is related with the topic treated in this paper, our focus is on determining the amount of aid that countries should allocate to a disaster-stricken country.

However, as far as the scope of researchers' standpoints is concerned, the research on aid standards is highly rare. Due to the diverse systems and processes of foreign aid and dissimilar institutional setup and affordable aid amount, there is no agreement on how much donors should lend once a disaster occurs. Taking the United States as an example, Perry and Travayiakis (2008) introduced the US government's response to foreign disasters in detail but did not discuss the standards of aid after disasters. Therefore, it is of originality to study the standards of international aid. Another example is the regulatory mechanism, Joshua et al. (2019) analyzed transparency and accountability affected populations and communities, rather than foreign donors.

The result showed that the transparency of financial flows was relatively high, but in the recovery stage, the transparency was low.

### *11.2.2 Estimations of Indirect Economic Loss Caused by Disasters*

(1) The definition of indirect economic loss caused by disasters. Different scholars hold different views on what indirect economic loss caused by disasters is. For example, Boisvert (1992) believed that indirect economic loss is the supply bottlenecks caused by direct economic loss or is the loss resulting from multiplier effect or propagation effect of the economic system caused by the decrease of demand. Gordon et al. (1997) argued that indirect economic loss is mainly caused by the broken traffic and industrial production capacity, including indirect impact and induced impact. However, Burrus et al. (2002) contended that indirect economic loss is the loss value resulting from the decrease in output after the damage or interruption of production. From the perspective of Haimes et al. (2005): Santos et al. (2004) and Growther et al. (2007): indirect economic loss was defined as the reduction of total output caused by disasters resulting from the inherent relevance of the economic system itself. Hal Cochrane (1996) said, "Indirect losses stem solely from forward and backward linked costs".

The World Bank contended that indirect loss is the decline in social production and income, and an increase in expenditure after disasters happen and before their recovery (UN-ECLAC/WB2003). According to the Committee on Assessing the Costs of Natural Disaster, National Research Council, in the short term, indirect economic losses caused by natural disasters include three types: (1) the losses of sales, salaries or profits caused by lack of function due to the material destruction of business structure; (2) the losses of purchase/shipment resulting from the closure of upstream and downstream industries due to direct material damage or destruction of infrastructure; (3) the losses duo to stop or drop in production of enterprises which cause a decrease in both income and expenditure, namely due to the multiplier effect or ripple effect.

The Indirect Loss Model of Hazus-MH based on The National Institute for Buildings Standards (NIBS) is employed to calculate the losses caused by supply shortages (forward linkages) anddemand reductions (backward linkages) due to disasters.

Assessment methods of earthquake-caused indirect economic loss (GB/T27932-2011) published by China Earthquake Administration pointed out that the indirect economic losses caused by an earthquake are "the economic losses brought by the indirect influence of the earthquake which has an impact on normal social economic activities, including the losses because of stop of production or reduction of output, loss of land price, and sections-related loss." A formula for the estimation of the indirect loss caused by earthquakes is given as Eq. (11.9).

Viewed from the above research, although the definitions are inconsistent, indirect economic losses all refer to the relevant loss brought by the breakup of economic activities resulting from the disruption caused by disasters. One of the main aspects of the paper is to study the indirect economic losses to other countries and regions brought by earthquakes, which can be measured by the correlation between industries from different countries. Therefore, the definition and methods given by The National Institute for Buildings Standards (NIBS) and Assessment methods of earthquake-caused indirect economic loss (GB/T 27932-2011) published by China Earthquake Administration are employed in this paper to make quantitative estimations of indirect economic losses caused by earthquakes. The calculation is based on the forward and backward correlation between industries in the world measured by the World Input-Output Database (WIOD): and a hypothesis of demand reductions (backward linkages) caused by Wenchuan earthquake is made in the paper.

(2) Quantitative estimations of indirect economic loss caused by disasters. Most of the scholars use Computable General Equilibrium (CGE) and Input-output Model for the quantitative estimations of indirect economic loss caused by disasters. For instance, Cochrane (1984) used the CGE model relatively early to simulate the impact of disasters on the regional economy. Okuyama et al. (1999) estimated the impact of earthquakes on areas occurred and other parts of Japan. Narayan employed the CGE model to assess the indirect economic losses brought by Hurricane Ami at Fiji Island. Tsuchiya et al. (2007) embedded the Traffic Flow Model in the regional CGE model to calculate the indirect effect caused by Niigata earthquake on adjacent areas via estimating the changes of freight flow and passenger flow there. Tirasirichai and Enke (2007) estimated the indirect loss due to damaged highway bridges by a regional CGE model. Hiroyuki Shibusawa et al. (2011) comprehensively divided Japan into 47 regions and constructed a dynamic CGE model containing regional commodity flows and regional investment dynamic modules to estimate of the indirect economic impact and regional distribution caused by earthquakes occurred in Tokai district, Japan. Particularly, Rose (2004) put forward the concept of "Resilience", based on which Rose and Liao (2005) calculated the economic losses caused by the interruption of Portland's urban water system to other sectors and regions after an earthquake with the CGE model. There are also other scholars who used different methods. Giving examples, Hanan et al. (2018) used the generalized Moment method (GMM) to study efficiency of disaster relief, the result showed that in a sample of 110 low - and middle-income countries, the higher the centrality of the health assistance network, the higher the child survival rate, if the amount of health assistance was controlled. Cejun et al. (2018) set up a multi-objective mixed integer nonlinear programming model, and provided a tool for decision makers to optimize the relief distribution network and inventory structure as well as alleviate the suffering of victims. Erik Alda et al. (2019) adopted data envelope-analysis (DEA) to analyze 106 countries receiving aid between 2010 and 2016, showing aid efficiency in 106 countries could be improved by an average of 20 to 50 per

cent. But this paper focuses on adopting the input-output method to study international aid.

Many scholars also used the input-output model to assess the indirect economic impact caused by disasters in various industrial sectors. For example, Haimes et al. (2005) put forward an inoperability input-output model to conduct a comparative analysis on situations of various departments in each region after disasters. Besides, Growher et al. (2007) assessed the economic losses to American basic industrial system caused by Hurricane Katrina and Rita and ordered different industries according to the degree of the impact based on the inoperability input-output model. Wu et al. (2017) assessed the indirect economic losses resulting from the Wenchuan earthquake in China on May 12th, 2008. Okuyama (2018) detaily stated the dynamic input-output models and their applications to estimate the indirect economic losses brought by natural disasters to various industries.

From the perspective of these two methods, faced with specific circumstances in each country, it is difficult to set parameters in different regions and industrial departments via CGE model because of its complex structure, massive scale, and numerous equations and parameters. The construction of the CGE model in different countries requires cooperation among researchers from all over the world, which poses obstacles to the assessment of indirect economic losses. On the contrary, the construction of the input-output model is relatively easy because it is the main core module of the CGE model and is based on the general equilibrium theory, thus theoretically maintaining the relative completeness and the conciseness practically. Besides, with the accessibility to data, it is suitable for estimating indirect economic losses caused by certain disasters to other related regions and countries. Therefore, the input-output model is applied in this paper to calculate the indirect economic losses caused by the Wenchuan earthquake to other countries.

## 11.3 Definitions, Steps and Indices

### *11.3.1 Working Definitions*

The principles and concepts involved in this study were defined below.

(1) The principles of international aid amount. The amount of aid should be matched with the indirect economic loss to a donor. In other words, the greater the indirect economic loss caused by a natural disaster to a donor is, the more the donor should aid. Additionally, the amount of aid should also match the donor's payment ability. Namely, the greater the donor's payment ability is, the more it should aid. The evaluation index can be expressed as formula (11.1).

(2) Direct economic loss. Only when the data on direct economic losses to sub-industrial sectors in other countries is obtained after a disaster, can indirect economic losses be calculated according to the inter-regional input-output

model. The overall economic losses and casualties are counted by the emergency database (EM-DAT) and so on after the disaster, but there is no data on direct economic losses to sub-industrial sectors. As a result, the direct economic losses caused by the Wenchuan earthquake of 2008 to industries (altogether 15 industrial sectors) in Sichuan assessed by the Chinese government were used in this study. In line with the industrial classification standards, the 15 sectors were decomposed into 56 industrial sectors on the WIOD table (see Table 11.1). Then based on the direct economic losses of these sectors after classification, the indirect economic losses were calculated according to Formula (11.13) (For specific data processing, please refer to the section of "5.2 Data description").

(3) Indirect economic loss. According to the statement in the section of "2.2 Estimations of indirect economic loss caused by disasters", in the present paper, the definition of indirect loss given by the Standardization Administration of China's (2011) was adopted. Due to data limitations, the indirect losses here mainly refer to the loss caused by earthquakes and other industrial-related losses.

(4) Payment ability. A country's payment ability to launch aid action is affected by a variety of factors, such as its aid budget, disposable fiscal revenue, and GDP. Nonetheless, it is difficult to get the data on other countries' aid budgets and disposable financial revenues. Furthermore, the payment ability is an absolute index which will be used to compare the world's GDP to figure out the recommended aid amount (see Eqs. (11.4)). Therefore, for the sake of data convenience and simplicity, GDP was used as an index to measure the payment ability of a country.

### *11.3.2 Research Steps*

(1) The direct economic losses were secured. Through the search for related documents, the economic losses brought by the May 12th Wenchuan earthquake to various industries in Sichuan were obtained.

(2) The indirect economic losses were calculated. The indirect economic losses caused by the May 12th Wenchuan earthquake to other countries were calculated based on the data on world input-output tables via Formula (11.13) after the economic losses caused by the earthquake to various industries in Sichuan Province were decomposed into 56 industrial sectors on the WIOD table.

(3) The amount of international aid from each country was calculated on the basis of its indirect economic loss. Assuming that the proportion of indirect economic losses in different countries is equal to the proportion of aid, a country's aid amount should be larger if its indirect economic loss is higher. On this basis, each country's aid amount was identified.

(4) The amount of international aid from each country was calculated on the basis of its payment ability. Assuming that the proportion of payment ability in different countries is equal to the proportion of aid, a country's aid amount

**Table 11.1** Comparison of 15 industries in "5.12 Wenchuan earthquake" and 56 industries in WIOD

| Industries in *China Statistical Yearbook* | Industries in *WIOD* |
|---|---|
| Agriculture | Crop and animal production, hunting and related service activities |
| Mining and Washing of Coal | Mining and quarrying |
| Extraction of Petroleum and Natural Gas | |
| Mining and Processing of Metal Ores | |
| Mining and Processing of Non-Metal Ores | |
| Manufacture of Foods and Tobacco | Manufacture of food products, beverages, and tobacco products |
| Production and Supply of Electric Power and Heat Power | Electricity, gas, steam and air conditioning supply |
| Production and Supply of Gas | |
| Production and Supply of Water | Water collection, treatment, and supply |
| Wholesale and retail trade | Wholesale and retail trade and repair of motor vehicles and motorcycles |
| | Wholesale trade, except motor vehicles and motorcycles |
| | Retail trade, except motor vehicles and motorcycles |
| Transportation and warehousing | Land transport and transport via pipelines |
| | Water transport |
| | Air transport |
| | Warehousing and support activities for transportation |
| Accommodation and food service activities | Accommodation and food service activities |
| Culture, sports, and entertainment | Publishing activities |
| | Motion picture, video and television programme production, sound recording and music publishing activities; programming and broadcasting activities |
| Information transmission, computer and software services | Telecommunications |
| | Computer programming, consultancy, and related activities; information service activities |
| Health, social security, and social welfare undertakings | Insurance, reinsurance and pension funding, except compulsory social security |
| Real estate | Real estate activities |
| Scientific research | Scientific research and development |
| Comprehensive technical service | Advertising and market research |
| | Other professional, scientific and technical activities; veterinary activities |

(continued)

**Table 11.1** (continued)

| Industries in *China Statistical Yearbook* | Industries in *WIOD* |
|---|---|
| | Administrative and support service activities |
| Public administration and social organization | Public administration and defence; compulsory social security |
| | Activities of extraterritorial organizations and bodies |
| Education | Education |
| Other social services | Human health and social work activities |
| | Other service activities |
| | Activities of households as employers; undifferentiated goods- and services-producing activities of households for own use |

*Note* Due to lack of data, The tourism industry in *China Statistical Yearbook* and the industries in *WIOD* as follows were not calculated: Manufacture of textiles, wearing apparel and leather products; Manufacture of wood and of products of wood and cork, except furniture; manufacture of articles of straw and plaiting materials; Manufacture of paper and paper products; Printing and reproduction of recorded media; Manufacture of coke and refined petroleum products; Manufacture of chemicals and chemical products; Manufacture of basic pharmaceutical products and pharmaceutical preparations; Manufacture of rubber and plastic products; Manufacture of other non-metallic mineral products; Manufacture of basic metals; Manufacture of fabricated metal products, except machinery and equipment; Manufacture of computer, electronic and optical products; Manufacture of electrical equipment; Manufacture of machinery and equipment n.e.c.; Manufacture of motor vehicles, trailers and semi-trailers; Manufacture of other transport equipment; Manufacture of furniture; other manufacturing; Repair and installation of machinery and equipment; Sewerage; waste collection, treatment and disposal activities; materials recovery; remediation activities and other waste management services; Construction; Postal and courier activities; Financial service activities, except insurance and pension funding; Activities auxiliary to financial services and insurance activities; Legal and accounting activities; activities of head offices; management consultancy activities; Architectural and engineering activities; technical testing and analysis; Forestry and logging; Fishing and aquaculture

should be more if its payment ability is greater. On this basis, each country's aid amount was located. Then the recommended amount of international aid was recalculated by considering both the indirect economic loss and payment ability of a country.

The flow chart of this study was shown in Fig. 11.1.

### 11.3.3 Evaluative Indices for Recommending the Amount of Aid

According to the above definitions and the research steps, the following evaluative indices and calculation formulae for the amount of aid were constructed:

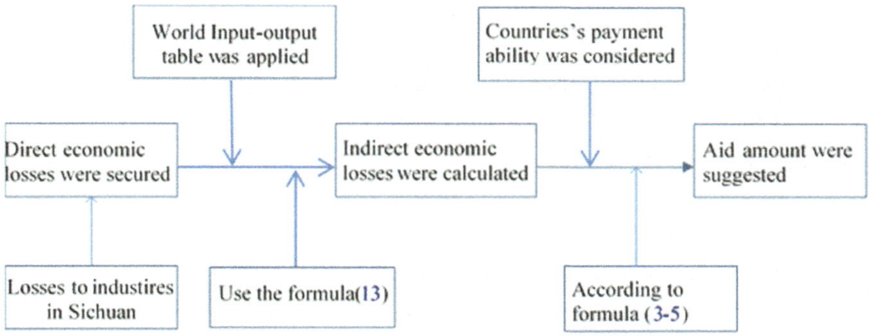


**Fig. 11.1** A flowchart of the study

(1) The formula for calculating the ratio of actual aid amount to the indirect economic loss to donor countries can be expressed as follows:

Index 1:

$$\text{Aid amount of a donor country}/\text{GDP of a donor country} \tag{11.1}$$

(2) The formula for calculating the ratio of actual aid amount to the payment ability of donor countries can be expressed as follows:

Index 2:

$$\text{Aid amount of a donor country}/\text{GDP of a donor country} \tag{11.2}$$

(3) If only the indirect economic loss to the donor countries is considered, the recommended aid amount can be expressed as follows:

Formula 1:

$$\begin{aligned}&\text{Amount of a country's recommended aid when considering its indirect economic loss}\\&= \text{Indirect economic loss to the country}\\&\quad /\text{Total indirect economic loss to all countries in the world}\\&\quad \times \text{Total amount of all countries' aid}\end{aligned} \tag{11.3}$$

(4) If only the payment ability of the donor countries is considered, the recommended aid amount can be expressed as follows:

Formula 2:

$$\begin{aligned}&\text{Amount of a country's recommended aid when considering its payment ability}\\&= \text{GDP of the country}\\&\quad /\text{Total GDP of all countries in the world}\end{aligned}$$

$$\times \text{ Total amount of all countries' aid} \tag{11.4}$$

(5) If both the indirect economic loss and payment ability of the donor countries are considered, the recommended aid amount can be expressed as follows:

Formula 3:

$$\begin{aligned}
&\text{Total amount of a country's recommended aid} \\
&= \text{Indirect economic loss to the country} \\
&\quad /\text{Total amount of the indirect economic losses to all countries} \\
&\quad \times \text{ Total amount of all countries' aid} \times \text{Weight 1} \\
&\quad + \text{GDP of the country/Total GDP of all countries in the world} \\
&\quad \times \text{ Total amount of all countries' aid} \times \text{Weight 2}
\end{aligned} \tag{11.5}$$

Among them, Weight 1 and Weight 2 can be assigned according to expert knowledge (the assignments are 0.75 and 0.25 respectively in this paper): and the sum of the two is 1.

## 11.4 Input-Output Model

As the last paragraph in Part of "2.2 Estimations of indirect economic loss caused by disasters" stated, the input-output model was chosen to calculate the indirect economic loss. Next, we will explain structure of international input-output table and detail calculation formulae.

International input-output tables are the empirical basis for the inter-regional input-output model. A typical input-output table is a matrix with columns and rows interlaced with each other. It depicts economic ties and distribution relations between sectors from the perspective of input sources of production and distribution direction of products, thereby comprehensively reflecting production, distribution, exchange, and consumption between sectors in different countries.

At present, most of the scholars employed *World Input-Output Tables of 2008* (*WIOD2008*) released by Timmer et al. (2015, 2016): the specific form of which was shown in Table 11.2. As was shown, there were $m$ different countries, and each country had $n$ different industrial sectors. The same classification of sectors applied to all countries. As for the intermediate input section, the main diagonal part denoted the internal economic structure of each country, while the non-main diagonal part denoted the economic and trade relations between countries. The final demand section consisted of sub-matrices of final demand from different countries to record the use of various sectors' products in different countries. Similarly, the added value section was also divided into several sub-matrices of added value in different countries to record their added value.

**Table 11.2** Inter-regional input-output table

| Output | | | Intermediate consumption | | | | | | | Final consumption | | | | | | Total output |
|---|---|---|---|---|---|---|---|---|---|---|---|---|---|---|---|---|
| | | | Country 1 | | | … | Country m | | | Country 1 | | … | Country m | | Export | |
| Input | | | Industry 1 | … | Industry n | … | Industry 1 | … | Industry n | Final consumption expenditure | Total investment forming | … | Final consumption expenditure | Total investment forming | | |
| Intermediate input | Country 1 | Country 1 | $X_{ij}^{rs}$ | | | | | | | $F_{ij}^{rs}$ | | | | | $S_i^r$ | $X_i^r$ |
| | | … | | | | | | | | | | | | | | |
| | | Country n | | | | | | | | | | | | | | |
| | … | … | | | | | | | | | | | | | | |
| | Country m | Country 1 | | | | | | | | | | | | | | |
| | | … | | | | | | | | | | | | | | |
| | | Country n | | | | | | | | | | | | | | |
| Value-added | | | $V_j^s$ | | | | | | | | | | | | | |

According to the row balance relationship in the input-output table, it holds the following balance equation:

$$\sum_{s=1}^{m}\sum_{j=1}^{n} x_{ij}^{rs} + \sum_{s=1}^{m}\sum_{k=1}^{2} f_{ik}^{rs} + s_i^r = x_i^r \text{ , } \forall r, i \tag{11.6}$$

$c_i^r = \sum_{s=1}^{m}\sum_{k=1}^{2} f_{ik}^{rs} + s_i^r$ represents the final consumption of industry $i$ in country $r$, and $x_i^r$ refers to the total output of industry $i$ in country $r$.

$$\sum_{s=1}^{m}\sum_{j=1}^{n} x_{ij}^{rs} + c_i^r = x_i^r \text{ , } \forall r, i \tag{11.7}$$

The relationship given in Eq. (11.7) can also be expressed in the matrix form as follows:

$$X_{ij}^{rs} E + C_i^r = X_i^r \tag{11.8}$$

where $X_{ij}^{rs}$ is the intermediate consumption matrix ($mn \times mn$): $E$ is a $mn \times 1$ column matrix, whose entries are identically 1 s, $C_i^r$ is the final consumption matrix ($mn \times 1$): and $X_i^r$ is the total output matrix ($mn \times 1$).

We now introduce the technical coefficient matrix $A$ (see illustration below): whose entries are defined as $a_{ij}^{rs} = x_{ij}^{rs}/x_j^s$, the ratios of the consumption of industry $j$ of country $s$ in industry $i$ of country $r$ to the total input of industry $j$ of country $s$ (also known as the intermediate consumption of the products by industry $j$ of country $s$ in industry $i$ of country $r$, abbreviated as an intermediate consumption coefficient. It should be noted that $A$ is a $mn \times mn$ matrix, as illustrated in the following:

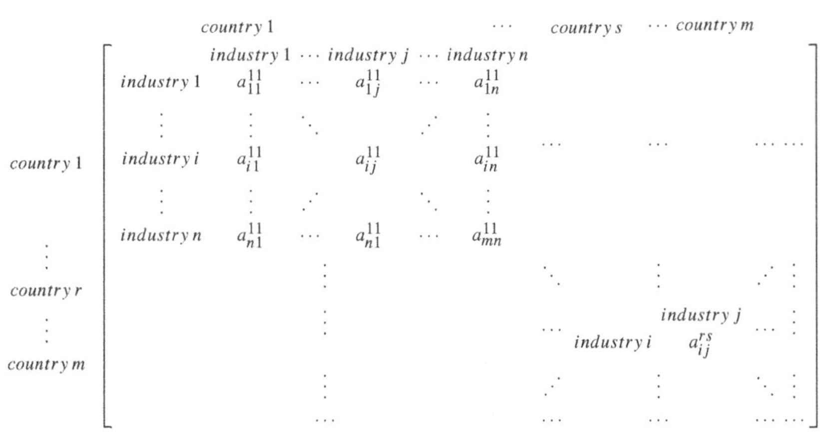


Matrix $A$ has the following two properties:

$$a_{ij}^{rs} \geq 0(\forall r, s = 1, 2, \cdots, m; \forall i, j = 1, 2, \cdots, n)$$

and $\sum_{r=1}^{m} \sum_{i=1}^{n} a_{ij}^{rs} < 1(\forall s = 1, 2, \cdots, m; \forall j = 1, 2, \cdots, n)$

In the inter-regional input-output table, the total input is equal to the total output of each industry. Since the matrix $X_i^r$ is the transpose of a matrix $X_j^s$. It holds that $X_{ij}^{rs}E = AX_i^r$. Then Formula (11.8) results in the following:

$$AX_i^r + C_i^r = X_i^r \tag{11.9}$$

which yields the matrix equation

$$(I - A)^{-1} C_i^r = X_i^r \tag{11.10}$$

where the matrix $(I - A)^{-1}$ is the Leontief inverse matrix.

The variable form of Formula (11.10) is:

$$(I - A)^{-1} \Delta C_i^r = \Delta X_i^r \tag{11.11}$$

Due to the correlation between regions, the variation of the final consumption $C_i^r$ will lead to the alteration of the total output $X_i^r$. In the disaster analysis, according to Wu et al. (2017): direct economic loss can be considered the final consumption reduction and indirect economic losses can be considered the total output reduction get rid of the final consumption reduction, According to (11): we will calculate the total output reduction, which results from the final consumption reduction. $\Delta X_i^r$ can be expanded as the following form:

$$\Delta X_i^r = \begin{bmatrix} \Delta x_1^1 \\ \vdots \\ \Delta x_i^1 \\ \vdots \\ \Delta x_n^1 \\ \vdots \\ \Delta x_1^r \\ \vdots \\ \Delta x_i^r \\ \vdots \\ \Delta x_n^r \\ \vdots \\ \vdots \end{bmatrix} \begin{matrix} industry\ 1 \\ \vdots \\ industry\ i \\ \vdots \\ industry\ n \\ \vdots \\ industry\ 1 \\ \vdots \\ industry\ i \\ \vdots \\ industry\ n \\ \vdots \\ \vdots \end{matrix} \begin{matrix} \\ \\ country\ 1 \\ \\ \\ \vdots \\ \\ \\ country\ r \\ \\ \vdots \\ country\ m \\ \\ \end{matrix} \tag{11.12}$$

where $\Delta x_i^r$ is an element of $\Delta X_i^r$, and it represents the total output loss value in the industry $i$ of country $r$, from the final consumption reduction $\Delta C_i^r$.

By adding together, the losses in the total outputs of all industries in each affected country, we can obtain the loss in the total output for the country. Then, we will get the indirect economic loss value of country by subtracting the final consumption reduction from the total output loss values. This can be illustrated in terms of the following equation (using the Wenchuan earthquake example):

$$\Delta X^r = \sum_{i=1}^{41} (\Delta x_i^r - \Delta c_i^r), r = 1, 2, \ldots, m \tag{11.13}$$

$\Delta X^r$ is the indirect economic loss value of country $r$. $\Delta x_i^r$ is an element of $\Delta X_i^r$ representing the total output loss values in industry $i$ of country $r$. $\Delta c_i^r$ is an element of the final consumption reduction $\Delta C_i^r$, and it represents the final consumption reduction in industry $i$ of country $r$.

## 11.5 Case and Data

### *11.5.1 Case Introduction*

The May 12th Wenchuan earthquake occurred at 14:28:01 China Standard Time (UTC + 8) on May 12th, 2008, measuring at 8.0 Ms on the Richter magnitude scale, 8.3 Mw on the moment magnitude scale and XI on the China seismic intensity scale. The earthquake's epicenter was located in Wenchuan County of Sichuan Province. The hardest-hit zone included 10 counties and cities in Sichuan Province, such as Wenchuan County; the harder-hit zone included 29 counties and cities in Sichuan Province, 8 counties, and cities in Gansu Province and 4 counties and cities in Shaanxi Province. According to the report by the Ministry of Civil Affairs of China, the Wenchuan earthquake caused 69,227 known deaths, 374,644 injured and 17,923 missing as of 12 o'clock on September 25th, 2008. Besides, this earthquake resulted in a direct economic loss of 845.2 billion yuan as of September 4th, 2008. To be specific, Sichuan suffered most, occupying 91.3% of the total loss; Gansu accounted for 5.8% of the total loss; Shaanxi took up 2.9% of the total loss. The Wenchuan earthquake was the most destructive earthquake since the founding of China and the most deadly one after the Tangshan earthquake. And because of the occurrence of the Wenchuan earthquake, it was approved by the State Council of China that May 12th be the national disaster prevention and disaster reduction day every year from 2009. Taking into account the huge impact of the May 12th Wenchuan earthquake on China and the great concern from countries all over the world, this disaster as a research case in this paper had better exemplary significance.

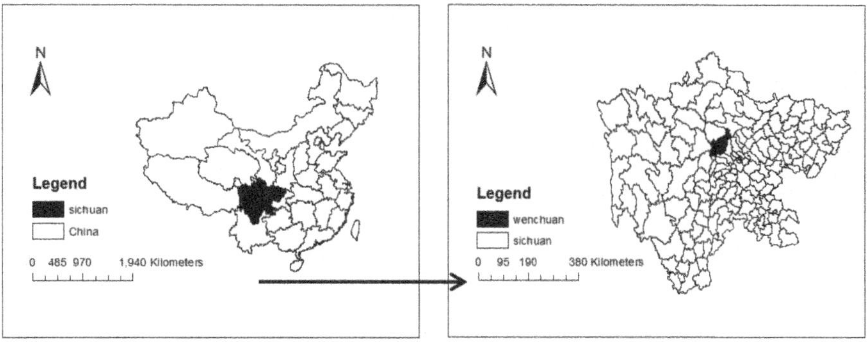


**Fig. 11.2** Location of Wenchuan County in China

Wenchuan County is located in the eastern edge of the Qinghai-tibet Plateau, northwest of Sichuan Province. At the end of 2007, Shenzhen has a total area of 8820 km$^2$ and a permanent population of 105, 436. Figure 11.2 showed the location of Wenchuan County in China.

### *11.5.2 Data Description*

(1) Direct economic losses brought by the Wenchuan earthquake. Since the May 12th Wenchuan earthquake occurred mostly in Sichuan Province, the economic losses to Sichuan Province were mainly considered in this paper. The data on direct economic losses to Sichuan Province came from the statistical data released by the Statistics Bureau of Sichuan, as well as the *Statistical System of Natural Disasters* released by the Ministry of Civil Affairs of China in 2008 and the relevant book account lists. According to the information provided by the Statistics Bureau of Sichuan, the total direct economic loss caused by the Wenchuan earthquake in Sichuan Province was as high as 737.197 billion yuan. There were 15 sectors suffering direct economic losses in Sichuan. To go into detail, the construction sector suffered the largest loss of 363.3 billion yuan, occupying 49.27% of the total direct economic loss; the second and third badly damaged sectors were the service sector and the transportation and warehousing sector, accounting for 16.61% and 10.17% of the total direct economic loss respectively.

Based on *International Standard Industrial Classification*, Revision 4 (ISIC Rev. 4): industries were classified into 56 sectors in world input-output tables. However, the 15 sectors with economic losses in Sichuan did not adhere strictly to this industrial classification method. Therefore, first of all, the 15 sectors in Sichuan were decomposed into 56 sectors in China according to the sector's name and connotation (the decomposition of industrial sectors was specified in Table 11.1). Then, in line with the proportion of the total output of the 15 sectors to the total output of the original 56 sectors, the direct losses were allocated to 56 industrial sectors in China. After that, the direct economic losses after classification served as the disturbance term $\Delta C_i^r$ were substituted into Formula (11.11) to calculate the indirect economic losses $\Delta X_i^r$ to different industries of every country.

(2) Other data. World input-output tables were offered by *WIOD2008*. The GDP data for countries in 2008 came from the World Bank's statistics. In addition, according to the website of the Ministry of Foreign Affairs of China, the data on the amount of aid from all countries and organizations after the Wenchuan earthquake were obtained.

## 11.6 Empirical Analysis

### *11.6.1 Analysis of Aid Situation*

The indirect economic losses to countries were calculated by Formula (11.13). And the actual aid amount and GDP data of all countries were collected. Then the aid situations of the world's main countries after the Wenchuan earthquake were obtained on the basis of Formulas (11.1) and (11.2). The results were shown in Table 11.3 as follows.

As could be seen from Table 11.3, the average and standard deviation of donation of these countries are 168.670 ten thousand dollars and 341.093, respectively. The countries with the ratio of aid amount to indirect economic loss above the average were as follows (in descending order): Indonesia, Australia, South Korea, Spain, Japan, Turkey, the United States, Italy, and Russia. In other words, these countries aided "too much". By contrast, the countries with the ratio of aid amount to indirect economic loss below the average were as follows (in ascending order): Lithuania, Estonia, Malta, Cyprus, Luxemburg and others up to 35 countries in total. Namely, these countries aided "too little".

From the ratio of donation to GDP ($10^{-4}$): the average and standard deviation are 0.016 and 0.017, respectively. The countries with the ratio of aid amount to GDP above the average were as follows (in descending order): Indonesia, Australia, South Korea, Romania, Hungary and others up to 15 countries in all. In other words, these countries aided "too much". The countries with the ratio of aid amount to GDP below the average were as follows (in ascending order): India, Finland, Lithuania, Latvia, Norway and others up to 26 countries in total. Namely, these countries aided "too little" (Fig. 11.3).

Next, the aid situation was reflected by the two above-mentioned indices in a comprehensive way. The results were presented in Fig. 11.4. In this figure, the horizontal axis denoted the ratio of aid amount to an indirect economic loss, and the vertical axis denoted the ratio of aid amount to GDP.

**Table 11.3** Evaluation results based on indirect economic losses and GDP data

| Country | Donation (ten thousand dollars) | Indirect economic losses (hundred million dollars) | Donation/Indirect economic losses ($10^{-4}$) | GDP of 2008 (hundred million dollars) | Donation/GDP ($10^{-4}$) |
|---|---|---|---|---|---|
| AUS | 617.806 | 598.795 | 1.032 | 10553.348 | 0.059 |
| AUT | 15.134 | 460.924 | 0.033 | 4302.943 | 0.004 |
| BEL | 56.452 | 618.577 | 0.091 | 5186.259 | 0.011 |
| BGR | 12.271 | 394.200 | 0.031 | 544.091 | 0.023 |
| BRA | 105.048 | 577.035 | 0.182 | 16958.245 | 0.006 |
| CAN | 120.405 | 1393.816 | 0.086 | 15491.312 | 0.008 |
| CHE | 24.671 | 568.905 | 0.043 | 1796.385 | 0.014 |
| CYP | 4.614 | 613.776 | 0.008 | 278.395 | 0.017 |
| CZE | 31.223 | 367.278 | 0.085 | 2357.186 | 0.013 |
| DEU | 229.278 | 1258.333 | 0.182 | 37523.656 | 0.006 |
| DNK | 26.586 | 538.549 | 0.049 | 3533.611 | 0.008 |
| ESP | 484.679 | 698.794 | 0.694 | 16350.154 | 0.030 |
| EST | 1.984 | 409.174 | 0.005 | 241.940 | 0.008 |
| FIN | 11.052 | 432.017 | 0.026 | 9362.282 | 0.001 |
| FRA | 99.832 | 1021.283 | 0.098 | 29234.657 | 0.003 |
| GBR | 191.545 | 961.015 | 0.199 | 28905.643 | 0.007 |
| GRC | 17.958 | 337.421 | 0.053 | 3544.608 | 0.005 |
| HRV | 9.138 | 391.881 | 0.023 | 704.815 | 0.013 |
| HUN | 53.462 | 340.602 | 0.157 | 1579.984 | 0.034 |
| IDN | 476.755 | 394.335 | 1.209 | 5432.539 | 0.088 |
| IND | 12.437 | 625.078 | 0.020 | 11869.528 | 0.001 |
| IRL | 39.843 | 697.881 | 0.057 | 2750.200 | 0.015 |
| ITA | 222.972 | 795.334 | 0.280 | 23907.292 | 0.009 |
| JPN | 997.366 | 1805.585 | 0.552 | 50379.085 | 0.020 |
| KOR | 468.949 | 612.433 | 0.766 | 10022.191 | 0.047 |
| LTU | 0.722 | 370.015 | 0.002 | 478.506 | 0.002 |
| LUX | 12.541 | 647.914 | 0.019 | 558.497 | 0.023 |
| LVA | 0.692 | 17.117 | 0.040 | 355.960 | 0.002 |
| MEX | 46.666 | 563.548 | 0.083 | 11012.753 | 0.004 |
| MLT | 2.268 | 478.836 | 0.005 | 89.772 | 0.025 |
| NLD | 98.803 | 653.167 | 0.151 | 9362.282 | 0.011 |
| NOR | 15.395 | 518.933 | 0.030 | 4625.544 | 0.003 |

(continued)

**Table 11.3** (continued)

| Country | Donation (ten thousand dollars) | Indirect economic losses (hundred million dollars) | Donation/Indirect economic losses ($10^{-4}$) | GDP of 2008 (hundred million dollars) | Donation/GDP ($10^{-4}$) |
|---|---|---|---|---|---|
| POL | 23.828 | 371.789 | 0.064 | 5338.158 | 0.005 |
| PRT | 57.525 | 354.719 | 0.162 | 2620.076 | 0.022 |
| ROU | 73.032 | 311.605 | 0.234 | 2081.816 | 0.035 |
| RUS | 121.850 | 440.246 | 0.277 | 16608.444 | 0.007 |
| SVK | 11.309 | 252.554 | 0.045 | 1003.246 | 0.011 |
| SVN | 7.246 | 376.121 | 0.019 | 555.899 | 0.013 |
| SWE | 23.369 | 610.913 | 0.038 | 5139.657 | 0.005 |
| TUR | 220.509 | 489.703 | 0.450 | 7643.357 | 0.029 |
| USA | 1868.270 | 5696.162 | 0.328 | 147185.820 | 0.013 |
| Average | 168.670 | 708.936 | 0.193 | 12377.320 | 0.016 |
| Standard deviation | 341.093 | 860.232 | 0.280 | 24278.626 | 0.017 |
| Total | 6915.487 | 29066.365 | 0.238 | 507470.000 | 0.014 |

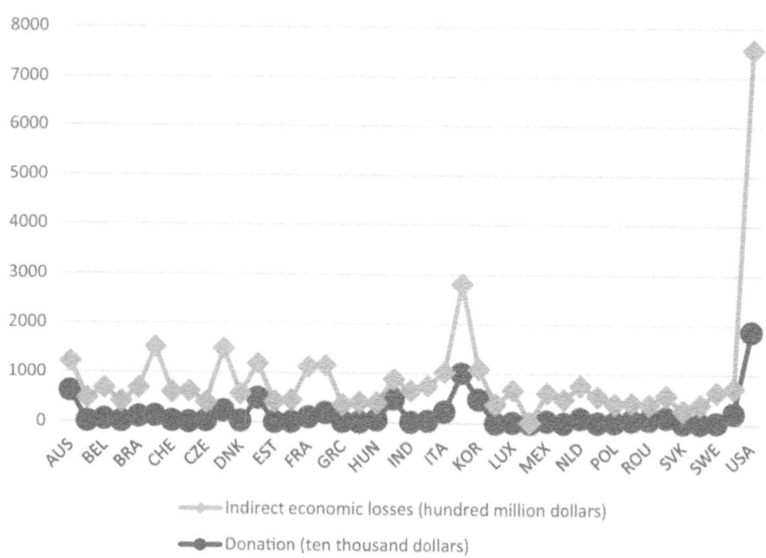


**Fig. 11.3** Compares the countries' donation and indirect economic losses

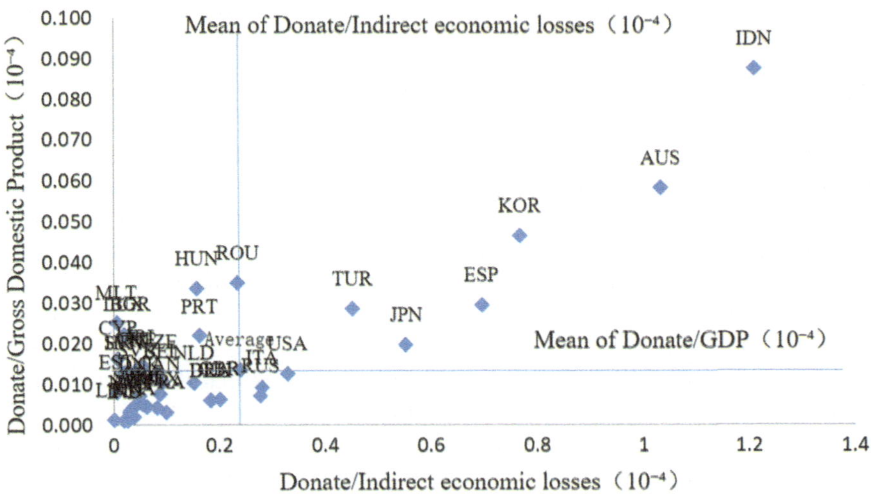


**Fig. 11.4** A comprehensive analyses of aid-GDP ratio and the aid-loss ratio, *Note*: The horizontal line meant the average ratio of aid amount to GDP (1/10000): measuring at 0.0136; the vertical line meant the average ratio of aid amount to indirect economic loss (1/10000): measuring at 0.238

With the average ratio of aid amount to GDP and the average ratio of aid amount to indirect economic loss forming two demarcation lines, the 41 donors were divided into four quadrants. Specifically speaking, the upper right, upper left, lower right, and lower left was the first, second, third and fourth quadrant respectively.

The first quadrant covered countries that aided more than they should (their ratio of aid amount to the indirect economic loss was above the average) and more than they could (their ratio of aid amount to GDP was above the average). There were 6 such countries, namely Indonesia, Australia, South Korea, Spain, Turkey, and Japan. The second quadrant covered countries that aided less than they should but more than they could, including Romania, Hungary, Malta, Bulgaria, Luxemburg, Portugal, Cyprus, Ireland and Chile up to 9 countries altogether. The third quadrant covered countries that aided more than they should but less than they could, including the United States, Italy and Russia up to 3 countries in all. The fourth quadrant covered countries that aided less than they should and less than they could, including Czech, Croatia, Slovenia, Slovakia, Belgium, Holland, Estonia, Canada, Denmark, Britain, Brazil, Germany, Greece, Poland, Sweden, Mexico, Austria, France, Norway, Latvia, Lithuania, Finland and India up to 23 countries in total.

### *11.6.2 Recommendation of Aid Amount*

According to the above analysis, the aid situation in the afore-mentioned countries seemed unfair. For this reason, according to Formula (11.3): (11.4): and (11.5):

the amount of the recommended aid from each country was calculated respectively under three conditions, namely when considering only the indirect economic loss, considering only the payment ability, and considering the both, as shown in the following table.

The above Table 11.4 gave recommended aid amounts for the 41 countries in consideration of their indirect economic losses and payment ability. Taking indirect economic losses into account, it was suggested that the United States, Japan, Canada, Germany, and France lend the largest aid, namely 13,552.34, 4,295.86, 3,316.18, 2,993.83 and 2,429.84 thousand U.S. dollars respectively and that Hungary, Greece, Romania, Slovakia, and Latvia lend the smallest aid, namely 810.36 802.79, 741.37, 600.88 and 40.73 thousand U.S. dollars respectively.

Taking payment ability into account, it was suggested that the United States, Japan, Germany, France, and Britain lend the largest aid, namely 20,057.6, 6,865.3, 5,113.5, 3,983.9, and 3,939.1 thousand U.S. dollars respectively, and that Lithuania, Latvia, Cyprus, Estonia, and Malta lend the smallest aid, namely 65.2, 48.5, 37.9, 33.0 and 12.2 thousand U.S. dollars respectively.

It could be seen that the recommended aid amount varied greatly with different evaluation indices. For instance, Luxemburg should aid 1,541.52 thousand U.S. dollars taking its indirect economic loss into account, or it could aid 76.1 thousand U.S. dollars taking its payment ability into account.

Given that this paper mainly considered indirect economic losses, the indirect economic loss to a country enjoyed a higher weight (for example, 3/4) while its payment ability had a lower weight (for example, 1/4) to offer the ultimate recommended amount for each country, as depicted in the last column of Table 11.3. It was suggested in the last that the United States, Japan, Germany, Canada, and France lend the largest aid, namely 15,178.66, 4,938.22, 3,523.75, 3,014.91 and 2,818.36 thousand U.S. dollars respectively and that Lithuania, Hungary, Romania, Slovakia, and Latvia lend the smallest aid, namely 676.56, 661.60, 626.95, 484.84 and 42.67 thousand U.S. dollars respectively.

The donation and suggest donation of countries can be seen in Fig. 11.5.

## 11.7 Conclusion

### 11.7.1 Implication and Contribution

Post-disaster assistance is an important factor for disaster reduction and sustainable development of communities. However, for lack of post-disaster assistance standards, not only the theorical study of disaster management is incomplete but also the unfairness potentially breeding among donor countries and the mutual aid is unregulated and unsustainable.

**Table 11.4** Suggest donation based on indirect economic losses and GDP

| Country | Donations for Wenchuan earthquake till July 7, 2008 (ten thousand dollars) | Suggest donation based on indirect economics losses (ten thousand dollars) | Suggest donation based on GDP (ten thousand dollars) | Suggest comprehensive donation based on indirect economic losses and GDP (ten thousand dollars) (Third column data × 0.75 + fourth column data × 0.25)) |
|---|---|---|---|---|
| AUS | 617.806 | 142.466 | 143.814 | 142.802 |
| AUT | 15.134 | 109.663 | 58.638 | 96.907 |
| BEL | 56.452 | 147.172 | 70.675 | 128.049 |
| BGR | 12.271 | 93.788 | 7.415 | 72.194 |
| BRA | 105.048 | 137.288 | 231.096 | 160.741 |
| CAN | 120.405 | 331.618 | 211.106 | 301.491 |
| CHE | 24.671 | 135.354 | 24.480 | 107.636 |
| CYP | 4.614 | 146.030 | 3.794 | 110.470 |
| CZE | 31.223 | 87.383 | 32.122 | 73.567 |
| DEU | 229.278 | 299.383 | 511.349 | 352.375 |
| DNK | 26.586 | 128.132 | 48.154 | 108.137 |
| ESP | 484.679 | 166.257 | 222.810 | 180.395 |
| EST | 1.984 | 97.351 | 3.297 | 73.838 |
| FIN | 11.052 | 102.786 | 127.583 | 108.985 |
| FRA | 99.832 | 242.984 | 398.392 | 281.836 |
| GBR | 191.545 | 228.645 | 393.908 | 269.961 |
| GRC | 17.958 | 80.279 | 48.304 | 72.284 |
| HRV | 9.138 | 93.236 | 9.605 | 72.327 |
| HUN | 53.462 | 81.036 | 21.531 | 66.160 |
| IDN | 476.755 | 93.821 | 74.031 | 88.873 |
| IND | 12.437 | 148.719 | 161.751 | 151.977 |
| IRL | 39.843 | 166.040 | 37.478 | 133.900 |
| ITA | 222.972 | 189.226 | 325.794 | 223.367 |
| JPN | 997.366 | 429.586 | 686.535 | 493.822 |
| KOR | 468.949 | 145.710 | 136.576 | 143.428 |
| LTU | 0.722 | 88.034 | 6.521 | 67.656 |
| LUX | 12.541 | 154.152 | 7.611 | 117.517 |
| LVA | 0.692 | 4.073 | 4.851 | 4.267 |
| MEX | 46.666 | 134.080 | 150.075 | 138.078 |

(continued)

**Table 11.4** (continued)

| Country | Donations for Wenchuan earthquake till July 7, 2008 (ten thousand dollars) | Suggest donation based on indirect economics losses (ten thousand dollars) | Suggest donation based on GDP (ten thousand dollars) | Suggest comprehensive donation based on indirect economic losses and GDP (ten thousand dollars) (Third column data × 0.75 + fourth column data × 0.25)) |
|---|---|---|---|---|
| MLT | 2.268 | 113.925 | 1.223 | 85.749 |
| NLD | 98.803 | 155.402 | 127.583 | 148.447 |
| NOR | 15.395 | 123.465 | 63.034 | 108.356 |
| POL | 23.828 | 88.456 | 72.745 | 84.530 |
| PRT | 57.525 | 84.395 | 35.705 | 72.221 |
| ROU | 73.032 | 74.137 | 28.370 | 62.695 |
| RUS | 121.850 | 104.744 | 226.330 | 135.141 |
| SVK | 11.309 | 60.088 | 13.672 | 48.484 |
| SVN | 7.246 | 89.487 | 7.575 | 69.010 |
| SWE | 23.369 | 145.349 | 70.040 | 126.522 |
| TUR | 220.509 | 116.511 | 104.159 | 113.423 |
| USA | 1868.270 | 1355.234 | 2005.757 | 1517.866 |
| Average | 168.670 | 168.670 | 168.670 | 168.670 |
| Standard deviation | 341.093 | 204.667 | 330.854 | 234.525 |
| Total | 6915.487 | | | |

Based on the above considerations, this paper proposes the map, indices and method to quantify the amount of aid that countries and multilateral organizations should allocate to disaster-stricken countries by considering both indirect economic loss and payment ability. The corresponding formulae and indices have been constructed. Then, taking the May 12th Wenchuan earthquake as an example, the international aid status in each country has been analyzed from the perspective of indirect economic loss and payment ability respectively, and the recommended amount of aid has also been calculated separately. Meanwhile, the total recommended amount when considering both aspects has been given as well. The main advantages of the proposed method are as follows:

(1) Objectively quantifiable. Different from the traditional idea of determining the amount of aid according to humanitarianism, strategic interests, and geographical proximity, the paper has focused on the angle of economic benefits and measured the amount of aid through indirect economic loss and payment ability. Such method proposes a clear calculation criterion to determine the amount of aid and will be objectively measurable.

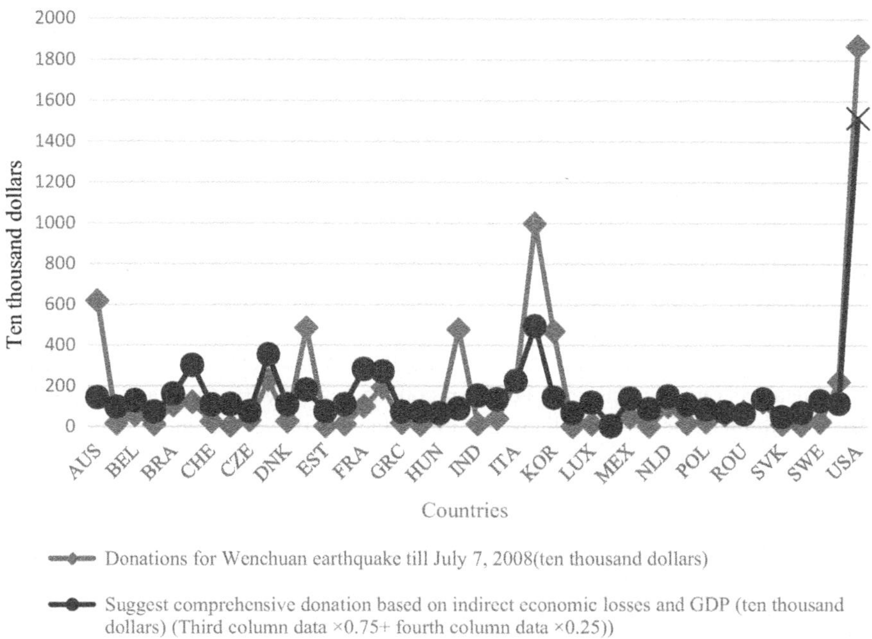


**Fig. 11.5** The donation and suggest donation of countries

(2) Simple calculation. The calculation idea and method of this study are concise and clear. The structure of the corresponding input-output tables is clear and the calculation steps are simple. Therefore, it will be easy to popularize and apply it in different settings.

### *11.7.2 Limitation and Prospective*

The inadequacies and future research include:

(1) Indirect economic loss calculated by input-output tables are too large. Because the input-output tables only consider the input-output relationship among all industries in a static and rigid way, it fails to take full account of the substitution relationship among various industrial sectors when a disaster occurs, causing high calculated results (Rose 2007). But the main purpose of this paper is to evaluate the relative value of international aid from the angle of indirect economic loss, so it will be unnecessary to calculate indirect economic loss accurately. In the later study, accurate methods might be proposed to measure the indirect economic loss.
(2) Consideration of indirect economic loss and payment ability at the same time remains uncertain. From the viewpoint of economic benefits, it is necessary to consider both indirect economic loss and payment ability. As a result, the

recommended aid amount considering the indirect economic loss has been set with a weight of 0.75 and the recommended aid amount considering payment ability has been set with a weight of 0.25 in this paper. But how to set the two weights is worth further thinking. Moreover, what other factors should be considered is equally worthy of follow-up research.

In addition, different reasons to explain why other scholars have not tried to determine the amount of aid from the perspective of indirect economic loss. First, due to the long geographical distance between the disaster-affected country and the donor, the indirect economic loss to the donor will hard to be noticed. Second, a disaster usually hits a local region of the donee. Despite a huge loss to the disaster-affected country, the caused economic disturbance is relatively small in other countries. Third, to delineate economic activities between countries with what tools and methods is also a difficult issue. Fourth, there are many factors that affect aid amount. Apart from indirect economic loss, strategic interests and others are also very vital factors. And then, the priority of these factors to determine the amount of international aid is worthy of further careful study.

Finally, it should be emphasized that national interests, democracy degree and donation operation mechanism of the donee should also be duly considered, though the original motivation for aid is humanitarianism. This paper has studied the issue of international aid merely from the perspective of indirect economic loss and payment ability. But it does not mean that these must be the only two factors considered in determining future international aid. The main purpose of this paper is to provide a new perspective for the study of international aid for disasters and to provide a quantifiable reference standard for other similar aid activities. In the future, research on aid motivation and effect can be carried out to develop and improve current evaluation systems for aid. In conclusion, this paper intends to play the effect of attracting valuable opinions.

**Acknowledgements** Ernesto DR Santibanez Gonzalez, Cuimei Wang also made great contributions to this manuscript. We express our heartfelt thanks to them. This research was supported by: National Social and Scientific Fund Program of China (18ZDA052; 17BGL142; 16ZDA047); The Natural Science Foundation of China (91546117, 71373131).

## References

Admasu, W. F., Boerema, A., Nyssen, J., Sewnet, A., et al. (2019). Uncovering ecosystem services on expropriated land : a participatory assessment in the case of urban expansion in Bahir Dar. *Northwest Ethiopia*, *9*(10).

Albala-Bertrand, J. M. (1993). Natural disaster situations and growth: A macroeconomic model for sudden disaster impacts. *World Development, 21,* 1417–1434.

Alda, E., Cuesta, J., Letters, E., et al. (2019). Measuring the efficiency of humanitarian aid. *Economy Letters*, 183.

Cardwell, R. et al. (2020). COVID-19 and international food assistance: policy proposals to keep food flowing: ScienceDirect. *World Development*, 135.

Alesina, A. F., & Dollar, D. (2000). Who gives foreign aid to whom and why. *Journal of Economic Growth, 5,* 33–63.
Bermeo, S. B. (2007). *Utility maximization and strategic development: A model of foreign aid allocation.* Princeton NJ, Mimeo: Department of Politics, Princeton University.
Birkland, T. A. (1997). *After Disaster: Agenda Setting, Public Policy, and Focusing Events.* Washington DC: Georgetown University Press.
Boisvert, R. (1992). Direct and indirect economic losses from lifeline damage. In: *Indirect Economics Consequences of a Catastrophic Earthquake.* Final Report by Development Technologies to the Federal Emergency Management Agency, Washington DC.
Brookshire, D. S., Chang, S. E., Cochrane, H., Olson, R. A., Rose, A., & Steenson, J. (1997). Direct and indirect economic losses from earthquake damage. *Earthquake Spectra, 13,* 683–701.
Bulte, E., Xu, L., & Zhang, X. (2018). Post-disaster aid and development of the manufacturing sector: Lessons from a natural experiment in China. *European Economics Review, 101,* 441–458.
Burnside, C., & Dollar, D. (2004). *Aid, policies, and growth: Revisiting the evidence.* In: Policy Research Working Paper 3251. Washington, DC.: The World Bank.
Burrus, R., Jr., Dumas, C. F., Farrell, C. H., Jr., & Hall, W.W. (2002). The impacts of low-intensity hurricanes on regional economic activity. *Nature Hazards Review, 3*(2), 118–125.
Cao, C., et al. (2018). A novel multi-objective programming model of relief distribution for sustainable disaster supply chain in large-scale natural disasters. *Journal of Clean Production,* 1422–1435.
Cao, C., Li, C., Yang, Q., Liu, Y., & Qu, T. (2018). A novel multi-objective programming model of relief distribution for sustainable disaster supply chain in large-scale natural disasters. *Journal of Cleaner Production, 174,* 1422–1435.
Cingranelli, D.L., & Pasquarello, T.E. (1985). Human rights practices and the distribution of U.S. foreign aid to Latin American countries. *American Journal of Political Science, 29*(3), 539.
Clemens, M. A., Radelet, S., & Bhavnani, R. (2004). *Counting chickens when they hatch: the short-term effect of aid on growth.* In: Working paper 44. Washington, DC.: Center for Global Development.
Cochrane, H. C. (1984). Knowledge of private loss and the efficiency of protection. In: Presented at the *Conference on the Economics of Natural Hazards and their Mitigation.* December. University of Florida.
Cochrane, H. C. (1996). Catastrophic earthquakes and the prospect of indirect loss. *Post- Earthquake Rehabilitation and Reconstruction,* 395–408.
Copelovitch, M. S. (2010). Master or servant? Common agency and the political economy of IMF Lending. *International Studies Quarterly , 54,* 49–77.
Doucouliagos, C., & Manning, E. (2009). *The allocation of development aid assistance: do new donors have old motives.* Economics Series, School of Accounting, Economics and Finance. Melbourne: Deakin University.
Dowling, J. M., & Hiemenz, U. (1985). Biases in the allocation of foreign aid: Some new evidence. *World Development, 13*(4), 535–541.
Drabek, T. E. (2003a). *Strategies for coordinating disaster responses.* Boulder, CO: Institute of Behavior Sciences.
Drabek, T. E. (2003). Strategies for coordinating disaster responses. *Disaster Prevention Management, 12*(5).
Dreher, A., & Jensen, N. M. (2007) Independent actor or agent? An empirical analysis of the impact of U.S. interests on International Monetary Fund conditions. *Journal Law of Economy, 50*(1), 105–124.
Dudley, L., & Montmarquette, C. A. (1976). Model of the supply of bilateral foreign aid. *American Economic Review, 66*(1), 132–142.
Eichenauer, V.Z., Fuchs, A., Kunze, S., et al. (2020). Distortions in aid allocation of United Nations flash appeals: Evidence from the 2015 Nepal earthquake. *World Development*, 136.
Fink, G., & Redaelli, S. (2011). Determinants of international emergency aid: humanitarian need only? *World Development, 39,* 741–757.

Furuoka, F. (2017). Determinants of China's and Japan's foreign aid allocations in Africa. *African Development Review, 29,* 376–388.
Ghanem, A. (2020). The impact of incentives for reconciliation in the Holy City–How international aid for the palestinians contributed to the expanding of israeli control over East Jerusalem. *Defence Peace Econ, 4,* 1–15.
Gordon, P., Moore, J. E., & Richardson, H. W. (1997). An integrated model of bridge performance, highway networks, and the spatial metropolitan economy: towards a general model of how losses due to earthquake impacts on lifelines affect the economy//NCEER-97-0005. In: *Proceedings of the Workshop on Earthquake Frontiers in Transportation Facilities.* Buffalo, N.Y.: National Center for Earthquake Engineering Research.
Growther, K. G., Haimes, Y. Y., & Taub, G. (2007). Systemic valuation of strategic preparedness through application of the inoperability input-output model with lessons learned from hurricane Katrina. *Risk Analysis, 27*(5), 1345–1364.
Habibzadeh, F., Yadollahie, M., & Kucheki, M. (2008). International aid in disaster zones: help or headache? *Lancet, 372*(9636), 374–374.
Haghi, M., Ghomi, S. M. F. T., & Jolai, F. (2017a). Developing a robust multi-objective model for pre/post disaster times under uncertainty in demand and resource. *Journal of Cleaner Production, 154,* 188–202.
Haghi, M., Ghomi, S. M. T. F., & Jolai, F. (2017). Developing a robust multi-objective model for pre/post disaster times under uncertainty in demand and resource. *Journal of Clean Production, 154,* 15, 188–202.
Haimes, Y. Y., Horowitz, B. M., Lambert, J. H., Santos, J. R., Lian, C., Crowther, K. G. (2005). Inoperability input-output model for interdependent infrastructure sectors I: Theory and methodology. *Journal of Infrastructure Systems, 11*(2), 67–79.
Hallegatte, S. (2008). An adaptive regional input-output model and its application to the assessment of the economic cost of Katrina. *Risk Analysis, 28*(3), 779–799.
Hallwright, J., & Handmer, J. (2019). Accountability and transparency in disaster aid: Cyclone Pam in Vanuatu. *International Journal of Disaster Risk Reduction,* 3.
Han, L., Koenig-Archi bugi, M., Opsahl, T. (2018). The social network of international health aid. *Social Science and Medicine,* 67–74.
Haraoka, T., Ojima, T., Murata, C., & Hayasaka, S. (2012). Factors influencing collaborative activities between non-professional disaster volunteers and victims of earthquake disasters. *PLoS ONE, 7*(10), 1–8.
Höffler, A., Outram, V. (2008). Need, merit or self-interest: What determines the allocation of aid? In: CSAE Working Paper. Oxford: Centre for the Study of African Economies
Huang, M., & Jianmei, H. (2020). Foreign aid study: Chinese schools and Chinese points. *The Pacific Review, 33*(3–4), 520–549.
Koch, S. (2017). International influence on forest governance in Tanzania: Analysing the role of aid experts in the REDD + process. *Forest Policy Economy, 83,* 181–190.
Kuziemko, I., & Werker, E. (2006). How much is a seat on the security council worth? Foreign aid and bribery at the United Nations. *Journal of Political Economy, 114,* 905–930.
Lauren, E., & Licari, F. (2020). Exploring the intersection between social determinants of health and unmet dental care needs using deep learning. *International Journal of Environmental Research and Public Health, 17*(19), 7286.
Lewin, K. M. (2020). Beyond business as usual: Aid and financing education in Sub Saharan Africa. *International Journal of Educational Development, 78,* 102247–102247.
Liam, C. K. (2017). Osimertinib as first-line treatment of egfr mutant advanced non-small-cell lung cancer. *Translational Lung Cancer Research, 6*(S1), S62.
Liao, H., Chi, Y., Zhang, J. (2020). Impact of international development aid on FDI along the Belt and Road. *China Economy Review,* 61.
Loayza, N., Olaberria, E., Rigolini, J., & Christiaensen, L. (2012). Natural disasters and growth: going beyond the averages. *World Development, 40,* 1317–1336.

Mahalik, M.K. et al. (2020). Assessing the effectiveness of total foreign aid and foreign energy aid inflows on environmental quality in India. *Energy Policy*, 149.

Maizels, A., & Nissanke, M. K. (1984). Motivations for aid to developing countries. *World Development, 12*(9), 879–900.

Michael, Dewald, et al. (1996). Comparative advantage and bilateral foreign aid policy. *World Development*, *24*(3), 549–556.

Nakhaei, M., Khankeh, H. R., Masoumi, G. R., Hosseini, M. A., Yekta, Z. P., Kurland, L., et al. (2015). Impact of disaster on women in Iran and implication for emergency nurses volunteering to provide urgent humanitarian aid relief: A qualitative study. *Australasian Emergency Nursing Journal, 18*(3), 165–172.

Neanidis, K. C., & Varvarigos, D. (2009). The allocation of volatile aid and economic growth: theory and evidence. *European Journal of Political Economy, 25,* 447–462.

Neumayer, E. (2003). Do human rights matter in bilateral aid allocation? A quantitative analysis of 21 donor countries. *Social Science Quarterly, 84*(3), 650–666.

Noy, I. (2009). The macroeconomic consequences of disasters. *World Development, 88,* 221–231.

Okuyama, Y. (2018). Dynamic input-output analysis. In: *Handbook of input–output analysis.*

Okuyama, Y., Sahin, S. (2009). *Impact estimation of disasters: A global aggregate for 1960 to 2007.* In: Policy Research Working Paper Series 4963, The World Bank.

Perry, M. C., Travayiakis, M. (2008). *The U.S. Foreign disaster response process: How it works and how it could work better.* The Institute for Foreign Policy Analysis, Inc.

Peters, B. G. (1998). Managing Horizontal Government: E Politics of Co-ordination. *Public Administration, 76*(2), 295–311.

Piotr, L. (2018). The impact of armed conflict and terrorism on foreign aid: A sector-level analysis. *World Development, 110,* 283–294.

Rajan, R. J., & Subramanian, A. (2008). Aid and growth: what does the cross-country evidence really show? *Review of Economics and Statistics, 90,* 643–665.

Raschkya, P. A. (2012). On the channel and type of aid: The case of international disaster assistance. *European Journal of Political Economy, 28*(1), 119–131.

Restivo, M., Shandra, J. M., & Sommer, J. M. (2017). The United States agency for international development and forest loss: A cross-national analysis of environmental aid. *The Social Science Journal, 55*(2), 171–181.

Richey, L. A., Ponte, S. (2020). Brand Aid and coffee value chain development interventions: Is Starbucks working aid out of business? *World Development*, 105193.

Rose, A. (2004). Economic principles, issues, and research priorities in hazard loss estimation. In: Y. Okuyama, & S. E. Chang (Eds), *Modeling spatial and economic impacts of disasters.* New York: Springer.

Rose, A., & Liao, S. Y. (2005). Modeling regional economic resilience to disasters: A computable general equilibrium analysis of water service disruptions. *Journal of Regional Science, 45*(1), 75–112.

Rose, A., Oladosu, G., & Liao, S. (2007). Regional economic impacts of a terrorist attack on the water system of Los Angeles: a computable general disequilibrium analysis. *Economy Costs Consequences Terror,* 291–316.

Santos, J. R., & Haimes, Y. Y. (2004). Modeling the demand reduction input output I-O inoperability due to terrorism of interconnected infrastructures. *Risk Analysis, 24*(6), 1437–1452.

Scobie, M. (2020). International aid, trade and investment and access and allocation. *International Environmental Agreements: Politics, Law and Economics*, 20.

Shibusawa, H., & Miyata, Y. (2011). Evaluating the dynamic and spatial economic impacts of an earthquake: a CGE application to Japan. *Regional Science Inquiry, 2,* 13–25.

Shields, R., & Menashy, F. (2017). The network of bilateral aid to education 2005–2015. *International Journal of Educational Development*, 64.

Skidmore, M., & Toya, H. (2002). Do natural disasters promote long-run growth. *Economic Inquiry, 40,* 664–687.

Suyeon, Yoo, Sungjin, et al. (2020). The image game: exploit kit detection based on recursive convolutional neural networks. IEEE. *Access*, 18808–18821.

Suzuki, M. (2020). Profits before patients? Analyzing donors' economic motives for foreign aid in the health sector. *World Development*,132.

Svensson, J. (2010). Aid, growth and democracy. *Economics Politics, 11*(3), 275–297.

Timmer, M. P., Dietzenbacher, E., Los, B., Stehrer, R., & Vries, G. J. D. (2015). An illustrated user guide to the world input-output database: the case of global automotive production. *Review of International Economics, 23,* 575–605.

Timmer, M. P., Los, B., Stehrer, R., & Vries, G. J. D. (2016). *An Anatomy of the global trade slowdown based on the WIOD 2016 release.* GGDC research memorandum, University of Groningen.

Tirasirichai, C., & Enke, D. (2007). Case study: Applying a regional CGE model for estimation of indirect economic losses due to damaged highway bridges. *The Engineering Economist, 52,* 367–401.

Townsend, R. (1994). Risk and insurance in village India. *Econometrica, 62,* 539–591.

Udry, C. (1994). Risk and saving in Northern Nigeria. *American Economic Review, 85*(5), 1287–1300.

United Nations International Strategy for Disaster Reduction. (2018). Extreme weather events affected 60 m people.

Wu, X. H., Xue, P. P., Guo, J., Ji, Z., Wei, G., & Ning, X. (2017). On the amount of counterpart assistance to be provided after natural disasters: from the perspective of indirect economic loss assessment. *Global Environment Change Part B Environment Hazards, 16*(1), 50–70.

Wu, X. H., Xu, Z., Liu, H., Guo, J., & Zhou, L. (2019). What Are the Impacts of Tropical Cyclones on Employment?–An Analysis Based on Meta-regression. *Weather Climate Society, 11*(2), 259–275.

Xiaoli, L., Benoliel, E., Peng, Y., Aneke, J., & Weigand, M. R. (2020). Genomic epidemiology of nontoxigenic corynebacterium diphtheriae from king county, washington state, usa between July 2018 and May 2019. *Microbial Genomics, 6*(12).

Yang, S., & Park, S. (2020). The effects of renewable energy financial incentive policy and democratic governance on renewable energy aid effectiveness. *Energy Policy*, 145.

Younas, J. (2008). Motivation for bilateral aid allocation. *European Journal of Political Economy, 24*, 661–674.

# Chapter 12
# Effectively Managing Counterpart Support Aid, for Damages Incurred from Natural Disasters, by Utilizing the Indirect Economic Losses

**Abstract** Counterpart support (strategically coordinated disaster aid through partnership) policies provide guidance for emergency management and reconstruction, focusing upon short time period after natural disasters. However, determination of the quantitative levels of counterpart support remains a key challenge area in the literature, and practice. The goal of the research is to fill such gaps by introducing an index framework consisting of an inter-regional input-output model (IRIO) and a resilience index, where appropriate measures of indirect economic losses are developed from an IRIO, and the indirect economic losses are achieved by using the provincial economic resilience assessment index system. To examine the internal validity, including systematic error or bias, we investigated the reliability of the adopting models, calculation methods and index systems. To explore the external validity of the proposed measures and resilience index over the widely applied IRIO framework, data from the 2008 Wenchuan earthquake, an 8.0Ms earthquake that devastated parts of China, was utilized for obtaining parameter values of the framework. A follow-up investigation found that the fairness of counterpart support has been substantially enhanced and the satisfaction has been noticeably improved.

**Keywords** Counterpart support · Natural disaster · Inter-regional input-output model · Indirect economic loss · Resilience and recovery · Internal and external validity

## 12.1 Background

Counterpart support in China was initiated by both the central and local governments as a policy framework, focused on narrowing regional economic gaps. Counterpart support, introduced in the 1950s, adopted in the early 1960s and developed in the 1980s, is still evolving in the new millennia. Counterpart support was fully implemented during the post-disaster reconstruction after the Wenchuan earthquake, 8.0Ms, on May 12, 2008, that killed 69,195 people, left 18,392 missing, and injured 374,176.

Shortly after the Wenchuan earthquake, the State Council issued *The Counterpart Support Scheme of Restoration and Reconstruction* on June 11, 2008 which

 
X. Wu and J. Guo, *Economic Impacts and Emergency Management of Disasters in China*,
https://doi.org/10.1007/978-981-16-1319-7_12

launched the counterpart support agenda for recovery and reconstruction. Counterpart designated 19 provinces (or municipalities directly under the central government, hereinafter referred to as provinces, or cities) in the Eastern and Central regions as counterpart support partners. Counterpart partners were required to quickly implement counterpart support, in pairs, based on the unified deployment of the central government. Specifically, selected provinces were obligated to transfer 1% of their local fiscal revenue to their partner counties, for three consecutive years (2008-2010).

### *12.1.1 Existing Problems*

China is a highly centralized society with a top-down governance structure (Zhang 2006). The current counterpart support policy, in such a circumstance, plays a more effective role for a faster reconstruction after disasters. However, the consequences, content and manifestation of the policy have received a lot of criticism, largely due to chaotic distributions of monetary donations and disaster relief products. For example, Ni et al. (2009) noted that the administrative system in counterpart support was inadequate, the participating provinces and cities lacked coordination, and the overall financial arrangements were unbalanced. Wang and Dong (2010) postulated that relevant laws and regulations were either unavailable or non-perfect, capital allocation and spending were seriously imbalanced. Cai (2012) commented that counterpart support is a non-institutionalized arrangement that does not have clear rules or procedures. Bulte et al. (2013) pointed out that the counterpart support interferes with the normal economic order of both sides, the policy does not necessarily play a real role for the recipient's long-term economic recovery, and the recipients may even develop into the Dutch disease. According to Wu (2012): the current counterpart support policy emphasized administrative obedience and humanitarian principles, and administrative roles are overly dominating. In particular, the driving mechanism, in terms of the economic interest, of the local government and relevant departments involved was unexplored, leading to the lack of a solid theoretical foundation for counterpart support policy.

In summary, many authors noticed the existing problems regarding the design of counterpart support policies, but most of their studies were confined to describing the phenomenon and giving speculative statements without developing appropriate quantitative measures, resulting in the lack of empirical support and validation.

### *12.1.2 Approach for Identifying and Solving the Problem*

The continuing development of counterpart support policies is based upon the perspective of political mobilization and humanitarian principles, which are equal in importance to the motivation of economic interests. However, the current counterpart policy fails to quantitatively measure the support levels of donors based on the insight of indirect economic losses, resulting in an unfair situation for both sides of the counterpart support program.

The objective of this paper is to develop a relatively complete and implementable framework for guiding and tracking the post-disaster operations more effectively, analyzing the counterpart support quantitatively, and providing concrete examples to illustrate and validate the support policies. These goals will be achieved with the following five steps.

i. The Inter-regional Input-output (IRIO) Model was utilized (Sect. 12.3.1).
ii. The resilience index of provincial economic systems, comprehensive computational procedure – Principal Component Analysis (PCA) and counterpart support evaluation index are introduced (Sects. 12.3.2 and 12.3.3).
iii. The indirect economic losses suffered by relevant provinces in the Wenchuan earthquake are calculated through the IRIO. The resilience of every provincial economic system is calculated and used to modify the indirect economic loss value for obtaining the actual indirect economic loss (Sect. 12.4).
iv. An index for accessing provincial counterpart support activities after the Wenchuan earthquake was developed according to the counterpart support value and the actual indirect economic loss (Sect. 12.4).
v. A study on the internal and external validity of the proposed counterpart support framework is given in Sect. 12.5.

Finally, the summary is provided in Sect. 12.6.

The following diagram illustrates the flowchart of the above contents.

## 12.2 Literature: Evaluation of Indirect Economic Losses and Resilience

The main objective of this paper is to develop an improved counterpart support framework, concerning approaches and methodologies. We begin with a review the current literature regarding the evaluation of indirect economic losses and assessment of resilience as these evaluations are the nucleus of this paper.

### *12.2.1 Indirect Economic Losses*

Currently, there are three types of core methods for assessing indirect economic losses. The first includes econometric models which focus on building indicators on hazards, demographic social and economic, while measuring the impact of disasters on economic development through changing coefficients of independent variables (Skidmore and Toya 2002; Noy and Nualsri 2007; Hallegatte and Dumas 2009; Kellenberg and Mobarak 2008; Coffman and Noy 2012; Heatwole and Rose 2013). The econometric models are relatively crude, and are difficult to characterize the affected channels of disasters but more suitable to assess the long-term economic impact of disasters.

The second contains input-output models which can be divided into the demand-driven I-O models (Jung et al. 2009; Okuyama and Santos 2014) and the supply-driven I-O models (Oosterhaven 1988; Dietzenbacher 1997; Leung et al. 2007; Ai and Polenske 2008; Park 2008) which are used for determining the reduction in the total output of the economic system due to the lowered demand ability or supply capacity of one (or more) sectors. Hashiguchi et al. (2017) made a research on the basis of OECD's annual ICIO tables, from 1995 to 2011, to find out 61 economies' relationship between final demand changes and production structures. They aimed at exploiting the resilience to economic shocks. As a result, production and final demand structures tended to be changed for reducing the negative feedbacks from final demand shocks. And countries those had the capacity of propping up economy by their own domestic service sectors tended to be more resilient to negative shocks. Luca and Georgios (2018) discussed how to incorporate different aspects of disaster modeling in the latest exploiting IO method. They took into consideration demand-sided and supply-sided perturbation triggers, static and dynamic representations, and especially the assessment of economic resilience. In this paper, they showed the relationships between IO method and the economic losses assessment connected to both natural disasters and man-made hazards. As a conclusion, the IO models in the context had advantages in terms of its moderate data requirements and combination with other analysis techniques. IO models could also play a relative role in policy supporting, particularly for impact analysis in large scale, and in determination of a cost-effective use of resources. Han and Goetz 2018 applied the concept of resilience and IO method to examine U.S. counties during the Great Depression. They mainly tested whether local economies which contain centralized industries was related to more resilient performance during the Great Depression empirically. IO method offered a centrality index for each industry. Pakoksung et al. 2019 combined a tsunami hazard map research and MRIO model to estimate the potential losses by Okinawa Island in a tsunami. They calculated tsunami flow characteristics by using the TUNAMI-N2 model while incorporating six earthquake fault scenarios around the area at first. The resulting map was overlaid with economic land use type and topography maps to identify vulnerable regions. Then, they extended the MRIO model combined with Chenery–Moses estimation method to assess the direct and indirect losses. Jin et al. 2020 took Guangdong Province as the research object to evaluate the damage caused by storm surge disasters through the static and dynamic IO method. They calculated the cumulative output loss under different recovery periods. The result indicated that the agricultural loss had serious effect on economy and the total loss, calculated by the static input-output model. And the total loss was greater than the one calculated by the dynamic input-output model. These models are suitable to assess short-term economic losses of linear systems, without considering the variation of inter-industry output coefficients in the long-term scenarios, changes in market prices, as well as the resilience of the affected regional economic systems (such as rescheduling production, and self-sufficiency). The calculated values are often relatively large and usually act as an upper boundary.

The third covers computable general equilibrium models (e.g. Narayan 2003; Rose and Guha 2004; Rose and Liao 2005; Chakkaphan and David 2007; Hirokazu and Satoshi 2008; Wei et al. 2012; Wang et al. 2014). Tanoue et al. (2020) developed a global framework to estimate the direct and indirect economic losses of river floods using a computable general equilibrium model and a global river and inundation model. The global river and inundation model can simulate the extent, depth, and period of floods. Then they applied the global river and inundation model to the 2011 Thailand flood and proved that this disaster has made $55.3 billion of total losses from 2011 to 2030. Gao et al. 2020 combined analytic hierarchy process (AHP) and geographic information system (GIS) to produce a comprehensive risk assessment from aspects of disaster, vulnerability, and resilience, with 11 indicators. Then, they introduced a method for calculating risk based on spatial and temporal cumulative patterns of typhoon-induced flood disasters,and involved the method in the basis of a computable general equilibrium. These models deal with the combined effects on different sectors by taking into account product substitution, supplements and price changes. But they fail to consider the inertia and transaction costs existing in the economic system. The calculated values are usually smaller and act as lower boundaries (Miller and Blair 2009; Hallegatte 2014).

The framework of this present paper is the indirect economic losses of the provinces and cities impacted by natural disasters. The IRIO method, one of the IO models, is to be employed. Compared with other models, the IRIO has a relatively simple structure to make it easier to understand and is capable of describing the impacts of disaster to interdependent provincial economic systems (Santos 2006).

Previously, some scholars already adopted IRIO in evaluating the indirect economic losses of disasters. For example, Hallegatte et al. (2011) calculated the impact of sea level rise and storm surges on coastal cities; Wu et al. (2012) assessed the economic losses of Wenchuan earthquake in 2008; Ranger et al. 2011 evaluated the potential impact of floods to Mumbai Under climate change scenarios. It is especially worth mentioning that, Hallegatte (2014) innovatively put forward an adaptive regional input-output (ARIO) inventory model to assess indirect economic losses of Hurricane Katrina. However, most researches employed primarily linear approaches, though few included the resilience in their models, often leading to over-estimated indirect economic losses. Irimoto et al. 2017 used transnational and interregional IO Model to evaluate economic damages cost of transport disruptions. The simulation result showed that the transport disruption in the Kanmon Straits caused damage to Japan, and the loss was approximately 36.3 billion. It also highlighted the disaster prevention in the Kanmon Straits, Kanto, and Huabei is helpful to final economic resilience. Liu et al. 2019 adopted ARIO model to assess the indirect economic losses caused by the sea ice disaster in Liaoning Province in China. The research revealed the indirect economic losses were 885 million yuan, and agriculture, food manufacturing, chemical industry department t were especially severe impacted.

To overcome the conventional linear approach idea in IRIO, and to avoid over-estimating indirect economic losses, this paper gives full consideration to the resilience of the associated provinces and cities, and builds the economic index system for the resilience recovery in the research framework, in an effort to obtain a more objective assessment on the indirect economic losses incurred from disasters. The evaluation index system is provided in Table 12.1.

### 12.2.2 Evaluation of Resilience

In the field of evaluating disaster losses, resilience has attracted wide attention (Kendra and Wachtendorf 2003; Manyena 2006; Tierney 2007; McEntire 2007; Eguchi and Adams 2007; Rose 2004; 2007a, b, 2007c, 2013a, b). Rose (2004, 2007c) referred to static economic resilience as the ability or capacity of a system to maintain functionality, when shocked. Regarding the system resilience, in a relatively complete fashion, Rose (2004, 2007c, 2013a, b) elaborated on the concept, connotation, extension, and evaluation index system. Courvisanos et al. (2016) had a study on Australian economy focusing on identifying regional economic resilience patterns by industry categories. They used a k-means algorithm data mining method to evaluate 13-year drought and the Global Financial Crisis impact on four groups of regions divided by function according to the 2001, 2006, and 2011 census data. Bruno (2019) made a literature review of economic resilience, focusing on the concepts and empirical methods, and then adopted a DSER (Dynamic Static Economic Resilience) model to create a two-dimensional index, to investigate Latin America and Caribbean's degree of regional economic resilience. The final conclusion of this investigation is that Mexico is one of the most resilient countries in the region and Paraguay is the least resilient countries,its economic resilience has kept a level of stagnation since 2000. Shymon et al. 2020 summarized arguments on bibliometric analysis of economic resilience by using the software VOSviewer (Visualizing scientific landscapes viewer). The core indicators of economic resilience assessment have proved to be macroeconomic stability, microeconomic market efficiency, governance and social development according to the generalization of the scientific papers. The following empirical data of European Union countries which have been classified on the six groups also confirmed the hypothesis of the economic resilience assessment core indicators. In addition, it is proved that no statistically significant difference among the indicators of economic resilience assessment according to the essential component.

But, so far, researchers have been sporadic on the resilience of provincial economic systems. In the literature assessing resilience, while qualitative descriptions have been given more considerations (Paton and Johnston 2006; Manyena 2006; Tierney 2007; Comfort 2010). Whittaker et al. (2020) made a comparative analysis on three past events and made secondary qualitative analysis to build a conceptual model of disaster management. The model they built, as a preparedness strategy, can improve the community resilience capabilities and reveal the potential implementation of social media. Finally, they also made a discussion on community empowerment related with resilience. Aksha and Emrich 2020 investigated community disaster resilience across Nepal. They quantified Nepal disaster resilience at village level, mainly using census data. By using DROP (Disaster Resilience of Place) model, they

**Table 12.1** The interregional input-output table*

| | | | intermediate consumption | | | | | | | final consumption | | | | | | |
|---|---|---|---|---|---|---|---|---|---|---|---|---|---|---|---|---|
| | | | region 1 | | | … | region m | | | region 1 | | … | region m | | export | total output |
| | | | industry 1 | … | industry n | … | industry 1 | … | industry n | final Consumption Expenditure | total investment forming | … | Final Consumption Expenditure | total investment forming | | |
| intermediate input | region 1 | industry 1 | | | | | | | | | | | | | | |
| | | … | | | | | | | | | | | | | | |
| | | industry n | | | | | | | | | | | | | | |
| | … | … | | | | | | | | | | | | | | |
| | region r | industry 1 | | | | | | | | | | | | | | |
| | | … | | | | | | | | | | | | | | |
| | | industry i | $X_{ij}^{rs}$ $_{mn\times mn}$ | | | | | | | $F_{ik}^{rs}$ $_{mn\times 2m}$ | | | | | $S_i^r$ $_{mn\times 1}$ | $X_i^r$ $_{mn\times 1}$ |
| | | … | | | | | | | | | | | | | | |
| | | industry n | | | | | | | | | | | | | | |
| | … | … | | | | | | | | | | | | | | |
| | region m | industry 1 | | | | | | | | | | | | | | |
| | | … | | | | | | | | | | | | | | |
| | | industry n | | | | | | | | | | | | | | |
| value added | | | $V_j^s$ $_{1\times mn}$ | | | | | | | | | | | | | |
| total input | | | $X_j^s$ $_{1\times mn}$ | | | | | | | | | | | | | |

* From *The theory and practice of making an interregional input-output table about the 30 provinces in China in 2007* (see Liu, Cheng & Tang, 2012)

* From *The theory and practice of making an interregional input-output table about the 30 provinces in China in 2007* (see Liu et al. 2012)

selected 22 variables as indicators of social, economic, community, infrastructure, and environmental resilience. The resilience was assessed for 3971 village development communities while using a PCA(Principal Component Analysis) method. Gong et al. 2020 analyzed the particular characteristics of the 2020 COVID crisis in China, and explored the particular characteristics' effects on regional recovery and potential resilience of the country. It was concluded that the combination of the characteristics of COVID, the institutional experience of dealing with epidemic crises, government support, and regional industrial structures, might affect the resilience rates of Chinese regions. Bnic et al. 2020 developed a risk-disaster-opportunity framework associated with a territorial system from a resilience perspective. This framework is used to analyze the social economic impacts by natural shocks. They designed a typology of natural disasters, presented a classification of long-run impacts, and made an empirical test with the worldwide EM-DATdatabase (Emergency Events Database). The researchers aimed at observing a positive social economic effect after disaster. Quantitative evaluations, especially with an appropriate index system, are very scarce. Zobel et al. 2020 discussed how to create a useful multi-dimensional indicator for a human system's resilience, and a way for visualizing and analyzing dimension's relationship. They also further discussed the issue of weighting dimension values and the impacts of a weighting scheme on the relative ranking in different scenarios. By analyzing dimension's relationship, people can take actions to strengthen the human system to defend the disaster. Sarker et al. (2020) have considered using big data to enhance disaster resilience management. It focused on the recent research explored to help people manage disaster by big data technology. It also highlighted the major principles of big data technology for disaster management such as open-source tools, strong infrastructure, developing local skills and so on.

Regional differences, in socio-economic geographical conditions, are remarkably large in China. Consequently, in the face of the disturbance caused by natural disasters, recovery capabilities across all provinces vary widely, with different patterns and variations in pace. To capture such differences, this paper puts forward an innovative evaluation index system for assessing individual provincial resilience for indirectly impacted provinces by a disaster.

Here, we point out that the provincial resilience is different from the direct hazard bearing bodies (such as Sichuan province) defined in the previously cited references (Rose et al. 2004, 2007c, 2013a, b). In this paper, provincial resilience refers to the system ability of recovering to normal levels in deploying various elements and resources, and reducing or eliminating indirect outside disturbances. Provincial resilience is broader than the concept of resilience defined for directly affected provinces, and its connotation is more abundant, including economic ability, government regulation and control ability, financial resources, scientific and technological levels, human resource management, infrastructure building, and enterprise competitive ability of indirect hazard bearing bodies. Moreover, the dependence of provincial resilience on the catastrophic events (such as earthquakes, floods, hurricanes, etc.) is not evident or clearly visible. According to Schmidt-Thomé et al. (2006): it is difficult to develop an index system for measuring the indirect resilience of hazard bearing bodies and it is also difficult to obtain relevant data. As shown in the research of Jacinto et al. (2020): they structured the concept of social resilience by a series of dimensions and indicators for resilience assessment of the society. They used text mining technology, basing on experts' surveys and bibliography reviews, to generate a specific indicators database. The results of this methodology, assisting with an online survey, express that four dimensions of the final database associate with social aspects (individuals, society, governance, and built Environment): when the other two refer to the environment and disaster. But there is still a gap to validate the indicators database through application to real case studies. Liu et al. 2020 took Wenchuan County as an example to analyze the disaster resilience's change rules effected by the spatial and temporal hazards aggregation effects. They collected ten years' data of 2008–2018 landslide geological hazards, and adopted the global autocorrelation coefficient and local autocorrelation coefficient to analyze the temporal trends and spatial patterns of earthquake-induced hazards. But they used only two disaster resilience indexes for analyzing and the two disaster resilience indexes were the compatibility coefficient of industrial and employment structure, and per capita GDP growth rate.

To fill such a gap, in this paper, we will elaborate, from economic capacity and six other aspects, an index system charactering the provincial resilience for after the indirect economic loss, and as far as possible provided with the explanation and justification for the meaning of resilience reflected by various sub-indicators (see Sect. 12.3.2). By combining the index system of economic resilience and the IRIO, we will be able to assess quantitatively the indirect economic losses for disaster affected provinces, particularly for the provinces impacted by the Wenchuan earthquake.

## 12.3 Models, Indicators and Data Specification

In this section, we first introduce the IRIO model. Then, the resilience index of provincial economic systems (Sect. 12.3.2): Principal Component Analysis and the evaluation index for counterpart support (PCA, see Sect. 12.3.3) are utilized for calculating the indirect economic losses suffered by relevant provinces and the resilience of each provincial economic system. Finally, the data used in the empirical analysis is introduced.

### *12.3.1 The Inter-regional Input-Output Model*

The inter-regional input-output Model (IRIO): put forward by American economist Isard in 1951 and also known as Isard model (1951, 1960): is an important tool for examining the economic relevance of different regions (Wu et al. 2012).

As the empirical basis of IRIO, the IRIO table is shown in Table 12.1. The table has $m$ different regions (often some natural geographic classification): and each region has $n$ different industries (such as agriculture, manufacturing, etc.). The classification method for industries, in different regions, is consistent. In the intermediate input section, the main, vertical section, represents the internal economic structure of each region, and the adjoining section describes economic and trade relations between the regions. The final consumption section provides final consumption sub matrices, from different regions, which respectively records the products' usage in the different industries of each region. Similarly, the value-added part is also divided into the added value sub matrices, which respectively record the added value of each region (Chen and Yang 2011).

In the intermediate input and intermediate consumption part of the table, $X_{ij}^{rs}$ is the intermediate consumption matrix, with dimensions $mn \times mn$, and $x_{ij}^{rs}$ is the general entry of $X_{ij}^{rs}$, representing the consumption of industry $j$ of region $s$ in industry $i$ of region $r$.

In the final consumption part, $F_{ik}^{rs}$ is the part of intermediate consumption matrix, with dimensions $mn \times 2m$. Each region has two items, final consumption expenditure and total investment forming, and $f_{ik}^{rs}$ is the general entry of $F_{ik}^{rs}$, representing the consumption of item $k$ of region $s$ in industry $i$ of region $r$. $f_{ik}^{rs}$ respectively represents the usage of the products in different region. $S_i^r$ is the export matrix, with dimensions $mn \times 1$, and is also a part of the intermediate consumption matrix, representing the export of industry $i$ in region $r$, and the general entry is denoted by $s_i^r$ .

The added value matrix, $V_i^s$ represents the added value of each region. For instance, $v_i^s$, the general entry of $V_i^s$, represents the added value of industry $i$ in region $s$.

$X_i^r$ is the total output matrix, with dimensions $mn \times 1$. Its general entry $x_i^r$ records the total output of industry $i$ in region $r$.

$X_j^s$ is the total input matrix, with dimensions $1 \times mn$. Its general entry $x_j^s$ records the total input of industry $j$ in region $s$. In the inter-regional input-output table, the total input and the total output are balanced, namely, the matrix $X_i^r$ is the transpose of matrix $X_j^s$ and vice versa.

The data of the IRIO table comes from *The theory and practice of making an inter-regional input-output table about the 30 provinces in China in 2007* (Liu et al. 2012). Regions represent provincial administrative units (or municipalities directly associated with the central government) in mainland China, including 30 provinces or cities in addition to Xinjiang, and every region has 30 industries. Of these 30 regions, Sichuan province is the disaster area, and the remaining 29 provinces or cities are outside the disaster, with various forms of trade with Sichuan province. Here, we have $m = 30$ (regions) and $n = 30$ (industries). The calculation of this 900 $\times$ 900 matrix was performed by making full use of the matrix operation function in Excel 2010.

According to the row balance relationship in the input-output table, it holds the following balance equation:

$$\sum_{s=1}^{m}\sum_{j=1}^{n} x_{ij}^{rs} + \sum_{s=1}^{m}\sum_{k=1}^{2} f_{ik}^{rs} + s_i^r = x_i^r, \forall r, i \tag{12.1}$$

Put $c_i^r = \sum_{s=1}^{m} \sum_{k=1}^{2} f_{ik}^{rs} + s_i^r$, which represents the final consumption of industry i in region r.

$x_i^r$ represents the total output of industry i in region r.

$$\sum_{s=1}^{m} \sum_{j=1}^{n} x_{ij}^{rs} + c_i^r = x_i^r \text{ , } \forall r, i \tag{12.2}$$

The relationship given in Eq. (12.2) can also be expressed in the matrix form as follows:

$$X_{ij}^{rs} E + C_i^r = X_i^r \tag{12.3}$$

where $X_{ij}^{rs}$ is the intermediate consumption matrix ($mn \times mn$): $E$ is a $mn \times 1$ column matrix, whose entries are identically 1 s, $C_i^r$ is the final consumption matrix ($mn \times 1$): and $X_i^r$ is the total output matrix ($mn \times 1$).

We now introduce the technical coefficient matrix $A$ (see illustration below): whose entries are defined as $a_{ij}^{rs} = x_{ij}^{rs} / x_j^s$, the ratios of the consumption of industry $j$ of region $s$ in industry $i$ of region $r$ to the total input of industry $j$ of region $s$ (also known as the intermediate consumption of the products by industry $j$ of region $s$ in industry $i$ of region $r$, abbreviated as an intermediate consumption coefficient). It should be noted that $A$ is a $mn \times mn$ matrix, as illustrated below:

$$
\begin{array}{cc}
 & \begin{array}{ccccccccc} \textit{region } 1 & & & & \cdots & & \textit{region } s & \cdots & \textit{region } m \end{array} \\
 & \begin{array}{ccccc} \textit{industry } 1 & \cdots & \textit{industry } j & \cdots & \textit{industry } n \end{array} \\
\begin{array}{c} \\ \textit{region } 1 \\ \\ \vdots \\ \textit{region } r \\ \vdots \\ \textit{region } m \end{array} &
\left[\begin{array}{cccccccccc}
\textit{industry } 1 & a_{11}^{11} & \cdots & a_{1j}^{11} & \cdots & a_{1n}^{11} & & & & \\
\vdots & \vdots & \ddots & \vdots & \cdot^{\cdot^{\cdot}} & \vdots & \cdots & & \cdots & \cdots\cdots \\
\textit{industry } i & a_{i1}^{11} & & a_{ij}^{11} & & a_{in}^{11} & & & & \\
\vdots & \vdots & \cdot^{\cdot^{\cdot}} & \vdots & \ddots & \vdots & & & & \\
\textit{industry } n & a_{n1}^{11} & \cdots & a_{n1}^{11} & \cdots & a_{mn}^{11} & & & & \\
 & & & \vdots & & & \ddots & & \vdots & \cdot^{\cdot^{\cdot}} \vdots \\
 & & & \vdots & & & & & \textit{industry } j & \vdots \\
 & & & & & & \cdots & \textit{industry } i & a_{ij}^{rs} & \cdots \vdots \\
 & & & \vdots & & & \cdot^{\cdot^{\cdot}} & & \vdots & \ddots \vdots \\
 & & & \cdots & & & \cdots & & \cdots & \cdots\cdots
\end{array}\right]
\end{array}
$$

Matrix $A$ has the following two properties:

$$a_{ij}^{rs} \geq 0 (\forall\ r, s = 1, 2, \ldots, m; \forall\ i, j = 1, 2, \ldots, n)$$

and $\sum_{r=1}^{m} \sum_{i=1}^{n} a_{ij}^{rs} < 1$ $(\forall\ s = 1, 2, \ldots, m;\ \forall\ j = 1, 2, \ldots, n)$

In the inter-regional input-output table, the total input is equal to the total output of each industry. Since matrix $X_i^r$ is the transpose of matrix $X_j^s$. It holds that $X_{ij}^{rs}E = AX_i^r$. Then Formula (12.3) results in the following:

$$AX_i^r + C_i^r = X_i^r \tag{12.4}$$

which yields the matrix equation

$$(I - A)^{-1}C_i^r = X_i^r \tag{12.5}$$

where the matrix $(I - A)^{-1}$ is the Leontief inverse matrix.

The variable form of Formula (12.5) is:

$$(I - A)^{-1}\Delta C_i^r = \Delta X_i^r \tag{12.6}$$

Due to the correlation between regions, the variation of the final consumption $C_i^r$ will lead to the alteration of the total output $X_i^r$. In the disaster analysis, according to Lu et al. (2002): direct economic loss can be considered as the final consumption reduction and indirect economic losses can be considered as the total output reduction with the removal of the final consumption reduction. According to (12.6): we will calculate the total output reduction, which results from the final consumption reduction. $\Delta X_i^r$ can be expanded as the following form:

$$\Delta X_i^r = \begin{bmatrix} \Delta x_1^1 \\ \vdots \\ \Delta x_i^1 \\ \vdots \\ \Delta x_n^1 \\ \vdots \\ \Delta x_1^r \\ \vdots \\ \Delta x_i^r \\ \vdots \\ \Delta x_n^r \\ \vdots \\ \vdots \end{bmatrix} \begin{matrix} industry\ 1 \\ \vdots \\ industry\ i \\ \vdots \\ industry\ n \\ \vdots \\ industry\ 1 \\ \vdots \\ industry\ i \\ \vdots \\ industry\ n \\ \vdots \\ \vdots \end{matrix} \begin{matrix} \\ \\ region\ 1 \\ \\ \\ \vdots \\ \\ \\ region\ r \\ \\ \vdots \\ region\ m \\ \\ \end{matrix} \tag{12.7}$$

where $\Delta x_i^r$ is an element of $\Delta X_i^r$, and it represents the total output loss value in the industry $i$ of region $r$, from the final consumption reduction $\Delta C_i^r$.

By adding together, the losses in the total outputs of all industries in each affected region, we can obtain the loss in the total output for the region. Then, we discover the indirect economic loss value of each region by subtracting the final consumption reduction from the total output loss values. This can be illustrated in terms of the following equation (using the Wenchuan earthquake example):

$$\Delta X^r = \sum_{i=1}^{31} (\Delta x_i^r - \Delta c_i^r), r = 1, 2, \ldots, m \tag{12.8}$$

$\Delta X^r$ is the indirect economic loss value of region $r$. $\Delta x_i^r$ is an element of $\Delta X_i^r$ representing the total output loss values in industry $i$ of region $r$. $\Delta c_i^r$ is an element of the final consumption reduction $\Delta C_i^r$, and it represents the final consumption reduction in industry $i$ of region $r$.

## 12.3.2 Resilience Index of Provincial Economic Systems

Based on the resilience of provincial economic systems, we take into account the scientific principle, integrity principle, data availability and comparability in developing the resilience index (Rose and Wei 2013b) for the relevant provincial economic systems.

Provincial Resilience Index refers to the ability of a province to mobilize existing resources, offset the indirect perturbation of disasters, and recover the economic-social system to return to normal levels after it is indirectly disturbed by disaster events. Such a capability evaluation system contains seven second-level indexes including economy, government, finance, technology, human resources, infrastructure and business, with 21 third-level indexes. Each such indicator is further explained below.

**Economic indicators**. Economic capacity is the basis for system resilience, and it determines whether or not a region is able to mobilize sufficient resources to offset the impact of disasters, and accomplish sustainable and healthy development of the region. In accordance with the data availability principle, we selected three indices reflecting regional economic income, Average financial income, Average wage of urban worker and Rural per capita net income, and three indices reflecting the capacity of regional economic growth, Per capita GDP, Total retail sales of consumer goods and Total investment in fixed assets.

**Government regulatory capacity indicators**. There are increasing evidences from the recent disasters that well aware and well-prepared local governments and local communities can minimize the impacts of disasters. China has a powerful government to dominate disaster management system. Regulatory governance is of growing importance in terms of day-to-day regulatory management, rule-making and enforcement; government regulatory capacity includes the level of government expenditure, Per capita fiscal expenditure and Fiscal expenditure as a share of

GDP, and the ability of protecting unemployed citizens and maintain social stability including providing insurance coverage for unemployed citizens.

**Financial indicators**. One of the major challenges that presented pressure was money, "money derives recovery," as well as the quickness of recovery to sustain the social and economic networks that were destroyed (Olshansky 2006). Regional financial capacity refers to the use of financial instruments to allocate social resources to offset the indirect impact of disasters and resume normal social production and daily life. We selected three indices: Credit balance of financing institution at the end of the year, Per capita savings deposits and Per capita insurance premium income.

**Science and technology investment category indicators**. Science and technology are an important factor in endogenous regional economic growth continue to play a recessive area returns to normal and key role. Here, the assessment is conducted mainly on the internal expenses of R&D budget and the number of employees engaged in the activities of science and technology.

**Human resource indicators**. Human resources are the key elements of regional economic development. Level of human resources for post-disaster economic recovery and growth in the deployment of resources plays a dominant role. Here, we use Per capita education spending, Number of college degree or above holders as a share of population of 6 years old and older and Average educational year.

**Infrastructural indicators**. Infrastructure, including roads, electricity, water, gas and other elements is to maintain economic operation of the system. Whether the region is directly or indirectly impacted by disasters, these factors have played an important role in the recovery of the system. Due to data limitation, we adopted the Passenger volume and Total electricity to reflect the level of regional infrastructure construction.

**Enterprise-class indicators**. Enterprises symbolize the viability of regional economic systems. The more the enterprises and the higher the quality, the higher the ability, in the face of external disturbances, the enterprises can supply and adjust the critical supplies automatically by following the market rules. To reflect the level of openness and the level of active financial activities of the regional economic system, here we selected two indexes reflecting respectively the number of foreign-funded enterprises and the number of scaled domestic enterprises.

These indicators are shown Table 12.2.

### *12.3.3 PCA and Counterpart Support Evaluation Index*

**Principal Component Analysis (PCA)**. It is a statistical procedure that uses an orthogonal transformation to convert a set of observations of possibly correlated variables into a set of values of linearly uncorrelated variables called principal components. The number of principal components is less than or equal to the number of original variables. This transformation is defined in such a way that the first principal component has the largest possible variance (that is, accounts for as much of the variability in the data as possible): and each succeeding component in turn has the highest

**Table 12.2** The resilience evaluation index system of provincial economic systems

| First-level index | Second-level index | Third-level index | Function |
|---|---|---|---|
| Resilience | Economic power | Average financial income | Reflect the economic foundation of regional economic system, as well as the reality and possibility of deploying resources |
| | | Average wage of urban worker | |
| | | Rural per capita net income | |
| | | Per capita GDP | |
| | | Total retail sales of consumer goods | |
| | | Total investment in fixed assets | |
| | Government | Per capita fiscal expenditure | Reflect the government management and the regulation effects on regional system resilience |
| | | Fiscal expenditure as a share of GDP | |
| | | The coverage of unemployment insurance | |
| | Financial | Credit balance of financing institution at the end of theyear | Reflect the capital of the regional economic system and financing ability |
| | | Per capita savings deposits | |
| | | Per capita insurance premium income | |
| | Science and technology | R&D expenses within budget | Reflect the regional economy system of science and technology innovation ability |
| | | Number engaged in the activities of science and technology | |
| | Human resources | Per capita education spending | Human resource advantage of regional economic system |
| | | Number of college degree or above holders as a share of population of 6 years old and older | |
| | | Average educational year | |

(continued)

**Table 12.2** (continued)

| First-level index | Second-level index | Third-level index | Function |
|---|---|---|---|
| | Infrastructure | Passenger volume | Reflect the supporting function in the infrastructure of the economy |
| | | Total electricity | |
| | Enterprise | The number of enterprises with foreign investment | Reflect the economic vitality of the regional economic system |
| | | The number of industrial enterprises above designated size | |

variance possible under the constraint that it is orthogonal to (i.e., uncorrelated with) the preceding components. Principal components are guaranteed to be independent if the data set is jointly, normally distributed. PCA is sensitive to the relative scaling of the original variables. In summary, PCA is a multivariate statistical analysis method by which a lesser number of reconstructed variables is combined from the original multiple variables through linear transformation. See Principal Component Analysis (Jolliffe 1986) and multivariate statistical analysis (He 2008) for details.

According to the resilience index, which has one first-level indicator, 7 second-level indexes, 21 third-level indexes, we use PCA method to evaluate the resilience of 31 provincial economic systems. The calculation was performed with SPSS 12.0.

**Counterpart Support Evaluation Index**. Following the above theoretical foundation, we introduce the concept of evaluation index, denoted by $E$, as the ratio of the amount of counterpart support received to the actual indirect economic losses, as shown below:

$$E = \frac{\text{the amount of counterpart support}}{\text{the actual indirect economic losses}} \tag{12.9}$$

Formula (12.1) will be used to calculate the ratio of counterpart support amount to the indirect economic losses. The actual indirect economic losses are obtained from the value of indirect economic losses calculated by using IRIO and then modified by the resilience (see Table 12.3 in Sect. 12.4).

### *12.3.4 Data Specification*

The data regarding direct economic loss as a result of the Wenchuan earthquake, in Sichuan province, originated from the Sichuan Province Bureau of Statistics, and *the State Statistical System of Natural Disasters* as well as the related parameter table released by The Ministry of Civil Affairs in 2008. The information provided by the Sichuan Province Bureau of Statistics indicates that the Wenchuan earthquake caused

**Table 12.3** The evaluation results based on the indirect economic losses

| The support | $\alpha$ | $\beta$ | Indirect economic loss (billion RMB) | The actual indirect economic loss (billion RMB) | Support amount (billion RMB) | $E$ | Suggest support value (billion RMB) |
|---|---|---|---|---|---|---|---|
| Beijing | 0.833 | 0.334 | 4.047 | 1.350 | 7.253 | 5.373 | 1.498 |
| Jiangsu | 0.912 | 0.270 | 15.535 | 4.195 | 11.000 | 2.622 | 4.655 |
| Shanghai | 0.814 | 0.349 | 9.801 | 3.417 | 8.250 | 2.414 | 3.792 |
| Guangdong | 1.000 | 0.200 | 25.756 | 5.151 | 11.200 | 2.174 | 5.716 |
| Fujian | 0.331 | 0.735 | 2.147 | 1.578 | 3.339 | 2.115 | 1.752 |
| Shandong | 0.706 | 0.435 | 13.333 | 5.798 | 12.000 | 2.070 | 6.434 |
| Zhejiang | 0.829 | 0.337 | 9.955 | 3.353 | 5.730 | 1.709 | 3.721 |
| Jiangxi | 0.146 | 0.883 | 1.196 | 1.056 | 1.300 | 1.231 | 1.172 |
| Shanxi | 0.224 | 0.821 | 3.032 | 2.488 | 2.150 | 0.864 | 2.762 |
| Liaoning | 0.445 | 0.644 | 7.838 | 5.048 | 4.027 | 0.798 | 5.602 |
| Hubei | 0.283 | 0.774 | 3.515 | 2.719 | 2.115 | 0.778 | 3.017 |
| Anhui | 0.208 | 0.834 | 3.560 | 2.968 | 2.130 | 0.718 | 3.294 |
| Hunan | 0.258 | 0.794 | 4.721 | 3.747 | 2.010 | 0.536 | 4.158 |
| Tianjin | 0.396 | 0.683 | 6.231 | 4.257 | 2.037 | 0.479 | 4.724 |
| Jilin | 0.180 | 0.856 | 2.098 | 1.795 | 0.820 | 0.457 | 1.992 |
| Heilongjiang | 0.201 | 0.839 | 4.672 | 3.921 | 1.550 | 0.395 | 4.351 |
| Henan | 0.367 | 0.706 | 10.982 | 7.757 | 3.000 | 0.387 | 8.609 |
| Chongqing | 0.164 | 0.869 | 6.370 | 5.532 | 1.700 | 0.307 | 6.140 |
| Hebei | 0.336 | 0.731 | 13.578 | 9.931 | 2.800 | 0.282 | 11.021 |

*Note* The data collected by the author based on public information. The support amount is the total amount from 2008 to 2010

direct economic losses as high as RMB 737.177 billion. Converting the input-output table of Sichuan province, included merging the 42 industries into 30 industries, 15 industries have a direct economic loss in this new table. Among them, the other services have the most severe losses, which reached RMB 480.987 billion, accounting for 65.25% of the total direct economic losses. Transportation and warehousing, food production and tobacco processing industry, and agricultural (including agriculture, forestry, animal husbandry and fishery) follow, and respectively account for 10.17%, 8.51%, and 4.95%.[1]

[1]The data comes from the research-*Major Natural Disaster Statistics and Indirect Economic loss Assessment: Based on the Study of Wenchuan Earthquake* (Sun 2011). The direct economic loss assessment in Wenchuan earthquake requires two steps: First, it should carry out the field survey according to the relevant national standards, which is the basis of the assessment work. Second, the direct economic loss is getting by using the specific methods in *The Fourth Part in Earthquake Field Work-Disaster Direct Loss Evaluation (GB/T18208.4-2005). (The national standard in china).*

The data in the inter-regional input-output table comes from *The Theory and Practice of Making an Inter-regional input-output table about the 30 Provinces In China In 2007* (Liu et al. 2012). The indirect economic loss of each province, and city, is calculated following Formula (12.5). Data regarding the amount of counterpart support given was derived from www.china.com.cn. In this study, the provinces, or cities, (including municipalities directly under the central government) are the subject of support. Considering the aforementioned situation, we add the aid given by Guangdong province and Shenzhen. Guangdong supported Wenchuan in Sichuan province and Shenzhen supported hard-hit areas in Shanxi Province after the 2008 Wenchuan earthquake.

Sichuan province experienced direct economic loss as a result of the Wenchuan earthquake, accounting for 91.3% of the total losses. Gansu and Shaanxi, respectively, account for 5.8 and 2.9%. Many provinces have recorded much smaller direct economic losses than Sichuan province. Thus, the direct economic loss caused by the Wenchuan earthquake is only considered for Sichuan province.

The data used to evaluate the resilience of provincial economic systems came from *the 2008 China statistical yearbook, 2008 statistical yearbook of provinces and cities,* and *science and technology of China statistics yearbook 2008.*

## 12.4 The Empirical Analysis

In order to provide empirical evidence, the Wenchuan earthquake was selected as a representative example for evaluating the compensation activities from all support provinces, or cities, during the post-disaster period of the earthquake.

The Wenchuan earthquake on May 12, 2008 was one of the most destructive earthquakes experienced by China. Here, we will evaluate the counterpart support activities in view of indirect economic loss of the Wenchuan earthquake. The research steps are as follows:

(i) Estimation of the indirect economic losses value. The indirect economic losses value of 30 provinces in China is calculated by using Formula (12.8).

(ii) Calculation and standardization of the resilience of each provincial economic system. According to the resilience index of provincial economic systems, use SPSS12.0 to conduct KMO and Bartlett sphere test of 21 indicators for 31 provinces and cities. The fact that KMO test coefficient is 0.824 and Bartlett sphere inspection's p value is less than 0.05 justify the use of PCA in data analysis. The comprehensive evaluation of efficiency of 84.56% exceeds the threshold of 80%, proving that the principal component analysis has a good dimension reduction effect, and can reflect the information of the original variables. Finally, we standardize the resilience of provincial economic systems, using the following Formula:

$$\alpha = \frac{x - x_{\min}}{x_{\max} - x_{\min}} \tag{12.10}$$

In Formula (12.10): $\alpha$ represents the standard value from the comprehensive evaluation of the resilience of a provincial economic system, $x$ stands for the synthetic appraisal value of the resilience of a provincial economic system, $x_{\min}$ is the minimum value of comprehensive evaluation value of the resilience of a provincial economic system, and $x_{\max}$ is the maximum value of comprehensive evaluation value of the resilience of a provincial economic system.

(iii) Modification of the indirect economic loss value of relevant provinces using resilience. In fact, the provincial economic system cannot be completely restored right after a disaster. According to Tierney (1995) and Rose and Lim 2002 we assume the provincial economic system is restored to 0.8 of the pre-quake levels[2]. Suppose the whole recovery of the provincial economic system is 1. After subtracting from 0.8 $\alpha$, we received the irrecoverable proportion of the system, denoted by $\beta$. We will obtain the actual indirect economic loss value by $\beta$ times, the indirect economic loss value calculated from step i).

$$\beta = 1 - 0.8\alpha \tag{12.11}$$

In Formula (12.11): $\beta$ is the irrecoverable proportion of economic system function, 0.8 is the largest ratio that a provincial economy system can be restored quickly after a disaster, and $\alpha$ is the comprehensive evaluation standard value of the resilience of a provincial economic system.

The actual indirect economic loss value of different affected regions is calculated by the following formula:

$$\Delta\hat{X}^r = \beta \times \Delta X^r \tag{12.12}$$

$\Delta X^r$ and $\beta$ are respectively from the Formulas (12.8) and (12.11). Then the total actual indirect economic loss value results from the final demand reduction of each industry in Sichuan province can is calculated by Formula (12.13):

$$\Delta\hat{X} = \sum_{r=1}^{m} \Delta\hat{X}^r \tag{12.13}$$

[2]Tierney (1995) learned for questionnaires that after Northridge Earthquake, the power system resilience of SAN Fernando valley, California, USA is 77.1%. Rose and Lim 2002 studied the same region after Northridge Earthquake. The research found that the direct static resilience in this region is 95% with the simulation model. At the same time, Rose & Lim also found that the market resilience is 79.3% with I-O model calculation. Based on the above research, we might as well simply assume that after the Wenchuan earthquake, the related provincial economic system can fully recover to 80% of pre-quake levels.

Through Formula (12.13): the total actual indirect economic losses in 29 provinces or cities (in addition to Sichuan province) are RMB 108.676 billion. During the three years, after the Wenchuan earthquake, the total counterpart support amount of 19 provinces or cities are RMB 84.411 billion. The counterpart support activities of 19 provinces or cities after the Wenchuan earthquake will be evaluated in the following.

(iv) According to the evaluation index $E$, we measure the counterpart support given by 19 provinces or cities after the Wenchuan earthquake. The calculation results are presented in Table 12.3.

Table 12.3 indicates that the total indirect economic loss of 19 counterpart supporters was RMB 148.368 million. The total actual indirect economic loss was RMB 76.063 million, and the total counterpart support was RMB 84.411 billion. According to *the post-earthquake counterpart support scheme* issued by the central government, the counterpart support amount of provinces and cities should not be less than 1% of their local fiscal revenue, in the previous year, for three years. Actually, the number of the continuous support for three years will exceed RMB 70 billion. In fact, in the three years after Wenchuan earthquake, the 19 other provinces or cities implement counterpart support projects 4,121, and provided the total counterpart support of RMB 84.411 billion. The total amount of counterpart support has reached the provisions of *the post-earthquake counterpart support scheme.*

Table 12.3 also orders the 19 provinces or cities by their $E$ values, with the top most five as Beijing (5.373): Jiangsu (2.622): Shanghai (2.414): Guangdong (2.174) and Fujian (2.115). The histogram representation is given in Fig. 12.1.

According to the above results, the support amounts given by Beijing, Jiangsu, Shanghai, Guangdong and Fujian are excessive. Whereas, the support amounts given

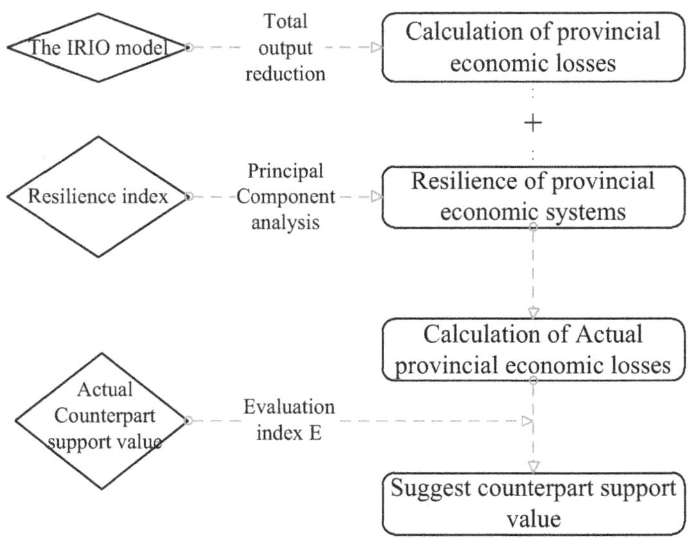


**Fig. 12.1** The flowchart for the proposed content

by Jilin, Heilongjiang, Henan, Chongqing and Hebei are insufficient. The counterpart framework is unfair to both sides.

Based on the above methods of calculation, during the rescue operations of Wenchuan Earthquake we computed the support amounts that should be provided by the counterpart partners (Table 12.3). The authors also inquired the participants of counterpart support (including Officials of Leadership Committee of Jiangsu Province Counterpart Support working in the Mianzhu earthquake disaster area; after Wenchuan earthquake, Jiangsu province was assigned to support Mianzhu city by the Central Government of China). Participants generally believe that the counterpart support should consider sufficiently the indirect economic loss and distribute proportionally the aids based on the indirect loss. Their positive feedback on the proposed counterpart support framework validates the fairness of the IRIO and resilience model and effectiveness of the approaches implemented in this study.

## 12.5 Internal Validity and External Validity

The proposed counterpart support framework is an analytical approach for assessing the damages of natural disasters, it comprises of the IRIO for indirect economic losses, resilience index and PCA for provincial resilience, index $E$ for level of support, and I-O data. The framework provides an approximation of the real-world problems, but there can produce deviations to a certain extent. As such, it is necessary to investigate the limitations, especially internal and external validity for promoting the proposed methodologies to similar disasters where counterpart support policies are critical for post-disaster operations.

**Internal validity**. This will focus in managing more precisely on identifying the actual dynamics in the case studied, including the IRIO for indirect economic losses, resilience index, and index E of support level. Suppose that the technical coefficient matrix $A$ (see Sect. 12.3.1) remains constant throughout the evolution process of a disaster event. The resilience assessment index, previously investigated by Hallegatte in 2014, index $E$ of level of support, proposed in the present paper, along with other measures utilized over the IRIO model constitute essentially an internal static and monetary assessment without implementing price changes, alternative, and substitute items concerning the shortage of goods in the economic system (Hallegatte 2014). This is true even if the resilience assessments of non-directly affected provinces were used to avoid the weakness of IRIO models (such as possible overestimation).

On the other hand, there are also several issues to be noted. First, the proposed resilience index (Sect. 12.3.2) may be subject to some limitations, including that, like those from other expert systems, computation results could be affected by the contents of the index and the employed calculation methods.

Second, simultaneously, errors or inaccuracy in the input data to the IRIO model, namely the data of IRIO tables, may lead to results different from the status of the real economic system. Moreover, it should be pointed out that, as China's input-output table data updated once every five years, the data of 2007 IRIO tables was utilized in the calculation. The Wenchuan earthquake occurred in 2008; 2007 IRIO data reflects an approximation of "supply and use" relationship among the regions before these disasters happened.

Third, the value of the counterpart support evaluation index $E$ is defined by dividing the total required disaster aid (Sichuan province) by the total actual indirect economic losses (19 provinces and cities): as given in Formula (12.1). However, as there is no available official statistical data, the disaster aid required by the disaster area (Sichuan province) is unknown. This was resolved by using the total support amount by the donors (19 provinces and cities).

Fourth, in determining the resilience ratios of provincial economic systems (see Formula (12.11)); we referred the research results by Tierney (1995) and:Rose and Lim 2002 and took the value 0.8. However, this value has some uncertainty. The smaller this value, the smaller the value of $\beta$, and the smaller the actual indirect economic loss $\Delta \hat{X}^r$ (Formula (12.12)). When the value of $E$ remains unchanged, the calculated support amounts of the donors (19 provinces and cities) will be smaller, and vice versa. But the rank according to the support amounts may vary. Moreover, it is also noticed from the computation that when the resilience ratio takes values 0.7 and 0.9, the counterpart support levels and rank change accordingly.

**External validity**. For studying the relevance or feasibility of the framework on similar disasters, i.e., for examining the external validity by a case study approach. Initially, as mentioned above, we substituted temporarily the $E$ values obtained from the Wenchuan earthquake for the 19 provinces (Formula (12.9)): and calculated approximate support amounts for the contributing provinces and cities. In future applications, when determining the supporting levels on similar disasters, one should first estimate the required amount from the affected areas, then according to the IRIO model compute indirect economic losses, calculate the values of evaluation index $E$, and then determine the support amounts for the provinces and cities. Moreover, for applications assessing economic losses from other natural disasters using the analytical framework proposed in this paper, researchers may utilize this model with caution: limitations of the IRIO as mentioned previously, completeness of the index system, availability of full data, and the accuracy of data.

## 12.6 Conclusions

This paper investigates quantitative measures of indirect economic losses incurred from natural disasters such as earthquakes. Subsequently, the paper reveals, in an innovative way, the driving mechanism behind the counterpart support policy: When the donors bestow monetary aid and urgent disaster relief goods to the disaster impacted areas, not only do the disaster impacted areas receive immediate counterpart assistance, but also the donors benefit economically by essentially helping reduce their own indirect economic losses. Therefore, donors should provide appropriate aid levels to the disaster affected regions/parties in accordance with the principle of proportionality.

Also, when implementing IRIO models assessing indirect economic losses, in order to overcome the conventional IRIO's linear approach idea and avoid over-estimations on the indirect economic losses, this paper gives a full consideration to the resilience of the associated provinces and cities, and establishes the economic index system for the resilience recovery.

Finally, the analytical framework, models and algorithms proposed in this paper may be used in the design of counterpart support policies and implementation programs for other large-scale earthquakes and natural disasters.

**Acknowledgements** Peipei Xue, Ji Guo, Zhonghui Ji, Guowei, Xueqiang Ning, Yujia Lou also made great contributions to this manuscript. We express our heartfelt thanks to them. This research was supported by: National Social and Scientific Fund Program of China (18ZDA052; 17BGL142;16ZDA047); The Natural Science Foundation of China (91546117,71373131, 71140014, 11371292). National Social and Scientific Fund Program (11CGL100): National Soft Scientific Fund Program (2011GXQ4B025): National Industry-specific Topics (GYHY200806017). This research was also supported by the Priority Academic Program Development of Jiangsu Higher Education Institutions.

## References

Ai, N., & Polenske, K. R. (2008). Socioeconomic impact analysis of yellow-dust storms: An approach and case study for Beijing. *Economic Systems Research, 20*(2), 187–203.

Aksha, S. K., & Emrich, C. T. (2020). Benchmarking community disaster resilience in Nepal. *International Journal of Environmental Research and Public Health, 17*(6), 1–22.

Bulte, E., Xu, L., & Zhang, X. Does aid promote or hinder industrial development? lessons from China. In: *The Northeast Universities Development Consortium Conference 2013 on development economics, Center for International Development at Harvard University*, Cambridge, MA, USA, 2-3 Nov 2013.

Bnic, A., Kourtit, K., & Nijkamp, P. (2020). Natural disasters as a development opportunity: a spatial economic resilience interpretation. *Review of Regional Research, 40,* 223–249.

Bruno, C. (2019) *Analysis of the regional economic resilience in Latin America and the caribbean from 2000 to 2017*. Universidade Federal de Ouro Preto.

Cai, J. (2012). *The counterpart support research between Chinese provinces within the framework of the horizontal fiscal balance theory*. Master's degree thesis of Fudan University, Shanghai.

Chakkaphan, T., & David, E. (2007). Case study: applying a regional CGE model for estimation of indirect economic losses due to damaged highway bridges. *The Engineering Economist: A Journal Devoted to the Problems of Capital Investment, 52*(4), 367–401.

Chen, X., & Yang, C. (2011). *Input-output technique*. Science Press.

Coffman, M., & Noy, I. (2012). Hurricane Iniki: Measuring the long-term economic impact of a natural disaster using synthetic control. *Environment and Development Economics, 17*(2), 187–205.

Comfort, L. K. (2010). *Designing Resilience*. University of Pittsburgh Pre.

Courvisanos, J., Jain, A., & Mardaneh, K. K. (2016). Economic resilience of regions under crises: A study of the Australian Economy. *Regional Studies, 50*(4), 629–643.

Dietzenbacher, E. (1997). In vindication of the Ghosh model: A reinterpretation as a price model. *Journal of Regional Science, 37,* 629–651.

Eguchi, R. T., & Adams, B. J. (2007). Improving resilience with remote sensing technologies. *TR News, 6*.

Gao, Z., Geddes, R. R., & Ma, T. (2020). Direct and indirect economic losses using typhoon-flood disaster analysis: An application to Guangdong Province, China. *Sustainability, 12*(21), 1–22.

Gong, H., Hassink, R., Tan, J., & Huang, D. (2020). Regional resilience in times of a pandemic crisis: The case of COVID in China. *Tijdschrift voor Economische en Sociale Geografie, 111*(3), 497–512.

Hallegatte, S., & Dumas, P. (2009). Can natural disasters have positive consequences? investigating the role of embodied technical change. *Ecological Economics, 68,* 777–786.

Hallegatte, S., Ranger, N., Mestre, O., Dumas, P., Corfee-Morlot, J., & Herweijer, C. (2011). Assessing climate change impacts, sea level rise and storm surge risk in port cities: a case study on Copenhagen. *Climatic Change, 104*(1), 113–137.

Hallegatte, S. (2014). Modeling the role of inventories and heterogeneity in the assessment of the economic costs of natural disasters. *Risk Analysis, 34,* 152–167.

Han, Y., & Goetz, S. J. (2018). Predicting US county economic resilience from industry input-output accounts. *Applied Economics, 51*(19–21), 2019–2028.

Hashiguchi, Y., Yamano, N., & Webb, C. (2017). Economic shocks and changes in global production structures: Methods for measuring economic resilience. *Ide Discussion Papers, 9,* 1–46.

Heatwole, N., & Rose, A. (2013). A reduced-form rapid economic consequence estimating model: Application to property damage from U.S. earthquakes. *International Journal of Disaster Risk Science, 4,* 20–32.

He, X. (2008). *Multivariate statistical analysis.* China Renmin University Press.

Hirokazu, T., & Satoshi, T. (2008). A framework for economic loss estimation due to seismic transportation network disruption: A spatial computable general equilibrium approach. *Natural Hazards, 44*(2), 253–265.

Irimoto, H., Shibusawa, H., & Miyata, Y. (2017). Evaluating the economic damages of transport disruptions using a transnational and interregional input-output model for Japan, China, and South Korea. *American Institute of Physics Conference Series, 1892*(110002), 1–6.

Isard, W. (1951). Inter-regional and regional input-output analysis: a model of a space-economy. *The Review of Economics and Statistics, 33,* 318–328.

Isard, W. (1960). *Methods of regional analysis: An introduction to regional science.* The MIT Press.

Jacinto, R., Reis, E., & Ferrão, J. (2020). Indicators for the assessment of social resilience in flood-affected communities: A text mining-based methodology. *Science of the Total Environment, 744*(140973), 1–17.

Jin, X., Sumaila, U. R., & Yin, K. (2020). Direct and indirect loss evaluation of storm surge disaster based on static and dynamic input-output models. *Sustainability, 12*(18), 1–25.

Jolliffe, I. T. (1986). *Principal component analysis.* New York: Spring-Verlag.

Luca, G., & Georgios, G. (2018). On input-output economic models in disaster impact assessment. *International Journal of Disaster Risk Reduction, 9*(30), 186–198.

Liu, W., Cheng, J., & Tang, Z. (2012). The theory and practice of inter-regional input-output table about 30 provinces in China in 2007. China Statistics Press.

Santos, Joost R. (2006). Inoperability input-output modeling of disruptions to interdependent economic systems. *Systems Engineering, 9*(1), 20–34.

Jung, J., Santos, J. R., & Haimes, Y. Y. (2009). International trade inoperability input-output model (IT-IIM): Theory and application. *Risk Analysis, 29*(1), 137–154.

Kellenberg, D., & Mobarak, A. M. (2008). Does rising income increase or decrease damage risk from natural disasters? *Journal of Urban Economics, 63,* 788–802.

Kendra, J. M., & Wachtendorf, T. (2003). Elements of resilience after the world trade center disaster: Reconstituting New York City's Emergency Operations Centre. *Disasters, 27*(1), 37–53.

Leung, M. F., Haimes, Y. Y., & Santos, J. R. (2007). Supply and output-side extensions to inoperability input-output model for interdependent infrastructures. *Journal of Infrastructure Systems, 13,* 299–310.

Liu, B., Han, S., Gong, H., Zhou, Z., & Zhang, D. (2020). Disaster resilience assessment based on the spatial and temporal aggregation effects of earthquake-induced hazards. *Environmental Science and Pollution Research, 27*(5), 29055–29067.

Liu, W., Cheng, J., & Tang, Z. (2012). *The theory and practice of inter-regional input-output table about 30 provinces in China in 2007*. China Statistics Press.

Liu, X., Yuan, S., Chen, Z., Song, L., Ma, Y., Wang, C., et al. (2019). Assessing the indirect economic losses of sea ice disasters: An adaptive regional input-output modeling approach. *International Journal of Offshore and Polar Engineering, 29*(4), 415–420.

Lu, C., Wei, Y., Fan, Y., & Xu, W. (2002). Quantitatively analytic model and application for the impact of natural disaster on national economy. *Journal of Natural Disasters, 11,* 15–20.

Manyena, S. B. (2006). The concept of resilience revisited. *Disasters, 30,* 434–450.

McEntire, D. A. (2007). *Disaster response and recovery: Strategies and tactics for resilience*. New Jersey: Wiley.

Miller, R., & Blair, P. (2009). *Input-output analysis: Foundations and extensions*. Cambridge: Cambridge University Press.

Narayan, P. K. (2003). Economic impact of the 2003 south pacific games on fiji. *Economic Papers: A Journal of Applied Economics and policy, 22*(3), 60–73.

Ni, F., Zhang, Y., & Yu, T. (2009). A preliminary study on the counterpart support of the Wenchuan earthquake. *Research on Economics and Management, 7,* 55–62.

Noy, I., & Nualsri, A. (2007). What do exogenous shocks tell us about growth theories? In: *Working Paper*. Santa Cruz Center for International Economics, pp 7-28.

Okuyama, Y., & Santos, J. R. (2014). Disaster impact and input-output analysis. *Economic Systems Research, 26*(1), 1–12.

Oosterhaven, J. (1988). On the plausibility of the supply driven input-output model. *Journal of Regional Science, 28*(2), 203–217.

Pakoksung, K., Suppasri, A., Matsubae, K., & Imamura, F. (2019). Estimating Tsunami economic losses of Okinawa Island with multi-regional-input-output modeling. *Geosciences (Switzerland), 9*(349), 1–21.

Park, J. Y. (2008). The economic impacts of a dirty-bomb attack on the Los Angeles and Long Beach port: applying supply-driven NIEMO. *Journal of Homeland Security and Emergency Management, 5*(1), 1–20.

Paton, D., & Johnston, D. M. *Disaster resilience: An integrated approach*. Charles C Thomas Publisher.

Ranger, N., Hallegatte, S., Bhattacharya, S., Bachu, M., Priya, S., & Dhore, K. (2011). An assessment of the potential impact of climate change on flood risk in Mumbai. *Climatic Change, 104*(1), 139–167.

Rose, A., & Lim, D. (2002). Business interruption losses from natural hazards: conceptual and methodological issues in the case of the Northridge earthquake. *Global Environmental Change Part B: Environmental Hazards, 4,* 1–14.

Rose, A. (2004). Defining and measuring economic resilience to disasters. *Disaster Prevention and Management, 13,* 307–314.

Rose, A., & Guha, G. S. (2004). Computable general equilibrium modeling of electric utility lifeline losses from earthquakes. *Modeling the Spatial Economic Impacts of Natural Hazards*:119–142.

Rose, A., & Liao, S. (2005). Modeling resilience to disasters: computable general equilibrium analysis of a water service disruption. *Journal of Regional Science, 45*(1), 75–112.

Rose, A., Oladosu, G., & Liao, S. (2007a). Business interruption impacts of a terrorist attack on the electric power system of Los Angeles: customer resilience to a total blackout. *Risk Analysis, 27,* 513–531.

Rose, A., Oladosu, G., & Liao, S. (2007b) Regional economic impacts of a terrorist attack on the water system of Los Angeles: a computable general disequilibrium analysis. *The Economic Costs and Consequences of Terrorism*, 291–316.

Rose, A. (2007c) Economic resilience to disasters: multidisciplinary origins and contextual dimensions. *Environmental Hazards: Human and Social Dimensions*, *7*, 1–16.

Rose, A., & Krausmann, E. (2013). An economic framework for the development of a resilience index for business recovery. *International Journal of Disaster Risk Reduction, 5,* 73–83.

Rose, A., & Wei, D. (2013). Estimating the economic consequences of a port shutdown: the special role of resilience. *Economic Systems Research, 25*(2), 212–232.

Sarker, M. N., Islam, M. S., Huq, M. E., Alam, G. M. M., Raihan, M. L. (2020) Big data-driven disaster resilience. *Information and Communication Technologies for Humanitarian Services, 8,* 165–185.

Schmidt-Thomé, P., Greivingb, S., Kallioa, H., Fleischhauerb, M., & Jarvaa, J. (2006). Economic risk maps of floods and earthquakes for European regions. *Quaternary International, 150*(1), 103–112.

Shymon, S., Kolomiets-Ludwig, E., Osiejewicz, J., Krawczyk, D., & Kaminska, B. (2020). The role of country brand in providing economic resilience. *Marketing and Management of Innovations, 1,* 303–311.

Skidmore, M., & Toya, H. (2002). Do natural disasters promote long-run growth? *Economic Inquiry, 40,* 664–687.

Sun, H. (2011). *Major natural disaster statistics and indirect economic loss assessment: based on the study of Wenchuan earthquake.* Master's degree thesis of Southwestern university of finance and economics, Chengdu.

Tanoue, M., Taguchi, R., Nakata, S., Watanabe, S., Fujimori, S., & Hirabayashi, Y. (2020). Estimation of direct and indirect economic losses caused by a flood with long-lasting inundation: application to the 2011 Thailand flood. *Water Resources Research, 56*(5), 1–39.

Tierney, K. J. (1995). *Impacts of recent US disasters on businesses: the 1993 midwest floods and the 1994 Northridge earthquake.* National Center for Earthquake Engineering Research, pp 189–222.

Tierney, K. J. (2007). 'From the margins to the mainstream? Disaster research at the crossroads. *Annual Review of Sociology, 33,* 503–525.

Wang, G., Li, X., Wu, X., & Yu, J. (2014). The rainstorm comprehensive economic loss assessment based on CGE model: using a July heavy rainstorm in Beijing as an example. *Natural Hazards.*

Wang, Y., & Dong, L. (2010). Preliminary study on China's local government's counterpart support mode after a disaster. *Contemporary World & Socialism, 1,* 131–136.

Wei, X., Li, N., Hu, A., Gao, Y., & Ji, Z. (2012). Assessing the economic impact of environmental disaster: a computable general equilibrium analysis. *China Population, Resources and Environment, 22*(11), 26–31.

Whittaker, S., Khalfan, M., M., A., and Ulhaq, I. 'Developing community disaster resilience through preparedness', International Journal of Critical Infrastructures, 2020, 16(1): 53.

Wu, J., Li, N., Hallegatte, S., Shi, P., Hu, A., & Liu, X. (2012). Regional indirect economic impact evaluation of the 2008 Wenchuan earthquake. *Environmental Earth Sciences, 65,* 161–172.

Wu, X. (2012) A meager opinion about building a new natural disaster relief system. *Journal of the Party School of the Central Committee of the C.P.C, 16*(4), 91–93.

Zobel, C. W., Baghersad, M., & Parker, B. R. (2020). Analytically comparing disaster resilience across multiple dimensions. *Socio-Economic Planning Sciences, 69*(100678), 1–14.

Zhang, X. (2006). Fiscal decentralization and political centralization in China: implications for growth and regional inequality. *Journal of Comparative Economics, 34*(4), 713–726.

# Chapter 13
# The Relationship Among Public Cognition, Perceived Value, and Meteorological Service Satisfaction

**Abstract** Clarifying the relationship between public cognition and satisfaction with meteorological service is an important way to adapt to and mitigate climate change. This paper first proposes an innovative concept on public meteorological cognition. Also, based on the survey data from 3,029 questionnaires on public cognition of meteorological disasters in Shenzhen city of China, the relationship among public cognition, perceived value, and meteorological service satisfaction is evaluated using a structural equation model (SEM). Research results demonstrate that: (1) Public cognition can significantly affect service satisfaction. (2) Shenzhen residents are generally satisfied with meteorological service, particularly during the typhoon season. However, the residents are dissatisfied with the availability of information on meteorological disaster warnings. (3) Both public meteorological cognition and perceived value of meteorological service significantly affect public satisfaction. (4) The public meteorological cognition can be improved by increasing the perceived value of meteorological service, which further enhances public satisfaction.

**Keywords** Meteorological Disaster · Public Cognition · Perceived Value · Service Satisfaction · Structural Equation Model

## 13.1 Introduction

The rapid climate warming and the frequent occurrence of meteorological disasters have posed a serious challenge to the sustainable development of the world as well as the ecological environment (Intergovernmental Panel on Climate Change, IPCC 2013). Meteorological disasters approximately account for 71% of the total economic losses caused by natural disasters (United Nations 2018). And China is one of the countries that experience the most frequent and severest natural disasters. On the other hand, continual meteorological disasters have facilitated the advancement of meteorological service. To increase public satisfaction, the meteorological department in China has been committed to improving meteorological service. Then, what is the public satisfaction with meteorological service? What are the factors that affect public satisfaction with meteorological service? What measures should be taken to enhance public satisfaction effectively? These are important issues for

 
X. Wu and J. Guo, *Economic Impacts and Emergency Management of Disasters in China*,
https://doi.org/10.1007/978-981-16-1319-7_13

the relevant governmental departments, the meteorological industry, and the public. However, relatively large-scale empirical research and data analysis is rare (Song and Du 2017; Song et al. 2018). To fill this gap, in the present situation and through an empirical study targeted at 3,029 Chinese residential families in Shenzhen city of China, this paper intends to analyze the relationship among public cognition, perceived value, and meteorological service satisfaction and to provide reference materials from communities and the public so as to carry out effective environmental disaster management.

Evaluations of satisfaction with products and services have attracted increasing attention in China and around the world because of developments in service industries and of growing public attention to service quality. Cardozo (1965) introduced the concept of "customer satisfaction" into business services in 1965. As studies on service quality emerged gradually in Western countries, enterprises and public institutions became aware of the significance of service quality and evaluated their service satisfaction. Subsequently, Sweden established the first satisfaction index model named Sweden Customer Satisfaction Barometer (SCSB). Based on SCSB, American Customer Satisfaction Index model (ACSI): Sweden Index of Customer Satisfaction (SICS): and European Customer Satisfaction Index (ECSI) were developed. These models are the existing mainstream satisfaction evaluation models in the world (Wang et al. 2011). At present, satisfaction evaluation models are widely used in all aspects of social life. For example, Xie and Zhang (2013) evaluated the job satisfaction of new generation employees by a structural equation model (hereafter referred to as SEM): and found that encouraging new generation employees to participate in enterprise supervision, management, and decision making can improve their participation intention and job satisfaction. Yen (2012) divided perceived value into three components: utilitarian value, social value, and hedonic value. Then he used mediated regression analysis to find that all three components of perceived value had positive relationships with cell phone users' loyalty. In a competitive market, it is vital to know the determinants of customer satisfaction. Park (2019) analyzed a vast amount of customer data and applied a structural equation modeling method. He empirically concluded that the quality of online airline services and in-flight customer experiences jointly decided customer satisfaction. Besides, there was a positive relationship between customer satisfaction and users' willingness to repurchase the service. However, the perceived cost value negatively affected users' willingness to repurchase service and customer satisfaction. In the financial services industry, customer satisfaction positively influenced both the future cost of customer service and customer value. Therefore, financial service providers needed to weigh the costs and benefits while improving customer satisfaction (Terpstra and Verbeeten 2014). In addition, satisfaction evaluations have also been used extensively in public service undertakings, especially in public health services. For instance, social care providers could improve service satisfaction by communicating in detail with receivers of social care services (Willis et al. 2016). Based on a partial least squares path model, Lobo et al. (2014) established a global satisfaction index and investigated user satisfaction with primary care services. The outcomes indicated that the most critical factors affecting user satisfaction were medical care and medical expenses. Also, opinions on health care equity and nursing service were significant determinants of user satisfaction. However, perceived accessibility negatively affected user satisfaction. In order to improve the quality of services, it is important for public service organizations to identify the range of services that have the most significant effect on citizen satisfaction. Based on rough sets theory, Alizadeh and Kianfar (2013) built a model of citizen satisfaction to ascertain the key factors that affected public service satisfaction. Ji and Hu (2013) introduced a satisfaction evaluation model into government public service assessment and evaluated the satisfaction with public services in 34 cities of China by combining the model with TOPSIS of entropy weight and cluster analysis. They found that several eastern coastal cities, including Xiamen, Qingdao, Hangzhou, Ningbo, and Dalian, showed the highest satisfaction levels. Nuviala et al. (2012) conducted many questionnaires to assess the perceived quality, satisfaction, and perceived value of sports service consumers. The findings indicated that perceived quality, consumer satisfaction with sports service, and perceived value were largely determined by several intangible factors, including the techniques of service personnel and easy access to sports information, and so on. Tan et al. (2017) investigated the factors influencing user loyalty in nonprofit organizations and the relationship among service experience, perceived quality, and user satisfaction. He referred to the research method of hotel customer satisfaction index and did a detailed questionnaire survey on library users. The results showed that service experience had a great effect on library user satisfaction and loyalty, but perceived service quality had little effect on user satisfaction and loyalty. Combining Bayesian networks and quantitative analysis, Wu et al. (2016) studied the effect of various aspects of service on consumer satisfaction with the quality of public transportation service. They pointed out that punctual arrival, reasonable waiting time, seating capacity, comfortable environment, and humanized considerations mainly affected customer satisfaction. To estimate overall customer satisfaction, some researchers have used importance weighting to combine the overall satisfaction with the importance of different satisfaction evaluation factors. Adding importance weighting to the satisfaction assessment was strongly supported by Hsieh (2012): and he evaluated the adequacy of importance weighting. He assigned different importance weightings to the satisfaction rating items and then summed the scores to get the overall satisfaction score. A few years later, Hsieh (2018) researched the adequacy and necessity of importance weighting in customer satisfaction evaluation again and assessed the importance of various home care services. The results demonstrated that people generally perceived different importance from home care service items, and the perceived importance of different service items was determined by the relationship between total satisfaction and satisfaction with each service item.

Currently, only a few empirical studies on the meteorological service satisfaction have been published. For illustration, Wang et al. (2011) established an SEM to evaluate public satisfaction with meteorological service. Wu et al. (2012) analyzed the effect of meteorological service on Shanghai-Nanjing Expressway by combining the method of willingness-to-pay (WTP) and structural equation modeling (SEM). Yuan et al. (2016) investigated the benefit and cost–benefit ratio of public meteorological services in China through multiple willingness-to-pay evaluation models. They demonstrated that the cost–benefit ratios in the northwest region were much lower than in the central and east regions. The result was consistent with the differences in economic conditions in the northwest, east, and central regions. In disaster risk evaluation, social vulnerability is a crucial evaluation indicator. According to the specific situation of a meteorological disaster site, Cai and Wei (2020) constructed a social vulnerability assessment index system. They also used the fuzzy interpretive structural modeling (FISM) method to establish structural relationships among social vulnerability assessment elements. Moreover, many scholars take typhoons as an example to research meteorological disasters. Zhong (2020) investigated the major elements in remedial services that affected public satisfaction after the government failed to disclose information during the typhoon. He employed structural equation modeling (SEM) and found that some internal intangible elements of remedial services such as outcome fairness, procedural fairness, interactional fairness, and information fairness primarily affected public satisfaction. Based on the framework of "data preparation-opinion mining-data analysis" and the combination of social network analysis and emotion analysis, Ma et al. (2020) identified the modes and features of the shift in public voice during Typhoon Mangkhut. They suggested that the official media's timely delivery of exact messages, more effective actions of leading public voice, and more concern for terrible human-caused events during typhoon disasters helped people cope with climate disasters better. However, existing studies have three limitations. First, they did not establish an SEM to evaluate meteorological service satisfaction. Second, most studies conducted questionnaire surveys to evaluate the satisfaction with meteorological service in inland cities, while few studies mounted a small-scale questionnaire or acquired a small amount of survey data concerning coastal regions where meteorological disasters are more frequent. Third, although the studies on public satisfaction evaluation are abundant in number, few scholars evaluated meteorological service satisfaction and its influencing factors from the perspective of public meteorological cognition.

Public knowledge of meteorological disasters and cognition of meteorological information can affect meteorological service satisfaction significantly. For instance, Getz (1978) reported that most respondents in New Jersey had a lower cognition of agrometeorological information because of the poor publicity and popularization of meteorological service, thereby resulting in the underuse of agrometeorological service in the state. Lellyett and Anaman (2010) observed that increasing public meteorological cognition and enhancing public self-protection capability could lead to a significant reduction in economic losses and casualties caused by meteorological disasters. In addition, taking a village in Zhejiang Province, China, as an example, Zhang et al. (2017) investigated the awareness, attitudes, and actions toward typhoon-related risks among residents in the countryside. They adopted various research methods, including questionnaire surveys, univariate and multivariate analysis, and the complementary log–log (CLL) model. The results indicated that rural residents were not fully aware of the risks of typhoons to their health and lives, and the actions of rural residents were not consistent with their awareness. Therefore, more educational activities and publicity campaigns were demanded to improve rural residents' abilities to protect themselves from meteorological disasters. Dube´ and Menon (2000) divided the service cognition of customers into positive and negative types; positive cognition resulted in positive evaluation and reaction to services, whereas negative cognition resulted in negative evaluation and reaction to services. De Ruyter and Bloemer (1999) stated that positive emotions could contribute to higher customer service satisfaction. Anderson et al. (2008) discovered a close relationship among customer service cognition, customer characteristics, and service satisfaction. Huang and Xu (2013) demonstrated that differences in personal cognition caused by different educational backgrounds could significantly affect the evaluation of public service satisfaction. Bayard and Jolly (2007) found that the awareness of farmers about environmental protection influenced their behavior and attitude; to be specific, higher cognition compelled farmers to participate in environmental improvement more positively and increased their satisfaction with environmental protection. Furthermore, there are numerous studies on perceived value, customer loyalty, and customer satisfaction. Su (2012) conducted an empirical study on the loyalty and satisfaction of tourists based on the cognition-emotion-behavior theory, and found that public service cognition had a significant effect on travel satisfaction of tourists; to go into detail, higher service cognition facilitated positive consumption emotion, higher service satisfaction, and loyalty. Joung et al. (2016) used structural equation modeling to test the relationships among perceived quality, perceived value, and customer satisfaction. The results revealed that both perceived quality and perceived value had remarkable influences on customer satisfaction. Besides, gender significantly influenced the relationship between perceived quality and perceived value. By applying partial least squares structural equation modeling (PLS-SEM) and electronic surveys, Wang et al. (2019) empirically analyzed the effect of perceived value and perceived risk on users' intention to carpool. The findings showed that users' perceived value and intention of ride-sharing were positively related, while high perceived risk reduced users' intention to share a ride. Roy et al. (2016) conducted an empirical study on the relationship among service equity, service quality, service efficiency and user satisfaction. They confirmed that service efficiency considerably affected service equity, service quality, and user satisfaction. In addition, Virvilaite et al. (2015) explored the relationship between consumer perceived value and customer loyalty. He assessed the overall perceived value in three components: functional value, sentimental value, and social value. Then he examined consumer loyalty from two perspectives: attitudinal loyalty and behavioral loyalty. The results indicated that all three components of perceived value positively affected customer loyalty. The functional value had the most significant effect on attitudinal loyalty, and sentimental value had the most significant effect on behavioral loyalty. Chou (2014) discussed the relationship among service value drivers, the users' perceived value, and user satisfaction in the semiconductor manufacturing service industry. He found a mismatch between users' perceived value and value drivers, and user satisfaction was more likely to be affected by line services than support services. Also, the type and geographical location of the client company played essential roles in the assessment of user satisfaction. All research results have confirmed the close relationship among public cognition, public perceived service quality, and satisfaction evaluation. Higher public meteorological cognition is accompanied by more accurate evaluation of meteorological service and meteorological service satisfaction, which are beneficial to proposing specific policy suggestions. China, which has experienced frequent meteorological disasters, is committed to the development of technologies and methods for the defense, monitoring, and emergency management of meteorological disasters. Therefore, an innovative concept of public meteorological cognition is proposed in this paper. Based on the survey data from 3,029 questionnaires on public cognition of meteorological security in Shenzhen, a quantitative analysis on the relationship among public meteorological cognition, perceived value, and meteorological service satisfaction will be conducted using SEM. This analysis hopes to provide substantial evidence for relevant theoretical research on meteorological disasters and operation services.

## 13.2 Method

### *13.2.1 Structural Equation Model (SEM)*

The SEM, known as covariance structural analysis model and linear structural relationship model, is an emerging statistical approach and research idea. SEM is a branch of applied statistics that has developed most rapidly over the past three decades. The model can search the intrinsic structural relationship among variables to verify the rationality of the structural relationship or model hypothesis. The model was suitable in this paper because it can depict the characteristics of latent variables and their relationship with observational variables. Therefore, SEM is also known as a latent variable analysis model (Hou et al. 2004).

Compared with traditional regression analysis, structural equation model has the following advantages. (1) Multiple dependent variables can be simultaneously considered and processed in structural equation analysis. (2) Measurement errors are allowed in the independent and dependent variables. (3) Factor structure and factor relationship can be evaluated simultaneously. (4) A measurement model with greater elasticity is allowed. (5) The fitting degree of the whole model can be estimated (Hou et al. 2004). This paper aims to investigate the relationship between multiple dependent and independent variables. Therefore, given the measurement errors existing in the data of each independent variable obtained by sampling survey, SEM model was suitable for the study.

SEM mainly studies two types of variables: observational and latent ones. SEM also involves exogenous and endogenous variables. The two SEM models here were measurement-related (a model between observational and latent variables) and structure-related (a model of latent variables).

The exogenous latent variables of SEM were represented by $\xi$, endogenous latent variables were represented by $\eta_1$ and $\eta_2$, and the error term of the structural model was represented by $\zeta$. Then, the SEM of meteorological service satisfaction could be expressed as $\eta = B\eta + \Gamma\xi + \zeta$. The equivalent matrix was

$$\begin{bmatrix} \eta_1 \\ \eta_2 \end{bmatrix} = \begin{bmatrix} \beta_{11} & 0 \\ \beta_{21} & \beta_{22} \end{bmatrix} \begin{bmatrix} \eta_1 \\ \eta_2 \end{bmatrix} + \begin{bmatrix} \gamma_1 \\ \gamma_2 \end{bmatrix} \xi + \begin{bmatrix} \zeta_1 \\ \zeta_2 \end{bmatrix},$$

where $\beta$ and $\gamma$ were path coefficients; $\beta_{ij}$ was the path coefficient of $\eta_j - \eta_i$, indicating the direct impact of $\eta_j$ (causal variable) on $\eta_i$ (outcome variable); and $\gamma_i$ was the path coefficient of $\xi - \eta_i$, indicating the direct impact of $\xi$ (causal variable) on $\eta_i$ (outcome variable).

$X = \Lambda_x \xi + \delta$ ($\Lambda_x$ was the factor loading of observational variable $X$ on the latent variable $\xi$) was the measurement equation of exogenous variables, whereas $Y = \Lambda_y \eta + \varepsilon$ ($\Lambda_y$ was the factor loading of observational variable $Y$ on the latent variable $\eta$) was the measurement equation of endogenous variables. $\delta$ and $\varepsilon$ were the vector matrices formed by the observation errors of $X$ and $Y$, respectively.

SEM involved some basic hypotheses, such as (1) $\varepsilon$ was uncorrelated with $\eta$, (2) $\delta$ was uncorrelated with $\xi$, (3) $\zeta$ was uncorrelated with $\xi$, (4) $\zeta$ was uncorrelated with $\eta$, and (5) no autocorrelation was found among $\zeta$, $\varepsilon$, and $\delta$. The basic idea of SEM was as follows: if $\Sigma$ was the initial theoretical covariance matrix of SEM and $S$ was the covariance matrix gained from samples, the free parameters in SEM could be estimated and corresponding coefficients could be calculated using $S$ to fit $\Sigma$. Meanwhile, the SEM degree of fitness could be tested through the hypothesis. All analyses were conducted using Statistic Package for Social Science (SPSS) and Analysis of Moment Structure (AMOS).

Based on previous research results and practical characteristics of this study, a model of influencing factors of meteorological service was proposed in this paper. The present model involved three latent variables, namely, public meteorological cognition, public perceived value of meteorological service (hereafter referred to as perceived value): and public satisfaction with meteorological service (hereafter referred to as satisfaction). Figure 13.1 presented the SEM framework.

### *13.2.2 Variables and Hypotheses*

In this paper, public meteorological cognition and perceived value were selected as two influencing factors of satisfaction to establish the corresponding SEM. Each latent variable was measured through several observational variables (Table 13.1).

Satisfaction is the meteorological department's ultimate service goal. The quality of meteorological service is determined via public evaluation and testing. The used questionnaire focused on six common meteorological disasters in Shenzhen (typhoon, storm, thunderstorm, heavy fog, high temperature, and cold wave): and their satisfaction scores were used as the observational variables of satisfaction in the model (Alam et al. 2018).

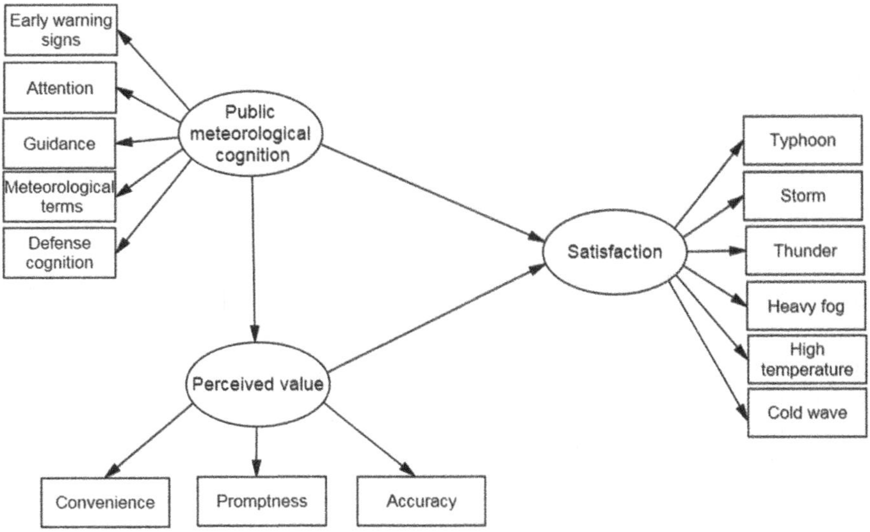


**Fig. 13.1** A framework of the SEM

(1) Public meteorological cognition

In a broad sense, satisfaction is determined by the quality of meteorological service and other factors. The receivers of meteorological service have different cognitions of the meteorological service due to their different backgrounds, which directly affect their satisfaction evaluations (Rahman et al. 2018). Therefore, this paper proposed the concept of an innovative latent variable public meteorological cognition.

According to cognitive psychology, public meteorological cognition depends on associated memories of meteorological disasters and services, including publicity of meteorological department, as well as paraphrasing and personal experiences of friends. These preconceived unique opinions and attitudes are known as public meteorological cognition. The cognitive competence of the public affects' perception and behavior to a large extent. For example, Xu et al. (2010) systematically analyzed the public cognition of seismic disasters in Nanzhen, Shanxi Province, and found that the public had an increased cognition of seismic disasters. Higher attention to disaster warning services provides the public with better self-protection skills and higher rationality to avoid disaster risks. Shan (2009) studied the effect of the new health policy of Shenzhen and found a significant impact of public medical cognition on public satisfaction with medical service. Based on the study of brand cognition, Li (2011) found that the cognitive competence of consumers could influence the perceived quality significantly, and that higher perceived quality led to higher perceived value, higher satisfaction with commodities, and greater purchase intention. These studies demonstrate the significant effect of public cognition on satisfaction evaluation.

**Table 13.1** Settings of latent variables and observational variables

| Latent variables | Observational variables | Questions |
|---|---|---|
| Public meteorological cognition | Early warning signs | Do you know the specific meanings of the Shenzhen early warning signs of meteorological disasters? (Q1) |
| | Attention | How much is your concern for meteorological security information? (Q2) |
| | Guidance | How useful is disaster prevention knowledge in your daily life? (Q3) |
| | Meteorological terms | Do you understand meteorological terms? (Q4) |
| | Defense cognition | Do you know how to defend yourself against meteorological disasters? (Q5) |
| Perceived value | Convenience | Is it convenient to obtain disaster meteorological information? (Q6) |
| | Promptness | Please evaluate the promptness of early warning about meteorological disasters. (Q7) |
| | Accuracy | Please evaluate the accuracy of disaster forecast. (Q8) |
| Satisfaction | Typhoon | Please give your scores for the meteorological service during a typhoon. (Q11) |
| | Storm | Please give your scores for the meteorological service during a storm. (Q12) |
| | Thunder | Please give your scores for the meteorological service during a thunderstorm. (Q13) |
| | Heavy fog | Please give your scores for the meteorological service during heavy fog. (Q14) |
| | High temperature | Please give your scores for the meteorological service during high temperature. (Q15) |
| | Cold wave | Please give your scores for the meteorological service during a cold wave. (Q16) |

Similarly, public meteorological cognition can significantly affect satisfaction. The satisfaction evaluation mainly involves two aspects: quality of meteorological service and public benefits (or losses) from meteorological service. These aspects are affected by different extents of public meteorological cognition. Public meteorological cognition includes attention, common meteorological knowledge, disaster risk perception, and self-protection. From the perspective of service quality, given the higher public meteorological cognition, the public is more aware of the necessity and importance of meteorological service and evaluates the service more objectively and reasonably. From the perspective of benefits, higher public meteorological cognition is equal to higher self-protection capability of the public. Losses caused by meteorological disasters are mainly determined by risk awareness and defensive measures of the public rather than the severity of disasters. Barnes et al. (2007) pointed out that improvement in public meteorological cognition could significantly increase the efficiency and accuracy of defensive measures. Prevention and reduction of casualty losses can increase public satisfaction, which is the meteorological service's ultimate goal. As a result, this paper proposed an innovative variable, public meteorological cognition, and analyzed its significant effect on satisfaction through data.

(2) Perceived value

Satisfaction depends on the meteorological cognition and the perceived value of the public. Public cognition of the risks of meteorological disasters, the significance of meteorological warning service, and the necessity of self-protection influence the public's perceived value and satisfaction (Miguel 2018).

The public perceived value refers to an essential perception that the public generates after accepting and using the meteorological service (Taylor and Kumar 2016). The practices of AT & T and Xerox confirm that the higher perceived value of customers has a significant role in their success. Reichheld and Sasser (1990) pointed out that improvement in the perceived value of customers on service quality could increase customer satisfaction, reduce customer defection, and increase business profits. Besides, Call (2009) declared that prompt and accurate meteorological disaster warnings were the major meteorological service provided by meteorological agencies to the public. In the present model, public perceived value included convenient access, promptness, and accuracy of meteorological warnings.

Based on the interpretations of SEM variables and their specific practical meanings, this paper proposed the following hypotheses:

- H1: "Public meteorological cognition" significantly affects "satisfaction."
- H2: "Public meteorological cognition" significantly affects "perceived value."
- H3: "Perceived value" significantly affects "satisfaction."

### 13.2.3 Samples and Data

Shenzhen is located on the east coast of the Pearl River Delta and is under the jurisdiction of Guangdong Province. At the end of 2017, Shenzhen has a total area of 1,997 km$^2$ and a permanent population of 12,528.3 thousand. Shenzhen city has 11 regions, including Futian (with an area of 78.66 km$^2$ and a permanent population of 1,561.2 thousand): Luohu (with an area of 78.75 km$^2$ and a permanent population of 102.72 thousand): Nanshan (with an area of 187.53 km$^2$ and a permanent population of 1,424.6 thousand): Yantian (with an area of 74.99 km$^2$ and a permanent population of 237.2 thousand): Baoan (with an area of 396.61 km$^2$ and a permanent population of 3,149 thousand): Longgang (with an area of 388.22 km$^2$ and a permanent population of 2,278.9 thousand): Longhua(with an area of 175.58 km$^2$ and a permanent population of 1,603.7 thousand): New Guangming (with an area of 155.44 km$^2$ and a permanent population of 596.8 thousand), Pingshan (with an area of 166.31 km$^2$ and a permanent population of 428 thousand): New Dapeng districts (with an area of 295.38 km$^2$ and a permanent population of 146.1 thousand): and Shenshan Special Cooperation Zone (with a permanent population of 75.7 thousand). Figure 13.2 showed the location of Shenzhen city in China.

Shenzhen enjoys a subtropical oceanic climate but is frequently hit by meteorological disasters, such as storm, typhoon, thunderstorm, high temperature, cold wave, heavy fog, dust-haze, drought, and hail. Due to the complex climatic conditions and frequent occurrence of meteorological disasters there, Meteorological Bureau of Shenzhen Municipality has attached great importance to public meteorological service.

Shenzhen was chosen as the research object for two reasons. Firstly, most meteorological bureaus at the provincial, municipal, and county level in China are under the vertical management of China Meteorological Administration. However, Meteorological Bureau of Shenzhen Municipality, as an exception, is directly managed by the local government, namely, the Shenzhen Municipal People's Government. Subsequently, Meteorological Bureau of Shenzhen Municipality has laid more emphasis on

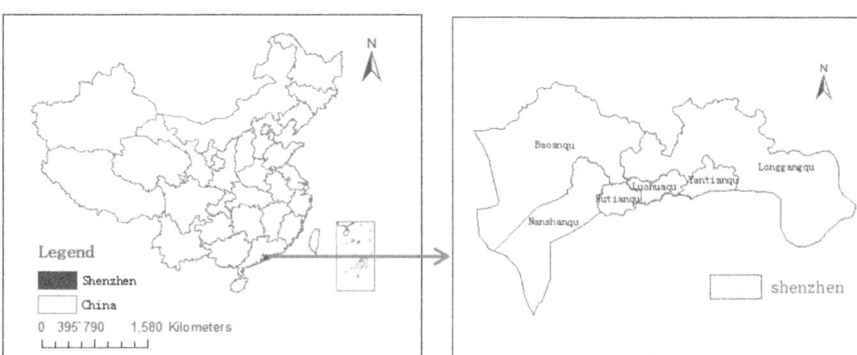


**Fig. 13.2** Location of Shenzhen city in China

providing high-quality meteorological service to the local citizens. There is no doubt that since the 1990s, Meteorological Bureau of Shenzhen Municipality, serving as an example, has outperformed other meteorological bureaus in terms of the service quality and content. Therefore, its management system and service level have led to a higher level of local meteorological service in China. This is one of the reasons why the meteorological service of Shenzhen was selected.

Secondly, Meteorological Bureau of Shenzhen Municipality provided abundant research data. To obtain a comprehensive understanding on public meteorological cognition, public satisfaction, and shortcomings of existing meteorological service, Shenzhen Meteorological Bureau conducted an "Investigation and Evaluation of Public Meteorological Cognition in Shenzhen" at the end of September 2012. The investigation covered 57 streets and 10 districts of Shenzhen City. In specific districts, the respondents received face-to-face interviews, read and recorded by investigators. A total of 3,109 questionnaires were sent. Collected survey data were processed using SPSS 25 and AMOS 25. Abnormal data were deleted and default values were corrected. Finally, 3,029 valid samples were collected, accounting for 97.42% of the sent questionnaires.

This investigation covered the entire Shenzhen City, including Futian, Luohu, Nanshan, Yantian, Baoan, Longgang, Longhua, New Guangming, Pingshan, and New Dapeng districts. These areas provided good representativeness because of the abundant and large-scale survey samples.

Descriptive statistics on the background information of respondents were provided in Table 13.2.

Judging from Table 13.2, samples in this questionnaire survey: (1) showed an almost balanced gender distribution (55.7% male and 44.3% female); (2) had a large proportion of the young and the middle-aged (18 to 45 years old): who could quickly respond to meteorological disasters, represented the major group of self-rescue and rescue work, and played essential roles in disaster prevention and reduction; (3) indicated higher meteorological cognition, because 98.6% of the respondents had an educational background of above primary school; (4) represented all income groups, with 6.8% of the respondents as high-income groups and 93.2% as low-income and middle-income groups, which was consistent with the actual situation; (5) exhibited consistent population distribution characteristics of Shenzhen. This questionnaire involved a large proportion of migrant workers (41.1%): which was in agreement with the frequent mobility of talents in Shenzhen because of its rapid economic development. In sum, this questionnaire survey covered all social classes via mass sample data, thereby representing the real public evaluation of and demand for meteorological service.

In the questionnaire survey, 14 indices and three latent variables were evaluated using the popular five-point Likert scale. A scale of 5 represented "great satisfaction," 4 represented "satisfaction," 3 represented "normal," 2 represented "dissatisfaction," and 1 represented "strong dissatisfaction." All of the responses to other questions were converted to a five-point Likert scale.

The mean value and standard deviation of observational variables in SEM were listed in Table 13.3.

**Table 13.2** Description of the background information of respondents

| Index | Items | Frequency | Proportion |
|---|---|---|---|
| Gender | Male | 1686 | 55.7% |
| | Female | 1343 | 44.3% |
| Age | <18 | 91 | 3.2% |
| | 18–30 | 1659 | 54.8% |
| | 31–45 | 823 | 27.2% |
| | 46–60 | 334 | 11.0% |
| | ≥61 | 116 | 3.8% |
| Educational background | Primary school or lower | 43 | 1.4% |
| | Junior high school | 575 | 19.0% |
| | Senior high school/technical secondary school | 1315 | 43.4% |
| | Junior college/higher vocational education | 729 | 24.1% |
| | Undergraduate or above | 367 | 12.1% |
| Annual income | ≤RMB 10,000 | 705 | 23.3% |
| | RMB 10,000–RMB 30,000 | 839 | 27.7% |
| | RMB 31,000–RMB 60,000 | 799 | 26.4% |
| | RMB 61,000–RMB 100,000 | 480 | 15.8% |
| | >RMB 100,000 | 206 | 6.8% |
| Career | Migrant workers | 1246 | 41.1 |
| | The staff of enterprises and public institutions | 620 | 20.5 |
| | Public officials | 78 | 2.6 |
| | Self-employed/individual business | 260 | 8.6 |
| | Emeritus and retired | 174 | 5.7 |
| | Freelancers | 466 | 15.4 |
| | Unemployed | 69 | 2.3 |
| | Students | 97 | 3.2 |
| | Practitioners in transportation industry | 6 | 0.2 |
| | Others | 13 | 0.4 |

As could be seen from Table 13.3, public satisfaction with the promptness of disaster warning reached as high as 3.86, indicating that the public had adequate time to adopt preventive measures against meteorological disasters to reduce unnecessary losses and casualties. Public satisfaction with the accuracy of disaster forecast reached 3.76. This result was related to the significant improvement in early-warning

**Table 13.3** Mean and standard deviation of observational variables

| Indices | Mean value | Standard deviation | Variance |
|---|---|---|---|
| Accuracy | 3.76 | 0.709 | 0.502 |
| Promptness | 3.86 | 0.714 | 0.510 |
| Convenience | 3.53 | 0.862 | 0.743 |
| Typhoon | 4.13 | 0.882 | 0.777 |
| Storm | 3.97 | 0.876 | 0.767 |
| Thunderstorm | 3.75 | 0.931 | 0.866 |
| Heavy fog | 3.71 | 0.919 | 0.845 |
| High temperature | 3.97 | 0.900 | 0.811 |
| Cold wave | 3.73 | 0.941 | 0.885 |
| Early warning signs | 3.03 | 0.969 | 0.938 |
| Guidance | 3.61 | 0.740 | 0.548 |
| Defense cognition | 3.62 | 0.735 | 0.540 |
| Attention | 3.54 | 0.914 | 0.835 |
| Meteorological terms | 4.11 | 0.731 | 0.534 |

techniques against meteorological disasters as China has focused substantial attention and investment on public meteorological service. However, the public was not satisfied with the convenience in accessing the meteorological disaster warning information because meteorological disasters (e.g., typhoon, storm, and thunderstorm) caused electricity and communication service outages. The early warnings against meteorological disasters became inaccessible to citizens in remote regions and in regions that experienced power and communication outages since these early warnings were mainly released through Television broadcast, the Internet, newspaper, telephone, and Short Messaging Service (SMS) in China.

From the perspective of public meteorological cognition, the public could understand meteorological terms. This view was closely related to the popularization of weather forecast in China. However, the public was less aware of early warnings against meteorological disasters. They were unaware of the severity of disasters based on the blue, yellow, orange, and red alarms. The public also had limited knowledge of defense skills. However, the public gradually became aware of the importance of defensive measures because of frequent meteorological disasters. Most people believed that the knowledge of defensive measures against meteorological disasters could provide self-protection guidance during disasters, thereby significantly decreasing the casualties and economic losses. Currently, the Republic in China still lacked knowledge of specific defensive measures to protect themselves against disasters.

According to the satisfaction evaluation during disasters, the public was highly satisfied with meteorological service during typhoons, relatively satisfied with the service during storms and high temperatures, but strongly dissatisfied with the service during heavy fogs, thunderstorms, and cold waves. This finding resulted from the frequent occurrence of typhoons and the deep impression of typhoons on Shenzhen citizens, which implied that public cognition might affect the satisfaction evaluation of the public.

### *13.2.4 Reliability and Validity Tests of the Questionnaire*

The reliability and validity of samples were tested before the exploratory factor analysis using SPSS and AMOS. Reliability refers to the stability and consistency of the questionnaire results when the same objects are investigated using the same method, and indicates whether the measuring tool (questionnaire or scale) can contribute a stable measurement to the test objects or variables. This study used Cronbach's alpha to test the reliability of the questionnaire. Observational variables with Cronbach's $\alpha < 0.35$ were deleted. The data reliability test results were listed in Table 13.4. Cronbach's $\alpha$ for public meteorological cognition, perceived value, and satisfaction value were 0.579, 0.635, and 0.908, respectively (all variables were within the acceptable range). Moreover, the Cronbach's $\alpha$ of the total scale reached 0.859, indicating the higher stability and reliability of the selected variables, as well as higher data reliability. The reliability and validity results were shown in Table 13.4.

Validity refers to the measurement accuracy of the measuring tools or means. The SPSS results were listed in Table 13.5. The Kaiser–Meyer–Olkin (KMO) test result was 0.903. The approximate chi-square value of Bartlett test of sphericity was 16,893.659 and the degree of freedom was 91, passing the significance test. This result demonstrated the existence of potential factor structure among variables, which was appropriate for factor analysis. Table 13.5 indicated the validity test result.

**Table 13.4** Reliability test

| | Items | Cronbach's alpha |
|---|---|---|
| Public meteorological cognition | 5 | 0.579 |
| Perceived value | 3 | 0.635 |
| Satisfaction | 6 | 0.908 |
| Reliability of the total scale | 14 | 0.859 |

**Table 13.5** Validity test

| KMO test | Bartlett test | | |
|---|---|---|---|
| 0.903 | Chi-square value | Degree of freedom | Significance level |
| | 16,893.659 | 91 | 0.000 |

## 13.3 Results

Like other statistical models, SEM also required overall test and evaluation after the parameter estimation. For the comprehensive evaluation of the goodness-of-fit of a model, the evaluation of model fitness also involved the fit indices of the model except the significance of estimated parameters. Table 13.6 suggested the results.

These goodness-of-fit indices demonstrated the preferable goodness-of-fit of the established SEM that had considerable practical significance to evaluate satisfaction and its influencing factors. The path coefficients were shown in Fig. 13.3.

In this paper, the SEM was tested mainly through absolute fit index, relative fit index, and parsimony fit index, and found good fit indices for the model. In the parsimony fit index, $\chi^2/\text{df}$ was 1.986. Figure 13.3 represented the influence relationships among latent variables. The three hypotheses were verified by path coefficients, critical ration (CR) and probability value (P).

The three hypotheses were all confirmed valid. First, the path coefficient of "public meteorological cognition-satisfaction" was 0.11, with a CR of 2.74 and P smaller than 0.01. This result indicated the significant positive effect of public meteorological cognition on satisfaction. Generally, higher public meteorological cognition led to better public understanding about the importance of meteorological disaster forecast service and higher satisfaction.

**Table 13.6** Fit indices of model

| Statistical test | Fit standard | Test result | Fit degree |
|---|---|---|---|
| *Absolute fit index* | | | |
| RMR | <0.05 | 0.010 | Supported |
| GFI | >0.90 | 0.995 | Supported |
| AGFI | >0.90 | 0.990 | Supported |
| *Incremental fit index* | | | |
| NFI | >0.90 | 0.994 | Supported |
| RFI | >0.90 | 0.989 | Supported |
| IFI | >0.90 | 0.997 | Supported |
| CFI | >0.90 | 0.997 | Supported |
| *Parsimony fit index* | | | |
| PGFI | >0.50 | 0.521 | Supported |
| CN | >200 | 2033 | Supported |
| $\chi^2/\text{df}$ | | 1.986 | Supported |
| AIC | Theoretical model value is smaller than both independent and saturated model values | 209 < 210 < 16,952 | Yes |
| CAIC | Theoretical model value is smaller than both independent and saturated model values | 560 < 946 < 17,050 | Yes |

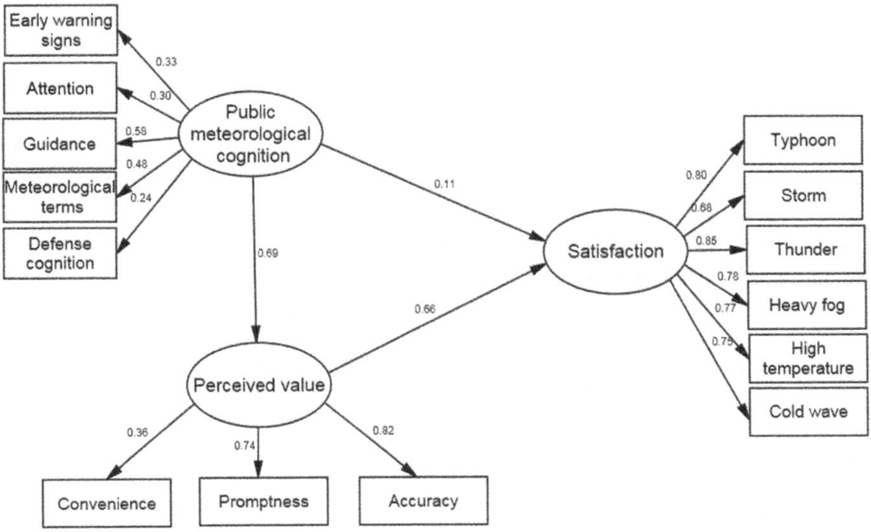


**Fig. 13.3** Results of the SEM

Second, the path coefficient of "public meteorological cognition-perceived value" was 0.69, with a CR of 10.587 and P smaller than 0.01. This result indicated the significant impact of public meteorological cognition on the perceived value.

Third, the path coefficient of "perceived value-satisfaction" was 0.66, with a CR of 12.716 and P smaller than 0.01. This result indicated that satisfaction was greater when the perceived value was higher.

Fourth, "public meteorological cognition" affected the "satisfaction" through "perceived value." Higher public meteorological cognition implied that the public understudied the necessity and significance of meteorological service and presented higher perceived value during the objective evaluation, thereby increasing the satisfaction correspondingly.

## 13.4 Discussion

Meteorological service plays an important role in the prevention and reduction of losses and casualties because of natural disasters that occur in China. Apart from the efforts of the meteorological department, disaster prevention and reduction also require public support and assistance (Meng and Xiong 2018; Wu et al. 2019). Therefore, this paper has proposed an innovative concept called public meteorological cognition. Public meteorological cognition has been tested by public cognition of early warnings, meteorological terms, defense security knowledge and guidance of defense knowledge in daily life, as well as by public attention to meteorological information.

Based on a questionnaire survey, SEM involving three latent variables and 14 observational variables has been established for the influencing factor analysis of public satisfaction with meteorological service. Data analysis using SPSS 25 and AMOS 25 has indicated that the observational variables in the measurement model significantly affect the latent variables, suggesting the higher target reliability of the measurement model. Path coefficients between latent variables in the structural model support the hypotheses, demonstrating the good overall degree of fit of the model. The model evaluation has confirmed the validity of hypotheses and tests, indicating the good evaluation effect of the SEM.

According to the established SEM, the following conclusions can be made:

(1) Public meteorological cognition significantly affects satisfaction. Higher public meteorological cognition implies higher attention and sensitivity to meteorological early warning service, which ensures sufficient time and energy to avoid disaster risks. Therefore, to highlight the significance of meteorological service and increase meteorological service benefit, we suggest that the meteorological department should reinforce management, optimize service, and enhance public cognition of meteorological knowledge and disaster risks.
(2) Public meteorological cognition positively affects the perceived value. Public meteorological cognition includes defense skills against disasters. Good defense skills enable the public to take appropriate self-protection measures calmly during disasters to significantly decrease casualties as well as economic losses. During the sudden onset of disasters, prompt and accurate early warning and good defensive skills may contribute to higher perceived value and objective evaluation of the meteorological service.
(3) Higher public meteorological cognition favors the increasing efficiency of meteorological service in China (Mi et al. 2016, 2019). The path coefficient of "perceived value-satisfaction" is 0.66, which indicates a proportional relationship between perceived value and satisfaction. Therefore, the meteorological department should improve its service continuously to increase public satisfaction. For example, electronic screens should be used to provide more humanized and easy-to-understand meteorological information.

Further research could be conducted from the following aspects:

(1) From the perspective of data resources, large data technology and methods could be used in the future to accurately define the public's demand and correspondingly provide excellent meteorological service. The development of communication technology and social media has facilitated the increasingly high accessibility to data. In addition to the traditional survey data mentioned in this paper, considerable information on public demand for meteorological service could also be collected by virtue of online social media including video image information, WeChat and Weibo. These multi-source heterogeneous data are typical "big data". If such data could be obtained and processed using data mining, semantic analysis, statistical correlation analysis and other methods, the precise demands of the public from differed regions and income groups for

meteorological service under various climate conditions will be gained. This could make valuable contributions to the improved service content and mode to be provided by meteorological departments.

(2) In terms of the analysis method, this paper mainly employed the SEM model to quantitatively analyze the relationship between multiple variables. Besides, the association rules mining method could also be used to investigate the difference existing in the demands of people with differed backgrounds for meteorological service; the neural network method be adopted to study the correlation between attribute variables (input variables) and assessment variables (output indicators) among multiple groups; and the spatial econometric model be employed to evaluate the correlation effect and spillover effect among the demands of people from different regions in Shenzhen. Undoubtedly, differential research methods can contribute greatly to the mining of more information from various aspects, thereby better facilitating the decision-making.

## 13.5 Implications for Conservation

The following are suggestions for meteorological service improvement:

(1) The research conclusion showed that improving the public awareness of disaster meteorological service is an immediate priority for meteorological departments. Our previous studies revealed that the public knew little about the hazards of disastrous weather and the importance of meteorological service, which is a vital cause of casualties and property losses. However, on the basis of the public's enhanced meteorological awareness, losses could only be avoided as a result of their further understanding of the scientific laws of meteorological disasters. A case in point is the forest fire that broke out at 17:00 on March 30, 2019 in Muli county, Liangshan Yi autonomous prefecture, Sichuan province. Thirty firefighters died in total. One of the reasons for the tragedy is the insufficient knowledge regarding the development rules and the harmfulness of fire under complex meteorological conditions. Therefore, both the public and the professionals including firefighters are in dire need of heightening their awareness concerning disasters.

(2) Enhance cooperation with broadcast, communication, urban construction, and important Web portals (Schattel and Bunge 2010) to deliver disaster warnings and important weather information to the public on time. Electronic billboards located in major urban areas are also excellent platforms for free and prompt meteorological warnings.

(3) Overcome existing technical and system bottlenecks in meteorological warning release and establish effective platforms to deliver warnings to the public in the coastal, remote, rural, as well as pasture areas (Sun et al. 2018).

(4) To provide better service to the public, as well as to minimize disaster losses, the meteorological department should continue to cooperate with units concerned,

provide full access to primary-level organizations and media, enhance accessibility of weather forecast and early warning information, and ensure that information reaches the whole country (Guo et al. 2019).

**Acknowledgements** Yanli Cao, Ge Gao, Yi Zou, Ji Guo, Yi Zhang also made great contributions to this manuscript. We express our heartfelt thanks to them. This research was supported by: National Social and Scientific Fund Program of China (18ZDA052; 17BGL142;16ZDA047); The Natural Science Foundation of China (91546117, 71373131).

## References

Alam, M. M., Wahid, A. N. M., & Siwar, C. (2018). Resilience, adaptation and expected support for food security among the malaysian east coast poor households. *Management of Environmental Quality: An International Journal, 29*(5), 877–902.

Alizadeh, A., & Kianfar, F. (2013). Developing a model for citizens' satisfaction with public sector services based on rough sets theory: A case study of tehran municipality. *Tehnicki Vjesnik-Technical Gazette, 20*(5), 795–802.

Anderson, S., Pearo, L. K., & Widener, S. K. (2008). Drivers of service satisfaction: Linking customer satisfaction to the service concept and customer characteristics. *Journal of Service Research, 10*(4), 365–381.

Barnes, L. R., Gruntfest, E. C., Hayden, M. H., Schultz, D. M., & Benight, C. (2007). False alarms and close calls: A conceptual model of warning accuracy. *Wea Forecasting, 22*(5), 1140–1147.

Bayard, B., & Jolly, C. (2007). Environmental behavior structure and socio-economic conditions of hillside farmers: A multiple-group structural equation modeling approach. *Ecological Economics, 62*(3–4), 433–440.

Cai, M., & Wei, G. (2020). A fuzzy social vulnerability evaluation from the perception of disaster bearers against meteorological disasters. *Natural Hazards, 103*(2), 2355–2370.

Call, D. A. (2009). An assessment of national weather service warning procedures for ice storms. *Weather and Forecasting, 24*(1), 104–120.

Cardozo, R. N. (1965). An experimental study of customer effort, expectation, and satisfaction. *Journal of Marketing Research, 2*(3), 244–249.

Chou, C. M. (2014). How does manufacturing service perceived value influence customer satisfaction? An investigation of global semiconductor industry. *International Journal of Production Research, 52*(17), 5041–5054.

De Ruyter, K., & Bloemer, J. (1999). Customer loyalty in extended service settings. *International Journal of Service Industry Management, 10*(3), 320–336.

Dube´, L., & Menon, K. (2000). Multiple roles of consumption emotions in post-purchase satisfaction with extended service transactions. *International Journal of Service Industry Management, 11*(3), 287–304.

Getz, R. R. (1978). A survey of New Jersey's agricultural weather service users. *Bulletin of the American Meteorological Society, 59*(10), 1297–1408.

Guo, J., Jin, J. J., Tang, Y. S., & Wu, X. H. (2019). Design of temperature insurance index and risk zonation for single-season rice in response to high-temperature and low-temperature damage: A case study of Jiangsu province, China. *International Journal of Environmental Research and Public Health, 16*(7), 1187.

Hsieh, C. M. (2012). Perceived importance of service elements in client satisfaction measures. *Journal of Social Service Research, 38*(4), 529–540.

Hsieh, C. M. (2018). Importance weighting in client satisfaction measures: Lessons from the life satisfaction literature. *Social Indicators Research, 138*(1), 45–60.

Huang, Y. M., & Xu, Y. Q. (2013). Analysis of the personal characteristics' impact on public services satisfaction. *Commercial Times, 23,* 96–98.

Hou, J. T., Wen, Z. L., Chen, Z. J., & Zhang, L. (2004). *Structural equation model and its application.* Beijing: Educational Science Publishing House.

IPCC AR5. (2013). Intergovernmental panel on climate change climate change fifth assessment report (AR5). London: Cambridge University Press, Cambridge.

Ji, J. M., & Hu, W. (2013). Evaluation on entropy weighted TOPSIS index of urban public service satisfaction in China: An empirical study based on lien survey of public service in chinese cities in 2012. *Journal of Shanghai Jiaotong University (Philosophy and Social Sciences), 21*(3), 42–51.

Joung, H. W., Choi, E. K., & Wang, E. (2016). Effects of perceived quality and perceived value of campus foodservice on customer satisfaction: moderating role of gender. *Journal of Quality Assurance in Hospitality & Tourism, 17*(2), 101–113.

Lellyett, S. C., & Anaman, K. A. (2010). Contingent valuation study of the public weather service in the Sydney metropolitan area. *Economic Papers a Journal of Applied Economics & Policy, 15*(3), 64–77.

Li, J. (2011). Brand cognition influence perceived quality empirical research, Master thesis, Beijing University of Post and Telecommunications, Beijing, China.

Lobo, A., Duarte, P., Carvalho, A., Rodrigues, V., Monteiro, M. J., & Alves, H. (2014). The association of equity, accessibility, and price with primary healthcare user's satisfaction. *Western Journal of Nursing Research, 36*(2), 191–208.

Ma, X. B., Liu, W., Zhou, X. Y., Qin, C. X., Chen, Y., Xiang, Y. F., et al. (2020). Evolution of online public opinion during meteorological disasters. *Environmental Hazards-Human and Policy Dimensions, 19*(4), 375–397.

Meng, S., & Xiong, D. (2018). Review and exploration of china subtropical climate change research based on scientometric analysis. *Tropical Conservation Science, 11,* 1–13.

Miguel, J. A. S. R. S. (2018). Climate change initiatives in Mexico: A review. *Management of Environmental Quality: An International Journal, 29*(6), 1042–1058.

Mi, Z., Zhang, Y., Guan, D., Shan, Y., Liu, Z., Cong, R., et al. (2016). Consumption-based emission accounting for Chinese cities. *Applied Energy, 184,* 1073–1081.

Mi, Z., Zheng, J., Meng, J., Zheng, H., Li, X., Coffman, D., et al. (2019). Carbon emissions of cities from a consumption-based perspective. *Applied Energy, 235,* 509–518.

Nuviala, A. N., Perez-Ordas, R., Osuna, M. B., Grao-Cruces, A., Nuviala, R. N., & Jurado, J. A. G. (2012). Quality, satisfaction and perceived value of users of public service sports. *Movimento, 18*(4), 11–32.

Park, E. (2019). The role of satisfaction on customer reuse to airline services: An application of big data approaches. *Journal of Retailing and Consumer Services, 47,* 370–374.

Rahman, S., Islam, M. S., Khan, M. N. H., & Touhiduzzaman, M. (2018). Climate change adaptation and disaster risk reduction (DRR) through coastal afforestation in South-Central Coast of Bangladesh. *Management of Environmental Quality: An International Journal.* https://doi.org/10.1108/MEQ-01-2018-0021.

Reichheld, F. F., & Sasser, W. E. (1990). Zero defections: Quality comes to services. *Harvard Business Review, 68*(5), 105–111.

Roy, S. K., Lassar, W. M., & Shekhar, V. (2016). Convenience and satisfaction: Mediation of fairness and quality. *Service Industries Journal, 36*(5–6), 239–260.

Schattel, J. L. J., & Bunge, R. (2008). The national weather service shares digital forecasts using web services. *Bulletin of the American Meteorological Society, 89*(4), 449–450.

Shan, L. (2009). A study of the behavior, satisfaction level, and their determinants of insurance participants after the enactment of Shenzhen new medical insurance policy. Master thesis, Central South University, Changsha, China.

Song, M., & Du, Q. (2017). Analysis and exploration of damage-reduction measures for flood disasters in China. *Annals of Operations Research, 3,* 1–16.

Song, M., Peng, J., Wang, J., & Dong, L. (2018). Better resource management: An improved resource and environmental efficiency evaluation approach that considers undesirable outputs. *Resources, Conservation and Recycling, 128,* 197–205.

Su, L. J. (2012). An association study on relationship between service cognitive elements, consumption emotions and tourist loyalty based on structural equation model. *Economic Management Journal, 7,* 112–123.

Sun, J., Wang, Z., & Li, G. (2018). Measuring emission-reduction and energy-conservation efficiency of chinese cities considering management and technology heterogeneity. *Journal of Cleaner Production, 175,* 561–571.

Tan, T. S., Chen, T. L., & Yang, P. H. (2017). User satisfaction and loyalty in a public library setting. *Social Behavior and Personality, 45*(5), 741–756.

Taylor, S., & Kumar, L. (2016). Global climate change impacts on pacific islands terrestrial biodiversity: A review. *Tropical Conservation Science, 9*(1), 203–223.

Terpstra, M., & Verbeeten, F. H. M. (2014). Customer satisfaction: Cost driver or value driver? Empirical evidence from the financial services industry. *European Management Journal, 32*(3), 499–508.

UN. (2018). UN office for disaster risk reduction in advance of international day for disaster reduction. *Economic Losses, Poverty & Disasters* 1998–2017.

Virvilaite, R., Piligrimiene, Z., & Kliukaite, A. (2015). The relations between consumer perceived value and loyalty. *Transformations in Business & Economics, 14*(1), 76–91.

Wang, G. Z., Du, J., Cao, J., & Liu, S. D. (2011). Meteorological services to the public satisfaction survey model based on SEM. *Journal of Applied Statistics and Management, 30*(3), 522–530.

Wang, Y., Gu, J. B., Wang, S. Y., & Wang, J. (2019). Understanding consumers' willingness to use ride-sharing services: The roles of perceived value and perceived risk. *Transportation Research Part C-Emerging Technologies, 105*(AUG.), 504–519.

Willis, R., Evandrou, M., Pathak, P., & Khambhaita, P. (2016). Problems with measuring satisfaction with social care. *Health & Social Care in the Community, 24*(5), 587–595.

Wu, J. X., Yang, M., Rasouli, S., & Xu, C. C. (2016). Exploring passenger assessments of bus service quality using bayesian networks. *Journal of Public Transportation, 19*(3), 36–54.

Wu, X. H., Sun, J., & Chen, Y. F. (2012). The value estimation of meteorological service in China based on contingent valuation. *Meteorological Monthly, 38*(1), 109–117.

Wu, X. H., X. Z., Liu, H., Guo, J., & Zhou, L. (2019). What are the impacts of tropical cyclones on employment? An analysis based on meta-regression. *Weather, Climate and Society, 11*(2), 259–275.

Xie, Y. H., & Zhang, Y. Q. (2013). Influence of employee participation on new generation employees' satisfaction. *Chinese Journal of Management, 10*(8), 1162–1169.

Xu, C. D., Zhou, Q., & Yu, Y. C. (2010). Research on the public perception and responses to the disaster of the MS8.0 Wenchuan earthquake-stricken area: A case study in Nanzheng in Southern Shanxi. *Journal of Seismological Research, 33*(3), 336–342.

Yen, Y. S. (2012). Exploring customer perceived value in mobile phone services. *International Journal of Mobile Communications, 10*(2), 213–229.

Yuan, H., Sun, M., & Wang, Y. (2016). Assessment of the benefits of the chinese public weather service. *Meteorological Applications, 23*(1), 132–139.

Zhang, W. C., Wang, W., Lin, J. F., Zhang, Y., Shang, X. P., Wang, X., et al. (2017). Perception, knowledge and behaviors related to typhoon: A cross sectional study among rural residents in Zhejiang, China. *International Journal of Environmental Research and Public Health, 14*(5), 12.

Zhong, Z. F. (2020). Research on the influence of remedial measures on public satisfaction after government information service failures in typhoon disasters: A case from China. *Ocean & Coastal Management, 190,* 7.

# Chapter 14
# A Comprehensive Estimation of the Economic Effects of Meteorological Services, Based on the Input-Output Method

**Abstract** Concentrating on consuming coefficient, partition coefficient and Leontief inverse matrix, relevant concepts and algorithms are developed for estimating the impact of meteorological services including the associated (indirect, complete) economic effect. Subsequently, quantitative estimations are particularly obtained for the meteorological services in Jiangxi province by utilizing the input-output method. It is found that the economic effects are noticeably rescued by the preventive strategies developed from both the meteorological information and internal relevance (interdependency) in the industrial economic system. Another finding is that the ratio range of input in the complete economic effect on meteorological services is about 1:108.27–1:183.06, remarkably different from a previous estimation based on the Delphi method (1:30–1:51). Particularly, economic effects of meteorological services are higher for non-traditional users of manufacturing, wholesale and retail trades, services sector, tourism and culture and art, and lower for traditional users of agriculture, forestry, livestock, fishery and construction industries.

**Keywords** Meteorological service · Direct (associated, complete, indirect) economic effect · Input-output model

## 14.1 Introduction

The production of sufficient food, fuel and fiber to meet the world's needs in a sustainable manner relies not only on the natural resources for growing them but also critically upon favorable weather conditions (Prokopy et al. 2013). In recent years, frequent severe weather conditions such as droughts, flood, heavy snowfalls and high temperatures, have increasingly raised governmental and public concerns about meteorological services. However, to promote the utilization of valuable meteorological services, benefits need to be demonstrated quantitatively and answers to relevant questions need to be convincible. Critical questions include those regarding the economic effects, their measures, and estimation methods and models. For example, what are some quantitative results regarding the economic effects saved from disastrous weathers due to accurate meteorological service forecasts? What are some meaningful and reasonable measures for estimating such benefits of meteorological

 
X. Wu and J. Guo, *Economic Impacts and Emergency Management of Disasters in China*,
https://doi.org/10.1007/978-981-16-1319-7_14

services? Unfortunately, there have been no effective methods and models established in the literature that can be employed by scientists for the desired estimation of the economic effects attributable to meteorological services. One difficulty is to correctly identify the economic effects saved from meteorological services as they are associated with each link of production or consumption. Another difficulty is to determine the costs operating the whole process of meteorological services that requires a wide range of considerations, including weather forecasting systems and assessment of many indirect costs. Still another difficulty is to describe a practical demand function—the demands of meteorological services can be highly implicit at present. Moreover, highly demanded assessment methods and models of economic effects benefited from meteorological services are also related to assessment policies, processes and practice (Pery et al. 2013).

Attempts in overcoming these difficulties were proposed by many researchers. Studies and exploratory trials have been carried out for exploring effective technologies and solutions both in China and abroad. These solutions can be roughly classified into three categories: Direct Field Investigation, Expert Knowledge and Qualitative Analysis, and Input-Output Assessment. Among the methods in the direct field investigation category, the focus is to measure the effects on the service objects that are rescued due to the use of meteorological services for users through the direct field investigation. Nguyen et al. (2013) calculated the economic effects of typhoon warning services in Vietnam. By designing questionnaires based on the contingent valuation method, Birol et al. (2006) estimated the economic effect of water resources management. Park et al. (2016) also calculated the economic value of the national meteorological service by conducting a contingent valuation survey in South Korea. Lee et al. (2014) used conjoint analysis and a discrete choice model to quantitatively measure the economic value of a pollen forecast system in South Korea. The pollen forecast system could be regard as a new meteorological information service. By using direct, indirect and reverse willingness-to-pay evaluation models, Yuan et al. (2016) estimated the benefit of the Chinese public weather service according to the nationwide survey conducted in China. By conducting a national face-to-face survey of registered farmers, Lin et al. (2019) used the contingent valuation method to estimate the economic value of meteorological information services in Taiwan for agricultural producers. Emanuel et al. (2012) explored the potential utility of seasonal Atlantic hurricane forecasts to a hypothetical property insurance firm. According to the economic data from interviewed users, Frei et al. (2014) calculated the economic value or benefit of weather forecasts used in the road transportation sector in Switzerland. Within the second category, Expert Knowledge and Qualitative Analysis, one calculates the effect brought by meteorological services using expert knowledge, Delphi method or alike, and then combining qualitative analysis measures and quantitative analysis results. Krieger and Green (2002) put forward the decision and optimization model of service effect estimation. Recently, Xu (2009) estimated meteorological service effects using the Delphi method. Integrating the experts' knowledge into the epidemiology-based exposure–response functions, Kan and Chen (2004) assessed the health based economic cost of particulate air pollution in urban areas of Shanghai of China. Recently, Zhang and Xi (2020) combined the methods of mixed group discussion and literature analysis to establish preliminary soil pollution value loss measurement indicators, and then used the Delphi method to modify, add, and delete indicators to obtain a set of feasible soil pollution value loss measurement indicator systems. By applying the multi-round Delphi method, Markou et al. (2020) brought impacts of climate change on crop production and water resources into the modeling effort on equal footing with cost values, and then quantified the economic impact of climate change on the agricultural sector of Cyprus. By selecting 47 experts to assess social and economic criteria and applying the Delphi method to rank and prioritize the indicators, Khashtabeh et al. (2020) assessed the economic effects of desertification control projects. Integrating the experts' knowledge into the preliminary evaluation index, Noh (2020) evaluated the economic value among the values of the library, and also attempted to measure the economic value of the library.

For the third category, Input-Output Assessment, researchers compute the associated effects brought by services using an input-output method. Chen and Yin (1992) proposed a computing method of indirect and complete economic effects. Using Input Occupancy Output techniques, Wang (1998) established an accounting method for estimating the complete forward and backward economic effects for all industries in the national economy. Hewings and Sonis (2009) proposed some concepts and algorithms relating to forward and backward linkage, correlative relations within industries and output multipliers in input-output analysis. Recently, Chen et al. (2013) estimated the associated social economic effects brought by oyster breeding in Taiwan, and Kerschner and Hubacek (2009) assessed the potential economic effects of peak oil using the input–output analysis. Hallegatte (2008) took into account of sector production capacities and of both forward and backward propagations within the economic system to assess the economic cost of Katrina. Taking indirect damages results into account, Mendoza-Tinoco et al. (2017) obtained an accurate assessment of total flooding costs and calculated the total economic burden of in the region of Yorkshire and The Humber. Understanding and quantifying total economic impacts of flood events, Sieg et al. (2019) coupled the direct economic impacts to a supply-side Input-Output model to estimate the indirect economic impacts. The study indicated that indirect economic impacts could be almost as high as direct economic impacts. By using input-output model to obtain ballpark estimate of losses, Khalid and Ali (2020) assessed the economic impact of natural disaster taking backward and forward linkages into account. Chang et al. (2014) presented an input-output analysis on how the port sectors impact a concerned economy using the South African case. Leontief price model was used for the scenario that what would occur if the price of port sector's cost was increased. Lin et al. (2020) estimated inter-regional payments for ecosystem services in Beijing-Tianjin-Hebei (BTH) region with the most serious environmental problem in China employing multi-regional input–output model. Garza-Gil et al. (2017) used an input-output model to quantify the social economic impact of fishing and aquaculture on Galicia. Adopting the input-output model, Jiang et al. (2019) assessed economic impacts of the geothermal industry in Beijing. Galbusera and Giannopoulos (2018) reviewed and discussed how different disaster modeling aspects had been incorporated in recent contributions exploiting input-output techniques. Meyer et al. (2013) examined different cost types, namely direct tangible damages, losses due to business interruption, indirect damages, intangible effects, and the costs of risk mitigation to assess the costs of natural hazards. They showed that the application of cost assessments in practice was incomplete and biased, as direct costs received a relatively large amount of attention, while intangible and indirect effects were rarely considered. By using adaptive regional Input-Output model, Huang et al. (2020) assessed the economic impact of climate change in China. Avelino and Dall'erba (2019) compared the economic impact of natural disasters generated by different input-output models. They started with the traditional Leontief model and then compared its assumptions and results with more complex methodologies, such as rebalancing algorithms, the sequential interindustry model and the dynamic inoperability input-output model. Chun et al. (2014) used input-output analysis to investigate the effect of hydrogen energy technology investment on the Korean economy for the period 2020–2040. The overall results revealed that the hydrogen sector could be characterized as intermediate primary production because of its high backward and forward linkage effects. Munjal (2013) measured the economic impact of the tourism industry in India using the tourism satellite account and input-output analysis. He also analysed the tourism industry's inter-linkages by placing it in the framework of the Input-Output Transactions Table and quantifying its overall impact on other industries through multiplier analysis. Suris-Regueiro and Santiago (2018a, b) assessed the possible socioeconomic impacts arising from a fishing supply shock, considering in equal measure the backward and forward linkages of fishing activity with other sectors. Within the methodological context of input-output analysis, Suris-Regueiro and Santiago (2018a, b) proposed a practical procedure considering forward and backward linkage to quantify socioeconomic impacts linked to supply shocks. Emonts-Holley et al. (2020) evaluated the values for various Input-Output Type II multipliers to a benchmark value calculated with the aid of social accounting matrix data. The results suggested that the variation in Type II IO multiplier values generated by these alternative methods was an empirically non-trivial issue. By using the Leontief Input-Output model, Rocco et al. (2020) indicated that an expansion of the electricity sector could contribute significantly to economic growth. Liu et al. (2020) explored the network relationship between electricity consumption and economic impact of eight industries in China using the input-output analysis. By disaggregating the aquaculture sector from Irelands 2010 Input-Output table and calculating the resultant Leontief inverse matrix, Grealis et al. (2017) estimated a number of economic multipliers for the aquaculture sector to calculate the potential indirect impacts of expansion. Lin et al. (2012) evaluated regional economic impacts using the input-output analysis developed by Leontief. These are just some of the existing researches achieved so far.

The Delphi method (a structured communication technique, originally developed as a systematic, interactive forecasting method which relies on a panel of experts), is frequently employed by researchers. As a subjective, qualitative method, the Delphi method is essentially a feedback anonymous letter of inquiry method, with several advantages such as full role of experts, brainstorming, and high accuracy. However, it should be noticed that this expert opinion method can be utilized only when there is a lack of sufficient information—due to its drawbacks including (1) no clear criteria regarding expert selection, (2) lack of rigorous scientific analysis of the results, and (3) the final convergence of views having a tendency to follow the crowd.

Moreover, except for a few case studies, most researchers only estimated the direct effects without investigating the indirect effects, which results in a gap in the literature of meteorological services. Moreover, most researchers simply combined field investigations and expert knowledge for estimating service effects in a single region, industry or enterprise; few studies utilized the input-output method to estimate the comprehensive service effects. Research, using input-output methods to calculate the associated and indirect economic effects, is rare. Chen and Yin (1992) and Wang (1998) respectively defined the concepts of indirect economic effect and complete economic effect and put forward corresponding algorithms.

Specifically, since the input-output table reflects more accurately the technical and economic relationships between industries in the national economy, it has become an ideal tool for calculating the associated and indirect economic effects of industries (Zhang and Zhao 2006). According to the principle of doing certain things and refraining from doing other things, we present assessment models for associated, indirect and complete economic effects based on the input-output table. Taking the meteorological service data in Jiangxi Province in 2007 as an example, we obtained a series of results regarding the economic effects of meteorological services.

Section 14.2 describes the concepts, principles and hypotheses. Section 14.3 introduces our estimation methods and algorithms. Section 14.4 illustrates our methods and algorithm with an actual example. The last section, Sect. 14.5, lays out the concluding remarks.

## 14.2 Concepts, Principles and Hypotheses

In this section we will define concepts that describe economic effects, and then introduce the principle of input-output table and several hypotheses.

### *14.2.1 Definition of Concepts*

Here we assume that the direct meteorological service object is industry $i$.

The direct economic effect of meteorological services is the increased economic effect due to the use of these meteorological services. To further explain this concept, assuming two similar industries, one utilizing the meteorological services and the other not, have similar input levels but with different outputs. The difference between the outputs that is beneficial from the use of the meteorological services is referred as the direct economic effect.

The associated economic effect of industry $i$ is the economic effect due to the demands of other industries for the products (or services) produced (or provided) by industry $i$, which is to be calculated through the interdependency coefficients.

The indirect economic effect of industry $i$ is the sum of economic effects for industry $i$ and other industries generated indirectly through an economic and technological relation.

The complete economic effect of industry $i$ is the increment of final output in all industries of national economy system brought by direct economic effect with the circulation of production–consumption.

### 14.2.2 Principle of the Input-Output Table

The input-output table describes resources of inputs and usages of outputs on all industries of the national economy in a matrix form for a period of time (usually one year). It reveals the quantitative relations which are not only interdependency but also mutually restraining for all industries of the national economy. As an important part of the national economic accounting system, the input-output table of China consists of three parts named as Quadrants I, II, III. This is illustrated in Table 14.1.

Interconnected, these three parts of input-output table fully and systematically reflect the interrelations of all industries of the national economy, during the production cycle—process from production to usage, by view of total quantity and structure of input-output. The following are some basic balance relationships in the input-output table:

(i) Line balance
Intermediate use + Final use + Others = Total output + Inflow
(ii) Column balance
Intermediate input + Increment = Total input
(iii) Gross balance
Total input = Total output
Total input in certain industry = Total output in this industry
Total intermediate use = Total Intermediate input
(iv) Interdependency between industries

The interdependency between industries can be expressed as follows:

$$x_i = \sum_j (a_{ij}x_j + c_j), i = 1, 2, \ldots, n \tag{14.1}$$

or in the matrix form: $X = AX + C$,

where $x_i$ is the total output of industry $i$, $c_i$ is the final demand of industry $i$, and $a_{ij}$ is the ratio of the input of industry $i$ over the total demand of industry $j$ ($1 \leq i, j \leq n$). Given $n$ industries, $a_{ij}$ characterizes the distribution of inputs contributed by the

**Table 14.1** Basic input-output table of China

| Input | | Output | | | | | | | | | | | | | | | | |
|---|---|---|---|---|---|---|---|---|---|---|---|---|---|---|---|---|---|---|
| | | Intermediate use | | | | Final use | | | | | | | | | | Inflow | Others | Total output |
| | | Farming forestry, animal husbandry and fishery | … | Public administration and social organization | Total intermediate use | Final consumption | | | | | Gross capital formation | | | Total | Total final use | | | |
| | | | | | | Resident consumption | | | Government consumption | Total | Fixed capital formation | Increase in inventory | Total | | | | | |
| | | | | | | Rural resident consumption | Urban resident consumption | Subtotal | | | | | | | | | | |
| Intermediate input | Farming forestry, animal husbandry and fishery<br>…<br>Public administration and social organization | Quadrant I | | | | Quadrant II | | | | | | | | | | | | |
| | Total intermediate input | | | | | | | | | | | | | | | | | |
| Increment | Laborers remuneration<br>Taxes on production<br>Depreciation of fixes assets<br>Operating surplus Total increment | Quadrant III | | | | | | | | | | | | | | | | |
| Total input | | | | | | | | | | | | | | | | | | |

n industries ($i = 1, 2, \ldots, n$) to the total input required by industry $j$ (Haimes et al. 2005). Matrix $A$ will be called the technical coefficient matrix.

### 14.2.3 Hypotheses of Input-Output Model

The input-output model is a simplification of the Walrasian general equilibrium model (Chen and Zhang 2005). There are three main hypotheses:

$H_1$: Pure industry. Assume that each industry only produces one kind of product with one production technology. Meanwhile no different production technology can be selected or mutually replaced in the process of production across different industries.

Models holding $H_1$ can reflect the composition of material consumption and the relation between production and technology more accurately.

$H_2$: Each technical coefficient is relatively fixed. Regardless of factors of technical progress and increase of labor productivity, assume that each direct consumption coefficient (i.e., technical coefficient). $a_{ij}$ is fixed in a given period, that is to say, ignore influences of relevant dynamic factors.

Here, dynamic factors include change of time, technology, price, industry or product structure among others. With $H_2$, the analysis will be much simplified.

$H_3$: Linear relation. Assume that there is a positive and proportional relationship between input and output in all industries of the national economy.

$H_3$ is closely related to $H_2$. On the premise that direct consumption coefficient $a_{ij}$ is fixed, there must be a positive and proportional relationship between consumption and production, fixed consumption in production ignored.

Despite exceeding the bounds of reasonable stipulations, these three hypotheses, presented in the forms subject to some ideal conditions, are fundamental in describing more general economic production relations and expanding the scope of input-output method, thus helpful for other researches as well.

## 14.3 Estimation Models of Associated, Indirect and Complete Economic Effects

### 14.3.1 Estimation Models of Associated Economic Effects

(1) Direct interdependency

The direct interdependency means the economic and technological relation between an industry and another industry which needs products or services from the former. It is usually measured by the direct distribution coefficient $h_{ij}(i, j = 1, 2, \ldots, n)$. $h_{ij}$ represents the proportion of the products or services directly used as intermediate products distributed from industry $i$ to industry $j$ in the total output. The formula calculating $h_{ij}$ is:

$$h_{ij} = \frac{x_{ij}}{X_i} \quad (i = 1, 2, \ldots, n, \ j = 1, 2, \ldots n) \tag{14.2}$$

where $x_{ij}$ denotes the products or services used as intermediate products distributed from industry $i$ to the latter and $X_i$ is the total output of industry $i$.

Clearly, the higher the direct distribution coefficient of an industry to another, the greater the direct interdependency of the former industry for the latter industry, and the more obvious direct driving effect.

(2) Complete distribution coefficient

The complete distribution coefficient $d_{ij}(i, j = 1, 2, \ldots, n)$ is the complete distribution of industry $j$ provided by per unit of value-added in industry $i$. It can be calculated on the basis of complete consumption coefficient. The matrix form formula calculating $d_{ij}$ is given by

$$D = (I - H)^{-1} - I \tag{14.3}$$

where $I$ is the $n$ by $n$ identity matrix and $H$ is the matrix of direct distribution coefficients, i.e., $H = (h_{ij})$. $(I - H)^{-1}$ describes the total accumulative distribution effect and it is similar to the Leontief inverse matrix $(I - A)^{-1}$.

The bigger the complete distribution coefficient, the greater the motivational effect of complete supply, and the bigger the complete interdependency between industries. Complete distribution coefficients not only reflect the direct impact among industries, but also reflect the indirect impact of every level, which is more comprehensive for analyzing relativity between industries.

(3) Associated economic effect

The associated contribution is the added value created by the service effect of an industry for the production of intermediate input. According to the balance relation of the input-output table and the theory of industry interdependency, the associated contribution of industry $i$ for the national economy is:

$$E_i = \sum d_{ij} Y_{ij} \tag{14.4}$$

Here, $d_{ij}$ is the complete distribution coefficient of industry $i$ for products of industry $j$, $Y_{ij}$ is the direct economic effect of meteorological service for industry $j$ due to industry $i$, and $E_i$ in (14.4) is called the associated economic effect of meteorological service from industry $i$.

### 14.3.2 Estimation Model of Indirect Economic Effect

Recall from Sect. 14.2.1, that the indirect economic effect is the economic effect brought indirectly through an economic and technological relation. According to the input-output model in Table 14.1, we can get the total output of one industry as follows:

$$\sum_{j=1}^{n} X_{ij} + Y_i = X \quad (i = 1, 2, \ldots, n) \tag{14.5}$$

Here, $X_{ij}$ is the intermediate consumption, representing the product value consumed in industry $j$ which is provided by industry $i$, $Y_i$ is the product value which is used as final use in industry $i$, and $X_i$ is the total output of industry $i$. By adding the direct consumption coefficients $a_{ij} = x_{ij}/X_j$ into the model, Eq. (14.5) can be turned into:

$$\sum_{j=1}^{n} a_{ij} X_j + Y_i = X_i \quad (i = 1, 2, \ldots, n) \tag{14.6}$$

The matrix form of (14.6) is $AX + Y = X$ where $A$ is the technical coefficient matrix (see Sect. 14.2.2), and hence we have

$$X = (1 - A)^{-1} Y \tag{14.7}$$

In the input-output table, service effects can be represented as the increase of final output, assuming that the final outputs of other industries are fixed. On the basis of the direct economic effect of a certain industry produced by services, we will explain the indirect effect as $\Delta X$ brought by the direct economic effect of an industry. Accordingly, Eq. (14.7) changes into the incremental form:

$$\Delta X = (I - A)^{-1} \Delta Y \tag{14.8}$$

Here, $\Delta X$ is the indirect effect of this industry brought by meteorological services, $(I - A)^{-1}$ is the Leontief inverse matrix, and $\Delta Y$ is the direct effect of this industry brought by services which is represented as the increase of final use.

### 14.3.3 Estimation Model of Complete Economic Effect

According to the previously established estimation model for the indirect economic effect, the increment of final use brought by the direct effect in the first round is $\Delta X = (I - A)^{-1} \Delta Y$.

The increase of output in the first round will improve resident income, thus increasing resident consumption, which will further lead to the increase of output in the second round. The whole process repeats itself in circle. Of course, there are some hidden assumptions. First, the economic system has an enormous amount of idle productive capacity so that there will not be induced investment in the process of circulation. Second, with the increasing resident income, the marginal propensity to consume is constant. Third, consumption structure does not change as consumption scale changes.

Assume that $\alpha = (\alpha_1, \alpha_2, \ldots, \alpha_n)$ denotes the vector of resident income structure in each industry ($\alpha_i$ is the ratio of laborers' remuneration in total output for industry $i$). Let $c$ denote the marginal propensity to consume. Then $c\alpha \cdot (I - A)^{-1}\Delta Y$ represents the increment for consumption brought by service effect in the first round. Let $w$ be the column vector of resident consumption structure coefficient in input-output table. Element $w_i$ in $w$ is the ratio of consumption of each industry in the total value of that column. So $wc\alpha(I - A)^{-1}\Delta Y$ is the resident consumption increment produced by the increase of final use in the first round. $(I - A)^{-1}wc\alpha(I - A)^{-1}\Delta Y$ is the output increment induced by the increase of final use in the initial state and first round, and so on. This production-consumption-production cycle will go on until the system reaches a new equilibrium. The foregoing is expressed by a mathematical equation as follows:

$$\Delta X = (I - A)^{-1}\Delta Y + (I - A)^{-1}wc\alpha(I - A)^{-1}\Delta Y + (I - A)^{-1}wc\alpha(I - A)^{-1}wc\alpha(I - A)^{-1}\Delta Y + \cdots \tag{14.9}$$

Then we can get:

$$\Delta X = (I - A)^{-1}[I - wc\alpha(I - A)^{-1}]^{-1}\Delta Y \tag{14.10}$$

## 14.4 The Empirical Analysis of Meteorological Service Effects in Jiangxi Province

In this section, we will utilize the data obtained from Jiangxi province in 2007 to illustrate the concepts and models introduced in this paper (Sect. 14.3). We employ the input-output method to estimate the economic effects of meteorological services based on the data given in the 2007 Input-output table of Jiangxi (2011).

### *14.4.1 Sample and Data*

Zou et al. (2008) conducted a research on the evaluation reports of meteorological services in Jiangxi from 2003 to 2007 using the traditional expert investigation method (Delphi method), while our purpose is, by utilizing the input-output model for the data supplied with the 2007 Input-output table of Jiangxi, to estimate quantitatively the economic effects rescued from the preventive strategies that are established based on the meteorological information and the interdependency between industrial economic systems. Our setting of the study is different from that of Zou, Lu and Dong, as outlined below.

(1) Data of input-output. They are from "Input-output table of Jiangxi in 2007" and "Input-output table of China in 2007", where the latter was compiled by the Economic Accounting Department of the National Bureau of Statistics of China in 2007. The table involves 2 branch classifications; one is a table of 42 industries, the other, a table of 135 industries. In this paper we use the data of 135 industries. According to the research of Gu et al. (2009), the resident marginal propensity to consume c in 2007 was 0.66.

(2) Data on the direct economic effect of meteorological services. Using the expert investigation method, Zou et al. (2008) estimated the meteorological service effect on agriculture, forestry, husbandry and fishery, transportation, construction, production and supply of electric power, gas and water, insurance, manufacturing, resident service and other services, wholesale and retail sale in Jiangxi province. To correspond to the names of 135 industries in input-output table, we process the same data but utilizing our comprehensive economic effect estimation method as follows:

(1) Zou, Lu and Dong synthesized agriculture, forestry, husbandry and fishery into one industry. In this paper we split it equally into five shares with the same average proportions of 3.61%.

(2) In Zou, Lu and Dong's study, there was only an average proportion of direct service effect for general "manufacturing". In this paper we use 54 kinds of manufacturing in the table of 135 industries with the same proportions of 0.512%.

(3) In Zou, Lu and Dong's study, there was only an average proportion of "insurance". Considering that "insurance" is a sub key of "finance" in the table of 135 industries, we equate "insurance" with "finance", whose ratio of meteorological service effect in total output is 1.943%.

(4) In Zou, Lu and Dong's study, there was only an average proportion of "transportation and warehousing". In this paper we treat 8 sub keys of "transportation and warehousing" in the table of 135 industries whose proportions are all 2.454% equally.

(5) In Zou, Lu and Dong's study, there was only a contribution rate of "resident service and other services". According to the table of 135 industries, "resident service and other services" will be subdivided into "resident service" and "other services", whose proportions are all 0.484%.

Specific results are provided in Appendix (Table 14.2).

It should be pointed out that the Delphi method is a structured communication technique, originally developed as a systematic, interactive forecasting method which relies on a panel of experts, thus subject to and dependent on the knowledge of the participating experts. Hence, this method is more subjective in nature.

Moreover, since the available meteorological service data sets for Jiangxi province from 2003 to 2007 are quite rich, the input-output method would be more appropriate. In fact, the Delphi (expert opinion) method is utilized only when there is a lack of sufficient information (due to its three drawbacks stated in Sect. 14.1).

In contrast, our estimation model (input-output method) for obtaining quantitative results regarding the comprehensive economic effects of meteorological services is established on the inhesion relevance among different industries, which is more objective and provides a practical setting for preventive strategies and other recommendations to rescue in the face of extreme weather conditions.

Specifically, since the input-output table reflects more accurately the technical and economic relationships between industries in the national economy (Zhang and Zhao 2006), it has become an ideal tool for calculating the associated and indirect economic effects of industries. According to the principle of doing certain things and refraining from doing other things, we present assessment models for associated, indirect and complete economic effects based on the input-output table. Taking the meteorological service data in Jiangxi Province in 2007 as an example, we obtained a series of results regarding the economic effects of meteorological services.

### 14.4.2 Results and Analysis

By utilizing the estimation equations of associated economic effect (Eq. 14.4), indirect economic effect (Eq. 14.8) and complete economic effect (Eq. 14.10), we summarize the results in Appendix (Table 14.3).

An analysis of Table 14.3 reaches the following conclusions:

Due to the technical and economic relations between industries, the direct economic effect of services can bring to all industries the associated, indirect and complete economic effects. The direct economic effect of meteorological service in Jiangxi Province in 2007 was 13882.63853 million RMB, which brought the associated economic effect of 39521.90571 RMB, indirect economic effect of 33991.28942 RMB and complete economic effect of 50105.33474 RMB. Three economic effects respectively increased by 1.847-fold, 1.448-fold and 2.609-fold.

The ratio range of input in associated economic effect in Jiangxi Province is about 1:85.41–1:145.197, the ratio range of input in indirect economic effect is about 1:73.44–1:124.848, the ratio range of input in complete economic effect is about 1:108.27–1:183.059, which are remarkably different from a previous estimation based on the Delphi method (stated below).

Ren (2009) studied the "Input-output table of China in 2007" for the whole country using the traditional Delphi method and concluded that the effect ratio range of input in output brought by meteorological services in China is 1:30–1:51.

In contrast, our results suggest that the associated, indirect and complete economic effects brought by meteorological services are so huge that more attention should be paid to this field.

(1) As observed from the calculation of associated economic effect brought by direct economic effect, the top five industries, in order of decreasing proportions of associated effect are refractory product manufacturing (1405.538-fold), special machinery for agriculture, forestry, husbandry and fishery manufacturing (158.467-fold), cement and gypsum product manufacturing (157.029-fold), brick, stone and other building material manufacturing (154.352-fold), ceramic product manufacturing (108.871-fold). The bottom five are construction (0.002-fold), other food manufacturing (0.030-fold), fishery (0.042-fold), animal husbandry (0.083-fold) and agriculture (0.144-fold).

Also, from the calculation of indirect economic effect brought by direct economic effect, the top 5 industries in order of decreasing increments are railway transport equipment manufacturing (15.316-fold), fertilizer manufacturing (8.698-fold), special machinery for agriculture, forestry, husbandry and fishery manufacturing (8.487-fold), pesticide manufacturing (7.896-fold), basic chemical raw material manufacturing (5.438-fold). The bottom five construction (0.035-fold), convenience food manufacturing (0.053-fold), fishery (0.060-fold), other food manufacturing (0.090-fold) and animal husbandry (0.148-fold).

Furthermore, as observed from the calculation of complete economic effect brought by direct economic effect, the top 5 industries in order of decreasing increments are railway transport equipment manufacturing (21.810-fold), fertilizer manufacturing (12.1651-fold), special machinery for agriculture, forestry, husbandry and fishery manufacturing (10.654-fold), pesticide manufacturing (10.602-fold) and wholesale and retail sale (9.113-fold). The bottom five are construction (0.069), fishery (0.231), warehousing (0.522-fold), service of agriculture, forestry, husbandry and fishery (0.546-fold) and animal husbandry (0.560-fold).

Thus, increments of indirect and complete economic effects on traditional meteorological service objects such as construction, agriculture, forestry, husbandry and fishery, and warehousing are comparatively low, while some industries such as railway transport, equipment manufacturing, and fertilizer manufacturing can reach more indirect and complete economic effects. Consequently, in the future, meteorological service should tilt toward to industries including railway transport, equipment manufacturing, and special machinery for agriculture, forestry, husbandry and fishery manufacturing, and provide more targeted fine services to improve their indirect and complete economic effects of meteorological service.

(2) As seen from the calculation of complete economic effect brought by indirect economic effect, the top five industries in order of decreasing increments are culture and art (577.222-fold), tobacco processing (67.673-fold), tourism (26.218-fold), weaving, dyeing and finishing (16.627-fold) and Public facilities management (14.027-fold). The bottom six are construction (0.033-fold),

cement and gypsum product manufacturing (0.078-fold), service of agriculture, forestry, husbandry and fishery (0.092-fold), refractory product manufacturing (0.122-fold), steel rolling processing (0.157-fold) and ferrous metal ore mining (0.157-fold). It indicates that owing to the production-consumption-production cyclic effect, the output multipliers of industries like culture and art, tobacco processing and tourism are bigger than those of construction, agriculture, forestry, husbandry and fishery and so on. The results are of course affected by multiple factors such as technical and economic relation, marginal propensity to consume, ratio of resident income in total output and so on. Because of the increasing relevance of industrial economic system, rapid development of public administration, social organization, education, technology, and the gradual reveal of effect on the policies of expanding domestic demand, the indirect and complete economic effects brought by meteorological service will continue to increase.

While Zou et al. (2008) estimated the ratio of meteorological services effect (input-output ratio) for various industries, they did not calculate the economic effects. As a result, we could not make a comparison between our results and theirs.

## 14.5 Concluding Remarks

In this paper we introduced the concepts of direct (associated, indirect, complete) economic effect. Focusing our research on the direct consuming coefficient, the complete consuming coefficient and Leontief inverse matrix, we have developed estimation methods for the associated, indirect and complete economic effects. Using the meteorological services in Jiangxi Province as a demonstrative example, the concepts and methods have been validated.

The main findings include:

(1) Higher interdependency between economic systems of different industries exist, implying that the associated, indirect and complete economic effects brought on by meteorological services could be much larger. For example, the ratio range of input in complete economic effect on meteorological services in Jiangxi Province is about 1:108.27–1:183.059, which is larger than that of previous estimation using Delphi method (1:30–1:51), suggesting that the society as a whole should pay more attention to meteorological services.

(2) Some industries with higher industrial connection ratios (Leontief inverse matrix), such as steel rolling processing, other non-metal ore mining and manufacturing, can achieve more associated, indirect and complete economic effects. It follows that more attention should be paid to the meteorological services of these industries.

(3) Increments of complete economic effect for some industries are relatively larger. These include railway transport, equipment manufacturing, fertilizer

manufacturing, special agriculture machinery manufacturing, forestry, livestock and fishery manufacturing, pesticide manufacturing, wholesale and retail sales and other services. Consequently, governments should engage meteorological services in these areas.

(4) Increments of indirect and complete economic effects on meteorological services traditionally directed to industries like construction, agriculture, forestry, livestock and fishery and warehousing are low. In the future, meteorological service providers should both expand their customer range and improve their quality of service in order to ultimately increase their comprehensive economic effects in these domains.

The algorithms developed in this paper are characterized by the following strengths:

(1) When used in estimating the economic effects of meteorological services, the algorithms make it possible to fully consider the intrinsic relationship between industries; calculated comprehensive values are more scientific and credible.
(2) The algorithms developed can rank the industries with the biggest increments and pick out highly sensitive industries. The results can provide references for development strategy and meteorological service investment decisions.
(3) The algorithms can also be used for loss from weather events, e.g., for the associated, indirect and complete economic loss of industrial economic systems caused by disasters or sudden crises (e.g. the impact estimation of "911" event on US aviation). Similarly, the impact estimation for different carbon reduction policies on industrial economic systems, goal programming and design of industrial regulations, all lend themselves to the use of the algorithms.

Finally, there are still some concerns regarding the concepts, algorithms and applications of associated, indirect and complete economic effect estimation mentioned. In particular, the assumption that the relevance within industries is linear, rigid and static may not reflect exactly reality of dynamic and complex industrial economic systems. To overcome such constraints assumed in the input-output method remains a major focus of future research.

**Acknowledgements** Guo Wei, Lingjuan Yang, Ji Guo, Huaguo Lu, Yunfeng Chen, Jian Sun, Mingyi Gao also made great contributions to this manuscript. We express our heartfelt thanks to them. This research was supported by: National Social and Scientific Fund Program of China (18ZDA052; 17BGL142; 16ZDA047); The Natural Science Foundation of China (91546117, 71373131, 71140014, 11371292). National Social and Scientific Fund Program (11CGL100), National Soft Scientific Fund Program (2011GXQ4B025), National Industry-specific Topics (GYHY200806017). This research was also supported by the Priority Academic Program Development of Jiangsu Higher Education Institutions.

# Appendix

See Tables 14.2 and 14.3.

**Table 14.2** Contribution rate of weather service in highly sensitive industries in Jiangxi Province, China (Measuring unit: %)

| Industry | Direct service effect in 2003–2007 | Contribution rate of meteorological service effect |
|---|---|---|
| Agriculture | 4.07–3.15 | 3.61 |
| Forestry | 4.07–3.15 | 3.61 |
| Animal husbandry | 4.07–3.15 | 3.61 |
| Fishery | 4.07–3.15 | 3.61 |
| Agriculture, forestry, husbandry and fishery | 4.07–3.15 | 3.61 |
| Convenience food manufacturing | 0.631–0.392 | 0.512 |
| Milk and dairy manufacturing | 0.631–0.392 | 0.512 |
| Condiments and fermentation products manufacturing | 0.631–0.392 | 0.512 |
| Other food manufacturing | 0.631–0.392 | 0.512 |
| Alcohol and wine manufacturing | 0.631–0.392 | 0.512 |
| Textile product manufacturing | 0.631–0.392 | 0.512 |
| Knitwear, weaving and its product manufacturing | 0.631–0.392 | 0.512 |
| Textile wearing apparel, footware, and cap manufacturing | 0.631–0.392 | 0.512 |
| Furniture manufacturing | 0.631–0.392 | 0.512 |
| Sport, cultural and educational supply manufacturing | 0.631–0.392 | 0.512 |
| Basic chemical raw material manufacturing | 0.631–0.392 | 0.512 |
| Fertilizer manufacturing | 0.631–0.392 | 0.512 |
| Pesticide manufacturing | 0.631–0.392 | 0.512 |

(continued)

**Table 14.2** (continued)

| Industry | Direct service effect in 2003–2007 | Contribution rate of meteorological service effect |
|---|---|---|
| Coating, printing ink, paint, and similar product manufacturing | 0.631–0.392 | 0.512 |
| Synthetic material manufacturing | 0.631–0.392 | 0.512 |
| Special chemical product manufacturing | 0.631–0.392 | 0.512 |
| Daily chemical product manufacturing | 0.631–0.392 | 0.512 |
| Pharmaceutical manufacturing | 0.631–0.392 | 0.512 |
| Chemical fiber manufacturing | 0.631–0.392 | 0.512 |
| Cement, lime and gypsum manufacturing | 0.631–0.392 | 0.512 |
| Cement and gypsum product manufacturing | 0.631–0.392 | 0.512 |
| Brick, stone and other building material manufacturing | 0.631–0.392 | 0.512 |
| Glass and glassware manufacturing | 0.631–0.392 | 0.512 |
| Ceramic product manufacturing | 0.631–0.392 | 0.512 |
| Refractory product manufacturing | 0.631–0.392 | 0.512 |
| Graphite and other non-metallic mineral product manufacturing | 0.631–0.392 | 0.512 |
| Non-ferrous metal and alloy manufacturing | 0.631–0.392 | 0.512 |
| Boiler and prime mover manufacturing | 0.631–0.392 | 0.512 |
| Metalworking machinery manufacturing | 0.631–0.392 | 0.512 |
| Hoist-transportation machine manufacturing | 0.631–0.392 | 0.512 |
| Pumps, valves, compressors and similar machinery manufacturing | 0.631–0.392 | 0.512 |

(continued)

**Table 14.2** (continued)

| Industry | Direct service effect in 2003–2007 | Contribution rate of meteorological service effect |
|---|---|---|
| Other common equipment manufacturing | 0.631–0.392 | 0.512 |
| Mining, metallurgy, building equipment manufacturing | 0.631–0.392 | 0.512 |
| Chemical, wood, nonmetal processing equipment manufacturing | 0.631–0.392 | 0.512 |
| Special machinery for agriculture, forestry, husbandry and fishery manufacturing | 0.631–0.392 | 0.512 |
| Other specialized equipment manufacturing | 0.631–0.392 | 0.512 |
| Railway transport equipment manufacturing | 0.631–0.392 | 0.512 |
| Automobile manufacturing | 0.631–0.392 | 0.512 |
| Vessel and floating facility manufacturing | 0.631–0.392 | 0.512 |
| Other transportation equipment manufacturing | 0.631–0.392 | 0.512 |
| Motor manufacturing | 0.631–0.392 | 0.512 |
| Transmission and distribution and control equipment manufacturing | 0.631–0.392 | 0.512 |
| Wire, cable, fiber optic cable and electrical equipment manufacturing | 0.631–0.392 | 0.512 |
| Household electric and non electric appliance manufacturing | 0.631–0.392 | 0.512 |
| Other electrical machinery and equipment manufacturing | 0.631–0.392 | 0.512 |
| Communication equipment manufacturing | 0.631–0.392 | 0.512 |
| Radar and radio equipment manufacturing | 0.631–0.392 | 0.512 |
| Electronic computer manufacturing | 0.631–0.392 | 0.512 |

(continued)

**Table 14.2** (continued)

| Industry | Direct service effect in 2003–2007 | Contribution rate of meteorological service effect |
|---|---|---|
| Electronic component manufacturing | 0.631–0.392 | 0.512 |
| Home audio-visual equipment manufacturing | 0.631–0.392 | 0.512 |
| Other electronic equipment manufacturing | 0.631–0.392 | 0.512 |
| Instrument manufacturing | 0.631–0.392 | 0.512 |
| Cultural and office machinery manufacturing | 0.631–0.392 | 0.512 |
| Craft and other product manufacturing | 0.631–0.392 | 0.512 |
| Production and supply of power and heat | 2.323–1.569 | 1.946 |
| Production and supply of gas | 2.323–1.569 | 1.946 |
| Production and supply of water | 2.323–1.569 | 1.946 |
| Construction | 2.513–1.769 | 2.141 |
| Railway transportation | 2.993–1.914 | 2.454 |
| Road transportation | 2.993–1.914 | 2.454 |
| City's public transportation | 2.993–1.914 | 2.454 |
| Water transportation | 2.993–1.914 | 2.454 |
| Air transportation | 2.993–1.914 | 2.454 |
| Pipeline transportation | 2.993–1.914 | 2.454 |
| Handling and other transport service | 2.993–1.914 | 2.454 |
| Warehousing | 2.993–1.914 | 2.454 |
| Wholesale and retail sale | 0.44–0.15 | 0.295 |
| Insurance | 2.279–1.607 | 1.943 |
| Resident service | 0.655–0.312 | 0.484 |
| Other service | 0.655–0.312 | 0.484 |

*Data source* Zou et al. (2008)

**Table 14.3** Results of economic effects (Measuring unit: Ten thousand RMB)

| Industry | Direct service effect | Associated economic effect | Indirect economic effect | Complete economic effect |
|---|---|---|---|---|
| Agriculture | 224274.860 | 32254.572 | 307400.052 | 415246.092 |
| Forestry | 45652.060 | 67369.404 | 68169.407 | 80815.325 |
| Animal husbandry | 157244.380 | 13094.821 | 180582.946 | 245308.922 |
| Fishery | 65774.200 | 2730.388 | 69725.861 | 80974.323 |
| Service of agriculture, forestry, husbandry and fishery | 22176.230 | 36522.675 | 31415.316 | 34289.819 |
| Coal mining and washing | / | 29468.833 | 64986.176 | 106900.696 |
| Oil and gas exploration | / | 2002.814 | 59147.069 | 96862.943 |
| Ferrous metal ore mining | / | 3.147 | 15374.575 | 17790.070 |
| Non-ferrous metal mining | / | 6192.810 | 27888.475 | 35079.747 |
| Other non-metal ore mining | / | 180479.691 | 27467.146 | 31787.500 |
| Grain grinding | / | 40438.204 | 8231.043 | 22338.272 |
| Feed processing | / | 76422.147 | 29632.467 | 39312.748 |
| Vegetable oil processing | / | 7223.678 | 3069.876 | 11041.238 |
| Sugar industry | / | 354.072 | 11.208 | 86.284 |
| Slaughtering and meat processing | / | 4688.495 | 3631.551 | 16511.096 |
| Aquatic product processing | / | 886.262 | 1136.525 | 6718.374 |
| Other food processing | / | 603.799 | 1374.011 | 16120.633 |
| Convenience food manufacturing | 1294.285 | 188.289 | 1363.028 | 7520.514 |
| Milk and dairy manufacturing | 541.542 | 175.256 | 716.447 | 4223.064 |
| Condiments and fermentation products manufacturing | 1733.750 | 595.822 | 2805.411 | 5249.706 |
| Other food manufacturing | 4296.243 | 129.679 | 4683.159 | 25718.227 |

(continued)

**Table 14.3** (continued)

| Industry | Direct service effect | Associated economic effect | Indirect economic effect | Complete economic effect |
|---|---|---|---|---|
| Alcohol and wine manufacturing | 3949.839 | 742.590 | 6565.676 | 20779.630 |
| Soft drink and refined tea processing | / | 368.611 | 729.371 | 3786.235 |
| Tobacco processing | / | 90.931 | 205.572 | 14109.853 |
| Cotton, chemical fiber textile and printing and dyeing finishing | / | 2263.104 | 11392.778 | 36670.132 |
| Weaving, dyeing and finishing | / | 424.478 | 308.375 | 5435.661 |
| Linen textile, silk spinning and finishing | / | 1519.773 | 2792.121 | 7674.866 |
| Textile product manufacturing | 2318.879 | 11662.786 | 7111.676 | 12948.707 |
| Knitwear, weaving and its product manufacturing | 3286.149 | 1361.131 | 4670.416 | 7287.079 |
| Textile wearing apparel, footware, and cap manufacturing | 7537.976 | 18570.466 | 19011.769 | 43126.773 |
| Leather, fur, feathers (fine hair) and its product manufacturing | / | 1591.953 | 9140.069 | 30904.725 |
| Timber, wood, bamboo, rattan, palm, and straw processing | / | 51003.512 | 23097.462 | 38102.199 |
| Furniture manufacturing | 7927.270 | 13202.959 | 11774.138 | 20665.662 |
| Paper and paper product manufacturing | / | 3417.195 | 20861.898 | 45138.795 |
| Printing and copying for recording medium | / | 2752.207 | 4972.889 | 17553.695 |
| Sport, cultural and educational supply manufacturing | 5552.497 | 12173.136 | 14409.494 | 22219.404 |
| Oil and nuclear fuel processing | / | 53732.201 | 45330.912 | 74672.808 |

(continued)

**Table 14.3** (continued)

| Industry | Direct service effect | Associated economic effect | Indirect economic effect | Complete economic effect |
|---|---|---|---|---|
| Coking | / | 134.923 | 30533.565 | 35546.660 |
| Basic chemical raw material manufacturing | 4313.508 | 7067.420 | 27771.611 | 37444.661 |
| Fertilizer manufacturing | 4776.596 | 113030.519 | 46324.485 | 60428.552 |
| Pesticide manufacturing | 3479.818 | 123788.558 | 30955.208 | 40371.197 |
| Coating, printing ink, paint, and similar product manufacturing | 2246.195 | 73507.519 | 12012.993 | 16516.688 |
| Synthetic material manufacturing | 4390.088 | 8384.865 | 20399.731 | 28660.573 |
| Special chemical product manufacturing | 5617.388 | 5959.214 | 32088.072 | 44742.483 |
| Daily chemical product manufacturing | 5380.403 | 3648.736 | 8484.226 | 20895.037 |
| Pharmaceutical manufacturing | 14668.068 | 4186.108 | 22027.422 | 29524.215 |
| Chemical fiber manufacturing | 5324.564 | 9295.692 | 13389.803 | 19345.855 |
| Rubber product manufacturing | / | 36257.879 | 16756.519 | 26013.082 |
| Plastic product manufacturing | / | 67906.036 | 19624.883 | 38499.650 |
| Cement, lime and gypsum manufacturing | 8157.829 | 185923.581 | 40322.398 | 49618.238 |
| Cement and gypsum product manufacturing | 1465.631 | 230146.363 | 7133.046 | 7690.405 |
| Brick, stone and other building material manufacturing | 934.492 | 144240.892 | 4230.565 | 7271.283 |
| Glass and glassware manufacturing | 3514.849 | 36133.173 | 16109.635 | 22741.921 |

(continued)

**Table 14.3** (continued)

| Industry | Direct service effect | Associated economic effect | Indirect economic effect | Complete economic effect |
|---|---|---|---|---|
| Ceramic product manufacturing | 1071.437 | 116648.089 | 3055.160 | 4717.192 |
| Refractory product manufacturing | 23.347 | 32815.366 | 108.039 | 121.212 |
| Graphite and other non-metallic mineral product manufacturing | 1815.357 | 23832.294 | 5177.474 | 6063.783 |
| Ironmaking | / | 123.489 | 2086.748 | 2427.965 |
| Steelmaking | / | 92.345 | 9490.169 | 11074.714 |
| Steel rolling processing | / | 253850.953 | 192794.942 | 223013.850 |
| Ferroalloy smelting | / | 915.104 | 8348.284 | 9723.447 |
| Non-ferrous metal and alloy manufacturing | 15380.644 | 8219.925 | 59352.409 | 72456.541 |
| Non-ferrous metal rolling process | / | 16988.377 | 35441.068 | 45998.841 |
| Metal product manufacturing | / | 46209.909 | 18022.247 | 31824.760 |
| Boiler and prime mover manufacturing | 1585.843 | 15390.963 | 5216.272 | 6956.593 |
| Metalworking machinery manufacturing | 1317.524 | 8476.230 | 4777.305 | 6708.909 |
| Hoist-transportation machine manufacturing | 751.089 | 560.301 | 1799.648 | 2400.930 |
| Pumps, valves, compressors and similar machinery manufacturing | 747.080 | 18494.049 | 3112.927 | 4196.952 |
| Other common equipment manufacturing | 2549.709 | 33004.312 | 15292.951 | 19117.583 |
| Mining, metallurgy, building equipment manufacturing | 1225.585 | 34734.644 | 5878.842 | 7334.650 |
| Chemical, wood, nonmetal processing equipment manufacturing | 153.743 | 1372.453 | 594.162 | 828.217 |

(continued)

**Table 14.3** (continued)

| Industry | Direct service effect | Associated economic effect | Indirect economic effect | Complete economic effect |
|---|---|---|---|---|
| Special machinery for agriculture, forestry, husbandry and fishery manufacturing | 542.986 | 86045.197 | 5151.476 | 6327.882 |
| Other specialized equipment manufacturing | 10897.859 | 7327.467 | 47018.932 | 66889.403 |
| Railway transport equipment manufacturing | 186.199 | 18862.441 | 3037.940 | 4247.180 |
| Automobile manufacturing | 6337.792 | 31957.175 | 31643.484 | 46873.349 |
| Vessel and floating facility manufacturing | 2552.346 | 5227.158 | 4394.514 | 5606.492 |
| Other transportation equipment manufacturing | 2430.771 | 535.248 | 2891.412 | 6278.044 |
| Motor manufacturing | 2773.806 | 27926.379 | 13458.015 | 17086.261 |
| Transmission, distribution and control equipment manufacturing | 1124.588 | 54310.877 | 6471.885 | 8334.190 |
| Wire, cable, fiber optic cable and electrical equipment manufacturing | 4094.003 | 114155.168 | 16208.657 | 21175.912 |
| Household electric and non electric appliance manufacturing | 4924.380 | 23225.400 | 7882.982 | 17166.417 |
| Other electrical machinery and equipment manufacturing | 10017.357 | 14318.681 | 21735.315 | 27076.277 |
| Communication equipment manufacturing | 2352.241 | 2951.962 | 4628.916 | 10437.479 |

(continued)

**Table 14.3** (continued)

| Industry | Direct service effect | Associated economic effect | Indirect economic effect | Complete economic effect |
|---|---|---|---|---|
| Radar and radio equipment manufacturing | 181.233 | 1602.207 | 281.370 | 326.689 |
| Electronic computer manufacturing | 1193.221 | 17732.838 | 4494.400 | 9978.567 |
| Electronic component manufacturing | 5151.759 | 6807.819 | 17136.031 | 27029.060 |
| Home audio-visual equipment manufacturing | 3591.788 | 1461.821 | 4379.862 | 20785.160 |
| Other electronic equipment manufacturing | 871.793 | 6197.221 | 1338.956 | 1758.516 |
| Instrument manufacturing | 3068.764 | 9233.189 | 12540.223 | 17682.669 |
| Cultural and office machinery manufacturing | 603.192 | 48454.565 | 2153.542 | 3659.179 |
| Craft and other product manufacturing | 3195.546 | 66736.291 | 11051.372 | 16906.321 |
| Scrap waste | / | 236.007 | 330.902 | 416.647 |
| Production and supply of power and heat | 86655.828 | 26555.778 | 232416.262 | 384403.028 |
| Production and supply of gas | 830.203 | 2633.266 | 1794.680 | 3742.844 |
| Production and supply of water | 7733.696 | 37911.991 | 12831.484 | 21718.429 |
| Construction | 384517.177 | 783.857 | 398017.605 | 411185.018 |
| Railway transportation | 44262.798 | 34882.827 | 139320.673 | 198323.547 |
| Road transportation | 100498.662 | 54551.412 | 180734.309 | 225390.320 |
| City's public transportation | 8640.534 | 20198.200 | 12884.220 | 16904.497 |

(continued)

**Table 14.3** (continued)

| Industry | Direct service effect | Associated economic effect | Indirect economic effect | Complete economic effect |
|---|---|---|---|---|
| Water transportation | 2287.128 | 14447.927 | 4474.668 | 7291.585 |
| Air transportation | 3791.430 | 19799.388 | 7387.494 | 11854.599 |
| Pipeline transportation | / | 0.000 | 0.000 | 0.000 |
| Handling and other transport service | 1992.648 | 10219.544 | 3805.300 | 5947.536 |
| Warehousing | 2736.210 | 9417.221 | 3598.809 | 4164.856 |
| The postal service | / | 22052.628 | 2228.910 | 4591.521 |
| Telecommunication and information transmission service | / | 12765.332 | 12776.421 | 39300.447 |
| Computer service | / | 2211.991 | 1412.032 | 2692.011 |
| Software | / | 517.298 | 70.752 | 184.895 |
| Wholesale and retail sale | 28363.365 | 33103.282 | 171367.334 | 286838.534 |
| Accommodation | / | 20236.829 | 7528.296 | 16449.092 |
| Catering | / | 22786.509 | 25574.979 | 49250.285 |
| Banking, security and other financial activity | / | 33651.299 | 46885.264 | 82681.399 |
| Insurance | / | 38477.101 | 5864.920 | 11096.667 |
| Real estate | / | 6902.654 | 18166.860 | 78204.631 |
| Leasing | / | 118605.765 | 835.384 | 2422.092 |
| Business service | / | 15666.721 | 6283.722 | 10785.177 |
| Tourism | / | 74.551 | 128.804 | 3505.748 |
| Research and experimental development | / | 117186.760 | 1598.279 | 1857.017 |
| Professional and technical service | / | 136052.891 | 4321.458 | 5614.004 |
| Science and technology exchange and promotion service | / | 20825.614 | 803.687 | 1126.383 |

(continued)

**Table 14.3** (continued)

| Industry | Direct service effect | Associated economic effect | Indirect economic effect | Complete economic effect |
|---|---|---|---|---|
| Geological exploration | / | 0.000 | 0.000 | 0.000 |
| Water management | / | 115937.570 | 2979.632 | 4471.497 |
| Environmental management | / | 9469.365 | 1190.529 | 2282.958 |
| Public facilities management | / | 523.006 | 110.174 | 1655.620 |
| Resident service | 2045.384 | 13369.132 | 5267.168 | 13544.352 |
| Other service | 3366.220 | 26964.684 | 20683.657 | 33635.381 |
| Education | / | 2670.063 | 8415.407 | 33121.785 |
| Health | / | 3211.955 | 15980.637 | 33957.909 |
| Social security | / | 7518.737 | 82.898 | 106.042 |
| Social welfare | / | 4109.687 | 92.954 | 114.111 |
| Press and publication | / | 30820.604 | 2182.198 | 4817.494 |
| Radio, television, film and motion picture | / | 158.709 | 148.309 | 1230.560 |
| Culture and art | / | 23.727 | 0.957 | 553.198 |
| Sport | / | 0.000 | 0.000 | 109.717 |
| Entertainment | / | 18301.346 | 4832.876 | 8490.062 |
| Public management and social organization | / | 3246.067 | 5919.578 | 7626.480 |
| Total | 1388263.853 | 3952190.571 | 3399128.942 | 5010533.474 |

# References

Avelino, A. F. T., & Dall'erba, S. (2019). Comparing the economic impact of natural disasters generated by different input-output models: An application to the 2007 Chehalis river flood (WA). *Risk Analysis, 39*(1), 85–104.

Birol, E., Karousakis, K., & Koundouri, P. (2006). Using economic valuation techniques to inform water resources management: A survey and critical appraisal of available techniques and an application. *Science of the Total Environment, 365,* 105–122.

Chang, Y. T., Shin, S. H., & Lee, P. T. W. (2014). Economic impact of port sectors on South African economy: An input-output analysis. *Transport Policy, 35,* 333–340.

Chen, H., & Yin, L. (1992). Calculation of indirect and complete economic effects. *Journal of UEST of China, 21*(3), 339–344.

Chen, Z., & Zhang, X. (2005). Research of several methodological issues of input-output analysis. *Quantitative & Technical Economics, 9,* 83–90.

Chen, T. A., Chang, T. C., Chiau, W. Y., & Shih, Y. C. (2013). Social economic assessment of coastal area Industrial development: An application of input-output model to Oyster Farming in Taiwan. *Ocean and Coastal Management, 73,* 153–159.

Chun, D., Woo, C., et al. (2014). The role of hydrogen energy development in the Korean economy: An input-output analysis. *International Journal of Hydrogen Energy, 39*(15), 7627–7633.

Economic Accounting Department of National Bureau of Statistics of China. (2011). 2007 input-output table of China. China Statistics Press.

Emanuel, K., Fondriest, F., & Kossin, J. (2012). Potential economic value of seasonal hurricane forecasts. *Weather, Climate, and Society, 4*(2), 110–117.

Emonts-Holley, T., Ross, A., & Swales, K. (2020). Estimating induced effects in IO impact analysis: Variation in the methods for calculating the Type II Leontief multipliers. *Economic Systems Research.* https://doi.org/10.1080/09535314.2020.1837741.

Frei, T., von Grunigen, S., & Willemse, S. (2014). Economic benefit of meteorology in the Swiss road transportation sector. *Meteorological Applications, 21*(2), 294–300.

Galbusera, L., & Giannopoulos, G. (2018). On input-output economic models in disaster impact assessment. *International Journal of Disaster Risk Reduction, 30,* 186–198.

Garza-Gil, M. D., Suris-Regueiro, J. C., & Varela-Lafuente, M. M. (2017). Using input-output methods to assess the effects of fishing and aquaculture on a regional economy: The case of Galicia, Spain. *Marine Policy, 85,* 48–53.

Grealis, E., Hynes, S., et al. (2017). The economic impact of aquaculture expansion: An input-output approach. *Marine Policy, 81,* 29–63.

Gu, B., Li, H., & Ye, H. (2009). Changes in urban and rural residents' marginal propensity to consume and the policy implication. *Journal of Financial Research, 3,* 199–206.

Haimes, Y. Y., Horowitz, B. M., Lambert, J. H., Santos, J. R., Lian, C., & Crowther, K. G. (2005). Inoperability Input-output Model (IIM) for interdependent infrastructure sectors. I: Theory and methodology. *Journal of Infrastructure Systems, 11*(2), 67–79.

Hallegatte, S. (2008). An adaptive regional input-output model and its application to the assessment of the economic cost of Katrina. *Risk Analysis, 28*(3), 779–799.

Hewings, G. J. D., & Sonis, M. (2009). Input–output analysis. In *International encyclopedia of human geography* (pp. 491–498).

Huang, C. F., Li, N., et al. (2020). Assessment of the economic cascading effect on future climate change in China: Evidence from agricultural direct damage. *Journal of Cleaner Production, 276,*.

Jiang, Y., Lei, Y. L., & Liu, J. (2019). Economic impacts of the geothermal industry in Beijing, China: An input-output approach. *Mathematical Geosciences, 51*(3), 353–372.

Kan, H., & Chen, B. (2004). Particulate air pollution in urban areas of Shanghai, China: Health based economic assessment. *Science of the Total Environment, 322,* 71–79.

Kerschner, C., & Hubacek, K. (2009). Assessing the suitability of input–output analysis for enhancing our understanding of potential economic effects of Peak Oil. *Energy, 34,* 284–290.

Khalid, M. A., & Ali, Y. (2020). Economic impact assessment of natural disaster with multi-criteria decision making for interdependent infrastructures. *Environment Development and Sustainability, 22*(8), 7287–7311.

Khashtabeh, R., Akbari, M., Kolahi, M., & Talebanfard, A. (2020). Assessing the effects of desertification control projects using socio-economic indicators in the arid regions of eastern Iran. *Environment, Development and Sustainability.* https://doi.org/10.1007/s10668-020-01065-6.

Krieger, A. M., & Green, P. E. (2002). A decision support model for selecting product/service effect positionings. *European Journal of Operational Research, 142,* 187–202.

Lee, J. W., Jang, J., Ko, K. K., & Cho, Y. (2014). Economic valuation of a new meteorological information service: Conjoint analysis for a pollen forecast system. *Weather, Climate, and Society, 6*(4), 495–505.

Lin, H. C., Kuo, Y. L., et al. (2012). Regional economic impact analysis of earthquakes in northern Taiwan and its implications for disaster reduction policies. *Natural Hazards, 61*(2), 603–620.

Lin, H. I., Liou, J. L., & Hsu, S. H. (2019). Economic valuation of public meteorological information services—A case study of agricultural producers in Taiwan. *Atmosphere, 10*(12), 753.

Lin, Y. S., Dong, Z. F., Zhang, W., & Zhang, H. Y. (2020). Estimating inter-regional payments for ecosystem services: Taking China's Beijing-Tianjin-Hebei region as an example. *Ecological Economics, 168*,.

Liu, D., Zeng, X. M., et al. (2020). A social network analysis regarding electricity consumption and economic growth in China. *Journal of Cleaner Production, 274*,.

Markou, M., Michailidis, A., et al. (2020). Applying a Delphi-type approach to estimate the adaptation cost on agriculture to climate change in Cyprus. *Atmosphere, 11*(5), 536.

Mendoza-Tinoco, D., Guan, D. B., et al. (2017). Flood footprint of the 2007 floods in the UK: The case of the Yorkshire and The Humber region. *Journal of Cleaner Production, 168,* 655–667.

Meyer, V., Becker, N., et al. (2013). Review article: Assessing the costs of natural hazards—State of the art and knowledge gaps. *Natural Hazards and Earth System Sciences, 13*(5), 1351–1373.

Munjal, P. (2013). Measuring the economic impact of the tourism industry in India using the Tourism Satellite Account and input-output analysis. *Tourism Economics, 19*(6), 1345–1359.

Nguyen, T., Robinson, J., Kaneko, S., & Komatsu, S. (2013). Estimating the value of economic effects associated with adaptation to climate change in a developing country: A case study of improvements in tropical cyclone warning services. *Ecological Economics, 86,* 117–128.

Noh, Y. (2020). A study of the evaluation of a library's economic value based on the users' and librarians' perceptions. *Electronic Library, 38*(3), 561–596.

Park, S. Y., Lim, S. Y., & Yoo, S. H. (2016). The economic value of the national meteorological service in the Korean household sector: A contingent valuation study. *Sustainability, 8*(9), 834.

Pery, A. P. R., Schuurmann, G., Ciffroy, P., Faust, M., Backhaus, T., Aicher, L., et al. (2013). Perspectives for integrating human and environmental risk assessment and synergies with socio-economic analysis. *Science of the Total Environment, 456–457,* 307–316.

Prokopy, L. S., Haigh, T., Mase, A. S., Angel, J., Hart, C., Knutson, C., et al. (2013). Agricultural advisors: A receptive audience for weather and climate information. *Weather, Climate, and Society, 5,* 162–167.

Ren, Z. (2009). *Evaluation method research of meteorological service effect*. Nanjing University of Information Science & Technology, Ph.D. dissertation.

Rocco, M. V., Tonini, F., et al. (2020). Electrification pathways for Tanzania: Implications for the economy and the environment. *Journal of Cleaner Production, 263*,.

Sieg, T., Schinko, T., et al. (2019). Integrated assessment of short-term direct and indirect economic flood impacts including uncertainty quantification. *PLoS One, 14*(4),

Suris-Regueiro, J. C., & Santiago, J. L. (2018a). Assessment of Socioeconomic impacts through physical multipliers: The case of fishing activity in Galicia (Spain). *Ecological Economics, 147,* 276–297.

Suris-Regueiro, J. C., & Santiago, J. L. (2018b). A methodological approach to quantifying socioeconomic impacts linked to supply shocks. *Environmental Impact Assessment Review, 69,* 104–110.

Wang, H. (1998). The computation of the forward and backward complete economic efficiency. *Systems Engineering, 6*(4), 53–56.

Xu, X. (2009). *Qixiang Fuwu Xiaoyi Pinggu Fangfa yu Fenxi Yanjiu.* China Meteorological Press.

Yuan, H. L., Sun, M., & Wang, Y. (2016). Assessment of the benefits of the Chinese public weather service. *Meteorological Applications, 23*(1), 132–139.

Zhang, W. Q., & Xi, Z. L. (2020). Application of Delphi method in screening of indexes for measuring soil pollution value evaluation. *Environmental Science and Pollution Research.* https://doi.org/10.1007/s11356-020-10919-5.

Zhang, Y., & Zhao, K. (2006). *Regional input-output analysis.* Beijing: Social Science Academic Press.

Zou, X., Lu, M., & Dong, B. (2008). Meteorological service effects evaluation report in Jiangxi from 2003–2007, 2008 Qixiang Fuwu Xiaoyi Pinggu Wenji (pp. 32–36).

# Part III
# Emission Allocation of Air Pollution

# Chapter 15
# Effect of Air Pollution on the Stock Yield of Heavy Pollution Enterprises in China's Key Control Cities Under Climate Change

**Abstract** Under the background of climate change, the haze days in China have increased significantly, which seriously hinders the sustainable development of society and arouses wide attention from the public. However, the researches on the effect of air pollution on the stock yield of heavy pollution enterprise in key control cities are quite limited. Thus, this paper collects the AQI (air quality index) of key control cities (over prefecture-level) in China and the stock yields of listed heavy pollution enterprises in these cities from 2011 to 2016, and through multi-discontinuities regression model, testes the effect of air pollution on the stock yield of heavy pollution enterprise. The results show that: (1) severe air pollution (AQI = 300) has a significant negative influence on stock yield and the results are robust; (2) there is a time effect in the influence of air pollution on stock yield and the negative influence has become significant since 2013. This paper gives a brief discussion on the cause of it and suggests that severe air pollution should be strictly controlled. Only by facing air pollution seriously, can we eliminate air pollution with collective wisdom and concerted efforts and achieve the sustainable development of city. Being the first study to look into the effect of air pollution on stock yield in key control cities in China, this paper provides empirical reference for government supervision departments, stock investors as well as enterprises.

**Keywords** Air pollution index · Heavy pollution enterprise · Stock yield · Multi-discontinuities regression

## 15.1 Introduction

Due to climate change, the air pollution in China is increasingly serious (Cai et al. 2017). It is estimated that, from 2001 to 2010, the annual premature death toll caused by air pollution increases from 418 to 514 thousand in China. According to the *Global Burden of Disease Study* conducted by the World Health Organization, the estimated premature death toll of China is higher and reaches 1.2 million in 2010.[1] Apart from health and lifespan, air pollution exerts adverse influences on other aspects

[1] https://www.healtheffects.org/Internationl/GBD-Press-Release.pdf.

 
X. Wu and J. Guo, *Economic Impacts and Emergency Management of Disasters in China*,
https://doi.org/10.1007/978-981-16-1319-7_15

of people's daily life as well, such as outdoor travel frequency, social interaction intention, and emotion. Through an analysis based on nationwide investigated data, Sexton (2012) found that when air quality warnings were given, the time people spent on outdoor activities would drop by 18%. Zheng et al. (2016) found that under sever air pollution, people were forced to dine out less often and they would get less satisfaction from dinning out. Chen et al. (2012) found that air pollution had a significant negative impact on productivity. Workers would feel distracted and down in the dumps during work. Besides, they would ask for leave frequently.

Air quality, which has attracted more and more attention from the public, will influence the psychology and behavior of people fully and thoroughly (Lundberg 1996; Lepori 2009). Similarly, environmental stress like weather change can influence stock market through investor sentiment. Saunders (1993) found there was a significant negative correlation between cloud coverage rate and stock yield. Hirshleifer and Shurnway (2003) verified the negative correlation between cloud coverage rate and stock yield. Lepori (2009) found that air pollution was negatively related to stock yield. Lu (2011) found weather index had no significant effects on stock yield while it could significantly influence the turnover rate and volatility. Guo and Zhang (2016), through a multivariate progressive empirical approach based on the data of air quality and stock market of Shanghai, found that the stock market tended to have higher yield, lower turnover rate and volatility with excellent air quality.

As air quality and economic behavior are closely related, this paper, based on and improved the researches of Saunders (1993) and Hirshleifer and Shurnway (2003), attempts to study the impacts of air pollution on investor sentiment and stock yield under climate change from the aspect of city. Based on the air quality data of key control cities in China and the stock yields of heavy pollution enterprises, this paper, through regression discontinuity, discusses how seriously and in which year will air pollution influence stock market. The main features of the present study are as follows: First, the object of study is the data of the listed companies in 100 key control cities in China. It can reduce the errors of results caused by the differences between samples and thus get more persuasive conclusions. Second, as people feel different about air pollution degree, the impacts of air pollution at different levels on the stock yield are examined through regression discontinuity. When AQI = 300, air pollution has a significant negative impact on stock yield. Third, as the Chinese government started to monitor air pollution and release the monitoring data officially in 2013, thus the year 2013 is regarded as a watershed. The results show that there has been a negative correlation between air pollution and stock yield since 2013.

This paper studies the effects of air pollution on the stock yield of heavy pollution enterprises in key control cities from different aspects, and then provides corresponding policy making suggestions on how to adapt to climate change and achieve sustainable development. The present study is a useful supplement to relevant researches. The rest of this paper is arranged as follows: the second part is literature review; the third part is introduction to indices and data; the fourth part is empirical analysis, and the last part is conclusions.

## 15.2 Literature Review

As stock yield is influenced by air pollution through investor sentiment, the literature review of this paper is divided into two parts, namely, the researches on the effect of air pollution on investor sentiment and the researches on the effect of investor sentiment on stock yield. A brief introduction to the ways air pollution affects stock yield and the reason for using regression discontinuity in this paper is given.

In terms of the researches on the effect of air pollution on investor sentiment, in 1903, Nelson pointed out that it would be rather difficult for investors to deal in shares in muggy and rainy weathers as confidently and freely as in dry and sunny weathers. People tended to be happy and optimistic in good weather. Air quality, as one of the index for weather conditions, would affect the emotions and feelings of people at some extent, and would further affect the transactions in stock market. Evans et al. (1987) believed air pollution would influence people's sentiment and sentiment would affect decision making. People would feel angrier, more depressed, and more helpless when exposed to severe air pollution. Zhou (1999) believed weather conditions, which human beings rely on for existence and development, highly restricted the activities of people. Weather conditions had attracted extensive attention from people because any change in weather would significantly influence people's life. Eagles (1994) found that the lack of sunshine would make people depressed or even lead to a rise in suicide rate. In stock market, the mental activities of investors would be influenced by the surrounding environment, for instance, weather conditions, and the mental activities would further influence the exchange of stock. Mehra and Sah (2002) found that a minor mood swing could lead to a significant fluctuation in capital price. Lucey and Dowling (2005) found that weather and biologic changes could affect the exchange of stock through influencing people's sentiment. Hsiao et al. (2020) combined econometric analysis and fuzzy logic-based examination to study the impact of local weather in China's stock market on investors sentiment and stock returns. The results indicated that investors were more positive about stocks and more likely to invest when the sunlight was stronger. A great quantity of psychological research showed that the air pollution impacted individual sentiment. Teng and He (2020) believed that actual air quality would affect investor behavior. The empirical results proved that the environment affected emotional response of investor to air pollution, which in turn affected trading behavior. Baylis et al. (2018) conducted a largest-scale investigation on the relationship between the emotions of human and meteorological conditions. The results of the research found that cold or hot temperatures, precipitation, cloud cover, humidity and smaller temperature ranges were all interrelated to deterioration of sentiment. Beecher et al. (2016) examined the relationship between weather condition or pollution and mental health. The initial research results pointed out that there was a certain relationship between weather pollution and changes in public mental health. Later, they came to a conclusion that the mental health problems of people increased with the decrease in sunshine hours. Peng et al. (2016) used geospatial methods to analyze personal happiness from weather data. They found that weather conditions and economic conditions were all associated with levels of happiness. Shahzad (2019) analyzed the impact of weather on stock returns. The humidity, temperature, air pressure, wind speed and state (clear, cloud, fog, rain, snow) of the stock market were used as weather variables to discuss the relationship with stock returns. The results revealed that the weather had a greater influence on China's capital market. In some cases, weather variables could also affect profitability. An et al. (2017) believed that air quality had tremendous effect on investor sentiment, and investor sentiment impacted stock market volatility. The GARCH model was used for empirical testing. The results suggested that air quality and investor sentiment could act on the stock market alone or together. According to these researches, serious air pollution could cause negative emotions on investors and their will of transaction would become weaker, through which the stock yield would be affected.

In terms of the researches on the influence of investor sentiment on stock yield, Forgas and Bower (1987) found that there was an emotion congruent effect in human being's behavior. In other words, when somebody feels happy, he/she is more likely to run into positive things, while when he/she feels upset, things around him/her are tend to be negative. Lee et al. (1991) came up with the "investor sentiment theory" which said that the expectations of trader on future earnings were easy to be affected by sentiment volatility. According to some psychological researches, the behavior decision-making and judgment of people can be affected by emotions. Wright and Bower (1992) put forward that people made positive evaluations on many things when they were in good moods, increasing investment and consumption for example. Isen (1993) proposed that people would simplify the cognitive processes to help themselves make decision when they were happy. Li and Wang (2002) and Song et al. (2003) gave objective evidence of the interaction between Chinese stock market and investor sentiment. Wu and Han (2007) found that investor sentiment could not only be used to predict the current stock yield but also the long-term (or intertemporal) stock yield. By constructing a firm-level index to measure individual mood caused by air pollution in the China's stock market, Wu and Lu (2020) studied how the personal investors sentiment affected stock pricing. Their findings suggested that the pessimistic individual investor reduced liquidity and volatility, which ultimately led to a decline in stock yields. Hu et al. (2015) explored how individual investors were notably affected by emotions and used a vector autoregression model to provide evidence for investor sentiment-driven transactions to increase market transaction frequency. Ying et al. (2020) demonstrated that sustainable cross-sectional changes in stock returns were explained by emotional fluctuations of the days of the week. Psychological research showed that Friday got a higher return than Monday because the mood on Friday was high while on Monday was low. Harding and He (2016) tested whether changes in investor sentiment would lead to changes in the determinants of stock prices. Their analysis results found that worsening sentiment would increase the risk aversion level of male investors compared to women. Lepori (2015) regarded the negative emotions caused by the end of the TV series as a mood-changing event. He found that when the proportion of Americans watching the TV finale increases, the US stock returns immediately decreased subsequently. Negative sentiment reduced the demand for risky assets. Abu et al. (2014)

explored whether intuitive measures of sentiment could explain the Monday effect—returns on Monday were negative on average. A greater number of investors were more pessimistic on Monday, and they became optimistic with the week progressing. Naeem et al. (2020) used the happiness index of Twitter as a representative of investor sentiment to examine the relationship between happiness and future market fluctuations. They found that Twitter's happiness significantly contributed to the future volatility of the sample countries. This discovery provided strong evidence for the nonlinear relationship between future stock market volatility and investors mood. Haritha and Rishad (2020) found that irrational emotions could significantly cause market volatility. Jin et al. (2020) proposed a stock market prediction model, where investor sentiment tendency was introduced. The authors believed that incorporating investor sentiment into stock forecasts could improve the accuracy of the model's prediction. The experimental results proved that the investors' emotional tendency was effective in improving the prediction results. Papakyriakou et al. (2019) believed that terrorist event could affect investor sentiment. By studying terrorist acts in seven countries from 1988 to 2017, they found that the stock market declined significantly on the day of the event or the following trading day, and the economic losses were significantly higher in the countries which had a higher sentiment decline after the event. Rahman and Shamsuddin (2019) examined the role of investor sentiment in explaining the countries' price-earning ratio. Optimistic investment sentiment tended to drive an excessively high P/E ratio. By analyzing the relationship between the P/E ratio and investor emotion in the G7 stock market, they came to a conclusion that the price-earnings ratio generally rose as investor sentiment improved. Dash and Maitra (2017) found that there was a significant impact of investor sentiment both on short-term and long-term returns. They used data from the Indian stock market to examine the relationship between stock yields and investor sentiment. Research provided support for the fact that no matter whether investors were short-term or long-term traders, their investment activities were related to emotions. Shi et al. (2018) used text mining strategies to identify individual investor sentiments, based on which they applied investor sentiment to the Chinese stock market. The research results emphasized that investor sentiment had a predictive effect on stock market returns. Other researches on the influences of investor sentiment on stock yield are conducted by Baker and Wurgler (2006), Kaplanski and Levy (2010), Levy and Yagil (2011), Wang and Sun (2004), Brown and Cliff (2004), Chen (2005), Ding and Suzhi (2005), Lin et al. (2006), and Shan (2011). Due to space limitations, the details of these researches will not be given.

Air pollution influences stock yield in different ways. Goetzmann et al. (2015) found that weather-based sentiment indicators can affect institutional investors' trading decisions as well as perceptions of mispricing, thereby affecting stock returns. This finding provided another channel for how weather affected stock returns. Lepori (2016) proved that air pollution effects only existed when trading was conducted on floor, meaning that the connection between air pollution effects and domestic stock yield was modulated by the trading floor community as a transmission mechanism. Guo and Zhang (2016) proposed that air quality affected the preference and decision-making of such stock market participants as supervision department, listed company, and local and non-local investors through policies (Oberndorfer and Andreas 2006; Mulatu et al. 2010; Fu et al. 2011; Kong et al. 2012), market expectations (Chen et al. 2011; Tan and Chen 2012; Banerjee 1992; Yang et al. 2004), and sentiment (Thaler 1993; Daniel et al. 1998; Bullinger 1990; Schottenfeld 1992; Nowakowicz-Debek et al. 2004; Coates and Herbert 2008; Hirshleifer 2001; Lin and Yu 2010) respectively. Then the trading behaviors (direction, quantity, and timing) are determined, through which the stock yield is affected eventually. It should be pointed out that policy, sentiment, and market expectation are closely related and influence each other. In addition, there are many literatures that showed the relationship between air pollution and stock yield. E.g. Huang et al. (2020) studied the impact of air pollution on the trading behavior of individual investors. They found that air pollution could make investors more influenced by attention-driven buying behavior and disposition effects, and proved that there was a negative correlation between air pollution and stock trading performance. Apergis and Gupta (2017) used the abnormal weather conditions in New York to predict the returns of the South African stock market. They found that the abnormal weather in New York could be used to predict the return of South African stocks, and the empirical results certified that abnormally deviated weather variables had a notable statistical negative impact on the return of South African stocks. Li and Peng (2016) discussed the impact of low sentiment caused by air pollution on stock returns. The results of the empirical study showed that there was a contemporaneous negative correlation between the air pollution level and the stock returns and a positive relationship with a two-day lag.

This paper conducts an empirical analysis with regression discontinuity model, through which endogency can be avoided effectively. Yu and Wang (2011) believed that regression discontinuity, second to random experiment, was an approach which could analyze the correlations between variables through the effective utilization of realistic constraint conditions. Lee (2008) proposed that regression discontinuity was widely applied as it could avoid the endogency in parameter estimation and faithfully reflect the correlations between variables. This paper attempts to find out whether the stock yield of enterprise will be affected when AQI reaches a certain threshold. Regression discontinuity is quite suitable for the case and thus is used in this paper.

## 15.3 Introduction to Indices and Data

The samples analyzed in this paper are the stock yields of listed heavy pollution enterprises in the key control cities in China between 2011 and 2016. The details of data and variables are as follows:

(1) Air Pollution Level. According to the notice released by the Ministry of Environmental Protection in the first half year of 2012, API (air pollution index) is replaced with AQI. Therefore, this paper uses AQI to evaluate the variables. Compared with API which only evaluates $SO_2$, $NO_2$, and $PM_{10}$, AQI is able to evaluate 3 more pollutants, namely, $PM_{2.5}$, $O_3$, and CO. Besides, AQI is has

a stricter standard by adopting a classification and rating system in limitation. Therefore, AQI monitors more pollutant indices than API and thus is more objective in evaluation results. The AQI Data of the key control cities are from the *Urban Ambient Air Quality Daily Report*[2] of the Ministry of Environmental Protection from Jan. 1, 2013 to Dec. 31, 2016.

(2) Discontinuity Selection. Stock yield and AQI, the explained variables of this paper, respectively are yearly measurement index and daily measurement index. For a unified analysis on the variables, this paper uses the method proposed by Xi and Liang (2015), namely selecting the yearly maximum values of API of key control cities. That's because the yearly maximum of API is able to reflect the pollution level. More importantly, it is easier to be perceived by the public than any other statistical characteristics. The yearly maximum and minimum values of AQI in this paper are 500 and 52 respectively. According to Table 15.1, the discontinuities between the maximum and the minimum are 100, 150, 200, and 300. Based on the method proposed by Xi and Liang (2015), this paper conducts a multi-discontinuities regression analysis on the yearly maximum of AQI.

(3) Control Variable. Arnott et al. (1989) proposed that foreign earnings, P/B ratio (price to book ratio), P/E ratio (price to earnings ratio), and enterprise scale were the four main influence factors of stock yield. Li and Liu (1997) conducted an empirical study on the basis of earnings per share. Chen et al. (2001) through cross-section multiple factor analysis, proposed that enterprise scale and P/B ratio had significant explanatory power to the stock yield on Chinese stock market. He (2001) put forward that the reciprocal of price to earnings ratio had a significant impact on stock yield. This paper, based on the above researches, selects the control variables of stock yield. They are enterprise scale, P/B ratio, stock yield, and the reciprocal of P/E ratio.

(4) Heavy Pollution Enterprise. In 2013, the Ministry of Environmental Protection issued the *Notice on Special Emission Limits on Air Pollutants*[3] which has classified 19 provinces into key control area. For the key control area, special limits for the key air pollutants in thermal power industry, iron and steel industry, petrochemical industry, cement industry, non-ferrous metals industry, and chemical industry as well as coal-fired boiler are applied. Therefore, the enterprises in the six industries in the 19 provinces can be used as the sample source. According to Liu and Liu (2015), the six industries can be further

[2]Website: https://datacenter.mep.gov.cn/report/air.daily/air.dairy_api.jsp.

[3]According to the *Notice on Special Emission Limits on Air Pollutants*, the six industries in major monitoring areas include thermal power industry, iron and steel industry, petrochemical industry, cement industry, non-ferrous metals industry, and chemical industry. The key control area contains 19 provinces (autonomous regions/municipalities). They are Beijing, Tianjin, Hebei, Shanghai, Jiangsu, Zhejiang, Guangdong, Liaoning, Shandong, Hubei, Hunan, Chongqing, Sichuan Province, Fujian, Shanxi, Shaanxi, Gansu, Ningxia, and Xinjiang.

divided into 12 heavy pollution industries.[4] The observation data are obtained in the following steps: first, selecting the data of the A-share listed heavy pollution enterprises which are located in key cities from CSMAR Solution and those of enterprises which have gotten special treatment are eliminated; second, selecting the stock yields of these listed heavy pollution enterprises between 2011 and 2016 from RESSET. Then we get 975 pieces of observation data after winsorizing the abnormal values in the stock yields and the adopted control variables.

## 15.4 Empirical Model, Results and Analysis

### *15.4.1 Empirical Model*

Based on the classification standard on AQI in China, a multi-discontinuities regression model is established (see Table 15.1).

The following study is to find out where there is a jump in the earnings management index of enterprise with AQI being around 100, 150, 200, and 300. The steps are as follows: First, determining the discontinuities (AQI = 100, AQI = 150, AQI = 200 and AQI = 300). Assuming that the samples near the discontinuities are random, these samples are identical in characteristics and have no significant differences. As a result, the omitted variable bias in empirical process is avoided (Hahn et al. 2001). Second, the samples over the discontinuities fall into treatment group and those under the discontinuities fall into control group. In the grouping of samples, the method proposed by Brollo et al. (2013) is used. The samples between different discontinuity intervals are divided into two parts from the middle. Those covered in $\left[\frac{Aj-1+Aj}{2}, A_j\right)$ belong to control group while those covered in $\left[A_j, \frac{Aj+Aj+1}{2}\right)$ belong to treatment group. Based on the research of Hahn et al. (2001), the regression discontinuity model is established:

$$y_{it} = \alpha^* D_{it} + \int \left(a_{it} - A_j\right) + D_{it}^* \int \left(a_{it} - A_j\right) + X\beta + \delta_t + \eta_i + \xi_z + \mu_{it} \tag{15.1}$$

[4]According to the *Industry Classification Standard for Listed Company* (2012 Edition) issued by China Securities Regulatory Commission, the above six industries are further divided into 12 sub-industries: B07 (petroleum and natural gas extraction), B08 (ferrous metal mining), B09 (nonferrous metal mining), C19 (leather and fur products and shoes), C25 (petroleum processing, coking, and nuclear fuel processing), C26 (manufacture of chemical raw materials and chemicals), C28 (manufacture of chemical fibers), C29 (rubber and plastics products), C30 (manufacture of non-metallic mineral), C31 (ferrous metal smelting and rolling), C32 (Non-ferrous metal smelting and rolling), and D44 (production and supply of electricity and heat).

**Table 15.1** Air quality index and the corresponding air quality level

| Air quality index | Air quality level | Air pollution level | Interpretation and suggestion |
|---|---|---|---|
| 0–50 | I | Excellent | The air is free from pollution and the air quality is satisfactory. Normal activities are suggested for all people |
| 51–100 | II | Good | The air quality is acceptable and only some extremely susceptible people will be slightly influenced by particular pollutants and they should have less outdoor activities |
| 101–150 | III | Lightly polluted | The symptoms of susceptible people will be slightly aggravated. Irritations occur to health people. Children, elders, and individuals with breathing and heat problems should reduce longtime-intense outdoor exercise |
| 151–200 | IV | Moderately polluted | The symptoms of susceptible people will be further aggravated. The heart and respiratory system of healthy people may be influenced. Individuals with heart and breathing problems should avoid longtime-intense outdoor exercise. Health people should restrict outdoor exercise |
| 201–300 | V | Heavily polluted | The symptoms of people who suffer from heart and lung diseases will be significantly aggravated and they will experience reduced endurance in activities. Symptoms occur to healthy people widely. Children, elders, and individuals with heart and lung diseases should stay indoors and stop outdoor exercise. Healthy people should reduce outdoor exercise |
| 300+ | VI | Severely polluted | Health people will experience reduced endurance in activities. There are strong symptoms which may trigger some illnesses. Children and elders should stay indoors and avoid exercise. Healthy people should avoid outdoor activities |

where $a_{it} \in \left[\frac{Aj-1+Aj}{2}, \frac{Aj+Aj+1}{2}\right]$, $D_{it} = 1\{a_{it}-A_j > 0\}$, $\gamma_{it}$ is the stock yield of Company $i$, $a_{it}$ is air quality index, $A_j$ is the $j$th discontinuity, and $a_{it}-A_j$ is the distance between Sample $i$ and Discontinuity $j$. $D_{it} = 1\{a_{it}-A_j > 0\}$, a treatment variable, is the function of Continuous Function $a_{it}$ and is determined by the difference between $a_{it}$ and discontinuity. When $a_{it}-A_j > 0$, $D_{it} = 1\{a_{it}-A_j > 0\}$ is 1, otherwise it is 0. $X$ refers to control variable, including Size (enterprise scale) and P/B ratio (price to book ratio). $\delta_t$ is time fixed effect (a time trend which does not change along with individual). $\eta_i$ is individual fixed effect (an individual difference which does not change with time). $\xi_z$ is discontinuity fixed effect. Error Term $\mu_{it}$ is the cluster of all industries. $f(a_{it}-A_j)$ is the function of Execution Variable $(a_{it}-A_j)$. $D^*_{it} f(a_{it}-A_j)$ refers to the function forms that may exist on both sides of control discontinuity. Formula (15.2) shows the discontinuity effect.

$$\gamma_{it} = \sum_{J=1}^{m} \alpha_J * D^*_{it} A_J + (1 + D_{it}) \int (a_{it} - A_j) + \int (a_{it} - A_j) * A_J + X\beta + \delta_t + \eta_i + \mu_{it} \quad (15.2)$$

where $a_J$ is the influence coefficient of air quality level on stock yield around Discontinuity $j$.

### 15.4.2 Empirical Results and Analysis

The overall discontinuity effect and separate discontinuity effect of air quality on stock yield from 2011 to 2016 are shown in Table 15.2.

Table 15.2 shows the regression results of the yearly maximum of AQI obtained through Formula 15.1. To enhance the robustness of the regression results, the linear function, quadratic function, and cubic function of AQI are regarded as control variables. As is shown in the 2–4 columns in Table 15.2, the stock yield will decrease by 0.0012–0.059 with each one increase in air quality level. When the discontinuity is 100 or 300 (AQI = 100 or AQI = 300), the air quality and stock yield are negatively related. However, when the discontinuity is 150 or 200 (AQI = 150 or AQI = 200), the air quality and stock yield are positively related. There is a significant negative effect on stock yield when AQI = 300 (confidence level is 5%). To improve the robustness of results, this paper, conducts regression test under different bandwidths. The omitted variable bias in empirical process is settled by assuming the samples near the discontinuities are randomly distributed. Considering the sample loss may be caused by small bandwidth and the variable omission may be caused by large bandwidth, this paper sets the bandwidth at 25 (half of the distance between two adjacent discontinuities) 25.[5] In empirical analysis, the bandwidths are reduced

[5]The bandwidths of the last two Discontinuities 200 and 300 are 50.

**Table 15.2** Discontinuity effect of stock yield from 2011 to 2016

| | Standard regression | | | Bandwidth = 20 | Bandwidth = 15 | Bandwidth = 10 |
|---|---|---|---|---|---|---|
| | Linear function | Quadratic function | Cubic function | | | |
| Overall discontinuity effect | −0.0012 (0.049) | −0.059 (0.076) | −0.046 (0.110) | −0.023 (0.083) | −0.047 (0.105) | −0.092 (0.174) |
| AQI = 100 | −0.217 (0.132) | −0.226 (0.141) | −0.131 (0.243) | −0.292 (0.156) | −0.197 (0.186) | 0.056 (0.043) |
| AQI = 150 | 0.0007 (0.060) | 0.023 (0.079) | 0.084 (0.089) | 0.063 (0.068) | 0.043 (0.092) | 0.042 (0.140) |
| AQI = 200 | 0.081 (0.060) | 0.107 (0.065) | 0.137 (0.087) | 0.057 (0.076) | 0.085 (0.096) | 0.219 (0.179) |
| AQI = 300 | −0.069 (0.061) | −0.162* (0.076) | −0.188* (0.098) | −0.214* (0.098) | −0.323* (0.159) | −0.834** (0.251) |
| Is control variable included | No | No | No | No | No | No |
| Sample size | 975 | 975 | 975 | 581 | 451 | 295 |

*Notes* (1) *, **, and *** respectively means Statistic t is significant at 5%, 2.5%, and 1% confidence levels; (2) the values stand for overall discontinuity effect and the regression coefficient of discontinuity. The values within brackets are standard deviations

to 15, 20, and 25 respectively. As is shown in the 5–7 columns in Table 15.2, the standard regression results and the local linear regression results of the three bandwidths obtained through linear function are quite close. The above analysis is based on the approach proposed by Xi and Liang (2015).

Server air pollution (AQI = 300) may cause considerable public concern. As a result, relevant government departments or supervision organizations will take corresponding measures to limit the emissions of heavy pollution enterprise, leading to the decline in stock yield. Besides, the stock yield of heavy pollution enterprise may also be reduced due to investor sentiment volatility. A robustness test is performed on the above results in the following section.

## 15.4.3 Robustness Test

### 15.4.3.1 Continuity of Execution Variable (AQI)

To find out whether the yearly maximum of AQI is controlled by local government, a continuity check on the execution variable $a_{it} - A_j$ (the distance between Sample $i$ and Discontinuity $j$) is made through the approach proposed by McCrary (2008) to detect the jumps at different discontinuities. The check results are shown in Fig. 15.1.

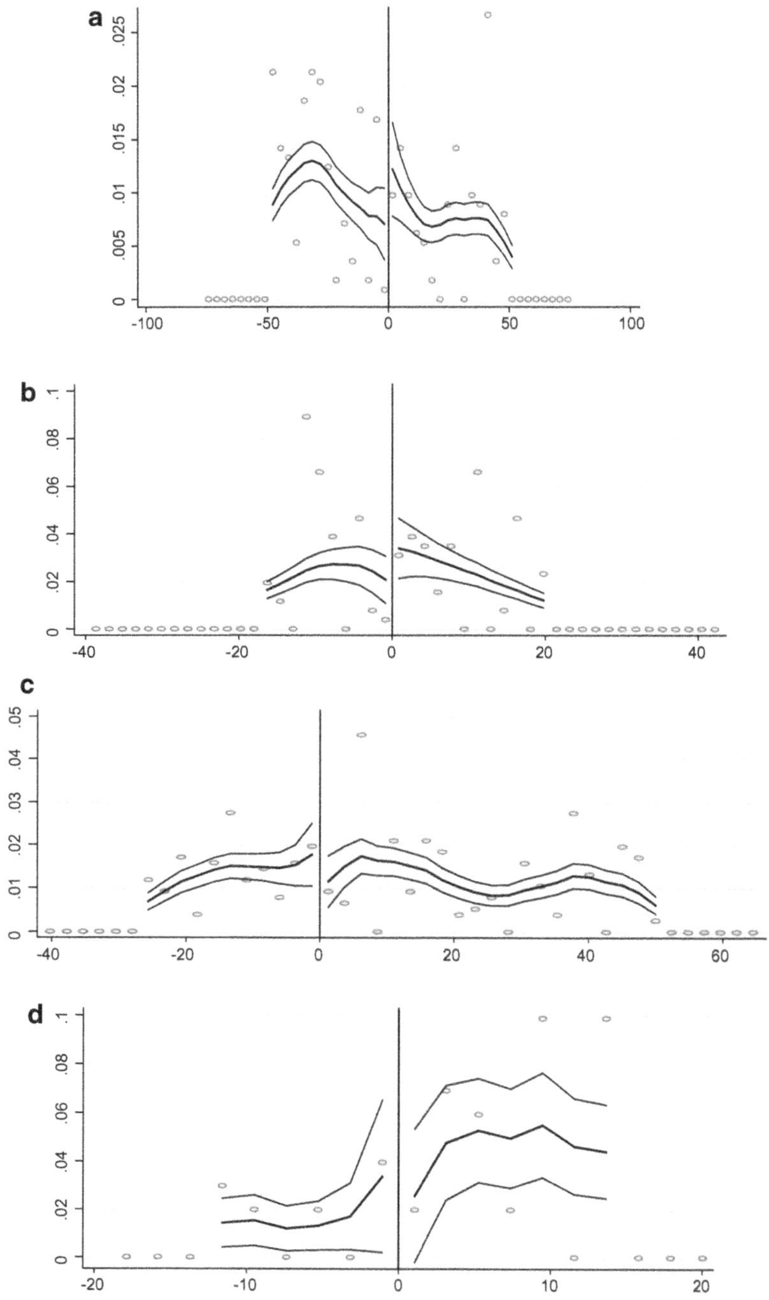


**Fig. 15.1** Check results of density function at Discontinuities 100 (**a**), 150 (**b**), 200 (**c**) and 300 (**d**)

It can be known from the check results that the confidence intervals of the estimation value of density function on both sides of the discontinuity overlap. That is to say the density function is continuous at the discontinuities. It indicates that the yearly maximum of AQI has not been controlled by local government.

#### 15.4.3.2 Continuity Check on Control Variable

A continuity check is performed on control variables so as to detect the jumps of control variables at different discontinuities, through which the effect of control variable on regression results can be known. The regression results are influenced by control variable if jumps are detected. Based on the model proposed by Xi and Liang (2015), there is:

$$x_{it} = \alpha * 1\{a_{it} - A_j)0\} + (1 + D_{it}) \int (a_{it} - A_j) + \delta_t + \eta_i + \xi_z + \mu_{it} \quad (15.3)$$

where $x_{it}$ refers to control variables. There are no jumps at discontinuity if $\alpha$ is small. The results are presented in Table 15.3.

**Table 15.3** Continuity check on control variable

| | Control variable (definition) | | | |
|---|---|---|---|---|
| | Size: the aggregate value is natural logarithm | | | |
| | P/B ratio (price to book ratio) | | | |
| | 1/P/E (1/price to earnings ratio) | | | |
| | EPS (earnings per share) | | | |
| | Linear function | | | |
| | Size | P/B ratio | 1/P/E | EPS |
| Overall discontinuity effect | −0.027<br>(0.039) | −0.375<br>(0.272) | 0.0003<br>(0.004) | 0.002<br>(0.028) |
| AQI = 100 | 0.109<br>(0.106) | 1.038<br>(0.750) | 0.007<br>(0.009) | 0.089<br>(0.075) |
| AQI = 150 | −0.047<br>(0.048) | −0.269<br>(0.340) | −0.005<br>(0.004) | −0.041<br>(0.034) |
| AQI = 200 | 0.022<br>(0.048) | −0.364<br>(0.334) | 0.004<br>(0.004) | −0.023<br>(0.034) |
| AQI = 300 | −0.096*<br>(0.048) | −0.406<br>(0.340) | 0.040<br>(0.004) | 0.009<br>(0.035) |
| Observation value | 975 | 965 | 839 | 969 |

*Notes* (1) *, **, and *** respectively means Statistic t is significant at 5%, 2.5%, and 1% confidence levels; (2) the values stand for overall discontinuity effect and the regression coefficient of discontinuity. The values within brackets are standard deviations

According to the check results on control variable at different discontinuities, when AQI = 300, Size is significant at 5% confidence level under linear function. However, it is not significant under other function forms such as quadratic function and cubic function. It indicates that Size is not robust and exerts little influence on regression results. Discontinuity effect doesn't show in P/B ratio (price to book ratio), 1/P/E (price to earnings ratio), and EPS (earnings per share) as they are not significant at each discontinuity. Therefore, Size, P/B ratio, 1/P/E and EPS can all be used as the control variable in this paper. However, the fact is that P/B ratio and 1/P/E significantly reduce the precision of regression results in empirical study. Thus, this paper only selects Size and EPS as control variables (see Table 15.4). It is obvious that the results in Table 15.4 and Table 15.2 are quite similar.

The following analysis is to find out where the effect of air pollution on stock yield will change in different years. Hu et al. (2014), using the API of Beijing before 2013, found that there were no significant correlations between air pollution and stock yield. Based on these findings, this paper conducts a regression analysis on the stock yields in different years when AQI = 300. The regression results are shown in Table 15.5.

When AQI = 300, the stock yields in different years under different function forms are shown in Table 15.5. It can be known from Table 15.5 that air quality has a positive influence on stock yield during 2011–2012 as well as 2011–2013. As the year increases, air pollution starts to exert a negative influence on stock yield. The

**Table 15.4** Discontinuity effect of stock yield from 2011 to 2016

| | Standard regression | | | Bandwidth = 20 | Bandwidth = 15 | Bandwidth = 10 |
|---|---|---|---|---|---|---|
| | Linear function | Quadratic function | Cubic function | | | |
| Overall discontinuity effect | 0.005<br>(0.049) | −0.060<br>(0.076) | −0.043<br>(0.108) | −0.017<br>(0.083) | −0.050<br>(0.106) | −0.085<br>(0.178) |
| AQI = 100 | −0.233<br>(0.132) | −0.246<br>(0.141) | −0.171<br>(0.242) | −0.304*<br>(0.156) | −0.215<br>(0.187) | 0.075<br>(0.450) |
| AQI = 150 | 0.012<br>(0.060) | 0.027<br>(0.079) | 0.087<br>(0.089) | 0.081<br>(0.069) | 0.037<br>(0.093) | 0.045<br>(0.144) |
| AQI = 200 | 0.087<br>(0.060) | 0.119<br>(0.065) | 0.150<br>(0.087) | 0.062<br>(0.076) | 0.106<br>(0.097) | 0.221<br>(0.182) |
| AQI = 300 | −0.069<br>(0.061) | −0.175*<br>(0.076) | −0.199*<br>(0.097) | −0.240*<br>(0.099) | −0.347*<br>(0.140) | −0.839**<br>(0.254) |
| Is control variable included | Yes | Yes | Yes | Yes | Yes | Yes |
| Sample size | 975 | 975 | 975 | 581 | 451 | 295 |

*Notes* (1) *, **, and *** respectively means Statistic t is significant at 5%, 2.5%, and 1% confidence levels; (2) the values stand for overall discontinuity effect and the regression coefficient of discontinuity. The values within brackets are standard deviations

**Table 15.5** Change of stock yield at AQI = 300

| Standard regression | | | | | | | | | |
|---|---|---|---|---|---|---|---|---|---|
| AQI = 300 | | | | | | | | | |
| | Year | | | | | | | | |
| | 2011–2012 | 2011–2013 | 2011–2014 | 2011–2015 | 2011–2016 | 2012–2016 | 2013–2016 | 2014–2016 | 2015–2016 |
| Linear function | 0.031** (0.103) | 0.045 (0.082) | −0.023 (0.067) | −0.065 (0.069) | −0.069 (0.061) | −0.110 (0.073) | −0.206* (0.092) | −0.240* (0.122) | −0.517* (0.231) |
| Quadratic function | 0.231 (0.128) | 0.064 (0.102) | −0.098 (0.087) | −0.177* (0.088) | −0.175* (0.076) | −0.244** (0.092) | −0.371** (0.112) | −0.397** (0.142) | −1.103** (0.324) |
| Cubic function | 0.406 (0.215) | 0.260 (0.153) | −0.059 (0.111) | −0.234* (0.113) | −0.199* (0.097) | −0.267* (0.113) | −0.427** (0.141) | −0.506** (0.175) | −1.153** (0.411) |

*Notes* (1) *, **, and *** respectively means Statistic t is significant at 5%, 2.5%, and 1% confidence levels; (2) the values stand for overall discontinuity effect and the regression coefficient of discontinuity. The values within brackets are standard deviations

influence is increasingly significant under different function forms. The year 2013 shows different characteristics in the regression. For example, the effect of air quality on stock yield is positive during 2011–2013 and becomes negative after 2013. Apart from that, there are more and more statistically significant coefficients after 2013. Therefore, the year 2013 can be regarded as a watershed.

In fact, Chinese government started to release the air quality data of major cities in 2013. On Jan. 1, 2013, China, according to the new air quality standard, officially released the key pollutants and AQI of Beijing-Tianjin-Hebei Region and 74 cities the first time, marking the completion of the first stage of monitoring task under new standard. The information is updated every hour so that the public can know about air quality in time. Haze is regarded as a serious environmental pollution problem for the first time in the report on natural disasters of 2013 released by the Disaster Reduction Center of Ministry of Civil Affairs. Public media started to make considerable reports on haze. In 2013, the News Broadcast, CCTV's national news program, gave an 8-munite report on the haze weather in China for the first time. In People's Daily, the official media of Chinese government, from 2011 to 2016, the pieces of reports on haze weather in 2011, 2012, 2013, and 2014 respectively are 3, 4, 40, and 26. The number increased sharply in 2013 and remained large in 2014. As the Chinese government and the public both pay high attention to haze weather, the air pollution has gradually developed into a social focus from an environmental problem since 2013. It indicates that the year 2013 is the first year for Chinese society to face the haze problem, which further proves the reliability of empirical results.

## 15.5 Conclusions

This paper collected the data of listed enterprises in six heavy pollution industries in the key control cities in China from 2011 to 2016 and analyzed the correlation between air quality and stock yield through regression discontinuity model. The empirical results show that, when the discontinuity is 300 (AQI = 300), there shows a significant negative effect on the stock yields of the listed enterprises. The results agree well with the investor sentiment theory which holds that severe air pollution may affect investor sentiment and make investors feel pessimistic about the expectations of stock market earnings, leading to the decline in stock yield. According to Guo and Zhang (2016), another possibility for the stock yield reduction is that supervision department has taken measures to restrict heavy pollution enterprises for the high emissions concerned by the public. No matter what causes the reduction of stock yield, server air pollution, surely has negative influences on the stock yield of listed enterprise according to the empirical results. The results also show that Discontinuity 300 (AQI = 300) can be regarded as a threshold at which air pollution starts to exert a significant negative effect on stock yield. Besides, the influences of air pollution on stock yield will change in different years. The year 2013 can be regarded as a watershed after which negative influences become significant gradually.

In view of the abovementioned findings, the following suggestions are made:

First, severe air pollution has a negative influence on economic development. As most of the key control cities in China are in the middle and later periods of industrialization, the emission of polluted air is high and air pollution cannot be eliminated in a short time. Consequently, when the air pollution passes a certain level, the city image, investment attraction, public sentiment, as well as earnings of listed enterprise will be impaired, which will further stunt the economic growth of city. Therefore, air pollution should never be neglected in order to maintain the economic growth of city.

Second, the harmfulness of air pollution should be faced seriously. There have been many research findings showed that air pollution had serious negative influences on people's health both physically and psychologically. This paper found that the real impact of air pollution on the society started to show in the year of 2013 when Chinese government faced the harm of air pollution. Due to the high attention the public paid on air pollution, haze, an environmental problem, has gradually developed into a political one which evaluates the governing capacity of Chinese government since 2016. The government, intentionally or unintentionally, starts to restrict the forecast and new report on haze weather. As a result, air pollution problem fades from the public view. It does not help to bury one's head in the sand while tackling the air pollution of city. Only by facing air pollution seriously, can the whole society eliminate air pollution with collective wisdom and concerted efforts.

At last, other less developed Chinese cities and foreign cities should learn a lesson from the key control cities in China during development. In fact, when the public realize the seriousness of air pollution, the society will try to exert pressure on government in different ways, resulting in the negative growth of economy. For example, in 2013, the Chinese government started the official monitoring on air quality and released the data of AQI, after which the stock yields of the heavy enterprises in key control cities decline. Therefore, the government should try to maintain equilibrium in economic development, public will, city image, and environmental protection, only by which can the city alleviate the negative effect produced by climate change and air pollution and achieve the sustainable development.

**Acknowledgements** Shanshan Chen, Ge Gao, Yanmin Liu also made great contributions to this manuscript. We express our heartfelt thanks to them. This research was supported by: National Social and Scientific Fund Program of China (18ZDA052; 17BGL142; 16ZDA047); The Natural Science Foundation of China (91546117, 71373131).

# References

Abu, B. A., Siganos, A., & Vagenas-Nanos, E. (2014). Does mood explain the monday effect? *Journal of Forecasting, 33*(6), 409–418.

An, N., Wang, B., Pan, P., et al. (2017). Study on the influence mechanism of air quality on stock market yield and volatility: Empirical test from China based on GARCH model. *Finance Research Letters, 26,* 119–125.

Apergis, N., & Gupta, R. (2017). Can weather conditions in New York Predict South African stock returns? *Research in International Business & Finance, 41,* 377–386.

Arnott, R. D., Kelso, C. M., et al. (1989). Forecasting factor returns an intriguing possilbility. *Journal of Portfolio Management, 16*(1), 28–35.

Baker, M., & Wurgler, J. (2006). Investor sentiment and the cross-section of stock returns. *The Journal of Finance, 61*(4), 1645–1680.

Banerjee, A. V. (1992). A simple model of herd behavior. *Quarterly Journal of Economics, 107*(3), 797–817.

Baylis, P., Obradovich, N., Kryvasheyeu, Y., et al. (2018). Weather impacts expressed sentiment. *Public Library of Science One, 13*(4), e0195750. https://doi.org/10.1371/journal.pone.0195750.

Beecher, M. E., Eggett, D., Erekson, D., et al. (2016). Sunshine on my shoulders: Weather, pollution, and emotional distress. *Journal of Affective Disorders, 205,* 234–238.

Brollo, F., Perotti, R., et al. (2013). The political resource curse. *The American Economic Review, 103*(5), 1759–1796.

Brown, G. W., & Cliff, M. T. (2004). Investor sentiment and the near-term stock market. *Journal of Empirical Finance, 11*(1), 1–27.

Bullinger, M. (1990). Environmental stress: Effects of air pollution on mood. Neuropsychological function and physical state. In S. Puglisi-Allegra, & A. Oliverio (Eds.), *Psychobiology of stress* (Vol. 54, pp. 241–250).

Cai, W. J., Li, K., Liao, H., Wang, H. J., et al. (2017). Weather conditions conducive to Beijing severe haze more frequent under climate change. *Nature Climate Change, 7,* 257–262.

Chen, Y. B. (2005). Mood fluctuations and volatility of asset prices. *Economic Research (China), 3,* 36–45.

Chen, Y., Jin, G. Z., Kumar, N., et al. (2012). Gaming in air pollution Data? Lessons from China. *Social Science Electronic Publishing, 12*(3), 1–43.

Chen, X. Y., Zhang, T. Y., & Chen, D. H. (2001). Cross sectional analysis of expected stock returns: Evidence from Chinese stock market. *Financial Research (China), 6,* 22–35.

Chen, S. F., Xie, W., & Zhu, X. Q. (2011). On Chinese investors' subjective concept of stock market under the expectation of adaptability. *Economic Theory and Economic Management (China), 7,* 76–79.

Coates, J., & Herbert, J. (2008). Endogenous steroids and financial risk taking on a London trading floor. *Proceedings of the National Academy of Sciences, 105*(16), 6167–6172.

Daniel, K., Hirshleifer, D., & Subrahmanyam, A. (1998). Investor psychology and security market under and overreactions. *Journal of Finance, 53*(6), 1839–1885.

Dash, S. R., & Maitra, D. (2017). Does sentiment matter for stock returns? Evidence from Indian stock market using wavelet approach. *Finance Research Letters, 26,* 32–39.

Ding, Z. G., & Suzhi, Z. (2005). Investor sentiment, intrinsic value estimation and stock price volatility. *World Management (China), 2,* 143–145.

Eagles, J. M. (1994). The relationship between mood and hours of sunlight in rapid cycling bipolar illness. *Biological Psychiatry, 36*(6), 422–424.

Evans, G. W., Jacobs, S. V., Dooley, D., & Catalano, R. (1987). The interaction of stressful life events and chronic strains on community mental health. *American Journal of Community Psychology, 15*(1), 23–34.

Fu, S. X., Zhang, B., & Zhang, W. B. (2011). Environmental regulation and "pollution heaven" effect of China's industrial regional distribution. *Journal of Shanxi Finance and Economics University (China), 7,* 8–14.

Forgas, J. P., & Bower, G. H. (1987). Mood effects on person – perception judgments. *Journal of Personality & Social Psychology, 53*(1), 53–60.

Goetzmann, W. N., Kim, D., Kumar, A., et al. (2015). Weather-induced mood, institutional investors, and stock returns. *Review of Financial Studies, 28*(1), 73–111.

Guo, Y. J., & Zhang, Y. H. (2016). Will air quality affect the stock market? *Journal of Financial Research (China), 2,* 71–85.

Hahn, J., Todd, P., & Van der Klaauw, W. (2001). Identification and estimation of treatment effects with a regression-discontinuity design. *Journal of Econometrica, 69*(1), 201–209.

Harding, N., & He, W. (2016). Investor mood and the determinants of stock prices: An experimental analysis. *Accounting & Finance, 56*(2), 445–478.

Haritha, P. H., & Rishad, A. (2020). An empirical examination of investor sentiment and stock market volatility: Evidence from India. *Financial Innovation, 6*(1), 34. https://doi.org/10.1186/s40854-020-00198-x.

He, Z. G. (2001). Empirical study on risk factors of Chinese stock market. *Economic Review (China), 3,* 81–85.

Hirshleifer, D. (2001). Investor psychology and asset pricing. *Journal of Finance, 56*(4), 1533–1597.

Hirshleifer, D., & Shurnway, T. (2003). Good day sunshine: Stock returns and the weather. *Journal of Finance, 58*(3), 1009–1032.

Hsiao, H. F., Xia, C. Y., Yuksel, S., & Dincer, H. (2020). Comparative analysis of investor sentiment with weather conditions using interval type 2 fuzzy hybrid decision making and regression methods: Evidence from Chinese stock market. *Economic Computation and Economic Cybernetics Studies and Research, 54*(3), 263–278.

Hu, W. Y., Huang, C. J., Chang, H. Y., et al. (2015). The effect of investor sentiment on feedback trading and trading frequency: Evidence from Taiwan intraday data. *Emerging Markets Finance & Trade, 51*(1), S111–S120.

Hu, X., Li, O. Z., & Lin, Y. (2014). *Particles, pollutions and prices* (pp. 1–60). Social Science Electronic Publishing.

Huang, J. K., Xu, N. H., & Yu, H. H. (2020). Pollution and performance: Do investors make worse trades on hazy days? *Management Science, 66*(10), 4455–4476.

Isen, A. M. (1993). Positive affect and decision making. In *Handbook of emotions* (pp. 261–277).

Jin, Z., Yang, Y., & Liu, Y. (2020). Stock closing price prediction based on sentiment analysis and LSTM. *Neural Computing and Applications, 32*(13), 9713–9729.

Kaplanski, G., & Levy, H. (2010). Sentiment and stock prices: The case of aviation disasters. *Journal of Financial Economics, 95*(2), 174–201.

Kong, D., Liu, S., & Dai, Y. (2012). Environmental policy, company environment protection, and stock market performance: Evidence from China. *Corporate Social Responsibility and Environmental Management, 21*(2), 100–112.

Lee, C., Shleifer, A., & Thaler, R. H. (1991). Investor sentiment and the closed-end fund puzzled. *The Journal of Finance, 46*(1), 75–109.

Lee, D. S. (2008). Randomized experiments from non-random selection in US House elections. *Journal of Econometricsm, 142*(2), 675–697.

Lepori, G. M. (2009). Environmental stressors, mood, and trading decisions: Evidence form ambient air pollution. Working papers series, Available at SSRN: http://ssrn.com/abstract=1284549.

Lepori, G. M. (2015). Investor mood and demand for stocks: Evidence from popular TV series finales. *Journal of Economic Psychology, 48,* 33–47.

Lepori, G. M. (2016). Air pollution and stock returns: Evidence from a natural experiment. *Journal of Empirical Finance, 35,* 25–42.

Levy, T., & Yagil, J. (2011). Air pollution and stock returns in the US. *Journal of Economic Psychology, 32*(3), 374–383.

Li, Y. X., & Liu, X. (1997). An empirical study on the impact of dividend policy on stock price. *Journal of Chongqing University (China), 20*(5), 78–82.

Li, Q., & Peng, C. H. (2016). The stock market effect of air pollution: Evidence from China. *Applied Economics, 48*(36), 3442–3461.

Li, X. D., & Wang, Y. N. (2002). An empirical study on the trading behavior of individual securities investors in China. *Economic Research (China), 11,* 54–63.

Lin, S., Yu, Q., Tang, Z. Y., et al. (2006). An experimental study on the "hot hand effect" and "gambler's fallacy" of Chinese investors. *Economic Research (China), 8*(2), 56–69.

Lin, S., & Yu, Q. (2010). Bounded rationality, animal spirits and market crashes: An experimental study of mood swings and trading behavior. *Economic Research (China), 8,* 115–127.

Liu, Y. G., & Liu, M. G. (2015). Haze affected heavily polluting enterprises earnings management? Based on the political cost hypothesis. *Accounting Research (China), 3,* 79–101.

Lu, J. (2011). Study on the weather effect of Chinese stock market. China Soft. *Science, 000*(006), 65–78,192.

Lucey, B. M., & Dowling, M. (2005). The role of feelings in investor decision-making. *Journal of Economic Surveys, 19*(2), 217–237.

Lundberg, A. (1996). Psychiatric aspects of air pollution. *Otolaryngology - Head and Neck Surgery, 114*(2), 227–231.

McCrary, J. (2008). Manipulation of the running variable in the regression discontinuity design: A density test. *Journal of Econometrics, 142*(2), 698–714.

Mehra, R., & Sah, R. (2002). Mood fluctuations, projection bias, and volatility of equity prices. *Journal of Economic Dynamic and Control, 26*(5), 869–887.

Mulatu, A., Gerlagh, R., Rigby, D., & Wossink, A. (2010). Environmental regulation and industry location in Europe. *Environmental and Resource Economics, 45*(4), 459–479.

Naeem, M. A., Farid, S., Faruk, B., et al. (2020). Can happiness predict future volatility in stock markets? *Research in International Business and Finance, 101298.* https://doi.org/10.1016/j.ribaf.2020.101298.

Nelson, S. (1903). *The ABC of stock market speculatio.* Fraser Publishing.

Nowakowicz-Debek, B., Saba, L., & Bis-Wencel, H. (2004). The effects of air pollutants on the cortisol and progesterone secretion in Polar Fox (Alopex lagopus). *Scientifur, 28*(3), 218–221.

Oberndorfer, U., & Andreas, Z. (2006). Environmentally oriented energy policy and stock returns: An empirical analysis. ZEW working paper, 06–079.

Papakyriakou, P., Sakkas, A., & Taoushianis, Z. (2019). The impact of terrorist attacks in G7 countries on international stock markets and the role of investor sentiment. *Social Science Electronic Publishing, 61,* 143–160.

Peng, Y. F., Tang, J. H., Fu, Y. C., et al. (2016). Analyzing personal happiness from global survey and weather data: A geospatial approach. *Public Library of Science One, 11*(4), e0153638. https://doi.org/10.1371/journal.pone.0153638.

Rahman, M. L., & Shamsuddin, A. (2019). Investor sentiment and the price-earnings ratio in the G7 stock markets. *Pacific Basin Finance Journal, 55,* 46–62.

Saunders, E. (1993). Stock prices and wall street weather. *American Economic Review, 83*(5), 1337–1345.

Schottenfeld, R. S. (1992). Psychologic sequelae of chemical and hazardous materials exposures. In J. B. Sullivan & G. R. Krieger (Eds.), *Hazardous materials toxicology* (pp. 463–470). Baltimore: Williams & Wilkins.

Sexton, A. L. (2012). Responses to air quality alerts: Do Americans spend less time outdoors? Human reactions and political economy. In *Association of Environmental and Resource Economists, 2nd Annual Summer Conference,* 3–5 June, Asheville, NC.

Shan, L. W. (2011). Psychology or substance: The impact of Wenchuan earthquake on China's capital market. *Economic Research (China), 4,* 121–134.

Shahzad, F. (2019). Does weather influence investor behavior, stock returns, and volatility? Evidence from the Greater China region. *Physica A-Statistical Mechanics and Its Applications, 523,* 525–543.

Shi, Y., Tang, Y. R., Cui, L. X., et al. (2018). A text mining based study of investor sentiment and its influence on stock returns. *Economic Computation and Economic Cybernetics Studies and Research, 52*(1), 183–199.

Song, J., Zhao, Y., & Wu, C. F. (2003). A model of leader-follower in the securities market. *Systems Engineering-Theory & Practice (China), 23*(1), 1–8.

Tan, S. T., & Chen, Y. Y. (2012). Investment experience can improve the income of investors: Based on the transaction records of investors. *Economic Research (China), 5,* 164–178.

Teng, M., & He, X. B. (2020). Air quality levels, environmental awareness and investor trading behavior: Evidence from stock market in China. *Journal of Cleaner Production, 244,* 118663. https://doi.org/10.1016/j.jclepro.2019.118663.

Thaler, R. H. (1993). *Advances in behavioral finance*. Princeton University Press.

Wang, M., & Sun, J. J. (2004). Stock market returns, volatility and the role of investor sentiment in China. *Economic Research (China), 10,* 75–83.

Wright, W. F., & Bower, G. H. (1992). Mood effects on subjective probability assessment. *Organizational Behavior and Human Decision Processes, 52*(2), 276–291.

Wu, Q., & Lu, J. (2020). Air pollution, individual investors, and stock pricing in China. *International Review of Economics & Finance, 67,* 267–287.

Wu, Y. R., & Han, L. Y. (2007). Incomplete rationality, investor sentiment and closed-end fund puzzle. *Economic Research (China), 3,* 117–129.

Xi, P. H., & Liang, R. B. (2015). The impact of air pollution on local environmental protection input–based on multiple breakpoint regression. *Statistical Research (China), 32*(9), 76–83.

Yang, X., Wang, X. Z., & Tang, X. X. (2004). Herding effects of individual and institutional investors in Chinese stock market. *The Journal of Tsinghua University (China), 12,* 1610–1614.

Ying, Q. W., Yousaf, T., ul Ain, Q., et al. (2020). Investor psychology, mood variations, and sustainable cross-sectional returns: A Chinese case study on investing in illiquid stocks on a specific day of the week. *Frontiers in Psychology, 11,* 173. https://doi.org/10.3389/fpsyg.2020.00173.

Yu, J. W., & Wang, C. C. (2011). Breakpoint regression and its application in economics. *Economic Perspectives (China), 2,* 125–131.

Zheng, S. Q., Zhang, X. N., & Sun, Y. (2016). The mechanism of the effect of air pollution on outdoor activities of urban residents. *Journal of Tsinghua University (China), 56*(1), 89–96.

Zhou, H. (1999). Study on the comprehensive index of the effect of climate change on human health. *Climate and Environmental Research (China), 4*(1), 121–126.

# Chapter 16
# Economic Losses and Willingness to Pay for Haze: The Data Analysis Based on 1123 Residential Families in Jiangsu Province, China

**Abstract** Haze pollution is a key obstacle for environmental management faced by China and many other developing countries. The survey on residential families' economic losses and willingness to pay (WTP) are regarded as an essential reference for the implementation of environmental policies for haze treatment. For Jiangsu Province of China, authors of this paper first conducted three qualitative interviews with respectively meteorologists, meteorological administrators, and residents, a questionnaire was then elaborately designed, and subsequent surveys of 1,123 families were administered in Jiangsu province. Further, authors investigated measurements of direct economic losses by using the contingent valuation method (CVM), and explored influential factors of WTP by utilizing the binary logistic regression. From this survey, the estimated total economic loss incurred by haze disasters and total treatment cost for haze-related diseases were respectively 22.38 billions (in RMB) and 8.4 billions for Jiangsu Province. 55.9% of residential families were willing to pay 11.6 billions RMB annually (51.97% of total loss) for haze treatment, leaving a shortage of 11.05 billions RMB, which the government is responsible to pay. These findings provide empirical information reflecting the opinions of communities and residential families, useful for the governments and industrial sectors to design environmental policies to meet the requirements of the public and control environmental pollution in an effective way to achieve sustainable development.

**Keywords** Environmental pollution · Economic loss · Willingness to pay · Contingent valuation method · Haze

## 16.1 Introduction

Environmental pollution and resource constraints have become key barriers for sustainable development faced by China and many other developing countries (Mi et al. 2017a, b; Mikulčić et al. 2019). As a frequent happening environmental pollution, haze has serious threats to living environment, human health and sustainable social development. A study by Lelieveld et al. (2015), estimated that outdoor air pollution in 2010, mostly by $PM_{2.5}$, leads to 3.3 (95% confidence interval 1.61–4.81) million premature deaths per year worldwide, predominantly in Asia. Perceiving the

 
X. Wu and J. Guo, *Economic Impacts and Emergency Management of Disasters in China*,
https://doi.org/10.1007/978-981-16-1319-7_16

information of the public and obtaining the support of the public are important for the harmonious and unified development of mankind, technology and environment (Mikulčić et al. 2017, 2019). But how much does the public know about haze pollution? How much is the public's willingness to pay (WTP)? A relatively large-scale empirical research and data analysis are rare (Song et al. 2018). Based on this situation, through the empirical research targeted at 1123 Chinese residential families, this paper analyzed economic losses incurred by haze pollution and evaluated the public's WTP of haze treatment, and also provided reference materials from communities and the public so as to carry out effective environmental management.

The importance of this study on economic losses caused by haze and willingness to pay lies in the following aspects: firstly, it provides data reference for the national haze control. Secondly, as for assessing the economic losses caused by haze, there are only fewer studies so far on large-scale field investigation, and this study can enrich the existing empirical studies. Thirdly, in the process of field research, this study helps people deepen their understanding of haze and achieve a more intuitive sense of economic losses caused by haze. It is also found that residents are willing to make their own efforts in controlling haze pollution, so as to play a role of scientific popularization.

### 16.1.1 Literatures About Economic Losses of Haze

Many recent studies have focused on evaluating the economic losses of haze. For example, in study of Gao et al. (2015), based on the results of Weather Research and Forecasting-Chemistry (WRF-Chem) model, the health impacts and health-related economic losses during the 2013 severe haze event in Beijing were calculated. Based on the $PM_{2.5}$ haze data of various provinces in China from 2004 to 2016, Zhao and Yuan (2020) analyzed the impact of haze pollution on the quality of China's economic development. Besides, this article used precipitation as an instrumental variable, then the loss of China's economic growth was estimated through a two-stage least squares framework. The research showed that haze pollution has severely reduced the quality of China's economic development. In this paper, Chen et al. (2020a, b) predicted the density of delicate particulate matter ($PM_{2.5}$). Based on the predicted density data, they then used the CGE and a well-designed exposure-response model to study the health effects of $PM_{2.5}$ pollution. Also, a social accounting matrix (SAM) was used to improve the accuracy of the parameter in the CGE model, and a recursive dynamic CGE model in the closed economy was used to evaluate the long-term economic loss caused by $PM_{2.5}$ pollution. The results showed $PM_{2.5}$ pollution seriously endangered economic system from 2013 to 2020. Chen et al. (2019) jointed econometrics and input-output models to calculate the cumulative economic losses of the industrial sector during the recovery period. Through a static model, it is estimated that the indirect economic loss caused by Beijing's representative haze pollution to the transportation industry in 2013 was 23.7 million yuan and the indirect industrial-related losses caused by the direct economic losses of haze pollution amounted to 102 million yuan. Hao et al. (2019) used the panel models to estimate the impact of haze pollution on the mortality rates of residents by macro data of 74 major cities in China. By using the value of the statistical life (VOSL) method, the reach found that the VOSL of haze pollution was 1.53 million yuan in China and the health cost of residents was equivalent to about 2% of cities' GDP. Based on 139 global countries statistics data and a geographical detector model, Liu and Dong (2020) analyzed the relationship between political corruption and haze pollution. Furthermore, the degree of corruption and per capita GDP were used as threshold variables to determine whether the nonlinear or linear relationship existed between haze pollution and crime. Qiu et al. (2018) investigated China's opinions on the benefits of economic growth and the drawbacks of haze pollution through an anonymous questionnaire with 29 questions. Hao et al. (2018) used urban panel data from 2013 to 2015 to estimate the impact of $PM_{2.5}$ concentration on per capita GDP through a well-designed simultaneous equation model. The results showed that haze pollution harmed economic development, while sustainable economic growth reduced the concentration of $PM_{2.5}$. Guo and Chen (2018) applied the Generalized addictive model (GAM) to analyze the association between ambient air pollutants and asthma patients with economic costs assessment, and found that the economic cost of asthma patient visits were attributed to $SO_2$, CO, $NO_2$, $PM_{10}$, $O_3$ and $PM_{2.5}$ with 101.30, 7.46, 17.15, 30.18, 6.39 and 34.50 million USD loss per year, respectively. Yang et al. (2018b) adopted a supply-driven input-output model to estimate the economic loss resulted from disease-induced working-time reduction across 30 Chinese provinces in 2012 using the most updated Chinese multiregional input-output table. Based on the related statistics data, Hou et al. (2019) analyzed the effects of haze to the social economy in Beijing by the mean-squared deviation weight method. Fan et al. (2019), by using logarithmic linear exposure-response function, monetized the economic losses relevant to health hazards by PM in the Jing-Jin-Ji region in China. Maji (2018) estimated the increased economic losses due to $PM_{10}$ by analyzing the average annual mortality caused by $PM_{2.5}$ in Mumbai and Delhi. Latif (2018) combined the literature on the impact of Malaysia's haze and analyzed the economic losses caused by the previous haze in Malaysia. Jaafar and Razi (2018) analyzed the literature on the impact of air pollution on health problems in Asia and believed that the impact of air pollution on the economy was huge. Othman et al. (2014) collected data of hospitalized patients with smog-related diseases in four hospitals, and analyzed the health impact and economic loss caused by haze in Kuala Lumpur and adjacent areas.

From our perspective, as for the effect of haze on the society and economy, most current studies are based on the assessment of the human health impact (World Health Organization 2000; Afroz et al. 2003; Sheldon and Sankaran 2017) and fewer have been conducted on flight delays, traffic accidents, and highway blockages caused by the extremely poor visibility due to haze (Mu and Zhang 2013; Othman et al. 2014). Also, fewer researchers studied the economic losses through a large-scale field investigation. To fill out such gaps, this article aimed multiple angles of losses and conducted a large-scale investigation.

### 16.1.2 Willingness to Pay and Its Application in Haze Reduction

Mitchell and Carson (2013) argued that the value of all goods can be measured by an individual's WTP for them. With the aim of assessing the economic value of the environment or natural resources, contingent valuation method (CVM) is used to construct a hypothetical market to directly ask individuals about their WTP for improving the environment or protecting natural resources. In 1963, CVM was used to evaluate the recreational value of the forest for the first time (Davis 1963). Arimah (1996) analyzed the WTP for improved environmental sanitation in a Nigerian City. Through a questionnaire survey of accidental sampling with 250 people face-to-face, researchers obtained some data, such as risk perception, WTP for haze management and self-protection, Sereenonchai et al. (2020) adopted the contingent valuation method (CVM), analysis of variance (ANOVA) and stepwise multiple linear regression to estimate those data. Lan et al. (2020) calibrated the willingness to pay (WTP) of residents to reduce haze exposure in China's Xi'an by the world's first Smog Free Tower. Based on CVM, (Ouyang et al. 2019) analyzed the factors influencing residents' WTP to alleviate haze in Shanghai's 16 districts. The result indicated that residents, living in areas were more affected by haze pollution, might not have a higher willingness to pay (WTP) for haze mitigation. Air pollution caused by haze could harm the skin of residents and affect their demand for anti-haze cosmetics. Therefore, based on 314 valid questionnaires, this article (Song et al. 2019) focused on residents' willingness to pay (WTP) for anti-haze cosmetics by the theory of customer perceived value. The conclusion suggested that people are willing to pay 56.1 yuan more per month to purchase anti-haze cosmetics. The required data was collected from 120 sample survey respondents through a structured questionnaire in the Faisalabad region. Ain et al. (2020) investigated the economic effect of air pollution on households (processing costs) and the main factors inducing individual's WTP for improved air quality. Based on a contingent valuation method (CVM), Munoz-Pizza et al. (2020) estimated the willingness to pay (WTP) for the urban greening scenario of Mexicali by simulating a non-existent market. Xie et al. (2020) analyzed China's greenhouse gas emission reduction policies and used WTP to estimate the economic benefits of improved air quality. The empirical results showed that the reduced $PM_{2.5}$ concentration could decrease the economic cost of \$406 billion and \$1206 billion by the 2030s and 2050s, respectively. Wang et al. (2016a, b) used dichotomous choices to assess the people's WTP for management and prevention of haze in Jiangsu. The result indicated that people's willingness to pay (WTP) for the prevention and control of haze was highly correlated with household monthly income and transportation. Bravo-Vargas et al. (2019) investigated the visitor's perceptions and WTP for pine control in Malalcahuello National Reserve. The reduction of haze is a typical non-market economic issue, so it is suitable to evaluate the economic benefits brought by haze reduction via the CVM (Carson et al. 2001; Wang and Mullahy 2006). Therefore, in this paper, this method was combined with WTP to assess how much the public is willing to pay for haze reduction.

The studies of public awareness and WTP for tackling haze have become an important aspect of environment management. Wang et al. (2016a, b) analyzed the awareness and willingness to pay for tackling smog pollution of 972 respondents in Zibo city in China. Lin et al. (2017) collected a sample of 390 and used a double-bounded dichotomous-choice survey design and the Kaplan-Meier-Turnbull method to infer the distribution of Singaporeans' WTP for haze mitigation. Based on CVM, Yang et al. (Yang, Ding, et al. 2018a) collected a sample of 1006 respondents and analyzed factors determining WTP and WTP amount. Their results showed that 53% of respondents were unwilling to pay for haze reduction. Xu and Shan (2018) used CVM and psychometric paradigm to investigate public risk perception and elicit WTP for reductions in health risk posed by fine particulate matter in Beijing, China. Huang et al. (2018) used CVM and statistical analysis to explore the willingness to pay/accept (WTP/WTA) for reductions in air pollution for the benefit of reducing health risks. Adopting the extended theory of planned behavior model and survey data collected from 425 respondents in China, Ru et al. (2019) revealed that young people's attitude towards reducing $PM_{2.5}$.

However, so far, large sample field researches with strict contingent valuation method are not sufficient. In response to these shortcomings, the research procedure and the survey questionnaire have been carefully designed (see Sect. 16.3), creating a noteworthy feature of this paper.

### *16.1.3 Willingness to Pay and Its Application in Other Aspects of Environmental*

Recently, willing to pay (WTP) have not only applications in haze reduction, but also in other parts of ecological protection. In the Arctic, Marine plastic pollution is a major ecological problem. Abate et al. (2020) used the contingent assessment method (CVM) to stimulate Norwegian households' willingness to pay (WTP) for decreasing plastic pollution in the oceans around Svalbard. Cicaiello et al. (2020) analyzed whether the production of polluting industries will affect willingness to pay (WTP) of individual on the environment. The Italy empirical results showed that: in "healthy" regions, increasing production in the polluting sectors would increase WTP for the environment. Khan et al. (2020) analyzed the transfer of benefits among the Three Basins of Wei River by evaluating the willingness to pay (WTP) for ecosystem services. The results of their research confirmed the diversity of public preferences in all three basins. Based on the micro survey data, He and Zhang (2020) studied the impact of environmental regulations on residents' willingness to pay (WTP) for environmental protection. Ito and Zhang (2020) estimated the willingness to pay for the clean air. The research found that a family was willing to pay $1.34 per year to remove air pollution ($PM_{10}$) and was ready to pay $32.7 per year to eliminate pollution caused by the Huai River heating policy. Based on the contingent valuation method (CVM), Xu et al. (2020) provided an economic assessment of the losses caused by the U. prolifera bloom from a cost-benefit perspective. The result suggested that each respondent was willing to pay 54.98 yuan per year on average. Dardanoni and Guerriero (2021) considered that discrete choice experiments were gradually used to evaluate environmental goods. The experiments never conducted with teenagers. These scholars designed and implemented such experiments to estimate willingness of children and young people aged 8–19 to pay for environmental protection projects. Based on household survey data, Jin and Li (2020) analyzed how high education levels contributed to WTP for relevant environmental improvements. Through regarding the formulation of the "Compulsory Education Law" as an instrumental variable, the result showed that higher education could increase the willingness to pay for environmental improvements.

## 16.2 Methods and Models

In this section, we introduce the methods and models that will be employed to assess the economic losses from haze disasters, including direct loss measurement (DLM) and willingness to pay (WTP).

### *16.2.1 Direct Loss Measurement (DLM)*

The common DLM includes VSL, COI, and direct inquiry. For example, the World Bank (Krupnick et al. 2006) once combined VSL and WTP to conduct a study on the residents of Chongqing and Shanghai in China, with the aim of calculating the economic loss caused by environmental disasters. The study was based on the framework of evaluating the health impact caused by each unit increase of the major pollutants, with the concentration-damage equation built based on toxicology or epidemiology. Lu et al. (2016) assessed that the four major ambient pollutants ($SO_2$, $NO_2$, $O_3$ and $PM_{10}$) in the PRD lead to the adverse health effects from 2010 to 2013 and applied the value of statistical life (VSL) and cost of illness (COI) methods to evaluate economic loss of mortality and morbidity. Bherwani et al. (2019) monetized the health effects in the year 2019 and 2020 by using the value of statistical life (VSL), cost of illness (COI), and per capita income (PCI) for disability-adjusted life years (DALY). Then they analyzed the reasons that four cities (Delhi, London, Paris, and Wuhan) decreased their health effects during the COVID-19 pandemic due to lower air pollution (AP) levels. Based on survey data of 338 cities in China, Diao et al. (2020) used the value of statistical life (VSL) and the cost of disease (COI) methods to calculate economic losses. The result showed that $PM_{2.5}$ pollution was still severe in 2015 and caused many people to suffer from a variety of health problems, especially related diseases and premature death. Economic development was accompanied by environmental issues, especially air pollution, which may have a negative impact on the health of residents. Han et al. (2019) used the value of statistical life (VSL) and the cost of disease (COI) methods to monetize economic losses. However, one can get more information if the influence mechanism and process of such phenomenon have been fully explained (Xie et al. 2014).

Given the difficulties involved in using VSL and COI, direct inquiry of the respondents about their economic losses in terms of health, transportation, and life is more convenient and reasonable. Consequently, our investigation was strategically conducted by directly collecting survey data regarding the economic loss caused by haze, with a pre-designed questionnaire developed from the following four aspects: additional medical expenses brought by diseases, extra loss due to bad traffic, extra loss due to flight delays caused by haze,[1] and extra spending in taking the protective measures against haze.

### 16.2.2 *Application of Binary Logistic Regression and WTP in Other Fields*

Sachin et al. (2020) evaluated the services of the mangrove ecosystem in the Uttara Kannada district of Karnataka, India. Then, the researchers analyzed the importance of mangroves and people's willingness to pay (WTP) for mangroves protection. By asking the interviewees about the polls, and applying the binary logistic regression model to analyze the interviewee's willingness to pay for the development and maintenance of mangroves. A total of 405 valid questionnaires were distributed to collect ES demand data, Chen et al. (2020a, b) analyzed people's primary ecosystem services (ES) requirements for Urban green infrastructures (UGI) by the binary logistic regression model. Mekonne et al. (2020) used a multi-stage sampling method to select a total sample of 480 healthcare providers. A Binary and multiple logistic regression analysis was performed to assess the relevant factor outcome variables. As a result, WTP for social health insurance (SHI) were only 132 (28.7%). There were many reasons not to adopt SHI. For instance, the government should pay the cost and choose to pay directly; the SHI plan cannot cover all health care costs, and health care providers had lost the interest in SHI wages. Zhang et al. (2020) estimated that the willingness of construction practitioners, knowing more about green housing (GH), to pay for GH in China. Through the use of questionnaires and face-to-face interviews, 180 construction participants in Jinan were surveyed, and nine critical factors related to practitioners' willingness to pay (WTP) were obtained. The author used a logistic regression model to analyze the collected data. Research findings showed that only 68 respondents are willing to pay for green housing (GH).

[1] When arranging the survey, the personnel involved in the survey have been explained that traffic in "extra loss due to bad traffic" refers to the daily ground traffic. The reason for this distinction is that the "extra loss due to flight delays" is more for business people, while the loss caused by daily ground traffic problems is more for daily life and work people. The two groups are different, with different payment capacity and willingness to pay for haze.

### 16.2.3 Willingness to Pay (WTP)

Possible deviations may exist when using the CVM. To prevent or minimize such drawbacks, particular processing methods were considered in our study, as described below.

(1) The respondents were fully informed of the research background to avoid information bias. Given that haze has become a well-known weather condition, the respondents have basic knowledge about the assessment object. However, in order to build a complete hypothetical market, the second part of the questionnaire (see Sect. 16.3.1) focused on the understanding of haze to strengthen the knowledge of haze for respondents. At the same time, the respondents were informed that the questionnaire was merely for academic purpose and had nothing to do with government agencies' actual work so that they are able to present their real opinions.

(2) A hypothetical situation was designed to avoid embedding bias (part-whole bias and scope effect). To reduce the bias caused by the uncertain scope of an assessment object, the background part asked respondents questions regarding their residential location, length of residence, and their activity areas. At the same time, when asking the respondents about their WTP, the phrase "in order to effectively improve the air quality of your city and reduce the harm of haze" was included in each question to help the respondents identify the scope of the assessment object. In the present survey, a hypothetical situation, a haze reduction special plan to be specific, was designed. In response to this plan, the respondents were asked to donate in line with their degree of being influenced and payment ability. Collected donations would be in the custody of the local government, and would be used for technological innovation, equipment improvement and production process reengineering of enterprises that discharge pollutants so as eventually reduce haze discharge.

(3) The questionnaire was carefully developed to avoid ordering bias. The familiarity of the respondents with the assessment object can reduce the ordering bias (Venkatachalam 2004). Carson et al. argued that the respondents must be reminded to read through all the questions and then provide their answers before and after asking them about their WTP (Carson et al. 2001); In turn, this leads to correct judgment and reduction of ordering bias. For this, the questionnaire features an added part about haze recognition. In addition, it adds a question in the WTP part ("What is the ratio of WTP expenses over the total annual income of your family?"). This question corresponds to the monthly family income in the first part, and reminds the respondents to give consistent answers throughout the questionnaire.

(4) The respondents were informed in advance to avoid export bias. The sequential bids and close-ended methods are combined in this study. The close-ended method uses the multiple bounded bidding. The number starts from 100 and increases sequentially until the respondents agree to it. If the respondent agrees with the first price, the price is raised and the respondent is asked again;

however, if he does not agree to the first price, it is reduced and he is asked again (see Sect. 16.3.1). In this way, the actual reaction of the respondents can be accurately obtained, thus avoiding the starting point bias and reducing the strategic bias. Prior to the survey, experts had been invited to a symposium and a pre-survey to negotiate a bid price (see Sect. 16.3.1).

(5) Students in this project were trained to avoid survey bias. Before the survey, 500 students who were engaged in this survey were trained. First, students participating in this project are required to ask their relatives and friends aged 18 years and above during their winter vacation. Second, each student sends and collects a maximum of three questionnaires to ensure the quality of the questionnaire and the authenticity of the data. Third, when choosing the respondents, students were required to survey 3 families with high, medium and low income respectively. Finally, students were meticulously trained in aspects of the research background, hypothetical payment situation, choice to pay willingly. In addition, questionnaires with inconsistent answers and many omissions are deleted.

It was worth mentioning that, there were some restrictions on the respondents' location, sex ratio and so on, so that the samples' structure reflects Jiangsu's population structure (See Table 16.1).

(6) Avoid hypothetical bias and strategic bias. Hypothetical bias refers to a situation where the decisions are not necessarily the same as those in the real market; strategy bias refers to a situation where the respondents answer WTP values against their real willingness by deliberately exaggerating or reducing the WTP value due to some reasons (Zha et al. 2013). A series of questions are designed from direct loss and WTP in the questionnaire to prevent these biases. Then, the obtained data are compared to analyze the reasons. At the same time, the reliability and validity of CVM are examined to further verify the reliability of the data (Wu et al. 2018).

## 16.3 Questionnaire Design, Survey Area and Data Collection

### *16.3.1 Questionnaire Design*

Before the questionnaire was designed, three qualitative interviews were respectively conducted, with 3 weather experts, 3 meteorological service administrators and 3 citizens. Through a symposium and a pilot questionnaire, the following aspects were explored. (1) What to be investigated? (2) How to investigate? (3) Whom to be investigated? Who are the right researchers? How to find the respondents? (4) How to design the background hypothesis? What are the assumptions? How to explain them to the respondents? (5) How to pay? How much the respondents are willing to pay? What is the payment method? Also include questions on the use of donations,

**Table 16.1** The comparison between the sample and the actual distribution

| Sample characteristics | | The proportion of subsamples (%) | The actual population distribution in 2013[a] (%) |
|---|---|---|---|
| Sex | Male | 50.7 | 50.3 |
| | Female | 49.3 | 49.7 |
| Age | 18–25 | 40.1 | 12.8 |
| | 26–40 | 17.5 | 21.8 |
| | 41–55 | 35.5 | 25.8 |
| | 56–70 | 4.5 | 18.4 |
| | ≧70 | 2.3 | 8.1 |
| Level of education[b] | Illiteracy | 1.8 | 5.0 |
| | Primary school | 3.9 | 24.1 |
| | Junior middle school | 15.0 | 39.3 |
| | Senior high school | 18.3 | 18.3 |
| | Bachelor degree or above | 60.8 | 13.3 |
| Source of samples | Nanjing city | 18.2 | 10.3 |
| | Wuxi city | 9.3 | 8.2 |
| | Xuzhou city | 4 | 10.8 |
| | Changzhou city | 5.7 | 5.9 |
| | Suzhou city | 6.6 | 13.3 |
| | Nantong city | 16.2 | 9.2 |
| | Lianyungang city | 2.9 | 5.6 |
| | Huaian city | 3.6 | 6.1 |
| | Yancheng city | 7.7 | 9.1 |
| | Yangzhou city | 7.3 | 5.6 |
| | Zhenjiang city | 4.0 | 4.0 |
| | Taizhou city | 9.3 | 5.8 |
| | Suqian city | 5.3 | 6.1 |

*Note* [a]The actual population distribution come from *Jiangsu statistical yearbook (2014)*. [b]In order to successfully complete the task, interviewees might have chosen households with relatively higher levels of education and with familiarity of the survey. This has led to a higher average education level of the surveyed sample than the local population. From another point of view, these people with higher education can better understand the questions in the questionnaire, and can express better the willingness of the surveyed group, and are more representative

and so on. Based on the interview results, the questionnaire was designed to include four parts, as described below.

In Part 1, we collected data about the social and economic characteristics of the respondents, including gender, age, income, education level, and family income. In Part 2, we collected information that determines the knowledge level of respondents in their understanding and evaluation of the impact of haze. In Part 3, we collected data regarding how haze influences the daily life of the respondents.

In Part 4, we asked respondents about whether or not they were willing to pay for haze remediation. The previous three parts explore general information of the public relevant to haze, gradually leading to the haze problem, and the losses incurred by the public due to haze-related reasons. Part 4 is the core of the questionnaire as it adopts the multiple bounded bidding CVM to guide the public to express their true WTP. The question is stated as follows:

> Implementation of the haze treatment plan will effectively improve the air quality in your city and reduce the harm of haze, but your family should pay __ RMB every year in the next five years. Would you support the plan?

Prior to conducting the actual questionnaire survey, we pre-surveyed the loss incurred by the public due to haze and their WTP. Based on the analysis of the pre-survey data, we provided 11 initial bids: 100, 200, 300, 400, 500, 600, 800, 1000, 1500, 2000, and 2500. Then, we show the 11 mark (100, 200, 300, 400, 500, 600, 800, 1000, 1500, 2000 and 2500) to respondents, and it is divided into two stages. Step 1: Start with 100 yuan and ask respondents if they are willing to take this price as their initial bid. Step 2: If the respondent agrees, 100 yuan is his $T_0$. If the respondent does not agree, ask him from 200 yuan. If he still does not agree, ask his willingness for 300 yuan until he agreed.

Then, $T_0$ is the initial bid determined by the respondent from the 11 bids. After determining $T_0$, it did further inquiry to obtain the value of $T_1$, and the interval between $T_0$ and $T_1$ was 50. For example, if the respondent offers 500 yuan as his initial bid, he will be asked if he is willing to raise the number to 550. If he answers no, then ask if he is willing to pay 525 yuan (If the answer is yes, it means that he is willing to pay 525 yuan. If the answer is no, it means he is willing to pay 500 yuan). If he answers yes, then we ask if he is willing to pay 575 yuan (If the answer is yes, it means that he is willing to pay 575 yuan. If the answer is no, it means he is willing to pay 550 yuan).

If the respondents did not support this plan, i.e., they expressed zero WTP, they were required to give the reasons briefly. The questions are designed as showing in the Fig. 16.1. Take $T_0 = 500$ RMB as an example.

### *16.3.2 Survey Areas*

On February 4, 2015, China's first assessment report on the public health' impact caused by long-time exposure to $PM_{2.5}$ was released. The report found that, in 2013, $PM_{2.5}$ pollution caused 25.7 million excess deaths in the 31 capital cities or municipalities directly associated with the central government, with an average excess mortality close to 1‰ (one thousandth). There are 12 cities that exceeded the average mortality rate, Nanjing (capital of Jiangsu Province), Shijiazhuang, Jinan, Changsha, Chengdu, Wuhan, Nanchang, Hefei, Tianjin, Harbin, Chongqing, and Shenyang in

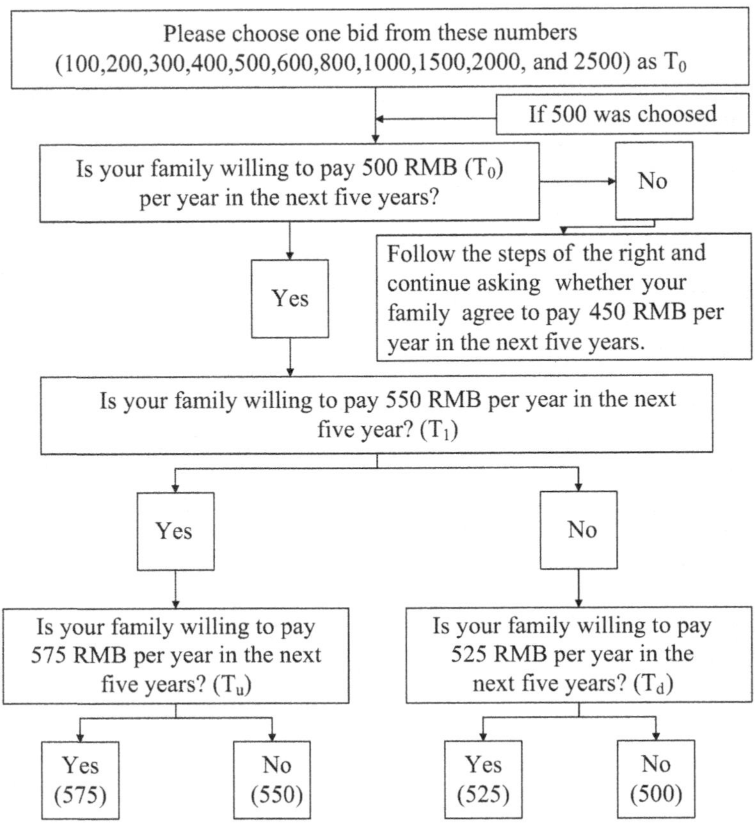


**Fig. 16.1** Question design of the multiple bounded bidding CVM

the order of decreasing rates. In contrast, according to the official data released by China, the national average mortality rate due to smoking exceeded 0.7‰ in 2012, and the national mortality rate caused by traffic accidents was 0.09‰.

In Jiangsu Province, a developed region located in the eastern coastal, more than 50% of the days in December of 2013 were detected as days with unacceptable air quality condition, including some key regions and 74 cities in Huaian, Suqian and Taizhou of Jiangsu Province. See details in Fig. 16.2. Haze conditions in Jiangsu Province vary from severe to less severe depending on the specific locations and this province provides a mixed and representative region for exploring different levels of impact by haze. Therefore, Jiangsu Province deserves an elaborate study regarding its hazy conditions.

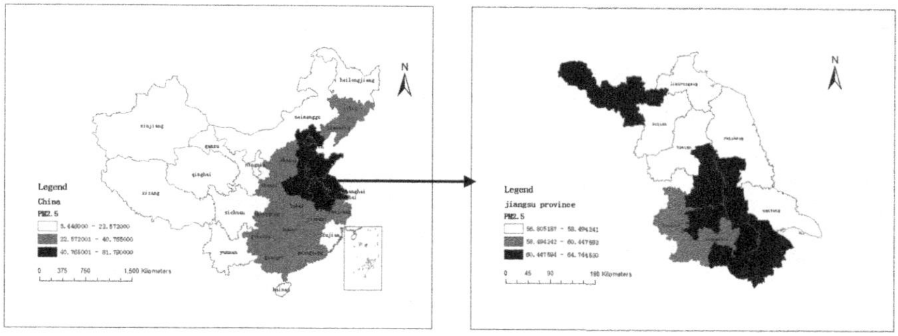


**Fig. 16.2** Location and average concentration of $PM_{2.5}$ of Jiangsu Province in China. *Note* The data come from "*A Data Center in NASA's Earth Observing System Data and Information System (EOSDIS)—Hosted by CIESIN at Columbia University*". https://sedac.ciesin.columbia.edu/data/sets/browse#opennewwindow

## *16.3.3 Survey Participants*

Before January of 2013, 400 college students were selected and trained on the survey setting and procedure. A total of 1500 questionnaires were distributed face to face throughout 13 prefecture-level cities of Jiangsu Province by these students during their winter vacation (from 15th January to 15th February).

The existing researches on the loss caused by haze at home and abroad are mostly limited to surveys with some small samples from limited areas (Forsyth 2014; Othman et al. 2014). The absence of information on a larger sample was striking. The survey in the current study covered a wider area with larger samples to provide strong data support for the loss research, which is rare and is an important contribution of the paper. After eliminating the questionnaires with incomplete answers, those whose respondents refused to answer the WTP questions and those from protesting questionnaires, 1,123 (74.9%) valid questionnaires were left. Cronbach's Alpha is used to calculate reliability value, which is 0.736. The validity value used KMO and Bartlett's Test to calculate is 0.701, both of which were acceptable.

In general, the proportions of gender, age, educational background, living area, duration of residency in the local places, and monthly family income are reasonable. The main characteristics of these 1,123 surveys are shown in Table 16.2.

**Table 16.2** Demographic data of the survey participants

| Item | | Frequency | Proportion (%) |
|---|---|---|---|
| Gender | Male | 569 | 50.7 |
| | Female | 554 | 49.3 |
| Age (years) | 18–25 | 450 | 40.1 |
| | 26–40 | 197 | 17.5 |
| | 41–55 | 399 | 35.5 |
| | 56–70 | 51 | 4.50 |
| | Above 70 | 26 | 2.30 |
| Education level[a] | No regular education | 20 | 1.8 |
| | Primary school | 44 | 3.9 |
| | Secondary school | 169 | 15.0 |
| | Senior high school and Technical secondary school | 206 | 18.3 |
| | College degree | 124 | 11.0 |
| | Bachelor's degree | 537 | 47.8 |
| | Master's degree and above | 23 | 2.0 |
| Activity areas | Urban areas | 566 | 50.4 |
| | Suburbs | 236 | 21.0 |
| | Outskirts and rural areas | 321 | 28.6 |
| Duration of residency | Less than 1 year | 113 | 10.1 |
| | 1–4 years | 152 | 13.5 |
| | 5–9 years | 74 | 6.6 |
| | 10–19 years | 227 | 20.2 |
| | 20 years and above | 557 | 49.6 |
| Monthly family income (RMB) | Below 3000 | 218 | 19.4 |
| | 3000–5999 | 444 | 39.5 |
| | 6000–10,000 | 275 | 24.5 |
| | 10000–20,000 | 98 | 8.7 |
| | Above 20,000 | 88 | 7.8 |

*Note* [a]In the questionnaire, the options of Level of Education are given different values as follows: No regular education = 1; Primary school = 2; Secondary school = 3; Senior high school and technical secondary school = 4; College degree = 5; Bachelor's degree = 6; Master's degree and above = 7. Education level is represented as the arithmetic mean

## 16.4 Empirical Analysis

### *16.4.1 Loss Caused by Haze*

The third part of the questionnaire gathers data about the impacts caused by haze. In 2013, Jiangsu Province' families experienced haze 8.12 times on the average[2], and the average loss was 917.62 RMB per family. It was assumed that the samples obtained from the survey can represent all the residents in Jiangsu Province (The following inference about the residents in Jiangsu Province was based on this hypothesis, which would not be repeated later due to limited space). It was further assumed that the public and the government work together on haze remediation and the maximum contribution is equal to the total loss. Given that the total loss caused by haze is 917.62 RMB per family and the WTP of the public is 476.83 RMB per family per year in the next five years, the government should bear 440.79 RMB per family per year in costs. See the details in Table 16.3.

Among the losses caused by haze, the average loss brought by haze-related diseases is the largest at 346.02 RMB per family. The main diseases caused by haze include cough, cold, rhino pharyngitis, bronchitis, among others. See the details in Fig. 16.3. Using the data from the Sixth National Population Census (2010), we multiply the average loss per family by the number of families, and calculate the sum of losses in Jiangsu Province (22.38 billion RMB) in 2013 (China 2011).

In one report for the haze disaster occurring in January of 2013 alone (in China, hazy weathers appear often in fall and winter), it affected 20 provinces and data from 27 cities in 14 of these provinces indicated that the emergency cares increased from 10 to 150%, with children and elders as most victims. A conservative estimation resulted in a direct economic loss of 118.88 RMB per family due to physical discomfort caused by the haze, with a total loss of 22.6 billion RMB in the 14 provinces (Mu and Zhang 2013). From 2000 to 2004, the health loss caused by $PM_{10}$ account for 3.6% of GDP in Beijing, about 4.3 billion RMB every year (Zhang et al. 2007).

In contrast, from our survey, in Jiangsu Province only, the prevalence of haze related diseases reached a high level of 79.96% (898 of the 1,123 respondents reported that at least one family member became sick at least once due to hazy weathers in 2013), with an average medical cost of 346.02 RMB per family, summing up to a total medical cost of 8.4 billion RMB for the whole province in 2013.

To further screen the factors that affect the WTP of the families for haze treatment, the sample from Jiangsu Province is subdivided as showed in Table 16.2.

(1) Residents in urban and rural areas. In terms of losses caused by haze, there is no significant difference between urban and rural areas. Meanwhile, in terms

[2]Since government departments only began to publish $PM_{2.5}$ values in 2013. Public information shows that $PM_{2.5}$ value in December 2013 can only be obtained at present. Therefore, this paper cannot get the number of haze occurrences in 2013 through official data. At the same time, the impression of the respondents on the haze in 2013 can be further deepened by asking the respondents.

**Table 16.3** Loss comparison of different samples in Jiangsu province

| Item | Type | | | | | | |
|---|---|---|---|---|---|---|---|
| | The whole Jiangsu Province | Rural Areas | Urban Areas | Below 25 years old | Above 25 years old | Living for less than 10 years in the local place | Living for more than 10 years in the local place |
| Education level[a] | 4.85 | 4.35 | 5.04 | 5.79 | 4.21 | 5.39 | 4.62 |
| Monthly family income (RMB)[a] | 7588.6 | 6772.59 | 7915.21 | 7386.67 | 7723.63 | 8088.76 | 7376.91 |
| Number of haze incidents in 2013[a] | 8.12 | 6.8 | 8.65 | 7.49 | 8.54 | 7.94 | 8.2 |
| Loss from diseases (RMB)[a] | 346.02 | 358.71 | 340.94 | 254.12 | 407.47 | 323.82 | 355.59 |
| Expenses for taking protective measures (RMB)[a] | 240.89 | 210.28 | 253.15 | 226.61 | 250.44 | 229.8 | 245.89 |
| Loss from flight delays (RMB)[a] | 118.21 | 119 | 117.89 | 152 | 95.62 | 152.81 | 103.44 |
| Loss from vehicle travel (RMB)[a] | 212.49 | 257.63 | 194.42 | 178.11 | 235.48 | 164.5 | 233.46 |
| Total loss caused by haze (RMB)[a] | 917.62 | 945.62 | 906.41 | 810.84 | 989.01 | 870.93 | 938.37 |
| WTP of the public (RMB)[a] | 476.83 | 419.31 | 501.39 | 417.68 | 514.43 | 444.38 | 488.8 |
| Sample size | 1123 | 321 | 802 | 450 | 673 | 339 | 784 |

*Note* (1) [a]These are arithmetic averages. (2) The loss caused by haze is statistically determined by the questions in the questionnaire, including 2.1 How much extra expense has been caused by diseases because of haze?_____ yuan (seeing a doctor, buying medicine, sick leave); 6.3 How much economic loss did your airtravel bring to you due to the haze? _____ yuan. 7.3 How much economic loss did the vehicle driving cause due to the influence of haze? _____ yuan. The three questions examined the costs due to illness, flight delays and vehicle driving caused by haze

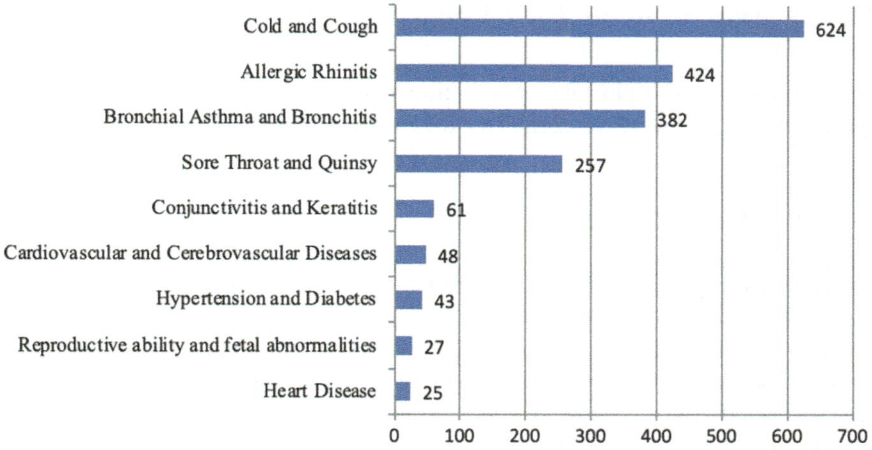


**Fig. 16.3** Diseases caused by haze. *Note* Horizontal axis: frequency; Vertical axis: disease type; Sample size: 1123

of taking protective measures against haze and WTP, the urban families spend more money and are more willing to pay for improving the hazy weather.

(2) Residents below and above 25 years. The average loss from diseases caused by haze to families of the respondents 25 years or older is 407.47 RMB per family, far higher than that of the families of those 25 years or younger (254.12 RMB per family). At the same time, the former is willing to pay 514.43 RMB per family for haze treatment, which is slightly higher than the latter (417.68 RMB per family).

(3) Residents for more than 10 years and less than 10 years. The respondents who have been living in the local places for more than 10 years are more sensitive to the changes brought about by the hazy weather; thus, their perceptions of haze, loss from haze-related diseases and WTP are greater.

(4) In terms of anti-haze measures, up to three options were allowed to choose. The chosen options and the corresponding proportions were as follows: wearing a preventive mask (56.9%), refraining from going outdoors (51.2%), using an air purifier (10.9%), adjusting the diet and clearing away the lung-heat (16.7%), washing the face and bare skin upon arrival at home (19.3%), buying green plants (15%) and taking no preventive measures (5.1%). As was shown, wearing a preventive mask and refraining from going outdoors took the first and second place respectively, indicating that haze had exerted negative influence on residents' daily life and travel.

### 16.4.2 Analysis of the Factors that Affect WTP

Recall that the data employed in this section include the survey results (1,123 valid questionnaires, see Sect. 16.3.2) and the losses due to haze conditions (Sect. 16.3.1).

#### 16.4.2.1 Model Selection

To describe the characteristics of factors that affect the public's willingness to pay, we estimate the log odds (e.g., $\ln \frac{p}{1-p} = A + BX$ where $1 - p = P(Y = 0) = 1 - P(Y = 1)$). With this setting, predictive variables are not required to meet a normal distribution (Dichotomous or interval or ratio), more explanatory variables can be selected to enhance the prediction accuracy of the model, with the probability significance, and the regression result of the logistic model has a stronger explaining power (Wu et al. 2019). The basic form of the logistic model is given as follows:

$$\ln \frac{p}{1-p} = \beta_0 + \beta_1 x_1 + \beta_2 x_2 + \cdots + \beta_k x_k \tag{16.1}$$

where $x_i$ s are the explanatory variables (these are the factors that influence the likelihood of WTP), $p$ is the occurrence probability of the event (WTP) when the independent variables $x_i$ take a sequence of given values, and $\beta_0, \beta_1, \ldots, \beta_k$ are the unknown parameters to be estimated (slopes, $\beta_i = 0$ means the variable has no effect on the log odds). Equation (16.1) can be converted into the following form describing the odds:

$$\frac{p}{1-p} = e^{\beta_0 + \beta_1 x_1 + \beta_2 x_2 + \cdots + \beta_k x_k} \tag{16.2}$$

where $\frac{p}{1-p}$ is known as the odds ratio. It follows from (16.2) that the calculation formula for $p$ is given by the following:

$$p = \frac{e^{\beta_0 + \beta_1 x_1 + \beta_2 x_2 + \cdots + \beta_k x_k}}{1 + e^{\beta_0 + \beta_1 x_1 + \beta_2 x_2 + \cdots + \beta_k x_k}}. \text{ (Wang and Guo 2001)} \tag{16.3}$$

#### 16.4.2.2 Dependent Variables

A question was included in Part 4 of the questionnaire to gauge the public's WTP with regards haze treatment. The question can be seen in Section "3.1 Questionnaire Design". Then, the amount that the respondents were willing to pay was used as a dependent variable.

#### 16.4.2.3 Explanatory Variables

Based on the research of demographics, the background factors of the respondents also affect the WTP. Combined with the above discussion, some typical influential factors, such as gender, age, educational level, marital status, activity areas, family background, degree of impact brought on by haze, and so on, were selected as the explanatory variables. Variable description, symbols, and reasons are listed in Table 16.4.

#### 16.4.2.4 Analysis of the Regression Results

To analyze the 1,123 valid questionnaires obtained from Jiangsu Province, SPSS 20.0 statistical software was used for the binary logistic regression. It can be seen from Table 16.5 that according to the statistical significance level, the public's willingness to pay for improving haze weather is affected by the following factors in turn: vehicle travel loss, disease loss, local residence time, education level and whether there are elderly people in the family. And the positive and negative of coefficient represents the direction that influences the willingness to pay. The results are presented in Table 16.5, where each coefficient is between the named predictor and the WTP.

It follows from Table 16.5 above, along with the relevant statistical significance of the employed statistics tests, that the WTP of the public for improving the hazy weather is primarily influenced by the following six factors:

(1) Loss from vehicle travel has a positive influence on the WTP. Travelers are easily exposed to hazy weathers as they experience more outdoor activities. In addition, Hazy weathers account for more frequent traffic congestions, car accidents and hence more loss. Consequently, they are more likely willing to pay for haze treatment.
(2) Expenses for taking protective measures (cost for masks, air purifiers, potted plants, improving diet and so on) are positively related to the WTP. Investment on preventive/protective actions and the investment for haze treatment are consistent, and hence people taking protective measures are more willing to pay for the haze treatment.
(3) Education level also has positive influence on WTP. Generally, respondents with higher educational levels are more demanding of the quality of life. Given their profound understanding of the harmful impacts of haze, they are more eager to pay for the treatment of haze pollution.
(4) Duration of residency is another positive factor on WTP. The longer the respondents live in the local places, the more they are willing to pay for haze treatment, due to long term good returns from paying for haze treatment, beneficial for their family members, relatives, friends, and future generations.
(5) The loss from diseases is another influential factor on WTP, in a negative way, indicating that families that have suffered more losses from haze-related diseases are less willing to pay for haze treatment. While families suffering

**Table 16.4** Definitions of the explanatory variables

| Influential factor | Definition | Influential factor | Definition |
|---|---|---|---|
| Gender | 1 = Male; 0 = Female | With children | 1 = Yes; 0 = No |
| Age | 1 = Between 18 and 25 years old;<br>2 = Between 26 and 40 years old;<br>3 = Between 41 and 55 years old;<br>4 = Between 56 and 70 years old;<br>5 = Over 70 years old | Concern on the hazy weather | 1 = Never concerned; 2 = Rarely concerned; 3 = Occasionally concerned; 4 = Often concerned; 5 = Greatly concerned |
| Education level | 1 = No regular education;<br>2 = Primary school;<br>3 = Secondary school;<br>4 = Senior high school and technical secondary school;<br>5 = College degree;<br>6 = Bachelor's degree;<br>7 = Master's degree and above | History of cigarette smoking | 1 = non-smoker; 2 = 0.5 packets/day;<br>3 = 1 packet/day; 4 = 2 packets/day;<br>5 = more than 2 packets/day |
| Marital status | 1 = Married;<br>0 = Unmarried | Health condition | 1 = Healthy; 0 = Have diseases |
| Activity areas | 1 = Urban areas; 2 = Suburban areas; 3 = Outskirts and rural areas | Loss from diseases | 1 = Yes; 0 = No |
| Duration of residency | 1 = Less than 1 year; 2 = 1 to 4 years;3 = 5 to 9 years;4 = 10 to 19 years; 5 = 20 years and above | Loss from flights | 1 = Yes; 0 = No |
| Monthly family income (RMB) | 1 = Below 3000; 2 = Between 3000 and 5999; 3 = Between 6000 and 10000; 4 = Between 10000 and 20000; 5 = Above 20000 | Loss from vehicle travel | 1 = Yes; 0 = No |
| With elderly members | 1 = Yes; 0 = No | Expenses for taking protective measures | 1 = Yes; 0 = No |

from haze related diseases are more eager for treating haze, due to their labor ability, employment status, income, financial ability, and the higher expenses incurred in the treatment of the families suffered the diseases, some of these families are not affordable for higher WTP. In our sample, medical costs

**Table 16.5** Regression results of the logistic model on factors affecting the WTP of the Sample in Jiangsu PROVINCE

| Influential factor | Regression coefficient | Standard deviation | Significance | Expected value |
|---|---|---|---|---|
| Gender | 0.053 | 0.137 | 0.698 | 1.054 |
| Age | 0.049 | 0.100 | 0.627 | 1.050 |
| Education level | 0.166** | 0.062 | 0.007 | 1.181 |
| Marital status | 0.047 | 0.214 | 0.825 | 1.048 |
| Activity areas | 0.091 | 0.080 | 0.252 | 1.096 |
| Duration of residency | 0.139** | 0.051 | 0.007 | 1.149 |
| Monthly family income | −0.053 | 0.057 | 0.357 | 0.949 |
| With elderly members | 0.271* | 0.137 | 0.048 | 0.763 |
| With children | 0.123 | 0.152 | 0.415 | 1.131 |
| Concern on the hazy weather | 0.031 | 0.066 | 0.635 | 1.032 |
| History of cigarette smoking | −0.040 | 0.082 | 0.630 | 0.961 |
| Health condition | −0.293 | 0.351 | 0.405 | 0.746 |
| Loss from diseases | −0.296* | 0.141 | 0.036 | 0.744 |
| Loss from flight delays | −0.134 | 0.290 | 0.645 | 0.875 |
| Loss from vehicle travel | 0.819*** | 0.180 | 0.000 | 2.269 |
| Expenses for taking protective measures | 0.518*** | 0.151 | 0.001 | 1.680 |
| Constant | −1.401 | 0.545 | 0.010 | 0.246 |

*Note* *, **, and *** represent significance levels of 5%, 1% and 0.1%, respectively

(346.02 RMB per family) from haze-related diseases account for the largest proportion of the total loss to public (Sect. 4.1).

(6) Having the elder members of the family can also influence WTP. Families with elder members are more willing to pay for haze treatment. Previous research found that haze can cause the progression of respiratory and heart diseases (Mu and Zhang 2013; Xie et al. 2014). In harsh environments, such as haze, the special population, such as the elderly and the children, is more susceptible to sickness because of their poor adaptability and strong vulnerability to haze. This action is closely connected with the influence of the Chinese national tradition of respect for the old.

#### 16.4.2.5 Regression Analysis of the Samples Subdivided from the Perspective of Demographics

When dividing the samples according to the monthly family income, we consider both the per capita income of urban households (5419.85 RMB) from Jiangsu Statistical Yearbook 2012 and the average monthly income of all respondents' families in this survey (7588.6 RMB), and the medium value of 6000 RMB is taken as a standard to divide the samples of Jiangsu Province into the high-income families (the monthly family income being more than 6000 RMB) and the low-income families (monthly family income being less than 6000 RMB).

To partition the population by age, age 25 was used to split the population into two groups. People younger than 25 years old are in the education and start-up stages and have limited economic autonomy. Thus, they have no exact cognition of the WTP problem; with certain behavior cognition and economic autonomy, the group of 25 years old and older can express their WTP objectives.

The samples obtained by the above process are regressed by employing Eq. (16.3). The results are shown in Table 16.6.

Results in Table 16.6 show great variations among the relevant factors that affect the WTP.[3]

(1) Regression results based on gender. From the regression results, for female respondents, education level, activity areas, loss from diseases, loss from vehicle travel and expenses for taking protective measures affect their WTP more greatly. In contrast, the duration of residency and vehicle travel have more influence for male respondents. These results may suggest that females are more sensitive to environmental hazards (e.g., haze).[4]

(2) Regression results based on family income. High-income families pay more attention to loss from diseases, loss from vehicle travel and expenses for protective measures. For low-income families, significant factors include education level and duration of residency. For these families with limited disposable income, they have no ability to migrate to other places to escape haze. Meanwhile, families with certain education levels and longer duration in local area are more aware about the harm of haze, which increases their WTP.

[3]This paper mainly studies the economic losses caused by haze and the willingness to pay, and the ability to pay has a great impact on the willingness to pay. Generally, the stronger the ability to pay, the greater the willingness to pay. Among many factors that affect the willingness to pay. The relations of residence time, marital status and ability to pay are not significant enough, while gender, age and income are more closely related to the ability to pay, so we choose these three factors as the classification criteria.

[4]Mendoza et al. (2014), when assessing the vulnerability of Cambodia, the Philippines and Vietnam to the impact of climate change, found that women were more closely connected with family life and more sensitive to the environmental changes they relied on from the analysis at the community and family levels. In order to study whether there are differences between men and women in their willingness to pay for haze, groups were subdivided according to gender. The results also show that women are more sensitive to environmental hazards.

**Table 16.6** Regression Results of the logistic model on factors affecting the WTP

| Influential factor | Dependent variables | | | | | |
|---|---|---|---|---|---|---|
| | Coefficient | | | | | |
| | Male | Female | Below 6000 RMB | Above 6000 RMB | Below 25 years | Over 25 years |
| Gender | – | – | 0.140 (0.436) | −0.032 (0.888) | −0.400 (0.063) | 0.351 (0.058) |
| Age | 0.033 (0.818) | 0.071 (0.632) | 0.069 (0.595) | 0.006 (0.971) | – | – |
| Education level | 0.103 (0.220) | 0.239* (0.013) | 0.323*** (0.000) | −0.054 (0.586) | 0.283 (0.078) | 0.161** (0.024) |
| Marital status | −0.145 (0.645) | 0.299 (0.338) | 0.243 (0.395) | −0.163 (0.631) | −0.483 (0.270) | 0.118 (0.723) |
| Activity areas | −0.117 (0.317) | 0.256* (0.024) | 0.161 (0.116) | 0.053 (0.690) | 0.151 (0.227) | −0.049 (0.650) |
| Duration of residency | 0.278*** (0.000) | 0.017 (0.811) | 0.215*** (0.001) | 0.042 (0.612) | −0.001 (0.984) | 0.331*** (0.000) |
| Monthly family income | −0.129 (0.115) | 0.014 (0.865) | – | – | 0.060 (0.486) | −0.138 (0.093) |
| With elderly members | −0.313 (0.116) | −0.224 (0.252) | −0.275 (0.135) | −0.222 (0.298) | −0.558** (0.008) | −0.042 (0.823) |
| With children | 0.296 (0.195) | −0.069 (0.741) | −0.007 (0.974) | 0.249 (0.301) | −0.224 (0.277) | 0.464** (0.004) |
| Concern on the hazy weather | −0.030 (0.743) | 0.066 (0.501) | −0.025 (0.781) | 0.117 (0.249) | −0.018 (0.866) | −0.022 (0.798) |
| History of cigarette smoking | −0.068 (0.465) | −0.129 (0.531) | 0.080 (0.486) | −0.200 (0.116) | 0.084 (0.652) | −0.122 (0.204) |
| Health condition | −0.265 (0.559) | −0.264 (0.642) | −0.825 (0.082) | 0.458 (0.434) | −0.437 (0.422) | 0.012 (0.980) |
| Loss from diseases | −0.240 (0.228) | −0.362* (0.080) | −0.148 (0.420) | −0.605** (0.009) | −0.291 (0.201) | −0.273 (0.144) |
| Loss from flight delays | −0.482 (0.269) | 0.147 (0.720) | −0.027 (0.939) | −0.031 (0.955) | 0.715 (0.139) | −0.663* (0.099) |
| Loss from vehicle travel | 1.022*** (0.000) | 0.602*(0.025) | 0.512* (0.028) | 1.304*** (0.000) | 0.494 (0.122) | 0.980*** (0.000) |
| Expenses for taking protective measures | 0.347 (0.096) | 0.743*** (0.001) | 0.491* (0.012) | 0.716** (0.004) | 0.572* (0.024) | 0.531*** (0.007) |
| Constant | −0.672 (0.366) | −1.945(0.024) | −2.71 (0.000) | −0.060 (0.944) | −1.445 (0.219) | −2.027 (0.003) |

(continued)

**Table 16.6** (continued)

| Influential factor | Dependent variables | | | | | |
|---|---|---|---|---|---|---|
| | Coefficient | | | | | |
| | Male | Female | Below 6000 RMB | Above 6000 RMB | Below 25 years | Over 25 years |
| Total sample | 569 | 554 | 662 | 461 | 450 | 673 |

*Note* *, **, and *** represent significance levels of 5%, 1% and 0.1%, respectively; the number in the brackets is the value of P

(3) Regression results based on age. Factors affecting the respondents' WTP vary largely by age. From Sect. 16.4.2.4, respondents younger than 25 years old pay more attention to having elderly members in the family, whereas those ages 25 years or older focus on having children in the family. These results imply that the health of the family is a main public concern when facing the threat of haze. In other words, elder members and children are the main reasons for engaging the public to pay for haze treatment.

## 16.5 Discussion on the Validation of the Model

Internal validity is a property of scientific studies, reflecting the extent to which a causal conclusion based on a study is warranted. Such warranty is constituted by the extent to which a study minimizes systematic error or "bias".

Accredited methods for achieving the internal validation (cross-validation) of the binary logistic regression (and other methods as well) include data splitting, repeated data-splitting, jackknife technique and bootstrapping (Cox and Snell 1989; Shao 1993). In addition to the qualitative interviews for determining independent variables and handling confounding variables, this study employed the data-splitting approach as it is a straightforward and fairly popular approach in which the whole data is randomly split into two parts—one for developing the model, and the other for measuring the performance of the model. More precisely, the internal validation is the process of assessing how the results of the binary logistic regression will generalize to an independent data set. Moreover, in the analysis of the WTP, we eliminated the outliers using the two-interquartile range interval. However, there are some limitations in the study: due to the focus of the project and the availability of data, bootstrapping procedure was not performed on data and external validity could not be investigated. Also, influential cases (i.e., some returned questionnaires) were neither eliminated nor technically processed.

## 16.6 Conclusions and Discussions

### *16.6.1 Conclusions*

Economic loss assessment is an important part of measuring the extent of environmental hazards, but only fewer isolated studies have been conducted to assess the economic losses incurred by haze. In this study, a large number of samples from the Jiangsu Province in China are investigated to obtain the vast amount of real and effective statistics. Economic losses and the prevalence (resp., medical costs) of diseases caused by haze disasters have been assessed, and the percentage of residents—willing to pay for haze treatment has been analyzed based on different partitions of the population by utilizing the CVM and the binary logistic regression model, with influential factors of the WTP explored.

The following is an exclusive summary of the findings from the sample:

(1) Losses brought by haze for Jiangsu Province. In 2013, the average loss incurred from haze weather was approximately 917.62 RMB per family; whereas the total economic loss of these families amounted to 22.38 billion RMB. Nationwide, it is estimated that in 2013 the corresponding figures were 884.62 RMB per family and 346.02 billion RMB in total.

(2) WTP for haze treatment. To treat haze, the families are willing to pay 476.83 RMB per family per year in the next five years; totaling to 11.6 billion RMB for the province. This amount is approximately 51.96% of the total losses. The government should pay the remainder of 440.79 RMB per family for haze treatment per year, totaling 11.05 billion RMB a year.

(3) Factors that affect the WTP. The urban respondents ages 25 years or older have been living in the residence for more than 10 years, females, and those who have babies or elder family members are more willing to pay for haze treatment, indicating that family is an important reason for people when they make decisions on whether or not to pay for haze treatment.

### *16.6.2 Discussions*

(1) The government's investment in haze treatment costs should be largely increased. In 2013, the public willingness to pay was 12.366 billion RMB and the total loss value in Jiangsu Province was 23.797 billion RMB respectively. However, the investment in the treatment of industrial waste gas in Jiangsu Province was only 5.62 billion RMB (see Table 16.7).

Let us assume that the government governance expenditure is equal to the sum of the willingness to pay by the public and the total loss caused by haze pollution. The actual expenditure from the government investment is far lower than the public's willingness to pay and the total loss, leaving a huge gap to fill. Hence,

**Table 16.7** Public willingness to pay and loss value and actual expenditure in Jiangsu Province

| Number | Items | Jiangsu province |
|---|---|---|
| (1) | Annual public willingness to pay for per family (Yuan) | 476.83 |
| (2) | Total annual haze loss for per family (Yuan) | 917.62 |
| (3) | Total number of households (10 thousand) | 2593.31 |
| (4) | Total annual public willingness to pay for all households (100 million RMB) ((1) × (3)) | 123.66 |
| (5) | Total annual haze loss for all households (100 million RMB) ((2) × (3)) | 237.97 |
| (6) | Actual expenditure from the government investment (100 million RMB) | 56.22* |

*Note* 1. (1)–(5) come from the section "5 Empirical Analysis"
2. *: It is "Expenditure on industrial waste gas treatment in Jiangsu Province", which come from *Jiangsu statistical yearbook (2014)*

government departments should increase substantial investments in environmental protection including waste gas treatment.

(2) Utilize big data resources and technologies, and increase the transparency of the environmental management. The public is the most direct victim of haze pollution, and on the other hand, the direct beneficiary of air quality improvement, the ultimate judge of pollution control, and at the same time a larger producer of the pollution. To accomplish the long-term governance, the public must be engaged with the full right to know and to participate with strong enthusiasm. At present, with the vigorous development of big data technology represented by the 5G technologies, people are rethinking the environmental management paradigm that uses massive data as a resource and big data technology as a research tool. In the aspects of air pollution monitoring, hazard assessment, governance and effectiveness evaluation, big data processing technologies and computation methods can be employed to analyze and process massive data to obtain scientific and deeper results. In the way of environmental management, through the multi-directional information exchange among the government, enterprises and the public, the transparency of the government and corporate pollution control behavior and the degree of public's awareness will be enhanced, and finally the goal of protecting the environment and serving the public is accomplished.

In this study, there are some aspects to be improved. Firstly, convenience sampling rather than randomized sampling was adopted. The overall inference about all Jiangsu residents' willingness to pay was based on the assumption that the obtained data can represent the population. Secondly, though the research background, payment assumption and other information were explained as clearly as possible during the survey to reduce any errors, it cannot be ensured that every respondent well understands the information due to the large number of students and respondents participating in the survey. Thirdly, the content of a haze reduction plan can greatly affect the willingness of respondents. An ideal special haze reduction plan was developed in this study, but it remains questionable whether this hypothetical plan is reasonable. The influence of the plan on the respondents depends on the rationality of the plan, the quality of the researchers and the understanding degree of the respondents. Therefore, each link of the survey is worth further investigation so as to carry out the research properly and obtain more accurate data.

Finally, the sample obtained from Jiangsu Province demonstrated the public's strong desire for the treatment of haze pollution as well as their willingness to pay. Greater understanding of the public's need through representative samples can help the government improve its technology innovation strategies including policies and investments, and promote communities to develop more effective emergency measures.

**Acknowledgements** Guo Wei, Yi Zou, Jinxing Lu also made great contributions to this manuscript. We express our heartfelt thanks to them. This research was supported by: National Social and Scientific Fund Program of China (18ZDA052; 17BGL142; 16ZDA047); The Natural Science Foundation of China (91546117, 71373131).

## References

Abate, T. G., Borger, T., Aanese, M., Aanese, M., Falk-Andersson, J., Wyles, K. J., et al. (2020). Valuation of marine plastic pollution in the European Arctic: Applying an integrated choice and latent variable model to contingent valuation. *Ecological Economics, 169*,.

Afroz, R., Hassan, M. N., & Ibrahim, N. A. (2003). Review of air pollution and health impacts in malaysia. *Environmental Research, 92*(2), 71–77.

Ain, Q., Ullah, R., Kamran, M. A., & Zulfiqar, F. (2020). Air pollution and its economic impacts at household level: Willingness to pay for environmental services in Pakistan. *Environmental Science and Pollution Research*. https://doi.org/10.1007/s11356-020-11023-4.

Arimah, B. C. (1996). Willingness to pay for improved environmental sanitation in a nigerian city. *Journal of Environmental Management, 48*(2), 127–138.

Arrow, K., & Solow, R. (1993). Report of the NOAA panel on contingent valuation. Washington, DC: National Oceanic and Atmospheric Administration.

Bherwani, H., Nair, M., Musugu, K., Gautam, S., Gupta, A., Kapley, A., et al. (2020). Valuation of air pollution externalities: Comparative assessment of economic damage and emission reduction under COVID-19 lockdown. *Air Quality, Atmosphere and Health, 13*(6), 683–694.

Bobinac, A., Exel, N. J. A. V., Rutten, F. F. H., & Brouwer, W. B. F. (2012). Get more, pay more? an elaborate test of construct validity of willingness to pay per QALY estimates obtained through contingent valuation. *Journal of Health Economics, 31*(1), 1–168.

Bravo-Vargas, V., García, R. A., Pizarro, J. C., & Pauchard, A. (2019). Do people care about pine invasions? Visitor perceptions and willingness to pay for pine control in a protected area. *Journal of Environmental Management, 229*(1), 57–66.

Carson, R. T., Flores, N. E., & Meade, N. F. (2001). Contingent valuation: Controversies and evidence. *Environmental & Resource Economics, 19*(2), 173–210.

Chen, J. B., Chen, K. Y., Wang, G. Z., Chen, R. R., Liu, X. D., & Wei, G. (2019). Indirect economic impact incurred by haze pollution: An econometric and input-output joint model. *International Journal of Environmental Research and Public Health, 16*(13), 2328.

Chen, K. Y., Wang, G. Z., Wu, L. Y., Chen, J. B., Yuan, S., Liu, Q., & Liu, X. D. (2020a). PM2.5 Pollution: Health and economic effect assessment based on a recursive dynamic computable general equilibrium model. *International Journal of Environmental Research and Public Health, 16*(24), 5102.

Chen, S. Y., Wang, Y. F., Ni, Z. B., Zhang, X. B., & Xia, B. C. (2020b). Benefits of the ecosystem services provided by urban green infrastructures: Differences between perception and measurements. *Urban Forestry & Urban Greening, 54*, 126774.

Cicaiello, L., Ercolano, S., Gaeta, G. L., & Pinto, M. (2020). Willingness to pay for environmental protection and the importance of pollutant industries in the regional economy. Evidence from Italy. *Ecological Economics, 177*, 10674.

Cox, D. R., & Snell, E. J. (1989). Analysis of binary data, 32. CRC Press.

Dardanoni, V., & Guerriero, C. (2021). Young people's willingness to pay for environmental protection. *Ecological Economics, 179*.

Davis, R. K. (1963). Recreation planning as an economic problem. *Natural Resources Journal, 3*, 239.

Desvousges, W. H., Hudson, S. P., & Ruby, M. C. (1996). *Evaluating CV performance: Separating the light from the heat, Bjornstad and Kahn. The contingent valuation of environmental resources: Methodological issues and research needs*. Cheltenham: Edward Elgar.

Diao, B. D., Ding, L., Zhang, Q., Na, J. L., & Cheng, J. H. (2020). Impact of urbanization on PM2.5-related health and economic loss in China 338 cities. *International Journal of Environmental Research and Public Health, 17*(3), 990.

Fan, F., Lei, Y., & Li, L. (2019). Health damage assessment of particulate matter pollution in Jing-Jin-Ji region of china. *Environmental Science and Pollution Research*,1–13.

Forsyth, T. (2014). Public concerns about transboundary haze: A comparison of Indonesia, Singapore, and Malaysia. *Global Environmental Change, 25*, 76–86.

Gao, M., Guttikunda, S. K., Carmichael, G. R., Wang, Y., Liu, Z., & Stanier, C. O. (2015). Health impacts and economic losses assessment of the 2013 severe haze event in Beijing area. *Science of the Total Environment, 511*, 553–561.

Guo, H. B., & Chen, M. X. (2018). Short-term effect of air pollution on asthma patient visits in Shanghai area and assessment of economic costs. *Ecotoxicology and Environmental Safety, 161*, 184–189.

Guo, J., Zhou, L., & Wu, X. (2018). Tendency of embodied carbon change in the export trade of chinese manufacturing industry from 2000 to 2015 and its driving factors. *Sustainability, 10*, 1–12.

Han, F., Lu, X. C., Xiao, C. C., Chang, M., & Huang, K. (2019). Estimation of health effects and economic losses from ambient air pollution in undeveloped areas: Evidence from Guangxi, China. *International Journal of Environmental Research and Public Health, 16*(15), 2707.

Hao, Y., Peng, H., Temulun, T., Liu, L. Q., Mao, J., Lu, Z. N., & Chen, H. (2018). How harmful is air pollution to economic development? New evidence from PM2.5 concentrations of Chinese cities. *Journal of Cleaner Production, 172*, 743–757.

Hao, Y., Zhao, M. Y., & Lu, Z. N. (2019). What is the health cost of haze pollution? Evidence from China. *International Journal of Health Planning and Management, 34*(4), 1290–1303.

He, L. Y., & Zhang, H. Z. (2020). Spillover or crowding out? The effects of environmental regulation on residents' willingness to pay for environmental protection. *Natural Hazards*. https://doi.org/10.1007/s11069-020-04326-9.

Hou, F. M., Wang, Y., & Zuo, F. Y. (2019). Environmental study on the social and economic impact of Beijing's haze problem: Based on DPSIR model. *Ekoloji, 28*(107), 1299–1307.

Huang, L., Li, J., & He, R. Y. (2018). Quantitative analysis of health risk perception, exposure levels, and willingness to pay/accept of PM2.5 during the 2014 Nanjing Youth Olympic games. *Environmental Science and Technology, 52*(23), 13824–13833.

Ito, K., & Zhang, S. (2020). Willingness to pay for clean air: Evidence from air purifier markets in China. *Journal of Political Economy, 128*(5), 1627–1672.

Jaafar, H., & Razi, N. A. (2018). A systematic review of financial implications of air pollution on health in Asia. *Environmental Science and Pollution Research, 25*(30), 30009–30020.

Jin, T. Y., & Li, M. (2020). Does education increase pro-environmental willingness to pay? Evidence from Chinese household survey. *Journal of Cleaner Production, 275*,.

Khan, S. U., Hayat, S., Xia, X. L., Liu, G. B., & Zhao, M. J. (2020). Improvisation of indigenous environmental benefit transfer and valuation for cleaner environment: Choice experiment across northwest China. *Journal of Cleaner Production, 274*,.

Krupnick, A., Hoffmann, S., Larsen, B., Peng, X., Tao, R., Yan, C., et al. (2006). *The willingness to pay for mortality risk reductions in Shanghai and Chongqing, China, Resources for the Future.* Washington, DC: The World Bank.

Lan, F., Lu, J. Z., Chen, J., Zhang, X. L., Zhao, Z. H., & Pui, D. Y. H. (2020). Willingness to pay for staying away from haze: Evidence from a quasi-natural experiment in Xi'an. *Journal of Environmental Management, 262*,.

Latif, M. T., Othman, M., Juneng, L., & Tangang, F. (2018). Impact of regional haze towards air quality in Malaysia: A review. *Atmospheric Environment, 177*, 28–44.

Lelieveld, J., Evans, J. S., Fnais, M., Giannadaki, D., & Pozzer, A. (2015). The contribution of outdoor air pollution sources to premature mortality on a global scale. *Nature, 525*, 367–371.

Lin, Y., Wijedasa, L. S., & Chisholm, R. A. (2017). Singapore's willingness to pay for mitigation of transboundary forest-fire haze from Indonesia. *Environmental Research Letters, 12*(2), 024017.

Liu, Y. J., & Dong, F. (2020). Corruption, economic development and haze pollution: Evidence from 139 global countries. *Sustainability, 12*(9), 3523.

Lu, X. C., Yao, T., Fung, J. C. H., & Lin, C. Q. (2016). Estimation of health and economic costs of air pollution over the Pearl River Delta region in China. *Science of the Total Environment, 566*, 134–143.

Maji, K. J., Dikshit, A. K., & Deshpande, A. (2017). Disability-adjusted life years and economic cost assessment of the health effects related to pm 2.5, and pm 10, pollution in Mumbai and Delhi, in India from 1991 to 2015. *Environmental Science and Pollution Research, 24*(5), 4709–4730.

Mekonne, A., Seifu, B., Hailu, C., & Atomsa, A. (2020). Willingness to pay for social health insurance and associated factors among health care providers in Addis Ababa, Ethiopia. *Biomed Research International*, 8412957.

Mendoza, M. E. T., The, B. D., Naret, H., Ballaran, V. G., & Arias, J. K. B. (2014). Assessing vulnerability to climate change impacts in cambodia, the Philippines and Vietnam: An analysis at the commune and household level. *Journal of Environmental Science & Management, 17*(2), 78–91.

Mi, Z. F., Meng, J., & Guan, D. B. (2017a). Chinese CO2 emission flows have reversed since the global financial crisis. *Nature communications, 8*(1), 1712.

Mi, Z., Meng, J., Guan, D., Shan, Y., Liu, Z., & Wang, Y. (2017b). Pattern changes in determinants of Chinese emissions. *Environmental Research Letters, 12* (7), 074003.

Mikulčić, H., Duić, N., & Dewil, R. (2017). Environmental management as a pillar for sustainable development. *Journal of Environmental Management, 203*(Pt 3), 867–871.

Mikulčić, H., Duić, N., Schlör, H., & Dewil, R. (2019). Troubleshooting the problems arising from sustainable development. *Journal of Environmental Management, 232*, 52–57.

Mitchell, R. C., & Carson, R. T. (2013). Using surveys to value public goods: The contingent valuation method. Routledge.

Mu, Q., & Zhang, S. Q. (2013). An evaluation of the economic loss due to the heavy haze during January 2013 in China. *China Environmental Science, 33*(11), 2087–2094.

Munoz-Pizza, D. M., Villada-Canela, M., Rivera-Castaneda, P., Reyna-Carranza, M.A., Osornio-Vargas, A., & Martinez-Cruz, A. L. (2020). Stated benefits from air quality improvement through urban afforestation in an arid city—A contingent valuation in Mexicali, Baja California, Mexico. *Urban Forestry & Urban Greening*, 126854.

National bureau of statistics of the People's Republic of China. The Sixth National Population Census, 2013. http://www.stats.gov.cn/tjsj/tjgb/rkpcgb/dfrkpcgb/201202/t20120228_30394.html.

Othman, J., Sahani, M., Mahmud, M., & Ahmad, M. K. (2014). Transboundary smoke haze pollution in Malaysia: Inpatient health impacts and economic valuation. *Environmental Pollution, 189*(43), 194–201.

Ouyang, X. L., Zhuang, W. X., & Sun, C. W. (2019). Haze, health, and income: An integrated model for willingness to pay for haze mitigation in Shanghai. *China. Energy Economics, 84,*.

Qiu, F., Wang, E., Fan, M., Liao, H., Wang, L. T., & Huang, Z. Y. (2018). A questionnaire case study of chinese opinions on the haze pollution and economic growth. *Sustainability, 10*(6), 1970.

Ru, X. J., Qin, H. B., & Wang, S. Y. (2019). Young people's behaviour intentions towards reducing PM2.5 in China: Extending the theory of planned behaviour. *Resources conservation and recycling, 141*, 99–108.

Sachin, S. M., Yadav, V. K., Pal, S., Karmakar, S., & Marti, V. S. (2020). Survey based economic evaluation of ecosystem services of mangrove from Uttar Kannada district of Karnataka. *India. Journal of Environmental Biology, 41*(5), 980–986.

Sereenonchai, S., Arunrat, N., & Kamnoonwatana, D. (2020). Risk perception on haze pollution and willingness to pay for self-protection and haze management in Chiang Mai Province, Northern Thailand. *Atmosphere, 11*(6), 600.

Shao, J. (1993). Linear model selection by cross-validation. *Journal of the American statistical Association, 88*(422), 486–494.

Sheldon, T. L., & Sankaran, C. (2017). The impact of indonesian forest fires on Singaporean pollution and health. *American Economic Review, 107*(5), 526–529.

Song, M., Peng, J., Wang, J., & Dong, L. (2018). Better resource management: An improved resource and environmental efficiency evaluation approach that considers undesirable outputs. *Resources, Conservation and Recycling, 128,* 197–205.

Song, Y., Guo, S., & Zhang, M. (2019). Assessing customers' perceived value of the anti-haze cosmetics under haze pollution. *Science of the Total Environment, 685,* 753–762.

Venkatachalam, L. (2004). The contingent valuation method: A review. *Environmental Impact Assessment Review, 24*(1), 89–124.

Wang, J. C., & Guo, Z. G. (2001). *Logistic regression models: Methods and application, 20.* Beijing: Higher Education Press.

Wang, H., & Mullahy, J. (2006). Willingness to pay for reducing fatal risk by improving air quality: A contingent valuation study in Chongqing. *China. Science of the Total Environment, 367*(1), 50–57.

Wang, G. Z., Song, Y. X., Chen, J. B., & Yu, J. (2016a). Valuation of haze management and prevention using the contingent valuation method with the sure independence screening algorithm. *Sustainability, 8*(4), 310.

Wang, Y. T., Sun, M. X., & Yang, X. C. (2016b). Public awareness and willingness to pay for tackling smog pollution in China: A case study. *Journal of Cleaner Production,112*(2), 1627–1634.

World Health Organization. (2000). Western Pacific Regional Office WHO/WPRO. Report on biregional workshop on health impacts of haze—Related air pollution, Kuala Lumpur. World Health Organization. Western Pacific Regional Office—WHO / WPRO.

Wu, X., Cao, Y., Xiao, Y., & Guo, J. (2018). Finding of urban rainstorm and waterlogging disasters based on microblogging data and the location-routing problem model of urban emergency logistics. *Annuals of Operations Research*, 1–32.

Wu, X. H., Xu, Z., Liu, H., Guo, J., & Zhou, L. (2019). What are the impacts of tropical cyclones on employment?—An Analysis Based on Meta-regression. *Weather Clim Soc, 11*(2), 259–275.

Xie, Y. B., Chen, J., & Li, W. (2014). An assessment of PM2. 5 related health risks and impaired values of Beijing residents in a consecutive high-level exposure during heavy haze days. *Chinese Journal of Environmental Science, 35*(1), 1–8.

Xie, Y., Wu, Y. Z., Xie, M. J., Li, B. D., Zhang, H., Ma, T., et al. (2020). Health and economic benefit of China's greenhouse gas mitigation by 2050. *Environmental Research Letters, 15*(10),

Xu, Z. H., & Shan, J. Z. (2018). The effect of risk perception on willingness to pay for reductions in the health risks posed by particulate matter 2.5: A case study of Beijing, China. *Energy & Environment, 29*(8), 1319–1337.

Xu, Z. H., Li, J. M., Yang, Z., & Shan, J. Z. (2020). Residents' willingness to pay for the elimination of Ulva prolifera bloom: A case study in Qingdao, China. *Journal of Environmental Planning and Management*. https://doi.org/10.1080/09640568.2020.1784114.

Yang, G., Wang, Y., Zeng, Y., Gao, G. F., Liang, X., Zhou, M., et al. (2013). Rapid health transition in China, 1990–2010: Findings from the global burden of disease study 2010. *The Lancet, 381*(9882), 1987–2015.

Yang, F., Ding, L., & Liu, C. (2018a) Haze attitudes and the willingness to pay for haze improvement: Evidence from four cities in Shandong Province, China. *International Journal of Environmental Research and Public Health, 15*(10).

Yang, X., Guan, D. B., & Jing, M. (2018b). Assessment of the pollution-health-economics nexus in China. *Atmospheric Chemistry and Physics, 18*(19), 14433-14443.

Zha, A. P., Qiu, J. W., & Huang, J. (2013). Several problems regarding contingent valuation method. *Tourism Tribune, 28*(4), 25–34.

Zhang, M. S., Song, Y., & Cai, X. H. (2007). A health-based assessment of particulate air pollution in urban areas of Beijing in 2000–2004. *Science of the Total Environment, 376*(1), 100–108.

Zhang, L., Chen, L. W., Wu, Z. Z., Xue, H., & Dong, W. L. (2018). Key factors affecting informed consumers' willingness to pay for green housing: A case study of Jinan, China. *Sustainability, 10*(6), 1711.

Zhao, Q., & Yuan, C. H. (2020). Did haze pollution harm the quality development? An empirical study based on China's PM2.5 concentrations. *Sustainability, 12*(4), 1607.

# Chapter 17
# Spatial Concentration, Impact Factors and Prevention-Control Measures of $PM_{2.5}$ Pollution in China

**Abstract** To improve the air pollution of China fundamentally, effective measures should be proposed based on the thorough understanding of the characteristics of air pollution. Based on spatial econometrics, this paper investigates the characteristics and analyzes the determinants of the spatial concentration of $PM_{2.5}$ pollution in China. Results show that: (1) $PM_{2.5}$ pollution is highly concentrated in central and Eastern China, covering 17 regions which accounts for 75% of the total population and GDP (Gross Domestic Product); (2) The $PM_{2.5}$ values in China show a significant spatial correlation. Provinces such as Shandong, Henan, Anhui, and Hubei are high in $PM_{2.5}$ concentration. Meanwhile, these provinces are high in population density, GDP, and coal consumptions, and have a large amount of civilian cars. (3) $PM_{2.5}$ pollution shows spatial spillover effects. A 1% increase in the $PM_{2.5}$ values of neighboring provinces will lead to a 0.78% increase in that of one province. (4) An upward U-shaped relationship is observed between the density of per capita GDP and $PM_{2.5}$, and the $PM_{2.5}$ value is far from the turning point of growth. With the further growth of the density of per capita GDP, the $PM_{2.5}$ value is expected to increase rapidly and continuously. (5) Based on the characteristics of spatial concentration and spatial spillover, this paper proposes several prevention-control measures for haze pollution, such as stressing on the treatment of air pollution in severely polluted provinces, avoiding moving pollution industries to neighboring areas, performing joint prevention and control nationwide. Air pollution may only be rooted by transforming the pattern of economic growth.

**Keywords** Haze · $PM_{2.5}$ · Spatial concentration · Impact factors

## 17.1 Introduction

In recent years, large-scale hazy weather has persistently occurred in China. This phenomenon has seriously endangered public health and caused huge economic losses (Chen et al. 2012; Mu and Zhang 2013). From 2000 to 2015, $PM_{2.5}$ concentration in developed countries such as Europe and the United States increased steadily, while in comparison, $PM_{2.5}$ concentration in China showed a trend of rapid growth (Cao et al. 2018). In January 2013, haze affected an area of more than 1.4 million



X. Wu and J. Guo, *Economic Impacts and Emergency Management of Disasters in China*,
https://doi.org/10.1007/978-981-16-1319-7_17

$km^2$ in Eastern and Northern China, resulting in over 800 million victims. Non-hazy weather lasted for only five days in this January. In February 2014, haze clouded 161 cities in Northern China, among which 51 cities, including Beijing, were polluted and 11 cities were seriously polluted. In 2015, $PM_{2.5}$ pollution contributed 40.3% to total stroke deaths, 33.1% to acute lower respiratory infections deaths, 26.8% to ischemic heart disease deaths, 23.9% to lung cancer deaths, respectively (Song et al. 2017). In 2016, $PM_{2.5}$ pollution resulted in 0.964 million mortality in China, accounting for 9.98% of total Chinese reported deaths. Simultaneously, the economic loss caused by $PM_{2.5}$ pollution reached 101.39 billion dollars, accounting for 0.91% of the whole national GDP (Kamal et al. 2018). Haze forced the closure of primary and secondary schools as well as that of highways and airports. Tian et al. (2018) evaluated $PM_{2.5}$-related health impacts from China's road transport sector in 2030, results showing that the road transport sector caused 163.64 thousand $PM_{2.5}$-related deaths annually and increased the per capita risk of falling ill by 0.37%. In 2012, the economic losses in China caused by $PM_{2.5}$ and other air pollutants amounted to nearly 2 trillion RMB (Zhang et al. 2013). From 2015 to 2017, the economic loss resulting from $PM_{2.5}$'s health loss respectively were 3205.05, 3223.51, and 3344.80 billion yuan, which accounted for 4.34%, 4.07% and 3.85% of the GDP of China, showing a relatively downward trend (Guan et al. 2019a). In general, the potential of $PM_{2.5}$ reduction in all Chinese cities was 42.6% without considering external sources, 40.4% when taking external sources into consideration (Cheng et al. 2019).

The Chinese government is used to taking stopgap measures for haze pollution. One way is to transfer the pollution source to other places to reduce the pollutant discharge. For example, Beijing moves its heavy polluting enterprises such as iron and steel plants to its neighboring regions like Tangshan (Hebei Province). Another way is to shut down pollution sources for some time before and after major events to get clean air temporarily, such as "APEC Blue", "Youth Olympic Blue", and "G20 Blue". However, it turns out to be an expedient which cannot solve haze pollution from the root. The haze in Tangshan floats back to Beijing, resulting in long-lasting hazy weather in Beijing. Once APEC, Youth Olympic Games, and G20 are over, the hazy weather will return. Therefore, effective prevention-control countermeasures should be proposed based on the characteristics of haze pollution. For example, more attention should be paid to $PM_{2.5}$ pollution on a national scale rather than a regional or urban scale (Peng et al. 2016). High-quality and long-term air quality monitoring facilities were essential for air pollution control (Fu and Chen 2017). Since household activity significantly influenced $PM_{2.5}$ emissions, household behavior-related measures should also be attached more importance (Shi et al. 2017). Dong et al. (2019) considered that the optimization of energy mix and energy intensity could effectively reduce $PM_{2.5}$ concentration. Additionally, upgrading industrial structure, promoting clean energy, applying innovative technology were also the dominant measures of $PM_{2.5}$ reduction (Fan and Xu 2020). Due to the $PM_{2.5}$'s spatial spillover effect, cooperative governance of $PM_{2.5}$ pollution between regions and even countries became an irresistible trend (Fu et al. 2020). While coordinating governance, differentiated regional policies should be formulated, considering the location, energy resources and environmental status (Su and Yu 2019).

To mitigate the negative impacts on public health and economic loss arising from $PM_{2.5}$ pollution, a large number of researches about $PM_{2.5}$ pollution's characteristics in China have been conducted. Firstly, $PM_{2.5}$ pollution in China presented significant spatial–temporal heterogeneity. Different regions and urban agglomerations had different characteristics of $PM_{2.5}$ pollution (Lu et al. 2017; He et al. 2019; Ji et al. 2019). From 2000 to 2015, the North China had a high concentration of $PM_{2.5}$, while the south-eastern China had a low concentration of $PM_{2.5}$ (He et al. 2018). Although most cities in eastern China had already reached a high level of $PM_{2.5}$, they were experiencing a decline of $PM_{2.5}$ in recent years, while cities in southern and south-western China with low $PM_{2.5}$ concentration experienced an increase (Zhao et al. 2019a, b). Secondly, China's $PM_{2.5}$ concentration presented obviously temporal variation. In the short term, the highest and lowest $PM_{2.5}$ respectively occurred in the evening and afternoon hours (Tânia et al. 2017). In the long term, $PM_{2.5}$ concentration varied with seasons (Xu et al. 2017; Li et al. 2019c). Its value tended to be higher in cold months, lower in warm months (Feng et al. 2015; Ming et al. 2017; Liu et al. 2019; Chen et al. 2019c; Guo et al. 2020). Thirdly, $PM_{2.5}$ pollution in China had a distinct spatial spillover effect. One area's $PM_{2.5}$ pollution could aggravate its surrounding areas' $PM_{2.5}$ pollution (Ma et al. 2016; Li et al. 2019c; Zheng et al. 2018). The haze pollution spillover effect was stronger in eastern China than in the western and central areas (Chen et al. 2019b). Du et al. (2019) considered that the spatial dependence of $PM_{2.5}$ pollution existed in the range of 200 km in Beijing-Tianjin-Hebei agglomeration. Simultaneously, $PM_{2.5}$ concentration in China was periodic in terms of time. Based on Empirical Mode Decomposition-Wavelet Analysis (EMD-WA) model, Wu et al. (2020b) found that $PM_{2.5}$ concentration in Yangtze River Delta region presented apparent periodicity, respectively seasonal, short, medium and long terms. Although a series of studies concerning $PM_{2.5}$'s characteristics in China have already been done, more researches are still needed to deepen the study and comprehension of $PM_{2.5}$. The purpose of this paper is to explore the characteristics of $PM_{2.5}$ further, so that providing more countermeasures for reducing haze pollution.

Haze is mainly composed of $PM_{10}$ (inhalable particles) and $PM_{2.5}$ (inhalable particles). With more previous researches conducted on the components of $PM_{2.5}$ and easier access to the observation data of $PM_{2.5}$, $PM_{2.5}$ is adopted as the object of this study instead of $PM_{10}$. $PM_{2.5}$ is structurally complicated. Most scholars have analyzed the components of $PM_{2.5}$ from the physical and chemical perspectives (Bates and Sizto 1987; Hussain et al. 2013; Tang et al. 2014; Thurston et al. 1994; Tan et al. 2003; Ma et al. 2012; An et al. 2013; Jansen et al. 2014), but little is known about the contribution of different components from the perspectives of time and space (Dong and Liang 2014; Wu et al. 2016a, b; Xie et al. 2014; Yang et al. 2010; Zhao et al. 2013). $PM_{2.5}$ is mainly generated by traffic emissions (Wang et al. 2015; Chen et al. 2017b; Zhang et al. 2017b; Mirella et al. 2019; Li et al. 2019b), straw burning in agricultural areas (Liu et al. 2017a), industrial emissions (Li et al. 2015), coal, biomass and oil combustion (Zhang et al. 2017c; Hao et al. 2018a, b; Guan et al. 2019b), residential emissions (Liao et al. 2017; ship emissions (Chen et al. 2017c, 2019a; Xu et al. 2018), mobile sources (Yin et al. 2017a, b) and so on. These pollutants are closely related to GDP (Gross Domestic Product), population, energy consumption, and industrial waste gas emission, respectively. We intend to use the density of the above variables as the substitution variables of the components of $PM_{2.5}$. We collect the data of $PM_{2.5}$ and variables from 2001 to 2010. Based on the analysis of the spatial spillover effect of $PM_{2.5}$, the contribution degrees of different components to $PM_{2.5}$ growth will be discussed via the spatial panel data model. To predict the possible turning point in the $PM_{2.5}$ growth curve, a Kuznets curve will be built by virtue of $PM_{2.5}$ values and the density of per capita GDP variables.

In recent years, a great number of studies regarding factors affecting $PM_{2.5}$ concentration were conducted by scholars. To some extent, $PM_{2.5}$ pollution was closely related to natural factors (Liu et al. 2017b; Guo et al. 2017; Jin et al. 2019; Zhang et al. 2020a, b; Wang et al. 2016; Wei et al. 2020). For example, by utilizing the ground monitoring data of 366 cities in China and geographic weighted regression (GWR), Chen et al. (2020b) considered that the increase of temperature and wind speed resulted in the decline of $PM_{2.5}$ pollution. Based on geographically and temporally weighted regression model (GTWR), Liu et al. (2020) found that the enhancement of precipitation could reduce $PM_{2.5}$ in Southeast China, while in southern, central and western China, rainfall and $PM_{2.5}$ concentrations presented a positive relationship.

However, $PM_{2.5}$ pollution was ultimately caused by a series of socioeconomic factors. Economic development was the crucial factor that seriously affected haze pollution (Chen et al. 2018; Du et al. 2018; Gan et al. 2020). The relationship between $PM_{2.5}$ concentration and economic development presented an inverted U-shaped curve, demonstrating the existence of the Environmental Kuznets Curve (EKC) in China (Hao et al. 2016; Cheng et al. 2017; Ding et al. 2019). Based on a quantile regression approach, Xu and Lin (2018) found that owing to the differences in fixed-asset investment and export trade, the impact of economic development on $PM_{2.5}$ pollution was the highest in all the quantile provinces. The high speed of urbanization in China could affect $PM_{2.5}$ pollution as well (Zhu et al. 2019; Zou et al. 2020; Feng and Wang 2020). Wang et al. (2018a) and Wu et al. (2018) demonstrated the existence of an inverted U-shaped EKC between $PM_{2.5}$ and urbanization in whole China, but an N-shaped EKC pattern in the developed eastern region. Based on econometric models, Shi et al. (2019) discovered that urbanization had a significant positive impact on $PM_{2.5}$ concentration in both medium-sized city and very large-sized cities. Environmental regulations could also affect $PM_{2.5}$ pollution. Based on Generalized Method of Moments (GMM) method and provincial data, Zhang et al. (2020a, b) discovered that command-controlled regulations and economic-incentive regulations had nonlinear relationship with $PM_{2.5}$ pollution, and the regression results of voluntary-consciousness regulations were not statistically significant. Additionally, other factors including international trade (Liang et al. 2017), population density (Ding et al. 2019), coal consumption (Xie et al. 2020), industrial structure (Zhang et al. 2020a, b), technological progress (Chen et al. 2020a), air pollution control policies (Cai et al. 2018), income (Ji et al. 2018), foreign direct investment (Cheng et al. 2020), R&D (Wu et al. 2020a), local government behavior (Zhang et al. 2020a, b) and industrial agglomeration (Li et al. 2021; Lu et al. 2021) also resulted in severe $PM_{2.5}$ pollution in China. The joint effort of natural and socioeconomic factors brought about $PM_{2.5}$ pollution, and the relationship between each factor and $PM_{2.5}$ presented spatially heterogeneous (Wang et al. 2018b, 2019). This paper verifies more detailed factors that affect $PM_{2.5}$ to provide a more targeted reference for the government to implement policies concerning $PM_{2.5}$ reduction.

The empirical study of this paper is based on the spatial panel data model first proposed by Anselin (1988). Based on panel data model, the dependent variable and error term of spatial lag are introduced into the spatial panel data model. Besides, spatial correlation is included in the spatial panel data model which takes into consideration not only spatial correlation but also temporal factors. Thus, this model makes up for the deficiency of the traditional panel data model and is widely applied in the researches on environmental economics. Based on the provincial panel data in China and via the spatial fixed effect model, Zhu et al. (2010) and Zhang (2014) studied the spatial dependence relationship among industrial pollutants and the Environmental Kuznets Curve between these pollutants and GDP per capita. After testing the transnational Environmental Kuznets Curve model according to the spatial lag model, Maddison (2006) found that both the $SO_2$ emission amount per capita and the $NO_x$ emission amount per capita are affected by the emission from neighboring countries. Based on the spatial panel model, Hossein and Kaneko (2013) discovered that environmental quality of countries spreads spatially to their neighbors through the flowing of institutional quality of countries. Burnett et al. (2013) explored the relationship among $CO_2$ emission of states in U.S.A., economic activity, and other factors through spatial panel econometric model, and found that economic distance plays an important role in interstate $CO_2$ emission. Via empirical analysis of spatial panel econometric model, Kang et al. (2016) verified that the relationship between economic development and $CO_2$ emissions was an inverted N-shaped curve. By comparing three types of spatial regression models, Spatial Durbin Model (SDM) was ultimately employed by Wang et al. (2017a, b) to estimate the spatial dependence of industrial pollutants' emission intensities. Their findings showed that an apparent spatial spillover effect existed in almost all the industrial sectors in terms of water and air pollutant emission intensities. By utilizing STIRPAT model and spatial panel regression model, Zhang et al. (2017a) explored that one province's environmental policies could influence its neighbor's policy-enacting due to spatial spillover effect. Combining dynamic spatial panel model and remote sensing data, Zhou et al. (2018) demonstrated the existence of $CO_2$'s spatial correlation at the city level of China. Integrating Spatial Durbin model (SDM) with provincial data, Huang (2018) discovered that the increase of direct investment from foreign countries, popularity density and industrial pollution treatment investment could effectively cause a reduction in $SO_2$ emissions. Based on spatial panel data model, Li et al. (2020) found that the spatial spillover effect was greater than the direct effect in terms of China's air pollution. By using spatial econometric model, Lv and Li (2021) explored the relationship between financial development and $CO_2$ emissions. Their findings indicated that a country's financial development played a fundamental role in the reduction of $CO_2$ emissions, and being surrounded by countries with good financial development could be helpful to a country's environmental performance. Taking $SO_2$ and $CO_2$ as the research objects, these studies analyzed their spatial effect, spatial dependence and spatial heterogeneity. Similar to $SO_2$ and $CO_2$, $PM_{2.5}$ is the product of human life and characterized by spillover-proneness in space. For the past few years, some studies have touched upon the spatial spillover effect of $PM_{2.5}$ from the perspective of spatial econometrics at present. For example, Nan et al. (2019) found that $PM_{2.5}$ concentration between regions could significantly affect each other by using spatial dynamic model. In particular, $PM_{2.5}$ in regions with high concentrations was more likely to spread to surrounding areas. Li et al. (2019a) examined the effect of environmental regulations on $PM_{2.5}$ pollution through the results of static and dynamic spatial panel model. They found an obvious spatial spillover effect and regional differences between Eastern and Western China. Bonding spatial econometric model with geographical and temporal weighted regression (GTWR), Fu and Li (2020) explored the relationship between socioeconomic factors (e.g., renewable energy consumption ratio, per $CO_2$ emission, urban population ratio) and $PM_{2.5}$ pollution globally. Using spatial econometric model, and electing economic geography matrix as spatial weight, Zhang et al. (2020a, b) found a significant positive correlation between $PM_{2.5}$ concentrations in various provinces in China. The spatial distribution was characterized by agglomeration. Therefore, we use spatial panel data model to analyze the spatial concentration of $PM_{2.5}$ as well as the Environmental Kuznets Curve of $PM_{2.5}$.

Similar to the studies by Zhu et al. (2010), Zhang (2014), Maddison (2006) and Ma and Zhang (2014), the present study consists of three steps. First, the Moran's I index proposed by Moran (1950) was used to test global spatial correlation of $PM_{2.5}$ (Sect. 17.2). Second, to further study the formation factors of $PM_{2.5}$ and their influence degrees, variables closely related to $PM_{2.5}$ values were selected and spatial correlation between these variables and $PM_{2.5}$ values was explored via spatial econometric model. We found that $PGDP^D$ affects $PM_{2.5}$ most (Sect. 17.3). According to the above results, we further studied the relationship between $PGDP^D$ and $PM_{2.5}$ by using the Kuznets Curve, and then summarized the research results and prevention-control measures (Sect. 17.4).

## 17.2 Spatial Correlation Analysis of $PM_{2.5}$ Concentrations

### *17.2.1 Data*

China began collecting formal statistical data about $PM_{2.5}$ in 2012, and has put great effort into data collection since ever. At present, besides observation data (such as Abas et al. 2004; Hossein et al. 2013), annual average values of $PM_{2.5}$ from 2001 to 2010 offered by Battelle Memorial Institute and Center for International Earth Science Information Network have also been adopted by many scholars (Ma and Zhang 2014); For example, after studying and preliminarily estimating the concentration of inhalable particulate matter in provinces of China based on satellite data, they came up with a table of "Annual average population-weighted $PM_{2.5}$ concentrations in provinces, municipalities and autonomous regions of China in 2001–2010"

**Table 17.1** Moran's I values of population-weighted $PM_{2.5}$ values in different provinces of China from 2001 to 2010

| Year | Moran's I | Expected value | Std-err | Z-stat | *p*-value |
|---|---|---|---|---|---|
| 2001 | 0.453 | −0.035 | 0.111 | 4.373 | 0.001 |
| 2002 | 0.446 | −0.035 | 0.119 | 4.026 | 0.001 |
| 2003 | 0.431 | −0.035 | 0.118 | 3.930 | 0.001 |
| 2004 | 0.425 | −0.035 | 0.119 | 3.851 | 0.001 |
| 2005 | 0.466 | −0.035 | 0.118 | 4.214 | 0.001 |
| 2006 | 0.429 | −0.035 | 0.112 | 4.138 | 0.001 |
| 2007 | 0.484 | −0.035 | 0.115 | 4.503 | 0.001 |
| 2008 | 0.444 | −0.035 | 0.117 | 4.111 | 0.001 |
| 2009 | 0.412 | −0.035 | 0.114 | 3.848 | 0.001 |
| 2010 | 0.427 | −0.035 | 0.117 | 3.893 | 0.001 |

*Note* $E(I) = -1/(n - 1)$, $n = 30$ (Chongqing and Sichuan are combined, and Hong Kong, Macao and Taiwan are excluded); 999 times of simulation by the Monte Carlo method

(obtained from Ref. (2012), and see Table A1). In this table, the $PM_{2.5}$ concentration index is indicated by the average concentration of exposure to air pollution in each province, and the population is weighted. Namely, each province is divided into certain grid regions ($0.1 \times 0.1$), or approximately 10 km × 10 km at mid-latitudes. Then, with the proportion of residents within a grid region to the total population of each province and municipality as the weight, the average population-weighted concentration of exposure to air pollution in each grid region is calculated. The population-weighted value fully considers different situations in sparsely populated low-polluted areas and densely populated high-polluted areas, pays more attention to the actual effects of fine particulate matter on residents, and is in line with Ma and Zhang (2014) and Wu et al. (2016a).

Therefore, population-weight $PM_{2.5}$ values in different provinces are adopted in this study, without considering Taiwan, Hong Kong and Macao, and combining Chongqing and Sichuan as one region due to data availability. Thereby, we use data of $PM_{2.5}$ in 30 administrative regions in 10 years.

### *17.2.2 Present Status of $PM_{2.5}$ Concentrations*

Haze pollution is quite severe in China. Judging from population-weighted values of $PM_{2.5}$, the average $PM_{2.5}$ values vary between 24.475 and 29.975 in China from 2001 to 2010. Fluctuations in $PM_{2.5}$ values are observed, but only at a modest rate. The value is the largest (29.975) in 2007 and the smallest (24.475) in 2010. Nevertheless, the smallest value is still higher than the air quality standard of 10 set by the WHO (World Health Organization). Only the $PM_{2.5}$ values of three regions are lower than the air quality standard. They are Hainan, Heilongjiang, and Tibet, which have the

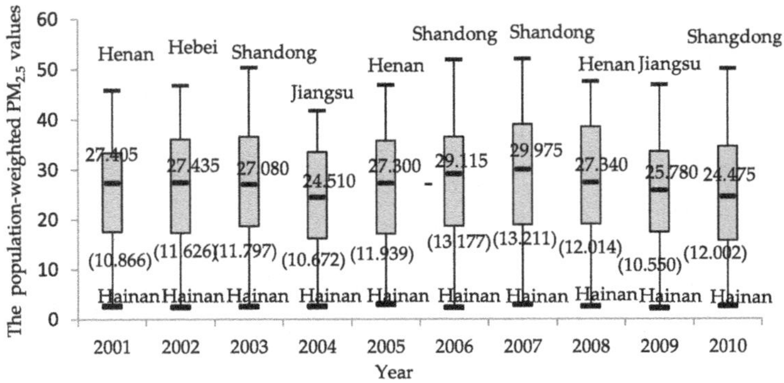


**Note:** On the top of each boxplot is the province with the largest population-weighted $PM_{2.5}$ value in a year, Below each boxplot is the province with the smallest population-weighted $PM_{2.5}$ value in the same year, The horizontal line in each boxplot represents the mean population-weighted $PM_{2.5}$ value in this year. Besides, the values in the brackets are the standard deviations of population-weighted $PM_{2.5}$ values in provinces from 2001 to 2010.

**Fig. 17.1** Boxplots of population-weighted $PM_{2.5}$ values in provinces of China from 2001 to 2010

lowest values for 10 years, 8 years, and 4 years, respectively. The $PM_{2.5}$ values of other provinces are all higher than the standard, among which Shandong, Henan, Jiangsu and Hebei have the highest values (approximately being 50, which is five times higher than the air quality standard) for 4 years, 3 years, 2 years and 1 year respectively. These values indicate severe air pollution. Those provinces are located in Central and Eastern China (Fig. 17.1). We can observe from the figures in brackets that,[1] the standard deviations of population-weighted $PM_{2.5}$ values in provinces from 2001 to 2010 fluctuate slightly. The maximum value and the minimum value are 13.211 (in 2007) and 10.550 (in 2009) respectively.

The $PM_{2.5}$ values exhibit an obvious spatial concentration phenomenon. Han et al. (2014) applied the annual average $PM_{2.5}$ values from 2001 and 2006 offered by Battelle Memorial Institute and Center for International Earth Science Information Network. They found that the $PM_{2.5}$ values in 350 prefecture-level cities of China are distributed in two bands[2]: one starts from the North of Hebei, passes through Beijing, Shaanxi, the Northwest of Henan and the South of Shaanxi, and ends at the Southeast of Sichuan; the other starts from Shanghai and Zhejiang in the East, passes through the South of Anhui, Henan, and Jiangxi and arrives at Guangxi and Guangdong. However, our findings are somewhat different: we found that the $PM_{2.5}$ values in different regions are distributed in blocks and highly agglomerated geographically. In other words, the regions with high $PM_{2.5}$ values (larger than the average value) are located in Central and Eastern China to form a large block area. The area covers

[1]The values in the brackets are the standard deviations of population-weighted $PM_{2.5}$ values of provinces from 2001 to 2010.

[2]Though $PM_{2.5}$ concentrations in 350 prefecture-level cities can be obtained, the social and economic data of these 350 cities are not available. Thus, the data of prefecture-level cities are not adopted in this paper.

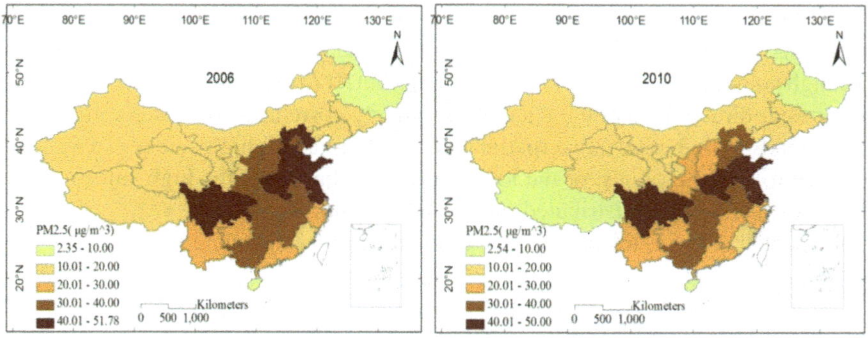


(a) (b)

**Fig. 17.2** Distribution maps of $PM_{2.5}$ values in different provinces of China in 2006 and in 2010

14 to 17 provinces. The population sizes and GDP values in these provinces account for three-fourths of the total amount in China, nearly covering all economically-developed provinces of China. At the same time, populations in these provinces are exposed to the threat of haze. The geographic distribution of $PM_{2.5}$ values in different provinces in 2006 and in 2010 is shown in Fig. 17.2a, b, respectively.

According to the above research, $PM_{2.5}$ values are obviously distributed in blocks, indicating that $PM_{2.5}$ concentrations are in a spatial correlation. Then, the spatial correlation degree is measured by spatial econometrics.

### *17.2.3 Global Spatial Correlation*

Toble (1970) proposed the first law of geography, holding that all things are spatially correlated. A shorter distance means a higher correlation degree; meanwhile, a longer distance means a lower correlation degree. The population distribution and economic development in China also exhibit spatial concentration. Accordingly, $PM_{2.5}$ values may share this feature. In the present study, Moran's I index proposed by Moran (1950) is adopted to test the global spatial correlation of $PM_{2.5}$ values. The calculation formula is:

$$I = \frac{n\sum_{i=1}^{n}\sum_{j=1}^{n} w_{ij}(A_i - \bar{A})(A_j - \bar{A})}{\sum_{i=1}^{n}\sum_{j=1}^{n} w_{ij}(A_i - \bar{A})^2} \tag{17.1}$$

where $n$ is the number of subject provinces, a total of 30 administrative regions, excluding Hong Kong, Macao, and Taiwan and combining Sichuan and Chongqing as a whole; $i$ and $j$ refer to each province; $A_i$ and $A_j$ refer to the population-weighted $PM_{2.5}$ values in the $i$th province and the $j$th province, respectively; $I$ is the index value used to measure the global spatial correlation. $I$ varies between $-1$ and 1.

If $I$ is positive, $A_i$ and $A_j$ change in the same direction and the data are positively correlated. A closer value to 1 corresponds to higher positive spatial autocorrelation. The high values (low values) of $PM_{2.5}$ are adjacent. If $I$ is negative, $A_i$ and $A_j$ change in opposite directions and the data are negatively correlated. A closer value to $-1$ corresponds to higher negative spatial autocorrelation. The high values of $PM_{2.5}$ are adjacent to the low values, or the low values are adjacent to the high values. If $I$ is close to 0, the data are distributed randomly without correlation.

$w_{ij}$, which refers to the spatial weight matrix, can be calculated as

$$w_{ij} = \begin{cases} 1, \text{ when provinces } i \text{ and } j \text{ have a common border or point} \\ 0, \text{ when provinces } i \text{ and } j \text{ have no common border or point} \\ 0, \text{ when } i = j \end{cases} \tag{17.2}$$

Adjacency means two regions have a common border or point. When calculating the spatial weight matrix, Sichuan and Chongqing are combined into one region. The global and local spatial correlations are calculated with GeoDA1.4.0.

From 2001 to 2010, the Moran's $I$ values in regions vary between the relatively stable values of 0.412 and 0.484, indicating that the $PM_{2.5}$ values in these provinces exhibit a positive spatial autocorrelation. In other words, the higher the $PM_{2.5}$ value of a province, the higher that of its adjacent province, and vice versa. The concomitant probabilities (p) of Moran's I are all smaller than 0.05, which suggests statistical significance.

Moran's $I$ value is the highest (0.484) in 2007 and the lowest (0.412) in 2009, which is basically close to the years with the highest and lowest average $PM_{2.5}$ values. Thereby, we can infer that these sequences exhibit a certain significant correlation at the level of 10%. $PM_{2.5}$ and Moran's I are positive correlation. The years with high average $PM_{2.5}$ values also have high Moran's values (0.412–0.484). As Moran's I is a measure of spatial autocorrelation, in the years with high average $PM_{2.5}$ values, the spatial correlation is strong. By contrast, in the years with low average values of $PM_{2.5}$, the spatial correlation is weak (Table 17.1).

The scatter diagram of Moran's I values in different regions from 2001 to 2010 can be divided into four quadrants with the average value as the axis. The first and third quadrants indicate high–high and low–low positive correlations, respectively. The second and fourth quadrants indicate low–high and high–low negative correlations, respectively. According to the scatter diagram of 2006 (Fig. 17.3a), the Moran's I values in about 15 regions are in the first quadrant every year, indicating large $PM_{2.5}$ values in spatial concentration. 11 regions are in the third quadrant, which indicates small $PM_{2.5}$ values in spatial concentration. 4 regions are in the second and fourth quadrants, showing negatively correlated $PM_{2.5}$ values not in any spatial concentration. Overall, the $PM_{2.5}$ values in most regions are in spatial concentration. In other words, the regions with high (or low) $PM_{2.5}$ values are adjacent (See Fig. 17.3a, b for details).

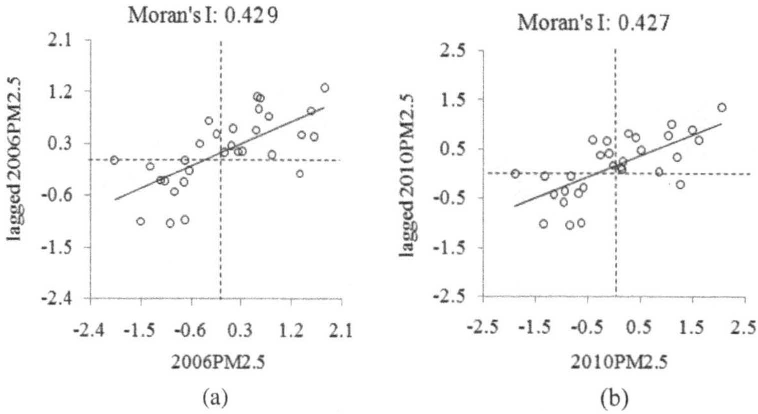


**Fig. 17.3** Moran's I scatter diagrams of $PM_{2.5}$ values in different regions in 2006 and in 2010. *Note* The vertical axis is used for the spatially averaged neighboring values and the horizontal for the value for the area at the center of the spatial average

### *17.2.4 Local Spatial Correlation*

A Moran's I scatter diagram can test overall agglomeration through local spatial autocorrelation, but it cannot test whether $PM_{2.5}$ values in some local regions exhibit agglomeration or not. Accordingly, a local indicator of spatial association (LISA) proposed by Anselin (1995) is adopted to test the local spatial autocorrelation of $PM_{2.5}$ values in different regions. The calculation formula of LISA of the area $i$ is:

$$I_i = \frac{(A_i - \bar{A})}{S^2} \sum_{j \neq i}^{n} w_{ij}(A_i - \bar{A}) \tag{17.3}$$

where $n$, $i$, and $j$ mean the same mentioned above; $S^2$ refers to the variance of population-weighted $PM_{2.5}$ values in 30 provinces; $I_i$ is the index value used to measure the spatial correlation of Area $i$. If $I_i > 0$, the high $PM_{2.5}$ values (or low values) in different parts of Area $i$ are adjacent. In other words, regions with high or low $PM_{2.5}$ values are agglomerated spatially. The spatial concentration diagrams of local $PM_{2.5}$ values in 2006 and in 2010 are shown below (Fig. 17.4a, b). Each diagram passes the test of significance level of 5% and is obtained after Monte Carlo simulations.

According to the above diagrams and the LISA diagram of other years, the $PM_{2.5}$ values in most regions of China exhibit obvious high–high or low–low spatial concentration. The provinces with high values are mostly concentrated in central and Eastern China, including Shandong, Henan, Anhui, and Hubei. The regions with low values are mostly concentrated in northwestern, north and northeastern of China. These regions include Xinjiang, Inner Mongolia, Heilongjiang, and Jilin. Table 17.2 lists the regions with high–high or low–low $PM_{2.5}$ agglomeration from 2001 to 2010. The

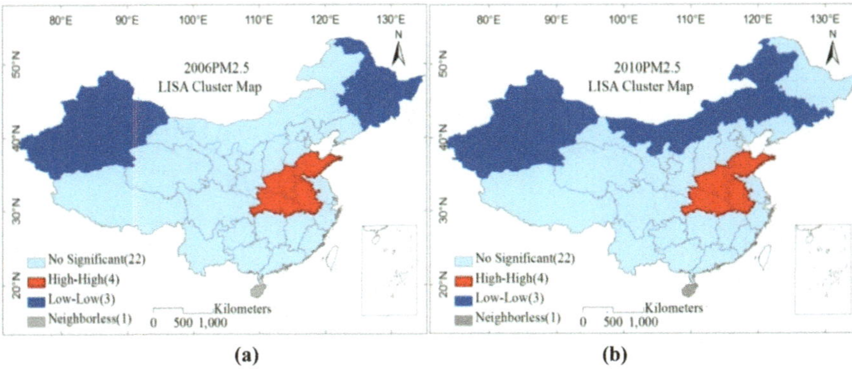


**Fig. 17.4** Local agglomeration diagrams of the $PM_{2.5}$ values in different regions of China in 2006 and 2010

**Table 17.2** Provinces with high–high or low–low spatial concentration in China from 2001 to 2010

| Year | High–high | Low–low |
|---|---|---|
| 2001 | Hubei, Henan, Shandong, Anhui | Xinjiang, Jilin, Heilongjiang |
| 2002 | Hubei, Henan, Shandong, Anhui, Tianjin | Xinjiang, Jilin |
| 2003 | Hubei, Henan, Shandong, Anhui, Hebei | Xinjiang |
| 2004 | Hubei, Henan, Shandong, Anhui, Hunan | Xinjiang, Jilin, Heilongjiang, Inner Mongolia |
| 2005 | Hubei, Henan, Shandong, Anhui, Hunan | Xinjiang, Jilin, Heilongjiang, Inner Mongolia |
| 2006 | Hubei, Henan, Shandong, Anhui | Xinjiang, Jilin, Heilongjiang |
| 2007 | Hubei, Henan, Shandong, Anhui | Xinjiang, Jilin, Heilongjiang, Inner Mongolia |
| 2008 | Hubei, Henan, Shandong, Anhui, Tianjin | Xinjiang, Jilin |
| 2009 | Hubei, Henan, Shandong, Anhui | Xinjiang, Jilin |
| 2010 | Hubei, Henan, Shandong, Anhui | Xinjiang, Jilin, Heilongjiang |

results pass the test of significance level of 5% and are obtained after Monte Carlo simulations.

The $PM_{2.5}$ values show obvious spatial concentration considering the following points. First, the provinces in central and Eastern China are located in the East Asian summer monsoon area with meteorological conditions of precipitation and wind speed/direction. In January 2013, hazy weather occurred in Eastern China (Anhui, and Shandong, Henan, Hubei) with strong intensity, great duration and large scope. The meteorological factor can explain the variance of diurnal variation of more than two thirds of hazy weather, and the variance contribution reaches 0.68 (Zhang et al. 2013). Second, central and eastern China has a dense population and a well-developed economy, leading to large waste gas emission, automobile exhaust and coal consumption, which explains high $PM_{2.5}$ values (Table 17.3). Shandong, Henan, Hubei and Anhui with high $PM_{2.5}$ values are considered as examples in the discussion below. The population sizes per $km^2$ in these provinces are many times larger than the average value of the country (obtained through dividing the sum of the total by the country's total area, the same below): Shandong (623 per $km^2$), Henan (563 per $km^2$), Anhui (426 per $km^2$), and Hubei (308 per $km^2$). The GDPs per $km^2$ are also more than two times larger than the average value of the country: Shandong (2546.809 ten thousand yuan per $km^2$), Henan (1382.776 ten thousand yuan per $km^2$), Anhui (884.705 ten thousand yuan per $km^2$), and Hubei (858.935 ten thousand yuan per $km^2$). In addition, the numbers of civilian cars per $km^2$ of these four provinces are in the top 50% of the country: Shandong (45.896 per $km^2$), Henan (23.936 per $km^2$), Anhui (15.019 per $km^2$), and Hubei (11.162 per $km^2$). Coal consumptions per $km^2$ are two times larger than the average value of the country (455.486 tons per $km^2$): Shandong (2427.041 tons per $km^2$), Henan (1559.880 tons per $km^2$), Anhui (957.459 tons per $km^2$), and Hubei (724.598 tons per $km^2$). Third, Jilin has a low $PM_{2.5}$ value in 2010, a population density of 147 per $km^2$, a GDP of 462.520 ten thousand yuan per $km^2$, a car number of 8.158 per $km^2$, and a coal consumption of 511.348 tons per $km^2$. These values are close to the national average and less than half of those of Anhui. Fourth, Ma and Zhang (2014) believed that haze in China is agglomerated in central and eastern China, which is related closely to their similar industrial structure. Arguably, it is difficult to obtain a clean-type, high-quality innovation-driven industry in the short term. Therefore, under the strong GDP examination by the central government, these provinces have to prioritize the manufacturing industry characterized by three highs (i.e., high pollution, high emission, and high consumption). Moreover, investors tend to choose central and eastern provinces with rich resources, large population and convenient transport for survival. To attract investors, the local governments dominantly or recessively race to relax the restrictions on the environment, which further intensifies the agglomeration of haze in these provinces.

## 17.3 Analysis of Spatial Influential Factors of $PM_{2.5}$ Concentrations

To further study the factors that contribute to $PM_{2.5}$ concentrations and the degrees of influence of different factors, the variables closely related to $PM_{2.5}$ concentrations are selected based on the previous analysis for the empirical analysis of the correlation between these variables and the $PM_{2.5}$ value.

**Table 17.3** Socio-economic indicator of provinces in China in 2010

| Province | $POP^D$ | $GDP^D$ | $COAC^D$ | $CAR^D$ |
|---|---|---|---|---|
| Shanghai | 3656 | 27247.587 | 9266.648 | 276.814 |
| Beijing | 1168 | 8400.941 | 1567.497 | 267.564 |
| Tianjin | 1150 | 8163.24 | 4251.918 | 139.974 |
| Jiangsu | 767 | 4037.571 | 2251.509 | 53.684 |
| Zhejiang | 534 | 2717.873 | 1367.633 | 53.149 |
| Guangdong | 580 | 2556.281 | 887.979 | 43.459 |
| Shandong | 623 | 2546.809 | 2427.041 | 45.896 |
| Henan | 563 | 1382.776 | 1559.88 | 23.936 |
| Liaoning | 230 | 1265.063 | 1158.905 | 20.310 |
| Fujian | 304 | 1214.931 | 579.245 | 16.247 |
| Hebei | 383 | 1086.535 | 1463.224 | 26.259 |
| Chongqing | 351 | 963.012 | 777.266 | 13.888 |
| Anhui | 426 | 884.705 | 957.459 | 15.019 |
| Hubei | 308 | 858.935 | 724.598 | 11.162 |
| Hunan | 310 | 757.222 | 534.624 | 9.965 |
| Hainan | 256 | 607.206 | 190.353 | 11.543 |
| Shanxi | 229 | 588.667 | 1910.755 | 15.86 |
| Jiangxi | 267 | 565.943 | 374.026 | 8.229 |
| Shaanxi | 182 | 492.387 | 566.076 | 9.272 |
| Jilin | 147 | 462.52 | 511.348 | 8.158 |
| Guangxi | 195 | 405.518 | 263.001 | 6.443 |
| Sichuan | 167 | 356.993 | 239.310 | 7.374 |
| Guizhou | 198 | 261.486 | 619.778 | 6.577 |
| Ningxia | 95 | 254.465 | 868.211 | 6.253 |
| Heilongjiang | 84 | 227.981 | 268.671 | 4.283 |
| Yunnan | 120 | 188.473 | 243.919 | 6.103 |
| Inner Mongolia | 21 | 98.664 | 228.267 | 1.588 |
| Gansu | 56 | 90.686 | 118.609 | 1.872 |
| Xinjiang | 17 | 32.756 | 48.833 | 0.766 |
| Qinghai | 8 | 18.696 | 17.592 | 0.429 |

*Note* (1) Indices of population and GDP are obtained from *China Statistical Yearbook* (2011), index of coal consumption comes from *China Energy Statistical Yearbook* (2011), and index of civilian cars is from *China Automotive Industry Yearbook* (2011). (2) $POP^D$: Density of population (per $km^2$). $GDP^D$: Density of GDP (ten thousand yuan per $km^2$). $COAC^D$: Density of coal consumptions (ton per $km^2$). $CAR^D$: Density of civilian cars (per $km^2$)

### 17.3.1 Data

We perform a quantitative analysis of the data in the 30 regions from 2001 to 2010. As mentioned previously, the major sources of $PM_{2.5}$ include industrial waste gas (dust), life waste gas (dust), vehicle exhaust (dust) and coal dust. The number of vehicles is difficult to obtain. On the one hand, the number of public cars cannot be obtained. On the other hand, though the number of civilian cars since 2005 is available for Chinese people, the short data sequence is not representative. As a result, this variable is not included in the analysis. In this study, population size, per capital GDP, coal consumption, and industrial waste gas emission are considered as the source variables of $PM_{2.5}$. The data of $PM_{2.5}$ values are obtained from Battelle Memorial Institute and CIESIN (2013). Those of population size, per capita GDP, and industrial waste gas emission are obtained from *China Statistical Yearbook,* and those of coal consumption are obtained from *China Energy Statistical Yearbook*. To reduce the heteroscedasticity with logarithmic values of variables, the logarithmic values of independent variables and dependent variables are adopted. The regression of the spatial panel data is calculated by Matlab2010a.

In addition, with the values in 2000 as the base year, the density of per capita GDP ($PGDP^D$) in different provinces are deflated according to the inflation rate with yuan per $km^2$ as the unit; the density of population size ($POP^D$) is measured in per $km^2$; the density of industrial waste gas emission in different provinces ($GWAS^D$) is measured in ten thousand normal $m^3$ per $km^2$; and the density of coal consumption ($COAC^D$) is measured in ton per $km^2$.

### 17.3.2 Model Setting

The $POP^D$, $PGDP^D$, $GWAS^D$, and $COAC^D$ in these provinces in the past years may have multicollinearity, which leads to information redundancy, and the multi-index multicollinearity of the spatial panel data have not been solved by Lesage and Pace (2014). Thus, regression is conducted between the above variables and the $PM_{2.5}$ value to identify the relationship between them.

(1) Traditional panel data model. The basic model is

$$lnPM_{2.5it} = \alpha_0 + \alpha_1 lnX_{it} + \mu_{it} \tag{17.4}$$

where $i$ refers to the province, $i = 1, 2, \ldots, 29$, $t$ refers to the year, $t = 1, 2, \ldots, 10$, $lnPM_{2.5it}$ refers to the $PM_{2.5}$ values in different provinces from 2001 to 2010, $lnX_{it}$ refers to $lnPOP^D_{it}$, $lnPGDP^D_{it}$, $lnCOAC^D_{it}$, $lnGWAS^D_{it}$, $\alpha_0$ refers to the intercept term; $\alpha_1$ refers to the coefficients of independent variables, and $\mu_{it}$ refers to the random error term, which could be decomposed as follows:

$$\mu_{it} = \delta_{it} + \vartheta_{it} + \varepsilon_{it} \tag{17.5}$$

where $\delta_{it}$ and $\vartheta_{it}$ refer to the random perturbations of time effect and individual effect, respectively, and $\varepsilon_{it}$ refers to the random error term. OLS (ordinary least squares) can be used for parameter estimation.

(2) Spatial lag panel data model. After introducing the spatial variable, the spatial error model assumes that the random error term $\varepsilon_{it}$ follows a normal distribution. Equation (17.4) can be rewritten as the spatial lag panel data model.

$$\begin{aligned} ln\mathrm{PM}_{2.5it} &= \alpha_0 + \alpha_1 lnX_{it} + \rho \sum W ln\mathrm{PM}_{2.5it} \\ &+ \delta_{it} + \vartheta_{it} + \varepsilon_{it}(\varepsilon_{it} \sim \mathrm{N}(0, \sigma_{it}^2)) \end{aligned} \quad (17.6)$$

where $W$ refers to the spatial weight vector matrix, $\sum W ln\mathrm{PM}_{2.5it}$ refers to the overall situation of $\mathrm{PM}_{2.5}$ in the areas around Province $i$ in Year $t$, $\rho$ is the degree of the spatial spillover effect, indicating the correlation coefficient of $\mathrm{PM}_{2.5}$ in the areas around Province $i$ with that in Province $i$ in Year $t$, $\sigma_{it}^2$ is the variance of $\varepsilon_{it}$.

(3) Spatial error panel data model. If the disturbance term shows spatial correlation, $\varepsilon_{it}$ does not necessarily follow a normal distribution. Equation (17.6) can be rewritten as the spatial error panel data model.

$$\begin{aligned} ln\mathrm{PM}_{2.5it} &= \alpha_0 + \alpha_1 lnX_{it} + \delta_{it} + \vartheta_{it} + \varepsilon_{it}, \\ \varepsilon_{it} &= \lambda \sum W\varepsilon_{it} + \varphi_{it}, \varphi_{it} \sim \mathrm{N}(0, \sigma_{it}^2) \end{aligned} \quad (17.7)$$

where $\varphi_{it}$ refers to the random error term of $\varepsilon_{it}$, which follows a normal distribution, and $\lambda$ is the spatial autocorrelation coefficient of $\varepsilon_{it}$.

GMM or ML (Anselin and Getis 1992) is used in estimating Eqs. (17.6) and (17.7). The empirical results are given and explained below.

### 17.3.3 Results of Empirical Analysis

To analyze the influence of different independent variables on the $\mathrm{PM}_{2.5}$ value and their contributions, five variables in 30 regions of China (excluding Hong Kong, Macao, Taiwan, and combining Chongqing and Sichuan) from 2001 to 2010 are selected to establish the spatial panel regression model. The dependent variable is $ln\mathrm{PM}_{2.5it}$, and the independent variables are $ln\mathrm{POP}_{it}^{\mathrm{D}}$, $ln\mathrm{PGDP}_{it}^{\mathrm{D}}$, $ln\mathrm{COAC}_{it}^{\mathrm{D}}$, $ln\mathrm{GWAS}_{it}^{\mathrm{D}}$. On the basis of Models (17.4), (17.6), and (17.7), the ML method is adopted. The results calculated by Matlab2010a are shown in Table 17.4.

When setting the threshold value of selecting the random effect or the fixed effect by Hausman test with Matlab2010a, $p > 0.05$ implies rejection of spatial fixed effect (Table 17.4). The Hausman test values of Equations (a) and (c) show that the random

**Table 17.4** The regression results of spatial panel data

| Parameter | | Independent variable and model | | | |
|---|---|---|---|---|---|
| | | Equation a: independent variable $lnPOP_{it}^{D}$ | Equation b: independent variable $lnPGDP_{it}^{D}$ | Equation c: independent variable $lnCOAC_{it}^{D}$ | Equation d: independent variable $lnGWAS_{it}^{D}$ |
| | | Spatial lag (random effect) | Spatial error (fixed effect) | Spatial lag (random effect) | Spatial error(fixed effect) |
| $\alpha_0$ | | 0.311* (0.088) | | 0.625*** (0.000) | |
| $\alpha_1$ | | 0.072** (0.016) | 0.180** (0.027) | 0.008 (0.439) | 0.019 (0.233) |
| $\rho$ | | 0.776*** (0.000) | | 0.781 (0.000) | |
| $\Lambda$ | | | 0.793*** (0.000) | | 0.801*** (0.000) |
| $R^2$ | | 0.990 | 0.978 | 0.990 | 0.977 |
| Log likelihood | | 314.179 | 413.469 | 312.143 | 411.735 |
| Random/fixed effect selection | Hausman test | −15.457*** (0.000) | −2.614 (0.270) | 6.964*** (0.031) | −3.289 (0.193) |
| | LR-test | 739.722*** (0.000) | 820.478*** (0.000) | 779.667*** (0.000) | 847.544*** (0.000) |

*Note* (1) *, **, and ***indicate significance at the levels of 10%, 5% and 1%, respectively; (2) The data in brackets are the adjoint p value. (3) Equation a: $lnPM_{2.5it} = \alpha_0 + \alpha_1 lnPOP_{it}^{D} + \rho\sum WlnPM_{2.5it} + \delta_{it} + \vartheta_{it} + \varepsilon_{it}$. (4) Equation b: $lnPM_{2.5it} = \alpha_0 + \alpha_1 lnPGDP_{it}^{D} + \delta_{it} + \vartheta_{it} + \varepsilon_{it}$. (5) Equation c: $lnPM_{2.5it} = \alpha_0 + \alpha_1 lnCOAC_{it}^{D} + \rho\sum WlnPM_{2.5it} + \delta_{it} + \vartheta_{it} + \varepsilon_{it}$. (6) Equation d: $lnPM_{2.5it} = \alpha_0 + \alpha_1 lnGWAS_{it}^{D} + \delta_{it} + \vartheta_{it} + \varepsilon_{it}$

effect model is desirable. The Hausman test values of Equations (b) and (d) show that the fixed effect model is recommendable.

According to the equations in Table 17.4, both $\rho$ and $\lambda$ are positive, which indicate that $PM_{2.5}$ has spatial spillover effect. In Equations (a) and (c), $\rho$ are 0.776, 0.781 respectively, which indicate that every 1% increase in the $PM_{2.5}$ value in the surrounding areas will cause the $PM_{2.5}$ value in the local place to increase by 0.776% and 0.781% respectively. In Equations (b) and (d), $\lambda$ is 0.793, 0.801, which indicates that the residual error term of $PM_{2.5}$ in the surrounding areas significantly affects that in the local place, with the residual error term referred to the factors except independent variables ($lnGWAS_{it}^{D}$, $lnPGDP_{it}^{D}$) that determine dependent variables; $\alpha_1$ shows that the factors such as the density of population size and per capita GDP are positive spatially correlated with $PM_{2.5}$ value. Meanwhile, the density of coal consumption and waste gas emission has no significant impact on the $PM_{2.5}$ value.

According to Equations (a) and (b), every 1% increase in the logarithmic values of the density of population size and per capita GDP will cause the logarithmic value of $PM_{2.5}$ to increase by 0.072% and 0.180% respectively. Among these variables, the density of per capita GDP has significant influence on $PM_{2.5}$. Thus, a higher density of per capital GDP in a region corresponds to a larger $PM_{2.5}$ value. However, according to Equations (c) and (d), the influence of the density of coal consumption and waste gas emission on $PM_{2.5}$ is not significant. This shows the following implications. First, the $PM_{2.5}$ value is affected by the density of the total amount rather than the economic structural factor. For example, the coefficients of the indicators ($POP^D$, $PGDP^D$) that represent the density of total amount are large and significant, whereas those of the indicators ($GWAS^D$, and $COAC^D$) that represent the density of structural factors are not significant. This suggests that per capita GDP composition, production mode, and people's consumption and lifestyles be adjusted and systematically designed to realize the change in the mode of economic growth. Second, the effect of the direct sources (waste gas emission and coal consumption) on $PM_{2.5}$ becomes insignificant because of the spatial spillover effect. According to Equation (c), the density of coal consumption is not a significant source indicator of $PM_{2.5}$ due to the spatial spillover effect of $PM_{2.5}$ in surrounding areas. According to Equation (d), the coefficient of another important source indicator of $PM_{2.5}$ (i.e., the density of waste gas emission) is also not significant because of the spatial spillover effect of society, economy, technology and other error elements in different regions.

Considering that the density of per capita GDP shows the greatest influence on $PM_{2.5}$, we use Kuznets curve to further study the relationship between $PGDP^D$ and $PM_{2.5}$. The steps and test are the same as earlier. Equations (17.4), (17.6), and (17.7) are consistent, but the independent variables are changed to $lnPGDP_{it}^D$ and $(lnPGDP_{it}^D)^2$. The parameter test shows that the spatial lag panel data model with the fixed effect should be adopted. The results are as follows:

$$lnPM_{2.5it} = \begin{matrix} -0.355lnPGDP_{it}^D & +0.034(lnPGDP_{it}^D)^2 & +0.789\sum WlnPM_{2.5it} \\ (0.025) & (0.009) & (0.000) \end{matrix} \tag{17.8}$$

The values in brackets are the concomitant probability of the parameter. $R^2 = 0.992$; Log likelihood = 415.323; LR-test = 984.505 ($P$-value = 0).

Thus, without considering the spatial lag term $\sum WlnPM_{2.5it}$ of the dependent variable $lnPM_{2.5it}$, a quadratic equation of one unknown between $lnPM_{2.5}$ and $lnGDP$ in the positive U shape is formulated. The $PM_{2.5}$ value in the surrounding significantly influences that in the local place with the coefficient of 0.789, implying that every 1% increase in the logarithmic value of $PM_{2.5}$ in the surrounding will increase that in the local region by 0.789%.

From the curve, the slope equation of $lnPM_{2.5it}$ to $lnGDP_{it}^D$ is:

$$\frac{\partial\, lnPM_{2.5it}}{\partial\, lnPGDP_{it}^D} = -0.355 + 0.068lnPGDP_{it}^D \tag{17.9}$$

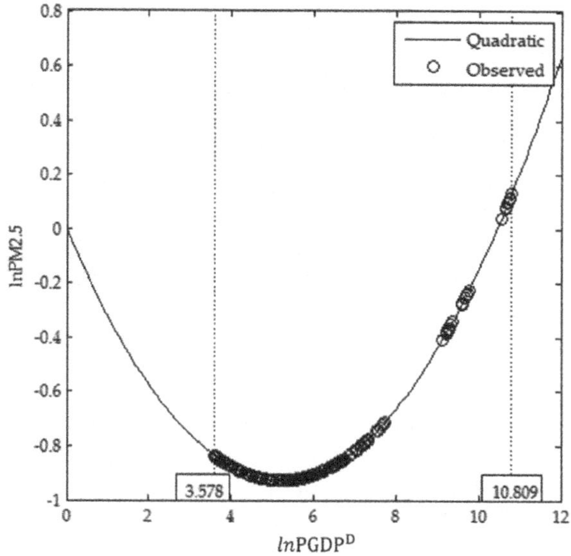


**Fig. 17.5** Curve relationship between $lnPM_{2.5}$ and $lnPGDP^D$

From the above formula, the $PM_{2.5}$ value is the lowest when the logarithmic value of the $PGDP^D$ is 5.221 (the $PGDP^D$ value is 185.043 yuan per $km^2$). From 2001 to 2010, the regions reaching the lowest point of the curve are Guangxi (from 2001 to 2004) and Guizhou (2007, 2009). In Fig. 17.4a, b, these regions have low $lnPM_{2.5}$ values and their spatial correlations are insignificant, which implicitly implies to some degree that social structure, industrial structure and consumption trends in these provinces are relatively logistically structured and of help in reducing the emission of $PM_{2.5}$.

The part between 3.578 and 10.809 in Fig. 17.5 shows that the curve section of $lnPM_{2.5it}$ and $lnPGDP_{it}^D$ is in different areas from 2001 to 2010. Therefore, if current trends continue, with the steady growth of the $PGDP^D$ in different areas, the $PM_{2.5}$ value will also rapidly increase. The so-called inverted U-shape inflection point does not appear. Hence, the rapid growth trend of $PM_{2.5}$ will be difficult to curb if the existing mode of economic growth is not changed fundamentally and the environmental pollution is not effectively controlled. In fact, the haze pollution with $PM_{2.5}$ as the representative continuously occurred at a large scale in different parts of China from 2011 and 2014 (Sun et al. 2016). The pollution is particularly serious in Northern, Central and Eastern China, which further verifies the conclusions of the present study.

## 17.4 Concluding Remarks

In recent years, the air pollution in China hasn't been improved fundamentally. The main reason lies in that there lacks adequate researches on the characteristics and impact factors of spatial concentration and spatial spillover. Thus, effective prevention-control plans cannot be made in time. This study has facilitated the overall and local spatial correlation analyses between $PM_{2.5}$ values in different provinces of China and variables indicating the sources of $PM_{2.5}$. These variables consist of the density of population size, per capita GDP, coal consumption, and industrial waste gas emission. Afterwards, the spatial panel data model has been built. We have the following concluding remarks:

(1) $PM_{2.5}$ pollution in China is increasingly grave. The $PM_{2.5}$ value each year is two to three times greater than the air quality standard of the WHO. The pollution concentrates in Central and Eastern China in blocks, covering 17 regions which accounts for 75% of the total population size and GDP of China.

(2) The $PM_{2.5}$ values in China show a significant spatial correlation. The regions with high $PM_{2.5}$ are agglomerated in masses with severe pollution, such as Hubei, Henan, Shandong, and Anhui. These regions had large population size, GDP, coal consumption, and number of civilian cars among all the provinces in China. The regions with low $PM_{2.5}$ are also agglomerated in masses. These provinces include Xinjiang, Jilin, Heilongjiang, and Inner Mongolia. The indicator values in these provinces are small.

(3) There shows spatial spillover effect in $PM_{2.5}$ pollution. A 1% increase in the $PM_{2.5}$ values of neighboring provinces will lead to a 0.78% increase in that of one province.

(4) The $PM_{2.5}$ value is affected by the total amount indicators. The density of the total amount indicators per capita GDP and population size significantly influences the $PM_{2.5}$ value, in which every 1% increase in the logarithmic values of $POP^D$ and $PGDP^D$, causing the logarithmic value of $PM_{2.5}$ to increase by 0.072% and 0.180% respectively. Both people's lifestyle and mode of per capita GDP growth influence $PM_{2.5}$.

(5) An upward U-shaped relationship is observed between $lnPM_{2.5}$ and $lnPGDP^D$. The $PM_{2.5}$ value is far from the turning point of growth. With the further growth of $PGDP^D$, the $PM_{2.5}$ value is expected to increase rapidly and continuously. The observation during 2011 and 2013 also verifies such a prediction. The values of $lnPGDP^D$ in regions including Guangxi (from 2001 to 2004) and Guizhou (2007, 2009) are closest to the lower portion of the Kuznets curve, and to some extent, this implies that in these provinces, social structure, industrial structure and consumption trends are relatively logistically structured, thus reducing the emission of $PM_{2.5}$. The deeper reason of such a phenomenon is worth of further studies in the future.

Thus, haze in China with $PM_{2.5}$ and $PM_{10}$ as representatives is typically distributed in blocks and exhibits significant spatial spillover effect. Thus, a province or region cannot fundamentally control $PM_{2.5}$ concentrations solely by transferring the polluting industries to adjacent provinces or strictly implementing the one-side $PM_{2.5}$ concentration control action. According to the characteristics of air pollution, prevention-control measures should be taken in the following ways. First, the central government of China shall focus on the haze pollution of severely-polluted provinces. Only by changing the structure of energy consumption and transforming the pattern of economic growth can theses provinces prevent air pollution from its source as well as bring the inflection point of air pollution growth forward. Second, local government shall stop transferring heavily-polluted industries to its neighboring areas. According to data analysis and empirical fact, there is special spillover effect in air pollution. It will only make situations worse for all involved by moving polluted sources to neighboring regions. Third, haze pollution shall be prevented and controlled with joint efforts. The "whole nation system" can be adopted in handling haze pollution. For example, to set up a special group led by the State Council and assisted by local government for the comprehensive treatment of haze pollution or implement "grid" management in pollution highly concentrated and severely polluted area (She and Chao 2012). Therefore, the advantages of Chinese government in public administration and "whole nation system" can be maximized to prevent and control pollution. Taxation and environmental regulation with laws and economic means are also applicable. Fourth, all individuals should be encouraged to practice an environmentally friendly way of living and participate in $PM_{2.5}$ concentration control. Only through the effective implementation of the above-mentioned measures can we reduce the threat of haze pollution and realize sustainable development.

**Acknowledgements** Yufeng Chen, Guizhi Wang, Yeming Gong, Zhiqing Tian also made great contributions to this manuscript. We express our heartfelt thanks to them. This research was supported by: National Social and Scientific Fund Program of China (18ZDA052; 17BGL142; 16ZDA047); The Natural Science Foundation of China (91546117, 71373131).

## References

Abas, M. R. B., Rahman, N. A., Omar, N. Y. M. J., Maah, M. J., Samah, A. A., Oros, D. R., et al. (2004). Organic composition of aerosol particulate matter during a haze episode in Kuala Lumpur, Malaysia. *Atmospheric Environment, 38,* 4223–4241.

An, J. L., Li, Y., Chen, Y., Li, J., Qu, Y., & Tang, Y. J. (2013). Enhancements of major aerosol components due to additional HONO sources in the North China Plain and implications for visibility and haze. *Advances in Atmospheric Sciences, 30,* 57–66.

Anselin, L. (1988). *Spatial econometrics: Methods and models* (p. 10). Kluwer Academic Publishers: Dordrecht, Holland.

Anselin, L. (1995). Local indicators of spatial association-LISA. *Geographical Analysis, 27,* 93–115.

Anselin, L., & Getis, A. (1992). Spatial statistical analysis and geographic information system. *The Annals of Regional Science, 26,* 19–33.

Bates, D. V., & Sizto, R. (1987). Air pollution and hospital admissions in Southern Ontario: The acid summer haze effect. *Environmental Research, 43,* 317–331.

Burnett, J. W., Bergstrom, J. C., & Dorfman, J. H. (2013). A spatial panel data approach to estimating U.S. state-level energy emissions. *Energy Economics, 40,* 396–404.

Cai, S. Y., Ma, Q., Wang, S. X., Zhao, B., Michael, B., Cohen, A., Martin, R. V., Zhang, Q. Q., Li, Q. B., Wang, Y. X., Hao, J. M., Joseph, F., Mohammad, H. F., & Burnett, R. T. (2018). Impact of air pollution control policies on future $PM_{2.5}$ concentrations and their source contributions in China. *Journal of Environmental Management, 227,* 124–133.

Cao, S. S., Zhao, W. J., Guan, H. L., Hu, D. Y., Mo, Y., Zhao, W. H., & Li, S. S. (2018). Comparison of remotely sensed $PM_{2.5}$ concentrations between developed and developing countries: Results from the US, Europe, China, and India. *Journal of Cleaner Production, 182,* 672–681.

Chen, R. J., Kan, H. D., Chen, B. H., Huang, W., Bai, Z. P., Song, G. X., & Pan, G. W. (2012). Association of particulate air pollution with daily mortality: The China air pollution and health effects study. *American Journal of Epidemiology, 175,* 1173–1181.

Chen, D. S., Liu, X. X., Lang, J. L., Zhou, Y., Wei, L., Wang, X. T., & Guo, X. R. (2017b). Estimating the contribution of regional transport to $PM_{2.5}$ air pollution in a rural area on the North China plain. *Science of the Total Environment, 583,* 280–291.

Chen, D. S., Wang, X. T., Nelson, P., Li, Y., Zhao, N., Zhao, Y. H., Lang, J. L., Zhou, Y., & Guo, X. R. (2017c). Ship emission inventory and its impact on the $PM_{2.5}$ air pollution in Qingdao Port, North China. *Atmospheric Environment, 166,* 351–361.

Chen, J., Zhou, C. S., Wang, S. J., & Li, S. J. (2018). Impacts of energy consumption structure, energy intensity, economic growth, urbanization on $PM_{2.5}$ concentrations in countries globally. *Applied Energy,* 94–105.

Chen, D. S., Tian, X. L., Lang, J. L., Zhou, Y., Li, Y., Guo, X. R., Wang, W. L., & Liu, B. (2019a). The impact of ship emissions on $PM_{2.5}$ and the deposition of nitrogen and sulfur in Yangtze River Delta, China. *Science of the Total Environment, 649,* 1609–1619.

Chen, S. M., Zhang, Y., Zhang, Y. B., & Liu, Z. X. (2019b). The relationship between industrial restructuring and China's regional haze pollution: A spatial spillover perspective. *Journal of Cleaner Production, 239,* 115808.

Chen, Q., Chen, Y., Luo, X. S., Hong, Y. W., Hong, Z. Y., Zhao, Z., & Chen, J. S. (2019c). Seasonal characteristics and health risks of $PM_{2.5}$-bound organic pollutants in industrial and urban areas of a China megacity. *Journal of Environmental Management, 245,* 273–281.

Chen, J., Wang, S. J., Zhou, C. S., & Li, M. (2020a). Does the path of technological progress matter in mitigating China's $PM_{2.5}$ concentrations? Evidence from three urban agglomerations in China. *Environmental Pollution, 254,* 113012.

Chen, X. Y., Li, F., Zhang, J. D., Zhou, W., Wang, X. Y., & Fu, H. J. (2020b). Spatiotemporal mapping and multiple driving forces identifying of $PM_{2.5}$ variation and its joint management strategies across China. *Journal of Cleaner Production, 250,* 119534.

Cheng, Z. H., Li, L. S., & Liu, J. (2017). Identifying the spatial effects and driving factors of urban $PM_{2.5}$ pollution in China. *Ecological Indicators, 82,* 61–75.

Cheng, X. S., Lu, K., Liu, W., & Xiao, D. (2019). Efficiency and marginal abatement cost of $PM_{2.5}$ in China: A parametric approach. *Journal of Cleaner Production, 235,* 57–68.

Cheng, Z. H., Li, L. S., & Liu, J. (2020). The impact of foreign direct investment on urban $PM_{2.5}$ pollution in China. *Journal of Environmental Management, 265,* 110532.

Ding, Y. T., Zhang, M., Qian, X. Y., Li, C. R., Chen, S., & Wang, W. W. (2019). Using the geographical detector technique to explore the impact of socioeconomic factors on $PM_{2.5}$ concentrations in China. *Journal of Cleaner Production, 211,* 1480–1490.

Dong, L., & Liang, H. W. (2014). Spatial analysis on regional air pollutions and $CO_2$ emissions in China: Emission pattern and regional disparity. *Atmospheric Environment, 92,* 280–291.

Dong, F., Zhang, S. N., Long, R. Y., Zhang, X. Y., & Sun, Z. Y. (2019). Determinants of haze pollution: An analysis from the perspective of spatiotemporal heterogeneity. *Journal of Cleaner Production, 222,* 768–783.

Du, G., Liu, S. Z., Lei, N., & Huang, Y. (2018). A test of environmental Kuznets curve for haze pollution in China: Evidence from the penal data of 27 capital cities. *Journal of Cleaner Production, 205,* 821–827.

Du, Y. Y., Wan, Q., Liu, H. M., Liu, H., Kelly, K., & Peng, J. (2019). How does urbanization influence $PM_{2.5}$ concentrations? Perspective of spillover effect of multi-dimensional urbanization impact. *Journal of Cleaner Production, 220,* 974–983.

Environmental Information Network. (2012). A panorama of air pollution in China seen from space. Retrieved February 21, 2012, from https://www.12369.com.cn/news/detail?id=1403.

Fan, X. M., & Xu, Y. Z. (2020). Convergence on the haze pollution: City-level evidence from China. *Atmospheric Pollution Research, 11,* 141–152.

Feng, Y. C., & Wang, X. H. (2020). Effects of urban sprawl on haze pollution in China based on dynamic spatial Durbin model during 2003–2016. *Journal of Cleaner Production, 242,* 118368.

Feng, J. L., Hu, J. C., Xu, B. H., Hu, X. L., Sun, P., Han, W. L., Gu, Z. P., Yu, X. M., & Wu, M. H. (2015). Characteristics and seasonal variation of organic matter in $PM_{2.5}$ at a regional background site of the Yangtze River Delta region. *Atmospheric Environment, 123,* 288–297.

Fu, H. B., & Chen, J. M. (2017). Formation, features and controlling strategies of severe haze-fog pollutions in China. *Science of the Total Environment, 578,* 121–138.

Fu, Z. Y., & Li, R. (2020). The contributions of socioeconomic indicators to global $PM_{2.5}$ based on the hybrid method of spatial econometric model and geographical and temporal weighted regression. *Science of the Total Environment, 703,* 135481.

Fu, M., Andrew Kelly, J., & Peter Clinch, J. (2020). Prediction of $PM_{2.5}$ daily concentrations for grid points throughout a vast area using remote sensing data and an improved dynamic spatial panel model. *Atmospheric Environment, 237,* 117667.

Gan, T., Liang, W., Yang, H. C., & Liao, X. C. (2020). The effect of economic development on haze pollution ($PM_{2.5}$) based on a spatial perspective: Urbanization as a mediating variable. *Journal of Cleaner Production, 266,* 121880.

Guan, Y., Kang, L., Wang, Y., Zhang, N. N., & Ju, M. T. (2019a). Health loss attributed to $PM_{2.5}$ pollution in China's cities: Economic impact, annual change and reduction potential. *Journal of Cleaner Production, 127,* 284–294.

Guan, Q. Y., Liu, Z. Y., Yang, L. Q., Luo, H. P., Yang, Y. Y., Zhao, R., & Wang, F. F. (2019b). Variation in $PM_{2.5}$ source over megacities on the ancient Silk Road, northwestern China. *Journal of Cleaner Production, 208,* 897–903.

Guo, J. P., Xia, F., Zhang, Y., Liu, H., Li, J., Lou, M. Y., He, J., Yan, Y., Wang, F., Min, M., & Zhai, P. M. (2017). Impact of diurnal variability and meteorological factors on the $PM_{2.5}$-AOD relationship: Implications for $PM_{2.5}$ remote sensing. *Environmental Pollution, 221,* 94–104.

Guo, B., Wang, Y. Q., Zhang, X., Y., 2020. Temporal and spatial variations of haze and fog and the characteristics of $PM_{2.5}$ during heavy pollution episodes in China from, et al. (2013). to 2018. *Atmospheric Pollution Research, 11*(10), 1847–1856.

Han, L. J., Zhou, W. Q., Li, W. F., & Li, L. (2014). Impact of urbanization level on urban air quality: A case of fine particles ($PM_{2.5}$) in Chinese cities. *Environmental Pollution, 194,* 163–170.

Hao, Y., & Liu, Y. M. (2016). The influential factors of urban $PM_{2.5}$ concentrations in China: A spatial econometric analysis. *Journal of Cleaner Production, 112,* 1443–1453.

Hao, Y., Peng, H., Temulun, T., Liu, L. Q., Mao, J., Lu, Z. N., & Chen, H. (2018a). How harmful is air pollution to economic development? New evidence from $PM_{2.5}$ concentrations of Chinese cities. *Journal of Cleaner Production, 172,* 743–757.

Hao, Y. F., Meng, X. P., Yu, X. P., Lei, M. L., Li, W. J., Shi, F. T., Yang, W. W., Zhang, S. J., & Xie, S. D. (2018b). Characteristics of trace elements in $PM_{2.5}$ and $PM_{10}$ of Chifeng, northeast China: Insights into spatiotemporal variations and sources. *Atmospheric Research, 213,* 550–561.

He, Q. S., Geng, F. H., Li, C. C., Yang, S. Q., Wang, Y. Y., Mu, H. Z., Zhou, G. Q., Liu, X. B., Gao, W., Cheng, T. T., & Wu, Z. (2018). Long-term characteristics of satellite-based $PM_{2.5}$ over East China. *Science of the Total Environment, 612,* 1417–1423.

He, J. H., Ding, S., & Liu, D. F. (2019). Exploring the spatiotemporal pattern of $PM_{2.5}$ distribution and its determinants in Chinese cities based on a multilevel analysis approach. *Science of the Total Environment, 659,* 1513–1525.

Hossein, H. M., & Kaneko, S. (2013). Can environmental quality spread through institutions? *Energy Policy, 56,* 312–321.

Hossein, M. Hosseini, & Shinji, K. (2013). Can environmental quality spread through institutions? *Energy Policy, 56,* 312–321.

Huang, T. J. (2018). Sulfur dioxide ($SO_2$) emissions and government spending on environmental protection in China: Evidence from spatial econometric analysis. *Journal of Cleaner Production, 175,* 431–441.

Hussain, S. Q., Ahn, S. Y., Park, H., Kwon, G., Raja, J., Lee, Y., et al. (2013). Light trapping scheme of ICP-RIE glass texturing by $SF_6$/Ar plasma for high haze ratio. *Vacuum, 94,* 87–91.

Jansen, R. C., Shi, Y., Chen, J. M., Hu, W. J., Xu, C., Hong, S. M., Li, J., & Zhang, M. (2014). Using hourly measurements to explore the role of secondary inorganic aerosol in $PM_{2.5}$ during haze and fog in Hangzhou, China. *Advances in Atmospheric Sciences, 31,* 1427–1434.

Ji, X., Yao, Y. X., & Long, X. L. (2018). What causes $PM_{2.5}$ pollution? Cross-economy empirical analysis from socioeconomic perspective. *Energy Policy, 119,* 458–472.

Ji, G. X., Tian, L., Zhao, J. C., Yue, Y. L., & Wang, Z. (2019). Detecting spatiotemporal dynamics of $PM_{2.5}$ emission data in China using DMSP-OLS nighttime stable light data. *Journal of Cleaner Production, 209,* 363–370.

Jin, J. Q., Du, Y., Xu, L. J., Chen, Z. Y., Chen, J. J., Wu, Y., & Ou, C. Q. (2019). Using Bayesian spatio-temporal model to determine the socio-economic and meteorological factors influencing ambient $PM_{2.5}$ levels in 109 Chinese cities. *Environmental Pollution, 254,* 113023.

Kamal, J. M., Wei-Feng, Y., Mohit Arora, S. M., & Shiva, N. (2018). $PM_{2.5}$-related health and economic loss assessment for 338 Chinese cities. *Environment International, 121,* 392–403.

Kang, Y. Q., Zhao, T., & Yang, Y. Y. (2016). Environmental Kuznets curve for $CO_2$ emissions in China: A spatial panel data approach. *Ecological Indicators, 63,* 231–239.

Lesage, J., & Pace, R. L. (2014). *Introduction to spatial econometrics* (pp. 99–100). Peking University Press: Beijing, China.

Li, X., Zhang, Q., Zhang, Y., Zheng, B., Wang, K., Chen, Y., Timothy, J., Wallington, Han, W. J., Shen, W., Zhang, X. Y., & He, K. B. (2015). Source contributions of urban $PM_{2.5}$ in the Beijing–Tianjin–Hebei region: Changes between 2006 and 2013 and relative impacts of emissions and meteorology. *Atmospheric Environment, 123,* 229–239.

Li, L., Liu, X. M., Ge, J. J., Chu, X. H., & Wang, J. (2019a). Regional differences in spatial spillover and hysteresis effects: A theoretical and empirical study of environmental regulations on haze pollution in China. *Journal of Cleaner Production, 230,* 1096–1110.

Li, R., Mei, X., Wei L. F., Han, X., Zhang, M. G., & Jing, Y. Y. (2019b). Study on the contribution of transport to $PM_{2.5}$ in typical regions of China using the regional air quality model RAMS-CMAQ. *Atmospheric Environment, 214,* 116856.

Li, Y., Xue, Y., Guang, J., Gerrit de L., Self, R., She, L., Fan, C., Xie, Y. Q., & Chen, G. L. (2019c). Spatial and temporal distribution characteristics of haze days and associated factors in China from 1973 to 2017. *Atmospheric Environment, 214,* 116862.

Li, L., Hong, X., & Wang, J. (2020). Evaluating the impact of clean energy consumption and factor allocation on China's air pollution: A spatial econometric approach. *Energy, 195,* 116842.

Li, X. H., Xu, Y. Y., & Yao, X. (2021). Effects of industrial agglomeration on haze pollution: A Chinese city-level study. *Energy Policy, 148,* 111928.

Liang, S., Katerina, S. S., Olivier, J., Sarang, S., Qu, S., Steven, J. S., & Xu, M. (2017). Consumption-based human health impacts of primary $PM_{2.5}$: The hidden burden of international trade. *Journal of Cleaner Production, 167,* 133–139.

Liao, J. W., Jin, A. Z., Zoë, A. C., Ajay, P., Tao, Y., Shan, M., Yang, X. D., Li, H. X., Liu, G. Q., & Kirk, R. S. (2017). The impact of household cooking and heating with solid fuels on ambient $PM_{2.5}$ in peri-urban Beijing. *Atmospheric Environment, 165,* 62–72.

Liu, Y. P., Wu, J. G., & Yu, D. Y. (2017a). Characterizing spatiotemporal patterns of air pollution in China: A multiscale landscape approach. *Ecological Indicators, 76,* 344–356.

Liu, H. M., Fang, C. L., Zhang, X. L., Wang, Z. Y., Bao, C., & Li, F. Z. (2017b). The effect of natural and anthropogenic factors on haze pollution in Chinese cities: A spatial econometrics approach. *Journal of Cleaner Production, 165,* 323–333.

Liu, J. Z., Li, W. F., & Wu, J. S. (2019). A framework for delineating the regional boundaries of $PM_{2.5}$ pollution: A case study of China. *Environmental Pollution, 235,* 642–651.
Liu, Q. Q., Wu, R., Zhang, W. Z., Li, W., & Wang, S. J. (2020). The varying driving forces of $PM_{2.5}$ concentrations in Chinese cities: Insights from a geographically and temporally weighted regression model. *Environment International, 145,* 106168.
Lu, D. B., Xu, J. H., Yang, D. Y., & Zhao, J. N. (2017). Spatio-temporal variation and influence factors of $PM_{2.5}$ concentrations in China from 1998 to 2014. *Atmospheric Pollution Research, 8,* 1151–1159.
Lu, W., Tam, V. W. Y., Du. L., & Chen, H. (2021). Impact of industrial agglomeration on haze pollution: New evidence from Bohai Sea Economic Region in China. *Journal of Cleaner Production, 280,* 124414.
Lv, Z. K., & Li, S. S. (2021). How financial development affects $CO_2$ emissions: A spatial econometric analysis. *Journal of Environmental Management., 277,* 111397.
Ma, L. M., & Zhang, X. (2014). The spatial effect of haze pollution in China and the impact from economic change and energy structure. *China Industrial Economic, 4,* 19–31.
Ma, J. Z., Xu, X. B., Zhao, C. S., & Yan, P. (2012). A review of atmospheric chemistry research in China: Photochemical smog, haze pollution, and gas-aerosol interactions. *Advances in Atmospheric Sciences, 29,* 1006–1026.
Ma, Y.-R., Ji, Q., & Fan, Y. (2016). Spatial linkage analysis of the impact of regional economic activities on $PM_{2.5}$ pollution in China. *Journal of Cleaner Production, 139,* 1157–1167.
Maddison, D. (2006). Environmental Kuznets curves: A spatial econometric approach. *Journal of Environmental Economics and Management, 51,* 218–230.
Ming, L. L., Jin, L., Li, J., Fu, P. Q., Yang, W. Y., Liu, D., Zhang, G., Wang, Z. F., & Li, X. D. (2017). $PM_{2.5}$ in the Yangtze River Delta, China: Chemical compositions, seasonal variations, and regional pollution events. *Environmental Pollution, 223,* 200–212.
Mirella, M., Ari, L., Gülcin, A., et al. (2019). $PM_{2.5}$ concentration and composition in the urban air of Nanjing, China: Effects of emission control measures applied during the 2014 Youth Olympic Games. *Science of The Total Environment, 652,* 1–18.
Moran, P. A. P. (1950). Notes on continuous stochastic phenomena. *Biometrika, 37,* 17–23.
Mu, Q., & Zhang, S. Q. (2013). An evaluation of the economic loss due to the heavy haze during January 2013 in China. *China Environmental Science, 33,* 2087–2094.
Nan, Y. Q., Fan, X. M., Bian, Y. C., Cai, H. Y., & Li, Q. (2019). Impacts of the natural gas infrastructure and consumption on fine particulate matter concentration in China's prefectural cities: A new perspective from spatial dynamic panel models. *Journal of Cleaner Production, 239,* 117987.
Peng, J., Chen, S., Lv, H. L., Liu, Y. X., & Wu, J. S. (2016). Spatiotemporal patterns of remotely sensed $PM_{2.5}$ concentration in China from 1999 to 2011. *Remote Sensing of Environment, 174,* 109–121.
She, L., & Cao, X. X. (2012). Reflections on the disaster emergency response capacity of China. *Management World, 7,* 176–177.
Shi, H. X., Fan, J., & Zhao, D. T. (2017). Predicting household $PM_{2.5}$-reduction behavior in Chinese urban areas: An integrative model of theory of planned behavior and norm activation theory. *Journal of Cleaner Production, 145,* 64–73.
Shi, K. F., Wang, F., Yang, Q. Y., Wang, L., Sun, X. F., & Li, X. F. (2019). Exploring the relationships between urban forms and fine particulate ($PM_{2.5}$) concentration in China: A multi-perspective study. *Journal of Cleaner Production, 213,* 990–1004.
Song, C. B., He, J. J., Wu, L., Jin, T. S., Xi, C., Li, R. P., et al. (2017). Health burden attributable to ambient $PM_{2.5}$ in China. *Environmental Pollution, 223,* 575–586.
Su, Y., & Yu, Y. Q. (2019). Spatial association effect of regional pollution control. *Journal of Cleaner Production, 213,* 540–552.
Sun, J., Wang, J. N., Wei, Y. Q., Li, Y. R., & Liu, M. (2016). The haze nightmare following the economic boom in China: Dilemma and tradeoffs. *International Journal of Environmental Research and Public Health, 13,* 402–414.

Tânia, F., Peilin, L., Nelson, B., et al. (2017). Trends of $PM_{2.5}$ concentrations in China: A long term approach. *Journal of Environmental Management,196,719–732.,.*

Tang, L. L., Zhang, Y. J., Sun, Y. L., Yu, H. X., Zhou, H. C., Wang, Z., et al. (2014). Components and optical properties of submicron aerosol during the lasting haze period in Nanjing. *Chinese Science Bulletin, 59,* 1955–1966.

Thurston, G. D., Iot, K., Hayes, C. G., Bates, D. V., & Lippmann, M. (1994). Respiratory Hospital admissions and summertime haze air pollution in Toronto, Ontario: Consideration of the role of acid aerosols. *Environmental Research, 65,* 271–290.

Tian, X., Dai, H. C., Geng, Y., Jeffrey, W., Wu, R., Xie, Y., & Hao, H. (2018). Economic impacts from $PM_{2.5}$ pollution-related health effects in China's road transport sector: A provincial-level analysis. *Environment International, 115,* 220–229.

Tobler, W. (1970). A computer movie simulating urban growth in the Detroit region. *Economic Geography, 46,* 234–240.

Tran, B. N., Ferris, J. P., & Chera, J. J. (2003). The photochemical formation of a titan haze analog. Structural analysis by x-ray photoelectron and infrared spectroscopy. *Icarus, 162,* 114–124.

Wang, Q. Z., Zhuang, G. S., Huang, K., Liu, T. N., Deng, C. R., Xu, J., Lin, Y. F., Guo, Z. G., Chen, Y., Fu, Q. Y., Joshua, S., Fu, & Chen, J. K. (2015). Probing the severe haze pollution in three typical regions of China: Characteristics, sources and regional impacts. *Atmospheric Environment, 120,* 76–88.

Wang, Q., Liu, M., Yu, Y. P., & Li, Y. (2016). Characterization and source apportionment of $PM_{2.5}$-bound polycyclic aromatic hydrocarbons from Shanghai city, China. *Environmental Pollution, 21,* 118–128.

Wang, C. R., Du, X. M., & Liu, Y. (2017a). Measuring spatial spillover effects of industrial emissions: A method and case study in Anhui province, China. *Journal of Cleaner Production, 141,* 1240–1249.

Wang, S. J., Zhou, C. S., Wang, Z. B., Feng, K. S., & Klaus, H. (2017b). The characteristics and drivers of fine particulate matter ($PM_{2.5}$) distribution in China. *Journal of Cleaner Production, 142,* 1800–1809.

Wang, X. M., Tian, G. H., Yang, D. Y., Zhang, W. X., Lu, D. B., & Liu, Z. M. (2018a). Responses of $PM_{2.5}$ pollution to urbanization in China. *Energy Policy, 123,* 602–610.

Wang, S. J., Liu, X. P., Yang, X., Zou, B., & Wang, J. Y. (2018b). Spatial variations of $PM_{2.5}$ in Chinese cities for the joint impacts of human activities and natural conditions: A global and local regression perspective. *Journal of Cleaner Production, 203,* 143–152.

Wang, J. Y., Wang, S. J., & Li, S. J. (2019). Examining the spatially varying effects of factors on $PM_{2.5}$ concentrations in Chinese cities using geographically weighted regression modeling. *Environmental Pollution, 248,* 792–803.

Wei, O. Y., Gao, B., Cheng, H. G., Zhang, L., Wang, Y. D., Lin, C. Y., & Chen, J. (2020). Airborne bacterial communities and antibiotic resistance gene dynamics in $PM_{2.5}$ during rainfall. *Environment International,* 105318.

Wu, J. N., Zhang, P., Yi, H. T., & Zhao, Q. (2016a). What causes haze pollution? An empirical study of $PM_{2.5}$ concentrations in Chinese Cities. *Sustainability, 8,* 132–146.

Wu, X. H., Tan, L., Guo, J., Wang, Y. Y., Liu, H., & Zhu, W. W. (2016b). A study of allocative efficiency of $PM_{2.5}$ emission rights based on a zero-sum gains data envelopment model. *Journal of Cleaner Production, 113,* 1024–1031.

Wu, J. S., Zheng, H. Q., Zhe, F., Xie, W. D., & Song, J. (2018). Study on the relationship between urbanization and fine particulate matter ($PM_{2.5}$) concentration and its implication in China. *Journal of Cleaner Production, 182,* 872–882.

Wu, W. Q., Zhang, M., & Ding, Y. T. (2020a). Exploring the effect of economic and environment factors on $PM_{2.5}$ concentration: A case study of the Beijing-Tianjin-Hebei region. *Journal of Environmental Management, 268,* 110703.

Wu, X. H., He, S. L., Guo, J., & Sun, W. H. (2020b). A multi-scale periodic study of $PM_{2.5}$ concentration in the Yangtze River Delta of China based on empirical mode decomposition-wavelet analysis. *Journal of Cleaner Production,* 124853.

Xie, Y. B., Chen, J., & Li, W. (2014). An assessment of $PM_{2.5}$ related health risks and impaired values in Beijing residents in a consecutive high-level exposure during heavy haze days. *Environmental Science, 35,* 1–8.

Xie, H., Ai, H. S., & Deng, Z. G. (2020). Impacts of the scattered coal consumption on $PM_{2.5}$ pollution in China. *Journal of Cleaner Production, 245,* 118922.

Xu, B., & Lin, B. Q. (2018). What cause large regional differences in $PM_{2.5}$ pollutions in China? Evidence from quantile regression model. *Journal of Cleaner Production, 174,* 447–461.

Xu, L. Z., Stuart, B., Chen, F., Li, J. B., Zhong, X. F., Feng, Y. J., Rao, Q. H., & Chen, F. (2017). Spatiotemporal characteristics of $PM_{2.5}$ and $PM_{10}$ at urban and corresponding background sites in 23 cities in China. *Science of the Total Environment, 559–600,* 2074–2084.

Xu, L. L., Jiao, L., Hong, Z. Y., Zhang, Y. R., Du, W. J., Wu, X., Chen, Y. T., Deng, J. J., Hong, Y. W., & Chen, J. S. (2018). Source identification of $PM_{2.5}$ at a port and an adjacent urban site in a coastal city of China: Impact of ship emissions and port activities. *Science of the Total Environment, 634,* 1205–1213.

Yang, J., Niu, Z. Q., Shi, C. E., Liu, D. Y., & Li, Z. H. (2010). Microphysics of atmospheric aerosols during winter haze/fog events in Nanjing. *Environmental Science, 31,* 1425–1431.

Yang, D. Y., Wang, X. M., Xu, J. H., Xu, C. D., Lu, D. B., Ye, C., Wang, Z. J., & Bai, L. (2018). Quantifying the influence of natural and socioeconomic factors and their interactive impact on $PM_{2.5}$ pollution in China. *Environmental Pollution, 241,* 475–483.

Yin, H., Massimo, P., & Xu, L. Y. (2017a). External costs of $PM_{2.5}$ pollution in Beijing, China: Uncertainty analysis of multiple health impacts and costs. *Environmental Pollution, 226,* 356–369.

Yin, X. H., Huang, Z. J., Zheng, J. Y., Yuan, Z. B., Zhu, W. B., Huang, X. B., & Chen, D. X. (2017b). Source contributions to $PM_{2.5}$ in Guangdong province, China by numerical modeling: Results and implications. *Atmospheric Research, 186,* 63–71.

Zhang, H. B. (2014). 'Robust' influence factors of environment pollution in China: An empirical analysis based on spatial panel data EBA model. Master Thesis, Hefei University of Technology, Anhui, China.

Zhang, X. Y., Zhang, X. Y., Sun, J. Y., Wang, Y. Q., Li, W. J., Zhang, Q., et al. (2013). Factors contributing to haze and fog in China. *Chinese Science Bulletin, 58,* 1178–1187.

Zhang, R. H., Li, Q., & Zhang, R. N. (2014). Meteorological conditions for the persistent severe fog and haze event over eastern China in January 2013. *Science China, 57,* 26–35.

Zhang, Q., Yang, J., Sun, Z. X., & Wu, F. (2017a). Analyzing the impact factors of energy-related $CO_2$ emissions in China: What can spatial panel regressions tell us? *Journal of Cleaner Production, 161,* 1085–1093.

Zhang, Y. P., Chen, J., Yang, H. N., Li, R. J., & Yu, Q. (2017b). Seasonal variation and potential source regions of $PM_{2.5}$-bound PAHs in the megacity Beijing, China: Impact of regional transport. *Environmental Pollution, 231,* 329–338.

Zhang, Z. Z., Wang, W. X., Cheng, M. M., Liu, S. J., Xu, J., He, Y. J., & Meng, F. (2017c). The contribution of residential coal combustion to $PM_{2.5}$ pollution over China's Beijing-Tianjin-Hebei region in winter. *Atmospheric Environment, 159,* 147–161.

Zhang, M., Liu, X. X., Sun, X. R., & Wang, W. W. (2020a). The influence of multiple environmental regulations on haze pollution: Evidence from China. *Atmospheric Pollution Research, 11,* 170–179.

Zhang, M., Sun, X., & Wang, W. W. (2020b). Study on the effect of environmental regulations and industrial structure on haze pollution in China from the dual perspective of independence and linkage. *Journal of Cleaner Production, 256,* 120748.

Zhao, X. J., Pu, W. W., Meng, W., Ma, Z. Q., Dong, F., & He, D. (2013). $PM_{2.5}$ pollution and aerosol optical properties in fog and haze days during autumn and winter in Beijing area. *Environmental Science, 34,* 416–423.

Zhao, L., Wang, L. T., Tan, J. H., Duan, J. C., Ma, X., Zhang, C. Y., Ji, S. P., Qi, M. Y., Lu, X. H., Wang, Y., Wang, Q., & Xu, R. G. (2019a). Changes of chemical composition and source apportionment of $PM_{2.5}$ during 2013–2017 in urban Handan, China. *Atmospheric Environment, 206,* 119–131.

Zhao, X. L., Zhou, W. Q., Han, L. J., & Locke, D. (2019b). Spatiotemporal variation in $PM_{2.5}$ concentrations and their relationship with socioeconomic factors in China's major cities. *Environment International, 133,* 105145.

Zheng, Z. F., Xu, G. R., Yang, Y. J., Wang, Y. T., & Li, Q. C. (2018). Statistical characteristics and the urban spillover effect of haze pollution in the circum-Beijing region. *Atmospheric Pollution Research, 9,* 1062–1071.

Zhou, C. S., Chen, J., & Wang, S. J. (2018). Examining the effects of socioeconomic development on fine particulate matter ($PM_{2.5}$) in China's cities using spatial regression and the geographical detector technique. *Science of the Total Environment, 619–620,* 436–445.

Zhu, P. H., Yuan, J. J., & Zeng, W. Y. (2010). Analysis of Chinese industry environmental Kuznets curve empirical study based on spatial panel model. *China Industrial Economic, 6,* 65–74.

Zou, Q. R., & Shi, J. (2020). The heterogeneous effect of socioeconomic driving factors on $PM_{2.5}$ in China's 30 province-level administrative regions: Evidence from Bayesian hierarchical spatial quantile regression. *Environmental Pollution, 264,* 114690.

# Chapter 18
# Study of Haze Emission Efficiency Based on New Co-opetition DEA

**Abstract** As haze intensifies in China, controlling haze emission has become a top priority in the country's environment protection endeavor. Since haze moves across different regions, it is necessary to develop a DEA (Data Envelopment Analysis) model underpinned by both competition and cooperation to evaluate the haze emission efficiency in different provinces. This study innovatively adopts the spatial econometrics to construct the co-opetition matrices of Chinese provinces, then builds the co-opetition DEA model that evaluates the haze emission efficiency of them, and finally uses the haze data for 2015 as an example to assess the applicability of the model. The results of the study include: First, compared with the traditional CCR model, this study constructs the co-opetition DEA cross-efficiency model that integrates haze's feature of cross-border moving, and is thus more in line with the reality of haze emission and movement. Second, compared with the efficiency value gained using the CCR model, the haze emission efficiency values for Tianjin and Guangdong, two decision-making units, register greater variance when using the DEA model. The reason might lie in that they have a different spatial transportation relationship with their surrounding provinces. Third, the haze emission efficiency of provinces, resulting from the evaluation based on the co-opetition DEA method, varies greatly: those with high efficiency are mostly inland provinces that have a slow-growing economy and adverse climatic conditions, while many of the provinces that have low efficiency are located in the relatively prosperous east China. The specific co-opetition DEA model constructed in this study enriches the research on the DEA model, which can be applied to the emission efficiency evaluation of similar pollutants that cross the border and can contribute empirical support to the haze reducing efforts of the government with its empirical results.

**Keywords** Haze · Co-opetition DEA · Cross efficiency · Spatial dependence matrices

## 18.1 Introduction

Although China's economy has been growing rapidly over the past forty-odd years since the introduction of the reform and opening-up policy, the country has meanwhile seen air quality deteriorate consistently, ranking as world's No. 1 emitter of nearly

 
X. Wu and J. Guo, *Economic Impacts and Emergency Management of Disasters in China*,
https://doi.org/10.1007/978-981-16-1319-7_18

every category of pollutants. Among them, the atmospheric compound pollution, represented by the particulate matter less than 2.5 microns in diameter (or $PM_{2.5}$): has become one of the significant environmental problems that constrain the country's balanced development between economy and environment. In December 2016, China experienced a haze that swept the largest area, lasted the longest, and had the highest intensity by the time for that year. Satellite monitoring showed the haze extended to affect 17 provinces or provincial-level cities, covering an area of 1.42 million square kilometers or over one-seventh of the territory.[1] In 2017, North China and the Huang-Huai area (regions between Yellow River and Huai River and around them) also saw the most extended haze weather since winter set in. Forecasts said that heavy haze would hit parts of Beijing, Tianjin, Hebei Province, Shanxi Province, Henan Province and Guanzhong, Shannxi Province, with the minimum visibility at less than 1 km. In response to it, dozens of cities in north China including Beijing, Tianjin and Shijiazhuang, the provincial capital of Hebei activated the highest weather emergency alarm—the Red Alert.[2] Once formed, haze is difficult to disperse, which severely impairs urban environment quality and easily breeds strong societal dissatisfaction. Hence, how to effectively control and address haze has become a severe problem in need of tackling in China's environmental governance.

Haze efficiency evaluation is the premise and basis of haze emission control. Air pollutants emission efficiency can reflect the relationship between the economic value created and the air pollution during the production and living process of economic units, thus showing embodying the equilibrium relationship between economic development and air environment protection. Seen from practical terms, calculating the haze emission efficiency and evaluating its results can help, on the one hand, find the problems existing in the economic development of different regions, like whether input indicators (capital, labor force) have been reasonably utilized (Zheng et al. 2007; Song et al. 2015). The redundant input indicators can be cut down to control haze emissions, and improvement measures can be summarized based on the research results. On the other hand, to reach the reduction target in haze emissions, local governments formulate their own "reducing haze" tasks. Given the development levels and production and technological level varies among different regions, a "one-size-fits-all" approach must not be adopted while specifying the "reducing haze" task for them, but differentiated haze measures should be developed in light of the economic development level and haze emissions efficiency of different regions (Miao et al. 2013). Only when the emission control is based on the evaluation of the emission efficiency, will it have a scientific basis and practical significance (Wu et al. 2018a).

[1]Strongest Haze in 2016 Hit China's 17 Provinces. See: https://www.baidu.com/link?url=rwof42FQOxCx01YMkwydY51_n0LT9ij9Sg5uX6UEizK&wd=&eqid=fce3f99d00065970000000035a33b8fb.

[2]Why is This Boot of Haze Affecting Beijing-Tianjin-Hebei Area Ferocious? See: https://news.weather.com.cn/2016/12/2633094.shtml

Haze has a spatial spillover effect. With China's economy thriving and urbanization accelerating, the pollutants emissions have kept increasing, aggravating the regional air pollution, which makes the cross-border movement of relevant pollutants the focus of attention from governments and scholars (Ren et al. 2014). Take the Beijing-Tianjin-Hebei region as an example, between 2012 and 2013, pollutants from another place contributed about 28 percent to 36 percent of the $PM_{2.5}$ amount of Beijing. In some instances of heavy air pollution, $PM_{2.5}$ that drift to Beijing accounted for over 50‰ of the city's total amount[3]. During the same period, about 10–15‰ of total amount of the particulate matter 10 microns or less in diameter ($PM_{10}$) in Tianjin came from another place, and 22–24‰ of the total amount of $PM_{2.5}$ came from outside.[4] For Shijiazhuang, Hebei Province, 23–30‰ of total $PM_{2.5}$ amount was originated externally, while the externally originated amount of $PM_{10}$ takes up 10 percent to 15 percent of the total amount for the same period.[5] Wind direction, temperature difference and other forces of nature cause the cross-regional moving of fine particles that form haze (Tai et al. 2010; Wang et al. 2014; Pan et al. 2015). Adjacent areas that have different haze density would display the relationship of "one depending on the other"—that is the area with the higher haze density will likely see its haze spill over to its neighboring area. The resulting spillover effect will usually change the distribution pattern of haze pollution in different regions. The larger the haze density difference between adjoining areas is, the more distinct the spatial spillover effect will be. Therefore, when evaluating the haze emission efficiency, the spatial correlation between the decision-making units should be considered. At present, some scholars have evaluated the haze emission efficiencies, such as Wu et al. (2016b) and Wang et al. (2017). However, little literature employs the correlational matrix to evaluate the spatial spillover relationship of haze emissions.

This study innovatively incorporates the spatial correlational matrix to construct the co-opetition DEA cross-efficiency model, thereby calculating the $PM_{2.5}$ emission efficiency of different decision-making units. First, the study takes the Chinese provinces as the decision-making units. Using $PM_{2.5}$ as the example (an undesirable output) (Saen 2010; Song et al. 2017a, b): it establishes the co-opetition relationship matrices of different provinces through calculating the $PM_{2.5}$ spatial dependence of 29 provinces of China. Then, considering that cross efficiency is non-unique, and the weight is not reasonable, a co-opetition DEA cross-efficiency model is constructed and introduced to make the model comply with reality. Lastly, the study sets the input and output indicators that affect $PM_{2.5}$ emissions, collects relevant data, and conducts the feasibility verification of the established model.

[3]Report of Chinese Academy of Social Sciences: Hebei Largest Source of Haze in Beijing and Addressing Haze Needs Coordinated Effort. See: https://www.xcf.cn/ddxg2/201611/t20161109_777662.htm.

[4]Environmental Protection Bureau of Tianjin: https://www.tjhb.gov.cn/news/news_headtitle/201410/t20141009_570.html.

[5]Environmental Protection Department of Hebei Province: https://www.hb12369.net/hjzw/hbhbzxd/dq/201409/t20140901_43629.html.

The rest of this paper is arranged as follows: the second part is literature review, the third part is the introduction to the model, the fourth part is empirical analysis, and the conclusions are given in the last part.

## 18.2 Literature Review

### *18.2.1 Evaluation of Emission Efficiency of Air Pollutants*

Existing literature that evaluates explicitly the haze emission efficiency is relatively rare. Many scholars calculate and evaluate environmental efficiency. For instance, Fleishman et al. (2009) employed the DEA model and used $NO_X$ and $SO_2$ as undesirable output to evaluate the emission efficiency of power plants in America, and also adopted the TOBIT model to test whether the $NO_X$ and $SO_2$ regulation policies have an impact on their DEA scores. Rashidi et al. (2015) added energy inputs, undesirable outputs and non-discretionary factors (precipitation average) into the analysis, and measured the eco-efficiency of countries in the organization for economic co-operation and development (OECD) countries. Sueyoshi and Yuan (2015a employed the DEA model and took $PM_{2.5}$ and $PM_{10}$ as undesirable output to evaluate the emission performance of 28 provinces and provincial-level municipalities of China. Camarero et al. (2013) examined the emission efficiency of three pollutants in 22 OECD countries from 1980 to 2008 and analyzed the convergence characteristics of efficiency. Guo et al. (2017a, b) used a dynamic DEA model to assess the emission efficiency of carbon dioxide from fossil fuels in OECD countries and China. Picazo-Tadeo et al. (2014) evaluated the GHG emission efficiency of 28 EU countries between 1990 and 2011 using the DEA, the directional distance function, and the Luenberger productivity indicator. Choi et al. (2012) used a non-radial DEA model to estimate the $CO_2$ emission efficiency in China. Zhou et al. (2010) used the Malmquist productivity index based on environmental DEA technology to calculate the carbon dioxide emissions performance of the world's top 18 emitters from 1997 to 2004. Song et al. (2013) utilized a Super-SBM model to measure and calculate the energy efficiency of BRICS, then applied bootstrap to modify the values based on DEA derived from small sample data, and finally measured the relationship between energy efficiency and carbon emissions. Song et al. (2016) used a non-radial DEA under natural and managerial disposability to measure the unified efficiency of 30 administrative regions in China and then evaluated their operational and environmental performances. Bang et al. (2019) used the DEA to evaluate the ecological efficiency of different industries in South Korea, then used Tobit regression method to analyze the key performance indicators and the characteristics in effective environmental reporting, finally reached important conclusions that industries characteristics have an important impact on ecological efficiency. To clarify the different characteristics of $CO_2$ emissions in various industries, Wang et al. (2020a) took Liaoning as a representative industry province, then assessed the $CO_2$ emission efficiency using DEA and Malmquist-Luenberger productivity index. Meng (2019) proposed a direction-distance function model to assess the carbon emission efficiency of 29 regions in China and further used non-parametric methods to estimate the cost of carbon emission reduction. Zhou et al. (2020) used hierarchy analysis solve the heterogeneity of time-varying data, then collected air quality daily data of 360 cities in China from January 2018 to August 2019, finally applied the window DEA model to measure the dynamic air quality index. The conclusion shows that influenced by monthly changes influenced air quality. Wang et al. (2019b) used stochastic frontier method to calculate the performance and reduction potential of carbon emission of 39 industrial sectors in the Beijing-Tianjin-Hebei area during the period 2010–2016, and then further put forward some suggestions for improvement on strengthening sustainable development through the calculation results. Lee and Choi (2018) proposed the non-radial meta-frontier Malmquist $CO_2$ emission performance index (NMMCPI) and used this new method to evaluated the GHG emission performance of manufacturing industries in Korean. Chen et al. (2020a, b, c, d) took into account both economic and environmental performance, then used the non-radial distance function to evaluate regional ecological efficiency of the non-ferrous metal industry in China from 2000 to 2016. Finally, the variation of regional technology gap ratio and the primary cause of ecological inefficiency were analyzed. Zhou et al. (2018) constructed a new DEA model, which combined integral with zero-sum gains constraints to analyses the current characteristics of air detection data, evaluate air quality, then further got results that there were big gaps in air quality among different cities. Iftikhar et al. (2018) realized that every economy is composed of production and distribution departments, then introduced an improved network DEA model and used this new model to calculate energy efficiencies and $CO_2$ emissions efficiencies of economies under free disposability assumption. At finally, the conclusion showed that inefficiencies in energy consumption and $CO_2$ emissions were due to economic and distributional inefficiencies. Wang et al. (2020a, b, c) took $PM_{2.5}$and $SO_2$ as the bad output under the total factor production framework, then use an improved context-dependent SBM-DEA model to assessed air pollution efficiencies of 30 provinces in China, finally showed the feasibility and effectiveness of context-dependent SBM-DEA model. Xu et al. (2020) combined DEA with logarithmic average index method to decompose the influencing factors of $PM_{2.5}$ emissions into multiple sub-factors, then analyzed the differences of influencing on $PM_{2.5}$ emissions by taking into account both time and space differences. Sueyoshi et al. (2015) took $PM_{2.5}$ and $PM_{10}$ as unexpected outputs and used DEA to evaluate regional performance under two conditions of natural disposal and management disposal. Li et al. (2018a, b) took employees, fixed assets and energy consumption as input indicators and took GDP, $PM_{2.5}$, $SO_2$ and $NO_2$ as output indicators, then used slacks-based measure (SBM) DEA model to evaluate the overall efficiencies and specific efficiencies of 31 cities. Chen et al. (2020a, b, c, d) used a Super-SBM model, which included resource consumption and bad output, to assess industrial environmental efficiency(IEE) in China, then analyzed affect factors and Spatio-temporal evolution of IEE by applying the spatial auto-correlation test and the spatial Durbin model. To integrate environmental, government and economy for analysis, Li et al. (2020a, b) used the dynamic and network SBM-DEA model to evaluate the annual energy and air pollution emission efficiencies of 30 provinces and municipalities in China from 2013 to 2016. Wang and Wang proposed an improved non-separable hybrid model to evaluate and explore the unified environmental efficiency of industries under natural and managerial disposability. Hermoso-Orzaez et al. (2020) used the DEA model to measure and compare the environmental efficiency of the 28 countries of the European Union (EU). Wang et al. (2019a) used an improved process-level DEA method to assess the environmental efficiency of the steel industry, then further analyzed the impact of various DEA models on efficiency values by comparing CCR-DEA, BCC-DEA, SBM-DEA and Bootstrap-DEA models. Li et al. (2020a, b) proposed an improved DEA model to calculated the environmental total factor productivity and the related composition of China from 2003 to 2013, and further explored the relationship between environmental efficiency and $PM_{2.5}$.

In recent years, scholars have begun to draw lessons from environmental performance assessment, using the DEA model to study the haze emission efficiency (Wu et al. 2018a). For example, Wu et al. (2016c) explored the efficiency of inter-provincial allocation of PM emission rights under the premise of a total fixed target. Guo et al. (2017a, b) comprehensively evaluated the environmental performance of 109 key environmental monitoring cities nationwide from three aspects of natural performance, management performance and scale performance through using the DEA environmental performance evaluation model, with $PM_{2.5}$ and $PM_{10}$ being the undesirable output. The regional differences were also analyzed.

After summarizing the previous studies, we find that the evaluation of the atmospheric environment efficiency focuses primarily on traditional air pollutants, such as $CO_2$. Few existing research adopts the Co-opetition DEA method to study the emission efficiency of haze, which has the characteristic of the transboundary movement. This study plans to probe into this—calculating the emission efficiency of haze more scientifically while at the same time providing suggestions for haze emission control.

### *18.2.2 Spatial Spillover Effect*

Haze results from the superposition of local pollution and pollution originating externally. Recent years saw environmental economists pay increasing attention to the study of the effect of space on environmental pollution (Anselin 2001). Under the influence of natural factors such as wind flow and water flow, the environmental quality of a particular area is bound to be negatively affected by the pollution discharge in a neighboring area. Also, human factors such as industrial transfer, cross-border trade and the externalities of environmental policies will further strengthen the spatial correlation of pollution emissions among regions (Poon et al. 2006). Scholars have verified the spillover effect of environmental pollution. For instance, Maddison (2006) used $SO_2$ and $NO_X$ as environmental quality indicators and found that there is a significant spatial spillover effect regarding air pollution and governance among

European countries. Poon et al. (2006) used a spatial econometric model to study $SO_2$ and soot, and find that there is also a spillover effect of air pollution among China's provinces. The research findings by analyzing two kinds of atmospheric pollutants, $CO_2$ and $PM_{10}$ showed that a country has a distinct cross-border spillover effect on its neighboring countries (Hosseini and Rahbar 2011). Zheng and Liu (2011) used the method of spatial econometrics to analyze the relationship between economic growth and carbon emissions in various provinces in China. The results showed that the carbon emissions of various provinces show a specific spatial space, and the autocorrelation provinces with the highest carbon emissions are mostly located in economically developed coastal areas. Wang and Wang (2013) applied $SO_2$ emission to characterize the environmental pollution level and used panel data from 30 provinces in China from 2000 to 2010 to do regression analysis. The regression analysis showed that there is spatial autocorrelation between $SO_2$ pollutant emissions and economic development. Chen et al. (2017) used the SDM model to study the impact of air pollution and spatial spillover effects on public health in 116 cities in China from 2006 to 2012. You and Lv (2018) studied the spatial effects of $CO_2$ emissions in 83 countries from 1985 to 2013. Yang and Xu (2020) proposed a theoretical Spatial Durbin model to examine the influence of air pollution on wage distortions, then utilize the Spatial Durbin Model to explain the impact mechanisms of air pollution on wage distortion by taking data from 289 cities in China from 1998 to 2006 as samples. These literatures mainly use spatial econometric methods and focus on the study of atmospheric pollutants such as $CO_2$ and $SO_2$.

In recent years, people have paid more attention to the spatial spillover effects of haze when studying the effects of haze on the economy and public life (Shi et al. 2014). Ma and Zhang (2014) used spatial econometric methods to analyze the interaction effects of haze pollution among the 31 provinces in China. The results show that the spillover effects of haze among provinces are apparent. Based on the environmental Kuznets curve, this paper discussed the haze pollution from the perspective of energy structure and spatial effect. Subsequently, Pan et al. (2015) studied the persistence and spatial spillover effects of haze pollution in the Beijing-Tianjin-Hebei region. The results showed that there was a spatial spillover effect of smog pollution among different cities in the Beijing-Tianjin-Hebei region. Pan et al. (2015) examined the persistence characteristics of the $PM_{2.5}$ index in a single city, and the spatial spillover effects of pollution between different cities in the region and the regional conversion model was used to distinguish between high pollution and the two states of low pollution studied the persistence characteristics of the $PM_{2.5}$ index. Based on Ma and Zhang (2014): Shao et al. (2016) used the dynamic spatial panel model and systematic generalized moment estimation method to identify the key factors affecting haze pollution and discuss the policies for haze control. Seven socio-economic factors, such as population density and R&D intensity, were investigated more comprehensively. The direct and indirect effects of various factors on haze pollution were calculated and compared. It was found that the haze pollution in China had noticeable spatial spillover effect and high-emission club agglomeration characteristics. Also, some other scholars have studied the spatial correlation of smog pollution (Tang et al. 2017). It is concluded that these scholars mainly use spatial measurement methods to verify the existence of smog spillover effects. Besides, some scholars analyze the factors that affect the haze spillover effect (Su et al. 2018; Cheng et al. 2017). For example, from the perspective of industrial space layout, Luo and Li (2018) introduced the transportation distance matrix and economic distance matrix into the spatial Dubin model and adopted the two sets of haze data of prefecture-level cities AOD and AQI to empirically test the effect of haze spills causing by the interaction between industrial agglomeration and transportation. The results showed that after the addition of traffic factors, the specialized agglomeration of the industry has significantly produced the regional transmission effect of smog pollution. Feng et al. (2020) investigated the spatial correlation of $PM_{2.5}$ in Beijing-Tianjin-Hebei, Yangtze River Delta and Pearl River Delta city clusters from 2016 to 2018, then analyzed the spatial spillover effect of environmental regulation on air pollution, finally discussed the influencing factors of spatial spillover effect on air pollution through the STIRPAT framework. Gan et al. (2020) took $PM_{2.5}$ as the representative of haze pollution and collected panel data of 287 cities in China from 1998 to 2016, then applied the spatial Durbin model to research the effects of economic and population accumulation on the spatial spillover of haze pollution. Zheng et al. (2020) firstly utilized spatial data analysis method to explored spatial spillover of haze pollution, then analyzed the influence of environmental regulation on haze pollution. The results proved that haze pollution has noticeable spatial spillover effect and the effect of environmental law on haze was also significant. Based on a collection of panel data from 21 cities in Guangdong province from 2005 to 2016, Liao et al. (2020) used the spatial econometric models with inverse distance weight to analyze the spatial–temporal evolution and affecting factors of haze pollution of 21 cities in Guangdong province. The last result demonstrated that haze pollution has evident spatial autocorrelation and spatial spillover effect in Guangdong province. From the perspective of spatial correlation, Chen et al. (2019) utilized the semi-parametric global vector auto-regression model (SGVAR) and environmental Kuznets curve to explore the spatial spillover effect of air pollution and the development of adjustment of industrial structure on haze pollution, and then get the conclusion that haze pollution in China has severe spatial spillover effect while the relationship between haze and economy presents a significantly inverted U shape. Li et al. (2019) firstly analyzed the influencing mechanism of environmental regulation on haze pollution, then used static and dynamic spatial panel data models, which based on panel data of 31 provinces from 2005 to 2015, to explore the geographical distribution characteristics of spatial spillover and hysteresis effects of environmental regulation on haze pollution. The last result indicated that spatial spillover and hysteresis effects of environmental law on haze pollution presented noticeable regional differences.

It is thus apparent that in studying haze pollution in China, the spillover effect cannot be neglected. Since haze pollution is a regional public problem with apparent geographical dependence and spillover of external effects, the issue of competition and cooperation (or co-opetition) among regions must be considered. However, how to define the co-opetition relationship among regions and which kind of method should be used to evaluate the relationship, thereby building a DEA model with a co-opetition relationship, become the critical point of this study.

### 18.2.3 Cross-Efficiency Evaluation Method

Cross-efficiency model is based on the traditional DEA model and evaluates the cross efficiency of decision-making units, or using two strategies—self-evaluation and peer evaluation—to evaluate the relative efficiency of the decision-making units. The traditional DEA method is based on the self-evaluation strategy, manifested by that the weighing is determined by decision-making units themselves to maximize their efficiency while minimizing others' efficiency (Wu et al. 2008). To overcome the self-evaluation flaws of the DEA method, Scholars proposed DEA models based on the peer evaluation strategy. The representative one is the DEA cross-efficiency method (An et al. 2018; Wu et al. 2018a). Concerning the cross-efficiency evaluation, some scholars have reflected on it from different approaches.

The study of cross efficiency evaluation is also an important and hot issue in DEA research. At present, the theoretical research on cross-efficiency evaluation usually includes two aspects; one is how to use cross-efficiency matrix to evaluate and rank all decision-making units (Li et al. 2018a, b). For example, Green et al. (1996) and others believe that the scoring model with confidence domain is essentially a cross-evaluation method. It is proved by a derivation that the weight of the CK model in the scoring process has been determined at the beginning of the selection of the DMUs, and then the cross-efficiency method is directly introduced into the scoring evaluation case to candidate cross-evaluation scoring matrix, and the ranking results are given by the maximum eigenvalue method. The essence of the viewpoint mentioned in the paper is the process of cross-evaluation, and the innovation of efficiency integration or scoring integration method points out another feasible way for the integration method in the theory of cross-efficiency. In recent years, many scholars have improved the traditional average cross-efficiency score to the weighted average. Wang and Chin (2011) considered the optimistic state of decision makers and used a sequential weighted average operator to integrate the cross-efficiency matrix. Wu et al. (2008, 2011) used the kernel theory and information entropy in the cooperative game to weight the average of the cross-efficiency matrix. Wang and Wang (2013) demonstrated the necessity of weighted average cross-efficiency by numerical examples and proposed three computational methods to determine the importance of each DMU.

On the other hand, because the weights of input and output variables are not unique in determining the CCR efficiency, the cross-efficiency matrix is not unique. Therefore, many scholars have proposed different quadratic models to determine the weights of input and output variables (Wu et al. 2018b). The benevolent and aggressive DEA models (Doyle and Green 1994) are most widely used, that is, when the efficiency of a DMU is maintained as the CCR efficiency, the efficiency of the remaining units is maximized or minimized to solve a group of weights. Liang et al. (2008b) draws on the relevant viewpoints of game theory, proposes the game cross-efficiency model and gives its Nash equilibrium solution. It is believed that the evaluated DMU can converge into the approved scores of all DMUs in the bargaining process. This value is also proved to be a Nash equilibrium solution. In order to solve the difficult problem of selecting the aggressive model and the benevolent model, Wang et al. (2010, 2011) proposed a neutral cross-efficiency model to reduce the number of zero weights of input and output variables. By introducing quadratic goals, the fault of non-unique cross efficiency may be reduced to some extent. In reality, however, there may be competition or hostility among some decision-making units, and cooperation or alliance among some other units (Liang et al. 2008a). The DEA cross-efficiency model considering competition and cooperation compensates for the deficiency of the cross-efficiency model in the multi-attribute comprehensive evaluation and improves the discrimination and rationality of the evaluation results, so it has been widely used (Tsai et al. 2013).

Recently, many researchers explored the cross-efficiency evaluation integrated other methods. For example, Wu et al. (2016a) proposed a DEA cross-efficiency evaluation approach based on Pareto improvement. Song et al. (2017a, b) improved the evaluation of cross efficiencies based on Shannon entropy weight. Liu et al. developed a concept of the aggressive game cross-efficiency and proposed an aggressive secondary model to minimize the cross-efficiencies of other DMUs. Liu et al. (2019) investigated the cross-efficiency evaluation in DEA by prospect theory. Based on a directional distance function, Lin (2019) studied the cross-efficiency evaluation capable of dealing with negative data. Han et al. (2018) presented an improved DEA cross model based on the information entropy for assessing carbon efficiency in industrial areas, then compared the proposed improved DEA model with the traditional DEA model through empirical analysis, finally found that this improved DEA cross model has a better efficiency discrimination ability than the traditional DEA model. Fan et al. (2020) added BWM and TOPSIS method to traditional DEA cross-efficiency model and developed an improved cross-efficiency evaluation model. The improved DEA cross-efficiency model can solve the convergence problem of cross efficiency. Kao and Liu (2019) established a relational DEA model for assessing the cross efficiencies of the system and divisions. Fan et al. (2019) considered the uncertainty of decision caused by information fuzziness and further proposed a new decision-making method. The new model worked out the uncertain problem on cross efficiency values and ranking of DMUs and also takes into account attitudes of decision-makers. At last, a typical example proved the validity and practicability of the proposed new model in the order. To solve the disadvantages from the traditional model of cross-efficiency, Chen et al. (2020a, b, c, d) established a new aggregation cross-efficiency method, then verified the validity and practicability of the new aggregation cross-efficiency method using this new method for aggregating the cross-efficiency of 27 industrial robots. Zhang et al. (2020) combined grey system theory with traditional DEA model and further constructed an improved DEA model for cross-efficiency, which solved the drawback of neglecting the weight of evaluation index in the traditional cross-efficiency DEA model, then used the improved model for evaluating operation efficiency more accurately in the actual case. To overcome the instability of evaluation in the traditional DEA cross-efficiency model, Wang et al. (2020c) proposed an improved DEA cross-efficiency model that can satisfy the stability and practicality of the evaluation, then verified the validity and rationality of the enhanced model through a particular example. Kao and Liu (2020) constructed a non-radical DEA cross-efficiency model and used the new non-radical DEA model for evaluating the efficiency of the robot in the production. The result proved that the new non-radical model could solve existing problem on negative efficiency score, differences between input and output radical efficiency scores under variable returns to scale in the traditional DEA model. To solve the problem of neglecting the significant differences in the traditional DEA cross-efficiency model, Sun et al. (2020) established the altruistic cross efficiency model based on the conservative point of view, then proved the validity and practicability of the new model through the case of a manufacturing system. Ding et al. (2020) proposed a modified cross-efficiency DEA model, which introduced undesired outputs and also took into account both self-evaluation and peer evaluation, then used the modified model to evaluate the green efficiency of marine economy in 11 coastal areas. Cui et al. (2020) constructed two improved DEA cross-efficiency model, which called Dynamic Benign Environment DEA and Dynamic Aggressive Environment cross-efficiency model respectively and then employed two improved models to evaluate the dynamic environmental efficiency of 29 airlines. The result showed the degree of competition and cooperation among airlines. Shi et al. (2019) constructed an improved cross-efficiency evaluation model that made every DMUs maintain a neutral attitude towards others DMUs. The result showed that the cross-efficiency values calculated by this improved model are more logical than the traditional cross-efficiency model. Chen et al. (2020a, b, c, d) considered both efficiency overestimation and technological heterogeneity and further established a modified, comprehensive DEA model by combining the traditional cross-efficiency DEA model with the meta-frontier analysis framework. This improved DEA model could decompose the cross-efficiency in detail and found detailed reasons about inefficiencies to further provided the more detailed reference for decision-makers. Chen et al. (2020a, b, c, d) proposed an improved DEA cross-efficiency model that can solve the problem of overestimating environmental efficiency. Then, this improved DEA cross-efficiency model was applied to assess environmental efficiency under the situation of both self-evaluation and peer evaluation. Davtalab-Olyaie and Asgharian (2021) constructed a multi-objective programming model for providing all Pareto-optimal cross-efficiency score sets under the self-prioritizing principle in cross efficiency evaluation. This proposed new model was converted to a non-linear single-objective program through the weighted sum technique for maximizing the average of cross-efficiency scores of all DMUs.

On the whole, how to evaluate the competition and cooperation relationship among DMUs is the core problem in the cross-efficiency models (Wu et al. 2016b). Yang et al. (2011) proposes an excellent competitive DEA cross-efficiency method, which divides all DMUs into several groups. The preference weights of each DMU can maximize the total efficiency of the allies and minimize the total efficiency of the adversaries. In this study, we need to further define the competitive and cooperative relationship between DMUs according to their spatial spillover relationship. Therefore, this study attempts to propose a new cross-efficiency model based on the competition-cooperation relationship with the spatial measurement method.

## 18.3 Co-opetition Dea Model Construction

### 18.3.1 Traditional Cross-Efficiency DEA Model

Assume that the technical efficiency of a group of n $\text{DMU}_\text{s}$ is measured and denoted as $DMU_j(j = 1, 2, \ldots, n)$; there are $m$ kinds of inputs of the $j$th decision-making unit, denoted as $x_{ij}(i = 1, 2, \ldots, m)$ and the input weights are expressed as $v_i(i = 1, 2, \ldots, m)$; there are $s$ kinds of desirable outputs for the $j$th decision-making unit, denoted as $y_{rj}(r = 1, 2, \ldots, s)$ : and the weights of desirable outputs are expressed as $u_r(r = 1, 2, \ldots, s)$; there are $t$ kinds of undesirable outputs for the $j$th decision-making unit, denoted as $b_{pj}(p = 1, 2, \ldots, t)$ : and the weights of undesirable outputs are expressed as $\varphi_p(p = 1, 2, \ldots, t)$.

First, by using the nonlinear distance transfer function $f(b) = \frac{1}{b}, b \neq 0$ to convert the undesired output $b_j$ into the expected outputs $b_j^{'}$.[6]. The principle of the above method of dealing with the unexpected output is to convert the undesirable output into the form of the desirable output whose value is bigger means better. The $d$th $(1 \leq d \leq n)$ decision-making unit currently to be measured is denoted as $DMU_d$ We add the expected outputs $b_j^{'}$ to the traditional DEA mosdel and the output-to-input ratio $\theta_d$ is expressed as:

$$\theta_d = \max \sum\nolimits_{r=1}^{s} u_{rd} y_{rd} + \sum\nolimits_{p=1}^{t} \varphi_{pd} b'_{pd}$$

$$s.t. \begin{cases} \sum_{i=1}^{m} v_{id} x_{ij} - \left( \sum_{r=1}^{s} u_{rd} y_{rj} + \sum_{p=1}^{t} \varphi_{pd} b'_{pj} \right) \geq 0, \; j = 1, 2, \ldots, n \\ \sum\limits_{i=1}^{m} v_{id} x_{id} = 1 \\ u_{rd} \geq 0, \; v_{id} \geq 0, \varphi_{pd} \geq 0, \; i = 1, 2, \ldots, m, \; r = 1, 2, \ldots, s, \; p = 1, 2, \ldots, t \end{cases} \tag{18.1}$$

Where $x_{id}, \; y_{rd}, \; and \, b_{pd}^{'}$ respectively represent the input, desirable output and undesirable output indicator of $DMU_d$; the $v_{id}, \; u_{rd} \; and \; \varphi_{pd}$ are respectively the weights of the input, desirable output and undesirable output indicator of $DMU_d$ Through model (18.1): the solution $(\theta_d^*, v_i d^*, u_r d^*, \varphi_p d^*)$ can be gained. $\theta_d^*$ is the optimal efficiency value of $DMU_d$ in the model (18.1).$v_{id}^*, \; u_{rd}^*$ and $\varphi_{pd}^*$ are the optimal weight of input, desirable output and undesirable output indicators of $DMU_d$ in the model (18.1). In the meantime, the optimal solution $\left(\theta_j^*, v_{ij}^*, u_{rj}^*, \varphi_{pj}^*\right)(j = 1, 2, \ldots, n, j \neq d)$ of the $DMU_j$ can also be obtained. Similarly, $\theta_j^*$ is the optimal efficiency value of $DMU_j$ in the model (18.1).

[6]The reasons for the transformation are as follows: First, treating the undesirable outputs as inputs directly cannot not reflect the true production process (Seiford and Zhu 2002); Second, it is hard to judge whether the undesirable output-$PM_{2.5}$, which is a kind of unique pollutant with complex components and a complicated formation process-is suitable for weak disposability assumption (Liu et al. 2010). Then, wu use such transformation utilized the information of original data and eliminated the subjective influence.

$v_i j^*, u^*_{rj}$ *and* $\varphi^*_{pj}$ are the optimal weight of input, desirable output and undesirable output indicators of $DMU_j$ in the model (18.1). $\theta_d$ represents the self-evaluation efficiency when the $d^{th}$ decision-making unit undergoes the optimal treatment. The cross efficiency of $DMU_d$ can be obtained through the following formula:

$$\theta^*_{jd} = \frac{\sum_{r=1}^{s} u^*_{rj} y_{rd} + \sum_{p=1}^{t} \varphi^*_{pj} b'_{pd}}{\sum_{i=1}^{m} v^*_{ij} x_{id}}, \ j = 1, 2, \ldots, n, \ j \neq d \tag{18.2}$$

Based on the model (18.1) and (18.2): the cross-efficiency values of all the decision-making units evaluated can be obtained, and the final cross efficiency value is the average value $\overline{\theta}^*_d$ of all the cross-efficiency $\overline{\theta}^*_d$.

$$\overline{\theta}^*_d = \frac{1}{n}\left(\sum\nolimits_{j=1, j\neq d}^{n} \theta^*_{jd} + \theta_d\right) \tag{18.3}$$

Cross efficiency is based on the peer evaluation strategy. With it, the average value of the preferred weights of all the decision-making units is taken as the public weight, and the efficiency of decision-making units under this public weight is cross efficiency. Therefore, cross efficiency can effectively avoid the subjective factors of decision-makers, thus making the evaluation results more widely recognized.

### *18.3.2 Co-opetition DEA model*

A general, actual situation is that there may be competition or hostile relations among some decision-making units. In this case, we cannot only evaluate the benevolent or aggressive models. Here, we take reference from Yang et al. (2011) idea and use a new cross-efficiency model based on co-opetition.

Assume that the technical efficiency of the $j$th decision-making unit is $DMU_j (j = 1, 2, \ldots, n)$ : and the $k$th decision-making unit is denoted as $DMU_k (k = 1, 2, \ldots, n)$ : a co-opetition relationship matrix $\{DMU_j, DMU_k\} (j \neq k)$ is thus established. If $DMU_j$ and $DMU_k$ are in a cooperative relationship, the coefficient is denoted as 1; if $DMU_j$ and $DMU_k$ are in competing relations, the coefficient is marked as $-1$; When the decision-making unit engages in self-evaluation, the coefficient is denoted as 0. So the DEA cross-efficiency model based on co-opetition is:

$$\hat{\theta}_d = \max \sum\nolimits_{r=1}^{s} u_{rd}\left(\sum\nolimits_{j=1}^{n} g_{jd} y_{rd}\right) + \sum\nolimits_{p=1}^{t} \varphi_{pd}\left(\sum\nolimits_{j=1}^{n} g_{jd} b'_{pd}\right)$$

$$
s.t.\begin{cases}
\sum_{r=1}^{s} u_{rd} y_{rd} + \sum_{p=1}^{t} \varphi_{pd} b'_{pd} - \theta_d^* \sum_{i=1}^{m} v_{id} x_{id} = 0 \\
\sum_{i=1}^{m} v_{id} \left( \sum_{j=1}^{n} x_{ij} \right) - (\sum_{r=1}^{s} u_{rd} \left( \sum_{j=1}^{n} g_{rd} y_{rj} \right) + \sum_{p=1}^{t} \varphi_{pd} \left( \sum_{j=1}^{n} b'_{pj} \right)) \geq 0 \\
\sum_{i=1}^{m} v_{id} \left( \sum_{j=1}^{n} x_{ij} \right) = 1 \\
\sum_{i=1}^{m} v_{id} x_{ij} - (\sum_{r=1}^{s} u_{rd} y_{rj} + \sum_{p=1}^{t} \varphi_{pd} b'_{pj}) \geq 0, \, j = 1, 2, \ldots, n \\
u_{rd} \geq 0, \, v_{id} \geq 0, \, \varphi_{pd} \geq 0, \, i = 1, 2, \ldots, m, \, r = 1, 2, \ldots, s, \, p = 1, 2, \ldots, t
\end{cases}
\tag{18.4}
$$

where $\overline{\theta}_d$ means co-opetition efficiency value of the $d$th decision-making unit $DMU_d$, which is the maximum value of the objective function. $g_{rd}$ is the co-opetition matrix, and $\theta_d^*$ is the efficiency value resulting from using the traditional cross-efficiency model (18.1).

### *18.3.3 Construction of Co-opetition Matrix*

There are many ways to build a relational matrix. For example, Sun (2013) constructed a qualitative spatial directional relationship model based on the directional relationship. Cao (2016) constructed a relational matrix according to the division of economic stages; if the two decision-making units are in the same stage of development, the coefficient of co-opetition is denoted as 1, and if they are not in the same stage, the coefficient is denoted as −1. Yang et al. (2011) used clustering analysis to divide decision-making units into several categories, and each category has inherent similarities in preference weights. Any two decision-making units, if falling under the same category, are allies to each other; if not, they are believed to be hostile to each other. The two decision-making units that are allies prefer similar weight system, and tend to accept the other one's preference; on the contrary, the two hostile decision-making units tend to negate each other's preference weighting system.

The cross-regional transmission of haze pollution has much to do with the geographical distribution of different regions. Haze in a region tends to occur locally first, before spreading to neighboring regions. Based on this, the interaction between decision-making units must be considered when analyzing the emission efficiency of haze. However, the interaction among the decision-making units is not entirely homogeneous. Moreover, given the interaction is also affected by the geographical location, the method of space metrology can be drawn on during research. Concerning the transboundary transmission of haze pollution, Ma et al. (2014) and Pan et al. (2015) have used space econometric models to study the spillover effects of haze pollution. They used the spatial relational matrix to evaluate the relationship between adjacent regions, which is a good reference for this study.

Haze is caused by both the local pollution and pollution transmitted from another region. There is a spatial spillover effect of the haze pollution among different areas, so the spatial econometric model can be used to analyze the regional correlation. Use the spatial econometrics tool in the ArcGIS software, and get Maron'I. The formula is as follows.

$$\mathrm{I_i} = \frac{(\mathrm{x_i} - \overline{\mathrm{x}})}{\mathrm{S}^2} \sum_{\mathrm{j=1}}^{\mathrm{n}} \mathrm{w_{ij}}(\mathrm{x_i} - \mathrm{x}) \tag{18.5}$$

$I_i$ is an index that measures the degree of correlation of $PM_{2.5}$ in area $i$and its surroundings. In $S^2 = 1/n \sum_{(i=1)}^{n} (x_i - \overline{x})^2$, $\overline{x} = \frac{1}{n} \sum_{i=1}^{n} x_i$, $x_i$ is the concentration of $PM_{2.5}$ in area $i$, $n$ is the number of areas, $w_{ij}$ is the spatial weight between area $i$ and area $j$, s and $w_{ij}$ is the spatial weight matrix. The setting principle of the element $w_{ij}$ in W is:

The principle of setting weight $\mathrm{w_{ij}}$:

$$w_{ij} = \begin{cases} 1, whenareaiandj\ adjion \\ 0, when\ area\ i\ and\ j\ dont\ adjion\ or\ i = j \end{cases} \tag{18.6}$$

$I_i > 0$ indicates that the region $i$ is positively correlated with the surrounding area, or that the regions with similar $PM_{2.5}$ are clustered together, manifested as high-high type agglomeration or low-low type agglomeration. $I_i < 0$ indicates a negative correlation, that is, areas with different concentrations of $PM_{2.5}$ are clustered together, exhibiting a high-low or low–high agglomeration.

Because haze's spatial spillover is closely related to geographic proximity, spatial econometric models are used to analyze the spatiotemporal correlations and spillover effects of haze in 29 provinces in China. That is, we calculate the spatial correlation of $PM_{2.5}$ according to Maron's I, construct the relational matrix, and then build a new co-opetition DEA model based on this (see the model (18.4)).

## 18.4 Empricial Analysis

### *18.4.1 Indicator Selection*

In using the DEA model to assess the emission efficiency of air pollutants, how to determine the input and output indicators is one of the key issues. Based on the previous studies, and according to the composition and origin of $PM_{2.5}$ (Ho et al. 2016; Liu et al. 2016; Wang et al. 2016b; Yang et al. 2016; Tolis et al. 2015; Zhang et al. 2016a; Qiao et al. 2015): and in light of the availability of data, the study selects capital, labor, sulfur dioxide ($SO_2$) emission, nitrogen oxide ($NO_X$) emission, soot emission and coal consumption as input indicators, and GDP and $PM_{2.5}$ respectively as desirable and undesirable output indicators. As the data of atmospheric environment capacity in Tibet, Chongqing, Hong Kong, Macau and Taiwan are not comprehensive enough, the data of the remaining 29 provinces, centrally-controlled municipalities and autonomous regions are made the research object. The specific indicators and data sources are as follows.

#### 18.4.1.1 Input Indicators

The selection of input indicators should have a clear theoretical basis and economic implications. Capital and labor input are essential to evaluating haze production and management efficiency. Input-side indicators of the traditional production function include capital and labor, and output-side indicators include, such as GDP. Later, scholars added factors that affect the GDP to the input-side such as energy, environment, and climate (Shi et al. 2008). This study also draws on this idea—adding to the input side environment and energy indicators related to the $PM_{2.5}$ output and adding $PM_{2.5}$ indicator to the output side. The production function expression is expanded as follows:

$$Y_i = A_i K_i^{\alpha} L_i^{\beta} C_i^{\gamma} \tag{18.7}$$

where, $Y_i$ represents the output of Region $i$, $A_i$ the Technology of Region $i$, $K_i$ the Capital input in Region $i$, $L_i$ the Labor input in Region $i$, and $C_i$ the environment and energy input related to $PM_{2.5}$ output in Region $i$. $\alpha$, $\beta$ and $\gamma$ are respectively the output elasticity of capital, labor and the environmental and energy input indicators related to $PM_{2.5}$.

Haze is the product of multi-stages with complicated physical–chemical reaction. So, we selected the essential factors leading to haze as input variables instead of undesirable output indicators. The factors include sulfur dioxide emissions ($SO_2$): nitrogen oxide emissions ($NO_X$): soot emissions, and coal consumption.

Sulfides and nitrogen oxides. Zhang et al. (2016b) found that secondary sulfate contributes significantly to the formation of haze and that the reduction of sulfur emission has a good correlation with the decrease in times of haze as well as reduction of $PM_{2.5}$ concentration. Gieré et al. (2006) also argued that coal-fired $SO_2$ and $NO_X$ undergo complex chemical reactions with other air pollutants, and change from gas pollutants into solid pollutants, which is the main reason for the increasing $PM_{2.5}$. Therefore, $SO_2$ and $NO_X$ emissions are taken as input indicators. Data on $SO_2$ and $NO_X$ emissions are from the *China Environmental Statistical Yearbook 2016*.

Smoke and dust. The primary sources of $PM_{2.5}$ are dust, construction dust, coal dust, smelting dust, sulfate, automobile dust, and coal dust contributes 30.34% to $PM_{2.5}$ (Huang et al. 2006). Gieré et al. (2006) held that coal-fired soot contains a large amount of $PM_{2.5}$, which has an important impact on the environment and health. Therefore, soot is selected as an input indicator. Data on smoke and dust come from the *China Environmental Statistical Yearbook 2016.*

Coal consumption. Zhang et al. (2013) collected and analyzed $PM_{2.5}$ samples of different seasons in Beijing from 2009 to 2010, and found that fire coal accounted for 18% of the sources of $PM_{2.5}$ affecting Beijing in different seasons. According to the emission patterns, the contributions of fire coal to $PM_{2.5}$ in the atmosphere can be divided into two categories: primary particles directly discharged, and secondary particles taking shape after being released into the atmosphere in a gaseous form such as $SO_2$, $NO_X$, and VOC (Shi 2013). Therefore, coal consumption should be included among the input indicators. Data on coal consumption come from the *China Environmental Statistical Yearbook 2016.*

SPSS was used to test the correlation of six input indicators (capital, labor force, $SO_2$, $NO_X$, soot and coal consumption) and outputs indicators (GDP and $PM_{2.5}$). The results are shown in Tables 18.1 and 18.2. From a statistical point of view, the

**Table 18.1** Correlation results of input indicators

| | | $SO_2$ | $NO_X$ | Soot | Coal | Capital | Labor |
|---|---|---|---|---|---|---|---|
| $SO_2$ | Pearson's correlation | 1 | 0.900** | 0.828** | 0.915** | 0.220 | 0.361 |
| | Significance (double tail) | | 0.000 | 0.000 | 0.000 | 0.252 | 0.054 |
| $NO_X$ | Pearson's correlation | 0.900** | 1 | 0.836** | 0.917** | 0.227 | 0.557** |
| | Significance (double tail) | 0.000 | | 0.000 | 0.000 | 0.237 | 0.002 |
| Soot | Pearson's correlation | 0.828** | 0.836** | 1 | 0.859** | 0.070 | 0.186 |
| | Significance (double tail) | 0.000 | 0.000 | | 0.000 | 0.720 | 0.334 |
| Coal | Pearson's correlation | 0.915** | 0.917** | 0.859** | 1 | 0.071 | 0.374* |
| | Significance (double tail) | 0.000 | 0.000 | 0.000 | | 0.716 | 0.046 |
| Capital | Pearson's correlation | 0.220 | 0.227 | 0.070 | 0.071 | 1 | 0.482** |
| | Significance (double tail) | 0.252 | 0.237 | 0.720 | 0.716 | | 0.008 |
| Labor | Pearson's correlation | 0.361 | 0.557** | 0.186 | 0.374* | 0.482** | 1 |
| | Significance (double tail) | 0.054 | 0.002 | 0.334 | 0.046 | 0.008 | |

*Note* * and ** are correlation were significant at 0.05 level and 0.01 level, separately

**Table 18.2** Correlation results of output indicators

| | | GDP | $PM_{2.5}$ |
|---|---|---|---|
| GDP | Pearson's correlation | 1 | 0.267 |
| | Significance (double tail) | | 0.161 |
| $PM_{2.5}$ | Pearson's correlation | 0.267 | 1 |
| | Significance (double tail) | 0.161 | |

correlation results of input indicators in Table 18.1 show that under the significance level of 0.01, there are strong correlation among $SO_2$, $NO_X$, soot, Labor force, and GDP. Meanwhile, there is no multiple collinear relationship between GDP and $PM_{2.5}$. From the economic meaning of index selection, this study attempts to find out the input indicators that affect haze pollution and then control haze emissions by cutting down the source indicators which cause haze. From previous studies, we can see that $SO_2$, $NO_X$, soot, and Coal are all the primary sources of haze pollution. If we remove the input indicators that produce multiple collinearities, the consequences will be as follows: on the one hand, this means that the index is not adequately selected; on the other hand, we would miss the main source indicators of haze pollution, so that we cannot solve the research purposes of this study. Therefore, we can not eliminate $SO_2$, $NO_X$, soot, and Coal.

#### 18.4.1.2 Output Indicators

Haze evaluation indicators. The main components of haze are $PM_{10}$ and $PM_{2.5}$. China started collecting official statistics on $PM_{2.5}$ since 2012, so available data is limited. In this study, the author adopts the global annual average of population-weighted $PM_{2.5}$ from 2001 to 2010 developed by the Battelle Memorial Institute and the Center for International Earth Science Information Network, and then considers a weighted approach to the following two factors: first, land area of provinces; second, the primary $PM_{2.5}$ atmospheric environment capacity of each province under the $PM_{2.5}$ standard-reaching constraint.

Atmospheric environment capacity. Drawing on the thinking of Guo et al. (2015): the study takes the maximum permissible emissions of primary $PM_{2.5}$ from 31 provinces (municipalities and autonomous regions) resulting from a simulated calculation by Xue et al. (2014) as the data source for this study. Then, considering the factors of land area and atmospheric environmental capacity of different provinces, the $PM_{2.5}$ concentration is processed, and a new $PM_{2.5}$ index is obtained as the output index of the study. The calculation process is shown in Table 18.3.

In summary, this study selects capital, labor, sulfur dioxide emission ($SO_2$): nitrogen oxide emission ($NO_X$): smoke and dust emissions and coal consumption as input indicators, and makes GDP and $PM_{2.5}$ respectively the desirable output and undesirable output indicators. The data is derived from the *China Statistical Yearbook 2016*, the *China Environmental Statistical Yearbook 2016* and the "China $PM_{2.5}$ Concentration Ranking in 2015" released by international environmental protection organization Greenpeace.[7] The definitions and accounting methods of each indicator are shown in Table 18.3 and the raw data of inputs and outputs are shown in Table 18.4.

[7]China $PM_{2.5}$ Concentration Ranking in 2015 by Greenpeace:https://www.greenpeace.org.cn/pm25-city-ranking-2015/.

**Table 18.3** Description of input and output indicators

| Indicator category | Indicator name | Accounting content | Unit |
|---|---|---|---|
| Input indicators | Sulfur dioxide emissions ($SO_2$) | Sulfur dioxide emissions | Ton |
| | Nitrogen oxide emissions ($NO_X$) | Total nitrogen oxides emissions | Ton |
| | Soot emissions | Total amount of soot emissions | Ton |
| | Coal consumption | Coal consumption | Ten thousand tons |
| | Car ownership<br>Capital (K)<br>Workforce (L) | Civil and private car ownership<br>Total investment in fixed assets<br>Employed population | Ten thousand vehicles<br>Hundred million yuan<br>Ten thousand people |
| Output indicators | $PM_{2.5}$ emissions | Atmospheric environment capacity of the one-time $PM_{2.5}$, which is obtained through $PM_{2.5}$ concentration weighted by population of each province multiplying by the area of each province, before dividing by the national $PM_{2.5}$ up-to-standard constraint | |
| | GDP | Gross National Product | Hundred million yuan |

## 18.4.2 Co-opetition Matrix

The ArcGIS software is used to calculate the spatial correlation of provinces. It can be seen from the figure below that the spatial clustering effect of China's particulate matter is apparent. The high pollution agglomeration mainly occurs in the Beijing-Tianjin-Hebei region and central China. High-high cluster covers mainly seven provinces, namely Beijing, Tianjin, Hebei, Shandong, Shanxi, Henan, and Hubei. Low-low cluster mainly involves Xinjiang and Jilin areas. The specific results are shown in Fig. 18.1.

How to quantitatively evaluate the spillover of haze among areas is also one of the critical issues in the study. However, no research combines the spillover effect of haze among different regions and the inter-regional co-opetition. When there is a spatial spillover effect, changes in haze pollution in the area will also have an impact on haze pollution in the neighboring areas. As for how to measure the strength of the spatial spillover relations, the study proposes three hypotheses:

Hypothesis 1: The two main bodies of spatial spillover are active output side and passive input side. If the current measurement decision unit is an active output side, it

**Table 18.4** Data of inputs and outputs

| Inputs | | | | | | | Outputs | |
|---|---|---|---|---|---|---|---|---|
| | | | | | | | Desirable outputs | Undesirable outputs |
| DMU | $SO_2$ emissions (t.) | $NO_X$emissions (t.) | Soot emissions (t.) | Coal consumption (10,00 tons) | Capital (100 million yuan) | Labor force (10,000 people) | GDP (100 million yuan) | $PM_{2.5}$ mcg/m$^3$ |
| Beijing | 71,171.67 | 137,627.14 | 49,386.55 | 1165.18 | 964.25 | 777.34 | 23,014.59 | 80.4 |
| Tianjin | 185,900.43 | 246,800.02 | 100,685.72 | 4538.83 | 163.87 | 294.78 | 16,538.19 | 71.5 |
| Hebei | 1,108,370.93 | 1,350,808.34 | 1,575,417.12 | 28,943.13 | 1044.58 | 643.65 | 29,806.11 | 77.3 |
| Shanxi | 1,120,643.18 | 930,750.79 | 1,448,903.7 | 37,115.1 | 720.97 | 440.27 | 12,766.49 | 56.4 |
| Inner Mongolia | 1,230,945.68 | 1,139,013.23 | 878,752.73 | 36,499.76 | 705.02 | 298.27 | 17,831.51 | 41 |
| Liaoning | 968,766.93 | 828,123.64 | 1,000,038.37 | 17,336.36 | 821.73 | 618.39 | 28,669.02 | 55 |
| Jilin | 362,928 | 501,664 | 447,329.49 | 9805.31 | 436.46 | 325.06 | 14,063.13 | 54.4 |
| Heilongjiang | 456,331.21 | 644,811.4 | 644,064.47 | 13,432.85 | 499.99 | 433.52 | 15,083.67 | 39.4 |
| Shanghai | 170,843.52 | 300,621.06 | 120,668.29 | 4728.13 | 501.61 | 637.23 | 25,123.45 | 53.9 |
| Jiangsu | 835,058.81 | 1,067,642.49 | 654,500.71 | 27,209.12 | 806.89 | 1552.08 | 70,116.38 | 56.6 |
| Zhejiang | 537,826.34 | 607,699.72 | 330,248.84 | 13,826.07 | 1658.55 | 1083.41 | 42,886.49 | 47.7 |
| Anhui | 480,072.79 | 721,008.59 | 545,916.71 | 15,671.32 | 1145.89 | 513.79 | 22,005.63 | 55.1 |
| Fujian | 337,881.74 | 379,021.84 | 341,663.62 | 7659.94 | 1498.67 | 663.08 | 25,979.82 | 28.7 |
| Jiangxi | 528,064.92 | 492,693.36 | 480,624.27 | 7698.24 | 678.02 | 480.49 | 16,723.78 | 42.8 |
| Shandong | 1,525,670.1 | 1,423,884.03 | 1,082,461.03 | 40,926.94 | 752.41 | 1236.72 | 63,002.33 | 66.4 |
| Henna | 1,144,252.03 | 1,262,371.87 | 846,125.01 | 23,719.94 | 1228.73 | 1125.85 | 37,002.16 | 80.7 |
| Hubei | 551,358 | 514,460.61 | 446,974 | 11,765.91 | 1050.37 | 712.33 | 29,550.19 | 65.9 |

(continued)

**Table 18.4** (continued)

| Inputs | | | | | | | Outputs | |
|---|---|---|---|---|---|---|---|---|
| | | | | | | | Desirable outputs | Undesirable outputs |
| DMU | $SO_2$ emissions (t.) | $NO_X$emissions (t.) | Soot emissions (t.) | Coal consumption (10,00 tons) | Capital (100 million yuan) | Labor force (10,000 people) | GDP (100 million yuan) | $PM_{2.5}$ mcg/m$^3$ |
| Hunan | 595,473.42 | 496,928.11 | 454,499.38 | 11,142.26 | 1331.43 | 579.15 | 28,902.21 | 52.5 |
| Guangdong | 678,341.35 | 996,899.19 | 347,785.72 | 16,587.32 | 1755.3 | 1948.04 | 72,812.55 | 34 |
| Guangxi | 421,198.7 | 373,435.2 | 355,865.28 | 6046.71 | 1207.52 | 405.41 | 16,803.12 | 40.2 |
| Hainan | 32,300.06 | 89,518.24 | 20,400 | 1071.92 | 209.71 | 100.36 | 3702.76 | 19.3 |
| Sichuan | 717,584.45 | 525,880.33 | 412,571.66 | 9288.9 | 1656.81 | 795.47 | 30,053.10 | 46.7 |
| Guihzou | 852,964.5 | 419,137.2 | 285,588.72 | 12,833.49 | 598.15 | 307.47 | 10,502.56 | 31.7 |
| Yunnan | 583,739.22 | 449,365.61 | 312,563.29 | 7712.85 | 1463.23 | 414.66 | 13,619.17 | 28 |
| Shaanxi | 735,017.21 | 627,366.16 | 603,648.92 | 18,373.61 | 1238.36 | 511.84 | 18,021.86 | 52 |
| Gansu | 570,621.39 | 387,271.54 | 295,439.86 | 6557.06 | 1101.91 | 261.76 | 6790.32 | 41.2 |
| Qinghai | 150,766 | 117,855 | 246,020.04 | 1508.12 | 609.03 | 62.71 | 2417.05 | 42.6 |
| Ningxia | 357,596.19 | 367,633.87 | 229,909.47 | 8907.37 | 307.03 | 73.12 | 2911.77 | 45.8 |
| Xinjiang | 778,330.32 | 736,504.76 | 595,916.68 | 17,359.28 | 1561.52 | 317.25 | 9324.80 | 53.7 |

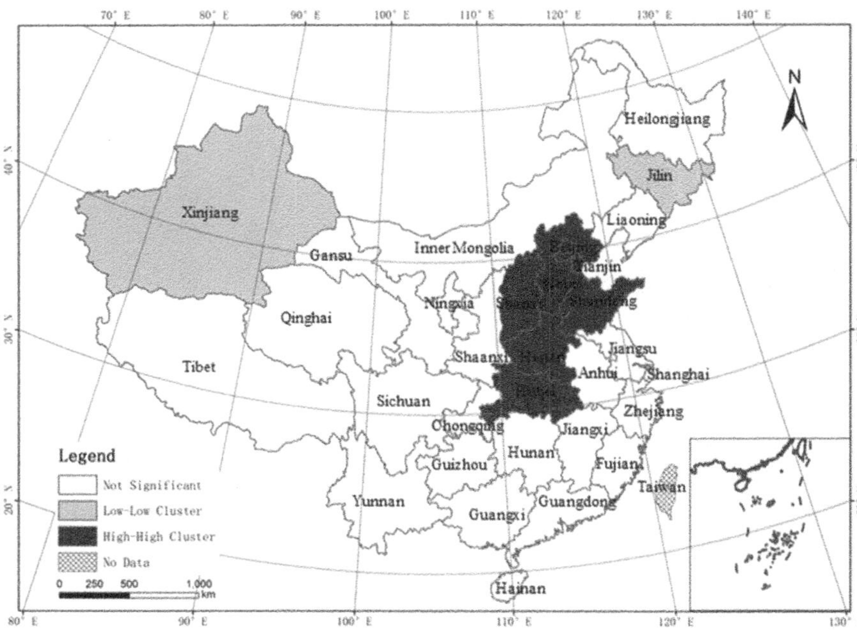


**Fig. 18.1** Distribution of moran'i of $PM_{2.5}$

is then in cooperation with the passive input side. If the current measurement decision unit is a passive input side, it is then in competition with the active output side.

Hypothesis 2: The spatial spillover of haze has the characteristics of geographical proximity transfer and transfer between high and low concentration. In other words, haze moves from high-high cluster to low-low cluster or regions where $PM_{2.5}$ is not significant or moves from low-low cluster to regions where $PM_{2.5}$ is not significant.

Hypothesis 3: The value of the co-opetition coefficient indicates the span of different grades of the haze co-opetition relationship. The larger the grade span, the higher the absolute value of the co-opetition. For example, 1 (−1): 0.5 (−0.5): and 0 are used to express the different strengths of the co-opetition coefficient.

According to the Moran'I index obtained above, assuming that haze spills over from high-high cluster to low-low cluster or regions where $PM_{2.5}$ is not significant, or from low-low cluster to regions where $PM_{2.5}$ is not significant, assuming that there is spatial proximity transfer of haze, that is haze moves to adjacent low-low cluster or regions where $PM_{2.5}$ is not significant, and the overall benefit of the active haze output side is positive and the overall benefit of the passive recipients is negative, the specific situation is as follows:

(1) If the two decision-making units are in the same cluster, the two units are believed to be cooperative, and the coefficient of co-operation is denoted as 1.
(2) If the two decision-making units are in different clusters:

When the two units are adjacent: First, when the $DMU_d$ is in a high-high cluster, $DMU_j$ is in a low-low cluster, the coefficient of co-opetition is denoted as 0.5 in the case that $DMU_d$ is in cooperation with $DMU_j$, and the coefficient is denoted as −0.5 in the case that $DMU_j$ is in a competitive relationship with $DMU_d$.

Second, when $DMU_d$ is in a low-low cluster, $DMU_j$ is in an area where $PM_{2.5}$ concentration in space is insignificant, co-opetition coefficient is denoted as 0.5 in the case that $DMU_d$ is in a cooperative relationship with $DMU_j$, and the coefficient is denoted as −0.5 in the case that $DMU_j$ is in a competitive relationship with $DMU_d$.

Third, when $DMU_d$ is in a high-high cluster, $DMU_j$ is in an area where $PM_{2.5}$ concentration in space is insignificant, co-opetition coefficient is denoted as 1 in the case that $DMU_d$ is in a cooperative relationship with $DMU_j$, and the coefficient is denoted as −1 in the case that $DMU_j$ is in a competitive relationship with $DMU_d$.

When the two decision-making units are not adjacent, it is considered that the two decision-making units are cooperative and the coefficient of co-opetition is denoted as 1.

(3) The self-evaluation coefficient of the decision-making unit is denoted as zero.

Take Inner Mongolia, a place where the $PM_{2.5}$ concentration is insignificant, as an example. It is close to high-high haze cluster where Beijing, Tianjin, Hebei and Shanxi provinces are located, and is adjacent to Hebei and Shanxi. Therefore, Inner Mongolia is in competition with Hebei and Shanxi provinces, with the co-opetition efficient denoted as −1. Inner Mongolia is not adjacent to Beijing and Tianjin, so it is in cooperation with Beijing and Tianjin, with the coefficient denoted as; the self-evaluation coefficient of Inner Mongolia is zero; Jilin is located in low-low cluster and adjacent to Inner Mongolia, so Inner Mongolia is in competition with Jilin, with the coefficient denoted as −0.5. The relationships between Inner Mongolia and Liaoning, Heilongjiang, Shanghai, Jiangsu, Zhejiang, Anhui, Fujian, Jiangxi, Shandong, Henan, Hubei, Hunan, Guangdong, Guangxi, Hainan, Sichuan, Guizhou, Yunnan, Shaanxi, Gansu, Qinghai, Ningxia and Xinjiang all satisfy the hypothesis of cooperative relationship, so the co-opetition coefficients are all 1. Hence the haze spatial spillover effect is linked with the co-opetition between the provinces, and the co-opetition relationship matrix between Inner Mongolia and other provinces is established.

The national co-opetition matrix $g_{rd}$ is constructed according to this, as shown in Table 18.5.

**Table 18.5** Coopetition matrix $g_{rd}$

| DMU | | Other given decision making units | | | | | | | | | | | | | | |
|---|---|---|---|---|---|---|---|---|---|---|---|---|---|---|---|---|
| | | Beijing | Tianjin | Hebei | Shanxi | Inner Mongolia | Liaoning | Jilin | Heilongjiang | Shanghai | Jiangsu | Zhejiang | Anhui | Fujian | Jiangxi | Shandong |
| Current decision-making units | Beijing | 0 | 1 | 1 | 1 | 1 | 1 | 1 | 1 | 1 | 1 | 1 | 1 | 1 | 1 | 1 |
| | Tianjin | 1 | 0 | 1 | 1 | 1 | 1 | 1 | 1 | 1 | 1 | 1 | 1 | 1 | 1 | 1 |
| | Hebei | 1 | 1 | 0 | 1 | 1 | 1 | 1 | 1 | 1 | 1 | 1 | 1 | 1 | 1 | 1 |
| | Shanxi | 1 | 1 | 1 | 0 | 1 | 1 | 1 | 1 | 1 | 1 | 1 | 1 | 1 | 1 | 1 |
| | Inner Mongolia | 1 | 1 | -1 | -1 | 0 | 1 | -0.5 | 1 | 1 | 1 | 1 | 1 | 1 | 1 | 1 |
| | Liaoning | 1 | 1 | -1 | 1 | 1 | 0 | -0.5 | 1 | 1 | 1 | 1 | 1 | 1 | 1 | 1 |
| | Jilin | 1 | 1 | 1 | 1 | 0.5 | 0.5 | 0 | 0.5 | 1 | 1 | 1 | 1 | 1 | 1 | 1 |
| | Heilongjiang | 1 | 1 | 1 | 1 | 1 | 1 | -0.5 | 0 | 1 | 1 | 1 | 1 | 1 | 1 | 1 |
| | Shanghai | 1 | 1 | 1 | 1 | 1 | 1 | 1 | 1 | 0 | 1 | 1 | 1 | 1 | 1 | 1 |
| | Jiangsu | 1 | 1 | 1 | 1 | 1 | 1 | 1 | 1 | 1 | 0 | 1 | 1 | 1 | 1 | -1 |
| | Zhejiang | 1 | 1 | 1 | 1 | 1 | 1 | 1 | 1 | 1 | 1 | 0 | 1 | 1 | 1 | 1 |
| | Anhui | 1 | 1 | 1 | 1 | 1 | 1 | 1 | 1 | 1 | 1 | 1 | 0 | 1 | 1 | -1 |
| | Fujian | 1 | 1 | 1 | 1 | 1 | 1 | 1 | 1 | 1 | 1 | 1 | 1 | 0 | 1 | 1 |
| | Jiangxi | 1 | 1 | 1 | 1 | 1 | 1 | 1 | 1 | 1 | 1 | 1 | 1 | 1 | 0 | 1 |
| | Shandong | 1 | 1 | 1 | 1 | 1 | 1 | 1 | 1 | 1 | 1 | 1 | 1 | 1 | 1 | 0 |
| | Henna | 1 | 1 | 1 | 1 | 1 | 1 | 1 | 1 | 1 | 1 | 1 | 1 | 1 | 1 | 1 |
| | Hubei | 1 | 1 | 1 | 1 | 1 | 1 | 1 | 1 | 1 | 1 | 1 | 1 | 1 | 1 | 1 |
| | Hunan | 1 | 1 | 1 | 1 | 1 | 1 | 1 | 1 | 1 | 1 | 1 | 1 | 1 | 1 | 1 |
| | Guangdong | 1 | 1 | 1 | 1 | 1 | 1 | 1 | 1 | 1 | 1 | 1 | 1 | 1 | 1 | 1 |
| | Guangxi | 1 | 1 | 1 | 1 | 1 | 1 | 1 | 1 | 1 | 1 | 1 | 1 | 1 | 1 | 1 |
| | Hainan | 1 | 1 | 1 | 1 | 1 | 1 | 1 | 1 | 1 | 1 | 1 | 1 | 1 | 1 | 1 |
| | Sichuan | 1 | 1 | 1 | 1 | 1 | 1 | 1 | 1 | 1 | 1 | 1 | 1 | 1 | 1 | 1 |
| | Guihzou | 1 | 1 | 1 | 1 | 1 | 1 | 1 | 1 | 1 | 1 | 1 | 1 | 1 | 1 | 1 |
| | Yunnan | 1 | 1 | 1 | 1 | 1 | 1 | 1 | 1 | 1 | 1 | 1 | 1 | 1 | 1 | 1 |
| | Shaanxi | 1 | 1 | 1 | -1 | 1 | 1 | 1 | 1 | 1 | 1 | 1 | 1 | 1 | 1 | 1 |

(continued)

**Table 18.5** (continued)

| DMU | | Other given decision making units | | | | | | | | | | | | | | |
|---|---|---|---|---|---|---|---|---|---|---|---|---|---|---|---|---|
| | | Beijing | Tianjin | Hebei | Shanxi | Inner Mongolia | Liaoning | Jilin | Heilongjiang | Shanghai | Jiangsu | Zhejiang | Anhui | Fujian | Jiangxi | Shandong |
| | Gansu | 1 | 1 | 1 | 1 | 1 | 1 | 1 | 1 | 1 | 1 | 1 | 1 | 1 | 1 | 1 |
| | Qinghai | 1 | 1 | 1 | 1 | 1 | 1 | 1 | 1 | 1 | 1 | 1 | 1 | 1 | 1 | 1 |
| | Ningxia | 1 | 1 | 1 | 1 | 1 | 1 | 1 | 1 | 1 | 1 | 1 | 1 | 1 | 1 | 1 |
| | Xinjiang | 1 | 1 | 1 | 1 | 1 | 1 | 1 | 1 | 1 | 1 | 1 | 1 | 1 | 1 | 1 |

| DMU | | Other given decision-making units | | | | | | | | | | | | | | |
|---|---|---|---|---|---|---|---|---|---|---|---|---|---|---|---|---|
| | | Hennan | Hubei | Hunan | Guangdong | Guangxi | Hainan | Sichuan | Guihzou | Yunnan | Shaanxi | Gansu | Qinghai | Ningxia | Xinjiang | |
| **Current decision making units** | Beijing | 1 | 1 | 1 | 1 | 1 | 1 | 1 | 1 | 1 | 1 | 1 | 1 | 1 | 1 | |
| | Tianjin | 1 | 1 | 1 | 1 | 1 | 1 | 1 | 1 | 1 | 1 | 1 | 1 | 1 | 1 | |
| | Hebei | 1 | 1 | 1 | 1 | 1 | 1 | 1 | 1 | 1 | 1 | 1 | 1 | 1 | 1 | |
| | Shanxi | 1 | 1 | 1 | 1 | 1 | 1 | 1 | 1 | 1 | 1 | 1 | 1 | 1 | 1 | |
| | Inner Mongolia | 1 | 1 | 1 | 1 | 1 | 1 | 1 | 1 | 1 | 1 | 1 | 1 | 1 | 1 | |
| | Liaoning | 1 | 1 | 1 | 1 | 1 | 1 | 1 | 1 | 1 | 1 | 1 | 1 | 1 | 1 | |
| | Jilin | 1 | 1 | 1 | 1 | 1 | 1 | 1 | 1 | 1 | 1 | 1 | 1 | 1 | 1 | |
| | Heilongjiang | 1 | 1 | 1 | 1 | 1 | 1 | 1 | 1 | 1 | 1 | 1 | 1 | 1 | 1 | |
| | Shanghai | 1 | 1 | 1 | 1 | 1 | 1 | 1 | 1 | 1 | 1 | 1 | 1 | 1 | 1 | |
| | Jiangsu | 1 | 1 | 1 | 1 | 1 | 1 | 1 | 1 | 1 | 1 | 1 | 1 | 1 | 1 | |
| | Zhejiang | 1 | 1 | 1 | 1 | 1 | 1 | 1 | 1 | 1 | 1 | 1 | 1 | 1 | 1 | |
| | Anhui | -1 | -1 | 1 | 1 | 1 | 1 | 1 | 1 | 1 | 1 | 1 | 1 | 1 | 1 | |
| | Fujian | 1 | 1 | 1 | 1 | 1 | 1 | 1 | 1 | 1 | 1 | 1 | 1 | 1 | 1 | |
| | Jiangxi | 1 | -1 | 1 | 1 | 1 | 1 | 1 | 1 | 1 | 1 | 1 | 1 | 1 | 1 | |
| | Shandong | 1 | 1 | 1 | 1 | 1 | 1 | 1 | 1 | 1 | 1 | 1 | 1 | 1 | 1 | |
| | Henna | 0 | 1 | 1 | 1 | 1 | 1 | 1 | 1 | 1 | 1 | 1 | 1 | 1 | 1 | |
| | Hubei | 1 | 0 | 1 | 1 | 1 | 1 | 1 | 1 | 1 | 1 | 1 | 1 | 1 | 1 | |
| | Hunan | 1 | -1 | 0 | 1 | 1 | 1 | 1 | 1 | 1 | 1 | 1 | 1 | 1 | 1 | |

(continued)

**Table 18.5** (continued)

| DMU | Other given decision making units | | | | | | | | | | | | | | |
|---|---|---|---|---|---|---|---|---|---|---|---|---|---|---|---|
| | Beijing | Tianjin | Hebei | Shanxi | Inner Mongolia | Liaoning | Jilin | Heilongjiang | Shanghai | Jiangsu | Zhejiang | Anhui | Fujian | Jiangxi | Shandong |
| Guangdong | 1 | 1 | 1 | 0 | 1 | 1 | 1 | 1 | 1 | 1 | 1 | 1 | 1 | 1 | |
| Guangxi | 1 | 1 | 1 | 1 | 0 | 1 | 1 | 1 | 1 | 1 | 1 | 1 | 1 | 1 | |
| Hainan | 1 | 1 | 1 | 1 | 1 | 0 | 1 | 1 | 1 | 1 | 1 | 1 | 1 | 1 | |
| Sichuan | 1 | 1 | 1 | 1 | 1 | 1 | 0 | 1 | 1 | 1 | 1 | 1 | 1 | 1 | |
| Guihzou | 1 | 1 | 1 | 1 | 1 | 1 | 1 | 0 | 1 | 1 | 1 | 1 | 1 | 1 | |
| Yunnan | 1 | 1 | 1 | 1 | 1 | 1 | 1 | 1 | 0 | 1 | 1 | 1 | 1 | 1 | |
| Shaanxi | -1 | -1 | 1 | 1 | 1 | 1 | 1 | 1 | 1 | 0 | 1 | 1 | 1 | 1 | |
| Gansu | 1 | 1 | 1 | 1 | 1 | 1 | 1 | 1 | 1 | 1 | 0 | 1 | 1 | -0.5 | |
| Qinghai | 1 | 1 | 1 | 1 | 1 | 1 | 1 | 1 | 1 | 1 | 1 | 0 | 1 | -0.5 | |
| Ningxia | 1 | 1 | 1 | 1 | 1 | 1 | 1 | 1 | 1 | 1 | 1 | 1 | 0 | 1 | |
| Xinjiang | 1 | 1 | 1 | 1 | 1 | 1 | 1 | 1 | 1 | 1 | 0.5 | 0.5 | 1 | 0 | |

## 18.5 Empirical Results

### *18.5.1 Evaluation and Analysis of Results*

According to the available data, use MATLAB software to calculate the co-opetition DEA model, and use the CCR model to calculate the haze emission efficiency of all provinces. The haze emission efficiency value of 29 provinces and cities in China and its ranking are obtained. See Table 18.6 for details.

(1) Efficiency Evaluation of Individual Provinces

It can be seen from Table 18.6 above that the efficiency value of the decision-making units for 2015 is not evenly distributed. Ningxia, Shanxi, Hainan, Xinjiang, and Qinghai are the top five provinces ranking regarding haze efficiency emission, with the efficiency values being 0.966, 0.959, 0.959, 0.958, and 0.957 respectively. Heilongjiang, Yunnan, Liaoning, Henan, and Shandong rank as the last five, with the haze emission efficiency values being 0.732, 0.661, 0.656, 0.625, and 0.611. Hence, the efficiency value varies significantly among different provinces. After examining the characteristics of these provinces, we can find that the provinces with higher haze emission efficiency are mostly economically underdeveloped inland provinces with unfavorable meteorological conditions, such as Ningxia, Xinjiang, and Qinghai; provinces with low haze emission efficiency are mostly the economically developed eastern regions like Jiangsu, Shandong and Liaoning. This is inconsistent with the conclusion of previous studies (Wang et al. 2016; He et al. 2016). A likely reason is that haze occurs mostly in winter in China (Pan et al. 2013; Xu et al. 2016; Yang 2017): and influenced by the Asian high pressure, wind in most parts of the country blow from the land to the Pacific Ocean - northwesterly wind. The wind speed has the effect of carrying and diluting the pollutants horizontally, and the wind direction causes the pollutants to move down the wind away from the pollutant source. The pollution transported from the areas with considerable pollution discharges upwind may lead to air pollution in the areas downwind where the discharge of pollutants is relatively small (Liu et al. 2017b): and regional and long-distance movement of pollutants has a significant impact on air quality (Coury 2007; Borge 2007; Wang 2010). We speculate that the result occurs because the strong winter monsoon "blows" the haze in inland areas to the economically developed eastern provinces. This study considers the trans-regional transport of haze and makes the conclusion new and more realistic.

Judging from the construction of the model, among the co-opetition matrices established based on the hypotheses, provinces whose coefficient is negative are 10 in number, including Inner Mongolia, Liaoning, Heilongjiang, Jiangsu, Anhui, Jiangxi, Hunan, Shaanxi, Gansu and Qinghai. Take Anhui and Liaoning as an example. Anhui is adjacent to the high-high cluster in the spatial correlation diagram and thus is in competition with Shandong, Henan and Hubei,

**Table 18.6** Haze emission efficiency value score of provinces and ranking

| DMU | CCR efficiency value | CCR efficiency value ranking | Co-opetition cross Efficiency Value | Co-opetition Cross Efficiency Value Ranking |
|---|---|---|---|---|
| Beijing | 0.985 | 17 | 0.944 | 13 |
| Tianjin | 0.999 | 7 | 0.874 | 19 |
| Hebei | 0.999 | 8 | 0.948 | 11 |
| Shanxi | 0.998 | 15 | 0.959 | 2 |
| Inner Mongolia | 0.999 | 13 | 0.954 | 8 |
| Liaoning | 0.673 | 26 | 0.656 | 27 |
| Jilin | 0.999 | 4 | 0.919 | 18 |
| Heilongjiang | 0.739 | 25 | 0.732 | 25 |
| Shanghai | 0.972 | 19 | 0.928 | 16 |
| Jiangsu | 0.848 | 22 | 0.762 | 24 |
| Zhejiang | 1 | 1 | 0.938 | 15 |
| Anhui | 0.999 | 3 | 0.946 | 12 |
| Fujian | 0.968 | 20 | 0.922 | 17 |
| Jiangxi | 0.999 | 12 | 0.952 | 9 |
| Shandong | 0.651 | 28 | 0.611 | 29 |
| Henan | 0.643 | 28 | 0.625 | 28 |
| Hubei | 0.829 | 24 | 0.809 | 23 |
| Hunan | 0.845 | 23 | 0.814 | 22 |
| Guangdong | 0.999 | 10 | 0.873 | 20 |
| Guangxi | 0.871 | 21 | 0.858 | 21 |
| Hainan | 0.972 | 18 | 0.959 | 3 |
| Sichuan | 0.999 | 6 | 0.942 | 14 |
| Guizhou | 0.997 | 16 | 0.957 | 6 |
| Yunnan | 0.662 | 27 | 0.661 | 26 |
| Shaanxi | 0.999 | 5 | 0.952 | 10 |
| Gansu | 0.999 | 9 | 0.955 | 7 |
| Qinghai | 0.999 | 11 | 0.957 | 5 |
| Ningxia | 1 | 1 | 0.966 | 1 |
| Xinjiang | 0.999 | 14 | 0.958 | 4 |

and the coefficient of co-opetition is $-1$. Compared with the traditional DEA model, the rank of the province's efficiency value obtained based on the co-opetition DEA model decreases by 9, because the co-opetition cross-coefficient in the model's expression acts on the numerator, and the mathematical meaning is that the entire efficiency value becomes smaller. In the spatial correlation diagram, Liaoning adjoins both the high-high cluster and low-low cluster, is adjacent to Hebei and Jilin, with the coefficients of co-opetition being respectively −1 and −0.5. By the same token, the co-opetition cross-coefficient in the model's expression acts on the numerator, and the mathematical meaning is that the entire efficiency value becomes smaller, and the empirical result shows that the co-opetition co-efficient value ranks one place lower than the CCR efficiency value. Aside from the co-opetition matrices of the abovementioned 10 provinces where there are negative coefficients, the co-opetition coefficients in other provinces are all non-negative. Take Beijing as an example. Beijing is in the Beijing-Tianjin-Hebei highly polluted area, and thus is in cooperation with other provinces, expressed as that the coefficient of co-opetition is positive. The mathematical meaning shows that the co-opetition efficiency increases and the empirical result is that the co-opetition efficiency value ranks four places higher than that of the CCR efficiency value. In this study, the spatial correlation matrix is introduced to build a co-opetition DEA cross-efficiency model to estimate the $PM_{2.5}$ emission efficiency of each decision-making unit. This way, the ranking of the decision-making units is also more reasonable.

(2) Further Evaluation by Region

The geographical zone dividing of China's more than 30 provinces and centrally-controlled municipalities produces eight regions[8]: East China, South China, Central China, North China, Northwest China, Southwest China, Northeast China and Hong Kong, Macau and Taiwan. Such a division is conducive to analyzing haze emission efficiency in all regions. Then, the rank-sum test is used to calculate the relationship of the co-opetition efficiency values in the eight different regions. The specific test methods and results are shown in Table 18.7.

Assume that the efficiency values are distributed in the same manner as the regions are categorized, the null hypothesis is rejected at a significance level of 0.05 through the K-W test, that is, there is a significant difference among the co-opetition efficiency values of the eight zones. Of the top 10 provinces ranked in terms of co-opetition cross efficiency value, five are in Northwest China, two belong to North China, and the remaining three are respectively in South China, Central China and Southwest China. Thus, regions along the northwesterly wind have higher emission efficiency, despite their poor economic development conditions; and though economically more developed, the regions located along the southeasterly wind have lower emission efficiency. The haze emission efficiency of each region is shown in Fig. 18.2.

According to the abovementioned K-W test results, it can be seen from Fig. 18.2 that there are differences among haze emission efficiency of different zones. The haze emission efficiency is generally high in Northwest China and North

[8]East China: Shandong, Jiangsu, Anhui, Zhejiang, Fujian and Shanghai; South China: Guangdong, Guangxi and Hainan; Central China: Hubei, Hunan, Henan and Jiangxi; North China: Beijing, Tianjin, Hebei, Shanxi and Inner Mongolia; Northwest China: Ningxia, Qinghai, Shaanxi, Gansu; Southwest China: Sichuan, Yunnan, Guizhou, Tibet, Chongqing; Northeast China: Liaoning, Jilin, Heilongjiang; HK, MC and TW: Hong Kong, Macau, Taiwan. Due to the lack of data, Chongqing, Tibet, Hong Kong, Macau and Taiwan are not taken into account.

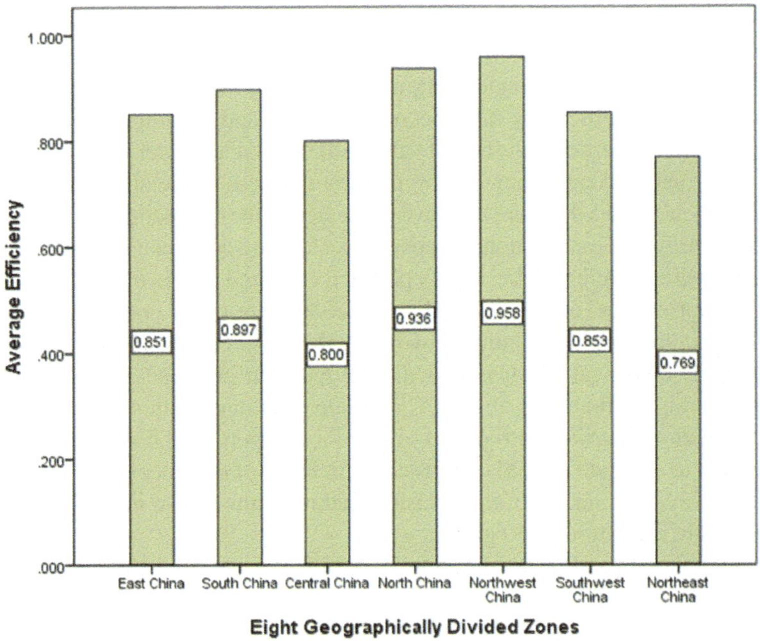


**Fig. 18.2** Ranking of haze emission efficiency value of eight zones

China, while the efficiency is generally low in Central China and Northeast China.

(3) Haze pollution in one region increases haze pollution in surrounding areas

According to Table 18.6, Beijing ranks 17th in terms of the traditional CCR efficiency, but sees its rank rose to 13th concerning co-opetition cross-efficiency value. Tianjin and Hebei, however, see their co-opetition cross-efficiency value rank decrease compared with the traditional CCR efficiency. Analysis of the Beijing-Tianjin-Hebei region shows that within the Beijing-Tianjin-Hebei region, as the cost of land, labor remuneration and other factors continued to rise and government regulation and control continued to increase in Beijing, heavy-polluting industries were relocated to surrounding regions. Tianjin, on the one hand, received food industry, study making and study products industry, ferrous and non-ferrous metal smelting and rolling processing industry and other traditional manufacturing industries to provide support and cooperation, and it, on the other hand, exported some of its modern manufacturing industries like transportation equipment, electrical machinery and equipment manufacturing. Benefitting from its cost advantages in resources, manpower and land and with the active promotion by the government, Hebei Province has undertaken a lot of high-input, high-polluting capital-intensive industries from Beijing and Tianjin, such as ferrous metal smelting and rolling processing industry, metal products industry, petroleum processing and coking industry, chemical raw materials and

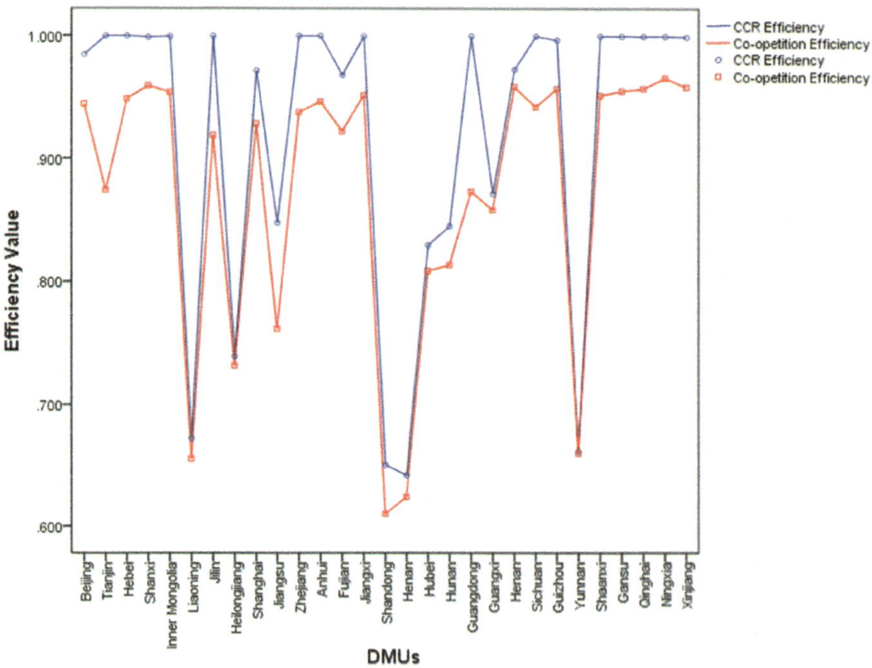


**Fig. 18.3** Efficiency value distribution

**Table 18.7** K-W test results

| Null hypothesis | Test method | Level of significance | Decision |
|---|---|---|---|
| No significant difference between efficiency value of different regions | Independent Sample Kruskal Walliss Test | 0.036 | Rejecting null hypothesis |

chemical products manufacturing over the past decade or so. To sum up, the cross-regional movement of haze causes a decline in the efficiency ranking of Hebei and Tianjin.

### *18.5.2 Method Validity Analysis*

The haze emission efficiency values of the 29 provinces obtained using the co-opetition DEA evaluation are entirely different from the traditional CCR efficiency values. Traditional CCR models cannot rank provinces with an efficiency value of 1. For example, Zhejiang and Ningxia have the same haze emission efficiency value of 1, and cannot be further ranked. Considering the co-opetition between decision-making units, the co-opetition coefficient matrix g (x) constructed in this study is more realistic for the calculation of cross-efficiency values. It can be seen from Table 18.6 that the haze emission efficiency values of all the provinces are less than 1 in the assessment results of the competing DEA model. For example, the DEA efficiency for Ningxia is one under the traditional CCR model, and its scores and ranks the same under the co-opetition cross efficiency model. For Zhejiang whose traditional CCR efficiency value is 1, its co-opetition DEA efficiency value is 0.938, ranking 15th. Hence, co-opetition DEA can help classify decision-making units at a more nuanced level.

According to the calculation results, the evaluation results of traditional CCR model and co-opetition DEA model can be obtained, as shown in Fig. 18.3.

As can be seen from the figure above, overall, compared with the traditional CCR model, the evaluation based on the co-opetition DEA model delivers basically same results, but consistently smaller efficiency values. Hence, the co-opetition DEA model constructed in this study is more realistic and takes into full consideration the cooperation and competition among the decision-making units under evaluation. The calculated haze emission efficiency is more accurate and can be better recognized. The ranking results are more reliable and reasonable.

## 18.6 Conclusions

(1) In this study, a co-opetition DEA cross-efficiency model is constructed using spatial econometrics method and with the spillover relationship between decision-making units, which overcomes the shortcoming of traditional DEA—setting all provinces and cities together as either in a competitive or cooperative relationship. Taking provinces in China as the decision-making units and taking $PM_{2.5}$ as an example (as undesirable output): the study calculates the spatial correlation of $PM_{2.5}$ in 29 provinces in China, making the evaluation results more realistic.

(2) The main conclusions of the empirical study include: First, haze emission efficiency for different provinces and municipalities in 2015 calculated using the co-opetition DEA method varies greatly. Provinces with higher haze emission efficiency are mostly inland provinces characterized by relatively slow economic development and poor meteorological conditions; while provinces that have lower haze emission efficiency are mostly economically developed eastern regions. Second, because of the significant interaction of air pollution with the surrounding area, and under the effect of haze cross-region movement, the two decision-making units, Tianjin and Guangdong, are significantly affected by the competition and cooperation, and the evaluation results of the traditional CCR model differ significantly from those resulting from co-opetition DEA model.

(3) Compared with the efficiency calculated by the traditional CCR model, the distribution trend of the efficiency values obtained using the model constructed in this study is the same as that of the traditional CCR model, but the cross-efficiency value of each decision-making unit is less than the traditional CCR efficiency value, and can be ranked in a more accurate, nuanced manner.

The main innovation of this study lies in that it tries to introduce the method of spatial econometrics into the construction of co-opetition DEA, which enriches the research scope of DEA. However, regarding future research, how to match the result of a spatial matrix with the actual situation of spatial spillover is worth further study. Other issues that deserve further study include:

(1) Better combine co-opetition with cross-efficiency evaluation methods. The existing research on cross efficiency is generally divided into two situations: First, assume that all decision-making units are all in a cooperative alliance; second, all decision-making units are assumed to be in a competitive rivalry. There is almost no existing research which considers that decision-making units are in competitive and cooperative relationships simultaneously. In response to this problem, this study introduces the cross-efficiency model based on co-opetition relationship matrix. However, in dealing with actual problems, the co-opetition relationship among decision-making units is very complicated, so how to expand the correlational matrix that describes the actual co-opetitive relations to solve more complex problems points the direction for future research.
(2) Construct the spatially weighted matrix of geo-economic distance. In this study, we analyze the spatial correlation characteristics of haze pollution by using the Moran 'I index. The spatial weight coefficient involved is the geographic distance weight matrix. Given the fact that the level of regional economic development is spatially correlated, the weight matrix of economic distance including industrial transfer and regional spillover may be considered, in order to enhance the robustness of the analysis results. This not only considers the spatial influence of geographical distance but also reflects the reality that there are spillovers and radiation effects between regions, which may reflect the degree of spatial correlation between decision-making units more thoroughly and objectively.

**Acknowledgements** Peng Zhao, Yufeng Chen, Zhanxin Ma, Zhiyong Ji also made great contributions to this manuscript. We express our heartfelt thanks to them. This research was supported by: National Social and Scientific Fund Program of China (18ZDA052; 17BGL142; 16ZDA047); The Natural Science Foundation of China (91546117, 71373131).

## References


An, Q., Wen, Y., & Ding, T. (2018). Resource sharing and payoff allocation in a three-stage system: Integrating network DEA with the Shapley value method. *Omega* (in Press). https://doi.org/10.1016/j.omega.2018.05.008.

Anselin, L. (2001). Spatial effects in econometric practice in environmental and resource economics. *American Journal of Agricultural Economics, 83*(3), 705–710.

Bang, Y. Y., Lee, D. S., & Lim, S. R. (2019). Analysis of corporate $CO_2$ and energy cost efficiency: The role of performance indicators and effective environmental reporting. *Energy Policy*, 133.

Borge, R., Lumbreras, J., & Vardoulakis, S. (2007). Analysis of long-range transport influences on urban $PM_{10}$ using two-stage atmospheric trajectory clusters. *Atmospheric Environment, 41*(21), 4434–4450.

Camarero, M., Castillo, J., Picazo-Tadeo, A. J., & Tamarit, C. (2013). Eco-efficiency and convergence in OECD countries. *Environmental & Resource Economics, 55*(1), 87–106.

Cao, Y. (2016). *Regional technical innovation efficiency evaluation and promotion strategies based on cross-efficiency model*. Shenyang University of Technology.

Chen, X., Shao, S., & Tian, Z. (2017). Impacts of air pollution and its spatial spillover effect on public health based on China's big data sample. *Journal of Cleaner Production, 142,*, 915–925.

Chen, X., & Lin, B. Q. (2020). Assessment of eco-efficiency change considering energy and environment: A study of China's non-ferrous metals industry. *Journal of Cleaner Production*, 277.

Chen, S., Zhang, Y., Zhang, Y., & Liu, Z. (2019). The relationship between industrial restructuring and china's regional haze pollution: a spatial spillover perspective. *Journal of Cleaner Production*, 239.

Chen, L., Wang, Y. M., & Huang, Y. (2020a). Cross-efficiency aggregation method based on prospect consensus process. *Annals of Operations Research, 288*(1), 115–135.

Chen, Y., Zhu, B., Sun, X., & Xu, G. (2020b). Industrial environmental efficiency and its influencing factors in china: Analysis based on the Super-SBM model and spatial panel data. *Environmental Science and Pollution Research, 27*(9), 44267–44278.

Chen, L., Wu, F. M., Wang, Y. M., & Li, M. J. (2020c). Analysis of the environmental efficiency in China based on the DEA cross-efficiency approach under different policy objectives. *Expert Systems, 37*(3).

Chen, L., Huang, Y., Li, M. J., & Wang, Y. M. (2020d). Meta-frontier analysis using cross-efficiency method for performance evaluation. *European Journal of Operational Research, 280*(1), 219–229.

Cheng, Z., Li, L., & Liu, J. (2017). Identifying the spatial effects and driving factors of urban $PM_{2.5}$ pollution in China. *Ecological Indicators*, 82: 61–75.

Choi, Y., Zhang, N., & Zhou, P. (2012). Efficiency and abatement costs of energy-related $CO_2$ emissions in China: A slacks-based efficiency measure. *Applied Energy, 98*, 198–208.

Coury, C., & Dillner, A. M. (2007). Trends and sources of particulate matter in the superstition wilderness using air trajectory and aerosol cluster analysis. *Atmospheric Environment*, 2017, 41(40): 9309–9323.

Cui, Q., & Li, Y. (2020). A cross efficiency distinguishing method to explore the cooperation degree in dynamic airline environmental efficiency. *Transport Policy, 99*, 31–43.

Davtalab-Olyaie, M., & Asgharian, M. (2021). On Pareto-optimality in the cross-efficiency evaluation. *European Journal of Operational Research, 288*(1), 247–257.

Ding, L., Yang, Y., Wang, L., & Calin, A. C. (2020). Cross efficiency assessment of china's marine economy under environmental governance. *Ocean & Coastal Management, 193*, 105245.

Doyle, J., & Green, R. (1994). Efficiency and cross efficiency in DEA: Derivations, meanings and the uses. *Journal of the Operational Research Society, 45*, 567–578.

Fan, J. P., Lan, J. R., Zhang, J., Wang, Z., & Wu, M. Q. (2019). A novel cross-efficiency evaluation method under hesitant fuzzy environment. *Journal of Intelligent & Fuzzy Systems, 36*(1), 371–383.

Fan, J. P., Guo, Z. W., & Wu, M. Q. (2020). An improvement of DEA cross-efficiency aggregation based on BWM-TOPSIS. *IEEE Access, 8,* 37334–37342.

Feng, T., Du, H. B., Lin, Z. G., & Zuo, J. (2020). Spatial spillover effects of environmental regulations on air pollution: Evidence from urban agglomerations in China. *Journal of Environmental Management*, 272.

Fleishman, R., Alexander, R., Bretschneider, S., & Popp, D. (2009). Does regulation stimulate productivity? The effect of air quality policies on the efficiency of US power plants. *Energy Policy, 37*(11), 4574–4582.

Gan, T., Yang, H. C., Liang, W., & Liao, X. C. (2020). *Do economic development and population agglomeration inevitably aggravate haze pollution in China?* Environmental Science and Pollution Research: New evidence from spatial econometric analysis.

Gieré, R., Blackford, M., & Smith, K. (2006). TEM Study of $PM_{2.5}$ emitted from coal and tire combustion in a thermal power station. *Environmental Science & Technology, 40*(20), 6235–6240.

Green, R. H., Doyle, J. R., & Cook, W. D. (1996). Preference voting and project ranking using DEA and cross-evaluation. *European Journal of Operational Research, 90*(3), 461–472.

Guo, X., Lu, C. C., & Lee, J. H. (2017a). Applying the dynamic DEA model to evaluate the energy efficiency of OECD countries and China. *Energy, 134,* 392–399.

Guo, J., Zhu, D. D., Wu, X. H., & Yan, Y. Z. (2017b). Study on environment performance evaluation and regional differences of strictly-environmental-monitored cities in China. *Sustainability*. https://doi.org/10.3390/su9122094.

Han, Y. M., Long, C., Geng, Z. Q., & Zhang, K. Y. (2018). Carbon emission analysis and evaluation of industrial departments in China: An improved environmental DEA cross model based on information entropy. *Journal of Environmental Management, 205,* 298–307.

He, F., Ma, D. D., & Zhu, L. Y. (2016). Measurement and factors of environmental technology efficiency in China under the constraint of haze—provincial panel data based on the SBM-undesirable model. *R&D Management, 28*(5), 34–43.

Hermoso-Orzaez, M. J., Garcia-Alguacil, M., & Terrados-Cepeda, J. (2020) Measurement of environmental efficiency in the countries of the European Union with the enhanced data envelopment analysis method (DEA) during the period 2005–2012. *Environmental Science and Pollution Research, 27*(13):15691–15715.

Ho, K. F., Ho, S. S. H., & Huang, R. J. (2016). Chemical composition and bioreactivity of $PM_{2.5}$, during 2013 haze events in China. *Atmospheric Environment, 126,* 162–170.

Hosseini, H. M., & Rahbar, F. (2011). Spatial environmental Kuznets curve for Asian countries: Study of $CO_2$ and $PM_{10}$, *37*(58), 1–14.

Huang, H. J., Liu, H. N., & Jiang, W. M. (2006). Physical and chemical characteristics and source apportionment of $PM_{2.5}$ in Nanjing. *Climatic and Environmental Research, 11*(6), 713–722.

Iftikhar, Y., Wang, Z., Zhang, B., & Wang, B. (2018). Energy and $CO_2$ emissions efficiency of major economies: A network DEA approach. *Energy, 147,* 197–207.

Kao, C., & Liu, S. T. (2019). Cross efficiency measurement and decomposition in two basic network systems. *Omega, 83,* 70–79.

Kao, C., & Liu, S. T. (2020). A slacks-based measure model for calculating cross efficiency in data envelopment analysis. *Omega*, 95.

Lee, H., & Choi, Y. (2018). Heterogeneity and its policy implications in GHG emission performance of manufacturing industries. *Carbon Management, 9*(4), 347–360.

Li, F., Zhu, Q., & Liang, L. (2018a). Allocating a fixed cost based on a DEA-game cross efficiency approach. *Expert Systems with Applications, 96,* 196–207.

Li, Y., Chiu, Y. H., Lu, L. C., & Chiu, C. R. (2018b). Evaluation of energy efficiency and air pollutant emissions in Chinese provinces. *Energy Efficiency, 12*(4), 963–977.

Li, L., Liu, X., Ge, J., Chu, X., & Wang, J. (2019). Regional differences in spatial spillover and hysteresis effects: A theoretical and empirical study of environmental regulations on haze pollution in china. *Journal of Cleaner Production, 230,* 1096–1110.

Li, Y., Chiu, Y. H., Wang, L. H., Zhou, Y., & Lin, T. Y. (2020a). Dynamic and network slack-based measure analysis of China's regional energy and air pollution reduction efficiencies. *Journal of Cleaner Production*, 251.

Li, G., Fang, C., & He, S. (2020b). The influence of environmental efficiency on $PM_{2.5}$ pollution: evidence from 283 Chinese prefecture-level cities. *Science of The Total Environment*, 141549.

Liang, L., Wu, J., & Cook, W. D. (2008a). Alternative secondary goals in DEA cross-efficiency evaluation. *International Journal of Production Economics, 113*(2), 1025–1030.

Liang, L., Wu, J., & Cook, W. D. (2008b). The DEA game cross-efficiency model and its nash equilibrium. *Operations Research, 56*(5), 1278–1288.

Liao, S. M., Wang, D., Liang, Z. J., Xia, C. Y., Guo, H., & Zhao, W. J. (2020). Spatial spillover effect and sources of city-level haze pollution in China: a case study of guangdong provinces. *Polish Journal of Environmental Studies, 29*(5), 3213–3223.

Lin, R. Cross-efficiency evaluation capable of dealing with negative data: A directional distance function-based approach. *Journal of the Operational Research Society*, 2019, DOI/https://doi.org/10.1080/01605682.2019.1567652.

Liu, W. B., Meng, W., Li, X. X., & Zhang, D. Q. (2010). DEA models with undesirable inputs and outputs. *Annals of Operations Research, 173*(1), 177–194.

Liu, B., Song, N., & Dai, Q. (2016). Chemical composition and source apportionment of ambient $PM_{2.5}$, during the non-heating period in Taian, China. *Atmospheric Research, 170*, 23–33.

Liu, W., Wang, Y. M., & Lv, S. (2017a). An aggressive game cross-efficiency evaluation in data envelopment analysis. *Annals of Operations Research, 259*(1–2), 241–258.

Liu, J., Wu, D., & Fan, S. (2017b). A one-year, on-line, multi-site observational study on water-soluble inorganic ions in $PM_{2.5}$ over the Pearl River Delta region, China. *Science of the Total Environment, 601*, 1720–1732.

Liu, H., Song, Y., & Yang, G. (2019). Cross-efficiency evaluation in data envelopment analysis based on prospect theory. *European Journal of Operational Research, 273*(1), 364–375.

Luo, N. S., & Li, J. M. (2018). Do industrial agglomeration and traffic links aggravate the spatial spillover effects of haze? ——Analysis from the perspective of spatial distribution of industries. *Industrial Economics Research, 4,* 5.

Ma, L. M., & Zhang, X. (2014). Spatial effects of regional air pollution and the impact of industrial structure. *China Population, Resources and Environment, 24*(7), 157–164.

Maddison, D. (2006). Environmental Kuznets curves: A spatial econometric approach. *Journal of Environmental Economics & Management, 51*(2), 218–230.

Meng, F. (2019). Carbon emissions efficiency and abatement cost under inter-region differentiated mitigation strategies: a modified ddf model. *Physica A: Statistical Mechanics and its Applications, 532*,

Miao, Z., Zhou, P., Wang, Y., & Sun, Z. R. (2013). Energy Saving, emission reduction and air pollutants emissions rights allocation research. *China Industrial Economy, 2014*(6), 31–43.

Pan, B. F., Wang, W., & Li, L. (2013). Analysis of the reason of formation and the characteristic of pollution about fog or haze at key cities in autumn and winter in China. *Environment and Sustainable Development, 38*(1), 33–36.

Pan, H. F., Wang, X., & Zhang, S. Y. (2015). Duration and spatial spillover effects of haze pollution—Evidence from Beijing-Tianjin-Hebei region. *China Soft Science, 12,* 134–143.

Picazo-Tadeo, A. J., Castillo-Giménez, J., & Beltrán-Esteve, M. (2014). An intertemporal approach to measuring environmental performance with directional distance functions: Greenhouse gas emissions in the European Union. *Ecological Economics, 100*(1), 173–182.

Poon, P. H., Casaa, I., & He, C. (2006). The impact of energy, transport and trade on air pollution in China. *Eurasian Geography and Economics, 47*(5), 568–584.

Qiao, T., Xiu, G., & Zheng, Y. (2015). Preliminary investigation of $PM_1$, $PM_{2.5}$, $PM_{10}$, and its metal elemental composition in tunnels at a subway station in Shanghai, China. *Transportation Research Part D Transport & Environment,, 41*, 136–146.

Rashidi, K., Shabani, A., & Saen, R. F. (2015). Using data envelopment analysis for estimating energy saving and undesirable output abatement: A case study in the Organization for Economic

Co-Operation and Development (OECD) countries. *Journal of Cleaner Production, 105,* 241–252.

Ren, Z. H., Wan, B. T., & Su, F. Q. (2004). Several characteristics of atmospheric environmental quality in China at Present. *Research of Environmental Sciences, 17*(1), 1–6.

Saen, R. F. (2010). Developing a new data envelopment analysis methodology for supplier selection in the presence of both undesirable outputs and imprecise data. *International Journal of Advanced Manufacturing Technology, 51*(9–12), 1243–1250.

Seiford, L. M., & Zhu, J. (2002). Modeling undesirable factors in efficiency evaluation. *European Journal of Operational Research, 141*(2), 16–20.

Shao, S., Li, X., & Cao, J. H. (2016). China's economic policy choices for governing smog pollution based on spatial spillover effects. *Economic Research Journal, 9,* 73–88.

Shi, D., Wu, L. X., Fu, X. X., & Wu, B. (2008). Study on regional differences and causes of energy efficiency in China—based on variance decomposition of stochastic frontier production function. *Management World, 2,* 35–43.

Shi, K., Liu, C. Q., & Wu, S. H. (2014). Self-organized evolution of trans-boundary $PM_{10}$ pollution in Zhoushan City. *Acta Scientiae Circumstantiate, 34*(5), 1125–1132.

Shi, H., Wang, Y., & Chen, L. (2019). Neutral cross-efficiency evaluation regarding an ideal frontier and anti-ideal frontier as evaluation criteria. *Computers & Industrial Engineering, 132,* 385–394.

Song, M. L., Zhang, L. L., Liu, W., & Fisher, R. (2013). Bootstrap-DEA analysis of BRICS' energy efficiency based on small sample data. *Applied Energy, 112*(C), 1049–1055.

Song, M. L., Zhang, J., & Wang, S. H. (2015). Review of the network environmental efficiencies of listed petroleum enterprises in China. *Renewable & Sustainable Energy Reviews, 43,* 65–71.

Song, M. L., Zhang, G. J., & Fang, K. N. (2016). Regional operational and environmental performance evaluation in China: Non-radial DEA methodology under natural and managerial disposability. *Natural Hazards, 84*(1), 243–265.

Song, M., Zhu, Q., Peng, J., & Santibanez Gonzalez, E. D. R. (2017a). Improving the evaluation of cross efficiencies: A method based on Shannon entropy weight. *Computers & Industrial Engineering, 112,* 99–106.

Song, M. L., Zhou, Y. X., Zhang, R. R., & Fisher, R. (2017b). Environmental efficiency evaluation with left–right fuzzy numbers. *Operational Research, 17*(3), 697–714.

Su, W., Liu, Y., & Wang, S. (2018). Regional inequality, spatial spillover effects, and the factors influencing city-level energy-related carbon emissions in China. *Journal of Geographical Sciences, 28*(4), 495–513.

Sueyoshi, T., & Yuan, Y. (2015). China's regional sustainability and diversified resource allocation: DEA environmental assessment on economic development and air pollution. *Energy Economics, 49*(8), 239–256.

Sun, W. (2013). Research on modeling and similarity of qualitative direction relations based on the direction relation matrix. Jilin University.

Sun, J. S., Wu, J., Wang, Y. M., Li, L., & Wang, Y. H. (2020). Cross-efficiency evaluation method based on the conservative point of view. *Expert Systems, 37* (4).

Tai, A. P. K., Mickley, L. J., & Jacob, D. J. (2010). Correlations between fine particulate matter ($PM_{2.5}$) and meteorological variables in the United States: implications for the sensitivity of $PM_{2.5}$ to climate change. *Atmospheric Environment, 44*(32), 3976–3984.

Tang, D. L., Li, L., & Hong, X. F. (2017). The spatial spillover effect of energy consumption on haze pollution in China—An empirical research based on the static and dynamic spatial panel data model. *Systems Engineering-Theory & Practice, 37*(7), 1697–1708.

Tolis, E. I., Saraga, D. E., & Lytra, M. K. (2015). Concentration and chemical composition of $PM_{2.5}$ for a one-year period at Thessaloniki, Greece: A comparison between city and port area. *Atmospheric Environment, 113,* 197–207.

Tsai, H., Wu, J., & Sun, J. (2013). Cross-efficiency evaluation of Taiwan's international tourist hotels under competitive and cooperative relationships. *Journal of China Tourism Research, 9*(4), 413–428.

Wang, Y. M., & Chin, K. S. (2011). The use of OWA operator weights for cross-efficiency aggregation. *Omega, 39*(5), 493–503.

Wang, Y. M., & Wang, S. (2013). Approaches to determining the relative importance weights for cross-efficiency aggregation in data envelopment analysis. *Journal of the Operational Research Society, 64*(1), 60–69.

Wang, X., & Wang, Y. (2020). Regional unified environmental efficiency of china: A non-separable hybrid measure under natural and managerial disposability. *Environmental Science and Pollution Research, 27*(22), 27609–27625.

Wang, F., Chen, D. S., & Cheng. S. Y. (2010) Identification of regional atmospheric $PM_{10}$ transport pathways using HYSPLIT, MM5-CMAQ and synoptic pressure pattern analysis. *Environmental Modelling & Software, 25*(8), 927–934.

Wang, Y. M., Chin, K. S., & Jiang, P. (2011). Weight determination in the cross-efficiency evaluation. *Computers & Industrial Engineering, 61*(3), 497–502.

Wang, S., Xiu, T. Y., Sun, Y., Meng, X. R., & Xu, J. C. (2014). The changes of mist and haze days and meteorological element during 1960–2012 in Xi'an. *Acta Scientiae Circumstantiae, 34*(1), 19–26.

Wang, X. Q., Ju, X., & Feng, B. (2016a). Analysis of performance variances of haze main precursors emissions among China's provinces. *Journal of Arid Land Resources and Environment, 30*(4), 190–196.

Wang, H. L., Qiao, L. P., & Lou, S. R. (2016b). Chemical composition of $PM_{2.5}$, and meteorological impact among three years in urban Shanghai, China. *Journal of Cleaner Production, 112*, 1302–1311.

Wang, K. L., Meng, X. R., & Yang, B. C. (2017). Regional differences and influencing factors of China's air pollution emission efficiency considering technological heterogeneity. *China Population, Resources and Environment, 27*(1), 101–110.

Wang, Y. H, Wen, Z. G, Cao, X. Z, Zhao, F; & Xu, J. J. (2019a). Environmental efficiency evaluation of China's iron and steel industry: A process-level data envelopment analysis. *Science of The Total Environment*, 707.

Wang, C., Zhan, J., Bai, Y., Chu, X., & Zhang, F. (2019b) Measuring carbon emission performance of industrial sectors in the Beijing–Tianjin–Hebei region, china: a stochastic frontier approach. *Science of The Total Environment, 685*, 786–794.

Wang, L., Xi, F., Yin, Y., Wang, J., & Bing, L. (2020a). Industrial total factor $CO_2$ emission performance assessment of Chinese heavy industrial province. *Energy Efficiency, 13*(1), 177–192.

Wang, K. L., Ding, L. L., Wang, J. M., & Yang, M. (2020b). Analysis of provincial total-factor air pollution efficiency in china by using context-dependent slacks-based measure considering undesirable outputs. *Natural Hazards, 104*(9), 1899–1921.

Wang, Q., Wei, K., Zhang, Y., & Wang, X. (2020c). Comprehensive cross-efficiency methods with common weight restrictions in data envelopment analysis. Asia-Pacific Journal of Operational Research,37(5).

Wu, J., Liang, L., & Zha, Y. C. (2008). Determination of the weights of ultimate cross efficiency based on the solution of nucleolus in cooperative game. *Systems Engineering-Theory & Practice, 28*(5), 92–97.

Wu, J., Sun, J., & Liang, L. (2011). Determination of weights for ultimate cross efficiency using Shannon entropy. *Expert Systems with Applications, 38*(5), 5162–5165.

Wu, J., Chu, J., Sun, J., & Zhu, Q. (2016a). DEA cross-efficiency evaluation based on Pareto improvement. *European Journal of Operational Research, 248*(2), 571–579.

Wu, X. H., Chen, Y. F., & Guo J. (2016b). Spatial concentration, impact factors and prevention-control measures of $PM_{2.5}$ pollution in China. *Natural Hazards, 86*, 1–18.

Wu, X. H., Tan, L., Guo, J., & Zhu, W. W. (2016c). A study of allocative efficiency of air pollutant emission rights based on a zero sum gains data envelopment model: Taking $PM_{2.5}$ as an example. *Journal of Cleaner Production, 113*, 1024–1031.

Wu, X., Chen, Y., Guo, J., & Gao, G. (2018). Inputs optimization to reduce the undesirable outputs by environmental hazards: a DEA model with data of $PM_{2.5}$ in China. *Natural Hazards, 90*(1), 1–25.

Wu, X. H., Chen, S. S., & Guo, J. (2018a). Effect of air pollution on the stock yield of heavy pollution enterprises in China's key control cities. *Journal of Cleaner Production, 170*(1), 399–406.

Wu, J., Yu, Y., Zhu, Q., An, Q. X., & Liang, L. (2018b). Closest target for the orientation-free context-dependent DEA under variable returns to scale. *Journal of the Operational Research Society, 69*(11), 1819–1833.

Xu, J., Chang, L., & Qu, Y. (2016). The meteorological modulation on $PM_{2.5}$ interannual oscillation during 2013 to 2015 in Shanghai, China. *Science of the Total Environment, 572,* 1138–1149.

Xu, S. C., Zhou, Y. F., Feng, C., Wang, Y., & Li, Y. F. (2020). What factors influence $PM_{2.5}$ emissions in China? An analysis of regional differences using a combined method of data envelopment analysis and logarithmic mean Divisia index. *Environmental Science and Pollution Research, 27*(27), 34234–34249.

Xue, W. B., Fei, F. U., Wang, J. N., Ke-Bi, H. E., Yu, L., & Yang, J. T. (2014). Modeling study on atmospheric environmental capacity of major pollutants constrained by $PM_{2.5}$ compliance of Chinese cities. *China Environmental Science, 34*(10), 2490–2496.

Yang, J., & Xu, L. (2020). How does china's air pollution influence its labor wage distortions? theoretical and empirical analysis from the perspective of spatial spillover effects. *Science of The Total Environment.*

Yang, F., Xia, Q., & Liang, L. (2011). DEA cross efficiency evaluation method for competitive and cooperative decision-making units. *Systems Engineering-Theory & Practice, 31*(1), 92–98.

Yang, H., Chen, J., & Wen, J. (2016). Composition and sources of $PM_{2.5}$, around the heating periods of 2013 and 2014 in Beijing: Implications for efficient mitigation measures. *Atmospheric Environment, 124,* 378–386.

Yang, S., Ma, Y. L., & Duan, F. K. (2017). Characteristics and formation of typical winter haze in Handan, one of the most polluted cities in China. *Science of the Total Environment, 613,* 1367–1375.

You, W., & Lv, Z. (2018). Spillover effects of economic globalization on $CO_2$ emissions: A spatial panel approach. *Energy Economics, 73,* 248–257.

Zhang, R., Jing, J., & Tao, J. (2013).Chemical characterization and source apportionment of $PM_{2.5}$ in Beijing: seasonal perspective. *Atmospheric Chemistry and Physics*, 13(14): 7053–7074.

Zhang, Y., Huang, W., & Cai, T. (2016a).Concentrations and chemical compositions of fine particles ($PM_{2.5}$) during haze and non-haze days in Beijing. *Atmospheric Research*, 174–175, 62–69.

Zhang, Y., Huang, W., Cai, T.(2016b). Fang, D.Q., Wang, Y.Q., Song, J., Hu, M., & Zhang, Y. X. Concentrations and chemical compositions of fine particles ($PM_{2.5}$) during haze and non-haze days in Beijing. *Atmospheric Research*, 174: 62–69.

Zhang, J., Chang, J.P., Lin, P., Song, M. Z., & Gong, Y. Q.(2020). Operation Efficiency Evaluation of the China-Europe Freight Train Based on Grey Cross-Efficiency DEA, Scientific Programming.

Zheng, C. D., & Liu, S. (2011). Empirical research of carbon emission and economic growth in China based on the spatial econometric analysis. *China Population, Resources and Environment, 21*(5), 80–86.

Zheng, L. X., & Zhou, M. (2020). spatial spillover effects of environmental regulation on haze pollution in china. *Journal of Environmental Protection and Ecology, 21*(2), 525–534.

Zheng, P. N., Chen, H. B., Chen, X. G., Zhou, D. B., & Zhang, B. Y. (2007). Study on distribution of reduction targets based on DEA model. *Chinese Journal of Environmental Engineering, 11*(1), 133–139.

Zhou, P., Ang, B. W., & Han, J. Y. (2010). Total-factor carbon emission performance: A Malmquist index analysis. *Energy Economics, 32*(1), 194–201.

Zhou, Z., Guo, X., Wu, H., & Yu, J. (2018). Evaluating air quality in china based on daily data: Application of integer data envelopment analysis. *Journal of Cleaner Production, 198,* 304–311.

Zhou, Z., Chen, Y., Song, P., & Ding, T. (2020). China's urban air quality evaluation with streaming data: A DEA window analysis. *Science of the Total Environment, 727,* 138213.

# Chapter 19
# Inputs Optimization to Reduce the Undesirable Outputs by Environmental Hazards: A DEA Model with Data of $PM_{2.5}$ in China

**Abstract** Currently, the hazy weather in China is increasingly serious. It is urgent for China to reduce haze emissions in environmental governance. A feasible way is to control haze emissions by optimizing the input sources. This paper proposed an innovative method in which the haze emission is controlled by readjusting input indicators. The output efficiency of input indicators in 29 provinces in China is calculated through 7 input indicators (namely, $SO_2$ emissions, $NO_X$ emissions, soot emissions, coal consumption, car ownership, capital, and labor force) as well as GDP (desirable output) and $PM_{2.5}$ emissions (undesirable output). The results showed that, the input indicators are excessive in redundancy on condition that $PM_{2.5}$ emissions and GDP are equal. The input indicators are high in redundancy rate except labor force. The redundancy rates of soot emissions, $SO_2$ emissions and coal consumption are relatively high and respectively are 78%, 67.18%, and 61.14%. Moreover, all the provinces are redundant in inputs except Beijing, Tianjin, and Shanghai which are optimal in input–output efficiency. The redundancy of middle and western provinces, such as Ningxia, Guizhou, and Shanxi, is relatively large. The ideas and methods proposed in this paper can provide a reference for the future researches that aim to reduce the input indicators of undesirable output and the empirical results can provide empirical support for the $PM_{2.5}$ abatement in China.

**Keywords** Environmental hazards · $PM_{2.5}$ · DEA model · Undesirable output · Reduction indicators

## 19.1 Introduction

Since the reform and opening-up which began about 30 years ago, the extensive mode of economic growth has brought excessive pollutant discharges to China. According to the British Petroleum (BP), *Statistical Review of World Energy* shows that China's total energy consumption accounted for 20.3% of the world in 2010, which is more than that of the United States to become the world's largest energy consumer. China's carbon emission amount is more than that of the United States in 2007, and becomes the largest Carbon emission in the world. At present, the air pollutant emission in China is high, with $SO_2$ (sulfur dioxide) and $CO_2$ (carbon dioxide), CO (carbon

 
X. Wu and J. Guo, *Economic Impacts and Emergency Management of Disasters in China*,
https://doi.org/10.1007/978-981-16-1319-7_19

monoxide), $NO_2$, HC (hydrocarbons) and industrial smoke dust emissions being much higher than the identification standard. The annual emissions of $SO_2$ and soot were nearly 20 million tons and 12 million tons in China, which is the world's biggest producer of emissions. As a consequence, China is higher than any other countries in the total emissions of most pollutants. The atmospheric pollution has been increasingly serious these years. According to the *Environmental Analysis of People's Republic of China* which was released jointly by Asian Development Bank and Tsinghua University in 2013, among the 500 big cities in China, those have reached the air quality standards set by the World Health Organization only account for 1% or less and among the 10 cities which are polluted the most heavily, 7 are in China (Asian Development Bank 2012). Continuous hazy weather and severely polluted air not only damage the health of citizen and government credibility but also impede the sustainable development of society as well as the construction of comprehensive well-off society. How to control air pollution through effective measures has been the primary concern for government and academics.

In terms of practice, the government hopes to control haze through national administrative power. The Chinese government pays high attention to the prevention and control of haze and has issued a series of policy papers. In September 2013, the State Council issued the *Air Pollution Prevention and Control Action Plan* (hereinafter referred to as the *Action Plan*) (People's Republic of China State Council 2013) which sets specific goals for the control of atmospheric pollution of different regions and formulates 35 measures for achieving the goals. The ultimate aim of the *Action Plan* is to get rid of hazy weather gradually and improve the air quality in five years or more. "We must strengthen the protection of ecological environment and resolve to take forceful measures to complete this challenging task", said the prime minister of China Li Keqiang in the *2014 Report on the Work of the Central People's Government*. According to the executive meeting of the State Council held in February 2015, besides improving the treatment policy of air pollution, three measures, namely, adjusting the energy structure, enhancing the tax incentive function, and establishing the responsibility assessing system of atmospheric pollution prevention and control, shall be taken immediately. The government shall play a significant role in controlling haze weather. The haze and smog should be reduced through the advance in technology as well as the adjustment of energy structure and industrial structure. However, there are no specific goals and ways for the adjustment of energy structure and industrial structure. Besides, the adjustment range is not clear yet. Thus, the administrative operability of these measures is low.

In terms of theoretical research, many scholars tend to reduce air pollutant emissions from the source. However, the source and formation of air pollutants are quite complicated. As for China, the sources of air pollutants mainly include stationary source (power plant, chemical plant, etc.), moving source (motor vehicle, off-road machines, etc.), non-point source (burning of solvent coatings, biomass, and agricultural waste, blowing dust, etc.), and natural source (vegetation). There is a great disparity in the emission characteristics as the emissions come from different industries and the production technology in one industry is quite different. The causes of pollution include fine particles directly from the abovementioned sources, ozone

($O_3$) converted from such gaseous pollutants as sulfur dioxide ($SO_2$), nitrogen oxide ($NO_X$), volatile organic compound ($VOC_s$), and ammonia ($NH_3$) after chemical action, and secondary particles (sulfate, nitrate, ammonium salt, organics, etc.). According to the historical monitoring data, secondary particle accounts for over 80% in $PM_{2.5}$ mass concentration in the serious air contamination accidents recently happened in Jiangsu Province. There are different pollutants whose formations interact with each other and coexist at high concentrations. The atmospheric pollution from different places influences each other. Besides, the rapid urbanization has greatly changed the regional special structure of urban agglomeration, which weakens the diffusivity of atmospheric boundary layer and increases the occurrence of adverse weather. These are the cause and source of atmospheric pollution in cities. The cause and source are so complicated, which makes it rather hard to prevent and control the atmospheric pollution. Therefore, it is a quite difficult and long-term job to reduce haze after sorting out its origin. Thus, the air pollution can be controlled by taking ideas from management science. More specifically, the emission reduction of air pollutants can be studied by using quantitative analysis tools. The advantage of this method lies in that it can provide empirical supports for the emission reduction targets set by government as well as the reduction range. Moreover, there is no need to sort out the source or formation of air pollutants. This method is of great practical significance and can offer reference for others.

This paper proposed a method which attempts to control haze emissions by cutting down the source indicators which cause haze. The provinces (or municipalities) of China are regarded as evaluation units. Taking $PM_{2.5}$ for example (undesirable output), the possible factors of $PM_{2.5}$ emissions are input indicators according to the data envelope analysis (DEA). On the basis of efficiency evaluation, the redundancy of input indicators is calculated. The redundant indexes are regarded as the reduction indicators which control $PM_{2.5}$ emissions. Those provinces with low input–output efficiency should formulate industrial policies suitable for increasing the input–output efficiency. Thus, the haze can be reduced by adjusting the reduction indicators. The advantage of the proposed method lies in that there is no need to consider the complicated source and formation of haze. With simple principle and easy access to data, the proposed method can provide some new ideas for the prevention and treatment of haze.

The rest of this paper is arranged as follows: the second part is literature review; the third part is the introduction to model, indicators, and data; the forth part is analysis of empirical results; the last part is conclusions and policy recommendations.

## 19.2 Literature Review

### *19.2.1 DEA and Its Application*

The Data Envelopment Analysis (DEA) which was first put forward by Cooper (Charnes et al. 1978) is a mathematical method which assesses the efficiency of evaluation unit through linear programming. Then, Banker et al. (1984) added the constraints of variable return to scale to the CCR model and further put forward the BCC model with the variable return to scale. Up to now, the CCR model and BCC model are still the most widely traditional models in DEA. Besides, both CCR and BCC model belongs to the radial model in DEA, these two kinds of the model only take into account increasing or reducing the proportion of all input-outputs and ignore the slack improvement section in measuring the inefficiency degree of each decision-making unit. To show the derelict part in efficiency value, Tone (2001) proposed a non-radial or Slack-Based Measure (SBM) DEA model, which also takes into account the undesired output. The advantages of DEA lie in that the weight of input indicators and output indicators can be ignored (Färe and Grosskopf 2004) and it is quite steady by evaluating through linear programming (Färe et al. 1996). Through the comparison between effective decision making unite (DMU) and ineffective DMU, the inefficient determinants can be better analyzed (Olatubi and Dismukes 2000). The disadvantage of DEA is that it is quite sensitive to the combination of abnormal values and input and output indicators (Tyteca 1997; Färe and Grosskopf 1996).

DEA has been widely applied in the field of environmental performance evaluation. High-quality achievements have been made in the generation of new ideas on DEA environmental performance evaluation (Dyckho and Allen 2001; Gomes and Lins 2008; Korhonen and Luptacik 2004; Kumar 2006; Liang et al. 2004; Oude Lansink and Silva 2003), the establishment of evaluation model (Pasurka 2006; Picazo-Tadeo et al. 2006; Ramanathan 2002; Bevilacqua and Braglia 2012; Zhang and Bartels 1998; Zhou et al. 2006a, 2006b; Sueyoshi and Goto 2001), and the application evaluation of model (Goto and Tsutsui 1998; Sueyoshi and Goto 2001; Hu and Wang 2006; Hu and Kao 2007; Zhou et al. 2006a, 2006b, 2008, 2012).

Subsequently, some scholars have also done some researches on environmental efficiency evaluation by improving the traditional DEA models. To solve subjectivity and uncertainty in traditional DEA cross model, Han et al. (2018) established an improved DEA cross model to assess the carbon emission efficiency of industrial sectors in China, then compared the improved DEA cross model with the traditional DEA model, finally got a conclusion that the enhanced DEA cross model has a more vital ability to discriminate efficiency. He et al. (2018a) constructed an SBM-DEA model with non-separable undesired output, then combined SBM-DEA with an integrated environmental efficiency index to assess environmental efficiencies of social and economic sectors in China. Cecchini et al. (2018) employed SBM-DEA to estimate the environmental efficiency of dairy farms, then compute the marginal cost of $CO_2$ emission reduction by utilizing the dual model of SBM-DEA. Xing et al. (2018) combined Economic Input–Output Life Cycle Assessment (EIO-LCA) with DEA model to evaluate the environmental efficiency and environmental impact level of 26 economic sectors in China, then further put forward some suggestions for improving ecological efficiency. Based on technological heterogeneity, Long et al. (2018) utilized a Meta-Frontier directional slacks-based measure to evaluate the environmental efficiencies of 192 thermal power plants, then further analyzed the trend of technology gap among provinces and further explored influencing factors of ecological efficiency using bootstrapped truncation regression. At finally, the conclusion indicated that reducing coal utilization rate and expanding technology were the keys to improving environmental efficiency. Ma et al. (2018) added the new constraint on $PM_{2.5}$ to the research framework of environmental efficiency assessment, then used the SBM-DEA model with the undesirable output to measure environmental efficiency with and without consideration of $PM_{2.5}$ based on provincial panel data from 2001 to 2012 in China. The results showed that ignoring $PM_{2.5}$ will result in significant environmental efficiency deviation. Wu et al. (2019) presented a new non-homogeneous DEA model. The new DEA model mainly solve the complexity of efficiency assessment caused by input–output non-homogeneity of different DMUs.

In recent years, some researchers, based on the ideas from environmental performance evaluation, have tried to assess the discharge efficiency of air pollutants through DEA. Soloveitchik et al. (2002) calculated the marginal cost of pollutants discharge reduction of the electric power department in Israel with DEA. Fleishman et al. (2009) evaluated the pollutant discharge efficiency of power plant in America though DEA model ($NO_X$ and $SO_2$ were regarded as undesirable outputs) and tested the effect of the regulation policies of $SO_2$ and $NO_X$ on the score of DEA with TOBIT model. Sueyoshi and Goto (2012) assessed the environmental performance of power plant in America with developed DEA. Sueyoshi and Yuan (2015) evaluated the pollutant discharge efficiency of 28 provinces and cities in China with DEA ($PM_{2.5}$ and $PM_{10}$ were regarded as undesirable outputs). Miao et al. (2013) put forward a non-radial allocation model for multiple undesirable outputs so as to study the distribution mechanism of regional air pollutant emission rights while taking into account both the energy-saving target as well as the haze reduction target and discussed the local distribution of the air pollutant emission rights of 30 Chinese provinces in 2015 through empirical analysis. Li et al. (2018) adopted the SBM-DEA model to evaluate overall efficiency of 31 cities and specific emission efficiencies of various undesirable outputs through a collection of data from 31 cities in china between 2013 and 2017, then explored the effects of undesired outputs on the overall efficiency and ranking of cities. Guo et al. (2015a), based on ZSG-DEA, regarded $PM_{2.5}$ as undesirable output and assessed the discharge efficiency of $PM_{2.5}$ of different provinces under the condition of constant total $PM_{2.5}$ emissions while taking the atmospheric environmental capacities of provinces into account. Other scholars also have evaluated the emission efficiencies of pollution gases through improved DEA models. Wang et al. (2018b) combined DEA model with Material Balance Principle (MBP) to construct an improved DEA model, then used the improved model to evaluate the environment and emission reduction efficiency. Based on DEA model window analysis, Zhang et al. (2018b) used the meta-frontier non-radial direction distance function to assess the carbon emission performance and energy efficiency of member countries, which participated in Clean Development Mechanism (CDM) projects from 1900 to 2015. They also further analyzed the effect of CDM on carbon emission performance and energy efficiency of CDM projects participants using quantile regression. Wu et al. (2018) presented an improved environmental DEA-based model to evaluate the energy utilization rate, $CO_2$ discharge efficiency and environmental-economic efficiency of APEC economies. Wang et al. (2019a) used the SBM-DEA model with Windows Analysis method to evaluate the carbon emission efficiency and emission reduction potential of provinces in China from 2003 to 2016, then used the panel Tobit model to explore the impact of abundance level of natural resources on emissions efficiency. Wang and Ma (2018) employed the Malmquist Index based on DEA model with bad outputs to measure and analyze the $CO_2$ emissions efficiencies of 13 cities in Jiangsu province during 2000–2014, then further employed a Tobit model to explore the influencing factors of $CO_2$ emissions efficiency. Yang et al. (2019b) used the DEA model and the Malmquist index to evaluate the carbon emission performance of the logistics industry in 16 prefecture-level cities in Yunnan province from both static and dynamic perspectives, respectively, then the Tobit model was used to explored influencing factors of the carbon emission performance in the logistics industry. Besides, some scholars further explored allocation of air pollution emissions based on evaluating efficiency air pollutants through DEA. Zhou et al. (2018) proposed an improved non-radical DEA method, containing multiple abatement factors, to evaluate the $CO_2$ emission performance of Cities in China, then established a composite index for a reasonable allocation of $CO_2$ emission quotas based on fairness and efficiency simultaneously. Cucchiella et al. (2018) used the DEA model to analyze the competitiveness of European Union member countries based on sustainable growth, then utilized the Zero Sum Gains (ZSG) DEA model for a new allocation quotas of $CO_2$ emission limits and energy consumption. He et al. (2018b) used the DEA method to measure the cost–benefit of cooperative emission in china, then provided the strategy of optimal cooperative partner selection utilizing minimizing the cooperative cost. Chen et al. (2018) analyzed the distribution efficiency of six industries in China using the EBM-DEA model, then make an optimal allocation of $CO_2$ emission quotas using the ZSG-DEA method and further establish the reasonable carbon emission allocation scheme. To achieve a scientific carbon emission scheme, Fang et al. (2019) constructed an improved ZSG-DEA model to present a strategy on $CO_2$ emission allocation based on a perspective of scientific and economic costs. Yang et al. (2019a) realized that efficiency maximization or invariance is difficult to achieve in the actual situation and then established an improved DEA method, which achieve a gradual improvement for efficiency and reduction in carbon emission, and then applied the improved DEA model to the allocation of carbon emission among provinces in China. Based on $CO_2$ emission reduction target in 2020, Cai and Ye (2019) firstly decomposed overall emission reduction target in China into provincial sub-targets, then adopted the ZSG-DEA method to put forward the optimal allocation scheme of carbon emissions in 30 Chinese provinces, finally measured the allocation efficiencies of provincial $CO_2$ emission quota through EBM-DEA Model. Xie et al. (2019) combine data envelopment analysis (DEA) with the max–min satisfaction to established an improved DEA allocation model, then applied this improved model to assess the utilization of carbon emission rights in different provinces. At last, the result indicated that the new model can achieved the efficiency evaluating and a fixed cost allocation for carbon emissions. Li et al. (2020) took both competition and cooperation into consideration and proposed an integrated cooperative game-data envelopment analysis (DEA) model, then combined the improved model with a practical computation procedure to further proposed a two-layer allocation method for allocating the $CO_2$ emission reduction quota for manufacturing industries in china. Based on heterogeneity between regions and industries, Yang et al. (2020) presented a multi-layer meta-frontier DEA method to evaluate dynamic performance, the inefficiency, reduction potential of $CO_2$ emission, and then further proposed $CO_2$ emission reduction paths for manufacturing industries.

It can be known from the above-mentioned studies that only a few researchers regarded PM as undesirable output and evaluated air pollutant emissions through DEA. No researchers have regarded the source of PM as input indicator and studied the redundancy of PM input indicators.

### *19.2.2 Components and Sources of $PM_{2.5}$*

The components and sources of $PM_{2.5}$ are hot issues in the researches on atmospheric pollution. Many researchers analyzed the chemical components and sources of $PM_{2.5}$ in different seasons and regions on the basis of optical characteristics. Zhang et al. (2016) studied the pollution characteristics of the air and the water-soluble components in the $PM_{2.5}$ of Xi'an in spring and summer. Yang et al. (2015) analyzed the components and sources of the $PM_{2.5}$ of Beijing in the summers of 2013 and 2014. Huang et al. (2014) studied the optical characteristics and chemical constituents of the $PM_{2.5}$ of the spring of 2012 in Shanghai. Zhao et al. (2014) studied the constituents and sources of organic acid in the $PM_{2.5}$ of Pearl River Delta region. Cheng et al. (2015) analyzed the chemical constituents and origins of the $PM_{2.5}$ and $PM_{10}$ in the air above Hong Kong's roads. Wei et al. (2014) studied the constituents and sources of the haze of 2013 in Handan, Hebei Province. Zhang et al. (2018a) conducted an in-depth identification of the source categories, source areas and pollution characteristics of $PM_1$ and $PM_{2.5}$ in autumn in Beijing. Cesari et al. (2018) explored sources and formation processes of $PM_{2.5}$ and $PM_{10}$ and how they changed with the seasons at the Environmental Climate Observatory in Lecce (southern Italy). Wang et al. (2018c) investigated the chemical characteristics and potential regional sources of $PM_{2.5}$ in the industrial urban areas of Ningbo city. Ryou et al. (2018) conducted an in-depth study of origin categories of $PM_{10}$ and $PM_{2.5}$ in South Korea from 2000 to 2017 by combining positive matrix factorization with chemical mass balance. Wang et al. (2018a) conducted an in-depth study of the leading chemical composition, formation principle and geographical origin of $PM_{2.5}$ in two core cities, Chengdu and Chongqing, in Sichuan province. Zhu et al. (2018) summarized 239 papers on PM sources published from 1987 to 2017, then summed up research methods on PM sources in these papers and further extracted primary sources of PM from different regions in China. Deng et al. (2018) used three receptor models, Principal Component Analysis Combining Multiple linear Regression (PCA-MLR), UNMIX and Positive Matrix Factorization (PMF), to identified contributions from various sources to $PM_{2.5}$, then analyzed and compared three receptor models according to three results of identifications. Ma et al. (2018) measured concentration, type, and activity of the components in $PM_{2.5}$ samples that collected in Beijing over one year. Jiang et al. (2018) collected 228 daily PM in Zhengzhou from the autumn in 2014 to the summer in 2015, then analyzed sources of pollution, characteristics of pollution and health risks in $PM_{2.5}$ and $PM_{10}$. Wang et al. (2019b) measured and studied the main components and sources of $PM_{2.5}$ under different haze seasons. Sun et al. (2019) collected $PM_{2.5}$ samples from 21 cities of 7 regions in China, then further analyzed chemical components of $PM_{2.5}$ models. Ahmad et al. (2019) collected daily $PM_{2.5}$ samples from Lahore in July 2018, then explored chemical compositions, sources and contribution areas of $PM_{2.5}$.

Other researches on the components and sources of $PM_{2.5}$ are from Zhang et al. (2011), Griffith et al. (2015), Zhao et al. (2015), Qiao et al. (2015), Zhang et al. (2016), Qiu et al. (2016), Chen et al. (2010), etc. Conclusions can be drawn from these researches that the chemical constituents of $PM_{2.5}$ are quite complicated. The major constituents include water-soluble inorganic salt, inorganic elements, elemental carbon, and organic carbon. The chemical constituents varies a lot due to geographical factors, energy structure, meteorological factors, and seasons (Sun et al. 2015). Based on the available data of $PM_{2.5}$, it can be concluded that $PM_{2.5}$ mainly comes in the following ways: coal, petroleum products (automobile exhaust), burning of construction waste and municipal waste, and thermal power plant (Duan et al. 2008; Kumar et al. 2013). Thus, based on the researches above and the availability of data, this paper selects $SO_2$ emissions, $NO_X$ emissions, soot emissions, coal consumption, car ownership, and labor force as the source indicators of $PM_{2.5}$.

## 19.3 Model and Indicators

### 19.3.1 *Non-radial Ultra-efficient DEA Model*

The first DEA model proposed by Charnes, Cooper and Rhodes in 1978 is known as CCR model (Charnes et al. 1978). The principle of the model is listed below.

The technical efficiency of decision-making unit (DMU) is written as $DMU_j$ $j = 1, 2, \ldots, n$, where $n$ is the number of decision-making units. The input of DMU is $x_i (i = 1, 2, \ldots, m)$, where $m$ is the number of inputs of each DMU. The weight of input is $v_i (i = 1, 2, \ldots, m)$. The output of DMU is $y_r (r = 1, 2, \ldots, q)$, where $q$ is the number of outputs of each DMU. The weight of output is $u_r (r = 1, 2 \ldots, q)$. Then the $k$th DMU can be written as $DMU_k$ whose ratio of output to input $h_k$ is:

$$h_k = \sum_{r=1}^{q} u_{rk} y_{rk} / \sum_{i=1}^{m} v_{ik} x_{ik} (v \geq 0, u \geq 0) \tag{19.1}$$

where $x_{ik}$, $y_{rk}$ and $y_{rk}$ refer to the input indicator and output indicator of $\text{DMU}_\text{k}$ respectively. $v_{ik}$, $u_{rk}$ and $v_{ik}$, $u_{rk}$ refer to the weight of the input indicator and output indicator of $\text{DMU}_\text{k}$ respectively. Let's assume that $h_k \in [0, 1]$. Thus, on condition that the return to scale of DMU is constant, DEA model can be expressed as (Bian 2006):

$$\begin{aligned}
&\text{Min}\left[\theta - \varepsilon\left(\sum_{i=1}^{m} s_i^- + \sum_{r=1}^{q} s_r^+\right)\right] \\
&\text{s.t.} \\
&\sum_{k=1}^{n} \lambda_k x_{ik} + s_i^- = \theta x_{ik}, i = 1, 2, \ldots, m, \\
&\sum_{k=1}^{n} \lambda_k y_{rk} - s_r^+ = y_{rk}, r = 1, 2, \ldots, q, \\
&s^-, s^+, \lambda_k \geq 0, k = 1, 2, \ldots, n
\end{aligned} \tag{19.2}$$

where $\theta$ is the effective value of $\text{DMU}_\text{k}$, $\varepsilon$ (Shi 2012) is the non-Archimedean infinite simal (usually $\varepsilon = 10^{-6}$), $s_i^-$ and $s_r^+$ are the slack variables of input and output respectively, and $\lambda_k$ is the linear combination coefficient of $\text{DMU}_\text{k}$. Model (19.2) is the basic DEA model in which the output remains unchanged while cutting down the resource input of DMU.

The technical efficiency obtained through CCR model contains part of the scale efficiency.[1] Banker and Charnes et al. (1984) developed CCR model into BCC model by replacing constant returns to scale with variable returns to scale. BCC model can evaluate the relative efficiency of DMU with variable returns to scale. The technical efficiency obtained through BCC model is known as Pure Technical Efficiency (PTE) as it has excluded the effect of scale. Thus, BCC model accords with the practical situation better than CCR model in evaluating the relative efficiency of DMU.

Compared with CCR model, BCC model has a constraint condition, namely $\sum_{j=1}^{n} \lambda_j = 1(\lambda_j \geq 0, j = 1, 2, \ldots, n)$. The constraint condition is to ensure the production scale of subpoint and that of DMU are on the same level. Suppose the $k$th is $\text{DMU}_\text{k}$, then the input–output efficiency of $\text{DMU}_\text{k}$ is:

$$\begin{aligned}
&\text{Min}\theta \\
&\text{s.t.}
\end{aligned}$$

[1] Comprehensive technical efficiency is composed of two parts. Comprehensive technical efficiency = pure technical efficiency × scale efficiency. Pure technical efficiency refers to the production efficiency which is influenced by the management and technology of enterprise. Scale efficiency refers to the production efficiency which is influenced by the scale of enterprise.

$$\sum_{k=1}^{n}\lambda_k x_{ik} \le \theta x_{ik}, i = 1, 2, \ldots, m,$$

$$\sum_{k=1}^{n}\lambda_k y_{rk} \ge y_{rk}, r = 1, 2, \ldots, q,$$

$$\sum_{k=1}^{n}\lambda_k = 1, \lambda_k > 0, k = 1, 2, \ldots, n \tag{19.3}$$

where $\theta$ is the relative efficiency of $\mathrm{DMU_k}$, $\lambda_k$ is the weight coefficient, and $x_{ik}$ and $y_{rk}$ respectively are the inputs and outputs of $\mathrm{DMU_k}$.

As for the environmental efficiency evaluation of DEA, the pollutants (such as waste water, exhaust gas, solid waste, etc.) of evaluation unit discharged from production are known as undesirable outputs (Luo 2012). Whereas the good outputs (such as total industrial output value, profit, etc.) are known as desirable outputs. The increase of undesirable outputs will reduce the efficiency of DMU. Thus, the way undesirable outputs are handled is the key to the evaluation of environmental efficiency.

Suppose there are $n$ decision making units and each DMU has $m$ inputs, $q$ desirable outputs, and $p$ undesirable outputs. Then the Inputs $X_k$, Desirable Outputs $Y_k$, and Undesirable Outputs $Z_k$ of $\mathrm{DMU_k}$ $k = 1, 2, \ldots, n$ can be expressed as follows respectively:

$$X_k = (x_{1k}, x_{2k}, \ldots, x_{mk})^T > 0 \tag{19.4}$$

$$Y_k = (y_{1k}, y_{2k}, \ldots, y_{qk})^T > 0 \tag{19.5}$$

$$Z_k = (z_{1k}, z_{2k}, \ldots, z_{pk})^T \ge 0 \tag{19.6}$$

where $x_{mk}$ refers to the inputs of $\mathrm{DMU_k}$, $y_{qk}$ refers to the desirable outputs of $\mathrm{DMU_k}$, $z_{pk}$ refers to the undesirable outputs of $\mathrm{DMU_k}$ ($k$ = 1, 2, …, $n$). The possibility set which contains undesirable outputs is:

$$T_G = \left\{(X, Y, Z)|X \ge \sum_{k=1}^{n}\lambda_k X_k, Y \le \sum_{k=1}^{n}\lambda_k Y_k, Z \ge \sum_{k=1}^{n}\lambda_k Z_k\right\}$$
$$\lambda_k \ge 0, k = 1, 2, \ldots, n \tag{19.7}$$

The undesirable output model can be classified into radial DEA model and non-radial DEA model (Xu and Sun 2014). Though radial DEA model has been widely used by researchers, it still has deficiencies. Firstly, in radial DEA model, the input variables of $\mathrm{DMU_j}$ are equal in changing ratio. That is to say, the efficiency changes through the variation of all input variables in the same proportion. It is often inconsistent with the practical situation. Secondly, radial DEA model fails to show the effect of decision maker's preference on factor inputs. Thirdly, radial DEA model fails to consider the effect of the non-radial slack variables $S^-$ and $S^+$ on the efficiency of $DMU_j$ ($S^-$ and $S^+$ refer to the input slack variable and output slack variable of DMU respectively). This paper attempts to calculate the redundancy of input indicators through slack variables and reduce haze emission by cutting down different input indicators. The non-radial DEA model is feasible as it has taking the variation of input variables in different proportions into consideration. Therefore, the non-radial DEA model which is based on undesirable outputs is adopted in this paper. The $\theta$ in Model (19.2) is replaced by $\sum_{i=1}^{m} \rho_i\theta_i / \sum_{i=1}^{m} \rho_i$, where $\rho_i$ refers to the preference of decision makers for the $i$th input variable in DMU ($\rho_i \in [0, 1]$). Suppose the $k$th DMU which is to be measured is $DMU_k$, and then the non-radial ultra-efficient DEA model can be expressed as:

$$\begin{aligned}
&\text{Min}\left[\sum_{i=1}^{m} \rho_i\theta_i / \sum_{i=1}^{m} \rho_i - \varepsilon\left(\sum_{i=1}^{m} s_i^- + \sum_{r=1}^{q} s_r^+\right)\right] \\
&\text{s.t.} \\
&\sum_{k=1}^{n} \lambda_k x_{ik} + s_i^- = \theta_i x_k, i = 1, 2, \ldots, m, \\
&\sum_{k=1}^{n} \lambda_k y_{rk} - s_r^+ = y_k, r = 1, 2, \ldots, q, \\
&s^-, s^+, \lambda_k \geq 0, k = 1, 2, \ldots, n
\end{aligned} \tag{19.8}$$

where $\theta_i$ is the effective value of $DMU_k$. The abovementioned model is calculated through DEA-SOLVER Pro5.

### 19.3.2 *The Input Redundancy and Redundancy Rate of DEA*

Assuming that the same set of input factors is used to produce the same set of output factors in n DMUs, the production possibility set of the DEA model can be expressed as Eq. (19.7). The use of the unequal "loose" constraint represents the free disposability of inputs and outputs, which means that if inputs x can produce output y, then more x + Δx inputs can also produce y; inputs x can also produce less output y − Δy. Based on the production possibility set $T_G$ in Eq. (19.7), the input and output of a particular decision-making unit DMU0 are expressed as follows:

$$x_{i0} = \sum_{j=1}^{n} \lambda_j x_{ij} + s_{i0}^-, \; y_{r0} = \sum_{j=1}^{n} \lambda_j r_{ij} + s_{r0}^+ \tag{19.9}$$

where $\lambda_j, s_{i0}^-, s_{r0}^+ \geq 0 x_{i0}$ and $y_{r0}$ are the input and output of a specific decision-making unit DMU0. $x_{ij}$ is the input of the i-th indicator of the j-th decision making unit, $y_{rj}$ is the output of the r-th indicator of the j-th decision making unit, $s_{i0}^-$ is the slack variable of input i, which represents the excessive amount of DMU0 on the i-th input factor, $s_{r0}^+$ is the slack variable of output r, which represents the insufficient amount of DMU0 on the r-th output factor.

The sum of the slack variables of an input factor $s_{0j}^-$, that is $\sum_{j=1}^{n} s_{0j}^-$, is called the input redundancy,[2] the ratio of which to the corresponding input indicator $\sum_{j=1}^{n} x_{0j}$ is defined as the total input redundancy rate, denoted by $\chi_{ij}$.

$$\chi_{ij} = \frac{\sum_{i=1}^{m} S_i^-}{\sum_{i=1}^{m} \sum_{j=1}^{n} x_{ij}}, i = 1, 2, \ldots, m;\ j = 1, 2, \ldots, n \tag{19.10}$$

The above formula represents the percentage of input variable savings. The comparison of the input redundancies (rates) of different decision-making units in the same period can be used to judge the input use efficiency of the decision making units comprehensively.

The input redundancy rate of each input factor can be obtained by dividing the slack variable of each input factor in the decision-making unit by the corresponding input factor value, denoted by $\gamma_{ij}$.

$$\gamma_{ij} = \frac{s_i^-}{x_{ij}}, \quad i = 1, 2, \ldots, m;\ j = 1, 2, \ldots, n \tag{19.11}$$

[2]According to formula (1), the reason for the difference of DEA efficiency can be divided into three aspects: (1) From the perspective of input. The denominators of formula (1) are the input indicators. From the calculation results of the input indicators, except Beijing, Tianjin and Shanghai, the decision making units of other provinces have one or more input indicators that are more than DEA effective input, resulting in DEA efficiency value less than 1. Take Hebei Province for example, the redundancy rates of $SO_2$ emissions, $NO_X$ emissions, soot emissions, coal consumption, car ownership, capital and labor force are 964686.041, 1157308.897, 1093714.577, 22252.012, 712.265, 8418.193 and 0 respectively, indicating that the amount of input must be reduced to achieve effective DEA. (2) From the perspective of output. It can be seen from the molecular part of GDP (desirable output) and $PM_{2.5}$ (undesirable output) (see Table 19.2) that the provinces with relatively low efficiency values are Gansu, Qinghai and other provinces that are relatively backward in economic development. The desirable output GDP of these provinces is quite low and the undesirable output $PM_{2.5}$ is relatively high, which is one of the reasons why DEA is not effective. However, since this paper focuses on the improvement of the DEA efficiency of each evaluation unit by reducing the input indicator, how to raise the desirable output (GDP) and reduce the undesirable output ($PM_{2.5}$) are not yet considered. Of course, this is the next step that needs to be studied. (3) Emission efficiency values are relative values. The DEA efficiency values of the DMUs obtained in Table 19.3 and the redundancies of the input indicators of DMUs obtained in Table 19.4 are relative values compared with other "leading" DMUs. As mentioned in this paper, the three DMUs in Beijing, Tianjin and Shanghai are on the frontier whose efficiency value is 1 and the efficiency values of other DMUs and the redundancies of their input indicators are relative to these DMUs on frontier.

### 19.3.3 *Index Selection*

#### 19.3.3.1 Production Function

There should be specific theoretical basis and economic meanings for the selection of input indicators. The production function proposed by Cobb–Douglas is a classical model of input and output. The production function can be expressed as:

$$Y = AL^{\alpha}K^{\beta}\mu \tag{19.12}$$

where $Y$ is gross output and $A$ is comprehensive technology level (enterprise's business management level, the quality of labor force, advanced technology, etc.). $L$ is the amount of contributed labor force. $K$ is contributed capital. $\alpha$ and $\beta$ respectively are the elastic coefficients of labor force input and capital input. $\mu$ is stochastic disturbance term. It can be concluded from the above expression that the principal factors that determine the system development level are fixed assets, comprehensive technology level, and the amount of contributed labor force.

In traditional production functions, indicators such as $K$ and $L$ are at the side of input whereas indicators like GDP are at the side of output. Influencing factors (such as energy, environment, and climate) of GDP were added to the side of input by scholars later on. Lei et al. (2014) added the Usage Amount of Raw Materials $r$, the Usage Amount of Energy $e$, the Input of Labor Force $l$, and the Input of Equipment Maintenance and Management $m$ into the side of input and developed C–D production function into:

$$q = kr^{\alpha}e^{\beta}l^{\theta}m^{\gamma} \tag{19.13}$$

where $\alpha$, $\beta$, $\theta$, and $\gamma$ are respectively the elastic coefficients of the Usage Amount of Raw Materials $r$, the Usage Amount of Energy $e$, the Input of Labor Force $l$, and the Input of Equipment Maintenance and Management $m$. Thus, this paper develops the production function by adding $PM_{2.5}$ at the side of output and indicators related to energy and environment at the side of input. The expression of the developed production function is:

$$Y_j = A_j K_j^{\alpha} L_j^{\beta} C_j^{\chi} \tag{19.14}$$

where $Y_j$ refers to the output of Region $j$, $A_j$ refers to the technology of Region $j$, $K_j$ refers to the capital input of Region $j$, $L_j$ refers to the labor input of Region $j$, and $C_j$ refers to the inputs of environment and energy related to the $PM_{2.5}$ output of Region $j$. $\alpha$, $\beta$, $\alpha$, $\beta$ and $\gamma$ are the output elasticity of capital, labor force, and the environment and energy related to $PM_{2.5}$ output respectively.

#### 19.3.3.2 Input Indicators of the Components and Sources of $PM_{2.5}$

The selection of proper environmental indicators and energy indicators is crucial for this study. Based on the previous relevant researches, this paper, after considering the components and sources of $PM_{2.5}$ together with the availability of data, chooses capital, labor force, $SO_2$ emissions, $NO_X$ emissions, soot emissions, coal consumption, and car ownership as input indicators.

Sulfide and Nitrogen Oxide. Ni (2013) proposed that the substances transformed from nitrogen oxide and sulfur oxide are major sources of $PM_{2.5}$. Sheng (2014) put forward that the secondary sulfate in particulate matters exerted an important influence on the formation of haze and there was a positive correlation between the reduction of haze and that of $PM_{2.5}$ concentration and sulfur emissions. Taking Alaska for example, secondary sulfur and nitrate have contributed 8%–20% and 3%–11% respectively to $PM_{2.5}$. The total amount of $SO_2$ emissions and $NO_X$ emissions is highly related to $PM_{2.5}$ concentration indicators. Thus, $SO_2$ and $NO_X$ are adopted and regarded as input indicator variables in this paper. The data are from the *China Statistical Yearbook on Environment-2013.*

Soot. According to the study of Huang et al. (2006), blowing dust, construction dust, coal dust, smelting dust, sulfate, and automobile dust are the main sources of $PM_{2.5}$. The contribution of coal dust to $PM_{2.5}$ accounts for 30.34%. Gieré et al. (2006) proposed that lots of $PM_{2.5}$ in the soot were from coal combustion and these fine particles did great damage to the environment and people's health. Therefore, soot is adopted in this paper. The data are from the *China Statistical Yearbook on Environment-2013.*

Coal Consumption. Gieré et al. (2006) also proposed that the $SO_2$ and $NO_X$ caused by coal combustion were the primary causes of $PM_{2.5}$. Because $SO_2$ and $NO_X$ will react with other pollutants in the air and then transform from gaseous pollutants into solid pollutants. Deng (2015) put forward that the CO emissions greatly increased in winter due to the burning of coal for heating and thus elevated the $PM_{2.5}$ concentration. Therefore, coal consumption is selected as input indicator. The data are from the *China Statistical Yearbook on Environment-2013.*

Car ownership. According to the *Annual Report on the Prevention and Control of Motor Vehicle Pollution in China-2013* (Vehicle Emission Control Center of MEP 2014) published by the Ministry of Environmental Protection, vehicle is the major contributor to pollution. The $NO_X$ and PM from vehicle exhaust account for over 90% and HC and CO account for over 70%. Motor vehicle pollution is the main source of air pollution in China. It is also the main cause of dust-haze pollution and photochemical smog pollution. Huo (2009) proposed that the $NO_X$ and CO discharged from motor vehicle respectively accounted for 43% and 83% in the air pollutants in cities. Zhang et al. (2014) put forward that $PM_{2.5}$ came both from the combustion of vehicle fuel and the reaction between automobile exhaust and other pollutants. Taking Beijing as an example, $PM_{2.5}$ concentration is the highest in morning peak (7:00–9:00) and evening peak (16:00–19:00) when there are most cars running on the road. Automobile exhaust is one of the main sources of $PM_{2.5}$

in Beijing. Therefore, civil car ownership is adopted as input indicator in this paper. The data are from the *China Statistical Yearbook on Environment-2013*.

#### 19.3.3.3 Output Indicators

According to the study of Guo et al. (2015b), GDP and $PM_{2.5}$ emissions are regarded as desirable output indicator and undesirable output indicator respectively. New $PM_{2.5}$ measurement indicators are obtained from $PM_{2.5}$ concentration after taking the land area of province and atmospheric environmental capacity into account. First, the population weighted $PM_{2.5}$ concentration of province, the land area of province, and the primary $PM_{2.5}$ atmospheric environmental capacity of province (constrained by the $PM_{2.5}$ standard) are normalized respectively. Then the undesirable output of $PM_{2.5}$ can be obtained by dividing the product of the normalized population weighted $PM_{2.5}$ concentration of province times the normalized land area of province by the normalized primary $PM_{2.5}$ atmospheric environmental capacity (see Table 19.1 for the calculation formula).

Evaluation indicator of haze. The main components of Haze are $PM_{10}$ and $PM_{2.5}$. The data are quite difficult to get as relevant departments in China started to collect the data of $PM_{2.5}$ in 2012. Thus, some researchers used the data observed by themselves (Abas et al.2004; Hossein and Kaneko 2013). Whereas, the data adopted in most of the previous studies were the global annual average $PM_{2.5}$ from 2001 to 2010. These data were released by the Battelle Memorial Institute and the Center for International Earth Science Information Network of Columbia University, and so were the population

**Table 19.1** The description of input and output indicators

| Indicator categories | Name of indicators | Accounting content | Unit |
|---|---|---|---|
| Input indicators | $SO_2$ emissions ($SO_2$) | $SO_2$ emissions | Ton |
| | $NO_X$ emissions ($NO_x$) | Total emissions of $NO_X$ | Ton |
| | Soot emissions | Total emissions of soot | Ton |
| | Coal consumption | Coal consumption | 10,000 tons |
| | Car ownership | Civil and private car ownership | 10,000 |
| | Capital (K) | Fixed-asset investment | 100 million yuan |
| | Labor force (L) | Employed population | 10,000 people |
| Output indicators | $PM_{2.5}$ emissions | Population weighted $PM_{2.5}$ concentration of province * land area of province/the primary $PM_{2.5}$ atmospheric environmental capacity (constrained by the $PM_{2.5}$ standard) | |
| | GDP | GNP | 100 million yuan |

weighted $PM_{2.5}$ emissions of provinces from 2001 to 2010. The factors are considered in the calculation of $PM_{2.5}$ emission efficiency. They are the land area of province (the data are from the *2001–2010 China Statistical Yearbook on Environment*) and the primary $PM_{2.5}$ atmospheric environmental capacity (Xue 2014a).

Atmospheric environmental capacity. Atmospheric environmental capacity refers to the maximum pollutant bearing capacity of one region or the allowable maximum air pollutant emissions on condition that the target value of atmospheric environment is reached (namely, maintaining ecological balance while not damaging people's physical health). Atmospheric environmental capacity is important for the control of air pollutant emissions as well as air quality management. Many scholars have conducted studies on the simulation and calculation of atmospheric environmental capacity with different environmental goals (Li 2005; Xue 2013, 2014a). Xue et al. (2014b), based on the 3rd generation air quality model WRF-CAMx and the national emission inventory of major air pollutants, developed an air-quality restrained iterative algorithm to assess the atmospheric environmental capacity. They calculated the maximum permissible emissions of primary $PM_{2.5}$ of 31 Chinese provinces (municipalities and autonomous regions). The analog calculation was conducted under the condition that the annual average $PM_{2.5}$ concentration of 333 prefecture-level cities in China meets the goal set by the Ambient Air Quality Standard (GB3095-2012). Thus, the data from Wang's research can be utilized in this study.

## 19.4 Empirical Analysis

### *19.4.1 Data Sources and Data Selection*

Based on the researches of Guo et al. (2015c) and Zheng et al. (2007), GDP and $PM_{2.5}$ are regarded as desirable output variable and undesirable output variable respectively. $PM_{2.5}$ emissions = population weighted $PM_{2.5}$ concentration of province * the land area of province/the primary $PM_{2.5}$ atmospheric environmental capacity (constrained by the $PM_{2.5}$ standard). $SO_2$ emissions, $NO_X$ emissions, soot emissions, coal consumption, car ownership, capital, and labor force are selected as input indicators. The definition and calculation method of the 7 input indicators are given below in Table 19.1.

It should be noted that only the data of environmental capacity of provinces from 2010 are available. Therefore, the data adopted in this paper are all from 2012 except those of atmospheric environmental capacity (from 2010) so as to make sure the data are reasonable and available. The data of input and output indicators of 2012 are listed in Table 19.2.

**Table 19.2** Data of inputs and outputs

| Inputs | | | | | | | | Outputs | |
|---|---|---|---|---|---|---|---|---|---|
| | | | | | | | | Desirable outputs | Undesirable outputs |
| DMU | $SO_2$ emissions (ton) | $NO_X$ emissions (ton) | Soot emissions (ton) | Coal consumption (1000 tons) | Car ownership (10,000) | Capital (100 million yuan) | Labor force (10,000 people) | GDP (100 million yuan) | $PM_{2.5}$ |
| Beijing | 93849.39 | 177493.41 | 66824.78 | 2270.00 | 899.11 | 6112.40 | 592.33 | 17879.40 | 53.65 |
| Tianjin | 224521.40 | 334222.59 | 84064.00 | 5298.00 | 406.66 | 7934.80 | 148.06 | 12893.88 | 39.65 |
| Hebei | 1341201.15 | 1761109.58 | 1235877.24 | 31359.00 | 1352.55 | 19661.30 | 641.27 | 26575.01 | 777.04 |
| Shanxi | 1301755.00 | 1243969.91 | 1070863.36 | 34551.00 | 600.40 | 8863.30 | 386.20 | 12112.83 | 294.63 |
| Inner Mongolia | 1384928.33 | 1418897.36 | 833010.10 | 36620.00 | 489.74 | 11875.70 | 360.88 | 15880.58 | 1339.91 |
| Liaoning | 1058712.30 | 1036321.95 | 726257.71 | 18219.00 | 719.70 | 21836.30 | 807.00 | 24846.43 | 258.48 |
| Jining | 403482.25 | 575851.78 | 264755.80 | 11083.00 | 379.68 | 9511.50 | 407.07 | 11939.24 | 261.36 |
| Heilongjiang | 514299.73 | 780611.37 | 699275.14 | 13965.00 | 461.24 | 9694.70 | 504.20 | 13691.58 | 696.77 |
| Shanghai | 228218.29 | 401617.86 | 87148.42 | 5703.00 | 353.82 | 5117.60 | 711.95 | 20181.72 | 13.01 |
| Jiangsu | 991966.79 | 1479608.69 | 443207.70 | 27762.00 | 1448.89 | 30854.20 | 2232.88 | 54058.22 | 253.76 |
| Zhejiang | 625766.42 | 808848.79 | 254029.81 | 14374.00 | 1416.90 | 17649.40 | 1546.22 | 34665.33 | 204.20 |
| Anhui | 519589.35 | 921267.88 | 462058.61 | 14704.00 | 526.54 | 15425.80 | 646.22 | 17212.05 | 464.00 |
| Fujian | 371251.34 | 467210.98 | 252635.35 | 8485.00 | 514.80 | 12439.90 | 652.73 | 19701.78 | 125.90 |
| Jiangxi | 567687.21 | 577095.16 | 357373.06 | 6802.00 | 351.22 | 10774.20 | 659.87 | 12948.88 | 264.99 |
| Shandong | 1748806.99 | 1738973.30 | 695266.81 | 40233.00 | 1904.72 | 31256.00 | 1375.02 | 50013.24 | 508.46 |

(continued)

**Table 19.2** (continued)

| Inputs | | | | | | | | Outputs | |
|---|---|---|---|---|---|---|---|---|---|
| | | | | | | | | Desirable outputs | Undesirable outputs |
| DMU | $SO_2$ emissions (ton) | $NO_X$ emissions (ton) | Soot emissions (ton) | Coal consumption (1000 tons) | Car ownership (10,000) | Capital (100 million yuan) | Labor force (10,000 people) | GDP (100 million yuan) | $PM_{2.5}$ |
| Henan | 1275909.33 | 1625897.69 | 599823.47 | 25240.00 | 1049.75 | 21450.00 | 865.51 | 29599.31 | 664.88 |
| Hubei | 622367.29 | 640007.89 | 349657.23 | 15799.00 | 521.09 | 15578.30 | 911.53 | 22250.45 | 495.85 |
| Hunan | 644959.47 | 607213.80 | 340723.52 | 12084.00 | 569.73 | 14523.20 | 721.93 | 22154.23 | 553.05 |
| Guangdong | 799223.24 | 1303428.77 | 328251.62 | 17634.00 | 1900.88 | 18751.50 | 1808.95 | 57067.92 | 213.33 |
| Guangxi | 504123.33 | 498255.64 | 299723.01 | 7264.00 | 377.02 | 9808.60 | 477.61 | 13035.10 | 290.31 |
| Hainan | 34136.86 | 103392.33 | 16605.57 | 931.00 | 98.14 | 2145.40 | 116.78 | 2855.54 | 34.00 |
| Sichuan | 864440.44 | 659004.69 | 295836.11 | 11872.00 | 902.11 | 17040.00 | 884.11 | 23872.80 | 1278.83 |
| Guizhou | 1041086.62 | 563538.70 | 294496.99 | 13328.00 | 296.57 | 5717.80 | 276.40 | 6852.20 | 366.70 |
| Yunnan | 672215.92 | 544346.30 | 390645.91 | 9850.00 | 602.32 | 7831.10 | 563.01 | 10309.47 | 421.27 |
| Shaanxi | 843755.44 | 808128.82 | 462050.81 | 15774.00 | 515.43 | 12044.50 | 420.50 | 14453.68 | 331.96 |
| Gansu | 572489.40 | 473381.80 | 207567.02 | 6558.00 | 219.31 | 5145.00 | 225.96 | 5650.20 | 542.29 |
| Qinghai | 153853.33 | 126058.73 | 156392.96 | 1859.00 | 84.91 | 1883.40 | 69.87 | 1893.54 | 779.84 |
| Ningxia | 406633.25 | 455404.94 | 198336.71 | 8055.00 | 119.84 | 2096.90 | 98.93 | 2341.29 | 80.88 |
| Xinjiang | 796128.41 | 819477.30 | 696125.97 | 12028.00 | 346.34 | 6158.80 | 211.68 | 7505.31 | 2164.42 |

*Note* The data of Chongqing, Tibet, Hong Kong, Macao, and Taiwan are not excluded from the table (the same below)

## 19.4.2 Results of Empirical Analysis

### 19.4.2.1 The Emission Efficiency Values of Each Province

Choose undesirable model in Mode Selection while using Dea Solver 5.0. The weight of good outputs and bad outputs respectively are 0.65 and 0.35. The emission efficiency of each province is calculated and the results are listed in Table 19.3.

The economic significance of DEA effective value:

(1) When $h_0 = 1$ and $S^+ = S^- = 0$, $DMU_0$ is DEA efficient. The input–output efficiency is optimal, in which case the Output $Y_0$ of $DMU_0$ obtained through the Input $X_0$ is highest.
(2) When $h_0 = 1$ and $S^+ \neq 0$ (or $S^- \neq 0$), $DMU_0$ is weak DEA efficient. In the economic system composed of $n$ decision making units, the Output $Y_0$ will remain unchanged after cutting down $S^-$ in Input $X_0$ or the Output $Y_0$ can increase by $S^+$ without changing the Input $X_0$.
(3) When $0 \leq h_0 < 1$, $DMU_0$ is DEA inefficient. The Output $Y_0$ of $DMU_0$ will remain unchanged after the input is cut down to only $h_0$ of the Input $X_0$.

It can be known from the Relative Efficiency $\theta$ in Table 19.3 that the provinces in China differ a lot in the $PM_{2.5}$ discharge efficiency. The provinces can be divided into three groups according to the $PM_{2.5}$ discharge efficiency. The three-decision making unites Beijing, Shanghai, Tianjin are in the first group as they are the highest in the input–output efficiency. With the value of 1 in efficiency, the three provinces (municipalities) are in the stochastic frontier. It indicates that the three provinces (municipalities) are harmonious in the relation between economy development and environment. Guangdong, Fujian, Hainan, Zhejiang, Jiangsu, Hunan, and Shandong are in the second group. The input–output efficiency of these 7 provinces are higher than the national average value $\overline{\theta} = 0.427$. The 7 provinces are close to the stochastic frontier. Hubei, Sichuan, Guangxi, Henan, Liaoning, Jilin, Hebei, Shaanxi, Inner Mongolia, Jiangxi, Anhui, Heilongjiang, Xinjiang, Qinghai, Gansu, Shanxi, Yunnan, Guizhou, and Ningxia are in the third group. The initial discharge efficiency of these 19 provinces is lower than the average value. The 19 provinces are far from the stochastic frontier. The input–output efficiency of Ningxia Province is only 0.187 which is the lowest.

As is shown in Table 19.3, municipalities such as Beijing, Shanghai, and Tianjin are high in $\theta$. These provinces (municipalities) are high in economic development level as well as resource allocation efficiency, thus they are higher in the input–output efficiency than other provinces. Provinces (such as Guangdong, Fujian, etc.) in eastern coastal China are lower in $\theta$ than Beijing, Shanghai, and Tianjin. Less developed provinces such as Guizhou and Ningxia are the lowest in $\theta$.

**Table 19.3** Analysis results of DEA model

| DMU | Score | Excess | | | | | | |
|---|---|---|---|---|---|---|---|---|
| DMU | | $SO_2$ emissions | NOx emissions | Soot emissions | Coal consumption | Car ownership | Capital | Labor force |
| Beijing | 1 | 0 | 0 | 0 | 0 | 0 | 0 | 0 |
| Tianjin | 1 | 0 | 0 | 0 | 0 | 0 | 0 | 0 |
| Hebei | 0.3305445 | 964686.04 | 1157308.9 | 1093714.6 | 22252.012 | 712.26545 | 8418.1927 | 0 |
| Shanxi | 0.2443169 | 1154235 | 992522.47 | 1014754.8 | 30906.472 | 363.84392 | 5166.741 | 0 |
| Inner Mongolia | 0.3282583 | 1154203.5 | 1052430.9 | 745991.35 | 31057.484 | 93.977625 | 4817.5777 | 0 |
| Liaoning | 0.3616026 | 759911.24 | 524287.65 | 612535.21 | 10823.016 | 243.1817 | 14478.906 | 0 |
| Jilin | 0.3403716 | 264851.03 | 334689.42 | 211894.42 | 7633.0901 | 162.05818 | 6269.4317 | 0 |
| Heilongjiang | 0.3023864 | 359473.04 | 508147.82 | 640152.35 | 10096 | 221.20323 | 6222.8438 | 21.202496 |
| Shanghai | 1 | 0 | 0 | 0 | 0 | 0 | 0 | 0 |
| Jiangsu | 0.4798068 | 380667.33 | 403845.74 | 209774.25 | 12486.095 | 501.15713 | 17146.332 | 325.86961 |
| Zhejiang | 0.4866069 | 233765.03 | 119005.92 | 104338.47 | 4578.1859 | 809.15759 | 8859.104 | 323.33208 |
| Anhui | 0.3230257 | 324952.59 | 578746.69 | 387733.78 | 9840.1766 | 224.78338 | 11061.237 | 39.03097 |
| Fujian | 0.5153438 | 137610.12 | 64442.919 | 163646.67 | 2689.5765 | 144.49897 | 6800.9432 | 0 |
| Jiangxi | 0.3245822 | 421259.09 | 319411.4 | 301457.39 | 3142.8737 | 124.20403 | 7490.6747 | 203.0727 |
| Shandong | 0.4340521 | 1083366.8 | 645196.6 | 443281.47 | 24000.843 | 798.72814 | 12654.128 | 0 |
| Henan | 0.361845 | 895355.32 | 991659.05 | 455477.58 | 15912.301 | 425.64587 | 11227.521 | 0 |
| Hubei | 0.398842 | 370755.45 | 197222.14 | 253575.65 | 9511.4132 | 131.00163 | 9936.1197 | 126.60147 |
| Hunan | 0.4484319 | 379143 | 151260.32 | 239542.67 | 5502.1853 | 146.24016 | 7999.0649 | 0 |
| Guangdong | 0.6937056 | 101489.19 | 116092.37 | 62925.404 | 406.26952 | 780.15179 | 1174.8266 | 0 |
| Guangxi | 0.3639831 | 356720.22 | 238856.1 | 243435.02 | 3580.5094 | 148.49245 | 6503.2114 | 17.771124 |

(continued)

**Table 19.3** (continued)

| DMU | Score | Excess | | | | | | |
|---|---|---|---|---|---|---|---|---|
| DMU | | $SO_2$ emissions | NOx emissions | Soot emissions | Coal consumption | Car ownership | Capital | Labor force |
| Hainan | 0.511637 | 10739.284 | 61204.532 | 5127.0801 | 352.48783 | 0 | 1291.712 | 19.197618 |
| Sichuan | 0.395056 | 594482.8 | 183934.04 | 192748.92 | 5125.9655 | 483.57907 | 10986.431 | 41.949869 |
| Guizhou | 0.2277646 | 963600.79 | 427179.37 | 264907.92 | 11391.688 | 176.43924 | 3980.2465 | 34.675123 |
| Yunnan | 0.238002 | 555634.7 | 339187.01 | 346127.7 | 6936.7246 | 421.57739 | 5216.8657 | 199.3231 |
| Shaanxi | 0.3283412 | 657377.94 | 497881.77 | 391367.22 | 11207.647 | 209.414 | 7020.2305 | 0 |
| Gansu | 0.2461862 | 508595.99 | 360942.36 | 183168.41 | 4961.3526 | 120.25235 | 3712.2448 | 26.638045 |
| Qinghai | 0.2519707 | 132440.86 | 88377.131 | 148216.3 | 1323.9188 | 51.713012 | 1403.2437 | 3.0716398 |
| Ningxia | 0.1872599 | 380157.55 | 408813.08 | 188226.58 | 7393.3925 | 78.79319 | 1503.205 | 16.336375 |
| Xinjiang | 0.2634279 | 697637.13 | 656688.25 | 658805.09 | 9620.8701 | 183.50873 | 3448.4174 | 0 |

#### 19.4.2.2 The Total Redundancy Rate

According to the results of formula (19.10), when the $PM_{2.5}$ emissions and GDP are equal, all the input indicators are redundant. The redundancy rates of all input indicators are over 50% except that of labor force and car ownership. The redundancy rate of soot emissions is 78.59%, which is the highest. The redundancy rates of $SO_2$ and coal consumption respectively are 67.18% and 61.14%. When $0 \leq h_0 < 1$, $DMU_0$ is DEA inefficient. In that case, the Output $Y_0$ of $DMU_0$ will remain unchanged after the input is cut down to only $h_0$ of the Input $X_0$. The cut shall focus on those input indicators which show redundancy. Therefore, soot emissions should be cut down firstly. $SO_2$ emissions, coal consumption, capital, $NO_X$ emissions, car ownership, and labor force should be cut down by 67.18%, 61.14%, 51.45%, 49.76%, 39.92% and 7.23% respectively. The results are listed in Table 19.4.

Redundancy means what we can cut. For example, the redundancy of $SO_2$ emissions is 13843111.05t, that is to say, if we want to achieve the DEA efficient, in the economic system composed of decision-making units, the Output $Y_0$ will remain unchanged after cutting down $S^-$ in input $SO_2$ emissions. Similarly, the redundancy of $NO_X$ emissions, soot emissions, coal consumption, car ownership, capital, and labor force are 11419333.97 tons, 9562926.33 tons, 262732.55 million tons, 7755.87 ten thousand cars, 184789.45 hundred million Yuan and 1398.07 ten thousand Yuan people respectively. And the results of redundancy are obtained by the summation of $S^-$, which are the slack variable of the 7 input indicators $SO_2$ emissions, $NO_X$ emissions, soot emissions, coal consumption, car ownership, capital, and labor force.

Some reasons why the above-mentioned results arise can be summarized as following: (1) High capital input. In the first ten years of the twenty-first Century, the United States capital formation rate is only about 20%, while the Chinese capital formation rate in the same period has been hovering around 40%, and the physical capital formation rate reached a staggering 48.6% in 2010, indicating that China's economy is still in the "high input, high output" stage, and that the capital input has a redundancy. (2) The employment population decreased and the quality of labor force is improved. Based on the 2012 statistical bulletin, the working age population is 937.27 million in the mainland, and the working age population has declined, which had a decrease of 3.45 million, in comparison with that at the end of last year. The quality of labor force in our country has been greatly improved in recent years, according to the 6th National Population Census. So, the labor force displays a lower redundancy.

#### 19.4.2.3 The Redundancy Rate of Input Indicators of Each Province

According to the formula (19.11), the redundancy rate of input can be obtained by dividing the slack variable of province's input indicator by the corresponding value of input indicator and the redundancy rate of output can be obtained by dividing the slack variable of province's output indicator by the corresponding value of output indicator. The results are listed in Table 19.5.

**Table 19.4** The redundancy (rate) of input indicators

| | $SO_2$ emissions | $NO_X$ emissions | Soot emissions | Coal consumption | Car ownership | Capital | Labor force |
|---|---|---|---|---|---|---|---|
| Inputs | 20607358.27 | 22950638.01 | 12168884.79 | 429704.00 | 19429.41 | 359181.60 | 19324.67 |
| Redundancy | 13843111.05 | 11419333.97 | 9562926.33 | 262732.55 | 7755.87 | 184789.45 | 1398.07 |
| Redundancy rate (%)_ | 67.18 | 49.76 | 78.59 | 61.14 | 39.92 | 51.45 | 7.23 |

**Table 19.5** The redundancy rate of input indicators of each province

| Inputs | | | | | | | | Outputs | |
|---|---|---|---|---|---|---|---|---|---|
| | | | | | | | | Desirable outputs | Undesirable outputs |
| DMU | $SO_2$ emissions (%) | NOx emissions (%) | Soot emissions (%) | Coal consumption (%) | Car ownership (%) | Capital (%) | Labor force (%) | GDP | $PM_{2.5}$ (%) |
| Beijing | 0 | 0 | 0 | 0 | 0 | 0 | 0 | 0 | 0 |
| Tianjin | 0 | 0 | 0 | 0 | 0 | 0 | 0 | 0 | 0 |
| Hebei | 71.93 | 65.71 | 88.50 | 70.96 | 52.66 | 42.82 | 0 | 0 | 93.90 |
| Shanxi | 88.67 | 79.79 | 94.76 | 89.45 | 60.60 | 58.29 | 0 | 0 | 95.92 |
| Inner Mongolia | 83.34 | 74.17 | 89.55 | 84.81 | 19.19 | 40.57 | 0 | 0 | 97.72 |
| Liaoning | 71.78 | 50.59 | 84.34 | 59.41 | 33.79 | 66.31 | 0 | 0 | 91.05 |
| Jilin | 65.64 | 58.12 | 80.03 | 68.87 | 42.68 | 65.91 | 0 | 0 | 96.50 |
| Heilongjiang | 69.90 | 65.10 | 91.55 | 72.30 | 47.96 | 64.19 | 4.21 | 0 | 98.73 |
| Shanghai | 0 | 0 | 0 | 0 | 0 | 0 | 0 | 0 | 0 |
| Jiangsu | 38.38 | 27.29 | 47.33 | 44.98 | 34.59 | 55.57 | 14.59 | 0 | 86.26 |
| Zhejiang | 37.36 | 14.71 | 41.07 | 31.85 | 57.11 | 50.19 | 20.91 | 0 | 89.05 |
| Anhui | 62.54 | 62.82 | 83.91 | 66.92 | 42.69 | 71.71 | 6.04 | 0 | 97.61 |
| Fujian | 37.07 | 13.79 | 64.78 | 31.70 | 28.07 | 54.67 | 0 | 0 | 86.48 |
| Jiangxi | 74.21 | 55.35 | 84.35 | 46.21 | 35.36 | 69.52 | 30.77 | 0 | 96.85 |
| Shandong | 61.95 | 37.10 | 63.76 | 59.65 | 41.93 | 40.49 | 0 | 0 | 85.84 |
| Henan | 70.17 | 60.99 | 75.94 | 63.04 | 40.55 | 52.34 | 0 | 0 | 94.38 |
| Hubei | 59.57 | 30.82 | 72.52 | 60.20 | 25.14 | 63.78 | 13.89 | 0 | 97.11 |

(continued)

**Table 19.5** (continued)

| Inputs | | | | | | | | Outputs | |
|---|---|---|---|---|---|---|---|---|---|
| | | | | | | | | Desirable outputs | Undesirable outputs |
| DMU | $SO_2$ emissions (%) | NOx emissions (%) | Soot emissions (%) | Coal consumption (%) | Car ownership (%) | Capital (%) | Labor force (%) | GDP | $PM_{2.5}$ (%) |
| Hunan | 58.79 | 24.91 | 70.30 | 45.53 | 25.67 | 55.08 | 0 | 0 | 96.32 |
| Guangdong | 12.70 | 8.91 | 19.17 | 2.30 | 41.04 | 6.27 | 0 | 0 | 72.97 |
| Guangxi | 70.76 | 47.94 | 81.22 | 49.29 | 39.39 | 66.30 | 3.72 | 0 | 97.10 |
| Hainan | 31.46 | 59.20 | 30.88 | 37.86 | 0 | 60.21 | 16.44 | 0 | 84.41 |
| Sichuan | 68.77 | 27.91 | 65.15 | 43.18 | 53.61 | 64.47 | 4.74 | 0 | 98.80 |
| Guizhou | 92.56 | 75.80 | 89.95 | 85.47 | 59.49 | 69.61 | 12.55 | 0 | 98.80 |
| Yunnan | 82.66 | 62.31 | 88.60 | 70.42 | 69.99 | 66.62 | 35.40 | 0 | 98.42 |
| Shaanxi | 77.91 | 61.61 | 84.70 | 71.05 | 40.63 | 58.29 | 0 | 0 | 94.44 |
| Gansu | 88.84 | 76.25 | 88.25 | 75.65 | 54.83 | 72.15 | 11.79 | 0 | 99.33 |
| Qinghai | 86.08 | 70.11 | 94.77 | 71.22 | 60.90 | 74.51 | 4.40 | 0 | 99.84 |
| Ningxia | 93.49 | 89.77 | 94.90 | 91.79 | 65.75 | 71.69 | 16.51 | 0 | 98.13 |
| Xinjiang | 87.63 | 80.14 | 94.64 | 79.99 | 52.99 | 55.99 | 0 | 0 | 99.53 |

Conclusions can be drawn from Table 19.5 that: (1) The input–output efficiency of Beijing, Tianjin, and Shanghai is 1 and the input–output redundancy is 0, thus there is no need to cut down the input indicators to control $PM_{2.5}$ emissions; (2) As for provinces such as Shangxi, Inner Mongolia, Jilin, and Heilongjiang, the redundancy rates of $NO_X$ emissions, coal consumption, and $SO_2$ emissions are in the top three; (3) As for provinces such as Hebei, Shandong, Henan, Yunnan, Shaanxi, and Ningxia, the redundancy rates of $NO_X$ emissions, $SO_2$ emissions, and coal consumption are in the top three; (4) As for provinces such as Liaoning, Fujian, Jiangxi, Hunan, Guangxi, Sichuan, and Qinghai, the input indicators which are high in the redundancy rate are $SO_2$ emissions, soot emissions, and capital; (5) In conclusion, provinces such as Guizhou, Shanxi, Yunnan, Qinghai, and Ningxia are relatively high in the redundancy rate of input indicator. The redundancy which needs to be cut down is large in amount.

Conclusions can also be drawn from Table 19.5 that: (1) High redundancy rates mainly appear in $SO_2$ emissions, soot emissions, and coal consumption whereas low redundancy rates mainly appear in labor force and capital; (2) The provinces which are high in the redundancy rates of $SO_2$ emissions, soot emissions and coal consumption mainly include Heibei, Shanxi, Inner Mongolia, Jilin, Heilongjiang, Shandong, Henan, Guizhou, Yunnan, Shaanxi, Gansu, Ningxia, and Xinjiang; (3) The redundancy rate of labor force is the lowest; except Jiangxi, Yunnan, and Zhejiang, the redundancy rates of labor force of other provinces are all below 20%; the redundancy rates of labor force of Beijing, Tianjin, Heibei, Shanxi, Inner Mongolia, Liaoning, Jilin, Shanghai, Fujian, Shandong, Henan, Hunan, Guangdong, Shaanxi, and Xinjiang are 0; (4) Provinces in eastern coastal China are relatively low in the redundancy rates of input indicators whereas those in central and western regions are relatively high. That's because the eastern coastal regions are well developed in economy and the production technology; moreover, these regions have more light industries than inland China, thus they have put more efforts in energy conservation and emission reduction; (5) These provinces listed in Table 19.5 all need to cut down the redundancy of input indicators (or output indicators) so as to improve the input–output efficiency except Beijing, Tianjin, and Shanghai.

Taking Jiangsu Province as an example, the redundancy rates of $SO_2$, $NO_X$, soot, coal consumption, car ownership, capital, and labor force respectively are 38.38%, 27.29%, 47.33%, 44.98%, 34.59%, 55.57%, and 14.59%. Therefore, $PM_{2.5}$ emissions of Jiangsu can be reduced by cutting down input indicators. The possible measures for $PM_{2.5}$ reduction are as follows: control the emissions of $SO_2$, $NO_X$ and soot; increase the utilization efficiency of coal and develop new energy so as to reduce the reliance on coal; develop new energy vehicles and promote the technological innovation in automobile industry; control car ownership through odd-and-even license plate rule and public transport so as to reduce motor vehicle pollution; increase the environmental benefit of fixed-asset investment so as to reduce the redundancy rate of capital. The $PM_{2.5}$ emissions will be effectively reduced if these measures are well taken.

## 19.5 Conclusions and Policy Recommendations

This paper, based on DEA model, proposed a method in which haze emissions can be controlled by cutting down input indicators. The 7 input indicators $SO_2$ emissions, $NO_X$ emissions, soot emissions, coal consumption, car ownership, capital, and labor force are adopted in this paper. The input–output efficiency of province was calculated with $PM_{2.5}$ as undesirable output indicator and GDP as desirable output indicator. The result shows that: (1) All the provinces are redundant in inputs except Beijing, Tianjin, and Shanghai; (2) All the listed input indicators are excessive in redundancy on condition that the $PM_{2.5}$ emissions and GDP are equal; all the input indicators are high in redundancy rate except labor force and car ownership; the redundancy rate of soot emissions is up to 78%.

Based on the research results of this paper, the suggestions for haze control are as follows.

The first suggestion is to increase the input–output efficiency. (1) As the input–output efficiency of Beijing, Tianjin, and Shanghai is 1, thus the three cities should maintain the harmonic relationship between economy development and environment. (2) Other local governments should strive to achieve the goal for haze reduction. Those western provinces which are low in input–output efficiency, especially Guizhou, Shanxi, Yunnan, Qinghai, and Ningxia, should formulate industrial policies suitable for the local situation. These provinces should inhibit energy-intensive and high-emission industries, close down backward production facilities, and promote the upgrading of traditional industries so as to achieve the haze reduction target as early as possible. For example, Shanxi Province should gradually eliminate backward steel and coal chemical industries. Shanxi should not over develop heavy chemical industries which contribute a lot to GDP and take practical and effective measures to control and reduce haze.

The second suggestion is to cut down the redundancy rate of input indicators. (1) The structure of energy consumption should be adjusted in order to reduce the redundancy of coal. One of the most effective ways to control haze is to cut down the use of fossil energy, especially coal. For example, the power plant should change the ways of power generating and depend less on coal. Nuclear energy and clean energy should be developed so as to alleviate the contradiction of energy between supply and demand as well as environmental pollution. (2) More efforts should be spent on the prevention and control of vehicle exhaust as it is one of the most important sources of haze. Chinese Academy of Sciences (2014) proposed that the contribution rate of vehicles to $PM_{2.5}$ ranged from 10 to 50%. In terms of vehicle exhaust pollution, equal efforts should be paid both on prevention and treatment. Relevant departments should make policies to eliminate old cars, inhibit the development of diesel vehicles, reduce traffic congestion, popularize high-efficiency technology and products against vehicle exhaust, promote the use of clean fuels, reduce the content of harmful matters (like sulfur) in fuels, strictly implement the tail gas emission standards of new vehicles, and develop high-capacity rail transit. (3) The treatment of $SO_2$ should be strengthened. Relevant departments should develop the treatment technology against $SO_2$ (like the fuel gas desulfurization technology used before, during, and after combustion), adjust energy structure, promote the use of coal briquette and clean energy (such as electricity, natural gas, coal gas, and liquefied petroleum gas), develop urban energy infrastructures which contribute to $SO_2$ reduction, and guide green consumption. Moreover, the domestic pollution sources should be governed strictly so as to control the emissions of pollutants (such as lampblack, volatile organic compound, and soot). For instance, the outdoor barbecue in densely-populated big cities should be restricted through issuing laws.

Thirdly, from a practical point of view, many provinces have also undertaken work to reduce the redundancy of inputs. For example, in 2011, Beijing included the project of changing fuel from coal to natural gas in the government program to reduce the amount of coal input. Given the large number of cars, in 2014, Beijing began to limit the number of cars and strictly control the discharge of motor vehicles on roads. In 2011, Tianjin promotes gas and other clean energy, aiming at reducing the consumption of coal. In Hebei Province, the remaining 23,562 coal-fired boilers will be eliminated by 30%, 30%, 40% in 2015, 2016, 2017 respectively to solve the problem of high coal redundancy. In 2014, in the control of motor vehicles, 811,400 yellow-label cars and old cars were eliminated in an effort to reduce the contribution of motor vehicle exhaust to the haze (Wu 2017a, 2017b). These measures control the output of haze by reducing the redundancy of the input indicators, which is consistent with the ideas presented in this paper.

It should be pointed out that there are limitations to this paper. First, the input indicators adopted in this paper are not typical enough. There are 7 input indicators, 1 desirable output indicator and 1 undesirable output indicator in this paper. As the input indicators are selected on the basis of previous studies, thus they may not be the most appropriate indicators. It is worth mentioning that the input–output efficiency of each evaluation province is not only related to these "hard" input indicators, but also the "soft" input indicators, such as the degree of industrial agglomeration, the arrangements of social system and the degree of economic export. As a result, the design of a reasonable indicator as well as the collection of data is the focus of study in the next step. Second, the results of this review are not exactly the same as those known by the public and the media. As found in this paper, the emission efficiency value of Beijing, Tianjin and Shanghai are 1, above the frontier. But it is known to all that the haze of Beijing and Tianjin has been criticized by the public and the media. So how to include the perception and commentary of the public and media into the input or output indicator system is also worthy of further study in the next step. Third, the indicators are poor in timeliness. Haze not only contains $PM_{2.5}$ but also $PM_{10}$ and other particles. As the data are hard to collect, only the data of $PM_{2.5}$ input and output indicators from 2012 are used in this paper. The data of the atmospheric environmental capacity of each province are all from 2010. These limitations are to be overcome in the future studies.

**Acknowledgements** Ji Guo, Ge Gao, Zhiyong Ji also made great contributions to this manuscript. We express our heartfelt thanks to them. This research was supported by: National Social and Scientific Fund Program of China (18ZDA052; 17BGL142; 16ZDA047); The Natural Science Foundation of China (91546117, 71373131).

## References

Abas, M. R. Bin, Rahman, N. A., Omar, N. Y. M. J., Maah, M. J., Samah, A. A., Oros, D. R., Otto, A., & Simoneit, B. R. T. (2004). Organic composition of aerosol particulate matter during a haze episode in Kuala Lumpur, Malaysia. *Atmospheric Environment, 38*(25), 4223–4241.

Asian Development Bank (2012). Toward an Environmentally Sustainable Future: Country Environmental Analysis of the People's Republic of China.

Ahmad, M., Cheng, S., Yu, Q., Qin, W., & Chen, J. (2019). Chemical and source characterization of $PM_{2.5}$ in summertime in severely polluted Lahore, Pakistan. *Atmospheric Research, 234,* 104715.

Bevilacqua, M., & Braglia, M. (2012). Environmental efficiency analysis for ENI oil refineries. *Journal of Cleaner Production, 10*(1), 85–92.

Banker, R. D., Charnes, A., & Cooper, W. W. (1984). Some models for estimating technical and scale inefficiencies in data envelopment analysis. *Management Science, 30*(9), 1078–1092.

Bian, Y. W. (2006). *Research on environmental efficiency evaluation method based on DEA theory.* University of Science and Technology of China.

Cai, W. G., & Ye, P. Y. (2019). A more scientific allocation scheme of carbon dioxide emissions allowances: The case from China. *Journal of Cleaner Production, 215,* 903–912.

Cecchini, L., Venanzi, S., Pierri, A., & Chiorri, M. (2018). Environmental efficiency analysis and estimation of $CO_2$ abatement costs in dairy cattle farms in Umbria (Italy): An SBM-DEA model with undesirable output. *Journal of Cleaner Production, 197,* 895–907.

Cesari, D., De Benedetto, G. E., Bonasoni, P., Busetto, M., Dinoi, A., Merico, E., et al. (2018). Seasonal variability of $PM_{2.5}$ and $PM_{10}$ composition and sources in an urban background site in Southern Italy. *Science of the Total Environment, 612,* 202–213.

Charnes, A., Cooper, W. W., & Rhodes, E. (1978). Measuring the efficiency of decision making units. *European Journal of Operational Research, 2*(6), 429–444.

Chen, L., He, F., & Wang, J. (2018). Allocative efficiency of carbon emission allowances among sectors in china. *Polish Journal of Environmental Studies, 27*(2), 557–563.

Chen, K., Yin, Y., Wei, Y. X., & Yang, W. F. (2010). Characteristics of carbonaceous aerosols in $PM_{2.5}$ in Nanjing. *China Environmental Science, 30*(8), 1015–1020.

Cheng, Y., Zhang, R. J., Lee, S. C., Gu, Z. L., Ho, K. F., Zhang, Y. W., et al. (2015). $PM_{2.5}$ and $PM_{10\text{-}2.5}$ chemical composition and source apportionment near a Hong Kong roadway. *Particuology,* (18), 96–104.

Chinese Academy of Sciences. (2014). Research group think that motor vehicles contribute 10–50% of $PM_{2.5}$, Reports for: https://www.gov.cn/jrzg/2014-01/02/content_2559005.htm.

Cucchiella, F., D"Adamo, I., Gastaldi, M., & Miliacca, M. (2018). Efficiency and allocation of emission allowances and energy consumption over more sustainable European economies. *Journal of Cleaner Production, 182,* 805–817.

Deng, L. (2015). *An analysis of the factors in Harbin during winter.* Northeast Forestry University.

Deng, J., Zhang, Y., Qiu, Y., Zhang, H., Du, W., Xu, L., et al. (2018). Source apportionment of $PM_{2.5}$ at the Lin'an regional background site in china with three receptor models. *Atmospheric Research, 202,* 23–32.

Duan, L. Y., Bian, J., & Zhu, Z. W. (2008). *Chemistry and society.* Beijing: Chemical Industry Press.

Dyckho, H., & Allen, K. (2001). Measuring ecological efficiency with data envelopment analysis (DEA). *European Journal of Operational Research, 132*(2), 312–325.

Färe, R., & Grosskopf, S. (1996). Intertemporal production frontiers: With dynamic DEA. *Journal of the Operational Research Society, 48*(6), 9–45.
Färe, R., & Grosskopf, S. (2004). Modeling undesirable factors in efficiency evaluation: Comment. *European Journal of Operational Research, 157*(1), 242–245.
Färe, R., Grosskopf, S., & Tyteca, D. (1996). An activity analysis model of the environmental performance of firms-application to fossil-fuel-fired electric utilities. *Ecological Economics, 18*(8), 161–175.
Fang, K., Zhang, Q., Long, Y., Yoshida, Y., Sun, L., Zhang, H., et al. (2019). How can china achieve its intended nationally determined contributions by 2030? A multi-criteria allocation of China's carbon emission allowance. *Applied Energy, 241*, 380–389.
Fleishman, R., Alexander, R., Bretschneider, S., & Popp, D. (2009). Does regulation stimulate productivity? The effect of air quality policies on the efficiency of US power plants. *Energy Policy, 37*(11), 4574–4582.
Gieré, R., Blackford, M., & Smith, K. (2006). TEM study of $PM_{2.5}$ emitted from coal and tire combustion in a thermal power station. *Environmental Science & Technology, 40*(20), 6235–6240.
Gomes, E. G., & Lins, M. P. E. (2008). Modelling undesirable outputs with zero gains DEA models. *Journal of the Operational Research Society, 59*(5), 615–623.
Goto, M., & Tsutsui, M. (1998). Comparison of productive and cost efficiencies among Japanese and US electric utilities. *Omega, 26*(2), 177–194.
Griffith, S. M., Huang, X. H. H., Louie, P. K. K., & Yu, J. Z. (2015). Characterizing the thermodynamic and chemical composition factors controlling $PM_{2.5}$ nitrate: Insights gained from two years of online measurements in Hong Kong. *Atmospheric Environment, 122*, 864–875.
Guo, J., Liu, H., Wu, X. H., & Wang, Y. Y. (2015a, 2015b, 2015c). Allocation of air pollutants emission rights based on zero-sum gains data envelopment analysis. *China Soft Science*, (11), 176–185.
Han, Y., Long, C., Geng, Z., & Zhang, K. (2018). Carbon emission analysis and evaluation of industrial departments in China: An improved environmental DEA cross model based on information entropy. *Journal of Environmental Management, 205*, 298–307.
He, Q., Han, J., Guan, D. B., Mi, Z. F., Zhao, H. Y., & Zhang, Q. (2018a). The comprehensive environmental efficiency of socioeconomic sectors in China: An analysis based on a non-separable bad output SBM. *Journal of Cleaner Production, 176*(3), 1091–1110.
He, W., Yang, Y., Wang, Z., & Zhu, J. (2018b). Estimation and allocation of cost savings from collaborative $CO_2$ abatement in china. *Energy Economics, 72*, 62–74.
Hosseini, H. M., & Kaneko, S. (2013). Can environmental quality spread through institutions? *Energy Policy, 56*, 312–321.
Hu, J. L., & Kao, C. H. (2007). Efficient energy-saving targets for APEC economies. *Energy Policy, 35*(1), 373–382.
Hu, J. L., & Wang, S. C. (2006). Total-factor energy efficiency of regions in China. *Energy Policy, 34*(17), 3206–3217.
Huang, H. J., Liu, H. N., Jiang, W. M., Huang, S. H., & Zhang, Y. Y. (2006). Physical and chemical characteristics and source apportionment of $PM_{2.5}$ in Nanjing. *Climatic and Environmental Research, 11*(6), 713–722.
Huang, Z. S., Xiu, G. L., Zhu, M. Y., Tao, J., & Yu, J. Z. (2014). Characteristics and sources of carbonaceous species in $PM_{2.5}$ in summer and winter in Shanghai. *Environmental Science & Technology, 37*(4), 124–129.
Huo, J. J. (2009). A brief analysis to control automobile exhaust pollution. *China Science and Technology Information*, (3), 23–27.
Jiang, N., Yin, S., Guo, Y., Li, J., Kang, P., Zhang, R., et al. (2018). Characteristics of mass concentration, chemical composition, source apportionment of $PM_{2.5}$ and $PM_{10}$ and health risk assessment in the emerging megacity in china. *Atmospheric Pollution Research, 9*(2), 309–321.
Korhonen, P. J., & Luptacik, M. (2004). Eco-efficiency analysis of power plants: An extension of data envelopment analysis. *European Journal of Operational Research, 154*(2), 437–446.

Kumar, S. (2006). Environmentally sensitive productivity growth: A global analysis using Malmquist-Luenberger index. *Ecological Economics, 56*(2), 280–293.

Kumar, P., Pirjola, L., Ketzel, M., & Harrison, R. M. (2013). Nanoparticle emissions from 11 non-vehicle exhaustsources—A review. *Atmospheric Environment, 67*(2), 252–277.

Lei, D., Chen, Z. H., & Deng, J. Q. (2014). Simplification of quasi-Cobb-Douglas production function and the optimization of resources distribution for circular economy. *System Engineering Theory and Practice, 34*(3), 683–690.

Li, Y. S. (2005). *Controlling technical guidelines for environmental capacity in cities*. Beijing: China Environmental Science.

Li, Y., Chiu, Y. H., Lu, L. C., & Chiu, C. R. (2018). Evaluation of energy efficiency and air pollutant emissions in Chinese provinces. *Energy Efficiency, 12*(4), 963–977.

Li, F., Emrouznejad, A., Yang, G. L., & Li, Y. J. (2020). Carbon emission abatement quota allocation in Chinese manufacturing industries: An integrated cooperative game data envelopment analysis approach. *Journal of the Operational Research Society, 71*(8), 1259-1288.

Liang, L., Wu, D., & Hua, Z. (2004). MES-DEA modelling for analyzing anti-industrial pollution efficiency and its application in Anhui Province of China. *International Journal of Global Energy Issues, 22*(2–4), 88–98.

Long, X. L., Wu, C., Zhang, J. J., & Zhang, J. (2018). Environmental efficiency for 192 thermal power plants in the Yangtze River Delta considering heterogeneity: A meta-frontier directional slacks-based measure approach. *Renewable and Sustainable Energy Reviews, 82,* 3962–3971.

Luo, Y. (2012). *DEA-based research on indicator selection and environmental performance measurement*. University of Science and Technology of China.

Ma, D., He, F., Li, G., & Chen, L. (2018). Estimation and comparative analysis of environmental efficiency in china, with and without consideration of haze. *Polish Journal of Environmental Studies, 27*(1), 201–211.

Miao, Z., Zhou, P., Wang, Y., & Sun, Z. R. (2013). Energy-saving, "Minus Haze" and assignment of atmospheric pollutant emissions. *China Industrial Economy,* (6), 31–43.

Ni, Y. (2013). *The $PM_{2.5}$ pollution prevention countermeasures study in Harbin*. Northeast Forestry University.

Olatubi, W. O., & Dismukes, D. E. (2000). A data envelopment analysis of the levels and determinants of coal-fired electric power generation performance. *Utilities Policy, 9*(2), 47–59.

Oude Lansink, A., & Silva, E. (2003). $CO_2$ and energy efficiency of different heating technologies in the Dutch glasshouse industry. *Environmental and Resource Economics, 24*(4), 395–407.

Pasurka, C. A., Jr. (2006). Decomposing electric power plant emissions within a joint production framework. *Energy Economics, 28*(1), 26–43.

People's Republic of China State Council. (2013). Air pollution prevention action plan (10).

Picazo-Tadeo, A. J., Reig-Martínez, E., & Hernández-Sancho, F. (2006). Directional distance functions and environmental regulation. *Resource and Energy Economics, 27*(2), 131–142.

Qiao, T., Xiu, G., Zheng, Y., Yang, J., Wang, L., Yang, J., et al. (2015). Preliminary investigation of $PM_1$, $PM_{2.5}$, $PM_{10}$, and its metal elemental composition in tunnels at a subway station in Shanghai, China. *Transportation Research Part D,* (41), 136–146.

Qiu, X. H., Duan, L., Gao, J., Wang, S. L., Chai, F. H., Hu, J., et al. (2016). Chemical composition and source apportionment of $PM_{10}$ and $PM_{2.5}$ in different functional areas of Lanzhou, China. *Journal of Environmental Science,* (40), 75–83.

Ramanathan, R. (2002). Combining indicators of energy consumption and $CO_2$ emissions: A cross-country comparison. *International Journal of Global Energy Issues, 17*(3), 214–227.

Ryou, H. G., Heo, J., & Kim, S. Y. (2018). Source apportionment of $PM_{10}$ and $PM_{2.5}$ air pollution, and possible impacts of study characteristics in South Korea. *Environmental Pollution, 240,* 963–972.

Sheng, T. (2014). *Research on characteristics of ratio and source of $PM_{2.5}$ and $PM_{10}$ in Kun Ming*. Kunming University of Science and Technology.

Shi, F. G. (2012). Research on technical efficiency in China based on non-radial and super-efficiency DEA model. *Statistics and Decision,* (14), 90–93.

Soloveitchik, D., Ben-Aderet, N., Grinman, M., & Lotov, A. (2002). Multiobjective optimization and marginal pollution abatement cost in the electricity sector—An Israeli case study. *European Journal of Operational Research, 140*(3), 571–583.

Sueyoshi, T., & Goto, M. (2001). Slack-adjusted DEA for time series analysis: Performance measurement of Japanese electric power generation industry in 1984–1993. *European Journal of Operational Research, 133*(2), 232–259.

Sueyoshi, T., & Goto, M. (2012) Returns to scale and damages to scale on U.S. Fossil fuel power plants: Radial and non-radial approaches for DEA environmental assessment. *Energy Economics, 34*(6), 2240–2259.

Sun, G. Q., Yang, H. N., Liu, X. C., Tao, Y., & Cheng, J. H. (2015). Distribution characteristics and sources analysis of water-soluble inorganic ions in $PM_{10}$ in Duyun City. *The Administration and Technique of Environmental Monitoring, 27*(6).

Sun, J., Shen, Z., Zhang, L., Lei, Y., Gong, X., Zhang, Q., et al. (2019). Chemical source profiles of urban fugitive dust $PM_{2.5}$ samples from 21 cities across china. *The Science of the Total Environment, 649,* 1045–1053.

Tone, K. (2001). A slacks-based measure of efficiency in data envelopment analysis. *European Journal of Operational Research, 130*(3), 498–509.

Tyteca, D. (1997). Linear programming models for the measurement of environmental performance of firms—Concepts and empirical results. *Journal of Productivity Analysis, 8*(2), 183–197.

Vehicle Emission Control Center of MEP. (2014). "China vehicle emission control annual report in 2013" has been issued by MEP. *Environment and Sustainable Development, 39*(1), 9–10.

Wu, X.H., Chen, Y.F., Guo, J. et al. (2017a) Spatial Concentration, Impact Factors and Prevention Control Measures of $PM_{2.5}$ Pollution in China. *Natural Hazards, 86*(1), 393–410.

Wu, X. H., Xue, P. P., Guo, J., et al. (2017b). On the amount of counterpart assistance to be provided after natural disasters: From the perspective of indirect economic loss assessment. *Environmental Hazards, 16*(1), 1–21.

Wu, T. H., Chen, Y. S., Shang, W., & Wu, J. T. (2018). Measuring energy use and $CO_2$ emission performances for APEC economies. *Journal of Cleaner Production, 183,* 590–601.

Wu, J., Li, M. J., Zhu, Q. Y., Zhou, Z. X., & Liang, L. (2019). Energy and environmental efficiency measurement of China's industrial sectors: A DEA model with non-homogeneous inputs and outputs. *Energy Economics, 78,* 468–480.

Wang, S., & Ma, Y. (2018). Influencing factors and regional discrepancies of the efficiency of carbon dioxide emissions in Jiangsu, China. *Ecological Indicators, 90,* 460–468.

Wang, H., Tian, M., Chen, Y., Shi, G., Liu, Y., Yang, F., et al. (2018a). Seasonal characteristics, formation mechanisms and source origins of $PM_{2.5}$ in two megacities in Sichuan basin, China. *Atmospheric Chemistry and Physics, 18*(2), 865–881.

Wang, K., Wei, Y. M., & Huang, Z. M. (2018b). Environmental efficiency and abatement efficiency measurements of China's thermal power industry: A data envelopment analysis based materials balance approach. *European Journal of Operational Research, 269*(1), 35–50.

Wang, W., Yu, J., Cui, Y., He, J., Xue, P., Cao, W., et al. (2018c). Characteristics of fine particulate matter and its sources in an industrialized coastal city, Ningbo, Yangtze River Delta, China. *Atmospheric Research, 203,* 105–117.

Wang, K., Wu, M., Sun, Y., Shi, X., Sun, A., & Zhang, P. (2019a). Resource abundance, industrial structure, and regional carbon emissions efficiency in China. *Resources Policy, 60,* 203–214.

Wang, M. M., Zheng, Y. J., Jing, T., Tian, J. Z., Chen, P. S., Dong, M. Y., et al. (2019b). Component determination and their formation of $PM_{2.5}$. *Science of Advanced Materials, 11*(5), 756–763.

Wei, Z., Wang, L.-T., Chen, M.-Z., Zheng, Y., et al. (2014). The 2013 Severe Haze over the Southern Hebei, China: $PM_{2.5}$ composition and source apportionment. *Atmospheric Pollution Research,* (5), 759–769.

Xu, P., & Sun, Y. H. (2014). Efficiency measure of undesirable outputs in DEA. *Journal of Quantitative Economics, 31*(1), 90–93.

Xie, Q. W., Hu, P., Jiang, A., Li, Y. J. (2019). Carbon emissions allocation based on satisfaction perspective and data envelopment analysis. *Energy Policy, 132,* 254–264.

Xing, Z. C., Wang, J. G., & Zhang, J. (2018). Expansion of environmental impact assessment for eco-efficiency evaluation of China's economic sectors: An economic input-output based frontier approach. *Science of the Total Environment, 635,* 284–293.

Xue, W. B., Wang, J. N., Yang, J. T., Lei, Y., Wang, Y. M., & Chen, X. (2013). Domestic and foreign research progress of air quality model. *Environment and Sustainable Development, 38*(3), 14–20.

Xue, W. B., Fu, F., Wang, J. N., He, K. B., & Hang, B. P. (2014a). Modeling study on atmospheric environmental capacity of major pollutants constrained by $PM_{2.5}$ compliance of chinese cities. *China Environmental Science, 34*(10), 2490–2496.

Xue, W. B., Fu, F., Wang, J. N., Tang, G. Q., Lei, Yu., Yang, J., et al. (2014b). Numerical study on the characteristics of regional transport of $PM_{2.5}$ in China. *China Environmental Science, 06,* 1361–1368.

Yang, H. N., Chen, J., Wen, J. J., Tian, H. Z., & Liu, X. G. (2015). Composition and sources of $PM_{2.5}$ around the heating periods of 2013 and 2014 in Beijing: Implications for efficient mitigation measures. *Atmospheric Environment,* (124), 378–386.

Yang, M., An, Q., Ding, T., Yin, P., & Liang, L. (2019a). Carbon emission allocation in China based on gradually efficiency improvement and emission reduction planning principle. *Annals of Operations Research, 278*(1–2), 123–139.

Yang, J., Tang, L., Mi, Z., Liu, S., Li, L., & Zheng, J. (2019b). Carbon emissions performance in logistics at the city level. *Journal of Cleaner Production, 231,* 1258–1266.

Yang, J., Cheng, J. X., & Huang, S. J. (2020). $CO_2$ emissions performance and reduction potential in China's manufacturing industry: A multi-hierarchy meta-frontier approach. *Journal of Cleaner Production, 255.*

Zhang, Y., & Bartels, B. (1998). The effect of sample size on the mean efficiency in DEA with an application to electricity distribution in Australia, Sweden and New Zealand. *Journal of Productivity Analysis, 9*(3), 187–204.

Zhang, C., Liu, H., Bressers, H. T. A., & Buchanan, K. S. (2011). Productivity growth and environmental regulations—Accounting for undesirable outputs: Analysis of China's thirty provincial regions using the Malmquist-Luenberger index. *Ecological Economics,* (70), 2369–2379.

Zhang, C. M., Lu, S. C., Song, Z. F., & Wang, Q. (2014). Research on motor vehicle ownership under the control of $PM_{2.5}$. *Highways & Automotive Applications,* (5), 30–32.

Zhang, Y., Huang, W., Cai, T., Fang, D., Wang, Y., & Song, J. (2016). Concentrations and chemical compositions of fine particles ($PM_{2.5}$) during haze and non-haze days in Beijing. *Atmospheric Research,* (174), 174–175, 62–69.

Zhang, Y., Lang, J., Cheng, S., Li, S., Zhou, Y., Chen, D., et al. (2018a). Chemical composition and sources of $PM_1$ and $PM_{2.5}$ in Beijing in autumn. *Science of the Total Environment, 630,* 72–82.

Zhang, Y. J., Sun, Y. F., & Huang, J. (2018b). Energy efficiency, carbon emission performance, and technology gaps: Evidence from CDM project investment. *Energy Policy, 115,* 119–130.

Zhao, M., Qiao, T., Huang, Z., Zhu, M., Wei, X., Xiu, G., et al. (2015). Comparison of ionic and carbonaceous compositions of $PM_{2.5}$ in 2009 and 2012 in Shanghai, China. *Science of the Total Environment,* (536), 695–703.

Zhao, X., Wang, X., Ding, X., He, Q., Zhang, Z., Liu, T., et al. (2014). Compositions and sources of organic acids in fine particles ($PM_{2.5}$) over the Pearl river delta region, South China. *Journal of Environmental Sciences, 26,* 110–121.

Zheng, P. N., Chen, H. B., Chen, X. G., Zhou, D. B., & Zhang, B. Y. (2007). Study on distribution of reduction targets based on DEA model. *Chinese Journal of Environmental Engineering, 11*(1), 133–139.

Zhou, Z., Liu, C., Zeng, X., Jiang, Y., & Liu, W. (2018). Carbon emission performance evaluation and allocation in Chinese cities. *Journal of Cleaner Production, 172,* 1254–1272.

Zhou, P., Ang, B. W., & Poh, K. L. (2006a). Decision analysis in energy and environmental modeling: An update. *Energy, 31*(14), 2604–2622.

Zhou, P., Ang, B. W., & Poh, K. L. (2006b). Slacks-based efficiency measures for modeling environmental performance. *Ecological Economics, 60*(1), 111–118.

Zhou, P., Ang, B. W., & Poh, K. L. (2008). Measuring environmental performance under different environmental DEA technologies. *Energy Economics, 30*(1), 1–14.

Zhu, Y., Huang, L., Li, J., Ying, Q., Zhang, H., Liu, X., et al. (2018). Sources of particulate matter in china: Insights from source apportionment studies published in 1987–2017. *Environment International, 115*, 343–357.

# Chapter 20
# A Study of Allocative Efficiency of $PM_{2.5}$ Emission Rights Based on a Zero Sum Gains Data Envelopment Model

**Abstract** It is an urgent task for China to control haze emission in environmental treatment. Emission right trading is a feasible way to achieve the reduction of pollutant emission on the premise that the total pollutant emission amount is under control, and the allocation of initial emission rights based on the target total amount is the key to emission right trading. In this paper, via the input-oriented ZSG-DEA model, the interprovincial allocative efficiency of $PM_{2.5}$ emission rights is investigated under the condition that the target total amount is fixed. The results showed that (1) after initial emission rights were allocated in accordance with the ZSG-DEA model, $PM_{2.5}$ emission amounts of all provinces would be in a new common DEA frontier so as to realize the overall Pareto optimality with a set total amount; (2) two factors, namely and areas and atmospheric environmental capacities of all provinces, were considered in the actual allocation to avoid the homogenization of all evaluated units found in the previous evaluation literature on allocative efficiency, thereby making the evaluation results more in line with the actual situations in all provinces. Such an investigation approach can provide guidance on the allocation of initial emission rights in emission right trading; and the research results can offer empirical support for haze-reducing work load conducted by central and local governments of China.

**Keywords** Air pollutant emission right · ZSG-DEA model · Emission right trading · Allocative efficiency · $PM_{2.5}$

## 20.1 Introduction

In recent years, foggy and hazy day shave greatly increased in China, arousing widespread concern at home and abroad (Yu et al. 2011). In January 2013, 30 provinces (autonomous regions and municipalities) in China were four times haze-shrouded, and Beijing only had five haze-free days. On January 14, 2014, the research report entitled "Towards an Environmentally Sustainable Future: A National Environmental Analysis of People's Republic of China" pointed out that only less than 1% of the 500 largest cities in China had achieved the air quality standards recommended by the World Health Organization; and seven out of the ten cities most polluted in the world belonged to China (Zhang and Crooks 2012). Lelieveld et al. (2015) and

 
X. Wu and J. Guo, *Economic Impacts and Emergency Management of Disasters in China*,
https://doi.org/10.1007/978-981-16-1319-7_20

Yang et al. (2013) estimated the premature deaths etc. that were caused by outdoor air pollution, mostly by $PM_{2.5}$. The outdoor pollution contributes to 3.3 (95% CI, 1.61–4.81) million premature deaths per year worldwide, predominantly in Asia. In China, the premature deaths hit 1.36 million, accounting for 41.2% of the world total.

Attaching great importance to the prevention and control of haze, our government has successively introduced a series of important policy-type documents, such as "A Comprehensive Working Scheme of Saving Energy and Reducing Emission in the Period of 'Twelfth Five'" (2011), "Planning of Prevention and Control of Atmospheric Pollution in the Key Areas in the Period of 'Twelfth Five'" (2012), "An Action Plan of Prevention and Control of Atmospheric Pollution" (2013) and the newly revised "Environmental Protection Law" (2015) and so on, in all of which the establishment of a regional coordination mechanism to coordinate regional environmental treatment has been proposed. In addition, the State Council has also signed target responsibility contracts with all provincial governments so as to conduct annual assessment and investigate accountability strictly. But from the perspective of treatment practice, haze treatment forcefully promoted through the use of administrative power can exert some effect only in the short run. Shutting down factories temporarily can only bring about transient haze reduction. Once the reins are loosened, hazy days will increase rapidly. "APEC Blue" in Beijing, 2014 and "Youth Olympic Blue" in Nanjing, 2014 are just two such cases (there are great differences of Chinese air quality before and after "APEC Blue", see Huang et al. 2015). In the long run, giving full play to market mechanism may be another way of effective haze treatment.

Recently, the emission right of air pollutants such as carbon and sulfur dioxide has opened up trade, both at home and in abroad. Naturally, as haze is an air pollutant just like carbon and sulfur dioxide, the emission right trading on haze is expected to be opened up as well. For instance, by analogy with the international mature experience and practice on carbon emission right trading we can control the total emission amount of haze typical components, allocate the initial emission rights at the local level, and trade surplus emission rights on the market. Such an approach takes into account both the overall target and the actual situations of all provinces, thus putting into play the autonomy of provinces. In contrast with the simple shutting down of pollution-eliciting enterprises, this approach is more feasible in haze control in the long run.

However, what amount will the initial haze emission right be for each province respectively? This is a gap in the current literature and practice. Different from carbon emission, the total amount of haze emission is difficult to calculate, and consequently, the development of certain indices utilized to calculate haze emission rights becomes one priority. Moreover, methods used to evaluate the haze emission efficiency of each province are desired.

Fortunately, $PM_{2.5}$ can serve as a representative variable of haze for all provinces (autonomous regions and municipalities) in China, and hence as an evaluation unit.

Under the condition that the nationwide total emission amount of $PM_{2.5}$ is fixed, indices such as the land area and the atmospheric environmental capacity are also considered to reallocate $PM_{2.5}$ emission rights of all provinces, thereby offering empirical support for $PM_{2.5}$ emission right trading and new ideas for our government's haze treatment.

## 20.2 Literature Review

### *20.2.1 Emission Right Trading Research*

Generally speaking, there are two types of regulation on such public goods as air pollutants: one is tax regulation (Baumol and Oates 1988), and the other is emission right trading (Nordhaus 2005).

Tax regulation, an essential tool used by the government, also plays a vital role in controlling air pollutant emissions. Many scholars have studied the effect of tax regulation on pollutant emission. For example, Ruth and Amato (2002) investigated the impact of carbon cost changes on output, energy consumption and carbon emissions, and compared the results of various climate change and technology policies. Malcolm and Zhang (2006) adopted realistic chemical engineering models and mathematical optimization techniques to evaluate different regulations, and the method could assess the impact of future regulatory scenarios for managers. Fischer and Newell (2008) evaluated various policies for reducing $CO_2$ emissions and promoting renewable energy innovation. And they used incentives to evaluate the relative performance of procedures. Rive (2010) proposed an improved CGE model to assess the costs and the co-benefits of implementing air quality and climate policies simultaneously. The results revealed that synergistic benefits were highly dependent on policy choices, and as greenhouse targets became more ambitious, their importance relative to total costs could decrease. Pelin and Kesidou (2011) used a recent OECD framework to examine the role of external policy tools and firm-specific internal factors in stimulating eco-innovation. Although tax regulation is simple and practicable and causes area relatively small loss of GDP, in view of its poor and uncertain effect on emission reduction, it is difficult to ensure the realization of emission reduction targets by relying singly on carbon tax policy (Shi et al. 2013).

For the emission right trading its theoretical basis includes "Property Rights Theory" and "Coase Theorem" put forward by Coase (1960). Afterwards, Dales (1968) for the first time formulated the concept of emission right trading. He suggested that emission rights of economic entities can be stipulated in the form of emission permits, and surplus emission rights can also be traded. For that matter, the method of stipulating emission rights in the form of permits is known as the initial allocation of emission rights (Burton and Sanjour 1969, 1970). Montgomery (1972) adopted mathematical economics theory to demonstrate the cost-efficiency and effectiveness of emissions trading in combating pollution. This research showed that the emission trading market could measure the standard of environmental quality. Tietenberg et al. (1992) systematically demonstrated the advantages of emissions trading over previous administrative directives in his work "Emissions Trading—Reform of Pollution Control Policy". Environmental Protection Agency (EPA) first applied emission right trading for the treatment of air and river pollution; subsequently, Germany, Australia, the United Kingdom and other countries carried out the practice of emissions trading in succession. Based on the Dales' theory of emission right trading, the National Environmental Protection Agency of the United States formulated and promulgated the "Control of Total Amount and Trade" rule in the late 70s, and implemented the "Acid Rain Program" in early 1995.

After entering into the twenty-first century, a growing number of scholars have paid attention to the allocation and trading of air pollutant emission rights. For example, Mackenzie et al. (2008) extended Böhringer and Lange's (2005) analysis of the initial allocation mechanism, based on relative performance comparisons between firms. The results showed that assigning permits depending on external factors (independent of output and emissions) could potentially achieve social optimality. Later, Mackenzie et al. (2009) outlined a license allocation contest (PAC), which assigned suitable licenses to companies based on their ranking relative. Under two scenarios of complete and incomplete information, Chavez et al. (2009) analyzed the implementation costs between the firm-specific emission standard system and the transferable emission permit system. The results showed that, in the presence of incomplete information, the cost of regulation based on specific emission standards for each firm was no less than that of a transferable emission permit system. Pickl et al. (2010) described one uncertain market's international procedure, which helped to establish optimal energy management and interactive resource planning processes under uncertain emission trading markets. Many scholars have also suggested that the Chinese government control air pollution by issuing emission permits. For example, Wu and Wang (2010) employed the economic approach to demonstrate the social benefits and social welfare brought by emissions trading. The results expressed that the implementation of emission right trading was an inevitable trend of market economy development. Zhang and Peng (2011) comprehensively analyzed the latest research progress of foreign emissions trading mechanism, and the research had an important guiding role for the domestic emissions trading mechanism. Jin et al. (2011) investigated the optimal regulatory strategy for achieving the fixed total emissions target in the emissions trading system. The results indicated that inducing complete compliance is the optimal strategy to realize the objective. Wei et al. (2011) carried out a statistical and analysis of atmospheric quality data in Urumqi. The results showed that: air pollution in Urumqi was still rather severe, and total control of urban air pollutants would be the primary means to control the city's air quality. To prevent acid rain, China first introduced the emissions right trading system in the 1990s. In April 2001, the National Environmental Protection Agency (NEPA) and the American Environmental Protection Association (AEPA) signed a collaborative project, entitled "Study on Promoting the Implementation of Total Sulfur Dioxide Emission Control and Emissions Right Trading Policies in China," and then carried out the "4 + 3 + 1" project. In September of that year, the first emissions trading case in China was implemented smoothly in Nantong City, Jiangsu Province, under the efforts of many parties. The trading parties were Nantong Tianshenggang Power Generation Co., Ltd. and Nantong Cellulose Fibers Co., Ltd. During 2001–2007, the total amount of $SO_2$ emission rights traded between the two parties reached 1800 tons. In 2003, Jiangsu Taigang Harbor Environmental Protection Power Generation Co., Ltd. achieved cross-site trading of $SO_2$ emission rights with Nanjing Shimonoseki Power Plant Co., Ltd., and this set a precedent for cross-regional trading in China. On November 10, 2007, the first emission right trading center was established and went public in Jiaxing, Zhejiang, China. In May 2008, Tianjin Climate Exchange was jointly set up by Tianjin Property Rights Exchange, CNPC Assets Management Co., Ltd. and Chicago Climate Exchange. These activities have played a certain role in promoting market trading of air pollutant emission rights.

$SO_2$ is the symbol of pollutant emission rights trading in haze management (Peng et al. 2014). $SO_2$ is one of the primary polluting energy sources in the emission rights trading now, so emission rights trading is suitable for haze management in China. And haze emission right is a typical public resource; consider emission right trading as an economic tool for haze control and environmental protection is necessary. However, the actual trading activities of haze emission rights have not come into existence in China so far. One of the main reasons is the lack of quantitative assessment aiming at the allocation of haze initial emission rights in China, which comprises the precise purpose of this study.

### *20.2.2 Research on the Allocation of Emission Rights of Air Pollutants*

As the implementation and expansion of emission right trading, the issue of the initial allocation of emission rights has gradually entered people's vision. In 1984, Hahn pointed out that in imperfectly competitive markets, the model chosen of emission rights initial allocation could make a decisive impact on the resource allocation efficiency. In 1990, the CAAA (Clean Air Act Amendment) of the United States first proposed three initial emission rights allocation models: free allocation, government pricing, and public auction. Among them, free allocation is a standard scheme adopted in the current emissions trading. The initial distribution of emission rights is directly related to the emission units' economic interests and affects the environmental capacity resource allocation efficiency. Thus, a large number of research results have emerged in the initial allocation of emission rights. For example, Zhou et al. (2013) constructed a nonlinear programming model to evaluate the economic performance of inter-provincial abatement allowance trading and allocated the initial emission rights of different provinces based on five equity criteria. The results showed that the inter-provincial emission reduction trading mechanism could reduce the Chinese total abatement cost over 40%. Park et al. (2011) used the Boltzmann distribution to allocate permits in emissions trading. The method described the most probable, natural, and fair distribution of emissions permits among multiple countries. To realize a globally equitable carbon emission space, Pan et al. (2014) proposed an allocation scheme based on cumulative emission per capita, and this allocation scheme simultaneously considered the historical emissions and future demand in both developed and developing countries. The research on the initial allocation of emission rights in China started late. For example, Feng and Wang (2014) introduced options into the initial allocation of carbon emission rights, and they studied the pricing issue of emission rights initial allocation using the Black–Scholes option pricing model. Wang et al. (2014) compared the domestic and international approaches on initial emission rights allocation and modified the Black–Scholes pricing model. Liao et al. (2015) simulated a specific case using baseline, grandfathering and Shapley values, and the case consists of the initial allocation of carbon emission allowances of three power plants in Shanghai, China.

Based on the importance of the initial allocation of emission rights, some scholars began to focus on the efficiency of the initial allocation of emission rights. The allocative efficiency of emission rights is an important factor in measuring the fairness and reasonability of emission right allocation. Domestic scholars Chen et al. (1998) and Ma et al. (1999, 2006) applied the linear programming method to the study of air pollutant allocation, but the interprovincial allocative efficiency of pollutant emission rights was not evaluated. Recently, DEA was increasingly used to evaluate the efficiency of air pollutant emissions. For example, Beltrán-Esteve and Picazo-Tadeo (2015) used the DEA model to analyze the environmental performance of the transport sector in 38 countries, during 1995–2009. The results indicated that environmental performance had improved significantly since the 1990s. Lee et al. (2014) used a slacks-based data envelopment analysis (SBM-DEA) model to assess the environmental efficiency of port cities and calculated the social and opportunity costs of air pollutant emissions in low-efficiency port cities. Picazo-Tadeo et al. (2014) proposed a DEA-based method to assess cross-period environmental performance on a specific pollutant management level. This method was used to determine the environmental performance of the EU-28 in terms of greenhouse gas emissions during 1990–2011.

Since air pollutant emission belongs to undesirable output, the more such output means the lower allocative efficiency and the less such output means the higher allocative efficiency. In contrast, the traditional DEA model presupposes output as desirable, so the more output means the higher allocative efficiency and the less output means the lower allocative efficiency. In order to make it possible for the DEA model to measure the environmental efficiency that even covers undesirable output, some scholars made favorable improvements on the traditional DEA model. For example, Färe et al. (1989) developed a performance measurement method suitable for general multiple output settings, and this method could distinguish the desirable outputs and non-desirable outputs. Hailu and Veeman (2001) extended the Chavas-Cox method to non-parametric analysis and provided a complete representation of the production technology by incorporating undesired outputs. The results showed the limitations of the traditional DEA method. Using the classification invariance property, Seiford and Zhu (2002) demonstrated that the standard DEA model could improve performance by increasing the desired output and decreasing the undesired output. This method maintained the linearity and convexity of DEA model. Tone (2001) proposed a slacks-based measure (SBM) of efficiency in DEA. This method could directly deal with the input excesses and the output shortfalls of the relevant decision-making units. Later, Tone (2004) modified the SBM proposed in Tone (2001) by considering the undesirable outputs. However, these improved DEA models treat the DMUs as independent decision-making units, which have limitations in the allocation of emission-reducing responsibility based on the target total amount. They fail to take into consideration the cooperation or competition among DMUs. Nevertheless, the allocation of emission-reducing responsibility based on the target total amount requires interdependent allocation of undesirable output among DMUs. Therefore, if some inefficient DMU wants to improve efficiency and reduce undesirable output, other DMUs are inevitably required to increase their undesirable output. At this moment, the original DEA model is inappropriate.

### 20.2.3 The ZSG-DEA Model

In view of this situation, Lins et al. (2003) proposed the ZSG-DEA model (Zero-sum Gains Data Envelopment Analysis, or ZSG-DEA for short) by considering the competition, cooperation and allocation of undesirable output among DMUs. This model can revise the allocation scheme of undesirable output in line with the DEA efficiency of each DMU, thereby further improving its DEA efficiency. Based on the framework of Kyoto Protocol, Gomes and Lins (2008) applied this model to reallocate the $CO_2$ emission right of each country. This method has been widely used in the evaluation of allocative efficiency among multiple decision-making units when the total emission amount is set. For example, Singh et al. (2014) extended the DEA model and reallocated the excess inputs without reducing the efficiency of other decision-making units. This method would help decision-makers to allocate the extra inputs rationally. Chiu et al. (2013) adopted a Super SBM-ZSG-DEA (Slacks-Based Measure Zero Sum Gains Data Envelopment Analysis) model to examine allocation equality. Lin and Ning (2011) utilized the ZSG-DEA model to evaluate the efficiency of carbon emission allocation in EU countries, and the results showed that the EU countries had low efficiency in carbon emission allocation. Zheng (2012) utilized the ZSG-DEA model to analyze the inter-provincial carbon emission reduction responsibilities in China. The results showed that some western provinces, such as Ningxia and Gansu, must reduce a large number of carbon emissions. To handle the issue of the constant total amount of resource allocation, Wang et al. (2013) proposed an improved zero-sum gains DEA model, and the model was used to allocate inter-provincial emission shares of China in 2020. The results showed that different provinces afforded different emission reduction burdens in terms of emission reduction intensity, energy intensity and non-fossil fuel increase quota. According to the " zero-sum benefit" idea, Miao et al. (2013) constructed an air pollutant emission rights allocation mechanism aimed at energy saving and emission reduction, and the model was used to allocate regional air pollutant rights. Hu and Fang (2010) employed the zero-sum gains DEA to measure the efficiency scores of securities firms, and the results indicated that the traditional DEA model underestimates the efficiency of securities firms. Sun et al.

(2012) provided a new approach to solving the problem of energy consumption quota allocation, based on the environmental DEA technology and ZSG-DEA. The results showed that the environmental regulation cost was significant reduced after allocation by ZSG-DEA. Given that the distribution of each province's $PM_{2.5}$ emission rights are based on the decrease of total emissions, such a method will be adopted in this paper as well.

It is worth noting that as far as the previous studies are concerned, the actual situation of each allocation unit was not taken into account in the related research literature on the allocation of pollutant emission rights base on the ZSG-DEA model; instead, all allocation units were homogenized, leaving the land area and the atmospheric environmental capacity of each allocation unit (here refers to the province, autonomous region or municipality) untouched upon. Therefore, from the perspective of allocative efficiency and considering each province's land area and atmospheric environmental capacity of one $PM_{2.5}$ emission that meets the national constraint of $PM_{2.5}$ emission amount, the ZSG-DEA model will be adopted in this paper so as to analyze the allocative efficiency of each province, autonomous region or municipality's $PM_{2.5}$ emission-reducing responsibility, and an efficient DEA allocative scheme will be attempted via iterative calculation in accordance with the ZSG-DEA model.

## 20.3 Model Setting, Data Source and Index Selection

### *20.3.1 Model Setting*

#### 20.3.1.1 Basic DEA Model

DEA (Data Envelopment Analysis) is a widely used method for efficiency evaluation of multiple input/output decision making units, and its core idea is to calculate the boundary of the maximum output or that of the minimum inputusing input and output data. In the beginning, Charnes et al. (1978) put forward the CCR (Charnes & Cooper & Rhodes) model with constant returns to scale. Later on, Banker et al. (1984) replaced the assumption of constant returns to scale in the CCR model by the assumption of variable returns to scale, thus developing the so-called BCC model (Banker & Charnes & Cooper, which can be further divided into two types, that is, the output-oriented type and the input-oriented type). For instance, the input-oriented BCC model used in evaluating the relative efficiency of target decision making unit $DMU_0$ via the basic DEA method can be expressed in the following formula (20.1) (if the convex constraint $\sum_i \lambda_i = 1$ is removed, it reduces to a CCR model).

$$Min\ h_0$$

$$
\begin{aligned}
& st.\ h_0 x_0 \geq \sum_i \lambda_i x_i \\
& \sum_i \lambda_i y_i \geq y_0 \\
& \sum_i \lambda_i = 1 \\
& \lambda_i \geq 0
\end{aligned}
\tag{20.1}
$$

In this formula, $h_0$ is the relative efficiency of $DMU_0$, $\lambda_i$ is the weight coefficient, and $x_i$ and $y_i$ are the input amount and output amount of $DMU_i$ respectively with $i = 0, 1, \cdots, n$.

#### 20.3.1.2 ZSG-DEA Model

In order to solve the regional allocation issue of the total air pollutant emission amount, Lins et al. (2003) and Gomes and Lins (2008) put forward the ZSG-DEA model. They proposed that several iterative calculations of input or output be carried out to make each DMU achieve its valid boundary of efficiency. In the input-oriented model, if $DMU_0$ is an invalid DEA decision making unit, its ZSG-DEA efficiency value is $h_{Z0}$. In order to achieve a valid DEA, $DMU_0$ must reduce the usage of input $x_0$.

According to the proportional increase strategy (Lins et al. 2003), the input-oriented BCC model used in evaluating the relative efficiency of decision-making unit $DMU_0$ via the ZSG-DEA method can be expressed in the following Formula (20.2).

$$
\begin{aligned}
& Min\ h_{Z0} \\
& st.\ h_{Z0} x_0 \geq \sum_i \lambda_i x_i \left( 1 + \frac{x_0 (1 - h_{Z_0})}{\sum_{i \neq 0} x_i} \right) \\
& \sum_i \lambda_i y_i \geq y_0 \\
& \sum_i \lambda_i = 1 \\
& \lambda_i \geq 0
\end{aligned}
\tag{20.2}
$$

where $x_0$ and $y_0$ are the input amount and output amount of $DMU_0$ respectively, $x_i$ and $y_i$ are the input amount and output amount of $DMU_i$ respectively, $h_{Z0}$ is the relative efficiency of $DMU_0$ under the ZSG-DEA method, and $\lambda_j$ is the weight coefficient. According to the $h_{Z0}$ value and relevant parameters in Formula (20.2), the allocation mode of $x_i$ among DMUs can be revised, thereby keeping the total amount of $x_i$ unchanged and improving efficiencies of all DMUs.

#### 20.3.1.3 Cooperation Among Decision Making Units

Generally speaking, the ZSG-DEA model involves a nonlinear programming issue, and some decision-making units with efficiency not equal to one form a cooperative set C. From the perspective of proportional increase strategy, when the decision-making units of the cooperative set achieve the target in the efficiency frontier through the proportional increase strategy, efficiencies of these decision-making units under the ZSG-DEA model are in proportion to their efficiencies under the original DEA model. Linset al. (2003) and Gomes et al. (2003, 2005) have already proved that there is a linear relationship between $h_{Zi}$ and $h_i$ under the condition of ZSG, as is shown in Formula (20.3):

$$h_{Zi} = h_i \left( 1 - \frac{\sum\limits_{j \in C} \left[ x_j \left( q_{ij} h_{Zi} - 1 \right) \right]}{\sum\limits_{j \notin C} x_j} \right), \tag{20.3}$$

where $j = 0, 1, \cdots, n$, C refers to a cooperative set formed by provinces whose undesirable output efficiencies are not equal to one, and $h_i$ and $h_{Zi}$ denote $DMU_i$'s initial efficiency and efficiency after allocation respectively, $q_{ij} = h_i / h_j$ stands for the ratio of traditional efficiency of province *i* to that of province *j*, and $x_j$ is the input amount of $DMU_j$. Through this formula, each province's efficiency that reaches the new ZSG frontier $h_{Zi}$ can be calculated.

### *20.3.2 Data Source and Index Selection*

In this paper, according to Gomes and Lins (2008), GDP, energy consumption amount, labor and capital are regarded as the output variables, and the undesirable output (Chinese province's population-weighted $PM_{2.5}$ concentration × provincial land area/atmospheric environmental capacity of one $PM_{2.5}$ emission that meets the national constraint of $PM_{2.5}$ emission amount) is chosen as the input variable. The significance of such considerations lies in the reasoning that with the same emission right, if decision making units enjoy higher GDP, larger energy consumption amount or more capital and labor, the allocative efficiency is relatively high; or in other words, with the same GDP, energy consumption amount or labor and capital, the allocation is more effective when allocated air pollutant emissions are fewer. With regard to the energy consumption amount, three types of fossil energy, namely coal, oil and natural gas, are employed to represent the resource endowment and energy consumption structure of each province.

#### 20.3.2.1 Input Indices

(1) The evaluation index of haze. Haze mainly consists of $PM_{10}$ and $PM_{2.5}$. Given the fact that the relevant data of $PM_{2.5}$ has not been collected until 2012 in China, it is extremely difficult to obtain a long-term accumulated data. At present, though some domestic and foreign scholars utilize the data obtained via self-observation (such as Abas et al. 2004; Hossein and Kaneko 2013), most of them adopt the global $PM_{2.5}$ annual average during the period of 2001–2010 jointly developed by Battelle Memorial Institute and Center for International Earth Science Information Network. Based on the research ideas of Van Donkelaar et al. (2010), such data get the regional $PM_{2.5}$ annual average under different humidities by inverting and analyzing remotely sensed aerosol optical depth through physical and chemical models. At the same time, their team members have also developed the population-weighted $PM_{2.5}$ value of each province in 2001–2010. The authors downloaded and worked out the $PM_{2.5}$ value of each province in China under the humidity of 35%[1] in 2001–2010. But in comparison with the population-weighted $PM_{2.5}$ value, the latter takes full account of the actual impact of the $PM_{2.5}$ value on populations of different densities, and therefore sounds more persuasive. Therefore, the population-weighted $PM_{2.5}$ value of each province is preferred here.
It is worth noting that in the reallocation of $PM_{2.5}$ emission and evaluation of $PM_{2.5}$ emission efficiency in this research, the following two factors are considered: one is the land area of each province (with data from *China Statistical Yearbooks* (2001–2010)), and the other is each province's atmospheric environmental capacity of one $PM_{2.5}$ emission that meets the national constraint of $PM_{2.5}$ emission amount (Xue et al. 2014).
(2) Atmospheric environmental capacity. Atmospheric environmental capacity refers to the maximum allowable air pollutant emission amount under the constraint of some environmental target (such as air quality standards or critical loads of acid deposition) in a region. It is an important basis for the control of the total air pollutant emission amount and air quality management. Many scholars have carried out calculations and simulations of atmospheric environmental capacity according to different environmental targets (Ren et al. 2000; Duan et al. 2002; Chai et al. 2006; Li 2005; Xue et al. 2014). Among them, Xue, by relying on the third generation of air quality model WRF-CAMx and the national emission inventory of air pollutants, developed an iterative algorithm of atmospheric environment capacity under the constraint of environmental quality, and simulated and calculated the maximum allowable emission amounts of one $PM_{2.5}$ emission of 31 provinces, municipalities and autonomous regions in China with the average $PM_{2.5}$ annual concentration of 333 prefecture-level cities in China reaching the ambient air quality standard (GB3095-2012) as the target. With proper calculation process and authoritative

[1] Humidity of 35% is more in line with the general situation of China. For more details, please see Han et al. (2014).

data sources, the atmospheric environment capacity of 29 provinces, municipalities and autonomous regions obtained through Xue's research can be used as the data source of atmospheric environmental capacity index in this paper.

(3) Input index about $PM_{2.5}$ emission. The total emission amount of $PM_{2.5}$ in one area is related to its $PM_{2.5}$ concentration, land area and $PM_{2.5}$ depth. However, its emission right of $PM_{2.5}$ is related to both the total emission amount of $PM_{2.5}$ and the atmospheric environment capacity. There is a positive correlation between the emission right of $PM_{2.5}$ and $PM_{2.5}$ concentration, land area as with $PM_{2.5}$ depth. While the emission right of $PM_{2.5}$ is negatively related to the atmospheric environment capacity. Given that the $PM_{2.5}$ depth is hard to measure, we can multiply the $PM_{2.5}$ concentration and the land area, and then divide it by the atmospheric environment capacity. Then the calculation results can reflect the $PM_{2.5}$ emission rights of each province to some extent. The calculation steps are shown as follows:

Firstly, each province's population-weighted $PM_{2.5}$ concentration, land area and atmospheric environmental capacity of one $PM_{2.5}$ emission that meets the national constraint of $PM_{2.5}$ emission amount are standardized respectively. Next, each province's standardized population-weighted $PM_{2.5}$ concentration is multiplied by its land area, and then divided by its atmospheric environmental capacity of one $PM_{2.5}$ emission that meets the national constraint of $PM_{2.5}$ emission amount. The final result is the value of undesirable output.

#### 20.3.2.2 Output Indices

Through an analysis of $PM_{2.5}$ source apportionment, Zheng et al. (2014) found that the main causes of $PM_{2.5}$ included combustion and secondary PM transformed in the atmosphere. Given that the combustion is mostly caused by the burning of fossil energy, the expenditure on each fossil energy is regarded as input index.

Energy consumption data are derived from *China Energy Statistical Yearbooks* (2001–2010) and fossil energy consumption amount mainly refers to coal, oil and natural gas consumption amount with data coming from each province's energy balance sheets (2001–2010). Labor remuneration is indicated by employees' average wage and capital input is replaced by fixed-asset investment. Data on employees' average wage, fixed-asset investment, provincial GDP are all derived from *China Statistical Yearbooks* (2001–2010), and the first three types of these data are converted into constant prices with data in 2000 as the benchmark.

Specific descriptions of indices are shown in Table 20.1.

The statistical characteristics of the variables are shown in Table 20.2. As can be seen from Table 20.2, the deviation of each index is large and the skewness and kurtosis are notablenotzero, thus the statistical regression method is not fit for this case. However, as a non-parametric statistics method, DEA is quite suitable for the input–output efficiency evaluation of abnormal distributed data, especially the

**Table 20.1** Specific descriptions of input and output indices

| Types of indices | Names of indices | Accounting content | Units |
|---|---|---|---|
| Output indices | Coal | Coal, coke | Million tons |
| | Oil | Crude oil, gasoline, kerosene, diesel oil, fuel oil | Million tons |
| | Gas | Natural gas consumption amount | Billion cubic meters |
| | Labor | Labor remuneration[a] | Yuan |
| | Capital | Fixed-asset investment | Billion yuan |
| | GDP | GDP | Billion yuan |
| Input index | $PM_{2.5}$ emission | $\frac{\text{Chinese province's population weighted PM2.5 concentration} \times \text{provincial land area}}{\text{Atmospheric environmental capacity of one PM2.5 emission that meets the national constraint of PM2.5 emission amount}}$ | |

[a]The labor remuneration indice is chosen here instead of the laborer number indice used in other studies. In the opinion of the authors, given the huge gap of laborer payment levels in all provincial regions, the labor remuneration indice can reflect the labor input situations in regional economical activity in a more authentic manner.

**Table 20.2** The descriptive statistics of indices

| Variable | Units | Mean | Maximum value | Minimum value | Standard deviation | Skewness | Kurtosis |
|---|---|---|---|---|---|---|---|
| Coal | Million tons | 9936.68 | 27,122.51 | 392.76 | 7345.74 | 1.15 | 0.61 |
| Oil | Million tons | 1844.03 | 6511.73 | 164.64 | 1693.32 | 1.60 | 1.99 |
| Natural gas | Billion $m^3$ | 19.20 | 100.74 | 0.77 | 19.97 | 2.67 | 9.44 |
| Labor remuneration | Yuan | 9336.56 | 18,238.27 | 6899.60 | 2871.74 | 1.79 | 2.89 |
| Fixed-asset investment | Billion yuan | 3305.28 | 8869.25 | 378.98 | 2232.98 | 1.02 | 0.58 |
| GDP | Billion yuan | 3892.30 | 12,213.16 | 330.94 | 2968.74 | 1.31 | 1.45 |
| Province's standardized population-weighted $PM_{2.5}$ concentration | $\mu g/m^3$ | 27.22 | 46.14 | 2.57 | 11.42 | −0.10 | −0.68 |
| Land area | Ten thousand $km^2$ | 28.62 | 166.00 | 0.63 | 35.81 | 2.75 | 8.16 |
| Atmospheric environmental capacity of one $PM_{2.5}$ emission that meets the national constraint of $PM_{2.5}$ emission amount are standardized respectively | Ten thousand tons | 20.77 | 42.67 | 2.79 | 11.16 | 0.12 | −0.51 |

efficiency evaluation of multi–input–multi–output system. These advantages show the rationality of DEA method the other way round.

Due to great dimensional differences of these indices, they need to be standardized. Accordingly, the Min–max standardization method is adopted, and the calculation formula is as follows:

$$b_i = \frac{p_i - \min(p_i)}{\max(p_i) - \min(p_i)}, \tag{20.4}$$

where $p_i$ represents the input/output index, and $i = 1, 2, 3 \ldots 29$, representing one of these 29 provinces[2] respectively. Input/output indices of some provinces turn to be zero after standardization. As a result, the zero values after standardization are

[2]The data of Chongqing and Sichuan are merged as one due to the data analysis. The data of other 29 provinces can be found in Table 20.2.

uniformly set as 0.0000001[3] in case initial emission efficiency will not be worked out.

## 20.4 Analysis of Empirical Results

By means of software DEA solver 5.0 and Matlab, each province's $PM_{2.5}$ initial emission efficiency and emission efficiency after allocation through the ZSG-DEA model are calculated, and the allocation result of each province's $PM_{2.5}$ emission right is secured, as is shown at length in Table 20.3. In the following table, $x_i$ denotes each province's $PM_{2.5}$ initial emission amount before allocation; $x_{Zi}$ represents each province's $PM_{2.5}$ emission amount after allocation through the ZSG-DEA model (when two factors, provincial land area and atmospheric environmental capacity of one $PM_{2.5}$ emission that meets the national constraint of $PM_{2.5}$ emission amount, are considered); $\Delta x_i$ stands for each province's $PM_{2.5}$ emission-reducing potential; $h_i$ stands for each province's $PM_{2.5}$ initial emission efficiency and $h_{Zi}$ stands for each province's emission efficiency after allocation through the ZSG-DEA model; $p_i$ denotes each province's population-weighted $PM_{2.5}$ initial concentration, and $p_{Zi}$ denotes each province's population-weighted $PM_{2.5}$ concentration after re-allocation. The calculation results are presented in Table 20.3.

(1) From the viewpoint of each province's $PM_{2.5}$ initial emission efficiency $h_i$, the average $PM_{2.5}$ initial emission efficiency, as can be derived from Table 20.3, is 0.4147, which indicates that the $PM_{2.5}$ emission efficiency in China on the whole is not high and there exists a great gap among some provinces in terms of $PM_{2.5}$ emission efficiency. Accordingly, provinces can be roughly divided into three categories.
The first category includes Beijing, Shanxi, Liaoning, Shanghai, Jiangsu, Shandong, Guangdong, Hainan, and Sichuan. Existing $PM_{2.5}$ emission efficiencies of these nine provinces are in a common frontier; and since these nine provinces well coordinate the relationship between economic development and environmental development, they can obtain more emission rights under the ZSG-DEA efficiency allocation system. The second category includes Heilongjiang, Zhejiang and Henan. Emission efficiencies of these three provinces are above the average efficiency and are near to the frontier. The third category includes Tianjin, Hebei, Inner Mongolia, Jilin, Anhui, Fujian, Jiangxi, Hubei, Hunan, Guangxi, Guizhou, Yunnan, Shaanxi, Gansu, Qinghai, Ningxia and Xinjiang. Initial emission efficiencies of these 17 provinces are below the average efficiency and are far away from the frontier. Among them, Gansu and Qinghai have the lowest emission efficiencies close to zero.

[3] This value is the value nearest to zero with software Dea Solver 5.0 still in operation. If the value is less than or equal to $10^{-8}$, the software Dea Solver 5.0will prompt a warning that reads as "range error", implying that the value is too small to be valid.

**Table 20.3** $PM_{2.5}$ emission efficiencies and allocation results

| Regions | Initial emission amount $x_i$ | Emission amount after allocation $x_{Zi}$ | Emission-reducing potential $\Delta x_i$ | Initial emission efficiency y $h_i$ | Emission efficiency after allocation $h_{Zi}$ | $PM_{2.5}$ initial concentration $p_i$ | $PM_{2.5}$ concentration after allocation $p_{Zi}$ |
|---|---|---|---|---|---|---|---|
| Beijing | 44,553.0396[a] | 44,557.6350 | 0.0000 | 1.0000 | 1.0000 | 33.1460 | 33.1490 |
| Tianjin | 0.1077 | 0.0000 | 0.1077 | 0.0000 | 1.0000 | 32.9290 | 2.5720 |
| Hebei | 0.2226 | 0.0791 | 0.1435 | 0.3552 | 1.0000 | 43.8070 | 17.2200 |
| Shanxi | 0.0631 | 0.0631 | 0.0000 | 1.0000 | 1.0000 | 26.8760 | 26.8790 |
| Inner Mongolia | 0.1775 | 0.0529 | 0.1246 | 0.2980 | 1.0000 | 13.4400 | 5.8110 |
| Liaoning | 0.0497 | 0.0497 | 0.0000 | 1.0000 | 1.0000 | 19.5230 | 19.5250 |
| Jilin | 0.0708 | 0.0037 | 0.0670 | 0.0526 | 1.0000 | 15.9990 | 3.2780 |
| Heilongjiang | 0.0783 | 0.0336 | 0.0447 | 0.4287 | 1.0000 | 9.3720 | 5.4880 |
| Shanghai | 0.0000 | 0.0000 | 0.0000 | 1.0000 | 1.0000 | 26.9410 | 26.9440 |
| Jiangsu | 0.1012 | 0.1012 | 0.0000 | 1.0000 | 1.0000 | 43.9370 | 43.9410 |
| Zhejiang | 0.0960 | 0.0521 | 0.0438 | 0.5432 | 1.0000 | 23.1580 | 13.7560 |
| Anhui | 0.1798 | 0.0167 | 0.1632 | 0.0927 | 1.0000 | 36.6940 | 5.7340 |
| Fujian | 0.0612 | 0.0000 | 0.0612 | 0.0000 | 1.0000 | 17.9100 | 2.5720 |
| Jiangxi | 0.1868 | 0.0000 | 0.1868 | 0.0000 | 1.0000 | 30.5220 | 2.5720 |
| Shandong | 0.1145 | 0.1145 | 0.0000 | 1.0000 | 1.0000 | 46.1440 | 46.1480 |
| Henan | 0.1977 | 0.0976 | 0.1001 | 0.4938 | 1.0000 | 45.0850 | 23.5670 |
| Hubei | 0.1854 | 0.0155 | 0.1699 | 0.0835 | 1.0000 | 37.7770 | 5.5120 |
| Hunan | 0.2273 | 0.0085 | 0.2188 | 0.0375 | 1.0000 | 33.0260 | 3.7130 |
| Guangdong | 0.0692 | 0.0692 | 0.0000 | 1.0000 | 1.0000 | 27.3320 | 27.3350 |
| Guangxi | 0.1160 | 0.0000 | 0.1160 | 0.0000 | 1.0000 | 37.5790 | 2.5720 |

(continued)

**Table 20.3** (continued)

| Regions | Initial emission amount $x_i$ | Emission amount after allocation $x_{Zi}$ | Emission-reducing potential $\Delta x_i$ | Initial emission efficiency y $h_i$ | Emission efficiency after allocation $h_{Zi}$ | $PM_{2.5}$ initial concentration $p_i$ | $PM_{2.5}$ concentration after allocation $p_{Zi}$ |
|---|---|---|---|---|---|---|---|
| Hainan | 0.0000 | 0.0000 | 0.0000 | 1.0000 | 1.0000 | 2.5720 | 2.5720 |
| Sichuan | 0.3816 | 0.3817 | 0.0000 | 1.0000 | 1.0000 | 38.7540 | 38.7580 |
| Guizhou | 0.1173 | 0.0082 | 0.1090 | 0.0701 | 1.0000 | 22.8590 | 3.9940 |
| Yunnan | 0.1868 | 0.0050 | 0.1818 | 0.0265 | 1.0000 | 28.5070 | 3.2600 |
| Shaanxi | 0.1504 | 0.0601 ara> | 0.0903 | 0.3993 | 1.0000 | 28.0820 | 12.7580 |
| Gansu | 0.2523 | 0.0000 | 0.2523 | 0.0000 | 1.0000 | 18.5630 | 2.5720 |
| Qinghai | 1.4696 | 0.0000 | 1.4696 | 0.0000 | 1.0000 | 14.4020 | 2.5720 |
| Ningxia | 0.1089 | 0.0000 | 0.1089 | 0.0000 | 1.0000 | 15.8590 | 2.5720 |
| Xinjiang | 0.9788 | 0.1426 | 0.8362 | 0.1456 | 1.0000 | 18.5700 | 4.9020 |
| Total | 44,558.9899 | 44,558.9899 | 4.5955 | | | | |

Note: In the fourth column, $\Delta x_i = x_i(1 - h_{Zi})$

[a]Input/output indices of some provinces fall to zero after standardization. To avoid the "range error" in calculation, the zero values after standardization are uniformly set at 0.0000001. Therefore, the value of Beijing is much bigger than those of other provinces.

It is worth mentioning that although $PM_{2.5}$ initial allocation efficiencies of Beijing and Shanghai are in the common frontier, and theoretically they may increase rather than decrease certain emission amounts through the ZSG-DEA efficiency allocation model. These two regions in reality still need to reduce their emission amounts owing to the fact that for one thing, these two large cities are regarded as super-municipalities in a traditional sense where $PM_{2.5}$ emission amounts and concentrations are high given the irrelatively small land areas; and for another, they belong to haze-prone areas influenced by haze diffusion originating from Hebei and other surrounding areas. Furthermore, $PM_{2.5}$ concentrations of Henan, Hebei, Hubei and other provinces are high while their $PM_{2.5}$ emission efficiencies are relatively low, indicating that, with excessively high $PM_{2.5}$ emission amounts in view of their energy consumption, labor remuneration, capital stock, provincial GDP, these provinces are under great pressure to improve emission-reducing technology, to change energy consumption structure and eventually to reduce haze emission.

(2) In terms of each province's emission amount after ZSG-DEA reallocation $x_{Zi}$, $x_{Zi}$ and $x_i$ differ greatly, though the total emission amount of all provinces stays the same. Compared with their $PM_{2.5}$ initial emission amounts $x_i$, emission amounts after allocation $x_{Zi}$ of Beijing, Shanxi, Liaoning, Jiangsu, Shanghai, Shandong, Guangdong, Hainan and Sichuan gain a total rise of 4.5955 units, with Beijing receiving the largest rise amount of nearly 4.5954 units; whereas emission amounts after allocation $x_{Zi}$ of Tianjin, Hebei, Henan, Inner Mongolia, Jilin, Heilongjiang, Zhejiang, Anhui, Fujian, Jiangxi, Hubei, Hunan, Guangxi, Guizhou, Yunnan, Shaanxi, Gansu, Qinghai, Ningxia and Xinjiang get a total drop of 4.5955 units, with Qinghai having the largest drop amount close to 1.4696 units. As can be seen from above, the total increase amount is equal to the total decrease amount, resulting in the unchanged total emission amount.

With regard to $PM_{2.5}$ emission concentration after allocation $p_{Zi}$, Shandong obtains the maximum growth of 0.0045 μg/cubic meter, whereas Guangxi gets the maximum cutback of 35.0068 μg/cubic meter.

(3) In respect of each province's $PM_{2.5}$ emission-reducing potential $\Delta x_i$, 20 provinces (Tianjin, Hebei, Inner Mongolia, Jilin, Anhui, Fujian, Jiangxi, Hubei, Hunan, Guangxi, Guizhou, Yunnan, Shaanxi, Gansu, Qinghai, Ningxia, Xinjiang, Heilongjiang, Zhejiang and Henan) have such haze-reducing potentials. All their $PM_{2.5}$ emission-reducing potentials $\Delta x_i$ can be calculated as 0.0103% of the total emission amount. Moreover, there also exist certain discrepancy between calculation results of some provinces' emission-reducing potentials and difference values derived from their $PM_{2.5}$ emission amounts before and after allocation (namely difference values between $x_i$ and $x_{Zi}$). For an illustration, Anhui's initial emission amount $x_i$ is 0.1798 units, and its emission-reducing potential $\Delta x_i$ is 0.1632 units. After allocation through the ZSG-DEA model, its reduction emission amount is 0.1632 units. Therefore, under the collective prevention and control mechanism of air pollutants, Anhui

should further reduce its air pollutant emission; otherwise, not only its ecological environment will be destroyed, but also its surrounding areas in the same climatic zone will be affected.

According to the $h_{Zi}$ value and relevant parameters in Formula (20.2), the mode for allocating $x_i$ among provinces can be revised, which will not only keep the total amount of $x_i$ unchanged, but also improve each province's emission efficiency. After many iterations, final emission efficiencies of all provinces reach one. At this time, no possible improvements can be made on each province's emission efficiency, and a fair allocation scheme of air pollutant emission rights is achieved.

Nevertheless, it should be noted that the hypothesis that the total emission amount is fixed does not mean that decision-making units cannot be encouraged to reduce emissions. Actually, in the long run, each province can still reduce its air pollutant emission by means of technological innovation or industrial restructuring, and can earn a profit by putting its surplus emission right on the market.

(4) Taking into consideration each province's land area and atmospheric environmental capacity of one $PM_{2.5}$ emission that meets the national constraint of $PM_{2.5}$ emission amount, all emission amounts are allocated through the ZSG-DEA model, thus making $PM_{2.5}$ emission amounts of all provinces in a new ZSG-DEA frontier and achieving a maximized overall technical efficiency. If there is a $PM_{2.5}$ emission right trading market, provinces with increased emission amounts are theoretically allowed to sell their surplus emission rights to those in need. Meanwhile, if provinces under the heavy emission-reducing pressure fail to further tap their haze-reducing potentials, they will face a double loss economically and environmentally.

## 20.5 Conclusion and Implication

In this paper, we considered each province's land area and atmospheric environmental capacity of one $PM_{2.5}$ emission that meets the national constraint of $PM_{2.5}$ emission amount in the actual allocation. Subsequently, with the input and output data of 29 provinces, the factor allocation level is calculated through the ZSG-DEA model assuming that the overall $PM_{2.5}$ emission efficiency is maximized, and, as the result, this procedure results in an allocation scheme of $PM_{2.5}$ emission amounts. This research approach can provide empirical support for the nationwide control of the total $PM_{2.5}$ emission amount and the $PM_{2.5}$ emission right trading among provinces, and also set abasis for the collective prevention and control policy of air pollutants among neighboring provinces. Based on this study, the following policy suggestions are made:

First, local governments should bear in mind their target responsibilities to reduce air pollutant emissions. Central and western provinces with relatively low emission efficiencies, such as Shanxi, Gansu, Xinjiang, Inner Mongolia, and Heilongjiang, should actively formulate industrial policies in line with their actual regional situations so as to curb the excessive growth of high energy-consumption and pollutant-emission sectors and to complete their minimal targets of “haze-reducing” work as soon as possible. In addition, provinces with relatively high $PM_{2.5}$ emission concentrations, such as Shandong, Henan and Hebei, should formulate their emission charging policies and emission permit systems in order to phase out backward steel industry and coal chemical industry, to accelerate the elimination of backward production capacity, and to promote the transformation and upgrading of traditional industries.

Second, the central government needs to establish among regions an interest coordinating mechanism and a collective prevention and control mechanism for $PM_{2.5}$ emission. The establishment of an interregional collective prevention and control mechanism depends upon the reasonable coordination and balance of regional interests. In other words, all regions should follow the fairness principle and efficiency principle to achieve mutual benefits and win–win cooperation. Given great interregional differences in economic development level, industrial structure and layout, environmental protection payment willingness, capital investment and pollution control level, and in haze emission amount, distribution, temporal and spatial variation, transmission intensity and diffusion rule, a “common but differentiated” collective prevention and control monitor system is set up according to emission target amounts and interregional differences on the basis of interregional unified supervision and law enforcement.

Third, the central government should promote interregional $PM_{2.5}$ emission right trading and establish an emission right compensative usage and trading system. $PM_{2.5}$ emission right trading can save regions ‘emission-reducing costs and improve their energy utilization efficiencies. Since 2007, relevant departments of the State Council have carried out pilot compensative usage and trading of emission rights in 11 provinces (autonomous regions and municipalities), including Jiangsu, Zhejiang, Hunan, Hubei, Henan, Hebei, Shanxi, Shaanxi, Inner Mongolia and Tianjin. In August 2014, “Guiding Opinions on Further Promoting Pilot Compensative Usage and Trading of Emission Rights “issued by the State Council pointed out that all pilot areas should fully finish checking and ratifying emission rights of existing emission enterprises by the end of 2015 and basically set up an emission right compensative usage and trading system by the end of 2017. The issue of this documents hall be conducive to give full play to the role of market mechanism in environmental protection and pollutant reduction, promote the reduction of total emission amount of major pollutants (including $PM_{2.5}$) and lay the foundation for the full implementation of the emission right compensative usage and trading system. The ZSG-DEA model being applied, this paper is also of some reference value for the initial allocation of $PM_{2.5}$ emission rights and the calculation of potential trading limits among regions.

Last but not least, the design of emission trading scheme should fully considerate the environment carrying capacity of each province. This paper adopts the environment capacity index of one $PM_{2.5}$ emission (Xue et al. 2014) which shows that the environment carrying capacities of each province differ greatly with Inner Mongolia ($42.67 \times 10^4$ tons) being the highest and Beijing ($2.79 \times 10^4$ tons) being the lowest.

We have also found that there was a flagrant contrast between the allocation with and without considering the environment capacity (due to space limitation, the calculation will not be shown in this paper). For this reason, the environment carrying capacity should be fully considered in the design of emission trading scheme of $PM_{2.5}$ as with other similar pollutants.

On the other hand, there are some limitations in the study, as discussed below.

First, the undesirable output index is too narrow and limited and therefore needs to be further expanded into multiple undesirable output indices under the ZSG-DEA model. There exist many kinds of undesirable output in the economy and environment system, and haze does not merely contain $PM_{2.5}$, and each kind of air pollutants has a different negative effect on the atmospheric environment. In this aspect, a multiple undesirable output model is called for. With the inclusion of correlation and degree of importance among multiple output indices and appropriate weights among the outputs, more comprehensive indices for measuring the degree of haze pollution can be developed.

Second, efficiency is emphasized in the above-mentioned allocation scheme and fairness of allocation is relatively not well dealt with. Due to distinct differences in the level of economic development, industrial structure, energy-saving potential, environmental capacity, and the national industrial layout among various regions, it is impossible for them to have an "equal" air pollutant emission target; instead they must bear "common but differentiated responsibilities". That is to say, all factors should be considered in the allocation of air pollutant emission rights with the aim of reasonably decomposing the total energy-saving and emission-reducing amount to various regions and sectors to ensure the fairness of allocation.

Third, the assessment criterion of environment capacity of each province (or region) needs a further elaboration. Due to data limitation, this paper adopts the atmospheric environmental capacity index provided by Xue et al. (2014). However, when considering the uncertain factors in Xue's research such as meteorological condition, emission inventory, and the assumption of $PM_{2.5}$ component equilibrium, further research should be carried out on how to overcome these uncertainties.

**Acknowledgements** Ling Tan, Ji Guo, Yingying Wang, Hui Liu, Weiwei Zhu, Mengke Zhao also made great contributions to this manuscript. We express our heartfelt thanks to them. This research was supported by: National Social and Scientific Fund Program of China (18ZDA052; 17BGL142; 16ZDA047); The Natural Science Foundation of China (91546117, 71373131).

## References

Abas, M. R. B., Rahman, N. A., Omar, N. Y., et al. (2004). Organic composition of aerosol particulate matter during a haze episode in Kuala Lumpur Malaysia. *Atmospheric Environment, 38*(25), 4223–4241.

Banker, R. D., Charnes, A. W., & Cooper, W. W. (1984). Some Models for estimating technical and scale efficiency in data envelopment analysis. *Management Science, 30,* 1078–1092.

Baumol, W. J., & W. E. Oates. (1988). The theory of environmental policy (2nd ed.). Cambridge: Cambridge University Press.
Beltrán-Esteve, M., & Picazo-Tadeo, A. J. (2015). Assessing environmental performance trends in the transport industry: Eco-innovation or catching-up? *Energy Economics, 51*(SEP.), 570–580.
Burton, E., & Sanjour, W. (1969). Multiple source analysis of air pollution abatement strategies. *Federal Accountant,* XVIII, 48–69.
Burton, E., & Sanjour, W. (1970). Applications of cost-effectiveness analysis to air pollution control. DHEW Contract No. CPA 22-69-17. Washington, DC: Ernst and Ernst.
Chai, F. H., Chen, Y. Z., et al. (2006). Study for regional air pollutants total amount control technologies and demonstration. *Research of Environmental Sciences, 4,* 163–171.
Charnes, A. W., Cooper, W. W., & Rhodes, E. (1978). Measuring the efficiency of decision making units. *European Journal of Operational Research., 2*(78), 429–444.
Chavez, C. A., Villena, M. G., & Stranlund, J. K. (2009). The choice of policy instruments to control pollution under costly enforcement and incomplete information. *Journal of Applied Economics, 12*(2), 207–227.
Chen, W. Y., Fang, D., Xue, D. Z., et al. (1998). Study on fair emission permital location approach in urban air pollution control. *Journal of Tsinghua University (Science and Technology), 7,* 50–53.
Chiu, Y. H., Lin, J. C., Hsu, C. C., et al. (2013). Carbon emission allowances of efficiency analysis: Application of super SBM ZSG-DEA model. *Journal of Environment Study., 22*(3), 653–666.
Böhringer, C., & Lange, A. (2005). On the design of optimal grandfathering schemes for emission allowances. *European Economic Review, 49*(8), 2041–2055.
Coase, R. H. (1960). The problem of social cost. *Journal of Law and Economics., 3*(1), 1–44.
Dales, J. H. (1968). *Pollution, property & prices: An essay in policy-making and economics.* Toronto: University of Toronto Press.
Montgomery, D. W. (1972). . Markets in licenses and efficient pollution control programs. *Journal of Economic Theory,* (5), 395–418.
Duan, L., Hao, J. M., et al. (2002). Estimating critical loads of sulfur and nitrogen for Chinese soils by steady state method. *Environment Science, 23*(2), 7–12.
Färe, R., Grosskopf, S., Lovell, C., et al. (1989). Multilateral productivity comparisons when some outputs are undesirable: A nonparametric approach. *Review of Economics and Statistics, 71*(1), 90–98.
Feng, L., & Wang, T. Q. (2014). Research on the pricing of initial allocation of carbon emission rights in China. *J. Study and Practice, 4,* 45–51.
Fischer, C., & Newell, R. G. (2008). Environmental and technology policies for climate mitigation. *Journal of Environmental Economics and Management, 55*(2), 142–162.
Gomes, E. G., & Lins, M. P. E. (2008). Modeling undesirable outputs with zero sum gains data envelopment analysis models. *Journal of the Operational Research Society, 59*(5), 616–623.
Gomes, E. G., Soares de Mello, J. C. C. B., & Lins, M. P. E. (2003). Buscase qüencial de alvos intermediários em modelos DEA com soma deoutputs constante (Step by step target search in Zero Sum Gains DEA models). *Investigação Operacional,* 23, 1–16.
Gomes, E. G., Soares de Mello, J. C. C. B., & Lins, M. P. E. (2005). Uniformizaçao da fronteira eficiente em modelos de Análise de Envoltória deDados com Ganhos de Soma Zero e Retornos Constantes de Escala (Uniform efficient frontier in Zero Sum Gains DEA CCR models). *Pesquisa Operacional,* 25, 261–277.
Hailu, A., & Veeman, T. S. (2001). Non-parametric productivity analysis with undesirable outputs: An application to the Canadian pulp and paper industry. *American Journal of Agricultural Economics, 83*(3), 605–616.
Hahn, R. (1984). Market power and transferable property rights. *Journal of General Information, 99*(4), 753–765.
Han, L. J., Zhou, W. Q., & Li, W. F., et al. (2014). Impact of urbanization level on urban air quality: A case of fine particles (PM2.5) in Chinese cities. *Environmental Pollution,* (194), 163–170.
Hossein, H. M., & Kaneko, S. (2013). Can environmental quality spread through institutions. *Energy Policy, 56*(2), 312–321.

Hu, J. L., & Fang, C. Y. (2010). Do market share and efficiency matter for each other? An application of the zero-sum gains data envelopment analysis. *Journal of the Operational Research Society, 61*(4), 647–657.
Jin, S., Sheng, Z. H., & Du, J. G. (2011). Analysis of government supervision strategy in the emission trading system. *Chinese Journal of Management Science, 4,* 174–182.
Huang, K., Zhang, X. Y., & Lin, Y. F. (2015). The "APEC Blue" phenomenon: Regional emission control effects observed from space. *Atmospheric Research, 164–165,* 65–75.
Lelieveld, J., Evans, J. S., Fnais, M., Giannadaki, D., & Pozzer, A. (2015). The contribution of outdoor air pollution sources to premature mortality on a global scale. *Nature, 525,* 367–371.
Lee, T., Yeo, G. T., & Thai, V. V. (2014). Environmental efficiency analysis of port cities: Slacks-based measure data envelopment analysis approach. *Transport Policy, 33*(4), 82–88.
Li, Y. S. (2005). *Technical guide for the total quantity control of atmospheric environmental capacity in urban area.* Beijing: China Environmental Science Press.
Liao, Z., Zhu, X., & Shi, J. (2015). Case study on initial allocation of shanghai carbon emission trading based on shapely value. *Journal of Cleaner Production, 103,* 338–344.
Lin, T., & Ning, J. F. (2011). Study on allocation efficiency of carbon emission permit in EUETS based on ZSG-DEA model. *The Journal of Quantitative & Technical Economics, 3,* 36–50.
Lins, M. P. E., Gomes, E. G., et al. (2003). Olympic ranking based on a zero-sum gains DEA model. *European Journal of Operational Research, 148*(2), 312–322.
Ma, X. M., Li, S. G., Luan, S. J., et al. (1999). Studies on urban total air pollutant emission control planning in China. *Acta Scientiarum Naturalium Universities Pekinensis, 2,* 265–230.
Ma, X. M., Wang, D. H., Yi, Z. B., et al. (2006). Study on the method of calculating and distributing the total amount of urban air pollutants. *Journal of Peking University (Natural Science Edition), 2,* 271–275.
Mackenzie, I. A., Hanley, N., & Kornienko, T. (2008). The optimal initial allocation of pollution permits: A relative performance approach. *Environmental and Resource Economics, 39*(3), 265–282.
MacKenzie, I. A., Hanley, N., & Kornienko, T. (2009). Using contests to allocate pollution rights. *Energy Policy, 37*(7), 2798–2806.
Malcolm, A., & Zhang, L. B. (2006). Case study on design of regulatory policies for sustainable emission reduction. *Computer Aided Chemical Engineering, 21,* 1119–1124.
Miao, Z., Zhou, P., Wang, Y., et al. (2013). Energy saving, emission reduction and air pollutants emission rights allocation research. *China Industrial Economics, 6,* 31–43.
Nordhaus, W. D. (2005). Life after Kyoto: Alternative approaches to global warming. *National Bureau of Economic Research.*
Pan, X., Teng, F., & Wang, G. Sharing emission space at an equitable basis: allocation scheme based on the equal cumulative emission per capita principle. *Applied Energy,* 113(Jan.), 1810–1818.
Park, J. W., Kim, C. U., & Isard, W. (2011). Permit allocation in emissions trading using the Boltzmann distribution. *Physica A: Statal Mechanics and Its Applications, 391*(20), 4883–4890.
Pelin, D., & Kesidou, E. (2011). Stimulating different types of eco-innovation in the UK: Government policies and firm motivation. *General Information, 70*(8), 1546–1557.
Peng, X. M., Ren, J., & Cheng, H. W. (2014). An exploration of haze issues based on environmental accounting perspective. *Manager Journal, 08,* 191–192.
Picazo-Tadeo, A. J., Castillo-Gimenez, J., & Beltran-Esteve, M. (2014). An intertemporal approach to measuring environmental performance with directional distance functions: Greenhouse gas emissions in the European Union. *Ecological Economics, 100*(Apr.), 173–182.
Pickl, S., Kropat, E., & Hahn, H. (2010). The impact of uncertain emission trading markets on interactive resource planning processes and international emission trading experiments. *Climatic Change, 103*(1–2), 327–338.
Ren, Z. H., Yu, X. Z., & et al. (2000). The Research on total amount control of air pollutant in China. In *Eighth National Conference on Atmospheric Environment, Kunming* (Vol. 10).
Rive, N. (2010). Climate policy in Western Europe and avoided costs of air pollution control. *Economic Modeling, 27*(1), 103–115.

Ruth, M., & Amato, A. (2002). Vintage structure dynamics and climate change policies: the case of US iron and steel. *Energy Policy, 30*(7), 541–552.
Seiford, L. M., & Zhu, J. (2002). Modeling undesirable factors in efficiency evaluation. *European Journal of Operational Research, 142*(1), 16–20.
Shi, M. J., Yuan, Y. N., Zhou, S. L., & et al. (2013). Carbon tax, cap-and-trade or mixed policy: Which is better for carbon mitigation? *Journal of Management Sciences in China,* (9), 9–19.
Singh, S., & Surya, S. M. (2014). Efficiency improvement strategy under constant sum of inputs. *Journal of Math Model Algor, 13*(4), 579–596.
Sun, Z. R., Zhou, D. Q., Zhou, P., et al. (2012). Quota Allocation of China' s energy conservation based on environmental ZSG-DEA. *Systems Engineering, 1,* 84–90.
Tietenberg, C., & Wu, G., Fan, H. Y. (1992). *Emission trading: Reform of pollution control policies.* Beijing: The Joint Publishing Company Ltd.
Tone, K. (2001). A slacks-based measure of efficiency in data envelopment analysis. *European Journal of Operational Research, 130*(3), 498–509.
Tone, K. (2004). *Dealing with undesirable outputs in DEA: A slacks-based measure (SBM) approach* (pp. 44–45). Toronto: Presentation at NAPW III.
Van Donkelaar, A., Martin, R. V., Brauer, M., et al. (2010). Global estimates of ambient fine particulate matter concentrations from satellite-based aerosol optical depth: Development and application. *Environment Health Prospect, 118*(6), 847–855.
Wang, K., Zhang, X., Wei, Y. M., & et al. (2013). Regional allocation of $CO_2$ emissions allowance over provinces in China by 2020. *Energy Policy, 54*(3), 214–229.
Wang, S. S., Li, N., & Wang, J. J. (2014). An application of black-Scholes model in pricing initial allocation of emissions. *Shanghai Environmental Sciences, 1,* 149–152.
Wei, Y., Jia, X. H., & Wei, Y. (2011). Total quantity control and reduction system for air pollution in Urumqi. *Journal of Arid Land Resources and Environment, 2,* 119–123.
Wu, P. Z., & Wang, Q. (2010). Economic Analysis on Emission Permits Trading. *China Population, Resources and Environment., 5,* 55–58.
Xue, W. B., Fu, F., & Wang, J. N. (2014). Modeling study on atmospheric environmental capacity of major pollutants constrained by PM2.5 compliance of Chinese cities. *China Environmental Science, 34*(10), 2490–2496.
Yang, G. H., Wang, Y., Zeng, Y. X., et al. (2013). Rapid health transition in China, 1990–2010: Findings from the Global Burden of Disease Study 2010. *Lancet, 381*(9882), 1987–2015.
Yu, X. N., Zhu, B., Yin, Y., et al. (2011). A comparative analysis of aerosol properties in dust and haze-fog days in a Chinese urban region. *Atmospheric Research, 99*(2), 241–247.
Zhang, L. F., & Peng, Y. Y. (2011). Research progress of emission trading mechanism. *Economic Perspectives, 4,* 135–140.
Zhang, Q. F., & Crooks, R. (2012). Toward an environmentally sustainable future: Country environmental analysis of the People's Republic of China. *China Financial & Economic Publishing House,* (11).
Zheng, L. Q. (2012). Sharing the carbon emission reduction responsibility across Chinese provinces: A zero sum gains DEA model. *Resources Science, 11,* 2087–2096.
Zheng, M., Zhang, Y. J., Yan, C. Q., et al. (2014). Review of PM2.5 source apportionment methods in China. *Acta Scientiarum Naturalium Universitatis Pekinensis, 6,* 1141–1154.
Zhou, P., Zhang, L., Zhou, D. Q., & Xia, W. J. (2013). Modeling economic performance of interprovincial co 2 emission reduction quota trading in china. *Applied Energy, 112*(16), 1518–1528.

# Part IV
# Environmental Performance Evaluation

# Chapter 21
# Efficiency Evaluation and PM Emission Reallocation of China Ports Based on Improved DEA Models

**Abstract** The emission of particulate matter (PM) and other atmospheric pollutants in port operations and shipping have caused a huge negative impact on the environment. Consequently, how to evaluate the environmental efficiency of ports and put forward corresponding countermeasures on this basis is becoming a more important issue than ever before from the perspectives of the government, academia, and society. We construct three data envelopment analysis (DEA) models to evaluate the environmental efficiency of ports under the circumstances of environmental control, non-environmental control and PM emission through inter-ports cooperation. The innovation of the DEA models constructed in this paper lies in: (1) Setting environmental control parameters to uniformly manipulate the situations of environmental control and non-environmental control, etc.; (2) Allowing non-equal proportional change of input index, expected output and non-expected output index; (3) Setting preference co-efficient for ports to admit favorable decisions; (4) Utilizing a distance formula of expected output under the situation of PM emission through inter-ports cooperation. Further, data from 11 major ports in China are collected to compare the expected output under different PM emission standards assuming the situation of environmental control and non-environmental control, port cooperation, and non-cooperative sewage discharge. The empirical results show that: (1) Ports in the eastern China (Shanghai, Ningbo, and Nanjing) have higher port efficiency; (2) Port cooperation can improve the overall expected output but it will lose its edge with the improvement of PM emission standards. (3) Ports follow the same trend of output loss regardless of favorable decisions. In the end, the author makes a summary, puts forward relevant policy suggestions and makes the recommendation for future research.

**Keywords** DEA · Environmental pollution · PM emission · Environmental efficiency · Reallocation · Efficiency evaluation

 
X. Wu and J. Guo, *Economic Impacts and Emergency Management of Disasters in China*,
https://doi.org/10.1007/978-981-16-1319-7_21

## 21.1 Introduction

As the great artery of the national economy, the waterway is the most important part of transportation around the world, but it can negatively impact the environment. According to *Third IMO GHG Study 2014-Final Report* from the International Maritime Organization (IMO),[1] international shipping, domestic shipping, and fishing produce about 1.45 million tons of PM as calculated by the top-down method, which is 7% higher in 2011 than in 2008. Especially in China, where water way transportation contributes to more frequent foggy and hazy weather at those ports. As a result, these unusual weather patterns attract society's attention. In 2017, there port from *China Ports Yearbook (CPY)* states that seven Chinese ports are the top ten in the world. This is exciting economic news but also alarming because it may exacerbate environmental changes in those ports. Although economic and social development is still the main task of national work at this present stage in China, the government has started tackling environmental problems and has taken actions to protect the environment such as releasing tighter regulation to limit the air pollutant emission near the harbor. For example, on Nov 30th 2018, the Chinese government enacted emission control regulations to protect the blue sky, facilitate green shipping, port development, and energy savings.

However, port pollution is not only an important environmental problem in China but also in other countries or cities. Because of that, most of them set up their strategies (which are not limited to PM) to reduce air pollution. For instance, Ulsan Metropolitan City defines its policy as a low carbon strategy to greenhouse gas (GHG) and to act as a global stronghold for the green industry (Mat et al. 2016). In some Emission Control Areas (ECAs), like the U.S. coast, the Baltic Sea and the English Channel, the government enacts a rule that vessels must burn low sulfur fuel when they enter these areas (Davarzani et al. 2016). Similarly, Yangtze River Delta cities in China have issued environmental policies to jointly limit air pollutants such as *Obligatory Targets of Environmental Protection* from Anhui Province (Yang et al. 2019). The IMO's Marine Environmental Protection Committee agrees that the sulfur content in vessel fuels required to be abated to 0.50% (5000 ppm) to protect the environment beginning 1st January 2020, known as Regulation 14 (Cullinane and Bergqvist 2014). Because of these strict rules, ports have to continue to increase investment to meet the government's requirements, negatively impacting profits.

The above facts raise some questions about how much governments should limit air pollutants and what ports can do to follow a more stringent set of rules. To solve these problems, scholars carried out some researches. For example, Chang and Park (2016) measured the output losses of Korean ports when the government imposed different levels of air pollution regulation. They suggested that this was a reason to issue a more temperate emission target by the local government at the beginning because the foregone cargo traffic increased more quickly than the emission reduction. Gobbi et al. (2019) tried to compare the impact of port emissions such as $NO_2$, $SO_2$, and $PM_{10}$ in Civitavecchia. The study illustrated that both ultrafine

[1] Abbreviations used in this paper are listed in Appendix A1 (Table A1).

particles and black carbon had a great impact in high concentrations at ports with non-environmental regulation (NER). One way for the port to comply with regulatory requirements was to cut down the emissions of auxiliary engines at berth. Yu et al. (2019) developed a multi-objective model to provide strategic planning to present an efficient way to use shore-side electricity. The other was to allow the substitution of air pollutants between different locations to maximize the expected output (Chen 2013; He et al. 2018). These studies, however, did not make a comprehensive analysis of output loss with respect to different ports' strategies.

Thus, to answer this question, three improved DEA models are established to measure port efficiency under the circumstances of environmental regulation (ER), non-environmental regulation (NER), and reallocation of PM emission permits through inter-ports cooperation. A comprehensive production model is extended from the directional distance function of Färe et al. (2007a, b) to incorporate both ER and NER and to allow all the inputs and outputs to be simultaneously and disproportionately changed. Then, a comprehensive emission model is generalized from the Chang and Park (2016) industry emission target model to allow non-proportional changes in inputs. Next, a comprehensive reallocation model is improved from the Zhou et al. (2013b) spatial allocation model to depict the output distance at different PM emission targets with the port's cooperative strategy. A preference co-efficient is set for ports in order to choose favorable decisions for all three improved models. Further, the data collected from the 11 Chinese main ports from 2012 to 2016 are divided into four areas for calculation. Finally, the empirical result is summarized to put forward correlative suggestions to port strategies and government policies.

The remainder of the paper is structured as follows: Sect. 21.2 (Literature review) is a review of studies about the environmental pollution of the transportation sector based on DEA models. Section 21.3 (Model) firstly introduces the existing DEA models (Färe model, Chang and Park model, and Zhou model). Then, three improved DEA models (the comprehensive production model, the comprehensive emission model, and the comprehensive reallocation model) are constructed to assess the environmental efficiency of ports under the circumstances of ER, NER, and reallocation of PM emission permits. In Sect. 21.4 (Case study), the improved DEA models are applied to calculate the environmental efficiency of 11 Chinese ports between 2012 and 2016. Section 21.5 (Conclusion) summarizes the paper and puts forward relevant policy suggestions and makes a recommendation for future research.

## 21.2 Literature Review

The literature has been proliferated to investigate the environmental pollution in transportation over the past decades. However, DEA becomes one of the most widely used non-parametric methods to evaluate public programs since an important study by Charnes et al. (1978).

Many scholars have evaluated the environmental efficiency of transportation systems (TS) from multiple perspectives. For example, He et al. (2018) centered on carbon dioxide and calculated the environmental efficiency of several major sectors including transportation part at the Chinese provincial level with non-separable non-expected output. Chang et al. (2013) investigated the environmental efficiencies of transportation systems (TS) of Chinese provinces. From the result, they found that the government could lower much carbon emissions at the provincial level because of the inefficiency of the Chinese transportation industry. Chang et al. (2014) measured the economic and environmental efficiency of a large number of global airlines. Sun et al. (2017) calculated the environmental efficiency of Chinese 17 ports, and their results suggested that policies should be implemented by following their respective circumstances to overcome their shortcomings. Kiani Mavi et al. (2019) measured transport efficiency with the Malmquist productivity index based on an improved DEA model. Egilmez and Park (2014) calculated the pollution emissions such as carbon emissions of manufacturing sectors, and compared their environmental performance and economic performance by an improved hierarchical methodology. Li et al. (2016) assessed the regional TS efficiency in China to dig out the reason of inefficiency. Pina and Torres (2001) analyzed the transport efficiency under the urban TS of public sectors and private sectors in the European Union. Baran and Górecka (2019) evaluated transport efficiency of road and rail freight in different counties in the European Union and analyzed the correlation between transport efficiency, GDP and $CO_2$ emissions. However, most of these studies evaluated the environmental efficiency based on only one year of data at the city or provincial level and rarely focused on the port. Since too many private cars would affect the air quality of the city, Sun et al. (2010) focused on the public transport and calculated the environmental efficiency of the ten Beijing bus transit stations based on the data of operation cost, number of employees, bus vehicles, etc. The results were provided to government decision-makers to promote the construction of public terminals and improve the efficiency of public transportation. To promote public health and environmental improvement, Porter et al. (2020) studied the relationship between cycling frequency and a range of environmental variables, such as bike lane length, population density, riding distance, tree coverage, parks, etc. Their research provided urban traffic managers with possible solutions for increasing green vehicles' usage to protect the urban environment. Djordjevi and Krmac (2019) used the non-radial DEA method and TOPSIS method respectively to calculate the environmental efficiency changes of road, railway, and aviation in Europe from 2006 to 2012. The results showed that compared with the non-radial DEA method, the TOPSIS method was more accurate in the transportation department's efficiency evaluation. Unlike the transport of ordinary goods, the transport of dangerous goods needed to consider more external traffic environment factors. Aiming at the problem of dangerous goods transport, Ma et al. (2013) developed a new integrated heuristic algorithm to optimize the problem of dangerous goods transport routes and made an empirical analysis with China's eastern and western case railways. Previous studies have calculated the energy and environmental efficiency of the U.S. transportation sector based on a series of basic parameters such as fuel type and operational efficiency provided by Reistad (1975). Bligh and Ugursal (2013) revised the basic parameters and reassessed the efficiency of the transportation sector based on the actual situation in the United States. In order to reduce the fuel consumption of ships, Tran (2019) set up a navigation environment model based on a fuzzy clustering algorithm and took bulk cargo ships as an example. The model involved variables such as wave height, wind speed and ship maneuvering type. It could be simulated according to different navigation environments to find out the best ship maneuvering speed and effectively reduce fuel consumption.

Some scholars carried out studies on energy efficiency and sustainability efficiency. Most of them concentrate on assessing the energy efficiency of various TS in cities. For example, Song et al. (2014) obtained the tendency of energy consumption of transportation and petroleum in Shanghai from 2000 to 2010 to dig out the influence factors on them. Hu et al. (2011) estimated the energy efficiency of lots of cities including Taipei, Yilan, and Taoyuan in Taiwan between 1998 and 2007 based on an improved four-stage DEA approach, and their result showed that the local governments must commit to changing inefficient cars to green energy cars with the central government help. Tian et al. (2020) assessed the sustainability efficiency of TS in Shaanxi province in China. Liu et al. (2016) calculated both energy and environment efficiency of TS including road and railway at the Chinese provincial level. The study showed that the energy structure and cleaner energy should be continuously adjusted and used in China. Cui and Li (2014) examined the energy efficiency of TS by proposing a novel three-stage DEA model. The study found that the energy efficiency of transportation is dependent on two points (transport structure and management measures). Guo et al. (2017) established an index system, easy to use to select both input and output, and provided an improved SBM model to assess the efficiency evaluation of the potential decrease of energy and pollution emission in China. Ramanathan (2000) obtained energy efficiency under different TS in India. Considering bad output, Li et al. (2016) evaluated transportation efficiency and sought the factors of transportation inefficiency in China. To design green-energy planning of transportation schemes for an air-conditioning manufacturer in China, Ji et al. (2016) constructed an improved model for suppliers, manufacturers, and retailers. Bi et al. (2014) were concerned about energy consumption and carbon dioxide emissions in China's transport sector. In order to provide policy advice on the sustainable development of China's transportation industry, they examined the environmental efficiency of the transportation industry in 30 provinces of China from 2006 to 2010 based on the DEA method. Their model could also provide potential carbon dioxide emission reduction for each province. Chen et al. (2018) focused on the harmful effects of rapid economic development, such as environmental pollution and energy consumption. The energy efficiency changes of 15 cities in the Yangtze River Delta from 2009 to 2013 were compared through the DEA window tool. They found that factors such as gross domestic product per capita reduced energy efficiency. Starting from the shortage of energy, Corlu et al. (2020) combined heuristic algorithm and artificial intelligence algorithm to calculate the environmental efficiency of transportation in China, the United States, OECD, the United States, and other countries and gave the path to improve the environmental efficiency. Talla Konchou et al. (2015) assessed Cameroon's transport energy efficiency and exergy efficiency from 2001 to 2010 using data from a variety of fuels, including crude oil, natural gas, diesel, and coal. The findings showed that Cameroon's transport energy efficiency was low. Based on the DEA method, Zhang et al. (2020) calculated the local transportation sector's carbon dioxide emission efficiency from 2008 to 2017 through each province's panel data in China. They believed that the central provinces had higher environmental efficiency, while the eastern regions had the most significant environmental efficiency improvement. Zhang et al. (2011) studied the changes in transport energy efficiency and exergy efficiency in China using transport energy data over a span of 30 years from 1980 to 2009. The results showed that transportation energy consumption in 2009 was twice as high as in 1980. The transportation sector used slightly more oil than China imports.

Recently, performance assessment is another hot topic discussed by scholars. Xiong et al. (2019) studied performance improvement of the transportation sector based on an improved distance friction minimization model. Wu et al. (2016a, b) constructed a novel parallel DEA model to assess the environmental efficiency of TS of all Chinese provinces along with energy consumption, and noticed that there were big dissimilarities between passenger and freight transportation subsystems. Particularly, they found that local governments should pay more attention to improving freight transportation. Lee et al. (2014) selected 11 main ports in the world to evaluate their environmental performance with oxide, sulfur oxide and carbon dioxide as undesirable output. Barros and Peypoch (2009) employed both operational and financial variables to compute the operational performance of the Association of European Airlines between 2000 and 2005. Zhou et al. (2013a, b) designed an improved DEA model to obtain the $CO_2$ emission performance at the Chinese provincial level under the transport sector. Bostian et al. (2018) measured the environmental performance with application in a paper company based on a novel directional distance model obtaining maximum expected outputs and minimum bad outputs. Lan and Lin (2005) constructed an improved DEA model to include environmental effects and then applied in performance evaluation of railways based on a newly four-stage DEA model to contribute to some policy suggestions. To monitor manufacturers' emissions from freight transport, Holden et al. (2016) constructed a newly context-dependent non-expected output DEA approach. Kim et al. (2011) evaluated the environmental efficiency with structure change imposed by the Kyoto Protocol in Korea in terms of gas emission reduction. Jeon et al. (2005) believed that the transportation sector's sustainable development could not be separated from the joint role of economic benefits, environmental protection, and social welfare. They established the transportation sector's utility and efficiency evaluation system and applied the evaluation method to provide managers with beneficial, sustainable development strategies based on these three factors. Due to the fuzziness, complexity and incomplete information of real-time traffic problems, Singh et al. (2017) first used neutral set to describe complex real-time traffic problems and proposed the optimal traffic efficiency model under neutral environment. Urban traffic congestion would not only affect travel efficiency but also brought about severe air pollution. Dai et al. (2017) studied the impact of connected vehicles, or second-pass vehicles, on the traffic system to ease congestion. They divided second-trip vehicles into two categories: those with information on the first trip and those without complete information. The results showed that second-trip vehicles with more multi-trip information could effectively improve traffic efficiency and alleviate traffic congestion. Bernardo (2012) applied the idea of a value stream map to transportation to reduce waste and improve efficiency. Ülengin et al. (2010) proposed a novel three-stage model to study transport policies' impact on the environment, economy, and transport efficiency. The cognitive mapping model was built up to determine the main factors of the interaction between traffic and the environment. Based on the above model, they suggested feasible measures conducive to green transportation promotion and development. Green sustainability was one of the more and more important goals of transportation development. To meet Louisiana's transportation needs, Kelle et al. (2019) built intermodal networks based on roads, waterways, and railroads and measured their respective environmental efficiencies. They found that the increase in road transport led to environmental pollution and more severe traffic jams. Wang et al. (2020) discussed in detail how transportation infrastructure affected energy efficiency in the industrial sector in both the short and long term and analyzed the relationship between economic, industrial agglomeration, and energy efficiency in terms of technology spillovers, economies of scale, and competition. Finally, the empirical analysis was carried out based on Chinese provinces' panel data from 2000 to 2017. Chen and Lei (2017) discussed the factors that produce carbon dioxide in transportation regarding direct impact, indirect impact, and overall impact. They found that transport intensity and energy consumption directly affect carbon dioxide emissions from the transport sector, while population size indirectly affected dioxide emissions and was positively correlated with them. Moreover, they argued that policies such as controlling the size of vehicles and using cleaner energy could effectively reduce carbon dioxide emissions. When using the traditional DEA method to evaluate the transportation department's efficiency, it was not easy to distinguish the efficiency decision unit. Therefore, based on the cooperative game model and cross-efficiency method, Omrani et al. (2016) proposed a new model to identify efficiency units. Using Iran as an example, they calculated 20 different provinces' transport efficiency and provided advice on sustainable development.

Researchers also focused on other aspects of green transportation system. For example, some scholars regarded walking as a means of transportation. Liao et al. (2017) discussed the impact of traffic conditions, distance traveled, and environmental awareness on the way people over 65 choose to walk. It was suggested that promoting public and individual environmental awareness is helpful to increase the walking rate. Dadpour et al. (2016) separated walking from physical activity and searched 11,777 relevant articles, defining four key factors that affected walking: safety, environmental aesthetics, social interaction, and efficiency. Based on these four factors, they conducted a walking survey among citizens aged between 18 and 65. The results showed that environmental aesthetics and social interaction had positive and negative effects on walking. Compared with the outdoor transportation that most researchers were concerned about, Scholz and Schabus (2017) focused on indoor intelligent transportation. They found the optimal transport path by building a visual network of in-store product transport linked to the manufacturer's data. The results showed that their network model could improve indoor transport efficiency and reduce pollution in factories. Previous scholars tended to evaluate traffic environmental efficiency based on historical data. Nevertheless, Sonmez et al. (2017)

were more concerned about the prediction of future environmental efficiency. They used the human-worker ant colony algorithm to predict the Turkish transport sector's environmental efficiency based on data from 1970 to 2013. The results showed that Turkey's transport energy consumption in 2034 was likely to double that of 2013. Wu et al. (2019) compared China's transportation sector's energy consumption with that of the United States. It was found that there was a weak decoupling between transportation energy consumption and economic growth in the long run, and the decoupling index of China was about ten times that of the United States. Finally, they explained the above decoupling phenomenon from energy density, structure, and population and gave corresponding policy suggestions. Automobile exhaust not only polluted the air but also might increase the accident rate. Oh et al. (2016) discussed the relationship between vehicle exhaust emissions and vehicle collisions from this new perspective. After analyzing the data of private automobile accidents in the United States, it was found that there was a significant positive correlation between automobile exhaust and collision. Some feasible measures to improve road safety and reduce automobile exhaust emissions were put forward. Palander et al. (2020) studied how to improve wood transportation's energy efficiency under the goal of carbon neutrality. They compared the amount of fuel used by different vehicle types to transport wood, based on 2018–2020 vehicle plan data from Stora Enso of Finland. The study found that the improvement of automobile technology would significantly reduce energy consumption and improve energy efficiency. Dewulf et al. (2004) studied the impact of the European railway RAVEL project on railways' environmental efficiency. The project incorporated factors affecting environmental pollution into product design. They saw the project as a good push for green railway standardization. Most studies used the IPCC's top-down approach to calculate local transport sector $CO_2$ emissions. Since this method was not very accurate, Sim et al. (2015) revised the original IPCC method based on the actual situation of traffic in South Korea and proposed a new method to calculate carbon dioxide emissions. The method could measure each mode of transportation's carbon dioxide emissions and provide environmental managers with more detailed environmental transportation policies. Li and Zhang (2019) took operational capacity and environmental regulation as constraints and put forward a novel logistics topology network to seek a regional logistics system's maximum carrying capacity. The network could contain multiple modes of transportation and provide optimal solutions for regional logistics system operation. Fewer scholars have discussed the relationship between street conditions and vehicle fuel consumption. Wang et al. (2014) analyzed data from 108 drivers driving in the Southeast Michigan area and concluded that narrow streets and densely populated areas could slow cars down, produce more pollution, and affect energy efficiency.

Considering a measurement of the output loss between ER and NER, Färe et al. (2007a, b) established a newly DEA model with the application in electric power plants to calculate the technical efficiency. Färe et al. (2007a, b) also calculated the output loss between ER and NER with a newly directional environmental distance approach. Comparing with the observed GDP and simulated GDP, Färe et al. (2012a, b) assessed the production technology of different OECD countries with different emissions targets. Chang et al. (2018) investigated whether ECAs' regulations influenced the efficiencies of ports operation in these areas. The results proved that ECA regulations reflected the views of the stakeholders that could hurt port efficiency. Haralambides and Gujar (2012) assessed the port service production for both expected outputs and non-expected outputs based on a novel eco-DEA approach. To measure the pollution abatement cost change indexes, Cui et al. (2018) constructed a newly DEA approach named Dynamic Environmental approach to split the indexes into small parts. Due to traditional coal transportation problems, such as high energy consumption, long transportation distance, and environmental pollution, Zhang et al. (2018) developed an optimal path model based on high-voltage transportation, which could help managers make the optimal transportation plan. Their results showed that although high-voltage transport was the preferred mode of transport, traditional coal transport would still play an essential role during China's 13th Five-Year Plan period. Wang et al. (2018) introduced the unexpected output (carbon dioxide emissions) and extended the Generalized Divisia Index Method to measure transportation efficiency for the first time. At the same time, they studied the elasticity of decoupling between transport and carbon dioxide emissions. They found that the added value of transport, consumption, etc., were the main factors influencing carbon dioxide emissions. Balasubramaniam et al. (2017) studied traffic pollution emissions and sustainability from the Internet of vehicles' perspective. Their study analyzed the pollution problem and focused on the relationship between traffic safety and sustainability. The results showed that accidents were related to the type and time of the vehicle.

Inspired by the previous work, some scholars have studied the emission reallocation questions. To cope with emission permits reallocation, Lozano et al. (2009) proposed a DEA approach that had three phases and examined it in the paper industry. Wu et al. (2016a, b) developed a novel DEA model for environmental performance improvement permitting resource reallocation between different decision-making units (DMUs) and allowing emission target change. Zhou et al. (2013b) set up a number of centralized DEA approaches to optimize $CO_2$ emissions at various conditions. The result showed that the Chinese government might use a modest emission reduction policy to achieve GDP growth and $CO_2$ emissions reduction.

While few papers study both the output loss and PM emission reallocation in the port sector by using the DEA model, this paper attempts to measure them simultaneously to achieve the desired behavior for ports and provide some helpful suggestions to the government.

We will generalize the Färe et al. (2007a, b) model to set environmental control parameters to incorporate both ER and NER, permit non-equal proportional change of input index, expected output and non-expected output index in existing models (Fare et al. 2007a, b; Chang and Park, 2016), establish a comprehensive reallocation model to measure expected output distance at different pollution emission targets based on Zhou et al. (2013b) spatial allocation model, and set preference co-efficient in all improved models for ports to choose favorable decisions. Last, the models are applied to 11 Chinese main ports for measurement.

## 21.3 Model

### 21.3.1 Environmental Technology

Considering a basic production process (port operation), producing expected outputs (standard container throughput) it inevitably delivers on-expected outputs such as suspended PM emissions or other emissions. The basic model called environmental technology can measure the expected output respectively under ER and NER.

Let $x = (x_1, \ldots, x_N) \in \mathfrak{R}_+^N$ denote the input vector, $y = (y_1, \ldots, y_S) \in \mathfrak{R}_+^S$ the vector of expected outputs, and $p = (p_1, \ldots, p_M) \in \mathfrak{R}_+^M$ the vector of non-expected outputs. Then the environmental technology introduced by Färe et al. (2007b) can be given as:

$$\mathrm{T} = \{(\mathrm{x}, \mathrm{y}, \mathrm{p}) : \mathrm{xcanproduce}(\mathrm{y}, \mathrm{p})\} \tag{21.1}$$

The environmental technology can be determined as output sets $P(x)$ or input sets $L(y, p)$:

$$(\mathrm{x}, \mathrm{y}, \mathrm{p}) \in \mathrm{T} \iff (\mathrm{y}, \mathrm{p}) \in \mathrm{P}(\mathrm{x}) \Leftrightarrow \mathrm{x} \in \mathrm{L}(\mathrm{y}, \mathrm{p}) \tag{21.2}$$

This environmental technology assumes two axioms which are null-jointness and weak disposability, as described in Eq. (21.3) and Eq. (21.4), respectively.

$$(\mathrm{y}, \mathrm{p}) \in \mathrm{P}(\mathrm{x})\mathrm{andp} = 0\mathrm{implyy} = 0 \tag{21.3}$$

$$(\mathrm{y}, \mathrm{p}) \in \mathrm{P}(\mathrm{x})\mathrm{and}0 \le \theta \le 1\mathrm{imply}(\theta\mathrm{y}, \theta\mathrm{p}) \in \mathrm{P}(\mathrm{x}) \tag{21.4}$$

Then, the environmental technology can be formulated via the DEA model as an environmental production function. Assume there are $k = 1, \ldots, K$ DMUs with inputs vector $x_k = (x_{1k}, \ldots, x_{Nk})$, expected output vector $y_k$, and non-expected outputs vector $p_k = (p_{1k}, \ldots, p_{Mk})$ for $\mathrm{DMU}_k$. $z_k(k = 1, \ldots, K)$ denote the intensity variables. The environmental production model for port $k'$ with single output under ER introduced by Färe et al. (2007a, b) is formulated as:

$$\mathrm{F}\left(\mathrm{x}^{\mathrm{k}'}, \mathrm{p}^{\mathrm{k}'}\right) = \max \sum_{\mathrm{k}=1}^{\mathrm{K}} \mathrm{z_k y_k}$$

$$\text{s.t.} \begin{cases} \sum_{\mathrm{k}=1}^{\mathrm{K}} \mathrm{z_k x_{nk}} \le \mathrm{x_{nk'}} \quad \mathrm{n} = 1, \ldots, \mathrm{N} \ (\mathrm{i}) \\ \sum_{\mathrm{k}=1}^{\mathrm{K}} \mathrm{z_k p_{mk}} = \mathrm{p_{mk'}} \quad \mathrm{m} = 1, \ldots, \mathrm{M} \ (\mathrm{ii}) \\ \mathrm{z_k} \ge 0 \quad \mathrm{k} = 1, \ldots, \mathrm{K} \ (\mathrm{iii}) \end{cases} \tag{21.5}$$

Furthermore, in order to measure the port's performance, Färe et al. (2007a, b) defined the directional output distance function (DODF) as:

$$\vec{D}(x, y, p; g_y, g_p) = Sup\{\beta : (y + \beta g_y, p - \beta g_p) \in P(x)\} \tag{21.6}$$

where the vector $g = (g_y, g_p)$ indicates the direction that the port would like to adjust the expected outputs and non-expected outputs, and $\beta$ describes the maximum increase of non-expected outputs. Assume expected outputs vector for $\text{DMU}_k$ is $y_k = (y_{1k}, \ldots, y_{Sk})$. Then the DODF can be evaluated for the port $k'$ with multiple outputs under ER by the following DEA model:

$$\vec{D}\left(x^{k'}, y^{k'}, p^{k'}; g_y, g_p\right) = \max \beta^{k'}$$

$$s.t. = \begin{cases} \sum_{k=1}^{K} z_k y_{sk} \geq y_{sk'} + \beta^{k'} g_{y_s} \sum_{k=1}^{K} z_k y_{sk} \geq y_{sk'} + \beta^{k'} g_{y_s} & s = 1, \ldots, S\ (i) \\ \sum_{k=1}^{K} z_k p_{mk} = p_{mk'} - \beta^{k'} g_{p_m} & m = 1, \ldots, M\ (ii) \\ \sum_{k=1}^{K} z_k x_{nk} \leq x_{nk'} & n = 1, \ldots, N\ (iii) \\ z_k \geq 0 & k = 1, \ldots, K\ (iv) \end{cases} \tag{21.7}$$

Equation (21.7) represents that the port could simultaneously and proportionally expand multiple expected outputs and reduce on-expected outputs. Referring to Färe et al. (2007a, b), the environmental production function and DOD Funder ER can be easily changed to NER to replace the strict equality of non-expected outputs constraints Eq. (21.5)-ii and Eq. (21.7)-ii with Eq. (21.8) and Eq. (21.9).

$$\sum_{k=1}^{K} z_k p_{mk} \leq p_{mk'} \tag{21.8}$$

$$\sum_{k=1}^{K} z_k p_{mk} \leq p_{mk'} - \beta^{k'} g_{p_m} \tag{21.9}$$

Let $\vec{DU}$ be a DOD Funder the NER. The output loss between ER and NER can be calculated by

$$D\vec{P}AC = \vec{DU}\left(x^{k'}, y^{k'}, p^{k'}; g_y, g_p\right) - \vec{D}\left(x^{k'}, y^{k'}, p^{k'}; g_y, g_p\right) \tag{21.10}$$

### 21.3.2 Previous Industry Emission Target Model

To better imitate the realistic world, Chang and Park (2016) extended the Färe et al. (2007a, b) model by adding the maximum PM emission target limits on the total emissions of industries. This model does not require proportionally change in expected outputs and non-expected outputs. It is defined as:

$$\rho = max \sum\nolimits_{k=1}^{K} \beta_k y_k$$

$$s.t. \begin{cases} \sum\nolimits_{h=1}^{K} z_{hk} y_h \geq y_k + \beta_k g_{y_k} \ \ k = 1, \ldots, K \ (i) \\ \sum\nolimits_{h=1}^{K} z_{hk} p_h = p_k - \tau_k g_{p_k} \ \ k = 1, \ldots, K \ (ii) \\ \sum\nolimits_{h=1}^{K} z_{hk} x_{nh} \leq x_{nk} \ \ n = 1, \ldots, N; k = 1, \ldots, K \ (iii) \\ \sum\nolimits_{k=1}^{K} \sum\nolimits_{h=1}^{K} z_{hk} p_h \leq P \ (iv) \\ z_{hk} \geq 0, \beta_k, \tau_k \geq 0 \ k = 1, \ldots, K \ (v) \end{cases} \tag{21.11}$$

where $P$ denotes the PM emission target for the industry. It can be controlled by the government to evaluate the maximum output of port $k$ at the PM emission target $P$. The output loss can be calculated by

$$\rho_{loss} = \rho\left(x, y, b; \sum\nolimits_{k=1}^{K} p_k\right) - \rho(x, y, b; P) \tag{21.12}$$

$$\text{for } \overline{P_{LB}} \leq P \leq \sum_{k=1}^{K} p_k \tag{21.13}$$

where $\overline{P_{LB}}$ is the lower bound of $P$, and $\sum\nolimits_{k=1}^{K} p_k$ denotes the total emission in the industry.

### 21.3.3 Previous Spatial Allocation Model

Furthermore, to ensure not exceeding the upper limit of the PM emission target, port could adopt a cooperative strategy to permit the substitution of PM emission between different DMUs to achieve the maximum of the aggregate expected outputs. Assume $\sigma$ as a control coefficient of PM emission (between zero to one) imposed by the government. Then the spatial reallocation model (SRM) is expressed by Zhou et al. (2013b) as:

$$SRM = max \sum_{k=1}^{K} \widehat{y}_k$$

$$\text{s.t.}\begin{cases} \sum_{h=1}^{K} z_{hk}x_{nh} \leq x_{nh} \;\; n = 1,\ldots,N;\; k = 1\ldots,K \;(i) \\ \sum_{h=1}^{K} z_{hk}y_h \geq \hat{y}_k \;\; k = 1,\ldots,K \;(ii) \\ \sum_{h=1}^{K} z_{hk}p_h = \hat{p}_k \;\; k = 1,\ldots,K \;(iii) \\ \sum_{h=1}^{K} \hat{p}_h = \sigma \bullet \sum_{h=1}^{K} p_h \;(iv) \\ z_{hk} \geq 0, \hat{y}_k \geq 0, \hat{p}_k \geq 0 \;\; h,k = 1,\ldots,K \;(v) \end{cases} \tag{21.14}$$

where $\hat{p}_k$ and $\hat{y}_k$ are decision variables, $z_{hk}$, $\hat{y}_k$ and $\hat{p}_h$ denoterespectively intensity variables, the expected outputs after PM emission reallocation between cooperative DMUs, and the optimal amount of PM emission permit to each DMUs. Equation (21.14)-(iv) could be controlled by the government to re-draft the number of total emissions to measure how much production should be reduced.

### 21.3.4 The Comprehensive Production Model

Equations (21.7), (21.11) and (21.14) are all useful models to measure the output loss under ER and NER and to deal with emission reallocation question, but there are still some problems. First, Eqs. (21.7) and (21.11) do not allow non-equal proportional change of input index, expected output and non-expected output index. However, the automated port may allow inputting less manpower or berths to get more standard container throughput with less PM emission. Second, three equations do not consider ports to adjust the direction vector in their favor. Third, Eq. (21.14) does not provide a distance function like DODF to measure the output loss directly. Last, Eqs. (21.11) and (21.14) can only measure single expected output and non-expected output at the same time. Thus, to generalize these functions, suppose that there are $k = 1, \ldots, K$ DMUs and then we improve Eq. (21.6) to describe the automated port operation as follows:

$$\vec{D}(x, y, p; g_x, g_y, g_p) = \mathrm{Sup}\{\beta : (y + \beta g_{y,p} - \beta g_p) \in P(x - \alpha g_x)\} \tag{21.15}$$

where $\beta, \tau$ and $\alpha$ indicate respectively the maximum feasible expansion of expected outputs $y_k = (y_{1k}, \ldots, y_{Sk})$, contraction of non-expected outputs $p_k = (p_{1k}, \ldots, p_{Mk})$, and inputs $x_k = (x_{1k}, \ldots, x_{Nk})$. The direction vector can be expressed as

$$g = \left(g_{x_k} = \psi_{nk}, g_{y_k} = \mu_{sk}, g_{p_k} = \zeta_{mk}\right) \tag{21.16}$$

We also assume

$$\sum_{n}^{N} \psi_{nk} + \sum_{s}^{S} \mu_{sk} + \sum_{m}^{M} \zeta_{mk} = 1, (\psi_{nk} \geq 0, \mu_{sk} \geq 0, \zeta_{mk} \geq 0) \tag{21.17}$$

where $g$ denotes the direction vector,$\psi$, $\mu$ and $\zeta$ are preference co-efficient controlled by port.[2] When Eq. (21.15) equals zero, it means that the product plan is situated on the frontier of the output sets. Then the comprehensive production model (CPM), incorporating ER and NER, can be formulated as:

$$\vec{CPM} = \max \sum_{k=1}^{K} \beta_k$$

$$s.t. \begin{cases} \sum_{h=1}^{K} z_{hk} y_{sh} \geq y_{sk} + \beta_k g_{y_k} \quad s = 1, \ldots, S; k = 1, \ldots, K \ (i) \\ (1-\delta) \bullet \sum_{h=1}^{K} z_{hk} p_{mh} = (1-\delta) \bullet (p_{mk} - \tau_k g_{p_k}) \quad m = 1, \ldots, M; k = 1, \ldots, K \ (ii) \\ \delta \bullet \sum_{k=1}^{K} z_{hk} p_{mh} \geq \delta \bullet (p_{mk} - \tau_k g_{p_k}) \quad m = 1, \ldots, M; k = 1, \ldots, K \ (iii) \\ \sum_{h=1}^{K} z_{hk} x_{nh} \leq x_{nk} - \alpha_k g_{x_k} \quad n = 1, \ldots, N; k = 1, \ldots, K \ (iv) \\ z_{hk} \geq 0, \beta_k, \tau_k, \alpha_k \geq 0, \delta = 0, 1 \quad h; k = 1, \ldots, K \ (v) \end{cases} \tag{21.18}$$

where $\delta$ denotes the environmental control parameter. If $\delta = 1$, the model represents NER. If $\delta = 0$, it expresses ER. The direction vector follows $g = (g_{x_k} = \psi_{nk}, g_{y_k} = \mu_{sk}, g_{p_k} = \zeta_{mk} | \sum_n^N \psi_{nk} + \sum_s^S \mu_{sk} + \sum_m^M \zeta_{mk} = 1, \psi_{nk} \geq 0, \mu_{sk} \geq 0, \zeta_{mk} \geq 0)$ is decided by the port. The comprehensive model allows all the inputs and outputs to be contracted or improved disproportionately by using different coefficients $(\beta, \tau, \alpha)$ and incorporates both ER and NER. Then the output loss between ER and NER can be measured by the following function:

$$\vec{\Delta y} = \vec{\text{CPM}}(1) - \vec{\text{CPM}}(0) \tag{21.19}$$

Figure 21.1 provides graphic explanations for Eq. (21.18). Assume there is an observed port (Point $A$) inside output set $P(x - \alpha g_x)$. It can choose any north-western directions to increase its technical efficiency to the production frontier. In Fig. 21.1, Point A increases the technical efficiency along the vertical direction to Point B, which locates at the frontier of output set $P(x - \alpha g_x)$. Then, the distance $AB$ measures the needed increasable expected output from technical inefficiency to technical efficiency under ER. Considering the observed port (Point $A$) being projected to point $B^{'}$,the distance $AB^{'}$ measures the needed increasable expected output under NER. Therefore, the distance $BB^{'}$ is calculated by Eq. (21.19) to evaluate the output loss between ER and NER. Figure 21.1 illustrates that environmental production technology produces fewer outputs than non-environmental production technology.

[2]Färe et al. (2013) assume the direction vector ($\psi + \mu + \zeta = 1$) endogenously. In this paper, we suppose the direction vector could be decided by ports in their best interests.

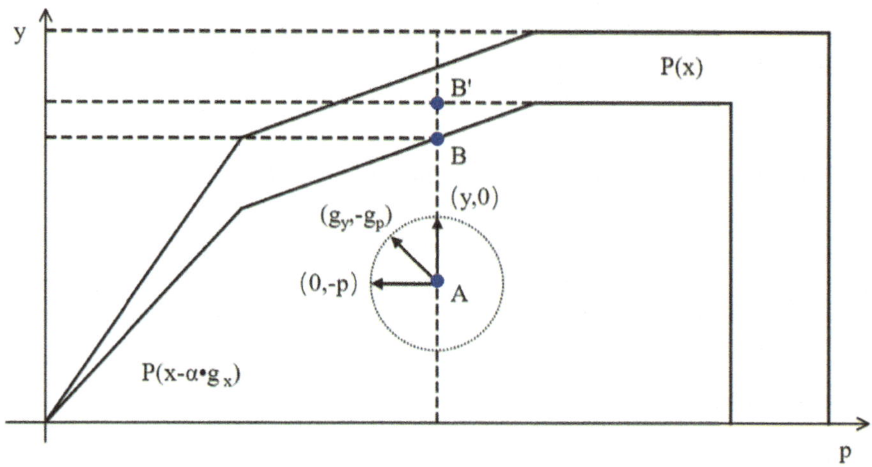


**Fig. 21.1** The comprehensive production model and DODF

## *21.3.5 The Comprehensive Emission Model*

Then, we improve the industry emission target model by forming a comprehensive emission model (CEM).

$$\vec{\text{CEM}}(\omega) = \max \sum_{k=1}^{K} \beta_k$$

$$\text{s.t}\begin{cases} \sum_{h=1}^{K} z_{hk} y_{sh} \geq y_{sk} + \beta_k g_{y_k} & s = 1, \ldots, S; k = 1, \ldots, K \\ \sum_{h=1}^{K} z_{hk} p_{mh} = p_{mk} - \tau_k g_{p_k} & m = 1, \ldots, M; k = 1, \ldots, K \\ \sum_{h=1}^{K} z_{hk} x_{nh} \leq x_{nk} - \alpha_k g_{x_k} & n = 1, \ldots, N; k = 1, \ldots, K \\ \sum_{k=1}^{K} \sum_{h=1}^{K} z_{hk} p_{mh} \leq \omega \cdot \sum_{k=1}^{K} p_{mk} & m = 1, \ldots, M \\ z_{hk} \geq 0, \beta_k, \tau_k, \alpha_k \geq 0 & h, k = 1, \ldots, K \end{cases} \tag{21.20}$$

where $\omega$(between zero to one) denotes the coefficient of actual PM emission ($\sum_{k=1}^{K} p_{mk}$), whichis controlled by the government.The direction vector follows $g = (g_{x_k} = \psi_{nk}, g_{y_k} = \mu_{sk}, g_{p_k} = \zeta_{mk} | \sum_n^N \psi_{nk} + \sum_s^S \mu_{sk} + \sum_m^M \zeta_{mk} = 1, \psi_{nk} \geq 0, \mu_{sk} \geq 0, \zeta_{mk} \geq 0)$, which is decided by the port. To achieve a reasonable environmental policy, coefficient $\omega$ could be used to help the government to check the change of increasable expected outputs with adjusting PM emission targets. Non-equal proportional change of input index, expected output and non-expected output index are allowed in a comprehensive emission model. This model can change multiple pollution targets at the same time.

### 21.3.6 The Comprehensive Reallocation Model

Next, a comprehensive reallocation model (CRM), improved from Zhou et al. (2013b),is established to measure the maximum increasable expected output in the context of PM emission reallocation of ports under different PM emission targets.

$$\vec{CRM}(\omega) = \max \sum_{k=1}^{K} (\beta_{1k} - \beta_{2k})$$

$$\text{s.t} \begin{cases} \sum_{h=1}^{K} z_{hk} y_{sh} \geq y_{sk} + (\beta_{1k} - \beta_{2k}) g_{y_k} & s = 1, \ldots, S; k = 1, \ldots, K \ (i) \\ \sum_{h=1}^{K} z_{hk} p_{mh} = p_{mk} - (\tau_{1k} - \tau_{2k}) g_{p_k} & m = 1, \ldots, M; k = 1, \ldots, K \ (ii) \\ \sum_{h=1}^{K} z_{hk} x_{nh} \leq x_{nk} - (\alpha_{1k} - \alpha_{2k}) g_{x_k} & n = 1, \ldots, N; k = 1, \ldots, K \ (iii) \\ \sum_{h=1}^{K} g_{p_h} (\tau_{1k} - \tau_{2k}) = (1 - \omega) \cdot \sum_{h=1}^{K} p_{mh} & m = 1, \ldots, M m = 1, \ldots, M \\ z_{hk}, \beta_{1k}, \beta_{2k}, \tau_{1k}, \tau_{2k}, \alpha_{1k}, \alpha_{2k} \geq 0 & k = 1, \ldots, K \end{cases}$$

(21.21)

where $(\beta_{1k} - \beta_{2k})$, $(\tau_{1k} - \tau_{2k})$ and $(\alpha_{1k} - \alpha_{2k})$[3] denote the change in expected outputs, non-expected outputs, and inputs after PM emission reallocation. $\omega$ (between zero to one) stands for the coefficient controlled by the government of actual PM emission ($\sum_{h=1}^{K} p_{mh}$). The direction vector follows $g = (g_{x_k} = \psi_{nk}, g_{y_k} = \mu_{sk}, g_{p_k} = \zeta_{mk} | \sum_{n}^{N} \psi_{nk} + \sum_{s}^{S} \mu_{sk} + \sum_{m}^{M} \zeta_{mk} = 1, \psi_{nk} \geq 0, \mu_{sk} \geq 0, \zeta_{mk} \geq 0)$, whichis decided by the port.

Figure 21.2 provides a simple graphic illustration of Eq. (21.21). Suppose there are three different ports (Points $A$, $B$, $C$) lying inside the production frontier. To achieve a maximum sum of standard container throughput, the three points increase the technical efficiency firstly to point to $R$, $F$ and $T$. Then an alliance is formed between the three portsto permit reallocation of PM emission. Points $R$, $F$ and $T$ move to the allocation efficiency Point $F$. The distance $CF$, $BF$ and $AF$ represent potential increasable expected output after PM emission reallocation along the direction vector.

[3]In the reallocation process, Eq. (21.21) allows DMUs to decrease or increase the expected outputs, non-expected outputs or inputs to reach the maximum sum of expected outputs of the alliance that means the coefficient may be negative or positive. Equation (21.21) can be easily changed to the northwestern model by defining $(\beta_{1k} - \beta_{2k}) \geq 0$, $(\tau_{1k} - \tau_{2k}) \geq 0$, and $(\alpha_{1k} - \alpha_{2k}) \geq 0$.

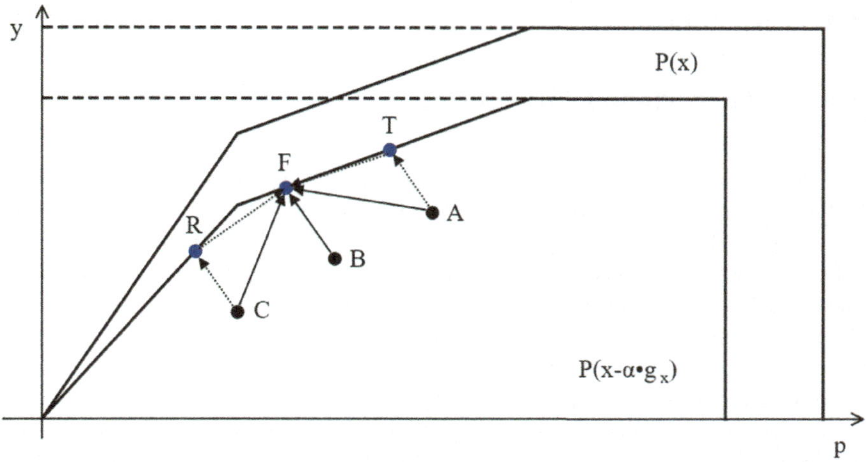


**Fig. 21.2** The comprehensive reallocation model

So, the total maximum expansion of the expected output of the alliance is calculated by Model (21). If the government requires a stricter PM emission target for the port industry, the alliance has to meet the requirement by finding a new optimal solution that minimizes the total distance.[4]

Then, the potential output loss between cooperative strategy and uncooperative strategy can be measured by

$$\vec{\Delta y'} = \vec{\mathrm{CRM}}(\omega) - \vec{\mathrm{CEM}}(\omega) \tag{21.22}$$

where the left side is the comprehensive reallocation model and the right side is the comprehensive emission model. It can be used to evaluate the output loss associated with cooperative strategy and uncooperative strategy at different PM emission targets. Equation (21.22) takes a value equal to or greater than zero at the condition of the same ports' preferences. If the result is equal to zero, it means that there is no room for improvement with a cooperative strategy. If the value is greater than zero, it is beneficial for ports to ally to seek a maximum sum of expected outputs.

In the next section, the data of 11 Chinese main ports are applied to these models to evaluate the efficiencies and assess the effects of different strategies.

[4]With issuing the stricter emission regulation, the value of the Eq. (21.21) will change from positive to negative.

## 21.4 Case Study

### 21.4.1 Description of Case Ports

There are about 20[5] major ports with container-handling capacity surpassing two-million twenty-feet equivalent unit (Teu) in China, which are located in the Bohai Bay, Yangtze River Delta, and Pearl River Delta. Eleven[6] of them are selected to evaluate the efficiency based on the improved DEA models because they are classified as above designated size ports and account for about 70–85%[7] of standard container throughput among all Chinese ports from 2012 to 2016. Figure 21.3 shows the geographical location of these 11 ports.

Considering possible cooperative strategies between different ports to maximize the sum of standard container throughput, the 11 ports are divided into 4 areas for simulation. The 4 areas are shown in detail in Table 21.1. The grouping is mainly based on geographical proximity and cooperation which has already been formed between ports in reality. For example, Tianjin port and Dalian port have signed a framework agreement on strategic in 2013.

### 21.4.2 Data Collection

Data for the 11 Chinese ports from 2012 to 2016 are collected to measure single expected output (standard container throughput) and single non-expected output (PM emission[8]). The inputs consist of labor, terminal length, berth quantity, and total assets. Table 21.2 lists the summary statistics of the 11 Chinese ports data.

The data of PM emission is estimated in this paper. The amount of PM emission in a port is split into two parts (vessel operation and terminal operation) to consider all the factors and calculated by

$$PM_{total} = PM_{vessel} + PM_{terminal} \tag{21.23}$$

For the vessel part, to reflect the influence of vessel operation and total transport distance on PM emission in a port, we will not calculate it based on a short distance (after vessel entering port[9]); Instead, we use water freight turnover volume to measure it. Then, it is formulated by:

5 The number is collected from CPY 2012–2016.

6 Eleven ports are listed companies in the Shanghai Stock Exchange that the data is easily obtainable.

7 The figure is calculated from CPY 2012–2016.

8 In this study, we mainly focus on PM emission and disregard other pollution such as $NO_X$ and $CO_2$.

9 Chang and Park (2016) evaluated $CO_2$ emission after vessel entering port from a specific location (harbor limit) to a quay wall.

**Fig. 21.3** Geographical locations of 11 Chinese ports

**Table 21.1** Eleven Chinese ports in four areas

| Area | Ports |
|---|---|
| 1 | Shanghai, Ningbo, Nanjing |
| 2 | Qingdao, Rizhao, Lianyungang |
| 3 | Tianjin, Dalian |
| 4 | Zhuhai, Guangzhou, Shenzhen |

**Table 21.2** Summary statistics (11 Chinese ports, 2012–2016)

| | Variable | Unit | Mean | Minimum | Maximum | Standard deviation |
|---|---|---|---|---|---|---|
| Input | Labor | Workers | 6147.1 | 529.0 | 20,748.0 | 5389.0 |
| | Terminal length | Meter | 36,844.7 | 11,236.0 | 86,089.0 | 21,851.9 |
| | Berth quantity | Pcs | 258.9 | 50.0 | 624.0 | 203.4 |
| | Total assets | RMB (in hundred millions) | 261.5 | 10.5 | 1167.9 | 264.6 |
| Expected output | Standard container throughput | 10,000 Teu | 1317.7 | 81.3 | 3713.0 | 1004.8 |
| Non-expected output | PM emission | Ton | 6700.8 | 339.7 | 28,771.3 | 7663.4 |

$$\mathrm{PM_{vessel}} = \mathrm{WFT{*}EF_i{*}H \div K_i} \tag{21.24}$$

where $WFT$ denotes water freight turnover volume,$EF_i$ the emission factor of specific fuel $i$,$H$ the transportation consumption of standard coal per kiloton • n mile by ocean carrier, and $K_i$ the standard coal coefficient of type $i$.To approximately evaluate vessel activities in transportation,$EF_i$ is chosen of large-sized ships based on PM emission of 2.7% Sulphur content HFO fuel with slow speed diesel from *Third IMO GHG Study 2014-Final Report.*

Freight throughput is selected to evaluate the PM emission for the terminal part considering that loading and discharging is the main activity of the port. Then the $PM_{terminal}$ can be calculated in a similar way by

$$\mathrm{PM_{terminal}} = \mathrm{FT} * \mathrm{EF}_i^{'} * \mathrm{H'} \div \mathrm{K}_i^{'} \tag{21.25}$$

where $FT$ represents the freight throughput, and $H^{'}$ stands for the port consumption of standard coal per million tons. Energy consumption of $PM_{terminal}$ is converted to general coal consumption ($K_i^{'}$) supposing thatthe primary machines (cranes)are driven by electricity with thermal power. Since there is no standard PM emission factor of coal, it is collected from Shen et al. (2015) under laboratory conditions.

All data sources for both inputs and outputs are listed in Appendix A2 (Table A2).

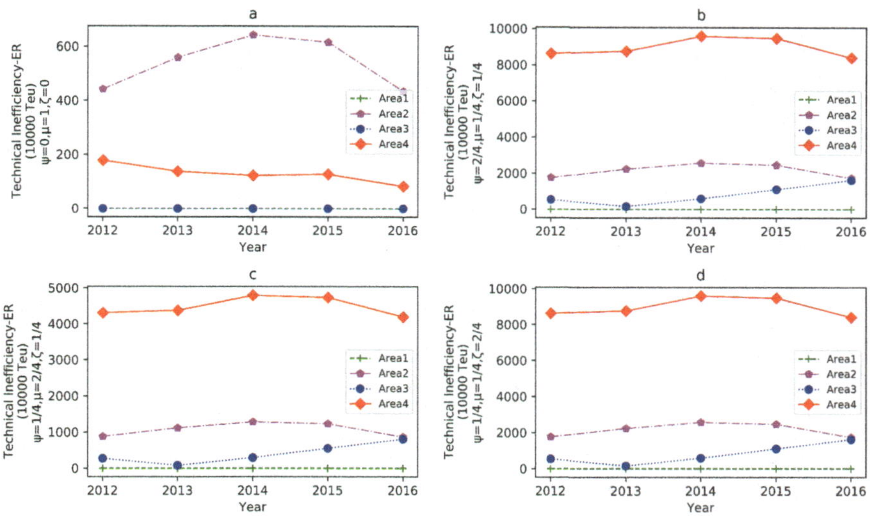


**Fig. 21.4** Technical inefficiency under ER (2012–2016)

### *21.4.3 Results and Discussions*

In this section, the environmental efficiency of port is first calculated under ER and NER with different kinds of preferences decided by the ports. Then, the efficiency is reassessed at different pollution regulation targets in the reallocation model. Finally, we can compare the output loss between PM reallocation and non-reallocation at the same PM emission target. With these results, the efficiency of different areas is shown to provide some helpful suggestions to ports and the government.

Figure 21.4 shows the results for Eq. (21.18) when $\delta = 0$.The maximum potential increasable standard container throughput iscalculated by the comprehensive production model of four kinds of preferences underER for four areas from 2012 to 2016. The preference co-efficient $\psi$ equally divides into the inputs index to make calculation easier.[10] As can be seen clearly, Fig. 21.4 (a) shows that Area 1 and Area 3 have zero standard container throughput to increase between 2012 to 2016 if they make the decisions as ($\psi = 0, \mu = 1, \zeta = 0$),which means they have higher technical efficiency. It is a slow downward trend from 2012 to 2016 for Area 4 that reflects it becomes more and more efficient. The most inefficient area is Area 2. If areas allow change of input index, expected output and non-expected output index to develop into technical efficiency, Fig. 21.4b–d depicts that all areas have more potential increasable expected output to grow. The potential increase mainly follows the direction vector of expected output. For example, the growth of expected output with the same weight ($\mu = \frac{1}{4}$) in Fig. 21.4b, d is two times than that in figure. (c) ($\mu = \frac{2}{4}$). However, it is noted that all areas follow the same trend regardless of

[10]This approach is used in this study.

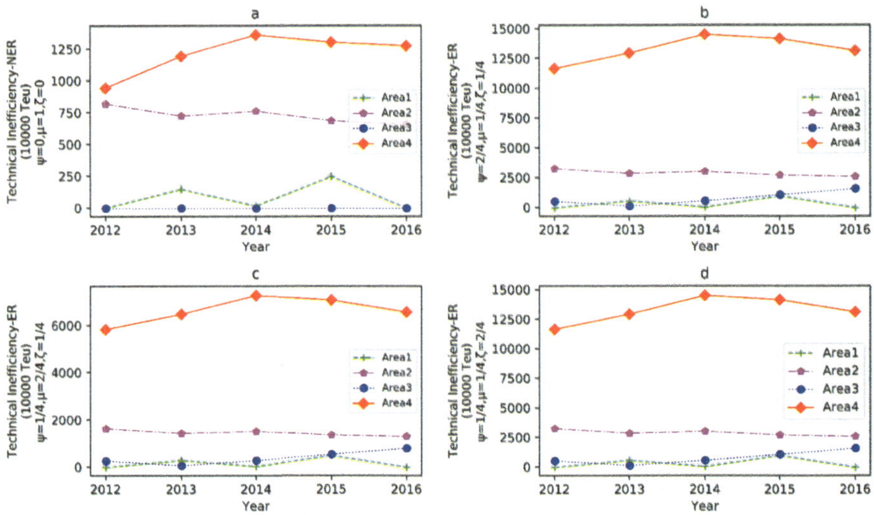


**Fig. 21.5** Technical inefficiency under NER (2012–2016)

the preferences chosen by the ports. In this case, only Area 1 has higher technical efficiency all the time and Area 4 becomes the most inefficient area.

Figure 21.5 describes the results for Eq. (21.18) when $\delta = 1$. Themaximum potential increasable standard container throughput is measured by the comprehensive production model of four kinds of preferences under NER for the four areas from 2012 to 2016. Figure 21.5 shows that no matter what preferences areas are chosen, in order to obtain technical efficiency, Area 4 has the most potential expected output to increase, which means it has the most technical inefficiency, while Area 2 comes in second. Area 1 still performs well under NER and its technical efficiency remains unchanged in most years. It is obtained similar conclusions from Fig. 21.5: Few growths of areas are expected in the vertical direction ($\psi = 0, \mu = 1, \zeta = 0$).Except for vertical direction, all areas still follow the same trend regardless of preferences chosen by the ports.

Figure 21.6 reveals the output loss between ER and NER of the four kinds of preferences (Eq. 21.19). We can clearly see that it has a dramatic increase in an output loss of Area 4 before 2014 and then stays high until 2016, implying that Area 4 bears a huge loss under ER than others in any directions. One potential reason is that the port resources have not been fully developed in Area 4 resulting in technical inefficiency. In particular, Area 3 has zero output loss from 2012 to 2016, which represents that it keeps the same technical inefficiency under ER and NER in any directions. Importantly, Fig. 21.6 shows that all areas have the same output loss trend no matter what preference areas chosen to respond to ER.

Figure 21.7 shows the results of Eq. (21.20) about the potential increasable standard container throughput for each area at different PM emission targets (ω from 1 to 0.3) of the four kinds of preferences. Figure 21.7 (a, e, i, m) represent that areas

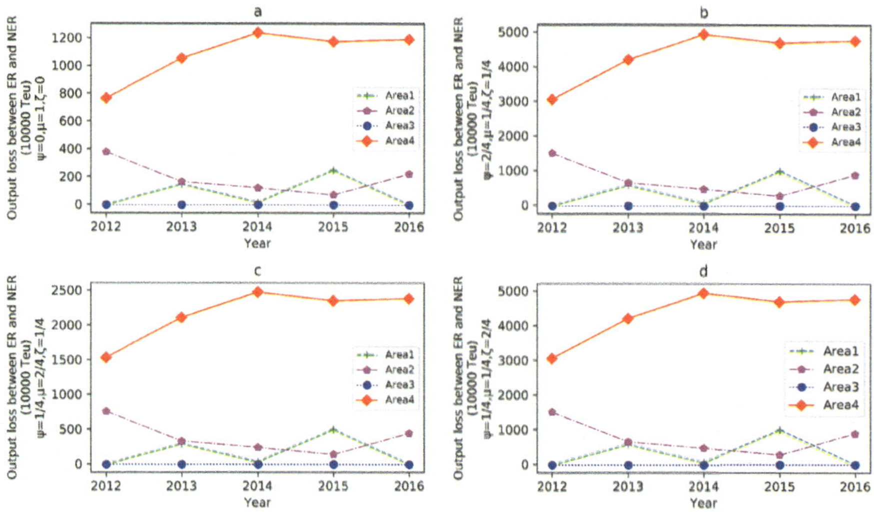


**Fig. 21.6** Output loss between ER and NER (2012–2016)

choose the vertical direction to respond to the government's ER. The rest of the pictures in Fig. 21.7 depicts that areas choose other directions to promote expected output under different PM emission targets. It can be obtained the following results from Fig. 21.7. First, even if stringent emission standard is in effect, almost areas still have potential increasable expected output as long as they are willing not to choose a vertical direction. Second, if the government raises the standards to promote emission reductions, all areas must abate activities to meet the pollution regulation. Third, Area 1 has zero increasable expected output from 2012 to 2016 with an initial emission target ($\omega = 1$) in any direction, and hence it has the highest technical efficiency again. Last, all areas have the same trend to decrease the expected output with the stricter ER except for the vertical direction.

Figure 21.8 shows the results of Eq. (21.21) about the potential increasable standard container throughput after PM reallocation of the four kinds of preferences at different PM emission targets (ω from 1 to 0.3), compared with the actual expected output. Figure 21.8 (a, e, i, m) represent that are as choose the vertical direction in the PM reallocation model. They have the same shape as Fig. 21.7a, e, i, m due to no change of PM emissions to each area. In other directions, it can be easily observed that all areas have huge potential increasable expected output after PM reallocation in most years. With raising the emission limit by the government, areas have the same trend to reduce the expected output in their preferred directions and value is from positive to negative. Comparing the two kinds of preference ($\psi = \frac{2}{4}, \mu = \frac{1}{4}, \zeta = \frac{1}{4}$) and ($\psi = \frac{1}{4}, \mu = \frac{2}{4}, \zeta = \frac{1}{4}$), all areas can efficiently reduce the amount of potential increasable expected output in a reallocation of PM emission with more weight given to $\mu$. However, input costs and a penalty for pollution should be taken into account in this decision.

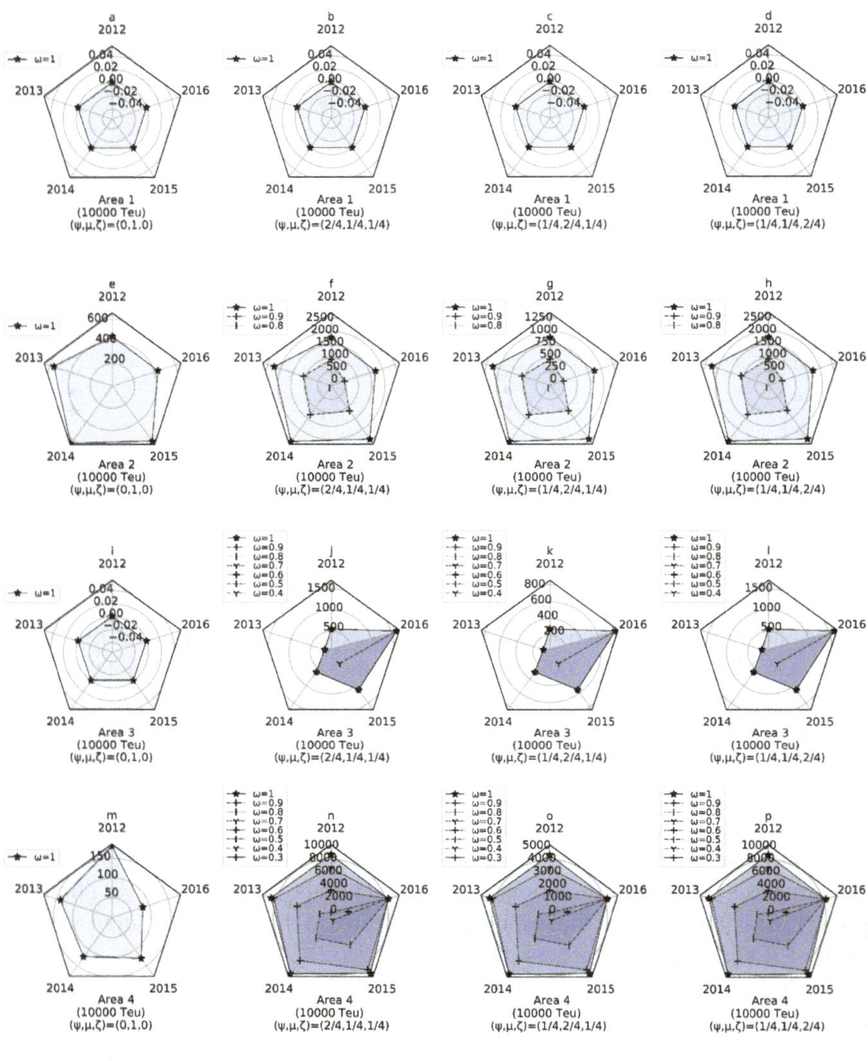


**Fig. 21.7** Potential increasable output at different PM emission targets for areas 1–4 (2012–2016)

Figure 21.9 shows the results of Eq. (21.22) about the output loss between cooperative strategy and uncooperative strategy for four areas. In the vertical direction (Fig. 21.9a, e, i, m), all areas have zero output loss because the value is the same between cooperative strategy and non-cooperative strategy. In other directions, output loss is foreseeable to increase in Area 1, Area 3 and Area 4 in most years. A possible explanation is that some members may become more and more inefficient and hence result in the false improvement with cooperation. For Area 2, the cooperation strategy is only valid in 2012. Therefore, efficient ports in Area 2 may consider dropping out of the alliance to seek new partners or the alliance kicks out the relatively inefficient

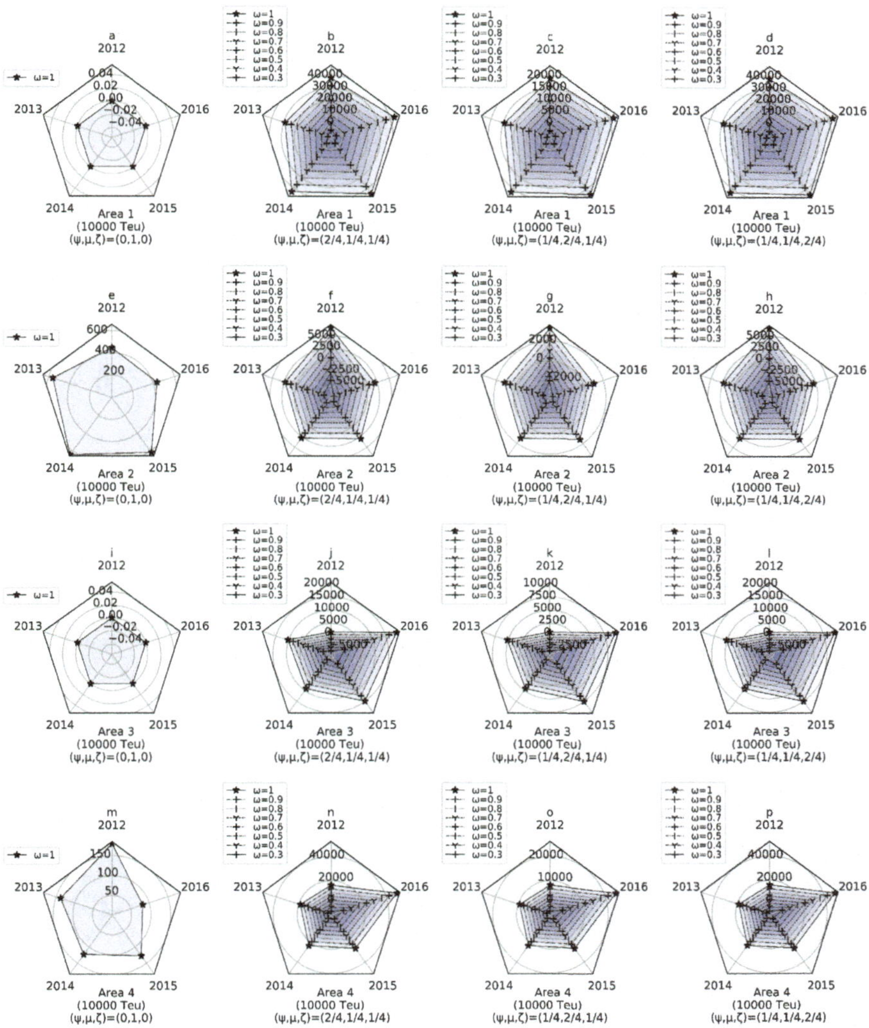


**Fig. 21.8** Potential increasable output after PM reallocation at different PM emission targets for areas 1–4 (2012–2016)

members to optimize the sum of the standard container throughput. Figure 21.9 also shows that cooperative strategy will lose ground to its uncooperative strategy (the value of output loss will gradually reduce to zero) when reducing the PM emission required by the government.

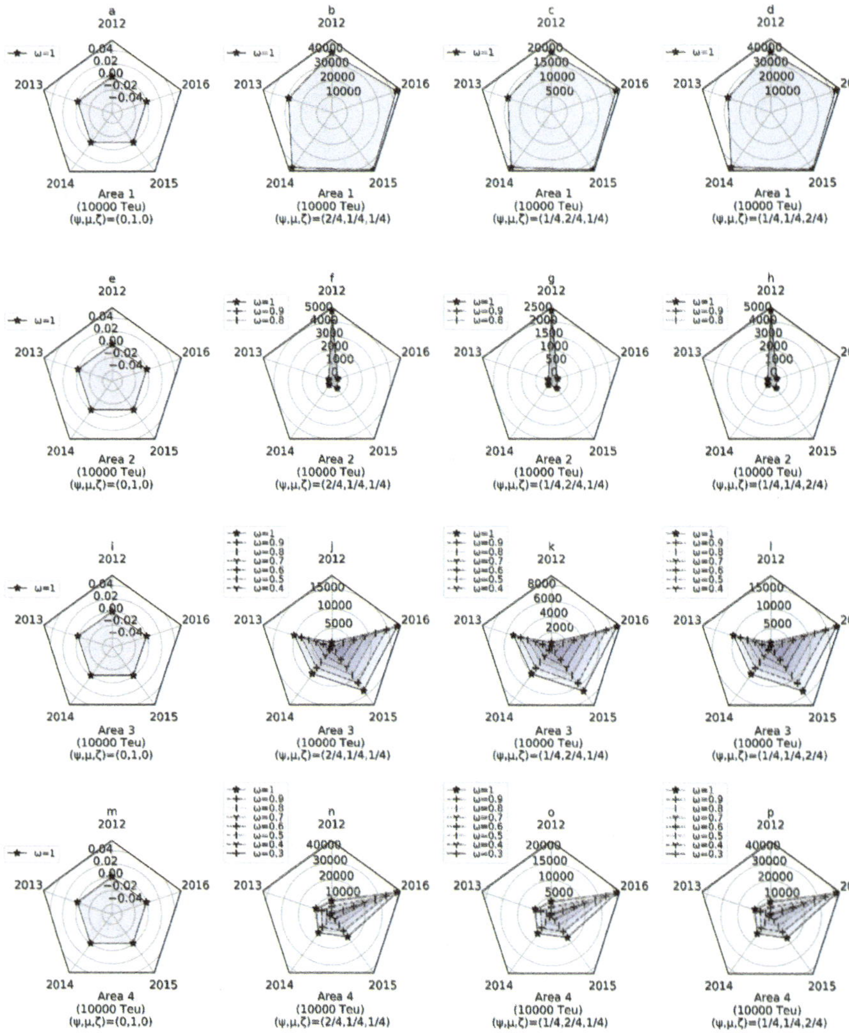


**Fig. 21.9** The output loss between cooperation and non-cooperation strategies for areas 1–4 (2012–2016)

## 21.5 Conclusion

In this study, to contribute some suggestions to the ports and government, a comprehensive production model, a comprehensive emission model, and a comprehensive reallocation model are developed to evaluate the environmental efficiency of 11 Chinese main ports. First, setting environmental control parameters in models to shift them between ER and NER easily. Second, non-equal proportional change of input index, expected output and non-expected output index is allowed in the improved models. Third, the preference co-efficient is set for ports to choose favorable decisions. Last, many earlier studies investigate and measure other emissions like $NO_x$ or $CO_2$ but we mainly focus on PM emission (calculated by water freight turnover volume and freight throughput), a top concern in China nowadays.

All models are applied to the 11 Chinese ports, and these ports are divided into four areas by using the port data from 2012 to 2016. Based on the findings, it is suggested: First, eastern ports in China (Area 1) generally have higher technical efficiency due to efficient production with relatively few input resources. To increase efficiency, the ocean carrier and port should perform their best to reduce transportation and port consumption of specific energy. For example, using cleaner vessels and improving port management is a way to approach the target.

Second, the port alliance can effectively increase the sum of expected output under ER. However, there usually exists a competition between the ports of the closest cities. The cities always make policies to attract more vessels to develop local GDP and reduce competitors' cargo volume. Although the competition mechanism will bring benefits to the port, its drawback is obvious. The port may abate some activities or increase more costs in pollution governance to keep current expected output with a tighter environmental policy issued by the government. If administrators can set up an effective mechanism to trigger spontaneous cooperation for ports, compared with uncooperative strategy, the alliance will possibly increase the total expected output under current pollution regulation or reduce the loss once the government makes a stricter emission policy. Although some members in the alliance will see reductions of expected output after cooperation, the whole alliance can be more resilient to deal with the foreseeable stricter environmental regulation.

Third, the ports cannot accept an overly restrictive pollution emission target no matter whether they ally or not. This is because, if the allowable discharge amount of the pollution emission is below a certain value, a port can only produce limited or even zero expected output. Thus, the local government or central government needs to balance the profit and damage caused by environmental pollution in the process of economic production to make a reasonable emission strategy. In this strategy, the current situation in China such as port facilities, vessel conditions, and international standards should be taken into account. In the opposite side, to some extent, inefficiency ports and old vessels are forced to be transformed by the strict standard.

Fourth, the ports have multiple decisions to deal with the ER. However, it will cause different results when ports assign different weights to input index, expected output index and non-expected output index. If the penalty for pollution emission is not high enough, ports usually assign more weights to the expected output index to ignore the penalty without decreasing the expected output. Therefore, the government needs to evaluate the validity of the environment policy to restrain ports' preferences.

Last but not least, the government may consider issuing some economic incentive policies to encourage ocean carriers and port enterprises to stimulate the use of high technologies in a greener way, thus reducing pollution emissions. Water transportation is the main mode of carrying goods for those ports and has a significant impact on the environment. Thus, it is necessary for the government to issue flexible policies to manage both vessels and ports. For example, cleaner energy, efficient waste gas treatment system, or other new technologies could be applied to those vessels and ports through government incentives. In other words, economic incentive policies, to a certain extent, can prevent environmental deterioration or even improve it.

There are still some limitations to this paper. First, it does not provide a method to determine the weight for preference co-efficient of ports exogenously. Further research is needed to assess multi-influenced factors such as the penalty for pollution emission and input costs. Second, the top-down method for calculating PM emissions is not very accurate. The bottom-up approach is recommended to achieve precise values. However, the bottom-up method is not addressed in this paper because our study covers 11 Chinese ports and most data like vessels' or cranes' power may not be obtained. Third, more valuable inputs may be included in the models for simulation if they can be readily available in the future. Finally, it is interesting to have a more in-depth discussion on the reallocation of emission permits by applying game theory to reveal the dilemma of ports' cooperative and uncooperative strategy.

**Acknowledgements** Zhijie Wang, Guo Wei, Thomas A. Dooling also made great contributions to this manuscript. We express our heartfelt thanks to them. This research was supported by: National Social and Scientific Fund Program of China (18ZDA052; 17BGL142; 16ZDA047); The Natural Science Foundation of China (91546117, 71373131).

# Appendix

## A1 Abbreviation

Abbreviations in this paper

| Full name | |
|---|---|
| China Ports Yearbook | CPY |
| Data envelopment analysis | DEA |
| Decision-making units | DMUs |
| Directional output distance function | DODF |
| Emission Control Areas | ECAs |
| Environmental regulation | ER |
| International Maritime Organization | IMO |
| Non-environmental regulation | NER |
| Particulate Matter | PM |
| Transportation systems | TS |
| Twenty-feet equivalent unit | Teu |

# Data Sources

Data sources for inputs and outputs

| Sources | Year | Data |
|---|---|---|
| Annual Report | 2012–2016 | Labor |
| | | Total assets |
| The National Bureau of Statistics of the People's Republic of China | 2012–2016 | Terminal length<br>Berth quantity |
| China Marine Statistical Yearbook<br>China Ports Yearbook | 2012–2016 | Standard container throughput |
| Statistical Communique of The People's Republic of China On the National Economic and Social Development | 2012–2016 | Water freight turnover volume |
| The National Bureau of Statistics of the People's Republic of China | | |
| China Ports Yearbook | 2012–2016 | Freight throughput |
| Third IMO GHG Study 2014-Final Report | 2014 | $EF_i$(Emission factor of fuel oil i)[a] |
| Shen et al. (2015) | 2015 | $EF_i^{'}$(Emission factor of general coal i)[b] |
| Statistics on the Development of Transportation Industry | 2012–2016 | $H$(transportation consumption of standard coal) |
| | | $H^{'}$(port consumption of standard coal) |
| China Energy Statistical Yearbook | 2012–2016 | $K_i$(The standard coal coefficient of fuel oil i) |
| | | $K_i^{'}$(The standard coal coefficient of general coal i)[c] |

[a]$Ef_i$ is chosen of large-sized ships based on PM emission of 2.7% Sulphur content HFO fuel with slow speed diesel from Third IMO GHG Study 2014-Final Report

[b]Since there is no standard PM emission factor of coal, it is collected from SHEN et al. (2015) under laboratory conditions.

[c]Energy consumption of $PM_{terminal}$ is converted to general coal consumption ($K_i^{'}$) supposing that the primary machines (cranes) are driven by electricity with thermal power.

# References

Balasubramaniam, A., Paul, A., Hong, W. H., Seo, H. C., & Kim, J. H. (2017). Comparative analysis of intelligent transportation systems for sustainable environment in Smart Cities. *Sustain.*, *9*, 1–12. https://doi.org/10.3390/su9071120.

Baran, J., & Górecka, A. K. (2019). Economic and environmental aspects of inland transport in EU countries. *Economic Research-Ekonomska Istrazivanja, 32,* 1037–1059. https://doi.org/10.1080/1331677X.2019.1578680.

Barros, C. P., & Peypoch, N. (2009). An evaluation of European airlines' operational performance. *International Journal of Production Economics, 122,* 525–533. https://doi.org/10.1016/j.ijpe.2009.04.016.

Bernardo, V. (2012). The transportation value stream map (TVSM) Bernardo Villarreal. *European Journal of Industrial Engineering, 6,* 216–233.

Bi, G., Wang, P., Yang, F., & Liang, L. (2014). Energy and environmental efficiency of china's transportation sector: A multidirectional analysis approach. *Mathematical Problems in Engineering.* https://doi.org/10.1155/2014/539596.

Bligh, D. C., & Ugursal, V. I. (2013). Exergy efficiency factors for transportation: Updated Reistad estimates. *International Journal of Exergy, 12,* 273–277. https://doi.org/10.1504/IJEX.2013.053390.

Bostian, M., Färe, R., Grosskopf, S., Lundgren, T., Weber, W. L. (2018). Time substitution for environmental performance: The case of Swedish manufacturing. *Empirical Economics, 54l,* 129–152. https://doi.org/10.1007/s00181-016-1180-7.

Chang, Y. T., Park, H., Jeong, J., & Lee, J. (2014). Evaluating economic and environmental efficiency of global airlines: A SBM-DEA approach. *Transportation Research Part D: Transport and Environment, 27,* 46–50. https://doi.org/10.1016/j.trd.2013.12.013.

Chang, Y. T., & Park, H. (2016). Measuring foregone output under industry emission reduction target in the transportation sector. *Transportation Research Part D: Transport and Environment, 49,* 138–153. https://doi.org/10.1016/j.trd.2016.08.017.

Chang, Y. T., Park, H. (Kevin), Lee, S., Kim, E. (2018). Have Emission Control Areas (ECAs) harmed port efficiency in Europe? *Transportation Research Part D: Transport and Environment, 58,* 39–53. https://doi.org/10.1016/j.trd.2017.10.018.

Chang, Y. T., Zhang, N., Danao, D., Zhang, N. (2013). Environmental efficiency analysis of transportation system in China: A non-radial DEA approach. *Energy Policy, 58,* 277–283. https://doi.org/10.1016/j.enpol.2013.03.011.

Charnes, A., Cooper, W. W., & Rhodes, E. (1978). Measuring the efficiency of decision making units. *European Journal of Operational Research, 2,* 429–444. https://doi.org/10.1016/0377-2217(78)90138-8.

Chen, C. M. (2013). A critique of non-parametric efficiency analysis in energy economics studies. *Energy Economics, 38,* 146–152. https://doi.org/10.1016/j.eneco.2013.03.009.

Chen, W., & Lei, Y. (2017). Path analysis of factors in energy-related $CO_2$ emissions from Beijing's transportation sector. *Transportation Research Part D: Transport and Environment, 50,* 473–487. https://doi.org/10.1016/j.trd.2016.11.027.

Chen, X., Gao, Y., An, Q., Wang, Z., & Neralić, L. (2018). Energy efficiency measurement of Chinese Yangtze River Delta's cities transportation: A DEA window analysis approach. *Energy Efficiency, 11,* 1941–1953. https://doi.org/10.1007/s12053-018-9635-7.

Corlu, C. G., De La Torre, R., Serrano-Hernandez, A., Juan, A. A., Faulin, J. (2020). Optimizing energy consumption in transportation: Literature review, insights, and research opportunities. *Energies,* 13. https://doi.org/10.3390/en13051115.

Cui, Q., & Li, Y. (2014). The evaluation of transportation energy efficiency: An application of three-stage virtual frontier DEA. *Transportation Research Part D: Transport and Environment, 29,* 1–11. https://doi.org/10.1016/j.trd.2014.03.007.

Cui, Q., Li, Y., & Lin, J. L. (2018). Pollution abatement costs change decomposition for airlines: An analysis from a dynamic perspective. *Transportation Research Part A: Policy and Practice, 111,* 96–107. https://doi.org/10.1016/j.tra.2018.03.014.

Cullinane, K., & Bergqvist, R. (2014). Emission control areas and their impact on maritime transport. *Transportation Research Part D: Transport and Environment, 28,* 1–5. https://doi.org/10.1016/j.trd.2013.12.004.

Dadpour, S., Pakzad, J., & Khankeh, H. (2016). Understanding the influence of environment on adults' walking experiences: A meta-synthesis study. *International Journal of Environmental Research and Public Health,* 13. https://doi.org/10.3390/ijerph13070731.

Dai, R., Lu, Y., Ding, C., & Lu, G. (2017). The Effect of connected vehicle environment on global travel efficiency and its optimal penetration rate. *Journal of Advanced Transportation.* https://doi.org/10.1155/2017/2697678.

Davarzani, H., Fahimnia, B., Bell, M., & Sarkis, J. (2016). Greening ports and maritime logistics: A review. *Transportation Research Part D: Transport and Environment, 48,* 473–487. https://doi.org/10.1016/j.trd.2015.07.007.

Dewulf, W., Duflou, J., & Ander, A. (2004). Toward a sector wide design for environment support system for the rail industry. *Environmental Management, 34,* 181–190. https://doi.org/10.1007/s00267-004-2921-5.

Djordjevi, B., & Krmac, E. (2019). Evaluation of energy-environment efficiency of european transport sectors: non-radial DEA and TOPSIS approach. *Energies.*

Egilmez, G., & Park, Y. S. (2014). Transportation related carbon, energy and water footprint analysis of U.S. manufacturing: An eco-efficiency assessment. *Transportation Research Part D: Transport and Environment, 32,* 143–159. https://doi.org/10.1016/j.trd.2014.07.001.

Färe, R., Grosskopf, S., Margaritis, D., & Weber, W. L. (2012). Technological change and timing reductions in greenhouse gas emissions. *Journal of Productivity Analysis, 37,* 205–216. https://doi.org/10.1007/s11123-011-0232-4.

Färe, R., Grosskopf, S., Whittaker G. X. (2012b) Directional output distance functions: Endogenous directions based on exogenous normalization constraints. *Journal of Productivity Analysis, 40,* 267–269. https://doi.org/10.1007/s11123-012-0333-8.

Färe, R., Grosskopf, S., & Whittaker, G. (2013). Directional output distance functions: endogenous directions based on exogenous normalization constraints. *Journal of Productivity Analysis, 40,* 267–269. https://doi.org/10.1007/s11123-012-0333-8.

Färe, R., Grosskopf, S., & Pasurka, C. A. (2007a). Pollution abatement activities and traditional productivity. *Ecological Economics, 62,* 673–682. https://doi.org/10.1016/j.ecolecon.2006.08.014.

Färe, R., Grosskopf, S., & Pasurka, C. A. (2007b). Environmental production functions and environmental directional distance functions. *Energy, 32,* 1055–1066. https://doi.org/10.1016/j.energy.2006.09.005.

Gobbi, G. P., Liberto, L. Di, Barnaba, F. (2019). Impact of port emissions on EU-regulated and non-regulated air quality indicators: The case of Civitavecchia (Italy). Science of the Total Environment, 134984. https://doi.org/10.1016/j.scitotenv.2019.134984.

Guo, X., Zhu, Q., Lv, L., Chu, J., & Wu, J. (2017). Efficiency evaluation of regional energy saving and emission reduction in China: A modified slacks-based measure approach. *Journal of Cleaner Production, 140,* 1313–1321. https://doi.org/10.1016/j.jclepro.2016.10.021.

Haralambides, H., & Gujar, G. (2012). On balancing supply chain efficiency and environmental impacts: An eco-DEA model applied to the dry port sector of India. *Maritime Economics & Logistics, 14,* 122–137. https://doi.org/10.1057/mel.2011.19.

He, Q., Han, J., Guan, D., Mi, Z., Zhao, H., & Zhang, Q. (2018). The comprehensive environmental efficiency of socioeconomic sectors in China: An analysis based on a non-separable bad output SBM. *Journal of Cleaner Production, 176,* 1091–1110. https://doi.org/10.1016/j.jclepro.2017.11.220.

Holden, R., Xu, B., Greening, P., Piecyk, M., & Dadhich, P. (2016). Towards a common measure of greenhouse gas related logistics activity using data envelopment analysis. *Transportation Research Part A: Policy and Practice, 91,* 105–119. https://doi.org/10.1016/j.tra.2016.06.001.

Hu, J. L., Lio, M. C., Yeh, F. Y., & Lin, C. H. (2011). Environment-adjusted regional energy efficiency in Taiwan. *Applied Energy, 88,* 2893–2899. https://doi.org/10.1016/j.apenergy.2011.01.068.

Jeon, C. M., Asce, S. M., Amekudzi, A., & Asce, M. (2005). Addressing Sustainability in Transportation Systems: Definitions, Indicators, and Metrics. *Journal of Infrastructure Systems, 11,* 31–50.

Ji, X., Wu, J., & Zhu, Q. (2016). Eco-design of transportation in sustainable supply chain management: A DEA-like method. *Transportation Research Part D: Transport and Environment, 48,* 451–459. https://doi.org/10.1016/j.trd.2015.08.007.

Kelle, P., Song, J., Jin, M., Schneider, H., & Claypool, C. (2019). Evaluation of operational and environmental sustainability tradeoffs in multimodal freight transportation planning. *International Journal of Production Economics, 209,* 411–420. https://doi.org/10.1016/j.ijpe.2018.08.011.

Kiani Mavi, R., Fathi, A., Farzipoor Saen, R., Kiani Mavi, N. (2019). Eco-innovation in transportation industry: A double frontier common weights analysis with ideal point method for Malmquist productivity index. *Resources, Conservation and Recycling, 147,* 39–48. https://doi.org/10.1016/j.resconrec.2019.04.017.

Kim, H. G., Choi, C. Y., Woo, J. W., Choi, Y., Kim, K., & Wu, D. D. (2011). Efficiency of the modal shift and environmental policy on the Korean railroad. *Stochastic environmental research and risk assessment, 25,* 305–322. https://doi.org/10.1007/s00477-010-0369-0.

Lan, L. W., & Lin, E. T. J. (2005). Measuring railway performance with adjustment of environmental effects, data noise and slacks. *Transportmetrica, 1,* 161–189. https://doi.org/10.1080/18128600508685645.

Lee, T., Yeo, G. T., & Thai, V. V. (2014). Environmental efficiency analysis of port cities: Slacks-based measure data envelopment analysis approach. *Transport Policy, 33,* 82–88. https://doi.org/10.1016/j.tranpol.2014.02.009.

Li, T., Yang, W., Zhang, H., & Cao, X. (2016). Evaluating the impact of transport investment on the efficiency of regional integrated transport systems in China. *Transport Policy, 45,* 66–76. https://doi.org/10.1016/j.tranpol.2015.09.005.

Li, Z., & Zhang, Y. (2019). Hierarchical evaluation algorithm of logistics carrying capacity based on transfer learning in multimedia environment. *Multimedia Tools and Applications, 78,* 4481–4501. https://doi.org/10.1007/s11042-018-6000-y.

Liao, Y., Huang, P. H., Hsiang, C. Y., Huang, J. H., Hsueh, M. C., Park, J. H. (2017). Associations of older Taiwanese adults' personal attributes and perceptions of the neighborhood environment concerning walking for recreation and transportation. *International Journal of Environmental Research and Public Health,* 14. https://doi.org/10.3390/ijerph14121594.

Liu, Z., Qin, C. X., & Zhang, Y. J. (2016). The energy-environment efficiency of road and railway sectors in China: Evidence from the provincial level. *Ecological Indicators, 69,* 559–570. https://doi.org/10.1016/j.ecolind.2016.05.016.

Lozano, S., Villa, G., & Brännlund, R. (2009). Centralised reallocation of emission permits using DEA. *European Journal of Operational Research, 193,* 752–760. https://doi.org/10.1016/j.ejor.2007.07.029.

Ma, C., Li, Y., He, R., Wu, F., Qi, B., & Ye, Q. (2013). Route optimisation models and algorithms for hazardous materials transportation under different environments. *International Journal of Bio-Inspired Computing, 5,* 252–265. https://doi.org/10.1504/IJBIC.2013.055473.

Mat, N., Cerceau, J., Shi, L., Park, H. S., Junqua, G., & Lopez-Ferber, M. (2016). Socio-ecological transitions toward low-carbon port cities: Trends, changes and adaptation processes in Asia and Europe. *Journal of Cleaner Production, 114,* 362–375. https://doi.org/10.1016/j.jclepro.2015.04.058.

Oh, C., Choi, J., & Jung, S. (2016). Proactive vehicle emissions quantification from crash potential under stop-and-go traffic conditions. *Transport Policy, 49,* 86–92. https://doi.org/10.1016/j.tranpol.2016.04.008.

Omrani, H., Shafaat, K., Alizadeh, A., X. (2016). Integrated data envelopment analysis and cooperative game for evaluating energy efficiency of transportation sector: A case of Iran. *Annals of Operations Research, 274,* 471–499. https://doi.org/10.1007/s10479-018-2803-5.

Palander, T., Haavikko, H., Kortelainen, E., Kärhä, K., & Borz, S. A. (2020). Improving environmental and energy efficiency in wood transportation for a carbon-neutral forest industry. *Forests, 11,* 1–17. https://doi.org/10.3390/f11111194.

Pina, V., & Torres, L. (2001). Analysis of the efficiency of local government services delivery. An application to urban public transport. *Transportation Research Part A: Policy and Practice,* 35, 929–944. https://doi.org/10.1016/S0965-8564(00)00033-1.

Porter, A. K., Kohl, H. W., Pérez, A., Reininger, B., Pettee Gabriel, K., & Salvo, D. (2020). Bikeability: Assessing the objectively measured environment in relation to recreation and transportation bicycling. *Environment and Behavior, 52,* 861–894. https://doi.org/10.1177/0013916518825289.

Ramanathan, R. (2000). A holistic approach to compare energy efficiencies of different transport modes. *Energy Policy, 28,* 743–747. https://doi.org/10.1016/S0301-4215(00)00072-0.

Reistad, G. M. (1975). Available energy conversion and utilization in the United States. *ASME J of Engineering for Power, 97,* 429–434.

Scholz, J., & Schabus, S. (2017). Towards an affordance-based ad-hoc suitability network for indoor manufacturing transportation processes. *ISPRS International Journal of Geo-Informatio,* 6. https://doi.org/10.3390/ijgi6090280.

Shen, G., Tao, S., Wei, S., Chen, Y., Zhang, Y., Huang, Y., et al. (2015). *NIH Public Access, 2015*(47), 2998–3005. https://doi.org/10.1021/es304599g.Field.

Sim, S., Oh, J., & Jeong, B. (2015). Measuring greenhouse gas emissions for the transportation sector in Korea. *Annals of Operations Research, 230,* 129–151. https://doi.org/10.1007/s10479-013-1452-y.

Singh, A., Kumar, A., & Appadoo, S. S. (2017). Modified approach for optimization of real life transportation problem in neutrosophic environment. *Mathematical Problems in Engineering.* https://doi.org/10.1155/2017/2139791.

Song, M., Wu, N., & Wu, K. (2014). Energy consumption and energy efficiency of the transportation sector in Shanghai. *Sustain., 6,* 702–717. https://doi.org/10.3390/su6020702.

Sonmez, M., Akgüngör, A. P., & Bektaş, S. (2017). Estimating transportation energy demand in Turkey using the artificial bee colony algorithm. *Energy, 122,* 301–310. https://doi.org/10.1016/j.energy.2017.01.074.

Sun, L., Rong, J., & Yao, L. (2010). Measuring transfer efficiency of Urban Public. *Journal of Urban Planning and Development, 136,* 314–319.

Sun, J., Yuan, Y., Yang, R., Ji, X., & Wu, J. (2017). Performance evaluation of Chinese port enterprises under significant environmental concerns: An extended DEA-based analysis. *Transport Policy, 60,* 75–86. https://doi.org/10.1016/j.tranpol.2017.09.001.

Talla Konchou, F. A., AloyemKaze, C. V., & Tchinda, R. (2015). An application of energy and exergy analysis at the transportation sector of Cameroon. *International Journal of Exergy, 18,* 129–141. https://doi.org/10.1504/IJEX.2015.072163.

Tian, N., Tang, S., Che, A., & Wu, P. (2020). Measuring regional transport sustainability using super-efficiency SBM-DEA with weighting preference. *Journal of Cleaner Production, 242,* 118474. https://doi.org/10.1016/j.jclepro.2019.118474.

Tran, T. A. (2019). A study of the energy efficiency management for bulk carriers considering navigation environmental impacts. *Journal of Intelligent & Fuzzy Systems, 36,* 2871–2884. https://doi.org/10.3233/JIFS-171698.

Ülengin, F., Kabak, Ö., Önsel, Ş, Ülengin, B., & Aktaş, E. (2010). A problem-structuring model for analyzing transportation-environment relationships. *European Journal of Operational Research, 200,* 844–859. https://doi.org/10.1016/j.ejor.2009.01.023.

Wang, X., Liu, C., Kostyniuk, L., Shen, Q., & Bao, S. (2014). The influence of street environments on fuel efficiency: Insights from naturalistic driving. *International Journal of Environmental Science and Technology, 11,* 2291–2306. https://doi.org/10.1007/s13762-014-0584-1.

Wang, Y., Zhou, Y., Zhu, L., Zhang, F., & Zhang, Y. (2018). Influencing factors and decoupling elasticity of China's transportation carbon emissions. *Energies, 11,* 1–29. https://doi.org/10.3390/en11051157.

Wang, N., Zhu, Y., & Yang, T. (2020). The impact of transportation infrastructure and industrial agglomeration on energy efficiency: Evidence from China's industrial sectors. *Journal of Cleaner Production, 244,* 118708. https://doi.org/10.1016/j.jclepro.2019.118708.

Wu, J., Chu, J., An, Q., Sun, J., & Yin, P. (2016). Resource reallocation and target setting for improving environmental performance of DMUs: An application to regional highway transportation systems in China. *Transportation Research Part D: Transport and Environment, 61,* 204–216. https://doi.org/10.1016/j.trd.2016.09.002.

Wu, J., Zhu, Q., Chu, J., Liu, H., & Liang, L. (2016). Measuring energy and environmental efficiency of transportation systems in China based on a parallel DEA approach. *Transportation Research Part D: Transport and Environment, 48,* 460–472. https://doi.org/10.1016/j.trd.2015.08.001.

Wu, Y., Zhu, Q., Zhong, L., & Zhang, T. (2019). Energy consumption in the transportation sectors in China and the United States: A longitudinal comparative study. *Structural Change and Economic Dynamics, 51,* 349–360. https://doi.org/10.1016/j.strueco.2018.12.003.

Xiong, B., Chen, H., An, Q., & Wu, J. (2019). A multi-objective distance friction minimization model for performance assessment through data envelopment analysis. *European Journal of Operational Research, 279,* 132–142. https://doi.org/10.1016/j.ejor.2019.05.007.

Yang, W., Yuan, G., & Han, J. (2019). Is China's air pollution control policy effective? Evidence from Yangtze River Delta cities. *Journal of Cleaner Production, 220,* 110–133. https://doi.org/10.1016/j.jclepro.2019.01.287.

Yu, J., Voß, S., & Tang, G. (2019). Strategy development for retrofitting ships for implementing shore side electricity. *Transportation Research Part D: Transport and Environment, 74,* 201–213. https://doi.org/10.1016/j.trd.2019.08.004.

Zhang, M., Li, G., Mu, H. L., & Ning, Y. D. (2011). Energy and exergy efficiencies in the Chinese transportation sector, 1980–2009. *Energy, 36,* 770–776. https://doi.org/10.1016/j.energy.2010.12.044.

Zhang, Y., Yu, Y., & Ma, T. (2018). System optimization of long-distance energy transportation in China using ultra-high-voltage power transmission. *Journal of Renewable and Sustainable Energy, 10*. https://doi.org/10.1063/1.5013177.

Zhang, Y. J., Jiang, L., & Shi, W. (2020). Exploring the growth-adjusted energy-emission efficiency of transportation industry in China. *Energy Econ., 90,* 104873. https://doi.org/10.1016/j.eneco.2020.104873.

Zhou, G., Chung, W., & Zhang, X. (2013). A study of carbon dioxide emissions performance of China's transport sector. *Energy, 50,* 302–314. https://doi.org/10.1016/j.energy.2012.11.045.

Zhou, P., Sun, Z. R., & Zhou, D. Q. X. (2013b). Optimal path for controlling $CO_2$ emissions in China: A perspective of efficiency analysis. *Energy Economics, 45,* 99–110. https://doi.org/10.1016/j.eneco.2014.06.019.

# Chapter 22
# Study on Environment Performance Evaluation and Regional Differences of Strictly-Environmental-Monitored Cities in China

**Abstract** With the rapid economic growth and development, the problem of environmental pollution in China's cities is becoming increasingly serious, and environmental pollution takes on a regional difference. There is, however, little comprehensive evaluation on the environmental performance and the regional difference of strictly-environmental-monitored cities in China. In this paper, the environmental performance of 109 strictly-environmental-monitored cities in China is evaluated in terms of natural performance, management performance and scale performance by Data Envelopment Analysis (DEA), incorporating $PM_{2.5}$ and $PM_{10}$ as undesirable outputs. The empirical results show that: (1) At present, the natural performance is quite high, while the management performance is noticeably low for most cities. (2) The gap between the level of economic development and environmental protection among cities in China is large, and the scale efficiency of big cities is better than that of smaller cities. The efficiency value of large-scale cities such as Beijing, Shanghai, Guangzhou, Shenzhen etc. is high, equaling 1; the value of smaller cities such as Sanmenxia, Baoding, Mudanjiang, Pingdingshan is low, close to 0, indicating that big cities are characterized by high environmental efficiency. (3) From the perspective of region, the level of environmental performance in China is badly uneven. For example, the environmental efficiency level of the Pan-Pearl River Delta region is superior to that of the Pan-Yangtze River region and the Bahia Rim region, whose values of environmental efficiency are 0.858, 0.658 and 0.622 respectively. The average efficiency of the Southern Coastal Economic Zone, Eastern Coastal Comprehensive Economic Zone, and the Comprehensive Economic Zone in the middle reaches of the Yangtze River is higher than that of other regions. Finally, the corresponding countermeasures and suggestions are put forward. The method used in this paper is applicable to the performance evaluation of cities, and the results of the evaluation reflect the differences of the environmental performance level between strictly-environmental-monitored cities and different regions in China, providing reference for the balanced environmental development of cities and regions.

**Keywords** DEA · Environment Performance · Strictly-environmental-monitored cities · $PM_{2.5}$ · $PM_{10}$



X. Wu and J. Guo, *Economic Impacts and Emergency Management of Disasters in China*,
https://doi.org/10.1007/978-981-16-1319-7_22

## 22.1 Introduction

With rapid economic growth, the problem of air pollution is increasingly serious. $PM_{2.5}$ and $PM_{10}$, the embodiment of air pollution, have arisen widespread public attention from the community. The Environmental Performance Index: 2016 report[1]released by Yale University has ranked the air quality in more than 180 countries in the world, with China ranking last but one. Among the index, China's exposure to nitrogen dioxide averaged at 15.29 (falling into the bottom five in the world), the average exposure to $PM_{2.5}$ was 2.256 (last-placed worldwide) and the $PM_{2.5}$ exceedance was 0 (the second worst out of 180). In addition, according to data from WHO, nearly 2.4 million people die of air pollution every year in China, of which about 300,000 are dead because of outdoor air pollutants.[2]$PM_{2.5}$ consists mainly of black carbon, sulfates, nitrates ($NO^{3-}$), ammonium, K($K^+$), Mg, Ca, Na, Cr etc., of which black carbon and $K^+$ may increase the risk of contracting asthma (Jung et al. 2017). Moreover, Cr poses the highest risk of developing carcinogenic (Awni et al. 2017). Thus, it can be seen that the problem of air pollution in China is extremely serious, and therefore studies on the environment performance evaluation are considerably significant and urgent.

At present, there are 113 strictly-environmental-monitored cities in China, but only 23.9% of them meet the national air quality standards. The development of a country depends mainly on the cities that can lead the country's future. Evaluating the environmental performance of strictly-environmental-monitored cities in China and regional comparative analysis can provide empirical support for cities' sustainable development. However, there is rare research on the methods and indicators that can be adopted to evaluate the environmental performance of strictly-environmental-monitored cities in China. In this paper, an advanced DEA method is employed to assess the natural performance and management performances of 109 strictly-environmental-monitored cities in China. The T-test is conducted to compare the regional differences in the environmental performance of different Chinese cities. Finally, relative suggestions concerning the management of Chinese environmental pollution are put forward.

The remaining parts are as follows: the second part is related literature review; the third part is about the model, indicators and data description; the third part is about the empirical results; the last part is about the conclusions and suggestions.

[1]https://research.iae.ac.cn/web/ShowArticle.asp?ArticleID=5399.

[2]https://www.who.int/quantifying_ehimpacts/national/countryprofile/china.pdf?ua=1.

## 22.2 Related Work and Literature Review

In recent years, the application of DEA model to environmental performance evaluation has been the mainstream approach. A great many of scholars have taken DEA model to evaluate environmental performance. Based on the pollutants involved in studies, the existing literature can be divided into the following two parts.

The first kind of researches, regarding $CO_2$, $SO_2$, $NO_2$, waste gas, waste water, and waste as undesirable outputs, focus on the analysis of the influence of air pollutants on energy efficiency and environmental performance (Wu et al. 2017; Hu et al. 2015; Wu et al. 2016a, b, c). Wu and Wu (2009), Hua et al. (2013), Sun et al. (2014), Wang et al. (2015a, b, c), Zha et al. (2016), Bian et al. (2013) and others, with the help of DEA method, studied issues relevant to energy efficiency given that $CO_2$, $SO_2$, $NO_2$ and waste gas were all undesirable outputs. Using pollutants as undesirable outputs, Zhang et al. (2016) made research on the environment performance of 30 provincial capitals in China with the application of REES(regional environmental efficiency SBM) model; Zaim and Taskin (2001) studied the environment performance and regulatory standards of OECD (Organization for Economic Co-operation and Development) countries regarding $CO_2$ emission as undesirable outputs; Lee et al. (2014) evaluated the environment performance of port cities from OECD countries after selected the emission of $NO_X$, $SO_2$ and $CO_2$ as undesirable output indexes. Li et al. (2012) improved the ISBM-DEA (Improved slacks-based measure-Data Envelopment Analysis) model and based on this, they made empirical research on the environment performance from 30 regions in China in the year 2009. Yang et al. (2012) used the DEA-SBM (Slacks Based Measure) method to evaluate the environment performance of city agglomerations in the northeastern region with pollutant emission as undesirable output index; Li et al. (2015) used the SEDEA (super-efficiency Data Envelopment Analysis) model and data from 30 provinces during 2000–2010 to analyze the efficiency of China's environment policies. The result showed that there were remarked differences of environment performance in different regions: the environment performance in eastern regions was apparently better than that in the middle and western regions. Yin et al. (2019) used a three-stage DEA model to evaluate China's provinces' energy efficiency in 2015, considering the unexpected output constraints of $CO_2$, $SO_2$, $NO_x$, smoke dust, and COD (chemical oxygen demand). The results showed that low-scale efficiency was the major constraint of China's energy environment efficiency. Among China's provinces, Beijing, Jiangsu, Shandong, Hunan, and Guangdong had high energy efficiency. Their environmental policies could provide a reference for other regions. Zhou et al. (2019) proposed the DEA model with wastewater and waste gas as undesirable outputs, then conducted an empirical study on China's industrial sectors' energy performance from 2010 to 2014. They analyzed how to improve each sector's efficiency through energy conservation and emission reduction based on the results. Accordingly, they proposed the specific target value for each sector: managers should increase desirable outputs and decrease undesirable outputs concurrently; policymakers should identify the different sectors' performance during past years. Iftikhar et al. (2018) applied the network DEA model to analyze the energy and $CO_2$ emissions efficiency of 19 major economies. They measured the efficiency from two perspectives: economic efficiency and distributive efficiency. The results indicated economic inefficiencies and distributive inefficiencies make China and the United States the two large energy users, respectively. Shang et al. (2020) assessed total factor energy efficiency in different China regions based on the SBM-DEA model. In order to calculate and compare total factor energy efficiency between different regions, they divided them into eight economic zones. It showed that the most efficient region was the Eastern Coastal Comprehensive Economic Zone, and the least efficient region was Greater Northwest Comprehensive Economic Zone. Yang and Wei (2019) analyzed the UTFEE (urban total factor energy efficiency) of 26 prefectural-level cities in China by applying game cross-efficiency DEA approach with the environmental constraints such as wastewater, $SO_2$, and SD (smoke and dust). On this basis, Tobit model was used to test 10 potential factors affecting efficiency. Lin et al. (2020) estimated and optimized 29 countries' energy structures based on the SBM-DEA model, considering per capita GDP as the good output and $CO_2$ as the bad output. The results showed that the overall efficiency of developed countries is higher than that of developing countries. However, inefficient countries could make significant progress through optimizing allocation. Zhang et al. (2019) evaluated the performance and resource allocation of 30 China's provinces for the period 2011–2015 utilizing a two-stage DEA model. From the perspective of time and space, they considered that most provinces were inefficient in pollution emission control and treatment. Hence improvement can be achieved by provinces by redistributing pollution treatment resources. Li et al. (2019) used the DNSBM (Dynamic, Network Slack Based Measure) model to study 30 China's provinces/municipalities 'energy and air pollution reduction efficiency. In the first production stage, labor, fixed asset, and energy consumption were regarded as the input variables, and GDP was the output variable. In the second treatment stage, treatment investment was the input variable, and $CO_2$, $SO_2$, $NO_2$ emissions reductions were the output variables. They found that second stage's efficiency was significantly lower than that of the first stage for most provinces/municipalities. The result implied that more effective measures should be taken to reduce air pollution. For example, learning advanced management experience of developed countries, improving industrial structure to adapt to local geographical conditions and climate characteristics, etc. Zhou et al. (2018) assessed the $CO_2$ emission performance of 71 cities in China by proposing a DEA method with multiple abatement factors. The results showed that the eastern region outperformed the central region, but the western region performed worst. What's more, they suggested that $CO_2$ emission performance was mainly influenced by technological progress. Therefore, emission reduction policies could be based on green technology and innovation. Jiang et al. (2020) proposed a DEA objective approach to solving the problem of improving the environmental efficiency in the process of resource redistribution, then made an empirical analysis of China's regional land transport system considering $CO_2$ emission as undesirable output. Zen et al. (2020) analyzed China's thermal power industry's environmental efficiency by a two-stage model. In their model, $CO_2$, $SO_2$, and soot were considered as undesirable outputs in the first stage.

Given the uncontrollable nature of $CO_2$, they only put $SO_2$ and Soot into the second abatement stage as inputs. Based on the results, they held that abatement efficiency was the key to environmental efficiency, especially the reduction of $SO_2$ and soot. Ouyang and Yang (2020) proposed a multiplicative network DEA model to calculate the regional energy and environmental efficiency of 27 OECD countries by treating $CO_2$ emission as undesired output. The empirical study proved that multiplicative DEA better explained the efficiency assignment of sequence structure and parallel structure than linear DEA. Sun et al. (2020) used a common weight DEA model to measure South Asia's environmental sustainability performance during 2001–2015. The most efficient to the least efficient countries were Bhutan, Nepal, Maldives, Afghanistan, Bangladesh, India, Sri Lanka, and Pakistan. Moreover, they proposed some policies to countries to improve cross-border trade in renewable energy. Allev et al. (2018) proposed some environmental indicators, including $CO_2$ emissions. Based on these indicators, they analyzed the environmental performance of European green mutual funds in a DEA framework, including DEA-F, DEA-S, DEA-C, DEA-G. Choosing the gas emissions as bad outputs including $NO_x$, $SO_x$ and GHG (greenhouse gases), Halkos and Petrou (2018) build up a novel DEA model to study the efficiency of the 28 European Union member states in 2008, 2010, 2012 and 2014. The empirical results showed that Germany, Ireland, and Britain were the three most efficient countries overall. Meanwhile, more efficient countries seem to have higher rates of recycling. Wang et al. (2019) made a research on the regional differences, dynamic evolution and influencing factors of China's provincial air pollution emission efficiency during 2006–2015 considering $SO_2$, $NO_x$ and dust as undesirable outputs. It showed that China had made impressive achievements in improving the efficiency of total factor air pollution emissions. However, there was still great potential for further improvement not only in narrowing regional disparities but also in promoting technological progress across regions. Chen et al. (2020) studied Chinese provinces' sustainability efficiency from 2000 to 2012, following a window-based multiplicative network DEA approach. It showed that there was obvious heterogeneity in environmental sustainability and ecological efficiency among different provinces and geographical regions in China. Therefore, the laws should be enacted in accordance with local conditions.

The second kind of researches also set $PM_{2.5}$ and $PM_{10}$ as research indexes on the basis of traditional pollutants. Reyes et al. (2016) used the RAMP (Regionalized Air quality Performance) Model to explore novel ways of visualizing and evaluating CMAQ (Community Multiscale Air Quality) model performance and errors for daily $PM_{2.5}$ concentrations across the continental United States. Gokhale and Raokhande (2008) used several models to evaluate roadside air quality and analyzed the prevailing meteorology and the temporal distribution of the measured daily average $PM_{10}$ and $PM_{2.5}$ concentrations in wintertime. Zhou and Zhou (2017) simulated the dynamic trends of gross domestic production (GDP), $PM_{2.5}$, and six air pollutant emissions between 2015 and 2030 in four different scenarios and calculate the results of AEC(Atmospheric environmental capacity) and AECC(Atmospheric environmental carrying capacity) constrained by GDP and $PM_{2.5}$. Kang et al. (2010) estimated real-time bias-adjusted $O_3$ and $PM_{2.5}$ air quality index forecasts and their performance evaluations over the continental United States. Sue Yoshi and Yuan (2015) applied DEA method to evaluate the environment performance of 28 provincial capitals in China after setting indexes like $PM_{2.5}$ and $PM_{10}$ as undesirable outputs; Feng and Wang (2015) used SBM model on the basis of non-radial perspective to incorporate the haze precursors as undesirable outputs into the energy efficiency framework of total factors in order to estimate the total-factor energy efficiency of the Beijing-Tianjin-Hebei region during 2003–2012 and analyzed the influencing factors of energy efficiency using Tobit model. He et al. (2016) estimated the provincial environment technology efficiency of China from 2001 to 2012 after incorporating haze into the research framework of environment technology efficiency and constructing the SBM regional model of undesirable outputs. Guo et al. (2015) discussed the provincial distribution efficiency of $PM_{2.5}$ emission permits under the premise of fixed total targets using ZSG-DEA (Zero-sum Gains Data Envelopment Analysis) model. Moutinh et al. (2020) used DEA and SFA-ML methods to compute 24 German cities' eco-efficiency. They found that Germany's best performing city was Aachen, Berlin, Bochum, Freiburg, and München. Furthermore, fractional regression was used to infer the factors influencing cities' efficiency. The results showed that excessive $PM_{10}$, temperature, $NO_2$ and rainfall had a significant impact on the efficiency. Ma et al. (2018) collected data from 30 Chinese mainland provinces from 2001 to 2012 to explore environmental efficiency based on the SBM-undesirable-VRS method with and without considering $PM_{2.5}$. The results showed that the unbalanced regional development in the eastern, central, and western regions. The authors believed that government could improve the inefficiency regions with large energy consumption, water consumption, and haze emissions by adjusting their inputs and the outputs. Wang et al. (2020) discussed the air pollution efficiency of China's 30 mainland provinces by using an improved context-dependent SBM (Slack Based Measure) approach with the undesirable outputs (e.g., $PM_{2.5}$). The results showed that the context-dependent SBM model was more feasible to evaluate the air pollution efficiency at a provincial level in Mainland China. Based on the result, achievable short-term air pollution reduction targets were proposed to the local government. Based on a DEA approach, Wu et al. (2018) proposed a method to control haze emission by readjusting input indicators. They calculated the efficiency of provinces with undesirable output ($PM_{2.5}$) and desirable output (GDP). It indicated that Beijing, Tianjin, and Shanghai had optimal input–output efficiency, while Midwestern China cities, such as Ningxia, Guizhou, and Shanxi, have excess inputs. Zhou et al. (2020) constructed a window DEA model with five air pollution indicators' daily data, including $PM_{2.5}$, $PM_{10}$, CO, NO, and $SO_2$. They found that China's urban air quality was heavily influenced by the change of the month. The most polluted provinces were concentrated in the continuous polluted areas centered in Shanxi province. Li et al. (2018) analyzed the overall efficiency score of 31 Chinese cities from 2013 to 2016. The total efficiency score of them in 2017 was also assessed using the Resample SBM model, considering the emission of $PM_{2.5}$ as one of the undesirable output indexes. The study proved that western cities incurred more environmental costs in the process of economic growth. Considering the differences between areas and periods, X et al. (2020) adopted the DEA-LMDI (data envelopment analysis and logarithmic mean Divisia index) method to explore and decompose the influencing factors of $PM_{2.5}$ emissions in China. The results showed that the regional EBT (environmental-based technology) effect was the critical factor to curb $PM_{2.5}$ emissions, and it was strong in east China and weak in northeast China. But the ESE (environmental-oriented scale efficiency), EME (environmental-oriented management efficiency), PSE (production-oriented scale efficiency), PME (production-oriented management efficiency) and PBT (production-based technology) had relatively small effects on $PM_{2.5}$ emissions. He et al. (2018) developed a comprehensive environmental efficiency index based on a DEA-SBM (Slacks Based Measure) model to estimate environmental efficiency by sectors including agriculture, power, industry, residential and transport. The results reflected that there were obvious differences in environmental efficiency between provinces and regions. Specifically, southern China had the best performance in agriculture, power, and industry, while eastern China outperformed in transport. Dong et al. (2020) utilized SE-SBM (super-efficiency slacks-based measure) model to calculate the EREHC (environmental regulation efficiency of haze control) values of 30 provinces, autonomous regions, and municipalities in China during 2003–2015. They demonstrated that EREHC values were largest in the eastern regions, followed by the western region, and lowest in the central region. However, most areas' efficiency showed an upward trend over the study period. Yu et al. (2020) studied China's 30 provinces' eco-efficiency by improving the matrix-type NDEA (network data envelopment analysis) model. The overall system included comprehensive output variables such as $CO_2$, $SO_2$, $PM_{10}$ was divided into the environmental subsystem, economy subsystem, and social subsystem. Zhang et al. (2020) employed the DEA-SBM model to estimate the prefectures' integrated environmental performance with GDP as desirable outputs and $PM_{2.5}$ as undesirable outputs. They also explored the effect of environmental regulation on $PM_{2.5}$ applying the DID model, and the results showed that the environmental regulation policy on $PM_{2.5}$ was effective.

Besides, scholars like W et al. (2016), Li and Cheng (2008), Ba et al. (2013), Wan et al. (2015) and Cheng (2008) also made lots of analysis on the environment performance evaluation and its differences between different regions on the condition that $CO_2$, $SO_2$, $NO_2$, waste gas, waste water, and waste were regarded as undesirable outputs. Limited by space, this paper will not enumerate those researches at length.

It can be seen from the above research that most existing studies selected provinces as research unites, which to certain degree limited the environment performance evaluation of China's cities, regions or even the whole. Moreover, most researches regarded single air pollutants like $CO_2$, $SO_2$, $NO_2$ and waste gas as undesirable outputs, while studies using undesirable outputs like $PM_{2.5}$ and $PM_{10}$ are rarely seen, let alone literature analysis on the regional differences of environmental pollution. In light of the above insufficiencies of previous studies, this paper has made comprehensive environment performance evaluation of 109 strictly-environmental-monitored cities in China[3] from the perspective of natural performance, management

[3]The 109 cities are strictly-environmental-monitored, noted by China Statistical Yearbook (except for Lasa, Haikou, Nanchong and Tongchuan while there lack data of Nanchong and Tongchuan).

performance as well as scale performance by Data Envelopment Analysis (DEA), incorporating $PM_{2.5}$ and $PM_{10}$ as undesirable outputs. What's more, the environmental performance differences of different regions have been further analyzed. It can be seen that this paper is a beneficial supplement to the existing research and is of great significance in terms of both the choice of objects and practical guides.

## 22.3 Model, Indexes and Data

### *22.3.1 DEA Model*

The method of data envelopment analysis (DEA) was proposed by Charnes, Coopor and Rhodes in 1978. The main principle of this method is to keep the input or output of the decision-making units (DMU) unchanged. The relatively efficient production frontier is determined by mathematical programming and statistics. Each decision-making unit is projected onto the production frontier of DEA and its relative effectiveness is evaluated by the degree of the deviation of the decision-making unit from the DEA frontier. This paper employed the DEA model put forward by Toshiyuki Sue Yoshi[4] to comprehensively evaluate the environment performance from the perspective of natural performance, management performance as well as scale performance, which is in line with the current situation that Chinese cities differ in economic growth, scale and geographical distribution and can better evaluate the environment performance of 109 strictly-environmental-monitored cities as well as other areas.

A brief introduction of the DEA environment performance evaluation model was put forward by Sue Yoshi and Yuan (2015). Due to space limitations, we will not introduce it detailly here.

[4]The main differences between this paper and Toshiyuki Sueyoshi (2015) are follows: The first is research object and data. Toshiyuki Sueyoshi selected provincial cities as the research object, while this paper has chosen 109 strictly-environmental-monitored cities as the research unit which to certain degree overcomes the limitation in evaluating the environmental performance of China's cities, regions or even the whole country. The second is empirical analysis and conclusion. Rather than emphasizing on the analysis of regional differences like Toshiyuki Suyoshi, this paper has discussed the environmental performance of Chinese cities both regionally and on the whole.In addition, it has also illustrated the environmental performance distribution of each city which can reflect the environmental performance of cities in each region in a more direct way. In general, the current environmental performance in China is quite low while the research result of Toshiyuki Sueyoshi tended to be rather positive. What's more, the empirical result of this paper differs from that of Toshiyuki Sueyoshi in that it is based on more scientific regional division with regional differential analysis. For instance, according to Toshiyuki Sueyoshi, the environmental performance of the eastern costal region (0.930) is better than that of the southern coastal region (0.629), while this research finds that the environmental performance of the costal economic regions is evidently higher than that of other regions and the environmental performance of the eastern coastal economic region is among the bottom ones. The environmental performance of the northern coastal economic region is rather lower, far from that given by Toshiyuki Sueyoshi, which is more in line with the reality.

### 22.3.2 T-test

The t-test, also known as student's t test proposed by British statistician Gossett, is to use the t distribution theory to infer the probability of the occurrence of difference so as to compare the two averages and to see whether the difference is significant. In this paper, the test of averages of two independent samples is used to test the difference of the data obtained from two non-related samples. Firstly, it is assumed that the two regions are independent, that is there is no correlation between the two experimental groups. Then the difference between the environmental performances of the two regions is analyzed.

$$t = \frac{\bar{X}_1 - \bar{X}_2}{\sqrt{\frac{(n_1-1)S_1^2+(n_2-1)S_2^2}{n_1+n_2-2}\left(\frac{1}{n_1}+\frac{1}{n_2}\right)}} \tag{22.1}$$

In the equation, $\bar{X}_1$, $\bar{X}_2$ are the averages of the two samples, $S_1^2$, $S_2^2$ are the variances, $n_1$, $n_2$ are the sample sizes. According to the calculation results, it can be determined whether the difference is significant by referring to the t distribution table. This statistical method will be used in Sect. 4.4.

### 22.3.3 Indexes

The outputs can be divided into the desirable one and the undesirable one in the DEA environment performance evaluation model. GDP, an ultimate fruit of regional production in certain period, can suitably embody the regional economic growth and therefore, it can be regarded as desirable output. On the basis of air pollutants, $PM_{2.5}$ and $PM_{10}$ are also taken into consideration. Given the data availability, the National Bureau of Statistics has categorized strictly-monitored indexes such as $NO_2$, $SO_2$, $PM_{2.5}$ and $PM_{10}$ in 109 strictly-environmental-monitored cities into undesirable outputs and the total population at the end of every year, investment in pollution control, total electricity consumption and the total expense of per capita consumption into input indexes, among which, the total population at the end of every year has something to do with the city scale and will influence its scale efficiency; While the total electricity consumption as well as total expense of per capital consumption is relevant to economic development and therefore, many researches regard these three indexes as input indexes. In addition, investment in pollution control can directly influence environment protection efficiency, and therefore, this paper also regards it as input index. The introduction of specific indexes is detailed as follows.

Input index: (1) total population at the end of the year: the number of population at 24 o'clock on Dec. 31 every year, measured by ten thousand; (2) investment in pollution control: the investment in pollution in certain time and area, measured by ten thousand yuan; (3) total electricity consumption: the total consumption of the whole city in a year, measured by ten thousand kwh; (4) per capita consumption expenditure: total spending on daily household life, measured by yuan.

Desirable output index: GDP: the ultimate fruit of production activities made by all permanent residents unites in some area during certain period, measured by hundred million yuan.

Undesirable output index: (1) mean annual concentration of $PM_{10}$, measured by $\mu/m^3$. $PM_{10}$ refers to particles whose diameter are less than or equal to 10 μm. (2) The mean annual concentration of $PM_{2.5}$, measured by $\mu/m^3$. $PM_{2.5}$ refers to particles whose diameter are less than or equal to 2.5 μm in aerodynamics. (3)$NO_2$: mean annual concentration, measured by $\mu/m^3$.(4) $SO_2$: mean annual concentration, measured by $\mu/m^3$.

### *22.3.4 Data*

This paper used the panel data collected from 109 strictly-environmental-monitored cities in 2014, among which, the data about $PM_{10}$, $PM_{2.5}$, $NO_2$ and $SO_2$ came from *China Statistical Yearbook* 2015, data about investment in pollution control from *The Almanac of China's Cities 2015*, and data about total population at the end of every year, total electricity consumption as well as GDP from *China City Statistical Yearbook 2015*. Data about per capital consumption expenditure came from the statistical yearbooks of each province. Since specific per capital consumption expenditure of some cities were not given by the statistical yearbooks; they were obtained through weighed average of data in the statistical bulletin. It can be seen from the data that, among all the cities, Shanghai has the largest GDP, total electricity consumption and per capita consumption expenditure, Chongqing has the largest population of 19.439 million, Wuhan spent 6334.429 billion yuan on pollution control, ranking first among all the cities. In addition, the concentrations of $PM_{2.5}$ and $PM_{10}$ in Baoding are the highest, 129 $\mu/m^3$ and 224 $\mu/m^3$, respectively. The concentrations of $NO_2$ and $SO_2$ in Zibo are the highest, 123 $\mu/m^3$ and 67 $\mu/m^3$, respectively. The specific data are shown in Table 22.1.

## 22.4 Empirical Result and Discussion

### *22.4.1 Empirical Results*

First of all, from the perspective of natural performance under variable return to scale, the performance values are all bigger than 0.2, most concentrated between 0.600 and 1.000. The natural performances in southern coastal cities are much higher compared with those in cities of Hebei, Shandong and Henan provinces. Cities with the highest

**Table 22.1** Data description of 109 strictly-environmental-monitored cities in 2014

| | Index | Unite | Minimum | Upper quartile | Median | Lower quartile | Maximum | Arithmetic average | Standard deviation |
|---|---|---|---|---|---|---|---|---|---|
| Input | Total population at the end of every year | Ten thousand people | 23.2 | 96.3 | 149.9 | 276.8 | 1943.9 | 240.85 | 272.6 |
| | Investment in pollution control | Ten thousand yuan | 15 | 13,997.6 | 33,157.6 | 74,270 | 633,442.9 | 57,916.22 | 80,358.01 |
| | Total electricity consumption | The thousand kwh | 93,942 | 597,249 | 1,108,120 | 1,877,765 | 13,465,607 | 1,725,849.2 | 2,089,113.6 |
| | Per capita consumption | Yuan | 4195.22 | 12,274 | 14,569.128 | 19,000.927 | 33,064.8 | 15,984.25 | 5444.74 |
| Desirable output | GDP | Hundred thousand yuan | 166,001 | 6,690,569 | 12,597,088 | 31,004,800 | 232,920,300 | 27,512,453 | 40,445,118 |
| Undesirable output | $PM_{2.5}$ | $\mu g/m^3$ | 29 | 52 | 65 | 74 | 129 | 64.53 | 19.12 |
| | $PM_{10}$ | $\mu g/m^3$ | 47 | 86 | 108 | 128 | 224 | 109.22 | 33.25 |
| | $SO_2$ | $\mu g/m^3$ | 8 | 24 | 31 | 50 | 123 | 37.37 | 20.31 |
| | $NO_2$ | $\mu g/m^3$ | 14 | 32 | 39 | 47 | 67 | 39.62 | 10.43 |

natural performance are Beijing, Dalian, Shanghai, Fuzhou, Shenzhen and Zhuhai. Their performance values are all 1. While Baoding, whose performance value is 0.318, is at the bottom in terms of natural performance.

Secondly, from the perspective of the natural performance under constant return to scale, Dalian, Shanghai, Guangzhou, Shenzhen, Changsha and Chengdu have the highest natural performance, the performance value being 1. While Sanmenxia has the lowest performance value of 0.018, followed by Jinzhou, Maanshan, Shizuishan and Jinchang. In general, the performance values of most cities are lower than 0.2, dominant by Shandong, Henan, Shanxi, Hebei and Liaoning provinces. The performance values of cities in the Yangtze River Delta are concentrated between 0.2 and 0.6, with lower efficiency on the whole.

Thirdly, the scale performance of most cities in Hebei, Henan, Shanxi, Liaoning, Gansu, Qinghai and Ningxia provinces is lower than 0.2, cities in the Yangtze River Delta have lower performance values and the scale performance in southern coastal cities is comparatively higher. Cities with the highest scale performance under natural performance are Dalian, Shanghai, Guangzhou, Shenzhen, Changsha and Chengdu, with the performance values being 1. Cities with the lowest scale performance are Sanmenxia, Mudanjiang, Shaoguan, Yangquan and Jiaozuo, with the performance values being lower than 0.1.

Fourthly, under variable massive loss, the management performance of each city is over ally higher with the highest being Shanghai, Fuzhou, Shenzhen, Quanzhou, Shantou, Wuhan and Chongqing. Their performance values are 1. The management performance of Baoding is the lowest, being merely 0.272. The management performance of cities in Guangdong and Fujian provinces is evidently higher than those in other provinces. And the management performance in some cities of Shandong, Henan and Hebei provinces is lower.

Fifthly, under constant massive loss, the management performance of Shanghai, Quanzhou, Shenzhen, Wuhan and Chongqing is the best with the performance values being 1. Mudanjiang has the lowest performance value, being only 0.161. The management performance in Qinhuangdao, Yanan, Yangquan and Anyang are also comparatively lower. As shown in the appendix Table 22.10, the management performance of some cities in Hebei, Shandong, Henan and Shanxi provinces are clearly lower than cities in other provinces.

Sixthly, from the perspective of scale performance under management performance, bigger cities such as Tianjin, Shanghai, Quanzhou, Shenzhen, Wuhan and Chongqing have higher performance values, being 1. Mudanjiang has the lowest scale performance and small cities like Yanan and Qujing also have lower scale performance. In general, the scale performance of cities in the southern and eastern coastal cities is much higher than that in the middle and western cities.

As can be seen above, the environment performance of big cities represented by provincial capitals is higher than other middle-or-small sized cities under whatever types of performance. What's more, cities with higher environment performance are clustered in provinces like Guangdong, Fujian, Shanghai, Jiangsu and Zhejiang, while cities with lower environment performance are gathered in such provinces as Hebei, Henan, Shandong, Shanxi, Gansu and Ningxia. In order to further expound the differences between various cities and regions, the following part will analyze the environment performance differences between big and small cities as well as different regions.

### 22.4.2 Overall Analysis on Environment Performance

As we can see from the environment performance of 109 strictly-environmental-monitored cities (see in Table 22.2), the management performance of most cities is lower than natural performance, which reveals that at present, most cities in China still put economic development at the first place while environmental protection at the second place. In addition, as Table 22.2 shows, the highest efficiency value is 1, while the lowest is only 0.018, which manifests that the environment performance between various cities is quietly different and the economic development does not get balance in hand with environmental protection. Natural performance, management performance and scale performance are comparatively lower on the whole, which shows the overall environment performance of cities in China is rather low.

**Table 22.2** Environment performance value description of 109 strictly-environmental-monitored cities in 2014

| | Natural performance under variable return to scale | Natural performance under constant return to scale | Scale performance under natural performance | Management performance under variable massive loss | Management performance under constant massive loss | Scale performance under management performance |
|---|---|---|---|---|---|---|
| Average | 0.714 | 0.373 | 0.485 | 0.618 | 0.526 | 0.845 |
| Standard deviation | 0.226 | 0.316 | 0.329 | 0.187 | 0.197 | 0.135 |
| Minimum | 0.318 | 0.018 | 0.018 | 0.272 | 0.161 | 0.310 |
| Upper quartiles | 0.524 | 0.113 | 0.178 | 0.491 | 0.391 | 0.773 |
| Medians | 0.706 | 0.256 | 0.425 | 0.577 | 0.503 | 0.881 |
| Lower quartiles | 1 | 0.596 | 0.776 | 0.704 | 0.588 | 0.939 |
| Maximum | 1.000 | 1.000 | 1.000 | 1.000 | 1.000 | 1.000 |

### 22.4.3 Regional Environment Performance Analysis

#### 22.4.3.1 Regional Division

In order to analyze the environment performance difference between different cities, the 109 strictly-environmental-monitored cities are sorted from three perspectives: provincial capitals or non-provincial capitals. The three regions division method based on economic distribution put forward by Sun and Liu (2005).[5] Eight economic regions including 30 provincial capitals divided by the development center of the State Council.[6]

Suppose there is no significant difference between provincial cities and non-provincial cities, there is also no significant difference between regions according to the division of "three regions" and "eight economic regions".

#### 22.4.3.2 Natural Performance, Management Performance and Scale Performance

Natural performance and management performance in various regions are evidently different which signifies that there are differences of economic development and environmental protection among regions.

Firstly, the average natural performance of provincial cities is 0.774, higher than 0.693 of non-provincial cities and the management performance of provincial cities is 0.670 higher than 0.600 of non-provincial provinces, which shows that provincial cities pay more attention to environmental protection. In addition, the efficiency value variance of provincial cities is less than non-provincial cities, which reveals

[5]The Pan-Yangtze river region: an economic region which connects the lower reaches of the Yangtze river economic center with the middle and upper yellow river delta economic region to form an economic center covering 15 cities in the Yangtze river delta and economically radioactive to more than 10 provinces like Hu, Su, Zhe, Wan, Yu, Shan, Gan, Ning, Qing and Jiang. The Pan-Pearl river delta region: an economic region that connects the Pearl river and Min river coastal economic regions with the upper and middle reach of the Yangtze river economic center to form a new economic center including 14 cities such as Guangzhou and Shenzhen, sub-centered at coastal cities in Fujian province like Xia, Zhang and Quan, wchich have a radioactive influence on Yue, Min, Qiong, Gui, Xiang, E, Gan, Yu, Gui, Dian, Chuan and Zang provinces. The great Bo sea surrounding area: an economic region that connects the city group in the Bo sea bay with the economic region located in the downstream area of the yellow river as well as the north China plain and the northeastern plain, including nine provinces like Jing, Jin, Liao, Lu, Ji, Jin, Ji, Hei and Meng.

[6]The southern coastal economic region includes Fujian, Guangdong and Hainan; the northern coastal comprehensive economic region includes Beijing, Tianjin, Hebei and Shandong; the eastern coastal comprehensive economic region includes Shanghai, Jiangsu and Zhejing; the middle yellow river comprehensive economic region includes Neimenggu, Henan, Shanxi and Shanxi; the middle Yangtze river comprehensive economic region includes Hubei, Hunan, Anhui and Jiangxi; the northeastern comprehensive economic region consists of Liaoning, Jilin and Heilongjiang; the southwestern comprehensive economic region includes Guangxi, Sichuan, Chongqing, Yunnan and Guizhou; the northwestern comprehensive economic region consists of Gansu, Qinghai, Ningxia and Xinjiang.

that the environment performance of provincial cities is less fluctuant than that of non-provincial cities, namely, the development gap between non-provincial cities is wider.

Secondly, among the three regional divisions, the efficiency value of Pan-Pearl River Delta is the highest, followed by Pan-Yangtze River Delta and greater Bo Sea surrounding area. The latter two are similar in terms of efficiency value. While the management performance average of the greater Bo sea surrounding area is the lowest, reflecting that this region attaches more importance to economic development and lacks efforts on environment protection. This conclusion accords with the current situation that air pollution happens more frequently and becomes increasingly serious in this region where heavy industry dominates. While this deviates from the environment evaluation made by Chen et al. (2015) according to the traditional regional division method of Beijing-Tianjin-Hebei, the Yangtze River delta and the Pearl River Delta.

Thirdly, in the eight regions division, the averages of natural performance and management performance in the southern costal economic region are the highest, being 0.948 and 0.943 respectively, which reflects that the southern coastal economic region attaches equal importance to both economic growth and environmental protection. The environment performance of southern coastal economic region is higher than that of other regions. While the management performance average of the same developed eastern coastal comprehensive economic region is 0.629, much lower than that of the southern coastal economic region, revealing that the environmental protection in the eastern costal comprehensive economic region is not as good as that in the southern coastal region. Besides, the management performance of the northern coastal comprehensive region is the lowest, being only 0.492, which reflects that the environmental protection situation in this region is worse. Please refer to Table 22.3 for more specific results.

The result also demonstrates that the natural performance under constant return to scale and the management performance under constant massive loss are much higher than those of non-provincial cities, which signifies that the economic development and environmental protection level of bigger cities are much higher than those of middle-and-small sized cities. Of the three regions, the efficiency of the Pan-pearl River Delta is the highest, followed by similar values of the Pan-Yangtze River Delta and great Bo Sea surrounding area. Among the eight regions, the efficiency of the southern costal economic region still tops, while the natural performance value of the northwestern comprehensive economic region is only 0.194, indicating that its economic development is much lower than other regions. The management performance average value of the middle yellow river comprehensive economic region is 0.415 which shows that its environment protection level is lower than other regions. Specific results are shown in Table 22.4.

In addition, the scale performance average of provincial cities under natural performance and management performance are 0.802 and 0.866 respectively, much higher than the responding 0.370 and 0.837 of non-provincial cities. The scale performance averages of southern coastal economic region, the eastern coastal comprehensive economic region, the middle Yangtze river comprehensive region and the northern

**Table 22.3** Environment performance value of each region under variable return to scale and variable massive loss

| Regional division | | Natural performance | | Management performance | |
|---|---|---|---|---|---|
| | | Arithmetic average | Standard deviation | Arithmetic average | Standard deviation |
| Provincial cities and non-provincial cities | Provincial cities | 0.774 | 0.211 | 0.670 | 0.184 |
| | Non-provincial cities | 0.693 | 0.229 | 0.600 | 0.185 |
| Three regions | Pan-Pearl River Delta | 0.858 | 0.171 | 0.740 | 0.198 |
| | Pan-Yangtze River Delta | 0.658 | 0.214 | 0.573 | 0.156 |
| | Greater Bo sea surrounding area | 0.622 | 0.219 | 0.538 | 0.137 |
| Eight economic regions | Northern coastal comprehensive economic region | 0.538 | 0.229 | 0.492 | 0.160 |
| | Northeastern comprehensive economic region | 0.743 | 0.180 | 0.566 | 0.100 |
| | Eastern coastal comprehensive economic region | 0.643 | 0.135 | 0.629 | 0.133 |
| | Southern coastal economic region | 0.948 | 0.085 | 0.943 | 0.094 |
| | The middle Yellow river comprehensive economic region | 0.642 | 0.253 | 0.508 | 0.116 |
| | The middle Yangtze river comprehensive region | 0.735 | 0.209 | 0.623 | 0.154 |
| | Greater southern comprehensive economic region | 0.888 | 0.129 | 0.700 | 0.181 |
| | Greater northern comprehensive economic region | 0.668 | 0.233 | 0.657 | 0.216 |

costal comprehensive region where lots of cities gather are clearly higher than those of other regions, which shows that bigger cities are able to make use of their city scale to promote economic development and environment protection and eventually to enhance their environment performance while for small cities, they are unable to

**Table 22.4** Environment performance value of each region under constant return to scale and constant massive loss

| Regional division | | Natural performance | | Management performance | |
|---|---|---|---|---|---|
| | | Arithmetic average | Standard deviation | Arithmetic average | Standard deviation |
| Provincial/non-provincial cities | Provincial cities | 0.654 | 0.294 | 0.586 | 0.202 |
| | Non-provincial cities | 0.271 | 0.257 | 0.505 | 0.1920 |
| Three regions | Pan-Pearl River Delta | 0.471 | 0.325 | 0.614 | 0.216 |
| | Pan-Yangtze River Delta | 0.326 | 0.279 | 0.508 | 0.181 |
| | Greater Bo sea surrounding area | 0.318 | 0.327 | 0.453 | 0.158 |
| Eight regions | Northern coastal comprehensive economic region | 0.344 | 0.325 | 0.428 | 0.172 |
| | Northeastern comprehensive economic region | 0.345 | 0.357 | 0.471 | 0.159 |
| | Eastern coastal comprehensive economic region | 0.406 | 0.237 | 0.588 | 0.147 |
| | Southern coastal economic region | 0.498 | 0.341 | 0.849 | 0.162 |
| | The middle yellow river comprehensive economic region | 0.261 | 0.316 | 0.415 | 0.128 |
| | The middle Yangtze river comprehensive economic region | 0.457 | 0.334 | 0.562 | 0.162 |
| | Southwestern comprehensive economic region | 0.459 | 0.328 | 0.518 | 0.172 |

(continued)

**Table 22.4** (continued)

| Regional division | | Natural performance | | Management performance | |
|---|---|---|---|---|---|
| | | Arithmetic average | Standard deviation | Arithmetic average | Standard deviation |
| | Northwestern comprehensive economic region | 0.194 | 0.201 | 0.559 | 0.261 |

get higher scale performance, which results in their low environment performance. Specific results can be referred to in Table 22.5.

### *22.4.4 Differences Between Regional Environment Performances*

In order to examine the differences between regional environment performances, t-test analysis is made on the natural performance under variable return to scale as well as on the management performance under variable massive loss. Tables 22.6, 22.7, 22.8 and 22.9 show the values of t-test and p under different regional divisions.

Table 22.6 shows the t-test value and p value of natural performance and management performance under variable return to scale and variable massive loss of provincial cities and non-provincial cities respectively. As we can see that the p values of natural performance and management performance are both greater than 0.05, the result is not significant and the test also fails, which means that there are no significant differences between provincial cities and non-provincial cities. This is due to the fact that air pollutants represented by $PM_{2.5}$ and $PM_{10}$ are likely to be influenced by air flow, wind direction and water vapor. All in all, they are more fluid compared with other kinds of environmental pollution (Wang et al. 2015a, b, c). This leads to the result that the air condition in a city will be influenced by surrounding cities and vice versa. And therefore, differences between cities are narrowed and the difference test fails.

In Table 22.7, the p values of natural performance and management performance in the Pan-Yangtze River Delta and Great Bo Sea surrounding area are 0.487 and 0.318 respectively. Both are higher than 0.05 and the value of t also fails the test, which reveals that there are no evident differences between Pan-Yangtze river delta and great Bo sea surrounding area. However, the p values of natural performance and management performance in the Pan-Pearl river delta, Pan-Yangtze river delta and the great Bo sea surrounding area are both 0, which means it passes the t-test, namely, there exist significant differences between the above regions: the economic growth

**Table 22.5** Scale performance value of each region

| Regional division | | Scale performance under natural performance | | Scale performance under management performance | |
|---|---|---|---|---|---|
| | | Arithmetic average | Standard deviation | Arithmetic average | Standard deviation |
| Provincial/non-provincial cities | Provincial cities | 0.802 | 0.244 | 0.866 | 0.119 |
| | Non-provincial cities | 0.370 | 0.276 | 0.837 | 0.140 |
| Three regions | Pan-Pearl River Delta region | 0.526 | 0.320 | 0.825 | 0.134 |
| | Pan-Yangtze River Delta Region | 0.470 | 0.327 | 0.875 | 0.121 |
| | Great Bo sea region | 0.458 | 0.345 | 0.833 | 0.146 |
| Eight economic regions | Northern coastal comprehensive region | 0.540 | 0.313 | 0.856 | 0.112 |
| | Northern comprehensive economic region | 0.438 | 0.398 | 0.821 | 0.195 |
| | Eastern coastal comprehensive region | 0.618 | 0.282 | 0.930 | 0.054 |
| | Southern coastal economic region | 0.511 | 0.334 | 0.894 | 0.119 |
| | The middle yellow river comprehensive economic region | 0.357 | 0.338 | 0.817 | 0.157 |
| | The middle Yangtze river comprehensive economic region | 0.566 | 0.323 | 0.898 | 0.060 |
| | The southwestern comprehensive economic region | 0.499 | 0.323 | 0.744 | 0.133 |

(continued)

**Table 22.5** (continued)

| Regional division | | Scale performance under natural performance | | Scale performance under management performance | |
|---|---|---|---|---|---|
| | | Arithmetic average | Standard deviation | Arithmetic average | Standard deviation |
| | The northwestern comprehensive economic region | 0.290 | 0.248 | 0.824 | 0.107 |

**Table 22.6** Environment performance t-test value and p value of provincial cities and non-provincial cities

| Grouping | Natural performance | Management performance |
|---|---|---|
| Provincial cities and non-provincial cities | 1.672 (0.098) | 1.765 (0.080) |

*Note* (1) Insignificant below the confidence level of 5%. (2) Within the bracket is the value of P

**Table 22.7** Environment performance t-test value and p value in three regions

| | Natural performance | | Management performance | |
|---|---|---|---|---|
| Grouping | Great Bo sea surrounding area | Pan-Pearl river delta region | Great Bo sea surrounding region | Pan-Pearl river delta region |
| Pan-Pearl river delta region | 0.698 (0.487) | −4.454* (0.000) | 1.006 (0.318) | −4.021* (0.000) |
| Great Bo sea surrounding region | | −5.129* (0.000) | | −5.000* (0.000) |

*Note* (1) *Significant below the confidence level of 5%. (2) Within the bracket is the value of p

and environmental protection in the Pan-Pearl river delta region is conspicuously better than that in the Pan-Yangtze river delta and the great Bo sea surrounding area.

Tables 22.8 and 22.9 are t-test values and p values of the natural performance under variable return to scale and management performance under variable massive loss. As the table shows, the p values of most regions (like the northeastern economic regions and the northern coastal comprehensive economic regions, southern coastal economic regions and northern coastal comprehensive economic regions) are less than 0.05, which signifies that the environment performance between these regions are significant, with that between the middle-and-southern coastal economic regions and other regions being the most evident. The p values of several regions (such as the middle yellow river comprehensive region and eastern coastal comprehensive

**Table 22.8** Natural performance t-test value and p value of eight regions

| | The northeastern | The eastern | The southern | The yellow river | The Yangtze river | The southwestern | The northwestern |
|---|---|---|---|---|---|---|---|
| The northern | −2.489* (0.020) | −1.542 (0.134) | −5.146* (0.000) | −1.283 (0.208) | −2.392* (0.023) | −5.458* (0.000) | −1.250 (0.225) |
| The northeastern | | 1.631 (0.116) | −3.129* (0.006) | 1.169 (0.252) | 0.103 (0.919) | −2.480* (0.020) | 0.772 (0.451) |
| The eastern | | | −6.089* (0.000) | 0.007 (0.994) | −1.427 (0.165) | −5.254* (0.000) | −0.325 (0.749) |
| The southern | | | | 3.513* (0.002) | 2.895* (0.009) | 1.253 (0.222) | 3.364* (0.005) |
| The yellow river | | | | | −1.131 (0.267) | −3.624* (0.001) | −0.237 (0.814) |
| The Yangtze river | | | | | | -2.501* (0.018) | 0.669 (0.512) |
| The southwestern | | | | | | | 2.987* (0.007) |

*Note* (1) *Significant below the confidence level of 5%. (2) Within the bracket is the value of p. (3) The northern coastal comprehensive economic region (the northern),the northeastern comprehensive economic region (the northeastern),the eastern coastal comprehensive economic region (the eastern),the southern coastal economic region (the southern),the middle yellow river comprehensive economic region (the yellow river),the middle Yangtze comprehensive economic region (the Yangtze river),the southwestern comprehensive economic region (the southern region) and the northwestern comprehensive economic region (the northwestern)

region, the middle yellow river comprehensive economic region and the northwestern comprehensive economic region) are greater than 0.05, and fail the significance test. In a word, there are significant differences between eight regions, namely, there exist significant environment performance differences between regions and the economic development as well as environmental protection differences between regions are remarked.

## 22.5 Conclusion and Suggestion

Regarding $PM_{2.5}$ and $PM_{10}$ as undesirable outputs, this paper has employed the DEA model method to evaluate the environment performance of 109 strictly-environmental-monitored cities from the perspective of natural performance, management performance and scale performance. The result shows that firstly, the natural performance of most cities is relatively higher while the management performance is significantly lower. This reveals that most cities in China still give priority to economic development while put environmental protection at the second place. Secondly, generally, the environment performance of 109 cities differs greatly: the

**Table 22.9** Management performance t-test value and p value of eight regions

| | The northeastern | The eastern | The southern | The yellow river | The Yangtze river | The southwestern | The northwestern |
|---|---|---|---|---|---|---|---|
| The northern | −1.355 (0.187) | −2.581* (0.015) | −7.702* (0.000) | −0.341 (0.735) | −2.264* (0.031) | −3.493* (0.001) | −2.050 (0.053) |
| The northeastern | | −1.317 (0.200) | −8.600* (0.000) | 1.394 (0.174) | −1.051 (0.304) | −2.240* (0.034) | −1.224 (0.239) |
| The eastern | | | −6.185* (0.000) | 2.865* (0.007) | 0.120 (0.905) | −1.254 (0.219) | −0.381 (0.708) |
| The southern | | | | 9.830* (0.000) | 5.569* (0.000) | 3.741* (0.001) | 3.576* (0.003) |
| The yellow river | | | | | −2.471* (0.019) | −3.904* (0.000) | −2.319* (0.029) |
| The Yangtze river | | | | | | −1.270 (0.214) | −0.426 (0.675) |
| The southeastern | | | | | | | 0.500 (0.622) |

*Note* (1) *Significant below the confidence level of 5%. (2)Within the bracket is the value of p. (3) The northern comprehensive economic region (the northern),the northeastern comprehensive economic region(the northeastern),the eastern coastal comprehensive economic region (the eastern),the southern coastal economic region (the southern),the middle yellow comprehensive economic region (the yellow river),the middle Yangtze river comprehensive economic region (the Yangtze river),the southwestern comprehensive economic region (the southwestern) and the northwestern comprehensive economic region (the northwestern)

environment performance of provincial cities is higher than that of non-provincial cities which signifies that the overall performance of bigger cities is better than that of smaller cities, for bigger cities can make use of their city scale to promote economic development and environmental protection. Thirdly, from the perspective of regional analysis, the environmental performance between regions is quietly different which reveals that the economic development and environmental protection between regions is imbalanced. The environment performance of Pan-Pearl river delta region is higher than those of the Pan-Yangtze river delta and great Bo Sea surrounding area. The efficiency averages of the southern coastal economic region, the eastern coastal comprehensive economic region, the middle Yangtze river comprehensive economic region and the northern coastal comprehensive economic region are all higher than those of other regions, showing that the economic development and environmental protection of these regions are better than those of such less developed regions as the middle yellow river comprehensive economic region, the southwestern comprehensive economic region as well as the northwestern comprehensive economic region.

The main differences between this paper and Toshiyuki Sueyoshi's research (2015) are as follows.

Firstly, the paper focuses on the environmental performance of 109 Chinese cities and discusses the general imbalance between economic development and environmental protection in Chinese cities.

Secondly, the previous research employed the fitting data, which is quite different from the real data. Compared with previous research, the results of this paper are more reliable.

Thirdly, this paper selects three kinds of classification methods: and the provincial capitals and non-provincial capitals, three regions and eight economic regions. The influence of the sizes of the cities on the balance the city's economic development and environmental protection is discussed, and the regional differences are analyzed. Previous studies focused on demonstrating regional differences and analyzing the differences, but the results were too optimistic. Therefore, this study is different from previous studies and the results are different from those of previous studies.

Based on the above conclusion, we can get the following policy enlightenment.

Firstly, pay more attention to enhancing the management level and environment performance. First of all, a full-fledged environment performance evaluation system should be established and the difference between the environment pollution consequence and the intended environment target should also be realized. The environment regulatory content, the inspectors' responsibility as well as corresponding punishment should be clearly defined in order to provide scientific decision-making foundation for governments and enterprises. In addition, in light of the current serious pollution, cities should select a proper development model based on their own comparative advantages to enhance their environment performance and government should restructure the industry, optimize the city expanding route and transform economic growth mode, introduce market regulation (Zhang et al. 2015), pay more attention to the transformation of old industrial cities and ensure the leading role of technical innovation in improving environment performance in order to promote the cities' sustainable development (Chen and Zhou 2014).

Secondly, place emphasis on the environmental protection of smaller cities. With the repaid urbanization, there exist lots of problems relevant to ecology, environment and economy (Yang 2014). The government should take positive measures for smaller cities (such as Sanmenxia, Baoding, Mudanjiang and Pingdingshan) with backward economy and low environment performance and encourage them to learn the precious experience about economic development and environmental protection from bigger cities (like Beijing, Guangzhou, Shenzhen and Shanghai). At the same time, the government should also respond to the mission of building of national central cities,[7] promote the construction of bigger cities, facilitate the development of small cities with the scale radiation function of bigger cities and channel talents, capital as well as pollution treatment equipment to middle and small sized cities. In addition, the government should give more policy support middle and small sized cities, promote

[7]National central city is the highest level of urban system put forward by Ministry of Housing and Urban–Rural Development in the National Urban System Planning in 2010. National central cities play a leading, radioactive and distributive role nationwide in terms of politics, economy, culture as well as foreign exchanges.

their economic development, improve their environment performance (Li 2009) to reach the ecological balance and sustainable development.

Thirdly, attach more importance to sustainable development. Different environmental protection strategies should be tailored to the features of less developed regions such as the middle yellow river comprehensive economic region, the southwestern comprehensive economic region and the northwestern comprehensive economic region (Wu et al. 2016a, b, c). Meanwhile, experience can be learned from the Pan-Pearl river delta to enhance more investments in technology and innovation, promote the development of high-end service industry, and integrate advanced manufacturing industry with the high-end service industry in order to realize the industrial structural optimizing and upgrading (Qi 2015). According to the emission reduction target, the government can make use of the emission right transaction and subsidies to reduce the pollutant emission allowance distributed to relevant industrial enterprises and allow enterprises to fulfill their emission targets by transacting emission rights. The government should also strengthen regional cooperation and set up special regional coordinative organizations to directly implement the management right or give advice towards surrounding regional coordination behavior (Sun 2007) to realize the coordinated and sustainable development between regions.

**Acknowledgements** Dongdong Zhu, Yaozhen Yan, Bin Lang also made great contributions to this manuscript. We express our heartfelt thanks to them. This research was supported by: National Social and Scientific Fund Program of China (18ZDA052; 17BGL142;16ZDA047); The Natural Science Foundation of China (91546117, 71373131). This research was also supported by the Priority Academic Program Development of Jiangsu Higher Education Institutions and the Flagship Major Development of Jiangsu Higher Education Institutions.

## Appendix

See Table 22.10.

**Table 22.10** Environmental performance 109 strictly-environmental-monitored cities

| Cities | Natural performance under variable return to scale | Natural performance under constant return to scale | Scale performance under natural performance | Management performance under variable massive loss | Management performance under constant massive loss | Scale performance under management performance |
|---|---|---|---|---|---|---|
| Beijing | 1.000 | 0.996 | 0.996 | 0.892 | 0.838 | 0.939 |
| Tianjin | 0.795 | 0.793 | 0.997 | 0.746 | 0.746 | 1.000 |
| Shijiazhuang | 0.397 | 0.225 | 0.566 | 0.429 | 0.339 | 0.790 |
| Qinhuangdao | 0.485 | 0.068 | 0.140 | 0.476 | 0.270 | 0.567 |

(continued)

**Table 22.10** (continued)

| Cities | Natural performance under variable return to scale | Natural performance under constant return to scale | Scale performance under natural performance | Management performance under variable massive loss | Management performance under constant massive loss | Scale performance under management performance |
|---|---|---|---|---|---|---|
| Tangshan | 0.343 | 0.186 | 0.543 | 0.542 | 0.540 | 0.997 |
| Baoding | 0.318 | 0.038 | 0.120 | 0.272 | 0.196 | 0.721 |
| Handan | 0.340 | 0.058 | 0.172 | 0.407 | 0.317 | 0.779 |
| Jinan | 0.709 | 0.686 | 0.968 | 0.415 | 0.392 | 0.945 |
| Qindao | 0.957 | 0.931 | 0.973 | 0.587 | 0.540 | 0.921 |
| Zibo | 0.333 | 0.216 | 0.649 | 0.350 | 0.305 | 0.872 |
| Zaozhuang | 0.385 | 0.182 | 0.472 | 0.356 | 0.325 | 0.914 |
| Yantai | 0.678 | 0.438 | 0.647 | 0.643 | 0.529 | 0.823 |
| Weifang | 0.386 | 0.134 | 0.346 | 0.491 | 0.436 | 0.888 |
| Jining | 0.362 | 0.106 | 0.293 | 0.397 | 0.347 | 0.874 |
| Taian | 0.637 | 0.327 | 0.513 | 0.396 | 0.357 | 0.902 |
| Rizhao | 0.477 | 0.121 | 0.254 | 0.480 | 0.370 | 0.770 |
| Shenyang | 0.782 | 0.761 | 0.973 | 0.548 | 0.537 | 0.979 |
| Dalian | 1.000 | 1.000 | 1.000 | 0.758 | 0.748 | 0.987 |
| Anshan | 0.702 | 0.121 | 0.172 | 0.539 | 0.511 | 0.948 |
| Fushun | 0.503 | 0.092 | 0.183 | 0.569 | 0.536 | 0.941 |
| Benxi | 0.528 | 0.077 | 0.146 | 0.599 | 0.567 | 0.947 |
| Jinzhou | 0.752 | 0.103 | 0.137 | 0.477 | 0.408 | 0.856 |
| Changchun | 0.883 | 0.791 | 0.896 | 0.491 | 0.351 | 0.716 |
| Jilin | 0.532 | 0.145 | 0.273 | 0.494 | 0.375 | 0.758 |
| Haeibin | 0.642 | 0.553 | 0.862 | 0.485 | 0.369 | 0.761 |
| Qiqihaer | 0.850 | 0.113 | 0.133 | 0.749 | 0.621 | 0.829 |
| Mudanjiang | 1.000 | 0.038 | 0.038 | 0.518 | 0.161 | 0.310 |
| Shanghai | 1.000 | 1.000 | 1.000 | 1.000 | 1.000 | 1.000 |
| Nanjing | 0.705 | 0.686 | 0.973 | 0.567 | 0.554 | 0.977 |
| Xuzhou | 0.543 | 0.343 | 0.631 | 0.518 | 0.428 | 0.827 |
| Lianyungang | 0.490 | 0.131 | 0.268 | 0.494 | 0.435 | 0.881 |
| Yangzhou | 0.706 | 0.596 | 0.844 | 0.534 | 0.500 | 0.936 |
| Nantong | 0.596 | 0.332 | 0.556 | 0.557 | 0.520 | 0.934 |
| Zhenjiang | 0.800 | 0.245 | 0.306 | 0.494 | 0.459 | 0.928 |
| Changzhou | 0.524 | 0.372 | 0.710 | 0.616 | 0.597 | 0.969 |
| Wuxi | 0.556 | 0.466 | 0.838 | 0.632 | 0.625 | 0.988 |
| Suzhou | 0.588 | 0.449 | 0.763 | 0.646 | 0.602 | 0.932 |

(continued)

**Table 22.10** (continued)

| Cities | Natural performance under variable return to scale | Natural performance under constant return to scale | Scale performance under natural performance | Management performance under variable massive loss | Management performance under constant massive loss | Scale performance under management performance |
|---|---|---|---|---|---|---|
| Hangzhou | 0.577 | 0.539 | 0.934 | 0.697 | 0.696 | 0.999 |
| Ningbo | 0.698 | 0.448 | 0.641 | 0.799 | 0.760 | 0.951 |
| Wenzhou | 0.721 | 0.193 | 0.268 | 0.704 | 0.602 | 0.855 |
| Huzhou | 0.634 | 0.105 | 0.165 | 0.593 | 0.509 | 0.858 |
| Shaoxing | 0.501 | 0.185 | 0.370 | 0.584 | 0.538 | 0.921 |
| Fuzhou | 1.000 | 0.759 | 0.759 | 1.000 | 0.767 | 0.767 |
| Xiamen | 0.897 | 0.472 | 0.526 | 0.896 | 0.845 | 0.943 |
| Quanzhou | 1.000 | 0.347 | 0.347 | 1.000 | 1.000 | 1.000 |
| Guangzhou | 1.000 | 1.000 | 1.000 | 0.887 | 0.864 | 0.975 |
| Shenzhen | 1.000 | 1.000 | 1.000 | 1.000 | 1.000 | 1.000 |
| Zhuhai | 1.000 | 0.330 | 0.330 | 0.976 | 0.916 | 0.939 |
| Shantou | 0.865 | 0.270 | 0.312 | 1.000 | 0.881 | 0.881 |
| Shaoguan | 0.771 | 0.064 | 0.083 | 0.724 | 0.464 | 0.641 |
| Zhanjiang | 1.000 | 0.244 | 0.244 | 1.000 | 0.900 | 0.900 |
| Xian | 0.661 | 0.610 | 0.923 | 0.519 | 0.485 | 0.933 |
| Baoji | 0.879 | 0.664 | 0.755 | 0.497 | 0.459 | 0.924 |
| Xianyang | 1.000 | 1.000 | 1.000 | 0.412 | 0.318 | 0.772 |
| Weinan | 1.000 | 0.496 | 0.496 | 0.441 | 0.273 | 0.619 |
| Yanan | 1.000 | 0.055 | 0.055 | 0.547 | 0.211 | 0.385 |
| Taiyuan | 0.497 | 0.245 | 0.493 | 0.694 | 0.676 | 0.974 |
| Datong | 0.702 | 0.098 | 0.139 | 0.682 | 0.388 | 0.570 |
| Yangquan | 0.408 | 0.032 | 0.078 | 0.409 | 0.294 | 0.719 |
| Changzhi | 0.499 | 0.039 | 0.078 | 0.467 | 0.420 | 0.899 |
| Linfen | 0.706 | 0.030 | 0.042 | 0.511 | 0.344 | 0.673 |
| Zhengzhou | 0.414 | 0.256 | 0.618 | 0.596 | 0.588 | 0.987 |
| Kaifeng | 0.434 | 0.056 | 0.128 | 0.451 | 0.411 | 0.912 |
| Luoyang | 0.397 | 0.113 | 0.285 | 0.459 | 0.411 | 0.895 |
| Pingdingshan | 0.362 | 0.038 | 0.106 | 0.352 | 0.316 | 0.898 |
| Jiaozuo | 0.382 | 0.034 | 0.089 | 0.465 | 0.442 | 0.951 |
| Anyang | 0.322 | 0.034 | 0.106 | 0.308 | 0.263 | 0.855 |
| Sanmenxia | 1.000 | 0.018 | 0.018 | 0.384 | 0.306 | 0.796 |
| Huhehaote | 1.000 | 0.970 | 0.970 | 0.700 | 0.585 | 0.837 |
| Baotou | 0.550 | 0.274 | 0.499 | 0.604 | 0.583 | 0.965 |
| Chifeng | 0.628 | 0.161 | 0.255 | 0.665 | 0.522 | 0.784 |
| Wuhan | 0.807 | 0.787 | 0.976 | 1.000 | 1.000 | 1.000 |

(continued)

**Table 22.10** (continued)

| Cities | Natural performance under variable return to scale | Natural performance under constant return to scale | Scale performance under natural performance | Management performance under variable massive loss | Management performance under constant massive loss | Scale performance under management performance |
|---|---|---|---|---|---|---|
| Jingzhou | 0.393 | 0.064 | 0.164 | 0.372 | 0.316 | 0.852 |
| Yichang | 0.578 | 0.386 | 0.668 | 0.738 | 0.731 | 0.990 |
| Changsha | 1.000 | 1.000 | 1.000 | 0.603 | 0.529 | 0.878 |
| Zhuzhou | 0.560 | 0.162 | 0.289 | 0.509 | 0.466 | 0.916 |
| Xiangtan | 0.517 | 0.116 | 0.224 | 0.448 | 0.391 | 0.873 |
| Yueyang | 0.604 | 0.332 | 0.550 | 0.587 | 0.535 | 0.912 |
| Changde | 1.000 | 1.000 | 1.000 | 0.700 | 0.647 | 0.923 |
| Zhangjiajie | 1.000 | 0.271 | 0.271 | 0.778 | 0.586 | 0.753 |
| Nanchang | 0.777 | 0.629 | 0.810 | 0.587 | 0.517 | 0.881 |
| Jiujiang | 0.888 | 0.389 | 0.438 | 0.659 | 0.563 | 0.855 |
| Hefei | 0.933 | 0.848 | 0.909 | 0.632 | 0.584 | 0.924 |
| Wuhu | 0.719 | 0.321 | 0.446 | 0.586 | 0.530 | 0.905 |
| Maanshan | 0.514 | 0.089 | 0.173 | 0.518 | 0.475 | 0.916 |
| Kunming | 1.000 | 0.888 | 0.888 | 0.902 | 0.588 | 0.652 |
| Qujing | 1.000 | 0.177 | 0.177 | 0.877 | 0.395 | 0.451 |
| Yuxi | 1.000 | 0.297 | 0.297 | 0.967 | 0.564 | 0.584 |
| Guiyang | 1.000 | 0.776 | 0.776 | 0.655 | 0.506 | 0.773 |
| Zunyi | 0.870 | 0.148 | 0.170 | 0.518 | 0.320 | 0.618 |
| Chengdu | 1.000 | 1.000 | 1.000 | 0.599 | 0.439 | 0.733 |
| Zigong | 1.000 | 1.000 | 1.000 | 0.585 | 0.466 | 0.797 |
| Panzhihua | 0.757 | 0.077 | 0.102 | 0.745 | 0.511 | 0.686 |
| Luzhou | 0.647 | 0.177 | 0.273 | 0.510 | 0.366 | 0.718 |
| Deyang | 1.000 | 0.208 | 0.208 | 0.564 | 0.408 | 0.723 |
| Mianyang | 0.751 | 0.204 | 0.272 | 0.655 | 0.533 | 0.814 |
| Yibin | 0.685 | 0.207 | 0.302 | 0.485 | 0.425 | 0.876 |
| Chongqing | 0.945 | 0.862 | 0.912 | 1.000 | 1.000 | 1.000 |
| Nanning | 0.866 | 0.598 | 0.691 | 0.707 | 0.459 | 0.649 |
| Liuzhou | \0.727 | 0.513 | 0.706 | 0.562 | 0.503 | 0.895 |
| Guilin | 0.848 | 0.240 | 0.283 | 0.572 | 0.461 | 0.806 |
| Beihai | 1.000 | 0.425 | 0.425 | 1.000 | 0.867 | 0.867 |
| Lanzhou | 0.485 | 0.156 | 0.323 | 0.501 | 0.341 | 0.680 |
| Jinchang | 1.000 | 0.036 | 0.036 | 0.935 | 0.864 | 0.924 |
| Xining | 0.463 | 0.083 | 0.178 | 0.472 | 0.389 | 0.824 |
| Yinchuan | 0.550 | 0.101 | 0.183 | 0.576 | 0.435 | 0.755 |
| Shizuishan | 0.625 | 0.041 | 0.065 | 0.577 | 0.459 | 0.796 |
| Wulumuqi | 0.552 | 0.375 | 0.679 | 0.541 | 0.425 | 0.787 |
| Kelamayi | 1.000 | 0.568 | 0.568 | 1.000 | 1.000 | 1.000 |

## References


Allevi, E., Basso, A., & Bonenti, F., et al. (2018). Measuring the environmental performance of green SRI funds: A DEA approach. *Energy Economics, 79*, 32–44.

Awni, A., Ankita, M., & Aparna, S., et al. (2017). Characterization, sources and health risk analysis of $PM_{2.5}$ bound metals during foggy and non-foggy days in sub-urban atmosphere of Agra. *Atmospheric Research, 197*, 121–131.

Bai, Y., Zhang, X., Hao, Y., et al. (2013). Research on regional environmental performance and its influential factors based on SBM-Malmquist-Tobit model. *Areal Research and Development, 32*(2), 90–95.

Bian, Y., He, P., & Xu, H. (2013). Estimation of potential energy saving and carbon dioxide emission reduction in China based on an extended non-radial DEA approach. *Energy Policy, 63*, 962–971.

Cheng, D. (2008). *Efficiency differences and its influential factors across provinces in China in the presence of environmental constraints* (pp. 32–41). Anhui: Hefei University of Technology.

Chen, X., & Zhou, Z. (2014). Urban environmental performance evaluation and decomposition of affecting factors based on variable return to scale. *China Soft Science, 10*, 121–128.

Chen, H., Hen, P., & Luo, Y. (2015). The research of Beijing-Tianjin-Hebei urban agglomerations' environmental efficiency and its influential factors. *Ecological Economy, 8*(31), 142–150.

Chen, Z., Kourtzidis, S., & Tzeremes, P., et al. (2020). A robust network DEA model for sustainability assessment: an application to Chinese Provinces. *Operational Research*, 1–28.

Dong, F., Zhang, S., Li, Y., et al. (2020). Examining environmental regulation efficiency of haze control and driving mechanism: Evidence from China. *Environmental Science and Pollution Research, 27*, 29171–29190.

Feng, B., & Wang, X. (2015). Research on energy efficiency considering the haze effect in Beijing-Tianjin-Hebei metropolitan region. *Journal of Arid Land Resources and Environment, 29*(10), 1–7.

Gokhale, S., & Raokhande, N. (2008). Performance evaluation of air quality models for predicting $PM_{10}$ and $PM_{2.5}$ concentrations at urban traffic intersection during winter period. *Science of the Total Environment, 394*(1), 9–24.

Guo, J., Liu, H., Wu, X., et al. (2015). Allocation of air pollutants emission rights based on zero-sum gains data envelopment analysis. *China Soft Science, 11*, 176–185.

Halkos, G., & Petrou, K. (2018). Assessing 28 EU Member States' environmental efficiency in national waste generation with DEA. *Journal of Cleaner Production, 208*, 509–521.

He, F., Ma, D., & Xu, X. (2016). Interval environmental efficiency across provinces in China under the constraint of haze with SBM-undesirable interval model. *Journal of Arid Land Resources and Environment, 30*(12), 28–33.

He, Q., Han, J., Guan, D., et al. (2018). The comprehensive environmental efficiency of socioeconomic sectors in China: An analysis based on a non-separable bad output SBM. *Journal of Cleaner Production, 176*, 1091–1110.

Hua, J., Ren, J., Xu, M., et al. (2013). Evaluation of Chinese regional carbon dioxide emission performance based on a three-stage DEA model. *Resources Science, 35*(7), 1447–1454.

Hu, J., Ying, Q., & Wang. Y., et al. (2015). Characterizing multi-pollutant air pollution in China: Comparison of three air quality indices. *Environment International, 84*, 17–25.

Iftikhar, Y., Wang, Z., Zhang, B., et al. (2018). Energy and $CO_2$ emissions efficiency of major economies: A network DEA approach. *Energy, 147*, 197–207.

Jiang, H., Wu, J., Chu, J., et al. (2020). Better resource utilization: A new DEA bi-objective resource reallocation approach considering environmental efficiency improvement. *Computers & Industrial Engineering, 144*, 1–11.

Jung, C, Young, L, & Hsu, H., et al. (2017). $PM_{2.5}$ components and outpatient visits for asthma: A time-stratified case-crossover study in a suburban area. *Environmental Pollution, 231*(Pt 1), 1085–1092.

Kang, D., Mathur, R., & Rao, S. (2010). Real-time bias-adjusted $O_3$ and $PM_{2.5}$ air quality index forecasts and their performance evaluations over the continental United States. *Atmospheric Environment, 44*(18), 2203–2212.

Lee, T., Yeo, G., & Thai, V. (2014). Environmental efficiency analysis of port cities: Slacks-based measure data envelopment analysis approach. *Transport Policy, 33*(4), 82–88.

Li, J. (2009). Eco-efficiency Differences and its influential factors across provinces in China. *South China Journal of Economics, 12,* 24–35.

Li, J., & Cheng, D. (2008). The Research on China's regional environmental efficiency difference and evolution rule-based on SBM model undesired output. *Industrial Technology Economy, 27*(11), 100–104.

Li, H., Wang, B., Xiong, B., et al. (2012). Empirical research on the regional environmental efficiency based on improved ISBM-DEA model. *Systems Engineering, 30*(7), 86–93.

Li, Y., Ouyang, H., Fang, K., et al. (2015). Evaluation of regional environmental efficiencies in China based on super-efficiency-DEA. *Ecological Indicators, 51,* 13–19.

Li, Y., Chiu, Y., & Lu, L. (2018). Energy and AQI performance of 31 cities in China. *Energy Policy, 122,* 194–202.

Li, Y., Chiu, Y., Wang, L., et al. (2019). Dynamic and network slack-based measure analysis of China's regional energy and air pollution reduction efficiencies. *Journal of Cleaner Production, 251,* 119546.

Lin, X., Zhu, X., Han, Y., et al. (2020). Economy and carbon dioxide emissions effects of energy structures in the world: Evidence based on SBM-DEA model. *Science of the Total Environment, 729,* 1–9.

Ma, D., He, F., & Li, G., et al. (2018). Estimation and Comparative Analysis of Environmental Efficiency in China, with and .without Consideration of Haze. *Polish Journal of Environmental Studies, 27*(1).

Moutinho, V., Madaleno, M., & Macedo, P. (2020). The effect of urban air pollutants in Germany: Eco-efficiency analysis through fractional regression models applied after DEA and SFA efficiency predictions. *Sustainable Cities and Society, 59,* 1–11.

Ouyang, W., & Yang, J. (2020). The network energy and environment efficiency analysis of 27 OECD countries: A multiplicative network DEA model. *Energy, 197,* 1–16.

Qi, M. (2015). Research on the performance of industrial transformation and upgrading in the Oearl river. *Social Scientist, 12,* 68–71.

Reyes, J., Xu, Y., & Vizuete, W., et al. (2016). Regionalized $PM_{2.5}$ community multiscale air quality model performance evaluation across a continuous spatiotemporal domain. *Atmospheric Environment, 148,* 258–265.

Shang, Y., Liu, H., & Lv, Y. (2020). Total factor energy efficiency in regions of China: An empirical analysis on SBM-DEA model with undesired generation. *Journal of King Saud Universityi—Science, 32*(3), 1925–1931.

Sueyoshi, T., & Yuan, Y. (2015). China's regional sustainability and diversified resource allocation: DEA environmental assessment on economic development and air pollution. *Energy Economics, 49,* 239–256.

Sun, H. (2007). A Study on the mechanism construct of regional coordination development. *Economic Geography, 27*(3), 362–365.

Sun, H., & Liu, C. (2005). The division in breadth ofChinese districts. *China Industrial Economy, 10,* 27–34.

Sun, S., Guo, Q., & Shao, Q. (2014). Study on provincial carbon emission's efficiency in China based on super-efficiency DEA model. *Yuejiang Academic Journal, 6,* 41–51.

Sun, H., Mohsin, M., Alharthi, M., et al. (2020). Measuring environmental sustainability performance of South Asia. *Journal of Cleaner Production, 251,* 1–13.

Wang, K., Wei, Y., & Huang, Z. (2015a). Potential gains from carbon emissions trading in China: A DEA based estimation on abatement cost savings. *Omegs, 63,* 48–59.

Wang, Q., Shen, T., & Qiu, J. (2015b). Environmental efficiency difference and influencing factors of China's three major city groups. *Urban Problems, 7,* 10–18.

Wang, Y., Liu, Y., & Li, J., et al. (2015c). The effect of $PM_{2.5}/PM_{10}$ variation based on precipitable water vapor and wind speed. *Journal of Catastrophology, 30*(1), 5–7.
Wang, K., Miao, Z., & Zhao, M., et al. (2019). China's provincial total-factor air pollution emission efficiency evaluation, dynamic evolution and influencing factors. *Ecological Indicators, 107*, 105578.1–105578.11.
Wang, K., Ding, L., & Wang, J., et al. (2020). Analysis of provincial total-factor air pollution efficiency in China by using context-dependent slacks-based measure considering undesirable outputs. *Natural Hazards, 104*(9).
Wu, Q., & Wu, C. (2009). Research on evaluation model of energy efficiency based on DEA. *Journal of Management Science, 22*(1), 3–112.
Wu, X., Chen. Y., & Guo, J. (2016a). Spatial concentration, impact factors and prevention-control measures of $PM_{2.5}$ pollution in China. *Natural Hazards, 86*, 1–18.
Wu, J., Yin, P., Sun, J., et al. (2016b). Evaluating the environmental efficiency of a two-stage system with undesired outputs by a DEA approach: An interest preference perspective. *European Journal of Operational Research, 254*(3), 1047–1062.
Wu, X., Cheng, H., & Wang, G. (2016c). Empirical study on evaluation and determinants of Chinese atmospheric environmental efficiency based on the Super-SBM model. *Yuejiang Academic Journal, 5*, 13–25.
Wu, X., Chen, S., & Guo, J. (2017). Effect of air pollution on the stock yield of heavy pollution enterprises in China's key control cities. *Journal of Cleaner Production*. https://doi.org/10.1016/j.jclepro. 2017.09.154.
Wu, X., Chen, Y., & Guo, J., et al. (2018). Inputs optimization to reduce the undesirable outputs by environmental hazards: a DEA model with data of $PM_{2.5}$ in China. *Natural Hazards, 90*, 1–25.
Xu, S., Zhou, Y., & Feng, C., et al. (2020). What factors influence $PM_{2.5}$ emissions in China? An analysis of regional differences using a combined method of data envelopment analysis and logarithmic mean Divisia index. *Environmental Science and Pollution Research, 27*(27), 34234–34249.
Yang, Y. (2014). Coupling and synergetic development of ecological-environment-economy in rapidly urbanizing regions: A review. *Ecology and Environmental Sciences, 23*(3), 541–546.
Yang, Z., & Wei, X. (2019). The measurement and influences of China's urban total factor energy efficiency under environmental pollution: Based on the game cross-efficiency DEA. *Journal of Cleaner Production, 209*, 439–450.
Yang, Q., Zhang, Y., & Li, Y. (2012). Research on environmental efficiency evaluation of urban agglomerations in northeast China based on DEA model. *Economic Geography, 32*(9), 51–60.
Yin, J., Cao, Y., & Tang, B. (2019). Fairness of China's provincial energy environment efficiency evaluation: Empirical analysis using a three-stage data envelopment analysis model. *Natural Hazards, 95*, 343–362.
Yu, S., Liu, J., & Li, L. (2020). Evaluating provincial eco-efficiency in China: An improved network data envelopment analysis model with undesirable output. *Environmental Science and Pollution Research, 27*, 6886–6903.
Zaim, O., & Taskin, F. (2001). Environmental efficiency in carbon dioxide emissions in the OECD: A non-parametric approach. *Resource and Energy Economics, 1*(23), 63–83.
Zeng, X., Zhou, Z., Liu, Q., et al. (2020). Environmental efficiency and abatement potential analysis with a two-stage DEA model incorporating the material balance principle. *Computers & Industrial Engineering, 148*, 1–13.
Zhang, Z., Lu, C., Chen, X., et al. (2015). Urban environmental performance and it's driving factors in China: Based on the super-efficiency DEA and panel regressive analysis. *Journal of Arid Land Resources and Environment, 29*(6), 1–7.
Zhang, J., Zeng, W., & Shi, H. (2016). Regional environmental efficiency in China: Analysis based on a regional slack-based measure with environmental undesirable outputs. *Ecological Indicators, 71*, 218–228.
Zhang, J., Wu, Q., & Zhou, Z. (2019). A two-stage DEA model for resource allocation in industrial pollution treatment and its application in China. *Journal of Cleaner Production, 228*, 29–39.

Zhang, N., Zhao, K., & Yu, Y. (2020). The effect of environmental regulation on air pollution, productivity, and factor structure: A quasi-natural experiment evidence from China. *Environmental Science and Pollution Research, 27,* 20392–20409.
Zha, Y., Zhao, L., & Bian, Y. (2016). Measuring regional efficiency of energy and carbon dioxide emissions in China: A chance constrained DEA approach. *Computers & Operations Research, 66,* 351–361.
Zhou, Y., & Zhou, J. (2017). Urban atmospheric environmental capacity and atmospheric environmental carrying capacity constrained by GDP-$PM_{2.5}$. *Ecological Indicators, 73,* 637–652.
Zhou, Z., Liu, C., Zeng, X., et al. (2018). Carbon emission performance evaluation and allocation in Chinese cities. *Journal of Cleaner Production, 172*(2), 1254–1272.
Zhou, Z., Xu, G., & Wang, C., et al. (2019). Modeling undesirable output with a DEA approach based on an exponential transformation: An application to measure the energy efficiency of Chinese industry. *Journal of Cleaner Production, 236*, 1–11.
Zhou, Z., Chen, Y., Song, P., et al. (2020). China's urban air quality evaluation with streaming data: A DEA window analysis. *Science of the Total Environment, 727,* 1–9.

# Chapter 23
# Tendency of Embodied Carbon Change in the Export Trade of Chinese Manufacturing Industry from 2000 to 2015 and Its Driving Factors

**Abstract** Manufacturing industry is an important part of the national industrial system, and usually an industry with high carbon content. However, few studies have been carried out on the total amount, structure and the trend of the embodied carbon emission in the international trade of the Chinese manufacturing industry. Based on the input–output method, the thesis proposes the coefficient of direct carbon emission and complete carbon emission and a method for calculating the embodied carbon of the export trade. It also calculates the coefficient of direct carbon emission and complete carbon emission for Chinese manufacturing sector from 2000 to 2015 and breaks down the embodied carbon change of export trade in the manufacturing industry to technological effect, structural effect and scale effect by using the method of structural decomposition. Several inspiring conclusions could be drawn from the thesis. For example: (1) The coefficient of both the direct carbon emission and the complete carbon emission has been decreasing significantly, indicating the achievements of the energy saving and emission reduction of the Chinese manufacturing industry. (2) The embodied carbon emission from the manufacturing exports remains high and presents a rising tendency. The main sectors that exports the embodied carbon includes "S10 mechanical equipment and instrument", "S9 metal products", "S6 chemical industry", etc., which should be the key sectors on reducing embodied carbon in exports. (3) The driving force of the embodied carbon exports lies in the scale effect of the manufacturing industry, on which the technical effect of the industry has a significant negative effect. The structural effect should have a positive influence that takes on a rising tendency; generally, this effect is only two thirds the scale effect. Finally, the corresponding policy suggestions have been made.

**Keywords** Import and export trade · Embodied carbon · Input–output method · Structural decomposition

## 23.1 Introduction

Manufacturing industry is a core component of a country's industrial system. With the capacity to encourage other industries, promote employment and increase tax income, it has been given priority by governments. As a manufacturing power, China has



X. Wu and J. Guo, *Economic Impacts and Emergency Management of Disasters in China*,
https://doi.org/10.1007/978-981-16-1319-7_23

proposed the initiative of "Made in China 2025". In 2017, the gross value of Chinese manufacturing industry is roughly equal to the total value of the US, Japanese and German manufacturing industries (Gong and Chen 2017). With a significant characteristic of "three highs and one low", namely, high investment, high consumption, high pollution and low cost, for a long period of time and high carbon content, Chinese manufacturing industry has become the key department for monitoring in the "Climax-reaching Plan" put forward by the Chinese government in 2014.

The high carbon characteristic of Chinese manufacturing industry will prompt the government to strengthen the environmental regulations upon which and thus affect the future development of the industry. However, Chinese manufacturing industry is an industry with frequent export trade and the flow of the embodied carbon between trades is significant. Most of the manufacturing industry in China manufactures for the purposes of export and leaves carbon in the country. As Levinson and Minier put it, pollution can flow with trade (Ederington 2004, 2005). The emission of carbon can also flow with trade. How much embodied carbon is emitted for the purpose of international trade and how should we calculate it? What changes have taken place during 2000 and 2015? Besides, Wang et al. (2017) deconstructed the factors of carbon emission in Guangdong province from 1990 to 2014 from the perspective of energy consumption. Wei et al. (2012) studied the dynamic changes of the cost of carbon emission reduction. Lugauer et al. (2014) and Zagheni (2011) proposes that changes of age structure would exert an effect on carbon emission. Therefore, factors that affected the dynamic changes of the embodied carbon in the Chinese manufacturing industry need to be calculated in detail, which, upon completion, could provide empirical evidence for Chinese government to carry out negotiations on carbon emission reduction with countries, formulate detailed plans for carbon emission reduction and import and export trade and ultimately make contributions to the sustainable development of Chinese manufacturing industry (Yang et al. 2017).

Based on the above considerations, the thesis proposes the coefficient of direct carbon emission and complete carbon emission and a method for calculating the embodied carbon of the export trade by applying the input–output method. It also calculates the coefficient of direct carbon emission and complete carbon emission for every Chinese manufacturing sector from 2000–2015 and decomposes the embodied carbon change of export trade in the manufacturing industry to technological effect, structural effect and scale effect by using the method of structural decomposition. Corresponding countermeasures and recommendations were proposed for the Chinese manufacturing industry for its transforming from "making" to "creating" and from "three highs and one low" to "sustainable development."

The rest of the paper is as follows: the second part is the thesis statement; the third part is the model construction; the fourth part is the data source and data processing; the fifth part is the analysis of the calculated embodied carbon; the sixth part is the analysis of the technology, structure and scale effects of the embodied carbon; the final part is the conclusion and further discussion.

## 23.2 Literature Review

Judging from current research, input–output method is used by scholars at home and abroad to calculate the embodied carbon. The study of scholars from different countries can be mainly divided into the following categories:

The first one is the study of embodied carbon in a specific region, for example, Li (2012) estimated the embodied carbon in the export trade of Xinjiang Province based on the input–output model of the non-competitive regional environment; Zhang and Zhou (2013) studied the embodied carbon in Beijing's domestic and foreign trade and its composition, industrial distribution and non-balance degree; Zhong (2013) calculated embodied carbon emission in the import and export trade of Guangdong Province by applying the input–output method; Mi et al. (2015) studied the embodied carbon emission of Beijing; Hasegawa et al. (2015) analyzed the carbon footprint of Japan by using the input–output model. Tian et al. (2014) analyzed the carbon footprint of China from the perspective of regional consumption and production. Through multi-regional input–output model, Fan et al. (2019a) used four years input–output data stepped over twenty years to establish an interprovincial carbon flow analysis framework of Hebei Province. The result showed provincial Trade had caused the transfer of embodied carbon emissions. By building environmentally extended multi-regional input–output model with an inter-provincial table of China, Fan et al. (2019b) explored that the consumption-based emission of Beijing-Tianjin-Hebei region was lower than production-based emission while the carbon emission in Beijing-Tianjin-Hebei region was closely related from the production-based emission. After examining the embodied carbon emissions in trade data of the Hong Kong special administrative region from 1990 to 2015, Huang et al. (2019) found out Hong Kong was a net carbon importer. Population density, GDP per capita, and trade openness played dominating roles in the embodied carbon emissions of Hong Kong. Through setting up a three-scale input–output model, Li et al. (2020a) distinguished local, domestic and foreign activities to point out that domestic imports dominated Beijing's total embodied energy use and to highlight the importance in order to consider the impacts of headquarter effect on Beijing's embodied energy use and redistribution pattern. By employing both single and multi-regional input–output tables to compare disparities in the embodied carbon emissions accounting in Tokyo, Long et al. (2020) indicated that the gap of emissions driven by Tokyo's final demand was considerably large and coal-generated emissions had been largely ignored by single-regional input–output table.

The second one is the study of carbon emissions in single countries. For example, Thomas et al. (2010) calculated the Net emissions of $CO_2$ of the United Kingdom from 1992 to 2004 by applying the multi-regional input–output model; Wang et al. (2020) analyzed that the progress in high- and new-technology industries contributed to reduce the gap of embodied carbon emissions in developed countries and in developing countries; Gao et al. (2020), through constructing a noncompetitive input–output model to measure the embodied carbon emissions between 2005 and 2017 in China, considered that China's direct carbon emissions had generally increased and there was significant heterogeneity among various industry sectors on efficiency of embodied carbon emissions. By using the multi-regional input–output model, Zhou et al. (2018) estimated the regional implied carbon emissions in China from 2002 to 2012 and proved that "pollution heaven" hypothesis happened in China, especially the growth of the inter-regional trade scale played a positive effect on the increase of embodied carbon emissions while technological progress played a negative effect on the increase of embodied carbon emissions. Guo et al. (2020) calculated the embodied carbon emissions by applying a multi-regional input–output model and identified the key driving factors of the embodied carbon emission by using structural decomposition analysis. Finally, he came to the conclusion that the mainly driving factors for the increase in embodied carbon emissions were household consumption and gross fixed capital formation while technical efficiency was the main factor contributed to the emission decline in Mongolia. Through using the global multi-regional input–output model, He and Hertwich (2019) accounted for direct and indirect, intermediate and final embodied carbon emissions to show that China had increased in both intermediate and final indirect carbon emissions compared to US and EU from 1995 to 2015. Based on non-competitive input–output models, Pu et al. (2020) measured China's embodied carbon emissions from international trade and interprovincial trade in order to demonstrate intermediate production technology, trade structure and total trade volume all promoted the growth of embodied carbon emissions. Through comparing embodied carbon emissions based on production principle and consumption principle in the eight major economic regions of China, Wang et al. (2019a) attested that the reduction of emission intensity in the production sector was the key factor to coordinate inter-provincial trade and regionally balanced development under open economic conditions. Based on the Multi-Scale Input–Output model, Results showed that different regions' present multi-carbon flow patterns categorized into resource supplier because of the regional heterogeneity in economic development and natural resource endowments (Hu et al. 2020). Manfred et al. (2010) discovered an obvious trend of rising in embodied carbon in the trade of the United Kingdom between 1994 and 2004 by applying the multi-regional input–output model; Yrjö et al. (2011) measured the embodied carbon in the trade of the Finnish food industry by using the EIO-LCA model; Bin et al. (2013) calculated the embodied carbon content of the Chinese import and export trade between 2000 and 2007 by using the Walras-Cassel model; Song (2012) calculated the embodied carbon emission in Chinese export trade between 2006 and 2009 by using the input–output model; Qiu and Li (2012) measured the embodied carbon emission of the Chinese import and export trade in the year 2000, 2005 and 2007 by using the input–output method. Yan et al. (2013) measured the embodied carbon of Chinese export trade by using the multi-regional input–output model and made a comparison of the responsibilities in production emission and consumption emission. Bin et al. (2013) calculated the $CO_2$ emission in China's international trade by using input–output method, based on competitive imports and non-competitive imports respectively.

The third one focused on revealing embodied carbon in bilateral countries and regions. For example, Wang et al. (2019b) calculated embodied carbon from 2000 to 2014 in the trade between China and Australia in order to study trends in the carbon emissions embodied in bilateral trade and to help policymakers of China and Australia specify more effective environmental policies. According to the relevant data from 2000 to 2015, Wang and Yang (2020) found the increase in real carbon emissions in China and India led to the growth in final demand. Thus, policymakers of China and India could curb carbon emission by reducing the carbon intensity coefficient effect. In addition, Wang et al. (2019c) based on the non-competitive input–output analysis to investigate the net carbon emissions embodied in trade between China and German. They found out the dominant reason of the growth of net carbon emission in bilateral trade was intermediate input structure effect of China and the country structure effect of Germany's final demand. Wang and Zhou (2019a) paid attention to the empirical research of embodied carbon emission between developed countries by assessing embodied carbon emissions in Germany-US trade from 2000 to 2015, and his study showed both Germany and the United States have tendencies to shift carbon emissions to developing countries. And then Wang and Zhou (2019b) established a structural analysis of carbon emissions embodied in US-Japan trade by using multi-regional input–output model and came to the conclusion that the economic losses of U.S. outweighed its environmental gains through carbon transfer with Japan. Meanwhile, Ji et al. (2020) paid attention to the empirical research of embodied carbon emission between developing countries by assessing embodied carbon emissions in China-Africa trade during 2000–2015, and his study showed the intensities of embodied carbon emission in both China and Africa were declining towards a rosy prospect and indicated a positive carbon emission efficiency of both sides. Long et al. (2018) compared the difference in imports and exports, production and consumption between China and Japan to analyze China's direct and complete carbon dioxide emissions intensity with Japan's and finally came to the conclusion that carbon emissions in all sectors of China were higher than that in Japan and China's emissions were mainly production-based emissions. Yu and Chen (2017) deemed that the China-South Korea trade diversion played dominating roles in reducing the global carbon emissions and easing the pressure of carbon emissions in China by calculating and decomposed the embodied carbon emissions in China-South Korea trade by using input–output models.

The fourth one is the research on carbon emissions of multiple countries and regions. For example, Glen et al. (2011) estimated the embodied trade carbon of 57 economic sectors in 113 countries by using the input–output method; Bin and Ang (2011) studied the embodied carbon emission in foreign trades of Asian countries by using the multi-regional input–output model; Wu et al. (2020) distinguished intermediate trade from final trade and based on the global multi-regional input–output account to explore that although China obtains a considerable economic trade surplus, its carbon trade deficit cannot be ignored; Jiang et al. (2020) built a multi-regional input–output model which embodied in international trade of 39 countries from 1995 to 2011 and calculated embodied carbon emissions was transferred globally through trade links; Zhong et al. (2018) analyzed carbon emissions embodied transfer for 39 countries from 1995 to 2011, based on the multi-regional input–output analytical framework, to prove that carbon emissions embodied in global trade primarily have flown from developing countries (or regions) to developed countries (or regions); Chen et al. (2018) whose study based on environmentally extended input–output analysis discovered that the economies were highly connected through embodied energy transfer and economies with large out-strength should encourage more companies to improve their energy efficiency and adopt more clean energy so as to improve the production of the exported goods and services. According to Kirsten et al. (2012) calculation under the guidance of the input–output model, the embodied import carbon of the OECD countries increased 80% from 1995 to 2005. Mi et al. (2016, 2017a, b) developed the inter-regional input–output table of China in 2012 and calculated the flow of the embodied carbon in China's import and export trade. On basis of the multi-regional input–output analysis between 1995 and 2011, Li et al. (2020b) depicted the characteristics of the global embodied carbon emissions transfer network and concluded that as the global trading network becomes more denser, the embodied carbon emissions problem between economies worse. Lu et al. (2020) proved that carbon emissions embodied had gradually moved from China and India to other the Belt and Road Initiative countries and the growth in final demand per capita was the most important driver for the growth of carbon emissions.

From the above analysis, it is observed that the input–output method is both a way to analyze the quantitative dependence between production and consumption of different sectors in the national economy and a research method (2012) to connect economic activities with environmental pollution, which can be used in calculating the embodied carbon in the export trades. What's more, input–output methods have a simple form, a clear principle, a reliable calculation result and avoid the problems of endogeneity, robustness, uncertain index settings, etc. in the parametric methods such as econometric mode. It is suitable for quantitative calculation of the embodied carbon in the input–output associations among different sectors. This paper therefore adopts the input–output method for research. From the research perspective, scholars at home and abroad focused mostly on the overall analysis on the national level but few on the analysis of the specific industries, with existing studies directing at industries like agriculture and petroleum but few at the import and export trade of Chinese manufacturing industries. Moreover, most of the existing researches calculated $CO_2$ emission of every sector by taking three kinds of primary fossil energy, namely, coal, petroleum and natural gas into account while few are concerning the eight kinds of primary and secondary fossil energy including coal, coke, crude oil, gasoline, kerosene, diesel, and fuel oil. Bin et al. (2013) are the limited scholars who calculated the above eight kinds of energy in theirs studies, but conducted for all industries.

In addition, most scholars only studied the embodied carbon of trade within the years of the input–output table, which could be disadvantageous in picturing the change of the embodied carbon in the long run. For the above reasons, the thesis proposes a way to calculate the coefficient of direct carbon emission and complete carbon emission and the embodied carbon in the export trade based on the input–output method. Take China's manufacturing industry for example, this paper calculated the direct carbon emission, complete carbon emission and the embodied carbon in the export trade of any sector between 2000 and 2015, analyzed the embodied carbon in the export trade from an overall level and a sectoral level, and further analyzed the trend of the driving factors of the embodied carbon changes in the export trade of the manufacturing industry. Finally, the corresponding suggestions of policy are proposed and are expected to provide some reference to the industry.

## 23.3 Research Method

### 23.3.1 Input–Output Model Building

Input–output method is the approach and method to analyze the quantitative relationship between input and output in a specific economic system. It is also called the industrial inter-sectoral analysis. It was first proposed by the American economist Wassily Leontief in 1936, the theoretical basis of which is Walras' general equilibrium theory. Based on the equilibrium relationship on input and output tables, an input–output mathematical model can be built between industries:

$$X = AX + Y \tag{23.1}$$

After tidying up:

$$X = (I - A)^{-1}Y \tag{23.2}$$

Among them, $A$ is the direct consumption coefficient or technical coefficient matrix. Each element $a_{ij} = \frac{x_{ij}}{X_j}$ in the matrix represents the number of products of the sector $i$ that need to be consumed as an intermediate product to produce one unit of $j$; $I$ is an identity matrix with all elements on the main diagonal being 1; $(I - A)^{-1}$ is Leontief's inverse matrix, representing the complete consumption coefficients; $X$ is the social final product matrix. $Y$ is the social final product matrix that contains other end products.

The application of input–output analysis can be extended to other areas such as labor, capital, energy, and carbon emissions. By building the input–output model that includes environmental factors, the relationship between export trade and $CO_2$ can be studied. Therefore, the thesis introduces the coefficient of direct carbon emission to construct the coefficient of the complete carbon emission, which is:

$$\hat{S} = S(I - A)^{-1} \tag{23.3}$$

Among which, S is one line of vectors $(1 \times n)$, whose element $S_j = \frac{E_j}{X_j}$($E_j$ represents the total $CO_2$ emission of sector $j$, $X_j$ represents the total output of sector $j$) represents the $CO_2$ emissions generated by the output of the production unit of sector $j$; $\hat{S}$ is the coefficient of the complete carbon emission, representing the total amount of the direct and indirect $CO_2$ produced by the output of the production unit.

The total amount of $CO_2$ emission generated to meet the final use:

$$F = S(I - A)^{-1}Y \tag{23.4}$$

More than 40–50% of China's export trade is processing trade. If the effect of the processing trade i.e. intermediate products consumed in the production process is not considered in calculating the embodied carbon in the export trade, the intermediate products needed in the production of the export products will be counted as the domestic production, leading to an overestimation of the embodied carbon in the Chinese export products. Therefore, the input of the domestic production process should be divided into two parts: domestic input and intermediate input in export trade. The corresponding coefficients of the direct consumption are:

$$A = A^m + A^d \tag{23.5}$$

Among them, $A^m$ is the import coefficient matrix, the element $a_{ij}^m$ of which represents the amount of intermediate input in the export trade of sector $i$ for every unit of output produced by sector $j$; $A^d$ is the coefficient of the direct consumption in the domestic input, the element $a_{ij}^d$ of which represents the amount of intermediate input in the domestic trade of sector $i$ for every unit of output produced by sector $j$. The embodied carbon in Chinese export trade can be represented as:

$$F^e = S(I - A^d)^{-1}Y^e \tag{23.6}$$

Among which, $S$ is the direct emission coefficient for China; $Y^e$ is the column vector of export.

### 23.3.2 The Building of the Structural Decomposition Analysis Model

In order to measure the driving factors of the embodied carbon changes in the export trade of the Chinese manufacturing industry. The thesis decomposes the embodied carbon changes into technological effect, structural effect and scale effect.

To expand $Y^e$ in formula (23.6):

$$Y^e = \frac{Y^e}{cY^e}(cY^e) \tag{23.7}$$

Among which, $cY^e$ is the total amount of export, $\frac{Y^e}{cY^e}(n \times 1)$ is the percentage of every sector's export amount in the total export amount. Let $Y_s^e = \frac{Y^e}{cY^e}$, $Y_v^e = cY^e$, $\hat{S} = S(I - A^d)^{-1}$, formula (23.6) can be rewritten as:

$$F^e = \hat{S}\, Y_s^e Y_v^e \tag{23.8}$$

According to formula (23.8), the embodied carbon changes in the export trade during the two phases (phase 0 and phase 1) can be written as:

$$\Delta F^e = F^e(1) - F^e(0) = \hat{S}(1)Y_S^e(1)Y_v^e(1) - \hat{S}(0)Y_s^e(0)Y_v^e(0) \tag{23.9}$$

Because of "non-unique problems", the application of structural decomposition in analyzing models could result in different decomposition forms. In order to solve the problem, the bilevel decomposition algorithm is adopted. The algorithm could average the effects of the dependent variables determined by the corresponding independent variables decomposed in both the first phase and the last phase, and finally obtain the effect of independent variables on the dependent variables.

If decomposition starts from the base period (i.e. phase 0), formula (23.9) could be written as:

$$\Delta F^e = \Delta \hat{S} Y_S^e(0)Y_v^e(0) + \hat{S}(1)\Delta Y_s^e Y_v^e(0) + \hat{S}(1)Y_s^e(1)\Delta Y_v^e \tag{23.10}$$

If decomposition starts from the calculation period (i.e. phase 1), formula (23.9) could be written as:

$$\Delta F^e = \Delta \hat{S} Y_S^e(1)Y_v^e(1) + \hat{S}(0)\Delta Y_s^e Y_v^e(1) + \hat{S}(0)Y_s^e(0)\Delta Y_v^e \tag{23.11}$$

Taking the average of formula (23.10) and formula (23.11):

$$\begin{aligned} \Delta F^e &= \frac{1}{2}\left[\Delta \hat{S} Y_s^e(0)Y_v^e(0) + \Delta \hat{S} Y_s^e(1)Y_v^e(1)\right] \\ &+\frac{1}{2}\left[\hat{S}(1)\Delta Y_s^e Y_v^e(0) + \hat{S}(0)\Delta Y_s^e Y_v^e(1)\right] \\ &+\frac{1}{2}\left[\hat{S}(1)Y_s^e(1)\Delta Y_v^e + \hat{S}(0)Y_s^e(0)\Delta Y_v^e\right] \end{aligned} \tag{23.12}$$

Formula (23.12) can be simplified as:

$$\Delta F^e = f(\Delta \hat{S}) + f(\Delta Y_s^e) + f(\Delta Y_v^e) \tag{23.13}$$

among which, $f(\Delta \hat{S}) = \frac{1}{2}\left[\Delta \hat{S} Y_s^e(0)Y_v^e(0) + \Delta \hat{S} Y_s^e(1)Y_v^e(1)\right]$ is the technological effect, which is the effect of the coefficient of the complete carbon emissions on the changes of the embodied carbon; $f(\Delta Y_s^e) = \frac{1}{2}\left[\hat{S}(1)\Delta Y_s^e Y_v^e(0) + \hat{S}(0)\Delta Y_s^e Y_v^e(1)\right]$ is the structural effect, which is the effect of the export structure on the changes of the embodied carbon; $f(\Delta Y_v^e) =$

$\frac{1}{2}\left[\hat{S}(1)Y_s^e(1)\Delta Y_v^e + \hat{S}(0)Y_s^e(0)\Delta Y_v^e\right]$ is the scale effect, which is the effect of the export amount on the changes of the embodied carbon.

## 23.4 Data Sources and Processing

According to formula (23.6), the following data is needed in the calculation of the embodied carbon in Chinese manufacturing industry: Leontief's inverse matrix of the domestic input, statistics on export trade and coefficients of the direct carbon emissions from every manufacturing sector.

### *23.4.1 Input–Output Tables and Export Trade Statistics*

Statistics of Leontief's inverse matrix of the domestic input $(I - A^d)^{-1}$ and statistics of the export trade are from the OECD database.

Input–Output Table: the input–output table in the database is different from the domestic one. The table in the database divided the domestic production input into two parts: domestic input and import input. The formula of the direct consumption coefficient could therefore be adopted directly to calculate $A^d$. Given the fact that the Chinese input–output table in the latest OECD database has only been updated to the year 2011 and the production structure and technology of one country changes little in a short period of time, the thesis receives enlightment from the research conducted by Zhong (2013), Wei (2012), Yan (2011), Guo and Weimei (2015)and replaces the table with that of the available table, i.e. the tables of 2011 to 2015 are replaced by that of 2011. In the same time, the input–output tables for the rest of the years remain unchanged.

Trade data: In order to coordinate with the sectors in the input–output table, the thesis adopts OECD bilateral trade data (BTD) and conduct research on the data selected within the year 2000 and 2015.

### *23.4.2 Coefficient of Direct Carbon Emission in the Manufacturing Sector*

The so-called coefficient of the $CO_2$ direct carbon emission is the amount of $CO_2$ emitted from the output unit of a certain sector. The statistics of the total output for sectors from 2000 to 2015 comes from Almanac of Chinese industrial economy 2001–2016. The energy consumption data of various industries comes from Chinese statistic almanac 2001–2016. The amount of $CO_2$ emission can be obtained from the total $CO_2$ emissions caused by various energy consumption. According to the

**Table 23.1** The value of energy's $NCV$ and $CEF$

| | Coal | Coke | Crude oil | Gasoline (Gj/Kg)) | Kerosene | Diesel | Fuel oil | Natural gas (Gj/m3) |
|---|---|---|---|---|---|---|---|---|
| NCV | 0.021 | 0.028 | 0.042 | 0.043 | 0.043 | 0.043 | 0.042 | 0.039 |
| CEF (Kg/Gj) | 26.0 | 29.2 | 20.0 | 20.2 | 19.6 | 20.2 | 21.1 | 15.3 |

*Source* Authors' calculations

energy consumption data of various industries in Chinese statistic almanac, the energy consumption of different industries can be divided into 9 categories. Given that the electricity energy ultimately comes from coal, oil, natural gas, etc., the thesis mainly measures the $CO_2$ emissions caused by the following 8 kinds of energy: Coal, coke, crude oil, gasoline, kerosene, diesel, fuel oil and natural gas.

In order to calculate the amount of $CO_2$ emitted by the above mentioned 8 kinds of energy, the thesis adopts the methodologies proposed in the Guidelines for National Greenhouse Gas Inventories (Chap. 6, vol. 2 (energy)) established by the Intergovernmental Panel on Climate Change (IPCC) in 2006:

$$\sum_{n=1}^{8} E_n = \sum_{n=1}^{8} C_n \times NCV_n \times CEF_n \times COF_n \times \frac{44}{12}, n = 1, 2, ..., 8 \tag{23.14}$$

Among which, $E$ stands for the $CO_2$ emission of the sector; $C$ is the consumption of various energy sources; $NCV$ is the net heating value of energy (the data comes from the average lower heating value in the Guidelines for National Greenhouse Gas Inventories (appendix 4)); $CEF$ is the carbon emission factor (the data comes from the Guidelines for National Greenhouse Gas Inventories (Table 1.3, Chap. 1, vol. 2 (energy))); $COF$ is the carbon oxidation factor, with the default value being 1; $\frac{44}{12}$ is the ratio of the relative molecular weight of carbon to the relative atomic weight of carbon; $n = 1, 2, ..., 8$ represent the above mentioned 8 kinds of energy respectively. The value of every kind of energy's $NCV$ and $CEF$ is shown in Table 23.1.

### *23.4.3 Division*

The Chinese input–output table in the OECD database contains 18 manufacturing sectors. The OECD bilateral trade database contains 30 manufacturing sectors. The energy consumption data and total output data of various industries contains 30 manufacturing sectors. To ensure the smooth calculation, the manufacturing sectors are summarized and merged into 12 sectors, as shown in Table 23.2.

**Table 23.2** Department consolidation

| Merged departments | Input–output table of OECD | The energy consumption table | Export trade table |
|---|---|---|---|
| S1 food, beverage and tobacco | Food products, beverages and tobacco | Farm and sideline products processing | Food beverages and tobacco |
| | | Food manufacturing | |
| | | Beverage manufacturing | |
| | | Tobacco industry | |
| S2 textile, clothing, leather and shoe-making | Textiles, textile products, leather and footwear | textile industry | Textiles leather and footwear |
| | | Textile clothing, shoes, hat manufacturing industry | |
| | | Leather, fur, feather (velvet) and its products | |
| S3 wood and wooden products | Wood and products of wood and cork | Wood processing and wood, bamboo, rattan, brown, grass manufacturing | Wood and cork |
| | | Furniture manufacturing | |
| S4 papermaking, printing, publishing, culture and education | Pulp, paper, paper products, printing and publishing | paper making and paper products industry | Pulp paper printing and publishing |
| | | The reproduction of printing and recording media | |
| | | Educational and sports goods | |
| S5 petroleum, coking, and nuclear fuel processing industries | Coke, refined petroleum products and nuclear fuel | Petroleum processing, coking and nuclear fuel processing | Coke refined petroleum and nuclear fuel |
| S6 chemical industry | Chemicals and chemical products | Chemical industry | Chemicals and chemical products |
| | | medicine manufacturing industry | Chemicals excluding pharmaceuticals |
| | | Chemical fiber manufacturing | Pharmaceuticals |
| S7 rubber and plastic products | Rubber and plastics products | Manufacture of rubber | Chemical rubber plastics and fuel |
| | | Manufacture of plastics | Rubber and plastics |
| S8 non-metallic mineral products | Other non-metallic mineral products | Manufacture of non-metallic mineral products | Non-metallic products |
| | | | Non-ferrous metals |

(continued)

**Table 23.2** (continued)

| Merged departments | Input–output table of OECD | The energy consumption table | Export trade table |
|---|---|---|---|
| S9 metal products | Basic metals | Ferrous metal smelting and rolling processing industry | Basic metals and fabricated metal products |
| | Fabricated metal products except machinery and equipment | Non-ferrous metal smelting and rolling processing industry | Basic metals |
| | | Manufacture of metal products | Iron and steel |
| | | | Fabricated metal products |
| S10 mechanical equipment and instrument | Machinery and equipment n.e.c | Manufacture of general-purpose machinery | Machinery and equipment |
| | Office, accounting and computing machinery | general and special equipment manufacturing | Machinery and equipment n.e.c |
| | Electrical machinery and apparatus n.e.c | Manufacture of electrical machinery & equipment | Electrical and optical equipment |
| | Radio, television and communication equipment | Communications equipment, computer and other electronic equipment manufacturing | Office accounting and computing machinery |
| | | | Electrical machinery and apparatus n.e.c |
| | Medical, precision and optical instruments | Instrumentation and culture, office machinery manufacturing | Radio TV communication equipment |
| | | | Medical precision and optical instrument |
| S11 transportation equipment | Motor vehicles, trailers and semi-trailers | transportation equipment manufacturing industry | Transport equipment |
| | | | Motor vehicles trailers and semi-trailers |
| | | | Other transport equipment |
| | Other transport equipment | | Shipbuilding |
| | | | Aircraft and spacecraft |
| | | | Railroad and transport equipment n.e.c |

(continued)

**Table 23.2** (continued)

| Merged departments | Input–output table of OECD | The energy consumption table | Export trade table |
|---|---|---|---|
| S12 other manufacturing industries | Manufacturing n.e.c; recycling | Handicraft article and other manufacturing | Manufacturing n.e.c and recycling |
| | | Waste resources and waste materials recycling and processing industry | |

*Source* Authors' calculations

## 23.5 Result and Analysis of Embodied Carbon Calculation

### *23.5.1 Coefficient of Direct Carbon Emission*

According to the total $CO_2$ emissions and the total output of various sectors, the direct carbon emission factors of various sectors of Chinese manufacturing industry from 2000 to 2015 can be calculated. The calculation results are shown in Table 23.3.

Several conclusions can be attained from Table 23.3.

The coefficient of the direct emission in the same year of different manufacturing sectors could differ greatly with an increasing trend. The sector with the largest coefficient of direct carbon emission for all years is "S5 petroleum, coking, and nuclear fuel processing industries". The sector with the smallest coefficient of direct carbon emission for all years is "S10 mechanical equipment and instrument". The largest coefficient was 72.767 times of the smallest coefficient in 2000; the number was 133.647 in 2005, 133.657 in 2010 and 197.667 in 2015, signifying an increasing trend of inter-sectoral direct emission coefficient. Take 2015 as an example, the four sectors with the largest coefficient of direct carbon emission in descending order are: "S5 petroleum, coking, and nuclear fuel processing industries", "S8 non-metallic mineral products", "S9 metal products" and "S6 chemical industry"; the four sectors with the smallest coefficient of direct carbon emission in ascending order are: "S10 mechanical equipment and instrument", "S11 transportation equipment", "S3 wood and wooden products", "S7 rubber and plastic products". Sectors with larger emission coefficient are mostly in the upstream of the industrial chain of the national economy. They provide necessary intermediate products or secondary energy to other sectors to other sectors and emitted more $CO_2$ in the direct production process. Therefore, there is an urgent need to improve their energy use efficiency and emission intensity.

From the perspective of time, the coefficient of direct carbon emission of every manufacturing sector dropped significantly. From 2000 to 2014, the four sectors with the biggest drop in descending order are: "S3 wood and wooden products", "S11 transportation equipment", "S10 mechanical equipment and instrument" and "S12 other manufacturing industries"; the four sectors with the smallest drop in ascending order are: "S5 petroleum, coking, and nuclear fuel processing industries", "S2 textile, clothing, leather and shoe-making", "S4 papermaking, printing, publishing, culture and education" and "S7 rubber and plastic products". It can be inferred that the manufacturing sectors have continuously raised the level of production technology

**Table 23.3** The coefficient of the direct carbon emission in Chinese manufacturing sectors (Kg/USD)

| Year<br>Sector | 2000 | 2001 | 2002 | 2003 | 2004 | 2005 | 2006 | 2007 | 2008 | 2009 | 2010 | 2011 | 2012 | 2013 | 2014 | 2015 |
|---|---|---|---|---|---|---|---|---|---|---|---|---|---|---|---|---|
| S1 | 0.332 | 0.410 | 0.335 | 0.291 | 0.222 | 0.192 | 0.153 | 0.123 | 0.117 | 0.099 | 0.084 | 0.081 | 0.078 | 0.075 | 0.074 | 0.071 |
| S2 | 0.176 | 0.235 | 0.198 | 0.177 | 0.188 | 0.157 | 0.139 | 0.117 | 0.107 | 0.094 | 0.082 | 0.078 | 0.073 | 0.071 | 0.068 | 0.064 |
| S3 | 0.289 | 0.301 | 0.253 | 0.242 | 0.204 | 0.116 | 0.124 | 0.092 | 0.089 | 0.074 | 0.058 | 0.042 | 0.031 | 0.026 | 0.024 | 0.021 |
| S4 | 0.822 | 0.735 | 0.663 | 0.573 | 0.624 | 0.483 | 0.515 | 0.421 | 0.397 | 0.378 | 0.325 | 0.321 | 0.289 | 0.276 | 0.265 | 0.260 |
| S5 | 6.747 | 8.929 | 9.261 | 8.178 | 7.741 | 7.235 | 5.503 | 5.043 | 4.090 | 4.596 | 3.837 | 3.628 | 3.534 | 3.416 | 3.376 | 3.301 |
| S6 | 1.731 | 1.964 | 1.906 | 1.659 | 1.238 | 0.858 | 0.968 | 0.797 | 0.736 | 0.656 | 0.507 | 0.407 | 0.386 | 0.372 | 0.364 | 0.358 |
| S7 | 0.150 | 0.228 | 0.177 | 0.157 | 0.159 | 0.138 | 0.106 | 0.084 | 0.089 | 0.080 | 0.070 | 0.065 | 0.060 | 0.055 | 0.051 | 0.046 |
| S8 | 3.003 | 3.268 | 2.869 | 2.778 | 2.965 | 4.854 | 1.979 | 1.518 | 1.488 | 1.286 | 0.981 | 0.781 | 0.702 | 0.683 | 0.651 | 0.624 |
| S9 | 2.624 | 2.951 | 2.888 | 2.509 | 1.848 | 2.009 | 1.608 | 1.294 | 1.044 | 1.139 | 0.995 | 0.872 | 0.762 | 0.685 | 0.603 | 0.545 |
| S10 | 0.093 | 0.101 | 0.089 | 0.071 | 0.057 | 0.054 | 0.044 | 0.036 | 0.033 | 0.036 | 0.029 | 0.027 | 0.023 | 0.021 | 0.019 | 0.018 |
| S11 | 0.145 | 0.166 | 0.131 | 0.100 | 0.100 | 0.103 | 0.070 | 0.054 | 0.054 | 0.044 | 0.034 | 0.031 | 0.031 | 0.028 | 0.027 | 0.025 |
| S12 | 0.300 | 0.551 | 0.388 | 0.387 | 0.459 | 0.134 | 0.223 | 0.152 | 0.138 | 0.110 | 0.086 | 0.075 | 0.072 | 0.070 | 0.065 | 0.062 |

*Source* Authors' calculations

and energy use during this period of time and some preliminary results of the energy saving and emission reduction have been achieved in one sector because of China's gradual emphasis on energy and environment.

### 23.5.2 *Coefficient of Complete Carbon Emission*

The coefficient of complete carbon emission of every manufacturing sector can be calculated according to formula (23.3), the results are shown in Table 23.4. Several conclusions could be attained from Table 23.4: the coefficient of the complete carbon emission in the same year of different manufacturing sectors also differs fairly large with an increasing trend. The sector with the largest coefficient of complete carbon emission for all years is "S5 petroleum, coking, and nuclear fuel processing industries" and the sector with the smallest coefficient being "S1 food, beverage and tobacco". The largest coefficient was 13.476 times of the smallest coefficient in 2000; the number was 22.701 in 2010 and 27.888 in 2015. Take 2015 as an example, the four sectors with the largest coefficient of complete carbon emission in descending order are: "S5 petroleum, coking, and nuclear fuel processing industries", "S8 non-metallic mineral products", "S9 metal products" and "S6 chemical industry"; the four sectors with the smallest coefficient of complete carbon emission in ascending order are: "S1 food, beverage and tobacco", "S2 textile, clothing, leather and shoe-making", "S3 wood and wooden products", "S12 other manufacturing industries". The sectors which have the largest complete emission coefficient coincides with the sectors which have the largest direct emission coefficient. The reason lies in the fact that the complete emission coefficient is the sum of the direct and indirect emission coefficients and the four sectors are the providers of intermediate products and secondary energy for other sectors, thus leading to the domination of the direct emission coefficient and the corresponding increase of the complete emission coefficient.

From the perspective of time, the coefficient of direct carbon emission of every manufacturing sector dropped continuously. From 2000 to 2014, the four sectors with the biggest drop in descending order are: "S1 food, beverage and tobacco", "S9 metal products", "S10 mechanical equipment and instrument" and "S12 other manufacturing industries"; the four sectors with the smallest drop in ascending order are: "S5 petroleum, coking, and nuclear fuel processing industries", "S4 papermaking, printing, publishing, culture and education", "S8 non-metallic mineral products" and "S2 textile, clothing, leather and shoe-making". The coefficient of complete carbon emission of every manufacturing sector drops more thanks to the implementation of the energy-saving and emission-reduction policy by a sector and their efforts made in eliminating outdated production capacity, improving energy efficiency, and reducing energy consumption per unit of production.

**Table 23.4** The coefficient of the complete carbon emission in Chinese manufacturing sectors (Kg/USD)

| Year<br>Sector | 2000 | 2001 | 2002 | 2003 | 2004 | 2005 | 2006 | 2007 | 2008 | 2009 | 2010 | 2011 | 2012 | 2013 | 2014 | 2015 |
|---|---|---|---|---|---|---|---|---|---|---|---|---|---|---|---|---|
| S1 | 0.542 | 0.658 | 0.570 | 0.497 | 0.400 | 0.378 | 0.312 | 0.256 | 0.235 | 0.213 | 0.177 | 0.156 | 0.145 | 0.138 | 0.327 | 0.125 |
| S2 | 0.709 | 0.876 | 0.808 | 0.712 | 0.647 | 0.552 | 0.508 | 0.428 | 0.384 | 0.357 | 0.296 | 0.287 | 0.275 | 0.264 | 0.242 | 0.223 |
| S3 | 1.051 | 1.193 | 1.116 | 1.002 | 0.843 | 0.654 | 0.598 | 0.489 | 0.434 | 0.418 | 0.340 | 0.331 | 0.32 | 0.31 | 0.28 | 0.275 |
| S4 | 1.465 | 1.457 | 1.359 | 1.183 | 1.165 | 1.121 | 1.120 | 0.926 | 0.847 | 0.817 | 0.688 | 0.650 | 0.64 | 0.625 | 0.611 | 0.584 |
| S5 | 7.301 | 9.645 | 9.995 | 8.826 | 8.343 | 7.590 | 5.778 | 5.291 | 4.293 | 4.820 | 4.023 | 3.824 | 3.753 | 3.654 | 3.586 | 3.486 |
| S6 | 2.920 | 3.389 | 3.316 | 2.896 | 2.279 | 1.810 | 1.843 | 1.547 | 1.391 | 1.303 | 1.029 | 1.025 | 1.022 | 1.014 | 0.952 | 0.867 |
| S7 | 1.171 | 1.441 | 1.357 | 1.191 | 1.013 | 1.049 | 0.775 | 0.655 | 0.578 | 0.583 | 0.484 | 0.425 | 0.385 | 0.375 | 0.367 | 0.358 |
| S8 | 4.283 | 4.794 | 4.360 | 4.111 | 4.188 | 5.578 | 2.510 | 1.970 | 1.877 | 1.685 | 1.310 | 1.285 | 1.254 | 1.184 | 1.175 | 1.64 |
| S9 | 4.553 | 5.228 | 5.145 | 4.488 | 3.473 | 2.486 | 1.976 | 1.612 | 1.308 | 1.422 | 1.231 | 1.213 | 1.182 | 1.175 | 1.154 | 1.098 |
| S10 | 1.321 | 1.532 | 1.489 | 1.298 | 1.058 | 0.824 | 0.672 | 0.556 | 0.472 | 0.491 | 0.411 | 0.405 | 0.385 | 0.356 | 0.345 | 0.336 |
| S11 | 1.330 | 1.555 | 1.479 | 1.274 | 1.066 | 0.910 | 0.736 | 0.605 | 0.520 | 0.525 | 0.437 | 0.427 | 0.415 | 0.405 | 0.385 | 0.376 |
| S12 | 1.236 | 1.649 | 1.454 | 1.322 | 1.245 | 0.696 | 0.697 | 0.547 | 0.477 | 0.454 | 0.371 | 0.362 | 0.357 | 0.342 | 0.337 | 0.315 |

*Source* Authors' calculations

### 23.5.3 The Embodied Carbon in the Export Trade on the Overall Level

According to formulas (23.6) and (23.14), the total amount of the embodied carbon in the export trade of Chinese manufacturing industry from 2000 to 2010 and the total amount of its $CO_2$ emission can be calculated, and the percentage of embodied carbon in the export trade in the total amount of $CO_2$ emission could thus be obtained. The results are shown in Table 23.5.

Several conclusions can be attained from Table 23.5.

The $CO_2$ emission in Chinese manufacturing industry has a rising trend in general. The amount of the emission has risen from 1.9332 billion tons in 2000 to 4.8805 tons in 2015, with an increase of 2.807 times. It is worth mentioning that the $CO_2$ emission of Chinese manufacturing industry increases 1.049 times between 2008 and 2009 under the circumstances of the global financial crisis.

The embodied carbon in Chinese manufacturing export trade from 2000 to 2008 marks a steady rise from 0.7617 billion tons in 2000 to 2.0992 billion tons in 2008, with an increase of 2.756 times. Influenced by the global economic crisis, the embodied carbon decreased between 2008 and 2009, but continued to creep up again from 2010 to 2015.

The embodied carbon of the Chinese manufacturing industry accounts for more than 35% of the $CO_2$ emission in the manufacturing industry, indicating that more than half of the Chinese $CO_2$ emission is not caused by the Chinese domestic consumption, but the import demand of China's trading partner countries.

### 23.5.4 The Embodied Carbon in the Export Trade on the Sectoral Level

By multiplying the coefficient of the complete carbon emission and the export trade volume of the sectors, the embodied carbon in the export trade of any sector could be calculated, the results are shown in Table 23.6.

The following conclusions can be attained from Table 23.6: the embodied carbon in the export trade of every manufacturing sectors from 2000 to 2015 marks an upward trend. It can be concluded that the major sectors that exports embodied carbon are: "S6 chemical industry", "S9 metal products" and "S10 mechanical equipment and instrument". Among them, the embodied carbon of the "S6 chemical industry" increased from 72.4 million tons in 2000 to 0.2135 billion tons in 2015; the embodied carbon of the "S9 metal products" increased from 0.1696 billion tons in 2000 to 0.4012 billion tons in 2015; the embodied carbon of "S10 mechanical equipment and instrument" increased from 0.3102 billion tons in 2000 to 0.8892 billion tons in 2015. Since the embodied carbon in the export trade is the product of complete carbon emission coefficient and the volume of export trade, it can be concluded that

**Table 23.5** The $CO_2$ emission in Chinese manufacturing industry and the embodied carbon in Chinese manufacturing export trade (100 million tons)

| Year | 2000 | 2001 | 2002 | 2003 | 2004 | 2005 | 2006 | 2007 | 2008 | 2009 | 2010 | 2011 | 2012 | 2013 | 2014 | 2015 |
|---|---|---|---|---|---|---|---|---|---|---|---|---|---|---|---|---|
| The embodied carbon in Chinese manufacturing export trade | 7.617 | 9.504 | 11.385 | 13.949 | 17.020 | 17.913 | 18.877 | 20.237 | 20.992 | 16.502 | 18.577 | 19.083 | 19.232 | 19.656 | 19.673 | 19.407 |
| The $CO_2$ emission in Chinese manufacturing industry | 19.332 | 19.186 | 20.600 | 23.902 | 29.699 | 33.273 | 37.154 | 39.755 | 42.951 | 45.057 | 48.805 | 50.205 | 51.203 | 52.387 | 53.648 | 54.269 |
| The embodied carbon accounts for the $CO_2$ emission (%) | 39.4 | 49.5 | 55.3 | 58.4 | 57.3 | 53.8 | 50.8 | 50.9 | 48.9 | 36.6 | 38.1 | 38 | 37.6 | 37.5 | 36.7 | 35.8 |

*Source* Authors' calculations

**Table 23.6** The embodied carbon in the export trade of Chinese manufacturing sectors (100 million tons)

| Year sector | 2000 | 2001 | 2002 | 2003 | 2004 | 2005 | 2006 | 2007 | 2008 | 2009 | 2010 | 2011 | 2012 | 2013 | 2014 | 2015 |
|---|---|---|---|---|---|---|---|---|---|---|---|---|---|---|---|---|
| S1 | 0.055 | 0.071 | 0.067 | 0.067 | 0.064 | 0.071 | 0.071 | 0.067 | 0.069 | 0.059 | 0.061 | 0.062 | 0.061 | 0.057 | 0.061 | 0.063 |
| S2 | 0.479 | 0.609 | 0.643 | 0.709 | 0.778 | 0.801 | 0.906 | 0.903 | 0.884 | 0.747 | 0.775 | 0.785 | 0.796 | 0.802 | 0.812 | 0.823 |
| S3 | 0.028 | 0.034 | 0.039 | 0.043 | 0.051 | 0.049 | 0.059 | 0.056 | 0.050 | 0.038 | 0.038 | 0.039 | 0.041 | 0.043 | 0.058 | 0.059 |
| S4 | 0.028 | 0.031 | 0.035 | 0.040 | 0.047 | 0.059 | 0.079 | 0.097 | 0.099 | 0.092 | 0.094 | 0.095 | 0.096 | 0.097 | 0.096 | 0.099 |
| S5 | 0.249 | 0.336 | 0.380 | 0.519 | 0.714 | 0.732 | 0.586 | 0.711 | 0.931 | 0.683 | 0.828 | 0.836 | 0.834 | 0.851 | 0.808 | 0.906 |
| S6 | 0.724 | 0.922 | 1.047 | 1.182 | 1.259 | 1.345 | 1.669 | 1.986 | 2.333 | 1.705 | 1.861 | 1.877 | 1.902 | 1.953 | 2.021 | 2.135 |
| S7 | 0.358 | 0.469 | 0.517 | 0.586 | 0.678 | 0.919 | 0.826 | 0.913 | 1.015 | 0.833 | 0.949 | 0.958 | 1.032 | 1.041 | 1.046 | 1.051 |
| S8 | 0.344 | 0.393 | 0.428 | 0.536 | 0.817 | 1.382 | 0.905 | 0.799 | 0.860 | 0.586 | 0.633 | 0.642 | 0.615 | 0.623 | 0.642 | 0.651 |
| S9 | 1.696 | 1.844 | 2.111 | 2.456 | 3.500 | 3.315 | 4.043 | 4.615 | 4.795 | 2.637 | 3.268 | 3.225 | 3.285 | 3.753 | 3.851 | 4.012 |
| S10 | 3.102 | 4.096 | 5.363 | 6.922 | 8.098 | 8.273 | 8.630 | 8.883 | 8.628 | 7.930 | 8.678 | 8.753 | 8.882 | 8.612 | 8.768 | 8.892 |
| S11 | 0.316 | 0.377 | 0.404 | 0.506 | 0.566 | 0.648 | 0.719 | 0.834 | 0.939 | 0.864 | 1.051 | 1.125 | 1.134 | 1.205 | 1.215 | 1.225 |
| S12 | 0.238 | 0.321 | 0.350 | 0.383 | 0.449 | 0.318 | 0.383 | 0.373 | 0.390 | 0.327 | 0.341 | 0.335 | 0.338 | 0.401 | 0.415 | 0.425 |

*Source* Authors' calculations

the main export sectors from 2000 to 2015 are: "S10 mechanical equipment and instrument", "S9 metal products" and "S6 chemical industry".

## 23.6 The Technological, Structural and Scale Effect of Embodied Carbon

### 23.6.1 *Three Kinds of Effect of Embodied Carbon*

Taking the year 2000 as the base period and 2001–2015 as calculation periods, the values of technological effect, structural effect and scale effect can be calculated respectively according to formula (23.13). The results are shown in Fig. 23.1.

From 2000 to 2015, the embodied carbon of China's manufacturing industry rose from 761.7 million tons to 2034.1 million tons, which was an increase of 1272.4 million tons. From Fig. 23.1, the following conclusions can be obtained:

(1) In the past years, the scale effect has a positive influence on the changes of the embodied carbon. In other words, the constant expansion of the export scale is the main engine that drives the increase of embodied carbon in export trade of the manufacturing industry. Even under the impact of financial crisis in 2009, scale effect still promoted the growth of embodied carbon as high as 1642.2 million tons.

(2) The improvement of emission coefficient has an offset effect on the increase of embodied carbon in export trades. From 2000 to 2015, the cumulative negative

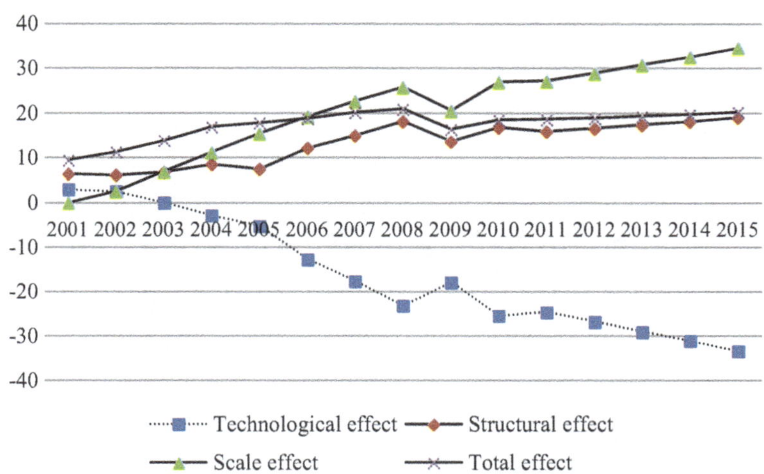


**Fig. 23.1** The technological effect and structural effect and the scale effect on the embodied carbon in Chinese manufacturing export trade (100 million tons) (*Source* Authors' calculations)

impact of technological effect on the embodied carbon growth in the manufacturing industry was—24,350.5 million tons. Technological effect measures the influence of the total carbon emission change on the embodied carbon in export trades, which indicates that the improvement of energy saving, emission reduction and productivity brought by production technology is of great benefit to inhibiting the increase of embodied carbon in exports of the manufacturing industry.

(3) In the past years, structural effect has a positive influence on the export of embodied carbon, but the influence is weaker than that of the scale effect. From 2000 to 2015, the cumulative influence exerted by structural effect on the embodied carbon growth in exports of manufacturing industry is 19931.94 million tons. The increasing trend of the structural effect shows that in the export structure of the manufacturing industry, the proportion contributed by carbon-intensive products to the total export trade volume witnesses a decrease.

### *23.6.2 Decomposition of Sectoral Structure of Embodied Carbon*

Taking 2000 as the base period and 2015 as the calculation period, this paper, on the level of sectors, decomposes the influence factors of the embodied carbon change in exports of the manufacturing industry into technological effect, structural effect and scale effect. The results are shown in Fig. 23.2.

From Fig. 23.2, the following conclusions can be attained:

(1) From the sector level, the embodied carbon in exports of every manufacturing sector has experienced a rise. Among them, "S10 mechanical equipment and

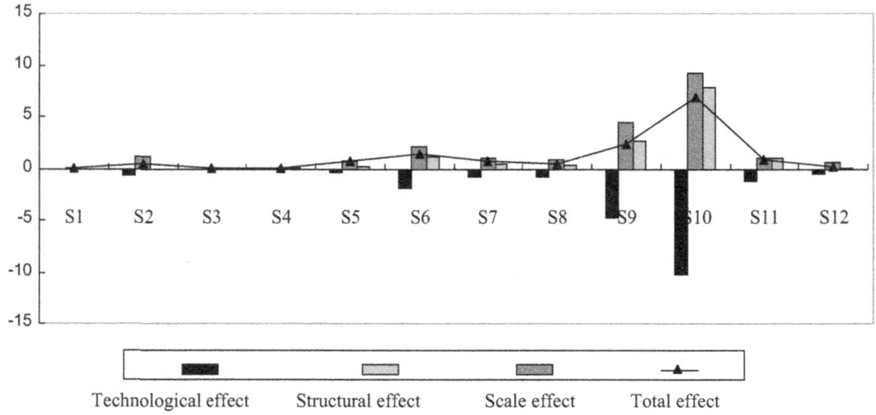


**Fig. 23.2** The technological effect, structural effect and scale effect on the level of sectors from 2000 to 2015 (100 million tons) ( *Source* Authors' calculations). *Note* (1) In the figure, S1–S12 represents a sector, and the sector name is referenced in Table 23.2

instrument" (698.5 million tons), "S9 metal products" (234.2 million tons) and "S6 chemical industry" (146.6 million tons) are the sectors that have the largest increase in the embodied carbon in export trades.

(2) Scale effect has a positive influence on all manufacturing sectors in terms of the rise of embodied carbon in export trades; technological effect exerts a negative effect on embodied carbon in export trades of all manufacturing sector. In other words, technological effect contributes to the decrease of embodied carbon in export trades; structural effect has diverse influence on the embodied carbon in export trades according to different manufacturing sectors. In the three sectors of "S10 mechanical equipment and instrument ", "S9 metal products" and "S6 chemical industry", the considerable increase of embodied carbon in export trades is mainly due to the joint influence of the scale effect and structural effect. Although the technological effect of the above three sectors can be used as a counterbalance, its influence is far below that of the scale effect and structural effect.

(3) The technological effect and structural effect of "S1 food, beverage and tobacco", "S2 textile, clothing, leather and shoe-making" are both negative, which is conducive to reducing embodied carbon in export trades; however, their negative effects cannot offset the influence of scale effect, leading to the increased embodied carbon in export trades of these two sectors.

From the above analysis, it can be perceived that from 2000 to 2015, the scale effect has a positive influence on the embodied carbon in export trades in all manufacturing sectors; the technological effect negatively influences embodied carbon in export trades of all sectors; the influence of structural effect differs according to various sectors. The structural effect indicates the influence of export proportion changes on the embodied carbon in export trades. Since it is inevitable that export proportion rises and falls in different sectors, the influence of the structural effect can be both positive negative.

## 23.7 Conclusions and Inspirations

The input–output method is a common method for evaluating embodied carbon. The thesis adopts an extended input–output method. By using the latest data in the OECD database, it calculates the coefficient of the direct carbon emission and complete carbon emission and the embodied carbon in the export trade of the Chinese manufacturing industry from 2000 to 2015 and decomposes the embodied carbon change of export trade in the manufacturing industry to technological effect, structural effect and scale effect by using the method of structural decomposition method. Several conclusions can be attained that although the embodied carbon of the Chinese manufacturing industry has shown a rising trend, the coefficient of the direct carbon emission and complete carbon emission have been declined in manufacturing sector. Scale effect has a positive influence on all manufacturing sectors in terms of the rise of embodied carbon in export trades; technological effect exerts a negative effect on embodied carbon in export trades of all manufacturing sector. The influence of the structural effect is relatively small but the overall trend of which is on the rise.

Based on the above conclusion, the following suggestions are made:

Optimize energy structure and improve energy efficiency. New energy and renewable resources should be vigorously developed and the proportion of coal and resources alike in energy consumption should be reduced. The east coast regions of China are rich in its wind energy and has a high potential of developing and using wind power. Other clean energy sources like the nuclear energy, bio-energy and solar energy are also prospective. What's more, whole society should combine the energy structure optimization with the increase of the energy-use efficiency, adopt the technology of energy saving and emission reduction, accelerate the reduction of overdependence the traditional manufacturing industries have on the energy sources like coal, improve the overall efficiency of the existing energy system, curb the overall consumption of coal continuously, limit and eliminate high-carbon industries and develop low-carbon industries.

Strengthen technology innovation and introduce clean production mechanism. The government should increase capital investment, encourage independent innovation, adjust the production structure so that the goal of energy saving and emission reduction could be achieved. The abundance of coal in China and its low price made it difficult for changing the coal-based energy consumption structure in China in the short term. Therefore, the technology of energy saving and emission reduction should be promoted and the energy consumption in the production be reduced. What's more, it is also necessary to positively introduce the Clean development mechanism (CDM) to reduce the carbon emission in the manufacturing industry of China. Developed countries are currently seeking opportunities to work with the CDM of the developing countries in order to achieve their goal of carbon emission reduction. The opportunity should be seized and the CDM program should be actively introduced to increase the efficiency of terminal energy use.

Transform the mode of trade growth and promote the structural adjustment of import and export products. The governments should control the products with low added value, high energy consumption and high emission at their sources and lead the product structure of the export products in the Chinese manufacturing industry towards one with high added value and low energy consumption. It is also necessary to encourage products export of manufacturing industries embraces low carbon emission and reduce the proportion of products export in manufacturing industries of high carbon emission. At the same time, efforts should be made to increase the environmental regulations and promote the technical progress of the clean energy to reduce the energy intensity and carbon-emission intensity of exports; to optimize the trade structure to reduce the proportion of energy and pollution-intensive products in the export products and facilitate the transformation in development mode of manufacturing industries from the quantitate expansion to quality-oriented growth; to lead the transformation and upgrade of processing trade and mitigate the negative effects of the fast development exerted on environment.

Construct the new mechanism of assigning responsibilities for greenhouse gas emission reduction. The current United Nations Framework Convention on Climate Change (UNFCCC) is based on a "producer-based" responsibility sharing mechanism, i.e., the carbon emission of one country contains all of the carbon emission of all products including those in the exports trade. The trading partner countries of China, while meeting their own consumer needs, bring Chinese manufacturing industry with huge pressure on emission reduction. Therefore, China should actively participate in the international climate change negotiation, promote the upgrade of the responsibility sharing mechanism, i.e., establish the "consumer-based" responsibility sharing mechanism, which could better reflect the principle of equitable distribution and be better accepted by other countries. Under the new mechanism of responsibility sharing, the developed countries should be responsible for their historical consumption and bear more responsibilities in emission reduction.

**Acknowledgements** Lei Zhou, Wanyi Wang also made great contributions to this manuscript. We express our heartfelt thanks to them. This research was supported by: National Social and Scientific Fund Program of China (18ZDA052; 17BGL142; 16ZDA047); The Natural Science Foundation of China (91546117, 71373131). The Ministry of Education Scientific Research Foundation for the returned overseas students (No. 2013-693, Ji Guo). This research was also supported by the Priority Academic Program Development of Jiangsu Higher Education Institutions.

**Conflicts of Interest** The authors declare no conflict of interest.

## References

Bin, S., & Ang, B. W. (2011). Input-output analysis of $CO_2$ emissions embodied in trade: The feedback effects. *Ecological Economics, 71,* 42–53.

Bin, S., Ang, B. W., & Melissa, L. (2013). Input-output analysis of $CO_2$ emissions embodied in trade and the driving forces: Processing and normal exports. *Ecological Economics, 88,* 119–125.

Chen, B., Li, J. S., Wu, X. F., Han, M. Y., Zeng, L., Li, Z., & Chen, G. Q. (2018). Global energy flows embodied in international trade: A combination of environmentally extended input–output analysis and complex network analysis. *Applied Energy, 210.*

Ederington, J., Levinson, A., & Minier, J. (2004). Trade Liberalization and pollution havens. *B.E. Journal: Advances in Economic Analysis and Policy, 4.*

Ederington, J., Levinson, A., & Minier, J. (2005). Footloose and pollution-free. *Review of Economics and Statistics , 87,* 92–99.

Fan, X. J., Wu, S. M., & Li, S. T. (2019a). Spatial-temporal analysis of carbon emissions embodied in interprovincial trade and optimization strategies: A case study of Hebei. *China. Energy, 185,* 1235–1249.

Fan, J. L., Meng, S., Wang, J. D., & Zhang, X. (2019b). Coordinated emission mitigation mechanism of Beijing-Tianjin-Hebei region in China: A perspective from $CO_2$ emissions embodied in domestic trade. *Energy Proceedings , 158,* 3893–3900.

Gao, P., Yue, S. J., & Chen, H. T. (2020). Carbon emission efficiency of China's industry sectors: From the perspective of embodied carbon emissions. *Journal of Cleaner Production, 13.*

Glen, P. P., Jan C. M., Christopher L., & Weber, O. E. (2011). Growth in emission transfers via international trade from 1990–2008. *Proceedings of the National Academy of Sciences of the United States of America, 108,* 8903–8908.

Gong, Z., & Chen, X. (2017). Analysis of interval data envelopment efficiency model considering different distribution characteristics—based on environmental performance evaluation of the manufacturing industry. *Sustainability, 9,* 2080.

Guo, J., & Weimei, Y. E. (2015). Measures and influencing factors of embodied carbon of manufacturing industries export trade in China. *Science and Technology Management Research , 329,* 214–222.

Guo, S., He, P., Bayaraa, M., & Li, J. S. (2020). Greenhouse gas emissions embodied in the Mongolian economy and their driving forces. *Science of the Total Environment, 714.*

Hasegawa, R., Kagawa, S., & Tsukui, M. (2015). Carbon footprint analysis through constructing a multi-region input–output table: A case study of Japan. *Journal of Economic Structures, 4,* 1–20.

He, K. H., & Hertwich, E. G. (2019). The flow of embodied carbon through the economies of China, the European Union, and the United States. *Resources Conservation and Recycling, 145,* 190–198.

Hu, J. M., Liu, G. Y., Meng, F. X., Hu, Y. C., & Casazza, M. (2020). Subnational carbon flow pattern analysis using multi-scale input-output model. *Ecological Modelling, 431.*

Huang, R., Lv, G. N., Chen, M., & Zhu, Z. Y. (2019). $CO_2$ emissions embodied in trade: Evidence for Hong Kong SAR. *Journal of Cleaner Production, 239.*

Ji, X., Liu, Y. F., Han, M. Y., & Meng, J. (2020) The mutual benefits from Sino-Africa trade: Evidence on emission transfer along the global supply chain. *Journal of Environmental Management, 263.*

Jiang, L., He, S. X., Tian, X., Zhang, B., & Zhou, H. F. (2020). Energy use embodied in international trade of 39 countries: Spatial transfer patterns and driving factors. *Energy, 195.*

Kirsten, S., Wiebe, M. B., Stefan, G., & Christian, L. (2012). Calculating energy-related $CO_2$ emissions embodied in international trade using a global input-output model. *Economic System Research , 24,* 113–139.

Li, L. (2012). Analyses of $CO_2$ emissions embodied in domestic and international trade for an open region: The case of Xinjiang. *Shanghai Journal of Economics, 2,* 13–23.

Li, Y. L., Chen, B., Chen, G. Q., Meng, J., & Hayat T. (2020). An embodied energy perspective of urban economy: A three-scale analysis for Beijing 2002–2012 with headquarter effect. *The Science of the total environment, 732.*

Li, Y. L., Chen, B., & Chen, G. Q. (2020). Carbon network embodied in international trade: Global structural evolution and its policy implications. *139.*

Long, R. Y., Li, J. Q., Chen, H., Zhang, L. L., & Li, Q. W. (2018). Embodied carbon dioxide flow in international trade: A comparative analysis based on China and Japan. *Journal of Environmental Management , 209,* 371–381.

Long, Y., Yoshida, Y., Liu, Q. L., Zhang, H. R., Wang, S. Q., & Fang. K. (2020). Comparison of city-level carbon footprint evaluation by applying single- and multi-regional input-output tables. *Journal of Environmental Management, 260.*

Lu, Q. L., Fang, K., Heijungs, R., Feng, K. S., Li, J. S., Wen, Q., Li, Y. M., & Huang, X. J. (2020). Imbalance and drivers of carbon emissions embodied in trade along the Belt and Road Initiative. *Applied Energy, 280.*

Lugauer, S., Jensen, R., & Sadler, C. (2014). An Estimate of the age distribution's effect on carbon dioxide emissions. *Economic Inquiry , 52,* 914–929.

Manfred, L., Richard, W., & Thomas, W. (2010). Uncertainty analysis for multi-region input-output models—a case study of the UK's carbon footprint. *Economic Systems Research , 22,* 43–63.

Mi, Z. F., Pan, S. Y., Yu, H., & Wei, Y. M. (2015). Potential impacts of industrial structure on energy consumption and $CO_2$ emission: A case study of Beijing. *Journal of Cleaner Production , 103,* 455–462.

Mi, Z., Zhang, Y., Guan, D., Shan, Y., Liu, Z., & Cong, R. (2016). Consumption-based emission accounting for Chinese cities. *Applied Energy, 184,* 1073–1081.

Mi, Z., Meng, J., Guan, D., Shan, Y., Song, M., Wei, Y. M., Liu, Z., et al. (2017a). Chinese $CO_2$ emission flows have reversed since the global financial crisis. *Nature Communications , 8,* 1712.

Mi, Z., Meng, J., Guan, D., Shan, Y., Song, M., Wei, Y. M., & Liu, Z. (2017b). Pattern changes in determinants of Chinese emissions. *Environmental Research Letters , 12,* 074003.

Pu, Z. N., Yue, S. J., & Gao, S. J. (2020) The driving factors of China's embodied carbon emissions. *Technological Forecasting & Social Change, 153.*

Qiu, Q., & Li, Q. Q. (2012). Accounting embodied carbon in foreign trade of China and the analysis of influential factors. *Economics and Management, 34,* 10–18.

Song, Y. Y. (2012). Empirical research on embodied carbon emissions of China's exports and impacting factors. Shandong University of Technology.

Thomas, W., Richard, W., Jan, C. M., Manfred, L., Guan, D. B., & Harris, R. (2010). A carbon footprint time series of the UK results from a multi-region input-output model. *Economic Systems Research , 22,* 19–42.

Tian, X., Chang, M., Lin, C., & Tanikawa, H. (2014). China's carbon footprint: a regional perspective on the effect of transitions in consumption and production patterns. *Applied Energy, 123,* 19–28.

Wang, Q., & Yang, X. (2020a). Imbalance of carbon embodied in South-South trade: Evidence from China-India trade. *Science of the Total Environment, 707.*

Wang, Q., & Zhou, Y. L. (2019a). Uncovering embodied $CO_2$ flows via North-North trade–a case study of US-Germany trade. *Science of the Total Environment , 691.*

Wang, Q, & Zhou, Y. L. (2019b). Imbalance of carbon emissions embodied in the US-Japan trade: Temporal change and driving factors. *Journal of Cleaner Production, 237.*

Wang, F., Wang, C., & Su, Y. (2017). Decomposition analysis of carbon emission factors from energy consumption in Guangdong province from 1990 to 2014. *Sustainability, 9,* 274.

Wang, Z. H., Li, Y. M., Cai, H. L., Yang, Y. T., & Wang, B. (2019). Regional difference and drivers in China's carbon emissions embodied in internal trade. *Energy Economics , 83,* 217–228.

Wang, S., Zhao, Y. H., & Wiedmann, T. (2019b). Carbon emissions embodied in China–Australia trade: A scenario analysis based on input–output analysis and panel regression models. *Journal of Cleaner Production, 220,* 721–731.

Wang, Q., Liu, Y., & Wang, H. (2019). Determinants of net carbon emissions embodied in Sino-German trade. *Journal of Cleaner Production , 235,* 1216–1231.

Wang, S. H., Tang, Y., Du, Z. H., & Song M. L. (2020). Export trade, embodied carbon emissions, and environmental pollution: An empirical analysis of China's high- and new-technology industries. *Journal of Environmental Management, 276.*

Wei, S. C. (2012). Eatimate of China's $CO_2$ emissions embodied in exports and study on the influences. Hunan University.

Wei, C., Ni, J., & Du, L. (2012). Regional allocation of carbon dioxide abatement in China. *China Economic Review , 23,* 552–565.

Wu, X. D., Guo, J. L., Li, C. H., Chen, G. Q., & Ji, X. (2020). Carbon emissions embodied in the global supply chain: Intermediate and final trade imbalances. *Science of the Total Environment, 707.*

Yan, Y. (2011). C02 emissions embodied in China's international trade. East China Normal University.

Yan, Y. F., Zhao, Z. X., & Wang, R. (2013). China's emission responsibility and trade-embodied emissions: A MRIO approach. *World Economy Study, 6,* 54–58.

Yang H. M., Wang Y., & Liu G. F. (2011). A Study on carbon emissions embodied in China' s import and export in 2002 and 2007. *Resources Science, 33,* 1563–1569.

Yang, B., Liu, C., & Su, Y. (2017). The allocation of carbon intensity reduction target by 2020 among industrial sectors in China. *Sustainability, 9,* 148.

Yrjö, V., Sirpa, K., Merja, S., Katajajuuri, J. M., Kirsi, U., Ilmo, M., Johanna, M., Juha, G., & Ari, N. (2011). Carbon footprint of food-approaches from national input-output statistics and a LCA of a food portion. *Journal of Cleaner Production, 19,* 1849–1856.

Yu, Y., & Chen, F. F. (2017). Research on carbon emissions embodied in trade between China and South Korea. *Atmospheric Pollution Research , 8,* 56–63.

Zagheni, E. (2011). The leverage of demographic dynamics on carbon dioxide emissions: Does age structure matter? *Demography, 48,* 371.

Zhang, W., & Zhou, Y. Y. (2013). Measurement of embodied $CO_2$ emission in trade and analysis on its misalignment of metropolitan area: Case of Beijing. *Technology Economics, 32,* 11–19.

Zhong, F. X. (2013). Empirical study on estimate of embodied carbon in Guangdong Province foreign trade and analysis of factors. Nanjing University of Information Science &Technology.

Zhong, Z. Q., Jiang, L., & Zhou, P. (2018). Transnational transfer of carbon emissions embodied in trade: Characteristics and determinants from a spatial perspective. *Energy, 147,* 858–875.

Zhou, D. Q., Zhou, X. Y., Xu, Q., Wu, F., Wang, Q. W., & Zha, D. L. (2018). Regional embodied carbon emissions and their transfer characteristics in China. *Structural Change and Economic Dynamics , 46,* 180–193.

The manufacturer's authorised representative in the EU is Springer Nature Customer Service Centre GmbH, Europaplatz 3, 69115 Heidelberg, Germany. If you have any concerns regarding our products, please contact ProductSafety@springernature.com

Printed and bound by CPI Group (UK) Ltd, Croydon, CR0 4YY

30/09/2026

02225295-0019